TORTS AND COMPENSATION

PERSONAL ACCOUNTABILITY AND SOCIAL RESPONSIBILITY FOR INJURY

Ninth Edition

■ ■ ■

Dan B. Dobbs

Regents Professor and Rosenstiel Distinguished Professor of Law Emeritus
James E. Rogers College of Law
The University of Arizona

Paul T. Hayden

William G. Coskran Professor of Law
Loyola Law School, Los Angeles
Loyola Marymount University

Ellen M. Bublick

Dan B. Dobbs Professor of Law
James E. Rogers College of Law
The University of Arizona

AMERICAN CASEBOOK SERIES®

WEST
ACADEMIC
PUBLISHING

American Casebook Series is a trademark registered in the U.S. Patent and Trademark Office.

To Dan B. Dobbs, whose work sets the standard.—P.T.H. & E.M.B.

To Diane, without whom my accomplishments would be fewer and far less meaningful.—P.T.H.

To my family, who continue to teach me the value of everything. And to my students, who make writing and teaching these materials a joy.—E.M.B.

PREFACE TO THE NINTH EDITION

For almost four decades, this casebook has been used as a teaching tool in law schools across the country. As with our previous eight editions, we present challenging contemporary cases and issues, without straying too far from the classic cases and the core of lawyering—thoughtful analysis and criticism. We want to engage students without mystifying them, and to collaborate with the professors who teach our book to spark students' lifelong interest in law in general, and in tort law in particular. One longtime characteristic of our book is the extent to which we engage with the tort law of our times.

This book deals centrally with injuries to persons. Reading about and discussing personal injury can be difficult. Many of the cases involve different forms of violence and harm. But tort law is the area of law designed to redress these injuries. Whether it does so adequately, or fails to live up to its role, is an important question for critical analysis. As such, students need to understand the real risks, harms, and conflicting interests that underlie legal responses. We try to present the subject of torts in a way that illuminates the problems to be addressed as well as the legal doctrines and reasoning that courts apply to them. Every case in the book concerns real people and real injuries—this book reflects that reality. Of course, much of the reality is leavened at times by the absurd and unexpected. A torts class using this book will be more than an exercise in solemn analysis of tragic situations. Our experience tells us that students and professors will enjoy discussing this material, and that, as in the complexities of life, smiles and laughter are neither rare nor inappropriate.

While the foundation of tort law is timeless, the common law, by its very nature, has never been static. Tort law is largely *state* law, which means that for every new legal question that arises, courts in various states will provide different answers and perspectives. Thus tort doctrine itself is continually being produced by our great experiment in federalism. Even within single states, we can see courts evolve in the way they apply their old legal doctrines or develop new law. Our casebook tries to reflect this dynamic process. Thus this edition includes developments in cases, topics and academic commentary that have occurred in the last few years. There are eighteen new main cases, many new case abstracts and hundreds of citations to newer cases.

Our primary criterion in selecting cases for inclusion in this book is whether they provide opportunities for analysis and for strengthening important lawyering skills such as reading, interpretation, evaluation and synthesis of legal materials. This book has never been merely a collection of illusory "majority rules." We hope students using this book will realize early on that both the cases and the notes aim to sharpen students' intellectual skills and enhance their understanding of legal process, as well as impart information.

Torts is a varied subject that crosses a wide range of types of conduct and types of injuries. However, personal injury torts remain the solid core of tort law for most first-year classes, and we focus mainly on such torts, including products liability. But most personal injuries are redressed through alternative means, such as workers' compensation, social security, or private insurance. A picture of injury law, therefore, includes those topics as well. And because we recognize the importance of economic torts to business litigation, we continue to develop the core rules of these torts. While the economic and dignitary torts materials are not intended to substitute for advanced courses, they provide an important introduction to that material.

A Note on Editing Conventions

The main "cases" reproduced in this (and almost any) casebook are opinions of judges, usually at the appellate levels. Such opinions are rarely succinct. They almost always include a good deal of matter on procedure and discuss many legal arguments that are not relevant to the ideas we want to highlight and develop. They also usually include many citations to cases as precedent or persuasive example. Editing is therefore necessary.

When we omit text in opinions, we indicate the omission by ellipses. Sometimes we summarize portions of a judicial opinion in our own language; we put that in brackets. We don't usually mark out omissions of citations of precedent and academic commentary at all, because such citations are so prevalent that every page would be cluttered with dots if we did. We likewise omit footnotes in opinions without marking the omission; when we retain footnotes we also retain their original numbering. Finally, in quoted cases, we usually omit any internal quotation marks to make materials more readable.

This edition contains numerous citations to the Restatement of Torts, and sometimes to the Restatement of Agency or other areas of relevant law. The Restatements of the Law are the product of the American Law Institute, a private law-reform group founded in 1923. The Restatements are not themselves law, but have proven quite influential with courts, many of which have voluntarily adopted the black-letter rules or commentary contained in Restatements. The newest torts Restatements are designated as Restatement (Third) of Torts, with subtitles to indicate the particular subject area covered—for instance, Liability for Physical and Emotional Harm, or Products Liability. Because the Restatement Third is not complete, the Restatement (Second) is still the most recent authority on some areas of tort law. Even in areas in which the Third Restatement exists, courts today may cite both the Second *and* Third Restatements, or pick either version over the other.

We hope that professors and students alike will learn from this book and enjoy the many thoughtful and thought-provoking cases presented here. As always, we have greatly enjoyed assembling them for you.

PAUL T. HAYDEN
ELLEN M. BUBLICK

March 2022

ACKNOWLEDGMENTS

We owe real thanks to many people who aided our work on this edition. Thanks particularly to Thomas Corrigan and Hannah Miller whose thoughtful and diligent work improved many chapters, and to Jefferson Abbey, Thomas Anagnostos, Neil Berglund, Laurel Comiter, Brian Fullmer, Jacqui Marzocca, Shawnee Melnick, and Carissa Pryor, whose research assistance and suggestions helped make this edition the best to date. Thanks also to David Jacobs for his careful edits of many chapters, to Andy Coan for his review of our work on qualified immunity, to Barbara Atwood for her assistance with issues of procedure, and to Jane Bambauer and Daniel Arellano for their insights on the defamation and privacy torts.

One of our great good fortunes has been the ability to collaborate with so many fine torts scholars from around the country who teach this book and have shared suggestions to improve it. For thoughtful suggested changes to the Ninth Edition we thank Hillel Bavli, Bari Burke, Anthony Dillof, Matthew Fraidin, Steven Friedell, Antonio Gidi, Abby Jones, Tom Mayo, Miranda McGowan, Kimberly Norwood, Chris Robertson, Deana Pollard Sacks, Roger Schechter, Barbara Stark, Merle Weiner, and Fred Yen. Many fine suggestions which have led us to change material also come from students who use our book. In this regard, we particularly thank Slam Dunkley, Russell Facente, Dawn Henry, Todd Proebsting, Michael Victor, Allison Weber, and Kate Zosky.

Paul adds kudos to the research librarians at Loyola Law School. Ellen also thanks Dean Miller for support for scholarship, Dave Heineking for workspace in Phoenix, Shaun Esposito for library research, and Barb Vandervelde and Bert Skye for help with this manuscript.

Paul and Ellen give special thanks to Dan Dobbs for his vision, his hard work, his advice, and his friendship. We also thank the outstanding professionals at West Academic, who improve our work, support our efforts, and are a great a pleasure to work with. Finally, we are grateful to our students, past and present, who continue to inspire, engage and teach us.

SUMMARY OF CONTENTS

PREFACE TO THE NINTH EDITION V

ACKNOWLEDGMENTS IX

TABLE OF CASES XXIX

PART 1. A FIRST LOOK AT TORTS

Chapter 1. Tort Law: Aims, Approaches, and Processes 3
§ 1. What Is Tort Law? 3
§ 2. The Goals of Tort Law 4
§ 3. Implementing Tort Law's Goals with Damages Awards 11

Chapter 2. Reading Torts Cases and Understanding Trial Procedure 19
§ 1. Looking for Facts, Rules, and Reasons 19
§ 2. Procedures at Trial 21

PART 2. INTENTIONAL TORTS

Chapter 3. Intentional Torts to Person or Property 37
§ 1. Battery 37
§ 2. Assault 58
§ 3. False Imprisonment 63
§ 4. Torts to Property 67
§ 5. Forcible Harms as Federal Civil Rights Violations: § 1983 Claims 77

Chapter 4. Defenses to Intentional Torts—Privileges 91
§ 1. Protecting Against the Plaintiff's Apparent Misconduct 91
§ 2. The Special Case of Consent 108
§ 3. Public and Private Necessity 120

PART 3. THE PRIMA FACIE CASE FOR NEGLIGENCE

Chapter 5. The Prima Facie Case for Negligence and the Element of Duty 131
§ 1. Theory and Elements of Negligence 131
§ 2. The General Duty of Care: The Reasonable and Prudent Person Standard 135
§ 3. Negligence Per Se: Using Safety-Related Rules to Specify Particular Tort Duties 152

Chapter 6. Breach of Duty 171
§ 1. Determining Breach 171
§ 2. Unstructured Weighing of Risks and Costs 180

§ 3. Structured Weighing of Risks and Costs 192
§ 4. Assessing Responsibility When More than One Person Is Negligent... 197
§ 5. Proving and Evaluating Conduct 201
§ 6. Evaluating Conduct Through Notice and Opportunity to Cure 212
§ 7. Violation of Private Standard or Common Custom 215
§ 8. Compliance with Statute 221
§ 9. Unspecified Negligence: Res Ipsa Loquitur 222

Chapter 7. Actual Harm and Factual Cause 237
§ 1. Actual Harm 237
§ 2. Factual Cause 241

Chapter 8. Scope of Liability (Proximate Cause) 273
§ 1. The Principle: Scope of Risk 273
§ 2. Assessing the Scope of the Risk... 290
§ 3. Intervening Causes 297

PART 4. DEFENSES TO THE NEGLIGENCE CASE

Chapter 9. Fault of the Plaintiff... 321
§ 1. Contributory Negligence: The Common Law Rule 321
§ 2. Adopting Comparative Fault Rules 323
§ 3. Applying Comparative Fault Rules.. 325
§ 4. All-or-Nothing Judgments After Comparative Fault.......................... 335
§ 5. Allocating Full Responsibility to the Defendant in the Interests of
    Policy or Justice.. 338
§ 6. Traditional Exceptions to the Contributory Negligence Bar................. 349

Chapter 10. Assumption of the Risk... 357
§ 1. Express Assumption of the Risk (Contractual) 357
§ 2. Primary Implied Assumption of the Risk 364
§ 3. Secondary Implied Assumption of the Risk...................................... 371

Chapter 11. Defenses Not on the Merits... 377
§ 1. Statutes of Limitation and Repose... 377
§ 2. Federal Preemption.. 395

PART 5. LIMITING OR EXPANDING THE DUTY OF CARE
ACCORDING TO CONTEXT OR RELATIONSHIP

Chapter 12. Carriers, Host-Drivers and Landowners........................... 403
§ 1. Carriers and Host-Drivers... 403
§ 2. Landowners' Duties to Entrants 407
§ 3. Landlords' Duty to Tenants... 434
§ 4. The Firefighter's Rule 437

Chapter 13. Duties of Health-Care Providers...................................... 445
§ 1. The Standard of Care in Medical Malpractice Actions........................ 445

§ 2. Informed Consent 458
§ 3. Res Ipsa Loquitur in Medical Malpractice Cases 467
§ 4. Statutory Reforms 474
§ 5. Elder Abuse in Nursing Homes and Other Care Facilities 484

Chapter 14. Family Members and Charities 489
§ 1. Family Members 489
§ 2. Charities 497

Chapter 15. Governmental Immunity 503
§ 1. Traditional Immunities and Their Passing: An Overview 503
§ 2. The Federal Tort Claims Act 504
§ 3. Immunity of States and Municipalities 523

PART 6. LIMITING THE DUTY OF CARE BASED ON RELATIONSHIPS OR THEIR ABSENCE

Chapter 16. Misfeasance and Nonfeasance 543
§ 1. The Misfeasance-Nonfeasance Distinction 543
§ 2. Nonfeasance and Exceptions: Affirmative Duties 553

Chapter 17. Contract and Duty 567
§ 1. Misfeasance in the Performance of a Contract: Liability for Physical
     and Economic Harm 567
§ 2. Nonfeasance in the Performance of a Contract and Liability for
     Physical Harm 572
§ 3. Scope of Duty Based on Undertaking 576
§ 4. Duty to Third Parties Based on Undertaking to Another 579
§ 5. Action as a Promise or Undertaking 585

Chapter 18. The Duty to Protect from Third Persons 589
§ 1. The General Rule and Its Exceptions 589
§ 2. Defendant's Relationship with the Plaintiff 597
§ 3. Defendant's Relationship with Dangerous Persons 614

PART 7. SPECIAL TYPES OF HARM

Chapter 19. Emotional Harm 637
§ 1. Intentional Infliction of Emotional Distress 637
§ 2. Negligent Infliction of Emotional Distress 647

Chapter 20. Prenatal Harms 675
§ 1. Prenatal and Preconception Injury 675
§ 2. Wrongful Birth, Conception, or Life 682

Chapter 21. Wrongful Death and Survival Actions 689
§ 1. Statutory Actions 690
§ 2. Damages 694

§ 3. Beneficiaries 703
§ 4. Defenses 705

PART 8. THE EBB AND FLOW OF COMMON LAW STRICT LIABILITY FOR PHYSICAL HARMS

Chapter 22. Vicarious Liability 711
§ 1. Respondeat Superior and Scope of Employment..................... 711
§ 2. Independent Contractors and Ostensible Agents 735
§ 3. Other Forms of Vicarious Responsibility................................ 748

Chapter 23. Common Law Strict Liability 753
§ 1. Historical Strict Liability for Trespassory Torts and the Advent of Fault Theory 753
§ 2. Strict Liability Today 754

Chapter 24. Tort Liability for Defective Products 777
§ 1. History, Rationales, and Scope of Products Liability 777
§ 2. Establishing a Prima Facie Case 799
§ 3. Defenses and Defeats 843

PART 9. PRACTICALITIES AND VALUES

Chapter 25. Apportionment and Settlement 871
§ 1. Apportionment Systems... 871
§ 2. Apportionment with Joint and Several Liability 874
§ 3. Apportionment in Jurisdictions with Several Liability 878
§ 4. Methods of Apportioning Liability: Special Contexts 892
§ 5. An Introduction to Settlements... 905

Chapter 26. Damages 913
§ 1. Compensatory Damages 913
§ 2. Punitive Damages 934

Chapter 27. Evaluating Tort Law 959
§ 1. Rules, Practices and Theories of Tort Law 959
§ 2. Tort Wars.. 960
§ 3. The Impact of Tort Law on the Injury Problem 963

PART 10. ALTERNATIVES TO TORT LAW

Chapter 28. Workers' Compensation 975
§ 1. Introduction 975
§ 2. Job-Related Injury... 983
§ 3. Workers' Compensation as the Exclusive Remedy 1003
§ 4. Tort Claims Against Third Parties 1010

**Chapter 29. Public Compensation Systems, Including Social
    Security** **1013**
§ 1. Compensation Schemes That Replace Tort Liability 1013
§ 2. Social Security Disability Benefits 1018

Chapter 30. Private Insurance Solutions **1029**

Chapter 31. Evaluating Injury Systems: A Discussion Agenda **1041**

PART 11. ECONOMIC AND DIGNITARY TORTS

**Chapter 32. Communication of Personally Harmful Impressions
    to Others** **1045**
§ 1. Defamation—Libel and Slander 1045
§ 2. Malicious Prosecution and Other Abuses of the Legal System 1068
§ 3. Privacy 1076
§ 4. Interference with Family Relationships 1082

**Chapter 33. Communication of Commercially Harmful
    Impressions to Others** **1085**
§ 1. Injurious Falsehood 1085
§ 2. Intentional Interference with Contract and Expectancy 1088
§ 3. Intellectual Property and Unfair Competition—Trademark
    Infringement 1097
§ 4. Misappropriation of Commercial Value 1103

Chapter 34. Misrepresentation and Other Misdealings **1107**
§ 1. Misrepresentation Causing Physical Harm 1107
§ 2. Misrepresentation in an Economic Context: Theories of Liability
    and Their Consequences 1114
§ 3. Reliance and Related Doctrines 1124
§ 4. Duty to Disclose 1130

INDEX 1137

TABLE OF CONTENTS

———

PREFACE TO THE NINTH EDITION... V

ACKNOWLEDGMENTS IX

TABLE OF CASES XXIX

PART 1. A FIRST LOOK AT TORTS

Chapter 1. Tort Law: Aims, Approaches, and Processes........................ 3
§ 1. What Is Tort Law?.. 3
§ 2. The Goals of Tort Law... 4
    A.   Some Broad (and Conflicting) Aims 4
        Dobbs, Hayden & Bublick, The Law of Torts 4
    B.   Approaches in Action: The Role of Fault.................................... 8
        Van Camp v. McAfoos 8
§ 3. Implementing Tort Law's Goals with Damages Awards 11
    Anderson v. Zamir 11

Chapter 2. Reading Torts Cases and Understanding Trial
Procedure 19
§ 1. Looking for Facts, Rules, and Reasons 19
§ 2. Procedures at Trial... 21

PART 2. INTENTIONAL TORTS

Chapter 3. Intentional Torts to Person or Property............................. 37
§ 1. Battery 37
    A.   Elements 37
        McElhaney v. Thomas 38
    B.   Dual or Single Intent.. 42
    C.   The Meaning of "Intent".. 46
        Garratt v. Dailey 46
    D.   Contact 52
    E.   Transferred Intent 56
§ 2. Assault 58
    Cullison v. Medley 58
§ 3. False Imprisonment 63
    McCann v. Wal-Mart Stores, Inc... 63
§ 4. Torts to Property 67
    A.   Trespass to Land 67
    B.   Conversion of Chattels—Trover 72
    C.   Trespass to Chattels.. 76

§ 5. Forcible Harms as Federal Civil Rights Violations: § 1983 Claims 77
   A.   Basic Contours: Federal Rights Violations 78
       42 U.S.C.A. § 1983 78
   B.   Qualified Immunity 82
       Rivas-Villegas v. Cortesluna 82

Chapter 4. Defenses to Intentional Torts—Privileges 91
§ 1. Protecting Against the Plaintiff's Apparent Misconduct 91
   A.   Self-Defense and Defense of Others 91
       Grimes v. Saban 91
   B.   Defense and Repossession of Property 97
       Katko v. Briney 97
       Brown v. Martinez 99
   C.   Arrest and Detention 100
       Gortarez v. Smitty's Super Valu, Inc. 100
   D.   Discipline 106
   E.   Observing Privileges 107
§ 2. The Special Case of Consent 108
   Wulf v. Kunnath 108
§ 3. Public and Private Necessity 120
   Surocco v. Geary 120
   Vincent v. Lake Erie Transportation Co. 124

PART 3. THE PRIMA FACIE CASE FOR NEGLIGENCE

**Chapter 5. The Prima Facie Case for Negligence and the Element
     of Duty 131**
§ 1. Theory and Elements of Negligence 131
   A.   The Fault Basis of Liability 131
       Oliver Wendell Holmes, The Common Law 131
   B.   Assessing Responsibility 132
   C.   Legal Elements of a Negligence Claim 133
   D.   Some Institutions of Negligence Practice 134
§ 2. The General Duty of Care: The Reasonable and Prudent Person
     Standard 135
   Stewart v. Motts 135
   Posas v. Horton 139
   Creasy v. Rusk 144
   Stevens v. Veenstra 149
§ 3. Negligence Per Se: Using Safety-Related Rules to Specify Particular
     Tort Duties 152
   O'Guin v. Bingham County 157
   Goldstein, Garber & Salama, LLC v. J.B. 164
   Getchell v. Lodge 167

Chapter 6. Breach of Duty 171
§ 1. Determining Breach 171
   A.   Intentional Torts or Intentional Acts That Involve Risk 172

B.   Foreseeability of Harm as a Prerequisite to Breach 174
     Pipher v. Parsell 174
C.   The Role of Judge and Jury 178
§ 2. Unstructured Weighing of Risks and Costs 180
     Indiana Consolidated Insurance Co. v. Mathew 180
     Stinnett v. Buchele 183
     Bernier v. Boston Edison Co. 187
§ 3. Structured Weighing of Risks and Costs 192
     United States v. Carroll Towing Co. 192
§ 4. Assessing Responsibility When More than One Person Is Negligent... 197
§ 5. Proving and Evaluating Conduct 201
A.   Proving Conduct 201
     Santiago v. First Student, Inc. 201
     Upchurch v. Rotenberry 203
§ 6. Evaluating Conduct Through Notice and Opportunity to Cure 212
     Renner v. Retzer Resources, Inc. 212
§ 7. Violation of Private Standard or Common Custom 215
A.   The Actor's Own Standard 215
B.   Custom 217
     The T.J. Hooper 218
§ 8. Compliance with Statute 221
§ 9. Unspecified Negligence: Res Ipsa Loquitur 222
A.   Origins and Basic Features 222
     Byrne v. Boadle 222
B.   Is Negligence More Probable than Not? 227
C.   Attributing Fault to the Defendant Rather than Others 231

Chapter 7. Actual Harm and Factual Cause **237**
§ 1. Actual Harm 237
     Right v. Breen 237
§ 2. Factual Cause 241
A.   The But-For Test of Causation 241
     Ziniti v. New England Central Railroad, Inc. 241
B.   Multiple Causes and Apportionment 247
C.   Problems with the But-For Test 249
     Landers v. East Texas Salt Water Disposal Company 249
D.   Alternatives to the But-For Test 252
     Lasley v. Combined Transport, Inc. 252
E.   Proof: What Harm Was Caused? 258
     Summers v. Tice 258
     Mohr v. Grantham 261

Chapter 8. Scope of Liability (Proximate Cause) **273**
§ 1. The Principle: Scope of Risk 273
     Thompson v. Kaczinski 274
     Palsgraf v. Long Island Railroad Co. 281

§ 2. Assessing the Scope of the Risk 290
     A.   Is Harm Outside the Scope of the Risk Because of the Manner
         in Which It Occurs? 290
         Ruiz v. Victory Properties LLC 290
     B.   Is Harm Outside the Scope of the Risk Because Its Extent Is
         Unforeseeable? 295
§ 3. Intervening Causes 297
     A.   Intentional or Criminal Intervening Acts 298
         Marcus v. Staubs 298
     B.   Negligent Intervening Acts 306
         Derdiarian v. Felix Contracting Corp. 306
         Torres v. JAI Dining Services (Phoenix) Inc. 310
         Marshall v. Nugent 311

PART 4. DEFENSES TO THE NEGLIGENCE CASE

Chapter 9. Fault of the Plaintiff 321
§ 1. Contributory Negligence: The Common Law Rule 321
     Butterfield v. Forrester 321
§ 2. Adopting Comparative Fault Rules 323
     New York Mckinney's Civ. Prac. Law § 1411 323
     Wisconsin Stat. Ann. § 895.045 323
§ 3. Applying Comparative Fault Rules 325
     A.   Apportioning Fault 325
         Pohl v. County of Furnas 325
     B.   Apportioning Responsibility 332
         Restatement (Third) of Torts: Apportionment of Liability 332
§ 4. All-or-Nothing Judgments After Comparative Fault 335
§ 5. Allocating Full Responsibility to the Defendant in the Interests of
     Policy or Justice 338
     Bexiga v. Havir Manufacturing Corp. 338
     Christensen v. Royal School District No. 160 343
§ 6. Traditional Exceptions to the Contributory Negligence Bar 349
     A.   The Rescue Doctrine 349
     B.   Last Clear Chance or Discovered Peril 349
     C.   Defendant's Reckless or Intentional Misconduct 350
     D.   Plaintiff's Illegal Activity 351
         Dugger v. Arredondo 351

Chapter 10. Assumption of the Risk 357
§ 1. Express Assumption of the Risk (Contractual) 357
     Moore v. Hartley Motors 361
§ 2. Primary Implied Assumption of the Risk 364
     Coomer v. Kansas City Royals Baseball Corp. 366
§ 3. Secondary Implied Assumption of the Risk 371
     Simmons v. Porter 371

Chapter 11. Defenses Not on the Merits.. 377
§ 1. Statutes of Limitation and Repose 377
    A.   Statutes of Limitation 378
        Crumpton v. Humana, Inc. 378
        Schmitz v. National Collegiate Athletic Ass'n 380
    B.   Statutes of Repose 392
        Durre v. Wilkinson Development, Inc. 392
§ 2. Federal Preemption.. 395
    Vreeland v. Ferrer 395

PART 5. LIMITING OR EXPANDING THE DUTY OF CARE ACCORDING TO CONTEXT OR RELATIONSHIP

Chapter 12. Carriers, Host-Drivers and Landowners....................... 403
§ 1. Carriers and Host-Drivers 403
    Ala. Code § 32–1–2 405
§ 2. Landowners' Duties to Entrants 407
    A.   Traditional Common-Law Duties............................... 407
        Catholic Diocese of El Paso v. Porter 407
    B.   Child Trespassers 414
        Bennett v. Stanley.. 414
    C.   Modifying the Traditional Common-Law Duties Owed to Entrants 419
        Rowland v. Christian... 419
    D.   Open and Obvious Hazards 423
        Kentucky River Medical Center v. McIntosh 423
    E.   Recreational-Use Statutes 430
§ 3. Landlords' Duty to Tenants 434
    Pagelsdorf v. Safeco Insurance Co. 434
§ 4. The Firefighter's Rule 437
    Minnich v. Med-Waste, Inc. 437

Chapter 13. Duties of Health-Care Providers.................................... 445
§ 1. The Standard of Care in Medical Malpractice Actions......................... 445
    Walski v. Tiesenga 445
    Vergara v. Doan.. 451
§ 2. Informed Consent 458
    Harnish v. Children's Hospital Medical Center 458
§ 3. Res Ipsa Loquitur in Medical Malpractice Cases................. 467
    Ybarra v. Spangard 467
    States v. Lourdes Hospital.. 471
§ 4. Statutory Reforms 474
    A.   The Medical Malpractice "Crisis" 474
    B.   Legislative Responses 476
    C.   State Constitutional Challenges to Statutory Reform ... 478

    D.   EMTALA Claims: Mandatory Emergency Treatment and
        Screening 480
        42 U.S.C.A. § 1395dd 480
§ 5. Elder Abuse in Nursing Homes and Other Care Facilities 484

Chapter 14. Family Members and Charities 489
§ 1. Family Members 489
    A.   The Traditional Family Immunities 489
    B.   The Contours of Parental Immunity 492
        Neel v. Sewell 492
§ 2. Charities 497

Chapter 15. Governmental Immunity 503
§ 1. Traditional Immunities and Their Passing: An Overview 503
§ 2. The Federal Tort Claims Act 504
    A.   Basic Scope and Limits 504
    B.   Discretionary Immunity 509
        Hajdusek v. United States 509
    C.   The *Feres* Doctrine 519
        Purcell v. United States 519
§ 3. Immunity of States and Municipalities 523
    A.   Under State Law 523
        Riss v. City of New York 523
        Harry Stoller and Co. v. City of Lowell 527
    B.   Under Federal Law: § 1983 535
        Navarro v. Block 536

PART 6. LIMITING THE DUTY OF CARE BASED ON RELATIONSHIPS OR THEIR ABSENCE

Chapter 16. Misfeasance and Nonfeasance 543
§ 1. The Misfeasance-Nonfeasance Distinction 543
    Boynton v. Kennecott Utah Copper, LLC 545
§ 2. Nonfeasance and Exceptions: Affirmative Duties 553
    Wakulich v. Mraz 557
    Podias v. Mairs 561

Chapter 17. Contract and Duty 567
§ 1. Misfeasance in the Performance of a Contract: Liability for Physical
    and Economic Harm 567
    Tingler v. Greystone Homes, Inc. 567
§ 2. Nonfeasance in the Performance of a Contract and Liability for
    Physical Harm 572
    Langlois v. Town of Proctor 572
§ 3. Scope of Duty Based on Undertaking 576
§ 4. Duty to Third Parties Based on Undertaking to Another 579
    A.   The Modern Rule 579
    B.   An Historical Perspective 582

§ 5. Action as a Promise or Undertaking 585

Florence v. Goldberg 585

Chapter 18. The Duty to Protect from Third Persons 589

§ 1. The General Rule and Its Exceptions 589

Brown v. USA Taekwondo 589

§ 2. Defendant's Relationship with the Plaintiff 597

Posecai v. Wal-Mart Stores, Inc. 597

Marquay v. Eno 603

Wright v. PRG Real Estate Management, Inc. 610

§ 3. Defendant's Relationship with Dangerous Persons 614

Tarasoff v. Regents of University of California 619

Brigance v. Velvet Dove Restaurant, Inc. 625

PART 7. SPECIAL TYPES OF HARM

Chapter 19. Emotional Harm 637

§ 1. Intentional Infliction of Emotional Distress 637

Chanko v. American Broadcasting Companies, Inc. 637

§ 2. Negligent Infliction of Emotional Distress 647

A. Emotional Distress from Direct Risks of Physical Harm 647

B. Emotional Distress Resulting from Injury to Another 651

Catron v. Lewis 651

Boucher v. Dixie Medical Center 658

C. Duties of Care to Protect Emotional Well-Being Independent of
Physical Risks 662

D. Negligent Infliction of Emotional Distress as an Ordinary
Negligence Claim? 667

E. Toxic Exposures: Fear of Future Harm 668

Potter v. Firestone Tire & Rubber Co. 668

Chapter 20. Prenatal Harms 675

§ 1. Prenatal and Preconception Injury 675

Remy v. MacDonald 675

§ 2. Wrongful Birth, Conception, or Life 682

Shull v. Reid 682

Chapter 21. Wrongful Death and Survival Actions 689

§ 1. Statutory Actions 690

Weigel v. Lee 690

§ 2. Damages 694

Laney v. Vance 694

Final Report of the Special Master for the September 11th Victim
Compensation Fund of 2001 699

§ 3. Beneficiaries 703

§ 4. Defenses 705

A. Contributory Negligence and Assumption of Risk 705

B. Statute of Limitations 706

PART 8. THE EBB AND FLOW OF COMMON LAW STRICT LIABILITY FOR PHYSICAL HARMS

Chapter 22. Vicarious Liability 711
§ 1. Respondeat Superior and Scope of Employment.................................. 711
    Cameron v. Osler.. 713
    Hinman v. Westinghouse Electric Co. 719
    Edgewater Motels, Inc. v. Gatzke 722
    Montague v. AMN Healthcare, Inc. 728
§ 2. Independent Contractors and Ostensible Agents 735
    Mavrikidis v. Petullo.. 735
    Pusey v. Bator.. 741
    O'Banner v. McDonald's Corp. 745
§ 3. Other Forms of Vicarious Responsibility... 748

Chapter 23. Common Law Strict Liability 753
§ 1. Historical Strict Liability for Trespassory Torts and the Advent of
    Fault Theory 753
§ 2. Strict Liability Today 754
    A.   Injuries Caused by Animals.. 755
          1.   Trespassing Animals 755
          2.   Abnormally Dangerous Animals.. 756
          3.   Wild Animals 757
    B.   Impoundments, Nuisances and Beyond....................................... 757
        Rylands v. Fletcher... 757
    C.   Abnormally Dangerous Activities 767
        Dyer v. Maine Drilling & Blasting, Inc. 767

Chapter 24. Tort Liability for Defective Products 777
§ 1. History, Rationales, and Scope of Products Liability 777
    A.   The Evolution of Liability Theories.. 777
    B.   Rationales for Strict Products Liability 781
    C.   Who Is Subject to Strict Liability? 784
        Loomis v. Amazon.com LLC 784
    D.   Excluding Stand-Alone Economic Harm: Products Liability's
        Economic Loss Rule... 794
        Moorman Mfg. Co. v. National Tank Co. 794
§ 2. Establishing a Prima Facie Case 799
    A.   Manufacturing Defects... 799
        Lee v. Crookston Coca-Cola Bottling Co. 799
    B.   Design Defects 806
        Knitz v. Minster Machine Co.. 809
        Genie Industries, Inc. v. Matak.. 813
        McCarthy v. Olin Corp. 820
    C.   Warning or Information Defects.. 826
        Liriano v. Hobart Corp. 826
    D.   Special Issues of Proof... 838

§ 3. Defenses and Defeats 843
   A. Comparative Fault and Assumption of Risk 843
        Bowling v. Heil Co. 843
   B. Misuse 848
        Hughes v. Magic Chef, Inc. 848
   C. Federal Preemption 857
        Doomes v. Best Transit Corp. 857
   D. The Government Contractor Defense 863
   E. Statutes of Limitation 865

PART 9. PRACTICALITIES AND VALUES

Chapter 25. Apportionment and Settlement 871
§ 1. Apportionment Systems 871
     Dobbs, Hayden & Bublick, The Law of Torts 871
§ 2. Apportionment with Joint and Several Liability 874
§ 3. Apportionment in Jurisdictions with Several Liability 878
   A. Abolishing or Limiting Joint and Several Liability 878
        Cal. Civ. Code § 1431.2 878
   B. Types of Actionable Conduct Subject to Apportionment 880
        Board of County Commissioners of Teton County v. Bassett 881
   C. Non-Parties at Fault 886
        Cramer v. Starr 886
§ 4. Methods of Apportioning Liability: Special Contexts 892
   A. Crashworthiness Cases: Causal or Fault Apportionment? 892
        D'Amario v. Ford Motor Co. 892
   B. Market Share Liability 897
        Hymowitz v. Eli Lilly & Co. 897
§ 5. An Introduction to Settlements 905
   A. Basic Rules 906
   B. Improvident Settlement 907
        Gleason v. Guzman 907

Chapter 26. Damages 913
§ 1. Compensatory Damages 913
   A. Proving and Computing Basic Damages 913
        Martin v. United States 916
   B. Lost Enjoyment of Life 921
   C. Adjustments in Damages 926
   D. Capping and Limiting Damages 929
        Cal. Civ. Code § 3333.2 929
        Md. Code Ann., Cts. & Jud. Proc. § 11–108 930
§ 2. Punitive Damages 934
   A. General Rules 934
        Dan B. Dobbs, The Law of Remedies 934
   B. Measurement of Punitive Damages 937
        State Farm Mut. Auto. Ins. Co. v. Campbell 940

   Mathias v. Accor Economy Lodging, Inc. 950

Chapter 27. Evaluating Tort Law **959**
§ 1. Rules, Practices and Theories of Tort Law 959
§ 2. Tort Wars 960
§ 3. The Impact of Tort Law on the Injury Problem 963

PART 10. ALTERNATIVES TO TORT LAW

Chapter 28. Workers' Compensation **975**
§ 1. Introduction 975
 A. The Employer's Tort Liability at Common Law 975
 B. The Adoption of Workers' Compensation 976
 C. Characteristics of the Statutes 977
 D. Coverage 978
 E. Benefits 979
§ 2. Job-Related Injury 983
 A. Arising Out of and in the Course of Employment 983
  Wait v. Travelers Indemnity Co. of Illinois 983
  Carvalho v. Decorative Fabrics Co. 990
 B. Accident, Injury and Disease 993
  Harris v. Board of Education of Howard County 995
 C. Multiple Exposure or Injury 1001
§ 3. Workers' Compensation as the Exclusive Remedy 1003
 Bowden v. Young 1004
§ 4. Tort Claims Against Third Parties 1010
 A. Co-Employees 1010
 B. The Statutory Employer and Borrowed Servants 1011
 C. Adjustments Among the Parties 1011

Chapter 29. Public Compensation Systems, Including Social
  Security **1013**
§ 1. Compensation Schemes That Replace Tort Liability 1013
 A. Taxing Industry and Eliminating Its Tort Liability 1013
 B. Taxing the Public to Protect Industries and Provide
  Compensation to Victims—the 9/11 Compensation System 1016
§ 2. Social Security Disability Benefits 1018
  42 U.S.C.A. § 423 1018
  Heckler v. Campbell 1023

Chapter 30. Private Insurance Solutions **1029**
New York Insurance Law 1032
New York Insurance Law 1033
Licari v. Elliott 1035

Chapter 31. Evaluating Injury Systems: A Discussion Agenda **1041**

PART 11. ECONOMIC AND DIGNITARY TORTS

Chapter 32. Communication of Personally Harmful Impressions to Others 1045
§ 1. Defamation—Libel and Slander 1045
    A. The Common Law Rules 1045
    B. The Constitutional Constraints of Free Speech 1053
        New York Times Co. v. Sullivan 1053
        Gertz v. Robert Welch, Inc. 1059
    C. Defamation in the Internet Age 1067
        Bublick, Bambauer & Arellano, Dobbs on Economic and Dignitary Torts 1067
§ 2. Malicious Prosecution and Other Abuses of the Legal System 1068
    A. Malicious Prosecution 1068
    B. Improper Civil Litigation 1071
    C. Abuse of Process 1074
§ 3. Privacy 1076
§ 4. Interference with Family Relationships 1082

Chapter 33. Communication of Commercially Harmful Impressions to Others 1085
§ 1. Injurious Falsehood 1085
    Brunson Communications, Inc. v. Arbitron, Inc. 1085
§ 2. Intentional Interference with Contract and Expectancy 1088
    Restatement (Third) of Torts: Liability for Economic Harm 1091
    Eldridge v. Johndrow 1091
§ 3. Intellectual Property and Unfair Competition—Trademark Infringement 1097
    Qualitex Co. v. Jacobson Products Co. 1099
§ 4. Misappropriation of Commercial Value 1103

Chapter 34. Misrepresentation and Other Misdealings 1107
§ 1. Misrepresentation Causing Physical Harm 1107
    Jowers v. BOC Group, Inc. 1107
§ 2. Misrepresentation in an Economic Context: Theories of Liability and Their Consequences 1114
    Ultramares Corp. v. Touche, Niven & Co. 1117
    Gauerke v. Rozga 1122
§ 3. Reliance and Related Doctrines 1124
§ 4. Duty to Disclose 1130
    Ollerman v. O'Rourke Co. 1130

INDEX 1137

TABLE OF CASES

The principal cases are in bold type.

———

5 Star, Inc. v. Ford Motor Co., 811
66 Fed. Credit Union v. Tucker, 680
985 Assocs., Ltd. v. Daewoo Electronics America, Inc., 841
20801, Inc. v. Parker, 632
A. O. Smith Corp. v. United States, 517
A.C., In re, 462
A.H. ex rel. C.H. v. Church of God in Christ, Inc., 733
A.R.B. v. Elkin, 55
A.W. v. Lancaster County Sch. Dist., 602, 608
AALAR, Ltd. v. Francis, 650
Abacus Fed. Sav. Bank v. ADT Sec. Servs., Inc., 575
Abdel-Samed v. Dailey, 457
Abel v. Eli Lilly & Co., 903
Abney v. Crosman Corp., 831
Abrams v. City of Chicago, 278
ACA Financial Guaranty Corp. v. Goldman, Sachs & Co., 1126
Accutane Litigation, In re, 837
Ackerson v. Bean Dredging LLC, 518
Adames v. Sheahan, 310, 713
Adams v. Board of Sedgwick County Com'rs, 624
Adams v. Murakami, 938
Adams v. State, 529
Adickes v. S.H. Kress & Co., 78
Aegis Ins. Services, Inc. v. 7 World Trade Co., L.P., 244
Affiliated FM Ins. Co. v. LTK Consulting Servs., Inc., 571
Agar Corp. v. Electro Circuits Int'l, LLC, 749
"Agent Orange" Product Liability Litigation, In re, 864
Aguallo v. City of Scottsbluff, 334
Ah Mook Sang v. Clark, 559
Ahlstrom v. Salt Lake City Corp., 721
Air & Liquid Systems Corp. v. DeVries, 836
Air Wisconsin Airlines Corp. v. Hoeper, 1050
Alarid v. Vanier, 169
Albala v. City of New York, 681
Albany Urology Clinic, P.C. v. Cleveland, 464
Alberts v. Schultz, 268
Alcala v. Marriott Intern., Inc., 618

Aldana v. School City of East Chicago, 233
Alderwoods (Pa.), Inc. v. Duquesne Light Co., 138
Aldorasi v. Crossroads Hosp. & Mgmt. Co., 545
Aleo v. SLB Toys USA, Inc., 161
Alexander v. Scheid, 267, 268
Ali v. City of Boston, 434
Ali v. Fisher, 750
Allen v. Lockwood, 176
Allenberg v. Bentley Hedges Travel Serv., Inc., 792
Allied Concrete Co. v. Lester, 924
Almonte v. Kurl, 268
Alphonse v. Acadian Ambulance Servs., Inc., 268
Alsteen v. Wauleco, Inc., 926
Alston v. Advanced Brands & Importing Co., 301
Amaral v. Cuppels, 70
Amazon.com, Inc. v. McMillan, 791
Ambers-Phillips v. SSM DePaul Health Center, 394
Ambling Management Co. v. Miller, 718
America v. Sunspray Condominium Ass'n, 240
American Biomedical Group, Inc. v. Techtrol, Inc., 74
American Future Systems, Inc. v. Better Business Bureau of Eastern Pennsylvania, 1064
American Optical Co. v. Weidenhamer, 831
American Radiology Services, LLC v. Reiss, 449
Amezcua v. Los Angeles Harley-Davidson, 364
Amos v. Lincoln Cty. Sch. Dist. No. 2, 211
Anaya v. Superior Court, 314
Andersen v. Khanna, 464
Anderson ex rel. Herren v. Iowa Dermatology Clinic, PLC, 391
Anderson v. Chicago Transit Authority, 404
Anderson v. Christopherson, 280
Anderson v. City of Bessemer, 328
Anderson v. Mandalay Corp., 731

Anderson v. Minneapolis, St. Paul & Sault Ste. Marie Railway, 251
Anderson v. PPCT Management Systems, Inc., 740
Anderson v. Soap Lake School Dist., 734
Anderson v. Stream, 495
Anderson v. Union Pac. R.R. Co., 231
Anderson v. Zamir, 11
Andreu v. Sec'y of Health & Human Services, 1015
Andrews v. Metropolitan Water Reclamation Dist. of Greater Chicago, 529
Angersola v. Radiologic Assocs. of Middletown P.C., 707
Angland v. Mountain Creek Resort, Inc., 371
Ann M. v. Pacific Plaza Shopping Center, 601
Arato v. Avedon, 465
Arbino v. Johnson & Johnson, 933
Arche v. United States of America, Department of the Army, 683
Archuleta v. City of Rawlins, 391
Ardinger v. Hummell, 151, 633
Argentine Republic v. Amerada Hess Shipping Corp., 647
Argereow v. Weisberg, 644
Armantrout v. Carlson, 697
Arnesen v. Rivers Edge Golf Club & Plantation, Inc., 1134
Arnoult v. Webster, 384
Aronberg v. Tolbert, 355
Arpin v. United States, 924
Arrant v. Graphic Packaging Intern., Inc., 1001
Arrington v. Wong, 481
Arroyo v. United States, 142, 152
Ascuitto v. Farricielli, 490
Ashcroft v. Iqbal, 509
Ashe v. Radiation Oncology Assocs., 462
Ashmore v. Hartford Hosp., 661
Atlanta Oculoplastic Surgery, P.C. v. Nestlehutt, 932
Atlantic Coast Airlines v. Cook, 650
Atlantic Coast Shipping Co. v. Stasiak, 998
Aubin v. Union Carbide Corp., 810, 817
Audler v. CBC Innovis Inc., 1119
Ault v. International Harvester Co., 840
Auslander Properties, LLC v. Nalley, 185
Auster v. Norwalk United Methodist Church, 155
Austin v. Kaness, 718

Aventis Pasteur, Inc. v. Skevofilax, 842
Averyt v. Wal-Mart, 922
Avila v. Citrus Community College Dist., 371
Avilla v. Newport Grand Jai Alai LLC, 1093
Ayers v. Jackson Twp., 388
B.B. v. County of Los Angeles, 333
B.D.H. v. Mickelson, 687
B.R. ex rel. Jeffs v. West, 277, 552
Babb v. Lee Cty. Landfill SC, LLC, 70, 71
Babes Showclub, Jaba, Inc. v. Lair, 440
Bader v. Johnson, 685
Badilla v. Midwest Air Traffic Control Service, Inc., 519
Bagley v. Mt. Bachelor, Inc., 360
Bailey v. C.S., 50
Bailey v. Schaff, 600, 613
Baker v. Bolton, 689
Baker v. Dorfman, 665
Baker v. Parsons, 1076
Baker v. Saint Francis Hosp., 733
Bakerman v. The Bombay Co., 1006
Baker-Smith v. Skolnick, 169
Baldasarre v. Butler, 737
Baldonado v. El Paso Natural Gas Co., 441
Ball v. United States, 515
Ball-Foster Glass Container Co. v. Giovanelli, 989
Baltimore & O.R. Co. v. Goodman, 156
Bank v. Mickels, 454
Banks v. Beckwith, 225
Banville v. Brennan, 71
Baptie v. Bruno, 534
Baptiste v. Bethlehem Landfill Co., 766
Barbie v. Minko Constr., Inc., 234
Barbre v. Pope, 457
Barclay v. Briscoe, 619, 721
Bard v. Jahnke, 756
Barillari v. City of Milwaukee, 527
Barker v. Kallish, 354
Barker v. Lull Engineering Co., 812
Barkley v. McKeever Enters., Inc., 104
Barneck v. Utah Dept. of Transp., 530
Barnes v. Gorman, 936
Barnes v. Paulin, 341
Barnes v. United States, 180
Barnett v. Clark, 730
Barnish v. KWI Building Co., 802
Barris v. County of Los Angeles, 484
Barry v. Quality Steel Prods., Inc., 317
Bartell v. State, 116
Barth v. Coleman, 883

Bartholomay v. Plains Grain & Agronomy, LLC, 1006

Bartholomew v. Wisconsin Patient's Comp. Fund, 698

Basic Energy Services, L.P. v. Petroleum Resource Mgmt. Corp., 741

Baska v. Scherzer, 56

Bass v. Gopal, Inc., 601

Bassett v. Lamantia, 533

Battalla v. State, 649

Baudanza v. Comcast of Massachusetts I, Inc., 325

Bauer v. Nesbitt, 632

Bauman v. Crawford, 170

Baumann v. Zhukov, 314

Baxter v. Bracey, 89

Baxter v. Ford Motor Co., 779

BDO Seidman, LLP v. Mindis Acquisition Corp., 1122

Beach v. University of Utah, 610

Bebry v. Zanauskas, 616

Beck v. Dobrowski, 172

Becker v. Mayo Found., 607

Beddingfield v. Linam, 616

Beggs v. State, Dep't of Social & Health Services, 163, 607

Behr v. Richmond, 1113

Bell ex rel. Bell v. Dawson, 561

Bell v. Grow With Me Childcare & Preschool LLC, 595

Bell v. Josselyn, 544

Below v. Norton, 1130

Benaquista v. Municipal Housing Authority, 278

Benham v. Morton & Furbish Agency, 436

Benik v. Hatcher, 437

Benjamin v. Wal-Mart Stores, Inc., 834

Bennett v. Napolitano, 422

Bennett v. Ohio Dep't of Rehab. & Correction, 65

Bennett v. Reynolds, 950, 954

Bennett v. Stanley, 414

Bennett, In re Estate of, 694

Benoit v. Saint-Gobain Performance Plastics Corp., 766, 926

Berberian v. Lynn, 147

Berberich v. Jack, 333, 883

Bergstrom v. Palmetto Health Alliance, 499

Berian v. Berberian, 650

Berman v. Laboratory Corp. of America, 1051

Berman v. Sitrin, 433

Bernardi Ortiz v. Cybex Int'l, Inc., 877

Bernie v. Catholic Diocese of Sioux Falls, 246

Bernier v. Boston Edison Co., 187

Bernson v. Browning-Farris Indus., 384

Bernstein v. Kapneck, 911

Berrier v. Simplicity Mfg., Inc., 808

Berry v. City of Chicago, 239

Bertrand v. Mullin, 1058

Best v. Taylor Mach. Works, 879

Bethel v. New York City Transit Auth., 405

Bettis v. Islamic Republic of Iran, 646

Betts v. Crawford, 369

Bevan v. Fix, 647

Bexiga v. Havir Manufacturing Corp., 338, 848

Bhinder v. Sun Co., 885

Bibbs v. Toyota Motor Co., 699

BIC Pen Corp. v. Carter, 802, 861

Bierman v. Weier, 1047

Bily v. Arthur Young & Co., 1120

Bishop v. TES Realty Trust, 436

Bitgood v. Greene, 324

Bittner v. American Honda Motor Co., 838

Bivens v. Six Unknown Named Agents of Federal Bureau of Narcotics, 508

BJ's Wholesale Club, Inc. v. Rosen, 361

Bjerk v. Anderson, 410

Bjerke v. Johnson, 346, 596

Black v. William Insulation Co., 619

Blackburn Ltd. P'ship v. Paul, 164

Blackwell v. Wyeth, 841

Blankenship v. American Ordnance Systems, LLS, 984

Blessing, In re Estate of, 704

Blondell v. Littlepage, 1089

Blue v. Environmental Engineering, Inc., 807

BMW of North America, Inc. v. Gore, 942

BNSF Railway Co. v. Eddy, 771

Board of County Com'rs v. Brown, 81, 536

Board of County Commissioners of Teton County v. Bassett, 881

Board of Trustees of Univ. of Dist. of Columbia v. DiSalvo, 302

Bob Allyn Masonry v. Murphy, 989

Bockrath v. Aldrich Chem. Co., Inc., 261

Bogdanski v. Budzik, 735

Bogie v. Rosenberg, 1081

Boiter v. South Carolina Dep't of Transp., 931

Boler v. Security Health Care, LLC, 706

Bolger v. Amazon.com, 787

Bolton v. United States, 508

Bonanno v. Centr. Contra Costa Transit Auth., 530
Bongiorno v. Americorp, Inc., 348
Bonhomme v. St. James, 1125, 1126
Bonito Boats, Inc. v. Thunder Craft Boats, Inc., 1097
Bonness v. Armitage, 386
Bonnette v. Conoco, Inc., 271
Bonte v. Bonte, 676
Boone v. Boone, 492
Bosco v. Janowitz, 207
Bouchat v. Balt. Ravens Ltd. P'ship, 1098
Boucher v. Dixie Medical Center, 658
Bourne v. Marty Gilman, Inc., 807
Bowden v. Young, 1004
Bowling v. Heil Co., 843
Bowyer ex rel. Eskra v. Adono, 749
Boyer v. Health Grades, Inc., 1076
Boyle v. Revici, 364
Boyle v. United Technologies Corp., 863
Boyle v. Wenk, 642
Boyles v. Kerr, 666
Boynton v. Kennecott Utah Copper, LLC, 545
Braaten v. Saberhagen Holdings, 836
Bracke v. Baza'r, Inc., 1001
Brackett v. Focus Hope, Inc., 993
Bradley v. Atlantic City Bd. of Educ., 1081
Bragan v. Symanzik, 430
Bragg v. Hi-Ranger, Inc., 838
Bramer v. Dotson, 665
Brand Mktg. Grp. LLC v. Intertek Testing Servs., N.A., Inc., 1119
Brandenburg v. Briarwood Forestry Services, LLC, 744
Brandon v. County of Richardson, 347, 642, 885
Branham v. Ford Motor Co., 938
Branham v. Stewart, 295
Braswell v. Cincinnati Inc., 831
Braswell v. Stinnett, 448
Bratton v. McDonough, 642
Bray v. St. John Health System, Inc., 601
Breast Implant Prod. Liab. Litig., In re, 793
Breese v. City of Burlington, 532
Brewer v. State, 123
Brian and Christie, Inc. v. Leishman Elec., Inc., 798
Brice, Estate of v. Toyota Motor Corp., 391
Bridges v. Park Place, Entn't, 629
Brigance v. Velvet Dove Restaurant, Inc., 625

Briggs v. Southwest Energy Production Company, 67
Bristol, City of v. Tilcon Minerals, Inc., 68
Britton v. Wooten, 301
Broadbent v. Broadbent, 492, 495
Broadnax v. Gonzalez, 680
Brogan v. Mitchell Int'l, Inc., 1113
Brokaw v. Winfield-Mt. Union Cmty. Sch. Dist., 177
Bronowicz v. Allegheny County, 1071
Bronsen v. Dawes County, 432
Brooks v. City of Huntington, 914
Brooks v. Lewin Realty III, Inc., 155
Brousseau v. Haugen, 86
Brown v. Delta Tau Delta, 599
Brown v. Dibbell, 466
Brown v. Kendall, 754
Brown v. Martinez, 99
Brown v. Merlo, 406, 421
Brown v. Mobley, 176
Brown v. Shyne, 163
Brown v. Soh, 359
Brown v. State, 240
Brown v. Superior Ct., 899, 902
Brown v. USA Taekwondo, 544, 589
Brown, Estate of v. Islamic Republic of Iran, 920
Brownback v. King, 504
Brueckner v. Norwich Univ., 650
Bruesewitz v. Wyeth LLC, 862
Bruncll v. Wildwood Crest Police Dept., 1001
Bruns v. City of Centralia, 143
Brunson Communications, Inc. v. Arbitron, Inc., 1085
Brunson v. Affinity Fed. Credit Union, 1070
Bryan R. v. Watchtower Bible & Tract Soc'y of N.Y., Inc., 554
Bryan v. United States, 509
Bufkin v. Felipe's Louisiana, LLC, 428
Bukowski v. Clarkson University, 360, 371
Bullard v. MRA Holding, LLC, 1105
Buono v. Scalia, 616
Burch v. Am. Family Mut. Ins. Co., 148
Burg v. Dampier, 875
Burgess v. Fischer, 80
Burgess v. Superior Court, 662
Burke v. Mesniaeff, 97
Burke v. Raven Electric, Inc., 982
Burke v. Spartanics, Ltd., 833
Burless v. W. Va. Univ. Hospitals, Inc., 747
Burnett v. Covell, 791

Burnett v. State Dept. of Natural Resources, 530
Burnette v. Eubanks, 697
Burningham v. Wright Medical Technology, Inc., 825
Burns v. Gagnon, 607
Burns v. Jaquays Mining Corp., 925
Burrell v. Meads, 409
Burton v. State, 418
Burton v. Twin Commander Aircraft LLC, 391
Bustamante v. Ponte, 254
Butler v. Acme Mkts., Inc., 138
Butterfield v. Forrester, 321
Butts v. United States, 449
Butz v. Economou, 509
Butz v. World Wide, Inc., 690
Bylsma v. Burger King Corp., 805
Byram v. Main, 769
Byrd Theatre Foundation v. Barnett, 498
Byrd v. Faber, 733
Byrd v. Richardson-Greenshields Securities, Inc., 1009
Byrne v. Boadle, 222, 472
C.A. v. William S. Hart Union High Sch. Dist., 606
C.C.H. v. Philadelphia Phillies, Inc., 346
C.H. v. Los Lunas Schools Bd. of Educ., 277, 302
Cabral v. Ralphs Grocery Co., 245
Cafazzo v. Cent. Med. Health Servs., Inc., 793
Cagey v. Commonwealth, 530
Caldwell v. Church, 69
Camacho v. Honda Motor Co., Ltd., 832
Cameron v. Osler, 713
Campbell Hausfeld/Scott Fetzer Co. v. Johnson, 852
Campbell v. General Motors Corp., 812
Camper v. Minor, 667
Campos v. Coleman, 661
Canavan v. Galuski, 750
Cannizaro v. Marinyak, 618
Canton, City of v. Harris, 538
Caporale v. C. W. Blakeslee & Sons, Inc., 773
Caprara v. Chrysler Corporation, 840
Carcamo-Lopez v. Doe, 353
Caris v. Mele, 827
Carnegay v. WalMart Stores, Inc., 104
Caro v. Weintraub, 1081
Caronia v. Philip Morris USA, Inc., 672
Carpue v. The London and Brighton Railway Company, 223

Carr v. Wm. C. Crowell Co., 729
Carrol v. Allstate Ins. Co., 667
Carroll Towing Co., United States v., 192
Carroll v. Sisters of Saint Francis, 674
Carroll v. United States, 518
Carruth v. Pittway Corp., 833
Carson v. Here's Johnny Portable Toilets, Inc., 1103
Carter v. Reynolds, 722
Carter v. Volunteer Apparel, Inc., 985
Carvalho v. Decorative Fabrics Co., 990
Cash v. Otis Elevator Co., 404
Cashion v. Smith, 1048
Castaneda v. Olsher, 592
Castillo v. E.I. Du Pont de Nemours & Co., Inc., 842
Castle Rock, Town of v. Gonzales, 539
Castro v. Melchor, 699, 923, 924
Cates v. Cates, 491
Catholic Diocese of El Paso v. Porter, 407
Catron v. Lewis, 650, 651
Catsouras v. Department of Cal. Highway Patrol, 1079
CB & I Constructors, Inc., United States v., 914
Cedar v. Johnson, 1083
Cedillo v. Sec'y of Health & Human Services, 1016
Cefaratti v. Aranow, 747
Ceja v. Rudolph & Sletten, Inc., 694
Centocor, Inc. v. Hamilton, 835
Cerny v. Cedar Bluffs Junior/Senior Pub. Sch., 149
Chadd v. United States, 515
Chaffee v. Seslar, 686
Chaffin v. Brame, 156
Chalifoux v. Radiology Associates of Richmond, Inc., 379
Chambers v. Vill. of Moreauville, 195
Chaney v. Team Technologies, Inc., 987
Chanko v. American Broadcasting Companies, Inc., 637
Chapman Custom Homes, Inc. v. Dallas Plumbing Co., 570
Chapman v. Cardiac Pacemakers, Inc., 706
Chapman v. Harner, 226
Chapman v. Mayfield, 630
Chapman v. Maytag Corp., 852
Chappell v. Wallace, 521
Charlton v. Mond, 1058
Chavez v. Carpenter, 703
Chavez v. Cedar Fair, LP, 403
Cheatham v. Pohle, 940
Chenault v. Huie, 680

Childress v. Boeing Aerospace Operations, Inc., 65
Childs v. Purll, 436
Chizmar v. Mackie, 665, 674
Christensen v. Royal School District No. 160, 343
Christensen v. Superior Court, 665
Christiana Care Health Care Services Inc. v. Carter, 716
Christiansen v. Providence Health System of Oregon Corp., 388
Christoff v. Nestle USA, Inc., 1104
Churchman v. Bay Area Rapid Transit Dist., 404
Cilley, Estate of v. Lane, 554
Cincinnati, City of v. Beretta U.S.A. Corp., 824
Cipollone v. Liggett Groups, Inc., 1111
Cities Service Co. v. State, 763
Citizens State Bank v. Timm, Schmidt & Co., 1120
Civetti v. Turner, 529
Clark County School Dist. v. Virtual Education Software, Inc., 1051
Clark v. Children's Memorial Hosp., 685
Clark v. Estate of Rice, 650
Clark v. Pfizer Inc., 1125
Clark v. South Carolina Dept. of Public Safety, 531
Clark v. St. Dominic-Jackson Memorial Hosp., 1110
Clarke v. Oregon Health Sciences University, 479
Clausen v. Icicle Seafoods, Inc., 915
Clay Elec. Coop., Inc. v. Johnson, 580
Clea v. Odom, 419
Clements v. Aramark Corp., 988, 998
Clinkscales v. Nelson Securities, Inc., 231, 289
Clinton Healthcare, LLC v. Atkinson, 412
Cloer v. Secretary of Health & Human Services, 385
Coan v. New Hampshire Dep't of Envtl. Servs., 432
Coburn v. City of Tucson, 180
Coburn v. Whitaker Constr. Co., 430
Cochran v. Brooke, 825
Cockerline v. Menendez, 230
Coffield v. Robinson, 384
Coffman v. Armstrong Intern., 836
Coghlan v. Beta Theta Pi Fraternity, 610
Cohen v. Alliant Enters., Inc., 715
Cohen v. Smith, 40
Colbert v. Moomba Sports, Inc., 656
Cole v. City of New Haven, 531
Cole v. Turner, 37

Coleman v. Court of Appeals of Maryland, 1009
Coleman v. East Joliet Fire Protection Dist., 533
Coleman v. Martinez, 624
Coleman v. Oregon Parks and Recreation Dept., 431
Coleman v. Soccer Ass'n of Columbia, 323
Coleson v. City of New York, 655
Colgate v. JUUL Labs, Inc., 163
Collins v. City of Harker Heights, 539
Collins v. City of Newton, 643
Collins v. COP Wyoming, LLC, 1004
Collins v. Eli Lilly & Co., 899
Collins v. Navistar, Inc., 853
Collins v. Plant Insulation Co., 891
Collins v. Scenic Homes, Inc., 300
Collins v. Superior Air-Ground Ambulance Service, Inc., 235
Collins v. United States, 516
Collum v. McCool, 601
Colosimo v. Gateway Community Church, 413
Colvin v. City of Gardena, 531
Combs v. Ohio Dept. of Natural Resources, Div. of Parks & Recreation, 434
Comedy III Prods., Inc. v. Gary Saderup, Inc., 1104
Coming Attractions Bridal & Formal, Inc. v. Texas Health Resources, 478
Commerce Bank v. Augsburger, 494
Commerce Ins. Co. v. Ultimate Livery Service, Inc., 631
Compuserve Inc. v. Cyber Promotions, Inc., 77
Connecticut Interlocal Risk Management Agency v. Jackson, 260
Conner v. Hodges, 660
Conner v. Quality Coach, Inc., 865
Connick v. Thompson, 539
Connolly v. Long Island Power Auth., 529
Conroy v. Regents of Univ. of Cal., 1125
Control Techniques, Inc. v. Johnson, 317
Cooke v. Allstate Management Corp., 611
Coomer v. Kansas City Royals Baseball Corp., 366
Cooper v. Rodriguez, 534
Cooper v. Thompson, 248
Cope v. Utah Valley State College, 533
Corcoran v. Banner Super Mkt., Inc., 234
Cordova v. City of Los Angeles, 530

Cormier v. City of Lynn, 608
Cornell v. 360 West 51st Street Realty, LLC, 842
Corvias Military Living, LLC v. Ventamatic, Ltd., 798
Cosgrove v. Commonwealth Edison Co., 228
Cotita v. Pharma-Plast, U.S.A., Inc., 848
Cottam v. CVS Pharmacy, 456
Cotten v. Wilson, 305
Cottingham ex rel. K.C. v. Sec'y of Health & Human Services, 1015
Cotton v. Wood, 223
Courtney v. Courtney, 749
Covenant Care, Inc. v. Superior Court, 488
Covey v. Brishka, 763
Covington v. George, 927
Cowan v. Hospice Support Care, Inc., 498
Cox Broadcasting Corp. v. Cohn, 1081
Cox v. Evansville Police Dep't, 730
Cox v. May Dep't Store Co., 235
Coyle v. Historic Mission Inn Corp., 138
Craft v. State ex rel. Wyoming Dep't of Health, 694
Cramer v. Starr, 201, **886**
Creasy v. Rusk, 144
Credit All. Corp. v. Arthur Andersen & Co., 1120
Crews v. Hollenbach, 373
Crichfield v. Grand Wailea Co., 433
Crisafulli v. Bass, 616
Cromer v. Children's Hosp. Med. Ctr., 445
Crookston v. Fire Ins. Exch., 940
Crosby v. Glasscock Trucking Co., Inc., 679
Crosstex North Texas Pipeline, L.P. v. Gardiner, 764
Crotta v. Home Depot, Inc., 877
Croyle ex rel. Croyle v. United States, 515
Crumpton v. Humana, Inc., 378
Cruz v. Daimler-Chrysler Motors Corp., 236
Cruz v. Johnson, 105
Cruz-Vazquez v. Mennonite General Hosp., Inc., 483
CSX Transp., Inc. v. Begley, 323
CSX Transp., Inc. v. Easterwood, 399
CSX Transp., Inc. v. Hensley, 673
CSX Transp., Inc. v. Miller, 248, 891
CTL Distribution, Inc., State v., 261
CTS Corp. v. Waldburger, 393
Cuc Thi Ngo v. Queen's Medical Center, 461

Cucinotta v. Deloitte Touch, LLP, 1052
Cuffy v. City of New York, 526
Cullison v. Medley, 58
Cummings v. Barber, 473
Curtis Publ'g Co. v. Butts, 1057
Curtis, Estate of v. South Las Vegas Medical Investors, LLC, 486
Customer Co. v. City of Sacramento, 123
Cyran v. Ware, 678
D.W. v. Bliss, 615
D'Amario v. Ford Motor Co., 892
Dakter v. Cavallino, 149
Daley v. A.W. Chesterton, Inc., 387
Daly v. General Motors Corp., 847, 880
Damon v. Moore, 1048
Daniel v. United States, 522
Daniels v. Senior Care, Inc., 185
Daniels v. Wiley, 436
Danos v. Boh Bros. Constr. Co., 1006
Dapo v. State, 395
Darby v. National Trust, 294
Dart v. Wiebe Mfg., Inc., 811
Dasha v. Maine Medical Center, 390
Daubert v. Merrell Dow Pharmaceuticals, Inc., 449, 841
Davenport v. Comstock Hills-Reno, 395
David v. Hett, 570
Davies v. Mann, 303
Davis Nursing Ass'n v. Neal, 489
Davis v. Cox, 1076
Davis v. Devereux Foundation, 731
Davis v. Dionne, 403
Davis v. Flatiron Materials Co., 909
Davis v. Frostburg Facility Operations, LLC, 451
Davis v. South Nasssau Communities Hosp., 625
De Leon Lopez v. Corporacion Insular de Seguros, 226
De Long v. County of Erie, 525
Dean v. Barrett Homes, Inc., 798
DeBusscher v. Sam's East, Inc., 229, 230
DeCarlo v. Eden Park Health Services, Inc., 236
Deckard v. Bunch, 629
Degener v. Hall Contracting Corp., 885
Deggs v. Asbestos Corp. Ltd., 706
Degliomini v. ESM Prods., Inc., 360
Del Lago Partners, Inc. v. Smith, 330, 350, 600
Delaney v. Baker, 488, 930
Delaney v. Deere & Co., 817
Delaney v. Reynolds, 303

Delfino v. Griffo, 629
Delgado v. Trax Bar & Grill, 587
Delta Airlines, Inc. v. Townsend, 632
DeLuca v. Bowden, 51
Demag v. Better Power Equipment, 422
Dempsey, United States v., 661, 662
Densberger v. United Tech's. Corp., 864
Denson v. Estate of Dillard, 144
Depuy Orthopaedics, Inc., In re, 818
Derdiarian v. Felix Contracting Corp., 306
DeRosa v. Remington Arms Co., 821
Derry v. Peek, 1115
Derwort v. Loomer, 403
Deschenes v. Transco, 1002
Destefano v. Children's Nat'l Med. Ctr., 664
Destefano v. Grabrian, 733
Deuley v. Dyncorp Int'l, Inc., 364
Devore v. American Eagle Energy Corp., 739
Dewald v. HCA Health Services of Tennessee, 747
DeWester v. Watkins, 633
Dezotell, In re Estate of, 704
Dhillon v. Crown Controls Corp., 820
Di Gildo v. Caponi, 415
Dias v. Brigham Med. Assocs., Inc., 740
Diaz v. Phoenix Lubrication Service, Inc., 576
Dick's Sporting Goods, Inc. v. Webb, 428
Dickens v. Puryear, 62
Dickens v. Sahley Realty Co., 228
Dickerson v. Strand, 1126
Didato v. Strehler, 684
Dietrich v. Northhampton, 678
Digicorp, Inc. v. Ameritech Corp., 1130
Dillard Dep't Stores, Inc. v. Silva, 105
Dillingham v. IBP, Inc., 924
Dillon v. Evanston Hospital, 270
Dillon v. Frazer, 15, 208
Dillon v. Legg, 619, 653
Dillon v. Twin State Gas & Electric Co., 258
DiMarco v. Lynch Homes-Chester County, Inc., 625
Dinsmoor v. City of Phoenix, 608
Dinsmore-Poff v. Alvord, 616
Diocese of Lubbock, In re, 645
District of Columbia v. Beretta U.S.A. Corp., 824
District of Columbia v. Howell, 920
District of Columbia v. Singleton, 229
District of Columbia v. Wesby, 86, 89

Dixon Mills Volunteer Fire Dept., Inc., Ex parte, 499
Dixon v. Ford Motor Co., 933
Dlouhy v. Kootenai Hosp. Dist., 453
Doan v. Banner Health, Inc., 655
Dobran v. Franciscan Medical Center, 665
Dobrovolny v. Ford Motor Co., 799
Doctors Hosp. of Augusta, LLC v. Alicea, 119
Dodd v. Hines, 120
Dodson v. S.D. Dep't of Human Servs., 331
Doe 1 v. Lake Oswego School Dist., 385
Doe 163 v. Quest Diagnostics, Inc., 477
Doe ex rel. Doe v. Baker, 734
Doe ex rel. Doe v. Wright Sec. Servs., Inc., 581
Doe Parents No. 1 v. State, Dep't of Educ., 193, 650
Doe v. Archdiocese of St. Paul, 389
Doe v. Coe, 734
Doe v. Corp. of President of Church of Jesus Christ of Latter-Day Saints, 643
Doe v. Guthrie Clinic, Ltd., 733
Doe v. Hagar, 1048
Doe v. Hartford Roman Catholic Diocesan Corp., 50, 618
Doe v. Holt, 490
Doe v. Internet Brands, Inc., 1053
Doe v. Isaacs, 935
Doe v. Johnston, 463
Doe v. Lawndale Elementary Sch. Dist., 606
Doe v. Linder Construction Co., 303
Doe v. Logan County Bd. of Educ., 606
Doe v. Newbury Bible Church, 713
Doe v. Roe, 389
Doe v. Saint Francis Hosp. & Medical Center, 734
Doe v. State, 713, 731
Doe v. Taylor Independent School Dist., 606
Doe v. Uber Technologies, Inc., 404
Doe, State v., 940
Doll v. Brown, 268
Donahue v. Ledgends, Inc., 359, 364
Donoghue v. Stevenson, 778
Donovan v. Philip Morris USA, Inc., 925
Donze v. General Motors, LLC, 808
Doomes v. Best Transit Corp., 857
Dorrell v. South Carolina Dept. of Transp., 745
Dorsey v. Reider, 633
Dorvil, Commonwealth v., 106

Dos Santos v. Coleta, 429
Doser v. Interstate Power Co., 403
Dotson v. Bernstein, 686
Double Quick, Inc. v. Moore, 302
Dougan v. Sikorsky Aircraft Corp., 926
Doull v. Foster, 255
Dowty v. Riggs, 648
Doyle v. Volkswagenwerk
   Aktiengesellschaft, 864
Dragomir v. Spring Harbor Hosp., 734
Draper v. Olivere Paving & Constr.
   Co., 713
DRD Pool Service, Inc. v. Freed, 698,
   933
Driscoll v. General Nutrition Corp.,
   1008
Duchess v. Langston Corp., 840
Dudley v. Offender Aid & Restoration
   of Richmond, Inc., 614
Dugger v. Arredondo, 351
Dun & Bradstreet, Inc. v. Greenmoss
   Builders, Inc., 1066
Duncan v. Corbetta, 217
Duncan v. Scottsdale Medical
   Imaging, Ltd., 117
Dupuy v. NMC Operating Co., 478
Durham v. Marberry, 699
**Durre v. Wilkinson Development,
   Inc., 392**
**Dyer v. Maine Drilling & Blasting,
   Inc., 767**
Dynamex Operations W. v. Superior
   Ct., 186
Eastin v. Broomfield, 929
Eaton v. Eaton, 225
Echols v. Lawton, 535
Ecker v. E & A Consulting Group, Inc.,
   244, 278, 301
Eckroth v. Pennsylvania Elec. Inc.,
   309
**Edgewater Motels, Inc. v. Gatzke,
   722**
Edson v. Barre Supervisory Union #
   61, 609
Edwards v. Fogarty, 706
Eggleston v. Pierce Cty., 123
Eichenwald v. Rivello, 52
Eighth Judicial Dist. Asbestos
   Litigation, In re, 793
Eiseman v. State, 610
Eklund v. Trost, 533
Elam v. Kansas City Southern Ry. Co.,
   399
Eldridge v. Johndrow, 1091
Elias v. Rolling Stone LLC, 1048
Elkerson, Estate of v. North Jersey
   Blood Ctr., 220
Ellinwood v. Cohen, 441
Elliott v. City of New York, 156

Ellis v. Estate of Ellis, 389, 491
Embarton v. GMRI, Inc., 391
English v. New England Medical
   Center, Inc., 499
Engquist v. Loyas, 920
Ennabe v. Manosa, 630
Enright v. Eli Lilly & Co., 682
Entergy Miss., Inc. v. Acey, 655
Erdelyi v. Lott, 1125
Eric J. v. Betty M., 615
Erie Ins. Co. v. Amazon.com, Inc., 791
Errico v. LaMountain, 232
Escola v. Coca Cola Bottling Co., 234,
   470
Escondido, Cal., City of v. Emmons, 89
Eskin v. Bartee, 655
Espina v. Jackson, 933
Espinoza v. Schulenburg, 440
Ess v. Eskaton Properties, Inc., 486
Estelle v. Gamble, 80
Etkind v. Suarez, 684
Eubanks, Estate of v. Eubanks, 704
Eugene, City of v. McDermed, 989
Evans v. Lorillard Tobacco Co., 819
Everett v. Littleton Construction Co.,
   603
Everitt v. Gen. Elec. Co., 217
Eversole v. Woods Acquisition, Inc.,
   228
Exner v. Sherman Power Construction
   Co., 772
Exxon Co., U.S.A. v. Sofec, Inc., 336
Exxon Mobil Corp. v. Albright, 671
Exxon Shipping Co. v. Baker, 950
Ezell v. Cockrell, 532
Fabre v. Marin, 894
Facebook, Inc. Internet Tracking
   Litigation, In re, 1078
Facler v. Genetzky, 662
Faile v. S.C. Dep't of Juvenile Justice,
   532
Fairchild v. Glenhaven Funeral
   Servs., 4
Fajardo v. City of Los Angeles, 539
Fancyboy v. Alaska Village Elec. Co-
   op., Inc., 298
Fandrey v. American Family Mut. Ins.
   Co., 288
Farhrendorff v. North Homes, Inc.,
   731
Farias v. Mr. Heater, Inc., 834
Farley v. Engelken, 929
Farmer v. B & G Food Enters., Inc.,
   440
Farmer v. Brennan, 80
Farmers Ins. Group v. County of
   Santa Clara, 713, 726, 730
Farrington v. Total Petroleum, Inc.,
   998

Farwell v. Keaton, 561
Fasolas v. Bobcat of New York, Inc., 803
Faul v. Jelco, Inc., 722
Favreau v. Miller, 436
Faya v. Almaraz, 674
Fazzaroli v. Portland School District No. 1J, 609
FCH1, LLC v. Rodriguez, 369
FDIC v. Meyer, 504
Fearing v. Bucher, 733
Feiereisen v. Newpage Corp., 988
Fein v. Permanente Medical Group, 932
Feld v. Borkowski, 371
Feltmeier v. Feltmeier, 379
Felton v. Lovett, 461
FEMA Trailer Formaldehyde Products Liability Litigation (Mississippi Plaintiffs), In re, 506
Fennell v. Maryland Hosp. Ctr., Inc., 267
Feres v. United States, 520
Fernandes v. DAR Dev. Corp., 339
Ferreira v. Child & Family Servs., 1047
Ferriter v. Daniel O'Connell's Sons, Inc., 661
Fiano v. Old Saybrook Fire Co. No. 1, Inc., 726
Fickle v. State, 530
Fields v. Hayden, 615
Figlar v. Gordon, 292
Fikes v. Furst, 1095
Fintzi v. N.J. YMHA-YWHA Camps, 183
First Midwest Bank v. City of Chicago, 78
First Midwest Bank v. Denson, 95
Fischer v. City of Sioux Falls, 413
Fisher v. Big Y Foods, Inc., 214
Fisher v. Carrousel Motor Hotel, Inc., 53
Fitzpatrick v. Natter, 208
Flannery v. United States, 924
Flax v. DaimlerChrysler Corp., 950
Florence v. Goldberg, 585
Flores v. Exprezit! Stores 98-Georgia, LLC, 631
Flores v. Santiago, 114
Florida Star, The v. B.J.F., 1081
Fojtik v. Hunter, 751
Folta v. Ferro Engineering, 1003
Fontaine v. Roman Catholic Church of Archdiocese of New Orleans, 667
Fontenot v. Taser Intern., Inc., 847
Foradori v. Harris, 923
Force v. American Family Mut. Ins. Co., 705

Ford Motor Co. v. Industrial Commission, 992
Ford Motor Co. v. Washington, 937
Fordham v. Oldroyd, 440
Foreman v. Callahan, 1027
Forma Sci., Inc. v. BioSera, Inc., 840
Forsman v. Blues, Brews & Bar-B-Ques, Inc., 58
Forsyth v. Joseph, 208
Fortres Grand Corp. v. Warner Bros. Entm't Inc., 1102
Foss v. Kincade, 187
Fossett v. Board of Regents of Univ. of Neb., 451
Foster Logging v. United States, 514
Foster v. Preston Mill Co., 772
Fowler v. Printers II, Inc., 1089
Fox v. Amazon.com, Inc., 791
Fox v. Ethicon Endo-Surgery, Inc., 384
Fox v. Mize, 733
Fraenkel v. Islamic Republic of Iran, 375
France v. Southern Equip. Co., 739, 741
Franklin Corp. v. Tedford, 1005, 1006
Franklin v. Gwinnett County Public Schools, 606
Frazier v. Drake, 141
Frederick v. Swift Transp. Co., 727
Freightliner Corp. v. Myrick, 859
Frey, Estate of v. Mastroiani, 254, 266
Frezzell v. City of New York, 531
Friedman v. Dozorc, 1074
Frost v. ADT, LLC, 575
Frost v. Salter Path Fire & Rescue, 992
Fruit v. Schreiner, 712
Frye v. United States, 842
Fuentes v. Alecio, 353
Fugate v. Fugate, 490
Funches v. Progressive Tractor & Implement Co., 245
Funchess v. Cecil Newman Corp., 612
Furry v. Miccosukee Tribe of Indians of Florida, 503
G.A.-H. v. K.G.G., 734
Gable v. Gable, 422
Gaines-Tabb v. ICI Explosives, USA, Inc., 807
Galanis v. CMA Management Co., 613
Galaxy Cable, Inc. v. Davis, 935
Galindo v. Town of Clarkstown, 411
Gallant v. MacDowell, 391
Gallo v. Barile, 1052
Galloway v. State, 361
Galveston City Ry. Co. v. Hewitt, 404
Gambardella v. Apple Health Care, Inc., 1057
Garback v. Lossing, 1080

Garcia v. Colorado Cab Co. LLC, 289
Gardner v. National Bulk Carriers, Inc., 267
Gardner v. Oregon Health Sciences Univ., 340
Garr v. City of Ottumwa, 244
Garratt v. Dailey, 9, **46**, 49, 951
Garrison v. Louisiana, 1061
Gates v. Richardson, 655
Gaubert, United States v., 511, 515
Gauerke v. Rozga, **1122**
Gaumer v. Rossville Truck and Tractor Co., 792
Gauvin v. Clark, 371
Gavin W. v. YMCA of Metro. Los Angeles, 359
Gaylord v. United States, 1098
Gaytan v. Wal-Mart, 741
Gebser v. Lago Vista Indep. Sch. Dist., 606
Geier v. American Honda Motor Co., 858, 859, 861
Gemmink v. Jay Peak Inc., 256
General Electric Co. v. Joiner, 841
General Electric Co. v. Niemet, 931
General Motors Corp. v. Hill, 428
General Motors Corp. v. Sanchez, 819, 847
Genie Industries, Inc. v. Matak, **813**
George v. Jefferson Hosp. Ass'n, 498
George v. Parke-Davis, 900
Georges v. State, 533
Georgia Dept. of Corrections v. Couch, 410
Georgia Dept. of Human Res. v. Bulbalia, 287
Georgia Dept. of Human Services v. Spruill, 530
Gerber v. Veltri, 45
Gertz v. Robert Welch, Inc., **1059**
Getchell v. Lodge, **167**
GGNC Administrative Services, LLC v. Schrader, 705
Giant Food, Inc. v. Mitchell, 192
Gibbs v. Blockbuster, Inc., 66
Gibson v. Gibson, 495
Gibson v. Leonard, 437
Gibson v. United States, 516
Giddings & Lewis, Inc. v. Industrial Risk Insurers, 798
Gieseke v. IDCA, Inc., 1094
Gift v. Palmer, 203
Gignilliat v. Gignilliat, Savitz & Bettis, L.L.P., 1104
Giles v. City of New Haven, 231, 471
Giles v. Wyeth, Inc., 838
Gillespie v. Edmier, 818

Gillespie v. Waterwheel Farms, Inc., 411
Gilmore v. Walgreen Co., 428
Gina Chin & Associates v. First Union Bank, 713
Ginsberg v. Quest Diagnostics, Inc., 686
Giordano v. Spencer, 95
Gipson v. Kasey, 602, 630
Gladon v. Greater Cleveland Regional Transit Authority, 410, 557
Glaser v. Mitchel, 69
Gleason v. Guzman, **907**
Glenn v. Peoples, 254, 445
Gniadek v. Camp Sunshine at Sebago Lake, Inc., 609
Goddard v. Farmers Ins. Co., 950
Godoy ex rel. Gramling v. I.E. du Pont de Nemours & Co., 804
Goff v. Elmo Greer & Sons Constr. Co., 954
Goforth v. Porter Medical Associates, Inc., 683
Goins v. Time Warner Cable Se., LLC, 142
Goldberg v. Horowitz, 455
Golden Spread Electric Coop., Inc. v. Emerson Process Management Power & Water Solutions, Inc., 798
Goldhagen v. Pasmowitz, 757
Goldstein, Garber & Salama, LLC v. J.B., **164**, 166
Goller v. White, 495
Gomez v. Superior Court, 404
Gonzales v. Mascarenas, 679
Gonzalez v. Johnson, 192, 303, 531
Gonzalez v. Mathis, 186, 739
Gonzalez v. Union Pac. R.R. Co., 324
Goodby v. Vetpharm, Inc., 662
Gooden v. City of Talladega, 192, 531
Gooden v. Coors Technical Ceramic Co., 989
Goodner v. Hyundai Motor Co., 819
Google, Inc. Privacy Policy Litigation, In re, 1079
Gordon-Couture, Estate of v. Brown, 431
Gore v. People's Savings Bank, 437
Gorman ex rel. Gorman, Estate of v. State, 1007
Gorman v. Abbott Labs., 903
Gortarez v. Smitty's Super Valu, Inc., **100**
Goss v. Allen, 151
Gouin v. Gouin, 62
Gould v. Ochsner, 73
Govich v. N. Am. Sys., Inc., 349
Grabowski v. Mangler, 991

Gracyalny v. Westinghouse Elec. Corp., 837
Graef v. Continental Indemnity Co., 994
Grager v. Schudar, 114
Graham v. Connor, 79, 80, 84
Grant v. Foster Wheeler, LLC, 257
Grant v. South Roxana Dad's Club, 430
Graves v. Estabrook, 656
Graves v. North Eastern Services, Inc., 334, 618
Graves v. Trudell, 99
Graves, Estate of v. City of Circleville, 533
Gray v. BellSouth Telecomm., Inc., 234
Great Atl. & Pac. Tea Co. v. Paul, 105
Greco v. Sumner Tavern, Inc., 600
Green v. Box Butte Gen. Hosp., 143
Green v. Gen. Petroleum Corp., 773
Green v. Monmouth Univ., 498
Green v. Pennsylvania Hosp., 747
Green v. Smith & Nephew AHP, Inc., 817
Greenberg v. Miami Children's Hospital Research Institute, Inc., 464
Greenberg, Trager & Herbst, LLP v. HSBC Bank USA, 1126
Greene v. Esplanade Venture Partnership, 656
Greene v. Tinker, 1049
Greenhill v. Vartanian, 391
Greenman v. Yuba Power Products, Inc., 780, 784, 795
Greenwald v. Van Handel, 354
Greenwood v. Anderson, 497
Gregoire v. City of Oak Harbor, 340
Gregory v. Carey, 924
Gregory v. Cott, 369
Gregory, In re Conservatorship of, 487
Greycas, Inc. v. Proud, 331
Griffin Industries, Inc. v. Jones, 792
Griggs v. Bounce N' Around Inflatables, L.L.C., 993
Grimes v. Kennedy Krieger Institute, Inc., 119, 466, 595
Grimes v. Saban, 91
Grimm v. Ariz. Bd. of Pardons & Paroles, 532
Gritzner v. Michael R., 617
Grodin v. Grodin, 676
Grotts v. Zahner, 656
Grover v. Stechel, 617
Grube v. Union Pac. R.R., 649
GTE Southwest, Inc. v. Bruce, 639
Guarantee Trust Life Ins. Co. v. Estate of Casper ex rel. Casper, 699

Gubbins v. Hurson, 226
Guerra v. State, 664
Guerrero v. Smith, 455
Guess v. Sharp Mfg. Co. of America, 1000
Guillory v. Saucier, 923
Gund v. County of Trinity, 979
Gunkel v. Renovations, Inc., 798
Gushlaw v. Milner, 579, 631
Gustafson ex rel. Reginella, Estate of v. Target Corp., 257
Gustafson v. Benda, 367
Guth v. Freeland, 665
H.R. Moch Co. v. Rensselaer Water Co., 548, 583
Habershaw v. Michaels Stores, Inc., 203
Hafer v. Melo, 535
Hagen Ins., Inc. v. Roller, 649
Hagenow v. American Family Mut. Ins. Co., 140
Hager v. M&K Construction, 980
Hagerty v. L. & L. Marine Services, Inc., 386
Hagler v. Coastal Farms Holdings, Inc., 233
Haight v. City & Borough of Juneau, 529
Haines v. Comfort Keepers, Inc., 54
Hairston v. Harward, 927
Hajdusek v. United States, **509**
Hale v. Beckstead, 428
Hale v. Ostrow, 245, 246
Halek v. United States, 187
Hall v. City of Newport, 618
Hall v. E.I. DuPont de Nemours & Co., 903
Hall v. Hilbun, 454
Hall, Estate of v. Akron Gen. Med. Ctr., 227
Halliday v. Sturm, Ruger & Co., 823, 856
Halsey, State ex rel. v. Phillips, 645
Hamil v. Bashline, 267
Hamilton v. Nestor, 650
Hammack v. White, 223
Hammer v. Ribi, 61
Hammerstein v. Jean Development West, 295
Hampton v. County of San Diego, 530
Hamric v. Wilderness Expeditions, Inc., 364
Hancock-Underwood v. Knight, 141
Handy v. Nejam, 411
Hanford Nuclear Reservation Litigation, In re, 771
Hansen v. Sea Ray Boats, Inc., 653
Happel v. Wal-Mart Stores, Inc., 456

Haralson v. Fisher Surveying, Inc., 955

Harb v. City of Bakersfield, 340

Hardee v. Bio-Medical Applications of South Carolina, Inc., 625

Harder v. Edwards, 66

Harder v. F.C. Clinton, Inc., 232, 487

Hardy v. New York City Health & Hospitals Corp., 484

Hardy v. Southwestern Bell Tel. Co., 270

Harlow v. Fitzgerald, 86

Harnish v. Children's Hospital Medical Center, 458

Harper v. Banks, Finley, White & Co., 998

Harrington v. Brooks Drugs, Inc., 661

Harrington v. Costello, 384

Harris v. Board of Education of Howard County, 995

Harris v. ShopKo Stores, Inc., 248, 296

Harris v. State, Dept. of Corrections, 1006

Harris v. Westin Management Co. East, 988

Harris-Fields v. Syze, 441

Harrison v. Roitman, 1051

Harrison v. Valentini, 379

Harry Stoller and Co. v. City of Lowell, 527

Hart v. State, 106

Harte v. Bd. of Commissioners of Cty. of Johnson, Kansas, 67

Hartwig v. Oregon Trail Eye Clinic, 673

Harvey v. Regional Health Network, Inc., 642

Harvey v. Strickland, 119, 462

Hastings v. Sauve, 756

Hatch v. Davis, 646

Hatfill v. New York Times Co., 1064

Havilah Real Property Services, LLC v. VLK, LLC, 1074

Hawkins v. Southwest Kansas Co-op Service, 1011

Hawkley, In re, 1073

Hayes v. D.C.I. Properties-DKY, LLC, 418

Hayes v. Decker, 842

Hayes v. Price, 348

Hayward v. Cleveland Clinic Found., 643

Haywood v. Drown, 79

HDI-Gerling Am. Ins. Co. v. Carlile Transportation Sys., Inc., 156

HealthSouth Corp., Ex parte, 448

Heath v. Sears, Roebuck & Co., 868

Heaven v. Pender, 620

Heckler v. Campbell, 1023

Hecksher v. Fairwinds Baptist Church, Inc., 712

Hedgepeth v. Whitman Walker Clinic, 649, 663

Hedlund v. State, 642

Hedlund v. Superior Court of Orange County, 624

Heiner v. Moretuzzo, 664

Heining v. Abernathy, 66

Helf v. Chevron U.S.A., Inc., 1006

Helling v. Carey, 450

Hellums v. Raber, 260

Helsel v. Hoosier Ins. Co., 657

Hemmings v. Pelham Wood Ltd. Liability Partnership, 613

Henderson Square Condominium Ass'n v. LAB Townhomes, LLC, 391

Henderson v. City of Columbus, 123

Henderson v. Woolley, 492

Henningsen v. Bloomfield Motors, Inc., 779

Henry v. Dow Chemical Co., 388

Henry v. Hamilton Equities, Inc., 436

Hensley v. Jackson County, 530

Henson ex rel. Hunt v. International Paper Co., 418

Henson v. Klein, 140, 335

Henson v. Uptown Drink, LLC, 370

Hernandez v. Barbo, 847

Hernandez v. Hillsides, Inc., 1080

Hernandez v. Mesa, 508

Hernandez v. Tokai Corp., 807

Herr v. Wheeler, 141

Herrington v. Gaulden, 580

Herron v. Hollis, 187

Hersh v. County of Morris, 988

Hersh v. E-T Enterprises, Ltd. Partnership, 429

Hesse v. Ashland Oil, Inc., 1003

Hester v. Vision Airlines, Inc., 939

Hewellette v. George, 490

Hewitt v. Palmer Veterinary Clinic, PC, 756

Hickerson v. Yamaha Motor Corp., 832

Hickingbotham v. Burke, 629

Hickle v. Whitney Farms, Inc., 155

Highfill v. Hale, 105

Hill v. City of Horn Lake, 740

Hill v. Cundiff, 641

Hill v. National Grid, 418

Hill v. Rhinehart, 874

Hill v. Sears, Roebuck & Co., 578

Hill v. Sparks, 148

Hill v. Superior Prop. Mgmt. Servs., Inc., 578

Hillerson v. Bismarck Public Schools, 363

Hilton v. Martin, 992

Hines v. Garrett, 302, 886

Hinkie v. United States, 523

Hinkle Metals & Supply Co. v. Feltman, 721

Hinman v. Westinghouse Electric Co., 719

HipSaver, Inc. v. Kiel, 1087

Hirpa v. IHC Hospitals, Inc., 456

Hislop v. Salt River Project Agric. Improvement & Power Dist., 656

HMC Hotel Props. II Ltd. P'ship v. Keystone-Tex. Prop. Holding Corp., 277

Hoch, Estate of v. Stifel, 955

Hodge, Ex parte, 394

Hofflander v. St. Catherine's Hosp., Inc., 147

Hoffman v. Capital Cities/ABC, Inc., 1104

Hoffman v. Young, 431

Hogan v. Winder, 1048

Hojnowski v. Vans Skate Park, 361

Holder v. Wilson Sporting Goods Co., 984

Holiday Motor Corp. v. Walters, 808

Holmes v. Levine, 298

Holodook v. Spencer, 495

Holston v. Sisters of Third Order of St. Francis, 924

Homer v. Long, 646

Honda of America Mfg., Inc. v. Norman, 818

Hood v. Ryobi America Corp., 853

Hoover v. New Holland North America, Inc., 855

Hope v. Pelzer, 90

Hopi Tribe v. Arizona Snowbowl Resort Ltd. Partnership, 766

Hopkins v. Miss. Valley Gas Co., 138

Hoppe v. Hoppe, 496

Hopper v. Swinnerton, 162

Horizon/CMS Healthcare Corp. v. Auld, 484, 485

Horne v. Elec. Eel Mfg., 364

Hornibrook v. Richard, 509

Horodyskyj v. Karanian, 1008

Horsley v. Rivera, 1066

Horst v. Deere & Co., 808

Horton v. Reaves, 51

Horwich v. Superior Court, 705

Hough v. McKiernan, 55

Howard v. Union Carbide Corp., 240

Howard v. University of Med. & Dentistry of N.J., 464

Howard v. Wal-Mart Stores, Inc., 230

Howard v. Zimmer, Inc., 162

Howell v. Hamilton Meats & Provisions, Inc., 928

Howerton v. Harbin Clinic, LLC, 640

Howlett v. Rose, 78

Hoyt v. Gutterz Bowl & Lounge L.L.C., 630

Hudgens v. Prosper, Inc., 120

Hudson v. GEICO Ins. Agency, Inc., 556

Hudson v. McMillian, 80

Hudson v. Old Guard Ins. Co., 151

Hudson-Connor v. Putney, 151

Huffman v. Sunshine Recycling, LLC, 66

Hughes v. Doe, 714

Hughes v. Magic Chef, Inc., 848

Hui v. Castaneda, 509

Hunt v. Zuffa LLC, 115

Hurst v. Capitell, 490

Hurst v. East Coast Hockey League, Inc., 369

Hustler Magazine Inc. v. Moral Majority Inc., 1099

Hustler Magazine v. Falwell, 645, 1065

Hutcherson v. City of Phoenix, 883

Hutchison v. Brookshire Bros., 54

Hutchison v. Fitzgerald Equip. Co., 578

Hutchison v. Luddy, 936

Huynh v. Phillips, 229

Hy Cite Corp. v. badbusinessbureau.com, L.L.C., 1072

Hymowitz v. Eli Lilly & Co., 681, **897**

Hysjulien v. Hill Top Home of Comfort, Inc., 642

Ileto v. Glock, Inc., 824

Indalecio v. Mobil Oil Marianas, Inc., 919

Indemnity Ins. Co. v. United States, 517

Indian Towing Co. v. United States, 506

Indiana Consolidated Insurance Co. v. Mathew, 180

Indiana Harbor Belt Railroad Co. v. American Cyanamid Co., 772

Industrial Indemnity Co. v. Industrial Accident Commission, 988

Ingram v. Drouin, 395

Integrated Direct Marketing, LLC v. May, 75

Intel Corp. v. Hamidi, 77

Internet Solutions Corp. v. Marshall, 1058

InTown Lessee Assocs., LLC v. Howard, 347

Ipsen v. Diamond Tree Experts, Inc., 441

Ironworkers Local Union 68 v. AstraZeneca Pharm., LP, 1125
Isik Jewelry v. Mars Media, Inc., 347
Iverson v. United States, 508
Iverson v. Vint, 763
Ives v. South Buffalo Railway Co., 977
Ivey v. Trans Global Gas & Oil, 1000
Izzarelli v. R.J. Reynolds Tobacco Co., 811
J&J Timber Co. v. Broome, 716
J.H. v. R&M Tagliareni, LLC, 437
J.S. v. R.T.H., 615
J'Aire Corp. v. Gregory, 1089
Jablonowska v. Suther, 657
Jablonski v. Ford Motor Co., 222, 838
Jack v. McFarland, 722
Jackman v. Cebrink-Swartz, 69
Jackson v. Axelrad, 149
Jackson v. Clark & Fay, Inc., 986
Jackson v. Nestle-Beich, Inc., 804
Jackson v. York Hannover Nursing Centers, 895
Jackson, City of v. Lewis, 531
Jacobson v. Ron, 289
Jagger v. Mohawk Mountain Ski Area, Inc., 371
Jakubowski v. Minn. Mining & Mfg., 803
James v. Kelly Trucking Co., 734
James v. Wormuth, 470
Janelsins v. Button, 111
Janis v. Nash Finch Co., 410
Jaramillo v. Weyerhaeuser Co., 792
Jarman v. HCR Manorcare, Inc., 488
Jarrell v. Kaul, 464
Jarrett v. Jones, 657
JBS Carriers, Inc., v. Washington, 354
Jefferson County Sch. Dist. R-1 v. Gilbert, 587
Jeffrey v. Cathers, 1087
Jeld-Wen, Inc. v. Gamble, 853
Jenkins v. C.R.E.S. Management, L.L.C., 601
Jenkins v. Jordan Valley Water Conservancy, 216
Jenkins v. Patel, 698
Jerista v. Murray, 229
Jett v. Ford Motor Co., 847
Jivan v. Economy Inn & Suites, 987
JLB Builders, L.L.C. v. Hernandez, 740
JLG Trucking, LLC v. Garza, 247
JMB Mfg., Inc. v. Child Craft, LLC, 1130
Johannensen v. New York City Dep't of Housing, Etc., 1000
Johme v. St. John's Mercy Healthcare, 988

John & Jane Roes, 1–100 v. FHP, Inc., 673
John Crane, Inc. v. Jones, 255, 257
John Doe 1 v. Archdiocese of Milwaukee, 379
John R. v. Oakland Unified School Dist., 391
John v. Philadelphia Pizza Team, Inc., 642
John v. St. Francis Hosp., Inc., 478
Johnson v. American Standard, Inc., 835
Johnson v. Jones, 116
Johnson v. Kokemoor, 463
Johnson v. Madison Cty. Court of Common Pleas, 67
Johnson v. Monsanto Co., 920
Johnson v. Morehouse Gen. Hosp., 330
Johnson v. Nextel Communications, Inc., 907
Johnson v. Ruark Obstetrics & Gynecology Assocs., P.A., 667
Johnson v. State, 650, 666
Johnson v. Wal-Mart Stores, Inc., 304
Johnson v. Wash. Gas Light Co., 211
Johnson, United States v., 520, 522
Johnstone v. City of Albuquerque, 305
Jones v. Brookshire Grocery Co., 215
Jones v. Clinton, 642
Jones v. Dirty World Entertainment Recordings LLC, 1053
Jones v. Healthsouth Treasure Valley Hosp., 747
Jones v. Nordictrack, Inc., 807
Jones v. Shipley, 62
Jordan v. Jewel Food Stores, Inc., 1103
Jordan v. Jordan, 244
Jordet v. Jordet, 1074
Jorge-Chavelas v. Louisiana Farm Bureau Cas. Ins. Co., 983
Joseph E. Seagram & Sons, Inc. v. McGuire, 853
Joseph v. State, 340
Josue v. Isuzu Motors Amer., Inc., 831
Jourdan River Estates, LLC v. Favre, 379
Jowers v. BOC Group, Inc., 1107
Jowers v. Lincoln Elec. Co., 1112
Juchniewcz v. Bridgeport Hosp., 336
June v. Union Carbide Corp., 246
Justice v. Lombardo, 534
K.H. v. J.R., 617
K.H. v. Morgan, 560
Kaiser v. Johnson & Johnson, 812, 817
Kaiser v. Millard Lumber, Inc., 1011
Kalata v. Anheuser-Busch Cos., 155
Kalenka v. Jadon, Inc., 631
Kallstrom v. United States, 657

Kansas State Bank & Trust Co. v. Specialized Transp. Servs., Inc., 885
Kaplan v. Mamelak, 117
Kappenman v. Klipfel, 433
Karas v. Strevell, 371
Karst v. Shur-Co., 832
Katamay v. Chicago Transit Authority, 404
Katko v. Briney, 97
Katrina Canal Breaches Litigation, In re, 517
Kaufman v. i-Stat Corp., 1125
Kaufman v. Langhofer, 662
Kawasaki Kisen Kaisha Ltd. v. Regal-Beloit Corp., 361
KBR, Inc., Burn Pit Litigation, In re, 519
KD v. Douglas Cty. Sch. Dist. No. 001, 607
Keans v. Bottiarelli, 926
Keller v. Koca, 618
Kellermann v. McDonough, 297
Kelley v. La Force, 73
Kelley v. Story Cty. Sheriff, 123
Kelley, Ex parte, 489
Kelly v. Berg, 141
Kelly v. Hartford Cas. Ins. Co., 471
Kelly v. VinZant, 464
Kemezy v. Peters, 938, 952
Kennedy v. Parrott, 118
Kenton v. Hyatt Hotels Corp., 923
Kentucky River Medical Center v. McIntosh, 423
Kerans v. Porter Paint Co., 1007
Kerkman v. Hintz, 455
Kerns v. Apfel, 1022
Kerr v. Corning Glass Works, 803
Kerr-McGee Corp. v. Hutto, 988
Kesner v. Superior Court, 553, 656
Kessel v. Leavitt, 1083
Khalifa v. Shannon, 1083
Khan v. Singh, 234, 473
Kilgore v. Shepard Co., 233
Kim ex rel. Alexander, Estate of v. Coxe, 633
Kim v. Lakeside Adult Family Home, 488
Kim v. United States, 516
Kimble v. Land Concepts, Inc., 950
Kinard v. Coats Co., Inc., 846
King v. Lens Creek Ltd. Partnership, 744
Kiowa Tribe of Oklahoma v. Mfg. Techs., Inc., 503
Kircher v. City of Jamestown, 586
Kiriakos v. Phillips, 161, 630
Kirk v. Denver Public Co., 940
Kirkbride v. Terex USA, LLC, 832
Kirlin v. Halverson, 731

Kiser v. A.W. Chesterton Co., 387
Kitowski v. United States, 521
Kivland v. Columbia Orthopaedic Group, LLP, 269, 305
Klasch v. Walgreen Co., 456
Klayman v. Zuckerberg, 1053
Klein v. Pyrodyne Corp., 773
Klein v. United States, 434
Kline v. 1500 Mass. Ave. Apartment Corp., 612
Kline v. Kline, 60
Klutschkowski v. PeaceHealth, 678, 932
K-Mart Corp. v. Gipson, 225
K-Mart Corp. v. Herring, 989
Knapton v. Monk, 756
Knepper v. Brown, 1113
Knick v. Township of Scott, Pennsylvania, 123
Knievel v. ESPN, 1048
Knitz v. Minster Machine Co., 809
Knowlton v. Ross, 65
Ko v. Maxim Healthcare Services, Inc., 655
Koch v. Norris Public Power District, 227
Koenig v. Koenig, 422
Koeppel v. Speirs, 1080
Koffman v. Garnett, 61
Kohl v. Kohl, 116
Kolson v. District of Columbia Dept. of Employment Services, 988
Komlodi v. Picciano, 305
Konchar v. Cebular, 136
Kordus v. Montes, 388
Kowalski v. Rose Drugs of Dardanelle, Inc., 456
Kramer v. Catholic Charities of the Diocese of Fort Wayne-South Bend, Inc., 216, 221
Krause v. Jones, 80
Kremen v. Cohen, 74
Krinitt v. Idaho Dep't of Fish & Game, 232
Krischer v. McIver, 462
Kruger v. Nebraska, 531
Kubert v. Best, 177
Kuchera v. Jersey Shore Family Health Center, 499
Kudlacik v. Johnny's Shawnee, Inc., 628
Kuligoski v. Brattleboro Retreat, 624
Kuligoski v. Rapoza, 740
Kumar v. Gate Gourmet, Inc., 41
Kumar v. Patel, 96
Kumho Tire Co., Ltd. v. Carmichael, 841
Kurns v. Railroad Friction Prods. Corp., 862

L.A.C. v. Ward Parkway Shopping Center Co., 601

Labadie v. Norwalk Rehabilitation Services, Inc., 989

Labatt Food Service, L.P., In re, 706

Labbe, Ex Parte, 716

Lacko, ex rel. Griswatch, Estate of v. Mercy Hosp., Cadillac, 483

LaCoste v. Pendleton Methodist Hosp., LLC, 477

Lageman ex rel. Lageman v. Zepp, 473

Laird v. Nelms, 507

Lake George Tort Claims, In re, 571

Lake v. D & L Langley Trucking, Inc., 324

Lake v. Memphis Landsmen, LLC, 861

Lakey v. Puget Sound Energy, Inc., 765

LaLonde v. County of Riverside, 84

Lam v. United States, 514

Lamont Bair Enterprises, Inc. v. City of Idaho Falls, 529

Lamprey v. Britton Const., Inc., 394

LAN/STV v. Martin K. Eby Constr. Co., 1130

Landeros v. Flood, 607

Landers v. East Texas Salt Water Disposal Company, 249

Landis v. Hearthmark, LLC, 496

Landry v. Bellanger, 884

Laney v. Vance, 694

Lang v. Holly Hill Motel, Inc., 156, 429

Langan v. St. Vincent's Hosp. of New York, 704

Langlois v. Town of Proctor, 337, **572**

Lanier v. Wal-Mart Stores, Inc., 215

Lanus v. United States, 522

Largey v. Rothman, 461

Larrimore v. American National Insurance Co., 290

Larsen v. Banner Health System, 664

Larsen v. Davis Cty. Sch. Dist., 118

Larson & Larson, P.A. v. TSA Indus., Inc., 386

Las Vegas, City of v. Evans, 1000

Lasley v. Combined Transport, Inc., 252

Lasley v. Hylton, 187

Laster v. Norfolk Southern Ry. Co., 418

Latimer v. Roaring Toyz, Inc., 1098

Latzel v. Bartek, 309

Laurel v. Prince, 673

Law v. Griffith, 928

Lawnwood Med. Ctr., Inc. v. Sadow, 1066

Lawrence v. Fox, 1118

Lawson v. City of Diboll, 433

Lawson v. Mitsubishi Motor Sales of Am., Inc., 229

Laybourn v. City of Wasilla, 1134

Lazenby v. Mark's Const., Inc., 439

Le v. Lautrup, 406

Leavitt v. Brockton Hospital, Inc., 280

Leavitt v. Twin Cnty. Rental Co., 581

LeBlanc v. Logan Hilton Joint Venture, 575

LeBlanc v. Snelgrove, 69

Lebron v. Gottlieb Mem'l Hosp., 932

Ledbetter v. Hunter, 479

Lee v. Crookston Coca-Cola Bottling Co., 799

Lee v. Luigi, Inc., 441

Lee v. State Farm Mut. Ins. Co., 650, 654

Leichtamer v. American Motors, Co., 806

Leichtman v. WLW Jacor Communications Inc., 55

Leighton v. City of New York, 679

Leining v. Foster Poultry Farms, Inc., 1114

Lemington Home for the Aged, In re, 1124

Lemoine v. Wolfe, 1071

Leonbruno v. Champlain Silk Mills, In re, 990

Leordeaunu v. American Protection Ins. Co., 989

LePage v. Horne, 149

LeRoy Fibre Co. v. Chicago, Milwaukee & St. Paul Ry. Co., 346

Levens v. Campbell, 1108

Levesque v. Doocy, 1048, 1057

Levin v. State, 445

Levine v. Russell Blaine Co., 218

Lewellen v. Franklin, 940

Lewellen v. Schneck Medical Center, 482

Lewis Operating Corp. v. Superior Court, 359

Lewis v. Ariens Co., 837

Lewis v. Dirt Sports LLC, 97

Lewis v. Lead Indus. Ass'n, 928

Lewis v. MBC Constr. Co., 922

Lexmark Int'l., Inc. v. Static Control Componenets, Inc., 1088

Libbey v. Hampton Water Works Co., 584

Libby v. Eighth Jud. Dist. Ct., 379

Liberty Mut. Ins. Co. v. Steadman, 643

Liberty v. State, Dept. of Transp., 433

Licari v. Elliott, 1035

Lickteig v. Kolar, 492

Lifson v. City of Syracuse, 141

Limones v. School District of Lee County, 178
Lincoln Elec. Co. v. McLemore, 383
Lincoln General Ins. Co. v. Detroit Diesel Corp., 799
Lincoln, City of v. County of Lancaster, 45, 111
Lindblom v. Sun Aviation, Inc., 162
Lindsey v. E & E Auto. & Tire Serv., Inc., 587
Lingenfelter v. Astrue, 1027
Lininger v. Eisenbaum, 684
Linnear v. Centerpoint Energy Entex/Reliant Energy, 229
Lippincott v. Whisenhunt, 1057
Lipsky, In re, 1088
Lipson v. Superior Court of Orange County, 441
Liriano v. Hobart Corp., 826, 830
Lisa M. v. Henry Mayo Newhall Mem. Hosp., 711, 732
Liszewski v. Target Corp., 600
Little v. Liquid Air Corp., 211
Livings, Estate of v. Sage's Investment Group, LLC, 429
LM v. United States, 507
Lodge v. Arett Sales Corp., 292
Loe v. Lenhardt, 773
Loge v. United States, 516
Lohnas v. Luzi, 379
Long v. Houser, 721
Loomis v. Amazon.com LLC, 784
Lopez v. Intercept Youth Services, Inc., 987
Lord v. Lovett, 265, 266
Lorenzo v. Wirth, 826
Los Angeles Unified Sch. Dist. v. S&W Atlas Iron & Metal Co., 68
Losee v. Clute, 778
Loughran v. The Phillies, 369
Louis v. Louis, 423
Louisville SW Hotel, LLC v. Lindsey, 919
Loungee Conservancy v. Citimortgage, 74
Lourim v. Swenson, 732
Love v. Walker, 448
Lovelace v. Anderson, 718
Lovely v. United States, 521
Lovick v. Wil-Rich, 837
Lowrey v. Montgomery Kone, Inc., 228
Lozano v. Montoya Alvarez, 392, 394
Lu v. United States, 375
Lucenti v. Laviero, 1006
Lucier v. Impact Recreation, Ltd., 436
Lugenbuhl v. Dowling, 466
Lumley v. Gye, 1088
Lundman v. McKown, 455
Lunsford v. Saberhagen Holdings, 807

Lusby v. Lusby, 490
Luthringer v. Moore, 773
Lydia v. Horton, 629, 633
Lyman v. Huber, 644
Lynch v. Scheininger, 682
Lyons v. Midnight Sun Transp. Servs., Inc., 140
M.D.C.G. v. United States, 505
Maas v. United States, 521
MacClatchey v. HCA Health Servs. of Fla., Inc., 228, 233
MacDermid v. Discover Fin. Servs., 644
MacDonald v. City Hosp., Inc., 933
MacDonald v. Thomas M. Cooley Law Sch., 1127
Mack v. Carmack, 679
Macke v. Patton, 704
MacPherson v. Buick Motor Co., 778, 794, 1118
Mader v. Duquesne Light Co., 16
Madison v. Home Products Corp., 793
Magee v. United States, 505
Maglin v. Tschannerl, 911
Mahon v. United States, 515, 518
Mahoney & Hagberg v. Newgard, 1050
Maison v. New Jersey Transit Corp., 403
Majca v. Beekil, 674
Majestic Realty Associates, Inc. v. Toti Contracting Co., 736
Malcolm v. Evenflo Co., 222
Maldonado v. Sinai Med. Group, Inc., 923
Malen v. MTD Products, Inc., 808
Maltais v. Equitable Life Assur. Soc'y of United States, 991
Manchester v. Drivers Management, LLC, 1000
Mancini v. City of Tacoma, 532
Maness v. Gordon, 389
Mann v. Northgate Investors, L.L.C., 437
Mann v. Shusteric Enterp., Inc., 629
Manners v. 5 Star Lodge & Stables, LLC, 413
Mannion & Mannion, Inc. v. Mendez, 726
Marcum v. Bowden, 629
Marcus v. Staubs, 298
Marks v. St. Luke's Episcopal Hosp., 478
Marmet Health Care Center, Inc. v. Brown, 359, 486
Marquay v. Eno, 603
Marshall v. Burger King Corp., 596
Marshall v. Burlington Northern, Inc., 400
Marshall v. Dodds, 394

Marshall v. Nugent, 311
Marshall v. Southern Railway Co., 156
Marsingill v. O'Malley, 461
Martell v. Driscoll, 632, 633
Martin Luther King, Jr., Ctr. for Soc.
    Change, Inc. v. Am. Heritage Prods.,
    Inc., 1104
Martin v. Abbott Labs., 900
Martin v. Brady, 534
Martin v. Christman, 757
Martin v. Herzog, 152, 830
Martin v. Marciano, 629
Martin v. Rhode Island Public Transit
    Auth., 1000
Martin v. Richey, 385
Martin v. Tug & Barge, Inc., 1094
Martin v. United States, 916
Martinez v. New Mexico Dept. of
    Transp., 530
Martinez v. Republic of Cuba, 116
Martinez v. Wilson, 351
Martinez v. Woodmar IV Condo.
    Homeowners Assoc., Inc., 613
Martin-McFarlane v. City of
    Philadelphia, 111
Maryea v. Velardi, 530
Maryland Cas. Co. v. Asbestos Claims
    Ct., 580
Massenburg v. City of Petersburg, 529
Massey v. Conagra Foods, Inc., 805
Massey v. Mercy Med. Ctr. Redding,
    455
**Mathias v. Accor Economy
    Lodging, Inc., 950**
Matthews v. Remington Arms Co., 852
Matthews v. Yoplait USA, Inc., 228
Matthies v. Mastromonaco, 464
Mattox v. State, Dept. of Corrections,
    596
Maupin v. Tankersly, 334
Maurer v. Speedway, LLC, 161
Mavrikidis v. Petullo, 735
Maxxim Shared Services, LLC, State
    ex rel. v. McGraw, 656
Maybee v. Jacobs Motor Co., 1134
Mayberry v. Dukes, 1007
Mayor of City of Garden City v.
    Harris, 431
McAdory v. Rogers, 932
McBride v. Bennett, 531
McCabe v. Am. Honda Motor Co., 813
McCahill v. New York Transportation
    Co., 296
McCann v. Hatchett, 989
**McCann v. Wal-Mart Stores, Inc.,
    63**
McCarthy v. Fuller, 1058
McCarthy v. Olin Corp., 820
McCathern v. Toyota Motor Corp., 811

McClung v. Delta Square Ltd. P'ship,
    602
McComish v. DeSoi, 218
McConnell v. United States, 521
McCoy v. Montgomery, 936
McCulley v. U.S. Bank of Montana,
    1115
McDermott v. State, 220
McDougald v. Garber, 915, 921
McDougall v. CRC Indus., Inc., 552
McDougall v. Lamm, 662
McGeehan, United States v., 1135
McGlone v. Hauger, 61
McGowan v. United States, 506
McGrath v. State Dept. of Public
    Safety, 1000
McGuire v. Curry, 618
McGuire v. Hodges, 209, 257
McIlroy v. Gibson's Apple Orchard,
    297
McKenzie v. Hawai'i Permanente
    Medical Group, Inc., 625
McKinley v. Casson, 348
McKinney v. Okoye, 1051
McKinnis v. Women & Infants Hosp.
    of R.I., 448
McKiver v. Murphy-Brown, LLC, 764
McKown v. Simon Property Group,
    Inc., 600
McLain v. Schweiker, 1021
McLaughlin Freight Lines, Inc. v.
    Gentrup, 227
McLean v. City of New York, 527
McLean v. Maverik Country Stores,
    Inc., 632
McLemore ex rel. McLemore v.
    Elizabeth Med. Investors, Ltd.
    P'ship, 936
McLeod v. Millette, 384
McMahon v. Craig, 662
McMahon v. Presidential Airways,
    Inc., 865
McNair v. Johnson & Johnson, 790
McNamara v. Honeyman, 339
McNamee v. A.J.W., 616
Mead v. SanofiAventis U.S., Inc., 207
Mead v. Sec'y of Health & Human
    Services, 1015
Meals v. Ford Motor Co., 924
Medcalf v. Washington Heights
    Condominium Ass'n, Inc., 278
Medina v. Hochberg, 625
Medtronic, Inc. v. Lohr, 860
Meek v. Montana Eighth Judicial
    Dist. Court, 927
Meinck v. City of Gastonia, 529
Melchor v. Singh, 278
Mellon Mortgage Co. v. Holder, 287

Memphis Community School Dist. v. Stachura, 81

Mengswater v. Anthony Kempler Trucking Inc., 302

Mensink v. American Grain, 412

Mercer v. Vanderbilt Univ., 340

Merck & Co., Inc. v. Garza, 257, 842

Meridian Medical Systems, LLC v. Epix Therapeutics, Inc., 750

Merit Energy Co. v. Horr, 740

Mesman v. Crane Pro Services, 812

Methodist Healthcare-Olive Branch Hosp. v. McNutt, 716

Metropolitan Property & Casualty Ins. Co. v. Deere & Co., 803

Metropolitan Stevedore Co. v. Rambo, 980

Mexicali Rose v. Superior Court (Clark v. Mexicali Rose), 804

Meyer ex rel. Coplin v. Fluor Corp., 388

Meyers v. Epstein, 118

Meyers v. Ferndale Sch. Dist., 279

Michaels v. CH2M Hill, Inc., 246, 310

Michaud v. Great Northern Nekoosa Corp., 656

Midler v. Ford Motor Co., 1104

Mik v. Federal Home Loan Mortgage Corp., 641

Mikolajczyk v. Ford Motor Co., 811, 812

Miles v. Burcham, 657

Milke v. Ratcliff Animal Hosp., Inc., 230

Milkovich v. Lorain Journal, 1065

Millea v. Erickson, 560

Miller v. Hartford Life Ins. Co., 1113

Miller v. Inglis, 438

Miller v. Rhode Island Hospital, 119

Miller v. Warren, 221

Millington v. Southeastern Elevator Co., Inc., 660

Milwaukee Auction Galleries Ltd. v. Chalk, 1129

Minnich v. Med-Waste, Inc., 437

Minns v. United States, 523

Mirand v. City of New York, 607

Miranda v. Said, 664

Mirapex Products Liab. Litigation, In re, 389

Mirkin v. Wasserman, 1125

Miron v. University of New Haven Police Dep't, 1052

Miskowiak v. Bethlehem Steel Co., 998

Mississippi Dep't of Transp. v. Nosef, 162

Missouri Pacific R.R. Co. v. Limmer, 400

Mita v. Guardsmark, LLC, 560

Mitchell Crane Services, Inc. v. Page, 301

Mitchell v. Cedar Rapids Community School Dist., 301

Mitchell v. Rochester Railway Co., 648

Mobil Oil Corp. v. Thorn, 581

Mobile Gas Serv. Corp. v. Robinson, 137

Moch Co. v. Rensselaer Water Co., 585, 1118

Mody v. Center for Women's Health, P.C., 447

Moeller v. Garlock Sealing Technologies, LLC, 841

Mohr v. Grantham, 261

Mole v. Jutton, 461

Molien v. Kaiser Foundation Hospitals, 650, 665

Monell v. Dep't of Social Services, 81, 536

Monk v. Temple George Associates, LLC, 601

Montague v. AMN Healthcare, Inc., 728

Montgomery v. Bazaz-Sehgal, 461

Montgomery v. Devoid, 75

Montgomery v. Montgomery, 1104

Montgomery v. Saleh, 533

Moody v. Delta W., Inc., 440

Mooney v. Johnson Cattle Co., Inc., 1095

Moore v. Crumpton, 617

Moore v. Ford Motor Co., 832

Moore v. Hartley Motors, 361

Moore v. Regents of the University of California, 74, 464

Moorman Mfg. Co. v. National Tank Co., 794, 1129

Moraca v. Ford Motor Co., 803

Moravec v. Moravec, 441

Morejon v. Rais Constr. Co., 226

Morgan & Pottinger, Attorneys, P.S.C. v. Botts, 1051

Morgan v. Scott, 217

Morguson v. 3M Co., 295

Morin v. Moore, 633

Morrell v. Hardin Creek, Inc., 437

Morris v. De La Torre, 600

Morris v. Giant Four Corners, Inc., 634

Morris v. Sanchez, 683

Morse v. Goduti, 422

Mortgage Specialists, Inc. v. Implode-Explode Heavy Indus., Inc., 1065

Morton v. Kirkwood, 79

Morway v. Trombly, 534

Moses ex rel. Moses, Estate of v. Sw. Va. Transit Mgmt. Co., 335

Moses v. Providence Hosp. & Med. Ctrs., Inc., 481

Moss Point School Dist. v. Stennis, 609

Motor Coach Industries, Inc. v. Khiabani ex rel. Rigaud, 832

Motyka v. City of Amsterdam, 529

Moyer v. United Dominion Industries, Inc., 853

Mrozka v. Archdiocese of St. Paul & Minneapolis, 936

Mueller v. Brannigan Bros. Restaurants & Taverns LLC, 734

Mueller v. Hill, 70

Mueller v. Tepler, 660

Mulhern v. Catholic Health Initiatives, 340

Mullen v. Zoebe, Inc., 441

Mullins v. Parkview Hospital, Inc., 41

Mummert v. Alizadeh, 706

Munroe v. Universal Health Serv., Inc., 617

Murdza v. Zimmerman, 751

Murphy v. Boston Herald, Inc., 1057

Murphy v. Lord Thompson's Manor, Inc., 667

Murray v. Indianapolis Public Schools, 323

Murray v. Oceanside Unified Sch. Dist., 1010

Murray v. Uber Technologies, Inc., 404

Murray v. UNMC Physicians, 448

Musta v. Mendota Heights Dental Center, 980

Mutual Pharmaceutical Co. v. Bartlett, 862

MV Transp., Inc. v. Allgeier, 735

Myers v. Crouse-Hinds Div. of Cooper Industries, Inc., 395

Myers v. United States, 517

NAACP v. Claiborne Hardware Co., 1096

Nabors Drilling, U.S.A. Inc. v. Escoto, 619

Nabors Well Servs., Ltd. v. Romero, 341

Nakamoto v. Kawauchi, 994

Nallan v. Helmsley-Spear, Inc., 600, 876

Nally v. Grace Community Church of the Valley, 455

Nalwa v. Cedar Fair, L.P., 405

Nam Soon Jeon v. 445 Seaside, Inc., 834

Nason v. Pruchnic, 16

Nasser v. Parker, 624

National Cas. Co. v. Northern Trust Bank, 676

National Property Holdings v. Westergren, 1127

Nationwide Mut. Ins. Co. v. Pasiak, 65

Navarette v. United States, 518

Navarro v. Block, 536

Navo v. Bingham Memorial Hosp., 454

NCAA Student-Athlete Name, & Likeness Licensing Litig., In re, 1104

Nealis v. Baird, 680

Needham v. Price, 490

Neel v. Sewell, 492

Neff v. Wal-Mart Stores E., LP, 66

Nei v. Burley, 1134

Neighbarger v. Irwin Industries, Inc., 440

Nelson v. Carroll, 63

Nelson v. Nason, 750

Nelson v. United States, 505

Neppel v. Development Homes, Inc., 641

Nestorowich v. Ricotta, 448

Network Automation, Inc. v. Advanced Sys. Concepts, Inc., 1102

Nevue v. Close, 911

New Hampshire Division for Children, Youth and Families, Petition of, 383

New Texas Auto Auction Services, L.P. v. Gomez, 791

New York City Asbestos Litigation, In re, 836

New York Times Co. v. Sullivan, 1053

New York, City of v. A-1 Jewelry & Pawn, Inc., 824

New York, City of v. Beretta U.S.A. Corp., 824

Newberry v. Allied Stores, Inc., 1067

Newmark v. Gimbels, Inc., 793

Newton v. Ellis, 545

Newton v. MJK/BJK, LLC, 765

Niang v. Dryades YMCA School of Commerce, Inc., 270

Nichol v. Stass, 497

Nicholasville Police Dep't, City of v. Abraham, 140

Nichols v. Progressive Northern Ins. Co., 629

Nicolay v. Stukel, 162

Nicolet, Inc. v. Nutt, 903

Nodak Mut. Ins. Co. v. Stegman, 691

Nolasco v. Malcom, 491

Nolechek v. Gesuale, 495

Norbeck v. Flathead County, 384

Norfolk & Western Railway v. Ayers, 672, 875

Norfolk Southern Railway Co. v. Shanklin, 400

Norgart v. Upjohn Co., 384

Norman v. Anderson Regional Med.
    Center, 449
Norman v. Borison, 1051
Norman v. Xytex Corp., 685
North Am. Med. Corp. v. Axiom
    Worldwide, Inc., 1102
North Pac. Ins. Co. v. Stucky, 661
Nostrame v. Santiago, 1094
Not Afraid v. State, 179
Nova Southeast University, Inc. v.
    Gross, 610
Novak Heating & Air Conditioning v.
    Carrier Corp., 235
Novak v. Capital Mgmt. & Dev. Corp.,
    600
Nowotny v. L & B Contract Indus.,
    Inc., 384
Nulle v. Krewer, 726
Nunez v. Carrabba's Italian Grill, Inc.,
    631
Nunez v. Professional Transit
    Management of Tucson, 405
O'Banner v. McDonald's Corp., 745
O'Brien v. Synnott, 118
O'Connell v. Biomet, Inc., 471
O'Connell v. Chasdi, 1010
O'Connell v. State, 498
O'Connor v. Burningham, 1064
O'Guin v. Bingham County, 157
O'Neil v. Crane Co., 836
O'Stricker v. Jim Walter Corp., 381
O'Sullivan v. Shaw, 430
Oakly Enterprises, LLC v. NPI, LLC,
    338
Ohio Farmers Ins. Co. v. Norman, 713
Okin v. Village of Cornwall-On-
    Hudson Police Dep't, 539
Oklahoma Tax Comm'n v. Citizen
    Band Potawatomi Indian Tribe of
    Oklahoma, 503
Okraynets v. Metropolitan Transp.
    Auth., 924
Old Island Fumigation, Inc. v. Barbee,
    774
Olier v. Bailey, 756
Oliva v. Nivar, 509
Ollerman v. O'Rourke Co., 1130
Olson v. Bismarck Parks and
    Recreation Dist, 433
Olson, United States v., 505
Omaha Healthcare Center, LLC v.
    Johnson, 486
One Indus., LLC v. Jim O'Neal Dist.,
    Inc., 1102
Onita Pacific Corp. v. Trustees of
    Bronson, 1116
Opati v. Republic of Sudan, 915
Opinion of the Justices, 1076

Ordinola v. University Physician
    Assocs., 479
Orientale v. Jennings, 15
Orleans, United States v., 518
Ornstein v. New York City Health &
    Hosp. Corp., 673
Orphan v. Pilnik, 461
Ortberg v. Goldman Sachs Group, 641
Ortega v. Kmart Corp., 215
Ortega v. Pajaro Valley Unified Sch.
    Dist., 391
Ortiz v. United States, 522
Osborn v. Haley, 508
Osborn v. Mason County, 532, 624
Osborn v. Twin Town Bowl, Inc., 630
Ostergren v. Cuccinelli, 1082
Otero v. Jordon Restaurant
    Enterprises, 745
Ouch v. Khea, 601
Ouellette v. Carde, 349
Oulette v. Beaupre, 384
Our Lady of Peace, Inc. v. Morgan, 732
Ovecka v. Burlington Northern Santa
    Fe R.R. Co., 727
Overseas Tankship (U.K.) Ltd. v.
    Mort's Dock & Eng'g Co. Ltd. (The
    Wagon Mound), 280
Owens Corning Fiberglass Corp. v.
    Parrish, 848
Owens v. Republic of Sudan, 646
Owens-Corning Fiberglass Corp. v.
    Ballard, 936
P.W. v. Children's Hosp. Colorado, 305
Pace v. State, 532
Pace v. Wal-Mart Stores East, LP, 214
Pacheco v. Ames, 230
Pacht v. Morris, 554
Packer v. Riverbend Communications,
    LLC, 410
**Pagelsdorf v. Safeco Insurance
    Co., 434**
Pages v. Seliman-Tapia, 96
Painter v. Amerimex Drilling I, Ltd.,
    722
Palandjian v. Foster, 447, 450
Palka v. Servicemaster Management
    Services Corp., 579
Pallares v. Seinar, 1075
Palmer ex rel. Palmer v. Walker
    Jamar Co., 707
Palmer v. Del Webb's High Sierra,
    1000
Palmer v. Zaklama, 1073
**Palsgraf v. Long Island Railroad
    Co., 281**
Pamela L. v. Farmer, 615
Papa John's Intern., Inc. v. McCoy,
    1070
Parillo v. Rhode Island Hosp., 707

Parish v. ICON Health and Fitness, Inc., 820
Parker v. Holiday Hospitality Franchising, Inc., 214, 745
Parker v. Mobil Oil Corp., 842
Parrish v. Latham & Watkins, 1073, 1074
Parsons v. Crown Disposal Co., 192
Parsons v. Smithey, 617
Partlow v. Stadler, 80
Passarello v. Grumbine, 448
Patch v. Hillerich & Bradsby Co., 834
Patterson v. Blair, 731
Pavik v. George & Lynch, Inc., 180
Pavlik v. Lane Ltd./Tobacco Exporters International, 834
Pavlou v. City of New York, 335
Pawlowski v. American Family Mut. Ins. Co., 757
Payne v. Gardner, 852
Payton v. Abbott Labs, 677
Payton v. United States, 531
Paz v. Brush Engineered Materials, Inc., 388, 650
Paz v. State of California, 580
Pehle v. Farm Bureau Life Ins. Co., 162
Pelitire v. Rinker, 114
Pelletier v. Fort Kent Golf Club, 331
Penn Harris Madison Sch. Corp. v. Howard, 350
Pensacola Motor Sales, Inc. v. Daphne Automotive, LLC, 1045
Penunuri v. Sundance Partners, Ltd., 359
Perez v. Wyeth Laboratories., Inc., 835
Perini Corp., State v., 395
Perius v. Nodak Mut. Ins. Co., 248
Perkins v. Wilkinson Sword, Inc., 853
Perl v. Meher, 1038
Perri v. Furama Restaurant, Inc., 187
Perrine v. E.I. du Pont de Nemours & Co., 925
Perrotti v. Gonicberg, 651
Perry v. S.N., 162, 607
Peters v. Forster, 745
Peters v. Menard, Inc., 105
Peters v. Wady Industries, Inc., 1010
Petersen v. Raymond Corp., 820
Peterson v. Cisco Systems, Inc., 727
Peterson v. Kings Gate Partners-Omaha I, L.P., 612
Peterson, Commonwealth v., 596
Petrovich v. Share Health Plan of Illinois, Inc., 748
PetSmart, Inc. v. Eighth Jud. Dist. Ct., 578
PF Chang's v. Industrial Com'n of Arizona, 992

Philadelphia Newspapers, Inc. v. Hepps, 1065
Philip Morris USA v. Williams, 955
Phillips v. Cricket Lighters, 854
Phillips v. Fujitec Am., Inc., 330
Phillips, State v., 95
Phipps v. Copeland Corp., 333
Picher v. Roman Catholic Bishop of Portland, 498, 500, 501
Piech v. Layendecker, 410
Pierson v. Ray, 86
Piltch v. Ford Motor Co., 808
Ping v. Beverly Enterprises, Inc., 706
Pinnacle Peak Developers v. TRW Investment Corp., 1127
Pino v. United States, 679
Pinter v. American Family Mut. Ins. Co., 440
Piper v. Goodring & Co., 73
Pipher v. Parsell, 174
Pippen v. NBCUniversal Media, LLC, 1048
Piselli v. 75th Street Med., 388
Pittman v. Western Engineering Co., 1003
Pitts v. Genie Industries, Inc., 803
Pittsburg Reduction Co. v. Horton, 313
Pixley v. Pro-Pak Industries, Inc., 1006
Planned Parenthood of the Columbia/Willamette, Inc. v. American Coalition of Life Activists, 63
Pletan v. Gaines, 531
PLIVA v. Mensing, 862
Ploof v. Putnam, 124, 125
Podias v. Mairs, 561
Podrygula v. Bray, 386
Pohl v. County of Furnas, 325
Pokis v. Buck Run Coal Co., 993
Pokora v. Wabash Ry., 156
Polanco v. Lombardi, 391
Polay v. McMahon, 1080
Polemis Case, 283
Polmatier v. Russ, 45
Polston v. Boomershine Pontiac-GMC Truck Inc., 808
POM Wonderful LLC v. Coca-Cola Co., 1088
Pommells v. Perez, 1038
Pooshs v. Philip Morris USA, Inc., 387
Popovich v. Allina Health System, 747
Posas v. Horton, 139
Posecai v. Wal-Mart Stores, Inc., 597
Post and Beam Equities Group, LLC v. Sunne Village Development Property Owners Ass'n, 764
Potter v. Chicago Pneumatic Tool Co., 802

Potter v. Firestone Tire & Rubber Co., 668
Poutman v. Wenatchee Valley Medical Center, P.S., 478
Powell v. Catholic Med. Ctr., 450
Prete v. Cray, 774
Price v. Kitsap Transit, 890
Price v. Purdue Pharma Co., 354
Primoris Energy Services Corp. v. Myers, 14
Prince v. Atchison, Topeka & Santa Fe Ry., 726
Pringle v. Valdez, 923
Progressive Halcyon Ins. Co. v. Philippi, 1010
Provoncha v. Vermont Motocross Ass'n, 363
Prows v. Indus. Comm'n of Utah, 992
Puckett v. Mt. Carmel Reg'l Med. Ctr., 277, 308
Puckrein v. ATI Transport, Inc., 741
Pullen v. West, 770
Purcell v. United States, 519
Purtle v. Shelton, 138
Purvis v. Grant Parish Sch. Bd., 329
Pusey v. Bator, 741
Pustejovsky v. Rapid-American Corp., 387
QBE Ins. Corp. v. Jinx-Proof Inc., 57
Qualitex Co. v. Jacobson Products Co., 1099
Quilez-Velar v. Ox Bodies, Inc., 812
Quinby v. Plumsteadville Family Practice, Inc., 226, 473
Quiroz v. ALCOA Inc., 288, 553
Quisenberry v. Huntington Ingalls Inc., 288
Qureshi v. Ahmed, 430
Qwest Servs. Corp. v. Blood, 16
R.R. v. New Life Community Church of CMA, Inc., 388
Ra v. Superior Court, 655
Racine v. Moon's Towing, 418
Raddin v. Macalaster Educ. Found., Inc., 57
Rael v. Cadena, 749
Raess v. Doescher, 60
Ragonese v. Racing Corp. of West Virginia, 411
Rains v. Bend of the River, 161
Rakestraw v. Gen. Dynamics Land Sys., Inc., 998
Rallis v. Demoulas Super Mkts., Inc., 176
Ramirez v. Nelson, 160
Ramirez v. Plough, Inc., 863
Ramkumar v. Grand Style Transp. Enters., Inc., 337
Ramon v. Nebo School Dist., 735

Ramos v. Brenntag Specialties, Inc., 836
Ramsey v. Georgia Southern Univ. Advanced Development Center, 836
Rand Res., LLC v. City of Carson, 1129
Randi W. v. Muroc Joint Unified Sch. Dist., 1113
Rappaport v. Nichols, 626
Rapuano v. Trustees of Dartmouth Coll., 606
Rascher v. Friend, 287
Rasmussen v. State Farm Mut. Aut. Ins. Co., 289
Ray Bell Const. Co. v. King, 989
RBC Capital Markets, LLC v. Jervis, 1124
Reardon ex rel. Estate of Parsons v. King, 734
Reardon v. Windswept Farm, 360
Reavis v. Slominski, 114
Reddick v. Chater, 1026
Redwing v. Catholic Bishop for the Diocese of Memphis, 618
Reed v. Hinderland, 751
Register.com v. Verio, Inc., 77
Rehn v. Secretary of Health & Human Services, 1015
Reicheneker v. Reicheneker, 411
Reid v. Pierce Cnty., 647
Reid v. Spadone Machine Co., 854
Reif v. Nagy, 72
Reilly v. Anderson, 749
Reis v. Volvo Cars of North America, 811
Reiser v. Coburn, 698
Reiter v. Dyken, 324
Remy v. MacDonald, 675
Renner v. Retzer Resources, Inc., 212
Renslow v. Mennonite Hospital, 680
Respublica v. De Longchamps, 40
Reyes-Colon v. United States, 516
Reynolds v. CB Sports Bar, Inc., 600
Reynolds v. Hicks, 629
Reynolds v. MacFarlane, 53
Reynolds v. W.H. Hinman Co., 767
RGR, LLC v. Settle, 335
Rice v. Collins Communication, Inc., 534, 584
Rice v. Diocese of Altoona-Johnstown, 391
Rice v. White, 560
Richardson v. Chapman, 924
Rickey v. Boden, 373
Rico v. Flores, 353
Ridgway Lane & Associates, Inc. v. Watson, 385
Ridings v. Maze, 657

Riegel v. Medronic, Inc., 862
Rieger v. Giant Eagle, Inc., 244
Riggs v. Georgia-Pacific LLC, 693
Right v. Breen, 237
Rippy v. Shepard, 633
Rismiller v. Gemini Ins. Co., 704
Risner v. Ohio Dept. of Transp., 530
Riss v. City of New York, 523, 585
Ritchie v. Glidden Co., 836
Ritchie v. United States, 522
Rittenour v. Gibson, 886
Rivas-Villegas v. Cortesluna, 82
Rivera v. Philip Morris, Inc., 832
Riviello v. Waldron, 711
Roberts v. Galen of Virginia, Inc., 483
Roberts v. State, 143
Roberts v. Williamson, 662
Robertson v. LeMaster, 619
Robins Dry Dock & Repair Co. v.
    Flint, 1118
Robins v. Harris, 113
Robinson v. District of Columbia, 217
Robinson v. LeCorps, 453
Robinson v. Lindsay, 151
Robinson v. Matt Mary Moran, Inc.,
    631
Robinson v. Reed-Prentice Division of
    Package Co., 855
Robinson v. Vivirito, 177
Rocha v. Faltys, 557
Rock Wool Mfg. Co., Ex parte, 1007
Rodebush v. Oklahoma Nursing
    Homes, Ltd., 731
Rodenburg v. Fargo-Moorhead Young
    Men's Christian Ass'n, 883
Rodgers v. Kemper Constr. Co., 730
Rodriguez v. Clark, 449
Rodriguez v. Del Sol Shopping Center
    Associates, L.P., 177, 596, 602
Rodriguez v. Kroger Co., 744
Rodriguez v. Primadonna Co., 629
Rodriguez v. Señior Frog's de la Isla,
    Inc., 920
Rodriguez v. Williams, 354
Roe v. Wade, 680
Rogers v. Louisville Land Co., 644
Roitz v. Kidman, 655
Rolf v. Tri State Motor Transit Co.,
    661
Rollo-Carlson ex rel. Flackus-Carlson
    v. United States, 507
Roman v. Estate of Gobbo, 144
Rome v. Flower Memorial Hospital,
    477
Romine v. Johnson Controls, Inc., 813
Romine v. Village of Irving, 178
Rondini v. Bunn, 305
Roop v. Parker Northwest Paving Co.,
    1073

Roos v. Morrison, 559
Root v. New Liberty Hosp. Dist., 484
Rosales v. Stewart, 615
Rose Crewboat Servs., Inc. v. Wood
    Res., LLC, 163, 166
Rosenberg v. MetLife, Inc., 1051
Rosenblatt v. Baer, 1064
Rosenbloom v. Metromedia, Inc., 1059
Ross v. Louise Wise Servs., Inc., 935
Ross v. Lowitz, 764
Roth v. Islamic Republic of Iran, 645
Roth v. Norfalco LLC, 400
Rothwell v. Nine Mile Falls School
    Dist., 1000
Rountree v. Boise Baseball, LLC, 364
Rowe v. Mazel Thirty, LLC, 439
Rowhouses, Inc. v. Smith, 257
Rowland v. Christian, 419, 589, 620
Roy v. City of Everett, 529
Roy v. State, 428, 429
Ruiz v. Killebrew, 449
Ruiz v. Tenet Hialeah Healthsystem,
    Inc., 445
**Ruiz v. Victory Properties LLC,
    290**
Rumbauskas v. Cantor, 1077
Russell v. Ingersoll-Rand Co., 706
Rustico v. Intuitive Surgical, Inc., 391
Rutherford v. Talisker Canyons Fin.,
    Co., 361
Ryan v. Napier, 49
Ryder v. Union Pacific R.R. Co., 400
Rye v. Women's Care Ctr. of Memphis,
    MPLLC, 668, 682
Rylands v. Fletcher, 757, 767
S K Peightal Eng'rs, LTD v. Mid
    Valley Real Estate Solutions V,
    LLC, 571
S&S Oil, Inc. v. Jackson, 373
Sacco v. High Country Indep. Press,
    Inc., 667
Sacramento, County of v. Lewis, 80
Sadler v. PacifiCare of Nev., 925
Saenz v. Whitewater Voyages, Inc.,
    706
Safeway Stores, Inc. v. Nest-Kart, 880
Safford Unified School Dist. No. 1 v.
    Redding, 82
Sagebrush Res., LLC v. Peterson, 77
Saine v. Comcast Cablevision of Ark.,
    Inc., 618
Sakiyama v. AMF Bowling Ctrs., Inc.,
    601
Saleh v. Damron, 680
Saleh v. Titan Corp., 518
SaleHoo Group, Ltd. v. ABC Co., 1065
Salerno v. Spectrum Med. Group, 450
Salica v. Tucson Heart Hosp.-
    Carondelet, L.L.C., 260

Salinas v. Vierstra, 365
Salinetro v. Nystrom, 244
Sallee v. Stewart, 433
Salt Lake City Corp. v. Labor Com'n, 989
Saltsman v. Sharp, 422
Samples v. Florida Birth-Related Neurological Injury Comp. Ass'n, 933
Samson v. Nahulu, 329
Sanatass v. Consolidated Investing Co., 745
Sanchez v. City of New York, 336
Sanchez v. Medicorp Health System, 748
Sanders v. Alger, 142, 148
Sanders v. United States, 517
Sanderson Farms, Inc. v. McCullough, 58
Sands ex rel. Sands v. Green, 388
Sangaray v. West River Assocs., LLC, 412
Sanislo v. Give Kids the World, Inc., 363
Santa Barbara, City of v. Superior Court, 361
Santa Rosa Health Care Corp. v. Garcia, 625
Santana v. Rainbow Cleaners, 624
Santana v. Zilog, Inc., 679
Santiago v. First Student, Inc., 201
Santiago v. Tanaka, 1134
Santor v. A & M Karagheusian, Inc., 794
Sapko v. State, 993
Saratoga Fishing Co. v. J.M. Martinac & Co., 798
Sardis v. Overhead Door Corp., 842
Sarna v. American Bosch Magneto Corp., 304
Sartin v. Estate of McPike, 246
Saucier ex rel. Mallory v. McDonald's Rests. of Mont., Inc., 118
Saucier v. Katz, 86
Saunders v. Smothers, 436
Sauve v. Winfree, 1011
Savage v. Three Rivers Med. Ctr., 233
Sawyer Brothers, Inc. v. Island Transporter, LLC, 650
Schack v. Schack, 657
Schaecher v. Bouffault, 1048
Schaefer v. Amer. Family Mut. Ins. Co., 697
Schaerrer v. Stewart's Plaza Pharmacy, Inc., 835
Schafer v. American Cyanamid Co., 1013
Schafer v. JLC Food Systems, Inc., 805

Schanne v. Addis, 1051
Scheer v. Rockne Motors Corp., 910
Schelling v. Humphrey, 618
Schenk v. Schenk, 490
Schirmer v. Mt. Auburn Obstetrics & Gynecology Assocs., Inc., 685
Schlumberger Technology Corp. v. Pasko, 383
Schmidt v. Mahoney, 625
Schmitz v. National Collegiate Athletic Ass'n, 380
Schoenfeld v. Quamme, 521
Scholz v. Delp, 1066
School of Visual Arts v. Kuprewicz, 76
Schork v. Huber, 686
Schroeder v. St. Louis County, 529
Schroeder v. Weighall, 479
Schueller v. Ad Art, Inc., 792
Schultz v. Foster-Glocester Reg'l Sch. Dist., 533
Schuster v. Altenberg, 624
Schuster v. City of New York, 525
Schwarz v. Philip Morris Inc., 956
SCI Texas Funeral Services, Inc. v. Nelson, 663
Sciarrotta v. Global Spectrum, 369
Scola v. JP Morgan Chase Bank, 411
Scott v. Harris, 79
Scott v. Matlack, Inc., 161
Scott v. Universal Sales, Inc., 614, 624
Scotton v. Landers, 909
Scurti v. City of New York, 422
Seaborne-Worsley v. Mintiens, 752
Seaton v. TripAdvisor LLC, 1087
Seavers v. Methodist Med. Ctr. of Oak Ridge, 225, 473
Sebelius v. Cloer, 1015
Sebra v. Wentworth, 71
Sedgwick CMS v. Valcourt-Williams, 987
Seely v. White Motor Co., 794
Seiller Waterman, LLC v. RLB Properties, Ltd., 1074
Sekerez v. Rush Univ. Med. Ctr., 465
Self v. Executive Comm. of Ga. Baptist Convention, 450
Sellers v. Township of Abington, 531
Senna v. Florimont, 1088
Sepaugh v. LaGrone, 495
September 11 Litigation, In re, 303, 854, 933, 1017
Sernovitz v. Dershaw, 684, 687
Service Oil, Inc. v. Gjestvang, 73
Sexton, Commonwealth v., 529
Shackil v. Lederle Labs., 904
Shadday v. Omni Hotels Management Corp., 602
Shakeri v. ADT Sec. Servs., Inc., 575
Shanks v. Upjohn Co., 812

Shansky v. United States, 511
Shantigar Found. v. Bear Mountain
  Builders, 892
Sharon P. v. Arman, 599
Sharrieff v. DBS Automotive Two,
  LLC, 246
Shaw v. Jendzejec, 679
Shaw v. Metro. Gov't of Nashville &
  Davidson Cty., 162
Shea v. Matassa, 632
Shealy v. Aiken County, 999
Shearer, United States v., 521
Shearin v. Lloyd, 379
Sheehan v. City of New York, 315
Sheehan v. San Francisco 49ers, Ltd.,
  1080
Sheffer v. Carolina Forge Co., 632,
  713, 727
Shell Oil Co. v. Writt, 1050
Shelton v. Kentucky Easter Seals Soc.,
  Inc., 410, 429
Shepherd v. Gardner Wholesale, Inc.,
  142
Sheppard-Mobley v. King, 680
Sheridan v. United States, 508
Sherman v. State Dep't of Public
  Safety, 733
Sheward, State v., 879, 932
Shine v. Vega, 462
Shipley v. City of New York, 665
Shipley v. Williams, 454
Shirley v. Glass, 633
Shivers v. United States, 514
Shoemake v. Fogel, Ltd., 495
Shotts v. OP Winter Haven, Inc., 486
Show v. Ford Motor Co., 813
Shuler v. Garrett, 461
Shuler v. United States, 514
Shull v. Reid, 682
Shumsky v. Eisenstein, 379
Sibbing v. Cave, 277
Sic v. Nunan, 176
Siegel v. Ridgewells, Inc., 651
Sikkelee v. Precision Airmotive Corp.,
  860
Sikorski's Case, 992
Silver v. Sportsstuff, Inc., 260
Simler v. Dubuque Paint Equip.
  Servs., Inc., 309
Simmons ex rel. Simmons v. Sacchetti,
  436
Simmons v. Himmelreich, 505
Simmons v. Homatas, 631
Simmons v. Porter, 371
Simpson v. Roberts, 679
Sinclair v. Block, 449
Sindell v. Abbott Labs, 899, 902
Sindi v. El-Moslimany, 642
Sinsel v. Olsen, 616

Sioux City & Pacific RR. Co. v. Stout,
  416
Siruta v. Siruta, 348
Sivit v. Village Green of Beachwood,
  940
Skilling v. United States, 1135
Skinner v. The London, Brighton and
  South Coast Railway Company, 223
Skrmetta v. Bayview Yacht Club, Inc.,
  1108
Slack v. Farmers Ins. Exch., 883
Slacum v. Jolley, 998
Sloan ex rel. Estate of Sloan v.
  Providence Health System-Oregon,
  314, 449
Slone v. Gen. Motors Corp., 853
Smaxwell v. Bayard, 615
Smith & Wesson Corp. v. City of Gary,
  824
Smith v. Anonymous Joint Enter.,
  1047
Smith v. Borello, 680
Smith v. Bryco Arms, 823
Smith v. California, 1056
Smith v. City of Stillwater, 531
Smith v. Cote, 684
Smith v. Crisp Regional Hosp., Inc.,
  483
Smith v. Cutter Biological, Inc., 903,
  904
Smith v. Eli Lilly & Co., 903
Smith v. Finch, 176, 194
Smith v. Lockheed Propulsion Co., 773
Smith v. London & South Western
  Railway, 297
Smith v. Massey-Ferguson, Inc., 372
Smith v. Meyring Cattle Co., L.L.C.,
  757
Smith v. R.J. Reynolds Tobacco Co.,
  351
Smith v. Richmond Memorial
  Hospital, 483
Smith v. Smith, 409, 497
Smith v. Toney, 656
Smith v. United States, 520, 698
Smith v. Wade, 81
Smith v. Wells, 153
Smith v. Whitaker, 699
Smothers v. Richland Mem'l Hosp.,
  912
Snell v. Norwalk Yellow Cab, Inc., 302
Snodgras v. Martin & Bayley, Inc.,
  631
Snowbarger v. Tri-County Elec. Coop.,
  989
Snyder v. Love, 395
Snyder v. LTG Lufttechnische GmbH,
  855
Snyder v. Michael's Stores, Inc., 1004

Snyder v. Phelps, 645, 1079
Snyder v. Sec'y of Health & Human
    Services, 1016
Soler, State v., 54
Sollin v. Wangler, 325
Sony BMG Music Entm't v.
    Tenenbaum, 1098
Sopha v. Owens-Corning Fiberglas
    Corp., 387
Sosa v. Alvarez-Machain, 507
Soto v. Bushmaster Firearms Intern.,
    LLC, 824
Soule v. Gen. Motors Corp., 807, 811,
    813
Sourbier v. State, 1011
South Cent. Reg'l Med. Ctr. v.
    Pickering, 674
South Coast Framing, Inc. v. Workers'
    Compensation Appeals Bd., 993
South Shore Baseball, LLC v.
    DeJesus, 366
South v. Maryland, 533
South v. Nat'l R.R. Passenger Corp.,
    554
Southeastern Pain Specialists, P.C. v.
    Brown, 451
Southern Alaska Carpenters Health &
    Sec. Trust Fund v. Jones, 1113
Sowers v. Forest Hills Subdivision,
    764
Spangler v. McQuitty, 693
Spann v. Shuqualak Lumber Co. Inc.,
    247
Spar v. Cha, 461, 462
Speed Boat Leasing, Inc. v. Elmer, 404
Spencer v. Health Force, Inc., 617
Spengler v. ADT Sec. Servs., Inc., 575
Spino v. John S. Tilley Ladder Co., 839
Spotts v. United States, 517
Spray, Gould & Bowers v. Associated
    Int'l Ins. Co., 391
Spurgeon v. Alabama Dep't of Human
    Resources, 497
Spurlock v. Townes, 732
Squeo v. Norwalk Hosp. Ass'n, 668
St. Amant v. Thompson, 1057
St. Louis, City of v. Benjamin Moore &
    Co., 903
St. Mary's Ohio Valley Heart Care,
    LLC v. Smith, 473
St. Onge v. MacDonald, 656
St. Paul Fire and Marine Insurance
    Company v. Sedona Contracting,
    Inc., 177
Staab v. Diocese of St. Cloud, 251
Stachulski v. Apple New England,
    LLC, 923
Stacy v. Rederiet Otto Danielsen, A.S.,
    647

Stahlecker v. Ford Motor Co., 852
Stallman v. Youngquist, 680
Stamboulis v. Stamboulis, 677
Stanley, United States v., 521
Stanton v. Metro Corp., 1046
Staples v. CBL & Associates, Inc., 602
Stark v. Ford Motor Co., 855
Starkenburg v. State, 532
State Auto Ins. Cos. v. B.N.C., 587
State Dept. of Corrections v. Cowles,
    532, 624
State Dept. of Envtl. Prot. v. Ventron
    Corp., 763
State Farm Fire & Cas. Co. v.
    Amazon.com, Inc., 791
State Farm Ins. Cos. v. Premier
    Manufactured Sys., Inc., 879
**State Farm Mut. Auto. Ins. Co. v.
    Campbell**, 905, 938, **940**, 951
State Farm Mut. Auto. Ins. Co. v. Ford
    Motor Co., 798
States v. Lourdes Hospital, 229,
    471
Steamfitters Local Union No. 602 v.
    Erie Ins. Exchange, 412
Stearns v. Metropolitan Life Ins. Co.,
    394
Steed v. Imperial Airlines, 704
Steed v. Rezin Orthopedics and Sports
    Medicine, S.C., 456
Stegemoller v. ACandS, Inc., 807
Steigman v. Outrigger Enterprises,
    Inc., 429
Steilen v. Cabela's Wholesale, Inc.,
    231
Steinhausen v. HomeServices of
    Nebraska, Inc., 1048
Stelluti v. Casapenn Enterprises,
    LLC, 357
Stelly v. Nat'l Union Fire Ins. Co., 254
Stenrich Group v. Jemmott, 1000
Stephens v. Crown Equipment Corp.,
    15
Stephens v. CSX Transp., Inc., 329
Stevens v. Veenstra, **149**
Stewart v. Federated Department
    Stores, Inc., 600
Stewart v. Motts, **135**
Stewart-Graves v. Vaughn, 466
Stieneke v. Russi, 1130
Stiner v. Amazon.com, Inc., 791
Stinnett v. Buchele, **183**
Stockberger v. United States, 555
Stocker v. State, 581
Stone v. York Haven Power Co., 433
Stopford v. Milton Town Sch. Dist.,
    138
Strait v. Crary, 152
Streifel v. Bulkley, 147

Strenke v. Hogner, 936
Strickland v. Medlen, 662
Stringfellow, United States v., 875
Strock v. Pressnell, 716
Strunk v. Zoltanski, 615
Stuard v. Jorgenson, 385
Stuart v. Freiberg, 1124
Sturbridge Partners, Ltd. v. Walker, 601
Sturdevant v. Kent, 315
Sullivan v. Abovenet Commc'ns, 215
Sullivan v. Boston Gas Co., 650
Sullivan v. Dunham, 772
Sullivan v. Zebley, 1022
Sullivant v. City of Oklahoma City, 123
Sullo v. Greenberg, 450
Summers v. Tice, 258, 897
Summit View, Inc. v. W. W. Clyde & Co., 772
Summy v. City of Des Moines, 308
Sumsion v. J. Lyne Roberts & Sons, Inc., 745
Sun Int'l. Bahamas, Ltd. v. Wagner, 955
Sun Oil Co. v. Robicheaux, Tex. Com. App., 249
Sun Val, LLC v. Com'r of Transp., 337
Sunday v. Stratton Corp., 370
Sundermann v. Hy-Vee, Inc., 428
Surette v. Islamic Republic of Iran, 920
Surles ex rel. Johnson v. Greyhound Lines, Inc., 600
Surocco v. Geary, 120
Susan B. Anthony List v. Driehaus, 1050
Sutowski v. Eli Lilly & Co., 903
Sutton v. Tomco Machining, Inc., 1010
Suvada v. White Motor Co., 794
Swanson v. Brewster, 928
Swartz v. Gale Webb Transp. Co., 270
Sweeney v. City of Bettendorf, 244
Synergies3 Tec Services, LLC v. Corvo, 734
Szydel v. Markman, 473
T & E Industries, Inc. v. Safety Light Corp., 774
Taber v. Maine, 521
Tabieros v. Clark Equip. Co., 832
Tadros v. City of Omaha, 329
Tam v. Eighth Judicial Dist. Court, 933
Tanja H. v. Regents of University of Calif., 610
Tanksley v. ProSoft Automation, Inc., 855
Tannerite Sports, LLC v. NBCUniversal News Grp., 1050

Tarasoff v. Regents of University of California, 619
Tarr v. Bob Ciasulli's Mack Auto Mall, Inc., 938
Taus v. Loftus, 1075
Taylor v. Cutler, 682
Taylor v. McNichols, 1074
Taylor v. Riojas, 90
Taylor v. Smith, 625
Taylor v. Vencor, Inc., 477
Teague ex rel. Martinosky, Estate of v. Crossroads Coop. Ass'n, 1007
Tedrick v. Community Resource Center, Inc., 624
Tegman v. Accident & Medical Investigations, Inc., 885
Telemundo Network Grp., LLC v. Azteca Int'l Corp., 1089
Tembenis v. Sec'y of Health & Human Servs., 693
Tennessee v. Garner, 84
Tenney v. Atlantic Assocs., 303
Terbush v. United States, 516
Terracon Consultants W., Inc. v. Mandalay Resort Grp., 1130
Terry v. Caputo, 842
Tetuan v. A.H. Robins Co., 937
Texas & P. Ry. v. Behymer, 220
The T.J. Hooper, 218
THI of Tex. at Lubbock I, LLC v. Perea, 931
Thibeault v. Larson, 686
Thing v. Lachusa, 654
Thoma v. Cracker Barrel Old Country Store, Inc., 214
Thomalen v. Marriott Corp., 762
Thomas v. Harrington, 749
Thomas v. Heard, 50
Thomas v. Mallett, 903
Thomas v. Sumner, 1052
Thomas v. Winchester, 778
Thompson v. County of Alameda, 532, 623
Thompson v. Hi Tech Motor Sports, Inc., 364
Thompson v. Kaczinski, 274
Thompson v. Winn-Dixie, 330
Thornhill v. Midwest Physician Ctr., 684
Thornton v. Garcini, 668
Thorsen v. Kaufmann's Dep't Stores, 66
Tibbetts v. Dairyland Ins. Co., 337
Tibert v. Nodak Mut. Ins. Co., 57
Tiller v. McLure, 641
Tillman v. Goodpasture, 684
Time, Inc. v. Firestone, 1064
Timothy G. v. State, Dept. of Health & Social Services, 389

Tincher v. Omega Flex, Inc., 811, 817
Tingler v. Greystone Homes, Inc., 567
Tobacco Cases II, In re, 861
Tobias v. Arteaga, 535
Tobin v. Federal Express Corp., 400
Tobin v. Norwood Country Club, Inc., 706
Todd v. Mass Transit Admin., 403
Toffoloni v. LPF Publ'g Grp., LLC, 1104
Toler v. Sud-Chermie, Inc., 1052
Tomlinson v. Metropolitan Pediatrics, LLC, 687
Tomlinson v. Puget Sound Freight Lines, Inc., 999
Toms v. Calvary Assembly of God, Inc., 773
Toney v. Chester Cnty. Hosp., 663
Too Much Media, LLC v. Hale, 1049, 1053
Toogood v. Rogal, 448
Toomer v. William C. Smith & Co., Inc., 128
Torres v. Goodyear Tire & Rubber Co., 790
Torres v. JAI Dining Services (Phoenix) Inc., 310
Tota v. Alexander's, 103
Touche Ross v. Commercial Union Ins., 1120
Touchet v. Hampton, 94
Toure v. Avis Rent A Car Systems, Inc., 1038
Townsend v. Legere, 335
Tracey v. Solesky, 615
Transue v. Aesthetech Corp., 825
Trevino v. Kent County, 208
Trinity Lutheran Church, Inc. of Evansville, Ind. v. Miller, 718
Triplett v. River Region Medical Corp, 296
Trowell v. Providence Hosp. & Med. Centers, Inc., 451
Trujeque v. Serv. Merch. Co., 233
Trujillo v. City of Albuquerque, 932
Truman v. Griese, 530
Truman v. Thomas, 466
Truong v. Hassan, 81
Tug Valley Pharmacy, LLC v. All Plaintiffs Below in Mingo Cty., 354
Tunkl v. Regents of University of California, 358
Turcios v. Debruler Co., 644
Turcotte v. Fell, 371
Turley v. ISG Lackawanna, Inc., 642
Turner v. Big Lake Oil Co., 764
Turner v. Cathedral Ministries, 410
Turner v. Jordan, 884

Turner v. Mandalay Sports Entertainment, LLC, 370
Turner v. State, 530
Twomey v. Commonwealth, 530
TXO Production Corp. v. Alliance Resources Corp., 949
Ty Inc. v. Perryman, 1102
Uloth v. City Tank Corp., 832
Ultramares Corp. v. Touche, Niven & Co., 1117
Union Carbide Corp. v. Industrial Com'n, 1001
Union Colliery Co. v. Industrial Commission, 992
Union Pac. Railroad Co. v. Ameron Pole Products LLC, 254
Uniroyal Goodrich Tire Co. v. Martinez, 839
United Blood Serv's, Div. of Blood Sys., Inc. v. Quintana, 450
United Food & Commercial Workers Int'l Union v. Wal-Mart Stores, Inc., 70
Universal Communication Systems, Inc. v. Lycos, Inc., 1053
University of Ariz. Health Sciences Ctr. v. Superior Court, 686
University of Texas v. Garner, 432
University of the Incarnate Word v. Redus, 526
Unruh-Haxton v. Regents of Univ. of Cal., 74
Upchurch v. Rotenberry, 203
Uzuegbunam v. Preczewski, 81, 913
Valcaniant v. Detroit Edison Co., 288
Valdez v. City of New York, 526
Valdez v. United States, 392
Valenzuela v. ADT Sec. Servs., Inc., 575
Van Camp v. McAfoos, 8
Van Dinter v. Orr, 1133
Van Gaasbeck v. Webatuck Cent. Sch. Dist. No. 1, 341
Vandermark v. Ford Motor Co., 785
Vanderpool v. State, 627
Vargas v. Inland Washington, LLC, 186, 745
Varig Airlines, United States v., 514
Vaughn v. First Transit, Inc., 534
Vaughn v. Ruoff, 114
Veatch v. City of Waverly, 66
Veazey v. Elmwood Plantation Assocs., Ltd., 885
Velazquez v. Jiminez, 457
Vendrella v. Astriab Family Ltd. Parnership, 757
Ventricelli v. Kinney System Rent A Car, Inc., 307

Veolia Water Indianapolis, LLC v.
    National Trust Ins. Co., 529
Verga v. Workers' Comp. Appeals Bd.,
    1000
Vergara v. Doan, 451
Verrastro v. Bayhospitalists, LLC,
    714, 716
Verrazono v. Gehl Co., 813
VIA Metropolitan Transit v. Meck, 404
Victorson v. Bock Laundry Machine
    Co., 866
Vince v. Wilson, 633
**Vincent v. Lake Erie
    Transportation Co., 124**
Viner v. Sweet, 243, 254
Vitale v. Henchey, 118
Vitro v. Mihelcic, 662
Voeller v. HSBC Card Services, Inc.,
    988
Vollaro v. Lispi, 879
Volunteers of Am. Colo. Branch v.
    Gardenswartz, 928
Volz v. Ledes, 878
Voris v. Molinaro, 661
Vredenburg v. Sedgwick CMS, 994
Vreeland v. Ferrer, 395
W.C. v. Secretary of Health & Human
    Services, 1015
Waco v. Kirwan, 432
Wadler v. City of New York, 440
Wagner v. International Railway, 289
Wagner v. State, 43
**Wait v. Travelers Indemnity Co. of
    Illinois, 983**
Waite v. Waite, 491
Wakulich v. Mraz, 557
Walcofski v. Lehigh Valley Coal Co.,
    993
Wald v. Grainger, 208, 920
Walderbach v. Archdiocese of
    Dubuque, Inc., 740
Waldrop v. Peabody Galion Corp., 867
Walker v. Chicago Housing Auth., 208
Wall v. Marouk, 478
Wall v. Stout, 454
Wal-Mart Stores, Inc. v. Alexander,
    660
Wal-Mart Stores, Inc. v. Wright, 215
Walsh v. BASF Corp., 842
Walski v. Tiesenga, 445
Ward Farms Partnership v. Enerbase
    Co-op. Resources, 1116
Ward v. Inishmaan Assocs. Ltd.
    Partnership, 612
Warr v. JMGM Group, LLC, 628
Warren v. Jeffries, 229
Warrick v. Stewart, 211
Wartluft v. Milton Hershey Sch. &
    Sch. Tr., 156

Washburn v. City of Federal Way, 533
Washington v. John T. Rhines Co., 663
Wassell v. Adams, 329
Waste Management of Texas, Inc. v.
    Stevenson, 1011
Watauga, City of v. Gordon, 57, 63
Watkins v. Ford Motor Co., 868
Watson v. Kentucky & Indiana Bridge
    & Railroad, 300
Watts v. Medicis Pharmaceutical
    Corp., 835
Weaver v. Ward, 753
Webb v. Special Electric Co., 836
Webber v. Butner, 348
Webber v. Deck, 177
Weber v. Stokely-Van Camp, Inc., 752
Wegleitner v. Sattler, 628
Wegner v. Milwaukee Mut. Ins. Co.,
    123
Weigel v. Lee, 690
Weigle v. SPX Corp., 833
Weinberg v. Dinger, 174
Weinstein v. Leonard, 1075
Weinstein v. Prudential Prop. & Cas.
    Ins. Co., 956
Welch v. Southland Corp., 885
Welch v. Sudbury Youth Soccer
    Association, Inc., 499
Welding Fume Prods. Liab. Litig., In
    re, 1107
Wells v. Oklahoma Roofing & Sheet
    Metal, L.L.C., 1006
Wells v. Tallahassee Mem'l Reg'l Med.
    Ctr., Inc., 891
Wende C. v. United Methodist Church,
    115
West v. East Tennessee Pioneer Oil
    Co., 634
West v. Jewett & Noonan Transp.,
    Inc., 764
West Virginia Regional Jail &
    Correctional Facility Authority v.
    A.B., 534
West Virginia Univ. Hospitals, Inc.,
    State ex rel. v. Scott, 487
Westby v. Gorsuch, 1116
Wheeling & Lake Erie RR. Co. v.
    Harvey, 416
Whelan v. Armstrong Intern. Inc., 836
Whirlpool Corp. v. Camacho, 841
Whisnant v. United States, 515
White v. Beeks, 461
White v. Ford Motor Co., 956
White v. Lembach, 462
White v. Many Rivers West Ltd.
    Partnership, 436
White v. Muniz, 42
White v. Revco Discount Drug Ctrs.,
    Inc., 718

White v. Samsung Elec. Am., Inc., 1104
White v. State, 440, 441
White v. University of Idaho, 45
Whitehead v. Food Max of Mississippi, Inc., 1073
Whitehead v. Toyota Motor Corp., 893
Whitley v. Albers, 80
Whitley v. Andersen, 41
Whitney v. California, 1055
Whitten v. Cox, 106
Whitworth v. Bynum, 406
Wick v. Henderson, 473
Wickersham v. Ford Motor Co., 305
Widenhouse v. Colson, 1083
Wiener v. Southcoast Childcare Ctrs., Inc., 288
Wilkins v. City of Haverhill, 432
Wilkow v. Forbes, Inc., 1067
Will v. Michigan Dept. of State Police, 78, 535
Williams Ford, Inc. v. Hartford Courant Co., 1125
Williams v. Booker, 464
Williams v. City of Chicago, 66
Williams v. City of Omaha, 531
Williams v. Glash, 912
Williams v. Hawkins, 391
Williams v. Kingery Constr. Co., 393
Williams v. Manchester, 271
Williams v. Philip Morris Inc., 779, 956
Williams v. RJ Reynolds Tobacco Co., 956
Williams v. State, 303
Williams v. Tharp, 1069
Williams v. Weatherstone, 609
Williamson v. Amrani, 463
Williamson v. Daniels, 616
Williamson v. Mazda Motor of America, Inc., 858, 859, 861
Williamson v. Waldman, 674
Willis v. Bender, 463
Willis v. Gami Golden Glades, LLC, 650
Willis v. Westerfield, 140, 337
Wilson Sporting Goods Co. v. Hickox, 807
Wilson v. Americare Systems, Inc., 486
Wilson v. Continental Ins. Cos., 610
Wilson v. Durrani, 394
Wilson v. Interlake Steel Co., 764
Wilson v. Kansas State University, 433
Wilson v. Kuenzi, 685
Wine-Settergren v. Lamey, 661
Winfrey v. GGP Ala Moana LLC, 234, 557

Winger v. CM Holdings, L.L.C., 156
Winn v. Pioneer Medical Group, Inc., 488
Winschel v. Brown, 354
Winterbottom v. Wright, 582
Wise v. Huntingdon County Housing Development Corp., 530
Wittenberg v. Robinov, 1129
Witthoeft v. Kiskaddon, 625
Wizinsky v. State, 530
Wlosinski v. Cohn, 462
Wolfe v. Schaefer, 1077
Wolston v. Reader's Digest Ass'n, Inc., 1064
Wood v. Groh, 138
Wood v. McGrath, North, Mullin & Kratz, P.C., 907
Wood v. Mercedes-Benz of Oklahoma City, 429
Woodley, In re, 693
Woodman v. Kera, LLC, 361
Woods v. Cole, 885
Woods v. Harry B. Woods Plumbing Co., 986
Woolley v. Henderson, 460
World Trade Center Bombing Litigation, In re, 530
Wotzka v. Minndakota Ltd. Parnership, 428
Wray v. Green, 176
Wright v. PRG Real Estate Management, Inc., 610
Wright's Case, 980
Wulf v. Kunnath, 108
Wurster v. Plastics Group, Inc., 838
Wuthrich v. King County, 530
Wyeth v. Levine, 837, 860
Wyeth, Inc. v. Weeks, 1113
Xcentric Ventures, LLC v. Borodkin, 1072
Yamaguchi v. Harnsmut, 729
Yanakos v. UPMC, 395
Yang v. Voyagaire Houseboats, Inc., 359
Yania v. Bigan, 557
Yates v. Hites, 141
Yates v. Mansfield Bd. of Educ., 607
Yates v. University of W.Va. Bd. of Trustees, 449
Yattaw v. City of East Providence, 432
Yazdianpour v. Safeblood Technologies, Inc., 1126
Ybarra v. Spangard, 467
Yearsley v. W.A. Ross Constr. Co., 518
Yearty v. Scott Holder Enterprises, Inc., 246
Yommer v. McKenzie, 763
Young v. Beck, 751

Young v. Salt Lake City School
    District, 608
Young v. United States, 516
Yount v. Deibert, 257
Yourtee v. Hubbard, 299
Z.J. v. Vanderbilt Univ., 156
Zach v. Nebraska State Patrol, 994
Zadeh v. Robinson, 87
Zehr v. Haugen, 686
Zeier v. Zimmer, Inc., 478
Zelig v. County of Los Angeles, 527
Zellmer v. Zellmer, 497
Zeran v. America Online, Inc., 1053
Zhao v. United States, 15
**Ziniti v. New England Central
    Railroad, Inc., 241**
Zirkle v. Winkler, 740
Zorilla v. Aypco Constr. II, LLC, 1121
Zsigray v. Langman, 641
Zuchowicz v. United States, 256
Zwart v. Penning, 70

TORTS AND COMPENSATION

PERSONAL ACCOUNTABILITY AND SOCIAL RESPONSIBILITY FOR INJURY

Ninth Edition

PART 1

A FIRST LOOK AT TORTS

■ ■ ■

CHAPTER 1

TORT LAW: AIMS, APPROACHES, AND PROCESSES

■ ■ ■

§ 1. WHAT IS TORT LAW?

Tort as wrongdoing. Torts are wrongs recognized by law as grounds for a lawsuit. These wrongs include an intentional punch in the nose and also a negligent car wreck. They include medical malpractice and some environmental pollution. The list of tortious wrongs is very long. All torts involve conduct that falls below some legal standard. In almost all cases, the defendant is in some sense at fault, either because he intends harm or because he takes unreasonable risks of harm.

Harm required. In all tort cases, the defendant's wrong results in a harm to another person (or entity, such as a corporation), that the law is willing to say constitutes a legal injury. The injured person is said to have a "cause of action," that is, a claim against the person who committed the tort. This claim can be pursued in court. Most of the cases in this book involve some kind of physical injury or threat of physical injury. Some torts, however, involve harm that is purely commercial and others involve intangible harm such as harm to reputation.

Torts, crimes, and contracts. A breach of contract is often grounds for a lawsuit, but a breach of contract is often not considered to be a tort at all. It must ordinarily be redressed under the rules for contracts, not the rules for torts. Some torts are also crimes. A punch in the nose is a tort called battery, but it may also be a crime. Sometimes a defendant who attacked the plaintiff is prosecuted criminally and is also held liable to the plaintiff for the tort. The two fields of law often overlap. However, they are not identical. Some acts that cause no harm at all to individuals might be crimes but not torts. Conversely, some acts cause harm and are torts but not crimes. That is because criminal law aims at vindicating public interests, while tort law aims at vindicating individual rights and redressing private harms.

Non-tort systems. Physical injuries inflicted by one person upon another are commonly addressed by tort law, but there are alternatives to tort law. Toward the end of this book, several chapters consider alternatives such as workers' compensation systems, which require employers to buy insurance and to pay for all on-the-job injuries even when the employer is not at fault. Non-tort systems are important for tort lawyers and also for those who wish to understand the way society deals with injuries. However, for now we are going to concentrate on the way injuries are addressed under tort law.

Common questions in tort law. Much of the law of torts is concerned with three questions: (1) what conduct counts as tortious or wrongful? (2) Did the conduct cause the kind of harm the law will recognize? (3) What defenses can be raised against liability if the defendant has committed a tort? The answers to these questions turn in part on why we have tort law and what its aims are.

§ 2. THE GOALS OF TORT LAW

A. SOME BROAD (AND CONFLICTING) AIMS

DOBBS, HAYDEN & BUBLICK, THE LAW OF TORTS
Vol. 1 §§ 10–14 (2d ed. 2011)

§ 10 Justice, policy, and process aims of tort law in summary

. . . *Morality or corrective justice.* Particular aims of tort law are usually erected under one of two large systems of thought. The first bases tort law on moral responsibility or at least on some idea that the defendant has in some important way wronged the plaintiff. It attempts to hold defendants liable for harms they wrongfully caused and no others. Good social effects may result when courts act to right the wrongs done by defendants, but in this system of thought that is not the point of imposing liability. Liability is imposed instead when and only when it is "right" to do so. As stated in a decision of the House of Lords, "The overall object of tort law is to define cases in which the law may justly hold one party liable to compensate another." *Fairchild v. Glenhaven Funeral Servs.,* [2002] 3 All E.R. 305, 2002 WL 820081 (H.L. 2002).

Social utility or public policy. The second large system of thought reverses the emphasis; it bases tort law on social policy or a good-for-all-of-us view. Social policy may coincide with justice in particular cases, but the dominant concern is not justice to the individual; it is to provide a system of rules that, overall, works toward the good of society.

Potential conflicts. The first two ways of looking at tort law are usually regarded as antithetical to each other. Although justice and policy often point to the same result, they do not always do so, and when they do not, one of these views must prevail or both must be compromised. The legal process view might also conflict with the aims of justice or those of policy.

Suppose a city, facing a raging and spreading fire, attempts to create a firebreak by blowing up a row of houses. Because time is critical, the city insists upon doing so before the plaintiff, who owns one of the houses, can remove his furniture. When the whole thing is over, the plaintiff claims damages from the city for the value of the furniture he could have saved. The city has acted for the good of its residents generally, but the plaintiff is the one who pays the costs. If the city's action is to be judged by a standard of social policy, some jurists might say the city should not be liable. On the other hand, if it is judged by corrective justice standards, the city should pay for the damage it caused in blowing up the houses. Otherwise, the city would get the advantage of its action (whatever that advantage might be) but would pay none of the costs. There are more subtle examples, but this one is enough to suggest the potential conflict between a decision based upon (supposed) social policy and one based upon justice to the individual. . . .

§ 11 Corrective justice, distributive justice, and policy

. . . For lawyers arguing cases, the question is not likely to be whether judges must wholly exclude policy or wholly exclude justice. Instead, advocacy requires lawyers to show judges why one approach or the other is most appropriate for the particular case. . . .

§ 12 Fault and other normative bases for liability

. . . *Fault and justice.* Tort law imposes liability upon defendants for conduct the law treats as wrong. In most instances, the conduct adjudged as wrong can be viewed as morally faulty conduct: it is intentional misconduct or at least unreasonably risky conduct likely to cause harm to others. In these cases, tort law seems to be commensurate in a general way with corrective justice ideals. The defendant's fault is a wrong that has harmed the plaintiff in some recognizable way; tort law, by subjecting the wrongdoer to a judgment that can be enforced against his assets, can put the accounts right between the parties.

Conversely, it can be argued that in a corrective justice scheme, it would be wrong to impose liability upon a defendant who is not at fault in causing the plaintiff's harm. Society may wish to compensate injured people by the use of public funds, but it cannot justly force one innocent individual to compensate another.

These views emphasize individual accountability for fault, accompanied by individual freedom to act without fault. They are consistent with an ideal of social responsibility for victims, however; they do not speak against government compensation for victims when the defendant is not at fault, only against compensation by the faultless defendant.

Strict liability and corrective justice. When tort law imposes liability without fault, does it go beyond the principle of corrective justice? At least *some* strict liability seems commensurate with corrective justice. For

to correspond

example, suppose a long-standing custom in our neighborhood permits any neighbor to borrow garden equipment from any other neighbor, but the custom is equally strong that if the equipment is damaged or lost while in the borrower's possession, the borrower must make the loss good. Suppose I borrow your lawnmower and without my fault it is damaged when a truck backs over it in my driveway. A rule that imposes liability upon me would be a strict liability rule because I was not at fault. Even so, liability seems to accord with corrective justice so long as you and I both know of the custom. . . . Whatever is to be said of strict liability theories of corrective justice, the great majority of tort cases turn on some kind of perception that the defendant is at fault in a significant way. At least for those cases, tort law begins with ideals of justice, even if those ideals may be modified by pragmatic, process, or policy considerations in particular cases.

§ 13 Compensation, risk distribution, fault

Compensation. Compensation of persons injured by wrongdoing is one of the generally accepted aims of tort law. Payment of compensation to injured persons is desirable. If a person has been wronged by a defendant, it is just that the defendant make compensation. Compensation is also socially desirable, for otherwise the uncompensated injured persons will represent further costs and problems for society. . . .

. . . *[R]isk distribution or loss spreading.* . . . [S]ome commentators have argued that tort liability should be strict or expansive in order to secure compensation for more injured persons. Some defendants if not all were seen as good "risk distributors" who should be liable for any harms they cause regardless of fault because they can "distribute" the costs of paying compensation. This means that some defendants, such as products manufacturers, could pay compensation for injuries they cause and then recoup some or all of those costs by raising the price of products. In this view, each individual purchaser of the products will pay a tiny fraction of the costs of injuries inflicted by those products and the injured person will not be compelled to bear the entire cost alone. Loss would thus cause less social dislocation. At the same time, an enterprise would be forced to internalize losses typically generated by the business itself.

Limited acceptance of risk distribution arguments. The common law of tort has not in fact generally adopted views that compensation is more important than corrective justice or that liability should be strict. Distribution arguments and strict liability have gone hand in hand, but only in certain kinds of cases. They have not supplanted fault as the most common basis for tort liability. . . .

§ 14 Fostering freedom, deterring unsafe conduct; economic analysis

Deterrence. Courts and writers almost always recognize that another aim of tort law is to deter certain kinds of conduct by imposing liability when that conduct causes harm. The idea of deterrence is not so much that an individual, having been held liable for a tort, would thereafter conduct himself better. It is rather the idea that all persons, recognizing potential tort liability, would tend to avoid conduct that could lead to tort liability. They might sometimes engage in the conduct in question, but only if they would get more out of it than the tort liability would cost. . . .

Deterrence: justice or social policy? Both systems of thought that emphasize justice and those that emphasize social policy goals can agree that deterrence is acceptable, but the two approaches might call for deterring quite different conduct. If you focus on conduct that is wrongful in the sense of being unjust to an individual, you might regard any given act as wrongful even though it is economically useful in society. If you focus on social policy, you might want to forgive defendants who cause harms by their socially useful activities. . . .

Economic analysis. [O]ne particular kind of social policy consideration is the economic one. If economics is defined broadly enough to include a consideration of all human wants and desires, then perhaps all social policies are in a sense economic policies. . . .

NOTE

Further reading. Many writers have analyzed tort law's goals and methods. Major contributions and differing views about justice vs. deterrence (or moral vs. economic analysis) are discussed in Gary T. Schwartz, *Mixed Theories of Tort Law: Affirming Both Deterrence and Corrective Justice*, 75 TEX. L. REV. 1801 (1997). For a more recent look at the tensions, see Lawrence A. Cunningham, *Traditional Versus Economic Analysis: Evidence from Cardozo and Posner Torts Opinions*, 62 FLA. L. REV. 667 (2010). There is also an admirably succinct summary in William E. Nelson, *From Fairness to Efficiency: The Transformation of Tort Law in New York, 1920–1980*, 47 BUFF. L. REV. 117 (1999). David A. Fischer, *Successive Causes and the Enigma of Duplicated Harm,* 66 TENN. L. REV. 1127 (1999), concludes that when courts have been forced to choose between the goals of fairness and efficiency, they have opted for fairness. Louis Kaplow and Steven Shavell argue in *Fairness versus Welfare*, 114 HARV. L. REV. 961 (2001), that courts err whenever they accord independent weight to notions of fairness such as corrective justice, and instead should focus on individual well-being. The materials in this book may help you determine for yourself whether either of these conclusions is well-founded.

Scholars have engaged in the "fairness versus efficiency" debate for several decades. Is it focused on the right questions? Cristina Carmody Tilley argues in *Tort Law Inside Out*, 126 YALE L.J. 1320 (2017), that tort doctrine is centrally concerned not with efficiency or morality, but rather with "community"; that is, that tort law "operates as a vehicle through which communities perpetually reexamine and communicate their values." And noting that the struggle between fairness and efficiency "has long shown signs of being tired," Nathaniel Donahue and John Fabian Witt argue that "a core function of many substantive tort doctrines is to structure and enable the private administration of rights and duties that the law of torts sets out." *Tort as Private Administration*, 105 CORNELL L.REV. 1093 (2020). The fact that almost all tort cases settle prior to trial, they argue, has exposed a "hidden function" of tort law, which is to shape the process by which private parties settle.

B. APPROACHES IN ACTION: THE ROLE OF FAULT

A great deal can be said about approaches to tort law and its goals, but for those without experience in reading actual cases and encountering actual tort problems, the goals are so abstract that they almost elude the grasp. The best approach may be to keep the goals or approaches in mind while reading cases.

VAN CAMP V. MCAFOOS

156 N.W.2d 878 (Iowa 1968)

BECKER, JUSTICE.

This case comes to us on appeal from the trial court's action in sustaining defendant's motion to dismiss. We are therefore limited to what can be gleaned from the pleadings.

In Division I of her petition plaintiff sues Mark McAfoos alleging in pertinent part, "That at said time and place defendant Mark McAfoos was operating a tricycle on said public sidewalk, and drove the tricycle into the rear of the plaintiff without warning, striking the right leg of the plaintiff thereby causing an injury to the Achilles' tendon of that leg.

"That as a direct and proximate cause of the defendant's action, plaintiff's tendon was injured and subsequently required surgery. . . ." [In another part of the petition the plaintiff alleged that Mark was three years, one month old.]

The trial court sustained the motion to dismiss as to Division I stating in part, "It is not alleged that the defendant was negligent. It is not alleged that the action of the defendant was willful or wrongful in any manner. Under these circumstances it is difficult to see how the Division as now set out states any basis upon which the plaintiff could recover."

The question presented is, did plaintiff plead a cause of action. . . .

I. Plaintiff's sole assignment of error as to Division I is "The trial court erred in failing to recognize categories of tort liability other than negligence, in evaluating the pleading in plaintiff's first division."

PA

. . . She stands firmly on the proposition that invasion of her person is in itself a wrong and she need plead no more. We do not agree. . . . In essence plaintiff urges a person has a right not to be injuriously touched or struck as she lawfully uses a public sidewalk. She was injuriously struck by Mark. Therefore Mark is liable. She argues that no more need be pleaded. It follows that no more need be proved in order to justify submission of the case. Plaintiff's posture satisfies us she would have us impose liability without fault. We are not prepared to extend this concept to childish acts (by children).

II. Plaintiff's reply brief states "If the absence of a single word or conclusory label remains the *sine qua non* of pleading a valid cause of action, we have restored today's jurisprudence to the specious procedural formalism of the 18th Century common courts."

PA

The trial court's ruling was not a return to legal formalism. Plaintiff makes it abundantly clear she insists on a right to recovery by proof of an accident caused by another, independent of fault or wrong doing. Where an essential element of the cause of action is missing, the question is not what may be shown under the pleading but whether a cause of action has been pled.

. . . Unless and until we are ready to recognize liability without fault for otherwise innocent childish actions, fault must be discernible in the pleading and in proof. . . Intentionally wrongful or negligently wrongful use of the tricycle is neither pled nor can it be made out from the bare allegation defendant "operated a tricycle on said public sidewalk and drove the tricycle into the rear of the plaintiff without warning." . . .

III. Plaintiff cites many cases from other jurisdictions holding a child of tender years may be liable *in tort. Garratt v. Dailey*, 46 Wash. 2d 197, 279 P.2d 1091. All of the foregoing cases involve the fault concept. Many turn on the question of whether the child could be guilty of the fault charged but each case has fault as one of the essential elements of liability. We need not disagree with those authorities. Whatever her motive, plaintiff has chosen to plead in such a way as to avoid bringing herself within the scope of those cases. . . .

Affirmed.

NOTES

1. **Overview.** Casebook editors may select cases and materials with more than one purpose in mind. At any given point, several themes may be in progress. *Van Camp* displays both a substantive and a procedural theme. The substantive or tort law theme has to do with the grounds for liability. The procedural theme has to do with how a tort cause of action is pleaded in court. In this case, why does the court consider only "what can be gleaned from the pleadings"? Most cases in this book will raise a number of issues that require

analysis and further thought. Notes like these should help you develop that analysis or furnish related information.

2.   **Historical strict liability and the rules today.** From the early days of tort law, about the 13th century until perhaps as late as the 18th century, anyone who acted affirmatively and directly (like Mark McAfoos) might be held liable for harm done, even though he was not at fault. In these cases the plaintiff used a form of action for suing called *Trespass*. The plaintiff would win unless the defendant had some special defense, called justification or excuse. An example of a defense would be self-defense. If the harm caused was indirect, on the other hand, the defendant was not responsible unless he was at fault in some way. If Mark McAfoos had left his tricycle on the walk and the plaintiff had bumped into it in the dark, this would have been an indirect harm and even in the early English law Mark would not have been liable without fault. Cases of indirect harm required the plaintiff in that period to select a form of action for suing called *Trespass on the Case*, or just *Case*. Does *Van Camp* implicitly or expressly reject the older rule that a defendant can be liable for direct harms even in the absence of fault?

3.   **What is fault?** What would it take to show fault in *Van Camp*? Suppose McAfoos said that he ran into Ms. Van Camp on purpose because he wanted to hear her get angry. If McAfoos caused the accident, how could it have happened without his fault? In *Van Camp,* the court upheld the dismissal of plaintiff's claim because no fault had been pleaded—neither "intentionally wrongful" nor "negligently wrongful" use of the tricycle. Both intentional misconduct and negligent misconduct can be forms of fault. Specific tort claims require pleading particular types of fault.

4.   **Tort law and the states.** With few exceptions, tort law is made by the courts and legislatures of the various states, not by the federal government. When you read *Van Camp* how can you tell which state court wrote the opinion? If *Van Camp* tells us that fault is required to maintain a battery claim in Iowa, do we know whether fault is required in Illinois?

5.   **Evaluation of the legal rule.** How does the rule or principle in *Van Camp* stack up against the aims of tort law? Is the fault-based rule in *Van Camp* just? Does it reflect socially desirable standards of deterring wrongdoing and compensating injured persons? What other sort of rule could the court have adopted? Evaluation of bases for a legal rule and alternatives to it is important to lawyers. It is one process by which lawyers begin to formulate legal arguments.

6.   **Grasping a principle.** *Van Camp* involved a child on a tricycle. But the principle or reason behind the case might apply to many other situations. One function of a lawyer is to recognize the possibility of applying the principle of a case to a new set of facts. Try it:

(a)   H becomes angry with his wife, W, and repeatedly hits her with his fist, breaking her jaw and bruising her face. Would the principle or idea in *Van Camp* either establish or exclude liability?

(b)   The defendant's yard has a tree near the sidewalk. The tree appears to be sound and healthy, but in fact it is rotten and it blows over in a wind. It strikes a passerby. Can you predict from *Van Camp* whether a court would impose liability?

§ 3. IMPLEMENTING TORT LAW'S GOALS WITH DAMAGES AWARDS

In a few cases the remedy for a tort is an injunction. That is, the court will order the defendant to cease committing a tort such as a nuisance or a continuing contamination of the plaintiff's land. In the overwhelming majority of injury cases, however, the remedy is compensatory damages, an award of money to compensate the injured person for the harms caused by the defendant's tortious conduct.

ANDERSON V. ZAMIR

931 N.E.2d 697 (Ill. App. 2010)

JUSTICE CHAPMAN delivered the opinion of the court:

Tiffany Anderson appeals from the trial court's September 19, 2008, denial of her motion for a new trial from a final judgment after a jury trial. . . .   *[handwritten: PH]*

On September 22, 2005, Tiffany was involved in a motor vehicle accident with Saadia Zamir. Tiffany was rear-ended. Her head hit the steering wheel. Tiffany's car was pushed forward into the car directly in front of her vehicle. Her vehicle was towed.   *[handwritten: F]*

Although sore immediately following the accident, she did not seek medical attention right after the accident. Later that day, Tiffany went to the hospital to try to obtain medical care related to a headache from which she had suffered since the accident. Her neck was also sore at this time. Overall, her symptoms had gotten worse since the time of the accident. That evening at the hospital, she was prescribed a neck brace and pain medication.   *[handwritten: F]*

Thereafter, she followed up with the medical clinic of the student health center at Southern Illinois University at Carbondale (SIU-C), where she was then a student. She testified that she complained of pain stemming from her lower back and running up into her neck, primarily on the left side of her body. . . . She was treated with pain medication and some physical therapy and home exercises for about six months. In the spring of 2006, she had a cervical MRI, which the radiologist determined was negative. In July 2006, Tiffany returned to the student health center medical clinic with specific left shoulder complaints. Tiffany was referred to Dr. Treg Brown, an orthopedic specialist at the clinic. An MRI of her left shoulder revealed a tear in the labrum of her left shoulder, and in   *[handwritten: F   9 months after accident]*

15 months after accident

December 2006, Tiffany underwent left shoulder surgery to repair the labrum tear. The surgery was orthoscopic and left Tiffany with several small scars on her left shoulder. After the surgery, Tiffany underwent physical therapy.

Tiffany provided testimony about the pain she experienced from the injuries and following the surgery. Tiffany testified to the activities in which she had engaged before the accident and the limitations she experienced due to these injuries.

PH

Tiffany filed suit against the Zamirs for personal injuries resulting from the accident. The Zamirs admitted liability. The case went to trial on the issue of damages only. The trial was held for two days beginning on July 21, 2008. Medical bills totaling $28,804 were admitted into evidence. At the conclusion of the trial, the jury awarded Tiffany a total of $12,500— only $5,000 for medical bills and the balance of $7,500 for pain and suffering. Tiffany filed a motion for a new trial, which the court denied on September 19, 2008. . . .

I

The trial court's ruling on a motion for a new trial should not be reversed on appeal unless the party who is seeking the new trial can affirmatively show that the court clearly abused its discretion. In determining whether the trial court abused its discretion, we must consider whether the jury's verdict was supported by the evidence and whether the complaining party was denied a fair trial.

given

The amount of money a jury awards "is peculiarly an issue of fact for the jury to determine" and is entitled to substantial deference. If the jury received proper instruction and otherwise had a reasonable basis for its award, the appellate court will not disturb the verdict. Although there is no precise formula for determining if a monetary award is fair and reasonable, the following factors should be considered: the extent of the injuries suffered and the degree of the permanency of those injuries, the plaintiff's age, the possibility of future difficulties, the amount of medical expenses involved, and the restrictions upon the plaintiff's life as a result of the injuries suffered. A jury's damages award cannot be overturned unless it is shown that the jury clearly ignored an established element of damages, that the verdict was the result of passion or prejudice, or that the award bears no reasonable relationship to the loss that was suffered.

In this case, liability was admitted, and essentially the cervical injury was conceded, along with damages related to that injury. What the defendants contested at the trial was the shoulder injury. The only medical evidence offered [by either party] at the trial was presented by Tiffany's [experts] in her case. The defendants' attorney merely cross-examined Tiffany's physicians and presented no independent evaluation of Tiffany's injuries, her medical care, her medical bills, or her prognosis. A review of the cross-examination of Tiffany's physicians reflects that neither physician wavered in his opinion relative to the cause of the shoulder injury. We find that the testimony of both physicians is of great importance to our consideration of the proof relative to the damages award. . . .

Dr. Perkins testified that Tiffany's shoulder injury was most probably caused by the September 2005 motor vehicle accident. Dr. Perkins explained that this late experience of symptoms is fairly common. Initially, the patient complains of cervical pain, and the patient simply does not experience the signs of laxity and shoulder pain until the cervical area starts to improve and the patient starts engaging in more activity.

Dr. Treg Brown testified at the trial that he had reviewed all of her records and found nothing in her records other than the motor vehicle accident to explain the shoulder injury that Tiffany sustained. . . . Dr. Brown testified that her surgical care and all the medical bills associated therewith were related to the motor vehicle accident.

. . . The jury does not have to believe a witness if the jury believes that the testimony is false based upon "all of the other evidence or the inherent improbability or contradictions in the testimony." However, the jury is also not allowed to arbitrarily reject unimpeached testimony. . . .

Tiffany's medical bills totaled $28,804, but the jury chose to ignore this uncontradicted evidence and award her only $5,000 for medical bills, presumably following the suggestion of the defendants' attorney that it award her damages only for her cervical injury. The defendants advanced the argument that the shoulder injury was not causally connected to the motor vehicle accident because of the delay between the motor vehicle accident and the report of specific shoulder pain. The defendants also sought to argue that the injury was related to a viral infection. While the propriety of asking these questions on cross-examination of the physicians is not in doubt, the problem is that neither physician agreed with the arguments advanced by the defendants' attorney. . . . Again, all the medical testimony introduced at the trial supported the theory that the shoulder injury was causally connected to the motor vehicle accident. No evidence contradicting this connection was introduced. The witnesses were not impeached, and they stood by their opinions of causation. Upon reviewing the testimony, we do not conclude that this medical testimony is inherently improbable.

We find that the jury's verdict simply bears no reasonable relationship to the injuries established by Tiffany at the trial, and accordingly, the damages award must be reversed. Furthermore, we conclude that the trial court abused its discretion in upholding this damages award in light of the only medical evidence introduced at the trial. . . . For the foregoing reasons, the judgment of the circuit court of Jackson County is hereby reversed, and the cause is remanded for a new trial on the issue of damages.

NOTES

1. **Compensatory damages components.** The injured person usually has the burden of proving that the defendant is liable. In *Anderson* the defendant admitted liability. Once liability is proved or admitted, a plaintiff is entitled to recover compensatory damages caused by the defendant's tortious conduct. Upon proper proof, a plaintiff is entitled to compensation for (1) lost wages and lost earning capacity, (2) medical expenses, (3) pain and suffering endured, including mental or emotional pain, and (4) any special or particularized damages that do not fit neatly within the other categories. The plaintiff can recover not only for such losses that have already occurred, but also for such losses that are reasonably certain to occur in the future, if the evidence demonstrates the likelihood of such future losses. *See* 3 DOBBS, HAYDEN & BUBLICK, THE LAW OF TORTS § 479 (2d ed. 2011).

The gist of the damages rules is that the defendant has wrongfully reduced the plaintiff's net assets, tangible and intangible, and should be required to restore them—that is, to restore the plaintiff to the condition the plaintiff was in before the tort, to the extent that can be done with money. Are the compensatory damages rules consistent with some or all of the broad goals of tort law?

2. **Measuring damages.** "Because the measure of damages in a personal injury case is not subject to mathematical calculation, each case must be measured by its own facts, and considerable latitude and discretion are vested in the jury." *Primoris Energy Services Corp. v. Myers*, 569 S.W.3d 745 (Tex. App. 2018). The amount of damages need not be proved with precision, but the amount cannot be based on speculation, either. Courts often say that the amount of damages must be proved to a "substantial certainty," or perhaps more accurately, to a "reasonable certainty." Pain and suffering and lost earnings and earning capacity are inherently impossible to prove with precision, but are routinely awarded to plaintiffs upon proper proof.

3. **Measuring pain and suffering.** One difficulty in assessing proper compensation is that for many of us, our main assets are not in the form of money or property but in the form of good health and freedom from pain. Although pain is not quantifiable, freedom from pain has economic value. We can see that in the expenditures people make to gain pleasure and avoid pain. You could also imagine that someone offered you money for the right to break your leg. If you would accept such an awful offer at all, you would almost certainly demand even more money if the break would entail pain. The amount of money you would demand to suffer pain is not the measure of a tortfeasor's liability (he is only liable for reasonable compensation, not what you would demand). Even so, if freedom from pain is an intangible asset, pain inflicted by a defendant represents a real loss and should be compensated somehow. How does the jury know how much to award for pain and suffering? How did Tiffany Anderson address that?

4. **Lost wages and earning capacity.** Where the plaintiff proves that the defendant's tort has caused a loss of wages—because, for example, the

plaintiff has not been able to work (or work as much) because of the injury—that is a category of compensable damages. *See, e.g., Dillon v. Frazer*, 678 S.E.2d 251 (S.C. 2009) (granting new trial on damages where jury disregarded uncontroverted evidence of $18,000 in lost wages and overtime pay). A plaintiff can also seek to recover damages for loss of future earning capacity, upon proof to a substantial certainty that the defendant's tort caused a diminution in plaintiff's power to earn money. *See, e.g., Stephens v. Crown Equipment Corp.*, 22 F.3d 832 (8th Cir. 1994). Thus even a person who was not employed at the time of injury may be able to recover for a loss of earning capacity. *See, e.g., Zhao v. United States*, 963 F.3d 629 (7th Cir. 2020) (affirming award of $2.6 million for lost earning capacity to a plaintiff injured at birth). Why do you think Tiffany Anderson was not awarded damages for lost wages or loss of earning capacity?

5. **Attorney's fees.** One of the most important institutional rules covering most litigation in the United States is that a losing party is not required to pay the winning party's attorney's fees as a line-item. Under this so-called American Rule, each party pays its own attorney's fees, win or lose, unless some special statute or law allows for fee-shifting. As a result, the almost universal system of litigation finance in this country is that plaintiffs' attorneys in torts cases are paid by contingent fees: they are paid nothing if they lose, and a percentage of the recovery if they win. The percentage may vary from around 25% to 40%, sometimes higher. The percentage may sound high, but considering the lawyer's investment of time and effort and the fact that the lawyer will be paid nothing in some cases, such fees are usually not a bad deal for the client who could not afford to pay a lawyer otherwise. State rules of professional responsibility prohibit lawyers from charging or collecting fees that are unreasonable, excessive or unconscionable. *See* ABA MODEL RULES OF PROFESSIONAL CONDUCT 1.5(a) (prohibiting unreasonable fees).

Given that a plaintiff's lawyer is likely to be paid a percentage of the damages obtained, why isn't the plaintiff left short of money for medical expenses and lost wages and earning capacity in every case?

6. **Judge and jury.** Determining the amount of damages is the jury's job, but as you can see from *Anderson* the trial judge and the appellate judges have important roles to play in the final outcome. Once the jury has fixed damages, can an aggrieved party win simply by arguing that the jury got the amount wrong? Is that what happened in *Anderson*?

7. **Judicial powers: additur, remittitur, and new trial.** Following an insufficient award of damages in a jury trial, a state court trial judge has the power to deny the plaintiff's motion for a new trial on the condition that the defendant consents to pay an increased award of damages; this power is called *additur*. The judge's power to deny defendant's motion for new trial if plaintiff remits part of an excessively high award is called *remittitur*. *See Orientale v. Jennings*, 218 A.3d 806 (N.J. 2019) (exploring history of those powers). The trial judge also has the power, and sometimes the duty, to order a new trial on damages, as you can see in *Anderson*. *See also Mader v.*

Duquesne Light Co., 241 A.3d 600 (Pa. 2020) (new trial may be ordered with respect to discrete categories of damages, excluding from retrial those types of damages that were properly awarded). Can a judge use the power of additur or remittitur, or grant a new trial on damages, based simply on the judge's opinion that the amount is too low or too high? Or based on the judge's view that a different jury would have come up with a different amount? *See Nason v. Pruchnic*, 204 A.3d 861 (Me. 2019).

8. **Criticisms of damages.** You may have heard or read many criticisms of tort law—that it is out of control, that Americans litigate trivial matters, that they are greedy, and that they seek something for nothing. No doubt greed shows up in lawsuits as well as in corporate board rooms and elsewhere. However, it is important to know that the studies available do *not* support the claim that litigation by individuals has increased or that juries often run amok. A 2008 report issued by the Bureau of Justice Statistics—as of 2021 the most recent of its kind—estimates the median award in tort cases at $24,000, slightly lower than the $35,000 median award in contract cases. In all cases, only 4% of plaintiffs received awards over one million dollars. In addition, from 1992 to 2005 the number of tort cases decreased by 40%. Did plaintiffs fare better with juries rather than judges? Quite to the contrary. *See* Lynn Langton & Thomas H. Cohen, BUREAU OF JUSTICE STATISTICS, U.S. DEP'T. OF JUSTICE, NCJ 223851, CIVIL BENCH AND JURY TRIALS IN STATE COURTS, 2005 (October 2008).

9. **Punitive damages.** In a few cases, juries are permitted to award punitive damages in addition to compensatory damages. Virtually all states authorize punitive damages only when a tortfeasor has acted maliciously or willfully or wantonly in causing injury. Punitive damages are intended to provide a measure of added deterrence and punishment for the wrongdoer's serious, even reprehensible, misconduct. They are measured not by what the plaintiff has lost, but rather by what will punish the particular defendant given the seriousness of wrongdoing, among other factors. *See Qwest Servs. Corp. v. Blood*, 252 P.3d 1071 (Colo. 2011) (upholding punitive damages award of $18 million against utility company found by the jury to have acted willfully and wantonly in failing to maintain a utility pole that collapsed and seriously injured a lineman). Punitive damages are explored in greater detail in Chapter 26.

NOTE: POPULAR CONCEPTIONS AND
MISCONCEPTIONS—THE McDONALD'S CASE

You should be cautious about forming judgments about all tort law based upon anecdotes or media presentations rather than an understanding of the whole tort system. One case that grabbed media attention and continues to generate criticism involved a large judgment for a woman who was burned by scalding coffee she got at a McDonald's drive-through. Sitting in the car, she held the container between her legs to take the top off and the coffee spilled. It was hot enough to inflict third degree burns—which covered her groin and genital area. Third degree burns can burn entirely through the skin and vessels and all the way to the bone. She was hospitalized, underwent skin grafts, had excruciating pain, and was permanently disfigured. She asked McDonald's to pay her $11,000 hospital bills, but McDonald's refused. She hired an attorney who demanded $90,000 in damages, but McDonald's refused that, too. Her lawyer then filed a suit and discovered that McDonald's intentionally kept its coffee hot enough to inflict third degree burns and in fact had known of at least 700 people who had been burned by its scalding coffee. Shriner's Burn Center had published warnings to the fast food industry about the severity of the burns from coffee at this temperature. The lawyer now demanded more in compensatory damages, and sought punitive damages as well. At trial, after hearing all of the evidence, the jury awarded the plaintiff $200,000 in compensatory damages, reduced to $160,000 because it decided that she was partly at fault in causing her own injuries. The jury then added $2.7 million in punitive damages, based on a finding that McDonald's was reckless or even malicious. While this was a large sum, it represented only about two days' of McDonald's revenues from coffee sales. The judge reduced the punitive award to $480,000, leaving the plaintiff with a total damages award of $640,000.

Media and web commentators often present a different picture. They often leave out the fact that most of the award was in the form of punitive damages—meant to punish, not to compensate, that the punitive damages award was reduced as part of the ordinary mechanisms of tort law (the judge's review), and that the coffee was not merely "hot," but capable of great harm, which it in fact caused quite needlessly. You can still read comments on the web in essence saying that "an old woman" spilled coffee on herself and got something for nothing, omitting to note that the jury reduced the compensatory damages by $40,000 for the plaintiff's supposed fault in spilling the coffee, and perhaps betraying a contempt for "old women." You'll want to judge for yourself, but as professionals we should base our analyses on more facts than appear in the popular media. You can find a summary of the McDonald's case in Mark B. Greenlee, *Kramer v. Java World: Images, Issues, and Idols in the Debate over Tort Reform*, 26 CAP. U. L. REV. 701 (1997).

CHAPTER 2

READING TORTS CASES AND UNDERSTANDING TRIAL PROCEDURE

• • •

§ 1. LOOKING FOR FACTS, RULES, AND REASONS

Reading cases to understand principles and predict law. This course presents real cases that involve individuals and sometimes organizations as plaintiffs, defendants, lawyers, and judges. The "cases" in this book are actually the explanations judges give for the legal decisions that they make. By carefully reading these judicial explanations, called opinions, good lawyers can learn the governing legal principles of tort law. They can also envision what other legal rules could develop from these principles. In addition, they can learn to identify recurring issues, distinguish seemingly similar cases, and find similarities in cases that are seemingly different. Why are these skills important? One reason is that in the United States, tort law develops through a common law system. That means a court decision in an individual case not only serves to resolve that case, but creates a rule to be followed in future cases. In order to make professional estimates about likely outcomes of a case if a client must sue or defend, an attorney will need to be able to read and understand prior case law. Also, an attorney who wishes to construct a sound legal argument must be able to compare the case before her with prior legal cases and principles.

Facts. The facts of a case are likely to influence the judge in deciding on appropriate legal rules. If the case is about a four-year-old who causes harm, the judge's observations about "the liability of children" may really be observations only about the liability of very young children. The facts that influence the judge's decision may be an explicit part of the case or an implicit part of the judge's reasoning. The scope of a rule will require interpretation on your part, and it means that you must understand the facts in the case very well indeed. When you identify the important facts of a case be sure to include all facts necessary to the judge's decision and to the legal elements of the case. For example, if a cause of action requires proof of actual physical harm, the fact that the defendant's achilles tendon was injured and required surgery will be an important fact to record. You may also include facts that demonstrate the overall context of the case and facts helpful to remembering the case.

19

Procedural posture. Reading cases well requires attention to both the substantive legal issues raised by the parties and the legal procedures through which those issues are raised. The legal procedure that triggered the court's ruling is important to understanding the substantive legal rule of the case—did the lower court dismiss the plaintiff's complaint before any evidence had been gathered, grant summary judgment for the defendant after reviewing all the material facts, or reverse a judgment against the defendant after a full trial and verdict? The allocation of decision-making power between judge and jury is a major process element in many tort cases. Suppose: (1) The defendant files a motion saying the judge should dismiss the plaintiff's claim without letting a jury decide it, but the judge denies the motion and lets the jury decide. (2) The jury decides for the defendant. (3) The judge upholds the jury's verdict. Process values explain this sequence. In item (1), by refusing to dismiss the case the judge is not saying that the plaintiff should win. The judge is saying instead that the decision on the particular issue in light of the facts stated should be made by the jury, not by the judge. So the jury's verdict either way will be upheld on those particular facts. In other cases, judges will take the case away from the jury, allocating power to themselves instead of the jury. The appropriate role of judge and jury is often a basic concern in applying legal rules. Typically, judges decide issues of law and juries resolve issues of fact. A reader of cases must pay attention to which procedure triggers the appeal. One example of a statement about the procedure of a case might be "summary judgment granted by the trial court and upheld by the appellate court."

Issues. The substantive issue raised by the litigants as shaped by the court will also affect the holding. It is helpful to recognize both the procedural issue—"should the trial court's motion for summary judgment be upheld?"—and the substantive question presented to the court—"is intent to harm required to show a battery?" Often the substantive issue will be the primary focus of analysis in classes other than procedure.

Holding. The holding of the court is the court's response to the issues raised by the parties. The procedural form of the holding might be as simple as "reversed." However, a fuller statement of the holding might also include the rule of law the court stated in response to the substantive issue raised in the case. For example, a statement of a holding that includes both the procedural holding and the rule of the case might be "Reversed, for the defendant; a battery cannot be proved without proof that the defendant intended harm or offense." The rules of law established by the court concerning the substantive issues, sometimes referred to as "the rules of a case," are helpful because they may be used to resolve similar cases later on. Sometimes a judge clearly earmarks a rule. More often, you must interpret what you read.

Reasoning. The rules in most judicial decisions are interpreted in part by following the judge's reasoning. Ideally, the judge's reasoning explains why the rule exists (or why the judge is creating the rule) and how it applies to the case. The judge's reasoning may include analogies to other cases or legal doctrines, reference to persuasive authorities like the Restatement or prominent treatises, and discussion of fairness or policy concerns. What the judge emphasizes in reasoning about the rule tells you a great deal about what the rule is and what its limits might be. Be sure to note the reasoning of arguments made in concurring and dissenting opinions as well as the majority's explanation.

Application of rules. Often, in the common law, attorneys are asked to apply the rule and reasoning of a decided case to a new factual situation or hypothetical. Although rules found in yesterday's cases will help resolve today's disputes, they usually will not do so simply or directly. You will find you must reason about how the rule is to be applied in other fact scenarios, including your client's situation.

Evaluation. After you read the case, take time to think about how the case you read relates to other cases you have examined. What does the case add? Why is it significant? Is the rule of the case just? Does it promote useful policy aims? Is the reasoning sound? Are there alternative solutions that would be preferable in terms of principle and policy? Does the rule of the case work effectively with other rules you have studied? This is your chance to reflect on connections between cases and the wisdom of rules as a whole.

Rules point lawyers to evidence required and arguments available. Frequently, the rules in yesterday's cases do not actually resolve today's disputes at all. Instead, their most important function is to point to evidence that lawyers will need to gather for a trial and to arguments lawyers will need to construct in presenting a claim or in defending it.

§ 2. PROCEDURES AT TRIAL

The cases you read are usually the decisions of appellate court judges. Less often they are decisions of trial court judges who occasionally decide to provide a written explanation of their decisions. Appellate court judges typically address facts that are raised in party briefs and reference a factual record assembled for summary judgment or a transcript of the trial. Since a judge's decision about tort law will come within a particular procedural context, it is necessary to have a basic understanding of trial procedure.

Trial procedure can be complicated, but the basic plan of a trial is very simple. It is designed to resolve two kinds of disputes. The first kind of dispute is about the facts, about what happened. Almost all trials involve at least some factual dispute. The second kind of dispute is about the law.

Most trials also involve disputes about what the legal rules are, or how they should apply to the particular case.

Below you will find a list of trial procedures. Although we've listed these procedures in the order in which they typically arise in a trial, some of the procedures—the ones marked with an asterisk—are the main procedural devices that raise the legal issues that appear in the tort cases in this book. The procedures that most frequently raise legal issues reflect the judge's role as a gatekeeper who screens out evidence that is improper and often screens out whole cases, preventing the evidence or the case from being considered by the jury. When the judge screens out the whole case, the jury decides nothing and lawyers say the case did not "get to the jury," meaning that the judge decided that the plaintiff must lose under some rule of law or that the plaintiff's evidence was insufficient to permit reasonable people to find the facts essential for the plaintiff to win. On occasion, a plaintiff can prevail on a motion for judgment without trial. One of the first questions lawyers are likely to ask when they evaluate a new case is: Can this case get to the jury?—meaning, will the judge screen the case out or will the jury be permitted to make the ultimate decision in the case?

You may want to look back at these pages as you encounter these procedures in cases. In the appendix following this section, we narrate a hypothetical case so you can see the procedures being applied.

For our discussion here, it may be helpful to imagine a very simple kind of case in which the plaintiff contends that the defendant struck him. Defendant denies this completely. How does this get to court and what happens there?

Complaint. Plaintiff's lawyer, having investigated the applicable law and facts, writes up a document called a complaint or petition. This document states the facts as claimed by the client. This document is formally filed with the court (in the court clerk's office) and a copy is served on (delivered to) the defendant, sometimes by an officer of the court such as the sheriff or the federal marshal. In most courts today, electronic filing is available and may be mandatory.

*The Motion to Dismiss or Demurrer. If the defendant believes that the plaintiff's complaint does not state facts that show a good legal claim, the appropriate response is to file a motion to dismiss the complaint for failure to state a claim upon which relief can be granted. This is a Rule 12(b)(6) motion under the Federal Rules of Civil Procedure. The effect of this motion is to say to the judge, "Take all the facts stated in the complaint as if they were proved; even so, they do not show a valid legal claim."

Since the facts alleged are temporarily assumed to be true for purpose of considering this motion, there is no factual dispute. The issue raised is one of law, for the judge to decide, not the jury. Suppose plaintiff's lawyer wrote up, filed and served a complaint stating not that the defendant struck the plaintiff, but instead that the defendant frowned at the plaintiff. Frowning is not a tort, so defendant's motion to dismiss would be sustained.

Conceivably the plaintiff's complaint would be rewritten or amended to add important allegations. This would usually be permitted. However, in most cases in this casebook, the issue is on appeal for the very reason that the plaintiff *cannot* add any provable facts that will help.

Notice that the motion to dismiss comes at a very early stage of the case—before the defendant has filed an answer or along with the defendant's answer. In other words, it comes before any time has been invested in developing proof or calling a jury.

If the motion to dismiss or demurrer is denied, the case will proceed and defendant will file an answer.

Answer. If the defendant has not moved to dismiss the complaint, or if the defendant's motion to dismiss is denied, the defendant must file a document taking a position on the complaint. Very often it is an "answer." An answer usually disputes some of the factual claims of the plaintiff. For example, if plaintiff's complaint states "Defendant struck the plaintiff in the face," the defendant might answer saying she denies that she struck the plaintiff. This reveals what facts are in dispute between the parties. Because the dispute is about the facts, the parties will gather evidence for presentation to a jury.

Discovery. Discovery is the portion of the case in which both parties gather information about the underlying claims. For example, the defendant might depose the plaintiff in order to obtain new information or reveal inaccuracies. Did the plaintiff seek medical treatment after the event? What did the plaintiff tell the doctor at the time? Discovery is not limited to gathering information from the parties. The parties may also seek information from others who know about the event. For example, if other people were in the room at the time that the defendant allegedly struck the plaintiff, the parties might interview those witnesses (sometimes under oath) and ask what they saw. The parties can investigate facts through written requests for documents as well as oral interviews. For example, either party could ask for written records of the plaintiff's doctor visit.

*The Motion for Summary Judgment. The motion to dismiss assumes all the facts stated in the complaint are true and argues that, even so, the complaint fails to show a good legal claim. On the other hand, the summary judgment motion, which occurs after the parties have gathered facts during the process of discovery, is based on a developed set of facts. If the moving party, almost always the defendant, shows that (1) there is no real dispute about important facts and (2) on the undisputed facts, the law compels judgment for the defendant, summary judgment will be granted.

Suppose the parties go through discovery and the plaintiff states, "he hit me," while the defendant states, "I did not." The defendant cannot get summary judgment because the truth of the fact he asserted is important to the controversy and is directly disputed by the plaintiff. It will be for the jury to decide which party is speaking truthfully. Even if one party has more witnesses than another, the dispute of fact is still for the jury to resolve.

Pretrial briefs and motions in limine. After a case is set for trial, the parties may want the judge to decide beforehand whether to include or exclude certain types of evidence and whether particular legal rules will apply. The parties may file motions or briefs asking the judge to shape the trial in a particular way. For example, in a motion in limine the defendant might ask the trial judge to keep out evidence that the defendant struck another person five years earlier on the ground that evidence of the earlier incident might prejudice the jury against the defendant.

Selection of a jury. When the case comes up for trial, prospective jurors are questioned by the judge and perhaps by the lawyers to determine whether they are biased about issues in the case or about one of the parties. Lawyers may "strike" or eliminate some prospects. Of those who remain, 12 (or sometimes six or eight) are then "put in the box" as jurors for the particular case.

Opening statements. At this point the judge will ask the plaintiff's lawyer to state the case for the plaintiff. This is not an argument but a preliminary view of the testimony the plaintiff will put on. Then the defendant's lawyer will make a similar opening statement.

Plaintiff's case. Next the plaintiff's attorney calls the first witness. By asking questions, the lawyer elicits answers that establish what the witness knows about the facts relevant to the case. After the witness is questioned by the plaintiff's lawyer, the defendant's lawyer has an opportunity to cross-examine the witness, by asking questions that may put the matters in a different light, or may give them a different emphasis, or may show that the witness was mistaken, lying, or biased. The two examinations of the witness thus can give the jury a basis for judging how much the witness really knew and how credible the witness might be. This process continues as the plaintiff's attorney calls each of the plaintiff's witnesses in turn.

*The Motion for Directed Verdict. Defendants usually move for a directed verdict (referred to as a motion for judgment as a matter of law in federal courts) at the end of the plaintiff's evidence and again when the defendant's evidence is completed. Such motions assert that the proof offered by the plaintiff is legally insufficient to warrant a jury's verdict for the plaintiff. More rarely, a plaintiff might move for directed verdict, but such a motion is seldom granted in view of the plaintiff's burden of proof.

The judge considers the evidence in the light most favorable to the plaintiff. That is, the judge takes into account all the reasonable inferences the jury would be allowed to draw from the testimony. Considering all the evidence in this light, the judge will grant the motion for a directed verdict if a jury of reasonable persons could not differ on the evidence, or if the facts taken in this favorable light do not establish any legal claims. The standard can be stated in other ways, but the basic idea is that the judge is not to take over the jury's role. So a directed verdict should be denied if there is room for reasonable jurors to disagree. This almost always involves some interaction of fact and law—do the facts, taken in a light favorable to the plaintiff, establish the elements required by law?

A motion for directed verdict is somewhat similar to a summary judgment motion, with a similar standard, but it is based on the *evidence produced in full at the trial*.

Defendant's case. When all of the plaintiff's witnesses have been examined and cross-examined, the defendant puts on witnesses who give the defense side of the story. These witnesses, answering questions on the defense counsel's examination, often give a different factual picture from that given by the plaintiff's witnesses. After each witness is examined, the plaintiff's counsel cross-examines.

*Objections to Evidence and Offers of Evidence. Not only before the trial, but also during the trial, the parties can object to evidence that is presented. Evidence that is not relevant to help prove any element involved in the case should be excluded by the judge, especially if the evidence is likely to mislead the jury or to be "prejudicial." A trial judge's admission of evidence over objection, or her refusal to admit evidence because of objection, raises legal issues. Rulings on admission of evidence are often rulings based on a specific principle of law.

Closing arguments. Plaintiff's lawyer, then defendant's lawyer, then plaintiff's lawyer in rebuttal, will make closing arguments to the jury. These are arguments, not statements of fact. They are aimed at persuading the jury, on the basis of the testimony, that one side or the other should be believed.

*Proposed Jury Instructions and Objections to Them. Instructions are *i.e.* the trial judge's statements of law to the jury. They tell the jury what it must consider and what facts must be found to exist before the plaintiff can recover, or before a defense applies. Instructions must accurately state the law. Lawyers must actively object to instructions they feel are incorrect statements of law, or propose instructions of their own. Once the judge listens to each party's suggested instructions and decides which are appropriate, the judge instructs or "charges" the jury. Thus, a judge might instruct the jury that if it finds that the defendant intentionally struck the plaintiff with intent to harm, it should bring in a verdict for the plaintiff.

Notice that this leaves the fact-finding to the jury and the legal rules to the judge. Since an instruction is supposed to represent a correct statement of the law, and one on which the jury will act, an erroneous statement of the law would be ground for appeal.

Jury Verdict. After receiving instructions from the judge, the jury members talk with each other and consider whether the evidence presented in the trial meets or does not meet the legal rules articulated by the judge. The jury reaches a verdict on the plaintiff's claim, and when applicable decides on an appropriate remedy. For example, if the jury finds that the defendant struck the plaintiff in a way that provides the plaintiff with a recognizable claim against the defendant, the jury might also award the plaintiff a sum of money it deems fair compensation.

*The Motion J.N.O.V.—A Renewed Motion for Judgment as a Matter of Law. The post-trial motion for judgment notwithstanding the verdict (also referred to as a renewed motion for judgment as a matter of law in federal courts) is a virtual renewal of the motion for directed verdict. (N.O.V. is for the Latin *non obstante veredicto*, meaning notwithstanding the verdict.) The motion asserts that the evidence is not legally sufficient to justify a jury verdict for the plaintiff. A judge who is unwilling to grant a directed verdict before the jury reaches its decision may grant a J.N.O.V. after the verdict is reported. There may be several reasons for this. For example, the judge may firmly believe the jury will find for the defendant even without a directed verdict. Or the judge may believe that the jury will come in with a verdict for the plaintiff, but that it will be small and reasonable. Afterwards, when the J.N.O.V. motion is presented, the judge may have some second thoughts. Another possibility is that the judge wants to have a jury verdict in case that can simply be reinstated if the appellate court reverses on appeal.

The legal issue presented by the J.N.O.V. motion is the legal sufficiency of the evidence. It should be decided according to the same standard that governs the directed verdict motion: that no reasonable jury could have arrived at the verdict.

*The Motion for New Trial. The parties are entitled not only to a trial but to one that is carried out without any serious legal error. Either attorney may therefore file a motion for a new trial due to error(s) made in the first one. If the judge agrees that an error was made and that there is a strong possibility the error prejudiced the jury, a new trial should be granted.

A second kind of new trial motion is unique. This asks the judge to grant a new trial, not because of error, but because the verdict is against the weight of the evidence or because the damages award was unconscionably high (or possibly unconscionably low). These motions really ask the judge to use something like discretion. The judge cannot substitute herself for the jury and make the ultimate decision in the case merely because she differs from the jury about what is right. Still, the judge does have considerable power to grant a *new trial*. If a new trial is granted, a new jury will hear the evidence. This may be done in many states because the first jury's verdict is against the weight of the evidence (though not legally wrong), or because the damages award was excessive. Judges do not often grant such motions, although they do sometimes grant a remittitur, conditioning the denial of the new trial motion on plaintiff's consent to receive a lower amount of damages than granted by the jury.

Appeals. When a case has been resolved by a judge or jury, a party may ask a higher court to review the determination. Typically, state court systems have two levels of courts of appeal—intermediate appellate courts and a state supreme court. If an intermediate appellate court affirms the trial court's ruling, the non-prevailing party can accept the appellate court ruling or appeal further to the state supreme court. In rare cases, where the case raises an issue of federal law, the tort issue can be appealed further to the United States Supreme Court. It is unusual for tort cases to be resolved by the United States Supreme Court because tort law is generally state law for which state courts are considered the final arbiter.

When an appellate court reverses a lower court's decision, the case typically returns to the place it left off in the trial process. For example, if the trial court dismisses the plaintiff's complaint and the court of appeals reverses the dismissal, the plaintiff will not necessarily prevail in the case. Instead, the case will be returned to the lower court and the defendant will have to answer the complaint, after which the discovery process will begin, and so forth.

Appendix: A Narrative Case with Procedural Rulings

The Complaint and Answer

Rosa Light makes an appointment with an attorney, Lawton. Careful questioning by Lawton develops the story summarized here: "Two months ago, when I was about eight months pregnant, I was at a dance with Bill Burton. He got angry with me because I danced with his brother, who is a terrible flirt. Anyway, Bill hit me in the stomach. Two or three weeks after that I had the baby. I had no permanent bad effects from the blow and the baby had no obvious injury, but I want to sue Bill. Can I?"

Lawton writes up a complaint for Rosa, asserting that Bill committed a battery against her. Lawton also writes up a complaint on behalf of the child, Adrian. This complaint alleges the same facts, and in addition says in part: "On information and belief it is alleged that the plaintiff Adrian Light felt the blow and suffered pain from it."

The complaint is then filed in the office of the clerk of the trial court and a copy is served on (or handed to) Bill. Bill's lawyer gets a different story. Bill says in substance: "I did try to pull my brother away from Rosa and when I did she came flying at me, trying to scratch me. I held her at arm's length—well, maybe I had to push a little—but didn't hit her in the stomach or anywhere else."

Bill's lawyer, Atwood, files a paper which combines two documents: First, Atwood files an "answer," in which he says Bill denies the facts alleged; Bill did not hit Rosa at all. This is extended to say that to the extent Bill touched Rosa at all, it was in justifiable self-defense. This answer raises factual issues to be decided by the trier of fact.

The Defendant Demurs or Moves to Dismiss

Atwood also includes in the papers a motion traditionally known as a *demurrer* at common law and as a *motion to dismiss* under Rule 12(b)(6) in federal courts and in most state courts. The paper asks the court to dismiss the claim of the child, Adrian, on the ground that even if the facts claimed by Rosa and Adrian were true, no law supports any claim by the child.

Judge Martinez Ponders and Decides

The *Light* file comes to Judge Rebecca Martinez in the usual course of her work as a trial court judge. Her first reaction is that the motion to dismiss the child's claim should be granted, since the facts alleged in the complaint do not appear to her to show a battery to the child, though undoubtedly the complaint states facts showing a battery to the mother. On second thought, she recognizes that the case is novel and she is loath to dismiss it without study. The memorandum submitted by Atwood on Bill's behalf argues: "An unborn child is not a person to whom a tort can be committed." Judge Martinez considers this argument and the cases cited by each party. She then concludes that the argument does not represent the law. Accordingly, she signs a formal order denying the motion to dismiss. The order is mailed to each lawyer.

Defense Planning: Discovery

"Does this mean we'll have to have a trial?" Bill asks. "Maybe," Atwood says, "but not necessarily. We could take depositions of witnesses and of the plaintiff, and maybe we could get some helpful stuff, maybe even an admission that the baby wasn't hurt. If we could get the plaintiff to admit that the baby wasn't hurt, we could file a motion for summary judgment, because I believe that if the baby wasn't hurt or at least offended, there wasn't any battery, even if the baby is a person who can sue for a tort before his birth."

Bill says, "But they won't admit that. They already said in their complaint that the baby felt pain." "You are right, but maybe we can do something even better. Maybe we can file an affidavit of a doctor saying that the baby felt nothing. Affidavits can't be used at trial as proof, but they can be used to show there is no real dispute about the facts. If the plaintiffs can't deny the affidavit by an affidavit of their own, the judge will have to say there is no dispute about the facts for a jury to decide, and that means she'll have to decide on the law."

The Defense Motion for Summary Judgment and Judge Martinez's Ruling

Atwood is able to get an affidavit, but it is not quite so good as he had hoped. The doctor gave an affidavit saying that the child might have felt a blow, but could not differentiate it from many other movements or feelings, or attribute it to a human being. Atwood files this affidavit along with his motion for summary judgment.

Judge Martinez begins working through the summary judgment motion in *Light v. Burton.* "I've already ruled that the baby, though not born at the time, is a person who could be victimized by a tort," she reflects. "But it is true that there is no battery if the plaintiff is not hurt or offended." She reads the affidavit from the defendant's doctor. "So the baby could not tell the blow was from a human source or distinguish it from other discomforts." The plaintiff, however, has filed a counter-affidavit from another doctor saying that, while it was true that before birth the baby could not distinguish one blow from another, it would feel pain as an unpleasant sensation if the blow was hard enough. Judge Martinez would be glad to get rid of the case, but she concludes that the defendant's affidavit does not really establish a fact helpful to the defendant. She writes a brief statement of her reasons for denying the summary judgment motion as follows:

> "The defendant's affidavit establishes that the baby could not distinguish this harm from other harms, but it does not establish that there is no harm. The plaintiff's affidavit supports the idea that the baby before birth could and did feel unpleasant sensations as the result of the blow, if there was a blow. The facts shown by the defendant and left undisputed by the plaintiff do not warrant judgment in his favor, since I hold that the child's feelings would constitute 'harm' under the law of battery. The case will have to go to trial, therefore, on the factual issues raised by the complaint and answer."

Pre-Trial, Trial, and Admission of Evidence

Before trial, defendant files a trial brief asking the court to apply the legal definition of physical harm supplied in the Restatement Third of Torts: Liability for Physical and Emotional Harm § 4. The judge rules that under prior case law, the state follows the rule in the Restatement Second of Torts, and that is the legal definition on which the jury will be instructed.

Months later, after a pre-trial conference in which the judge attempts to get issues clarified and to encourage settlement, the case is scheduled for trial and a jury is impaneled.

Rosa Light's attorney, Lawton, begins putting on his case. After Rosa has testified to the main events stated in her complaint, Lawton asks:

Q. What happened after Bill Burton hit you?

A. He pulled his brother by the arm outside.

Q. What did you do?

A. I went to the window and watched while Bill beat his brother up. Then I got sick.

At this point Atwood stands up and says, "We object, Your Honor. This testimony should be stricken as prejudicial and the jury cautioned." Judge Martinez says, "Overruled. Go on Mr. Lawton."

Motions for Directed Verdict

The trial proceeds in normal fashion. The plaintiff's witnesses are examined and cross-examined. When the plaintiff's case is completed, the defendant's attorney approaches the bench. "We move for a directed verdict as to the infant plaintiff, Your Honor," Atwood says in a voice the jury could not hear. "The plaintiff has failed to prove an essential element of the case: harm or offense. There is no offense without consciousness. As to harm, the Restatement Second of Torts requires "physical impairment of the condition of another's body, or physical pain or illness." [§ 15]. There is no testimony even remotely supporting the idea that there was physical pain or illness. We do not think the Supreme Court of this state would accept a passing discomfort as 'harm,' and this is the most the testimony would support." Lawton answers: "Doctor Veillicht testified, Your Honor, that the child in the womb could feel a blow like that attributed to the defendant and would feel it as a negative thing, pain in the sense that the baby would try to avoid it." Judge Martinez: "I'm going to deny the motion and instruct the jury as to the definition of harm."

After Judge Martinez denies the motion for directed verdict, the defendant proceeds to introduce his evidence, and again witnesses are examined and cross-examined. When the defendant completes his proof, Atwood again moves for directed verdict and it is again denied.

Closing Arguments and Instructions to the Jury

The lawyers then give their closing arguments, summarizing the evidence favorable to each side and discounting evidence against them, each trying to persuade the jury that his client was telling the truth. In addition, Lawton talks considerably about the importance of damages. Atwood urges the jury to keep things in perspective.

After the closing arguments, there is a recess for lunch. Judge Martinez asks the lawyers to meet with her in chambers before resuming the afternoon session. In chambers, she reminds them that they had previously submitted proposed instructions to the jury, had also previously seen the instructions she expected to give, and had made their "record" of objections and requests about those instructions.

"Now the evidence always takes a few unexpected turns," she adds, "and I think I had better add an instruction. "I've been worried about the question of harm to the fetus. There is no evidence of any pathological harm. As you know, Mr. Atwood, I refused to grant your motion for directed verdict, which you made on the ground that there was no harm as a matter of law. The definition of harm our Supreme Court has previously applied is the Restatement Second's definition. I think there may be enough evidence to get to the jury on this, but I do think we need a very careful statement to the jury. Does either of you have a proposed instruction?"

"I do not, Your Honor; whatever you think will suit us," Lawton says.

"I do have one," Atwood says, and he passes copies. His proposed instruction would tell the jury that before the infant plaintiff could recover, it would be necessary to find that harm was done and that harm would require either an identifiable physical symptom or sign, or some identifiable medical condition, and that it could not be a transitory feeling.

"We would object to that, of course," Lawton comments.

"Yes, I think that may be too strong," the judge says, "but maybe something along those lines." She begins writing on the instruction proposed by Atwood and comes up with this:

"You are instructed as to the infant plaintiff there can be a recovery only if there is a battery as the Court has already defined that term to you. As to the infant plaintiff, this will require, in addition to an intentional unpermitted blow by the defendant, that the infant plaintiff has suffered harm. Harm is defined to include any physical impairment of the body, physical pain, or illness. It is not necessary that there be any permanent ill-effects, but on the other hand a trivial and transitory feeling on the part of the fetus would not constitute harm for this purpose."

Lawton objects to the last clause, and his objection is written down as part of the record. Atwood objects to the instruction so far as it fails to require some identifiable medical condition or the pain of a conscious, living being. This objection is also noted. The judge and lawyers then return to the courtroom for the remainder of the trial.

The Jury's Verdict

Judge Martinez duly instructs the jury, which then adjourns to the privacy of the jury room. For the lawyers it is a waiting time. When the bailiff announces that the jury is coming in, Judge Martinez takes the bench. The lawyers go to their tables and the jury files in.

"Have you reached a verdict?" Judge Martinez asks.

"We have, Your Honor," the foreman says.

"Please hand it to the bailiff." The bailiff hands the paper to the judge. The form has been provided by the judge and filled in or crossed out by the jury. "We the jury," Judge Martinez reads out loud, "find for the plaintiff Rosa Light in the sum of $10,000 and for the plaintiff Adrian Light in the sum of $5,000." "Is this your verdict?"

"It is, Your Honor."

Judge Martinez thanks the jurors for their services, explains their obligation to return for further jury duty at a later date, discharges them, and adjourns the court.

J.N.O.V. and New Trial Motions and the Final Judgment

One motion, or pair of motions, remains to be asserted by the defendant's lawyer, Atwood. He files a written motion two days later, in two parts. The first part moves for "Judgment N.O.V."—a judgment notwithstanding the verdict. The second part moves in the alternative for a new trial for errors committed in the trial, and especially the error in the instruction on the battery to the child.

Judge Martinez denies the motions and enters a judgment on the verdict. The judgment is usually the last formal order. It is signed by the judge and reflects the jury's verdict. Here it provides that the plaintiff Rosa should have and recover from the defendant $10,000 and that the plaintiff Adrian should have and recover from the defendant $5,000.

Getting to the Appeal

These are the kinds of events that have occurred before the appeal. At this point the appeal process takes over. Here Atwood files notice of appeal, and in the course of the next few months provides the Appellate Court with excerpts from the trial record and files a brief arguing that the trial judge committed error in a number of respects. You can test yourself by determining what specific rulings or actions by the judge might constitute grounds for appeal. You can check the footnote for an answer.[1]

The Appellate Court Decides

Having seen Atwood's brief for the appellant, Lawton files a brief for the appellee. The Appellate Court schedules oral arguments for some

---

[1] Each of the procedural devices is the basis for a potential appeal. The judge, Atwood argues, should have granted the motion to dismiss, the motion for summary judgment, and the directed verdict motion; she should have instructed the jury as Atwood requested, and should not have admitted the evidence to which he objected. Each of these arguments is supported by propositions of law, for which Atwood argues in his appellate brief.

months later and after those are heard, the judges of the appellate court and their law clerks research the law further. They hold conferences about the case and draft an opinion. The various judges comment on the proposed opinion and finally they agree on a final draft. If a judge still disagrees he or she may write a dissent. The opinion is then formally announced and a copy is sent to the lawyers. This "opinion," or formal explanation of the court's decision, is then published in "advance sheets" and by on-line services (such as Westlaw), and finally in an official state volume as well as a "regional reporter." (Which regional reporter a case is reported in depends on which state court decided the case.) Each published opinion is given a citation so it can be found easily by lawyers and others researching the law in the library or on-line. For example, the appeals court's decision in *Light v. Burton* (which is a fictional case, of course) might be reported in volume 665 of the Northwest Reporter, Second Series, beginning on page 87. If the deciding court was the Court of Appeals of Michigan, and if the opinion was filed in 2004, the citation would look like this: 665 N.W.2d 87 (Mich. Ct. App. 2004). A court's published opinion is the "case" with which law study begins, in an effort to isolate principles and rules, and to learn how arguments can be constructed to persuade judges.

REFERENCES: THOMAS A. MAUET & DAVID MARCUS, PRETRIAL (10th ed. 2019); PAUL BERGMAN, TRIAL ADVOCACY IN A NUTSHELL (6th ed. 2016); STEVEN H. GOLDBERG & TRACY WALTERS MCCORMACK, THE FIRST TRIAL (WHERE DO I SIT? WHAT DO I SAY?) IN A NUTSHELL (3d ed. 2016); KENNEY F. HEGLAND, TRIAL AND CLINICAL SKILLS IN A NUTSHELL (5th ed. 2015).

PART 2

INTENTIONAL TORTS

■ ■ ■

CHAPTER 3

INTENTIONAL TORTS TO PERSON OR PROPERTY

■ ■ ■

Every type of tort claim has its own *elements*, or particular points that a plaintiff must prove in order to succeed on that claim. A plaintiff must first allege facts that would establish each of these required elements—in other words, a "prima facie case," or a case good "on the face of it." If the plaintiff does not, the judge will dismiss the complaint. But making allegations is not enough to win. The plaintiff must then go on to *prove* the prima facie case of some particular tort. The plaintiff bears the burden of proof on each element, meaning that if the plaintiff fails to prove a prima facie case, the defendant will win even without putting on a defense. In this chapter we will explore the required elements of a number of intentional tort claims. In the next chapter we will see a number of defenses that may allow the defendant to escape liability even when a prima facie case has been proved.

There are many types of tort claims. Conceptually, one way to organize these claims is to group them along two dimensions—the interests they protect, and the levels of culpability they require. In terms of interests, tort actions can protect against (1) physical injury to person or property; (2) dignitary and emotional harm; and (3) economic harm. With respect to culpability, tort rules may impose liability for intentional wrongdoing (intent or malice), negligence (lack of reasonable care), and even, in some cases, no failure to use care by the defendant (strict liability). Thomas C. Grey, *Accidental Torts*, 54 VAND. L. REV. 1225 (2001). Our exploration of tort claims begins with causes of action that protect against intended physical injury to person or property.

§ 1. BATTERY

A. ELEMENTS

"The least touching of another in anger is a battery. . . . If any of them use violence against the other, to force his way in a rude inordinate manner, it is a battery. . . ." *Cole v. Turner*, 6 Mod. Rep. 149, 90 Eng. Rep. 958 (Nisi Prius 1704).

MCELHANEY V. THOMAS

405 P.3d 1214 (Kan. 2017)

STEGALL, JUSTICE:

[Charles Thomas and Emma McElhaney were students at Clay County High School. Thomas played on the baseball team, and McElhaney was the team's manager. The day of the incident, both were in the parking lot headed toward the team bus to travel to a game. Thomas, driving his parents' truck, saw McElhaney, who was walking with another teammate, Andrew Hecker. Thomas approached McElhaney and Hecker from behind. McElhaney heard the truck and moved toward the curb to avoid being hit. The front-passenger tire of the truck then rolled onto McElhaney's feet, trapping her, and making her fall to the ground. When Thomas backed up, McElhaney realized she could neither stand nor walk. Thomas drove McElhaney to the bus to receive medical aid and she was then taken to a hospital.]

The basic facts are not in dispute. Instead, the parties' disagreement centers on Thomas' state of mind. McElhaney testified that... Thomas said, "Oh, my gosh, I'm so sorry. I just meant to bump you." In an affidavit, Adam Slagle, [a passenger in Thomas's truck] likewise claimed Thomas said that "he only meant to bump into Emma with his truck.".... Thomas, however, denied ever saying he meant to bump McElhaney. He maintains he merely pulled too close to McElhaney while attempting to park.

[Plaintiff pleaded the intentional tort of battery and sought punitive damages. The district court dismissed that cause of action on the ground that] even if the plaintiff's evidence is viewed in a light most favorable to her, the statement by the defendant that "I only meant to bump into you" does not rise to the level of an intentional tort. Although to act (bump) may have been intentional the resulting injury or intent to injure was not intentional.... I believe it's simply horseplay.... The [appellate court] affirmed the district court's rulings.... [T]he panel concluded that "[t]here is simply no evidence to support a claim that Thomas had any intent to injure McElhaney."... [T]he Court of Appeals found that under either a judgment on the pleadings standard or a summary judgment standard, Thomas was entitled to prevail on McElhaney's battery claim as a matter of law....

ANALYSIS

Boiled down, we perceive the essence of the matter to be whether an "intent to bump" another person with a Ford F-150 truck, if proved, can establish the legally requisite culpable state of mind to sustain both a battery and a punitive damages claim.... Therefore, in whatever procedural format the question is embedded (motion for punitive damages, motion for judgment on the pleadings, motion for summary judgment, etc.) the outcome turns on the answer to a purely legal question over which we exercise plenary review—viz., must McElhaney plead and produce evidence that Thomas intended to cause physical injury or bodily harm in order to present her battery and punitive damages claims to a jury?. . .

It has regularly been said that an intention to injure is a prerequisite in battery cases. Or, as we stated more recently, the actor must have intended both the act and to cause some kind of injury or damage. . . . [A prior Kansas case] "is consistent with the Restatement (Second) of Torts § 13 (1965), which states that a person will be subject to liability for battery if he or she 'acts intending to cause a harmful or offensive contact with the person of the other' and 'a harmful contact with the person of the other directly or indirectly results.' "

We do not shy from our prior holdings that an intent to injure is a necessary element of the civil tort of battery in Kansas. But the precise nature of the injurious intent necessary to sustain a battery claim must be understood in light of the personal interests protected by the common law tort of battery:

"The original purpose of the courts in providing the action for battery undoubtedly was to keep the peace by affording a substitute for private retribution. The element of personal indignity involved always has been given considerable weight. Consequently, the defendant is liable not only for contacts which do actual physical harm, but also for those relatively trivial ones which are merely offensive and insulting. Spitting in the face is a battery, as is forcibly removing the plaintiff's hat, or any other contact brought about in a rude and insolent manner. . . .

The defendant may be liable when intending only a joke. . . . The plaintiff is entitled to protection according to the usages of decent society, and offensive contacts, or those which are contrary to all good manners, need not be tolerated. At the same time, in a crowded world, a certain amount of personal contact is inevitable, and must be accepted." Prosser and Keeton on Torts § 9, 41–42 (5th ed. 1984). . . .

The "intent to injure" element of a civil battery claim can be satisfied in alternative ways—either by (1) an intent to cause a harmful bodily contact, that is, to cause the other physical injury; or by (2) an intent to cause an offensive bodily contact, that is, to invade the other's reasonable sense of personal dignity. Both states of mind are sufficiently culpable to justify imposing civil battery liability for damages. . . .

Given this, we have no difficulty concluding that McElhaney satisfied her initial burden of pleading and producing some evidence that Thomas acted with an intent to injure. Even if he did not intend to cause any physical harm to McElhaney, the intent to bump her with a Ford F-150 truck is sufficient, by itself, to allow a reasonable jury to conclude that he acted with an intent to offend—to invade McElhaney's reasonable sense of personal dignity. The district court erred by effectively granting summary judgment against McElhaney on her intentional tort claim. . . . McElhaney was entitled to present her claim for punitive damages to the jury solely by virtue of her battery claim. . . .

———————

COHEN V. SMITH, 648 N.E. 2d 329 (Ill. App. Ct. 1995). Patricia Cohen was admitted to St. Joseph Memorial Hospital ("Hospital") to deliver her baby via cesarean section. Cohen and her husband allegedly informed her physician, who in turn advised the Hospital staff, that the couple's religious beliefs prohibited Cohen from being seen unclothed by a male. Cohen's doctor assured her husband that their religious convictions would be respected. During Cohen's cesarean section, Roger Smith, a male nurse on staff at the Hospital, allegedly observed and touched Cohen's naked body. Cohen and her husband filed suit against Nurse Smith and the Hospital. The trial court allowed defendants' motions to dismiss. *Held,* we reverse.

"Liability for battery emphasizes the plaintiff's lack of consent to the touching. . . . Protecting personal integrity has always been viewed as an important basis for battery. . . . As early as 1784, a Pennsylvania defendant was prosecuted for striking the cane of a French ambassador.

The court furthered the distinction between harmful offensive batteries and nonharmful offensive batteries: "As to the assault, this is, perhaps, one of that kind, in which the insult is more to be considered than the actual damage; for, though no great bodily pain is suffered by a blow on the palm of the hand, or the skirt of the coat, yet these are clearly within the definition of assault and battery, and among gentlemen too often induce duelling and terminate in murder." (Respublica v. De Longchamps (Pa.1784), 1 Dall. 111, 1 L.Ed. 59, in Gregory, Kalven, & Epstein, Cases & Materials on Torts 904–905 (1977).). . . .

Although most people in modern society have come to accept the necessity of being seen unclothed and being touched by members of the opposite sex during medical treatment, the plaintiffs had not accepted these procedures and, according to their complaint, had informed defendants of their convictions. . . . A person's right to refuse or accept medical care is not one to be interfered with lightly. . . . Accepting as true the plaintiffs' allegations . . . we conclude that the trial court erred in dismissing both the battery and the intentional infliction of emotional distress counts.

NOTES

1.   **Elements.** What are the elements of a cause of action for battery? What sources would you look to in order to find these elements?

2.   **Lack of intent to harm.** Perhaps the paradigm of battery is an intentional punch in the nose. The defendant in *McElhaney* argued that he

lacked an intent to harm the plaintiff physically, yet the court held that the case must go to the jury. Looking closely at the required elements of battery, why isn't the argument of lack of intent to harm a winning claim?

3.   **Testing the rules.** How should the following cases be resolved?

(a)   The defendant surgeon was performing a gall-bladder operation. He became frustrated with the operation itself and with the plaintiff, a scrub nurse, who defendant thought was making mistakes. When the plaintiff handed defendant an instrument he considered inappropriate, he became so exasperated that he grabbed her shoulder and pulled her face down toward the surgical opening, saying, "Can't you see where I'm working? I'm working in a hole. I need long instruments." In plaintiff's suit, defendant argued that he was not liable because of the absence of evidence that he intended to inflict personal injury. *Snyder v. Turk,* 627 N.E.2d 1053 (Ohio Ct. App. 1993).

(b)   Plaintiffs' employer refused to allow plaintiffs to bring their own meals to work or let them leave the workplace for meals. Plaintiffs let the employer know that because of religious reasons they could not eat beef-pork meatballs. The employer said it would switch to turkey meatballs, which it did, but it then switched back to beef-pork without letting the employees know. *Kumar v. Gate Gourmet, Inc.,* 325 P.3d 193 (Wash. 2014). *See also* RESTATEMENT (THIRD) OF TORTS: INTENTIONAL TORTS TO PERSONS § 103 illus. 6 (Tentative Draft No. 1, 2015).

4.   **Offense.** The Restatement Third of Torts provides that a contact is offensive if either: "(a) the contact offends a reasonable sense of personal dignity; or (b) the contact is highly offensive to the other's unusually sensitive sense of personal dignity, and the actor knows that the contact will be highly offensive to the other." Under section (b), liability will not be imposed if it "would violate public policy" or if "requiring the actor to avoid the contact would be unduly burdensome." RESTATEMENT (THIRD) OF TORTS: INTENTIONAL TORTS TO PERSONS § 103 (Tentative Draft No. 1, 2015). In *Cohen,* could the defendant argue that liability would violate public policy?

5.   **Procedure: motion to dismiss in *Cohen*.** The plaintiff in *Cohen* prevailed in overturning the trial court's dismissal. Does that mean that the plaintiff won the case? What if, on remand, the plaintiff can produce no evidence that Nurse Smith knew of Patricia Cohen's wishes? *See Mullins v. Parkview Hospital, Inc.,* 865 N.E.2d 608 (Ind. 2007) (emergency medical technician student intubated the plaintiff and lacerated her esophagus but did not know that plaintiff had refused consent to have student-learners participate in her care; summary judgment granted for the student, but not for the doctors and their practices).

6.   **Procedure: summary judgment in *McElhaney*.** The defendant in *McElhaney* originally persuaded the trial court to grant a motion to dismiss.

Because the motion incorporated evidence, the Kansas Supreme Court treated it as a summary judgment motion. How does a motion to dismiss differ from a motion for summary judgment? What happens after the summary judgment ruling has been reversed?

B. DUAL OR SINGLE INTENT

WHITE V. MUNIZ, 999 P.2d 814 (Colo. 2000). Barbara White placed her 83-year-old grandmother, Helen Everly, in an assisted living facility. Every had progressive dementia of the Alzheimer type. Within a few days of admission, Everly became agitated and occasionally acted aggressively toward others. Sherry Lynn Muniz, a shift supervisor tried to change Everly's adult diaper. Initially Everly refused to allow Muniz to change her diaper, but eventually Muniz thought that Everly relented. However, as Muniz reached toward the diaper, Everly struck Muniz on the jaw and ordered her out of the room. Muniz sued Everly and White as her representative for assault and battery. After the evidence was presented, the trial judge instructed the jury in part as follows:

> "The fact that a person may suffer from Dementia, Alzheimer type, does not prevent a finding that she acted intentionally. You may find that she acted intentionally if she intended to do what she did, even though her reasons and motives were entirely irrational. However, she must have appreciated the offensiveness of her conduct."

So instructed, the jury found for Everly and White. The Court of Appeals held the instruction to be error and reversed. *Held,* affirmed.

"State courts and legal commentators generally agree that an intentional tort requires some proof that the tortfeasor intended harm or offense. . . . More recently, some courts around the nation have abandoned this dual intent requirement in an intentional tort setting, that being an intent to contact and an intent that the contact be harmful or offensive, and have required only that the tortfeasor intend a contact with another that results in a harmful or offensive touching. . . . These courts would find intent in contact to the back of a friend that results in a severe, unexpected injury even though the actor did not intend the contact to be harmful or offensive. . . .

Because Colorado law requires a dual intent, we apply here the Restatement's definition of the term. As a result, we reject the arguments of Muniz and find that the trial court delivered an adequate instruction to the jury. Operating in accordance with this instruction, the jury had to find that Everly appreciated the offensiveness of her conduct in order to be liable for the intentional tort of battery. It necessarily had to consider her mental capabilities in making such a finding, including her age, infirmity, education, skill, or any other characteristic as to which the jury had evidence. We presume that the jury "looked into the mind of Everly," and reasoned that Everly did not possess the necessary intent to commit an assault or a battery.

Reasoning

A jury can, of course, find a mentally deficient person liable for an intentional tort, but in order to do so, the jury must find that the actor intended offensive or harmful consequences. As a result, insanity is not a defense to an intentional tort according to the ordinary use of that term, but is a characteristic, like infancy, that may make it more difficult to prove the intent element of battery. . . .

WAGNER V. STATE, 122 P.3d 599 (Utah 2005). While waiting in a department store customer-service line, plaintiff Tracy Wagner was suddenly attacked from behind by Sam Geise, a mentally disabled patient who was brought to the store and accompanied by State employees as a part of a state mental health treatment program. Wagner sued the State for failing to supervise Geise. By statute, the State could not be liable for the patient's conduct if that conduct "arose out of battery." In her suit against the state, plaintiff asserted that Geise's conduct could not legally constitute a battery because battery requires the actor to intend harm or offense through his deliberate contact, an intent Mr. Giese was mentally incompetent to form. The State, on the other hand, argues that the only intent required for battery is simply an intent to make a contact. *Held*, trial court's dismissal of plaintiff's claim against the government is affirmed.

F

PH

"Utah has adopted the Second Restatement of Torts to define the elements of [battery], including the element of intent. . . . [We] agree with the State that only intent to make contact is necessary. . . . We hold that the actor need not intend that his contact be harmful or offensive in order to commit a battery so long as he deliberately made the contact and so long as that contact satisfies our legal test for what is harmful or offensive. . . .

*Rule 3
Reasoning*

[A dual intent rule is practically unworkable.] For example, a man who decides to flatter a woman he spots in a crowd with an unpetitioned-for kiss, one of the examples of battery Prosser provides, would find no objection under the Wagners' proposed rule so long as his intentional contact was initiated with no intent to injure or offend. He would be held civilly liable for his conduct only if he intended to harm or offend her through his kiss. A woman in such circumstances would not enjoy the presumption of the law in favor of preserving her bodily integrity; instead, her right to be free from physical contact with strangers would depend upon whether she could prove that the stranger hoped to harm or offend her through his contact. So long as he could show that he meant only flattery and the communication of positive feelings towards her in stroking her, kissing her, or hugging her, she must be subjected to it and will find no protection for her bodily integrity in our civil law."

NOTES

1. **Single vs. dual intent.** As you can see, state courts are divided about whether battery requires a plaintiff to prove merely 1) that the defendant intended to contact, or also 2) that the defendant intended to harm or offend by that contact. Courts that adopt a single intent rule and courts that adopt a dual intent rule both trace the origins of those rules to the Restatement Second of Torts and Dean Prosser's treatise, which suggests that those authorities are themselves unclear about this requirement.

2. **Subjective standard.** Both single and dual intent are judge by subjective standards—what the defendants themselves actually intended. "This subjective-intent requirement should be contrasted with negligence, which contains an objective-fault requirement." RESTATEMENT (THIRD) OF TORTS: INTENTIONAL TORTS TO PERSONS § 102 (Tentative Draft No. 1, 2015). An objective-fault requirement would ask, *not* what Everly or Geise themselves actually intended, but rather what a reasonable person in those situations would have intended.

3. **An intent to contact but not to harm or offend.** Single intent would seem to favor plaintiff recoveries when the defendant intended to cause a harmful or offensive contact but the plaintiff cannot prove that the defendant intended the harm or offense. In what kinds of cases might this matter? Look at *White* and *Wagner*. In both cases, because of mental disabilities, the plaintiffs might be unable to prove that the defendants who caused the harmful contact actually intended the harm. These difficulties may also arise in cases involving child defendants. In many other cases, as when a defendant punches a plaintiff in the nose, the difference between single and dual intent will not matter. The Restatement Third of Torts adopts a single intent rule because the rule "affords greater protection to the plaintiff's interest in bodily integrity" and is consistent with a number of cases, particularly in the medical battery context. However, the Restatement acknowledges that "a dual-intent approach is more consistent with the view that liability for battery should exist only when the actor is especially culpable." RESTATEMENT (THIRD) OF TORTS: INTENTIONAL TORTS TO PERSONS § 102 cmt. b (Tentative Draft No. 1, 2015).

4. **Some examples.** Would battery liability exist in a dual intent jurisdiction? In a single intent jurisdiction?

> (a) "Stephanie approaches Carol, a new coworker in her office, from behind. 'You look tense!' Stephanie declares, and immediately begins giving Carol a vigorous neck massage. When Carol objects, Stephanie promptly ends the massage. The massage injures Carol's neck and requires her to miss several weeks of work. RESTATEMENT (THIRD) OF TORTS: INTENTIONAL TORTS TO PERSONS § 102 cmt. b, illus. 2.

> (b) A deputy sheriff "made physical contact" with a police officer, who the deputy considered to be a friend. The contact to the officer's shoulder, which was variously described, ranging from

"lighter than a pat with an open palm" to a "closed fist punch." Unbeknownst to the deputy, the police officer had recently undergone surgery on the shoulder. The contact injured the officer's shoulder, causing more than $63,000 in expenses for the injuries. All of the parties agreed that the touching was "an intentional act." *City of Lincoln v. Cty. of Lancaster,* 898 N.W.2d 374 (Neb. 2017).

(c)   A law professor who had been at odds with his colleague grabbed the other professor's shoulder in a "strong and tight fashion." See *Gerber v. Veltri,* 203 F.Supp.3d 846 (N.D. Ohio 2016).

5.   **Justice and policy.** Does the single intent rule or the dual intent rule produce a more just outcome in these illustrations? Which rule represents better policy? The issue has provoked strong reactions from judges. *See White v. University of Idaho,* 797 P.2d 108 (Idaho 1990) (Bistlin, J., dissenting) ("The Court's opinion has a chilling effect on any thought of ever again tapping a dancing gent on the shoulder to ask, 'May I?' Today it is learned that so doing is a battery even though no harm or offense is intended. One lives and learns."). Scholars have also disputed the point. For an argument in favor of the single-intent rule, see Kenneth W. Simons, *A Restatement (Third) of Intentional Torts?,* 48 ARIZ. L. REV. 1061 (2006). For an argument that the dual-intent rule is better advised, see 1 DOBBS, HAYDEN & BUBLICK, THE LAW OF TORTS § 35 (2d ed. 2011). In a single intent battery state, would you expect other limitations to do more work—cutting back plaintiff recovery when the defendant had no intent to harm or offend? In the Restatement Third, as we will see in the chapter, doctrines of apparent and presumptive consent take on a more active role.

6.   **Proving intent.** If defendant says, "I did not mean to harm or offend the plaintiff," is the case over in a dual-intent jurisdiction? The *White v. Muniz* court wrote: "Juries may find it difficult to determine the mental state of an actor, but they may rely on circumstantial evidence in reaching their conclusion. . . . For example, a person of reasonable intelligence knows with substantial certainty that a stone thrown into a crowd will strike someone and result in an offensive or harmful contact to that person. Hence, if an actor of average intelligence performs such an act, the jury can determine that the actor had the requisite intent to cause a harmful or offensive contact, even though the actor denies having such thoughts."

NOTE: LIABILITY OF PEOPLE WITH MENTAL ILLNESS

Why is a person with a mental illness potentially liable for an intentional tort at all? Unlike the criminal law, the tort law does not generally recognize "insanity" as a defense. In *Polmatier v. Russ,* 537 A.2d 468 (Conn. 1988), defendant Russ shot his father-in-law Arthur Polmatier, causing his death. Russ was found not guilty by reason of insanity on a murder charge in criminal court, but in the tort action, a judgment was entered for the plaintiff even though Russ could not make a rational choice, and shot his father-in-law for "crazy" or schizophrenic reasons (including Russ' beliefs that Polmatier was a spy for the red Chinese and that Russ was a supreme being who could make his bed fly out of the window). According to the court "[a]n insane person may have an intent to invade the interests of another, even though his reasons and motives for forming that intention may be entirely irrational." Because Russ intended to shoot Polmatier, plaintiff was entitled to prevail.

Not all countries hold the "insane" liable for intentional torts. The German Civil Code § 827, for instance, excludes civil responsibility for one who is unable to exercise free will, except where he caused his own temporary disability by use of alcohol or similar means. Other countries are more nuanced still. In Mexico, for example, the Código Civil para el Distrito Federal § 1911 provides that the incompetent person is liable *unless* some other person such as a guardian is liable.

Should people with diminished mental capacity be held to the same rules of liability as others?

C. THE MEANING OF "INTENT"

GARRATT V. DAILEY
279 P.2d 1091 (Wash. 1955)

HILL, JUSTICE. . . .

Brian Dailey (age five years, nine months) was visiting with Naomi Garratt, an adult and a sister of the plaintiff, Ruth Garratt, likewise an adult, in the back yard of the plaintiff's home, on July 16, 1951. It is plaintiff's contention that she came out into the back yard to talk with Naomi and that, as she started to sit down in a wood and canvas lawn chair, Brian deliberately pulled it out from under her. The only one of the three persons present so testifying was Naomi Garratt. (Ruth Garratt, the plaintiff, did not testify as to how or why she fell.)

The trial court, unwilling to accept this testimony, adopted instead Brian Dailey's version of what happened, and made the following findings:

"III. . . . [T]hat while Naomi Garratt and Brian Dailey were in the back yard the plaintiff, Ruth Garratt, came out of her house into the back yard. Some time subsequent thereto defendant, Brian Dailey, picked up a lightly built wood and canvas lawn chair which was then and there located in the back yard of the above described premises, moved it sideways a few feet and seated himself therein, at which time he discovered the plaintiff, Ruth Garratt, about to sit down at the place where the lawn chair had formerly been, at which time he hurriedly got up from the chair and attempted to move it toward Ruth Garratt to aid her in sitting down in the chair; that due to the defendant's small size and lack of dexterity he was unable to get the lawn chair under the plaintiff in time to prevent her from falling to the ground. That plaintiff fell to the ground and sustained a fracture of her hip, and other injuries and damages as hereinafter set forth.

"IV. That the preponderance of the evidence in this case establishes that when the defendant, Brian Dailey, moved the chair in question *he did not have any wilful or unlawful purpose* in doing so; that *he did not have any intent to injure the plaintiff, or any intent to bring about any unauthorized or offensive contact with her person* or any object appurtenant thereto; that the circumstances which immediately preceded the fall of the plaintiff established that *the defendant, Brian Dailey, did not have purpose, intent or design to perform a prank or to effect an assault and battery upon the person of the plaintiff.*" (Italics ours, for a purpose hereinafter indicated.)

It is conceded that Ruth Garratt's fall resulted in a fractured hip and other painful and serious injuries. To obviate the necessity of a retrial in the event this court determines that she was entitled to a judgment against Brian Dailey, the amount of her damage was found to be $11,000. Plaintiff appeals from a judgment dismissing the action and asks for the entry of a judgment in that amount or a new trial.

The authorities generally, but with certain notable exceptions, state that when a minor has committed a tort with force he is liable to be proceeded against as any other person would be.

In our analysis of the applicable law, we start with the basic premise that Brian, whether five or fifty-five, must have committed some wrongful act before he could be liable for appellant's injuries. . . .

It is urged that Brian's action in moving the chair constituted a battery. A definition (not all-inclusive but sufficient for our purpose) of a battery is the intentional infliction of a harmful bodily contact upon another. The rule that determines liability for battery is given in 1 RESTATEMENT TORTS, 29, § 13, as:

"An act which, directly or indirectly, is the legal cause of a harmful contact with another's person makes the actor liable to the other, if

"(a) the act is done with the intention of bringing about a harmful or offensive contact. . . ."

In the comment on clause (a), the Restatement says:

> *"Character of actor's intentions.* In order that an act may be done with the intention of bringing about a harmful or offensive contact . . . , the act must be done for the purpose of causing the contact . . . or with knowledge on the part of the actor that such contact . . . is substantially certain to be produced." See, also, Prosser on Torts 41, § 8.

We have here the conceded volitional act of Brian, i.e., the moving of a chair. Had the plaintiff proved to the satisfaction of the trial court that Brian moved the chair while she was in the act of sitting down, Brian's action would patently have been for the purpose or with the intent of causing the plaintiff's bodily contact with the ground, and she would be entitled to a judgment against him for the resulting damages.

The plaintiff based her case on that theory, and the trial court held that she failed in her proof and accepted Brian's version of the facts rather than that given by the eyewitness who testified for the plaintiff. After the trial court determined that the plaintiff had not established her theory of a battery (i.e., that Brian had pulled the chair out from under the plaintiff while she was in the act of sitting down), it then became concerned with whether a battery was established under the facts as it found them to be.

In this connection, we quote another portion of the comment on the "Character of actor's intention," relating to clause (a) of the rule of the Restatement heretofore set forth:

> "It is not enough that the act itself is intentionally done and this, even though the actor realizes or should realize that it contains a very grave risk of bringing about the contact or apprehension. Such realization may make the actor's conduct negligent or even reckless but unless he realizes that to a substantial certainty, the contact or apprehension will result, the actor has not that intention which is necessary to make him liable under the rule stated in this section."

A battery would be established if, in addition to plaintiff's fall, it was proved that, when Brian moved the chair, he knew with substantial certainty that the plaintiff would attempt to sit down where the chair had been. If Brian had any of the intents which the trial court found . . . that he did not have, he would of course have had the knowledge to which we have referred. The mere absence of any intent to injure the plaintiff or to play a prank on her or to embarrass her, or to commit an assault and battery on her would not absolve him from liability if in fact he had such knowledge.

Without such knowledge, there would be nothing wrongful about Brian's act in moving the chair and, there being no wrongful act, there would be no liability.

While a finding that Brian had no such knowledge can be inferred from the findings made, we believe that before the plaintiff's action in such a case should be dismissed there should be no question but that the trial court had passed upon that issue; hence, the case should be remanded for clarifications of the findings to specifically cover the question of Brian's knowledge, because intent could be inferred therefrom. If the court finds that he had such knowledge the necessary intent will be established and the plaintiff will be entitled to recover, even though there was no purpose to injure or embarrass the plaintiff. If Brian did not have such knowledge, there was no wrongful act by him and the basic premise of liability on the theory of a battery was not established.

It will be noted that the law of battery as we have discussed it is the law applicable to adults, and no significance has been attached to the fact that Brian was a child less than six years of age when the alleged battery occurred. The only circumstance where Brian's age is of any consequence is in determining what he knew, and there his experience, capacity, and understanding are of course material. . . .

The cause is remanded for clarification, with instructions to make definite findings on the issue of whether Brian Dailey knew with substantial certainty that the plaintiff would attempt to sit down where the chair which he moved had been, and to change the judgment if the findings warrant it. . . .

NOTES

1.   **Subsequent history of the case.** On remand, the trial court found that the plaintiff was in the act of sitting down when Brian moved the chair, and that Brian knew this. In a bench trial, on the basis of the substantial certainty test, the judge found for the plaintiff. This was affirmed on the second appeal, *Garratt v. Dailey*, 304 P.2d 681 (Wash. 1956).

2.   **Defining intent.** What is the definition of intent accepted by the *Garratt* court? Imagine that defendant hates the plaintiff, sees him at a distance and hurls a stone, hoping to hit the plaintiff but believing that success is extremely unlikely. The stone does in fact hit the plaintiff, however. Is this a battery? Is the intent involved the same intent on which Brian Dailey was held liable?

3.   **The Restatement definition.** The Restatement Third of Torts defines "intent to produce a consequence" as either 1) a "purpose of producing that consequence" or 2) "knowing that the consequence is substantially certain to result." RESTATEMENT (THIRD) OF TORTS: LIABILITY FOR PHYSICAL AND EMOTIONAL HARM § 1 (2010). What if a police officer orders a dog to "bite and hold" a suspect? Would this be intent under the Restatement definition? *Ryan v. Napier*, 425 P.3d 230 (Ariz. 2018).

4. **Distinguishing intent from negligence.** Legal fault usually takes the form of intent or the form of negligence. Negligence is a large subject, to be considered beginning in Chapter 5. In general, negligence is conduct that creates an unreasonable risk of harm. Driving too fast would be an example.

5. **Reckless, willful and wanton conduct.** Between intent and negligence, courts sometimes identify another level of fault—willful and wanton, or reckless conduct. The Restatement Third defines recklessness as a particularly lopsided risk-benefit calculation: "[w]hen a person's conduct creates a known risk that can be reduced by relatively modest precautions." RESTATEMENT (THIRD) OF TORTS: LIABILITY FOR PHYSICAL AND EMOTIONAL HARM § 2 cmt. a (2010). Similarly, the Connecticut Supreme Court has written, "Recklessness requires a conscious choice of a course of action either with knowledge of the serious danger to others involved in it or with knowledge of facts which would disclose this danger to any reasonable man, and the actor must recognize that his conduct involves a risk substantially greater . . . than that which is necessary to make his conduct negligent." *Doe v. Hartford Roman Catholic Diocesan Corp.*, 119 A.3d 462 (Conn. 2015). While line-drawing can be difficult, courts must sometimes distinguish recklessness or wanton misconduct from either intent or negligence, for certain rules of damages or for different statutes of limitation. For example, conduct that falls short of intentional wrongdoing may still be reckless or wanton so that punitive damages would be justified.

6. **Levels of intent.** Can you distinguish between *Garratt v. Dailey* intent on the one hand and recklessness or negligence on the other? Test it out: Defendant became highly intoxicated and drove his car on the wrong side of the highway, causing a head-on collision that seriously injured the plaintiff. Is that *Garratt v. Dailey* intent, recklessness or just negligence? See *Thomas v. Heard*, 256 So.3d 644 (Ala. 2017) (driver, under the influence of alcohol and prescription drugs, failed to stop at a stop sign).

NOTE: CHILD LIABILITY

1. *General rule.* As recognized in *Garratt v. Dailey*, in most states children may be liable for torts they commit as long as the injured plaintiff can prove the required elements, including intent. That is, in most states a child cannot escape tort liability simply because of young age. *See, e.g., Bailey v. C.S.*, 12 S.W.3d 159 (Tex. App. 2000) (four-year old may be liable for battery, as "there is currently no specific age at which minors are immune from liability for intentional torts as a matter of law"). Does *Van Camp v. McAfoos* (Chapter 1) stand in opposition to this general rule?

2. *Young children.* In some states, however, particularly young children are "conclusively presumed to be incapable of harmful intent."

Under the "rule of sevens," age seven is frequently used as the cut-off point. *See, e.g., DeLuca v. Bowden,* 329 N.E.2d 109 (Ohio 1975).

3.   *Other solutions.* Will small children always be liable in states that do not grant blanket immunity to children under a particular age? Notice that the child's age would be relevant to show either that he could not or did not form an adequate intent to touch, to offend, or to harm. What about holding a child liable for intended *physical harms*, but not for intended *offense*? This was approved in *Horton v. Reaves,* 526 P.2d 304 (Colo. 1974).

NOTE: PARENTAL LIABILITY FOR THE TORTS OF THEIR MINOR CHILDREN

Why should a person injured by the tortious action of a child not just sue the child's parents and seek damages from them? The answer is that such a lawsuit is possible only if a statute authorizes such a suit—in which case the statutory requirements for recovery must be met—or if the parents are themselves at fault in some way. That is, the common law rule is that parents are not vicariously liable for the torts of their children simply by virtue of being parents.

Statutes imposing liability on parents for their children's torts exist in virtually every state, but they are usually limited in two significant ways: First, the child's tort must have been committed willfully or wantonly. Second, the damages that may be obtained are limited. Some states cap damages at a very low amount, while others are less restrictive. *Compare* CONN. GEN. STATS. ANN. § 52–572 (capping damages at $5,000 for injury to persons or property) *with* FLA. STAT. ANN. § 741.24 (providing no cap on damages for theft and destruction of property but limiting recovery to the amount of actual damages incurred).

Plaintiffs who sue parents for the parents' own fault will often allege that the parents negligently supervised their child, and that this caused the plaintiffs' harm. Such claims are very difficult to win. Indeed, such a claim failed in *Van Camp v. McAfoos* because the plaintiffs did not prove that the parents were at fault. On the other hand, what if a parent tells his minor child, "throw a rock at Susie's dad," and the child does so, hitting the target. Would *that* be actionable?

If parents often are not legally liable for a child's torts, how can the injured plaintiff hope to see any money in a suit against a child? Often the parents' insurance policy may cover minor children living in the household. Such a policy would pay any judgment rendered against the child.

D. CONTACT

EICHENWALD V. RIVELLO, 318 F.Supp.3d 766 (D. Md. 2018). Plaintiff Kurt Eichenwald is an author and award-winning journalist for the New York Times who suffers from epilepsy. During the 2016 election, Plaintiff was often critical of then-candidate Donald J. Trump and expressed those views in his writing and on his Twitter account. John Rivello, a Maryland resident who went by the twitter handle @jewgoldstein replied to one of Plaintiff's tweets with a Graphic Interchange Format ("GIF") that contained an animated strobe image flashing at a rapid speed and the message "YOU DESERVE A SEIZURE FOR YOUR POSTS." When Plaintiff clicked on the notification button on his twitter, Rivello's tweet "immediately loaded" and displayed the GIF, causing plaintiff to suffer a severe seizure at his home in Texas. Criminal investigation revealed that the defendant knew of plaintiff's epilepsy and had discussed with others his desire to cause plaintiff to suffer a seizure. Plaintiff brought a claim for battery among other torts. Defendant moved to dismiss.

Held, motion to dismiss denied. "[H]owever one characterizes Plaintiff's claim, the facts as pled constitute some form of a tort. The fundamental purposes of our tort system are to deter wrongful conduct, shift losses to responsible parties, and fairly compensate deserving victims. . . . A battery undoubtedly requires some physical contact. . . . [P]hysical contact need not be with the physical body of the plaintiff, and it need not be *direct* physical contact. . . . Plaintiff has alleged that light waves emitted from the GIF touched Plaintiff's retina, generated an electric signal, and caused a seizure. Taking, as the Court must, Plaintiff's allegations as true, including his characterization of the science and Plaintiff's physical condition, there was physical contact. . . . Defendant's tweet, activating certain harmful capabilities of the transmitting computer, converted the computer into a weapon to inflict physical injury. The computer and the tweet were no longer merely a mode of communication. . . . The strobe GIF was a physical tool.[1] . . . The Court [has not found] a case in which a Texas court found a battery under the circumstances presented here. . . . But the Court also has not found any Texas case establishing that the use of a laser-beam, or a sonic weapon, constitutes a battery. Yet if a person used a laser to intentionally blind another, or a sonic weapon to intentionally cause permanent hearing loss, the Court is confident that a Texas court would find a battery, even though the contact at issue was "only" a beam of light or a sound wave. . . . The broad sweep of Texas tort precedents provides firm ground on which to find that this unique fact pattern, if proven, qualifies as "battery.". . .

---

[1]   Effectively, and under the law, the scenario alleged is no different from that where a tortfeasor is alleged to have picked up a computer, thrown it at a Plaintiff, and caused an impact that injured the Plaintiff's brain.

NOTES

1.   **Indirect contact.** Often there is no dispute about whether contact occurred between the plaintiff and the defendant; think of the punch in the nose. But "contact" means more than the defendant's body directly touching the plaintiff's body. Imagine a defendant who fires a bullet into the plaintiff's body and seeks to escape liability for battery on the ground that there was no touching. Would courts accept the defendant's argument? Now consider a defendant who shakes the limb of a tree on which the plaintiff is sitting, but does not touch the plaintiff. A classic case on this point is *Fisher v. Carrousel Motor Hotel, Inc.*, 424 S.W.2d 627 (Tex. 1967). The plaintiff, Fisher, was a mathematician attending a meeting on telemetry equipment. He and the others at the meeting adjourned for lunch in the defendant's hotel. As the plaintiff was about to be served, he was approached by the manager, who "snatched the plate from Fisher's hand and shouted that he, a Negro, could not be served in the club." The court said: "[T]he intentional grabbing of plaintiff's plate constituted a battery. The intentional snatching of an object from one's hand is as clearly an offensive invasion of his person as would be an actual contact with the body." *See also Reynolds v. MacFarlane*, 322 P.3d 755 (Utah Ct. App. 2014).

2.   **Animus and harm.** Important to the *Eichenwald* decision was a firm conviction that tort law is designed to penalize "conduct outside the bounds of a civil society, conduct that should be punished so as to deter its repetition, and conduct that causes a compensable harm." That defendant intended to cause physical injury to the plaintiff may have mattered as much or more to the outcome than a technical definition of "contact." Would it be a battery if someone without epilepsy opened the defendant's GIF and was offended?

3.   **The new tort of purposeful infliction.** In recognition that liability for an intentional tort may sometimes be appropriate even in the absence of physical contact, the Restatement Third of Torts recently adopted a new tort of "purposeful infliction of bodily harm." The tort is established if: "(a) the actor purposely causes bodily harm to the other, either by the actor's affirmative conduct or by the actor's failure to prevent bodily harm when the actor has a duty to prevent such harm; and (b) the other does not effectively consent to the otherwise tortious conduct of the actor."

4.   **Examples.** In the following examples, would the conduct be sufficient to establish battery? Purposeful infliction of bodily harm? Both?

> (a)   D, a neighbor of elderly E, knows that E has left him a small inheritance in his will. One evening, as D is visiting E's house, E has a heart attack and reaches for his phone to call 911. Deciding that this is his chance to obtain the inheritance promptly, D snatches the phone away before E can reach it, and watches E die. RESTATEMENT (THIRD) OF TORTS: INTENTIONAL TORTS TO PERSONS § 104 illus. 7 (Tentative Draft No. 1, 2015).

(b) An in-home assistant stole jewelry and prescription pain pills from her elderly patient and, to hide the theft, substituted different pills that had not been prescribed. The patient suffered pain because of the deprivation of pain medication. *Haines v. Comfort Keepers, Inc.,* 393 P.3d 422 (Alaska 2017) (statutory claim).

5. **Creating the tort.** Eichenwald pleaded the new purposeful intentional infliction tort but the court did not decide the question. The court said: the mere fact that plaintiff's claim for purposeful infliction "is novel does not defeat it. . . . This is a developing area of the law. . . . It is not the place of a federal court, particularly one in Maryland, to interfere with a developing body of state tort law in Texas." Should courts adopt the purposeful infliction tort?

6. **The focus on purpose.** The focus of purposeful infliction is on the culpability of the defendant in purposefully causing bodily harm. What if a defendant does something that is not wrongful in itself—for example, moves a chair from the office of an employee with a bad back—but does it with a purpose to cause the employee back pain? Should this otherwise legitimate conduct become actionable because of the defendant's bad intent? Is there any problem with conditioning suit on wrongful intent in the absence of objectively wrongful action? Is the moved chair case the same as the *Eichenwald* case?

7. **Civil conspiracy.** Some cases that involve infliction of harm without contact by the defendant, involve contact made by other persons. The *Eichenwald* court cited *Hutchison v. Brookshire Bros.*, 284 F.Supp.2d 459 (E.D. Tex. 2003). In *Hutchinson*, a store owner allegedly asked a police officer to force the plaintiff to siphon gasoline from the plaintiff's car (plaintiff had accidentally over-pumped). The Court found that the store owner supplied the suggestion, encouragement and implements to siphon the gas, so that a battery claim against the owner could survive summary judgment (and viable actions existed against the police officer and the store as well). A case in which battery is inflicted through another person may give rise to a claim of civil conspiracy. Although elements can vary, the gist of the civil conspiracy action is 1) an agreement between two or more persons to commit a tort, 2) an overt act toward accomplishment of the wrong, and 3) damages.

8. **Civil law and criminal law.** Battery can be both a tort and a crime. At times statutes direct a state court to use the same or similar tests for the two contexts. *See State v. Soler*, 140 A.3d 755 (R.I. 2016). *Eichenwald* applied Texas law which looks to the statutory definition of criminal assault for the definition of a civil battery. Tex. Pen. Code Ann. § 22.01(a)(1), (3).

9. **Choice of law.** The *Eichenwald* court, though located in Maryland, applied the law of Texas, plaintiff's home state. In tort cases, "the rule of *lex loci delicti*" is well established. Under that rule, the law of the place where the tort was committed governs. Here the plaintiff was harmed (suffered a seizure) in Texas.

NOTE: DAMAGES FOR BATTERY

1.   *No need for physical harm.* What damages may be recovered by a plaintiff who prevails on a battery claim? Battery protects an interest in being free from an intentionally inflicted harmful or offensive contact. The plaintiff who wins a battery case has proved an invasion of this protected interest, and is thereby entitled to damages to compensate for that invasion or loss. Battery is one of the so-called "trespassory torts," that group of torts (also including assault, false imprisonment, and some property torts) that are accomplished by the use of some physical force and are regarded as harmful in and of themselves. These torts "are actionable even if the plaintiff has no proven physical harm." 1 DOBBS, HAYDEN & BUBLICK, THE LAW OF TORTS § 28 (2d ed. 2011). Sometimes it is said that with these trespassory torts, damages are "presumed" to flow from the tort itself. Do the cases above help explain why this is the rule?

2.   *Nominal damages.* A plaintiff who suffers only trivial harm or offense may still be entitled to some money. In *Leichtman,* a case in which a talk-show host blew cigar smoke in the face of an anti-smoking advocate in order to humiliate him, the court allowed the claim and wrote, "No matter how trivial the incident, a battery is actionable, even if damages are only one dollar." *Leichtman v. WLW Jacor Communications Inc.,* 634 N.E.2d 697 (Ohio 1994).

3.   *Economic damages.* If the intentional contact causes economic damages such as medical expenses or lost wages or earning capacity, those damages are readily recoverable upon proper proof. Thus a plaintiff who suffers a head injury from an intentional punch by the defendant may collect damages to compensate for any resulting medical expenses, rehabilitation, and wage loss. *See Hough v. McKiernan,* 101 A.3d 853 (R.I. 2014) ($925,000 for battery victim who suffered a swollen skull, a piece of which had to be removed and stored in his abdomen for three months before being put back in place, and who had to relearn how to walk and talk).

4.   *Pain and suffering and emotional distress damages.* When emotional distress results from a trespassory tort like battery, assault, or false imprisonment, damages for the distress are readily recoverable whether or not the plaintiff has suffered physical harm. How are such damages measured? As one court said, the plaintiff who proves assault or battery can recover "compensatory damages for bodily pain, humiliation, mental anguish and other injuries that occur as a necessary and natural consequence of the tortious conduct. The measure of damages is simply that which is fair and reasonable." *A.R.B. v. Elkin,* 98 S.W.3d 99 (Mo. Ct. App. 2003) ($100 was not reasonable amount of damages to son and daughter for father's physical and sexual abuse). A battery that is offensive but not physically harmful, then, can give rise to a substantial damages award.

5.   *Punitive damages.* In addition to compensatory damages, courts may allow punitive damages against an intentional tortfeasor who is guilty of "malice" or wanton misconduct, as the court held possible on remand in *McElhaney.*

E. TRANSFERRED INTENT

BASKA V. SCHERZER, 156 P.3d 617 (Kan. 2007). Celeste Baska had given her daughter Ashley, a high school senior, permission to organize a scavenger hunt and party. Around midnight, a fight broke out between Harry Scherzer, Jr. and Calvin Madrigal. Baska yelled at the boys to stop fighting. When they did not, Baska placed herself between them and was punched in the face, losing several teeth and receiving injuries to her neck and jaw. Baska sued Madrigal and Scherzer for personal injuries. In depositions, both Madrigal and Scherzer testified that they did not intend to strike or injure Baska. Instead, each testified that it was his intent only to strike and injure the other defendant. Madrigal and Scherzer then filed motions for summary judgment based on the one-year statute of limitations for assault and battery. [The statute of limitations for negligence actions was longer and would not have barred the plaintiff's claim]. *Held*, motions granted; Baska's cause of action was an action for assault and battery, not negligence.

"[T]he doctrine of transferred intent states that '[t]he tort of battery or of assault and battery may be committed, although the person struck or hit by the defendant is not the one whom he intended to strike or hit.' The comments to the Restatement (Second) of Torts, in describing the intent necessary for battery, explain:

> 'The intention which is necessary to make the actor liable [for civil battery] is not necessarily an intention to cause a harmful or offensive contact or an apprehension of such contact to the plaintiff himself or otherwise to cause him bodily harm. It is enough that the actor intends to produce such an effect upon some other person and that his act so intended is the legal cause of a harmful contact to the other. It is not necessary that the actor know or have reason even to suspect that the other is in the vicinity of the third person whom the actor intends to affect and, therefore, that he should recognize that his act, though directed against the third person, involves a risk of causing bodily harm to the other so that the act would be negligent toward him.' Restatement (Second) of Torts § 16, comment b (1964). . . .

The undisputed facts in this case show that the defendants intended to strike and cause harm to one another. When Baska intervened and stepped between the two boys, she was 'unintentionally' struck by punches intended for the defendants. Had the defendants struck each other and brought suit, they would be liable to one another for assault and battery. Under the doctrine of transferred intent, which has long been recognized in this state, the fact that the defendants struck the plaintiff does not change the fact that their actions (punching) were intentional. . . . [Failure to initiate her action within one year of the fight bars her action by reason of the one-year statute of limitations.] The trial court correctly granted defendant's motion for summary judgment."

H/D, Reasoning

NOTES

1.   **Transferred intent.** The doctrine of transferred intent has wide acceptance. This case demonstrates one form of transferred intent. How would you state the rule?

2.   **The extended liability principle.** The defendant who commits an intentional tort, at least if it involves conscious wrongdoing, is liable for all damages caused, not merely those intended or foreseeable. We will call this the extended liability principle. This principle explains the result in most transferred intent cases, as where the defendant intends a battery to one person and then accidentally causes a battery to another as well.

3.   **The "irony" of transferred intent.** Sometimes, classifying a tort as an intentional tort may help the plaintiff. For example, judgments in intentional tort cases may be more difficult for a defendant to discharge in bankruptcy. However, the Restatement Third of Torts calls it "somewhat ironic" that "intentional torts are generally deemed considerably more serious than torts of mere negligence," and yet "in certain circumstances the plaintiff is worse off if the tort committed against the plaintiff is classified as intentional rather than negligent." RESTATEMENT (THIRD) OF TORTS: LIABILITY FOR PHYSICAL AND EMOTIONAL HARM § 5 cmt. a (2010). How could a plaintiff be worse off with a judgment against the defendant for an intentional tort in contrast to a negligent or reckless tort? Did the transferred intent rule help the plaintiff in *Baska*?

4.   **The effects of classifying a tort as intentional.** One reason plaintiffs are worse off when the tort against them is classified as intentional is that many insurance policies pay judgments for negligent and reckless acts, which are considered "accidents," but exclude coverage for "intentional acts," thereby limiting the plaintiff's potential source of recovery. *See, e.g., Tibert v. Nodak Mut. Ins. Co.*, 816 N.W.2d 31 (N.D. 2012). An insurance company may seek declaratory judgment that the insured's conduct was intentional rather than negligent, freeing the insurer from any duty to defend or indemnify the insured. *See, e.g., QBE Ins. Corp. v. Jinx-Proof Inc.*, 6 N.E.3d 583 (N.Y. 2014). Similarly, a government may have waived immunity for some negligent acts but retained immunity for intentional torts. *See City of Watauga v. Gordon*, 434 S.W.3d 586 (Tex. 2014). Another reason is that statutes of limitations for intentional torts are often shorter than are statutes of limitations for negligent torts. *Raddin v. Macalaster Educ. Found., Inc.*, 175 So.3d 1243 (Miss. 2015)

(one-year statute of limitations barred battery claims against prep school dean).

5. **Underpleading.** Because of these adverse effects for plaintiffs, plaintiffs sometimes try to "underplead" intentional tort cases and style them as claims for negligence. *See* Ellen Smith Pryor, *The Stories We Tell*, 75 TEX. L. REV. 1721 (1997). Plaintiffs seeking to avoid adverse effects are frequently in the odd position of minimizing the wrongs committed against them. *See Forsman v. Blues, Brews & Bar-B-Ques, Inc.*, 903 N.W.2d 524 (N.D. 2017) (bar patron, knocked down by a drunk customer, fractured her leg and argued that "no evidence exists to infer an intent to injure"). But even when plaintiff underpleads an intentional tort—asserting a claim of negligence—the court can determine whether the case is truly an intentional tort and apply the shorter statute of limitations for intentional torts. See *Sanderson Farms, Inc. v. McCullough*, 212 So.3d 69 (Miss. 2017) (plaintiff claimed that from one foot away, defendant "mashed the gas" on his truck, repeatedly striking plaintiff; assault and battery would have been the appropriate tort actions).

6. **Accepting or rejecting extended liability in light of policy rationales.** If the purpose of the transferred intent rule is to afford broad recovery to people injured in situations in which harms were at least to some extent intended, might courts choose to employ the transferred intent rule only when the rule would effectuate those policies? For an argument that the transferred intent doctrine often works against plaintiffs and should be abolished or at least limited, *see* Vincent R. Johnson, *Transferred Intent in American Tort Law*, 87 MARQ. L. REV. 903 (2004). Would there be any other way to address the problems of ironic adverse effects when the more wrongful tort is proved?

§ 2. ASSAULT

CULLISON V. MEDLEY
570 N.E.2d 27 (Ind. 1991)

KRAHULIK, JUSTICE.

Dan R. Cullison (Appellant-Plaintiff below) petitions this Court to accept transfer of this cause in order to reverse the trial court's entry of summary judgment against him and in favor of the Appellees-Defendants below (collectively "the Medleys"). . . .

According to Cullison's deposition testimony, on February 2, 1986, he encountered Sandy, the 16-year-old daughter of Ernest, in a Linton, Indiana, grocery store parking lot. They exchanged pleasantries and Cullison invited her to have a Coke with him and to come to his home to talk further. A few hours later, someone knocked on the door of his mobile home. Cullison got out of bed and answered the door. He testified that he saw a person standing in the darkness who said that she wanted to talk to him. Cullison answered that he would have to get dressed because he had been in bed. Cullison went back to his bedroom, dressed, and returned to the darkened living room of his trailer. When he entered the living room and turned the lights on, he was confronted by Sandy Medley, as well as by father Ernest, brother Ron, mother Doris, and brother-in-law Terry Simmons. Ernest was on crutches due to knee surgery and had a revolver in a holster strapped to his thigh. Cullison testified that Sandy called him a "pervert" and told him he was "sick," mother Doris berated him while keeping her hand in her pocket, convincing Cullison that she also was carrying a pistol. Ron and Terry said nothing to Cullison, but their presence in his trailer home further intimidated him. Primarily, however, Cullison's attention was riveted to the gun carried by Ernest. Cullison testified that, while Ernest never withdrew the gun from his holster, he "grabbed for the gun a few times and shook the gun" at plaintiff while threatening to "jump astraddle" of Cullison if he did not leave Sandy alone. Cullison testified that Ernest "kept grabbing at it with his hand, like he was going to take it out," and "took it to mean he was going to shoot me" when Ernest threatened to "jump astraddle" of Cullison. Although no one actually touched Cullison, his testimony was that he feared he was about to be shot throughout the episode because Ernest kept moving his hand toward the gun as if to draw the revolver from the holster while threatening Cullison to leave Sandy alone.

As the Medleys were leaving, Cullison suffered chest pains and feared that he was having a heart attack. Approximately two months later, Cullison testified that Ernest glared at him in a menacing manner while again armed with a handgun at a restaurant in Linton. On one of these occasions, Ernest stood next to the booth where Cullison was seated while wearing a pistol and a holster approximately one foot from Cullison's face. Shortly after the incident at his home, Cullison learned that Ernest had previously shot a man. This added greatly to his fear and apprehension of Ernest on the later occasions when Ernest glared at him and stood next to the booth at which he was seated while armed with a handgun in a holster.

Cullison testified that as a result of the incident, he sought psychological counseling and therapy and continued to see a therapist for approximately 18 months. Additionally, Cullison sought psychiatric help and received prescription medication which prevented him from operating power tools or driving an automobile, thus injuring Cullison in his sole proprietorship construction business. Additionally, Cullison testified that he suffered from nervousness, depression, sleeplessness, inability to concentrate and impotency following his run-in with the Medleys. . . .

[Cullison sued the Medleys for a number of torts, including assault. The defendants moved for summary judgment on all claims. The trial court granted the motion and the appeals court affirmed.]

... In count two of his complaint, Cullison alleged an assault. The Court of Appeals decided that, because Ernest never removed his gun from the holster, his threat that he was going to "jump astraddle" of Cullison constituted conditional language which did not express any present intent to harm Cullison and, therefore, was not an assault. Further, the Court of Appeals decided that even if it were to find an assault, summary judgment was still appropriate because Cullison alleged only emotional distress and made no showing that the Medleys' actions were malicious, callous, or willful or that the alleged injuries he suffered were a foreseeable result of the Medleys' conduct. We disagree.

It is axiomatic that assault, unlike battery, is effectuated when one acts intending to cause a harmful or offensive contact with the person of the other or an imminent apprehension of such contact. It is the right to be free from the apprehension of a battery which is protected by the tort action which we call an assault. As this Court held approximately 90 years ago in *Kline v. Kline* (1901), 158 Ind. 602, 64 N.E. 9, an assault constitutes "a touching of the mind, if not of the body." Because it is a touching of the mind, as opposed to the body, the damages which are recoverable for an assault are damages for mental trauma and distress. "Any act of such a nature as to excite an apprehension of a battery may constitute an assault. It is an assault to shake a fist under another's nose, to aim or strike at him with a weapon, or to hold it in a threatening position, to rise or advance to strike another, to surround him with a display of force. . . ." W. PROSSER & J. KEETON, PROSSER AND KEETON ON TORTS § 10 (5th ed. 1984). Additionally, the apprehension must be one which would normally be aroused in the mind of a reasonable person. *Id.* Finally, the tort is complete with the invasion of the plaintiff's mental peace.

The facts alleged and testified to by Cullison could, if believed, entitle him to recover for an assault against the Medleys. A jury could reasonably conclude that the Medleys intended to frighten Cullison by surrounding him in his trailer and threatening him with bodily harm while one of them was armed with a revolver, even if that revolver was not removed from the . . . holster. Cullison testified that Ernest kept grabbing at the pistol as if he were going to take it out, and that Cullison thought Ernest was going to shoot him. It is for the jury to determine whether Cullison's apprehension of being shot or otherwise injured was one which would normally be aroused in the mind of a reasonable person. It was error for the trial court to enter summary judgment on the count two allegation of assault. . . .

[Reversed in part and remanded.]

NOTES

1.   **Applying *Cullison*.** In *Raess v. Doescher*, 833 N.E.2d 790 (Ind. 2008), "defendant [a cardiovascular surgeon], angry at the plaintiff about

reports to the hospital administration about the defendant's treatment of other perfusionists [individuals who operate the heart/lung machine during open heart surgeries], aggressively and rapidly advanced on the plaintiff with clenched fists, piercing eyes, beet-red face, popping veins, and screaming and swearing at him. The plaintiff backed up against a wall and put his hands up, believing that the defendant was going to hit him, '[t]hat he was going to smack the s**t out of me or do something.' Then the defendant suddenly stopped, turned, and stormed past the plaintiff and left the room, momentarily stopping to declare to the plaintiff 'you're finished, you're history.'" Under *Cullison*, would these facts, if proved, entitle the plaintiff to recover on the assault claim? What about a city administrator's claim that a council member seemed like he was about to hit her? *Hammer v. Ribi*, 401 P.3d 148 (Idaho 2017).

2. **Assault and battery.** "Assault" has a technical meaning in tort law. Newspapers may use the term as a euphemism for sexual battery. Even judges may use the term assault to mean a battery. But the two torts are different. One can find cases, especially older ones, that say, "Every battery necessarily involves an assault." *McGlone v. Hauger*, 104 N.E. 116 (Ind. Ct. App. 1914). Can this be an accurate formulation? Suppose the defendant struck a sleeping plaintiff with a baseball bat. Would that be an assault? In *Koffman v. Garnett*, 574 S.E.2d 258 (Va. 2003), a 260-pound football coach slammed a 144-pound 13-year-old student to the ground to demonstrate proper tackling technique. Because the student "had no warning of an imminent forceful tackle," the pleadings were insufficient to state a claim for assault.

3. **Apprehension.** What does "apprehension" mean? One common meaning of that word is "fear," and certainly the plaintiff in *Cullison* was probably fearful. But apprehension in the context of assault does not mean some generalized fear, but rather an awareness of an imminent touching that would be a battery if completed. *See* 1 DOBBS, HAYDEN & BUBLICK, THE LAW OF TORTS § 39 (2d ed. 2011). The Restatement Third of Torts now asks if "the actor's affirmative conduct causes the other to anticipate an imminent, and harmful or offensive, contact with his or her person." RESTATEMENT (THIRD) OF TORTS: INTENTIONAL TORTS TO PERSONS § 105 (Tentative Draft No. 1, 2015).

4. **Actual or reasonable apprehension?** The *Cullison* court asks the jury to decide whether Cullison's apprehension that he would be shot was "one which would normally be aroused in the mind of a reasonable person." Should the question be whether a reasonable person would have anticipated an imminent harmful or offensive contact or whether Cullison himself did? The Restatement Third of Torts recommends a subjective standard except when the claim stems primarily from the defendant's words. *Id.* § 105 cmt. d. Which would *Cullison* be?

5. **"Words alone."** Courts have sometimes said that words alone cannot count as an assault. But isn't it almost impossible to imagine words alone, divorced from any act at all? Suppose someone stands perfectly still at the entrance to a dark alley. The person is masked, holding a gun, and says: "I am now going to shoot you dead." Surely this could be reasonably understood

as a threat of imminent bodily harm. Maybe "words alone" is a an inaccurate shorthand or misnomer. Perhaps it means that the plaintiff must reasonably apprehend an immediate touching and that in most cases words alone will not suffice to create such an apprehension. This is how the Restatement Third of Torts interprets the rule. *Id.* § 105 cmt. g. *See Jones v. Shipley*, 508 S.W.3d 766 (Tex. App. 2016) (school chaperone told a 2nd grade student "I will get you" while shaking her finger; "the critical inquiry is whether a reasonable person under the circumstances would consider the words and conduct to be an objective threat of imminent bodily injury").

6. **Words negating intent to effect immediate touching.** Sometimes acts seem threatening but the threat is countered by words. The defendant draws back his arm as if to strike, but at the same time says "If the police officer were not here, I'd punch your nose." The words clearly mean he is *not* going to punch your nose. If there are no facts to make it reasonable to believe that the defendant will strike you in spite of the police officer's presence, this does not look like an assault.

7. **Words offering a choice of tortious alternatives.** Suppose the defendant says in a menacing way "I won't beat you to a pulp if you give me your basketball tickets; otherwise you are going to be pretty bloody." Is this an assault, even though the threatened battery can be avoided by complying with the aggressor's demands? *Cf. Gouin v. Gouin*, 249 F.Supp.2d 62 (D. Mass. 2003) (estranged married defendant said to plaintiff, during an argument about their son, "You can either do it my way or I can beat you half to death.").

8. **The meaning of "imminent."** To state a claim for assault, the plaintiff must have been placed in apprehension of an "imminent" harmful or offensive touching. What does that phrase mean? The Restatement Third of Torts says "imminent is not limited to immediate. . . . [I]mminence means that the conduct will occur without significant delay." RESTATEMENT (THIRD) OF TORTS: INTENTIONAL TORTS TO PERSONS § 105 cmt. e (Tentative Draft No. 1, 2015). In *Dickens v. Puryear*, 276 S.E.2d 325 (N.C. 1981), the plaintiff, a 31-year-old man, "shared sex, alcohol and marijuana" with defendant's 17-year-old daughter. The defendant and some of his friends lured the plaintiff into a rural area, where they beat him, handcuffed him to a piece of farm machinery, and threatened him with castration while brandishing knives. The court had no problem labeling many of these acts as batteries and assaults. But the defendant also "told plaintiff to go home, pull his telephone off the wall, pack his clothes, and leave the state of North Carolina; otherwise he would be killed." He was then freed, and sued the defendant almost three years later in a North Carolina court. Was this last threat imminent for the purposes of assault? What do you see as the strongest arguments on each side?

9. **Revisiting transferred intent.** In *Baska v. Scherzer* above, the defendant intended a battery against Person A but instead struck Person B (the plaintiff), thus committing a battery on the plaintiff based on the doctrine of transferred intent. A second form of transferred intent occurs when a defendant intends to commit one tort and ends up committing another. As the

court held in *Nelson v. Carroll,* 735 A.2d 1096 (Md. 1999), one who intends an assault but "touches this person in a harmful or offensive manner and claims the touching was inadvertent or accidental, is liable for battery." *See also City of Watauga v. Gordon*, 434 S.W.3d 586 (Tex. 2014) ("Liability in battery moreover extends to harmful bodily contacts even though only offensive contacts were intended.").

NOTE: RELATED STATUTORY CLAIMS

Legislatures have crafted some causes of action that allow plaintiffs to sue for damages on particular facts that might also give rise to common-law actions for assault. For example, the federal Free Access to Clinic Entrances Act (FACE), 18 U.S.C.A. § 248, creates a civil claim against anyone who by threat, force, or physical obstruction intentionally injures, intimidates, or interferes with a person seeking to obtain or provide "reproductive health services." In *Planned Parenthood of the Columbia/ Willamette, Inc. v. American Coalition of Life Activists,* 290 F.3d 1058 (9th Cir. 2002), defendants published "wanted" posters, describing plaintiffs as murderers (because they provided abortions) and giving names and addresses. When such posters had been posted about other abortion providers, the providers had been murdered, but not by the defendants. Should the court permit the jury to find a threat in violation of the statute and uphold an award of damages to the abortion providers?

Statutes in a number of states create a claim against stalkers who follow or stalk someone. The California statute creates a statutory tort called stalking based on a pattern of conduct the "intent of which was to follow, alarm, place under surveillance, or harass the plaintiff," with resulting reasonable fear by the plaintiff for herself or an immediate family member. In addition, the defendant must either make a credible threat or violate a restraining order. CAL. CIV. CODE § 1708.7.

§ 3. FALSE IMPRISONMENT

MCCANN V. WAL-MART STORES, INC.
210 F.3d 51 (1st Cir. 2000)

BOUDIN, CIRCUIT JUDGE.

This case involves a claim for false imprisonment. On December 11, 1996, Debra McCann and two of her children—Jillian, then 16, and Jonathan, then 12—were shopping at the Wal-Mart store in Bangor, Maine. . . . [T]he McCanns went to a register and paid for their purchases. One of their receipts was time stamped at 10:10 p.m.

As the McCanns were leaving the store, two Wal-Mart employees, Jean Taylor and Karla Hughes, stepped out in front of the McCanns' shopping cart, blocking their path to the exit. Taylor may have actually put her hand on the cart. The employees told Debra McCann that the children were not allowed in the store because they had been caught stealing on a prior occasion. In fact, the employees were mistaken; the son of a different family had been caught shoplifting in the store about two weeks before, and Taylor and Hughes confused the two families.

Despite Debra McCann's protestations, Taylor said that they had the records, that the police were being called, and that the McCanns "had to go with her." Debra McCann testified that she did not resist Taylor's direction because she believed that she had to go with Taylor and that the police were coming. Taylor and Hughes then brought the McCanns past the registers in the store to an area near the store exit. Taylor stood near the McCanns while Hughes purportedly went to call the police. During this time, Debra McCann tried to show Taylor her identification, but Taylor refused to look at it. . . .

Although Wal-Mart's employees had said they were calling the police, they actually called a store security officer who would be able to identify the earlier shoplifter. Eventually, the security officer, Rhonda Bickmore, arrived at the store and informed Hughes that the McCanns were not the family whose son had been caught shoplifting. Hughes then acknowledged her mistake to the McCanns, and the McCanns left the store at approximately 11:15 p.m. . . .

The jury awarded the McCanns $20,000 in compensatory damages on their claim that they were falsely imprisoned in the Wal-Mart store by Wal-Mart employees. Wal-Mart has now appealed. . . .

Although nuances vary from state to state, the gist of the common law tort is conduct by the actor which is intended to, and does in fact, "confine" another "within boundaries fixed by the actor" where, in addition, the victim is either "conscious of the confinement or is harmed by it." . . .

While "confinement" can be imposed by physical barriers or physical force, much less will do—although how much less becomes cloudy at the margins. It is generally settled that mere threats of physical force can suffice, and it is also settled . . . that the threats may be implicit as well as explicit, and that confinement can also be based on a false assertion of legal authority to confine. Indeed, the Restatement provides that confinement may occur by other unspecified means of "duress." . . .

The evidence, taken favorably to the McCanns, showed that Wal-Mart employees . . . told the McCanns that they had to come with the Wal-Mart employees and that Wal-Mart was calling the police, and then stood guard over the McCanns while waiting for a security guard to arrive. The direction to the McCanns, the reference to the police, and the continued presence of the Wal-Mart employees (who at one point told Jonathan McCann that he could not leave to go to the bathroom) were enough to induce reasonable people to believe either that they would be restrained physically if they sought to leave, or that the store was claiming lawful authority to confine them until the police arrived, or both.

H/D

Wal-Mart asserts that under Maine law, the jury had to find "actual, physical restraint," a phrase it takes from [*Knowlton v. Ross*, 95 A. 281 (Me. 1915).] While there is no complete definition of false imprisonment by Maine's highest court, this is a good example of taking language out of context. In *Knowlton*, the wife of a man who owed a hotel for past bills entered the hotel office and was allegedly told that she would go to jail if she did not pay the bill. . . . The court noted that the defendants did not ask Mrs. Knowlton into the room (another guest had sent for her), did not touch her, and did not tell her she could not leave. The court also said that any threat of jail to Mrs. Knowlton was only "evidence of an intention to imprison at some future time." In context, the reference to the necessity of "actual, physical restraint" is best understood as a reminder that a plaintiff must be actually confined—which Mrs. Knowlton was not.

Taking too literally the phrase "actual, physical restraint" would put Maine law broadly at odds with not only the Restatement but with a practically uniform body of common law in other states that accepts the mere threat of physical force, or a claim of lawful authority to restrain, as enough to satisfy the confinement requirement for false imprisonment (assuming always that the victim submits). It is true that in a diversity case, we are bound by Maine law, as Wal-Mart reminds us; but we are not required to treat a descriptive phrase as a general rule or attribute to elderly Maine cases an entirely improbable breadth. . . .

H/D and reasoning

Affirmed.

NOTES

1.   **Elements.** "False imprisonment occurs when a person confines another intentionally without lawful privilege and against his consent within a limited area for any appreciable time, however short." *Bennett v. Ohio Dep't of Rehab. & Correction*, 573 N.E.2d 633 (Ohio 1991). In addition, it is usually said that the plaintiff must have been aware of the confinement at the time or else must have sustained actual harm. Notice that bad motive is not one of the elements, only intent.

2.   **Example.** Suppose plaintiff is restrained by an armed and masked intruder who demands a combination to the safe. Then, when the employer returns and discovers that the intruder is an old friend, the employer prevents the employee from leaving the house or calling police for several hours? False imprisonment claim against the employer as well as the intruder? *Nationwide Mut. Ins. Co. v. Pasiak*, 173 A.3d 888 (Conn. 2017).

3.   **Confinement.** Confinement implies limited range of movement and it is not enough to exclude the plaintiff from some place such as a bar or restaurant. Suppose the plaintiff is locked in a room but knows of a safe and reasonable means of escape. Is plaintiff confined? *Cf. Childress v. Boeing Aerospace Operations, Inc.*, 8 Wash.App.2d 1054 (Ct. App. 2019) (security

guards wrongfully surround plaintiff's car with their cars, but plaintiff finds an escape route by lightly hitting a car without causing damage and driving away). Suppose the defendant refuses to stop a moving car, the doors of which are not locked. Is his passenger confined?

4. **Confinement by threats or duress.** (a) *Threats or demands.* When the claim is confinement by explicit or implicit threat or duress, factual details are critical. Suppose that in *McCann* the store guards had not mentioned police but had said, "You must wait until our supervisor arrives." Suppose instead that they had said "if you leave, we'll see that you are prosecuted." You can think of many variations. The central issue is whether the facts show confinement. (b) *Assertion of authority.* Submission to an officer's assertion of arrest under colorable legal authority is sufficient to show confinement. (c) *Duress of goods.* The defendant grabs the plaintiff's pants from a dressing room and refuses to return them. Plaintiff wishes to leave but doesn't want to leave without her pants. Is this an implicit threat that results in confinement? *See Thorsen v. Kaufmann's Dep't Stores*, 55 Pa. D. & C.4th 565 (Com. Pl. 2000), *aff'd*, 832 A.2d 552 (Pa. Super. 2003).

5. **Instigating confinement.** A defendant who, by a falsehood, instigates a confinement, or induces another person to unlawfully detain another, may also be subject to liability for false imprisonment. *See Gibbs v. Blockbuster, Inc.*, 318 S.W.3d 157 (Mo. Ct. App. 2010). Providing accurate information to law enforcement does not make a person liable for a subsequent confinement. Put differently, there may be a privilege to report to law enforcement. *Huffman v. Sunshine Recycling, LLC*, 826 S.E.2d 609 (S.C. 2019) (defendant cooperated with law enforcement investigation of whether metal brought in for recycling was stolen from utility and relayed information believed to be true). As we will see in Chapter 4 on defenses, there is also a shopkeepers' privilege to detain a person reasonably believed to have committed theft, in a reasonable manner and for a reasonable period of time. *Neff v. Wal-Mart Stores E., LP*, 113 N.E.3d 666 (Ind. Ct. App. 2018).

6. **Damages.** False imprisonment is a trespassory tort, so the plaintiff can recover damages even if plaintiff sustains no actual harm. Actual harm is required, however, to support a claim where the plaintiff was not aware of the confinement at the time it took place. The Restatement supposes a case in which defendant locks a baby in a bank vault with a time lock. The baby is not conscious of confinement but has difficulty breathing, so recovery is permitted for actual harm. Restatement (Second) of Torts § 42 & cmt. b, illus. 3 (1965).

7. **False arrest.** When an officer of the law improperly arrests a person, the tort is usually called false arrest. The rules requiring confinement are the same. *Veatch v. City of Waverly*, 858 N.W.2d 1 (Iowa 2015). An essential element to establishing claims of false arrest and false imprisonment is the lack of probable cause. *Heining v. Abernathy*, 295 So.3d 1032 (Ala. 2019). In cases of false arrest, the plaintiff may be able to bring a federal civil rights claim. In *Williams v. City of Chicago*, 733 F.3d 749 (7th Cir. 2013), the plaintiff smelled smoke, saw that his neighbor's house was on fire, and went to the porch of the burning house to "bang on the door to rouse anyone who might be inside." For this act of courage he was arrested for arson and criminal trespass,

though the charges were quickly dismissed. He sued the arresting officers under 42 U.S.C. § 1983 for false arrest, and the district court granted summary judgment for the defendants. Reversing, the court of appeals said that if the plaintiff's "mere presence outside the burning house were enough to arrest someone for arson, imagine the disincentives for neighbors to help each other. . . . [N]one of the circumstances of the fire supported a reasonable belief that he had committed either arson or criminal trespass. Williams has offered sufficient evidence . . . that [the officers] arrested him without probable cause." Civil rights claims are described briefly in section 5 below.

8. **Excessive confinement.** If a person is appropriately confined as an initial matter, but has been confined for an excessive period of time, the person can have a claim of false arrest or imprisonment. In *Harte v. Bd. of Commissioners of Cty. of Johnson, Kansas*, 864 F.3d 1154 (10th Cir. 2017), a SWAT team carrying Glocks, assault rifles, battering rams, and more entered into the plaintiffs' home early one morning intending to arrest people for growing marijuana. The SWAT team screamed at the family but found nothing after searching the whole house for 20 minutes. They then continued to search for two hours. The Hartes sued for assault, false arrest, and trespass. They were denied trespass and assault claims, because the troopers obtained a search warrant and had qualified immunity, even though they withheld information in the search warrant affidavit. However, the court of appeals reversed the district court's judgment on false arrest. The detention was unreasonable after a certain time. *See also Johnson v. Madison Cty. Court of Common Pleas*, 77 N.E.3d 978 (Ohio 2017) (false arrest claim could be brought "against the state agency calculating the terms of [prisoner's] confinement and actually confining him" for alleged miscalculation of sentence).

§ 4. TORTS TO PROPERTY

We just examined intentional torts to persons. Many torts involve intentional invasions of property interests. One might, for example, be defrauded in a way that causes loss of property. Only three torts, however, involve direct application of force to property and thus furnish substantial analogy to personal injury cases such as those involved in battery, assault, or false imprisonment. These torts are trespass to land, conversion of chattels, and trespass to chattels.

A. TRESPASS TO LAND

BRIGGS V. SOUTHWEST ENERGY PRODUCTION COMPANY, 224 A.3d 334 (Pa. 2020). The Briggs own property adjacent to land leased by Southwestern Energy Production Company for natural gas extraction through hydraulic fracturing. The Briggs claimed that Southwestern Energy obtained oil and gas from beneath the surface of their land and sued for trespass. *Held,* Defendant Southwestern Energy's summary judgment motion granted. The "rule of capture" is "[a] fundamental principle of oil-and-gas law holding that there is no liability for drainage of oil and gas from under the lands of another so long as there has been no trespass. The reference to 'the lands of another' in the above quote does not suggest a developer may invade the subsurface area of a neighboring property by drilling at an angle rather than vertically (referred to as slant drilling or slant wells), or by drilling horizontally beneath the surface. This is because the title holder of a parcel of land generally owns everything directly beneath the surface. Rather, and as suggested by the "no trespass" predicate, it refers to the potential for oil and gas to migrate from the plaintiff's property to the developer's land when extracted from a common pool or reservoir spanning both parcels. In Pennsylvania, a trespass occurs when a person who is not privileged to do so intrudes upon land in possession of another, whether willfully or by mistake. . . . Plaintiffs assume it is physically impossible to cause drainage of oil or gas from a neighbor's property via hydraulic fracturing without effectuating a physical intrusion onto that property. . . . [T]he rule of capture remains extant in Pennsylvania, and developers who use hydraulic fracturing may rely on pressure differentials to drain oil and gas from under another's property, at least in the absence of a physical invasion. . . . *Dissent*, "The practice [hydraulic fracturing] exploits natural shale fractures and creates new ones, and with present technology, much remains mysterious about precisely what happens so far beneath the surface. However, I do not view this uncertainty as a basis to absolve developers from trespass liability if a plaintiff can prove the fluids and proppants they intentionally injected into their wellbores travelled horizontally across property lines."

NOTES

1. **Elements.** To prevail on a claim for trespass to land, the plaintiff must prove that the defendant intentionally entered land in the possession of another, or caused a thing or a third person to do so. As such, the plaintiff must prove an ownership or a possessory interest in the land, and an intentional and tangible invasion, intrusion or entry by the defendant onto that land that harms the plaintiff's interest in exclusive possession. No harm to the land need be shown. *See, e.g., City of Bristol v. Tilcon Minerals, Inc.*, 931 A.2d 237 (Conn. 2007); *see also* 1 DOBBS, HAYDEN & BUBLICK, THE LAW OF TORTS § 49 (2d ed. 2011). Is the definition of trespass in *Briggs* similar?

2. **Intentional entry.** Intentional entry onto the plaintiff's land might be accomplished by personal entry or by intentionally causing an object to enter the land. *Los Angeles Unified Sch. Dist. v. S&W Atlas Iron & Metal Co.*, 506 F.Supp.3d 1018 (C.D. Cal. 2020) (injunction based on plaintiff's likelihood of success on trespass case; metal scrap yard operator abutting the school was "responsible for metal objects being released onto Plaintiff's property. Plaintiff has cited multiple instances of metal projectiles from Defendants' property landing onto Plaintiff's property."). The right of the landowner extends downward beneath the surface and to at least a reasonable height above ground, so that if one were to dig beneath the surface or fly very close to the

ground this would also constitute a trespass. How could "slant drilling" be an intentional entry? What does the *Briggs* majority view as different about slant drilling and the case before it?

3.   **Aerial intrusions.** Because trespass law has been interpreted to include landowner rights to a certain height above the property, intentionally flying a drone over the property could be considered a trespass. Indeed, some courts have so held. See, e.g., *Glaser v. Mitchel,* 2019 WL 5800428 (Cal. Ct. App. 2019) (trespass based on the conduct of retained experts in surreptitiously taking photographs of property by sending a pre-programmed drone flying over it). The question is often presented as a privacy tort, specifically, intrusion on seclusion. *Jackman v. Cebrink-Swartz,* 2021 WL 2171745 (Fla. Dist. Ct. App. 2021) (certifying question regarding surveillance activities of drones and video cameras on neighboring properties). To deal with issues raised by drones, the National Commission on Uniform State Laws is drafting a Uniform Tort Law Relating to Drones Act. The Act originally established a 200-foot shelf above a landowner's property within which the presence of a drone constituted a per se injury. After objection from the drone industry, the Act embraced a multifactor test that would consider: "the amount of time the drone was over the landowner's property; the altitude of operation; the number and frequency of times that the drone has been operated over the property; the time of day of the operation; the operator's purpose in operating the drone over the property; physical damage caused by the drone operation; economic damage caused by the drone operation; whether or not the drone was seen or heard over the property; whether or not the drone captured audio, video, or photographs; and whether or not the landowner has regularly allowed the operation of drones over the property." Ronnie R. Gipson Jr., *The Rise of Drones and the Erosion of Privacy and Trespass Laws*, 33 No. 3 AIR & SPACE LAW. 1 (2020). How would you evaluate the different proposals?

4.   **Limited rights.** In one situation intentional *entry* is not required. This occurs when one unintentionally enters, as where a car goes out of control without fault, and then the defendant refuses to leave. The refusal to leave is now considered a trespass. Also, if the landowner grants an entrant limited rights to enter, that does not give the entrant permanent rights. In *LeBlanc v. Snelgrove*, 133 A.3d 361 (Vt. 2015), the plaintiff granted a boathouse owner a limited right to enter a section of the plaintiff's property for the purpose of making repairs to the boathouse. That did not entitle the boathouse owner to build a permanent retaining wall several feet high and extending 25 feet onto the plaintiff's property.

5.   **The object of intent.** The object of the defendant's intent need not be "to trespass." It is enough that the defendant intended to enter the land. Once intent to enter is shown, the defendant does not escape liability merely because the defendant did not intend to harm the plaintiff's property or even to interfere with the plaintiff's rights of possession. Similarly, it is no defense that the defendant reasonably believes that the land is the defendant's own or that there is a right to be there. In *Caldwell v. Church*, 802 S.E.2d 835 (Ga. Ct. App. 2017), the Caldwells sold their bar and grill to Virginia Church. The

Caldwells believed that Church had breached an oral agreement in her operations of the bar and grill, so the Caldwells entered the premises, evicted Church, and changed the locks on the doors. They then ran the business without her permission. The Georgia Court of Appeals held that the Caldwells committed trespass when they changed the locks and operated the plaintiff's bar and grill without permission.

6.   **Intent to enter.** Is there intent to enter if the defendant does not have a purpose to enter the plaintiff's land but is substantially certain of entry? In *Amaral v. Cuppels*, 831 N.E.2d 915 (Mass. App. Ct. 2005), plaintiffs occupied newly constructed homes near the ninth tee of a pre-existing golf course. One plaintiff collected over 1800 golf balls that had landed on her property in a five-year period. When the golf course did not resolve the problem, plaintiff sued the course owner for trespass, seeking monetary and injunctive relief. The court declared that "the projection of golf balls from the defendant's property onto the plaintiffs' properties constitutes a continuing trespass," because the golf balls deprive plaintiffs of the exclusive possession of their land. The court rejected defendants' argument that plaintiffs had to accept the incursions because they had moved in after the golf course was built. The court wrote, "[t]o the extent that the ordinary use of the defendants' golf course requires land beyond the course boundaries to accommodate the travel of errant shots, it is incumbent on the defendants to acquire either the fee [ownership] in the additional land itself, or the right to use the additional land for that purpose."

7.   **Trespass and nuisance.** Many trespass cases also raise issues of nuisance, which is a separate tort. According to a passage from Dean Prosser the distinction between the torts of trespass and nuisance is that "trespass is an invasion of the plaintiff's interest in the exclusive possession of his land, while nuisance is an interference with his use and enjoyment of it. The difference is that between walking across his lawn and establishing a bawdy house next door; between felling a tree across his boundary line and keeping him awake at night with the noise of a rolling mill." *Amaral v. Cuppels*, 831 N.E.2d 915 (Mass. App. Ct. 2005). In *United Food & Commercial Workers Int'l Union v. Wal-Mart Stores, Inc.*, 162 A.3d 909 (Md. 2017), Wal-Mart sued the union for conducting in-store "flash mobs" and blocking "ingress and egress to parking lots, parking spaces, vehicular traffic, and store entrances." The court framed the trespass question as whether the union's conduct "exceeded the scope of Walmart's limited invitation to the public to enter its property for shopping purposes," and framed the nuisance question as whether the conduct "interfered with Walmart's use and enjoyment of its land."

8.   **Tangible invasion.** Trespass historically requires a tangible invasion onto the plaintiff's property. *Mueller v. Hill*, 345 P.3d 998 (Idaho 2015) (plaintiff could maintain trespass claim against defendant who blasted rocks and debris onto land, dumped dirt and rocks on land, and caused increased water runoff onto land). *Cf. Zwart v. Penning*, 912 N.W.2d 833 (S.D. 2018) (foreign water but not natural accumulations can be trespass). Intangible intrusions, as by noise, odor or light alone, are dealt with as cases of nuisance. *Babb v. Lee Cty. Landfill SC, LLC*, 747 S.E.2d 468 (S.C. 2013) ("Without the

dimensional test [requiring invasion through a physical tangible object], even the most ephemeral intrusion—the exhaust from a passing car, the sound waves from neighbors talking, or even a sneeze that carry onto one's land— would constitute a trespass and an entitlement to at least nominal damages.").

9. **Remedies for trespass: damages.** Because trespass is another traditional trespassory tort (as we have already seen, so are battery, assault, and false imprisonment), a trespasser will be liable for at least nominal damages even if no physical harm is done. When the defendant's trespass physically damages the land, the plaintiff can get damages measured either by the cost of repair or by the diminution in the value of the premises resulting from the tort. Upon proper proof the plaintiff can also get compensatory damages for loss of use of the land and for emotional distress or annoyance caused by the trespass. *See* 1 DOBBS, HAYDEN & BUBLICK, THE LAW OF TORTS § 56 (2d ed. 2011). South Carolina recently held that "damages for permanent trespass or nuisance in [the state] are limited to the full market value of the property." *Babb v. Lee Cty. Landfill SC, LLC*, 747 S.E.2d 468 (S.C. 2013). Could such a rule, in effect, permit private takings?

10. **Remedies for trespass: injunctive relief.** Where damages are inadequate, as where trespasses are continuing or will be repeated, the plaintiff may be entitled to an injunction to stop the trespassing or to force a trespasser to leave or remove something placed on the plaintiff's land. *See Banville v. Brennan*, 84 A.3d 424 (R.I. 2014) (ordering removal of defendant's building on plaintiff's land and upholding $50,000 award).

11. **Remedies: punitive damages.** Punitive damages may be awarded if the trespass is deliberate or "malicious." *See, e.g., Sebra v. Wentworth*, 990 A.2d 538 (Me. 2010) (plaintiff proved that defendants trespassed maliciously when they continued to use the plaintiff's driveway as an easement in disregard of a prior judgment, entitling plaintiff to punitive damages).

12. **Extended liability.** The trespasser is liable for damages directly caused by trespass, even if the trespasser could not foresee that harm. Suppose the defendant knows he is trespassing on a farm, and throws his cigarette into what appears to be a puddle of water. The "water" is really gasoline that leaked from a tractor, and it spreads a fire that burns down the farmer's barn. The extended liability rule makes the trespasser liable for loss of the barn.

13. **Hypotheticals.**

(a) An unidentified cat perches atop a fence that divides the Plunkett property from the Durfee property. The cat sets up an intolerable caterwauling in the middle of the night and Durfee hurls a shoe at the cat from her side of the line. The cat dodges and continues its serenade, but the shoe falls on Plunkett's property. Do these facts make a prima facie case of trespass?

(b) John Dangle took off from a mountain point in a hang-glider. He passed over Pergolesi's land at a height of 250 feet. Shortly thereafter a shotgun blast from an unidentified source ripped holes in the glider's surfaces and Dangle lost control. He landed safely in Burger's back yard. No damage was done to Burger's property. Is Dangle a trespasser as to either Pergolesi or Burger? What if he decides to set up camp there after the landing?

B. CONVERSION OF CHATTELS—TROVER

REIF V. NAGY, 106 N.Y.S.3d 5 (App. Div. 2019). Mr. Grunbaum became a victim of Nazi persecution who was arrested in 1938 and murdered in the Dachau Concentration Camp in 1941. Prior to his arrest, Mr. Grunbaum was a prolific art collector who owned hundreds of works of art, including many by Egon Schiele. . . . Mr. Grunbaum was forced to execute a power of attorney to his wife when he was sent to a concentration camp, and she was forced to declare his art collection in his absence as ordered by the Nazis. The Defendants, Richard Nagy and Richard Nagy Ltd. purchased two of Mr. Grunbaum's Schiele drawings, which they claim were originally sold by Mr. Grunbaum's sister-in-law, Mathilde Lukacs, to a gallery in Switzerland, and changed hands many times thereafter. The plaintiffs, the heirs of Mr. Grunbaum, emailed the Defendants demanding that the artworks be returned to them, and when their requests were refused they brought claims of conversion and replevin against the Defendants. Because the drawings allegedly were sold by his sister-in-law, the Defendants claimed they have good title to the artworks. *Held,* for the plaintiffs.

"An action for replevin requires the plaintiff to show legal title or a superior right of possession. Relatedly, an action for conversion requires the plaintiff to prove that the property is in the unauthorized possession of another who acted to exclude the plaintiff's rights. . . . As the heirs to Mr. Grunbaum, plaintiffs have made a threshold showing that they have an arguable claim of a superior right of possession to the Artworks, and that the Artworks are in the unauthorized possession of another who is acting to exclude plaintiffs' rights. Plaintiffs have therefore established to this Court's satisfaction that they have a *prima facie* case of both replevin and conversion. . . . New York protects the rightful owner's property where that property had been stolen, even if the property is in the possession of a good faith purchaser for value. A thief cannot convey good title. While defendants argue that they purchased the Artworks in good faith, title remains with the original owner or his heirs absent a valid conveyance of the works. As defendants have not shown that Mr. Grunbaum ever voluntarily transferred the Artworks to Ms. Lukacs, they cannot credibly allege that she owned them. . . .

NOTES

1. **Conversion.** Conversion is defined by the Restatement Second as an "intentional exercise of dominion over a chattel which so seriously interferes with the right of another to control it that the actor may justly be required to

pay the other the full value of the chattel." RESTATEMENT (SECOND) OF TORTS § 222A (1965). Dubbs steals Pedrick's watch. This is a conversion and Dubbs is a converter. He has, as it is said, "converted the watch to his own use." In other words, Dubbs has exercised substantial "dominion" over the watch and interfered with Pedrick's ability to control it. *See Gould v. Ochsner*, 354 P.3d 965 (Wyo. 2015) (ranch owner who refused to return a cattle brand was liable for conversion). As in *Reif v. Nagy* above, "a thief cannot convey good title" is a common refrain.

2.   **Remedies.** In a case in which property has been converted, a party can sue for the value of the watch at the time and place of the taking. *See, e.g., Serv. Oil, Inc. v. Gjestvang*, 861 N.W.2d 490 (N.D. 2015). In the earlier common law the form of action used to redress this conversion was known as trover. The plaintiff may also sue for replevin, a procedure by which seized goods are provisionally restored to their owner pending the outcome of the action to determine rights. Consequently, in the United States, converted art and other property may be returned to its original owner. *See Piper v. Goodring & Co.*, 2019 WL 7049263 (D. Ariz. 2019) (return of a rare 1954 Ferrari that had disappeared in Mexico and been sold by a girlfriend "suspected of murdering" the owner and several other "prior love interests," when the Ferrari showed up on an auction block in Scottsdale, Arizona). In 2016, Congress passed the Holocaust Expropriated Art Recovery Act of 2016 (HEAR Act), specifically to "ensure that claims to artwork and other property stolen or misappropriated by the Nazis are not unfairly barred by statutes of limitations but are resolved in a just and fair manner."

3.   **Intent.** As in the case of trespass to land, there is no requirement that the defendant be conscious of wrongdoing. One who takes another's watch in the honest belief that it is the person's own is still a converter if the dominion thus exercised is sufficiently substantial and the act interferes with another's right to exercise control. *See Kelley v. La Force,* 288 F.3d 1 (1st Cir. 2002) (even if police officers believed they were putting Pub into possession of its rightful owner, they still acted with intent to deprive plaintiff, the rightful owner of the Pub, of possession).

4.   **How conversion is accomplished.** In each of the following cases, suppose the defendant reasonably but mistakenly believes he has a right to deal with the property.

(a)   Defendant decides to burn his copy of a torts casebook and throws it in the fire. By mistake he got the plaintiff's copy instead.

(b)   Defendant restaurant holds a coat checked by A and also one checked by B. By mistake defendant gives B's coat to A, who disappears and is never found. B's coat is far more valuable than A's.

5.   **Substantial dominion?** One of the more difficult issues is what constitutes substantial dominion. It is clear that dominion is exercised in all

the above cases, including where the property is damaged by the defendant. But in other cases defendant merely takes the property for a short period of time, as in the case of a joyride. If he takes a car for a joyride and it is destroyed in the process, he is no doubt liable. But suppose he takes it and returns it. Is this a conversion? These facts and many variations on them raise questions of degree which cannot be resolved firmly on principle. The American Law Institute concludes that it is all a matter of how serious the interference is. Since a finding of conversion will mean that the defendant pays the full value of the chattel, the ALI concluded that the interference should be serious enough to justify imposing such liability and that a number of factors were important including:

(a) extent and duration of control;

(b) the defendant's intent to assert a right to the property;

(c) the defendant's good faith;

(d) the harm done; and

(e) expense or inconvenience caused.

See RESTATEMENT (SECOND) OF TORTS § 222A (1965). "Conversion would not apply where the '[i]ntention [is] good, the duration brief, the event harmless.' " *Loungee Conservancy v. Citimortgage*, 48 A.3d 774 (Me. 2012) (lender secured wrong home for foreclosure but provided access code to lockbox immediately upon notification of the error).

6. **New forms of property.** What types of property may be converted? The traditional common law rule was that conversion would lie only for tangible personal property. Thus neither land nor intangible property such as paper money or promissory notes could be converted. The rules today seem more liberal. *See* 1 DOBBS, HAYDEN & BUBLICK, THE LAW OF TORTS § 63 (2d ed. 2011). One can convert shares of stock or bonds and other documents which are strongly identified with the right itself. Cases have recognized some other expansions. Can a domain name be converted? *See Kremen v. Cohen*, 337 F.3d 1024 (9th Cir. 2003) (yes, the plaintiff had a property interest in the sex.com domain name). What if a doctor takes and without authorization sells or uses the plaintiff's egg or pre-embryo? *See Unruh-Haxton v. Regents of Univ. of Cal.*, 76 Cal.Rptr.3d 146 (Ct. App. 2008) (conversion claim survived a demurrer); *but cf. Moore v. Regents of Univ. of Cal.*, 793 P.2d 479 (Cal. 1990) (conversion claim does not lie for the unauthorized use of a patient's blood cells for commercial purposes).

7. **Conversion of electronic data.** Courts have taken very different stances on whether copying and use of confidential data can be a conversion or should be actionable only under other economic torts. In *American Biomedical Group, Inc. v. Techtrol, Inc.*, 374 P.3d 820 (Okla. 2016), the court wrote that "Oklahoma does not recognize the tort of conversion of intangible property in

the same manner as it does for personal property." Consequently, the claim was actionable under theories of misappropriation and breach of contract but not conversion. In *Integrated Direct Marketing, LLC v. May*, 495 S.W.3d 73 (Ark. 2016), the Arkansas Supreme Court held that an employee who copied a company's electronic data could be liable for conversion. "Under Arkansas law, intangible property, such as electronic data, standing alone and not deemed a trade secret, can be converted if the actions of the defendant are in denial of or inconsistent with the rights of the owner or person entitled to possession."

8. **Aiding and abetting.** Conversion may be accomplished by aiding and abetting another's conversion. In *Montgomery v. Devoid*, 915 A.2d 270 (Vt. 2006), a son stole $80,000 in cash, giving some to his father, who also stored some vehicles the son had stolen. The Court held that the father might be found liable along with the son.

9. **Serial conversions.** Dubbs steals Pedrick's watch, then sells the watch to Byer. Dubbs is a converter and so is Byer, since both have exercised substantial dominion and have intended to do so. Pedrick could sue either or both, though he could collect only once.

10. **Bona fide purchasers.** Byer in the preceding illustration is liable even if she buys in good faith, that is, even if she is a bona fide purchaser for value and without notice of Pedrick's rights. The theory is that Byer cannot purchase from Dubbs anything more than what Dubbs legally possesses. Dubbs has no title and thus cannot transfer title to Byer.

There is one special wrinkle in this rule. If Dubbs does not steal the watch but tricks Pedrick into selling it to him, then Dubbs *does* get title. Since Dubbs got it by a trick or fraud, Pedrick could go to court and have the sale voided; he could get his watch back because of Dubbs' fraud. However, he is not *required* to do this. He may do nothing at all and keep the money Dubbs paid him. At any rate, until Pedrick does go to court, Dubbs has title to the watch.

11. **The Uniform Commercial Code.** A comprehensive statute enacted in almost all states regulates many commercial dealings. One provision of the code covers this kind of case: Orwell takes his bike to the Merchant Bike Shop for repair. The bike shop repairs the bike but before Orwell returns, sells it to Dalzell. Under the rules stated above, Dalzell would be liable, since Merchant had no title to pass. The UCC, however, provides that if goods are entrusted to the possession of a merchant who deals in goods of that kind, the merchant has the legal power to transfer all the rights of the "entrustor." Is Dalzell liable or not? Suppose Orwell had stolen the bike, then taken it to Merchant for repair. Would Dalzell be liable? *See* 1 DOBBS, HAYDEN & BUBLICK, THE LAW OF TORTS § 72 (2d ed. 2011).

C. TRESPASS TO CHATTELS

SCHOOL OF VISUAL ARTS V. KUPREWICZ, 771 N.Y.S.2d 804 (Sup. Ct. 2003). The defendant, a former employee of the School of Visual Arts, allegedly caused large volumes of pornographic emails and unsolicited job applications to be sent to the plaintiff, resulting in depleted hard disk space, drained processing power, and other adverse affects on plaintiff's computer system. The school and its director of human resources brought suit against the defendant for trespass to chattels. In the trial court, *held*— motion to dismiss the trespass to chattels claim denied.

"To establish a trespass to chattels, [plaintiff] must prove that Kuprewicz intentionally, and without justification or consent, physically interfered with the use and enjoyment of personal property in [plaintiff]'s possession, and that [plaintiff] was harmed thereby. Thus, one who intentionally interferes with another's chattel is liable only if there results in harm to 'the owner's materially valuable interest in the physical condition, quality, or value of the chattel, or if the owner is deprived of the use of the chattel for a substantial time.' RESTATEMENT (SECOND) OF TORTS § 218, cmt. *e*. Furthermore, to sustain this cause of action, the defendant must act with the intention of interfering with the property or with knowledge that such interference is substantially certain to result. . . . The Court concludes that accepting these factual allegations as true, SVA has sufficiently stated a cause of action for trespass to chattels, and has alleged facts constituting each element of this claim. . . . It is important to note that by this decision, the Court does not hold that the mere sending of unsolicited e-mail communications will automatically subject the sender to tort liability. The Court merely concludes that . . . accepting [plaintiff]'s factual allegations of damage to its computer systems, the complaint states a valid cause of action for trespass to chattels."

NOTES

1. **Elements.** Trespass to chattels involves something short of a conversion. It is committed by "intentionally (a) dispossessing another of the chattel, or (b) using or intermeddling with a chattel in the possession of another." Restatement (Second) of Torts § 217 (1965). Liability is based on actual damage, either in the form of actual harm to the chattel itself or an interference with the plaintiff's access or use. *See* 1 DOBBS, HAYDEN & BUBLICK, THE LAW OF TORTS § 60 (2d ed. 2011).

2. **Hypotheticals.** Is there a trespass to chattel, a conversion, or no tort at all in the following cases?

    (a) Defendant pets the plaintiff's dog although the plaintiff has repeatedly told him not to do so. The dog is not harmed.

    (b) Defendant leans against the plaintiff's car.

(c)   Defendant takes the car for a joyride against the plaintiff's will, and puts the dog in the front seat with him.

(d)   Defendant, angered at the dog's barking, kicks the dog, then pushes the car over a cliff, causing substantial damages.

3.   **Expansions of the tort.** Trespass to chattels has traditionally involved the plaintiff's tangible chattel. "An actionable claim for trespass to chattels or personal property generally requires dispossession of the property, impairment of the condition, quality or value of the property, loss of use of the property, or other harm." *Sagebrush Res., LLC v. Peterson*, 841 N.W.2d 705 (N.D. 2014) (landowners who had complained about oil and gas operators' activities to a state commission did not cause dispossession, loss of use, or impairment of the property's value or condition; claim against landowners by operators failed). However, as in *School of Visual Arts,* some modern cases have held that clogging a company's email or computer systems with large amounts of unwanted email or other electronic interference can count as a trespass to chattels. *See, e.g., Register.com v. Verio, Inc.*, 356 F.3d 393 (2nd Cir. 2004) (defendant's use of a "search robot" that could overtax plaintiff's servers); *Beyond Sys., Inc. v. Kraft Foods, Inc.*, 777 F.3d 712 (4th Cir. 2015) (sending spam email would be a trespass to chattels under state statutes, but plaintiff consented, precluding recovery); *but cf. Intel Corp. v. Hamidi*, 71 P.3d 296 (Cal. 2003) (sending spam email not a trespass to chattels where it interferes with neither possessor's use or possession of a legally protected right in the plaintiff's computer system itself).

§ 5.   FORCIBLE HARMS AS FEDERAL CIVIL RIGHTS VIOLATIONS: § 1983 CLAIMS

We have pointed out that most tort law is the common law of various states. But there are a few federal statutes that create tort claims. One of the most important of these is found in one section of the Civil Rights Act of 1871, 42 U.S.C.A. § 1983. The federal claims under that statute are usually known as "section 1983 claims."

The facts involved in § 1983 claims often parallel the common law intentional tort claims we have seen in this chapter, where they involve the direct application of force. But a § 1983 claim requires proof that is quite different from that required to establish a common law intentional tort claim. While the history, scope and policy of § 1983 claims is addressed more fully in Civil Rights courses, we sketch the contours of the tort here. As we will see in Part A of this section, § 1983 claims have different elements than intentional tort claims. And as we will see in Part B of this section, an individual defendant sued under § 1983 may assert a powerful defense created by the Supreme Court, called qualified immunity, that is not available in a common-law tort claim.

A. BASIC CONTOURS: FEDERAL RIGHTS VIOLATIONS

42 U.S.C.A. § 1983

Every person who, under color of any statute, ordinance, regulation, custom, or usage, of any State or Territory or the District of Columbia, subjects, or causes to be subjected, any citizen of the United States or other persons within the jurisdiction thereof to the deprivation of any rights, privileges, or immunities secured by the Constitution and laws, shall be liable to the party injured in an action at law, suit in equity, or other proper proceeding for redress. . . .

NOTES

1. **Coverage.** Notice the parameters in the statute itself: a plaintiff has a § 1983 claim only where (1) the defendant, a person, (2) acts under color of state law, and (3) subjects the plaintiff to a deprivation of federal rights.

(a) A "person" means an individual, although the Supreme Court has held that a municipality may be considered a "person" as well. See the note on municipal liability below. But a state or a state agency is not a "person," and thus cannot be held liable for damages under § 1983. *Howlett v. Rose*, 496 U.S. 356 (1990); *Will v. Michigan Dept. of State Police*, 491 U.S. 58 (1989).

(b) A person acts "under color of state law" if, at the time of the wrongful act, that person was exercising power made possible by state law. The typical defendant is a state officer, such as a police officer, being sued in the officer's individual capacity. Every act done by a public employee is not "under color of state law," however; "the action must be 'related in some way to the performance of the duties of the state office.'" *First Midwest Bank v. City of Chicago*, 988 F.3d 978 (7th Cir. 2021) (no § 1983 liability because off-duty police officer who shot plaintiff during a purely personal argument was not acting under color of state law at the time of the shooting). Under some circumstances a private person may be found to have acted under color of state law. See *Adickes v. S.H. Kress & Co.*, 398 U.S. 144 (1970) (private person who conspired with state officers to enforce custom of racial segregation).

Because the statute refers only to those who act under color of *state* law, neither the federal government nor federal officers are subject to its terms— instead, special statutes and rules apply to federal governmental defendants. *See* Chapter 15.

(c) The "federal rights" involved in § 1983 suits are often rights guaranteed by the United States Constitution. Most of the cases alleging a wrongful use of force by state actors assert a violation of either (1) the Fourth Amendment, which prohibits "unreasonable searches and seizures"; (2) the Eighth Amendment, which prohibits the infliction of "cruel and unusual punishments"; or (3) the Fourteenth Amendment, which prohibits a state from depriving "any person of life, liberty, or property, without due process of law."

However, a deprivation of federal statutory rights under color of state law can also be actionable.

2.   **Why raise a section 1983 claim?** Many § 1983 cases involve actions that also constitute common law torts. *See, e.g., Morton v. Kirkwood*, 707 F.3d 1276 (11th Cir. 2013) (shooting an unarmed driver who raised his hands when he heard officer shout; excessive force in violation of the Fourth Amendment and a battery as well). If the facts of a case would allow a claim for a common law tort such as battery, assault, false imprisonment, trespass, or conversion, why would a plaintiff bring a § 1983 claim and not only the common law claim? Perhaps the most important reason is that another section of the federal Civil Rights Act allows a prevailing plaintiff to recover attorneys' fees from a losing defendant in a § 1983 case—something not available in the vast majority of common law tort claims. Second, the plaintiff may prefer a federal forum; The plaintiff may choose to bring a § 1983 case in either federal or state court. *See Haywood v. Drown*, 556 U.S. 729 (2009).

3.   **The constitutional tests.** What a plaintiff must prove to establish a violation of constitutional rights depends upon the particular constitutional provision that applies, which turns on the kind of right that was allegedly violated.

(a)   *The Fourth Amendment.* In the Fourth Amendment context, the test is whether the defendant's search or seizure was "unreasonable," which normally means a search or seizure either involving excessive force, or effected without either a warrant or probable cause to believe a crime has been committed. *See, e.g., Scott v. Harris*, 550 U.S. 372 (2007); *Graham v. Connor*, 490 U.S. 386 (1989); *Tennessee v. Garner*, 471 U.S. 1 (1985). Many civil rights cases alleging police brutality invoke the Fourth Amendment.

In *Graham v. Connor*, local police detained Dethorne Graham, a diabetic, after he had rushed into a convenience store to buy orange juice to counteract an insulin reaction and had then hurried out after seeing a number of people in line ahead of him. Graham's explanations were ignored; he was handcuffed and thrown forcefully into a police car, suffering multiple injuries. He was released when the officers determined that Graham had done nothing wrong. Graham sued the officers under § 1983 for using excessive force. The Court held that the claim was properly analyzed under the Fourth Amendment's "reasonableness" standard, which "is an objective one: the question is whether the officers' actions are 'objectively reasonable' in light of the facts and circumstances confronting them, without regard to their underlying intent or motivation." Proper application of the standard, said the Court, "requires careful attention to the facts and circumstances of each particular case, including the severity of the crime at issue, whether the suspect poses an immediate threat to the safety of the officers or others, and whether he is actively resisting arrest or attempting to evade arrest by flight." The Court vacated a defense judgment and remanded for reconsideration.

The Fourth Amendment's "reasonableness" standard means that even officers using deadly force may be found not to have violated a constitutional right at all, given the totality of circumstances. *See Partlow v. Stadler*, 774 F.3d 497 (8th Cir. 2014) (firing shots at plaintiff after he exited his apartment holding a shotgun was reasonable when police were forced to make a split-second judgment); *Krause v. Jones*, 765 F.3d 675 (6th Cir. 2014) (use of deadly force to subdue decedent was reasonable, given circumstances of decedent's pointing a gun at police).

(b) *The Eighth Amendment.* An Eighth Amendment violation requires a showing that the defendant inflicted "cruel and unusual" punishment on the plaintiff. Eighth Amendment cases typically involve plaintiffs who have been convicted of a crime and were in jail or prison at the time they were allegedly mistreated by corrections officers. Proving a violation has a subjective component; the plaintiff must show that the force was applied wantonly, in bad faith, sadistically, or maliciously. *See Whitley v. Albers*, 475 U.S. 312 (1986). In *Hudson v. McMillian*, 503 U.S. 1 (1992), the Court held that prison officials violated the Eighth Amendment's "cruel and unusual" standard when they used sadistic or malicious force against a prisoner, regardless of the amount of physical harm done to the prisoner: "Otherwise, the Eighth Amendment would permit any physical punishment, no matter how diabolic or inhuman, inflicting less than some arbitrary quantity of injury." But, said the Court, the force used must be objectively wrong, a violation of contemporary standards of decency.

Cruel and unusual punishment may also be found where the conditions of confinement are especially harsh, as in *Farmer v. Brennan*, 511 U.S. 825 (1994) (housing a prisoner where she was in serious danger of being raped by others). And the Court has held that "deliberate indifference to serious medical needs of prisoners constitutes the 'unnecessary and wanton infliction of pain' . . . proscribed by the Eighth Amendment." *Estelle v. Gamble*, 429 U.S. 97 (1976).

(c) *The Fourteenth Amendment.* The Fourteenth Amendment's substantive due process guarantee has been applied in some § 1983 cases, but the Supreme Court has indicated that where a more specific provision of the Bill of Rights can be applied, it should be—displacing the Fourteenth Amendment in many cases. *See, e.g., Graham v. Connor*, 490 U.S. 386 (1989) (holding that the Fourth Amendment's "reasonableness" standard should be used in an excessive force case, rejecting a more general claim based on the Fourteenth Amendment). But where a more specific amendment does not "cover" the conduct, the case can proceed as one based on substantive due process. See *Burgess v. Fischer*, 735 F.3d 462 (6th Cir. 2013) (in an excessive force case, Fourth Amendment applies if the plaintiff is a free person; the Eighth Amendment applies if the plaintiff is a convicted person; and the Fourteenth Amendment's more general standard applies when the plaintiff "does not fall clearly within either category," such as a person in pre-trial detention).

Where the Fourteenth Amendment is applied, the plaintiff must prove that the defendant's act "shocks the conscience of the court," which usually requires proof that the defendant had the intent to injure the plaintiff. *See, e.g., County of Sacramento v. Lewis*, 523 U.S. 833 (1998) (high-speed police chase that resulted in death of passenger on a motorcycle being pursued through a residential neighborhood; officer was merely reckless, so Fourteenth Amendment was not violated); *Truong v. Hassan*, 829 F.3d 627 (8th Cir. 2016) (affirming summary judgment for city bus driver alleging violation of passenger's substantive due process rights, where there was no proof that driver intended to injure the passenger when he ejected passenger for failure to pay the fare).

4. **Damages in § 1983 cases.** Damages in a § 1983 case are "ordinarily determined according to principles derived from the common law of torts." See *Memphis Community School Dist. v. Stachura*, 477 U.S. 299 (1986). Accordingly, a jury is not permitted to award damages based on its own assessment of the "abstract value" of the constitutional right that was violated; rather, an award of compensatory damages must be "grounded in determination of plaintiffs' actual losses." *Id.* Where no physical harm is proved, nominal damages (typically one dollar) may be available. *Uzuegbunam v. Preczewski*, 141 S.Ct. 792 (2021) (violation of First Amendment rights). Punitive damages may be awarded by a jury in a § 1983 case where the defendant's misconduct "involves reckless or callous indifference to the federally protected rights of others." *Smith v. Wade*, 461 U.S. 30 (1983).

NOTE: MUNICIPAL LIABILITY

Recall that § 1983 itself says that only a "person" may be liable under the statute. In *Monell v. Dep't of Social Services,* 436 U.S. 658 (1978), the Court held that a municipality may also be held liable under § 1983, but only where the plaintiff proves that a "policy or custom" of the municipality caused the violation of plaintiff's federal rights. The *Monell* Court made clear that municipal liability could not be based on the doctrine of *respondeat superior*; that is, a town or city could not be held vicariously liable as the employer of the individual who violated the plaintiff's constitutional rights. Rather, a municipal defendant is liable under § 1983 only "for its own violations." In *Board of County Com'rs v. Brown*, 520 U.S. 397 (1997), the Court held that to win a so-called *Monell* claim against a municipality, the plaintiff must prove both that the challenged "policy or custom" demonstrates the municipality's "fault," and that that the municipality's action was the "moving force" behind the violation of the plaintiff's federal rights.

Although municipalities are not vicariously liable under § 1983 for the civil rights violations of its employees, in most cases where a law enforcement officer is held personally liable, the municipality indemnifies the officer. One study of judgments and settlements between 2006 and 2011 showed that governments paid 99.98% of the dollars that plaintiffs recovered in such suits, and the officers themselves "almost never contributed." Joanna C. Schwartz, *Police Indemnification*, 89 N.Y.U. L. REV. 885 (2014). Does this fact undermine the deterrent effect of section 1983 liability?

B. QUALIFIED IMMUNITY

SAFFORD UNIFIED SCHOOL DIST. NO. 1 V. REDDING, 557 U.S. 364 (2009). Savana Redding, a 13-year-old middle school student, was summoned from her math class to the office of Assistant Principal Kerry Wilson. Redding was shown her day planner, in which knives, lighters, and a cigarette were found; she denied they were hers. Wilson then told Redding that he had received a report that she was giving ibuprofen and naproxen pills (common painkillers) to fellow students in violation of school rules. She denied knowledge of that as well, and agreed to allow a search of her backpack. No pills were found. Wilson then told a female administrative assistant to take Redding to the nurse's office "to search her clothes for pills." The administrative assistant and the female school nurse had her remove most of her clothes, "exposing her breasts and pelvic area to some degree." Again, no pills were found. Redding's mother sued the school and the three school officials under § 1983 for conducting a strip search in violation of Redding's Fourth Amendment right to be free of unreasonable searches. The defendants asserted qualified immunity, arguing that even if the search did violate Redding's constitutional rights, such a right was not "clearly established" at the time of the search. *Held*, the strip search was unreasonable and thus violated the Fourth Amendment, but the school officials cannot be held liable. While a previous decision of the Court said that public school officials must "limit the intrusiveness of a search in light of the age and sex of the student and the nature of the infraction, . . . lower courts have reached divergent conclusions regarding how [that case's] standard applies to such searches." The "differences of opinion" expressed in lower courts "are numerous enough, with well-reasoned majority and dissenting opinions, to counsel doubt that we were sufficiently clear in the prior statement of law. We conclude that qualified immunity is warranted."

RIVAS-VILLEGAS V. CORTESLUNA
142 S.Ct. 4 (2021)

PER CURIAM. . . .

At issue here is whether [police officer Daniel] Rivas-Villegas is entitled to qualified immunity because he did not violate clearly established law. The undisputed facts are as follows. A 911 operator received a call from a crying 12-year-old girl reporting that she, her mother, and her 15-year-old sister had shut themselves into a room at their home because her mother's boyfriend, Cortesluna, was trying to hurt them and had a chainsaw. The girl told the operator that Cortesluna was "always drinking," had "anger issues," was "really mad," and was using the chainsaw to "break something in the house." A police dispatcher relayed this information along with a description of Cortesluna in a request for officers to respond.

Rivas-Villegas heard the broadcast and responded to the scene along with four other officers. The officers spent several minutes observing the home and reported seeing through a window a man matching Cortesluna's description. One officer asked whether the girl and her family could exit the house. Dispatch responded that they "were unable to get out" and confirmed that the 911 operator had "hear[d] sawing in the background" and thought that Cortesluna might be trying to saw down the door.

After receiving this information, Rivas-Villegas knocked on the door and stated loudly, " 'police department, come to the front door, Union City police, come to the front door.' " Another officer yelled, "he's coming and has a weapon." A different officer then stated, "use less-lethal," referring to a beanbag shotgun. When Rivas-Villegas ordered Cortesluna to "drop it," Cortesluna dropped the "weapon," later identified as a metal tool.

Rivas-Villegas then commanded, "come out, put your hands up, walk out towards me." Cortesluna put his hands up and Rivas-Villegas told him to "keep coming." As Cortesluna walked out of the house and toward the officers, Rivas-Villegas said, " 'Stop. Get on your knees." Plaintiff stopped 10 to 11 feet from the officers. Another officer then saw a knife sticking out from the front left pocket of Cortesluna's pants and shouted, " 'he has a knife in his left pocket, knife in his pocket,' " and directed Cortesluna, "don't put your hands down," "hands up." Cortesluna turned his head toward the instructing officer but then lowered his head and his hands in contravention of the officer's orders. Another officer twice shot Cortesluna with a beanbag round from his shotgun, once in the lower stomach and once in the left hip.

After the second shot, Cortesluna raised his hands over his head. The officers shouted for him to " 'get down,' " which he did. Another officer stated, " 'left pocket, he's got a knife.' " Rivas-Villegas then straddled Cortesluna. He placed his right foot on the ground next to Cortesluna's right side with his right leg bent at the knee. He placed his left knee on the left side of Cortesluna's back, near where Cortesluna had a knife in his pocket. He raised both of Cortesluna's arms up behind his back. Rivas-Villegas was in this position for no more than eight seconds before standing up while continuing to hold Cortesluna's arms. At that point, another officer, who had just removed the knife from Cortesluna's pocket and tossed it away, came and handcuffed Cortesluna's hands behind his back. Rivas-Villegas lifted Cortesluna up and moved him away from the door.

Cortesluna brought suit under 42 U.S.C. § 1983, claiming, as relevant here, that Rivas-Villegas used excessive force in violation of the Fourth

Amendment. The District Court granted summary judgment to Rivas-Villegas, but the Court of Appeals for the Ninth Circuit reversed.

The Court of Appeals held that "Rivas-Villegas is not entitled to qualified immunity because existing precedent put him on notice that his conduct constituted excessive force." In reaching this conclusion, the Court of Appeals relied solely on *LaLonde* v. *County of Riverside*, 204 F.3d 947 (9th Cir. 2000). The court acknowledged that "the officers here responded to a more volatile situation than did the officers in *LaLonde*." Nevertheless, it reasoned: "Both *LaLonde* and this case involve suspects who were lying face-down on the ground and were not resisting either physically or verbally, on whose back the defendant officer leaned with a knee, causing allegedly significant injury."

Judge Collins dissented. As relevant, he argued that "the facts of *LaLonde* are materially distinguishable from this case and are therefore insufficient to have made clear to every reasonable officer that the force Rivas-Villegas used here was excessive."

We agree and therefore reverse. Even assuming that controlling Circuit precedent clearly establishes law for purposes of § 1983, *LaLonde* did not give fair notice to Rivas-Villegas. He is thus entitled to qualified immunity.

Qualified immunity attaches when an official's conduct does not violate clearly established statutory or constitutional rights of which a reasonable person would have known. A right is clearly established when it is sufficiently clear that every reasonable official would have understood that what he is doing violates that right. Although this Court's case law does not require a case directly on point for a right to be clearly established, existing precedent must have placed the statutory or constitutional question beyond debate. This inquiry must be undertaken in light of the specific context of the case, not as a broad general proposition.

Specificity is especially important in the Fourth Amendment context, where . . . it is sometimes difficult for an officer to determine how the relevant legal doctrine, here excessive force, will apply to the factual situation the officer confronts. Whether an officer has used excessive force depends on "the facts and circumstances of each particular case, including the severity of the crime at issue, whether the suspect poses an immediate threat to the safety of the officers or others, and whether he is actively resisting arrest or attempting to evade arrest by flight." *Graham v. Connor*, 490 U.S. 386, 396 (1989); see also *Tennessee v. Garner*, 471 U.S. 1, 11 (1985) ("Where the officer has probable cause to believe that the suspect poses a threat of serious physical harm, either to the officer or to others, it is not constitutionally unreasonable to prevent escape by using deadly force"). However, *Graham*'s and *Garner*'s standards are cast at a high level of generality. In an obvious case, these standards can "clearly establish" the answer, even without a body of relevant case law." But this is not an obvious case. Thus, to show a violation of clearly established law, Cortesluna must identify a case that put Rivas-Villegas on notice that his specific conduct was unlawful.

Cortesluna has not done so. Neither Cortesluna nor the Court of Appeals identified any Supreme Court case that addresses facts like the ones at issue here. Instead, the Court of Appeals relied solely on its precedent in *LaLonde*. Even assuming that Circuit precedent can clearly establish law for purposes of § 1983, *LaLonde* is materially distinguishable and thus does not govern the facts of this case.

In *LaLonde*, officers were responding to a neighbor's complaint that LaLonde had been making too much noise in his apartment. When they knocked on LaLonde's door, he "appeared in his underwear and a T-shirt, holding a sandwich in his hand." LaLonde testified that, after he refused to let the officers enter his home, they did so anyway and informed him he would be arrested for obstruction of justice. One officer then knocked the sandwich from LaLonde's hand and "grabbed LaLonde by his ponytail and knocked him backwards to the ground." After a short scuffle, the officer sprayed LaLonde in the face with pepper spray. At that point, LaLonde ceased resisting and another officer, while handcuffing LaLonde, "deliberately dug his knee into LaLonde's back with a force that caused him long-term if not permanent back injury."

The situation in *LaLonde* and the situation at issue here diverge in several respects. In *LaLonde*, officers were responding to a mere noise complaint, whereas here they were responding to a serious alleged incident of domestic violence possibly involving a chainsaw. In addition, LaLonde was unarmed. Cortesluna, in contrast, had a knife protruding from his left pocket for which he had just previously appeared to reach. Further, in this case, video evidence shows, and Cortesluna does not dispute, that Rivas-Villegas placed his knee on Cortesluna for no more than eight seconds and only on the side of his back near the knife that officers were in the process of retrieving. LaLonde, in contrast, testified that the officer deliberately dug his knee into his back when he had no weapon and had made no threat when approached by police. These facts, considered together in the context of this particular arrest, materially distinguish this case from *LaLonde*.

Precedent involving similar facts can help move a case beyond the otherwise hazy borders between excessive and acceptable force and thereby provide an officer notice that a specific use of force is unlawful. On the facts of this case, neither *LaLonde* nor any decision of this Court is sufficiently similar. For that reason, we grant Rivas-Villegas' petition for certiorari and reverse the Ninth Circuit's determination that Rivas-Villegas is not entitled to qualified immunity.

It is so ordered.

NOTES

1. **How did we get here? The history of qualified immunity.** The Supreme Court created the qualified immunity defense in *Pierson v. Ray*, 386 U.S. 547 (1967), protecting officers from liability for damages as long as they acted in "good faith." The defense was reformulated 15 years later in *Harlow v. Fitzgerald*, 457 U.S. 800 (1982), to eliminate any inquiry into subjective good faith; instead, said the Court, the defense should "turn primarily on objective factors." More specifically, the *Harlow* Court held that only where the defendant's conduct violated "clearly established statutory or constitutional rights of which a reasonable person would have known" could discovery even proceed; if the plaintiff failed to make such proof, the defendant was entitled to judgment as a matter of law. In 2001 the Court mandated a two-step sequence for resolving government officers' qualified immunity claims: first, the court must determine whether the defendant violated the plaintiff's constitutional rights; if so, then the court must next address whether the unconstitutionality of the defendant's conduct was "clearly established" at the time of the wrongful act. *Saucier v. Katz*, 533 U.S. 194 (2001).

Less than a decade later, a unanimous Court receded from *Saucier,* holding that a court can address the two questions—(1) whether the right was violated and (2) whether that right was "clearly established"—in any order it wants. *Pearson v. Callahan*, 555 U.S. 223 (2009). The Court recognized that "there will be cases in which a court will rather quickly and easily decide that there was no violation of *clearly established* law before turning to the more difficult question whether the relevant facts make out a constitutional question at all." This remains the law. *See, e.g., City of Talequah, Okla. v. Bond*, 142 S.Ct. 9 (2021) (per curiam) ("We need not, and do not, decide whether the officers violated the Fourth Amendment in the first place. . . . On this record, the officers plainly did not violate any clearly established law. . . . Neither the panel majority nor the respondent have identified a single precedent finding a Fourth Amendment violation under similar circumstances.").

At the time of writing, the *Rivas-Villegas* case was the most recent U.S. Supreme Court precedent on the qualified immunity.

2. **"Fair notice."** In *Pearson, supra* Note 1, the Court said that qualified immunity "balances two important interests—the need to hold public officials accountable when they exercise power irresponsibly and the need to shield officials from harassment, distraction, and liability when they perform their duties reasonably." The Court has made clear that the point of qualified immunity is to allow a § 1983 case to proceed against an individual officer only when "the officer had fair notice that her conduct was unlawful. . . . The relevant, dispositive inquiry in determining whether a right is clearly established is whether it would be clear to a reasonable officer that his conduct was unlawful in the situation he confronted." *Brousseau v. Haugen*, 543 U.S. 194, 199 (2004). In *District of Columbia v. Wesby*, 138 S.Ct. 577 (2018), the Court said that then-existing "precedent must be clear enough that every reasonable official would interpret it to establish the particular rule the

plaintiff seeks to apply. . . . The rule's contours must be so well defined that it is clear to a reasonable officer that his conduct was unlawful in the situation he confronted."

Qualified immunity rests on an assumption that government officials actually know about prior court decisions that constrain their authority. But if officials don't know of prior court decisions and have no reasonable way of knowing, does that reality undercut the doctrine? *See* Joanna C. Schwartz, *Qualified Immunity's Boldest Lie*, 88 U. CHI. L. REV. 605 (2021) (reporting findings of a study on the training of California police officers, showing that they do not receive such training, and that even if they did, "the notion that officers would consider the facts and holdings of these cases in the moments leading up to a use of force defies human-error research, common sense, and the Supreme Court's own assertions about law enforcement officers' ability to apply intricate rules while doing their jobs").

3.   **Judicial criticism of qualified immunity.** In a recent opinion in *Zadeh v. Robinson*, 928 F.3d 457 (5th Cir. 2019), Judge Don R. Willett expressed his "unease with the real-world functioning of modern immunity practice." He wrote:

> To some observers, qualified immunity smacks of unqualified impunity, letting public officials duck consequences for bad behavior—no matter how palpably unreasonable—as long as they were the *first* to behave badly. Merely proving a constitutional deprivation doesn't cut it; plaintiffs must cite functionally identical precedent that places the legal question "beyond debate" to "every" reasonable officer. Put differently, it's immaterial that someone acts unconstitutionally if no prior case held such misconduct unlawful. This current "yes harm, no foul" imbalance leaves victims violated but not vindicated. Wrongs are not righted, and wrongdoers are not reproached.
>
> . . . [C]ourts of appeals are divided—intractably—over precisely what degree of factual similarity must exist. How indistinguishable must existing precedent be? On the one hand, the Supreme Court reassures plaintiffs that its caselaw "does not require a case directly on point for a right to be clearly established." On the other hand, the Court admonishes that "clearly established law must be 'particularized' to the facts of the case." How to square these abstract instructions? Take Dr. Zadeh. Effectively, he loses since no previous panel has ever held this exact sort of search unconstitutional. In day-to-day practice, the "clearly established" standard is neither clear nor established among our Nation's lower courts.
>
> Two other factors perpetuate perplexity over "clearly established law." First, many courts grant immunity without first determining whether the challenged behavior violates the Constitution. They avoid scrutinizing the alleged offense by skipping to the simpler second prong: no factually analogous precedent. Forgoing a knotty

constitutional inquiry makes for easier sledding, no doubt. But the inexorable result is "constitutional stagnation"—fewer courts establishing law at all, much less *clearly* doing so. Section 1983 meets Catch-22. Plaintiffs must produce precedent even as fewer courts are producing precedent. Important constitutional questions go unanswered precisely because no one's answered them before. Courts then rely on that judicial silence to conclude there's no equivalent case on the books. No precedent = no clearly established law = no liability. An Escherian Stairwell. Heads government wins, tails plaintiff loses.

Second, constitutional litigation increasingly involves cutting-edge technologies. If courts leapfrog the underlying constitutional merits in cases raising novel issues like digital privacy, then constitutional clarity—matter-of-fact guidance about what the Constitution requires—remains exasperatingly elusive. Result: gauzy constitutional guardrails as technological innovation outpaces legal adaptation.

. . . A strange-bedfellows alliance of leading scholars and advocacy groups of every ideological stripe—perhaps the most diverse amici ever assembled—had joined forces to urge the Court to fundamentally reshape immunity doctrine. Even in this hyperpartisan age, there is a growing, cross-ideological chorus of jurists and scholars urging recalibration of contemporary immunity jurisprudence.

Indeed, it's curious how this entrenched, judge-created doctrine excuses constitutional violations by limiting the statute Congress passed to redress constitutional violations. Count me with Chief Justice Marshall: "The government of the United States has been emphatically termed a government of laws, and not of men. It will certainly cease to deserve this high appellation, if the laws furnish no remedy for the violation of a vested legal right." . . .

928 F.3d at 479–81 (Willett, J., concurring in part and dissenting in part).

4. **Academic criticism.** Scholarly criticism of the qualified immunity doctrine has been similarly withering. *See, e.g.*, Devon W. Carbado, *Blue on Black Violence: A Provisional Model of Some of the Causes*, 104 GEO. L.J. 1479 (2016) (identifying qualified immunity as a "fundamental barrier to holding police officers accountable," and thus a major factor contributing to police violence against African-Americans); Joanna C. Schwartz, *The Case Against Qualified Immunity*, 93 NOTRE DAME L. REV. 1797 (2018) (noting that "the Court's recent qualified immunity decisions make it seem nearly impossible to find clearly established law that would defeat the defense"); William Baude, *Is Qualified Immunity Unlawful?*, 106 CAL. L. REV. 45, 82 (2018) (noting that in the 35 years after the *Harlow* decision, the Court decided 30 qualified immunity cases but found official conduct to violate clearly established law only twice).

5.   **What "clearly established" means.** In the years since the *Pearson* decision, the Court's definition of "clearly established law" has evolved "both in terms of what sources can clearly establish the law and how factually similar prior court decisions must be to the case at hand." Schwartz, *Boldest Lie*, *supra* Note 3 (reviewing this evolution in detail). As illustrated by the *Rivas-Villegas* opinion above, the plaintiff cannot prevail against a defendant's assertion of qualified immunity without identifying at least one prior decided case—and perhaps a "body of relevant case law," see *District of Columbia v. Wesby*, 138 S.Ct. 577 (2018)—that holds on "sufficiently similar" facts that the defendant's conduct violates the constitution. This formulation of qualified immunity requires a court to engage in the kind of analysis we see in the primary case, parsing the facts of both the case before it and the facts of purportedly similar earlier reported cases in granular detail.

In *City of Escondido, Cal. v. Emmons*, 139 S.Ct. 500 (2019), two officers "forcibly apprehended" Marty Emmons, the father of a domestic violence complainant, when he disobeyed an order not to close the door of his daughter's apartment and "tried to brush by" Officer Craig. Emmons sued the officers under § 1983 for using unreasonable force. The Supreme Court held that "the clearly established right must be defined with specificity," especially in a Fourth Amendment case, and concluding that the Ninth Circuit's "formulation of the clearly established right was far too general. . . . [T]he Ninth Circuit's [prior] case law involved police force against individuals engaged in *passive* resistance. The Court of Appeals made no effort to explain how that case law prohibited Officer Craig's actions in this case. That is a problem under our precedents." The Court remanded to the Ninth Circuit, holding that it had "failed to properly analyze whether clearly established law barred Officer Craig from stopping and taking down Marty Emmons in this manner as Emmons exited the apartment."

As Professor Schwartz has noted, in recent years "circuit courts have granted officers qualified immunity even when prior precedent held that almost identical conduct was unconstitutional." She cites the example of *Baxter v. Bracey*, 751 Fed. App'x 869 (6th Cir. 2018), a case in which police officers released their police dog on a suspect who was sitting down with his hands up. A prior Sixth Circuit decision had held that releasing a dog on a suspect who was lying down violated the Fourth Amendment. But that earlier decision, the panel held, did not clearly establish that it was unconstitutional to release a dog on a suspect who was sitting down with his hands raised. Schwartz, *Boldest Lie*, supra Note 2, at 617–18.

6.   **"Obvious" constitutional violations.** The *Rivas-Villegas* Court mentions the one category of cases in which a plaintiff does not need to identify a prior decision on similar facts in order to prevail. These are the rare "obvious" cases in which officers would be "on notice" that their conduct would be unconstitutional based on a "general constitutional rule already identified in the decisional law," even without a prior decision specifically declaring it so. There are few such cases, and in each of them the misconduct of the defendants was extreme. Most have arisen under the Eighth Amendment.

For example, in *Hope v. Pelzer*, 536 U.S. 730 (2002), prison guards handcuffed an inmate to a hitching post on two occasions, once for seven hours without regular bathroom or water breaks. The Court held that a reasonable officer would know that this "obvious cruelty" was a violation of the Eighth Amendment, even though there was no prior decision directly on point: "officials can still be on notice that their conduct violates established law even in novel factual circumstances."

More recently, in *Taylor v. Riojas*, 141 S.Ct. 52 (2020) (per curiam), an inmate was confined for six days in a pair of "shockingly unsanitary" cells, the first of which had a floor and walls covered in feces and the second of which was frigidly cold and had a clogged floor drain to dispose of bodily wastes. The Court held that "no reasonable correctional officer could have concluded that, under the extreme circumstances of this case, it was constitutionally permissible to house Taylor in such deplorably unsanitary conditions for such an extended period of time. . . . Confronted with the particularly egregious facts of this case, any reasonable officer should have realized that Taylor's conditions of confinement offended the Constitution."

Is it clear to you when particular misconduct would be "obviously unlawful" from the perspective of a "reasonable officer?" For a sustained argument that courts should more frequently recognize "obvious" violations as a way to soften the immunity, see Alexander J. Lindvall, *Qualified Immunity and Obvious Constitutional Violations*, 28 GEO. MASON L. REV. 1047 (2021) (noting that recent reported cases from lower courts show that "officers' conduct only seems to be getting more and more egregious").

7. **Abolishing or reforming immunity.** In March 2021, the U.S. House of Representatives passed the George Floyd Justice in Policing Act of 2021, H.R. 1280, 117th Cong. § 102 (2021)., which would eliminate the qualified immunity defense for law-enforcement officers. The bill died in the Senate, however, and thus has not become law.

Would eliminating qualified immunity deter misconduct by state actors or lead to a flood of frivolous claims? For a sustained analysis see Joanna C. Schwartz, *After Qualified Immunity*, 120 COLUM. L. REV. 309 (2020) (reporting on a study that indicates that eliminating qualified immunity would clarify constitutional law, reduce the costs of litigation, and shift the focus of § 1983 cases to the critical question of whether government officials have exceeded their constitutional authority).

Are there other modifications that should be made in the doctrine, short of an abolition? Some have suggested that if the Court retains the "clearly established" requirement, it should at least allow for rights to be defined in a broader way, and move away from its insistence on factually similar conduct. See Schwartz, *Boldest Lie*, supra Note 2. Would that be preferable?

REFERENCES: 1 DOBBS, HAYDEN & BUBLICK, THE LAW OF TORTS §§ 28–79 (2d ed. 2011); DOBBS, HAYDEN & BUBLICK, HORNBOOK ON TORTS §§ 4.1–6.15 (2d ed. 2016).

CHAPTER 4

DEFENSES TO INTENTIONAL TORTS—PRIVILEGES

■ ■ ■

Even when the plaintiff states and proves facts sufficient to state a prima facie case for an intentional tort, the defendant might still prevail by proving a defense or privilege. The privileges explored in this chapter are for the most part affirmative defenses, meaning that the defendant has the burden of pleading and proving them. These defenses do not usually challenge the elements of the plaintiff's prima facie case; rather, they supply a legal reason or justification for the defendant's actions that render those actions non-tortious. We see three sets of privileges: first, those that attempt to justify the defendant's conduct as a response to the apparent misconduct of the plaintiff; second, the special case of consent; and third, the privileges of public and private necessity, which are based on policy rather than the plaintiff's apparent conduct or misconduct.

§ 1. PROTECTING AGAINST THE PLAINTIFF'S APPARENT MISCONDUCT

A. SELF-DEFENSE AND DEFENSE OF OTHERS

GRIMES V. SABAN
173 So.3d 919 (Ala. 2014)

BRYAN, JUSTICE.

[Sarah Grimes sued Kristen Saban, alleging assault and battery. Grimes argued that the beating she sustained by Saban left her with head injuries, anxiety, migraines and a deformed nose. Saban argued that Grimes instigated the altercation "by uttering hateful words to Saban" and that Saban acted in self-defense. Saban moved for summary judgment, which the trial court granted.]

In its summary-judgment order, the circuit court stated:

"Findings

"In the early morning hours of August 29, 2010, Grimes and Saban, along with some mutual girlfriends, returned to Saban's apartment after a night of socializing at a local bar. As they sat in the kitchen discussing the night's events, an argument ensued between Grimes and Saban, which prompted Saban to leave the room, go upstairs to her bedroom, and lock her door.

"While in her room, Saban posted on Facebook, "No one likes Sarah, yayyyyy!" apparently in reference to Grimes. Sometime later, Grimes saw this post, became angry, went to Saban's bedroom and began yelling and pounding on the locked door, demanding the post be removed. When Saban opened the door to her bedroom and attempted to show Grimes her phone and that the post had been removed, Grimes advanced toward Saban, got within inches of Saban's face, and continued yelling. As Saban pushed Grimes away, Grimes grabbed Saban by the throat, and the physical altercation began.

"Conclusions

"Saban was in her home, locked in her bedroom, when Grimes sought out Saban and initiated the confrontation. Grimes's response to Saban's Facebook post was unreasonable and excessive. . . . When Saban opened the door to an angry Grimes within inches of her face, it was reasonable for Saban to believe imminent use of unlawful physical force by Grimes was about to be used against her. Saban had a right to be in her home, had no duty to retreat and had the right to stand her ground. Therefore, Saban was justified in using physical force to defend herself from what she reasonably believed to be the use of unlawful physical force by Grimes. Furthermore, Saban was justified in using a degree of force that she reasonably believed was necessary to repel Grimes's use and threat of physical force.

"Due to these facts, Alabama Code § 13A–3–23 presumes that Saban's actions were justified and necessary to repel the use of physical force against her. Grimes failed to present evidence to rebut this presumption. Therefore . . . Saban's Motion for Summary Judgment is hereby GRANTED. . . ."

Grimes appealed. Grimes argues that the circuit court erred in entering a summary judgment in favor of Saban because, she says, genuine issues of material fact exist as to whether Saban acted in self-defense, under § 13A–3–23, Ala. Code 1975. Section 13A–3–23 provides, in pertinent part:

(a) A person is justified in using physical force upon another person in order to defend himself or herself or a third person from what he or she reasonably believes to be the use or imminent use of unlawful physical force by that other person, and he or she may use a degree of force which he or she reasonably believes to be necessary for the purpose. . . .

(b) A person who is justified under subsection (a) in using physical force, including deadly physical force, and who is not engaged in an unlawful activity and is in any place where he or she has the right to be has no duty to retreat and has the right to stand his or her ground.

(c) Notwithstanding the provisions of subsection (a), a person is not justified in using physical force if: . . .

> (2) He or she was the initial aggressor, except that his or her use of physical force upon another person under the circumstances is justifiable if he or she withdraws from the encounter and effectively communicates to the other person his or her intent to do so, but the latter person nevertheless continues or threatens the use of unlawful physical force.

(d) A person who uses force, including deadly physical force, as justified and permitted in this section is immune from criminal prosecution and civil action for the use of such force, unless the force was determined to be unlawful.

The [conclusions made by the trial court] . . . are supported by Saban's deposition testimony and by the affidavits of [other friends present on the evening of the incident], which she attached to her motion for a summary judgment. However, they are disputed by Grimes's deposition testimony, which was attached to Grimes's brief filed in opposition to Saban's summary-judgment motion. . . .

Grimes testified in her deposition that after she banged on Saban's door, insisting that Saban take down the Facebook post, Saban opened the door and came out of her bedroom to show Grimes that the post had been removed. Grimes testified that [the two were in the hall and] . . . Grimes had backed away from Saban's door when Saban came out of her room. . . . Grimes also testified in her deposition that, after Saban told her that the Facebook post had been removed, she said to Saban "something to the effect of 'I don't care, okay, but we're done,' and I called her crazy." Grimes testified that Saban then used both of her hands and shoved Grimes into [an] open door frame. . . . According to Grimes, when she put her hands on Saban's throat and chest to push her away, Saban started punching her and hit her in the face more than five times."

Grimes testified that, after the first punch, she told Saban that she was calling the cops. Grimes stated: "I'm not sure how many blows were after that. I did not swing back. I know I had my arm up to defend myself. She had a grip on my hair. And we were somehow moving along the wall. . . . [A friend] at this point . . . tried to pull her off, and it wasn't working. And at some point, the closer we got towards the living room, [another friend], who was asleep, got up out of bed and they somehow managed to pull Saban off of me." . . .

When viewed in the light most favorable to Grimes and when all reasonable inferences are drawn in favor of Grimes, Grimes's deposition testimony raises genuine issues of material fact as to whether Saban reasonably believed the use of force was necessary to defend herself against Grimes, whether Saban used a degree of force she reasonably believed was necessary, and whether Saban was the initial aggressor in the altercation. . . . Thus, the circuit court erred in entering a summary judgment in Saban's favor based on § 13A–3–23. In so holding, we should not be understood as expressing a view as to the merits of the underlying claims or affirmative defenses; we merely hold that there remain genuine issues of material fact for resolution by the fact-finder so as to preclude the entry of a summary judgment.

H/D
Reasoning

REVERSED AND REMANDED.

NOTES

1. **Elements of the self-defense privilege.** The trial court in *Grimes* erred by crediting the defendant's story. Does that mean the plaintiff will prevail? Which party must prove that the defendant acted in self-defense? To whom must that party prove that she acted in self-defense?

2. **Provocation.** Provocation is generally not sufficient to raise the self-defense privilege. As you can glean from *Grimes*, insults and arguments, for example, do not justify a physical attack by the insulted defendant. How can we distinguish acts that create the reasonable appearance of an attack from mere provocation? What facts did the trial and appellate courts recite to support one conclusion or the other?

In *Touchet v. Hampton*, 1 So.3d 729 (La. App. 2008), Touchet was terminated from his employment with Hampton's car dealership. Some weeks after being terminated, Hampton began to receive disturbing phone calls from Touchet, in which Touchet "cursed him, threatened him, and told him that he knew where he lived." Touchet left several threatening voice mail messages as well. Hampton decided to go to Touchet's new place of business (an RV center) to tell him to stop the harassing phone calls. When Hampton entered Touchet's office, Touchet's back was to him. According to Hampton, Touchet "quickly turned around in his chair and yelled "F[--k] you, Hampton." Hampton then struck Touchet a number of times, until one of Touchet's co-workers pulled him off. Touchet sued Hampton for battery, and Hampton asserted self-defense, claiming that at the moment he began to hit Touchet, he "was startled and scared because it appeared as if Touchet 'was going to him me, what he said he was going to do.' " Do you think Hampton proved he acted in self-defense?

3. **The "initial aggressor" rule.** Statutes in a number of states, as we see in *Grimes*, provide that if the defendant was the initial aggressor then self-defense may not be invoked by that defendant in either a criminal proceeding or a civil suit. Most such statutes go on to say, however, that where the initial aggressor has withdrawn from the encounter and communicates that to the

other person, that limitation is lifted. *See, e.g.*, KAN. STAT. ANN. 2019 Supp. §§ 21–5226(b) & (c). This has been called a "safe harbor" provision. *See State v. Phillips*, 479 P.3d 176 (Kan. 2021) (criminal case). It has been applied most often in criminal cases. Does this rule add anything to the common-law elements of the defense?

4.   **Mistake.** What if a defendant reasonably believes that he is being attacked, but is mistaken? Would a self-defense privilege still be available? *See* RESTATEMENT (SECOND) OF TORTS § 70 (1965).

5.   **Excessive force.** The privilege extends only to the use of reasonable force. Any excessive force is unprivileged and the defendant is liable for it. A defendant who retaliates or continues the "defense" after the fight is over is likewise liable. Defining excessive force is a matter of degree and depends very much on the facts of each case. If Grimes' testimony is believed, could this be an excessive force case?

6.   **Assault or imprisonment in self-defense.** The Restatement specifically recognizes that one may be privileged, given appropriate facts, to commit what otherwise would be an assault or a false imprisonment in self-defense. *See* RESTATEMENT (SECOND) OF TORTS § 67 (1965). One point of special interest is the rule in § 70 of the Second Restatement that the defendant may be privileged to put the plaintiff in apprehension of a harmful or offensive bodily contact even though the contact itself would not be privileged. Would this authorize defendant to point a gun at the plaintiff to forestall a punch in the nose, even though the defendant would not be privileged to fire it?

7.   **"Reasonable" deadly force.** The quantum of force considered reasonable in self-defense will vary with the facts. *See, e.g., Giordano v. Spencer*, 888 P.2d 915 (Nev. 1995) (punching plaintiff twice was a reasonable amount of force in self-defense, where plaintiff, with "a wild look in his eyes," raised his fists and used profanity at defendant). Is deadly force ever reasonable? The general rule is that the defendant's privilege to use that amount of force extends only so far as reasonably necessary to prevent death or serious bodily harm. *See First Midwest Bank v. Denson*, 562 N.E.2d 1256 (Ill. App. Ct. 1990) (upholding jury verdict for 67-year-old landlord who shot and killed evicted tenant whom landlord believed was about to push him down the stairs).

8.   **Retreat.** The defendant who is attacked is usually not required to retreat or otherwise avoid the need for self-defense. When the defendant is threatened with sexual attack, or force likely to cause death or serious bodily harm, the defendant is privileged to respond with reasonable deadly force. However, some states require reasonable retreat before deadly force is used when the defendant is not at home. *See, e.g.,* CONN. GEN. STATS. ANN. § 53a–19(b); RESTATEMENT (SECOND) OF TORTS § 65 (1965). Others have no such requirement. 1 DOBBS, HAYDEN & BUBLICK, THE LAW OF TORTS § 81 (2d ed. 2011). "Stand Your Ground" laws, now in place in some form in about half the states, declare that there is no duty to retreat before using force, in one's home or in any other place where one has a right to be.

NOTE: "STAND YOUR GROUND" STATUTES

Starting in 2005, states (including Alabama) began to adopt "Stand Your Ground" laws that remove the duty to retreat before using force, even deadly force, in self-defense. As of 2015, two dozen states had adopted a statutory "no duty to retreat" law; 18 of these states provide civil immunity and seven grant immunity from criminal prosecution. *See* NAT'L TASK FORCE ON STAND YOUR GROUND LAWS, AM. BAR ASS'N, FINAL REPORT AND RECOMMENDATIONS 42–43 (2015) ("ABA Report"). In the civil-immunity states, this means that a defendant may be declared immune from suit in a pre-trial hearing before a jury is ever impaneled, if the judge finds the use of force was justified. *See, e.g., Pages v. Seliman-Tapia*, 134 So.3d 536 (Fla. Dist. Ct. App. 2014) (defendant immune in suit for assault and battery, on ground that he had a reasonable fear for his disabled wife's safety in a parking-lot altercation with the plaintiff).

If a defendant is determined to be immune from prosecution in a criminal case on the basis of the Stand Your Ground law, does that finding bind a civil plaintiff in a subsequent tort suit, thus barring the civil claim as well? In *Kumar v. Patel*, 227 So.3d 557 (Fla. 2017), the court held that it did not. The court stressed that it would be unfair and would violate basic collateral estoppel rules to do so, because the civil plaintiff was not a party to the criminal proceeding. The court also relied on a 2017 amendment to Florida's statute that created different burdens of proof for criminal and civil proceedings. "Even in a case where the State could not prove by clear and convincing evidence that the defendant was not entitled to immunity," the court said, "the criminal defendant may not be able to prove by a preponderance of the evidence that he is entitled to immunity in the civil case."

Do "Stand Your Ground" laws represent good policy? The ABA Report cited above, which was issued after a thorough investigation of such laws across the United States, concludes that they "may cause more problems than they are solving." ABA Report, *supra,* at 19. Empirical data show that states with such laws experienced an *increase* in homicides since adopting such laws, and have not shown any decrease in theft, burglary, or assault crimes. The Report further finds that application of the laws "is unpredictable, uneven, and results in racial disparities." *Id.* at 2. Specifically in Stand Your Ground states, "a white shooter who kills a black victim is 350 percent more likely to be found justified than if the same shooter killed a white victim." *Id.* at 13. Based on its national investigation and research, the ABA Task Force recommended that "states that desire to combat violent crime" should not adopt such laws, and those "states that desire to reduce their overall homicide rates" should repeal them. *Id.*at 2.

NOTE: DEFENSE OF OTHERS

At one time, the privilege to defend a person other than one's self was limited to defending family members and servants. This restrictive view has little support today, although some states, including California, retain such limits. *See* CAL. CIV. CODE § 50 (dating to 1872: use of reasonable force allowed "to protect from wrongful injury the person or property of oneself, or of a spouse, child, parent, or other relative, or member of one's family, or of a ward, servant, master, or guest"). Today, most jurisdictions recognize that people may defend others on the same basis that they may defend themselves. *See, e.g., Burke v. Mesniaeff*, 220 A.3d 777 (Conn. 2019) (affirming jury verdict for defendant who reasonably believed that plaintiff, his former wife, was about to use physical force against houseguests when he forcibly removed her from the house); *Lewis v. Dirt Sports LLC*, 259 F.Supp.3d 1039 (D. Ariz. 2017) (defendant mother acted reasonably to protect son and another child by stepping between them and plaintiff, a 6-foot-tall adult, and "holding out her arms against plaintiff").

What if the defendant's belief that force is needed to protect another is reasonable, but mistaken? For example, suppose a defendant sees A striking B. Believing that B is being attacked, the defendant seizes A and delivers a stunning blow. B then runs off. It turns out that A was a police detective attempting to carry out a lawful arrest which B was resisting. A sues the defendant for battery. Can the defendant claim a privilege? The rule embodied in the Restatement Second of Torts § 76 says yes, as long as the defendant's belief that B was being attacked and needed help was reasonable, even if mistaken, and the amount of force used was reasonable. Some courts, however, have held that a mistake, even a reasonable one, destroys the privilege, leaving the defendant liable for battery.

B. DEFENSE AND REPOSSESSION OF PROPERTY

KATKO V. BRINEY

183 N.W.2d 657 (Iowa 1971)

MOORE, CHIEF JUSTICE.

[Defendant Bertha Briney inherited an unoccupied farm house. For ten years there were a series of housebreaking events, with damage to this property. She and her husband boarded up the windows and posted no trespass signs and eventually they set up a shotgun trap in one of the rooms. The gun was rigged to an old iron bed, barrel pointed at the door. A wire ran from the doorknob to the trigger. It was pointed to hit the legs of an intruder. Mr. Briney admitted he was "mad and tired of being tormented," but said he did not intend to injure anyone. There was no warning of the gun. The plaintiff and one McDonough had been to the house before. They were looking for old bottles and jars. They broke into

F

PH

the house, and plaintiff started to enter the bedroom. The shotgun went off, and much of his right leg, including part of the tibia, was blown away. He spent 40 days in the hospital. The jury found for the plaintiff in the sum of $20,000 actual damages and $10,000 punitive damages.]

Plaintiff testified he knew he had no right to break and enter the house with intent to steal bottles and fruit jars therefrom. He further testified he had entered a plea of guilty to larceny in the nighttime of property of less than $20 value from a private building. He stated he had been fined $50 and costs and paroled during good behavior from a 60-day jail sentence. . . .

The main thrust of defendants' defense in the trial court and on this appeal is that "the law permits use of a spring gun in a dwelling or warehouse for the purpose of preventing the unlawful entry of a burglar or thief.". . .

Instruction 6 stated: "An owner of premises is prohibited from willfully or intentionally injuring a trespasser by means of force that either takes life or inflicts great bodily injury; and therefore a person owning a premise is prohibited from setting out 'spring guns' and like dangerous devices which will likely take life or inflict great bodily injury, for the purpose of harming trespassers. The fact that the trespasser may be acting in violation of the law does not change the rule. The only time when such conduct of setting a 'spring gun' or a like dangerous device is justified would be when the trespasser was committing a felony of violence or a felony punishable by death, or where the trespasser was endangering human life by his act."

The overwhelming weight of authority, both textbook and case law, supports the trial court's statement of the applicable principles of law.

Rule   Restatement of Torts, section 85, page 180, states: "The value of human life and limb, not only to the individual concerned but also to society, so outweighs the interest of a possessor of land in excluding from it those whom he is not willing to admit thereto that a possessor of land has . . . no privilege to use force intended or likely to cause death or serious harm against another whom the possessor sees about to enter his premises or meddle with his chattel, unless the intrusion threatens death or serious bodily harm to the occupiers or users of the premises. . . . A possessor of land cannot do indirectly and by a mechanical device that which, were he present, he could not do immediately and in person.". . .

H/D   Affirmed.

NOTES

1.   **Reasonable force.** Both the self-defense privilege and the privilege to defend property similarly allow a defendant to use "reasonable" force. Why,

then, might the amount of force used be found to be excessive in one context but not another?

2. **Home invasion.** Would the case have been different if the trespasser had been entering the defendants' dwelling while the defendant was at home? Might a different common law privilege apply? *See Graves v. Trudell*, 765 N.Y.S.2d 104 (App. Div. 2003).

3. **Warnings and other barriers.** Would you favor a rule that permitted spring guns if there were large, clear warning signs? How about electrified fences or trained attack dogs? In deciding how to structure a rule on this subject, should you consider the possibility that a child or a police officer with a warrant might enter and be killed or grievously wounded if deadly force were permissible?

BROWN V. MARTINEZ

361 P.2d 152 (N.M. 1961)

MOISE, JUSTICE.

[Plaintiff, a 15-year-old boy, and two other boys visited the defendant's garden patch for the purpose of stealing watermelons. On the next night, the boys returned to the defendant's farm for the same purpose. Hearing the boys in the patch, defendant came out of his house with a rifle, and called to the boys to get out. Seeing two boys running toward the southwest corner of the property, defendant fired the gun toward the southeast to scare them. However, plaintiff was in the southeast corner of the property and the bullet struck him in the back of the left leg. The trial court dismissed the plaintiff's claim.]

. . . Our examination of the authorities convinces us that the question of the reasonableness of resort to firearms to prevent a trespass or to prevent commission of an unlawful act not amounting to a felony is one of law for the court, and that such conduct is not excusable.

Dean Prosser in his Handbook of the Law of Torts, states the rule thus:

"The reasonableness of the force used is usually a question of fact for the jury. But as in the case of self-defense, the law has marked out certain limitations. The force used must be of a kind appropriate to the defense of the property. A push in the right direction may be proper where a slap in the face is not. *And, since the law has always placed a higher value upon human safety than upon mere rights in property, it is the accepted rule that there is no privilege to use any force calculated to cause death or serious bodily injury where only the property is threatened.* The defendant may use the force reasonably necessary to overcome resistance and expel the intruder, and if in the process his own safety is threatened, he may defend himself, and even kill if necessary but in the first instance a mere trespass does not justify such an act." (Emphasis ours.)

There is no suggestion in the proof here that appellee in any way felt his safety was threatened. Accordingly, under the facts as proven and found, the appellee acted improperly and is liable for injuries caused in using a gun in the manner he did, and with such unfortunate consequences, in order to drive away trespassers on his property, or to protect his watermelons, or to scare the intruders. . . .

[Reversed and remanded for a determination of damages.]

NOTES

1. **Privileged acts.** Did the defendant in *Brown* perform any unprivileged act? What tort did he intend? Does the law of transferred intent help the plaintiff here?

2. **Recapture of chattels.** You might see *Brown v. Martinez* as more about recapturing chattels (watermelons) than it is about defending property before the defendant has lost possession. Any privilege to regain possession of chattels is quite limited; in general, the owner must resort to the courts for a remedy rather than using self-help. *See* 1 DOBBS, HAYDEN & BUBLICK, THE LAW OF TORTS § 91 (2d ed. 2011). If the defendant acts in "fresh pursuit," however, he is privileged to use a reasonable amount of force to defend possession. The privilege is lost if the defendant is mistaken about the need for force—for example, if he is wrong about the fact that the plaintiff has actually taken the chattel. *Id.*; *see also* RESTATEMENT (SECOND) OF TORTS §§ 100, 103 (1965).

3. **Repossession of land.** Many courts, operating under statutes, invoke similar rules when the owner of land has lost or given up possession of his real property: he must seek recovery in the courts, not by use of force, even by the use of reasonable force. The cases are divided, however, and some permit the owner with right to possession to use force, limited always to reasonable force. *See* 1 DOBBS, HAYDEN & BUBLICK, THE LAW OF TORTS § 90 (2d ed. 2011).

C. ARREST AND DETENTION

GORTAREZ V. SMITTY'S SUPER VALU, INC.
680 P.2d 807 (Ariz. 1984)

FELDMAN, JUSTICE.

[Ernest Gortarez, age 16, and his cousin, Albert Hernandez, age 18, were shopping in defendant's store around 8:00 p.m. While Hernandez was paying for a $22.00 power booster in the automotive department, Gortarez picked up a 59-cent vaporizer used to freshen the air in cars. Gortarez asked the clerk, Robert Sjulestad, if he could pay for it in the front of the store when he finished shopping, and the clerk said yes. Sjulestad had a "hunch" that Gortarez was going to steal the vaporizer, and followed them around the store and watched them as they shopped. Sjulestad never saw them dispose of or pay for the vaporizer, and when they left the store told the assistant manager, Scott Miller, and the security guard, Daniel Gibson, that "[t]hose two guys just ripped us off." Gibson, Miller and two other store employees ran out of the store to catch Gortarez and Hernandez. Gibson confronted Hernandez and began to search him, without saying what he was looking for. Hernandez did not resist and kept denying that he had taken anything. When Gortarez saw Gibson grab Hernandez, he yelled at Gibson to leave his cousin alone. A struggle ensued and Gibson put Gortarez in a choke hold, holding him even after Gortarez told the men that he had left the vaporizer in the store. The two cousins were released after a check-out boy told the store employees that he had found the vaporizer in one of the "catch-all baskets" at an unattended check-out stand in the store. Gortarez required medical treatment for injuries suffered from the choke hold. He and his parents sued Smitty's and Gibson for false arrest and false imprisonment, assault, and battery. At the close of the evidence in a jury trial, the court directed a verdict for the defendants on the false arrest and false imprisonment count. The jury returned a verdict for Gibson on assault and battery. The court of appeals affirmed, and the plaintiffs appealed.]

Historical Perspective

At common law, a private person's privilege to arrest another for a misdemeanor was very limited. . . . Arizona has codified the common law. So far as relevant here, the statute provides that a private person may make an arrest for a misdemeanor when the person to be arrested has committed a misdemeanor amounting to a breach of the peace in the presence of the person making the arrest. Thus, at common law and by statute, the privilege to arrest for misdemeanors without a warrant is limited to those misdemeanors which constitute a breach of the peace. [A mistaken belief that a breach of the peace has been committed does not confer a privilege under this statute.] In the case of misdemeanors such as shoplifting, there is no breach of the peace, and no common law privilege to arrest. [There is a common law privilege to use reasonable force to recapture a chattel "while in fresh pursuit," but the property owner must be correct that the person has stolen the chattel.]

Thus, privileges for misdemeanor arrest traditionally available at common law recognize no privilege to arrest for ordinary "shoplifting." Under this rule a shopkeeper who believed that a customer was shoplifting was placed in an untenable position. Either the shopkeeper allowed the suspect to leave the premises, risking the loss of merchandise, or took the risk of attempting to recapture the chattel by detaining the customer, facing liability for the wrongful detention if the person had not stolen merchandise.

As Prosser noted, shoplifting is a major problem, causing losses that range into millions of dollars each year. There have been a number of decisions which permit a business person for reasonable cause, to detain a customer for investigation. This privilege, however, is narrow; it is "confined to what is reasonably necessary for its limited purpose." . . .

The developing, common law "shopkeeper's privilege" described by Prosser was incorporated into the second Restatement of Torts with the addition of section 120A—Temporary Detention for Investigation:

> One who reasonably believes that another has tortiously taken a chattel upon his premises, or has failed to make cash payment for a chattel purchased or services rendered there, is privileged, without arresting the other, to detain him on the premises for the time necessary for a reasonable investigation of the facts.

Comment (a) states that this section is necessary to protect shopkeepers from the dilemma we have just described. Comment (d) explains that the privilege differs from the privilege to use reasonable force to recapture a chattel, because it protects the shopkeeper who has made a reasonable mistake regarding the guilt of the suspect. As noted in Comment (g), the privilege is one of detention only.

We have not had occasion to pass upon the applicability of the Restatement rule. Instead Arizona has adopted the shopkeeper's privilege by statute, which provides in pertinent part:

> C. A merchant, or his agent or employee, *with reasonable cause, may detain* on the premises *in a reasonable manner and for a reasonable time* any person suspected of shoplifting . . . *for questioning or summoning a law enforcement officer.*
>
> D. Reasonable cause is a defense to a civil or criminal action against a peace officer, merchant or an agent or employee of such merchant for false arrest, false or unlawful imprisonment or wrongful detention.

A.R.S. § 13–1805 (emphasis supplied).

The trial court was evidently of the view that by the terms of subsection D, reasonable cause, alone, was a defense. We disagree; we believe that the statutory shopkeeper's privilege, like that described in the Restatement, involves all of the elements noted in subsection C. Subsections C and D of § 13–1805 must be read together. . . .

To invoke the privilege, therefore, "reasonable cause" is only the threshold requirement. Once reasonable cause is established, there are two further questions regarding the application of the privilege. We must ask whether the purpose of the shopkeeper's action was proper (*i.e.,* detention for questioning or summoning a law enforcement officer). The last question is whether the detention was carried out in a reasonable manner and for a reasonable length of time. If the answer to any of the three questions is negative, then the privilege granted by statute is inapplicable and the actions of the shopkeeper are taken at his peril. . . .

Reasonable Cause

. . . [F]or the purposes of this privilege, reasonable cause and probable cause seem equivalent. Reasonable cause is not dependent on the guilt or innocence of the person, or whether the crime was actually committed. *Tota v. Alexander's,* 314 N.Y.S.2d 93, 95 (1968). In *Tota,* the court stated that one may act on what proves to be an incorrect belief provided the facts show that the belief was reasonable. . . .

In the case at bench, the facts supporting reasonable cause are as follows: the clerk saw Gortarez with the item when he asked if he could pay for it at the front. The clerk followed the two young men through the store, and did not see them either deposit the item or pay for it as they left. Although the question of reasonable cause in the instant case may have been close we defer to the trial court's better opportunity to see and judge the credibility of witnesses and uphold it on the specific finding that conflicting inferences could not be drawn from the facts and that reasonable cause existed as a matter of law.

Purpose of the Detention

The statute provides this privilege for the express and limited purpose of detention for investigation by questioning or summoning a law enforcement officer. A finding of detention for the proper purpose could not have been made as a matter of law on the state of the evidence before the trial judge, since there was no evidence of either questioning or summoning of officers. At best, this was a question for the jury, because although there was no questioning, it is possible that the intent of the employee was to question or call officers.

Reasonableness of the Detention

Assuming there was reasonable cause for the detention, and that the detention was for a proper purpose, the privilege still may not attach if the merchant does not detain in a reasonable manner and for a reasonable time. . . . Comment (h) to § 120A of the Restatement (Second) of Torts states that . . .

> Reasonable force may be used to detain the person; but . . . the use of force intended or likely to cause serious bodily harm is never privileged for the sole purpose of detention to investigate, and it becomes privileged only where the resistance of the other makes it necessary for the actor to use such force in self-defense. In the ordinary case, the use of any force at all will not be privileged until the other has been requested to remain; and it is only where there

is not time for such a request, or it would obviously be futile, that force is justified.

The Arizona statute is essentially a codification of the common law shopkeeper's privilege. The limitations on the use of force are obviously wise. We hold that the principle quoted is applicable to our statutory requirement that the detention be carried out in a "reasonable manner."

Under the restrictions given above, there was a question whether the use of force in the search of Hernandez, and, more importantly, in the restraint of Gortarez, was reasonable. There was no request that the two young men remain. No inquiry was made with regard to whether Hernandez had the vaporizer. Gibson testified that Hernandez gave no indication of resistance and made no attempt to escape. The possible theft of a 59-cent item hardly warrants apprehension that the two were armed or dangerous. There was, arguably, time to make a request to remain before Gibson seized Hernandez and began searching him. Also, there is no indication that such a request would *obviously* have been futile. The evidence adduced probably would have supported a finding that the manner of detention was unreasonable as a matter of law. At best, there was a question of fact; there was no support for the court's presumptive finding that as a matter of law the detention was performed reasonably.

[The court erred in its findings on the reasonableness of both the purpose and the manner of detention.] This requires reversal and retrial. At the new trial evidence on the three issues should be measured against the principles set forth in this opinion. . . .

NOTES

1.   **The common law rule and statutes.** Many states, such as Arizona, have adopted statutes that codify the merchant's common law privilege as summarized in the Restatement Second of Torts § 120A, quoted in *Gortarez*. *See, e.g.*, ALA. CODE § 15–10–14; GA. CODE ANN. § 51–7–60. Thus whether under the common law or under a statute, a merchant's privilege to detain a suspected shoplifter turns on the reasonableness of the merchant's suspicion, as well as the time and manner of detention. *See, e.g.*, *Barkley v. McKeever Enters., Inc.*, 456 S.W.3d 829 (Mo. 2015) (en banc) (applying statute: merchant is protected from civil and criminal liability where the detention was be carried out in a reasonable manner and for a reasonable time). Both the shopkeeper's reasonable belief that the plaintiff has engaged in shoplifting and the reasonableness of the time and manner of the detention are jury questions. *See Carnegay v. WalMart Stores, Inc.*, 839 S.E.2d 176 (Ga.App.2020) (reversing summary judgment for merchant on false imprisonment claim and remanding). Do flexible "reasonableness" standards provide sufficient guidance or should statutes state more specifically what a shopkeeper may or may not do? Do flexible standards strike a good balance between the rights of

the shopkeeper and the rights of the suspected shoplifter, or do they leave too many cases for the jury?

2. **Mistake.** Under the common law rule and most statutes, the shopkeeper is privileged to act even if reasonably mistaken about the fact that the plaintiff has taken goods without paying. *See, e.g., Dillard Dep't Stores, Inc. v. Silva,* 148 S.W.3d 370 (Tex. 2004). A few states require the shopkeeper to be correct—that is, they do not allow the shopkeeper to utilize this privilege unless the plaintiff did actually take the goods in question. Would this be a better rule? *See Great Atl. & Pac. Tea Co. v. Paul,* 261 A.2d 731 (Md. 1970) (refusing to adopt the Restatement's rule on reasonable mistake); *cf. Cruz v. Johnson,* 823 A.2d 1157 (R.I. 2003) (shopkeeper's privilege statute requires that the store guard actually observe shoplifting). If Arizona had such a "no mistake" rule in place with regard to shoplifting, how might it have changed the analysis in *Gortarez*?

3. **Reasonable manner of detention.** The *Gortarez* court, in discussing the reasonableness of the manner of detention, makes note of the fact that the item believed stolen was of little value (a 59-cent vaporizer). How might the analysis differ if the item had been worth, say, $5,000? Even if the item believed stolen had been valuable, what other facts might lead a jury to conclude that the manner of the detention in *Gortarez* was unreasonable?

4. **Inducing another person to detain.** A person who reports a suspected crime (shoplifting, for example), resulting in another person's detention, may also be sued for false imprisonment, but is granted a privilege to make such a report to appropriate authorities if he acted in good faith and made no knowing, malicious, or false statements. *See Highfill v. Hale,* 186 S.W.3d 277 (Mo. 2006).

5. **A merchant's recapture of chattels.** The common law grants no special privilege to merchants to recapture chattels once possession has been lost; the rules we saw in the Notes after *Brown v. Martinez,* above, apply to merchants as well. Thus if a thief runs out of a store with a stolen item, the store's guard is privileged to recapture it if he does so immediately or in fresh pursuit and uses a reasonable amount of force. Once possession has been lost, however, the detective cannot forcibly recapture it from the thief a week later. The store instead will be forced to sue or to invoke criminal processes. With respect to consumer goods, where the seller seeks to repossess because of the buyer's default, the law forbids the seller from using physical force at all. 1 DOBBS, HAYDEN & BUBLICK, THE LAW OF TORTS § 91 (2d ed. 2011).

6. **Statutory variation: pursuit off the premises.** In *Peters v. Menard, Inc.,* 589 N.W.2d 395 (Wis. 1999), the court applied a statute to extend the shopkeeper's privilege to allow merchants to follow suspected shoplifters off the premises in order to detain them, as long as the merchant had reasonable cause to suspect shoplifting, and both the manner and the length of time of the detention were reasonable. The court said that a contrary rule "would invite shoplifters to flee and increase the risk of harm to merchants and innocent customers." In that case, the thief stole a drill from the defendant's

hardware store, and was pursued for about seven minutes by the store's security guard into a flooded river, where he drowned.

7. **Using force to detain trespassers.** What if a landowner threatens or uses force and detains a trespasser? In *Whitten v. Cox,* 799 So.2d 1 (Miss. 2000), the three plaintiffs drove a pickup truck onto land occupied legally by the defendant Whitten, who was a municipal judge. The plaintiffs were crossing Whitten's land to get to land leased by one of their relatives. Whitten shouted for the truck to stop. When it did not, he fired several shots from a .45 caliber handgun, either into the air or at the truck. At one point he shot out one of the back tires and ordered the three men to get out. Whitten was in the presence of other men who were all armed with loaded assault rifles. Whitten told all three plaintiffs that they were under arrest for trespassing and handcuffed one of them, Cox. According to Cox, Whitten asked the two other plaintiffs whether they thought Cox could swim in the nearby bayou with those handcuffs on. Cox also said that Whitten pulled the bill of his cap down over his eyes and knocked his sunglasses off. Whitten and his companions escorted the three plaintiffs back to a camp Whitten occupied, and Whitten unsuccessfully tried to reach the Sheriff. At this point Whitten recognized Cox as the brother of someone who leased neighboring property, and the plaintiffs were freed. The plaintiffs sued Whitten for battery, assault and false imprisonment. Whitten claimed he asserted a valid privilege to arrest and detain them as trespassers. The case went to a jury. According to the court, "If the force used in the arrest of a suspected misdemeanant [and trespassing is a misdemeanor] is unreasonable and excessive, this may render the arrest and detention invalid." Was Whitten's use of force to stop the trespassers reasonable? Was his detention of them after he had stopped them reasonable?

D. DISCIPLINE

Where children are permitted to sue parents for torts, parents still enjoy a privilege to discipline, and to use force and confinement to do so. The limits of this force are ill-defined. The Restatement says parents may use reasonable force as they reasonably believe necessary. *See* RESTATEMENT (SECOND) OF TORTS § 147 (1965); 1 DOBBS, BUBLICK & HAYDEN, THE LAW OF TORTS § 104 (2d ed. 2011). Courts have more commonly articulated standards for appropriate discipline in the context of the criminal law. *See, e.g., Hart v. State,* 93 N.E.3d 803 (Ind. Ct. App. 2018) (affirming father's conviction for battery against child where jury could conclude that father "neither had a reasonable belief that force was necessary nor was the force used reasonable"); *see also* RESTATEMENT OF CHILDREN AND THE LAW § 3.24 (Tent. Draft No. 1, 2018) (parents privileged to use reasonable corporal punishment; rule applicable to criminal and child-custody proceedings).

In *Commonwealth v. Dorvil,* 32 N.E.3d 861 (Mass. 2015), the Massachusetts Supreme Judicial Court wrote: "we hold that a parent or guardian may not be subjected to criminal liability for the use of force against a minor child under the care and supervision of the parent or guardian, provided that (1) the force used against the minor child is reasonable; (2) the force is reasonably related to the purpose of safeguarding or promoting the welfare of the minor, including the prevention or punishment of the minor's misconduct; and (3) the force used neither causes, nor creates a substantial risk of causing, physical harm (beyond fleeting pain or minor, transient marks), gross degradation, or severe mental distress."

Those who are in charge of someone else's children also enjoy a similar disciplinary privilege. Teachers and school bus drivers are the most obvious examples. However, it may be that the teacher would not enjoy the same latitude for punishment that courts would recognize in a parent. Suppose a child is spanked by her parent for misbehavior and again by her teacher for additional misbehavior. Apart from local school board regulations affecting corporal punishment, what factors should a court consider in determining whether either the parent or the teacher is liable in tort?

What if "to calm him down" a teacher holds down on the floor a twelve-year-old child who has Asperger's syndrome? What if an 8-year-old with attention deficit disorder and mild mental retardation is repeatedly locked in a "seclusion room" by herself when she misbehaves at school? Some false imprisonment lawsuits have arisen from those sorts of responses.

E. OBSERVING PRIVILEGES

Many common law privileges have the effect of resolving the issues in the case by matter of reasonableness and degree. In self-defense, the issue is frequently whether the defendant reasonably believed that defense was necessary and then whether he used the amount of force reasonable to cope with the apparent threat. In the case of schoolroom punishment, teachers, being privileged to inflict some punishment, are liable only if they go too far. In false imprisonment cases a defendant might be privileged to detain for investigation for a short time, but not for long. All such cases involve matters of reasonableness and hence matters of degree.

Notice how those cases differ from cases in which a defendant commits a "kissing battery"—he kissed the plaintiff, a stranger, or touched the plaintiff in a private place. This is an offensive battery and it is no defense to say the touching did not last long, that the force used was minimal, or that the injury was not great. Thus in common law actions, there are cases in which "degree" is not important, and other cases in which, because the issue of privilege is injected, degree becomes quite significant.

§ 2. THE SPECIAL CASE OF CONSENT

WULF V. KUNNATH
827 N.W.2d 248 (Neb. 2013)

CASSEL, J. . . .

During the noon hour on October 23, 2007, nurses Susan C. Wulf, Paula Kehm, and Chelsea Crocker were seated at their desks in the nurse's workroom, when Sharad Kunnath, M.D., and Crystal Knight, M.D., joined them. They joked around, and the atmosphere was lighthearted. The group discussed upcoming snow removal that might occur while Kunnath was out of the country, and Wulf commented that it would be funny to see Kunnath using a snowblower. According to Kunnath, he said, "Hey, [Wulf], don't make fun of me," and tapped Wulf on the nape of her neck. He intended to make the contact at issue, but he did not intend to hurt Wulf. Wulf described the contact as "a strike on the back of [her] neck." Knight testified that Kunnath touched Wulf in the middle of the back of the head with the palm of his hand in "a playful, joking manner . . . something that you would do to a friend or a relative if they are making fun of you." Crocker testified that Kunnath "playfully tapped [Wulf] on the back of the neck." The laughing and joking in the workroom continued for a few more minutes.

Wulf's reaction to the contact is in dispute. She testified that her head moved forward rapidly a significant distance, that she dropped the telephone she was holding, and that she said, "Oh, my God, that hurt." She immediately felt pain in the back of her head and neck and suffered nausea, dizziness, and blurred vision. Kehm also recalled Wulf saying, "Ow, that hurt." [Knight, Kunnath and Crocker did not recall Wulf making any comments and did not observe anything leading them to believe that she had been injured.]

Within minutes of the incident, Wulf began an initial assessment on a patient, but she began to feel dizzy and nauseated. As she left the patient's room, she encountered nurse Kathy Krussel, who saw Wulf crying and rubbing her neck. Wulf told Krussel that Kunnath hit her in the neck. Krussel took Wulf into a treatment room, and Wulf reported that her neck hurt, that she had pain going down her arm, that she was nauseated, and that she was seeing spots. Kehm brought Wulf some ice, which Wulf placed on the back of her neck. Wulf was later moved out of the treatment room to a nurse practitioner's office, where she remained for the rest of the day. As Wulf walked to her car, she got more nauseated and felt as if she were going to pass out. Wulf drove herself to an emergency room.

Wulf, who was 58 years old at the time of trial, testified that in her career, she had never been struck in a similar manner. In her 30 years as a nurse, she had never seen a doctor "swat" somebody in the back of the head, never felt that she needed to announce to doctors that she did not want to be swatted in the back of the head, and never believed that she had consented to a doctor's swatting her on the back of the head by not saying anything. Although Krussel did not recall seeing anybody "thump" or "tap" others at the office, she testified that she would "[p]robably not" find it strange if that occurred. The office atmosphere was that of a close-knit group, who joked and teased one another. Wulf testified that the group had a familial—like relationship. Kunnath testified that he and Wulf had a very collegial and close relationship, that Wulf was like a mother to him, and that they would joke and tease. Wulf testified that prior to the incident, Kunnath had "[t]hump[ed]" her on two or three occasions while walking in the hallway. She said that they were "good-natured" thumps, as a brother would do to a sister. Wulf never complained about the thumping, never asked Kunnath not to do it again, and did not find it to be offensive conduct.

Wulf saw her physician, Anthony L. Hatcher, M.D., approximately 1 week after the incident. At that time, Wulf complained of neck pain and pain radiating down her right arm. Wulf told Hatcher that she was struck in the back of the head, but she did not say how hard she was hit. Based on the history that Wulf provided Hatcher, he opined that "her pain was related to the injury that occurred." Upon Hatcher's referral, Wulf saw Michael C.H. Longley, M.D., an orthopedic spine surgeon, on May 8, 2008, for her complaints of neck and right arm pain. Wulf informed Longley that she received a "substantial blow" to the back of the head. Longley testified that Wulf had "a tendency to magnify symptoms and exaggerate complaints." Ultimately, Wulf underwent two surgeries. When Longley was asked whether he believed it was more likely true that Wulf's pain was a result of being struck in October 2007, he answered that precise etiology for Wulf's ongoing symptoms was unclear. But he testified that the condition of the disk degeneration and spinal stenosis was clearly preexistent, so the condition itself was not caused by the October 2007 incident. . . .

At the close of all evidence, Wulf moved for a directed verdict on the issues of battery and injury. The district court overruled the motion. The jury subsequently returned a verdict for Kunnath, and the court entered judgment accordingly. Wulf timely appeals. . . .

ANALYSIS

. . . It is undisputed that Kunnath touched Wulf and that he intended to do so. Thus, Wulf contends that the district court should have directed a verdict in her favor on the issue of battery and that the court should have instructed the jury that a battery occurred, rather than allowing the jury to determine the issue. We disagree. . . .

In Nebraska, the intentional tort of "battery" is defined as an actual infliction of an unconsented injury upon or unconsented contact with another. Consent ordinarily bars recovery, because it "goes to negative the existence of any tort in the first instance." W. Page Keeton et al., Prosser and Keeton on the Law of Torts § 18 at 112 (5th ed.1984). It does so by destroying the wrongfulness of the conduct between the consenting parties. Consent is willingness in fact for conduct to occur. It may be manifested by action or inaction and need not be communicated to the actor. Apparent consent—words or conduct reasonably understood by another to be intended as consent—is as effective as consent in fact. . . .

Viewed in the light most favorable to Kunnath, the record contains evidence to demonstrate that Wulf consented to the contact by Kunnath. "The time and place, and the circumstances under which the act is done, will necessarily affect its unpermitted character, and so will the relations between the parties." Keeton et al., § 9 at 42. Evidence established that the contact occurred over the noon hour while doctors and nurses were joking around. Further, Kunnath and Wulf had a familial-like relationship. Such evidence tends to weaken Wulf's claim that the contact was nonconsensual. Moreover, "[s]ilence and inaction may manifest consent where a reasonable person would speak if he objected." *Id.*, § 18 at 113. Evidence showed that Kunnath had "thumped" Wulf on prior occasions at work—contact which Wulf testified was not offensive to her—and that Wulf never objected to the thumps by Kunnath. Further, Wulf never asked Kunnath not to thump her. "It is only when notice is given that all such conduct will no longer be tolerated that the defendant is no longer free to assume consent." *Id.* at 114. Based upon this evidence, reasonable minds could conclude that Wulf consented to Kunnath's contact and, thus, that no battery occurred. Accordingly, the district court did not err by denying Wulf's motion for directed verdict or by submitting the issue of battery to the jury, and the jury's verdict was not clearly wrong. . . .

AFFIRMED.

NOTES

1. **Actual vs. apparent consent.** "Actual consent to an act is a subjective willingness for the act to occur. Apparent consent is conduct, including words, that are reasonably understood by another as a reflection of consent. Either actual or apparent consent is effective to relieve the actor of responsibility for the acts addressed." DOBBS, HAYDEN & BUBLICK, HORNBOOK ON TORTS § 8.2, at 165 (2d ed. 2016). Do you agree with the court that reasonable minds could have concluded that Wulf consented to Kunnath's contact? Would the consent at issue be actual or apparent consent? What facts can you marshal to support your position?

2. **Silence as consent.** In the case of consent to sexual contact, jurisdictions have adopted different standards. "The view that 'NO means NO' is generally understood as requiring criminal liability, tort liability, or student disciplinary sanctions when an actor persists in initiating sexual intercourse

despite the actor's partner expressing objection to that conduct by words or conduct." KENNETH W. SIMONS, ACTUAL, APPARENT, HYPOTHETICAL, AND IMPLIED-IN-LAW CONSENT IN TORT LAW (forthcoming 2022). Other jurisdictions require affirmative consent, sometimes referred to by the standard "Only YES means YES." "This view is usually taken to mean that a person does not give legally effective consent to sexual intercourse unless the person expresses willingness to engage in intercourse (either by words or conduct), even if the person has given legally effective consent to lesser sexual intimacy during the same encounter with the actor. Such a standard gives protection to potential victims who express neither willingness nor unwillingness to engage in sexual intercourse." *Id.* Does *Wulf* imply that outside the context of sexual contact, silence can sometimes be construed as consent to contact?

3.   **Consent and battery: single vs. dual intent.** Recall that some jurisdictions require a plaintiff to prove only an intent to touch in order to satisfy the intent element of battery, whereas others require proof of both an intent to touch and an intent that the touching be harmful or offensive. If the defendant reasonably believed that the plaintiff consented to the touching at issue, how would defendant's argument for consent play out under both the single-intent and the dual-intent battery approaches? For an in-depth analysis of this question, see Nancy J. Moore, *Intent and Consent in the Tort of Battery: Confusion and Controversy*, 61 AM. U. L. REV. 1585 (2012). *See also Martin-McFarlane v. City of Philadelphia*, 299 F.Supp.3d 658 (E.D. Pa. 2017) ("Under Pennsylvania law, battery is defined as an intentional 'harmful or offensive contact with the person of another.' The fact that contact occurs without consent is sufficient to establish that it is offensive, and no intent to harm the plaintiff need be established.").

4.   **Apparent consent as lack of fault by the defendant.** Why should the plaintiff be barred from recovery on the basis of consent when plaintiff has not actually consented? In the usual case, the main reason is that the defendant who acts on a reasonable understanding of appearances is simply not a wrongdoer. The consent does not relieve the defendant of liability for a tort; defendant is simply not a tortfeasor at all. *See City of Lincoln v. County of Lancaster*, 898 N.W.2d 374 (Neb. 2017) (deputy sheriff "made physical contact" with a police officer friend; unbeknownst to the deputy, the police officer had recently undergone surgery on the shoulder). Does the addition of apparent consent to single intent battery effectively render it the same as dual intent battery? RESTATEMENT (THIRD) OF TORTS: INTENTIONAL TORTS TO PERSONS § 16 (Tent. Draft No. 4, 2019) ("Apparent consent exists if the actor reasonably believes that the other person actually consents to the conduct, without regard to whether the person does actually consent.").

5.   **Consent to the act.** Certainly, Wulf did not consent to a serious neck injury, or the aggravation of a serious neck injury. Nor could Kunnath have reasonably understood that she was consenting to such harm. Why doesn't Wulf's lack of consent to the actual harm matter? As one court put it, "Where the plaintiff consented to the battery itself, the consent extends to ordinary consequences stemming from it." *Janelsins v. Button*, 648 A.2d 1039 (Md. Ct.

Spec. App. 1994). Thus "the defendant is not liable for an intentional tort so long as his acts are those consented to, even if harmful consequences result. . . . Put differently, a consent is not normally interpreted to contain the implicit condition, 'I consent provided I am not hurt.'" DOBBS, HAYDEN & BUBLICK, HORNBOOK ON TORTS § 8.4, at 170 (2d ed. 2016).

6. **Context.** How would the analysis in differ, if at all, if Wulf had been a newly hired employee who did not know that Kunnath and her other co-employees had engaged in this kind of physical horseplay with each other for years without objection?

7. **Substantially different conduct.** Imagine that the employees described in *Wulf* were actually willing to allow colleagues to play harmless pranks on them, including light slaps on the head. Would consent to such contacts bar a claim for battery if one employee poured hot coffee over another employee's head "in jest?" The rule is that consent "extends to conduct that is not substantially different in nature from the conduct that the person is willing to permit." RESTATEMENT (THIRD) OF TORTS: INTENTIONAL TORTS TO PERSONS § 14(a) (Tent. Draft No. 4, 2019). The comment to this Restatement Third section gives the example of a handshake at a business meeting. If the defendant shakes plaintiff's hand "with somewhat more force than usual," consent to the act of shaking hands would bar a battery claim. But where the defendant "squeezes plaintiff's hand with such extraordinary force as to break plaintiff's hand, plaintiff's actual consent to a normal handshake does not preclude [defendant's] liability for battery." *Id.*, cmt. *b.*

8. **Presumed consent.** The newest Restatement creates a distinct third category of consent. In addition to actual and apparent consent the Restatement would add "presumed" consent, which would exist "if (1) under prevailing social norms, the actor is justified in engaging in the conduct in the absence of the other person's actual or apparent consent, and (2) the actor has no reason to believe that the person would not have actually consented to the conduct if the actor had requested the person's consent." RESTATEMENT (THIRD) OF TORTS: INTENTIONAL TORTS TO PERSONS § 16 (b) (Tent. Draft No. 4, 2019). The quintessential example would be a passenger on a bus pushing past other passengers in order to get to a seat. Is "presumed consent" about consent at all, or a sort of social privilege to engage in minor, unobjected to, customary touchings?

9. **Hypotheticals.** Would consent exist in any of the following scenarios?

(a) You are picnicking by a stream with a friend when the friend suddenly slaps you firmly on the back to kill a mosquito.

(b) You are at the movie theater and the person in front of you is talking on a cell phone as the movie starts. Annoyed, you reach out and tap the person on the shoulder and ask that the caller stop talking. The caller is subjectively offended and says so. *Cf.*

RESTATEMENT (THIRD) OF TORTS: INTENTIONAL TORTS TO PERSONS § 16, cmt. d, illus. 6 (Tent. Draft No. 4, 2019).

(c)   You play basketball in an amateur league sponsored by your local YMCA. A player on your team, whom you don't know well, makes an outstanding play, and you congratulate the other player with a gentle slap on the bottom, which is a customary act among basketball players. But unknown to you, the other player finds the contact extremely offensive. *See id.*, illus. 7.

(d)   Same facts as above, but you know that the player you slapped finds a gentle slap to the bottom extremely offensive. *See id.*, illus. 11.

10.   **Consent and false imprisonment.** Consent commonly arises as an issue in cases where a plaintiff has been detained for suspected shoplifting and sues for false imprisonment. *See* Chapter 3 § 3. If the plaintiff is asked to follow a store guard into a room and is interrogated by store employees, can plaintiff sue for false imprisonment if plaintiff does not protest? What if the customer agrees at first, but upon realizing why the customer is being asked to follow the guard, says he does not want to go anywhere because he has done nothing wrong? Does his initial consent to follow the guard carry through to the end of the detention?

———————

ROBINS V. HARRIS, 769 N.E.2d 586 (Ind. 2002). As described by the appellate court, in *Robins v. Harris,* 740 N.E.2d 914 (Ind. Ct. App. 2000), plaintiff Tammy Robins was a female inmate at a county jail and defendant Michael Soules was a new corrections officer on the third shift. According to Soules, when he met Robins she and another inmate, Martha Custer, flashed him by lifting up their shirts and exposing their breasts. Later that evening, Soules ordered a lock down, requiring all inmates to stay in their cells. Soules first summoned Custer out of her cell and upon her return then summoned Robins. He grabbed Robins by the arm and brought her into the shower room where she performed fellatio on him. Robins filed suit, alleging battery. Soules originally denied the allegations but two days later admitted to the sexual contact and resigned his position. He subsequently pled guilty to misdemeanor official misconduct in exchange for dismissal of a felony charge. In the tort action, Soules claimed he was not liable and raised an affirmative defense of consent. The court of appeals held that several parties were potentially subject to liability and that the inmate's alleged consent to the sexual contact was no defense. In the Indiana Supreme Court, "affirmed except as to the availability of the consent defense to the claim of battery," on which point the majority issued no opinion.

SULLIVAN, J., dissenting. "[T]he Court of Appeals said: 'We also note that consent is not available as a defense to Robins's sexual assault claim.

Under I.C. § 35–44–1–5(b), a [jailer] may not claim consent as a defense for sexual misconduct with a detainee. Given Robins's general lack of autonomy as an inmate, it would be incongruous to withhold the defense of consent in the criminal context but to allow Soules the defense in a civil claim.' I agree with this analysis. Our Legislature has made a public policy determination that the position of authority a jailer holds over a prisoner dictates that there be no exception for consent in our criminal law to the rule against sexual contact between jailer and prisoner. Our state's civil law should further the public policy objective the Legislature has adopted in the criminal context."

NOTES

1. **Duress or coercion.** Consent will not be given effect where it was obtained by duress or coercion that is intended to and does prevent the plaintiff from exercising free choice. DOBBS, HAYDEN & BUBLICK, HORNBOOK ON TORTS § 8.9 (2d ed. 2016). Thus a plaintiff who agrees to be sterilized only after being threatened that her children will be taken away from her if she does not has not given effective consent to the procedure. See *Vaughn v. Ruoff*, 253 F.3d 1124 (8th Cir. 2001).

2. **Relationship between the parties.** The power relationship between the parties may affect the analysis of whether the plaintiff consented to the defendant's conduct. For example, where the plaintiff is in jail, and the defendant a jailer, an issue is likely to arise as to whether the defendant could reasonably believe that the plaintiff was consenting to sexual contact. *See, e.g., Grager v. Schudar*, 770 N.W.2d 692 (N.D. 2009) ("[W]hen consent to a sexual act by a person in official custody or detained in a treatment facility, prison, or other institution is at issue in a situation where the actor has supervisory authority, disciplinary control or care over the detained person, the jury must be instructed that it must consider all of the factors limiting the detained person's ability to control the situation or to give consent in deciding whether the detained person effectively consented to the sexual act."). Should courts leave this question to juries, or was Justice Sullivan right in his dissenting opinion in *Robins* that a per se rule forbidding the consent defense in this context would represent better policy?

3. **Other power imbalances.** What about relationships that involve other power imbalances? Should employers be permitted to claim that an employee who is dependent for a job, wage increase, or promotion consented to sexual intercourse? *Reavis v. Slominski*, 551 N.W.2d 528 (Neb. 1996) (employer-employee). Federal statutes against employment discrimination can also come into play in these situations. Some state statutes forbid all sexual contact between mental health professionals and their patients. Under these statutes, the patient's consent is not legally effective to bar a claim against the therapist. *See Flores v. Santiago*, 986 N.E.2d 1216 (Ill. App. Ct. 2013). Would the situation be similar or different with a religious counselor? *Pelitire v. Rinker*, 270 So.3d 817 (La. App. 2019) (priest-parishioner; fact issue regarding

consent); *Wende C. v. United Methodist Church*, 827 N.E.2d 265 (N.Y. 2005) (pastor-parishioner).

———————

HUNT V. ZUFFA LLC, 361 F.Supp.3d 992 (D. Nev. 2019). Mixed martial arts fighter brought claim of battery against his competitor for use of banned performance enhancing drugs. The plaintiff, Hunt, believed that he would have avoided injury if not for the doping. *Held*, dismissed. "[I]t is well established that one who enters into a sport, game or contest may be taken to consent to physical contacts consistent with the understood rules of the game. Thus, the boxer who steps into the ring consents to his opponent's jabs, and likewise, Hunt implicitly consented to [defendant] Lesnar's blows. Hunt counters that his fight with Lesnar exceeded the scope of his consent, which he contends didn't extend to fighting a doping fighter. But the fact that Lesnar allegedly violated the rules of the sport does not automatically negate Hunt's consent. . . . The fact that Lesnar was allegedly doping violated the bout rules established by [mixed martial arts associations] but does not alone establish that his conduct exceeded the ordinary range of activity in an MMA fight. As Hunt's own allegations demonstrate, doping is an unfortunately common issue in MMA and was a risk he perceived. And although he argues that doping empowered Lesnar to move faster and hit harder, Hunt doesn't allege that Lesnar's conduct during the bout was somehow atypical—such as throwing Hunt out of the octagon or using "packed gloves" or a weapon. Nor does Hunt claim that his injuries exceeded those typical of an MMA bout. Accordingly, I find that Hunt consented to his fight with Lesnar, which precludes civil-battery liability."

NOTES

1.   **Scope of consent.** Consent does not bar a plaintiff's claim for any tortious conduct that is outside the scope of the plaintiff's consent. Why was the defendant Lesnar's conduct in *Hunt* not outside the scope of the plaintiff's consent? How did the court characterize the scope of plaintiff's consent? Do you agree with that characterization?

2.   **Consent procured by fraud.** Courts recognize that, in a general way, consent procured by fraud is not valid. Fraud is generally defined as a false representation of material fact designed to induce the plaintiff's reliance. If the plaintiff's consent was based on a mistake about a material fact concerning the nature of the transaction or conduct at issue, and the defendant was or should have been aware that the plaintiff was mistaken, any such consent will not be given legal effect. DOBBS, HAYDEN & BUBLICK, HORNBOOK ON TORTS § 8.8 (2d ed. 2016). Eating a chocolate from a box of poisoned candy seems like a mistake about the nature and quality of the contact. *See* 1 DOBBS, HAYDEN & BUBLICK, THE LAW OF TORTS § 111 (2d ed. 2011). Similarly, if a plaintiff agrees to a manipulation of her body based on the defendant's

representation that it is for medical purposes when it is in fact only for the defendant's sexual gratification, consent will not bar a tort claim against the defendant. See *Bartell v. State*, 82 N.W. 142 (Wis. 1900).

3.   **STIs.** Where defendants know that they have sexually transmitted infections but neither warn sexual partners nor provide protection, several cases have imposed liability. *E.g., Johnson v. Jones*, 344 P.3d 89 (Or. Ct. App. 2015) (genital herpes not revealed; consent obtained by material nondisclosure is not consent at all). Could substantial certainty of an STI be enough? See *Doe v. Johnson,* 817 F.Supp. 1382 (W.D. Mich. 1993) (defendant claimed to have had unprotected sex with more than 2,000 partners). Is high-risk sexual activity always enough to establish constructive knowledge? *Kohl v. Kohl,* 149 So.3d 137 (Fla. Dist. Ct. App. 2014) (no; husband's extramarital relations with prostitutes is not enough to establish actual or constructive knowledge).

4.   **Material facts?** What misrepresentations count as fraudulent so as to vitiate consent? In *Martinez v. Republic of Cuba*, 221 F.Supp.3d 276, 286 (N.D.N.Y. 2016), defendant married and had sex with the plaintiff while acting within the scope of his employment as a Cuban spy. Plaintiff sued Cuba claiming that this was battery under Florida law on the basis that she would not have agreed to have sexual intercourse with defendant if she had known that he was a Cuban spy. The state trial court agreed that this was a battery and not barred by consent, and entered a default judgment in plaintiff's favor. Plaintiff then filed an action in federal court seeking to enforce the judgment against Cuba under a federal statute allowing certain tort claims against foreign sovereigns. The federal district court held that the state trial court's interpretation of battery law was a "stretch," and thus there was no subject-matter jurisdiction over Cuba in American courts. Florida cases involving consent to sex procured by fraud or concealment, it said, were distinguishable. "Unlike the plaintiffs in [those cases], here [plaintiff] did not contract a sexually transmitted disease or suffer any kind of physical injury as a result of the alleged battery. The Florida state court cited no authority remotely supporting the view that deception about one's occupation can vitiate consent to sexual intercourse. . . . This is in marked contrast to the state of the law regarding battery claims arising out of the knowing transmission of sexually transmitted diseases to individuals who are unaware of their partner's condition." Do you agree with the Florida state court or the later federal court?

5.   **Revocation of consent.** Subject only to the slightest qualification, the plaintiff can revoke consent at any time by communicating the revocation to the defendant. Thus a landowner who has consented to another person's presence on the land could order the person to leave; a visitor who does not leave becomes a trespasser. A person who consents to intimate contact with another can have a change of heart and revoke consent; if that is communicated to the other person, any further contact would become tortious. *See* 1 DOBBS, HAYDEN & BUBLICK, THE LAW OF TORTS § 108.

6.   **Consent to crime.** When the plaintiff is injured during an illegal activity in which plaintiff has agreed to participate (such as an illegal boxing

match), courts have struggled to find a consistent approach to the issue of consent. Some have held consent to a crime is invalid, so that the tort claim can proceed. Others have said that that the plaintiff's consent bars the tort claim. The Restatement's rule is that the plaintiff's consent is a bar just as in any other case. RESTATEMENT (THIRD) OF TORTS: INTENTIONAL TORTS TO PERSONS § 14 (Tent. Draft No. 4, 2019)). However, if the statute makes the conduct illegal in order to protect the plaintiff from her own consent, as might be the case with a statutory rape law for example, the plaintiff's consent should not bar her claim. *Id.* Suppose a statute makes it unlawful to hire a child under 15 for work near industrial machinery. Should the child's consent be a bar? *See id*; 1 DOBBS, HAYDEN & BUBLICK, THE LAW OF TORTS § 116 (2d ed. 2011).

KAPLAN V. MAMELAK, 162 Cal.App.4th 637 (2008). A patient sued his doctor for medical malpractice and battery, claiming that the doctor operated on the wrong herniated disks in his back. The trial court granted the doctor's demurrer to the battery claim, and the jury found for the doctor on the malpractice claim. *Held*, reversed and remanded. A doctor who operates on a patient without that patient's consent commits a battery. Here the doctor "may have committed battery by operating on appellant's T6–7 and T7–8 disks when he did not have permission to operate on any disk other than T8–9." While "the law will deem a patient to have consented to a touching that, although not literally covered by the patient's express consent, involves complications inherent to the procedure, . . . a battery occurs if the physician performs a 'substantially different treatment' from that covered by the patient's expressed consent." These issues are for the jury, making the grant of demurrer improper.

NOTES

1. **Scope of consent in "medical battery" cases.** Many cases of "medical battery"—claims of battery made against doctors who performed a medical procedure on the plaintiff—involve allegations that the doctor exceeded the scope of the patient's consent. For example, in *Duncan v. Scottsdale Medical Imaging, Ltd.*, 70 P.3d 435 (Ariz. 2003), a patient who was about to get a magnetic resonance imaging (MRI) exam from the defendant needed a painkiller as part of that procedure. Duncan, the patient, allegedly told the nurse that she would accept only demerol or morphine, and the nurse assured her that only one of those particular drugs would be administered. On the day of the MRI, however, another nurse informed Duncan that she would be receiving a synthetic drug that was similar to demerol and morphine. Duncan objected strenuously and urged the nurse to call her doctor. After the nurse assured her "that the medication had been changed to morphine" Duncan finally agreed to the procedure. In fact, Duncan was injected with the synthetic drug, and suffered serious complications including vocal cord dysfunction, vomiting, severe headache, and post-traumatic stress syndrome.

Duncan sued for battery. Held, Duncan's "general authorization of an injection does not defeat her battery claim because her consent was limited to certain drugs. . . . The relevant inquiry here is not whether the patient consented to an injection; the issue is whether the patient consented to receive the specific drug that was administered."

What about a hospital patient who consents to a blood draw without being told that it was for a non-medical law-enforcement purpose? *See O'Brien v. Synnott*, 72 A.3d 331 (Vt. 2013). What if the plaintiff consented to an operation by Dr. A, but it was performed by Dr. B? *See Vitale v. Henchey*, 24 S.W.3d 651 (Ky. 2000); *Meyers v. Epstein*, 232 F.Supp.2d 192 (S.D.N.Y. 2002).

2. **The emergency exception.** The ordinary rule—that it is battery when a doctor treats a patient without the patient's consent, or in excess of the scope of a patient's consent—may not apply when the doctor must act in an emergency and obtaining consent is not possible. *See, e.g., Kennedy v. Parrott*, 90 S.E.2d 754 (N.C. 1956) (finding implied consent for a doctor to "extend the operation to remedy any abnormal or diseased condition in the area of the original incision" when the patient is incapable of giving consent and no one else with authority to consent is available). The Restatement Third of Torts generally provides: "If an actor engages in otherwise tortious intentional conduct for the purpose of preventing or reducing a risk to the life or health of another, the actor is not liable to the other," assuming reasonable belief in the need for treatment and no knowledge that plaintiff does not consent. RESTATEMENT (THIRD) OF TORTS: INTENTIONAL TORTS TO PERSONS § 17 (Tent. Draft No. 6, 2021).

3. **Incapacity to consent: minors.** Minors as a class are often thought to lack capacity to consent, although there is not a blanket rule that covers every situation; courts will sometimes look at the individual facts, to see if the particular minor has the experience and intelligence to consent to the particular act involved in the case. *See* 1 DOBBS, HAYDEN & BUBLICK, THE LAW OF TORTS § 109 (2d ed. 2011). Although courts are split, it is generally assumed that minors may consent to a number of touchings appropriate to their age. Probably two eight-year-olds can effectively consent to a football game in which touching is inevitable. Older minors can consent to more serious touchings, such as routine medical attention. The hospital emergency room that administers first aid to a 16-year-old with a broken arm is presumably protected from any claim of battery if the teenager consents. But many states impose criminal liability for sexual conduct with a minor. See *Larsen v. Davis Cty. Sch. Dist.*, 409 P.3d 114 (Utah 2017) ("Under our law, there are certain types of physical contact that are harmful and offensive as a matter of law, and to which no person can legally consent"; by law minors cannot consent to sexual contact with an adult teacher or a person who is 10 or more years older).

4. **Incapacity to consent: adults.** Incapacity of an adult is usually established only by showing that the particular adult could not manage his own affairs, or, in consent cases, that he did not understand the nature and character of the act. In *Saucier ex rel. Mallory v. McDonald's Rests. of Mont.*,

Inc., 179 P.3d 481 (Mont. 2008), an employee who was intellectually challenged engaged in a sexual relationship with her manager at McDonald's for nearly two months. In a suit against McDonald's and the manager, a neuropsychologist opined that "while [plaintiff] has the ability to seek out or reject sexual advances, she possesses an 'extremely limited capacity' to appreciate the consequences attendant to a sexual relationship." The Montana Supreme Court held that a genuine issue of material fact remained as to plaintiff's ability to consent. Summary judgment on the battery claim was denied.

5.   **Substituted consent.** An adult family member or guardian may be empowered to give consent for medical treatment on behalf of a minor or an incapacitated adult. *Drs. Hosp. of Augusta, LLC v. Alicea*, 788 S.E.2d 392 (Ga. 2016) ("a primary purpose of the Advance Directive Act is to ensure that in making decisions about a patient's health care, it is the will of the patient or her designated agent, rather than the will of the health care provider, that controls"). Many issues arise concerning substituted consent. In *Harvey v. Strickland*, 566 S.E.2d 529 (S.C. 2002), an adult patient, preparing for an operation, signed a form saying he refused to accept a blood transfusion for religious reasons. During the operation, the doctor determined that the patient needed a transfusion and called the patient's mother for permission, which she granted. When sued by the patient for battery, the doctor claimed that the patient had once said he would "consider" a transfusion. Can we say that this patient impliedly consented to substituted consent by his mother? The court said the case presented a jury question on that issue. Could a parent effectively consent to a medical experiment to be performed upon her child when the child is healthy and will derive no health benefit from the experiment? See *Grimes v. Kennedy Krieger Institute, Inc.*, 782 A.2d 807 (Md. 2001). Can a doctor rely on such consent?

6.   **Standards for substituted consent.** Substituted consent is almost a sub-specialty in itself. When someone is appointed as guardian for a person who is incompetent or unable to give or withhold consent, should the guardian make the decision (a) in the best interests of the patient or (b) on the basis of what the patient herself would do if she were competent?

7.   **Incompetence to give or withhold consent.** What if a person is intoxicated at the time of emergency treatment—should the doctor be required to obtain consent? In *Miller v. Rhode Island Hospital*, 625 A.2d 778 (R.I. 1993), the plaintiff had consumed many, many drinks before he was in an automobile collision. The trauma team at the emergency room, fearing internal bleeding, insisted on performing a peritoneal lavage. When plaintiff objected, doctors strapped him to a gurney, anesthetized him and performed the lavage. The plaintiff sued for battery. The court thought that competence to consent (or refuse consent) should be measured by the plaintiff's ability to understand the condition, nature and effect of the proposed treatment or its rejection. When the plaintiff was unable to understand the nature of the treatment due to his intoxication, doctors were not required to attempt to obtain his consent.

8. **Informed consent in medical malpractice cases.** A battery claim may be appropriate where the patient either did not consent at all, or when the treatment the doctor provided was different than the one to which the patient consented. But where the gist of the claim is that the doctor failed to obtain the patient's informed consent by not adequately explaining the procedure's risks and alternatives, that is a species of medical malpractice based in negligence. *See, e.g., Dodd v. Hines,* 229 So.3d 89 (Miss. 2017) (genuine issue of material fact in negligence claim whether plaintiff gave informed consent to remove her ovaries); DOBBS, HAYDEN & BUBLICK, HORNBOOK ON TORTS § 21.9 (2d ed. 2016).

A Mini-Problem for Review

"On May 29, 2007, Mr. Christopherson [a supervisor at Prosper, Inc.] asked for volunteers for a new motivational exercise. He offered no explanation to his team members regarding the nature of the exercise. In his search for volunteers, Mr. Christopherson challenged the loyalty and determination of his team members. Mr. Hudgens volunteered to be a part of the exercise to prove his loyalty and determination. Mr. Christopherson then led his team members to the top of a hill near Prosper's office. Once on the hill, Mr. Christopherson ordered Mr. Hudgens to lie down, facing up, with his head pointed downhill. Mr. Christopherson ordered other team members to hold Mr. Hudgens down by his arms and legs. Mr. Christopherson then slowly poured water from a gallon jug over Mr. Hudgens's mouth and nose so that he could not breathe. Mr. Hudgens struggled and tried to escape but, at Mr. Christopherson's direction, the other team members held him down. After concluding the exercise, Mr. Christopherson instructed his team members that they should work as hard at making sales as Mr. Hudgens had worked at trying to breathe." *Hudgens v. Prosper, Inc.,* 243 P.3d 1275 (Utah 2010). Based on these facts, Mr. Hudgens filed a Complaint alleging a number of intentional torts. What intentional torts do you see? If the defendants argued that Mr. Hudgens consented to their conduct, how would you analyze that argument?

§ 3. PUBLIC AND PRIVATE NECESSITY

SUROCCO V. GEARY
3 Cal. 69 (1853)

MURRAY, CHIEF JUSTICE, delivered the opinion of the Court.

This was an action, commenced in the court below, to recover damages for blowing up and destroying the plaintiffs' house and property, during the fire of the 24th of December, 1849.

Geary, at that time Alcalde [mayor] of San Francisco, justified, on the ground that he had the authority, by virtue of his office, to destroy said building, and also that it had been blown up by him to stop the progress of the conflagration [extensive fire] then raging.

It was in proof, that the fire passed over and burned beyond the building of the plaintiffs', and that at the time said building was destroyed, they were engaged in removing their property, and could, had they not been prevented, have succeeded in removing more, if not all of their goods.

The cause was tried by the court sitting as a jury, and a verdict rendered for the plaintiffs, from which the defendant prosecutes this appeal under the Practice Act of 1850.

The only question for our consideration is, whether the person who tears down or destroys the house of another, in good faith, and under apparent necessity, during the time of a conflagration, for the purpose of saving the buildings adjacent, and stopping its progress, can be held personally liable in an action by the owner of the property destroyed. . . .

The right to destroy property, to prevent the spread of a conflagration, has been traced to the highest law of necessity, and the natural rights of man, independent of society or civil government. "It is referred by moralists and jurists to the same great principle which justifies the exclusive appropriation of a plank in a shipwreck, though the life of another be sacrificed; with the throwing overboard goods in a tempest, for the safety of a vessel; with the trespassing upon the lands of another, to escape death by an enemy. It rests upon the maxim, Necessitas inducit privilegium quod jura privata."

The common law adopts the principles of the natural law, and places the justification of an act otherwise tortious precisely on the same ground of necessity.

This principle has been familiarly recognized by the books from the time of the saltpetre case, and the instances of tearing down houses to prevent a conflagration, or to raise bulwarks [walls] for the defense of a city, are made use of as illustrations, rather than as abstract cases, in which its exercise is permitted. At such times, the individual rights of property give way to the higher laws of impending necessity.

A house on fire, or those in its immediate vicinity, which serve to communicate the flames, becomes a nuisance, which it is lawful to abate, and the private rights of the individual yield to the considerations of general convenience, and the interests of society. Were it otherwise, one stubborn person might involve a whole city in ruin, by refusing to allow the destruction of a building which would cut off the flames and check the progress of the fire, and that, too, when it was perfectly evident that his building must be consumed. . . .

The counsel for the respondent has asked, who is to judge of the necessity of the destruction of property?

This must, in some instances, be a difficult matter to determine. The necessity of blowing up a house may not exist, or be as apparent to the owner, whose judgment is clouded by interests, and the hope of saving his property, as to others. In all such cases the conduct of the individual must be regulated by his own judgment as to the exigencies of the case. If a building should be torn down without apparent or actual necessity, the parties concerned would undoubtedly be liable in an action of trespass. But in every case the necessity must be clearly shown. It is true, many cases of hardship may grow out of this rule, and property may often in such cases be destroyed, without necessity, by irresponsible persons, but this difficulty would not be obviated by making the parties responsible in every case, whether the necessity existed or not.

The legislature of the State possess the power to regulate this subject by providing the manner in which buildings may be destroyed, and the mode in which compensation shall be made; and it is to be hoped that something will be done to obviate the difficulty, and prevent the happening of such events as those supposed by the respondent's counsel.

In the absence of any legislation on the subject, we are compelled to fall back upon the rules of the common law.

The evidence in this case clearly establishes the fact, that the blowing up of the house was necessary, as it would have been consumed had it been left standing. The plaintiffs cannot recover for the value of the goods which they might have saved; they were as much subject to the necessities of the occasion as the house in which they were situate; and if in such cases a party was held liable, it would too frequently happen, that the delay caused by the removal of the goods would render the destruction of the house useless.

The court below clearly erred as to the law applicable to the facts of this case. The testimony will not warrant a verdict against the defendant.

Judgment reversed.

NOTES

1. **Public necessity: scope of the privilege.** The rule applied in *Surocco* is reflected in the Restatement Second of Torts § 196 (privileging interference with land) and § 263 (privileging interference with chattels). The privilege of public necessity protects against actual harms done, where public rather than merely private interests are involved, the defendant had a reasonable belief that action was needed, and the action he took was a reasonable response to the need. The privilege protects not only public officials but also private citizens who act in the public interest. *See* 1 DOBBS, HAYDEN & BUBLICK, THE LAW OF TORTS § 118 (2d ed. 2011). The "essence of the doctrine

is that the government is acting under pressure of public necessity and to avert impending peril." The rule still applies today. *See Brewer v. State*, 341 P.3d 1107 (Alaska 2014) (burning plaintiff's vegetation to deprive advancing wildfires of fuel was justified by public necessity, barring tort claim as well as takings claim).

2. **Policy.** Does the public necessity privilege represent good policy? Does it make any difference in your assessment whether the defendant is a private actor as opposed to a government employee?

3. **Injustice to the property owner?** Even if the privilege serves a useful purpose in freeing the helpful citizen from liability, does it work an injustice in making the private property owner sacrifice his property to the public good?

4. **Constitutional takings clauses.** In part to address a perceived injustice to the property owner, some states have held that where the defendant is a "state actor" who destroys property for the public good in an emergency, the state itself should compensate the property owner under the Takings Clause of the state constitution. These clauses generally provide that no private property shall be taken for public use without just compensation. *See, e.g., Wegner v. Milwaukee Mut. Ins. Co.*, 479 N.W.2d 38 (Minn. 1991) (when police used flash-bang grenades against suspected felons who had run into plaintiff's house, Minnesota's Takings Clause required payment; "At its most basic level, the issue is whether it is fair to allocate the entire risk of loss to an innocent homeowner for the good of the public.").

I like that

The Fifth Amendment to the U.S. Constitution contains a similar takings clause. Prior to 2019, the Supreme Court had held that a plaintiff whose property was taken had no federal claim until a state court had denied the claim under state law. But the Court reversed course in *Knick v. Township of Scott, Pennsylvania*, 139 S.Ct. 2162 (2019), holding that a property owner has an actionable Fifth Amendment takings claim when the government takes the owner's property without paying for it, and therefore may bring a claim under § 1983 in federal court without first exhausting state remedies.

5. **What is a taking?** California itself has reaffirmed *Surocco* even where the defendant is a government actor, however, holding that the Takings Clause of its state constitution does not extend to police destruction or seizure of property, even if done to benefit the public. *Customer Co. v. City of Sacramento*, 895 P.2d 900 (Cal. 1995). Some other states have followed this analysis, holding that police destruction or seizure of property is not a constitutional "taking." *See, e.g., Eggleston v. Pierce Cty.*, 64 P.3d 618 (Wash. 2003); *Kelley v. Story Cty. Sheriff*, 611 N.W.2d 475 (Iowa 2000); *Sullivant v. City of Oklahoma City*, 940 P.2d 220 (Okla. 1997). Also, "it must be shown that there was an invasion of property rights that was intended or was the foreseeable result of authorized governmental action." *Henderson v. City of Columbus*, 827 N.W.2d 486 (Neb. 2013). Accordingly, a homeowner's house was not "taken or damaged for public use" when it was flooded by raw sewage

during a rainstorm because there was no showing that a government actor knew of or could foresee the damage to private property.

6.   **Insurance.** Might *Surocco* be justified today on the ground that fire insurance is commonly purchased by all landowners and that it is a cheap and efficient way of dealing with the loss by fire?

———————

PLOOF V. PUTNAM, 71 A. 188 (Vt. 1908). The defendant owned an island in Lake Champlain. The plaintiff, with his wife and two children, were sailing a sloop on the lake when a violent tempest arose. To avoid destruction of the sloop and injury to himself and his family, the plaintiff moored the boat at the defendant's dock. The defendant, through his servant, unmoored the boat. The sloop and its contents were destroyed and the people in it injured. The plaintiff claimed that unmooring the sloop was a trespass to it and that the defendant had a duty to permit the sloop to remain moored there. *Held,* for the plaintiff. "There are many cases in the books which hold that necessity . . . will justify entries upon land and interferences with personal property that would otherwise have been trespasses. . . . If one have a way over the land of another for his beasts to pass, and the beasts, being properly driven, feed the grass by morsels in passing, or run out of the way and are promptly pursued and brought back, trespass will not lie. A traveler on a highway who finds it obstructed from a sudden and temporary cause may pass upon the adjoining land without becoming a trespasser because of the necessity. An entry upon land to save goods which are in danger of being lost or destroyed by water or fire is not a trespass. . . . One may sacrifice the personal property of another to save his life or the lives of his fellows. . . . It is clear that an entry upon the land of another may be justified by necessity for mooring the sloop."

VINCENT V. LAKE ERIE TRANSPORTATION CO.

124 N.W. 221 (Minn. 1910)

O'BRIEN, J.

Secured

The steamship Reynolds, owned by the defendant, was for the purpose of discharging her cargo on November 27, 1905, moored to plaintiff's dock in Duluth. While the unloading of the boat was taking place a storm from the northeast developed, which at about 10 o'clock P.M., when the unloading was completed, had so grown in violence that the wind was then moving at 50 miles per hour and continued to increase during the night. There is some evidence that one, and perhaps two, boats were able to enter the harbor that night, but it is plain that navigation was practically suspended from the hour mentioned until the morning of the 29th when the storm abated, and during that time no master would have been justified in attempting to navigate his vessel, if he could avoid doing so. After the discharge of the cargo the Reynolds signaled for a tug to tow her from the dock, but none could be obtained because of the severity of the storm. If the lines holding the ship to the dock had been cast off, she would doubtless have drifted away; but, instead, the lines were kept fast, and as soon as one parted or chafed it was replaced, sometimes with a larger one. The vessel lay upon the outside of the dock, her bow to the east, the wind and waves striking her starboard quarter with such force that she was constantly being lifted and thrown against the dock, resulting in its damage as found by the jury, to the amount of $500.

We are satisfied that the character of the storm was such that it would have been highly imprudent for the master of the Reynolds to have attempted to leave the dock or to have permitted his vessel to drift away from it. . . . Nothing more was demanded of them than ordinary prudence and care, and the record in this case fully sustains the contention of the appellant that, in holding the vessel fast to the dock, those in charge of her exercised good judgment and prudent seamanship. . . .

The appellant contends by ample assignments of error that, because its conduct during the storm was rendered necessary by prudence and good seamanship under conditions over which it had no control, it cannot be held liable for any injury resulting to the property of others, and claims that the jury should have been so instructed. An analysis of the charge given by the trial court is not necessary, as in our opinion the only question for the jury was the amount of damages which the plaintiffs were entitled to recover, and no complaint is made upon that score.

The situation was one in which the ordinary rules regulating property rights were suspended by forces beyond human control, and if, without the direct intervention of some act by the one sought to be held liable the property of another was injured, such injury must be attributed to the act of God, and not to the wrongful act of the person sought to be charged. If during the storm the Reynolds had entered the harbor, and while there had become disabled and been thrown against the plaintiffs' dock, the plaintiffs could not have recovered. Again, if while attempting to hold fast to the dock the lines had parted, without any negligence, and the vessel carried against some other boat or dock in the harbor, there would be no liability upon her owner. But here those in charge of the vessel deliberately and by their direct efforts held her in such a position that the damage to the dock resulted, and, having thus preserved the ship at the expense of the dock, it seems to us that her owners are responsible to the dock owners to the extent of the injury inflicted. . . .

In Ploof v. Putnam, 71 Atl. 188, the Supreme Court of Vermont held that where, under stress of weather, a vessel was without permission moored to a private dock at an island in Lake Champlain owned by the defendant, the plaintiff was not guilty of trespass, and that the defendant was responsible in damages because his representative upon the island unmoored the vessel, permitting it to drift upon the shore, with resultant injuries to it. If, in that case, the vessel had been permitted to remain, and the dock had suffered an injury, we believe the shipowner would have been held liable for the injury done.

Theologians hold that a starving man may, without moral guilt, take what is necessary to sustain life; but it could hardly be said that the obligation would not be upon such person to pay the value of the property so taken when he became able to do so. And so public necessity, in times of war or peace, may require the taking of private property for public purposes; but under our system of jurisprudence compensation must be made.

Let us imagine in this case that for the better mooring of the vessel those in charge of her had appropriated a valuable cable lying upon the dock. No matter how justifiable such appropriation might have been, it would not be claimed that, because of the overwhelming necessity of the situation, the owner of the cable could not recover its value.

This is not a case where life or property was menaced by any object or thing belonging to the plaintiff, the destruction of which became necessary to prevent the threatened disaster. Nor is it a case where, because of the act of God, or unavoidable accident, the infliction of the injury was beyond the control of the defendant, but is one where the defendant prudently and advisedly availed itself of the plaintiffs' property for the purpose of preserving its own more valuable property and the plaintiffs are entitled to compensation for the injury done.

Order affirmed.

LEWIS, J. I dissent. . . . In my judgment, if the boat was lawfully in position at the time the storm broke, and the master could not, in the exercise of due care, have left that position without subjecting his vessel to the hazards of the storm, then the damage to the dock, caused by the pounding of the boat, was the result of an inevitable accident. . . .

I am of the opinion that one who constructs a dock to the navigable line of waters, and enters into contractual relations with the owner of a vessel to moor at the same, takes the risk of damage to his dock by a boat caught there by a storm, which event could not have been avoided in the exercise of due care, and further, that the legal status of the parties in such a case is not changed by renewal of cables to keep the boat from being cast adrift at the mercy of the tempest.

NOTES

1.   **Private necessity: scope of the privilege.** Can you glean the scope of the private necessity privilege from reading *Ploof* and *Vincent* together? How

does the private necessity privilege differ from the public necessity privilege? What might justify the difference? *See* 1 DOBBS, HAYDEN & BUBLICK, THE LAW OF TORTS § 117 (2d ed. 2011).

2. **Contractual rights.** Presumably the shipowner and dock owner made some consensual arrangement about the use of the dock. If the shipowner had the right to continued use of the dock under that arrangement, can it be said that by renewing the lines he took any benefit he was not entitled to?

3. **An economic perspective.** Does it matter whether courts adopt a legal rule that requires a boat owner to pay for damage to the dock or a rule that does not require such payment? It might not matter to whether the parties achieve an efficient allocation of resources. In his 1960 article entitled *The Problem of Social Cost*, 3 J. OF LAW & ECON. 1, economist Ronald Coase explained why. Parties can bargain around any legal rule in order to reach an efficient allocation of resources. Imagine for example that the boat is worth $500. If it goes out in the storm its full value will be lost. If it stays tethered to the dock, it will cause $1000 of damage to the dock. Given those damage estimates, the efficient allocation of resources would be to forgo the value of the boat rather than cause greater injury to the dock. Of course, the parties will reach this efficient result—letting the boat go—if the boat owner has to pay for damage done to the dock. In that scenario, the owner would face the choice of incurring a $500 loss or a $1000 loss, and would let the boat go in order to incur the lesser loss. However, if the boat owner does not have to pay for the damage to the dock, might the owner choose a $1000 loss to the dock owner rather than a $500 cost of the boat owner's own? Perhaps not. Given the opportunity to bargain, the dock owner could pay the boat owner an amount of money between $500 and $1000 to let the boat go and both parties would be better off.

At times, however, the legal rule may indeed matter to whether the parties reach the efficient result. When barriers to bargaining are high, such as when significant transaction and information costs are present, the parties may not be able to bargain effectively. In addition, the legal rule may matter a great deal to the parties themselves. The distribution of legal entitlements will affect the distribution of wealth between them. Under the rule that requires the boat owner to pay for damage, the owner will have a $500 loss from letting the boat go. If the boat owner is not required to pay for damage, the boat owner will at worst have no loss, and at best will have a gain of $500.

4. **The role of fault.** Is *Vincent* contrary to *Van Camp v. McAfoos*, the child tricyclist case we saw in Chapter 1? After all, the court recognized that the captain was not at fault, yet imposed liability.

5. **Scope of private necessity.** For some purposes, "a trespasser is one 'who enters or remains upon land in the possession of another without a privilege to do so created by the possessor's consent or otherwise.' Thus a person entering pursuant to a lawful privilege is not a trespasser under D.C. law." Would the necessity privilege justify a person climbing over a fence to

chase after his dog or would such a person be a trespasser without a privilege? *See Toomer v. William C. Smith & Co., Inc.*, 112 A.3d 324 (D.C. 2015).

6. **Necessity to take a life?** The driver of a school bus with twenty children on board is coming down a mountain road. On her left is a sheer precipice. On her right is solid rock. As the bus picks up speed, a car coming up the hill traveling very fast appears in the bus's lane. It is now clear that the driver must act. If she stays where she is, a collision will ensue. If she turns left, she will take the children over the cliff. She can turn right before gaining any more speed, but if she does so she will certainly strike two children waiting at the bus stop. This would kill the two children or seriously maim them, but it will probably save most of those on the bus. On the rationale of *Vincent* would the driver be liable for the deaths of the two children? Professor George Christie, in *The Defense of Necessity Considered from the Legal and Moral Points of View*, 48 DUKE L.J. 975 (1999), analyzes the positions of a number of philosophers. He himself thinks that an intentional killing to save a greater number of lives is not privileged.

REFERENCES: 1 DOBBS, HAYDEN & BUBLICK, THE LAW OF TORTS §§ 80–119 (2d ed. 2011); DOBBS, HAYDEN & BUBLICK, HORNBOOK ON TORTS §§ 7.1–7.21 (2d ed. 2016).

PART 3

THE PRIMA FACIE CASE FOR NEGLIGENCE

■ ■ ■

CHAPTER 5

THE PRIMA FACIE CASE FOR NEGLIGENCE AND THE ELEMENT OF DUTY

▪ ▪ ▪

§ 1. THEORY AND ELEMENTS OF NEGLIGENCE

A. THE FAULT BASIS OF LIABILITY

OLIVER WENDELL HOLMES, THE COMMON LAW
1881 Howe ed. 1963 pp. 76–78

The general principle of our law is that loss from accident must lie where it falls, and this principle is not affected by the fact that a human being is the instrument of misfortune. But relatively to a given human being anything is accident which he could not fairly have been expected to contemplate as possible, and therefore to avoid. In the language of the late Chief Justice Nelson of New York: "No case or principle can be found, or if found can be maintained, subjecting an individual to liability for an act done without fault on his part. . . . All the cases concede that an injury arising from inevitable accident, or, which in law or reason is the same thing, from an act that ordinary human care and foresight are unable to guard against, is but the misfortune of the sufferer, and lays no foundation for legal responsibility." . . .

A man need not, it is true, do this or that act,—the term act implies a choice,—but he must act somehow. Furthermore, the public generally profits by individual activity. As action cannot be avoided, and tends to the public good, there is obviously no policy in throwing the hazard of what is at once desirable and inevitable upon the actor.

The state might conceivably make itself a mutual insurance company against accidents, and distribute the burden of its citizens' mishaps among its members. There might be a pension for paralytics, and state aid for those who suffered in person or estate from tempest or wild beasts. As between individuals it might adopt the mutual insurance principle *pro tanto*, and divide damages when both were in fault, as in the *rusticum judicium* of the admiralty, or it might throw all loss upon the actor irrespective of fault. The state does none of these things, however, and the prevailing view is that its cumbrous and expensive machinery ought not to be set in motion unless some clear benefit is to be derived from disturbing the status quo. State interference is an evil, where it cannot be shown to be a good. Universal insurance, if desired, can be better and more cheaply accomplished by private enterprise. The undertaking to redistribute losses simply on the ground that they resulted from the defendant's act would not only be open to these objections, but, as it is hoped the preceding discussion has shown, to the still graver one of offending the sense of justice. Unless my act is of a nature to threaten others, unless under the circumstances a prudent man would have foreseen the possibility of harm, it is no more justifiable to make me indemnify my neighbor against the consequences, than to make me do the same thing if I had fallen upon him in a fit, or to compel me to insure him against lightning.

NOTES

1.   **Role of fault.** Holmes says that loss from accidents should generally lie where it falls. Why require fault in order to reallocate losses?

2.   **Role of government.** What things might the government do for mishaps and why does Holmes say these things should not be done?

3.   **Tort law's role today.** Governmental programs such as Social Security Disability Insurance provide greater assistance to individuals today than was available in Holmes' day. Does the existence of social welfare programs change the way you think about Holmes' arguments? The need for tort law?

B. ASSESSING RESPONSIBILITY

American tort law is typically requires fault, such as negligence. Tort law attempts to assess responsibility for actions and deter misconduct. On closer inspection, assessing fault turns out to be a difficult, time-consuming, and expensive task.

As we have seen in earlier chapters, intentional torts are defined in highly structured ways. In effect, the law of intentional torts prohibits specific acts like intentional touchings or intentional confinement of another person. By contrast, the tort of negligence is not defined by specific forbidden acts. Instead, negligence may be any conduct that creates an unreasonable risk of harm to others. It is actionable as a tort when that risk comes to fruition and causes actual harm of a foreseeable type. Assessing legal responsibility in negligence cases requires the consideration of a number of important concepts, including:

1. *Fault.* Intentionally harming another person is surely fault. But what is negligence? What about driving a car at 80 m.p.h.? Should we examine motives, states of mind, or merely external conduct? What if the defendant is in a hurry? Or does not understand the risk?

2. *Causation of harm.* A person who causes no harm is not legally responsible, no matter how bad the act. Imagine that defendant drives 90

m.p.h., but does not strike anyone. Plaintiff is offended, but not harmed. This will not suffice in the case of negligence, since actual damage is an element of the plaintiff's case.

3. *Fixing the scope of responsibility.* A person is not legally responsible for every harm that occurs because of the person's negligence, though the rule might be otherwise for intentional torts. Suppose Jim, who has promised to babysit at 7:00 p.m., is negligent in coming late. The parents, concluding that Jim would soon be there, leave the child alone. While the child is alone, he burns himself. Jim is undoubtedly negligent and responsible for something. In a sense he has caused the harm, since if he had not been late, the child would not have been burned. The law may well decide, however, that the injury was not within the scope of Jim's responsibility.

4. *A duty to take responsibility.* In many instances it will be possible to find that a defendant has failed to behave reasonably, that the defendant's conduct has caused harm, and that the harm caused is the very kind that was risked by his negligent conduct. Yet not every problem is the defendant's responsibility. Suppose you know your neighbor fails to watch his toddler and consequently that there is a risk the child will run into the street and be injured. You *could* watch the child when you are not busy, but perhaps you should be free to decide that for yourself. If so, we will say you are under no duty to the child, even if a reasonable person would have tried to avoid injury to him.

C. LEGAL ELEMENTS OF A NEGLIGENCE CLAIM

Courts have developed a general formula for the negligence claim. To receive compensation, the plaintiff must allege and prove facts establishing five elements:

(1) The defendant owed the plaintiff a legal duty. For example, the defendant had a responsibility to use reasonable care while driving.

(2) The defendant, by behaving negligently, breached that duty. For example, the defendant may have driven through a red light.

(3) The plaintiff suffered actual harm. For example, the plaintiff's car was injured, and her leg was broken.

(4) The defendant's negligence was an actual cause of this harm. For example, had it not been for the defendant driving through the red light, the plaintiff would not have suffered the injury to her car and leg. And,

(5) The defendant's negligence was a "proximate cause" of this damage or, as is sometimes said, the damage is within the "scope of liability" of the defendant. For example, the very risk that made

driving through the red light wrongful was the risk that defendant would hit the traveler with the right of way in the intersection.

Different courts may state these five required elements in slightly different ways, but the differences are matters of style, not substance. All courts require the plaintiff to sustain the burden of proving each of the five elements. All courts also agree that if the plaintiff fails to meet the burden of proving any one of them, the plaintiff cannot recover.

The plaintiff may be able to prove these five elements in a range of different negligent acts. The red-light running is but one illustration.

D. SOME INSTITUTIONS OF NEGLIGENCE PRACTICE

As we explore the detailed meanings of negligence, we must recognize several important legal institutions or problems that condition negligence law. These are practices we must have in mind when we try to understand what it really means to impose liability for negligence.

1. *Litigation finance—attorney's fees.* As we know from Chapter 1, each party must pay the party's own attorney. This has led to the contingent fee, under which the plaintiff may retain an attorney without payment of any fee unless the plaintiff wins the case. If the plaintiff wins, the attorney will share in the recovery, usually between 25% to 50%. In large, time-consuming cases, large awards for pain and suffering or for punitive damages are required if an attorney is to take the case, for otherwise the attorney won't be paid enough to make the case economically feasible.

2. *Liability insurance.* Although liability insurance for automobiles may be compulsory, the policy limit—the sum available to pay for injuries—is likely to be too low to cover the full cost of severe injury.

3. *The role of settlement.* The number of personal injury trials is small. However, the number of personal injuries is large. The volume of routine negligence claims in, say, auto accidents, is vast. Almost all injury claims are settled without trial. To come up with a reasonable estimate of a case's settlement value, lawyers for each side must determine what facts will be proved if the case goes to court and what legal rules will affect the outcome. Accordingly, lawyers must know the rules and also how they are likely to be applied in court. Although lawyers approach the cases as adversaries, they must make neutral, balanced judgments about how the case will appear to the judge and jury. The lawyer who relies on a rule that represents injustice or bad policy may find that the judge will reject the rule or that the jury will find a way not to apply it. Lawyers, and students, must make careful evaluation of the rules announced in cases.

In the following chapters, we explore each of the five elements of the negligence case in turn.

§ 2. THE GENERAL DUTY OF CARE: THE REASONABLE AND PRUDENT PERSON STANDARD

"Although it was not required in early English law, in order to establish a negligence cause of action today, the plaintiff must show that the defendant owes her a duty of care. 'A duty, in negligence cases, may be defined as an obligation, to which the law will give recognition and effect, to conform to a particular standard of conduct toward another.' . . . [D]uty is a question for the judge. . . . In general, when an actor's conduct, creates, maintains, or continues a risk of physical harm, he ordinarily has a duty of care. When such a duty is owed, the standard of care to be applied is ordinarily reasonable care under the circumstances." DOBBS, HAYDEN & BUBLICK, HORNBOOK ON TORTS § 10.1 (2d ed. 2016).

Under the general standard of reasonable care, an actor must exercise the care that would be exercised by a reasonable and prudent person under the same or similar circumstances to avoid or minimize risks of harm to others. *the standard*

This chapter begins with the ordinary situation in which an actor owes a duty of care and the standard is reasonable care. After we have reviewed the usual situation in which an actor owes a duty of reasonable care, we will see in later chapters that, in some contexts, actors may owe no duty at all. Also, courts sometimes modify the standard of care for particular contexts like medical negligence.

STEWART V. MOTTS
654 A.2d 535 (Pa. 1995)

MONTEMURO, JUSTICE. . . .

The sole issue presented before us is whether there exists a higher standard of "extraordinary care" for the use of dangerous instrumentalities over and above the standard of "reasonable care" such that the trial court erred for failing to give an instruction to the jury that the Appellee should have used a "high degree of care" in handling gasoline. Because we believe that there is but one standard of care, the standard of "reasonable care," we affirm. *I/ PH H/D*

The pertinent facts of this case are simple and were ably stated by the trial court:

On July 15, 1987, Plaintiff, Jonathon Stewart, stopped at Defendant, Martin Motts' auto repair shop and offered assistance to the Defendant in repairing an automobile fuel tank. In an effort to start and move the car with the gasoline tank unattached, the Plaintiff suggested and then proceeded to pour gasoline into the carburetor. The Defendant was to turn

the ignition key at a given moment. While the exact sequence of events was contested, the tragic result was that the car backfired, caused an explosion and resulted in Plaintiff suffering severe burns to his upper body.

[In Stewart's suit against Motts, the plaintiff asked the judge to instruct the jury in part "that gasoline due to its inflammability, is a very dangerous substance if not properly handled. . . . With an appreciation of such danger, and under conditions where its existence reasonably should have been known, there follows a high degree of care which circumscribes the conduct of everyone about the danger. . . ." The judge refused to so instruct and the jury returned a verdict for the defendant.]

We begin our discussion by reaffirming the principle that there is but one standard of care to be applied to negligence actions involving dangerous instrumentalities in this Commonwealth. This standard of care is "reasonable care" as well stated in the Restatement (Second) of Torts: "The care required is always reasonable care. The standard never varies, but the care which it is reasonable to require of the actor varies with the danger involved in his act and is proportionate to it. The greater the danger, the greater the care which must be exercised. . . ." Restatement (Second) of Torts § 298 comment b (1965). . . .

Properly read, our cases involving dangerous agencies reaffirm these well accepted principles found in the Restatement. In *Konchar v. Cebular*, 333 Pa. 499, 3 A.2d 913 (1939) . . . we recognized that the question of the plaintiff's contributory negligence was to be determined using the reasonable care standard in light of the particular circumstances of the case. One such circumstance, we acknowledged, was that gasoline, a dangerous substance, was involved requiring that the reasonably prudent person exercise a higher degree of care under these circumstances. Taken in context, our statement that the plaintiff was under a "high duty of care" did nothing more than reaffirm the general principle that the care employed by a reasonable man must be proportionate to the danger of the activity.

. . . We do not believe that [our other] cases created a heightened or extraordinary standard of care above and beyond the standard of reasonable care for handling dangerous agencies. When we referred to a "higher degree of care" in these cases, we were not creating a second tier of "extraordinary care" over and above ordinary or reasonable care. Instead, we were simply recognizing the general principle that under the reasonable care standard, the level of care must be proportionate to the danger involved. Our use of the language "higher degree of care" merely stated the common sense conclusion that the use of a dangerous agency would require the reasonably prudent person to exercise more care. . . .

In summation, this Commonwealth recognizes only one standard of care in negligence actions involving dangerous instrumentalities—the standard of reasonable care under the circumstances. It is well established by our case law that the reasonable man must exercise care in proportion to the danger involved in his act.

With these principles in mind we must next examine the jury instructions in this case. The trial judge explained to the jury that negligence is "the absence of ordinary care which a reasonably prudent person would exercise in the circumstances here presented." The trial judge further explained: "It is for you to determine how a reasonably prudent person would act in those circumstances. Ordinary care is the care a reasonably prudent person would use under the circumstances presented in this case. It is the duty of every person to use ordinary care not only for his own safety and the protection of his property, but also to avoid serious injury to others. What constitutes ordinary care varies according to the particular circumstances and conditions existing then and there. The amount of care required by law must be in keeping with the degree of danger involved. . . ."

We find that this charge, when read as a whole, adequately instructed the jury. The charge informed the jury that the proper standard of care was "reasonable" or "ordinary" care under the circumstances in accordance with the law of this Commonwealth. The charge properly instructed the jury that the level of care required changed with the circumstances. The charge also informed the jury that the level of care required increased proportionately with the level of danger in the activity. We find nothing in this charge that is confusing, misleading, or unclear. From these instructions, the jury had the tools to examine the circumstances of the case and determine that the defendant was required to exercise a "higher degree of care" in using the dangerous agency of gasoline. . . .

For the reasons set forth above, we affirm the order of the Superior Court.

NOTES

1. **The general standard of care.** *Stewart* applies the general standard of care for negligence cases. When a plaintiff sues a defendant on a negligence theory, the defendant is held to the standard of care that would be exercised by a reasonable person under the same or similar circumstances at the time of the alleged negligence. *See Mobile Gas Serv. Corp. v. Robinson*, 20 So.3d 770 (Ala. 2009) ("[C]are commensurate with the dangers involved . . . is the same degree of care and vigilance which persons of skill and prudence observe under like circumstances.").

2. **Dangerous instrumentalities: the orthodox view.** *Stewart* also states the orthodox view for negligence cases involving the use of dangerous instrumentalities: (a) the standard of care remains the reasonable and prudent person standard, but (b) if the foreseeable danger is high, the reasonable

person will ordinarily exercise a greater degree of care than if the foreseeable danger is low. *E.g., Butler v. Acme Mkts., Inc.,* 426 A.2d 521 (N.J. Super. Ct. App. Div. 1981), *aff'd,* 445 A.2d 1141 (N.J. 1982). The *standard* thus remains the same whether danger is high or low. What changes with the danger is the *amount of care* that a reasonable person would take. *E.g., Purtle v. Shelton,* 474 S.W.2d 123 (Ark. 1971) (trial judge in hunting-injury case was correct to refuse to instruct the jury that the defendant should have used a "high degree of care commensurate with the dangers involved"; "The duty enunciated in an instruction should be ordinary care under the circumstances, and the contention that the circumstances dictate a high degree of caution should be left to arguments of counsel.").

3.   **Reasonable care in dangerous situations.** Many courts have recognized the heightened danger inherent in providing electricity or gas. Still, those utilities that provide such services are almost always held to the standard of reasonable care rather than to some different, higher standard. *See Alderwoods (Pa.), Inc. v. Duquesne Light Co.,* 106 A.3d 27 (Pa. 2014) (electric utility fulfilled duty of reasonable care by warning customer of risks while reconnecting electric lines to building); *Hopkins v. Miss. Valley Gas Co.,* 866 So.2d 514 (Miss. Ct. App. 2004) (gas company satisfied duty of care by warning customer about storing gasoline next to reconnected water heater). What about a situation involving a black widow spider? *See Coyle v. Historic Mission Inn Corp.,* 24 Cal.App.5th 627 (2018) ("[T]he parties are disputing what reasonable care means. . . . Given that dispute, and that there is evidence that could support a finding . . . that the spraying of pesticide or posting of warning signs was needed, it is not the role of the court to decide what reasonable care means in the circumstances of this case. It is for the jury to decide.").

4.   **Reasonable care with vulnerable plaintiffs.** In cases involving vulnerable plaintiffs, such as minors, courts hold that while factors related to the plaintiff's vulnerability are relevant, the duty of reasonable care remains the same. *See Stopford v. Milton Town Sch. Dist.,* 202 A.3d 973 (Vt. 2018) ("[T]he duty of ordinary care requires schools to take age, circumstances, and a student's disposition into account in exercising reasonable care, but these factors do not raise the duty owed . . . beyond one of ordinary care.")

5.   **Departures from the orthodox view.** Courts do not always observe the orthodox view; some have held instead that when the danger is greater, the standard itself is higher. *See Wood v. Groh,* 7 P.3d 1163 (Kan. 2000) (citing cases); 1 DOBBS, HAYDEN & BUBLICK, THE LAW OF TORTS § 141 (2d ed. 2011).

6.   **Judge and jury.** Why does it matter whether the standard itself changes as the degree of foreseeable danger rises? What impact might an instruction based on such a conception have on the jury?

POSAS V. HORTON

228 P.3d 457 (Nev. 2010)

DOUGLAS, JUSTICE. . . .

Appellant Emilia Posas was driving in her car when a woman pushing a stroller began to cross the street in the middle of traffic, directly in front of Posas's car. Posas stopped suddenly to avoid hitting the jaywalking pedestrian. Respondent Nicole Horton was driving immediately behind Posas and hit the rear of Posas's car with the front-end of her car. . . . Horton was three to four feet behind Posas's vehicle right before the accident occurred, and she did not see the pedestrian cross in front of Posas. Horton testified, "yeah, obviously, I was following too close, I rearended her . . . you know, I made a mistake." . . . As a result of the accident, Posas filed a personal injury action against Horton. Despite Posas's objection during the settling of jury instructions, the jury was given a sudden-emergency instruction. The sudden-emergency instruction stated:

> A person confronted with a sudden emergency which he does not create, who acts according to his best judgment or, because of insufficient time to form a judgment fails to act in the most judicious manner, is not guilty of negligence if he exercises the care of a reasonably prudent person in like circumstances.

The jury returned a verdict in favor of Horton, finding her free from liability for the accident. Posas moved for a new trial, which the district court denied. This appeal followed.

Posas argues that the district court erred in giving the sudden-emergency instruction to the jury. We agree. . . .

In order to be entitled to the sudden-emergency jury instruction, the proponent must show there is sufficient "evidence to support a finding that [the proponent] had been suddenly placed in a position of peril through no negligence of his or her own, and in meeting the emergency . . . acted as a reasonably prudent person would in the same or a similar situation. There must be evidence of a sudden and unforeseeable change in conditions to which a driver was forced to respond to avoid injury." In determining the standard of reasonable care, the Restatement (Second) of Torts further states, "[t]he fact that the actor is not negligent after the emergency has arisen does not preclude his liability for his tortious conduct which has produced the emergency." The Restatement (Third) of Torts: Liability for Physical and Emotional Harm § 9 (2010) also supports this principle. . . . The types of emergencies that courts have found to warrant a sudden-emergency instruction include a "dust cloud, a moving object, a sudden blocking of the road, the sudden swerving of another vehicle, blinding lights, a dense patch of fog," an unexpected brake failure, and a stopped vehicle without emergency flashers activated at night. . . .

DA

Horton argues that she met the burden for the sudden-emergency instruction because the emergency was created by the pedestrian suddenly and unexpectedly crossing the street, that she did not cause the pedestrian to cross the street, and that Horton and Posas each acted as a reasonable person would have by braking to keep from hitting the pedestrian. However, Horton's own testimony belies that fact in light of her statement that she "was following too close." Thus, we conclude that Horton cannot appropriately claim that she faced a sudden emergency. She placed herself in a position of peril through her own negligence.

H/D

[As discussed in a prior case] certain so-called emergencies should

Rule

be anticipated, and the actor must be prepared to meet them when he engages in an activity in which they are likely to arise. Thus, under present day traffic conditions, any driver of an automobile must be prepared for the sudden appearance of obstacles and persons in the highway, and of other vehicles at intersections.

Id. (quoting W. Page Keeton, et al., *Prosser and Keeton on the Law of Torts* § 83 (5th ed.1984)). . . . The instruction tended to mislead or confuse the jury, and the error was prejudicial. . . . But for the error, as to the use of reasonable care by Horton, a different result may have been reached by the jury. . . . Accordingly, we reverse the judgment of the district court and remand for a new trial consistent with this opinion.

H

NOTES

1. **Relevance of emergency.** Is the *fact* of emergency irrelevant under the rule enunciated in *Posas*? If you represented a defendant in such a case, could you use that fact in determining what sum to offer in settlement, or in what to say to the jury in closing argument?

2. **Separate instructions.** Several courts have now said that the idea behind the emergency instruction is adequately covered by the instruction defining the reasonable care standard and that the separate emergency instruction should never be given. *See Lyons v. Midnight Sun Transp. Servs., Inc.,* 928 P.2d 1202 (Alaska 1996) ("We believe that the sudden emergency instruction is a generally useless appendage to the law of negligence. With or without an emergency, the standard of care a person must exercise is still that of a reasonable person under the circumstances."); *Willis v. Westerfield,* 839 N.E.2d 1179 (Ind. 2006) ("The emergency is simply one of the circumstances to be considered."); 1 DOBBS, HAYDEN & BUBLICK, THE LAW OF TORTS § 144 (2d ed. 2011). Nevertheless, some courts still feel these instructions need to be given to the jury. *See Hagenow v. American Family Mut. Ins. Co.,* 846 N.W.2d 373 (Iowa 2014) (analyzing a driver's stroke as an emergency, warranting an emergency instruction, but also noting that "the sudden emergency doctrine is merely an expression of the reasonably prudent person standard of care"). *See also City of Nicholasville Police Dep't v. Abraham,* 565 S.W.3d 639 (Ky. Ct. App. 2018).

3. **The Third Restatement.** The Restatement takes no position about whether an emergency instruction is appropriate, but it would take the fact of emergency into account. According to the Restatement: "If an actor is confronted with an unexpected emergency requiring rapid response, this is a circumstance to be taken into account in determining whether the actor's resulting conduct is that of the reasonably careful person." RESTATEMENT (THIRD) OF TORTS: LIABILITY FOR PHYSICAL AND EMOTIONAL HARM § 9 (2010). The fact of emergency is taken into account because it may indicate that "opportunities for deliberation have been limited by severe time pressure." *Id.* cmt. a. Yet if the emergency faced by the actor is due to the actor's own prior negligence, the defendant is liable for the plaintiff's harm notwithstanding the reasonableness of the defendant's later conduct. *Id.* cmt. d. If Horton had not been following Posas too closely, would the pedestrian's entry into the roadway count as a sudden emergency?

4. **Definition of emergency.** What constitutes an "emergency" remains a relevant question in those states that allow emergency instructions in some cases. The usual definition is a sudden, unexpected and unforeseen happening or condition that calls for immediate action, and that was not created by the party asserting the emergency. *See, e.g., Herr v. Wheeler*, 634 S.E.2d 317 (Va. 2006). In *Lifson v. City of Syracuse,* 958 N.E.2d 72 (N.Y. 2011), the court concluded that sun glare that temporarily blinded the defendant motorist was not a "sudden and unexpected circumstance," and thus the trial court erred in giving an emergency instruction. On the other hand, in *Frazier v. Drake*, 357 P.3d 365 (Nev. Ct. App. 2015), the court found an emergency where a bee suddenly flew into a truck's cabin and landed on the driver's eye. The court in *Kelly v. Berg*, 870 N.W.2d 481 (Wis. Ct. App. 2015), said "one of the elements of the emergency doctrine is that the time in which action is required is short enough to preclude a deliberate and intelligent choice of action. . . . In other words, the person's reaction to the danger must be 'practically instinctive or intuitive.' " Under that reasoning, the court held that an emergency instruction was improper where the plaintiff ran outside to separate fighting dogs, because she "had time to contemplate her course of conduct before acting."

5. **Emergency and incapacitation.** What if a defendant suffered a sudden unforeseeable stroke? In such a case, should an emergency instruction be offered or should the court say that the defendant is simply not negligent by a standard of reasonable care because even a reasonably careful person could not do anything differently in such a case? *See Hancock-Underwood v. Knight*, 670 S.E.2d 720 (Va. 2009).

6. **Proof of sudden emergency.** The gist of the sudden emergency instruction is that the party employing it had to make quick decisions. If the party cannot prove an emergency condition existed, the argument cannot be employed. See *Yates v. Hites*, 102 N.E.3d 901 (Ind. Ct. App. 2018) (car accident allegedly caused by "black ice" on the road that caused the driver to lose control of her vehicle and cross the centerline; reversed for insufficient evidence that black ice existed on the roadway at that time). Similarly, if the party did not

perceive the danger and react at all, doctrine is inapplicable. *Goins v. Time Warner Cable Se., LLC*, 812 S.E.2d 723 (N.C. App. 2018) (cyclists injured by a fallen power line; sudden emergency doctrine was inapplicable because the cyclists did not perceive the power line before colliding with it).

SHEPHERD V. GARDNER WHOLESALE, INC., 256 So.2d 877 (Ala. 1972). Plaintiff Roxie Shepherd tripped over a raised concrete slab in the sidewalk in front of defendant's business. Shepherd suffered from cataracts, leaving her with 20/100 vision in one eye and 20/80 in the other. "[A] person with impaired vision is not required to see what a person with normal vision can see. Such would be impossible, and one is not guilty of negligence by using the public sidewalks with the physical inability to see what a person with normal vision can see. A person laboring under a physical disability such as defective vision is not required to exercise a higher degree of care to avoid injury than is required of a person under no disability. Ordinary care in the case of such a person is such care as an ordinarily prudent person with a like infirmity would have exercised under the same or similar circumstances."

NOTES

1. **Role of physical impairments.** *Shepherd* reflects the rule on the role of physical disabilities in setting the standard of care in negligence cases. The newest Restatement provides that "The conduct of an actor with physical disability is negligent only if it does not conform to that of a reasonably careful person with the same disability." RESTATEMENT (THIRD) OF TORTS: LIABILITY FOR PHYSICAL AND EMOTIONAL HARM § 11(a) (2010). *See also Sanders v. Alger*, 394 P.3d 1083 (Ariz. 2017) (man with cerebral palsy owed caregiver the duty "of a reasonable person under the circumstances, and those circumstances include his physical disabilities and limitations"). What if the general rule were otherwise? As Judge Posner wrote: "A blind person who, while using the blind person's white cane, is hit at an intersection, when a sighted person would easily have dodged the vehicle hurtling toward him driven by the defendant, is not deemed negligent if he was being as careful as it is reasonable to expect a blind person to be, bearing in mind the cost to the blind of holding them to the same standard of care in crossing streets as sighted persons. Otherwise a blind person would lose the protection of tort law when he ventured to cross a street." *Arroyo v. United States*, 656 F.3d 663 (7th Cir. 2011) (Posner, J., concurring).

2. **Effect of the physical impairment rule on the plaintiff.** Is the rule an advantage for the physically disabled, or does the rule actually cut both ways? What if a person is blind, gets into a car and drives, and causes an accident because he cannot see. Posit that a sighted person would not have caused the accident at all. Does the physical impairment rule free the blind person from liability on those facts? What, exactly, is the standard of care on such facts? *See* RESTATEMENT (THIRD) OF TORTS: LIABILITY FOR PHYSICAL AND

EMOTIONAL HARM § 11 cmt. b (2010); *cf. Roberts v. State,* 396 So.2d 566 (La. Ct. App. 1981) (blind man knocked over the plaintiff in a crowded post office).

3. **Effect of the physical impairment rule on the defendant.** If the plaintiff is not negligent for failing to see an obstacle, is the defendant necessarily negligent for failing to correct it? What would happen if both the plaintiff and the defendant were not negligent? *See Bruns v. City of Centralia,* 21 N.E.3d 684 (Ill. 2014) (uneven sidewalk was an open and obvious danger that city had no duty to fix). In some cases, federal and state disability accommodation statutes may play a role in determining defendants' obligations. In other cases, as a matter of common law the defendant may be expected to take greater care in light of plaintiff's disability. For example, in *Green v. Box Butte Gen. Hosp.,* 818 N.W.2d 589 (Neb. 2012), hospital staff permitted a paraplegic patient to transfer himself from his wheelchair to shower chair, during which transfer patient fell to the floor, injuring his shoulder. Whether the hospital's conduct breached a standard of care was a factual issue for the jury's consideration.

4. **Old age.** Cases hold that old age, as such, is not taken into account in setting the standard of care. What if old age produces particular physical disabilities, however, such as an inability to move quickly as a hazard approaches? Should that be taken into account?

5. **Exceptional physical ability.** Suppose, instead of having a physical infirmity, the actor has strength and agility not possessed by normal persons, or that the actor's reaction time is exceptionally good. How would you express the standard of care owed by such a person?

6. **Intoxication.** What is to be done about an intoxicated person? Suppose one is wildly intoxicated, but drives in a perfect way. Injury results, though the driving is flawless. Presumably the law should not attempt to judge the ultimate worth or character of persons, but should judge conduct instead. The general rule is that an intoxicated person owes the same care as a sober person, and that if his overt conduct would be negligence in a sober person, it is also negligence in a drunken one. What can be made of this? Can it be reconciled with the rule that one considers physical impairments as one of the circumstances? Is it possible that in the case of voluntary intoxication the risk is taken when intoxicants are consumed, rather than later when the defendant drives?

7. **Sudden incapacitation.** Courts have uniformly held that where a person's alleged negligence is caused by a sudden physical incapacitation that is not foreseeable, there should be no liability. The standard of care, of course, is that of a reasonable and prudent person under the same or similar circumstances. Thus, for example, if a reasonable and prudent person would have had no notice of the sudden seizure or heart attack, and that incapacitation caused the conduct that led to the plaintiff's injury, the defendant is not legally responsible. RESTATEMENT (THIRD) OF TORTS: LIABILITY FOR PHYSICAL AND EMOTIONAL HARM § 11 cmt. d (2010). Many courts place the burden of proving sudden incapacitation on the defendant. *See, e.g.,*

Roman v. Estate of Gobbo, 791 N.E.2d 422 (Ohio 2003) (driver of vehicle died from sudden heart attack and caused accident). What if a person has a serious medical condition and has been warned by doctors not to drive, but does so anyway, suffers a seizure, and causes an accident? How does the standard of care work in that case? *Cf. Denson v. Estate of Dillard*, 116 N.E.3d 535 (Ind. Ct. App. 2018) (decedent who drove into a house during a heart attack was not liable despite having recently had a heart attack because medical personnel had not recommended driving restrictions and, thus, the heart attack causing the accident was not "reasonably foreseeable")

8.   **Contributory negligence.** The common law called a plaintiff's negligence "contributory negligence" and held that it barred the plaintiff's recovery completely. In most states today, the contributory negligence of a plaintiff operates to reduce the plaintiff's recovery of damages, but does not necessarily bar recovery completely. The focus of contributory negligence is often on the idea that the plaintiff should take reasonable care for herself, not on her failure to take care for others. The difference between plaintiff and defendant negligence is a slight one, and the standard of care is often the same, whether the risks were to self or others. RESTATEMENT (THIRD) OF TORTS: LIABILITY FOR PHYSICAL AND EMOTIONAL HARM § 3 cmt. a (2010); RESTATEMENT (THIRD) OF TORTS: APPORTIONMENT OF LIABILITY § 3 cmt. b (2000). Some thinkers say that the objective standard of reasonable care should not apply to unreasonable risks to self. Can you formulate an argument for or against this view?

CREASY V. RUSK

730 N.E.2d 659 (Ind. 2000)

SULLIVAN, JUSTICE. . . .

In July, 1992, Lloyd Rusk's wife admitted Rusk to the Brethren Healthcare Center ("BHC") because he suffered from memory loss and confusion and Rusk's wife was unable to care for him. Rusk's primary diagnosis was Alzheimer's disease. Over the course of three years at BHC, Rusk experienced periods of anxiousness, confusion, depression, disorientation, and agitation. Rusk often resisted when staff members attempted to remove him from prohibited areas of the facility. On several occasions, Rusk was belligerent with both staff and other residents. In particular, Rusk was often combative, agitated, and aggressive and would hit staff members when they tried to care for him. . . .

On May 16, 1995, Creasy and another certified nursing assistant, Linda Davis, were working through their routine of putting Rusk and other residents to bed. Creasy knew that Rusk had been "very agitated and combative that evening." By Creasy's account:

[Davis] was helping me put Mr. Rusk to bed. She was holding his wrists to keep him from hitting us and I was trying to get his legs to put him to bed. He was hitting and kicking wildly. During this time, he kicked me several times in my left knee and hip area. My lower back popped and I yelled out with pain from my lower back and left knee.

F

. . . Rusk moved for summary judgment and the trial court granted his motion. Creasy appealed. The Court of Appeals reversed, holding "that a person's mental capacity, whether that person is a child or an adult, must be factored [into] the determination of whether a legal duty exists." . . .

PH

[T]he generally accepted rule in jurisdictions other than Indiana is that mental disability does not excuse a person from liability for "conduct which does not conform to the standard of a reasonable man under like circumstances." Restatement (Second) of Torts § 283B; accord Restatement (Third) of Torts § 9(c) (Discussion Draft Apr. 5, 1999) ("Unless the actor is a child, the actor's mental or emotional disability is not considered in determining whether conduct is negligent."). People with mental disabilities are commonly held liable for their intentional and negligent torts. No allowance is made for lack of intelligence, ignorance, excitability, or proneness to accident. See Restatement (Second) of Torts § 283B cmt. c.

Legal scholars and authorities recognize that it is "impossible to ascribe either the volition implicit in an intentional tort, the departure from the standard of a 'reasonable' person which defines an act of ordinary negligence, or indeed any concept of 'fault' at all to one who . . . is by definition unable to control his [or her] own actions through any exercise of reason." Rather, the Restatement rule holding people with mental disabilities liable for their torts was founded upon public policy considerations.

The public policy reasons most often cited for holding individuals with mental disabilities to a standard of reasonable care in negligence claims include the following.

What other cases are saying

(1) Allocates losses between two innocent parties to the one who caused or occasioned the loss. . . .

(2) Provides incentive to those responsible for people with disabilities and interested in their estates to prevent harm and "restrain" those who are potentially dangerous. . . .

(3) Removes inducements for alleged tortfeasors to fake a mental disability in order to escape liability. . . .

(4) Avoids administrative problems involved in courts and juries attempting to identify and assess the significance of an actor's disability. As a practical matter, it is arguably too difficult to account for or draw any "satisfactory line between mental deficiency and those variations of temperament, intellect, and emotional balance."

(5) Forces persons with disabilities to pay for the damage they do if they "are to live in the world." A discussion draft for the Restatement (Third) of Torts rephrases this policy rationale and concludes: "[I]f a person is suffering from a mental disorder so serious as to make it likely that the person will engage in substandard conduct that threatens the safety of others, there can be doubts as to whether this person should be allowed to engage in the normal range of society's activities; given these doubts, there is nothing especially harsh in at least holding the person responsible for the harms the person may cause by substandard conduct." Restatement (Third) of Torts § 9 cmt. e (Discussion Draft April 5, 1999). . . .

Since the 1970s, Indiana law has strongly reflected policies to deinstitutionalize people with disabilities and integrate them into the least restrictive environment. National policy changes have led the way for some of Indiana's enactments in that several federal acts either guarantee the civil rights of people with disabilities or condition state aid upon state compliance with desegregation and integrationist practices. See, e.g., Individuals with Disabilities Education Act, 20 U.S.C. §§ 1400 et seq. (1994) (requiring that children with disabilities receive a free appropriate public education in the least restrictive environment in states that accept allocated funds) (originally enacted in 1975 as the Education for All Handicapped Children Act, P.L. 94–142 (amending the state education grant program under the 1970 Education for the Handicapped Act, P.L. 91–230; requiring states to provide a free appropriate public education to all children with disabilities in order to receive state grant funds)); Americans with Disabilities Act, 42 U.S.C. § 12132 (1994), and implementing regulation 28 C.F.R. § 35.130(d) (1999) (providing that a public entity shall administer services, programs, and activities in the most integrated setting appropriate to the needs of qualified individuals with disabilities); Fair Housing Act, 42 U.S.C. § 3604 (1994) (prohibiting discrimination based on "handicap" in the sale or rental of a dwelling).

These legislative developments reflect . . . a determination that people with disabilities should be treated in the same way as non-disabled persons.

[T]he Restatement rule may very well have been grounded in a policy determination that persons with mental disabilities should be institutionalized or otherwise confined rather than "live in the world." It is clear from our recitation of state and federal legislative and regulatory developments that contemporary public policy has rejected institutionalization and confinement for a "strong professional consensus in favor of . . . community treatment . . . and integration into the least restrictive . . . environment." . . . We observe that it is a matter of some irony that public policies favoring the opposite ends—institutionalization and confinement on the one hand and community treatment and integration into the least restrictive environment on the other—should nevertheless yield the same common law rule: that the general duty of care imposed on adults with mental disabilities is the same as that for adults without mental disabilities.

Rule

. . . We hold that a person with mental disabilities is generally held to the same standard of care as that of a reasonable person under the same circumstances without regard to the alleged tortfeasor's capacity to control or understand the consequences of his or her actions.

H/D

[However, one employed to take care of a patient known to be combative because of Alzheimer's disease has no complaint for injuries sustained in doing so. As to such a caretaker the duty of care is a one-way street, from caretaker to patient, not the other way around. Hence Rusk is not liable on these facts.]

NOTES

1. **Other cases.** *Accord*, that a mentally disabled person, involuntarily hospitalized, does not owe a duty of care to his professional caregiver and hence is not liable for negligence or recklessness causing the caregiver harm, *Streifel v. Bulkley*, 224 A.3d 539 (Conn. App. 2020); *Berberian v. Lynn*, 845 A.2d 122 (N.J. 2004). Cases that state a subjective standard for mentally deficient plaintiffs seem to be in reality cases based on the limited duty a confined disabled person owes to his caregiver. However, *Hofflander v. St. Catherine's Hosp., Inc.*, 664 N.W.2d 545 (Wis. 2003), clearly states a subjective standard for situations like the one in *Creasy v. Rusk*. On the court's analysis, would *Creasy* have come out differently if Rusk had injured a person who was in the hospital visiting another patient?

2. **"Defense" vs. "standard of care."** Sometimes insanity is discussed as a possible "defense," but it seems clear that the underlying issue is about the standard of care, not about defenses. The view of the Restatement (Third) of Torts § 11(c) (2010), the Restatement (Second) of Torts § 283B (1965), and the prevailing orthodoxy, is that neither insanity nor mental deficiency relieves the actor from liability, and that the actor's conduct must conform to the general standard of care of a reasonable person under similar external circumstances. Can the defendant meet that standard?

3. **Mental and psychological limitations.** Low intelligence and other mental or psychological limitations are treated the same way. Thomas is a sane man of low intelligence. He has never connected the danger of fire with his storage of rags, newspapers, and paint thinner in his garage. A fire originates in his garage and spreads to his neighbor's house. The jury will be instructed that Thomas is held to the care of a reasonable and prudent person. He does not escape liability because he did "the best he could do," or because he behaved as well as others of similar intelligence would have. Why might the tort law hold him to an objective standard of reasonable care?

4. **Considering rationales.** In its policy reasoning, the court in *Creasy* notes that the standard it adopts "[a]llocates losses between two innocent

parties to the one who caused or occasioned the loss." Is this the typical rule in tort law? In the *Van Camp* case from Chapter 1? Are the rules of liability for insane and mentally deficient persons based upon justice? Deterrence? The *Creasy* court suggests that policies supporting the "opposite ends" of community treatment and institutionalization nevertheless lead to the same common law rule. Can that be right?

5.   **Consistency?** Are the rules for mental disability at odds with the rules for physical disability? Can you harmonize or justify the difference in the law's treatment of these two situations? What about a mental disability that clearly springs from a physical disability—such as mental retardation that results from cerebral palsy? Should that condition be taken into account in setting the standard of care? *See Sanders v. Alger*, 394 P.3d 1083 (Ariz. 2017) (man with cerebral palsy and developmental disabilities owed caregiver the duty "of a reasonable person under the circumstances, and those circumstances include his physical disabilities and limitations"); *Burch v. American Family Mut. Ins. Co.*, 543 N.W.2d 277 (Wis. 1996).

6.   **Persons with superior knowledge.** What is to be done about a person with superior knowledge or mental ability, who can appreciate and act on some risk which reasonable and prudent persons, not having the special knowledge, would ignore?

––––––––––

HILL V. SPARKS, 546 S.W.2d 473 (Mo. Ct. App. 1976). Wayne Sparks was an operator of earth-moving machinery and had several seasons experience with a machine known as an earth scraper. At an exhibit of such machines he drove one, instructing his sister to stand on a ladder on the machine. It hit a mound of dirt and, because of its large rubber tires, bounced back. Sparks' sister was thrown forward in front of the left wheel and was run over before Sparks could stop the machine. She died almost instantly. This is an action for her death. "[Sparks], as an operator, with several seasons experience with earth scrapers, was familiar with the propensities of such machines. . . . He had heard decedent's husband, upon observing a boy riding on the scraper ladder during the demonstration, tell a Liberty Equipment employee to get the boy off the scraper because if he fell he would fall right under the wheel. Despite his knowledge and experience, appellant directed his sister to ride as a passenger on the ladder while he operated the machine. . . . 'The standard of the reasonable man requires only a minimum of attention, perception, memory, knowledge, intelligence, and judgment in order to recognize the existence of the risk. If the actor has in fact more than the minimum of these qualities, he is required to exercise the superior qualities that he has in a manner reasonable under the circumstances.' 2 Restatement of Torts (2d) § 289. . . . The evidence in this case presented an issue submissible to the jury of whether . . . appellant met the requisite standard of care."

NOTES

1. **Special training.** A high school sports coach has received special courses dealing with injured students. Would the standard of care require the coach of a small high school team to use this special knowledge in deciding whether to keep an injured player in a football game? *See Cerny v. Cedar Bluffs Junior/Senior Pub. Sch.*, 628 N.W.2d 697 (Neb. 2001), *on appeal after remand*, 679 N.W.2d 198 (Neb. 2004); *cf. Dakter v. Cavallino*, 866 N.W.2d 656 (Wis. 2015) (driver of semi tractor-trailer had duty to exercise degree of care appropriate for his profession or trade).

2. **Experts' knowledge of risk.** With babies, sudden infant death syndrome (SIDS) is a small risk. Allowing babies to sleep on their stomachs multiplies the risk—the risk is at least double, maybe as much as 12 times as great as the risk when babies sleep on their backs. If a baby dies from SIDS after the daycare center has placed her to sleep on her stomach, would the plaintiff need some kind of testimony to show that the daycare center should have known of the risk? What if the daycare center admits that it knew about a recommendation of the American Academy of Pediatrics against prone sleeping because of the risk of SIDS associated with it? *LePage v. Horne*, 809 A.2d 505 (Conn. 2002).

3. **Expertise when the actor is not acting in her capacity as an expert.** A medical doctor's special training will certainly be taken into account where the doctor is a defendant in a medical malpractice case, a situation we address at length in Chapter 13. But what if a doctor is a plaintiff in a lawsuit, claiming an injury caused by another doctor's negligence in failing to diagnose the plaintiff's condition when the plaintiff was a patient? Should the plaintiff's special knowledge and training be taken into account in determining whether he was contributorily negligent in failing to tell the defendant doctor about all of his symptoms? *See Jackson v. Axelrad*, 221 S.W.3d 650 (Tex. 2007).

STEVENS V. VEENSTRA

573 N.W.2d 341 (Mich. Ct. App. 1998)

MURPHY, PRESIDING JUDGE. . . .

As a fourteen-year-old, defendant Aaron Veenstra took a driver's education course offered through the Calumet Public School system. Veenstra had skipped four grades in elementary school and graduated from high school early. He was taking driver's education so that he would have transportation to college. Before the driver's education course, Veenstra had never driven an automobile on a public road in a developed area. On the first day of the driving portion of the class, Veenstra stopped the automobile he was driving at an intersection. When the traffic cleared, Veenstra made a right turn. However, Veenstra turned too sharply and headed at plaintiff who was getting out of his parked automobile. Both Veenstra and the driving instructor attempted to turn Veenstra's automobile away from plaintiff. Veenstra testified that as he was heading for plaintiff, he may have hit the accelerator instead of the brake. As a result, Veenstra's automobile struck plaintiff.

At trial, over plaintiff's objection, the trial court gave the following instruction:

A minor is not held to the same standard of conduct as an adult. When I use the words "ordinary care" with respect to the minor, Aaron S. Veenstra, I mean that degree of care which a reasonably careful minor of age, mental capacity and experience of Aaron S. Veenstra would use under the circumstances which you find existed in this case. It is for you to decide what a reasonably careful minor would do or would not do under such circumstances.

Utilizing this instruction, the jury found that Veenstra was not negligent.

On appeal, plaintiff claims that the trial court's instruction was improper and mandates reversal. We agree. . . .

Generally, in the context of negligence actions, the capability of minors, seven years of age or older, is not determined on the basis of an adult standard of conduct, but rather is determined on the basis of how a minor of similar age, mental capacity, and experience would conduct himself. However, Michigan "has a longstanding policy of holding all drivers, even minors, to an adult standard of care." A minor who engages in an adult activity that is dangerous, e.g., driving an automobile, is charged with the same standard of conduct as an adult. . . .

Veenstra and the trial court consider this case to be distinguishable from prior cases holding that minors driving automobiles are held to an adult standard of conduct and call for an exception to that rule. . . . Veenstra defines the activity he was involved in as not simply driving an automobile, but driving an automobile as part of a driver's education course to satisfy the legislative requirements placed upon those under eighteen years of age seeking to obtain an operator's license, and claims that because he was engaged in an activity, which by definition is limited to minors, he was not engaged in an adult activity and should not be held to an adult standard of conduct. We disagree.

One rationale behind holding a minor driving an automobile to an adult standard of conduct is that, because of the frequency and sometimes catastrophic results of automobile accidents, it would be unfair to the public to permit a minor operating an automobile to observe any standard of care other than that expected of all others operating automobiles. It would seem illogical to think that the dangers associated with driving are lessened when the activity is undertaken by a minor with little or no experience. While we concede that Veenstra was attempting to satisfy requirements placed only upon minors, we do not think that changes the nature of, or danger associated with, driving an automobile. . . .

While the process of learning involves unique dangers, for which some allowance may be justified for beginners undertaking some activities, when the probability of, or potential harm associated with, a particular activity is great, anyone engaged in the activity must be held to a certain minimum level of competence, even though that level may lie beyond the capability of a beginner. See 2 Restatement Torts, 2d, § 299, comment d, pp. 71–72. In other words, some activities are so dangerous that the risk must be borne by the beginner rather than the innocent victims, and lack of competence is no excuse. We believe that driving an automobile is such an activity, and that anyone driving an automobile, regardless of age, must be held to the same standard of competence and conduct.

Reasoning

Reversed and remanded for a new trial. . . . H

NOTES

1. **General rule for children.** *Stevens* discusses the general rule: a child accused of negligence is held to the standard of care of a reasonably careful child of the same age, intelligence, and experience. 1 DOBBS, HAYDEN & BUBLICK, THE LAW OF TORTS §§ 134–36 (2d ed. 2011). Is the ordinary child standard purely subjective?

2. **Applying the adult standard.** Alaska extended the adult standard to cover a 14-year-old's decision to permit another minor to drive a car with deadly results. *Ardinger v. Hummell*, 982 P.2d 727 (Alaska 1999). Courts have imposed the adult standard almost exclusively in cases of minors operating motorized vehicles. So a 13-year-old might be held to an adult standard when operating a snowmobile. *Robinson v. Lindsay*, 598 P.2d 392 (Wash. 1979). Similarly, a 12-year-old might be held to an adult standard while operating a motor boat, but only to a child standard while operating a bicycle. *Hudson v. Old Guard Ins. Co.*, 3 A.3d 246 (Del. 2010). What should be the standard when a 14-year-old allows an 11-year-old to operate a golf cart? *See Hudson-Connor v. Putney*, 86 P.3d 106 (Or. Ct. App. 2004). Meager authority has imposed the adult standard when a minor uses firearms. *See Goss v. Allen,* 360 A.2d 388 (N.J. 1976).

3. **Alternatives.** Should children be held only to the child standard when they are engaged in "carefree" activities appropriate to their development but to the adult standard when they engage in "inherently dangerous" or "adult" activities? Or should other factors enter into the equation as well? Suppose an adult rides on a snowmobile with an operator he knows to be 10 years of age. Would it be reasonable to demand and expect an adult standard of care of the child? RESTATEMENT (THIRD) OF TORTS: LIABILITY FOR PHYSICAL AND EMOTIONAL HARM § 10 cmt. f (2010).

4. **Policy reasons for the ordinary standard of reasonable care.** As Judge Posner has written: "The goal of the average-person rule (to give it

the more perspicuous name), in instrumental terms, is to provide an additional incentive, beyond that of moral duty or concern with personal safety, to avoid injuring people (or being injured). A driver who falls below the average of care, and as a result injures someone, is subject to tort liability; it is hoped that the threat will motivate drivers to be careful to avoid injuring others (or themselves). . . . But this motivational system works only if potential injurers and potential victims are capable of exercising the care of the average person, or if incapable can at least avoid situations in which they are likely to cause or suffer injury. Drivers have to be licensed, and this excludes, in principle anyway, the least competent persons." *Arroyo v. United States*, 656 F.3d 663 (7th Cir. 2011) (Posner, J., concurring). Would this policy be an argument for or against an adult standard in *Veenstra*?

5.   **Risks to self.** Should the result differ in a case of contributory negligence when the child's conduct poses risks to himself? In *Strait v. Crary*, 496 N.W.2d 634 (Wis. Ct. App. 1992), a 16-year-old who was drinking alcohol while riding in a truck attempted to climb out the window of the moving truck. He fell out and suffered a broken leg. The court used the child standard in determining whether he was guilty of contributory negligence. This was a dangerous activity. Why not use the adult standard?

6.   **The rule of sevens.** A few courts still say that minors over 14 are presumed capable of negligence, those between seven and 14 are presumed incapable of it, and those below seven are incapable of negligence as a matter of law. The rule of sevens is not so common now, but most states hold that children of very young years, three and under, are simply incapable of negligence. The Restatement (Third) of Torts § 10(b) provides that children under five are incapable of negligence.

7.   **Trial problems.** Even though Veenstra was driving a car, the trial court held that the adult standard did not apply. What made the lawyers try to distinguish this case and argue for application of a child standard here?

§ 3. NEGLIGENCE PER SE: USING SAFETY-RELATED RULES TO SPECIFY PARTICULAR TORT DUTIES

MARTIN V. HERZOG, 126 N.E. 814 (N.Y. 1920). Defendant, driving at night, crossed over the center line on a curve and struck a buggy occupied by decedent, causing his death. In a wrongful death action the defendant contended that decedent was negligent in driving without lights. A statute provided in part: "Every vehicle on wheels whether stationary or in motion, while upon any public street . . . shall have attached thereto a light or lights to be visible from the front and from the rear from one hour after sunset to one hour before sunrise. . . . A person violating the provisions of this section shall be guilty of a misdemeanor punishable by a fine not to exceed ten dollars." The trial judge charged the jury that decedent's violation of the statute could be considered as evidence of contributory negligence but not as negligence in itself. The jury found for the plaintiff. The Appellate Division reversed for new trial. In the Court of Appeals, by Cardozo, J., *held*, the Appellate Division is affirmed. "We think the unexcused omission of the statutory signals is more than some evidence of negligence. It is negligence in itself. . . . Yet the jurors were instructed in effect that they were at liberty in their discretion to treat the omission of lights either as innocent or as culpable. They were allowed to 'consider the default as lightly or gravely' as they would. They might as well have been told that they could use a like discretion in holding a master at fault for the omission of a safety appliance prescribed by positive law for the protection of a workman. Jurors have no dispensing power, by which they may relax the duty that one traveler on the highway owes under the statute to another."

SMITH V. WELLS, 212 A.3d 554 (Pa. Super. 2019). Defendant Andrew Wells was driving down the Pennsylvania Turnpike. Plaintiff Richard Smith, who was driving in front of him, saw that traffic was braking, and stopped. Defendant, by his own admission, "didn't stop quick enough . . . and rear-ended the car in front of me," creating a four-car pile-up. Defendant's lawyer, in his opening statement to the jury, said "the collision was Mr. Wells' fault . . . no question about it." The defense rested entirely on an argument that the wreck was not the actual cause of Smith's injuries, as Smith had been in three prior automobile accidents. "Smith moved for a directed verdict that Mr. Wells negligently drove his vehicle and so breached the standard of care as a matter of law. The trial court denied that motion and authored a verdict slip asking the jury:

> Do you find that Defendant Adam Wells was negligent?
>
> Yes _____ No _____

. . . The jury answered that question in the negative. Smith moved for judgment notwithstanding the verdict (JNOV) on the question of negligence, which the trial court denied." On appeal, *held:* the trial court's refusal to award plaintiff judgment as a matter of law was error. "[A]ll the other drivers conformed their speed to the mandates of the General Assembly, which has legislated as follows:

> No person shall drive a vehicle at a speed greater than is reasonable and prudent under the conditions and having regard to the actual and potential hazards then existing, *nor at a speed greater than will permit the driver to bring his vehicle to a stop within the assured clear distance ahead.* . . .

7[5] Pa.C.S.A. § 3361 (emphasis added). By its plain language, violation of this statute's second clause establishes Mr. Well's negligence per se. That clause prohibits anyone from driving at any 'speed greater than will permit the driver to bring his vehicle to a stop within the assured clear distance ahead.' Our legislature used the disjunctive conjunction 'nor.' Thus, the clause following 'nor' operates independently of the first clause's focus upon a 'reasonable and prudent' driving speed 'under the conditions . . . and potential hazards' of a roadway. . . . Section 3361 . . . prohibits two distinct forms of illegal driving. The first is driving at any speed that is unreasonable and imprudent for the conditions and hazards of the road. The second is driving at any speed that prevents a driver from fully braking before striking a car, pedestrian, or other object ahead. The latter violation, if committed, gives rise to negligence per se on the part of the driver striking the car, pedestrian, or other object ahead, because the legislature intended to protect all of them when it enacted Section 3361. Here, Mr. Wells drove at a speed that made it impossible for him to stop his vehicle within the assured clear distance ahead, because that distance ahead ended where Mr. Smith's bumper began."

NOTES

1.   **Negligence per se.** What is the function of the negligence per se doctrine? Notice the jury decision in each case, and the ultimate disposition after appeal. What is Justice Cardozo's concern in *Martin* with a jury being allowed to determine that a statutory violation was only evidence of plaintiff's negligence, rather than negligence in itself?

2.   **Negligence per se and negligence as a matter of law.** Is the court in *Smith* saying that there is a rule of law that a driver must be able to drive at a speed that will permit the driver to stop within the clear distance ahead, whether or not a reasonable person would be able to do so? Or is the court saying that defendant was guilty of negligence "as a matter of law," that is, that there is no room for reasonable jurors to differ about this conclusion? Or both? What's the difference?

3.   **A statute's effect on the duty of care.** The position taken in *Smith* and in *Martin* is the one followed by the Restatement and most courts, namely, that the unexcused violation of such statutes is, subject to some qualifications, "negligence per se." This means that violation of the statute actually determines the actor's negligence. Said another way, when a court applies the negligence per se rule to a statute, the statute itself supplants the usual common law standard of care, and violation of the statute establishes the element of duty and guides the element of breach. *See* RESTATEMENT (THIRD) OF TORTS: LIABILITY FOR PHYSICAL AND EMOTIONAL HARM § 14 (2010).

4.   **Types of statutes covered by the negligence per se rule.** In a negligence per se case, the legislature has neither expressly nor impliedly provided for civil liability. For example, a statute might set a speed limit for vehicles on the highway, prescribing a civil or criminal penalty for violation but not mentioning anything at all about the liability of a violator to someone harmed by a crash caused by speeding. In such a case, the court has discretion to choose whether or not to apply the statute as the standard of care, through the doctrine of negligence per se doctrine.

5. **Purpose of negligence per se.** Why might courts, exercising their common law authority, treat an actor's violation of safety-related statutes as negligence per se? The Third Restatement provides three rationales. "First, even when the legislature has not chosen to attach a liability provision to the prohibition it has imposed, as a matter of institutional comity it would be awkward for a court in a tort case to commend as reasonable that behavior that the legislature has already condemned as unlawful. Second, in ordinary tort cases, so long as reasonable minds can differ, the responsibility for determining whether a person's conduct is negligent is vested in the jury. One major reason for this is to take advantage of community assessments in making the negligence determination. Yet when the legislature has addressed the issue of what conduct is appropriate, the judgment of the legislature, as the authoritative representative of the community, takes precedence over the views of any one jury. Third, it must be recognized that the negligence standard encounters difficulty in dealing with problems of recurring conduct. When each jury makes up its own mind as to the negligence of that conduct, there are serious disadvantages in terms of inequality, high litigation costs, and failing to provide clear guidance to persons engaged in primary activity." RESTATEMENT (THIRD) OF TORTS: LIABILITY FOR PHYSICAL AND EMOTIONAL HARM § 14 cmt. c (2010).

6. **Jurisdictional variations.** Some states make violation of such a statute some *evidence of negligence* that may be considered by the jury, rather than regarding the statute as setting the standard of care. *See, e.g.*, WASH. REV. CODE § 5.40.050; *Brooks v. Lewin Realty III, Inc.*, 835 A.2d 616 (Md. 2003); *Kalata v. Anheuser-Busch Cos.*, 581 N.E.2d 656 (Ill. 1991). This puts the ultimate decision on the negligence issue with the jury. California's rule is different still: Evidence Code § 669 says that when a statute applies and a person has violated it, the failure of that person to exercise due care is presumed. The burden is then placed upon the violator to rebut that presumption.

7. **Negligence per se versus statutes that create a private right of action.** Negligence per se is not applicable to all statutes. First, the doctrine applies only to statutes that declare conduct unlawful but are silent as to civil liability—statutes that either do not expressly provide for civil liability or which "cannot be readily interpreted as impliedly creating a private right of action." RESTATEMENT (THIRD) OF TORTS: LIABILITY FOR PHYSICAL AND EMOTIONAL HARM § 14 cmts. b & c (2010). Where a statute itself provides for civil liability, creating a private right of action, the court must simply apply it. For example, a statute might provide that generators of hazardous wastes must dispose of them only in certain permitted ways, and that a person injured by unpermitted disposal has a statutory cause of action for damages against the waste generator. *See, e.g.*, *Hickle v. Whitney Farms, Inc.*, 64 P.3d 1244 (Wash. 2003) (applying WASH. REV. CODE § 70.95.240). Or a statute could provide that the owner or keeper of a dog that damages the property or person of another must pay compensation to the person whose property or person is harmed. *See, e.g.*, *Auster v. Norwalk United Methodist Church*, 943 A.2d 391

(Conn. 2008) (applying CONN. GEN. STAT. § 22–357). In such cases the court simply applies and enforces the statutory right.

When civil legislation expressly excludes a private cause of action for physical injury, courts are unlikely to use the statute as negligence per se. *See Wartluft v. Milton Hershey Sch. & Sch. Tr.*, 400 F.Supp.3d 91 (M.D. Pa. 2019) (ADA); *Z.J. v. Vanderbilt Univ.*, 355 F.Supp.3d 646 (M.D. Tenn. 2018) (Clery Act specifically states that its provisions do not give rise to private cause of action against educational institutions).

8. **Statutory instruments covered by the rule.** Courts usually apply the negligence per se rule to violations of city ordinances and even to violations of administrative regulations as well as to state and federal statutes. *See, e.g., HDI-Gerling Am. Ins. Co. v. Carlile Transportation Sys., Inc.*, 426 P.3d 881 (Alaska 2018) (applying negligence per se to federal statute requiring truckers to use flashers or deploy triangles when stopped); *Winger v. CM Holdings, L.L.C.*, 881 N.W.2d 433 (Iowa 2016) (breach of safety-related requirement— here a guardrail height rule—in a municipal ordinance is negligence per se); *Mize v. Mentor Worldwide LLC*, 265 Cal.Rptr.3d 468 (Ct. App. 2020) (failure to report breast implant failures to the FDA; plaintiff injuries are the type that FDA regulations sought to prevent and plaintiff was in the class protected). A few courts, however, hold that violation of an ordinance or administrative regulation is merely some evidence of negligence. *See Lang v. Holly Hill Motel, Inc.*, 909 N.E.2d 120 (Ohio 2009) (violation of administrative regulation is evidence of negligence only); *Elliott v. City of New York*, 747 N.E.2d 760 (N.Y. 2001) (violation of ordinances is evidence of negligence only).

9. **Judge-made rules.** In *Martin* and *Smith*, the court applied a statute as per se negligence, as is most usual today. However, courts have crafted similar rules of law on their own. *See Marshall v. Southern Railway Co.*, 62 S.E.2d 489 (N.C. 1950) (car hit an unlighted trestle; car must be able to stop within the range of its lights). Almost all rules of this kind have come to grief, or have caused it. *Chaffin v. Brame*, 64 S.E.2d 276 (N.C. 1951) (car hit an unlighted truck left on the highway; question was reasonable care). Justice Holmes once took the view that it was contributory negligence not to stop, look, and listen at a railroad crossing and that, if vision was impaired, one might be expected to get out of the car and walk to the edge of the track to assess the danger. *Baltimore & O. R. Co. v. Goodman*, 275 U.S. 66 (1927). Justice Cardozo was later able gently to push this decision aside, pointing to some of the injustices that could result. "Illustrations such as these," he said, "bear witness to the need for caution in framing standards of behavior that amount to rules of law. The need is the more urgent when there is no background of experience out of which the standards have emerged. They are then, not the natural flowering of behavior in its customary forms, but rules artificially developed and imposed from without." *Pokora v. Wabash Ry.*, 292 U.S. 98 (1934). Despite the statutory basis of the standard in *Smith,* should that case have come out differently, as in *Chaffin,* if defendant had run into an unlighted truck on the highway?

O'GUIN V. BINGHAM COUNTY

122 P.3d 308 (Idaho 2005)

TROUT, JUSTICE.

Frank and Leslie O'Guin, acting as individuals and as legal guardians of Frank O'Guin Jr. (the O'Guins), appeal the district court's grant of summary judgment in favor of Bingham County, Bingham County Commissioners and Bingham County Public Works, (collectively the County). Because the district court erred in its determinations regarding the negligence *per se* claim, we reverse the grant of summary judgment. *PH*

On July 7, 1999, Shaun and Alex O'Guin were killed while playing at the Bingham County landfill. Apparently, a section of the pit wall collapsed and crushed the children. Their older brother, Frank Jr., initially *F* discovered their bodies at the bottom of the pit. Earlier that day, the children had been eating lunch at Ridgecrest Elementary School as part of a summer lunch program. As they started walking home, the children went through an unlocked gate at the back of the schoolyard and through a privately owned empty field. The empty field is situated between the landfill and the schoolyard. The border between the empty field and the landfill was unobstructed. At the time of the children's death, the landfill was open to the public one day a week. It was closed on the day the children were killed and no landfill employees were present on the site.

[The O'Guins sued the County for negligence, claiming among other things that the County was negligent per se, relying on Idaho statutes and federal regulations. The trial court granted the County's motion for *PH* summary judgment on the count of negligence per se, and the O'Guins appealed.]

Generally, the question of whether a duty exists is a question of law, over which we exercise free review. Negligence *per se,* which results from the violation of a specific requirement of law or ordinance, is a question of law, over which this Court exercises free review.

The dispute in this case focuses on the duty or standard of care the *I* County owed to the O'Guin children. . . . In Idaho, it is well established that statutes and administrative regulations may define the applicable standard of care owed, and that violations of such statutes and regulations may constitute negligence *per se.* A court may adopt 'as the standard of conduct of a reasonable man the requirements of a legislative enactment or an administrative regulation. The effect of establishing negligence *per* *what* *se* through violation of a statute is to conclusively establish the first two *negligence per* elements of a cause of action in negligence. Negligence *per se* lessens the *se is* plaintiff's burden only on the issue of the 'actor's departure from the standard of conduct required of a reasonable man.'" Thus, the elements of duty and breach are taken away from the jury.

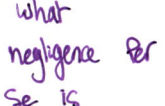

In order to replace a common law duty of care with a duty of care from a statute or regulation, the following elements must be met: (1) the statute or regulation must clearly define the required standard of conduct; (2) the statute or regulation must have been intended to prevent the type of harm the defendant's act or omission caused; (3) the plaintiff must be a member of the class of persons the statute or regulation was designed to protect; and (4) the violation must have been the proximate cause of the injury.

As to the first element, the district court found, and we agree, that the statute and regulations in this case clearly define the County's standard of conduct. . . . These regulations require the County to fence or otherwise block access to the landfill when an attendant is not on duty. The Legislature has specifically declared it to be "unlawful" to fail to comply with the landfill rules. In this case, the record reveals that on July 7, 1999, some of the landfill boundaries were not fenced or blocked. There is also evidence that the landfill was closed and no attendant was on duty on July 7, 1999. Therefore, the district court was correct that the regulations clearly define the County's required standard of conduct, and the County failed to meet that standard.

The second element asks whether the death of the O'Guin children is the type of harm the statute and regulations were intended to prevent. Idaho Code Section 39–7401(2) states:

> [I]t is the intent of the legislature to establish a program of solid waste management which complies with 40 CFR 258 and facilitates the incorporation of flexible standards in facility design and operation. The legislature hereby establishes the solid waste disposal standards and procedures outlined herein and a facility approval process for the state of Idaho, the political subdivisions thereof, and any private solid waste disposal site owner in order to facilitate the development and operation of solid waste disposal sites, to effect timely and responsible completion of statutory duties and to ensure protection of human health and the environment, to protect the air, land and waters of the state of Idaho.

This section demonstrates the legislature's desire to ensure the "protection of human health" in the "development and operation of solid waste disposal sites." It also makes specific reference to 40 C.F.R. § 258. . . . Section 258.25 of the Code of Federal Regulations states "[o]wners or operators of all municipal solid waste landfill units must control public access . . . by using artificial barriers, natural barriers, or both, as appropriate to protect human health." . . . "[P]rotection of human health" . . . certainly includes possible injury or death to people on the facility grounds. Operators of a landfill have a duty not only to prevent illegal dumping and unauthorized vehicular traffic, but to control public access as well.

... These statutes and rules demonstrate that the Legislature intended to safeguard both human health and safety. The injury to the safety of the O'Guin children is the type of harm the Idaho statute and regulations were intended to prevent because the children's deaths relate directly to control of public access and protection of human health and safety.

As to the third element, the O'Guin children are members of the class of persons the regulations were designed to protect. The regulations state "[u]nauthorized vehicles and persons shall be prohibited access to the site." As trespassers, the O'Guin children were certainly "unauthorized persons" and the regulations do not differentiate between the unauthorized person who comes to the landfill to dump improper materials and the unauthorized person who comes to the landfill to play. Furthermore, the regulations require the landfill "be fenced or otherwise blocked to access when an attendant is not on duty." This regulation demonstrates the connection between the requirement that the landfill perimeter be fenced or blocked and the protection of persons whose access is unauthorized. Therefore, the regulations controlling access were designed to protect the human health and safety of the unauthorized person who comes to a landfill when an attendant is not on duty and the O'Guin children fit within that category.

met

Finally, as to the fourth element, there is at least a disputed issue of fact created by an affidavit in the record, as to whether the County's violation of the statute and regulations resulted in the O'Guin children's deaths.

After concluding the regulations established a duty and that the County had breached that duty, the district court held "the O'Guins' allegations of negligence *per se* do not change the duty owed by the County to trespassers." This was error. There was no need for the district court to look to the common law duty owed to trespassers once it determined the statutory duty applied. Liability may become established upon proof that the violation of the statute caused the injuries of the plaintiff and the plaintiff's subsequent damages. A statute that adequately defines the required standard of care "supplants the reasonable person standard encompassed in the concept of ordinary negligence." . . . .

Ruling

. . . Standing alone, the regulations in this case are sufficient to satisfy the duty element for a negligence *per se* action. The O'Guins' use of statutory obligations to establish the County's duty under a negligence *per se* action replaces the common law duty of landowners to trespassers. . . . The district court's grant of summary judgment is vacated and the case remanded for further proceedings. . . .

H/D

JUSTICE EISMANN, Dissenting.

I cannot concur in the majority opinion because the regulations cited therein as supporting a claim of negligence *per se* were clearly not intended to prevent the type of harm involved in this case. . . .

The majority opinion relies upon IDAPA 58.01.06.005.02 and 40 C.F.R. 258.25 as providing the applicable standard of care. Neither of those regulations is intended to prevent trespassers from injuring themselves through an accident at a landfill. They are intended to prevent trespassers from dumping or salvaging materials that may be harmful to health or the environment. . . .

The concern is illegal dumping of wastes that are dangerous to human health and the environment. The word "health" is not normally construed to include freedom from accidents. Rather, it simply means "freedom from disease or abnormality." The majority can reach its conclusion only by redefining the word "health" to include "safety." Such redefinition is not supported either by Idaho law or by the federal regulations. . . .

The [federal] regulation only requires barriers to prevent "unauthorized vehicular traffic and illegal dumping of wastes." The required barriers need not be able to keep out trespassing pedestrians who may accidentally injure themselves at the landfill. . . . [T]he regulation was not intended to require municipal solid waste disposal facilities to fence out trespassing pedestrians. . . .

NOTES

1. **The class of persons and type of harm tests.** As the Idaho court explains in *O'Guin*, a threshold requirement for a statute to be given per se effect is that the injured person must be in a class of persons that the statute is designed to protect, and the type of harm that the actor's conduct causes must be a type that the statute is designed to protect against. These requirements are fairly uniform from state to state. *See* RESTATEMENT (THIRD) OF TORTS: LIABILITY FOR PHYSICAL AND EMOTIONAL HARM § 14 cmts. f & g (2010). As California's high court puts it, the negligence per se rule "arises from a tortfeasor's failure to exercise due care in violation of a statute designed to protect a class of persons, of which the injured party is a member, from the type of injury sustained." *Ramirez v. Nelson*, 188 P.3d 659 (Cal. 2008). *See* 1 DOBBS, HAYDEN & BUBLICK, THE LAW OF TORTS §§ 151–55 (2d ed. 2011).

2. **Judicial applications of the class of persons and type of harm tests.** As you might glean from the *O'Guin* case, there is a good deal of flexibility built in to the determination of whether the injured person is in the protected class and whether the type of harm that occurred is of the same type that the statute was designed to protect against. How does the court in *O'Guin* determine who is in the protected class, and what types of harm the statute was designed to protect against? How do we know whether the majority or the dissent is correct about what the legislature intended?

3. **Judicial adoption of statutes and judicial discretion.** *Must* the court consider legislative purpose to protect a certain class of persons or to protect against a certain type of harm? Remember that the statutes used in negligence per se cases do not themselves create, either expressly or impliedly, tort causes of action. Many courts would agree, therefore, with the statement that the fact the legislature has enacted such a statute "does not necessarily mean that the courts must adopt it as a standard of civil liability. Decisions regarding the proper civil standard of conduct rest with the courts. Thus, the courts must ultimately decide whether they will adopt a statutory standard to define the standard of reasonable persons in specific circumstances." *Rains v. Bend of the River*, 124 S.W.3d 580 (Tenn. Ct. App. 2003) (in an action brought by parents based on their 18-year-old son's suicide by firearm, refusing to adopt as negligence per se a statute that banned the sale of ammunition to minors); *see also Maurer v. Speedway, LLC*, 774 F.3d 1132 (7th Cir. 2014) (plaintiff failed to show that she fell within a class of persons a municipal ordinance on the required width of walkways was intended to protect, so the ordinance was inadmissible).

4. **Judicial ability to determine the scope of a statute's per se application.** If the court is free to adopt the legislative standard as one that reflects what reasonable people would do, what difference does it make that the legislature wrote the particular statute narrowly? To think about this, suppose the statute provides that heavy machinery used at construction sites must automatically make back-up noises when in reverse gear, and that the statute is for the protection of workers at the job site. If the machine in violation of the statute backs over an unsuspecting architecture student who is on the premises to be shown how a building is constructed, he may have no negligence per se claim. *Cf.* RESTATEMENT (SECOND) OF TORTS § 286 illus. 1 (1965). Yet the contractor violated the statute. It would have cost him no more to have complied with it for the purpose of protecting everyone than for the purpose of protecting workers on the job. Besides this, the legislature might have thought back-up beepers were needed "because of danger to workers," without really intending to exclude the possibility of saving other persons as well. These things might suggest that the class of person/class of risk rule should not be used to limit liability. But they might also suggest that the courts should use very general classifications, or, conceivably, that statutory violations should be treated as evidence of negligence even where negligence per se does not apply. In *Scott v. Matlack, Inc.*, 39 P.3d 1160 (Colo. 2002), the court faced a federal statute and regulations specifying workplace safety practices required for the benefit of the employer's employees. The court held that the safety regulations could be admitted in evidence to show industry safety customs not only for employees—the class of persons protected by the statute—but also for independent contractors on the work site.

5. **Statutes used as per se rules.** Varied statues have been given per se effect. *See Aleo v. SLB Toys USA, Inc.*, 995 N.E.2d 740 (Mass. 2013) (federal regulation governing swimming pool slides); *Kiriakos v. Phillips*, 139 A.3d 1006 (Md. 2016) (state regulation barring allowing an individual under 21 to

possess or consume alcohol); *Howard v. Zimmer, Inc.*, 299 P.3d 463 (Okla. 2013) (federal regulation under the Medical Device Amendments to the FDCA); *Miss. Dep't of Transp. v. Nosef*, 110 So.3d 317 (Miss. 2013) (specific law requiring warning signs to be placed around highway culverts; denial of motion to dismiss by Mississippi Department of Transportation pursuant to the general discretionary duty to place traffic-control signs).

6. **Statutes intended to protect the public at large.** One might think that if a court determines that the class protected by a statute is the public at large, the plaintiff will always fit within it. But many courts have held that a statute that does not create a duty to an identifiable class—a subset of the general public, in other words—cannot be given per se effect. *See, e.g., Pehle v. Farm Bureau Life Ins. Co.*, 397 F.3d 897 (10th Cir. 2005). *See also* 1 DOBBS, HAYDEN & BUBLICK, THE LAW OF TORTS § 153 (2d ed. 2011).

7. **The "defining the standard of conduct" requirement.** Why does the *O'Guin* court say that a statute cannot be given negligence per se effect unless it "clearly defines the required standard of conduct?" Could any statute be given per se effect if it did not? *See Shaw v. Metro. Gov't of Nashville & Davidson Cty.*, 596 S.W.3d 726 (Tenn. Ct. App. 2019) (refusing to apply negligence per se to a local code which only provided "general guidance" in "non-specific terms" about keeping public areas free from hazards after the plaintiff slipped and fell on allegedly unmaintained pavement).

8. **Establishing breach of the per se rule.** The *O'Guin* court says the effect of establishing negligence per se "is to conclusively establish the first two elements of a cause of action in negligence." According to the court, "the elements of duty and breach are taken away from the jury." Is that always true? What if the defendant claimed that the landfill boundaries actually had been fully fenced or blocked? Establishing negligence per se requires the plaintiff to prove that the statute to be applied was in fact violated. *Lindblom v. Sun Aviation, Inc.*, 862 N.W.2d 549 (S.D. 2015) (absent an admission of statutory violation, negligence per se is a question for finder of fact); *see also Nicolay v. Stukel*, 900 N.W.2d 71 (S.D. 2017) (rejecting argument that paying a traffic ticket after an accident constitutes an admission). In *Hopper v. Swinnerton*, 317 P.3d 698 (Idaho 2013), the plaintiffs failed to prove that the defendants violated the statute establishing the crime of child custody interference. Therefore, the negligence per se analysis could not proceed. How does the jury's role in determining breach differ when the defendant owes a statutory duty rather than only a duty of reasonable care?

9. **Rejecting statutory standards that impose new duties.** "[T]he defendant in most negligence per se cases already owes the plaintiff a pre-existing common law duty to act as a reasonably prudent person, so that the statute's role is merely to define more precisely what conduct breaches that duty." *Perry v. S.N.*, 973 S.W.2d 301 (Tex. 1998). When the statute creates a wholly new obligation and does not in itself purport to create a new cause of action, courts tend to give the statute no tort law effect at all. That was the case in *Perry*, where the statute required people to report known cases of child

abuse. Since no common law obligation of this sort existed, and the statute did not purport to create a new cause of action, the court denied recovery to children whose abuse might have been avoided if a timely report had been made. Although many courts do not give negligence per se effect to child-abuse reporting statutes, in *Beggs v. State, Dep't of Soc. & Health Servs.*, 247 P.3d 421 (Wash. 2011), the court held that such a statute implied a cause of action against a mandatory reporter who failed to report suspected abuse.

10. **The "causation" requirement.** Many cases say that the negligence per se rule does not impose liability for violation of a statute unless violation is a "proximate" cause of the plaintiff's harm. At times courts use the term "proximate cause" to mean both factual (but-for) cause and scope of liability—concepts addressed in upcoming chapters. For example, what if a third child testified that he saw the O'Guin children enter the landfill by climbing over the fence in a place that was fenced in accordance with statute?

11. **Licensing statutes.** Should courts adopt licensing statutes as standards of care? Perhaps the most famous case on this topic is *Brown v. Shyne*, 151 N.E. 197 (N.Y. 1926). The plaintiff alleged that the defendant held himself out to practice medicine, that his treatments paralyzed her, and that he had no license to practice medicine. The New York Court of Appeals held that the plaintiff could not get to the jury on this allegation but would instead be required to allege and prove negligence by ordinary means. Might it matter whether a physician lacks a license because she has not yet fully satisfied the state's residency requirement or because she has no medical training? RESTATEMENT (THIRD) OF TORTS: LIABILITY FOR PHYSICAL AND EMOTIONAL HARM § 14 cmt. h (2010). For a recent case, see *Colgate v. JUUL Labs, Inc.*, 402 F.Supp.3d 728 (N.D. Cal. 2019) ("Where a statutory provision does not define a standard of care but merely imposes an administrative requirement, such as the requirement to obtain a license or to file a report to support a regulatory scheme, violation of such requirement will not support a negligence per se claim").

12. **Common law negligence and negligence per se.** What would happen if the majority in *O'Guin* had determined that negligence per se did not apply? Notice that the plaintiff can claim negligence on ordinary common law principles even if the statute has no effect. That is, a plaintiff can claim both negligence per se and negligence for the same incident. If the court determines that negligence per se does not apply, the standard of care "defaults" back to the reasonable and prudent person standard. See *Rose Crewboat Servs., Inc. v. Wood Res., LLC*, 425 F.Supp.3d 668 (E.D. La. 2019) (common law negligence claim was an alternative to negligence per se claim; unlighted obstruction in the water could be negligence per se and/or negligence). In *O'Guin*, the standard of care landowners owe to trespassers may be lower than reasonable care in some cases, as we will see in Chapter 12. Indeed, the lower court in *O'Guin* determined that the common law standard of care the defendant landfill owed to the child trespassers was only a duty to refrain from willful and wanton acts, which had not been demonstrated. If the plaintiff is a trespasser who is not owed an ordinary duty of reasonable care

under the common law, showing that negligence per se rules apply becomes particularly significant to the plaintiff. In *Blackburn Ltd. P'ship v. Paul*, 90 A.3d 464 (Md. 2014), a child trespasser fell into the swimming pool at an apartment complex as a result of the defendant's failure to comply with a state regulation on barriers around pools. The child was in a specific class of persons the statute was designed to protect, said the court, reversing the trial court's grant of summary judgment for the defendant on the negligence per se claim.

GOLDSTEIN, GARBER & SALAMA, LLC v. J.B.

797 S.E.2d 87 (Ga. 2017)

HINES, CHIEF JUSTICE. . . .

Plaintiff/appellee J.B. was injured when certified registered nurse anesthetist ("CRNA") Paul Serdula sexually assaulted her in a surgical suite in the dental practice of defendant/appellant GGS. Serdula was hired by GGS as an independent contractor through anesthesia staffing agency Certified Anesthesia Providers; in accordance with its standard practice, that agency conducted an independent credentialing process on Serdula prior to placing him in any medical or dental facilities.

On September 16, 2009, J.B. came to GGS's offices for an outpatient dental procedure. Serdula administered anesthesia to J.B. and kept her in a heavily sedated state for approximately two hours, which included a 35-minute break between two phases of her procedure. At some point, J.B. was left alone with Serdula, and Serdula made three brief video recordings of himself sexually molesting her. These videos of J.B., as well as videos of Serdula sexually molesting other anesthetized patients, were later discovered when Serdula's hidden cell phone was found recording employees in GGS's office restroom. Prior to the crimes committed by Serdula against J.B., GGS had no knowledge of anything in Serdula's record that indicated he might sexually molest or otherwise harm a patient.

J.B. filed suit against GGS and Serdula, but withdrew her claims against Serdula after he pled guilty to numerous criminal charges related to his sexual assaults on patients and was sentenced to life in prison; she continued her suit against GGS, including claims for negligence per se and professional negligence. At trial, a jury found in favor of J.B., and the trial court entered judgment on that verdict. On appeal, the Court of Appeals affirmed the trial court, and this Court granted GGS's petition for a writ of certiorari. . . .

[T]he Court of Appeals erred in its analysis regarding negligence per se. As that Court noted, J.B.'s claim of negligence per se rested upon GGS's violation of permitting requirements of OCGA § 43–11–21.1,[6] which

---

[6]   OCGA § 43–11–21.1 reads:

governs when dentists may administer general anesthesia, or have it administered by a CRNA under a dentist's supervision. Although it was admitted that the dentists who were employees or agents of GGS did not have the permits required by OCGA § 43–11–21.1 (a), that alone does not establish negligence per se. Rather, negligence per se arises when a statute is violated, the person injured by the violation is within the class of persons the statute was intended to protect, and the harm complained of was the harm the statute was intended to guard against.

Although J.B. falls within the class of persons intended to be protected by OCGA § 43–11–21.1, the question is whether sexual assault is the type of harm the statute is intended to guard against. Although nothing in OCGA § 43–11–21.1 suggests that such harm is contemplated thereby, the Court of Appeals looked elsewhere in the same chapter of the Code in which OCGA § 43–11–21.1 is found, and identified purported authority for its finding that sexual assault is a harm that OCGA § 43–11–21.1 "was intended to guard against." In that regard, the Court of Appeals noted that OCGA § 43–11–2 (e)7 states that "such unlicensed activities as are mentioned in this chapter are a menace and a nuisance dangerous to the public health, safety, and welfare," and found that term was broad enough to encompass the injuries suffered here.

We disagree. Rather, the language of OCGA § 43–11–21.1 shows that its concern is to avoid medical complications that may arise in a dental setting from improper use of anesthesia due to improper training and experience, or inadequate equipment. In this context, the term "health, safety, and welfare" does not implicate the remote, nonmedical injuries suffered by J.B. Indeed, that this is so is evident by examining the precedent that the Court of Appeals cited for its conclusion that the term encompasses essentially all "unreasonable risks"; [the case cited by the Court of Appeals] dealt with medical injuries of the sort that the statutes involved were intended to prevent.

Accordingly, the Court of Appeals also erred in denying GGS's motion for directed verdict on the issue of negligence per se, and must be reversed on this basis as well.

Judgment reversed.

NOTES

1. **Type of harm.** When the statute does not specify the harms sought to be avoided, how are those harms to be understood? Is the type of harm to be

(a) No dentist shall administer general anesthesia on an outpatient basis unless such dentist has been issued a permit by the board under the conditions specified in this Code section. Such permit shall be subject to biennial renewal at the time the dentist is required to renew his or her license to practice dentistry. It shall be the responsibility of the dentist to provide such information as the board may require and to pay the separate initial issuance and renewal fees for the permit as may be established by the board. . . .

prevented "medical complications" or risks to the patient's health, safety and welfare"? Lawyers in a negligence per se case face a challenging task—establishing the type of harm that the statute is intended to guard against. If you represented plaintiff, how might you argue that sexual assault was a problem the licensing statute was designed to prevent? If you represented defendant, how might you argue that it was not?

2.   **The court of appeals' view.** The court of appeals in *Goldstein* upheld plaintiff's negligence per se claim on a different analysis of the harms to be avoided. *Goldstein, Garber & Salama, LLC v. J.B.*, 779 S.E.2d 484 (Ga. Ct. App. 2015). The appellate court's reasoning was that OCGA § 43–11–21.1 governs the qualifications required for a dentist to supervise a certified registered nurse anesthetist administering general anesthesia. Because the dentists did not meet those statutory qualifications, had not undergone the training required of dentist supervisors, and did not know how to read an anesthesia chart, they were "unable to recognize J.B.'s inappropriate level of sedation" (as an expert witness had opined). The facts they recounted were that the patient had been kept under heavy sedation for two hours between procedures, which "not only rendered her a more vulnerable target, but also constituted a violation of the standard of care and placed her at unnecessary risk of medical complications." The court of appeals also noted expert testimony "that the dental profession is aware that assaults like the one J.B. suffered do occur and actively seeks to prevent them. . . . And there was expert testimony that the requirement for monitoring an anesthetized patient existed to safeguard patient safety, among other reasons." Because the statute itself "does not list the harms it intends to guard against," and the "legislative intent behind this statute is set out expressly in another Code section within the chapter," which said only that unlicensed activities "are a menace and a nuisance dangerous to the public health, safety, and welfare." OCGA § 43–11–2(e), the court interpreted this broad language to encompass "both medical and non-medical dangers that could arise where, as here, a dentist is incapable of adequately supervising a certified registered nurse anesthetist, including the increased risk of a patient to abuse when the patient is placed under a greater level of sedation than necessary for a greater amount of time than necessary."

3.   **Common law negligence and negligence per se.** What happens when negligence per se does not apply? Notice that the plaintiff can claim negligence on ordinary common law principles even if the statute has no effect. That is, a plaintiff can claim both negligence per se and negligence for the same incident. If the court determines that negligence per se does not apply, the standard of care "defaults" back to the reasonable and prudent person standard. *See Rose Crewboat Servs., Inc. v. Wood Res., LLC*, 425 F.Supp.3d 668 (E.D. La. 2019) (common law negligence claim was an alternative to negligence per se claim; unlighted obstruction in the water could be negligence per se and/or negligence).

4.   **Reasonable care under the circumstances.** According to the Georgia Court of Appeals "there was no evidence that GGS knew of Serdula's previous assaults on patients," and "no evidence indicating that GGS should

have known of them." However, the Court of Appeals also noted the dental community's awareness that sexual assaults of anesthetized patients occur, and that it considers the assaults preventable events that should never happen. What should a reasonable dental practice do to prevent incapacitated patients from being sexual assaulted in its office? The Georgia Supreme Court in *GGS* also reversed the $3.7 million jury verdict for the plaintiff on her common law negligence claim on the ground that the sexual assault was unforeseeable, which defeated the element of proximate cause (an element that focuses on the type of harm and class of persons risked by the defendant's negligence).

GETCHELL V. LODGE

65 P.3d 50 (Alaska 2003)

FABE, CHIEF JUSTICE.

On the morning of January 16, 1998, Joyce Getchell and Barbara Lodge drove to work on the Kenai Spur Highway. Getchell headed south on the highway towards Kenai. Lodge headed north towards Nikiski. A thin layer of ice covered the unsanded road; the morning was dark. There was a dispute at trial about what happened next. However, because we draw all factual inferences in favor of the non-moving party when reviewing motions for JNOV and new trial, what follows is Lodge's account.

Because of the darkness, the icy road conditions, and the possibility of moose crossing the highway, Lodge was driving at about forty-five miles per hour, even though the speed limit was fifty-five. A moose emerged out of the darkness from Lodge's right and tried to cross the road as Lodge neared Mile 20 of the highway. Lodge hit her brakes as hard as she could. She testified that her car skidded immediately and began to rotate in a counterclockwise direction. Lodge lost control of her car as it continued to rotate and slide. Ultimately, the car crossed the center line of the road. The car finished rotating and came to a stop in the southbound lane. As Getchell headed south towards Mile 20, driving between forty-five and fifty-five miles per hour, she saw a car in her lane. Getchell hit the passenger side of Lodge's car. The impact injured Getchell's ankle, requiring surgery. . . .

Getchell brought a personal injury negligence action against Lodge. . . . Superior Court Judge Harold M. Brown conducted a three-day jury trial . . . . The jury found Lodge not negligent. . . .

Getchell argues that the trial court erred in denying her motions for JNOV and new trial, contending that reasonable jurors could have only concluded that Lodge acted negligently. Getchell structures her argument around the tort consequences of Lodge's alleged violation of two Alaska traffic regulations.[9] Getchell contends that because Lodge crossed the center lane of traffic into Getchell's lane she violated 13 AAC 02.085 and 13 AAC 02.050. Because Lodge violated these traffic regulations, Getchell argues, the burden of proof shifted to Lodge to show by a preponderance of the evidence that her conduct was excused. . . .

Getchell is correct that Lodge can only claim excuse if she handled her moose-avoidance maneuver and the resulting skid in a non-negligent manner. However, contrary to Getchell's argument, there is evidence in the record that Lodge did not purposefully steer into the oncoming lane and that the skid was not caused by her negligence. . . . Lodge [and her accident reconstruction expert] testified that she did not steer into the other lane.

In addition . . . Lodge testified that she slammed on her brakes to avoid a moose in her lane. According to Lodge, her brakes locked and she skidded into Getchell's lane. Reasonable jurors could have concluded that the presence of the moose in the road excused Lodge's skid into the oncoming lane of traffic. Skidding to avoid a moose is the type of excuse contemplated by § 288A of the Restatement (Second) of Torts . . . . Comment h of this section aptly describes this situation:

> *Emergency.* As in other cases of negligence (see § 296), the violation of an enactment or regulation will ordinarily be excused when the actor is confronted with an emergency which is not caused by his own misconduct.

It is plausible that the jury concluded that the moose created an emergency situation for Lodge and that they therefore excused the unfortunate consequences of her attempt to avoid the moose.

The jury also heard other evidence from which it could have reasonably concluded that Lodge was not negligent. Lodge points out that she had very little time to react after she saw the moose in the road. Lodge's accident reconstruction expert, James Stirling, expressed his opinion that Lodge had approximately "three-point-some seconds before" she would have

---

[9] . . . A plaintiff who establishes that a defendant violated a traffic regulation makes a prima facie case that the defendant acted negligently. The defendant then bears the burden to prove affirmatively that his violation was excused. . . . "Excuse" is a fluid concept. We have adopted the Restatement (Second) of Torts's position on excused violations of traffic regulations. Section 288(A) provides:

> (1) An excused violation of a legislative enactment or an administrative regulation is not negligence.
>
> (2) Unless the enactment or regulation is construed not to permit such excuse, its violation is excused when
>
>> (a) the violation is reasonable because of the actor's incapacity;
>>
>> (b) he neither knows nor should know of the occasion for compliance;
>>
>> (c) he is unable after reasonable diligence or care to comply;
>>
>> (d) he is confronted by an emergency not due to his own misconduct;
>>
>> (e) compliance would involve a greater risk of harm to the actor or to others.

RESTATEMENT (SECOND) OF TORTS § 288(A) (1965).

collided with the moose. According to Stirling, Lodge's perception of the danger, before she took any evasive action, would have consumed one-and-a-quarter to one-and-a-half seconds. Thus, Lodge argues, she had one-and-a-half seconds at most to slow the car down and correct the slide. Stirling testified that "[g]iven the surface and how slick it was, and given the speed of 45 miles an hour, [Lodge's attempts to correct her car's rotation] would have had to have been almost instantaneous to stop. . . . I would think she would have to perform higher than the average driver to do it." Based upon this testimony, reasonable jurors could have concluded that "Lodge was unable after reasonable care to comply with [13 AAC 02.085 and 13 AAC 02.050]." . . . Because we find that there was evidence from which reasonable jurors could have differed in their judgment of the facts as to whether Lodge acted negligently, we AFFIRM the trial court's denial of Getchell's motions for JNOV and new trial. . . .

DA

Reasoning

H/D

NOTES

1. **Excuses for a statutory violation.** In a number of cases, courts that ordinarily recognize the per se rule have held that a statutory violation was excused. This has been the holding, for example, where the statute required good brakes, but the brakes suddenly failed without the driver's fault. Courts have the discretion to decide whether or not to allow an excuse in a negligence per se case while the jury will make the factual determination of whether the violation was excused. *See, e.g., Baker-Smith v. Skolnick*, 249 Cal. Rptr. 3d 514 (Ct. App. 2019) ("To determine whether excuse could be a defense in a negligence per se case, California law weighs the benefits and burdens of accident precautions.").

2. **The Restatement list.** The Third Restatement has reworked and clarified the list of excuses from the Second Restatement quoted in *Getchell*. It now provides that a violation of a statute is "excused and not negligent" if (a) the violation is reasonable in light of the actor's childhood, physical disability, or physical incapacitation; (b) the actor exercises reasonable care in attempting to comply with the statute; (c) the actor neither knows nor should know of the factual circumstances that render the statute applicable; (d) the actor's violation of the statute is due to the confusing way in which the requirements of the statute are presented to the public; or (e) the actor's compliance with the statute would involve a greater risk of physical harm to the actor or to others than would noncompliance. RESTATEMENT (THIRD) OF TORTS: LIABILITY FOR PHYSICAL AND EMOTIONAL HARM § 15 (2010).

3. **Implications.** If no excuses were permitted, might the effect be a kind of strict liability? On the other hand, if excuses are not limited, is the negligence per se rule in effect scuttled? In *Alarid v. Vanier*, 327 P.2d 897 (Cal. 1958), the court said: "In our opinion the correct test is whether the person who has violated a statute has sustained the burden of showing that he did what might reasonably be expected of a person of ordinary prudence, acting under

similar circumstances, who desired to comply with the law." What effect, if any, does such an approach give to the statute?

4. **Child's standard in negligence per se cases.** Which prevails when a child violates a statute, the common law child standard of care or the statutory standard? In other words, does the negligence per se rule apply to children? In *Bauman v. Crawford*, 704 P.2d 1181 (Wash. 1985), the court said: "We hold that a minor's violation of a statute does not constitute proof of negligence per se, but may, in proper cases, be introduced as evidence of a minor's negligence." Why would holding children to the statutory standard be such a bad idea, especially where they are engaged in childish activities like walking across a street or riding a bicycle?

5. **Non-excuses.** Case law and the Third Restatement recognize that negligence per se has been applied, typically and traditionally, only to "unexcused" statutory violations, a formulation we saw in *Martin v. Herzog, supra*. Is it a valid excuse for a person to say that he did not agree with the statute's provisions? Or to argue that he was ignorant of the law? Or what if the violator can prove that people customarily violate the statutory provisions? No is the answer to all of these questions. *See* RESTATEMENT (THIRD) OF TORTS: LIABILITY FOR PHYSICAL AND EMOTIONAL HARM § 15 cmt. a (2010).

PROBLEM

Lind v. Maigret

Driving his car on a mountain highway, Maigret hit a fog bank and slowed. A large boulder rolled down the hillside and struck the rear of Maigret's car from the side. The impact spun Maigret's car around. Maigret did not react skillfully. He went into a state of shock when he felt the impact, gripping the steering wheel and closing his eyes. When his car came to a stop, the engine was stalled. He was unable to start it. The car was projecting across most of one lane of traffic in fairly thick fog. At this point it was hit by a truck driven by Lind. That impact caused serious injury to Lind. A statute provided that "no person shall stop, park, or leave standing any vehicle, whether attended or unattended, upon the roadway." Another statute provided that "every person driving a motor vehicle shall exercise care for the safety of others at all times."

Lind has proposed negligence per se instructions to the judge, who asks you, as Maigret's counsel, whether you have any objections or views on the subject. What is your position based on authority in this section?

CHAPTER 6

BREACH OF DUTY

■ ■ ■

§ 1. DETERMINING BREACH

It is up to the court to determine whether the defendant owes the plaintiff a duty, and what standard of care applies—most often, the duty of reasonable care under the circumstances.

Once the court determines that defendant owes plaintiff a duty, it is the jury's job to decide whether or not that duty was breached by the defendant's failure to exercise the requisite amount of care. The defendant who breaches the duty of care is said to be negligent. Negligence is overt conduct that creates unreasonable risks that a reasonable person would avoid. A typical jury instruction on breach explains the concept to the jury as follows: "Negligence is the failure to use reasonable care. Negligence may consist of action or inaction. Negligence is the failure to act as a reasonably careful person would act under the circumstances." Revised Arizona Jury Instructions—Civil (5th ed. 2013).

Notice that the term used in the instruction is "negligence." The "negligence" term is used both to refer to the entire cause of action and, because breach is at the heart of the negligence claim, to refer to the breach element alone.

In the common law, the jury determines the use, or failure to use, reasonable care under the circumstances. "What precautions are 'reasonable' depends upon the risk of harm involved and the practicability of preventing it." *Weinberg v. Dinger*, 524 A.2d 366 (N.J. 1987).

The level and type of care that is reasonable in a given situation is not obvious. In common law negligence cases, the content of the norm of reasonable care comes from "the finder of fact's own general normative sense of the situation, informed by individual experience and by the evidence submitted by the parties." Kenneth S. Abraham, *The Trouble with Negligence*, 54 VAND. L. REV. 1187, 1190 (2001).

When a jury's determines breach its job is both normative and factual. The finder of fact "simultaneously determines for itself what would constitute reasonable behavior under the circumstances and then applies this norm to the situation at hand." *Id.* at 1191.

Professor Abraham gives the example of a homeowner who shovels snow after a storm but does not succeed in removing all the snow. When a guest later slips on the ice and brings a negligence claim, the jury must decide what the facts were—how much ice was removed, how much ice was left, how visible the ice was to people using the steps, and so forth. The jury must also answer the normative question—how much snow is *reasonable* to remove. Conversely, when is it *unreasonable* not to remove snow?

We all have intuitions about what conduct is reasonable or unreasonable—driving 25 miles over the speed limit, driving while talking on a cell phone, driving at all. In this chapter, we are going to explore constructs that guide the issue of breach. These constructs underlie juror intuitions. They also guide lawyers' presentations of evidence. Finally, the constructs inform judges' decisions about whether to admit evidence, let a case go to the jury, and review of verdicts, among other choices.

Note that unreasonable conduct may include both acts and a failure to act when action is required. However, a mere state of mind is not conduct. If the defendant daydreams but drives properly in all respects, defendant might be careless in the lay sense, but is not legally negligent. As the Seventh Circuit succinctly stated in *Beck v. Dobrowski*, 559 F.3d 680, 682 (7th Cir. 2009): "Negligence is not a state of mind; it is a failure . . . to come up to the specified standard of care."

A. INTENTIONAL TORTS OR INTENTIONAL ACTS THAT INVOLVE RISK

Legal professionals think of intentional torts in contrast with negligence. Keep in mind that an intentional *act* is not necessarily an intentional *tort*. For example, if you intentionally drive at a very high speed you may be taking an unreasonable risk; if you do so and collide with another car, you'd be negligent. What else would be necessary to show you were chargeable with an intentional tort rather than negligence?

PROBLEM

Brown v. Stiel

The Stiel Company, a construction contractor, decided to build a building for its own use. It provided an architect with the basic design elements, and plans were drawn which Stiel then followed in building. Stiel chose a design in which the major structural components were steel. It rejected a design based on poured concrete in favor of steel beams because the steel beam construction was, in the particular situation, much cheaper and quicker. However, as Stiel knew, the kind of steel beam construction proposed generally caused or was associated with accidents which caused death or serious injury. In fact, it was known (through statistics) that for a building the size of Stiel's, approximately three workers or others would be killed or paralyzed or otherwise seriously injured. The concrete building also involved predictable injuries; but, for a building this size, the prediction was that only one person would be injured. Stiel nevertheless chose the riskier steel construction because of time and cost differences.

There was a collapse of some steel beams and John White, an employee of Stiel who had done steel work for many years, fell to the ground and suffered a broken back and permanent paralysis from the neck down. The same collapse dropped a steel beam on Billy Brown, a delivery person for a nearby deli. Billy Brown was on the premises bringing an order for the supervising architect when the beam fell. Brown lost a leg as a result of the building's collapse.

NOTES

1. **Intentional acts and intentional harms.** Did Stiel Co. commit an intentional tort? Consider whether this case differs from a case in which the defendant throws a brick from the roof of a building into a crowd below.

2. **Injury as a cost of business.** Suppose a court holds that no intentional tort is shown in this problem. Even so, maybe Stiel ought to pay for the harm done as a matter of justice or social policy. If certain costs are more or less inevitable in a business, maybe those costs should be regarded as a cost that business should bear as a part of its overhead. If a construction company expects that its own construction vehicles will periodically collide and sustain damage, it will budget for this cost and charge sufficient amounts to cover this cost as well as all others. Should the same be done when it comes to human costs?

3. **Workers' compensation.** Workers' compensation statutes proceed upon the theory that work-connected injuries may generally be regarded as a part of the employer's cost of doing business—the human "breakage," analogous to broken plates in a restaurant. Since such losses are more or less inevitable in a statistical sense, the employer simply budgets for them— charging sufficiently for its work to cover the costs.

4. **Plaintiffs not covered by workers' compensation.** Is there any justification for holding Stiel liable to White for workers' compensation but not holding Stiel liable to Brown?

5. **A negligence action.** Assuming that Brown cannot recover workers' compensation from Stiel because he was not an employee, and that he cannot recover from the deli because the workers' compensation statute did not cover businesses with very few employees, would Brown nevertheless have an action under common law tort theory? Consider the introductory comments about negligence as well as the cases that follow.

B. FORESEEABILITY OF HARM AS A PREREQUISITE TO BREACH

Risks of harm are unreasonable when a reasonable and prudent person would foresee that harm might result and would avoid conduct that creates the risk. Conversely, "[t]o act non-negligently is to take reasonable precautions to prevent the occurrence of foreseeable harm to others." *Weinberg v. Dinger*, 524 A.2d 366 (N.J. 1987). If no harm is foreseeable, would any precautions be required? Foreseeability of harm is the beginning, but not the end, of the breach analysis.

PIPHER V. PARSELL
930 A.2d 890 (Del. 2007)

HOLLAND, JUSTICE.

The plaintiff-appellant, Kristyn Pipher ("Pipher"), appeals from the Superior Court's judgment as a matter of law in favor of the defendant-appellee, Johnathan Parsell ("Parsell"). Pipher argues that the Superior Court erred when it ruled that, as a matter of law, Parsell was not negligent. We agree and hold that the issue of Parsell's negligence should have been submitted to the jury.

On March 20, 2002, around 6 p.m., Pipher, Parsell and Johnene Beisel ("Beisel"), also a defendant, were traveling south on Delaware Route 1 near Lewes, Delaware, in Parsell's pickup truck. All three were sitting on the front seat. Parsell was driving, Pipher was sitting in the middle, and Beisel was in the passenger seat next to the door. They were all sixteen-years-old at the time.

As they were traveling at 55 mph, Beisel unexpectedly "grabbed the steering wheel causing the truck to veer off onto the shoulder of the road." Parsell testified that Beisel's conduct caused him both shock and surprise. Although Beisel's conduct prompted him to be on his guard, Parsell further testified that he did not expect Beisel to grab the wheel again. Nevertheless, his recognition of how serious Beisel's conduct was shows he was aware that he now had someone in his car who had engaged in dangerous behavior.

Parsell testified that he did nothing in response to Beisel's initial action. Approximately thirty seconds later, Beisel again yanked the steering wheel, causing Parsell's truck to leave the roadway, slide down an embankment and strike a tree. Pipher was injured as a result of the collision.

Pipher's testimony at trial was for the most part consistent with Parsell's testimony. Pipher recalled that the three occupants in the vehicle were talking back and forth and that the mood was light as they drove south on Route 1. She also testified that after Beisel yanked the steering wheel for the first time, Parsell was able to regain control of the truck. According to Pipher, despite the dangerous nature of the conduct, Parsell and Beisel just laughed about it like it was a joke. Pipher testified she felt that Beisel grabbed the steering wheel a second time because Parsell "laughed it off" the first time.

At trial, Parsell acknowledged that he could have taken different steps to try to prevent Beisel from grabbing the steering wheel a second time. First, Parsell acknowledged, he could have admonished Beisel not to touch the steering wheel again. Second, he acknowledged that he could have pulled over to the side of the road and required Beisel to get into the back seat. Third, Parsell acknowledged that he could have warned Beisel that he would put her out of the vehicle.

The trial judge concluded that, as a matter of law, Parsell had no duty to do anything after Beisel yanked the wheel the first time because it would be reasonable for the driver to assume that it would not happen again. The trial judge also ruled that (1) there was no negligence in failing to discharge the dangerous passenger and (2) that failing to admonish the dangerous passenger was not negligence. . . .

A driver owes a duty of care to her or his passengers because it is foreseeable that they may be injured if, through inattention or otherwise, the driver involves the car she or he is operating in a collision. Almost forty-five years ago, this Court held that a minor who operates a motor vehicle on the highways of Delaware will be held to the same standard of care and "must accord his [or her] own passengers the same diligence and protection which is required of an adult motorist under similar circumstances.". . .

Pipher argues that after Beisel grabbed the steering wheel initially, Parsell was on notice that a dangerous situation could reoccur in the truck. Pipher further argues that once Parsell had notice of a possibly dangerous situation, he had a duty to exercise reasonable care to protect his passengers from that harm. Finally, Pipher concludes that Parsell was negligent when he kept driving without attempting to remove, or at least address, that risk. . . .

In general, where the actions of a passenger that cause an accident are not foreseeable, there is no negligence attributable to the driver. But, when actions of a passenger that interfere with the driver's safe operation of the motor vehicle are foreseeable, the failure to prevent such conduct may be a breach of the driver's duty to either other passengers or to the public. Under the circumstances of this case, a reasonable jury could find that Parsell breached his duty to protect Pipher from Beisel by preventing Beisel from grabbing the steering wheel a second time.

The issue of Parsell's alleged breach of duty to Pipher, the foreseeability of Beisel's repeat conduct, and the proximate cause of

Reasoning

Pipher's injuries were all factual determinations that should have been submitted to the jury. Accordingly, the judgment of the Superior Court, that was entered as a matter of law, is reversed. This matter is remanded for further proceedings in accordance with this opinion.

NOTES

1.   **An alternate scenario.** Would the trial court have been correct in ruling that there was no breach of duty as a matter of law if Beisel had caused the accident the first time she grabbed the wheel? Why would that be a different case? *Cf. Brown v. Mobley,* 488 S.E.2d 710 (Ga. Ct. App. 1997) (no evidence that eventual conduct of intoxicated passenger should have been anticipated).

2.   **Facts related to breach.** Given Beisel's prior conduct, should the breach issue have gone to a jury? What facts should a jury consider on remand? State the strongest arguments for both the plaintiff and the defendant on the breach issue.

3.   **Foreseeability as a prerequisite for breach.** Foreseeability of some type of harm is central to the issue of whether a person's conduct breached the standard of reasonable care. An actor can be negligent only if the actor's conduct created a foreseeable risk and a reasonable person would have recognized that risk. *See Rallis v. Demoulas Super Mkts., Inc.,* 977 A.2d 527 (N.H. 2009); *Smith v. Finch,* 681 S.E.2d 147 (Ga. 2009). Suppose a college professor does not warn the students to avoid putting their fingers in the room's electrical sockets. Would you foresee any harm from the professor's failure to warn? Any breach issue for the jury?

4.   **When harm is unforeseeable.** When a reasonable person in the defendant's circumstance would not foresee any danger, the defendant is "simply not negligent." *Allen v. Lockwood,* 156 So.3d 650 (La. 2015) (unpaved grassy church parking area that had been used for decades without incident did not create an unreasonable risk of harm). In *Sic v. Nunan,* 54 A.3d 553 (Conn. 2012), the plaintiff argued that a motorist, who was lawfully stopped in his own lane of travel while awaiting an opportunity to make a left turn, should have kept the wheels of his vehicle straight to ensure that if he was hit from behind he would not be propelled into the travel lane of oncoming traffic. However, the court held that a reasonable driver in the defendant's position was "not required to anticipate the potential that he would be rear-ended by another motorist or to guard against that eventuality by positioning his wheels in a particular direction." The *Sic* court reached this decision based on lack of foreseeability as a matter of *duty*, but the court in *Wray v. Green,* 126 A.3d 476 (R.I. 2015), found no evidence of *breach* where the defendant was stopped behind the left-turning plaintiff and a third car shoved him into the plaintiff's car.

5.   **Evaluating foreseeability.** If instead of distracting the driver from inside the car (as in *Pipher*) the friend sends text messages from another location which distract the driver, is injury foreseeable? The New Jersey

Superior Court in *Kubert v. Best*, 75 A.3d 1214 (N.J. Super. Ct. App. Div. 2013), was called on to decide such a case. The court noted "[i]t is foreseeable that a driver who is actually distracted by a text message might cause an accident and serious injuries or death, but it is not generally foreseeable that every recipient of a text message who is driving will neglect his obligation to obey the law and will be distracted by the text." Consequently, the court held that "the sender of a text message can potentially be liable if an accident is caused by texting, but only if the sender knew or had special reason to know that the recipient would view the text while driving and thus be distracted."

6. **The Third Restatement on foreseeability.** Under the Restatement (Third) of Torts, "the assessment of the foreseeability of a risk is no longer part of the duty analysis, but is to be considered when the [fact finder] decides if the defendant failed to exercise reasonable care." RESTATEMENT (THIRD) OF TORTS: LIABILITY FOR PHYSICAL AND EMOTIONAL HARM § 7 cmt. j (2010). This means that when there is some evidence that the risk was foreseeable, the question is typically one for the jury to resolve in terms of breach. *See Brokaw v. Winfield-Mt. Union Cmty. Sch. Dist.*, 788 N.W.2d 386 (Iowa 2010) (because reasonable minds could disagree with respect to factual questions, issue of whether basketball coach should have foreseen that player would strike opposing team player should be left to jury decision). The Third Restatement's conception continues to gain some adherents. *See, e.g., Rodriguez v. Del Sol Shopping Ctr. Assocs., L.P.*, 326 P.3d 465 (N.M. 2014) ("Foreseeability is a fact-intensive inquiry relevant only to breach of duty and legal cause considerations."); *but see Robinson v. Vivirito*, 86 A.3d 119 (N.J. 2014) (foreseeability is a "critical, but not dispositive" factor that "often subsumes many factors deemed relevant to the recognition of a duty"). Why does it matter if a court addresses foreseeability as an element of duty or leaves the question to a determination of breach?

7. **Foreseeability as a piece of the analysis.** To say that harm is foreseeable is just the a first step in the breach analysis. The jury must determine not only foreseeability but also reasonableness as a whole. "To establish breach, the factfinder must be able to determine what a reasonably prudent person would foresee, what an unreasonable risk of injury would be, and what would constitute an exercise of ordinary care in light of all the surrounding circumstances." *Webber v. Deck*, 433 F.Supp.3d 237 (D.N.H. 2020); *St. Paul Fire and Marine Ins. Co. v. Sedona Contracting, Inc.*, 474 F.Supp.3d 1211 (D.N.M. 2020).

NOTE: THE LANGUAGE OF FORESEEABILITY AND RISK

Focus for a moment, not on the ideas, principles, or rules, but on the *language* courts often use to express themselves about negligence and how we must read and understand that language.

"Courts often use the term 'foreseeable' as a shorthand expression. They might say, for example, that a defendant is negligent if harm was foreseeable. Such statements should not ordinarily be taken in a literal way. Harm is a foreseeable consequence of almost all acts, but courts definitely do not mean that *all* acts are negligent. Courts are likely to use the term 'foreseeable' to mean that harm was not only foreseeable but also too likely to occur to justify risking it without added precautions. . . . Along the same lines, when courts say that harm is unforeseeable, they may mean that although harm was actually foreseeable on the facts of the case, a reasonable person would not have taken action to prevent it because the risk of harm was low, and harm was so improbable that a reasonable person would not have taken safety precautions. Put differently, to say that harm was unforeseeable often seems to mean only that the foreseeable harm was not probable enough to require precaution, meaning ultimately that the defendant's conduct was not unreasonably risky." DOBBS, THE LAW OF TORTS § 143 (2001).

"The conclusion that harm would have been foreseeable to a reasonable person is entirely distinct from the conclusion that probability of harm was great enough to require care; and both these things are distinct from the conclusion that the actor's conduct was unreasonable in light of all the relevant factors. Clarity requires separation of those issues and the term foreseeability alone is not up to the job." 1 DOBBS, HAYDEN & BUBLICK, THE LAW OF TORTS § 159 (2d ed. 2011).

Consider the court's language in *Romine v. Village of Irving*, 783 N.E.2d 1064 (Ill. App. Ct. 2003). Police officers ejected two unruly, intoxicated people from a fair, knowing that those people were from out of town. Once ejected, the intoxicated people drove their car negligently, causing injuries to the plaintiff. The plaintiff included the police officers in the suit for damages on the ground that the police officers should have arrested the intoxicated persons to prevent their dangerous driving. The court said that police officers could not foresee criminal acts in general and in particular drunken driving by intoxicated persons they ejected from a fair. Can either of these statements be taken literally? Surely police can foresee criminal activity in general—after all, they are hired to prevent it and to arrest its perpetrators. And intoxicated driving seems not only foreseeable but as the court itself said, all too common. So what might the court have been trying to say when it used the "foreseeability" locution?

C. THE ROLE OF JUDGE AND JURY

LIMONES V. SCHOOL DISTRICT OF LEE COUNTY, 161 So.3d 384 (Fla. 2015). At approximately 7:40 p.m. on November 13, 2008, fifteen-year-old Abel Limones, Jr., suddenly collapsed during a high school soccer game. Thomas Busatta, the coach for East Lee County High School, immediately ran onto the field to check his player. Within three minutes of the collapse Able appeared to stop breathing and lost consciousness. Busatta, who was certified in the use of an automated external defibrillator (AED), testified that he yelled for an AED. The AED in the possession of Riverdale High School was actually at the game facility located at the end of the soccer field, but it was never brought on the field to Busatta. Emergency responders revived Abel [with an AED], but not until 8:06 p.m., twenty-six minutes after his initial collapse. Although Abel survived, he suffered a severe brain injury due to a lack of oxygen. . . . As a result, he now remains in a nearly persistent vegetative state that will require full-time care for the remainder of his life. Limones' parents brought an action against the county school board for negligence. The trial court entered summary judgment in favor of the school board. *Held*, reversed and remanded for trial. "[A] clearly recognized common law duty existed. . . . [S]chool employees must reasonably supervise students during activities that are subject to the control of the school. . . . 'Reasonable care under the circumstances' is a standard that may fluctuate with time, the student's age and activity, the extent of the injury, the available responder(s), and other facts. Advancements with technology and equipment available today, such as a portable AED, to treat an injury were most probably unavailable twenty years ago, and may be obsolete twenty years from now. We therefore leave it to the jury to determine, under the evidence presented, whether the particular actions of Respondent's employees satisfied or breached the duty of reasonable care owed. . . . [W]e reject the decision of the Second District to narrowly frame the issue as whether Respondent had a specified duty to diagnose the need for or use an AED on Abel. . . . Such a narrow definition of duty, a purely legal question, slides too easily into breach, a factual matter for the jury. . . . It is a matter for the jury to determine under the evidence whether Respondent's actions breached that duty and resulted in the damage that Abel suffered. "

NOTES

1. **Duty to use an AED?** Why does the Florida Supreme Court think it's a problem for the lower courts to decide whether the school district had a "duty to use an AED on Able"? What is the problem with describing the duty this way and how does it influence the procedural outcome of the case? How should the duty be described?

2. **Judge vs. jury.** Courts sometimes talk about the duty in very specific terms rather than leave the question of breach to the jury to assess. *See Not Afraid v. State*, 362 P.3d 71 (Mont. 2015) (requiring plaintiff to establish the standard of care that would be exercised by a governmental entity in placing, installing, and maintaining concrete barriers on a roadway). Although the creation of specific duties seems an outdated way of taking cases from the jury, you can still find cases that take such an approach. The underlying problem is to allocate decision-making power between judge and jury. The jury is to decide facts (Was the stop light red?). It is also to make

certain value judgments (Did the defendant's failure to stop amount to negligence?). It also determines credibility of witnesses, as we will see.

3. **Usurping the jury's role in breach.** Where a landowner or city fails to trim bushes, leaving an intersection obscured and leading to traffic accidents, courts have sometimes said the defendant had "no duty to trim the bushes" or the like. Such cases swipe any judgment about reasonable care from the jury. As the court in *Coburn v. City of Tucson*, 691 P.2d 1078 (Ariz. 1984), explained, many tort cases argue "that the city is, or is not, under a duty to post warning signs, remove obstructions from the road or sidewalks, install traffic control devices, fix potholes, and the like. We believe that an attempt to equate the concept of 'duty' with such specific details of conduct is unwise. . . . We see no benefit and considerable danger in attempting to analyze cases [in terms of duty]." A judge who uses specific details of conduct in the duty analysis may be found to have usurped the jury's role. *See Pavik v. George & Lynch, Inc.*, 183 A.3d 1258 (Del. 2018) (judge "took for itself the inherently fact-bound question" of whether defendant should have provided warning signs about road conditions).

4. **Duty or breach?** A woman fell while taking off her shoes before going through airport security, and sued the Transportation Safety Administration (TSA) for negligence in not providing her a chair. The record showed that "of the thousands of passengers passing through the security screening measures at the airport prior to plaintiff's injury, no similar incidents had occurred." The trial court granted summary judgment for the defendant, holding that the injury was not foreseeable and TSA did not have a duty to provide a chair. *See Barnes v. United States*, 485 F.3d 341 (6th Cir. 2007). In light of *Pipher* and *Limones*, how would you analyze this issue on appeal?

§ 2. UNSTRUCTURED WEIGHING OF RISKS AND COSTS

INDIANA CONSOLIDATED INSURANCE CO. v. MATHEW

402 N.E.2d 1000 (Ind. Ct. App. 1980)

HOFFMAN, JUDGE.

Appellant Indiana Consolidated Insurance Company seeks review of the finding that Robert D. Mathew (Mathew) did not act in a negligent manner so as to be liable for damages done to his brother's garage when a Toro riding lawnmower that Mathew was starting caught fire. Appellant insured the garage and premises under a homeowner's insurance policy and is pursuing this claim against Mathew by virtue of its subrogation rights.[1]

---

[1]   A fire insurer or collision insurer who pays its insured's loss "stands in the shoes" of the insured for the purpose of suing any tortfeasor whose tortious acts caused the loss.—Eds.

[T]he facts favorable to Mathew disclose that on May 1, 1976 Mathew's brother was out of town for the weekend. The two brothers lived across the street from each other and took turns mowing both lawns. In the late afternoon Mathew decided to mow both lawns and went to his brother's garage where a twelve horsepower Toro riding lawnmower was stored. The mower was approximately eight years old, was kept in good mechanical condition, and had required only minor tune-ups and belt replacements for the rotary mower assembly. Mathew pulled the mower away from the side wall of the garage and after checking the gas gauge filled the lawnmower approximately three-fourths full with gasoline using a funnel. He then went back across the street to his home for approximately twenty minutes. Upon returning to the garage Mathew started the lawnmower. However, he noticed a flame in the engine area under the hood and immediately shut the engine off. He opened the hood and saw a flame four to five inches tall under the gas tank. Using some clean towels Mathew tried to snuff out the flame but was unsuccessful. He could find no other means to extinguish the fire. The flames continued to grow and the machine began spewing gasoline, so he ran to his home to call the fire department. He returned to find the garage totally engulfed in flames.

At trial Mathew testified that he was afraid to try to push the flaming machine outside the garage for fear that the tank would explode in his face.

Indiana Consolidated brought this action against Mathew alleging that he breached a duty owed to his brother to exercise due care in starting the lawnmower and therefore stands liable for the damages resulting from his negligence. After a bench trial the court below entered the following finding, to-wit:

> The Court having heretofore taken this matter under advisement and having considered the evidence introduced in the trial of this cause and being sufficiently advised, now enters Findings as follows: The Court now finds . . . that there is no evidence of negligence on the part of the defendant, Robert D. Mathew, and that the plaintiff should take nothing by its complaint.

> IT IS THEREFORE ORDERED, ADJUDGED AND DECREED BY THE COURT that the plaintiff, Indiana Consolidated Insurance Company, take nothing by its complaint; and Judgment is entered for and on behalf of the defendant, Robert D. Mathew. Costs of this action are taxed to the plaintiff.

On appeal appellant contends that the judgment is contrary to law because Mathew was negligent in filling the gas tank, in starting the mower in an enclosed area, and in failing to push the flaming mower out of the garage. The standard by which Mathew's conduct is to be measured is whether he exercised the duty to use due care in operating the mower that an ordinary prudent man would exercise under the same or similar circumstances.

The record amply supports the finding that Mathew did not act in a negligent manner in filling the gas tank. He testified that he did so carefully, with the use of a funnel. He did not fill the tank full, and he was adamant in his belief that he did not spill any gasoline. He hypothesized that even had any gas been spilled it would have evaporated in the cool air during the twenty-minute period before he started the mower. Appellant is merely asking this Court to reweigh the evidence in regard to any gasoline spillage due to Mathew's admission on cross-examination that he could have spilled some fuel. The trier of fact resolved this issue in favor of Mathew, finding that he exercised due care in fueling the mower, and it must remain undisturbed upon appeal. Appellant is again reminded that any conflicts in testimony when appeal from a negative judgment is taken must be resolved in favor of the appellee.

Appellant's contention that Mathew should be held liable for the act of negligently starting the mower inside the garage is also without merit. It cannot seriously be contended that the evidence shows that Mathew acted other than a reasonably prudent man in pulling the mower out into an open area of the garage and starting it. The mower was a riding type that was of considerable weight and size. Garages are designed to permit the starting of motorized vehicles such as automobiles and are commonly used for such purpose. That this particular mower would catch fire at this particular time was not reasonably foreseeable. As one is not required to anticipate that which is unlikely to happen, the trial court did not err in determining that Mathew was not negligent in starting the mower inside the garage.

Appellant's further allegation that Mathew negligently failed to push the flaming mower out of the garage area is refuted by the evidence that the machine was spewing gasoline and that he was afraid for his safety should the tank explode. Mathew therefore chose to leave and summon help from the local fire department. One who is confronted with a sudden emergency not of his own making is not chargeable with negligence if he acts according to his best judgment. The sudden emergency doctrine requires the person so confronted to do that which an ordinary prudent man would do under like circumstances. Mathew's course of action can be deemed an exercise of ordinary prudence. The law values human life above property. Greater risk of one's person is justified to save life than is reasonable in protecting property. If Mathew had tried to push the riding mower ten feet into an open area the machine might have exploded and caused much graver damage to his person than was suffered by the destruction of the garage. Contrary to appellant's position several jurisdictions have ruled that one may be deemed negligent in voluntarily risking life or serious injury for the purpose of saving mere property. . . .

The judgment is not contrary to law and is therefore affirmed.   H/D

NOTES

1. **Specific acts of negligence.** When alleging breach, a party must say what the allegedly negligent party should have done differently. "Usually, the precaution identified by a party in seeking to establish the actor's negligence will consist of some way in which the actor could have modified the activity engaged in." RESTATEMENT (THIRD) OF TORTS: LIABILITY FOR PHYSICAL AND EMOTIONAL HARM § 3 cmt. j (2010). In *Indiana Consolidated*, which specific acts of the defendant were allegedly negligent?

2. **Factors that guide the breach evaluation.** This case involved a bench trial in which the judge is the finder of fact. Although unusual (the jury is typically the finder of fact), bench trials are easier to see the fact-finder's thought process because the court explains the decision in an opinion, rather than just issuing a verdict. What factors permitted the trial court, as finder of fact, to find that the defendant was not negligent?

3. **Burden of alternative conduct.** How can you measure the costs or burdens of alternative conduct, such as pushing the lawnmower out of the garage to then start it? If a child fell on wet grass while participating in a relay race at defendant's camp, what would be the cost of precaution? *See Fintzi v. N.J. YMHA-YWHA Camps*, 765 N.E.2d 288 (N.Y. 2001).

STINNETT V. BUCHELE

598 S.W.2d 469 (Ky. Ct. App. 1980)

BREETZ, JUDGE.

This is a tort action filed by an employee against his employer for injuries sustained during the course and scope of his employment. The lower court granted summary judgment to the employer on the ground that there was no showing that the injury was caused by the negligence of the employer. We affirm.   PH

The accident which gave rise to this suit was also the subject of a workmen's compensation claim. The Workmen's Compensation Board denied benefits because the employee, being employed in agriculture, was exempt from the coverage of the Workmen's Compensation Act. We have today, by separate and non-published opinion, affirmed the board in that regard. . . .

Earl S. Buchele is a practicing physician in Hardinsburg, Kentucky. He hired Alvin Stinnett as a farm laborer in January 1976. In September of that year Mr. Stinnett undertook to repair the roof on a barn located at one of Dr. Buchele's farms known as the Cloverport Farm. The repairs were to consist of nailing down the edges of the roof that had been loosened by the wind and painting the roof with a coating. Stinnett was severely injured when he fell from the roof while applying the coating with a paint roller.

Stinnett urges in his brief to this court that Dr. Buchele was negligent for failing to comply with occupational and health regulations and also for his failure to provide a safe place to work. Dr. Buchele denies both of those assertions, and, additionally, argues that Stinnett was contributorily negligent as a matter of law. We do not reach the issue of contributory negligence. . . .

Nor do we find any evidence to be submitted to the jury that Dr. Buchele was negligent in failing to provide Stinnett with a safe place to work. We agree with Stinnett when he states that Dr. Buchele had the obligation to furnish him:

> . . . a place reasonably safe having regard for the character of work and reasonably safe tools and appliances for doing the work. The measure of duty is to exercise ordinary or reasonable care to do so. The standard is the care exercised by prudent employers in similar circumstances.

We also agree with the sentence immediately preceding the quotation from that same opinion: "An employer's obligation to its employee is not the frequently impossible duty of furnishing absolutely safe instrumentalities or place to work."

Although we may consider that painting a barn roof is dangerous work, we cannot say that Dr. Buchele can be held liable for failing to provide a safe place to work solely because he asked Stinnett to work on the roof. We hold, therefore, that there was no showing of any negligence on the part of Dr. Buchele arising solely out of the fact that he had asked Stinnett to paint the barn roof.

Stinnett next argues . . . that a reasonable and prudent employer would have provided safety devices of some kind even though not required to by force of statute or regulation and that the question whether Dr. Buchele measured up to the standards of an ordinarily careful and prudent employer is one for the jury. . . . The liability of the employer:

> . . . rests upon the assumption that the employer has a better and more comprehensive knowledge than the employees, and ceases to be applicable where the employees' means of knowledge of the dangers to be incurred is equal to that of the employer. 53 Am. Jur. 2d, Master and Servant, § 160.

Stinnett had been in the painting business with his brother-in-law for two years before he began working for Dr. Buchele. Although the record is not clear whether Stinnett, his brother-in-law or both did the painting, they did paint a church steeple and an undetermined number of barn roofs. On occasion safety belts and safety nets had been used while painting the barn roofs. Stinnett was injured on a Sunday. Dr. Buchele was not present and he did not know that Stinnett was going to work on the barn roof on that particular day. Dr. Buchele had, however, purchased the material that Stinnett was applying to the roof when he fell. Stinnett did not ask Dr. Buchele to procure a safety net nor did he check to see if one was available. He admitted he could have used a safety rope around his waist but he did not think any were available. . . .

In short, we find no evidence of negligence on the part of Dr. Buchele to submit to a jury.

NOTES

1. **Workers' compensation exclusions.** Although workers' compensation statutes have been adopted everywhere, they do not include all workers within their benefits. Statutes may exclude agricultural employees, domestic employees, and casual employees, for example. One special case is that of the worker on interstate railroads. Under the Federal Employers Liability Act, 45 U.S.C.A. §§ 51 *et seq.*, called FELA, these workers have expanded tort rights, but no workers' compensation. In general, workers not covered by compensation laws must, like Mr. Stinnett, seek recovery under the tort system

2. **Expecting reasonable care from others.** How did the court conclude that Dr. Buchele was not negligent? Was it unforeseeable that Stinnett might fall off the roof if he did not have safety equipment? The theory of *Stinnett* is that a defendant who uses reasonable care can typically assume that others will use reasonable care as well. A more straightforward application of the principle arises in the context of driving. As jury instructions in some states provide, "A driver is entitled to assume that another motorist will proceed in a lawful manner and obey the laws of the road—unless it should become apparent to that driver, acting as a reasonably careful person, that the other motorist is not going to obey the laws of the road." Rev. Ariz. Jury Inst. Negligence 4 (2013). If in *Stinnett* the plaintiff had suffered from serious dementia—was likely to forget where he or she was—and the defendant knew it, should the result have been different? *See Daniels v. Senior Care, Inc.*, 21 S.W.3d 133 (Mo. Ct. App. 2000).

3. **Special expertise.** Another idea in *Stinnett* is that as between a worker with experience in a particular type of work, and an employer in an unrelated field, it is reasonable for the employer to rely on the person with expertise to take appropriate safety precautions. In *Auslander Props., LLC v. Nalley*, 558 S.W.3d 457 (Ky. 2018), the Kentucky Supreme Court described a similar holding this way: "We agree that when an employer sends its own employees into harm's way to perform any task regardless of the nature of the business, the employer must apprise itself of, and comply with, any safety regulation applicable to that task. . . . But when the employer engages the services of an independent contractor for a task alien to the core function of the employer's business, the employer is relying upon the special expertise and

ability of the contractor to know and obey the applicable safety standards of that activity. . . . [S]pecialized work like climbing rooftops and ladders, or climbing into the tree itself, to cut branches requires specialized knowledge and skills beyond what is reasonably expected of an ordinary property rental business."

4. **Independent contractors.** When a worker is classified as an "independent contractor" rather than as an employee, many adverse consequences follow. The vastly inferior treatment of independent contractors is a reason that contemporary courts are leery of the classification. *See Dynamex Operations W. v. Superior Ct.*, 416 P.3d 1 (Cal. 2018); RESTATEMENT (THIRD) OF AGENCY § 1.01 & § 7.07 (2006) (discarding the term 'independent contractor,' and adopting a broader view of who is an employee). But even courts wary of the classification invoke it to permit reduced care for such workers. *See Gonzalez v. Mathis*, 493 P.3d 212 (Cal. 2021) (homeowner not liable when window washer fell from roof). As the *Gonzalez* court wrote, "There is a strong presumption under California law that a hirer of an independent contractor delegates to the contractor all responsibility for workplace safety. This means that a hirer is typically not liable for injuries sustained by an independent contractor or its workers while on the job. . . . [T]he presumption originally stemmed from the following rationales: First, hirers usually have no right to control an independent contractor's work. Second, contractors can factor in the cost of safety precautions and insurance coverage in the contract price. Third, contractors are able to obtain workers' compensation to cover any on-the-job injuries. Finally, contractors are typically hired for their expertise, which enables them to perform the contracted-for work safely and successfully. *See* RESTATEMENT (THIRD) OF TORTS: LIABILITY FOR PHYSICAL AND EMOTIONAL HARM § 57, com. c, p. 402." However, the *Gonzalez* court identified "two limited circumstances in which the presumption is overcome": 1) when the hirer "retains control over any part of the independent contractor's work and negligently exercises that retained control" and 2) "if the landowner knew, or should have known, of a concealed hazard on the property that the contractor did not know of and could not have reasonably discovered, and the landowner failed to warn."

5. **Responsibility for workplace injuries.** In many contexts, workplace safety is highly regulated. Employers may be required to take safety precautions. *Vargas v. Inland Washington, LLC*, 452 P.3d 1205 (Wash. 2019) (genuine issue of material fact as to whether general contractor breached any common law duty it had to subcontractor's employee). In the context of painters, window washers, and other short-term employees, is there any reason to worry about relying on the workers for safety precautions? What if window washers don't, in fact, factor safety precautions and insurances costs into their contract price, don't have the option to get workers' compensation, and don't have special expertise about work safety? What if the workers do not have the resources to purchase safety equipment or insurance or are concerned about being fired if they ask for safety equipment?

6. **Social vs. individual responsibility for injuries.** Even if Dr. Buchele was not at fault, Mr. Stinnett was injured. Injured persons may not be able to work at all and may have substantial medical and other needs. Apart from human sympathy, is there any reason to consider this as a social problem rather than Stinnett's individual problem? If society ought to respond in some fashion, does that indicate that Dr. Buchele as an individual ought to bear Mr. Stinnett's loss? What other options exist?

7. **The obviousness of danger.** "[T]he obviousness of a risk may make the likelihood of its materializing so slight that there is no need to try to eliminate the risk." *Halek v. United States,* 178 F.3d 481 (7th Cir. 1999). Perhaps it is not unreasonable to fail to take action to lessen a risk to someone that is so patently obvious that the other person can be relied upon to avoid it. Is that an explanation for the *Stinnett* holding?

8. **Expecting care by third persons.** In some cases, a reasonable person may not breach a duty when the person reasonably relies on another to protect the plaintiff. If parents accompany a child to a backyard party and know of the swimming pool there, can the host reasonably think the risk of injury to the child is low in spite of the dangers of a pool? Why? *See Herron v. Hollis*, 546 S.E.2d 17 (Ga. Ct. App. 2001). If parents accompany a child to a host's backyard and allow the child to use a zip line, does the host create an unreasonable risk by failing to take special precautions for the child's use? *See LaForce v. Dyckman*, 132 N.E.3d 1015 (Mass. App. Ct. 2019). What if the parents do not know the host has a zip line that can be reached by a small child? *Cf. Perri v. Furama Rest., Inc.*, 781 N.E.2d 631 (Ill. App. Ct. 2002).

Some courts reach their conclusions in terms of duty rather than breach. *See, e.g., Justin M. v. Beadle*, 142 N.Y.S.3d 213 (App. Div. 2021) (homeowner at work owed no duty to protect child visiting home on a snow day); *Foss v. Kincade*, 766 N.W.2d 317 (Minn. 2009) (homeowner owed no duty to protect child in home who was under mother's supervision); *Lasley v. Hylton*, 764 S.E.2d 88 (Va. 2014) (host who let guest's two daughters, ages 8 and 12, drive his all-terrain vehicles owed no duty and breached no duty to a child guest when "a child's parent is present and supervising, and knows or should know of open and obvious risks associated with an activity," and the child participates in that activity "with the parent's permission"). Is it right to say that the defendants had no duty? Why might it matter if the issue is framed as one of duty rather than breach? Could both the defendant and the parent have breached a duty to the child?

BERNIER V. BOSTON EDISON CO.

403 N.E.2d 391 (Mass. 1980)

KAPLAN, JUSTICE.

About 2:30 p.m., May 24, 1972, the plaintiffs Arthur Bernier, Jr., and Patricia J. Kasputys, then eighteen and fifteen years old, were let out of school and, after going to Kasputys's house, sauntered to an ice cream parlor on Massachusetts Avenue in Lexington Center, one of the town's major shopping areas. A half hour later, Alice Ramsdell entered her 1968 Buick Skylark automobile parked, pointed east, on the south side of Massachusetts Avenue (which here runs west-east), in the last metered space about fifteen to twenty feet short of where the avenue meets Muzzey Street, a one-way street beginning at the avenue and running south. No traffic signals were posted at the junction with Muzzey Street.

As Ramsdell started her car, she noted, checking her rear-view and side-view mirrors, that there was a car—later identified as a Cadillac convertible driven by John Boireau—some seventy-five feet behind her. She wanted to make a right turn on Muzzey Street. Just before pulling out, Ramsdell observed that the Cadillac was much closer to her than before. Boireau, too, wished to turn right onto Muzzey Street. As there were no cars ahead of her before the intersection, Ramsdell thought she could make the turn before the Cadillac interfered.

As Ramsdell was pulling left slightly away from the curb, Boireau passed her traveling (as he said) about five miles an hour. Whether Ramsdell's car then "bolted" out and struck Boireau's car as he was negotiating the right turn, or Boireau turned into Ramsdell's car as the two attempted to make the turn, was the subject of conflicting testimony. So, too, the estimates of Ramsdell's speed on impact with Boireau varied from five to thirty miles an hour. Both drivers said they recognized the trouble and braked, but not before a minor collision occurred some ten to fifteen feet into the Muzzey Street intersection, Boireau's right front fender being slightly dented by contact with Ramsdell's left front fender.

What might have been a commonplace collision turned into a complicated accident. On impact, Ramsdell, a woman of sixty-nine, hit her head against her steering wheel and suffered a bloody nose. She testified she "lost complete control of that car." Dazed, she unknowingly let her foot slip from the power brake to the gas pedal. In the result, after veering right around Boireau's car and perhaps slowing slightly, she accelerated across the remaining twenty feet of Muzzey Street, bounced to the south sidewalk, about nine feet wide, of Massachusetts Avenue, and moved about fifty-five feet down the sidewalk. On this passage the car scraped the front of a camera store, hit and levelled a parking meter, struck and damaged extensively the right rear section of a Chevrolet Chevelle automobile (the third parked car beyond Muzzey Street), knocked down an electric light pole owned by the defendant Boston Edison Company (Edison), and struck the plaintiffs who had left the ice cream parlor and were walking side by side west, into the face of the oncoming car. There was much confusion at trial whether, after hitting the meter and car, Ramsdell first hit the pole and then the plaintiffs, or first the plaintiffs and then the pole, but no one denied she hit all three. The car came to a stop two to three feet over the stump of the pole with its left wheels in the gutter and its right wheels on the sidewalk, and in contact with the Chevelle.

The electric light pole, when hit, fell away from Ramsdell's car toward the east, struck a Volkswagen automobile parked along Massachusetts Avenue (the fourth car from Muzzey Street), and came down across the legs of Bernier. Boireau was able with help to lift the pole off Bernier. Bernier's thighs and left shin bone were broken, the latter break causing a permanently shortened left leg; and he had other related injuries. Kasputys lay within two feet of the pole further in from the curb than Bernier. There was no eyewitness testimony that she had been struck by the pole. She was unconscious and vomiting. She suffered a skull fracture on the right side of her head where pieces of metal and length of wire were found imbedded, and developed permanent pain in her left lower leg.

[Bernier and Kasputys sued Ramsdell, Boireau, and Edison. The claims against Edison alleged that it had negligently designed, selected, constructed and maintained the pole. The jury found against Ramsdell and Edison. Edison appeals.]

[T]he gravamen of the plaintiffs' case, as it appeared at trial, was that Edison had failed through negligence to design a pole that was accommodated reasonably to foreseeable vehicular impacts so as to avoid pedestrian injuries, and that the continued use of the pole created an unreasonable risk of such injuries.

As designer or codesigner of the pole and in control of its maintenance, Edison "must anticipate the environment in which its product will be used, and it must design against the reasonably foreseeable risk attending the product's use in that setting." Certainly the evidence showed that a risk of automobiles colliding with Edison poles—in particular No. 6 poles—was not only foreseeable but well known to the company. About 100 to 120 Edison poles a year were knocked down in such collisions in Edison's "Northeast Service Center" which included Lexington. . . . A so-called "knock down truck" worked steadily replacing downed poles in the district and installing new ones, and there were estimates by employees that in their years of field work they had replaced "thousands" of Edison poles. One employee said he had been personally involved in replacing at least a hundred poles of the type involved in the accident at bar.

As in the case of vehicles, design should take into account "foreseeable participation in collisions". And for the speeds to be encountered and consequences entailed in collisions, one analyzes the whole "setting." This was a busy shopping area with heavy pedestrian and vehicular traffic.

. . . Edison installed this No. 6 pole on February 3, 1949. It was of reinforced concrete, twenty-six feet nine inches in height, and ran from an eight inch base to a 5 3/8 inch top diameter. Four anchor bolts held it to a base that extended 4 2/3 feet below the surface. The pole was hollow, allowing for feeder wires to come from an underground cable up to the luminaire. Implanted in the concrete shaft were six vertical steel rods, each .375 (3/8) inch thick. Total weight of the pole and luminaire structure was 1,200 pounds.

What precautions were taken in the design to guard against the risk of pedestrian injury through collapse of a No. 6 pole upon impact by a vehicle? According to the evidence, the problem was not seriously adverted to. . . . Overall, the major considerations in Edison's design of poles (including their materials) seemed to be cost, adaptability to Edison's existing system of power supply and connecting apparatus, and capacity of Edison employees to install the poles safely.[4]

. . . To begin with, since injuries might be serious (as the present case indeed indicated), the likelihood of accidents need not be high to warrant careful consideration of safety features.

The plaintiffs' major witness concerning design safety was Howard Simpson, who had a doctorate in engineering and practiced as a consulting structural engineer. His qualifications as an expert on the strength of reinforced concrete were unchallenged. In his opinion, the concrete of the thickness specified for No. 6 poles lacked "ductility," the quality which would allow a pole, when struck by a car, to absorb part of the impact and bend without breaking. No. 6 would shatter when hit with sufficient force; indeed, one of the Edison supervisors testified about No. 6 that the concrete "all crumbles at the point of impact." As the exposed steel rods could not then support the weight of the pole, it would fall. As to the force sufficient to break No. 6 in this fashion, Simpson testified that the pole would succumb to a 1968 Buick Skylark with a passenger, spare tire, and full gas tank going as slowly as six m.p.h. A medium-sized truck weighing 10,000 pounds could level No. 6 when traveling at 1.5 m.p.h.

Simpson went on to say that the strength of the pole could have been substantially improved by using steel rods of larger diameter or by placing steel "hoops" or "spirals" perpendicular to those vertical rods. In his opinion the latter device would have enabled the pole to withstand the impact of the Buick at 11 m.p.h.—an important advance, as a car going 9 m.p.h. has an energy considerably greater than that at 6 m.p.h. Such hoops and spirals had been in use since the early 1900's in columns for buildings. Simpson calculated the cost per pole of the hoops at $5.75 and the spirals at $17.50.

We should add here that there was evidence from Edison employees of the existence of other pole-types, possibly of greater strength, that would

---

[4] It is fair to mention, however, that one engineer thought metal poles might have been passed over because they would tend to become electrified when downed and subject pedestrians to shock. Another thought pedestrian safety was adequately handled by having a reputable manufacturer fabricate the poles. There was some indication that Edison did not install so-called "breakaway" poles in areas such as Lexington Center because of danger to pedestrians.

at least have warranted comparison by Edison with the No. 6 pole in respect to safety values. Various metal poles (aluminum and steel) might have deserved such study. Edison's own No. 26, of prestressed concrete, designed in 1968, might have been an improvement. . . .

Edison argues that a finding of negligence here left it in the grip of a "polycentric" problem. If it chose to protect pedestrians by using stronger poles, motorists might be more seriously injured when they hit poles which did not break. If it chose to protect motorists, pedestrians would claim recovery when poles fell on them. No designer or owner, Edison added, is required to make or use a product wholly accident-free. There is some disingenuousness in this argument as the evidence shows Edison paid scant attention in the design of the No. 6 pole to the safety either of motorists or pedestrians. But we think there is nothing in the argument to relieve Edison of a duty to take precautions against knock-downs by cars, and it would seem reasonable for Edison to consider pedestrian safety with particular seriousness. Persons in a car are protected by a metal and glass shield sometimes three times as heavy as the pole's entire weight; pedestrians are exposed. Whether drivers are hurt any less by impact at similar speeds with poles that topple than with poles that bend rather than fall is unknown to us and apparently to Edison as well. To be sure, many more cars will hit poles than poles will hit pedestrians, but a six m.p.h. threshold for cars, and less for trucks, seems little protection indeed.

. . . Here the jury could rationally find negligence of design and maintenance. They could find that the vehicular speed at which No. 6 would topple was grievously low, creating an unacceptable risk of grave injury to persons at the scene (who in shopping areas such as Lexington Center might be numerous). The impact resistance of the pole could have been improved by relatively minor alterations available at the time and not inconveniencing Edison or the public, or possibly by the use of another type of pole with greater resistance. In balancing all the pertinent factors, the jury made a judgment as to the social acceptability of the design. . . .

Judgments affirmed.

NOTES

1. **Negligence factors.** What factors are important to the court's belief that negligence was proved?

2. **Building a case.** Lawyers must introduce evidence to build their case. What evidence did the plaintiffs supply to show that Edison could foresee cars colliding with poles and poles falling? That precautions existed? What evidence did Edison introduce to support the reasonableness of its conduct? What other evidence could it have offered?

3. **Unquantified risk and benefit.** Do you have a good idea just how risky it was to use these poles? How much benefit was there in using these

poles? To whom did the benefit, if any, flow? Suppose 1,500 people a year are injured by falling poles. Suppose it would cost $3,000–$5,000 to replace each pole with a breakaway pole that would greatly reduce, if not eliminate, these injuries. However, there are 88 million poles nationwide. Should it be left to a jury to decide in individual cases whether the failure to furnish breakaway poles was negligent? Should precautions be required when they are inexpensive, like the hoops and spirals, but not otherwise?

4.   **Social utility of the conduct.** What difference does it make to the negligence analysis if the defendant's conduct has social utility or value? In *Parsons v. Crown Disposal Co.*, 936 P.2d 70 (Cal. 1997), the plaintiff was thrown from the horse he was riding when the defendant's garbage truck, operating in a normal manner, startled the horse with loud noises. Affirming a summary judgment for the defendant, the court said that the main factor in the case is the social value of defendant's conduct. Because garbage collection activity is a vital public service and a matter of high social utility, the defendant is not negligent merely because he uses a machine that produces noises necessary to its regular operation, even though fright of horses might be foreseeable. *See also, e.g., Giant Food, Inc. v. Mitchell*, 640 A.2d 1134 (Md. 1994) (defendant's attempted "hot pursuit" recovery of stolen property did not expose other store customers to any unreasonable risk of harm; the "degree of risk of harm to invitees must be weighed against the privilege" to protect one's property); *Gooden v. City of Talladega*, 966 So.2d 232 (Ala. 2007) (police officer not negligent for engaging in a high-speed chase where the speeding motorist posed "a clear and immediate threat to the safety of other motorists"). *But see Gonzalez v. Johnson*, 581 S.W.3d 529 (Ky. 2019) (police officer's pursuit could be negligent if not of "sufficient social value" where injury or damage occurs).

§ 3. STRUCTURED WEIGHING OF RISKS AND COSTS

UNITED STATES V. CARROLL TOWING CO.

159 F.2d 169 (2d Cir. 1947)

L. HAND, CIRCUIT JUDGE.

[Proceedings in admiralty involving several different entities interested in the collision and sinking of a barge, the Anna C. The Conners company owned the barge, which was loaded with flour. Grace Line employees, operating the Carroll Towing Company tug, negligently caused the Anna C to break adrift. She was carried by wind and tide against a tanker, whose propeller broke a hole in her bottom. Conners' bargee was not on board, and the damage was not reported to anyone. Had there been a bargee there, the Grace Line employees, who had pumps available, could have saved the Anna C; as it was, she careened, dumped her cargo of flour, and sank. The court first held that Grace Line and Carroll Towing were liable, and then considered whether the absence of a bargee on board the Anna C was negligence that reduced recovery to Conners.]

It appears from the foregoing review that there is no general rule to determine when the absence of a bargee or other attendant will make the owner of the barge liable for injuries to other vessels if she breaks away from her moorings. . . . It becomes apparent why there can be no such general rule, when we consider the grounds for such a liability. Since there are occasions when every vessel will break from her moorings, and since, if she does, she becomes a menace to those about her; the owner's duty, as in other similar situations, to provide against resulting injuries is a function of three variables: (1) The probability that she will break away; (2) the gravity of the resulting injury, if she does; (3) the burden of adequate precautions. Possibly it serves to bring this notion into relief to state it in algebraic terms: if the probability be called P; the injury, L; and the burden, B; liability depends upon whether B is less than L multiplied by P: i.e., whether $B < PL$. Applied to the situation at bar, the likelihood that a barge will break from her fasts and the damage she will do, vary with the place and time; for example, if a storm threatens, the danger is greater; so it is, if she is in a crowded harbor where moored barges are constantly being shifted about. On the other hand, the barge must not be the bargee's prison, even though he lives aboard; he must go ashore at times. . . . In the case at bar the bargee left at five o'clock in the afternoon of January 3rd, and the flotilla broke away at about two o'clock in the afternoon of the following day, twenty-one hours afterwards. The bargee had been away all the time, and we hold that his fabricated story was affirmative evidence that he had no excuse for his absence. At the locus in quo—especially during the short January days and in the full tide of war activity—barges were being constantly "drilled" in and out. Certainly it was not beyond reasonable expectation that, with the inevitable haste and bustle, the work might not be done with adequate care. In such circumstances we hold—and it is all that we do hold—that it was a fair requirement that the Conners Company should have a bargee aboard (unless he had some excuse for his absence), during the working hours of daylight.

NOTES

1. **Risk-utility.** As we have seen, many cases approve risk-utility balancing to determine negligence, although very often in a form less structured than the formula Judge Hand advanced. *See, e.g., Doe Parents No. 1 v. State, Dep't of Educ.,* 58 P.3d 545 (Haw. 2002); *see also* 1 DOBBS, HAYDEN & BUBLICK, THE LAW OF TORTS § 160 (2d ed. 2011).

2. **Specific alternative conduct.** We have also seen in this chapter that the party asserting negligence first identifies some specific act of negligence, by pointing to what the defendant did or did not do and identifying some specific safer conduct that might have been pursued. If the alternative

conduct was safer, the court will want to know how much safer and something about its costs. What was the specific alternative conduct Judge Hand was considering in *Carroll Towing*? How would Judge Hand determine the risks and costs?

3. **A hypothetical.** Suppose that, by not having a bargee on board at all times, the barge would break loose and cause damage to itself or others about once a year, and that the average damage would be $25,000. Suppose also that the cost of keeping a bargee on board at all times to prevent this would be an average of $30,000 a year. Judge Hand seems to say this would be a case of no negligence, and Judge Posner says this is correct because the function of the fault system is to impose liability rules that will bring about "efficient" or cost-justified rules of safety. A rule that required the barge owner to spend $30,000 to save $25,000 would be inefficient and not cost-justified. *See* Richard A. Posner, *A Theory of Negligence*, 1 J. LEG. STUDIES 29, 32 (1972).

4. **Probability and severity of harm.** Consider the hypothetical variation of *Carroll Towing* given in Note 3. Where does probability come in? The answer is that it is built into the "average." Suppose the probability is that the barge without a full-time bargee will break loose once every *other* year with the damage of $25,000. The probability of harm is reduced, and this will be reflected in a new average—$12,500 instead of $25,000. Try working this out the other way—by supposing that the barge will break loose *twice* a year. Would it then be negligent not to have a full-time bargee? Might the same type of analysis work with respect to severity of harm? *See Smith v. Finch*, 681 S.E.2d 147 (Ga. 2009) (reasonable care "often requires the consideration of unlikely but serious consequences").

5. **Risk-utility and physical injury.** In light of this kind of thinking, reconsider the *Brown v. Stiel* problem. Does the *Carroll Towing* formula assist in structuring your analysis? Does the test's usefulness wane where the defendant's conduct risked physical injury or death rather than just property damage?

6. **Duty and breach.** Judge Hand says in *Carroll Towing* that "the owner's duty . . . is a function of three variables. . . ." Does it seem to you that he is really assuming a *duty* of reasonable care and then addressing the question of *breach* of that duty? The Third Restatement says that the major factors in analyzing whether conduct is negligent are "the foreseeable likelihood that the person's conduct will result in harm, the foreseeable severity of any harm that may ensue, and the burden of precautions to eliminate or reduce the risk of harm." *See* RESTATEMENT (THIRD) OF TORTS: LIABILITY FOR PHYSICAL AND EMOTIONAL HARM § 3 (2010).

———

NOTE: APPLYING THE RISK-UTILITY FORMULA

1. *Estimating risks.* Everything we do carries *some* risk. In applying the Hand formula, how do we know the degree of risk attributable to the defendant's activity? One answer might be that Hand was not proposing a formula into which actual numbers could be substituted for the "algebra." Instead, Hand might have been proposing only a model, an indication about the nature of the decision or estimate we need to make. Do the cases preceding *Carroll Towing* suggest that courts were estimating costs or benefits of the defendant's conduct compared to some supposedly safer alternative?

2. *Estimating costs or benefits.* How do you *know* how much a safety precaution would cost or how much the activity benefits people? Almost any activity has *some* benefit and almost any safety precaution has *some* costs, although one safety precaution—a warning of danger—is usually almost costless, so that under *Carroll Towing* a warning might be due even if the danger is small. *See* RESTATEMENT (THIRD) OF TORTS: LIABILITY FOR PHYSICAL AND EMOTIONAL HARM § 18 (2010). However, implementing a warning system might well have costs. For example, the company might have to design a computer-controlled system to blow train whistles at crossings. *See* Izhak Englard, *The System Builders: A Critical Appraisal of Modern American Tort Theory*, 9 J. LEGAL STUD. 27 (1980). Costs like this one, and benefits, are often much easier to reduce to numbers than are risks. That is so because many costs can be identified in dollar-numbers. Benefits can also be identified in dollar-numbers by asking about the earnings, savings, or increase in capital value effected by the activity.

3. *Judicial application of the BPL factors.* Applying a risk-utility test to a breach question when the plaintiff tripped over a deviation in the sidewalk, the court in *Chambers v. Village of Moreauville,* 85 So.3d 593 (La. 2012), wrote: "a municipality . . . is only liable for conditions that create an unreasonable risk of harm. Here, the utility of the sidewalk is high. Additionally, it would be fiscally exorbitant to require municipalities to correct all sidewalk deviations of one-and-one-quarter to one-and-one-half inches. Further, the risk of harm created by the deviation is low; there has never been a reported complaint about the deviation in the approximately forty years it has been in existence, the area of the sidewalk is well traveled, the deviation is relatively small, and it developed due to natural causes. Additionally, the deviation was readily observable, and [the plaintiff] failed to exercise the requisite standard of care while traversing this particular area of the sidewalk. Accordingly, we find the condition does not present an unreasonable risk of harm."

4. *The forgotten gopher hole.* As you leave your house one morning, on the way to try a tort case, you observe that a burrowing animal has dug a hole in your yard, very close to the sidewalk. Recognizing that the hole is

a risk to anyone who might step off the sidewalk, you make a mental note to fill the hole or barricade it as soon as you get home. But at the end of a long, hard day before a hostile jury, an irascible judge, and an unappreciative client, you have forgotten the hole. You plop in front of the television. In the meantime, a neighbor on his way to bring you a misdelivered copy of *Torts Illustrated* steps off the sidewalk in the dark, and breaks his ankle as he falls into the hole. Are you negligent? Does *Carroll Towing* help you decide? Might the risk-utility formula be more helpful for evaluating some types of negligence than others? *See* RESTATEMENT (SECOND) OF TORTS § 289 (1965) (memory of the reasonable person is required). Professor Latin points out that many routine cases involve nothing more than mistake and momentary inattention. Howard Latin, *"Good" Warnings, Bad Products, and Cognitive Limitations,* 41 U.C.L.A. L. REV. 1193 (1994).

5.   *Variable probabilities and information costs.* Look back at *Indiana Consolidated Ins. Co. v. Mathew.* What if leaving the burning mower in the garage created a 90% probability of fire damage to the garage of about $10,000 and no more, but a 5% probability of fire totally destroying the house at a loss of $100,000, a 4% probability of a fire spread that would cause losses of more than a million dollars, and a 1% probability of no harm. Does it seem preposterous to say that the jury should somehow factor all this into its negligence decision? Suppose the homeowner does not know how to estimate those probabilities. Information about the existence and degree of risk is itself an item of cost.

NOTE: EVALUATING THE RISK-UTILITY ASSESSMENT

1.   *What values?* What values or tort goals does the risk-utility assessment foster? Since everything we do carries some degree of risk, one argument for a risk-utility assessment is that it provides deterrence in the "right" amount. Relatedly, it maximizes community resources, for the community is richer if its members do not spend $10 to save someone else $5.

2.   *Objections.* Although economically oriented lawyers often like the risk-utility formula as Hand expressed it in *Carroll Towing*, there has been a strong current of objection to it so far as it emphasizes wealth or money. One approach says that basic liberties—freedom of action and security— are primary and take precedence over considerations of wealth. Under this approach, security from harm would be weighed against freedom of action, one basic liberty against another, but losses of liberty would not be offset by increases in wealth. *See* Gregory C. Keating, *Reasonableness and Rationality in Negligence Theory,* 48 STAN. L. REV. 311, 383 (1996).

3. *Alternatives to the risk-utility formula?* If you reject a weighing of risks and utilities, costs and benefits, how could you judge whether the defendant is negligent? Consider: Juries could judge (1) intuitively that "it seems negligent"; (2) solely by statutory prescriptions such as speed limits; (3) by hard-and-fast rules developed by judicial prescriptions, like the rule that you are always negligent if you drive so that you cannot stop within the range of your vision; (4) by custom of the community or the business involved; (5) by a moral rule that imposes liability if the defendant did anything more risky than defendant would have done to prevent the same harm to defendant's own self or property. How does the *Carroll Towing* formula stack up among the alternatives? On the risk-utility balance generally, *see* 1 DOBBS, HAYDEN & BUBLICK, THE LAW OF TORTS §§ 160–62 (2d ed. 2011).

§ 4. ASSESSING RESPONSIBILITY WHEN MORE THAN ONE PERSON IS NEGLIGENT

Many tort cases involve at least two tortfeasors who contribute to the harm done. To analyze and evaluate such cases properly, we need to understand as clearly as possible that liability of one person does not necessarily exclude liability of another. Equally, we need to understand how responsibility is apportioned—that is, who will pay what for damages caused. We deal with more advanced issues about this topic later on. For now, we can set out the structure of apportionment you should have in mind as we begin to read negligence cases.

In considering the rules set out in this section, you might want to have in mind a case like *Bernier v. Boston Edison Co.*, covered in the last section.

(1) **Comparative fault.** If Mrs. Ramsdell had been injured and sued Boston Edison, the rules in most states would allow her to recover, but with her damages reduced in proportion to her fault. The plaintiff's recovery is not ordinarily reduced to reflect her fault when the defendant is guilty of an intentional tort, but recovery is nowadays generally reduced in negligence and strict liability cases. The idea is that each faulty party must bear his or her share of the losses. The defendant's liability is correspondingly reduced so that he pays less than all of the plaintiff's damages. In some cases, the plaintiff actually recovers nothing at all, even though the defendant is also negligent in a substantial way.

(2) **Apportionment among defendants.** What would happen in the suits by Bernier and Kasputys against Boston Edison and Ramsdell if those defendants were chargeable with 80% and 20% of the fault respectively? Since both are negligent, it looks as if both should share in payments to the plaintiff. Ideally, then, Boston Edison would pay 80% of the damages for Bernier's permanently shortened leg and Kasputys' permanent pain and other injuries. Correspondingly, Ramsdell would pay 20% of those

damages. Tort law recognizes this ideal by adopting one of two systems to accomplish it. One of these systems, called the joint and several liability system, also tries to accommodate some other ideals.

(3) **Joint and several liability.** "Joint and several liability" sounds mysterious, but it means that the plaintiff can enforce her tort claim against either tortfeasor. She can actually obtain a judgment against both, but she cannot collect more than her full damages. Although it looks as if Kasputys had very substantial damages indeed, let's suppose for convenience that her damages came to $10,000. Under the rule of joint and several liability, the plaintiff might enforce that judgment entirely against either Boston Edison or against Ramsdell. But that is not the end of the story.

(4) **Contribution.** If Boston Edison paid the entire judgment of $10,000, it would be paying more than its fair share of the damages relative to Ramsdell. Under the joint and several liability system, most states would allow Boston Edison to obtain *contribution* from Ramsdell so as to make its payment proportional to its fault. Under today's rules, if Ramsdell's fault were 20% of the whole and Boston Edison's fault were 80%, Boston Edison should recover contribution from Ramsdell equal to 20% of the damages, $2,000. What is the net cost to Boston Edison after recovery of contribution? Do the rules of joint and several liability plus the rules of contribution carry out the goals of tort law?

Example of Joint and Several Liability With Contribution

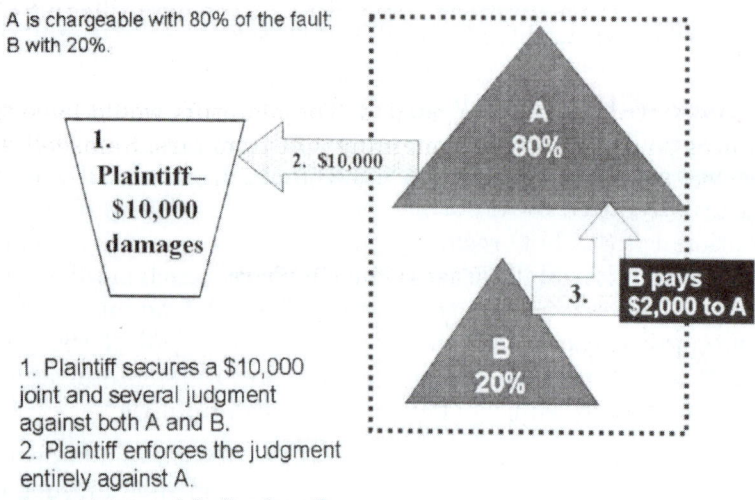

In the diagram, the plaintiff is not at fault and recovers all her losses resulting from the injury. Defendant A, although initially liable for all the losses, eventually recoups contribution from B. The net result is that A, who is chargeable with 80% of the fault, ultimately pays 80% of the plaintiff's damages, and B, with 20% of the fault, pays 20%. The principle applies, of course, without regard to the amount of the damages.

(5) **Insolvent or immune tortfeasors.** Suppose hypothetically that Mrs. Ramsdell had no insurance and no personal assets from which Kasputys could collect a judgment. Or suppose that Mrs. Ramsdell for some reason was immune to tort liability. (As bad as it sounds, it is true that some wrongdoers are free to commit torts without any liability.) On these suppositions, the joint and several liability rule means that the plaintiff would recover her damages from Boston Edison but that as a practical matter Boston Edison could not recover contribution, either because Mrs. Ramsdell had an immunity or because she had no assets with which to pay contribution. The joint and several liability system, then, in effect requires the solvent tortfeasor, Boston Edison, to pick up and pay the insolvent, uninsured, or immune tortfeasor's share. In such a case, the law's ideal— payment proportioned to fault—is not achieved. What other important goal is being accommodated by the joint and several liability system?

(6) **Several liability and comparative fault apportionment among tortfeasors.** An alternative scheme of apportionment has been enacted in a substantial number of states. We'll call it several liability, proportionate share liability, or comparative fault liability. In the several or proportionate share systems, the trier of fact makes a comparative fault apportionment of liability. This several liability system differs from joint liability in that no tortfeasor is liable for more than his proportionate share. On our hypothetical assumptions about *Bernier*, the plaintiffs there would collect only 80% of their damages from Boston Edison in a several liability system, because Boston Edison's fault was only 80% of the whole set of faults. Thus contribution is not needed. The plaintiffs would have to take their chances on collecting the remaining 20% from Mrs. Ramsdell. If Mrs. Ramsdell for any reason could not pay, the plaintiffs would bear 20% of their own losses.

B Cannot Pay His Share

P's loss

| P | | B | B's fault: 20% | If P is not at fault and A |
| | | A | A's fault: 80% | and B are, who should pick up B's share–P or A? |

(7) **Evaluating the two systems for apportioning loss.** When tortfeasor A is fully insured and tortfeasor B has neither insurance nor assets, which system is more consistent with tort goals, the joint and several liability system or the comparative apportionment system?

(8) **Recapping.** This is a lot of specialized information to absorb at one time. Maybe the best recap is to try your hand at applying the rules for sharing damages liabilities. Suppose:

(a) Patricia, a single mother often up at night with her child, is sleepy while driving to work. Dunn, driving a truck, attempts to cross the street in front of Patricia. Patricia was probably slow in hitting her brakes. She broadsided Dunn's truck. Dunn wasn't injured but Patricia was. The jury finds that Dunn's fault was 90%, Patricia's 10%, and that her damages come to $10,000. What amount of money must Dunn (or his liability insurance company) pay under the rules followed in most states?

(b) Agatha and Bert are each driving a car. Both are negligent and they collide in a city intersection. The force of the collision causes Bert to lose control. Consequently, his car strikes a pedestrian, Paul. Paul's injury results in medical expense, loss of wages, and pain. The jury assesses his damages at $100,000 and finds that Agatha's negligence was 75% of the whole, while Bert's was only 25%. (i) In a joint and several liability system, suppose that both Agatha and Bert are insured for liability or otherwise able to pay, but Paul enforces the judgment solely against Bert. What does Bert pay and what contribution rights does he have? (ii) If Agatha is insolvent and uninsured, what is Bert's position in a joint and several liability system? (iii) In a several liability system with comparative fault apportionment?

(9) **Additional variations.** This section focuses on two main systems for apportioning loss—several liability and joint and several liability. In truth, states employ a number of additional variations. The Restatement (Third) of Torts lists three more typical ways in which states apportion liability. *See* RESTATEMENT (THIRD) OF TORTS: APPORTIONMENT OF LIABILITY §§ 18–21 (Tracks A-E) (2000). These approaches are: 1) *Type of damages.* Some jurisdictions retain joint and several liability, but only for certain elements of damage such as economic harm. Parties are severally liable for noneconomic harm. 2) *Threshold percentage.* Other jurisdictions retain joint and several liability only if the defendant's assigned percentage of responsibility exceeds a certain threshold percentage such as 50%. If the defendant is assigned a lesser percentage of responsibility, several liability would apply. 3) *Reapportionment of uncollectible shares.* Still other jurisdictions assign responsibility but then reallocate the losses if an allocated share of the damages cannot be collected. If the plaintiff is unable to collect one defendant's share of the judgment, that share is reallocated among the remaining parties in the same ratio as that of the percentage shares of fault assigned to them. *See* 1 DOBBS, HAYDEN & BUBLICK, THE LAW OF TORTS § 487 (2d ed. 2011). In example 8 (b) imagine that $50,0000 of plaintiff's damages are for economic losses and $50,000 for noneconomic

losses. Also imagine that the fault of Agatha is 30%, the fault of Bert 40%, and the fault of Paul 30%. If Bert is insolvent, what amount would Agatha pay in a jurisdiction with (1) a type of damage system, (2) a threshold percentage system of 50%, or (3) a reapportionment system?

(10) **Bases of liability included in the apportionment.** Traditionally, comparative negligence compared the negligent conduct of one defendant with the negligent conduct of the plaintiff, and later, of other defendants. More recently, some jurisdictions have elected to compare negligence with strict liability, recklessness, and, in some circumstances, even intentional torts. With important limitations, particularly in the realm of intentional torts, the Third Restatement embraces such a view. *See* RESTATEMENT (THIRD) OF TORTS: APPORTIONMENT OF LIABILITY § 1 cmt. b (2000). Apportionment that involves different bases of liability raises a number of complicated issues which will be addressed in Chapter 25.

(11) **Parties included in the apportionment.** In a number of jurisdictions, a jury is asked to apportion the liability not just of plaintiffs and defendants who are parties in the case, but also of non-parties who are at fault. *See, e.g., Cramer v. Starr*, 375 P.3d 69 (Ariz. 2016). Suppose that the plaintiff sues another driver for a rear-end collision that caused her injury and required her to undergo a subsequent surgery. The driver defendant asks that responsibility be apportioned not only to the plaintiff and defendant, but also to the doctor who performed the plaintiff's spinal-fusion surgery after the accident. The jury apportions 20% of the responsibility for plaintiff's back injury to the negligent driver and 80% to the non-party surgeon. In a several liability jurisdiction, what would plaintiff recover? Is this a desirable result?

§ 5. PROVING AND EVALUATING CONDUCT

The plaintiff must prove each element of the case by a preponderance of the evidence, that is, by the greater weight of the evidence. Negligence, for example, must be shown to be more probable than not. The trier of fact, in other words, must reasonably believe that the probability of negligence exceeds one-half. David Kaye, *Probability Theory Meets Res Ipsa Loquitor*, 77 MICH. L. REV. 1456, 1467 (1979).

A. PROVING CONDUCT

SANTIAGO V. FIRST STUDENT, INC.

839 A.2d 550 (R.I. 2004)

PER CURIAM. . . .

[Defendant operates a school bus. Plaintiff alleged that in 1997, when she was in the eighth grade and being transported on one of defendant's buses, it collided with a car at an intersection the plaintiff cannot now identify. Defendant moved for summary judgment and "provided an affidavit prepared by its safety coordinator asserting that there were no company records confirming that an accident had even occurred" in November 1997.]

When plaintiff was deposed as part of pretrial discovery in this case, she testified that she could not remember the street or the neighborhood where the accident occurred. She also admitted that she "could [not] find [the] street today if [she] wanted to." The plaintiff did, however, offer a brief description of her recollection of the events. She remembered that the bus was driving on a one-way street approaching a stop sign. According to plaintiff, she saw the unidentified vehicle approaching the intersection, coming toward the bus from the right. She was then jerked forward when the bus driver applied the brakes and the bus collided with the unidentified vehicle. As a result of the collision, plaintiff says, the right side of her face hit the seat in front of her. Police did not respond to the accident and, consequently, there is no police report describing the incident.

Admitting that she did not see the collision occur, plaintiff was unable to offer any details about it. She was unable to say whether the unidentified car had a stop sign. She did not know whether the bus was damaged or the extent of the damage to the other vehicle, other than that its side mirror was knocked off. . . .

[The trial judge granted summary judgment for the defendant.]

Reviewing the evidence in the light most favorable to plaintiff, we must accept her assertion that she was injured in an accident. To assign negligence to defendant based on the evidence in the record, however, would impermissibly cross the line from reasonable inference and venture into the realm of rank speculation. The plaintiff admitted that she did not see how the collision occurred. Although she testified that a stop sign controlled the flow of traffic coming from the bus's direction, she does not allege that the bus driver failed to stop at the sign as directed. The plaintiff is unable to describe any actions on the part of the driver of the unidentified vehicle or unidentified bus driver relating to the accident. Indeed, there is no evidence of the interaction between the bus and the unidentified car, except that the two vehicles collided. Furthermore, plaintiff can provide no other witnesses capable of offering a meaningful description of the accident.

. . . The plaintiff attempts to justify a lack of evidence to support her case by pointing to the nature of the accident. . . . The fact that the plaintiff's case may be extremely difficult to prove, however, does not relieve her of the burden of presenting sufficient evidence to demonstrate the existence of a material question of fact. The plaintiff has not met that burden in this case and the defendant, therefore, is entitled to judgment as a matter of law.

[Affirmed.]

NOTES

1. **Evidence of negligence.** Is there evidence sufficient to get the plaintiff to the jury on the issue of breach in the following cases?

(a) The defendant was driving on a street 30 feet wide in clear weather. No cars were parked on the side. He ran into a three-year-old child in the street. No one saw how the child got in the street and no one saw the impact itself. The plaintiff asserts a claim on behalf of the child. *Gift v. Palmer*, 141 A.2d 408 (Pa. 1958).

(b) The plaintiff claims that she slipped on a shiny floor. She did not testify "that her fall was occasioned by any foreign substance on the floor, or that polish or wax had been negligently applied to the floor by defendant." *Habershaw v. Michaels Stores, Inc.*, 42 A.3d 1273 (R.I. 2012).

2. **Defendant's alternative conduct.** Could a reasonable person listen to the proof in the *Santiago, Gift,* and *Habershaw* cases and state exactly how the defendant should have altered his conduct to make it safer?

UPCHURCH V. ROTENBERRY

761 So.2d 199 (Miss. 2000)

PITTMAN, PRESIDING JUSTICE, for the Court. . . .

On the night of October 5, 1992, the decedent, Timothy Adam Upchurch, was riding in the passenger seat of Teresa Rotenberry's car while Rotenberry was driving. Adam was the only passenger in the car. The car was traveling west on Highway 182 in Oktibbeha County, Mississippi when Rotenberry lost control of her vehicle. Upchurch claims Teresa left the road suddenly without warning, causing injuries and damages to the decedent that resulted in his death. [The plaintiff sued for the wrongful death of her son. The jury found for the defendant. The plaintiff moved for Judgment N.O.V. The trial court denied the motion and this appeal followed.]

[There were no eyewitnesses except Rotenberry. One expert, Rosenhan, however, testified from evidence at the scene that Rotenberry's vehicle traveled in a straight line from the point it left the road to the point it hit the tree 160 feet away, that there were no scuff or skid marks, and that the vehicle's speed when it hit the tree was 60 mph.]

The speed the vehicle was traveling when it struck the tree, as well as, whether the vehicle left any marks either on the roadway or the area between leaving the road and striking the tree is . . . disputed in this case. Rotenberry's expert, Thomas Shaeffer, testified that there were tire marks which began on the road and proceeded off the road, through the grass, and down toward the tree. Shaeffer identified these marks as yaw marks. Shaeffer defines yaw marks as a mark a tire makes when it is still rotating but not traveling in the direction that it is oriented. . . .

On direct examination, Shaeffer testified that the car was traveling approximately 25 to 35 mph when it hit the tree. However, on cross examination, Shaeffer testified that the car was going 42 to 50 mph when it made impact with the tree.

Rotenberry introduced into evidence photographs to corroborate the conclusions of Shaeffer. . . .

Shaeffer also testified that he observed small pebbles wedged between the rim and tire on both the front left and rear left wheels of the vehicle. This is additional evidence that the vehicle made an extreme right hand turn. All of the evidence presented at trial by Shaeffer was consistent with the vehicle making an evasive maneuver to the right in order to avoid an object on the roadway. Shaeffer's final determination was that the car struck the tree and flipped over on its top, which undoubtedly caused additional damage to the vehicle.

Rotenberry testified as an adverse witness. Throughout the discovery proceedings and at the trial itself, Rotenberry testified that she could not remember the events leading up to the accident including a two-day period just prior to the accident. However, on November 13, 1992 (about 5 weeks after the accident), Rotenberry did sign a written statement detailing the accident. In this statement, Rotenberry testified that a large animal, either a deer or a dog, ran across the road and into her lane ultimately causing her to leave the road. . . .

In her brief, Upchurch raises the issue that Kirk Rosenhan, plaintiff's expert, testified that he smelled alcohol on the defendant at the accident scene. However, on direct examination of Rosenhan the following exchange occurred.

Q. Did you get close to Teresa Rotenberry?

A. Not really.

Q. Did you get close enough to smell her?

A. No, I didn't.

Q. Did you smell any odor of intoxicant on her?

A. Uh, not on her. . . .

On redirect examination after an overnight recess, Rosenhan changed his testimony to say that he had not been specific as to the driver of the vehicle the day before and that he did smell alcohol on the driver the night of the accident. The above exchange, however, makes it clear that Rosenhan was perfectly specific on direct examination in denying that he smelled alcohol on Rotenberry at the scene of the accident. It is noteworthy that Rosenhan did testify on direct examination that he smelled alcohol in the area. Also, the presence of beer in the car is not disputed in the facts of this case.

Larry Guyton, a trooper with the Mississippi Highway Patrol, also testified for the plaintiff. Officer Guyton testified that he arrived on the scene after Rotenberry had been taken away by ambulance. Officer Guyton spoke to Rotenberry by telephone in her hospital room two days after the accident, October 7th, and again on October 8th. Rotenberry was able to remember the accident at this point. She appeared alert during the conversation. Officer Guyton testified that Rotenberry told him that she was traveling westbound on Highway 182 near Starkville when she saw an animal coming into her lane from the opposite side of the road. She swerved to the right to avoid hitting the animal. In Officer Guyton's opinion, Rotenberry appeared to be telling him the truth.

Further, Officer Guyton testified on direct examination that Rotenberry told him that she had two beers earlier in the evening at a place called "The Landing" on Highway 182 near Starkville. On cross examination, however, Officer Guyton testified that Rotenberry did not tell him about drinking beer or about being at The Landing. He just asked her how the accident occurred, and she told him. Further, he stated that he did not put anything in his accident report concerning drinking or about being at The Landing. He continued by testifying that Rotenberry had not told him anything different than what was in his report. . . .

[T]his Court concludes that reasonable and fairminded jury members could reach different conclusions. Consequently, the jury verdict stands, and the motion for JNOV is denied.

This Court will not intrude into the realm of the jury by determining the credibility of a witness and making findings of fact. The jury is the judge of the weight of the evidence and the credibility of the witnesses. Through her statement and the testimony of other witnesses, Rotenberry offered evidence explaining the events of that tragic night. The jury considered this evidence, weighed it, and found in favor of Rotenberry. . . .

This Court has been even more specific regarding the realm of the jury concerning the credibility of witnesses in stating:

> The demeanor or bearing, the tone of voice, the attitude and appearance of the witnesses, all are primarily for inspection and review by the jury. The jury not only has the right and duty to determine the truth or falsity of the witnesses, but also has the right to evaluate and determine what portions of the testimony of

any witness it will accept or reject; therefore, unless it is clear to this Court that the verdict is contrary to the overwhelming weight of the credible testimony, this court will not set aside the verdict of a jury.

. . . According to its duty, the jury concluded that Rotenberry acted reasonably in swerving to the right to avoid an animal and that she did not have time to avoid a tree which lay only 160 feet (or slightly over 53 yards) from where Rotenberry left the road. The jury makes such fact determinations, not this Court. . . .

The resolution of disputed facts such as this is a duty that devolves upon the jury sitting as finders of fact. They are charged with listening to the witnesses, observing their demeanor, and coming to their own conclusions of which evidence they find more credible. Our system of jurisprudence has determined that citizen jurors, employing their native intelligence and collective life experiences, are best qualified to make those judgments. Absent some clear indication that the jurors in a particular case somehow ignored that duty, neither the trial court, nor this Court reviewing the record on appeal, are permitted to interfere in the conclusions reached by these jurors.

NOTES

The Process of Determining Fault

1.   **Small physical miscalculations—fault or not?** Lawyers often find it difficult to obtain facts necessary for an assessment of fault. One reason is that injuries are often caused by tiny miscalculations, hard for the actor to appreciate and almost impossible for a jury to understand at a later date. For instance, a car traveling at 50 m.p.h. travels about 75 feet per second. The time for drivers to react to an emergency, such as a child darting into the road, varies considerably. About half of all drivers take nearly a second to respond, but some take two seconds. *See* LEON ROBERTSON, INJURIES, CAUSES, CONTROL STRATEGIES AND PUBLIC POLICY 42 (1983). If a driver hits a child 100 feet from the point of observation, a reaction time for hitting the brakes of one second might have been sufficient to avoid the impact, but a reaction time of two seconds would not. Or again, what about the fact that a driver may lose part of her field of vision as she gets older—and with no way to be aware of this? Studies seem to indicate that loss of visual field is commonly associated with auto injuries, yet the topic does not come up in the cases. *See id.* at 62.

2.   **Accuracy of testimony.** A second problem in obtaining facts for making a judgment about fault lies with the accuracy of testimony. A very considerable body of information indicates that witnesses are generally inaccurate in a number of particulars. Part of this lies in perception of events, which is especially difficult if they occur quickly, only once, and with violence or stress. *See* ELIZABETH LOFTUS, EYEWITNESS TESTIMONY (1979).

3. **Using traffic rules to test "fault."** A social scientist studying the process of settling tort claims in automobile accident cases has said that, in practice, evaluation of claims consists chiefly in discovering traffic violations and that though "formal tort law" concerns issues of duty, foreseeability, reasonable care and a "fine weighing" of negligence, in most auto cases a traffic violation is the central issue. H. LAURENCE ROSS, SETTLED OUT OF COURT 20 (2d ed. 1980). If this is so, is it merely a result of the negligence per se rule? *See* RESTATEMENT (THIRD) OF TORTS: LIABILITY FOR PHYSICAL AND EMOTIONAL HARM § 14 cmt. d (2010) ("[T]he conduct of motorists is extensively dealt with by statutes and regulations; accordingly, in most highway-accident cases, findings of negligence depend on ascertaining which party has violated the relevant provisions of the state's motor-vehicle code."). Does this make it any more or any less important to find out exactly what the conduct was?

4. **Changing safety environments.** As some of these paragraphs show, the process of determining fault in tort cases is difficult at best. This leads to the idea that if you try to deal with vehicle safety after injury has occurred, you must look for fault, but that if you try to prevent accidents before they occur, you might try to change the environment. For example, roads may be better designed or signals more visible. Another approach to automobile safety left the tort system altogether. This sought to require auto makers to provide safer automobiles through regulations issued by the National Highway Traffic Safety Administration.

The Credibility Rule

5. **Jury role.** Credibility of witnesses is almost always a question for the jury. Consider this case: conflicting testimony and circumstances indicated that a jaywalking pedestrian emerged in front of a driver suddenly and without warning. Although three eyewitnesses had seen the pedestrian waiting to cross the street, the driver did not. Upholding a jury verdict that the defendant driver was not negligent for failing to observe the pedestrian, the trial judge stated that, based on the evidence presented, she "could not conclude that [the driver] was speeding or doing anything—such as reading a map or looking for a radio station—that would have distracted his attention from the road ahead." *Mead v. SanofiAventis U.S., Inc.*, 62 A.3d 512 (R.I. 2013). *See also Bosco v. Janowitz*, 903 N.E.2d 756 (Ill. App. Ct. 2009) ("It is the function of the jury to weigh contradictory evidence, judge the credibility of witnesses, and draw ultimate conclusions as to the facts of a case."). Standard instructions tell juries to determine credibility of witnesses for themselves, considering factors such as the witnesses' demeanor and other factors mentioned in *Upchurch. See, e.g.,* Ill. Pattern Jury Instructions—Civil § 1.01, ¶ 4 (2007 ed.).

6. **Lawyers' roles.** What is the role of the lawyers in this? Would you expect simply to gather favorable witnesses together, put their testimony on, and quit? What else *could* you do?

7. **Credibility, directed verdicts and new trials.** Given the credibility rule, should the plaintiff be entitled to a directed verdict in her favor if the defendant puts on no evidence at all, or if his evidence does not contradict

the plaintiff's? Some courts take the view that if the plaintiff offers testimony that is not only uncontradicted, but is clear and self-consistent, a directed verdict for the party having the burden of proof—usually the plaintiff—is permissible. *See, e.g., Trevino v. Kent County,* 936 S.W.2d 488 (Tex. App. 1996). Similarly, in *Wald v. Grainger,* 64 So.3d 1201 (Fla. 2011), the court said that the jury was not free to reject undisputed expert testimony that the plaintiff's thigh injury was permanent, where both plaintiff's and defendant's experts agreed on the point. *See also Dillon v. Frazer,* 678 S.E.2d 251 (S.C. 2009) (holding that trial judge abused his discretion in failing to grant a new trial when jury awarded $6,000 for undisputed damages of at least $30,000 and admitted liability).

FORSYTH V. JOSEPH, 450 P.2d 627 (N.M. Ct. App. 1968). Decedent was an occupant of a car struck by the Villa truck. The trial court found Villa to be negligent, partly because of excessive speed. There was evidence that Villa skidded 129 feet before the impact. *Held,* affirmed. "The speed limit was 55 miles per hour. The court found he was exceeding this speed and was traveling at the rate of 55 miles per hour at the point of impact. These findings are supported by the evidence. Even Villa testified that his speed 'at the point of impact' was 55 miles per hour. In addition thereto, we have the skid marks to which reference is above made, the force of the impact which knocked the Joseph vehicle about 20 or 25 feet and spun it about 90 degrees, and the continued momentum of Villa's vehicle, which carried it through the fence and into the open field where it came to a rest."

NOTES

1.   **Use of circumstantial evidence.** Circumstantial evidence—which is to say evidence of one fact that permits an inference of another fact—is often the most important evidence in tort cases. Although circumstantial evidence must be weighed case by case, in general it is entitled to as much weight as direct evidence. *Fitzpatrick v. Natter,* 961 A.2d 1229 (Pa. 2008). Almost all negligence cases involve at least some factual inferences. The inference may, of course, assist the defendant rather than the plaintiff. What inference would you draw if the proof showed defendant stopped his car in 33 feet?

2.   **Circumstantial evidence and legal conclusions.** Ordinary circumstantial evidence is evidence of one fact that tends to establish some other fact. What if a man steps onto the roof of an elevator to effect a repair, suddenly utters, "S * * *," and disappears from view as the elevator door closes, followed by a loud "boom"? *See Walker v. Chicago Housing Auth.,* 30 N.E.3d 539 (Ill. App. Ct. 2015) (bench trial). The trier of fact may reasonably infer that he slipped on oil on the roof of the elevator and fell to his death, despite the fact that no one actually saw him fall. *Id.*

3.   **An alert.** In the *Forsyth* case, perhaps Villa did not literally mean he was traveling 55 at the point of impact. What else might he have meant? What

is the responsibility of the lawyer about such a matter? Notice that Villa's admission was considered against him.

4.   **Judge and jury.** Questions of fact and questions of credibility are for the jury to decide. What about *inferences* of fact, such as those involved in *Forsyth?* The answer is that the jury is also the decision maker as to inferences, provided there is room for reasonable persons to draw or reject those inferences. "If the evidence adduced at trial is conflicting on a material point, or if reasonable persons may draw different conclusions from the evidence, or if a conclusion is dependent on the weight the fact finder gives to the testimony, a judge may not substitute his or her conclusion for that of the jury merely because he or she would have reached a different result." *McGuire v. Hodges*, 639 S.E.2d 284 (Va. 2007).

5.   **Evidence to assist in drawing inferences.** In many instances one might reject an inference of fact simply for lack of knowledge. Suppose the evidence is that the defendant left skid marks of 137 feet, and that his car was at a complete stop at the end of the marks. Do you know how fast he was going? What evidence could be introduced to assist a-judge or jury in drawing an inference about speed?

NOTE: WITNESSES' OPINIONS

1.   *Non-expert opinion.* Witnesses are not usually permitted to give opinions on "ultimate" issues that are reserved for jury decision in the case. For example, a witness would not be permitted to testify, "In my opinion, the defendant was negligent." The witness is required instead to state facts within his knowledge, for instance, "I saw the defendant run the red light." A few statements that might be classed as opinions are permitted, however, as a kind of shorthand or summing up of direct experience. An eyewitness may be permitted to estimate speed, distance, or intoxication, for example. It would be difficult to express any more accurately the facts on which it is based, and juries are likely to understand that the impression or estimate is no more than that.

2.   *Expert opinion.* Experts are usually allowed to give expert opinion or conclusions within the field of their expertise, provided the testimony is likely to be helpful to the jury on an issue in the case. For example, an orthopedic surgeon, examining a plaintiff who has tingling in the fingers and pain in the shoulder and neck, may infer that the patient suffers from some impingement on a nerve in the 6–7 cervical interspace of the neck. In the same way, investigating officers are usually allowed to give opinions about speed, distance, direction, and point of impact from evidence at the scene of a motor vehicle collision. But even this simple kind of testimony may be excluded if it is not helpful to the jury or the jury can readily determine the issue by interpreting the facts for themselves.

Expert opinion testimony raises serious issues. One very common problem is that experts often differ. One expert may testify that in her opinion the plaintiff suffers a serious paralysis that is irremediable, while another may testify that in his opinion the plaintiff is not injured at all or, if injured, will recover speedily. Juries have little basis for resolving such conflicts of opinion except on the basis of a feeling that one expert is more impressive than another—which perhaps suggests one of the reasons that courts are reluctant about opinion testimony in the first place.

A second problem with expert testimony is that the witness may not in fact be an expert at all with respect to his particular testimony; or that the expert may be an expert in some sense but still offer an opinion that is only speculation.

Another problem with expert testimony is that it may overwhelm the jury. Experts are often prestigious by reason of their professional status, and some are more or less professional witnesses whose presence and demeanor may be highly impressive. The seemingly independent status of the expert witness may suggest a disinterested appraisal, which may lend this testimony even more weight in the jury's mind, though in fact some experts become quite partisan.

NOTE

Should we be skeptical about our ability to resolve disputes by judging negligence? Chance plays a big role in determining whether you will recover if you are injured. There may be no witness to the event other than the defendant himself; the evidence may be conflicting; and witnesses on your side may be unappealing personalities and disliked by jurors, while witnesses on the other side may be pleasant and convincing.

PROBLEM

Kibler v. Maddux

You have been retained by the parents of Tommy Kibler, 4 years of age, to bring suit for Tommy's injuries. On January 6, Linda Rodriguez called Mrs. Kibler and invited Tommy to come play with her son, also 4, at her house. It was rainy and Mrs. Kibler dressed him in a slicker and took him to the Rodriguez home about 2:30. She asked Mrs. Rodriguez to call when she was ready for Tommy to come home, saying she would pick him up rather than let him cross the street alone. She had trained him to wait for her at the curb. About 4:00, Mrs. Rodriguez called and told Mrs. Kibler she would dress Tommy in his slicker and take him to the curb where Mrs. Kibler would meet him. It was anticipated that Mrs. Kibler would arrive slightly before or at the same time as Tommy, but she slipped and fell on her slippery sidewalk and walked rather slowly and painfully. Tommy arrived at the curb and waited for his mother, looking in the direction she was to come from.

In the meantime, Irene Maddux was proceeding north on Spruce Street driving her car. She arrived at the crest of a slope and at that point she could see Tommy standing at the curb in his yellow slicker about 400–500 yards away. She proceeded on towards that point, driving at 20 m.p.h. because of the rain, slippery roads, and gathering dusk. She watched Tommy constantly as she approached. When she reached a point she thinks was about 15 feet from Tommy, he suddenly ran out in front of her. It later became clear that he had waited somewhat longer for his mother than he expected to, and that when he saw her coming, he ran toward her. Maddux hit the brakes and also swerved to the right, but her left front fender struck Tommy and knocked him about 30 feet, causing some considerable injury.

Both sides have taken depositions and all the facts stated above are established. Defendant Maddux has moved for summary judgment on the basis of these admitted or established facts. How do you evaluate your case? What arguments can you make?

NOTES

1.　**Determining negligence claims.** In many cases, as in *Kibler*, it is possible to point to more than one act or omission that might constitute negligence. On occasion, lawyers fail to perceive their best claims of negligence and argue only the most obvious. Suppose the trial judge decided to hold a brief oral argument on the defendant's motion for summary judgment, and you have an opportunity to state in what respects Ms. Maddux could be found negligent by the trier. Would your primary argument be that she was driving too fast considering the weather?

2.　**Jury evaluation.** Courts are reluctant to decide negligence cases on summary judgment motions in some cases. Why is this? "An inherently normative issue . . . is not generally susceptible to summary judgment: the evidence requires that a jury balance the [safety precautions] against the nature and extent of the risk." *Little v. Liquid Air Corp.*, 952 F.2d 841 (5th Cir. 1992). In other words, juries are often called upon to decide not merely bare facts but also to make normative evaluations of the conduct involved. *See also Amos v. Lincoln Cty. Sch. Dist. No. 2*, 359 P.3d 954 (Wyo. 2015) (during a community basketball game at school, a lunchroom bench propped against the wall fell on a 5-year-old and killed him; the court reversed summary judgment for the defendant on the ground that "even where the material facts are undisputed, the question of whether a defendant breached its duty is generally one left to the finder of fact"). Of course, where facts are in dispute, summary judgement is also inappropriate. *See Johnson v. Wash. Gas Light Co.*, 109 A.3d 1118 (D.C. 2015) (fact question whether utility replaced access cover after maintenance or left utility hole uncovered).

But when the trial court concludes that the jury verdict is against the great weight of the evidence, the court can overturn it. *Warrick v. Stewart*, 29

N.E.3d 1284 (Ind. Ct. App. 2015) ("The trial judge sits as a 'thirteenth juror' and must determine whether in the minds of reasonable men a contrary verdict should have been reached. As the thirteenth juror, the trial judge 1) hears the case along with the jury, 2) observes witnesses for their credibility, intelligence, and wisdom, and 3) determines whether the verdict is against the weight of the evidence." The trial court determined that motorcyclist was not speeding when a dog darted into the street. Trial court motion to set aside verdict upheld.).

§ 6. EVALUATING CONDUCT THROUGH NOTICE AND OPPORTUNITY TO CURE

RENNER V. RETZER RESOURCES, INC.

236 So.3d 810 (Miss. 2017)

RANDOLPH, PRESIDING JUSTICE, for the Court. . . .

[O]n August 13, 2012, seventy-six-year-old John Renner ('Renner') was traveling from Jackson, Mississippi, to his home in St. Louis, Missouri. He, his wife, and two other family members stopped at a McDonald's in Winona. . . . After he received his order, Renner set his food down at a table and walked to the condiment station. . . . Before returning to his table, he thought one of the McDonald's employees spoke to him. Renner turned and faced the counter before realizing the employee was speaking to another customer. As Renner turned back around to return to his table, his left foot struck a protruding leg of a highchair, causing him to fall and suffer injury to his face and left shoulder. After the fall, Renner heard one of the McDonald's employees ask another what the highchair was doing there, and to move it. . . . [Renner sued McDonald's and Retzer Resources (the owner and operator of the McDonalds), among others. The circuit court granted summary judgment for the defendants, reasoning that "[t]he presence of a highchair in a restaurant like McDonald's is clearly a normal and usual condition that an invitee could expect to encounter."]

Greta Siegel was an eyewitness to the fall. Siegel, originally from Winona and a former Dean of Students at a college in California, was a frequent patron of the Winona McDonald's. Siegel visited McDonald's often in order to use its Wi-Fi connection. On the morning of the fall, Siegel was seated in a booth catty-corner to the location of the accident. Siegel's attention was directed that way when she heard a loud noise. She saw Renner fall and land on the floor. She also saw Renner's left foot tangled in the leg of a highchair. Siegel then heard a McDonald's employee immediately instruct other McDonald's employees to move the highchairs away from that area.

Siegel testified that she was not surprised that Renner had tripped at the condiment station, because the highchairs are obscured from view behind a "half wall," and because the legs of the highchairs protrude out farther than the tops of the highchairs. When questioned about the visibility of the highchairs, Siegel testified that, "[w]hat is hidden is the way that bottom juts out, because as you walk up to the chairs, obviously, they are there, but what you wouldn't expect is for a . . . piece of it to be sticking out." When asked about the particular morning of Renner's fall and whether the highchairs were sticking out into the aisle, Siegel confirmed that they were and described the placement of the chairs as a "big hazard." Siegel previously had seen other McDonald's customers bump into the highchairs at the same location where Renner fell. . . .

Siegel had complained several times about the location of the highchairs to a manager and to other McDonald's employees prior to this accident. Siegel testified that after complaining about the chairs, the employees would move them away from the corner, but still leave them on the same wall. However, Siegel also testified that, since the accident, the chairs remain in the same location.

Velencia Hubbard, the shift manager of McDonald's at the time of the accident, did not dispute any of Siegel's testimony. She opined that she thought the chairs were properly stored and did not believe they were out of place.

To recover in a trip-and-fall case, a plaintiff must "(1) show that some negligent act of the defendant caused his injury; or (2) show that the defendant had actual knowledge of a dangerous condition and failed to warn the plaintiff; or (3) show that the dangerous condition existed for a sufficient amount of time to impute constructive knowledge to the defendant, in that the defendant should have known of the dangerous condition."

Renner established sufficient facts, which, if believed, would defeat a motion for summary judgment. It would be a question for the finder of fact whether the defendants had actual knowledge of the alleged dangerous condition and failed to warn Renner, or whether the defendants had constructive knowledge of the alleged dangerous condition (another issue for a jury). Renner offered the deposition testimony of Siegel, who testified that the legs of the highchairs protrude into the aisle and are obscured from view behind a "half wall." Siegel claimed personally to have witnessed at least three customers bump into or kick the highchairs. Siegel testified that she repeatedly had alerted several McDonald's employees about her concerns regarding the alleged hidden nature and dangerous condition of the highchairs. . . .

The trial court's opinion fails to account for the testimony of Siegel and concluded that, because highchairs normally are present in restaurants, an invitee could expect to encounter them. The trial judge's opinion erroneously supplanted the facts in the record with his own opinion regarding the location of the highchairs This is a role for jurors. "The trial court's function on a Rule 56 motion for summary judgment is not to resolve disputed factual issues, but rather to determine whether issues of fact exist to be tried.". . .

[Reversed and remanded.]

NOTES

1.   **Three common theories of liability.** Lawyers have developed several means of attempting to prove a defendant's negligence when the plaintiff slips on foreign substances in the defendant's place of business. The plaintiff can show negligence on the part of the defendant by proving either that: (a) the defendant created and failed to take reasonable actions to abate the hazard, as where a waiter spills sauce on the floor; (b) the defendant did not directly create the condition but discovered or should have discovered a condition created by others (often called 'constructive notice') and failed to take reasonable steps to prevent injury from that condition; or (c) the defendant's mode or method of business operations made it foreseeable that others would create a dangerous condition, and the defendant failed to take reasonable measures to discover and remove it, as where a grocery's bean bin is constructed so that customers will regularly cause loose beans to fall on the floor, or where customers help themselves at a drink station. *See, e.g., Fisher v. Big Y Foods, Inc.*, 3 A.3d 919 (Conn. 2010); *Thoma v. Cracker Barrel Old Country Store, Inc.*, 649 So.2d 277 (Fla. Dist. Ct. App. 1995) (restaurant patron slipped on drops of clear liquid; wait staff was carrying trays with beverages; witnesses did not see anyone spill anything on the floor); *cf. Parker v. Holiday Hosp. Franchising, Inc.*, 446 S.W.3d 341 (Tenn. 2014) (a property owner cannot be held liable on a premises liability theory unless "the plaintiff proved . . . either that the condition was caused or created by the [owner] or if the condition was created by someone other than the [owner], that the [owner] had actual or constructive notice that the condition existed prior to the accident"; bench in a handicap-accessible shower collapsed, plaintiff had shown neither).

2.   **Evidence that the defendant should have discovered.** What was the evidence in *Renner* that defendants knew of the hazardous condition? How would a plaintiff prove that the defendant should have known of a hazardous condition, such as a foreign substance spilled on the floor? The chief method approved by the courts is to show that the substance had been there for a relatively long time. The jury is then permitted to conclude that a reasonable person should have discovered and remedied it. When such proof is presented, courts may say that the defendant was on constructive notice of the danger, meaning only that defendant should have discovered it. Getting evidence of this kind may be difficult, and when the evidence shows instead that some hazard was only present for a brief period of time, the plaintiff will have failed to prove constructive notice. Consequently, in *Pace v. Wal-Mart Stores E., LP*, 337 F.Supp.3d 513 (E.D. Pa. 2018), evidence that an employee was unloading boxes of grapes twenty minutes before a plaintiff slipped on

grapes was insufficient as a matter of law to prove constructive notice. Another method of showing constructive notice is to show prior accidents. *See Sullivan v. Abovenet Commc'ns*, 112 A.3d 347 (D.C. 2015) (evidence that a pedestrian had tripped on uneven surface surrounding manhole cover two weeks earlier raised fact issue as to whether the contractor had constructive notice of the defect).

3. **Evaluating reasonableness.** The main focus of this segment of the book is the evaluation of conduct. If we infer that loose green beans that fell out of the grocery store bin have been on the floor for an hour, we are left with the problem of evaluating the defendant's conduct. In some cases you might doubt whether courts or juries really have any way of saying that a reasonable and prudent store operator would have discovered a slippery substance on the floor within 15 minutes. On this issue consider: (a) The plaintiff can show the volume of customer traffic in the area where she fell. Would that be relevant to show that inspections by the storekeeper should have been more frequent? *See Jones v. Brookshire Grocery Co.*, 847 So.2d 43 (La. Ct. App. 2003). (b) Can the risk-utility test be applied in *Renner*? Could you evaluate the conduct as negligent or not by considering the consumer's reasonable expectations instead?

4. **Judicial help for the plaintiff.** Clearly slip-and-fall plaintiffs have serious proof problems. Some courts have developed corollary rules to help the plaintiff a little. In *Ortega v. Kmart Corp.,* 36 P.3d 11 (Cal. 2001), the court suggested leeway for the plaintiff when it said: "Whether a dangerous condition has existed long enough for a reasonably prudent person to have discovered it is a question of fact for the jury, and the cases do not impose exact time limitations. Each accident must be viewed in light of its own unique circumstances." A few courts have shifted the burden of proof to the shopkeeper to exculpate itself once the plaintiff has shown a fall due to a foreign substance. *See, e.g., Lanier v. Wal-Mart Stores, Inc.*, 99 S.W.3d 431 (Ky. 2003).

§ 7. VIOLATION OF PRIVATE STANDARD OR COMMON CUSTOM

A. THE ACTOR'S OWN STANDARD

WAL-MART STORES, INC. V. WRIGHT, 774 N.E.2d 891 (Ind. 2002). A woman slipped on a puddle of water in the outdoor garden area of a Wal-Mart store. She sued for her injuries, alleging that Wal-Mart was negligent in the maintenance, care and inspection of the premises. The parties stipulated to the admission of a number of Wal-Mart's employee documents assembled as a "Store Manual." Several of the provisions detailed procedures for dealing with spills and other floor hazards. At the end of the trial, the plaintiff tendered a jury instruction that said: "You may consider the violation of any rules, policies, practices and procedures contained in these manuals and safety handbook along with all of the other evidence and the Court's instructions in deciding whether Wal-Mart was negligent.

The violation of its rules, policies, practices and procedures are a proper item of evidence tending to show the degree of care recognized by Wal-Mart as ordinary care. . . ." The trial judge gave the instruction over Wal-Mart's objection. The jury found for the plaintiff, reducing her damages for her own comparative fault.

Held, the instruction was improper and the verdict must be reversed. "[Y]ou can set standards for yourself that exceed ordinary care and the fact that you've done that shouldn't be used, as this [instruction] says, as evidence tending to show the degree that you believe is ordinary." Wal-Mart's "rules and policies may exceed its view of what is required by ordinary care in a given situation. Rules and policies in the Manual may have been established for any number of reasons having nothing to do with safety and ordinary care, including a desire to appear more clean and neat to attract customers, or a concern that spills may contaminate merchandise. The law has long recognized that failure to follow a party's precautionary steps or procedures is not necessarily failure to exercise ordinary care. . . . 1 Dan B. Dobbs, The Law of Torts § 165 (2000). We think this rule is salutary because it encourages following the best practices without necessarily establishing them as a legal norm." The instruction is also erroneous for suggesting that jurors could apply "Wal-Mart's subjective view—as evidenced by the Manual—rather than an objective standard of ordinary care."

NOTES

1. **Private standards.** Why does the court believe that not giving internal safety rules the force of legal norms "encourages following the best practices"?

2. **Reasonable care and private standards.** Why not use a company's own standard to set the legal standard? In *Jenkins v. Jordan Valley Water Conservancy*, 321 P.3d 1049 (Utah 2013), the water conservancy's decision to replace a pipe could not be used to establish the standard of care for negligence purposes. The court wrote: "An internal determination that a pipeline should be replaced does not establish a tort law duty to do so. Internal decisions may be made for any number of reasons—convenience, caution, maximization of budget, mistake—having little to do with the standard of care. Thus, the resolution of this issue cannot be narrowly focused, as the court of appeals put it, on the decision to delay three years before replacing the pipeline. Instead, the critical issue is whether the applicable standard of care required the District to replace the pipeline near the Jenkins home. And we cannot see how the Jenkinses could show that it did without expert testimony." *See also Kramer v. Catholic Charities of the Diocese of Fort Wayne-South Bend, Inc.*, 32 N.E.3d 227 (Ind. 2015) (charity's own informal practice of conducting preplacement adoption checks did not create a responsibility for agency to make such checks).

3. **The Restatement view.** The Restatement Third takes a "flexible position" on the admissibility of evidence regarding the actor's departure from its own standard. RESTATEMENT (THIRD) OF TORTS: LIABILITY FOR PHYSICAL AND EMOTIONAL HARM § 13 cmt. f (2010). That practice may be relevant to foreseeability or risk, feasibility of precautions, or the plaintiff's reliance on a particular type of care. However, even when the evidence is admissible "it does not set a higher standard of care for the actor." *See Morgan v. Scott*, 291 S.W.3d 622 (Ky. 2009) (car dealership's internal rule requiring an employee to accompany a test driver did not create a duty of care to a third party injured by test driver); *Everitt v. General Elec. Co.*, 979 A.2d 760 (N.H. 2009) (internal policy regarding procedures to be followed in dealing with impaired employees did not create duty to the public).

B. CUSTOM

DUNCAN V. CORBETTA, 577 N.Y.S.2d 129 (App. Div. 1991). "The plaintiff William C. Duncan was injured when he began to descend a wooden exterior stairway at the defendant's residence and the top step collapsed. The court erred by precluding the plaintiffs' expert from testifying that it was common practice to use pressure-treated lumber in the construction of such stairways, even though the nonpressure-treated lumber used was permissible under the applicable building code. Proof of a general custom and usage is admissible because it tends to establish a standard by which ordinary care may be judged even where an ordinance prescribes certain minimum safety requirements which the custom exceeds. However, no significant prejudice resulted from the error. The plaintiffs failed to establish that the defendant had a role in the design or construction of the stairway." Judgment for defendant affirmed.

NOTES

1. **General rule.** Evidence that the defendant violated customary safety precautions of the relevant community is usually sufficient to get the plaintiff to the jury. The Third Restatement says that a person's "departure from the custom of the community, or of others in like circumstances, in a way that increases the risk" is evidence of that person's negligence "but does not require a finding of negligence." RESTATEMENT (THIRD) OF TORTS: LIABILITY FOR PHYSICAL AND EMOTIONAL HARM § 13(b) (2010).

2. **Customary statutory violations.** In *Duncan v. Corbetta*, the court was willing to say that a defendant who complied with all the safety requirements of a statute might still be negligent if he failed to follow a safety custom. What if a litigant who failed to comply with a statute or ordinance wants to introduce evidence that the law is customarily violated, that is, that custom tends to show that violation is reasonable conduct? Judges generally disfavor such a use of custom evidence. *See, e.g., Robinson v. District of Columbia*, 580 A.2d 1255 (D.C. 1990) (rejecting party's argument that it was reasonable to disobey traffic law by jaywalking outside the marked crosswalk,

as allegedly shown by "common practice of pedestrians at the location of the accident").

3. **What custom proves.** Existence of a safety custom might conceivably prove a number of different things. It might, for example, prove that harm was foreseeable, which is to say that the activity was recognizably risky; it might prove that the defendant knew or should have known of the risk; and it might prove that the risk was an "unreasonable" one unless the customary precaution is taken, or at least that it was unreasonable in the opinion of the community in general.

4. **Custom other than safety custom.** What if the custom is well-established and even widespread, but there is no evidence whether the custom arose from safety considerations or from convenience? In *Levine v. Russell Blaine Co.*, 7 N.E.2d 673 (N.Y. 1937), the plaintiff injured her hand on a rough, bristly rope for which defendant was responsible. There was an infection and later the arm had to be amputated. The plaintiff sought to introduce evidence that by custom the rope supplied should have been a smooth one. The court said:

> A smoother rope might have advantages other than greater safety. Its customary use might be due to these advantages, and might not show a general recognition that risk of injury would arise from use of a rougher rope. Proof of such custom or practice would then be insufficient, standing alone, to show negligence . . . but the chain of proof might, in this case, have been completed if evidence of customary use of a different rope had been supplemented by expert evidence explaining how and why one kind of rope may cause a foreseeable risk of injury which others customarily avoid.

5. **Safety manuals.** Could a plaintiff introduce into evidence safety manuals or codes promulgated by private or governmental organizations to show that the defendant, in failing to follow such manuals or codes, fell below the standard of reasonable care? Many courts have allowed such evidence. *See, e.g.*, *McComish v. DeSoi*, 200 A.2d 116 (N.J. 1964) (holding that safety codes were admissible as evidence of what was customarily done, although they did not set the standard of care). Some safety codes prepared by trade associations or industry groups have been adopted by statute or ordinance. Many city ordinances, for example, adopt a building or electrical code prepared by industry. In such a case, the privately prepared safety code takes on the force of a statute or ordinance and is not only admissible but may set the standard of care.

THE T.J. HOOPER

60 F.2d 737 (2d Cir. 1932)

L. HAND, CIRCUIT JUDGE.

The barges No. 17 and No. 30, belonging to the Northern Barge Company, had lifted cargoes of coal at Norfolk, Virginia, for New York in

March, 1928. They were towed by two tugs of the petitioner, the "Montrose" and the "Hooper," and were lost off the Jersey Coast on March tenth, in an easterly gale. The cargo owners sued the barges under the contracts of carriage; the owner of the barges sued the tugs under the towing contract, both for its own loss and as bailee of the cargoes; the owner of the tug filed a petition to limit its liability. All the suits were joined and heard together, and the judge found that all the vessels were unseaworthy; the tugs, because they did not carry radio receiving sets by which they could have seasonably got warnings of a change in the weather which should have caused them to seek shelter in the Delaware Breakwater en route. He therefore entered an interlocutory decree holding each tug and barge jointly liable to each cargo owner, and each tug for half damages for the loss of its barge. The petitioner appealed, and the barge owner appealed and filed assignments of error. . . .

[Radio broadcasts gave forecasts of coming heavy weather. Reasonable masters would have put in at a safe harbor had they received the broadcasts. The masters of these tugs did not receive the broadcasts] because their private radio receiving sets, which were on board, were not in working order. These belonged to them personally, and were partly a toy, partly a part of the equipment, but neither furnished by the owner, nor supervised by it. It is not fair to say that there was a general custom among coastwise carriers so to equip their tugs. One line alone did it; as for the rest, they relied upon their crews, so far as they can be said to have relied at all. An adequate receiving set suitable for a coastwise tug can now be got at small cost and is reasonably reliable if kept up; obviously it is a source of great protection to their tows. Twice every day they can receive these predictions, based upon the widest possible information, available to every vessel within two or three hundred miles and more. Such a set is the ears of the tug to catch the spoken word, just as the master's binoculars are her eyes to see a storm signal ashore. Whatever may be said as to other vessels, tugs towing heavy coal laden barges, strung out for half a mile, have little power to maneuver, and do not, as this case proves, expose themselves to weather which would not turn back stauncher craft. They can have at hand protection against dangers of which they can learn in no other way.

Is it then a final answer that the business had not yet generally adopted receiving sets? There are, no doubt, cases where courts seem to make the general practice of the calling the standard of proper diligence; we have indeed given some currency to the notion ourselves. Indeed in most cases reasonable prudence is in fact common prudence; but strictly it is never its measure; a whole calling may have unduly lagged in the adoption of new and available devices. It never may set its own tests, however persuasive be its usages. Courts must in the end say what is required; there are precautions so imperative that even their universal disregard will not excuse their omission. But here there was no custom at all as to receiving sets; some had them, some did not; the most that can be urged is that they had not yet become general. Certainly in such a case we need not pause; when some have thought a device necessary, at least we may say that they were right, and the others too slack. . . . [H]ad [the tugs] been properly equipped, they would have got the Arlington reports. The injury was a direct consequence of this unseaworthiness.

Decree affirmed.

NOTES

1. **The standard of the industry.** In *Estate of Elkerson v. North Jersey Blood Ctr.*, 776 A.2d 244 (N.J. Super. Ct. App. Div. 2001), a man died, allegedly as a result of receiving a transfusion of blood tainted with hepatitis. In the suit against the blood bank that had supplied the blood, the plaintiff's evidence showed that a better test was available to detect hepatitis. But evidence also showed that no blood banks used the better test. The trial judge instructed the jury that the defendant was to be judged by the standard practice of the blood banking industry at the relevant time. So instructed, the jury found that the defendant was not negligent. If you represented the plaintiff, what proposition would you assert in your brief on appeal?

2. **Custom as evidence.** Earlier decisions sometimes held that (a) evidence of custom was wholly inadmissible; or (b) on the contrary, custom represented the sole standard of care. As *The T.J. Hooper* would suggest, these older rules are largely obsolete. *See* RESTATEMENT (THIRD) OF TORTS: LIABILITY FOR PHYSICAL AND EMOTIONAL HARM § 13(a) (2010) ("An actor's compliance with the custom of the community, or of others in like circumstances, is evidence that the actor's conduct is not negligent but does not preclude a finding of negligence.") In *McDermott v. State,* 113 A.3d 419 (Conn. 2015) a bystander was killed by a falling tree but was standing a few feet outside the industry-standard two tree lengths from the cutting site. The lower court held that the industry custom represented the standard of care, but the Connecticut Supreme Court reversed. The industry standard was admissible with respect to the standard of care but was not conclusive. "The trier of fact is not bound by the industry standard, but rather should consider it in light of the totality of the evidence presented in the case."

3. **Custom and reasonable care.** As Justice Holmes famously put it in *Tex. & P. Ry. v. Behymer*, 189 U.S. 468 (1903), "what usually is done may be evidence of what ought to be done, but what ought to be done is set by the standard of reasonable prudence, whether it is usually complied with or not." Why say that reasonable care trumps custom? Does that decision make sense in *T.J. Hooper*?

4. **Custom and the standard of care.** If you have reservations about the risk-utility rule of *Carroll Towing*, how about using custom as the standard of care and the test of negligence? Would this policy be wise at least in the case

of sophisticated parties? Should the court in *T.J. Hooper* have let custom serve as a standard for those sophisticated parties?

§ 8. COMPLIANCE WITH STATUTE

As discussed in Chapter 5, statutes can sometimes define the duty of care. In these cases, violation of statutes can sometimes be determinative of an actor's negligence under the doctrine of negligence per se, and in other cases the statutory violation may provide evidence of negligence. Does an actor's compliance with statute preclude a finding of negligence?

MILLER V. WARREN, 390 S.E.2d 207 (W.Va. 1990). The plaintiffs awoke in their motel room to find it filled with smoke. They attempted to get out, but the door was too hot to touch. They suffered serious burns before they were rescued. In a suit against the motel, the plaintiffs asserted that the motel should have had smoke alarms in the rooms. The fire code did not require such alarms, however. The trial judge instructed the jury: "compliance with the fire codes under the law meets the standard of care and duty required of the defendant as it relates to the installation or lack of installation of safety devices unless other circumstances appear which would require additional care in order to comply with the requirements to use ordinary care in attendant circumstances." The jury, so instructed, found for the defendant. *Held*, reversed and remanded for new trial. "Failure to comply with a fire code or similar regulation constitutes prima facie negligence, if an injury proximately flows from the non-compliance and the injury is of the sort the regulation was intended to prevent. [But] [c]ompliance with a regulation does not constitute due care per se. Compliance with the appropriate regulations is competent evidence of due care, but not conclusive evidence of due care. If the defendants knew or should have known of some risk that would be prevented by reasonable measures not required by the regulation, they were negligent if they did not take such measures. It is settled law that a statute or regulation merely sets a floor of due care. Circumstances may require greater care, if a defendant knows or should know of other risks not contemplated by the regulation."

NOTES

1. **The effect of statutory compliance.** Statutory requirements usually reflect a minimum standard of care, not a maximum obligation. Courts traditionally agree that compliance with statute or regulation is not a defense. Compliance with statute is some *evidence* of reasonable care, even though it is not conclusive. *See Kramer v. Catholic Charities of the Diocese of Fort Wayne-South Bend, Inc.,* 32 N.E.3d 227 (Ind. 2015) (compliance is evidence of care; Catholic charities checked putative father registry when child was 31 days old, in accordance with state law). RESTATEMENT (THIRD) OF TORTS: LIABILITY FOR

PHYSICAL AND EMOTIONAL HARM § 16 (2010). Does this remind you of another negligence doctrine? Why wouldn't evidence of compliance with statute be dispositive on the issue of breach?

2. **Compliance and fault.** Evidence of compliance with statute typically suggests that a defendant was not negligent. *Jablonski v. Ford Motor Co.*, 955 N.E.2d 1138 (Ill. 2011) ("conformance to industry standards is relevant, but not dispositive on the issue of negligence," thus car company's compliance with statute in design of vehicle was probative but not dispositive on issue of negligence). That industry standards require less care than the plaintiff seeks "is but one piece of information" in a negligence analysis.

3. **Concerns about compliance evidence**. As with custom, some courts are cautious about admitting evidence of compliance with statute, lest the jury treat it as a standard of care. In *Malcolm v. Evenflo Co.*, 217 P.3d 514 (Mont. 2009), a four-month-old boy suffered fatal brain injuries from a rollover accident. The court barred from jury consideration, as more prejudicial than probative, evidence that the defendant's child safety seat complied with minimum federal standards. However, that ruling concerned the plaintiff's strict liability claim. Statutory compliance evidence was permitted with respect to the fault-based question of punitive damages.

§ 9. UNSPECIFIED NEGLIGENCE: RES IPSA LOQUITUR

"Some circumstantial evidence is very strong, as when you find a trout in the milk." H.D. THOREAU, JOURNAL, November 11, 1850 (B. Torrey ed. 1906).

A. ORIGINS AND BASIC FEATURES

BYRNE V. BOADLE
2 H. & C. 722, 159 Eng. Rep. 299 (Exch. 1863)

[Plaintiff gave evidence that he was walking in Scotland Road when he lost all recollection. Witnesses testified that a barrel of flour fell on him. The defendant's shop was adjacent and the barrel appeared to have fallen or to have been dropped from the shop. The trial judge "nonsuited" the plaintiff, taking the view that the plaintiff had put on no evidence of negligence. The plaintiff's attorney then sought review in a higher court by obtaining a "rule nisi to enter the verdict for the plaintiff. . . ." What follows includes a portion of the argument by Charles Russell for the defendant before Barons Channell, Bramwell, Pigott and Chief Baron Pollock of the Exchequer Court.]

Charles Russell now showed cause. First, there was no evidence to connect the defendant or his servants with the occurrence. . . . Surmise ought not to be substituted for strict proof when it is sought to fix a defendant with serious liability. The plaintiff should establish his case by affirmative evidence.

Secondly, assuming the facts to be brought home to the defendant or his servants, these facts do not disclose any evidence for the jury of negligence. The plaintiff was bound to give affirmative proof of negligence. But there was not a scintilla of evidence, unless the occurrence is of itself evidence of negligence. There was not even evidence that the barrel was being lowered by a jigger-hoist as alleged in the declaration. [Pollock, C.B. There are certain cases of which it may be said res ipsa loquitur, and this seems one of them. In some cases the Courts have held that the mere fact of the accident having occurred is evidence of negligence, as, for instance, in the case of railway collisions.] On examination of the authorities, that doctrine would seem to be confined to the case of a collision between two trains upon the same line, and both being the property and under the management of the same Company. Such was the case of Skinner v. The London, Brighton and South Coast Railway Company (5 Exch. 787), where the train in which the plaintiff was ran into another train which had stopped a short distance from a station, in consequence of a luggage train before it having broken down. In that case there must have been negligence, or the accident could not have happened. Other cases cited in the textbooks, in support of the doctrine of presumptive negligence, when examined, will be found not to do so. Amongst them is Carpue v. The London and Brighton Railway Company (5 Q.B. 747), but there, in addition to proof of the occurrence, the plaintiff gave affirmative evidence of negligence, by showing that the rails were somewhat deranged at the spot where the accident took place, and that the train was proceeding at a speed which, considering the state of the rails, was hazardous. . . . Later cases have qualified the doctrine of presumptive negligence. In Cotton v. Wood (8 C.B.N.S. 568), it was held that a Judge is not justified in leaving the case to the jury where the plaintiff's evidence is equally consistent with the absence as with the existence of negligence in the defendant. In Hammack v. White (11 C.B.N.S. 588, 594), Erle, J., said that he was of opinion "that the plaintiff in a case of this sort was not entitled to have the case left to the jury unless he gives some affirmative evidence that there has been negligence on the part of the defendant." [Pollock, C.B. If he meant that to apply to all cases, I must say, with great respect, that I entirely differ from him. He must refer to the mere nature of the accident in that particular case. Bramwell, B. No doubt, the presumption of negligence is not raised in every case of injury from accident, but in some it is. We must judge of the facts in a reasonable way; and regarding them in that light we know that these accidents do not take place without a cause, and in general that cause is negligence.] The law will not presume that a man is guilty of a wrong. It is consistent with the facts proved that the defendant's servants were using the utmost care and the best appliances to lower the barrel with safety. Then why should the fact that accidents of this nature are

sometimes caused by negligence raise any presumption against the defendant? There are many accidents from which no presumption of negligence can arise. [Bramwell, B. Looking at the matter in a reasonable way it comes to this—an injury is done to the plaintiff, who has no means of knowing whether it was the result of negligence; the defendant, who knows how it was caused, does not think fit to tell the jury.] Unless a plaintiff gives some evidence which ought to be submitted to the jury, the defendant is not bound to offer any defense. This plaintiff cannot, by a defective proof of his case, compel the defendant to give evidence in explanation. [Pollock, C.B. I have frequently observed that a defendant has a right to remain silent unless a prima facie case is established against him. But here the question is whether the plaintiff has not shewn such a case.] In a case of this nature, in which the sympathies of a jury are with the plaintiff, it would be dangerous to allow presumption to be substituted for affirmative proof of negligence.

Littler appeared to support the rule, but was not called upon to argue.

Pollock, C.B. We are all of opinion that the rule must be absolute to enter the verdict for the plaintiff. The learned counsel was quite right in saying that there are many accidents from which no presumption of negligence can arise, but I think it would be wrong to lay down as a rule that in no case can presumption of negligence arise from the fact of an accident. Suppose in this case the barrel had rolled out of the warehouse and fallen on the plaintiff, how could he possibly ascertain from what cause it occurred? It is the duty of persons who keep barrels in a warehouse to take care that they do not roll out, and I think that such a case would, beyond all doubt, afford prima facie evidence of negligence. A barrel could not roll out of a warehouse without some negligence, and to say that a plaintiff who is injured by it must call witnesses from the warehouse to prove negligence seems to me preposterous. [The other Barons concurred.]

NOTES

1.   **The function of res ipsa loquitur.** Consider how res ipsa loquitur evidence differs from ordinary circumstantial evidence. Using *Byrne* as a model, can you state exactly what *Byrne* has permitted that has not been permitted in earlier decisions?

2.   **Showing negligence.** The judges in *Byrne*, which is more or less the original res ipsa loquitur case, repeatedly referred to the commonsense interpretation of the facts before them—the accident, they felt, "spoke for itself," and what it said was that the defendant must have been negligent.

3.   **Specific requirements.** Modern courts have developed rules for the application of res ipsa loquitur. States differ as to their particular requirements. Traditionally, in order for res ipsa to apply, the plaintiff has to show three things: (1) the accident which produced a person's injury was one

which ordinarily does not happen in the absence of negligence, (2) the instrumentality or agent which caused the accident was under the exclusive control of the defendant, and (3) the circumstances indicated that the untoward event was not caused or contributed to by any act or neglect on the part of the injured person. *See, e.g., Eaton v. Eaton*, 575 A.2d 858 (N.J. 1990). The Second Restatement refined this traditional test, providing that a plaintiff must prove: (1) the event is of a kind which ordinarily does not occur in the absence of negligence; (2) other responsible causes, including the conduct of the plaintiff and third persons, are sufficiently eliminated by the evidence; and (3) the indicated negligence is within the scope of the defendant's duty to the plaintiff. RESTATEMENT (SECOND) OF TORTS § 328D (1965). Are these requirements materially different from each other? The Third Restatement offers still another formulation—that negligence can be inferred when the accident causing harm is a type that "ordinarily happens as a result of the negligence of a class of actors of which the defendant is the relevant member." RESTATEMENT (THIRD) OF TORTS: LIABILITY FOR PHYSICAL AND EMOTIONAL HARM § 17 (2010). We should expect variation in local rules, but always remember that a different articulation may be intended to express substantially the same ideas.

NOTE: PROCEDURAL INCIDENTS AND EFFECTS OF RES IPSA LOQUITUR

1. *Sufficiency-of-evidence issue.* The application of res ipsa loquitur means that, on the negligence issue, the plaintiff will survive a motion for summary judgment and get to the jury, which can then decide the case either way. Once the judge determines that reasonable people can conclude that negligence is probable, the jury is permitted to infer negligence but it is not required to do so. *Seavers v. Methodist Med. Ctr. of Oak Ridge*, 9 S.W.3d 86 (Tenn. 1999) (res ipsa loquitur "permits, but does not compel, a jury to infer negligence from the circumstances of an injury;" it allows an inference of negligence, but it does not alter the burden of proof or the standard of care).

2. *Instructing on res ipsa.* If the plaintiff has adduced evidence from which the jury could conclude that the elements of res ipsa loquitur are present, then trial judges commonly give a res ipsa loquitur instruction to the jury. The instruction "merely tells the jury that if they do find the existence of these elements then they may draw the inference of negligence," not that they must do so. *K-Mart Corp. v. Gipson*, 563 N.E.2d 667, 670 (Ind. Ct. App. 1990); *see also Banks v. Beckwith*, 762 N.W.2d 149, 153 (Iowa 2009) ("If reasonable minds might differ about whether the injury could result from surgery in the absence of negligence, the court should instruct on res ipsa.").

3. *Permissible inference effect.* Most courts hold that res ipsa creates a permissible inference that the jury may draw if it sees fit, and further that res ipsa does not shift the burden of persuasion from the plaintiff. Thus even if the defendant introduces no evidence at all, the jury may reject the inference and bring in a verdict for the defendant. Juries do in fact sometimes decide for defendants on res ipsa loquitur claims. *See, e.g., Gubbins v. Hurson*, 987 A.2d 466 (D.C. 2010).

4. *Abnormally strong inferences of negligence.* To say that the inference of negligence is merely permitted, not required, is to say that the plaintiff who makes out a permissible inference case would not be entitled to summary judgment. But could there be cases so strong that the permissible inference becomes a mandatory inference so that the trial judge would grant summary judgment after all? In *Morejon v. Rais Constr. Co.*, 851 N.E.2d 1143 (N.Y. 2006), the court said in dictum that "when the plaintiff's circumstantial proof is so convincing and the defendant's response is so weak that the inference of defendant's negligence is inescapable," it would be proper for the trial court to grant summary judgment or a directed verdict for the plaintiff in a res ipsa case. This occurred in *Quinby v. Plumsteadville Family Practice, Inc.*, 907 A.2d 1061 (Pa. 2006), where a quadriplegic patient fell off an examination table at the doctor's office and subsequently died. The court found that no reasonable jury could believe that this occurred for any reason other than the defendant's leaving the patient unattended and unrestrained. We see another example in *De Leon Lopez v. Corporacion Insular de Seguros*, 931 F.2d 116 (1st Cir. 1991), where two women gave birth to twins in the University Hospital at Puerto Rico Medical Center. The hospital somehow switched one twin from each set, so that each mother went home with two children, but only with one of her own. The mistake was discovered after a year and a half. The court thought that occasions for directing a verdict for the plaintiff were "hen's-teeth rare," but nevertheless affirmed such a ruling.

5. *The presumption effect.* A small number of courts say that res ipsa loquitur is *not* merely a common sense assessment of evidence which permits an inference of fault, but that, instead, it creates a "presumption" of negligence. The term "presumption" can be used loosely or can have technical meanings, explored in evidence courses. Courts usually mean that once the presumption applies, the defendant has the burden of showing he is *not* negligent.

Sometimes courts describe the presumption as (a) shifting the *burden of persuasion* or (b) shifting the *burden of production* (meaning production of evidence), or the burden of going forward with evidence. *See* 1 DOBBS, HAYDEN & BUBLICK, THE LAW OF TORTS § 170 (2d ed. 2011) (describing presumptions and their effects). On the side of shifting the burden of production, rather than shifting the burden of persuasion, see *Chapman v.*

Harner, 339 P.3d 519 (Colo. 2014). *Chapman* overruled earlier precedent and explained that res ipsa is like other rebuttable presumptions: once the defendant produces sufficient evidence, "the presumption is destroyed and only a permissible inference of negligence remains."

6. *Rebuttal by defendant.* Suppose the defendant does in fact offer proof about his conduct. What does this do to the res ipsa loquitur inference? Can the plaintiff still get to the jury? Suppose in *Byrne* the defendant offers proof that a trucker unaffiliated with the defendant was loading the flour and negligently dropped it. Suppose instead that the defendant proved it did everything normally, exercised all precautions about the flour storage, and cannot understand why the injury took place? Would the results be different under these two versions of the defendant's proof? The defendant's rebuttal evidence might be disbelieved by the trier, so the judge cannot appropriately remove res ipsa loquitur from the case merely because the defendant has offered alternative explanations or other rebuttal evidence. *See McLaughlin Freight Lines, Inc. v. Gentrup*, 798 N.W.2d 386 (Neb. 2011) (although cattle owner testified that he secured and latched the gate to his cattle pen, when cattle had escaped and were on the highway where they caused an accident, a reasonable jury could determine that cattle do not escape a steel enclosure in the absence of negligence). However, in *Estate of Hall v. Akron Gen. Med. Ctr.*, 927 N.E.2d 1112 (Ohio 2010), the Ohio court held that the defendant's rebuttal evidence would eliminate the likelihood of negligence established by the plaintiff's evidence and rejected the use of res ipsa loquitur, even though the jury, if permitted to decide, might have rejected the defendant's evidence on res ipsa loquitur.

B. IS NEGLIGENCE MORE PROBABLE THAN NOT?

KOCH V. NORRIS PUBLIC POWER DISTRICT, 632 N.W.2d 391 (Neb. Ct. App. 2001). The defendant's high-voltage line broke and fell, starting a fire that did considerable damage to the plaintiff's property. The weather was sunny and dry, and winds at 40 mph were ordinary. There was some inconclusive evidence that the line might have been shot by a bullet, but other evidence suggests that a bullet did not cause the line to fall. *Held,* the plaintiff may rely on res ipsa loquitur. "[P]ower lines do not normally fall without fault on behalf of the company that maintains them and . . . res ipsa loquitur is applied in the absence of a substantial, significant, or probable explanation. . . . It seems clear that power lines should be built and maintained so they do not fall without the intervention of nature or a person and that therefore if a line falls without explanation, it must have been negligently constructed or maintained."

COSGROVE V. COMMONWEALTH EDISON CO., 734 N.E.2d 155 (Ill. App. Ct. 2000). On a stormy night, the electric company's power lines were seen to be sparking in the alley behind the plaintiffs' house. At some point the power line was seen to fall. A few hours after the sparking was noticed, a fire occurred in the alley. Evidence indicated that a leak in a buried gas line was ignited by the sparks. The fire injured the plaintiffs. *Held*, the plaintiff cannot rely on res ipsa loquitur as to the electric company but can rely on it as to the gas company. "Other forces [besides negligence] may cause a downed power line, such as wind, lightning, storm, or an animal chewing through the wire." But a "ruptured gas line feeding a fire does not ordinarily occur in the absence of negligence. Gas mains are buried beyond the reach and interference of the general public, and the probability is great that breaks therein are occasioned by defects in the pipes or improper utilization thereof. In the ordinary course of events, gas explosions and fires do not occur; when one does occur, an inference of fault is justifiable. This inference may be explained or rebutted. However, even if the gas company is blameless, its superior knowledge of the facts at hand and its responsibility to the community create a duty to come forward and make an explanation."

NOTES

1. **Judging probabilities.** In determining the probabilities that the defendant was somehow negligent, judges draw on their common experience in life, rarely on actual data. *See Eversole v. Woods Acquisition, Inc.,* 135 S.W.3d 425 (Mo. Ct. App. 2004). The reasoning in *Koch* and *Cosgrove* is fairly typical. And once the trial judge believes jurors have the common life experience to make the judgment, the question will be passed to the jury for its verdict. On the jury's role in determining probabilities, see *MacClatchey v. HCA Health Servs. of Fla., Inc.,* 139 So.3d 970 (Fla. Dist. Ct. App. 2014) (whether a framed picture on the wall of a patient's hospital room would have fallen in the absence of the hospital's negligence was a question of fact for the jury; summary judgment for defendant reversed); *Matthews v. Yoplait USA, Inc.,* 835 S.E.2d 393 (Ga. Ct. App. 2019) (whether sharp metal fragments would be in a yogurt container in the absence of the yogurt company's negligence; summary judgment for defendant reversed). Some courts seem to go beyond requiring a probability of negligence and require a certainty. *See Dickens v. Sahley Realty Co.,* 756 S.E.2d 484 (W. Va. 2014) (affirming summary judgment for the defendant in a res ipsa case: "The doctrine applies only in cases where defendant's negligence is the only inference that can reasonably and legitimately be drawn from the circumstances.").

2. **Res ipsa, probability, and experts.** "[W]hen no fund of common knowledge would enable a layperson to reasonably draw such a conclusion, the plaintiff may present expert testimony that such an event usually does not occur without negligence," and the fact that experts for the defendant offer conflicting opinions does not rule out res ipsa loquitur. *Lowrey v. Montgomery*

Kone, Inc., 42 P.3d 621 (Ariz. Ct. App. 2002); *accord States v. Lourdes Hosp.*, 792 N.E.2d 151 (N.Y. 2003). But no expert will be needed where a lay jury can decide the issue based on common knowledge. *See, e.g., Jerista v. Murray*, 883 A.2d 350 (N.J. 2005) (automatic door suddenly closed on plaintiff).

3.   **Res ipsa and "ordinary accidents."** If res ipsa applies only when a permissible inference arises that the event would not ordinarily occur without negligence, does that mean that res ipsa is inapplicable to "ordinary accidents" that often occur without negligence? Some courts have said just that. *See, e.g., Linnear v. Centerpoint Energy Entex/Reliant Energy*, 966 So.2d 36 (La. 2007). In *Huynh v. Phillips*, 95 So.3d 1259 (Miss. 2012), the plaintiff was in the process of getting her nails buffed when "something" hit her eye causing a cornea injury. She provided no evidence that the buffer caused the eye injury or that the thing that hit her eye ordinarily would not have done so had the manicurist used proper care in operating the buffer. As such, no presumption of negligence arose under a theory of res ipsa loquitur.

4.   **Plaintiff's failure to offer available proof?** Suppose plaintiff, a child, is injured by a parked car that suddenly rolls backward. Plaintiff alleges that defendant failed to set the handbrake. The car might have had a defect, or children sitting in it waiting for parents might have touched it. Res ipsa? *See Warren v. Jeffries*, 139 S.E.2d 718 (N.C. 1965). Would it help the plaintiff to put on evidence that the car was examined immediately after the accident by a qualified mechanic and that the examination revealed nothing throwing light on the occurrence?

5.   **Inferences.** Sometimes a court will draw an inference against the plaintiff for failure to introduce some testimony. In *Lawson v. Mitsubishi Motor Sales of Am., Inc.*, 938 So.2d 35 (La. 2006), the court held that res ipsa was inappropriate where plaintiffs' experts had tampered with material evidence in a car-crash case, preventing the discovery of "direct evidence [that] would have been available to prove or disprove the plaintiff's theory" of the accident. For res ipsa to apply, the court said, "plaintiffs need to sufficiently exclude inference of . . . the responsibility of others besides defendant in causing the accident." In other cases, the defendant's questionable handling of evidence may be used by the court to bolster the plaintiff's res ipsa argument. *See, e.g., DeBusscher v. Sam's East, Inc.*, 505 F.3d 475 (6th Cir. 2007) (portable basketball goal on display in store fell on the plaintiff; the fact that the defendant sent the goal to the claims department without checking the ballast level showed that "evidence of the true explanation for the accident was more readily accessible" to the defendant).

6.   **Examples.** In a number of cases, the plaintiff or witnesses called by the plaintiff appear to have extensive knowledge of relevant facts, but never offer any testimony about them. Where a plaintiff apparently has access to evidence but fails to introduce it, an inference may arise that the absent evidence was unfavorable to the plaintiff. *See, e.g., District of Columbia v. Singleton*, 41 A.3d 717 (Md. 2012). In *Singleton*, a bus left the road and crashed into a tree on a dry sunny day. The bus passengers, who were asleep at the

time of collision, sought to apply res ipsa loquitur without calling at trial the bus driver or other known eyewitnesses to the accident, or introducing evidence of the police accident report. The court felt this "tactical decision to avoid reasonably available eyewitnesses" and other evidence supported the conclusion that res ipsa loquitur should be unavailable. What inference arises from the fact that 99.95% of healthy dogs recover from surgery? In *Milke v. Ratcliff Animal Hosp., Inc.*, 120 So.3d 343 (La. Ct. App. 2013), the plaintiff sued the vet for negligence, arguing res ipsa loquitur. The court ruled that the 99.95% statistic was insufficient to establish "that the .05% mortality is due to negligence." This was especially true when "the plaintiff declined a necropsy that might have revealed the cause of death."

7.   **Judge Posner's bus example.** In *Howard v. Wal-Mart Stores, Inc.*, 160 F.3d 358 (7th Cir. 1998), Judge Posner discussed a hypothetical case in which the plaintiff was struck by a bus. At that location, 51% of all buses are owned by company A and 49% by company B. Does the plaintiff make out a case against A by showing these facts plus negligence and causation? "If the 51/49 statistic is the plaintiff's only evidence, and he does not show that it was infeasible for him to obtain any additional evidence, the inference to be drawn is not that there is a 51 percent probability that it was a bus owned by A that hit the plaintiff. It is that the plaintiff either investigated and discovered that the bus was actually owned by B (and B might not have been negligent and so not liable even if a cause of the accident, or might be judgment-proof and so not worth suing), or that he simply has not bothered to conduct an investigation. If the first alternative is true, he should of course lose; and since it may be true, the probability that the plaintiff was hit by a bus owned by A is less than 51 percent and the plaintiff has failed to carry his burden of proof. If the second alternative is true—the plaintiff just hasn't conducted an investigation—he still should lose. A court shouldn't be required to expend its scarce resources of time and effort on a case until the plaintiff has conducted a sufficient investigation to make reasonably clear that an expenditure of public resources is likely to yield a significant social benefit. This principle is implicit in the law's decision to place the burden of producing evidence on the plaintiff rather than on the defendant."

8.   **Defendant's superior knowledge.** Sometimes courts say or imply that res ipsa cannot be invoked unless the defendant has superior knowledge. *See, e.g., Pacheco v. Ames,* 69 P.3d 324 (Wash. 2003); *DeBusscher v. Sam's East, Inc.*, 505 F.3d 475 (6th Cir. 2007) (Michigan law). Other courts give mixed accounts. *Cockerline v. Menendez*, 988 A.2d 575 (N.J. Super. Ct. App. Div. 2010). If res ipsa is a matter of assessing the probability that defendant is negligent, is superior knowledge by the defendant really necessary? Suppose the defendant runs off the road in a car, injures the plaintiff, and has amnesia. The plaintiff, on the other hand, remembers everything she saw in perfect, horror-stricken detail. No res ipsa?

9.   **Specific evidence of negligence.** What if the plaintiff relies on res ipsa loquitur, but also produces specific evidence of the defendant's negligence? Under the traditional rule, still followed in some jurisdictions, the plaintiff is

not permitted to do that. *See Anderson v. Union Pac. R.R. Co.*, 890 N.W.2d 791 (Neb. 2017), when chair that employee sat in collapsed, plaintiff showed some evidence that bolts had failed. Denying the res ipsa claim, the court held, "if specific acts of negligence are alleged or there is direct evidence of the precise cause of the accident, the doctrine of res ipsa loquitur does not apply." The more modern approach allows a plaintiff to put on proof of the defendant's particular negligent conduct while relying on res ipsa loquitur in the alternative—as long as the specific evidence does not provide a "complete explanation" of the accident. *See Steilen v. Cabela's Wholesale, Inc.*, 906 N.W.2d 913 (S.D. 2018) (product fell from shelving; "A plaintiff does not waive instructions on res ipsa loquitur by trying to establish specific acts of negligence through introduction of some evidence which does not clearly and definitely establish the exact cause of injury."); *Clinkscales v. Nelson Sec., Inc.*, 697 N.W.2d 836 (Iowa 2005) (allowing res ipsa theory in a restaurant grease-fire case). Why would res ipsa loquitur not be needed, or allowed, when the plaintiff's evidence provides a complete explanation of what occurred?

C. ATTRIBUTING FAULT TO THE DEFENDANT RATHER THAN OTHERS

GILES V. CITY OF NEW HAVEN, 636 A.2d 1335 (Conn. 1994). Plaintiff, an elevator operator, sued Otis Elevator Company (defendant), for its negligent failure to inspect, maintain and repair an elevator compensation chain. On the date plaintiff sustained injuries, the elevator began to shudder and shake, and the compensation chain fell to the bottom of the elevator shaft with a loud crash. Fearing for her safety, the plaintiff reversed the direction of the elevator, directed it to the nearest floor, and jumped from the cab sustaining additional injuries. At the time the plaintiff suffered her injuries, the defendant had a long-standing exclusive contract with the building owner to maintain and inspect the elevator and its component parts. The elevator was installed by the defendant approximately sixty-one years before the accident. The parties disputed whether the compensation chain had broken before plaintiff rapidly changed the direction of the elevator, or because plaintiff had done so. The Appellate Court concluded that the plaintiff had presented sufficient evidence to warrant presentation of the question of negligence under the doctrine of res ipsa loquitur to the jury.

Held, affirmed. "The defendant challenges the application of the res ipsa loquitur doctrine to this case because in its view the plaintiff failed to demonstrate that the defendant had exclusive control over the elevator. Specifically, the defendant argues that because plaintiff operated the elevator and controlled its movement and its chain's sway, she could not benefit from the doctrine notwithstanding defendant's own duty to maintain and inspect the elevator and to warn of any dangerous propensity. We disagree. . . . [I]n describing the extent of the defendant's control of the use of the instrumentality [that caused the event], we have never held that any use whatsoever of the instrumentality by the plaintiff would automatically preclude application of res ipsa loquitur. So restrictive an interpretation would substantially undermine the efficacy of the doctrine. Rather, our previous discussions of use were meant to reflect the idea of management and control, factors that help to limit the application of the res ipsa loquitur doctrine to those situations in which the defendant's negligence was more probably than not the cause of the plaintiff's injuries. . . . The point of requiring control by the defendant is, as indicated by Prosser, to provide the basis for an inference that whatever negligence was involved may properly be charged to the defendant. . . .' If the jury could reasonably find that defendant's control was sufficient to warrant an inference that the defendant was more likely responsible for the incident than someone else, even in the absence of proof of absolute exclusivity and control over the instrumentality by the defendant, the trial court must allow the jury to draw that inference. [In this case, the court concluded, that they could. Moreover, Connecticut's adoption of comparative negligence compels the conclusion that res ipsa can apply to a case even where the plaintiff's negligence contributed to the injury, as cases from at least seven other states have also held.] [T]he plaintiff was entitled to have a jury consider her claim that the defendant's negligence was the cause of her personal injuries."

NOTES

1. **Verbal obeisance to the control rule.** Many courts routinely list the defendant's exclusive control over the instrumentality of harm as one of the elements the plaintiff must prove to establish a res ipsa loquitur case. However, in many cases courts apply the rule loosely, so that the plaintiff can get to the jury on res ipsa loquitur even when the defendant did not truly have exclusive control.

2. **Contemporary view of control rule.** *Giles* reflects a contemporary view of the control rule, perhaps one that makes the words used to express the rule correlate with the application or outcome. Thus "control" is only one way of establishing the important point that the negligence was probably that of the defendant, not that of someone else. It is enough if, control or no control, instrument or no instrument, the defendant was one of the persons who was probably negligent. *See Harder v. F.C. Clinton, Inc.*, 948 P.2d 298 (Okla. 1997); *Errico v. LaMountain*, 713 A.2d 791 (R.I. 1998).

If the evidence does not suggest that the negligence was probably that of the defendant, res ipsa is not appropriate. For example, in *Krinitt v. Idaho Dep't of Fish & Game*, 357 P.3d 850 (Idaho 2015), a clipboard flew out of a three-person helicopter and hit the tail rotor, causing the helicopter to crash. Evidence showed that that clipboard came out of the helicopter door where the Fish & Game employee was sitting. Res ipsa loquitur applied. The court wrote: "Evidence conclusively showing the control or management of the instrumentality causing the injury is not required. It may be established by either direct or circumstantial evidence, and by such reasonable and logical inferences as may be drawn therefrom. The evidence must afford a rational basis for concluding that the cause of the accident was probably such that defendant would be responsible for any negligence connected with it. That does not mean that the possibility of other causes must be altogether eliminated, but only that their likelihood must be so reduced that the greater probability lies at the defendant's door." But when the evidence does not suggest the defendant's negligence, the control rule may bar the res ipsa claim. *See Savage v. Three Rivers Med. Ctr.*, 390 S.W.3d 104 (Ky. 2012) (citing the control rule and noting that sponge left inside patient could have been from any one of three different surgeries).

3. **Absurd control arguments?** At one time, the control rule was taken quite literally. In *Kilgore v. Shepard Co.*, 158 A. 720 (R.I. 1932), the plaintiff sat down on a chair in defendant's store. It collapsed and she was injured. The court rejected res ipsa loquitur on the ground that the defendant was not in exclusive control of the chair, the plaintiff herself being in "control" when she sat upon it. In line with *Giles*, courts today apply res ipsa to cases of injury resulting from taking a seat on chairs, bar stools, and even bleachers. See *e.g., Trujeque v. Serv. Merch. Co.*, 872 P.2d 361 (N.M. 1994). In *Aldana v. School City of East Chicago*, 769 N.E.2d 1201 (Ind. Ct. App. 2002), a bus with child passengers went off the clear, dry highway, then fishtailed back on two wheels, throwing passengers against and under seats. Oncoming traffic prudently stopped and no other vehicle was involved. The defendant argued that res ipsa loquitur was inapplicable because the road, "which was part of the instrumentality, was not within the control of the driver" and in particular that there were some holes in the road. How should the court respond?

4. **Instrumentalities accessible to the public.** When, as in *Giles*, an instrumentality is more or less accessible to the public, numerous persons may have interfered with the instrumentality, so the defendant is not literally in exclusive control. In some cases, courts bar the claim. For example, where a heavy item of merchandise in a store fell on the plaintiff's foot, and "could have fallen because of the action of another customer," the court wrote that "it is not possible to say that the manner in which defendant shelved the [items] is the more likely explanation for plaintiff's injury." *Hagler v. Coastal Farms Holdings, Inc.*, 309 P.3d 1073 (Or. 2013). Nevertheless, *Giles* is not alone in invoking res ipsa loquitur in public accessibility cases. *See MacClatchey v. HCA Health Servs. of Fla., Inc.*, 139 So.3d 970 (Fla. Dist. Ct. App. 2014) (framed picture fell from hospital wall; fact that room was open to many people did not bar the claim).

5. **Exploding-bottle cases.** Under a liberal formulation of the control requirement, the plaintiff might show that any fault in the case was attributable to the defendant merely by excluding other causes. Suppose the plaintiff buys a soft drink from a grocery, takes it home, and suffers an injury when the bottle "explodes." The bottler obviously was not in control at the time of injury. Nor do we know when the negligence was likely to have occurred. The grocer or a customer might well have dropped the bottle, causing a chip

for which the bottler is not responsible. In a leading case, *Escola v. Coca Cola Bottling Co.*, 150 P.2d 436 (Cal. 1944), the California Supreme Court held that the plaintiff could use res ipsa loquitur by showing that the defendant had control at the time of the probable negligence, and that this could be shown by excluding the negligence of others. Thus the plaintiff might show that the bottle had not been subjected to any unusual treatment in the grocery store, and on making such proof would be permitted to use res ipsa loquitur. As the New York Court of Appeals put it in a non-bottling case, "the exclusive control requirement is thus subordinated to its general purpose, that of indicating that it *probably* was the defendant's negligence which caused the accident." *Corcoran v. Banner Super Mkt., Inc.*, 227 N.E.2d 304 (N.Y. 1967).

6.   **Eliminating the plaintiff's fault.** Courts have often said that the plaintiff must show that she herself was not at fault or did not contribute to the injury. In retrospect, this looks like a specific instance of the control rule and shares its purpose. If so, then the real point is to show that the fault was at least in part attributable to the defendant. If this is right, the control rule and its subsidiary rule about plaintiff-fault merely point to evidence that will be important but not conclusive. Is *Giles* consistent with this view?

Some contemporary cases continue to say that a plaintiff must prove that she did not voluntarily or actively participate in causing her injury, but often only in listing elements of res ipsa loquitur without applying the rule, much less considering it in the light of change in the control rule. *E.g.*, *Gray v. BellSouth Telecomm., Inc.*, 11 So.3d 1269 (Miss. Ct. App. 2009); *Barbie v. Minko Constr., Inc.*, 766 N.W.2d 458 (N.D. 2009). Some courts, rather than abandoning the "no contribution" rule entirely, seem to have softened it so that, at a minimum, it no longer requires the plaintiff to carry the burden of persuading the jury that she was not at fault. *See, e.g., Khan v. Singh*, 975 A.2d 389, 394 (N.J. 2009) (requiring only that there be "no indication in the circumstances that the injury was the result of the plaintiff's own voluntary act or neglect").

7.   **Plaintiff's fault and defendant's breach.** Plaintiff's fault can blend with the issue of the defendant's breach. *In Winfrey v. GGP Ala Moana LLC*, 308 P.3d 891 (Haw. 2013), the pregnant plaintiff was on the roof of a shopping mall acting in an odd manner and saying unusual things (for example, that a baby was stuck in the exhaust duct). After refusing to get down from the roof and jumping onto the duct, she became stuck in it. Sometime after she was removed from the duct she died of hyperthermia and respiratory compromise. Because the death could have occurred without the mall owner's negligence, res ipsa loquitur did not apply. The facts in *Winfrey* suggest plaintiff fault, but can you see why the comparative fault issue might not be reached? As in *Stinnett*, based on an expectation that the plaintiff could care for herself, the defendant might have breached no duty at all.

8.   **Effect of comparative fault systems.** Some courts apparently assume that the plaintiff-fault rule was a rule of contributory negligence. These courts have concluded that, with the advent of comparative fault, under

which any contributory negligence will reduce but not bar the plaintiff's claim, the plaintiff-fault limit on res ipsa should be abolished or modified. *See e.g., Cox v. May Dep't Store Co.*, 903 P.2d 1119 (Ariz. Ct. App. 1995).

COLLINS V. SUPERIOR AIR-GROUND AMBULANCE SERVICE, INC., 789 N.E.2d 394 (Ill. App. Ct. 2003). Laura Collins, an elderly, bedridden woman who was unable to speak, lived with her daughter, Eva. Eva admitted her to Alden Wentworth Rehabilitation and Health Care Center for five days while the daughter was out of town. An ambulance service, Superior, transported Laura to Alden and returned her home after five days. When Laura was returned home, Eva discovered that she was suffering. A doctor quickly confirmed that Laura was (a) dehydrated and (b) had a broken leg. Suit was brought by Laura against both Superior and Alden. After Laura died, the suit was continued by Laura's estate. The estate relied upon res ipsa loquitur. "Superior argues that, because there were two defendants, plaintiff cannot, and does not, plead that it was Superior alone that controlled the instrumentality of the injury, a requirement necessary for a successful cause of action for *res ipsa loquitur.* However, this requirement frustrates the essence of *res ipsa loquitur,* which allows proof of negligence by circumstantial evidence when the direct evidence concerning the cause of injury is primarily within the knowledge and control of the defendant. . . . Under these specific facts, we conclude that where there are only two defendants who had consecutive control over plaintiff, and either one could have caused plaintiff's injuries, and both are named in the complaint, the complaint is sufficient for pleading purposes to raise the inference of negligence under the doctrine of *res ipsa loquitur.*"

NOTES

1. **The special problem of multiple actors.** Res ipsa loquitur does not ordinarily assist the plaintiff when two or more defendants are in control of the relevant instrumentality at different times. In such a case of serial or consecutive control, the occurrence of injury does not usually tend to show which defendant was negligent, much less that both were. *See Novak Heating & Air Conditioning v. Carrier Corp.*, 622 N.W.2d 495 (Iowa 2001). That is, where two or more defendants have been in serial control, "further information is typically needed in order to establish that any one of [them] was probably the negligent party," and the burden of coming forward with that information is on the plaintiff. RESTATEMENT (THIRD) OF TORTS: LIABILITY FOR PHYSICAL AND EMOTIONAL HARM § 17 cmt. f (2010).

2. **The vehicular collision example.** The plaintiff proves his automobile was struck by defendant's and that he, plaintiff, was injured. Is this a res ipsa loquitur case? When there are two moving vehicles there seems no basis for deciding that the driver of one is more likely at fault than the other. Is the case any different if the plaintiff is not one of the drivers but is instead

a pedestrian injured by flying debris from a collision between A and B? The traditional answer has been no. *See* Fleming James, *Proof of Breach in Negligence Cases*, 37 VA. L. REV. 179, 209–12 (1951).

3. **Questioning** *Collins.* In the light of the preceding paragraphs, how can we explain *Collins*? Is it more likely than not that both defendants were negligent? *Cf.* RESTATEMENT (THIRD) OF TORTS: LIABILITY FOR PHYSICAL AND EMOTIONAL HARM § 17 cmt. f (2010) ("If two parties have an ongoing relationship pursuant to which they share responsibility for a dangerous activity, and if an accident happens establishing the negligence of one of the two, imposing res ipsa loquitur liability on both is proper."). Some of the complications of multiple actor cases are considered in Chapter 13 in connection with the use of res ipsa loquitur in medical malpractice cases.

4. **Elder care.** In a number of recent cases, res ipsa loquitur has been used when a vulnerable person in the care of another has been injured. In *DeCarlo v. Eden Park Health Services, Inc.*, 887 N.Y.S.2d 315 (App. Div. 2009), an 87-year-old woman with severe osteoporosis and a host of other medical conditions, while a nonambulatory resident of defendant's nursing home facility, suffered fractures of her left ankle and right femur, the immediate cause of which is unknown. In light of evidence that these types of fractures did not happen in the course of normal activities and the defendant had not documented that the woman had any visitors, res ipsa loquitur was an appropriate theory for the jury.

5. **A defective product**. Where front airbags in a minivan activated and injured the owner who was cleaning the car at the time, would res ipsa be available against the dealership? The manufacturer? *See Cruz v. Daimler-Chrysler Motors Corp.*, 66 A.3d 446 (R.I. 2013) (res ipsa may suggest negligence on the part of one defendant and not another).

PROBLEM

Cashman v. Van Dyke

Darrick Van Dyke testified that he came home from work at 9:00 p.m. and his house was cold. He went downstairs and lit the furnace. He smelled no odor and noticed nothing unusual. He went to bed around 11:00 p.m. and awoke to an explosion with his house on fire. He was seriously injured by the fire and neighbor Marguerite Cashman's home next door burned down as well.

You represent Cashman. Do you have a res ipsa loquitur case against anyone? Must you do further investigation? What lines of investigation, if any, would you pursue?

REFERENCES: 1 DOBBS, HAYDEN & BUBLICK, THE LAW OF TORTS §§ 141–176 (2d ed. 2011); DOBBS, HAYDEN & BUBLICK, HORNBOOK ON TORTS §§ 12.1–13.7 (2d ed. 2016).

CHAPTER 7

ACTUAL HARM AND FACTUAL CAUSE

■ ■ ■

§ 1. ACTUAL HARM

The third element of a negligence prima facie case is that the plaintiff must suffer legally cognizable harm, frequently referred to as actual damages. The plaintiff who proves that the defendant's conduct was negligent, but fails to show that actual damages resulted from it, will lose the case.

RIGHT V. BREEN
890 A.2d 1287 (Conn. 2006)

KATZ, J.

In May, 2000, the plaintiff had stopped his automobile at a red traffic light when it was struck from behind by a vehicle driven by the defendant. There was minor damage to the plaintiff's vehicle, but no physical injuries were reported at the accident scene. Thereafter, the plaintiff brought this action, alleging that, as a result of the defendant's negligence, he had suffered bodily injury leading to both economic and noneconomic damages.[1] . . .

[At trial, plaintiff presented evidence that his injuries resulted from the collision. The defendant, however, presented evidence that the injuries resulted from the plaintiff's five previous automobile accidents.] Using a verdict form provided by the plaintiff, the jury returned a verdict of zero economic damages and zero noneconomic damages. . . .

The plaintiff then filed motions to set aside the verdict and for additur, arguing that, under Connecticut case law, he was entitled to at least nominal damages because he had suffered a technical legal injury that admittedly had been caused by the defendant. The defendant objected to the motions, arguing that . . . although she had admitted to causing the collision, she had denied the causal relationship between the collision and the plaintiff's alleged injuries. The trial court granted the plaintiff's motions, setting aside the jury's verdict and awarding the plaintiff $1,

---

[1] Neither the plaintiff's complaint nor his amended complaint sought recovery for the damage done to his automobile.

based upon the abundant appellate case law cited. [The trial court also awarded plaintiff $467.10 in costs as the prevailing party.]

The defendant appealed from the judgment of the trial court. . . . [Although the Appellate Court described our prior precedents, which apparently required an award of nominal damages] as "inconsistent and troubling," it observed that it was not at liberty to overrule or discard [those] precedents and, accordingly, affirmed the trial court's judgment. . . . This certified appeal followed. . . .

The defendant contends that, because causation and actual injury are essential elements of a negligence claim, a plaintiff's claim of negligence must fail entirely if he cannot establish these elements. . . .

The plaintiff responds that there is no need to revisit [a prior case which holds that defendant's admission of liability establishes a technical legal injury which entitles the plaintiff to damages] because [of] General Statutes § 52–195(b).[6] . . . Specifically, the plaintiff contends that, by filing an offer of judgment of $1 under § 52–195, a defendant may protect herself from an award of costs based on a technical legal injury and a consequent award of nominal damages. We agree with the defendant that a plaintiff must establish all of the elements of a negligence claim, including causation and actual injury, in order to recover and, therefore, the technical legal injury concept does not apply to a negligence action. . . .

Connecticut common law requires proof of actual damages to support a cause of action sounding in negligence. . . . [N]one of our cases has held that a plaintiff may prevail in a negligence action without alleging and proving actual damage. . . . [T]his was the rule at common law. . . . No contrary authority is cited and the common law rule, ancient as it may be, has been approved by contemporary commentators.

Although the rule making actual damage an element of a cause of action in negligence may have originated in the common law distinction between trespass and trespass on the case, we are not inclined to obliterate the distinction between intentional and unintentional conduct in terms of legal consequences which it serves to implement. Where the plaintiff's right has been intentionally invaded, its vindication in a court of law and the award of nominal and even exemplary damages serves the policy of deterrence in a real sense. It is difficult to imagine what purpose would be furthered by permitting anyone who is jostled in a crowd or otherwise suffers some unintended contact with his person or injury to his dignity to set in motion the judicial machinery necessary for a recovery of nominal

---

[6]   General Statutes § 52–195 addresses offers of judgment and provides in subsection (b) that, "[u]nless the plaintiff recovers more than the sum named in the offer of judgment, with interest from its date, he shall recover no costs accruing after he received notice of the filing of such offer, but shall pay the defendant's costs accruing after he received notice. Such costs may include reasonable attorney's fees in an amount not to exceed three hundred fifty dollars." [Statutory amendments changed this to "offers of compromise" rather than "judgment."]

damages. That judges and juries have more important business to occupy them is as true today as it was in ancient times when the rule originated. There is nothing arcane about the wisdom of not cluttering the courts with trivia. . . .

[C]onduct that is merely negligent, without proof of an actual injury, is not considered to be a significant interference with the public interest such that there is any right to complain of it, or to be free from it.

The judgment of the Appellate Court is reversed and the case is remanded to that court with direction to reverse the judgment of the trial court . . . and to modify the order of costs accordingly.

BERRY V. CITY OF CHICAGO, 181 N.E.3d 679 (Ill. 2020). Plaintiff sued the city for negligence, claiming that it breached its "duty of reasonable care in supplying water to its residents" when it undertook work to replace water mains and meters in such a way as to increase the risk of exposure to lead, and when it then failed to warn residents of those risks; and that this negligence caused "an increased risk of harm" from lead exposure. The trial court dismissed for failure to allege a "present injury." The intermediate appeals court reversed. In the Illinois Supreme Court, *held*: the dismissal was proper. "The rule . . . that an increased risk of harm is not, itself, an injury, is consistent with the traditional understanding of tort law. Almost anything that a person does while living and working in the world can create a risk of harm to others. The long-standing and primary purpose of tort law is not to punish or deter the creation of this risk but rather to compensate victims when the creation of risk tortiously manifests into harm. *See, e.g.*, Oliver Wendell Holmes Jr., *The Common Law* 144 (1881). . . . Further, there are practical reasons for requiring a showing of actual or realized harm before permitting recovery in tort. Among other things, such a requirement establishes a workable standard for judges and juries who must determine liability, protects court dockets from becoming clogged with comparatively unimportant or trivial claims, and reduces the threat of unlimited and unpredictable liability."

NOTES

1. **Purposes of the "actual harm" requirement.** What do the courts in *Right* and *Berry* say is the purpose of the requirement that a plaintiff in a negligence case prove an actual injury?

2. **Damages recoverable in a personal injury case.** Recall the elements of damages from Chapter 1—past and future medical expenses, loss of wages or earning capacity, pain and suffering (including emotional harm), and damages for any other specifically identifiable harm, such as special expenses necessary to travel for medical care. Punitive damages are generally

not recoverable in a negligence case, absent a showing of heightened wrongfulness, because entitlement to punitive damages depends on proof of the defendant's bad state of mind, variously described as willful, wanton, reckless, or malicious.

3. **Physical harm.** In *Right*, plaintiff *alleged* a form of legally cognizable harm—physical injury to his body. He just failed to *prove* any such harm, which was fatal to his case. *See Brown v. State*, 182 A.3d 597 (Vt. 2018) (on similar facts, no recovery where plaintiff failed to prove that she suffered any injuries from an auto accident involving defendant). Clearly, as a categorical matter, proven physical harm satisfies the actual harm requirement of a negligence prima facie case. *See* DOBBS, HAYDEN & BUBLICK, HORNBOOK ON TORTS § 14.1 (2d ed. 2016). "Physical harm" can mean either the physical impairment of the human body, or of real property, or tangible personal property. RESTATEMENT (THIRD) OF TORTS: PHYSICAL AND EMOTIONAL HARM § 4 (2010). A comment to the Restatement explains that "any detrimental change in the physical condition of a person's body or property counts as harmful impairment; there is no requirement that the detriment be major." *Id.*, cmt. c. Whether a specific kind of injury constitutes cognizable harm is a question of law for the court; pure emotional harm, or pure economic harm, without any physical injury to person or property, may not be considered legally cognizable in a negligence action. Where legally cognizable harm is proved, measuring the damages caused by such harm is a question of fact for the jury.

4. **Close cases.** In some cases, there is an argument about whether the plaintiff's claimed "harm" is, in fact, sufficient to support a negligence claim. Suppose a condo owner sues his condo association for negligence, claiming that the association's failure to enforce a smoking ban exposed him to secondhand smoke. Is that, standing alone, a sufficient allegation of actual harm? *See America v. Sunspray Condominium Ass'n*, 61 A.3d 1249 (Me. 2013) (affirming dismissal of complaint, because of plaintiff's failure to identify the extent of this exposure, or its effects on him). How might the plaintiff have alleged, then proved, that he suffered harm beyond mere "exposure" to a harmful substance? *See Howard v. Union Carbide Corp.*, 50 So.3d 1251 (La. 2010) (plaintiffs exposed to a chemical leak that was proved to have caused short-term watery eyes, nose and throat irritation, coughing and headaches; harm was compensable, albeit for small amount of damages, where claimants themselves and expert witnesses testified that they suffered such symptoms after exposure to toxin).

5. **Nominal damages.** Nominal damages are damages in name only— usually one dollar or six cents. While they are properly awarded in some kinds of cases where a plaintiff cannot prove damages to a reasonable certainty using any other measure, they are not proper in negligence cases "because plaintiff has no valid claim at all until a legally recognized loss is demonstrated." DAN B. DOBBS & CAPRICE L. ROBERTS, LAW OF REMEDIES § 3.3, at 225 (3d ed. 2018).

6.　**Statutory offer of judgment or compromise.** Statutes like the one mentioned in *Right* are designed to encourage defendants to make settlement offers. For the defendant, filing notification of an offer of judgment or compromise can make good sense. If the plaintiff does not recover a judgment that exceeds the amount of the defendant's offer, the defendant may not be required to pay certain costs of the plaintiff and may be entitled to recover some costs of its own from after the time the offer was made. The statutes may help plaintiffs get more viable settlement offers from defendants. Plaintiffs, however, face greater financial risk if they don't accept what can sometimes be very low offers.

§ 2. FACTUAL CAUSE

The fourth element of a negligence prima facie case is factual cause, also called actual cause or cause in fact. The plaintiff must prove, not only that plaintiff suffered legally cognizable harm, but that the harm was in fact caused by the defendant. Factual cause is a simple concept in most cases, but may be complicated in others.

A.　THE BUT-FOR TEST OF CAUSATION

ZINITI v. NEW ENGLAND CENTRAL RAILROAD, INC.

207 A.3d 463 (Vt. 2019)

ROBINSON, J.

[Plaintiff, a college student, was seriously injured when his car was struck by a train at a railroad crossing shortly after he had crossed over a covered bridge. At the time of the collision, there was a "crossbuck" railroad-crossing sign posted on the left side of the road. A crossbuck sign "consists of two rectangularly shaped signs that cross each other perpendicularly . . . [and] have a white background and black lettering that reads: 'RAILROAD CROSSING'." He sued New England Central Railroad ("NECR") for negligence, alleging among other things that that the crossbuck sign "was inadequate to warn motorists of the crossing," and that NECR should have installed a crossback sign on the right side of the road, along with another "advance warning" sign. The court granted defendant's motion for summary judgment with respect to that claim, on the ground that "even if plaintiff established that the failure to place those particular warning devices was a breach of NECR's duty of care, he could not establish that those particular omissions caused or contributed to the collision." A jury found for NECR on the remaining claims. Plaintiff argued on appeal that the court erred in granting defendant's summary judgment motion.]

. . . We conclude that defendant was entitled to summary judgment with respect to plaintiff's negligence claims resting on the absence of a crossbuck on the right and an advance warning sign because we conclude that plaintiff cannot meet his burden of proving the essential element of causation with respect to either claim.

Even assuming the absence of an advance warning sign or NECR's failure to place a crossbuck on the righthand side of the road amounted to a breach of the railroad's duty of care, plaintiff could not prove defendant's liability for negligence without evidence that the collision would not have occurred had either of the signs been in place. Common law negligence has four elements: a legal duty owed by defendant to plaintiff, a breach of that duty, actual injury to the plaintiff, and a causal link between the breach and the injury. With respect to the element of causation, a plaintiff alleging negligence must show both "but-for" and proximate causation. The former requires a showing that the harm would not have occurred "but for" the defendant's conduct such that the tortious conduct was a necessary condition for the occurrence of the plaintiff's harm. . . .

Although causation is normally left for the jury to determine, it may be decided as a matter of law where the proof is so clear that reasonable minds cannot draw different conclusions or where all reasonable minds would construe the facts and circumstances one way.

No reasonable jury could conclude that the absence of a crossbuck sign on the right caused or contributed to the collision. We reach this conclusion because a crossbuck sign on the right would not have provided approaching motorists with any warning of the crossing beyond the warning already provided earlier by the crossbuck sign on the left, which was clearly visible to motorists exiting the covered bridge. In addition, we reject plaintiff's theory of causation—that the absence of a crossbuck on the right should have triggered NECR to provide a flagger at the crossing and thus caused or contributed to the collision.

On the first point, the extensive photographic evidence submitted by the parties demonstrates unequivocally that the crossbuck sign on the lefthand side of the road was plainly visible to motorists approaching from the east immediately upon exiting the covered bridge and heading for the crossing. It is also plainly evident from the photographs that a crossbuck sign on the righthand side of the crossing would not have been immediately visible to a motorist upon exiting from the bridge and thus would not have provided any earlier, or meaningfully additional, notice of the crossing. For these reasons, we conclude that plaintiff cannot overcome the first hurdle of showing but-for causation.

Plaintiff's theory of causation in response to this evidence requires multiple steps. Plaintiff cites deposition testimony in which NECR's corporate designee acknowledged that NECR's internal rules require stopping and flagging at crossings where mandated signs are missing. Because a mandated sign—a crossbuck sign on the right—was missing in this case, plaintiff argues that pursuant to NECR's internal rules it was required to stop and flag at the crossing. Had NECR provided a flagger, the collision would not have happened. In plaintiff's view, evidence of NECR's failure to stop and flag the noncompliant crossing could have provided the jury with the necessary causal link to establish NECR's negligence on the basis of its alleged failure to place a required crossbuck.

To the extent that plaintiff's stop-and-flag argument is an alternative theory of negligence, the trial court did not preclude him from presenting it to the jury. That is, plaintiff was free to present evidence that the standard of care at this intersection required a flagger, or a flagger in the absence of certain other warning signs or devices.

But insofar as plaintiff's theory of liability is that the railroad breached its duty of care by failing to put a crossbuck on the righthand side of the road, the question before this Court is whether *that* failure was a but-for cause of the collision—that is, "a necessary condition for the occurrence of the plaintiff's harm." In other words, if NECR had not failed to place the crossbuck on the righthand side of the road, would the accident have happened? . . .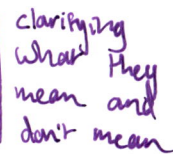

For similar reasons, we affirm the trial court's summary judgment as it relates to the advance warning sign. . . . We conclude that, given the specific configuration of the roadway approaching this crossing, including the layout of the road, the covered bridge, and the surrounding topography, an advance warning sign further in advance of the crossing would not have provided approaching motorists with any meaningful additional notice of the crossing. Thus, no reasonable jury could conclude that the lack of an advance warning sign was a cause of the accident. We do not mean to imply that the absence of an advance warning sign—which is intended as a supplemental visual signal cautioning motorists of an upcoming railroad crossing—can never legally contribute to the cause of a collision. But, in this case we have not found, and plaintiff has not directed us to, anything in the record suggesting that a reasonable juror could conclude that the absence of an advance warning sign was a cause of this collision. For that reason, the trial court did not err in deciding the question as a matter of law. . . .

Affirmed.

NOTES

1. **But-for as a hypothetical or counterfactual test.** "Determining causation always requires evaluation of hypothetical situations concerning what might have happened, but did not. . . . [T]he very idea of causation necessarily involves comparing historical events to a hypothetical alternative." *Viner v. Sweet*, 70 P.3d 1046 (Cal. 2003). The but-for rule thus requires the trier of fact to imagine an alternate scenario that never happened, that is, to

imagine what *would* have happened without the defendant's negligence. Do you see any problems with this?

2.   **Linking the negligent act to the harm.** Proving factual cause requires the plaintiff to identify exactly how the defendant's conduct was negligent. To count as a factual cause under the but-for test, the plaintiff must prove that her harm would not have occurred had the defendant not acted negligently. *See, e.g., Rieger v. Giant Eagle, Inc.*, 138 N.E.2d 1121 (Ohio 2019) (directed verdict for defendant should have been granted where plaintiff failed to adduce evidence on how defendant's alleged failure to train customers on how to use motorized carts was a factual cause of one customer crashing into another in the store). In other words, factual cause is not established if the plaintiff's harm would have occurred even if the defendant had acted non-negligently. Case examples abound. *See, e.g., Jordan v. Jordan*, 257 S.E.2d 761 (Va. 1979) (defendant backed out of the driveway without looking in her rearview mirror, however, her husband was squatting behind the rear bumper where he wouldn't have been seen even if she had looked); *Sweeney v. City of Bettendorf*, 762 N.W.2d 873 (Iowa 2009) (plaintiff alleged that defendant city was negligent in failing to provide adult supervision near children attending a minor league baseball game, resulting in a child being struck by a flying bat, but failed to prove that the child would not have been hit if the city had provided such supervision); *Salinetro v. Nystrom*, 341 So.2d 1059 (Fla. Dist. Ct. App. 1977) (plaintiff alleged that doctor was negligent in not asking her whether she was pregnant before ordering x-rays that allegedly harmed the fetus, but testified that if he had asked, she would have said no).

3.   **Negligence that is not considered a cause.** Whether a reasonable jury could find that defendant's negligence was an actual cause of plaintiff's harm depends on the facts of a particular case. In *Ziniti,* is the court saying that better signage could never avert an accident? In some cases, factual cause is not established because it appears that even extra precautions by the defendant would not have prevented the harm. For example, in *Aegis Ins. Services, Inc. v. 7 World Trade Co., L.P.*, 737 F.3d 166 (2d Cir. 2013), plaintiffs claimed that defendants negligently designed and constructed a building that collapsed when terrorists attacked the World Trade Center on 9/11/01. Affirming summary judgment for defendants on factual cause grounds, the court stressed the "unprecedented constellation of events" that day, and concluded that "7WTC would have collapsed regardless of any negligence ascribed by plaintiffs' experts to the design and construction of 7WTC." And in *Garr v. City of Ottumwa*, 846 N.W.2d 865 (Iowa 2014), plaintiff homeowners sued the City when their home was flooded, claiming the City's negligence in approving an upstream residential development and golf course was a factual cause of their harm. Reversing a jury verdict for the homeowners, the court concluded that "no reasonable efforts by the City to control upstream drainage, or other flood control measures, could have prevented the flooding" when over six inches of rain fell in 24 hours and water on the highway near plaintiffs' home was 25 feet deep—one of the worst floods in state history. *See also Ecker v. E & A Consulting Group*, 302 Neb. 578 (Neb. 2019) (affirming summary

judgment for defendant where plaintiff homeowners alleged that defendant's negligence in designing and building a drainage system caused their homes to flood, but evidence showed that even if the system had been built as plaintiff argued, "the rain event was still so significant that the homeowners properties would have flooded").

4. **Framing the hypothetical.** The focus of the hypothetical is on the *happening* of the defendant's negligent act, not the *reasons* the act was negligent. In *Cabral v. Ralphs Grocery Co.*, 248 P.3d 1170 (Cal. 2011), the driver of a car died in a rear-end collision with a tractor-trailer parked on the side of the freeway. The defendant claimed that parking the rig on the side of the road could not be a factual cause of harm "because the same collision would have occurred had Horn [the rig's driver] stopped for emergency rather than personal reasons." The court disagreed with defendant's analysis: "The negligent conduct plaintiff claimed caused her husband's death was Horn's stopping his tractor-trailer rig at the site. The counterfactual question relevant to but-for causation, therefore, is what would have happened if Horn had not stopped his tractor-trailer rig there, not what would have happened if Horn had had a better reason to stop. . . . [S]topping by the side of a freeway for an emergency might be just as dangerous to other motorists as stopping for a snack, but an emergency stop will not create liability because it is justified. While potential liability differs in the two situations (emergency and non-emergency), causation does not."

5. **Judge and jury.** Factual cause is a question of fact for the jury. Why did the *Ziniti* court hold that it was a question that the judge could properly answer? In *Hale v. Ostrow*, 166 S.W.3d 713 (Tenn. 2005), plaintiff was seriously injured when she tripped over a chunk of concrete on the sidewalk. She sued the owners of an adjacent vacant lot, alleging that they were negligent in allowing bushes to block the sidewalk, forcing her to try to walk around the obstruction. She testified in her deposition that "but for the bushes overgrowing the sidewalk, [she] would not have looked up to check for traffic, as she would not have needed to step into the street." The trial court granted summary judgment for defendants, but the Tennessee Supreme Court reversed. The court quoted her deposition testimony, then asked, "Might she nevertheless have tripped over the concrete and suffered the same injury? Indeed she might have." Thus there was a "genuine issue of material fact as to whether the overgrown bushes on the Ostrows' property were a cause in fact of her injury," making summary judgment inappropriate.

6. **Proof of causation.** Many courts have held that a plaintiff cannot escape summary judgment simply by suggesting that there is a *possibility* that something the defendant did caused the plaintiff's harm. In *Funches v. Progressive Tractor & Implement Co.*, 905 F.3d 846 (5th Cir. 2018), plaintiff was injured when his vehicle collided with a piece of farm equipment being towed by a pickup truck as the two vehicles passed each other on the highway. He sued, among others, the company that leased the equipment to the truck driver, alleging that the company was negligent "for failing to warn the pickup truck's driver of the dangers associated with towing the equipment with a

pickup instead of a tractor." Affirming a summary judgment for the defendant, the court agreed with the trial judge that even if the driver had been properly warned and had used a tractor to haul the equipment, "there was no evidence that this change in method would have made a difference." Plaintiff's factual cause argument, said the court, "amounts to mere conjecture—the possibility of causation." *See also Sharrieff v. DBS Automotive Two, LLC*, 242 So.3d 944 (Miss. App. 2018) ("Testimony that the crash would have been 'different' in some way—but 'we don't know' how—is insufficient to create a genuine issue of material fact."); *Sartin v. Estate of McPike*, 475 P.3d 522 (Wash. App. 2020) (in claim alleging negligence by transit company in failing to monitor the medical condition of a company driver who lost consciousness and collided with plaintiff's vehicle, summary judgment for the company was appropriate where it was "speculation" as to whether the driver would have passed a medical test had one been given).

7. **Factual and proximate cause distinguished.** (a) *Substantive difference*. Conceptually, factual cause is very different from proximate cause. Some thinking is that the factual cause issue is truly a factual issue in the sense that it does not entail policy decisions. Proximate cause, by contrast, is primarily a policy judgment about the scope of liability. In *June v. Union Carbide Corp.*, 577 F.3d 1234 (10th Cir. 2009), the court explained: "Ordinarily, a cause is a 'factual cause' only if it is a but-for cause, *see* [Restatement (Third) of Torts: Liability for Physical and Emotional Harm] § 26, although there is a potential exception ... when there are multiple causes, *see id.* § 27." In addition, "the harm must be among the 'harms that result from the risks that made the actor's conduct tortious.' *Id.* § 29. Traditionally, this second component has been referred to as 'proximate cause,' a term that has baffled law students (to say nothing of jurors, lawyers, and judges) for generations; but the Restatement (Third) has wisely redescribed the subject matter as 'scope of liability.'"

(b) *Terminology*. Because of the substantive difference between factual and proximate cause (scope of liability), many jurisdictions are careful to address the two concepts separately. *See, e.g., Bernie v. Catholic Diocese of Sioux Falls*, 821 N.W.2d 232 (S.D. 2012) ("In order to prevail in a suit based on negligence, a plaintiff must prove duty, breach of that duty, proximate and factual causation, and actual injury."). Some courts, as we see in *Ziniti*, say that "causation" is a single element, with two components, factual cause and proximate cause. *Accord, Michaels v. CH2M Hill, Inc.*, 257 P.3d 532 (Wash. 2011) ("Proximate cause can be divided into two elements: cause in fact and legal cause."); *Yearty v. Scott Holder Enterprises, Inc.*, 824 S.E.2d 817 (Ga. App. 2018). In other words, while all courts distinguish factual and proximate cause, they may use different verbal formulations to do so. Courts that combine the two concepts into one element may sometimes cause confusion. We address scope of liability (proximate cause) in the next chapter.

8. **Multiple causes.** What if Plaintiff proves that but-for the negligence of defendant A and defendant B, the plaintiff would not have been harmed. This was the situation in *Hale v. Ostrow*, 166 S.W.3d 713 (Tenn. 2005)

discussed in Note 1. If one landowner-defendant's bush had not overgrown the sidewalk, plaintiff might not have stepped into the street and tripped. Similarly, if another landowner-defendant's sidewalk had not been "crumbled" and in disrepair, plaintiff would not have fallen and crushed her hip. Would it be a problem to find that two defendants' conduct was a cause of plaintiff's injury. In Hale, the court explained, "It is not necessary that the defendants' act be the *sole* cause of plaintiff's injury, only that it be *a* cause." As such, courts sometime reject jury instructions that ask jurors whether defendant's conduct was "*the*" cause of an injury, rather than "*a*" cause.

B. MULTIPLE CAUSES AND APPORTIONMENT

NOTE: LIABILITY OF TWO OR MORE PERSONS

1. *Two persons causing separate or divisible injuries: causal apportionment.* Under the but-for rule, more than one actor's conduct can be causal. In some cases, tortfeasor A may cause a broken arm while tortfeasor B causes a broken leg. So far as the two injuries are separate, liability can be apportioned by causation. Each tortfeasor will be liable for the harms that tortfeasor caused. This explains why evidence of a second accident caused by another person is admissible as relevant to factual causation. *See, e.g., JLG Trucking, LLC v. Garza*, 466 S.W.3d 157 (Tex. 2016).

2. *Two persons causing a single indivisible injury: fault apportionment.* In some injuries, however, both tortfeasors' conduct contributes to a single injury. Suppose A negligently runs into a horse and then negligently leaves the carcass on the highway where it might cause a second accident. B then negligently runs into the carcass, causing injury to his passenger, P. But-for A's negligence, the second collision would not have occurred, as there would have been no horse on the road. But-for B's negligence, the second collision would not have occurred because he would have stopped or taken evasive action to avoid hitting it. The negligent acts of both A and B are but-for causes of the plaintiff's single injury and both are subject to liability. *See Spann v. Shuqualak Lumber Co. Inc.*, 990 So.2d 186 (Miss. 2008) (lumber company's negligence in causing a dense fog of emissions, along with the negligence of other drivers, can be factual cause of collision). How do we assign liability for harm to the tortfeasors in these multiple defendant cases? The question is which fault-apportionment rule to use, joint and several liability with possible contribution, or proportionate fault liability. When contribution is based on the relative fault of the tortfeasors, both these systems are forms of a fault-apportionment approach.

3. *Glancing back.* Before we go on, glance back at the two preceding paragraphs to see how simple they really are. If we can say that A caused only a broken arm and B only a broken leg, we can simply apportion

liability to causes. A is liable only for the broken arm because he caused that harm and no other. But conversely, if an indivisible injury is caused in fact by two or more persons, we cannot apportion liability by causation. We must instead use some form of fault apportionment.

4.   *Some defendants' conduct not a but-for cause of all injury.* Now suppose that C, a doctor, negligently makes both injuries worse, so that each break takes a week longer to heal than necessary. Can you work out (a) who is causally responsible for the broken arm and its delayed healing? (b) how joint and several liability would apply or not to the claims arising from the broken arm? Here is a start: A's negligence is a but-for cause of the broken arm. His negligence is likewise a but-for cause of the delayed healing, isn't it? *See, e.g., Cooper v. Thompson*, 353 P.3d 782 (Alaska 2015). The negligence of the doctor, C, is not a but-for cause of the broken arm but is a but-for cause of the added harm. How would joint and several liability work?

5.   *Liability for aggravation of a preexisting injury.* If the tortfeasor aggravates the plaintiff's preexisting disability, the tortfeasor is ideally liable only for the aggravation—a causal apportionment. *Perius v. Nodak Mut. Ins. Co.*, 782 N.W.2d 355 (N.D. 2010) ("When a defendant's negligence aggravates a preexisting injury, the defendant must compensate the victim for the full extent of the aggravation but is not liable for the preexisting condition itself."). This apportionment should be done by the jury, which will often require expert medical testimony. *Harris v. ShopKo Stores, Inc.*, 308 P.3d 449 (Utah 2013). When the tortious harm caused by the defendant combines with the preexisting condition such that a causal apportionment is not possible, joint liability or several liability may apply. *See CSX Transp., Inc. v. Miller*, 46 So.3d 434 (Ala. 2010) (where jury was unable to apportion liability between aggravation of injury and preexisting injury, liability for entire injury was appropriate).

6.   *Liability without but-for causation.* Under some circumstances a defendant is liable for harm to the plaintiff even though the defendant's negligent or illegal conduct was not a but-for cause of the harm. This is the case with *respondeat superior* liability: the telephone company is liable for its driver's on-the-job negligent driving that causes the plaintiff's injury. Such liability is not based upon the telephone company's negligence at all, but on the idea that, as a matter of policy, it should be liable for its employee's harmful torts. The same idea applies to partners in some circumstances, each being liable for the other's act. Analogously, those who act in a conspiracy or "in concert" to cause harm are all liable for the harm caused, even though only one of the conspirators is a direct cause of harm. At least one person's conduct must be a but-for cause of harm in such cases. If he is, the others are liable because they are deemed responsible for his acts. These paragraphs show that the conduct of two or more persons can be but-for causes and thus liable in some degree for the same harm. (The

amount of liability depends upon whether the state follows joint and several liability or proportionate share liability.)

What is to be said about but-for cause if the independent acts of either A or B would be sufficient to cause the full harm even if the other had not acted at all?

C. PROBLEMS WITH THE BUT-FOR TEST

LANDERS V. EAST TEXAS SALT WATER DISPOSAL COMPANY
248 S.W.2d 731 (Tex. 1952)

CALVERT, JUSTICE.

[Plaintiff owned a small lake, which he had cleaned and stocked with fish at considerable expense. He alleged that on or about April 1 the pipe lines of the East Texas Salt Water Disposal Company broke and some 10 to 15 thousand barrels of salt water flowed over his land and into the lake, killing the fish and causing other damages. He alleged that the other defendant, Sun Oil Company, on or about the same day also caused large quantities of salt water and also oil to flow into his lake, killing the fish. He alleged that each defendant was negligent.]

Did the plaintiff in his pleading allege facts which, if established by evidence, made the defendants jointly and severally liable for plaintiff's damages? From the face of the petition it appears that there was no concert of action nor unity of design between the defendants in the commission of their alleged tortious acts, an absence said by the court in the case of Sun Oil Co. v. Robicheaux, Tex. Com. App., 23 S.W.2d 713, 715, to be determinative of the non-existence of joint liability. In that case the rule was thus stated:

"The rule is well established in this state, and supported by almost universal authority, that an action at law for damages for torts cannot be maintained against several defendants jointly, when each acted independently of the others and there was no concert or unity of design between them. In such a case the tort of each defendant is several when committed, and it does not become joint because afterwards its consequences, united with the consequences of several other torts committed by other persons in producing damages. Under such circumstances, each tortfeasor is liable only for the part of the injury or damages caused by his own wrong; that is, where a person contributes to an injury along with others, he must respond in damages, but if he acts independently, and not in concert of action with other persons in causing such injury, he is liable only for the damages which directly and proximately result from his own act, and the fact that it may be difficult to define the damages caused by the wrongful act of each person who independently contributed to the final result does not affect the rule.". . .

The rule of the *Robicheaux* case, strictly followed, has made it impossible for a plaintiff, though gravely injured, to secure relief in the nature of damages through a joint and several judgment by joining in one suit as defendants all wrongdoers whose independent tortious acts have joined in producing an injury to the plaintiff, which, although theoretically divisible, as a practical matter and realistically considered is in fact but a single indivisible injury. As interpreted by the Courts of Civil Appeals the rule also denies to a plaintiff the right to proceed to judgment and satisfaction against the wrongdoers separately because in such a suit he cannot discharge the burden of proving with sufficient certainty, under pertinent rules of damages, the portion of the injury attributable to each defendant. . . . In other words, our courts seem to have embraced the philosophy, inherent in this class of decisions, that it is better that the injured party lose all of his damages than that any of several wrongdoers should pay more of the damages than he individually and separately caused. If such has been the law, from the standpoint of justice it should not have been; if it is the law now, it will not be hereafter. The case of Sun Oil Co. v. Robicheaux is overruled. Where the tortious acts of two or more wrongdoers join to produce an indivisible injury, that is, an injury which from its nature cannot be apportioned with reasonable certainty to the individual wrongdoers, all of the wrongdoers will be held jointly and severally liable for the entire damages and the injured party may proceed to judgment against any one separately or against all in one suit. . . .

There is, of course, no joint liability for damages for the loss of trees and grass killed by the salt water escaping from the pipe line owned by East Texas Salt Water Disposal Company before such water entered the lake. . . .

NOTES

1. **The but-for test applied to *Landers*.** Apply the but-for test to *Landers*. How does that test work if you believe the two bodies of salt water entered the plaintiff's lake at the same time? But-for the salt water spilled by the Disposal Company, would the plaintiff have avoided harm? Must you conclude that neither defendant caused the plaintiff's harm?

2. **Causation and divisible injury.** How does the but-for test work if you believe that one body of salt water reached the lake first? If, as the court suggests, trees and grass on one side of the lake were injured only by salt water from the Salt Water Disposal Company, would both parties have been an actual cause of that loss? Would liability for that damage be apportioned in a different way than would liability with respect to the fish?

3. **Causation and apportionment of indivisible injury.** There are at least two issues in *Landers*: whether each party's negligence can be said to have been a factual cause of the plaintiff's harm, and if so, for what portion of the damages each defendant should be liable. At the time *Landers* was decided joint and several liability for an indivisible injury was the norm and thus the *Landers* case treats these two issues as one. In a jurisdiction that has several liability, would it be possible to say in a case like *Landers* that the negligence of both parties was a factual cause of the plaintiff's full harm but that each party would be severally liable for damages? *See Staab v. Diocese of St. Cloud*, 813 N.W.2d 68 (Minn. 2012) (both property owner and plaintiff's husband were negligent for injuries caused when plaintiff's nonmotorized wheelchair went over unmarked drop off and threw plaintiff on to pavement; jury found property owner 50% at fault and plaintiff's husband 50% at fault, and thus under state's several liability statute property owner owed 50% of the damages).

4. **"Duplicative" causation.** Professor Richard Wright works out a modified and more complicated version of the but-for rule. Applying his rule, he draws a distinction between "preempted cause" and "duplicative cause." If each of the two salt flows in Landers was sufficient to kill all of the fish and would have done so regardless of the other flow, the two flows are "duplicative" causes. Professor Wright thinks cause should be defined in such a way that we would recognize the defendant's salt flow as a cause even if some other flow would have killed the fish anyway, and applies the same idea to all duplicative cause cases. *See* Richard Wright, *Causation in Tort Law*, 73 CAL. L. REV. 1735 (1985). Wright recognizes, however, that a straight but-for rule would not get this result.

5. **"Preemptive" causation.** Professor Wright's "preempted cause" category is illustrated by a case in which one tortfeasor poisons the victim's tea. Just as the victim puts the tea to his lips, the other tortfeasor shoots him dead. Death would have followed from the poison even if the second tortfeasor had fired no shot at all, just as one salt flow would have killed the plaintiff's fish even if no other flow had existed. But the two cases are not alike under Professor Wright's test. The victim died of a gunshot wound, not poison. The poisoner's conduct is not a cause.

6. **Negligent and non-negligent causes.** What should be the result in *Landers* if instead of two negligent causes sufficient to cause the full harm, one of the sufficient causes was negligent and another was not negligent? In *Anderson v. Minneapolis, St. Paul & Sault Ste. Marie Ry.*, 179 N.W. 45 (Minn. 1920), plaintiff's property was burned by a fire. Plaintiff's proof tended to show that the fire was set by defendant's engine. Defendant, however, offered proof tending to show that there were other fires in the area that might have originated from other and perhaps non-negligent causes. The trial judge instructed in part: "If you find that other fires not set by one of the defendant's engines mingled with one that was set by one of the defendant's engines, there may be difficulty in determining whether you should find that the fire set by the engine was a material or substantial element in causing plaintiff's damage.

If it was, the defendant is liable; otherwise, it is not. . . ." The jury, so charged, found for the plaintiff.

If but-for causation does not work in some kinds of cases, what test or tests might be better to achieve the goals of tort law?

D. ALTERNATIVES TO THE BUT-FOR TEST

LASLEY V. COMBINED TRANSPORT, INC.

261 P.3d 1215 (Or. 2011)

WALTERS, J. . . .

Plaintiff, decedent's father, brought this case against defendants Combined Transport, Inc. (Combined Transport) and Judy Clemmer (Clemmer). On the day that decedent died, a truck owned and operated by Combined Transport lost part of its load of large panes of glass on the I-5 freeway. During the clean-up, traffic backed up and decedent was stopped. Clemmer drove into decedent's pickup, causing leaks in its fuel system. The ensuing fire killed decedent. Combined Transport denied that it was negligent and that its conduct foreseeably resulted in decedent's death. Clemmer admitted that she was negligent in driving at an unreasonable speed and in failing to maintain a proper lookout and control. Clemmer also admitted that her negligence was a cause of decedent's death. Based on the pleadings, the trial court granted plaintiff's motion *in limine* to exclude evidence that Clemmer was intoxicated at the time of the collision. The jury rendered a verdict against both defendants, finding Combined Transport 22 percent at fault and Clemmer 78 percent at fault for plaintiff's damages.

Combined Transport appealed and the Court of Appeals reversed, concluding that the trial court had erred in excluding the evidence of Clemmer's intoxication. The Court of Appeals held that that evidence was relevant to two issues: . . . "whether Combined Transport's negligence was a substantial factor in causing decedent's death and . . . [how to] apportion fault between defendants. . . ."

We allowed plaintiff's petition for review. . . . We begin with the question of whether evidence of Clemmer's intoxication was relevant on the issue of causation. . . . [B]oth parties accept the premise that, when the negligence of multiple tortfeasors combines to produce harm, each tortfeasor whose negligence was a cause of the harm may be held liable. The parties also agree that it is factual, not legal cause, at issue in this case. . . . Combined Transport acknowledges, correctly, that the "substantial factor" test is a test of factual cause . . . :

> "Causation in Oregon law refers to causation in fact, that is to say, whether someone examining the event without regard to legal

consequences would conclude that the allegedly faulty conduct or condition in fact played a role in its occurrence.". . . Rule

Combined Transport contends that the "substantial factor" test expresses a "concept of relativity" that permits a jury to consider the degree to which the conduct of a particular defendant was a factor in causing the harm and to relieve a defendant of liability if its conduct was insignificant or insubstantial when compared to the conduct of others. . . .

It may be possible to imagine a circumstance in which one defendant's act is a factual cause of a plaintiff's harm in the sense that the harm would not have occurred absent the defendant's conduct, but in which that defendant's conduct is so insignificant, when contrasted with the conduct of a second defendant, that the first defendant's conduct should not be deemed a cause of the plaintiff's harm. However, for the reasons that we shall explain, that circumstance is not presented here. . . .

In this case, both the conduct of Clemmer and the conduct of Combined Transport were substantial factors in contributing to decedent's death. Clemmer admitted that her conduct in driving her car into decedent's pickup with such force that leaks in its fuel system caused the pickup to ignite was a substantial factor in causing decedent's death. The jury found that Combined Transport's conduct in spilling a load of glass panes on the freeway caused decedent to bring his pickup to a stop. Based on expert testimony that, had decedent been moving at or close to the speed limit when Clemmer hit him, the impact of the collision would not have been as great, decedent's truck would not have ignited, and decedent would not have died, the jury found that Combined Transport's conduct also was a substantial factor in causing decedent's death. The additional fact that Combined Transport sought to prove—that Clemmer was intoxicated at the time of the collision—could not make Clemmer's conduct any more significant or Combined Transport's conduct any less significant in that causation analysis.

Combined Transport's primary argument—that evidence of Clemmer's intoxication could establish that her conduct was more significant in the causation analysis—confuses causation and negligence. In deciding whether a defendant's act is a factual cause of a plaintiff's harm, the effect of the defendant's conduct, and not whether that conduct fell below the expected standard of care, is the relevant consideration. So, for instance, if Clemmer had been sober, driving at a reasonable rate of speed, keeping a proper lookout, and maintaining control of her car on the night of decedent's death, and if she had, nevertheless, collided with decedent's stationary pickup with such force that the truck ignited and decedent died, Clemmer's conduct would have been a cause of his death. That would be so even though Clemmer was not negligent and could not be held liable to plaintiff. . . .

Combined Transport argues . . . that evidence of Clemmer's intoxication was relevant to demonstrate that Combined Transport's conduct was less significant in the causation analysis. Combined Transport contends that it was entitled to prove that, because Clemmer was intoxicated, she would have collided with decedent's pickup and killed him, even if he had not been stopped on the freeway. . . .

Although Combined Transport's alternative argument may have merit in the abstract, it fails on the record before us. Combined Transport did not proffer evidence that showed that, because Clemmer was intoxicated, she inevitably would have killed decedent, even if his pickup had not been stationary.

[The intoxication evidence, though irrelevant to the issue of causation, is relevant to the issue of apportionment of fault].

NOTES

1. **"Substantial factor": broad use.** The substantial factor test was recommended by both the First and Second Restatements of Torts, leading a number of courts to adopt it as a general standard of factual cause. *See, e.g., Estate of Frey v. Mastroiani*, 463 P.3d 1197 (Haw. 2020) ("As we have consistently applied the substantial factor test, we have rejected other tests for legal causation, particularly the widely-used 'but for' rule."). *Lasley* suggests that the substantial factor test is broadly used in Oregon. California also uses a substantial factor formulation, but has made clear that the but-for test is subsumed within it. As one court recently explained, "California has adopted the "substantial factor" test for cause in fact determinations. Under that test, a defendant's conduct is a cause of a plaintiff's injury if: (1) the plaintiff would not have suffered the injury but for the defendant's conduct; or (2) the defendant's conduct was one of multiple causes sufficient to cause the alleged harm." *Union Pac. Railroad Co. v. Ameron Pole Products LLC*, 43 Cal.App.5th 974 (2019). This verbal formulation seems to track the Restatement Second §§ 431 & 432(1). This use of the "substantial factor" terminology, then, does not mean that it displaces the but-for test in all cases. Indeed, California has long held that but-for cause is the proper test in all cases except for those in which there were multiple sufficient causes of harm, *see Viner v. Sweet*, 70 P.3d 1046 (Cal. 2003), and many other courts have agreed.

2. **"Multiple cause" cases.** At times courts say that the substantial factor test, rather than the but-for test, necessarily applies whenever there is more than one "cause of injury." *Bustamante v. Ponte*, 529 S.W.3d 447 (Tex. 2017). *See also Stelly v. Nat'l Union Fire Ins. Co.*, 266 So.3d 395 (La. Ct. App. 2019) ("multiple causes of injury"); *Glenn v. Peoples*, 185 So.3d 981 (Miss. 2015) ("multiple tortfeasors"). Of course, this needn't be so. The but-for test works well in many multiple defendant cases, as in the case of tortious conduct by two actors, each of which is necessary to the harm that happened but neither of which is alone sufficient to produce it. An example would be the case of the dead horse negligently left in the road and the negligent driver who runs into

it. Both of the defendants are but-for causes of the harm to the passenger who is injured in the resulting car accident. Would the but-for test have worked well in *Lasley* too?

3. **The Third Restatement's formulation.** The Restatement Third rejects the substantial factor test, not only in the two-sufficient-cause cases, but altogether, finding it both "confusing" and "misused" by courts. RESTATEMENT (THIRD) OF TORTS: LIABILITY FOR PHYSICAL AND EMOTIONAL HARM § 26 cmt. j (2010). It instead provides that if tortious conduct of one tortfeasor, A, fails the but-for test only because there is another set of conduct also sufficient to cause the harm, then A's conduct is still a factual cause of that harm. *Id.* § 27. *See Doull v. Foster*, 163 N.E.3d 976 (Mass. 2021) (expressly adopting the Restatement Third approach). Would the newest Restatement test have worked in *Landers* and *Anderson*?

4. **Judicial concern.** Even before the publication of the Restatement Third, a number of courts expressed concern about the substantial factor test. In *John Crane, Inc. v. Jones*, 604 S.E.2d 822 (Ga. 2004), a case that sought recovery for a mill employee's exposure to asbestos, the Georgia Supreme Court wrote of "very real problems with applying a 'substantial factor' standard." According to the court, "In the analysis of a negligence action, the plaintiff must satisfy the elements of the tort, that is, the plaintiff must show a duty, a breach of that duty, causation, and damages. It would be a departure from the analysis to add the requirement that the causal connection must be substantial. Once the term 'substantial factor' is employed in the general negligence law vocabulary, there is the danger that it will be used not only to describe a general approach to the legal cause issue, but will turn into a separate and independent hurdle that the plaintiff will have to overcome in addition to the standard elements of a claim of negligence. So too, has there been great difficulty and disparity in the courts' definition of 'substantial factor.' "

In *Doull v. Foster, supra* Note 3, the Massachusetts high court rejected the substantial factor test entirely. The Restatement Second's formulation, the court said, "blurred the line between factual and legal causation" by attempting to "merge and confuse the but-for standard and the substantial factor test." 163 N.E.3d at 985. Even where there are multiple causes of harm, the court said, the but-for test usually works well: "If a defendant's conduct was necessary to bring about a harm, and the harm would not have occurred without the defendant's conduct, that defendant should be treated as a factual cause of harm." In those "rare cases presenting the problem of multiple sufficient causes"—the kinds of cases where the use of the but-for test would result in all of the defendants escaping liability—the court held that the Restatement Third approach should be used. "In such cases," the court concluded, "where there are multiple, simultaneously operating, sufficient causes, the jury do not have to make a but-for finding" to decide that a defendant's negligence is a factual cause of the harm. 163 N.E.3d. at 991.

Is "substantial factor" a test or measure of anything at all? Does the Third Restatement's approach provide greater clarity?

5. **Trivial contributions.** The Third Restatement provides that "when an actor's negligent conduct constitutes only a trivial contribution to a causal set that is a factual cause of harm," the harm is not considered within the scope of liability. RESTATEMENT (THIRD) OF TORTS: LIABILITY FOR PHYSICAL AND EMOTIONAL HARM § 36 (2010). The example the Restatement provides is of a person exposed to asbestos for 40 years from one source and for a single day from another. Dean Prosser gave the illustration of a match thrown into a forest fire. These illustrations seem easy in the extreme. But what about exposure to one asbestos source for 40 years and to another for two years? Can you see why the Restatement now treats this issue as one of policy under scope of liability rather than as an issue of factual cause?

NOTE: INCREASED RISK SHOWING CAUSATION

Suppose the defendant negligently constructs stairs that are too steep and negligently fails to light them. The plaintiff falls down them in the dark and is injured. Can you say the condition of the premises was a cause of the plaintiff's harm? After all, the plaintiff might fall for many reasons. Many cases are like this, particularly when the defendant *fails* to provide a safety measure. The defendant negligently fails to have a lifeguard on duty at a motel. A child drowns. Would a lifeguard have saved the child? In many cases like this, courts permit juries to find that the defendant's negligent act or omission was a factual cause of the plaintiff's harm.

Can we say those cases represent a principle or rule that when the defendant negligently creates a risk of the very harm that befell the plaintiff, causation is established, or at least that an inference of causation is permitted? In *Zuchowicz v. United States,* 140 F.3d 381 (2d Cir. 1998), Judge Calabresi, a most eminent torts scholar, referring to opinions of Cardozo and Traynor, said:

> [T]hey stated that: if (a) a negligent act was deemed wrongful *because* that act increased the chances that a particular type of accident would occur, and (b) a mishap of that very sort did happen, this was enough to support a finding by the trier of fact that the negligent behavior caused the harm. Where such a strong causal link exists, it is up to the negligent party to bring in evidence denying *but for* cause and suggesting that in the actual case the wrongful conduct had not been a substantial factor.

Judge Calabresi further refined this conception in *Gemmink v. Jay Peak Inc.,* 807 F.3d 46 (2d Cir. 2015) ("[T]he greater the risk that the defendant's conduct will result in the harm the plaintiff suffered, the more likely that a jury will be allowed to find that such conduct was the cause of that harm."), and *Estate of Gustafson ex rel. Reginella v. Target Corp.*, 819 F.3d 673 (2d Cir. 2016) (under New York law, where there is no "direct evidence of the likelihood of causation," the first question is whether the defendant's negligence "increase[d] the chances of plaintiff's injury, and by how much?").

Courts often decide cases without mentioning the inference of causation that may be drawn from increased risk. In *McGuire v. Hodges*, 639 S.E.2d 284 (Va. 2007), a thirty-month-old child was found floating in a pool. The pool was fenced but had a gate that lacked a proper latching device. The homeowner argued that plaintiff failed to show how the child accessed the pool and thus the jury's verdict was based on "conjecture and speculation." However, the court held that the circumstantial evidence in the case was sufficient to support the jury's verdict for the plaintiff. "Testimony at trial described an unlocked gate, secured only by a chain, which the young boy was attempting to open shortly before he was found floating in the pool. . . . The only evidence directly supporting as fact that the gate was well secured at the time of the drowning was the testimony of [the homeowner]," which the "jury was free to discredit." Similarly, in *Yount v. Deibert*, 147 P.3d 1065 (Kan. 2006), boys playing with fire inside a house that was later engulfed in flames created an inference of causation for the jury to consider.

At times, evidence of exposure can be used to create an inference of causation. *Rowhouses, Inc. v. Smith*, 133 A.3d 1054 (Md. 2016) (childhood exposure to lead-based paint in apartment unit). In *John Crane, Inc. v. Jones*, 604 S.E.2d 822 (Ga. 2004), in which the plaintiff contracted mesothelioma because of occupational exposure to asbestos dust, to show factual cause "plaintiff must identify the asbestos-containing product of a particular defendant and show that [he] worked in proximity to [use of that product]." Where the plaintiff cannot prove exposure to the defendant's particular asbestos-containing product, however, the case will be lost on factual cause grounds. *See Grant v. Foster Wheeler, LLC*, 140 A.3d 1242 (Me. 2016) (evidence "too speculative" to support a finding that the plaintiff encountered asbestos fibers from defendant's product while working as a ship-factory cleaner decades ago).

Courts have developed other sorts of intermediate tests to create an inference of causation for particular contexts. *See Merck & Co., Inc. v. Garza,* 347 S.W.3d 256 (Tex. 2011) (in products liability suit alleging harm from prescription drug Vioxx, "when parties attempt to prove general causation using epidemiological evidence, a threshold requirement of reliability is that the evidence demonstrate a statistically significant doubling of the risk"; the plaintiff must also show that he or she is similar to the subjects in the studies, and that other plausible causes are excluded with reasonable certainty).

E. PROOF: WHAT HARM WAS CAUSED?

Liability for negligence attaches only when factual cause links the defendant's negligence to the plaintiff's injury. Consequently, how we define the harm to the plaintiff and the negligence of the defendant can be important parts of the causation question.

In *Dillon v. Twin State Gas & Electric Co.*, 163 A. 111 (N.H. 1932), the defendant's negligence in failing to insulate a wire caused a 14-year-old boy to be electrocuted just as he slipped off of a bridge and was about to fall into a river in which he would have been killed or seriously injured. Did the electrocution cause the loss of the boy's whole life, or simply the loss of a few additional minutes of it?

SUMMERS V. TICE
199 P.2d 1 (Cal. 1948)

CARTER, JUSTICE.

Each of the two defendants appeals from a judgment against them in an action for personal injuries. Pursuant to stipulation the appeals have been consolidated.

Plaintiff's action was against both defendants for an injury to his right eye and face as the result of being struck by bird shot discharged from a shotgun. The case was tried by the court without a jury and the court found that on November 20, 1945, plaintiff and the two defendants were hunting quail on the open range. Each of the defendants was armed with a 12 gauge shotgun loaded with shells containing 7 1/2 size shot. . . . The view of defendants with reference to plaintiff was unobstructed and they knew his location. Defendant Tice flushed a quail which rose in flight to a ten foot elevation and flew between plaintiff and defendants. Both defendants shot at the quail, shooting in plaintiff's direction. At that time defendants were 75 yards from plaintiff. One shot struck plaintiff in his eye and another in his upper lip. Finally it was found by the court that as the direct result of the shooting by defendants the shots struck plaintiff as above mentioned and that defendants were negligent in so shooting and plaintiff was not contributorily negligent. . . .

The one shot that entered plaintiff's eye was the major factor in assessing damages and that shot could not have come from the gun of both defendants. It was from one or the other only.

It has been held that where a group of persons are on a hunting party, or otherwise engaged in the use of firearms, and two of them are negligent in firing in the direction of a third person who is injured thereby, both of those so firing are liable for the injury suffered by the third person, although the negligence of only one of them could have caused the injury. Both drivers have been held liable for the negligence of one where they engaged in a racing contest causing an injury to a third person. These cases speak of the action of defendants as being in concert as the ground of decision, yet it would seem they are straining that concept and the more reasonable basis appears in Oliver v. Miles, supra. There two persons were hunting together. Both shot at some partridges and in so doing shot across the highway injuring plaintiff who was traveling on it. The court stated they were acting in concert and thus both were liable. The court then stated: "We think that . . . each is liable for the resulting injury to the boy, although no one can say definitely who actually shot him. *To hold otherwise would be to exonerate both from liability, although each was negligent, and the injury resulted from such negligence.*" . . .

When we consider the relative position of the parties and the results that would flow if plaintiff was required to pin the injury on one of the defendants only, a requirement that the burden of proof on that subject be shifted to defendants becomes manifest. They are both wrongdoers negligent toward plaintiff. They brought about a situation where the negligence of one of them injured the plaintiff, hence it should rest with them each to absolve himself if he can. The injured party has been placed by defendants in the unfair position of pointing to which defendant caused the harm. If one can escape the other may also and plaintiff is remediless. Ordinarily defendants are in a far better position to offer evidence to determine what one caused the injury. . . .

Cases are cited for the proposition that where two or more tortfeasors acting independently of each other cause an injury to plaintiff, they are not joint tortfeasors and plaintiff must establish the portion of the damage caused by each, even though it is impossible to prove the portion of the injury caused by each. In view of the foregoing discussion it is apparent that defendants in cases like the present one may be treated as liable on the same basis as joint tortfeasors, and hence the last cited cases are distinguishable inasmuch as they involve independent tortfeasors.

In addition to that, however, it should be pointed out that the same reasons of policy and justice [which] shift the burden to each of defendants to absolve himself if he can—relieving the wronged person of the duty of apportioning the injury to a particular defendant—apply here where we are concerned with whether plaintiff is required to supply evidence for the apportionment of damages. If defendants are independent tortfeasors and thus each liable for the damage caused by him alone, and, at least, where the matter of apportionment is incapable of proof, the innocent wronged party should not be deprived of his right to redress. The wrongdoers should be left to work out between themselves any apportionment. Some of the cited cases refer to the difficulty of apportioning the burden of damages between the independent tortfeasors, and say that where factually a correct division cannot be made, the trier of fact may make it the best it can, which would be more or less a guess, stressing the factor that the wrongdoers are not in a position to complain of uncertainty. . . .

The judgment is Affirmed.

NOTES

1.   **The harm caused.** One negligent tortfeasor in *Summers* caused the harm to the plaintiff's eye. What harm did the other tortfeasor's negligence cause? In evidentiary terms, was the plaintiff worse off because there were two negligent defendants rather than one? In a recent hunting case, a hunter shot at a deer. Another member of his hunting party then shot in the same direction and injured a person from another group. Even though the first hunter's bullet did not hit the injured plaintiff, the court found that the first hunter also could be liable to the plaintiff if (1) his shooting was negligent and (2) it was reasonably foreseeable that shooting in that direction would encourage his companion to shoot that way negligently too. *See Hellums v. Raber,* 853 N.E.2d 143 (Ind. Ct. App. 2006).

2.   **Alternative causation.** The *Summers v. Tice* approach has been widely adopted by courts in "alternative cause" or "alternative liability" cases. *See Conn. Interlocal Risk Management Agency v. Jackson,* 214 A.3d 841 (Conn. 2019) (noting that "at least some version of the doctrine 'has been accepted by virtually all jurisdictions,'" *quoting* Mark Geistfeld, *The Doctrinal Unity of Alternative Liability and Market-Share Liability,* 155 U. PA. L. REV. 447 (2006)). In the alternative-cause cases, all tortfeasors are negligent, but only one of them has caused the plaintiff's harm. The difficulty is that it is impossible to determine which one is the cause, usually because their "tortious conduct was substantially simultaneous in time and of the same character." *Silver v. Sportsstuff, Inc.,* 14 N.Y.S.3d 421 (App. Div. 2015). The doctrine was originally rooted in joint and several liability, but has been adopted even in jurisdictions that have adopted several liability. *See Salica v. Tucson Heart Hosp.-Carondelet, L.L.C.,* 231 P.3d 946 (Ariz. Ct. App. 2010) (citing *Summers* with approval and holding that to avoid the " 'unfairness of denying the injured person redress simply because he cannot prove how much damage each [tortfeasor] did, when it is certain that between them they did all,' tortfeasors are left to apportion damages among themselves when causation is potentially indeterminable"). Indeed, the argument for allowing the alternative causation rule may be stronger when the effect of the rule is not to assign full liability to the negligent defendant but instead to allow the negligent defendant who potentially has a causal role to be counted as one defendant in the broader apportionment. 1 DOBBS, HAYDEN & BUBLICK, THE LAW OF TORTS § 193 (2d ed. 2011).

3.   **Shifting the burden of proof on causation.** A and B, each acting negligently, separately cause injury to the plaintiff. As a practical matter, the plaintiff cannot show how much of the injury was caused by A and how much by B. Under traditional rules, A and B are jointly and severally liable. Does this work when a large number of defendants contribute to harm? Suppose the

plaintiff was exposed at work to various identified products of 55 different defendants, that toxins from these products entered his body, and "that each toxin that entered his body was a substantial factor in bringing about, prolonging, or aggravating" cancer. Would such facts sufficiently show causation? *See Bockrath v. Aldrich Chem. Co.,* 980 P.2d 398 (Cal. 1999). If your answer is "yes," what exactly is left to be decided in the case, if anything?

4. **The Restatement view.** Under the RESTATEMENT (THIRD) OF TORTS: LIABILITY FOR PHYSICAL AND EMOTIONAL HARM § 28 (2010), "When the plaintiff sues all of multiple actors and proves that each engaged in tortious conduct that exposed the plaintiff to a risk of harm and that the tortious conduct of one or more of them caused the plaintiff's harm but the plaintiff cannot reasonably be expected to prove which actor caused the harm, the burden of proof, including both production and persuasion, on factual cause is shifted to the defendants." Notice that while *Summers v. Tice* involved only two defendants, neither the Third Restatement nor the Second limits the rule to two defendants. The Connecticut Supreme Court applied *Summers v. Tice* to three defendants, each of whom negligently disposed of cigarettes in an abandoned mill, causing a fire, in *Conn. Interlocal v. Jackson,* supra Note 2.

5. **Harm by one of seven.** In *State v. CTL Distribution, Inc.,* 715 So.2d 262 (Fla. Dist. Ct. App. 1998), one or more truckers spilled a hazardous substance when making deliveries of that substance at a certain business. The state environmental agency sued the seven truckers who delivered the substance. It proved that one of them, CTL, had once spilled the substance and argued that *Summers v. Tice* would authorize liability for all seven. How would you rule on causation if you were the judge? Under the Restatement, might the case be different if the state could prove that all seven had spilled a hazardous substance, only one of which caused the harm?

MOHR V. GRANTHAM

262 P.3d 490 (Wash. 2011)

OWENS, J. . . .

[O]n the afternoon of August 31, 2004, Mrs. Mohr suffered a hypoglycemic event that caused her to run her car into a utility pole at approximately 45 m.p.h. She was taken by ambulance to the emergency room at Kadlec Medical Center (KMC). Having visible lacerations on her face from the car accident, Mrs. Mohr was given a neurological assessment upon arrival, at around 4:00 p.m., and a computerized tomography (CT) scan of her brain about an hour later. These tests were overseen or authorized by Dr. Dale Grantham, who was charged with Mrs. Mohr's care at KMC on August 31. The results were normal.

Following those neurological tests, however, Mrs. Mohr reported and was observed to have neurological symptoms, including being wobbly on her feet and having severe pain after being administered pain medication. Dr. Grantham informed one of Mrs. Mohr's physician sons, Dr. Brandt

Mohr, by phone that he would carry out another neurological assessment before discharging her. He did not. Instead, he prescribed a narcotic, Darvocet, and sent Mrs. Mohr home with her husband. At that point, Mrs. Mohr could not walk herself to or from the car and had to be carried to bed by her husband when they arrived home. The Mohrs were not given discharge instructions that included specific information about head injuries.

Mrs. Mohr was again transported to KMC by ambulance just after 7:00 a.m. on September 1, 2004. . . . However, Dr. Dawson [the attending physician that morning] did not provide any anticoagulant or antithrombotic treatment or therapy. . . .

Before the transfer [to the intermediate care unit at 11:30 a.m.], Mrs. Mohr's two physician sons had arrived at KMC to be by her side. They tried to get both Dr. Dawson and then, after her transfer, Dr. Watson to order a CT angiogram. A CT angiogram was not done until 2:30 p.m., after the Mohr sons had Dr. Watson repeatedly paged. Then, although the results were available at 3:27 p.m., Dr. Watson was not located or informed until 4:50 p.m. that the CT angiogram showed a dissected carotid artery. He still did not order anyone to administer anticoagulant therapy, antiplatelet agents, or any other treatment. Dr. Watson had prescribed aspirin around 2:00 p.m. but did not order its immediate administration.

Mrs. Mohr's sons finally arranged a transfer and transport to Harborview Medical Center. . . . Only shortly before her transport at 6:00 p.m. on September 1, 2004, was Mrs. Mohr finally given aspirin, though it had to be administered in suppository form because, by then, she could no longer swallow.

Mrs. Mohr is now permanently brain damaged; a quarter to a third of her brain tissue was destroyed. In particular, the portions of her brain that were damaged are involved with motor control, sensation, and spatial reasoning.

Mrs. Mohr and her husband filed suit, claiming that Mrs. Mohr received negligent treatment, far below the recognized standard of care. They argue that the doctors' negligence substantially diminished her chance of recovery and that, with nonnegligent care, her disability could have been lessened or altogether avoided. The Mohrs' claim relies, at least in part, on a medical malpractice cause of action for the loss of a chance. In support of their claim, the Mohrs presented the family's testimony, including her two sons who are doctors, and the testimony of two other doctors, Kyra Becker and A. Basil Harris. The testimony included expert opinions that the treatment Mrs. Mohr received violated standards of care and that, had Mrs. Mohr received nonnegligent treatment at various points between August 31 and September 1, 2004, she would have had a 50 to 60 percent chance of a better outcome. The better outcome would have been no disability or, at least, significantly less disability.

On April 16, 2009, the Benton County Superior Court granted summary judgment for the defendants on the basis that the Mohrs did not show "but for" causation. . . . The Mohrs appealed, and the Court of Appeals certified the case for our review. . . .

In the medical malpractice context, is there a cause of action for a lost chance of a better outcome? . . .

Whether there is a cause of action for a lost chance of a better outcome in the medical malpractice context is a question of law, which we review de novo. . . .

[In our opinion in *Herskovits*, in which an allegedly negligent failure to diagnose lung cancer likely diminished the plaintiff's chance of long-term survival from 39 percent to 25 percent, we found that Herskovits's lost chance was actionable. In *Herskovits,*] the lead opinion, signed by two justices, and the concurring opinion, which garnered a plurality, agreed on the fundamental bases for recognizing a cause of action for the loss of a chance. The lead opinion explained:

> To decide otherwise would be a blanket release from liability for doctors and hospitals any time there was less than a 50 percent chance of survival, regardless of how flagrant the negligence.

The plurality similarly noted that traditional all-or-nothing causation in lost chance cases " 'subverts the deterrence objectives of tort law.' " Both opinions found that "the loss of a less than even chance is a loss worthy of redress." With emphasis, the lead opinion agreed, stating that " '[n]o matter how small that chance may have been—and its magnitude cannot be ascertained—no one can say that the chance of prolonging one's life or decreasing suffering is valueless.' "

> The lead and plurality opinions split over *how,* not whether, to recognize a cause of action. . . . [T]he lead opinion held that the appropriate framework for considering a lost chance claim was with a "substantial factor" theory of causation. . . .

The "substantial factor test" is an exception to the general rule of proving but for causation and requires that a plaintiff prove that the defendant's alleged act or omission was a substantial factor in causing the plaintiff's injury, even if the injury could have occurred anyway.

Rather than looking to the causation element, the plurality opinion in *Herskovits* focused instead on the nature of the injury. . . . The plurality found it more analytically sound to conceive of the injury as the lost chance. . . .

[T]he *Herskovits* majority's recognition of a cause of action in a survival action has remained intact since its adoption.... Washington courts have, however, generally declined to extend *Herskovits* to other negligence claims [including legal malpractice, contaminated food claims, and asbestos exposure]. Such limitation is common: "[T]he courts that have accepted lost opportunity as cognizable harm have almost universally limited its recognition to medical-malpractice cases." RESTATEMENT (THIRD) OF TORTS: LIABILITY FOR PHYSICAL AND EMOTIONAL HARM § 26 cmt. n at 356–57 (2010).... Since *Herskovits,* the majority of states that have considered the lost chance doctrine have adopted it, although with varying rationales. Several states have rejected the doctrine....

We find no *persuasive* rationale to distinguish *Herskovits* from a medical malpractice claim where the facts involve a loss of chance of avoiding or minimizing permanent disability rather than death.... [T]he same underlying principles of deterring negligence and compensating for injury apply....

Now nearly 30 years since *Herskovits* was decided, history assures us that *Herskovits* did not upend the world of torts in Washington, as demonstrated by the few cases relying on *Herskovits* that have been heard by Washington appellate courts.

We hold that *Herskovits* applies to lost chance claims where the ultimate harm is some serious injury short of death. We also formally adopt the reasoning of the *Herskovits* plurality. Under this formulation, a plaintiff bears the burden to prove duty, breach, and that such breach of duty proximately caused a loss of chance of a better outcome. This reasoning of the *Herskovits* plurality has largely withstood many of the concerns about the doctrine, particularly because it does not prescribe the specific manner of proving causation in lost chance cases. Rather, it relies on established tort theories of causation, without applying a particular causation test to *all* lost chance cases. Instead, the loss of a chance is the compensable injury....

In *Herskovits,* both the lead and concurring opinions discussed limiting damages. This is a common approach in lost chance cases, responsive in part to the criticism of holding individuals or organizations liable on the basis of uncertain probabilities. RESTATEMENT (THIRD) OF TORTS: LIABILITY FOR PHYSICAL AND EMOTIONAL HARM § 26 cmt. n at 356 ("Rather than full damages for the adverse outcome, the plaintiff is only compensated for the lost opportunity. The lost opportunity may be thought of as the adverse outcome discounted by the difference between the ex ante probability of the outcome in light of the defendant's negligence and the probability of the outcome absent the defendant's negligence."). Treating the loss of a chance as the cognizable injury "permits plaintiffs to recover for the loss of an opportunity for a better outcome, an interest that we agree should be compensable, while providing for the proper valuation of such an interest." *Lord v. Lovett,* 146 N.H. 232, 236, 770 A.2d 1103 (2001). In particular, the *Herskovits* plurality adopted a proportional damages approach, holding that, if the loss was a 40 percent chance of survival, the plaintiff could recover only 40 percent of what would be compensable under the ultimate harm of death or disability (i.e., 40 percent of traditional tort recovery), such as lost earnings. This percentage of loss is a question of fact for the jury and will relate to the scientific measures available, likely as presented through experts. Where appropriate, it may otherwise be discounted for margins of error to further reflect the uncertainty of outcome even with a nonnegligent standard of care. . . .

Interpreting the facts in the light most favorable to the Mohrs, they have made a prima facie case under the lost chance doctrine. . . . [W]e reverse the order of summary judgment and remand to the trial court for further proceedings.

MADSEN, C.J. (dissenting). . . .

It is a fundamental principle that in a medical malpractice action the plaintiff must prove causation of the plaintiff's actual physical (or mental) injury before tort liability will be imposed. To avoid the difficulty posed by this requirement, the majority recognizes a cause of action for which the plaintiff does not have to prove that "but for" the physician's negligence, the injury would not have occurred. . . . The majority simply redefines the injury as the lost chance. With this semantic leap—essentially a fiction— the causation problem is fixed.

But in reality the problem remains. No matter how the lost chance cause of action is characterized, the plaintiff is freed of the requirement of proving causation because, no matter how the action is described, the end result is that liability is imposed based on *possibilities* and not on probabilities. . . .

As the [District Court of Alaska] in *Crosby* correctly responded, "[i]f a plaintiff's chance of recovery was reduced from 20 percent to 10 percent, then permitting recovery for that 10 percent loss enables a plaintiff to recover damages even when the plaintiff's actual physical injury was *not* more likely than not caused by a defendant's alleged negligence." . . .

The "deterrence" justification identified by the majority is in fact unrelated to preventing harm-causing negligence. As Benjamin Cardozo famously explained long ago, " 'negligence in the air' " is not actionable. Physicians, and indeed individuals involved in thousands of actions, are negligent every day without legal consequence because, despite the involvement or presence of others, their acts *do not actually cause harm* to the other persons.

The Texas Supreme Court aptly observed, when it "reject[ed] the notion that the enhanced deterrence of the loss of chance approach might be so valuable as to justify scrapping [the] traditional concepts of causation," that *"[i]f deterrence were the sole value to be served by tort law, we could dispense with the notion of causation altogether and award damages on the basis of negligence alone."*. . .

Moreover, the goal of compensation is not served, either, because there is no way to prove a physician's acts or omissions in fact caused the actual physical harm, rather than the actual harm resulting from the preexisting condition. . . .

If there is to be any change in this law, it should come from the legislature, after appropriate hearings, collection of data, and consideration of competing interests. . . . [T]he legislature is best positioned to consider the myriad of public policy matters implicated by the lost chance doctrine. . . .

The lost chance doctrine also gives rise to other questions. "For instance, what is a 'late diagnosis'? Does a diagnosis missed this week, but made next week, rise to the level of diminished chance?". . . What about in the very case before this court, where we are not considering the passage of weeks, or even days, but of hours? . . .

The ramifications of the majority's opinion are unknown but potentially far-reaching. The majority opinion has the potential to alter health care in this state, as physicians would have to contemplate whether to provide an unprecedented level of care to avoid liability for even a slightly diminished *chance* of a better outcome. As noted, even a small percentage of chance can equal a substantial award. At the same time, it is no secret that health care insurance coverage is already strained, for those who even have such insurance, and adopting this doctrine cannot help but impact the nature and extent of insurance reimbursement for potential tests and treatments ordered as an eventual result of the majority's decision to expand liability to an unprecedented degree in this state.

All of these matters are public policy considerations for the legislature. . . .

NOTES

1. **Choosing a rule.** The *Mohr* majority and dissent present three different approaches that a court might take in deciding lost opportunity claims. What are the two approaches addressed by the majority? What is the approach suggested by the dissent? These approaches were also discussed in *Lord v. Lovett*, 770 A.2d 1103 (N.H. 2001), a lost opportunity case cited by the *Mohr* court and involving negligent misdiagnosis of a spinal cord injury. What are the merits of the different approaches? *See, e.g., Estate of Frey v. Mastroiani,* 463 P.3d 1197 (Haw. 2020) (discussing the approaches at length,

but declining to adopt loss of chance as an "independent and separately compensable cause of action).

2. **The traditional rule.** Remember that the plaintiff must prove each element of her case by a preponderance of the evidence. This means the "greater weight" of the evidence—more likely than not. Translated into numbers, the traditional rule would require plaintiff to persuade the trier that the probabilities are greater than 50% that each element is established. Some courts insist that this rule should then preclude recovery when a patient dies after a physician's misdiagnosis increases the patient's chance of death when the patient had only a 50–50 chance of living anyway. *E.g., Fennell v. Maryland Hosp. Ctr., Inc.*, 580 A.2d 206 (Md. 1990). In a few states, legislatures have selected the traditional rule, abrogating court decisions to the contrary. *See* MICH. COMP. LAWS § 600.2912a(2) ("In an action alleging medical malpractice, the plaintiff cannot recover for loss of an opportunity to survive or an opportunity to achieve a better result unless the opportunity was greater than 50%."); S.D. CODIFIED LAWS § 20–9–1.1.

3. **Relaxed causation tests.** Some courts, either by their words or deeds, have relaxed the plaintiff's burden of proof of causation in cases when a physician causes the loss of a chance of 50% or less. The causation requirement is relaxed by permitting plaintiffs to submit their cases to the jury upon demonstrating that the increased risk created by defendant's negligence was a substantial factor or that the defendant's conduct "destroyed a substantial possibility" of achieving a more favorable outcome. In this group, courts permit juries to award full damages, as if the plaintiff had proved causation by a preponderance of the evidence. *See, e.g., Hamil v. Bashline,* 392 A.2d 1280 (Pa. 1978).

4. **Duty-to-try analysis.** A similar but more striking approach appeared in *Gardner v. National Bulk Carriers, Inc.,* 310 F.2d 284 (4th Cir. 1962). Gardner, a seaman on board a ship at sea, was called to stand watch at 11:30, but he could not be found. He had last been seen five or six hours earlier. The ship notified the Coast Guard but did not attempt to return to those areas of the sea where, at any time during the five hours, he might have fallen overboard. In a suit for Gardner's death, the defendant argued that factual cause had not been shown, since a search probably could not have found a man who had gone overboard hours earlier. But the Fourth Circuit held that the duty of the captain was to make every reasonable effort. "It was less than a duty to rescue him, but it was a positive duty to make a sincere attempt at rescue. . . . [C]ausation is proved if the master's omission destroys the reasonable possibility of rescue." The court apparently envisioned full liability for the seaman's death.

5. **Quantified value-of-the-chance approach.** Still another approach is to say that causal rules are not changed. Instead, the lost opportunity for a better outcome is *itself* the injury for which the negligently injured person may recover. *See Alexander v. Scheid,* 726 N.E.2d 272 (Ind. 2000) (in case involving delay in cancer diagnosis; "We think that loss of chance

is better understood as a description of the injury. . . . If a plaintiff seeks recovery specifically for what the plaintiff alleges the doctor to have caused, i.e., a decrease in the patient's probability of recovery, rather than for the ultimate outcome, causation is no longer debatable. Rather, the problem becomes one of identification and valuation or quantification of that injury."). Under this approach, if the *chance* of survival was 40% and the defendant's negligence more likely than not eliminated that *chance,* then the defendant would be liable for the loss he has caused—the chance. In damages, this is presumably 40% of the damages for which the defendant would be liable if he caused death. This value-of-the-chance theory has now gained substantial support, primarily as a result of a 1981 article, Joseph H. King, Jr., *Causation, Valuation and Chance in Personal Injury Torts*, 90 YALE L. J. 1353 (1981); *see* Lauren Guest, David Schap & Thi Tran, *The Loss of Chance Rule as a Separate Category of Damages in Medical Malpractice: A State-by-State Analysis*, 21 J. LEGAL ECON. 53 (2015) (finding that as of 2014, 24 states had adopted such an approach, while 17 had rejected it).

6.   **What *must* be proved by a preponderance of the evidence under quantified approach.** Under the lost chance rule, are there some things that still *must* be proved by a preponderance of the evidence, that is, under a more-likely-than-not standard? *See Almonte v. Kurl,* 46 A.3d 1 (R.I. 2012) (although court might consider loss of chance under an appropriate factual scenario, plaintiff had not presented any expert testimony that emergency room doctor's negligence caused patient's suicide within 36 hours of discharge or caused a loss of a chance for a better outcome). What if the plaintiff proved that there was a 40% chance that the patient had a 30% chance? *See Alphonse v. Acadian Ambulance Servs., Inc.*, 844 So.2d 294 (La. Ct. App. 2003); *Alberts v. Schultz*, 975 P.2d 1279 (N.M. 1999). Some courts have concluded, particularly in the loss of chance context, that the loss must be "substantial" before it is compensable. However, others have rejected this view. In *Alexander v. Schied,* 726 N.E.2d 272 (Ind. 2000), the court wrote "Because we measure damages by probabilizing the injury, the likelihood that plaintiffs will bring claims for trivial reductions in chance of recovery seems small. If, in the future, we face a volume of insignificant claims, perhaps such a rule will become necessary. For now, we are content to rely on basic economics to deter resort to the courts to redress remote probabilities or insubstantial diminutions in the likelihood of recovery." What are the economics that would deter claims for trivial reductions?

7.   **Reducing damages to reflect probability where causation is more likely than not.** "If the patient in our example was entitled to 25 percent of his full damages because he had only a 25 percent chance of survival, he should be entitled to 75 percent of his damages if he had a 75 percent chance of survival—not 100 percent of his damages on the theory that by establishing a 75 percent chance he proved injury by a preponderance of the evidence. He proves injury in both cases, but in both cases the injury is merely probabilistic and must be discounted accordingly." *Doll v. Brown,* 75 F.3d 1200 (7th Cir. 1996) (Posner, J.). *See also* John Makdisi, *Proportional Liability: A*

Comprehensive Rule to Apportion Tort Damages Based Probability, 67 N.C. L. REV. 1063 (1989) (supporting general use of lost chance or probabilistic causation). How would this change the "normal" rules of causation? How would juries determine these percentages? Some courts have rejected the idea that a probabilistic approach should be used where the injury is more probable than not. *See Kivland v. Columbia Orthopaedic Group, LLP*, 331 S.W.3d 299 (Mo. 2011) (where the plaintiff can prove that it is more likely than not that the defendant's negligent medical care caused the patient's death, the recovery should be based on the state's wrongful death statute and "loss of chance" has no application at all).

Evaluating the Approaches

8. **Deterrence.** Which rule (if any) seems to provide the most appropriate deterrence? Take a look at the hypothetical facts and table below.

Three Cancer Patients

Each patient has a 1/3 or 33.33% chance of survival if properly treated. The defendant negligently treats each one and all three die. In each case, damages for wrongful death would have been $100,000 if the negligence is treated as a cause of the harm. We cannot in fact know which one would have lived had proper treatment been provided, but the overwhelming likelihood is that one would have lived. An omniscient trier of fact would know which one (line four).

	Recovery	Total Liability
Traditional rule	$0.0	$0.0
Relaxed causation	$100,000 each	$300,000
Lost chance	$33,333.33 each	$100,000
Omniscient trier	$100,000 to one estate	$100,000

9. **Lost chance liability in other contexts?** " 'Loss of a chance' is a novel theory of causation commonly used by courts in the United States in medical misdiagnosis cases. Yet the theory has a vastly broader potential application than this. In fact, it could be applied in virtually every case of questionable causation." David A. Fischer, *Tort Recovery for Loss of a Chance,* 36 WAKE FOREST L. REV. 605 (2001). Should the doctrine apply outside medical malpractice cases? Professor Fischer explores the question and concludes that case-by-case policy analysis will be required. You might think that courts could appropriately limit the lost chance recovery to cases in which the defendant owed a duty to maximize the plaintiff's chances. That would certainly cover

physicians who are hired for the very purpose of maximizing chances. Would the reasoning extend to other professionals like attorneys? So far, as mentioned in *Mohr,* courts have applied value of the chance reasoning mainly to physician-patient cases. *See Niang v. Dryades YMCA School of Commerce, Inc.,* 286 So.3d 506 (La. App. 2019) ("[L]oss of chance of survival claims are not applicable to non-medical malpractice cases."); *Hardy v. Southwestern Bell Tel. Co.,* 910 P.2d 1024 (Okla. 1996) (refusing to extend loss-of-chance theory "beyond the established boundary of medical malpractice").

DILLON V. EVANSTON HOSPITAL, 771 N.E.2d 357 (Ill. 2002). A catheter was inserted into the plaintiff's body in the course of a medical procedure. As planned, it was removed, except that a portion broke off and remained in her body. Neither her doctor nor the hospital so advised her. Much later, she discovered that the remaining portion had worked its way in two pieces into her heart, one part floating freely in the heart, the other with its tip embedded in the wall of the right ventricle. In the plaintiff's suit against doctor and hospital, the jury found for the plaintiff and awarded damages for past and future pain and suffering and also damages for increased risk of future harm. *Held,* judgment for plaintiff on increased risk is permissible, but the case is reversed for more adequate instruction. "[T]heories of lost chance of recovery and increased risk of future injury have similar theoretical underpinnings." However, the trial judge's instruction on the increased risk damages requires reversal because it failed to require (a) evidence of increased risk of future harm and (b) damages proportioned to the probability that the risks of future harm would materialize.

NOTES

1.   **Partial criticism of *Dillon.*** In *Swartz v. Gale Webb Transp. Co.,* 215 S.W.3d 127 (Mo. 2007), the court said that *Dillon*'s approach, which requires the jury "to quantify the percent of risk it finds and separately award damages for it," was unduly complex. Instead, the jury should be allowed to "consider all evidence of past and present injuries, including the increased risk of future injury that those present injuries create, as well as future injuries that the jury finds are reasonably certain to occur, and to award a single sum of damages for such injuries." In *Swartz,* a medical expert testified that the plaintiff suffered a back injury that carried with it "at least a 25 percent chance, and perhaps a 50 percent chance, of requiring surgery in the future." All parties agreed that this testimony did not establish that she will need future surgery, and thus that she could not recover "the costs of the possible future back surgery." However, said the court, this chance of future complications "makes it a worse injury than a back injury that has a lesser chance of future complications requiring surgery or that had fully healed at

the time of trial," so admitting the testimony for the jury's consideration of damages was not an abuse of discretion.

2. **Present injury.** In an Illinois case subsequent to *Dillon*, the defendant negligently caused a car accident with a pregnant woman. The woman required x-rays and medication which doctors told her could cause disabilities in the fetus. Because of these risks and risks to her own health from continuing the pregnancy—a pelvic bone fracture which could not be fixed during a pregnancy—she elected to terminate the pregnancy. The Illinois Supreme Court denied recovery under its wrongful death act on the ground that the fetus' increased risk of future harm was not a present injury for which the fetus could have brought an action for damages against the defendant. The court distinguished *Dillon* on the ground that the catheter embedded in plaintiff's heart was a present injury. *See Williams v. Manchester,* 888 N.E.2d 1 (Ill. 2008). If the woman would have continued the pregnancy absent the accident, wasn't the defendant's negligence a cause of the fetus' death?

3. **Small risks.** Where the plaintiffs had only slight exposure to asbestos and only a small increased risk of future harm, Louisiana held there could be no recovery for the increased risk. *Bonnette v. Conoco, Inc.,* 837 So.2d 1219 (La. 2003). Professor King concludes that the courts are divided on whether to apply the loss of chance approach to future consequences that may not in fact ever occur. Joseph H. King, Jr., *"Reduction of Likelihood" Reformulation And Other Retrofitting of The Loss-of-a-Chance Doctrine,* 28 U. MEM. L. REV. 491 (1998).

AN END NOTE: LIABILITY WITHOUT CAUSATION?

From a moral or normative point of view, would it be wrong to hold a defendant liable when he has committed negligent acts but, fortuitously, has not caused harm? From the point of view of deterring unsafe conduct, would liability without causation be a good idea? *See* Margaret A. Berger, *Eliminating General Causation: Notes Towards a New Theory of Justice and Toxic Torts,* 97 COLUM. L. REV. 2117 (1997). Consider this possible rule for liability without proof of causation: The defendant is liable without proof that his conduct caused legal harm if, but only if

(1) the defendant has acted negligently; and

(2) the negligence created an identifiable risk; and

(3) the plaintiff was one of the persons subjected to that risk; and

(4) the plaintiff actually suffered harm of the kind risked by the defendant.

REFERENCES: DOBBS, HAYDEN & BUBLICK, HORNBOOK ON TORTS §§ 14.1–14.11 (2d ed. 2016); 1 DOBBS, HAYDEN & BUBLICK, THE LAW OF TORTS §§ 183–197 (2d ed. 2011); DAVID W. ROBERTSON,

THE COMMON SENSE OF CAUSE IN FACT, 75 TEX. L. REV. 1765, 1780 (1997); SYMPOSIUM, CAUSATION IN THE LAW OF TORTS, 63 CHI-KENT L. REV. 397 (1987).

CHAPTER 8

SCOPE OF LIABILITY (PROXIMATE CAUSE)

■ ■ ■

§ 1. THE PRINCIPLE: SCOPE OF RISK

The final element that a plaintiff must prove in a negligence case is that plaintiff's harm fell within the scope of defendant's liability, in other words, that the harm resulted from the risks that made the defendant's conduct negligent in the first place. In more traditional language, the scope-of-liability concept has been termed "proximate cause" or "legal cause." Where reasonable people could disagree, the scope of liability issue is an issue of fact for the jury.

Scope-of-liability determinations involve case-specific inquiries into whether the defendant should be held legally responsible to the plaintiff. Even when the defendant was negligent and in fact caused the harm to the plaintiff, the defendant is not liable if the actual harm was not within the scope of the risk the defendant created.

Why would it be either just or good policy to hold that a defendant is not liable for harm defendant has, in fact, negligently caused? Suppose that the defendant is Dr. Dayden, a surgeon who performed a vasectomy operation upon Mr. Fallow some years ago. Because the vasectomy was negligently performed, Mr. Fallow sired a child, William. When William reached the age of six, he set fire to the plaintiff's garage. The plaintiff has now sued William, Mr. Fallow, and Dr. Dayden. The plaintiff can show that Dr. Dayden negligently performed the vasectomy and that Dayden's negligence in fact was one of the causes of William's conception and birth. The plaintiff can also show that plaintiff's garage would not have been burned but for William's existence. As such, Dr. Dayden's negligence in the vasectomy operation could be a cause in fact of the fire.

Probably all lawyers would agree that the surgeon is not liable for the burning of the garage. The reasons for this outcome may be expressed in different ways. Many judicial opinions are likely to emphasize "causation," the attenuated causal link between the surgeon's negligence and the harm ultimately done by William. Yet while causation is often the conventional locution, the underlying idea seems to be more precise and more principled: Liability for negligence is liability for the unreasonable risks the defendant created, not for reasonable risks or for those that were unforeseeable. We don't think a vasectomy is negligently performed because it might cause a fire, so the fire loss was outside the risks that led us to think Dr. Dayden was negligent. (Although a connection between unwanted children and higher crime rates has been argued. See STEVEN LEVITT & STEPHAN DUBNER, FREAKONOMICS (2006)).

Judges express themselves in many different ways on scope of liability issues. Ask yourself in each case whether the reason for relieving the defendant of liability was merely one of practicality or policy. Or is the reason a moral one, grounded in justice, for limiting an actor's liability to harms that result from unreasonable risks?

THOMPSON V. KACZINSKI

774 N.W.2d 829 (Iowa 2009)

HECHT, JUSTICE.

James Kaczinski and Michelle Lockwood resided in rural Madison County, near Earlham, on property abutting a gravel road. During the late summer of 2006, they disassembled a trampoline and placed its component parts on their yard approximately thirty-eight feet from the road. Intending to dispose of them at a later time, Kaczinski and Lockwood did not secure the parts in place. A few weeks later, on the night of September 16 and morning of September 17, 2006, a severe thunderstorm moved through the Earlham area. Wind gusts from the storm displaced the top of the trampoline from the yard to the surface of the road.

Later that morning, while driving from one church to another where he served as a pastor, Charles Thompson approached the defendants' property. When he swerved to avoid the obstruction on the road, Thompson lost control of his vehicle. His car entered the ditch and rolled several times. Kaczinski and Lockwood were awakened by Thompson's screams at about 9:40 a.m., shortly after the accident. When they went outside to investigate, they discovered the top of their trampoline lying on the roadway. Lockwood dragged the object back into the yard while Kaczinski assisted Thompson.

Thompson and his wife filed suit, alleging Kaczinski and Lockwood breached statutory and common law duties by negligently allowing the trampoline to obstruct the roadway. Kaczinski and Lockwood moved for summary judgment, contending they owed no duty under the circumstances because the risk of the trampoline's displacement from their yard to the surface of the road was not foreseeable. The district court granted the motion, concluding Kaczinski and Lockwood breached no duty and the damages claimed by the plaintiffs were not proximately caused by the defendants' negligence. The Thompsons appealed. We transferred the case to the court of appeals, which affirmed the district court's ruling. We granted the Thompsons' application for further review. . . .

[Defendant had no statutory duty to avoid obstructing a highway right-of-way because that duty applied only to an intentional obstruction. However, defendants did owe a common law duty of reasonable care. We turn next to the issue of causation, raised by the district court.]

We have held causation has two components: cause in fact and legal cause. The decisions of this court have established it is the plaintiff's burden to prove both cause in fact and legal (proximate) cause. The latter component requires a policy determination of whether "the policy of the law must require the defendant to be *legally responsible* for the injury." . . .

"Tort law does not impose liability on an actor for all harm factually caused by the actor's tortious conduct." Restatement (Third) ch. 6 Special Note on Proximate Cause. . . . [T]he drafters of the Restatement (Third) have clarified the essential role of policy considerations in the determination of the scope of liability. "An actor's liability is limited to those physical harms that result from the risks that made the actor's conduct tortious." *Id.* § 29. This principle, referred to as the "risk standard," is intended to prevent the unjustified imposition of liability by "confining liability's scope to the reasons for holding the actor liable in the first place." As an example of the standard's application, the drafters provide an illustration of a hunter returning from the field and handing his loaded shotgun to a child as he enters the house. *Id.* cmt. *d,* illus. 3. The child drops the gun (an object assumed for the purposes of the illustration to be neither too heavy nor unwieldy for a child of that age and size to handle) which lands on her foot and breaks her toe. Applying the risk standard described above, the hunter would not be liable for the broken toe because the risk that made his action negligent was the risk that the child would shoot someone, not that she would drop the gun and sustain an injury to her foot.

The scope-of-liability issue is fact-intensive as it requires consideration of the risks that made the actor's conduct tortious and a determination of whether the harm at issue is a result of any of those risks. When, as in this case, the court considers in advance of trial whether

> the plaintiff's harm is beyond the scope of liability as a matter of law, courts must initially consider all of the range of harms risked by the defendant's conduct that the jury *could* find as the basis for determining [the defendant's] conduct tortious. Then, the court can compare the plaintiff's harm with the range of harms risked by the defendant to determine whether a reasonable jury might find the former among the latter.

The drafters advance several advantages of limiting liability in this way. First, the application of the risk standard is comparatively simple. The standard "appeals to intuitive notions of fairness and proportionality by limiting liability to harms that result from risks created by the actor's wrongful conduct, but for no others." It also is flexible enough to "accommodate fairness concerns raised by the specific facts of a case."

Foreseeability has previously played an important role in our proximate cause determinations. . . . The drafters of the Restatement (Third) explain that foreseeability is still relevant in scope-of-liability determinations. . . . Properly understood, both the risk standard and a foreseeability test exclude liability for harms that were sufficiently unforeseeable at the time of the actor's tortious conduct that they were not among the risks—potential harms—that made the actor negligent. . . .

Although the risk standard and the foreseeability test are comparable in negligence actions. . . [the Restatement drafters] explain that a foreseeability test "risks being misunderstood because of uncertainty about what must be foreseen, by whom, and at what time."

We find the drafters' clarification of scope of liability sound and are persuaded by their explanation of the advantages of applying the risk standard as articulated in the Restatement (Third), and, accordingly, adopt it.

Our next task, then, is to consider whether the district court erred in concluding the harm suffered by the Thompsons was, as a matter of law, outside the scope of the risk of Kaczinski and Lockwood's conduct. We conclude the question of whether a serious injury to a motorist was within the range of harms risked by disassembling the trampoline and leaving it untethered for a few weeks on the yard less than forty feet from the road is not so clear in this case as to justify the district court's resolution of the issue as a matter of law at the summary judgment stage. A reasonable fact finder could determine Kaczinski and Lockwood should have known high winds occasionally occur in Iowa in September and a strong gust of wind could displace the unsecured trampoline parts the short distance from the yard to the roadway and endanger motorists. Although they were in their home for several hours after the storm passed and approximately two-and-a-half hours after daybreak, Kaczinski and Lockwood did not discover their property on the nearby roadway, remove it, or warn approaching motorists of it. On this record, viewed in the light most favorable to the Thompsons, we conclude a reasonable fact finder could find the harm suffered by the Thompsons resulted from the risks that made the defendants' conduct negligent. Accordingly, the district court erred in deciding the scope-of-liability question as a matter of law in this case. . . . Accordingly, we reverse the district court's dismissal of this claim and remand this case for trial. . . .

NOTES

1. **Applying the risk rule.** "An actor's liability is limited to those physical harms that result from the risks that made the actor's conduct tortious." RESTATEMENT (THIRD) OF TORTS: LIABILITY FOR PHYSICAL AND

EMOTIONAL HARM § 29 (2010). Look at the facts in *Thompson*. Some kind of risk or foreseeable harm makes the court think that the defendant might have been negligent. What kind of risks did the defendant's conduct create? Did the harm that transpired result from those risks?

2. **Formulations of the principle.** Take a few minutes to consider the idea that the harm that occurred to the plaintiff must be of the same general nature as the foreseeable risk created by the defendant's negligence. Evaluate the following as alternative statements of the idea. (1) Liability must be rejected unless a reasonable person would have reasonably foreseen and avoided harm of the same general kind actually suffered by the plaintiff. (2) The defendant who negligently creates a risk to the plaintiff is subject to liability when that risk or a similar one results in harm, but not when some entirely different risk eventuates in an entirely different harm. Is the example of a hunter who hands a gun to a young child who drops it on her toe helpful in illustrating the risk rule? What is the range of harms that made the hunter's conduct negligent in that situation?

3. **Foreseeability in scope of risk and in breach.** The *Thompson* court says that foreseeability plays an important role in scope of liability, but we previously saw that it played a role in breach as well. Is the concept of foreseeability completely redundant in the two settings? Some courts have said that in breach we are concerned with the broader question of whether the defendant's conduct foreseeably risks some type of harm to someone such that the conduct should have been avoided. In scope of liability we are concerned with whether the defendant's conduct foreseeably risked the type of harm that actually happened to the plaintiff in the case at hand. So the foreseeability inquiry is more focused and specific in the scope of liability context. As one federal judge said of the Supreme Court of New Mexico's rulings on foreseeability in the duty/breach context and the scope of liability/proximate cause context: "[T]he former is a minimal threshold *legal* requirement for opening the courthouse doors, whereas the latter is part of the much more specific *factual* requirement that must be proved to win the case once the courthouse doors are open." *C.H. v. Los Lunas Schools Bd. of Educ.*, 852 F.Supp.2d 1344 (D.N.M. 2012). *See also B.R. and C.R. v. West*, 275 P.3d 228 (Utah 2012).

4. **Two ways of stating the elements of the plaintiff's case.** We have been careful in this book to state the factual cause element separately from the scope-of-liability or proximate cause element. In *Thompson,* the court began by referring to "causation" in its two parts, but then carefully separated the distinct elements. Many courts merge the two concepts by saying that the term proximate cause includes both factual cause and foreseeability. *Sibbing v. Cave*, 922 N.E.2d 594 (Ind. 2010); *Puckett v. Mt. Carmel Reg'l Med. Ctr.*, 228 P.3d 1048 (Kan. 2010); *HMC Hotel Props. II Ltd. P'ship v. Keystone-Tex. Prop. Holding Corp.*, 439 S.W.3d 910 (Tex. 2014). Viewing proximate cause as a conglomeration of elements risks confusion: when a court speaks of "proximate cause," it may not be clear whether the court is referring to the factual cause

component, or the scope of liability component. We aim to avoid this confusion by keeping the two elements separate.

5. Applying the rule in *Thompson*.

(a) In *Melchor v. Singh*, 935 N.Y.S.2d 106 (App. Div. 2011), a worker used his employer's ladder. The ladder had old, worn feet and the worker placed bricks under the feet to help stabilize it. He had asked his supervisor for sandbags or another worker to hold the ladder steady, but did not receive either to assist him. While he was working, the bottom of the ladder slid away from the building and he was injured. Do you think the defendant's negligence in providing a deficient ladder was a proximate cause of the plaintiff's injuries? What tests would you use to guide your analysis?

(b) In *Ecker v. E & A Consulting Grp., Inc.*, 924 N.W.2d 671 (Neb. 2019), plaintiffs had backyards abutting a creek. A consulting company completed a study recommending that the sanitary district construct a berm at 100-year flood levels to avoid flooding in nearby homes. Such a berm was built but had some low spots. A storm that exceeded the 100-year flood level occurred, flooding plaintiffs' houses. Assuming the berm was defective because of its failure to meet the 100-year flood level protections, was it a proximate cause of the flooding of plaintiffs' homes when the water exceeded the 100-year level?

(c) *Medcalf v. Washington Heights Condominium Ass'n*, 747 A.2d 532 (Conn. App. Ct. 2000), the plaintiff went to visit her friend Skiades. When plaintiff arrived she called on the intercom from outside the building to ask Skiades to buzz her in. Because the building's buzzer system was broken, Skiades walked downstairs to let plaintiff in. Before Skiades got to the front door, plaintiff was attacked. If the building was negligent in failing to maintain the telephone security intercom system, was the harm that occurred "of the same general nature as the foreseeable risk created by defendant's negligence?" What risks might you have foreseen from the broken intercom system? A similar case is *Benaquista v. Municipal Housing Authority*, 622 N.Y.S.2d 129 (App. Div. 1995), where the defendant failed to maintain an intercom and the apartment owner was injured walking downstairs to admit a visitor.

ABRAMS V. CITY OF CHICAGO, 811 N.E.2d 670 (Ill. 2004). The plaintiff, suing for herself and the estate of her deceased child, alleged that the defendant was negligent in failing to send an ambulance to take her to the hospital for delivery of the child when her contractions were 10 minutes apart. As a result of this failure, a friend took her in a car. The friend drove through a red light, horn sounding, and was struck by Gregory Jones, driving at 75 m.p.h. Jones had been drinking and using cocaine. The plaintiff was left in a coma for two weeks and her child died. The trial court granted summary judgment for the defendant on the ground that the defendant's failure to provide an ambulance was not a proximate cause of the injuries. The intermediate court reversed. On review, *held*, the intermediate court erred, and the trial court's grant of summary judgment is affirmed. "[W]e conclude as a matter of law that the City could *not* have reasonably anticipated that a refusal to send an ambulance when labor pains are 10 minutes apart would likely result in plaintiff's driver running a red light at the same time that a substance-impaired driver was speeding through the intersection on a suspended license. Millions of women in labor make it safely to the hospital each year by private transportation. . . . While all traffic accidents are to some extent remotely foreseeable, this is not the kind of harm that was sufficiently foreseeable. . . ."

NOTES

1. **Step 1: identifying the risks that called for more care.** "I'd better send an ambulance to this caller; otherwise, she might use a private car which would be in a collision." Would a reasonable dispatcher ever think that? If your answer is no, maybe you've decided that the risks created by the failure to dispatch an ambulance did not include car collisions. In that case, the plaintiff's injury and the child's death would not be within the scope of the risk we would have in mind when we said the defendant was negligent, so the conclusion is, "not within the scope of liability."

2. **Answering the scope of liability question.** Could reasonable people differ on whether negligent failure to send an ambulance for a pregnant woman might easily result in speeding to the hospital because of the delay? If the answer to that question is "yes," then scope of liability would be a question for the judgment of the jury on the foreseeability issue.

3. **Defining the scope of liability by reference to the reason for liability.** In *Meyers v. Ferndale Sch. Dist.*, 481 P.3d 1084 (Wash. 2021) a student was killed by a vehicle during an off-campus walk along the side of the road with his P.E. class. The 25 students were walking with their backs to traffic when the driver of a car fell asleep at the wheel, lost control of the car, and struck the decedent and three other students. The student's estate claimed that the defendant school district was negligent because the walk did not comply with internal policies and safety precautions. The trial court granted summary judgment for the defendant on duty and proximate cause grounds. The Washington Supreme Court disagreed held that summary judgment should not have been granted. The question on proximate cause is "whether as a matter of policy the connection between the ultimate result and the act or omission of the defendant is too remote or insubstantial to impose liability." According to the Court, duty, which "includes the underlying policy considerations for imposing liability," is the start of the proximate cause analysis. In this case, the scope of the district's duty to its students is to protect them from "reasonably anticipated dangers," and factual issues remained on whether the negligence of the vehicle's driver was reasonably foreseeable, making summary judgment on proximate cause grounds improper.

4. **Examples.** Try the idea on some other facts.

(a)　Defendant negligently pollutes a bay with oil. One risk is that the oil will cling to docks and have to be cleaned off. Fire is not a foreseeable risk, however, because everyone involved reasonably believes that the oil cannot catch fire on the cold waters of the bay. Their belief, though reasonable, proved wrong and by a fluke, the oil caught fire and burned the plaintiff's docks. If the scope-of-risk rule enunciated and applied in *Thompson* controls here, can the plaintiff recover? *Overseas Tankship (U.K.) Ltd. v. Mort's Dock & Engineering Co. Ltd. (The Wagon Mound),* [1961] A.C. 388 (Privy Council 1961).

(b)　Last year, the plaintiff received a blood transfusion. Blood was supplied by the defendant blood bank, ABO. Neither ABO nor anyone else at that time knew that blood could carry an obscure disease, tortosis, much less any way to test for it. However, ABO and other blood banks knew that blood could carry a devastating disease, contractosis, and that blood could readily be tested for that disease. No such test was made. The blood received by the plaintiff carried tortosis, from which the plaintiff now suffers. If ABO had screened the blood for contractosis, it would have found signs of that disease and would have rejected the blood for that reason. If ABO was negligent in not screening for contractosis is it liable to the plaintiff for tortosis?

(c)　In violation of hospital policy, a hospital released a patient without an escort after the patient had received sedating medication. The patient got into a pedestrian-automobile accident and police were called. On his way to the scene of the accident, the police officer's cruiser was struck by another vehicle, permanently injuring the officer. The officer sued the hospital for its negligent release of the patient. Was the accident of the same general type that the hospital should have foreseen and taken reasonable measures to prevent? *Leavitt v. Brockton Hospital, Inc.,* 907 N.E.2d 213 (Mass. 2009).

5.　**Policy or justice: the risk rule or directness.** Maybe the scope-of-risk rule as articulated in *Thompson* and *Abrams* is wrong. It sometimes relieves a faulty defendant at the expense of the innocent plaintiff, doesn't it? For this reason, older cases sometimes held that the defendant would be liable, even for unforeseeable harms, so long as they were "direct" and no new tort by someone else intervened. Directness language sometimes creeps into cases today. For example, in *Anderson v. Christopherson*, 816 N.W.2d 626 (Minn. 2012), plaintiff fell and suffered a broken hip when he tried to separate an attacking unleashed dog from his own dog. The court wrote that whether the attacking dog's conduct was a proximate cause of plaintiff's injury depended on whether the injury was "a direct and immediate result" of the dog's conduct. In a case like this where the dog did not attack the plaintiff directly, there was a fact question as to whether plaintiff's "intervention into the fight was voluntary." If it was, proximate cause would not be established. Is such a doctrine preferable?

6.　**Policy or justice: justification for the risk rule.** If the scope-of-risk rule is right, what exactly is its justification? Consider: (1) The rule is purely pragmatic. Liability must stop somewhere. The but-for causation test would leave people exposed to continuous liability as long as they lived. (2) The risk rule is just, or at least logical. If liability is imposed only for negligence and negligence creates only a risk of harm A, then liability should be limited to harm A. Any other result would be a species of strict liability, that is, liability for harms as to which the defendant created no unreasonable risks. *See* 1 DOBBS, HAYDEN & BUBLICK, THE LAW OF TORTS § 199 (2d ed. 2011).

PALSGRAF V. LONG ISLAND RAILROAD CO.
162 N.E. 99 (N.Y. 1928)

CARDOZO, C.J.

Plaintiff was standing on a platform of defendant's railroad after buying a ticket to go to Rockaway Beach. A train stopped at the station, bound for another place. Two men ran forward to catch it. One of the men reached the platform of the car without mishap, though the train was already moving. The other man, carrying a package, jumped aboard the car, but seemed unsteady as if about to fall. A guard on the car, who had held the door open, reached forward to help him in, and another guard on the platform pushed him from behind. In this act, the package was dislodged, and fell upon the rails. It was a package of small size, about fifteen inches long, and was covered by a newspaper. In fact it contained fireworks, but there was nothing in its appearance to give notice of its contents. The fireworks when they fell exploded. The shock of the explosion threw down some scales at the other end of the platform many feet away. The scales struck the plaintiff, causing injuries for which she sues. [The case was submitted to a jury, which returned a verdict for the plaintiff. The Appellate Division affirmed the judgment for the plaintiff.]

The conduct of the defendant's guard, if a wrong in its relation to the holder of package, was not a wrong in its relation to the plaintiff, standing far away. Relatively to her it was not negligence at all. Nothing in the situation gave notice that the falling package had in it the potency of peril to persons thus removed. Negligence is not actionable unless it involves the invasion of a legally protected interest, the violation of a right. Proof of negligence in the air, so to speak, will not do. . . . Negligence is the absence of care, according to the circumstances. The plaintiff, as she stood upon the platform of the station, might claim to be protected against intentional invasion of her bodily security. Such invasion is not charged. She might claim to be protected against unintentional invasion by conduct involving in the thought of reasonable men an unreasonable hazard that such invasion would ensue. These, from the point of view of the law, were the bounds of her immunity, with perhaps some rare exceptions. . . . If no hazard was apparent to the eye of ordinary vigilance, an act innocent and harmless, at least to outward seeming, with reference to her, did not take to itself the quality of a tort because it happened to be a wrong, though apparently not one involving the risk of bodily insecurity, with reference to some one else. . . .

The risk reasonably to be perceived defines the duty to be obeyed, and risk imports relation; it is risk to another or to others within the range of apprehension. This does not mean, of course, that one who launches a destructive force is always relieved of liability, if the force, though known to be destructive pursues an unexpected path. "It was not necessary that the defendant should have had notice of the particular method in which an accident would occur, if the possibility of an accident was clear to the ordinarily prudent eye." Some acts, such as shooting are so imminently dangerous to any one who may come within reach of the missile however unexpectedly, as to impose a duty of provision not far from that of an insurer. Even today, and much oftener in earlier stages of law, one acts sometimes at one's peril. Under this head, it may be, fall certain cases of what is known as transferred intent, an act willfully dangerous to A resulting by misadventure in injury to B. These cases aside, wrong is defined in terms of the natural or probable, at least when unintentional. The range of reasonable apprehension is at times a question for the court, and at times, if varying inferences are possible, a question for the jury. Here, by concession, there was nothing in the situation to suggest to the most cautious mind that the parcel wrapped in newspaper would spread wreckage through the station. If the guard had thrown it down knowingly and willfully, he would not have threatened the plaintiff's safety, so far as appearances could warn him. His conduct would not have involved, even then, an unreasonable probability of invasion of her bodily security. Liability can be no greater where the act is inadvertent. . . .

The law of causation, remote or proximate, is thus foreign to the case before us. The question of liability is always anterior to the question of the measure of the consequences that go with liability. If there is no tort to be redressed, there is no occasion to consider what damage might be recovered if there were a finding of a tort. We may assume, without deciding, that negligence, not at large or in the abstract, but in relation to the plaintiff, would entail liability for any and all consequences, however novel or extraordinary. There is room for argument that a distinction is to be drawn according to the diversity of interests invaded by the act, as where conduct negligent in that it threatens an insignificant invasion of an interest in property results in an unforeseeable invasion of an interest of another order, as, e.g., one of bodily security. Perhaps other distinctions may be necessary. We do not go into the question now. The consequences to be followed must first be rooted in a wrong.

The judgment of the Appellate Division and that of the Trial Term should be reversed, and the complaint dismissed, with costs in all courts.

ANDREWS, J. (dissenting.) . . .

[1: Duty runs to the world at large and negligence
toward one is negligence to all]

The result we shall reach depends upon our theory as to the nature of negligence. Is it a relative concept—the breach of some duty owing to a particular person or to particular persons? Or where there is an act which unreasonably threatens the safety of others, is the doer liable for all its proximate consequences, even where they result in injury to one who would generally be thought to be outside the radius of danger? This is not a mere dispute as to words. We might not believe that to the average mind the dropping of the bundle would seem to involve the probability of harm to the plaintiff standing many feet away whatever might be the case as to the owner or to one so near as to be likely to be struck by its fall. If, however, we adopt the second hypothesis, we have to inquire only as to the relation between cause and effect. We deal in terms of proximate cause, not of negligence. . . .

But we are told that "there is no negligence unless there is in the particular case a legal duty to take care, and this duty must be one which is owed to the plaintiff himself and not merely to others." Salmond Torts (6th Ed.) 24. This I think too narrow a conception. Where there is the unreasonable act, and some right that may be affected there is negligence whether damage does or does not result. That is immaterial. Should we drive down Broadway at a reckless speed, we are negligent whether we strike an approaching car or miss it by an inch. The act itself is wrongful. It is a wrong not only to those who happen to be within the radius of danger, but to all who might have been there—a wrong to the public at large. . . .

It may well be that there is no such thing as negligence in the abstract. "Proof of negligence in the air, so to speak, will not do." In an empty world negligence would not exist. It does involve a relationship between man and his fellows, but not merely a relationship between man and those whom he might reasonably expect his act would injure; rather, a relationship between him and those whom he does in fact injure. If his act has a tendency to harm some one, it harms him a mile away as surely as it does those on the scene. . . .

In the well-known *Polemis* Case, [1921] 3 K.B. 560, Scrutton, L.J., said that the dropping of a plank was negligent, for it might injure "workman or cargo or ship." Because of either possibility, the owner of the vessel was to be made good for his loss. The act being wrongful, the doer was liable for its proximate results.[1] . . .

---

[1] The facts that made these statements significant were probably known to many of Judge Andrews' readers. Workers on deck negligently caused a wooden plank to fall into the hold, no doubt risking injury to workmen below, to goods, or even to the ship, but not foreseeably risking a fire. Nevertheless, the wood somehow sparked a fire that destroyed the ship and those responsible for the workmen's negligence were held liable for this startling result.—Eds.

The proposition is this: Every one owes to the world at large the duty of refraining from those acts that may unreasonably threaten the safety of others. Such an act occurs.... Unreasonable risk being taken, its consequences are not confined to those who might probably be hurt....

[2: Liability is limited by proximate cause, not by defining the scope of duty or negligence]

The right to recover damages rests on additional considerations. The plaintiff's rights must be injured, and this injury must be caused by the negligence. We build a dam, but are negligent as to its foundations. Breaking, it injures property down stream. We are not liable if all this happened because of some reason other than the insecure foundation. But, when injuries do result from our unlawful act, we are liable for the consequences. It does not matter that they are unusual, unexpected, unforeseen, and unforeseeable. But there is one limitation. The damages must be so connected with the negligence that the latter may be said to be the proximate cause of the former.

[3: Proximate cause is determined by several factors, not by the scope of the defendant's negligence]

These two words have never been given an inclusive definition. What is a cause in a legal sense, still more what is a proximate cause, depend in each case upon many considerations, as does the existence of negligence itself. Any philosophical doctrine of causation does not help us. A boy throws a stone into a pond. The ripples spread. The water level rises. The history of that pond is altered to all eternity. It will be altered by other causes also. Yet it will be forever the resultant of all causes combined. Each one will have an influence. How great only omniscience can say. You may speak of a chain, or, if you please, a net. An analogy is of little aid. Each cause brings about future events. Without each the future would not be the same. Each is proximate in the sense it is essential. But that is not what we mean by the word. Nor on the other hand do we mean sole cause. There is no such thing.

Should analogy be thought helpful, however, I prefer that of a stream. The spring, starting on its journey, is joined by tributary after tributary. The river, reaching the ocean, comes from a hundred sources. No man may say whence any drop of water is derived. Yet for a time distinction may be possible. Into the clear creek, brown swamp water flows from the left. Later, from the right comes water stained by its clay bed. The three may remain for a space, sharply divided. But at last inevitably no trace of separation remains. They are so commingled that all distinction is lost.

As we have said, we cannot trace the effect of an act to the end, if end there is. Again, however, we may trace it part of the way. A murder at Serajevo may be the necessary antecedent to an assassination in London twenty years hence. An overturned lantern may burn all Chicago. We may follow the fire from the shed to the last building. We rightly say the fire started by the lantern caused its destruction.

A cause, but not the proximate cause. What we do mean by the word "proximate" is that, because of convenience, of public policy, of a rough sense of justice, the law arbitrarily declines to trace a series of events beyond a certain point. This is not logic. It is practical politics. Take our rule as to fires. Sparks from my burning haystack set on fire my house and my neighbor's. I may recover from a negligent railroad. He may not. Yet the wrongful act as directly harmed the one as the other. We may regret the line was drawn just where it was, but drawn somewhere it had to be. We said the act of the railroad was not the proximate cause of our neighbor's fire. Cause it surely was. The words we used were simply indicative of our notions of public policy. Other courts think differently. But somewhere they reach the point where they cannot say the stream comes from any one source. . . .

There are some hints that may help us. The proximate cause, involved as it may be with many other causes, must be, at the least, something without which the event would not happen. The court must ask itself whether there was a natural and continuous sequence between cause and effect. Was the one a substantial factor in producing the other? Was there a direct connection between them, without too many intervening causes? Is the effect of cause on result not too attenuated? Is the cause likely, in the usual judgment of mankind, to produce the result? Or, by the exercise of prudent foresight, could the result be foreseen? Is the result too remote from the cause, and here we consider remoteness in time and space. . . . Clearly we must so consider, for the greater the distance either in time or space, the more surely do other causes intervene to affect the result. When a lantern is overturned, the firing of a shed is a fairly direct consequence. Many things contribute to the spread of the conflagration—the force of the wind, the direction and width of streets, the character of intervening structures, other factors. We draw an uncertain and wavering line, but draw it we must as best we can. . . .

Once again, it is all a question of fair judgment, always keeping in mind the fact that we endeavor to make a rule in each case that will be practical and in keeping with the general understanding of mankind. . . .

In fairness he would make good every injury flowing from his negligence. Not because of tenderness toward him we say he need not answer for all that follows his wrong. We look back to the catastrophe, the fire kindled by the spark, or the explosion. We trace the consequences, not indefinitely, but to a certain point. And to aid us in fixing that point we ask what might ordinarily be expected to follow the fire or the explosion.

This last suggestion is the factor which must determine the case before us. The act upon which defendant's liability rests is knocking an apparently harmless package onto the platform. The act was negligent. For its proximate consequences the defendant is liable. If its contents were broken, to the owner; if it fell upon and crushed a passenger's foot, then to him; if it exploded and injured one in the immediate vicinity, to him also. . . . Mrs. Palsgraf was standing some distance away. How far cannot be told from the record—apparently 25 or 30 feet, perhaps less. Except for the explosion, she would not have been injured. We are told by the appellant in his brief, "It cannot be denied that the explosion was the direct cause of the plaintiff's injuries." So it was a substantial factor in producing the result—there was here a natural and continuous sequence—direct connection. The only intervening cause was that, instead of blowing her to the ground, the concussion smashed the weighing machine which in turn fell upon her. There was no remoteness in time, little in space. And surely, given such an explosion as here, it needed no great foresight to predict that the natural result would be to injure one on the platform at no greater distance from its scene than was the plaintiff. Just how no one might be able to predict. Whether by flying fragments, by broken glass, by wreckage of machines or structures no one could say. But injury in some form was most probable.

Under these circumstances I cannot say as a matter of law that the plaintiff's injuries were not the proximate result of the negligence. That is all we have before us. The court refused to so charge. No request was made to submit the matter to the jury as a question of fact, even would that have been proper upon the record before us.

NOTES

1.   **Integrating *Palsgraf* and *Thompson*.** Reading *Palsgraf* and *Thompson* together, we can say that the defendant is liable only for harms within the scope of the risks defendant negligently created. More specifically, the defendant is liable only (a) for types of injuries foreseeably risked by his negligence and (b) to classes of persons foreseeably risked by his negligence. In other words, the defendant is not liable unless a reasonable person in defendant's circumstances should have foreseen that defendant's conduct risked injuries of the same general type that occurred to a general class of persons within which the plaintiff is found. Professors John Goldberg and Ben Zipursky call the *Palsgraf* rule a "substantive standing or proper-plaintiff principle." That is, a "requirement that the defendant breach a duty of care owed to the plaintiff (or a person situated as was the plaintiff in relation to the defendant's conduct), instead of breaching a duty of care owed only to someone else." RECOGNIZING WRONGS 201 (2020).

2.   **Was the defendant negligent?** Could Cardozo have just as easily said that the defendant was not negligent at all, towards anyone? If a reasonable person would foresee no harm to anyone as a result of the person's conduct we do not need to reach the proximate cause issue. Why not?

3. **Foreseeable injury.** If some kind of harm could have been foreseen in *Palsgraf*, to what class of persons should the guard have foreseen injury? Suppose the guard's push caused the man with the package to knock over a passenger who was already on the train. Would harm to that passenger have been foreseeable? Was Mrs. Palsgraf within that same class of persons? Modern cases often free a defendant from liability where the plaintiff is not within a class foreseeably risked by the negligent conduct. *See, e.g., Mellon Mortgage Co. v. Holder*, 5 S.W.3d 654 (Tex. 1999) (woman raped in defendant Mellon's parking garage by a policeman who had pulled her over several blocks away was "not a member of [a] class . . . that Mellon could have reasonably foreseen would be the victim of a criminal act in its garage"). However, the Restatement (Third) of Torts now suggests that no separate reference need be made to unforeseeable plaintiffs. Could you characterize the harm in *Palsgraf* as a different type of harm than that risked by the conductor's negligence? *See* RESTATEMENT (THIRD) OF TORTS: LIABILITY FOR PHYSICAL AND EMOTIONAL HARM § 29 cmt. n, illus. 9 (2010).

4. **Cardozo's duty/negligence locution compared to proximate cause language.** In *Palsgraf*, Cardozo seemed concerned with scope of risk but did not invoke the concept of proximate cause by that name. Instead, Cardozo concluded that "[r]elatively to her it was not negligence at all," because no harm to her was foreseeable. Although expressed in terms of duty or negligence, the rule is just like one that asserts the defendant's conduct is not a proximate cause when the defendant could not foresee harm to persons situated like the plaintiff. However, who decides duty and who decides proximate cause?

5. **Jury role.** Scope of risk is a matter that must necessarily be determined on the facts of each case. Consequently, when the question is about the scope of risk, the question is usually one for the jury so long as reasonable people could differ. *Rascher v. Friend*, 689 S.E.2d 661 (Va. 2010) ("[W]hether an act was a proximate cause of an event is best determined by a jury. This is so simply because the particular facts of each case are critical to that determination."); *Georgia Dep't of Human Res. v. Bulbalia*, 694 S.E.2d 115 (Ga. Ct. App. 2010). Why did Cardozo, then, refuse to permit a jury to decide foreseeability in *Palsgraf*?

6. **Andrews: rejecting the duty/negligence locution.** Judge Andrews, dissenting, tried to establish two points. First, he argued that a person who is negligent to *any* class of persons is negligent to everyone who is in fact injured. He rejected Cardozo's effort to deal with the issue as one of duty or negligence. Instead, for Andrews, the issue became one of proximate cause.

7. **Andrews: the limited role of foreseeability in proximate cause determinations.** Andrews' second point was that proximate cause was *not* a matter of foreseeability alone. For Andrews, proximate cause was a matter of a host of factors. Since it was not foreseeability alone that determined proximate cause for Andrews, he would not allow the railroad to escape

liability for its supposed negligence merely because no reasonable person would expect the package to cause harm to someone a distance away.

8. **Adopting a scope of risk or foreseeability approach.** When courts are concerned with the scope-of-risk question, they have often adopted Andrews' proximate cause locution but Cardozo's foreseeability test. The result is that decisions on proximate cause today almost always emphasize foreseeability in some form as a limitation on liability. They are thus scope-of-risk cases. Only a few cases continue to reflect some affinity with Andrews' view that liability could be imposed for types of harm or to classes of person who were not reasonably foreseeable victims, and even these may find policy reasons against liability beyond the scope of the risk in particular cases. *See Fandrey v. American Family Mut. Ins. Co.*, 680 N.W.2d 345 (Wis. 2004).

9. **Limits based on *Palsgraf*.** Cardozo invoked a scope-of-risk rule, but expressed it by saying either that the railroad was not negligent toward Mrs. Palsgraf or by saying it owed her no duty of care. Some courts today use this "no duty" or "limited duty" terminology in adjudicating scope-of-risk questions based on foreseeability, saying a defendant owes no duty of care if the type of harm is not foreseeable. *See Wiener v. Southcoast Childcare Ctrs., Inc.*, 88 P.3d 517 (Cal. 2004); *Valcaniant v. Detroit Edison Co.*, 679 N.W.2d 689 (Mich. 2004).

The disaggregation of duty—duty *to the plaintiff*—is also language from Cardozo's *Palsgraf* opinion that courts have used to limit duty. In *Quiroz v. ALCOA Inc.*, 416 P.3d 824 (Ariz. 2018), Ernest Quiroz died of mesothelioma, allegedly as a result of 18 years of exposure to asbestos fibers carried home on his father's work clothes. Ernest's family's sued his father's employer. Holding that "the employer owed no duty to the public regarding secondary asbestos exposure," the court quoted Cardozo: " 'Proof of negligence in the air, so to speak, will not do. . . . One who seeks redress at law does not make out a cause of action' by merely showing he has been injured, or that another has engaged in wrongful conduct; rather, 'plaintiff must show . . . a wrong to herself; i.e., a violation of her own right, and not merely a wrong to some one else, nor conduct wrongful because unsocial, but not a wrong to any one.' " Could you agree with Cardozo's foreseeability principle, and even his use of the duty locution, yet still disagree with its use in *Quiroz*? *See Quisenberry v. Huntington Ingalls Inc.*, 818 S.E.2d 805, 810 (Va. 2018) (duty to child in second-hand asbestos exposure case, citing *Palsgraf*, "the existence of a duty does not depend on proving a particular relationship . . . in the vast majority of negligence actions, the parties were strangers at the time of the incident, and the action is based upon the broad duty . . . not to injure others by acts of omission or commission"). To what class of persons do you foresee harm when you send toxic chemicals home with an employee?

NOTE: THE RESCUE DOCTRINE

How does the risk rule work in this kind of case: Defendant negligently creates a risk to *A*. *B*, who was not subject to the risk or who escaped it, attempts to rescue *A* and is hurt in the process. Defendant, having created a risk to *A*, is liable to A. Is defendant also liable to *B*? *Palsgraf* might lead one to answer that defendant is not liable to B, or that the issue would turn on whether rescue would be foreseeable in the particular situation at the time defendant was guilty of negligence. Judge Cardozo's own answer, however, was otherwise.

In *Wagner v. International Railway*, 133 N.E. 437 (N.Y. 1921), the railway permitted passengers to stand in between the cars while the train was moving over a high trestle. One of them fell off into a gorge as the train rounded a curve. The plaintiff attempted to climb down to locate the victim, who was his cousin. In the course of this attempt, the plaintiff himself was injured. Cardozo, speaking in his Delphic manner, held that the railway was liable to the rescuer. "Danger invites rescue," he said, suggesting, perhaps, that rescue is foreseeable or is foreseeable as a matter of law. But he added a few sentences later: "The wrongdoer may not have foreseen the coming of a deliverer. He is accountable as if he had." The latter statement might be read as rejecting any criterion of foreseeability, or it might be read to mean only that a reasonable person would have foreseen rescue, whether the defendant subjectively foresaw it or not.

Whatever Cardozo meant, the cases have generally agreed that the rescuer can recover from the defendant whose negligence prompts the rescue if the rescuer had a reasonable belief that the victim was in peril. *See, e.g., Rasmussen v. State Farm Mut. Auto. Ins. Co.*, 770 N.W.2d 619 (Neb. 2009); *Clinkscales v. Nelson Secs., Inc.*, 697 N.W.2d 836 (Iowa 2005).

Rescue does not always involve physical intervention. In *Garcia v. Colorado Cab Co. LLC*, 467 P.3d 302 (Colo. 2020), a cab driver was being beaten by an angry and inebriated passenger. The plaintiff rescuer shouted at the passenger to stop and the passenger then turned his aggression toward the plaintiff, running the intervenor down with the car and causing severe injuries. Plaintiff qualified as a rescuer by whom the cab company could be sued for negligence for not installing driver partitions or security cameras despite 44 attacks on cab drivers in the prior three years.

Should the rescue doctrine apply when the rescuer is attempting to save property rather than persons? In *Jacobson v. Ron*, 2009 WL 144992 (Tex. App. 2009), defendant purchased property from plaintiff's family trust and began demolishing the building before paying off the note. Plaintiff was injured while attempting to rescue the building and stop demolition. What result?

NOTE: VIOLATION OF STATUTE AND "PROXIMATE CAUSE"

As we saw in Chapter 5, in most states, violation of a non-tort statute is "negligence per se," but this rule is conditioned upon a finding that the statute was designed to protect against the type of harm that occurred and the class of persons to which the plaintiff is a member.

A well-known and very clear example of this is *Larrimore v. American National Insurance Co.*, 89 P.2d 340 (Okla. 1939). A statute forbade laying out poisons. The defendant provided a rat poison to its tenant, a coffee shop. The coffee shop put the poison near the coffee burner. The plaintiff was injured when she lit the burner because the poison exploded due to its phosphorous content. The trial judge, as trier of fact, found for the defendant. The Supreme Court of Oklahoma affirmed, commenting:

> It is not enough for a plaintiff to show that the defendant neglected a duty imposed by statute. He must go further and show that his injury was caused by his exposure to a hazard from which it was the purpose of the statute to protect him. . . . Those only to whom [the statutory] duty is due and who have sustained injuries of the character its discharge was designed to prevent can maintain actions for its breach.

The court is stating the fundamental scope-of-risk rule as applied to a statutory liability, isn't it?

§ 2. ASSESSING THE SCOPE OF THE RISK

A. IS HARM OUTSIDE THE SCOPE OF THE RISK BECAUSE OF THE MANNER IN WHICH IT OCCURS?

RUIZ v. VICTORY PROPERTIES LLC

107 A.3d 381 (Conn. 2015)

PALMER, J. . . .

The plaintiff Olga Rivera (Olga) commenced this negligence action, both in her individual capacity and as next friend and parent of the named plaintiff, Adriana Ruiz (Adriana), against their landlord, the defendant, Victory Properties, LLC. . . .

[Th]e defendant owned and managed a six-family apartment building. . . . Children who lived in the apartment, along with other visiting children, regularly used the apartment's backyard as a playground, even though it was in very poor condition. In particular, it contained discarded home furnishings and appliances, and an abandoned motor vehicle in a state of complete disrepair. In addition, as a result of the deteriorating concrete sidewalks and retaining walls, chunks of concrete were lying about, along with piles of construction material, trash and rocks. Parents of the children playing in this area were concerned because the children would play with the debris, including the broken concrete. The defendant's owner, who also served as the apartment manager, was aware of the condition of this area because a tenant had complained to him about it, and he personally observed the area when he visited the property each month to collect rent money. Nevertheless, the defendant made no effort to remove or cordon off the debris so that children playing in the area would not have access to it. . . .

On May 14, 2008 . . . 10 year-old Luis Cruz (Luis) . . . decided that he wanted to see if he could break a piece of concrete. To that end, at about 4 p.m., Luis picked up a piece of concrete from the backyard that weighed approximately eighteen pounds, carried it up to his family's third floor apartment, and dropped it from the window or balcony of that apartment to the ground below. Luis saw his cousin Adriana below and yelled, urging her to get out of the way, but the rock struck her on the head, causing very serious injuries, including a crushed skull, traumatic brain injury and paralysis on her right side. As a result of these injuries, Adriana had two surgeries and had been hospitalized for nearly two months.

The plaintiffs subsequently commenced this action against the defendant, alleging that the defendant was negligent in failing to remove the loose concrete and other debris from the backyard of the apartment building, and that this negligence was a cause of Adriana's injuries because it was a substantial factor in producing those injuries. The defendant filed a motion for summary judgment. . . . The trial court granted the defendant's motion, concluding that the defendant did not owe Adriana a duty of care because a reasonable landlord in the defendant's position, knowing that there were pieces of broken concrete and other debris in the backyard of the apartment building, would not have foreseen that a child would injure another child by "lugging a piece of concrete up to the balcony of the building and pitching it off, onto the head of the other child. . . ." The trial court further concluded that permitting a jury to find liability under the facts of this case "would likely discourage landlords from renting apartments to families with young children. It would surely drive up the economic costs associated with maintaining and insuring rental properties, without a concomitant benefit of safeguarding against conditions and hazards that are much more prevalent than the one here." . . .

The Appellate Court reversed the trial court's judgment, concluding that the trial court, in evaluating whether Adriana's injuries were foreseeable, failed to consider whether the harm that she suffered was within the general scope of the risk created by the defendant's failure to remove potentially dangerous debris from the backyard and, instead, improperly focused on the specific manner in which the injuries occurred. In other words, the Appellate Court determined that the trial court had framed the nature of the risk in too narrow of terms. In its view, the risk of harm created by the defendant's conduct was not, as the trial court had concluded, a child carrying a piece of concrete to a third floor apartment and dropping it to the backyard below but, rather, that of a child "getting hurt by a large piece of concrete thrown by another child," conduct that, according to the Appellate Court, a fact finder reasonably could find to be foreseeable. . . .

[We] affirm the judgment of the Appellate Court. . . . [The Court first addressed the land owner's duty. It then turned to the issue of proximate cause]. . . . Because actual causation, in theory, is virtually limitless, the legal construct of proximate cause serves to establish how far down the causal continuum tortfeasors will be held liable for the consequences of their actions. . . . [T]he inquiry fundamental to all proximate cause questions [is] whether the harm that occurred was of the same general nature as the foreseeable risk created by the defendant's negligence. . . .

[A]s this court previously has explained, "[as] long as harm of the general nature as that which occurred is foreseeable there is a basis for liability even though the manner in which the accident happens is unusual, bizarre or unforeseeable." *Lodge v. Arett Sales Corp.,* 246 Conn. 563, 587, 717 A.2d 215 (1998) (*Berdon, J.,* dissenting) (focus of foreseeability inquiry should be "on the general nature of the harm and not the specific manner in which the injury occurred or the conduct of a third party"); *Figlar v. Gordon,* 133 Conn. 577, 581–82, 53 A.2d 645 (1947) (foreseeability "does not mean that one charged with negligence must be found actually to have foreseen the probability of harm or that the particular injury which resulted was foreseeable, but the test is, would the ordinary man in the defendant's position, knowing what he knew or should have known, anticipate that harm of the general nature of that suffered was likely to result"). Thus, as the Appellate Court further explained, "[a]lthough a jury might find it not foreseeable that a ten year old child would carry a large [piece of concrete] up to a third floor balcony, throw it off, and hit someone below, defining the harm of the general nature in that way as a matter of law would be too specific; it would transform the general nature of the harm into the specific way in which the harm occurred." *Ruiz v. Victory Properties, LLC,* supra, at 127, 43 A.3d 186.

Comment (i) to § 29 of the Restatement (Third) of Torts underscores this point: "Courts often respond to efforts by advocates to employ excessive detail in characterizing the type of harm in order to make it appear more unforeseeable with the dictum that the manner of harm is irrelevant. Factfinders, no doubt, respond to these efforts with their own judgment and common sense to decide the appropriate specificity with which to assess the scope of liability." 1 Restatement (Third), Torts, Liability for Physical and Emotional Harm § 29, comment (i), p. 504 (2010). . . .

In the present case, the defendant does not dispute that the risk of harm created by its failure to remove the buckets, trash, broken concrete pieces and other debris from the backyard was that children playing in the area might trip on them or throw them at other children. The types of injuries one would expect to result from this type of behavior run the gamut from cuts and bruises to broken bones, concussions and even fractured skulls. Adriana's injuries, although severe, fall squarely along this continuum of harm. That they occurred in an unusual manner, namely, by a child dropping a piece of concrete into the backyard playground from a third floor balcony instead of throwing it while in the backyard, does not alter this fundamental fact. We therefore agree with the Appellate Court that Adriana's injuries were sufficiently foreseeable that it was inappropriate for the trial court to foreclose the foreseeability question as a matter of law. . . . Conclusions of proximate cause are to be drawn by the jury and not by the court. . . . The judgment of the Appellate court is affirmed.

ZARELLA, J., with whom McDONALD, J., joins, dissenting. . . .

In my view, the trial court correctly concluded that the defendant, the property owner in this case, did not have a legal duty to prevent ten year old Luis Cruz from taking an eighteen pound piece of cinder block (cinder block) from the backyard of his apartment building, carrying the cinder block up to the balcony of his third story unit, and dropping it on the named plaintiff, Adriana Ruiz, also a tenant in the building, because such conduct was not a reasonably foreseeable consequence of the defendant's leaving the cinder block in the yard. Additionally, public policy dictates that it would be imprudent to allow a jury to hold the defendant responsible for Cruz' conduct, as the majority does today. . . . What further makes the plaintiff's injuries not reasonably foreseeable is the intentional nature of Cruz' conduct. . . . Finally, the harm that the plaintiff suffered was not reasonably foreseeable because there is no evidence in the record that the defendant knew or should have known that either Cruz or other tenants had a propensity for throwing objects from their balconies. . . .

The majority unduly broadens the foreseeability inquiry to a level of generality at which every conceivable accident involving the cinder block that Cruz used to injure the plaintiff would be deemed foreseeable. While it is true that the foreseeability inquiry should not narrowly focus on the manner in which the plaintiff was injured, it is incorrect to suggest that the circumstances giving rise to the plaintiff's injuries are never relevant. To the contrary, the majority concedes that determining the foreseeability of a plaintiff's injuries involves a fact-sensitive inquiry; and a survey of our case law reveals that we often have considered the manner in which a plaintiff's injuries occurred to be highly relevant to the foreseeability inquiry. . . . Section 29 of the Restatement (Third) of Torts . . . supports the view that the manner in which a plaintiff is injured is relevant to the foreseeability analysis, as comment (*o*) to that section provides: "Some aspects of the manner in which the harm occurs *are* relevant to a determination of the scope of an actor's liability. . . . [T]he manner of harm can be of critical importance in determining whether the harm is within the scope of liability. . . ." § 29, comment (*o*), pp. 509–10. . . .

[L]ogically, this makes sense. If the manner in which the plaintiff was injured was irrelevant, as the majority concludes, then the defendant could have been held liable even if Cruz had brought the cinder block to his third story unit and left it there for three days before deciding to throw it off the balcony. Likewise, according to the majority, the defendant could have been held liable if Cruz had taken the cinder block from the backyard, carried it to a different apartment building, and injured someone there. Such absurd results demonstrate that the manner of the harm is, as the Restatement (Third) of Torts indicates, crucial to determining the foreseeability of a plaintiff's injury. . . . I would conclude, as a matter of law, that protecting the plaintiff from Cruz was outside the scope of the defendant's legal duty.

NOTES

1. **Manner of harm vs. type of injury.** There is obviously much room for judicial judgment in characterizing the risks that are foreseeable. Courts often say that in order to hold a defendant liable, the precise manner of harm need not be foreseeable if the general type of harm was foreseeable. How does the majority in both the Supreme Court and Appellate Court in *Ruiz* characterize the type of harm? How does the dissent and the trial court before it characterize the type of harm? Which is most persuasive to you?

2. **Level of generality.** How foreseeable the harm is may depend on the level of generality with which it is described. If the type of harm risked in *Ruiz* was a child being injured by the mishandling of the broken concrete, isn't that the type of harm that occurred? If the type of harm is instead described very specifically, as by the dissent in its opening line, the type of harm risked might be different from that which occurred. What is the appropriate level of generality to use for characterizing the risk of harm? The Restatement (Third) of Torts leaves these matters to factfinders' "judgment and common sense." RESTATEMENT (THIRD) OF TORTS: LIABILITY FOR PHYSICAL AND EMOTIONAL HARM § 29 cmt. i (2010). Do you think common sense would lead all factfinders to the same conclusion? Does this make the role of the jury more important? Does it also make the lawyers' role more important?

3. **Another example.** In *Darby v. National Trust*, [2001] P.I.Q.R. 27 (C.A., Civ.), a healthy adult man drowned in a murky pond on the grounds of a large English estate owned by the National Trust and held open for recreational use. The plaintiff (the man's wife and estate) sued the National Trust, claiming that it was negligent in failing to prevent swimming in the pond, either by posting signage or by providing in-person warnings by rangers. The plaintiff relied in part on an expert witness who testified that the ponds

on the estate were particularly unsuited for swimming because of the risk of swimmers contracting Weils disease, "an unpleasant and occasionally fatal condition transmitted from rats' urine." The judges of the English Court of Appeal held that the defendant was not liable, one of them concluding, "Unpleasant though Weils disease, I have no doubt, is, it was not the kind of risk or damage which Mr Darby suffered, and any duty to warn against Weils disease, cannot, in my judgment, support a claim for damages resulting from a quite different cause." If one risk of swimming in this murky pool was death (perhaps from Weils disease), and death did in fact occur (albeit from drowning), is the court making liability turn on the way that the death occurred?

4. **Unforeseeable third-party actions.** Some courts do appear to require foreseeability of many details about the manner in which an injury occurred. In such cases the negligent defendant escapes responsibility even when defendant should have foreseen the precise injury that occurred, because defendant could not foresee the precise *manner* in which it occurred. In *Morguson v. 3M Co.*, 857 So.2d 796 (Ala. 2003), the defendant manufactured a heart-lung machine, but its design left it possible that it would be wrongly connected with potentially deadly results. That, in fact, happened. In an operation on the decedent, the perfusionist set up the machine so the blood flowed the wrong way and the patient died. The court focused on the fact that although the machine's design made misconnection and death foreseeable, the perfusionist's later specific acts in failing to check the connection then falsely claiming he had, were not. That was enough to hold that the defendant was not responsible. Do you foresee any problems with such an approach? We will see more about foreseeability of particular details in the intervening cause section.

5. **Next friend.** A "next friend" is a "person who appears in a lawsuit to act for the benefit of an incompetent or minor plaintiff, but who is not a party to the lawsuit and is not appointed as a guardian." *Branham v. Stewart*, 307 S.W.3d 94 (Ky. 2010) (quoting BLACK'S LAW DICTIONARY (8th ed. 2004)). In *Ruiz*, the parent is suing the tortfeasor for the benefit of the injured child, and independently for her own loss.

B. IS HARM OUTSIDE THE SCOPE OF THE RISK BECAUSE ITS EXTENT IS UNFORESEEABLE?

HAMMERSTEIN V. JEAN DEVELOPMENT WEST, 907 P.2d 975 (Nev. 1995). Plaintiff, about 70 years of age, was a guest at the defendant's hotel. As the hotel knew, he was a diabetic. Walking up and down stairs was bad for him, but there were no rooms on the ground floor and besides, there was an elevator. In the early morning hours a fire alarm went off. Elevators were locked and plaintiff had to walk down from the fourth floor. In doing so he twisted his ankle. Much later, on returning to his room, he found a blister on his foot. This eventually became a gangrenous infection probably because of his diabetes, which interferes with circulation in the lower extremities. There was in fact no fire and the fire alarm system had gone off without a fire on numerous occasions but had never been corrected. *Held,* summary judgment for the defendant was error. "It should have been foreseeable to Nevada Landing that if its fire alarm system was unreasonably faulty, harm to a certain type of plaintiff, i.e., one of its guests, could result. Also, this particular variety of harm, injuring an ankle or foot on the way down a stairwell, is a foreseeable variety of harm in this circumstance. The extent of the infection on Hammerstein's leg may not have been foreseeable, but the underlying injury should have been."

NOTES

1. **The thin-skull rule.** The term "thin skull" or "eggshell skull" is widely used in tort law in reference to some variant on the following facts. Defendant negligently strikes the plaintiff. The blow is such that a normal person would suffer only slight injury, such as a bruise. The plaintiff, however, has an unusually thin skull, a fact the defendant does not know. As a result of the minor blow, the plaintiff suffers terrible injuries. If the defendant is in fact guilty of tort—that is, if defendant was negligent or guilty of intentional harm—then the fact that the harm was much worse than anyone would have expected does not limit his liability. This is the thin-skull rule. It is often generalized by saying that the defendant "takes the plaintiff as he finds him," that is, with whatever extra damages the plaintiff might have because the plaintiff has a "thin skull," or has diabetes, or is pregnant, or suffers hemophilia, or is otherwise pre-disposed to suffer more. A leading case is *McCahill v. New York Transportation Co.*, 94 N.E. 616 (N.Y. 1911). There the defendant ran into the plaintiff, who suffered a broken thigh. In the hospital plaintiff began to suffer delirium tremens, from which he died. This resulted only because of a pre-existing alcoholic condition. The defendant took the plaintiff as he found him and was held liable for his death.

2. **Liability for the aggravation of the preexisting condition.** The thin-skull rule does not make the tortfeasor liable for the preexisting condition itself; rather, the rule calls for liability for any *aggravation* of that original condition that is caused by the defendant's negligence, even where that aggravation was unforeseeable. *See Harris v. ShopKo Stores, Inc.*, 308 P.3d 449 (Utah 2013).

3. **No liability without fault.** The thin-skull cases do not impose liability without fault. The defendant's act must have been one that would cause some harm to an ordinary person, or the defendant must have been at fault because defendant knew or should have known of the plaintiff's susceptible condition. *See Triplett v. River Region Medical Corp.*, 50 So.3d 1032 (Miss. Ct. App. 2010) (thin-skull rule does not cover injuries stemming from the aggravation of preexisting conditions if the patient fails to inform her doctors of the preexisting condition prior to surgery). The thin-skull rule merely holds that the defendant does not escape liability for the unforeseeable

personal reactions of the plaintiff, once negligence or intentional fault is established.

4.   **A broader principle.** The thin-skull rule may reflect a broader principle, and indeed that is the way the court in *Hammerstein* articulated its holding: a defendant may be liable for the full extent of a plaintiff's harm, even where the extent of that harm was unforeseeable, where the other elements of a prima facie case are established. In a famous English case, *Smith v. London & South Western Railway*, L.R. 6 C.P. 14 (1870), a judge articulated the principle quite well:

> If a man fires a gun across a road where he may reasonably anticipate that persons will be passing, and hits someone, he is guilty of negligence, and liable for the injury he has caused; but if he fires in his own wood, where he cannot reasonably anticipate that any one will be, he is not liable to any one whom he shoots, which shews that what a person may reasonably anticipate is important in considering whether he has been negligent; but if a person fires across a road when it is dangerous to do so and kills a man who is in the receipt of a large income, he will be liable for the whole damage, however great, that may have resulted to his family, and cannot set up that he could not have reasonably expected to have injured any one but a labourer.

The thin-skull principle is well-settled. *See* RESTATEMENT (THIRD) OF TORTS: LIABILITY FOR PHYSICAL AND EMOTIONAL HARM § 29 cmt. p (2010). Is it consistent with the scope-of-risk rule?

§ 3. INTERVENING CAUSES

NOTE: SCOPE OF RISK AND NATURAL AND CONTINUOUS SEQUENCE

Imagine this case: Tortfeasor A leaves an unlighted excavation in the sidewalk. Tortfeasor B negligently jostles the plaintiff, causing him to fall into the excavation.

"The proximate cause of an injury is that which, in a natural and continuous sequence, unbroken by any efficient intervening cause, produces an injury, and without which the injury would not have occurred."

These words and others very similar have been used in literally hundreds of American cases. Many courts continue to define "proximate cause" in terms of a "natural and continuous sequence unbroken by any intervening cause." *See, e.g., McIlroy v. Gibson's Apple Orchard,* 43 A.3d 948 (Me. 2012); *Kellermann v. McDonough,* 684 S.E.2d 786 (Va. 2009). This language has done quite a bit to obscure issues and principles. For one thing, courts have recognized repeatedly, and we ourselves have seen, that there may be many tortfeasors who are all liable and thus all proximate causes. When judges speak of "the" proximate cause rather than "a" proximate cause, they may be pushing the jury to an unconscious bias against finding both tortfeasors liable. *See, e.g., Holmes v. Levine*, 639 S.E.2d 235 (Va. 2007) (jury instruction that the plaintiff had to prove that defendant's negligence was "*the* proximate cause of the death of [decedent]" was reversible error, where evidence indicated that there could be other proximate causes of the death).

When tortfeasors act in sequence, the first tortfeasor often argues that the second tortfeasor's act is an "intervening cause" that "supersedes" the first tortfeasor's liability entirely. Courts often use metaphorical rather than principled language here: a superseding cause breaks the causal chain.

The emphasis on intervening causes and causal chains has obscured the more fundamental scope-of-risk principle: An intervening act of some second tortfeasor should relieve the first tortfeasor of liability only when the resulting harm is outside the scope of the risk negligently created by the first tortfeasor. An "intervening cause that lies within the scope of the foreseeable risk, or has a reasonable connection to it, is not a superseding cause." *Fancyboy v. Alaska Village Elec. Co-op., Inc.*, 984 P.2d 1128 (Alaska 1999).

A. INTENTIONAL OR CRIMINAL INTERVENING ACTS

MARCUS V. STAUBS
736 S.E.2d 360 (W.Va. 2012)

PER CURIAM: . . .

This case involves a single-car automobile accident which resulted in the death of 14-year-old Samantha Staubs (hereinafter "Samantha") and serious injury to her sister, 13-year-old Jessica Staubs (hereinafter "Jessica"). Both were passengers in a vehicle stolen and driven by 14-year-old Misty Johnson (hereinafter "Misty"), who was intoxicated. [The alcohol was obtained when 18-year-old defendant Jonathan "Ray" Marcus, picked up some of the girls to take them to a party and on the way drove the group across the West Virginia/Virginia line to a convenience store. At the store, defendant's 26-year-old friend Steven Woodward went in alone and bought four, forty-ounce containers of "Hurricane" brand malt liquor. There was conflicting testimony about whether Marcus had asked Woodward to purchase alcohol for the girls and whether Marcus knew that alcohol was being purchased for that purpose. At the party the girls began drinking the alcohol. A parent came home and told the girls they could not stay the night. There was testimony that Samantha called Marcus for a ride, which he declined to provide.]

Finding no one available to pick them up, Misty and Samantha left [the] house stating they were going to steal a car. They returned minutes later with a truck they stole from neighbor Mack Jenkins and retrieved Kelly and Jessica. Minutes later, with Misty at the wheel and Samantha an unsecured front passenger, the vehicle hit an embankment. Samantha was killed; Jessica sustained a head injury. . . .

Respondent Lori Ann Staubs filed suit as the mother and next friend of Jessica Staubs and as Administratrix of the Estate of Samantha Staubs against petitioner [Marcus] and others. Respondent alleged that petitioner and Woodward negligently "provided" alcohol to the minors. . . .

[Both parties] took the position that the material facts were undisputed. . . . [T]he trial court entered an order denying petitioner's motion for summary judgment and granting respondent [Staub's] cross-motion for summary judgment. . . . The trial court then made the following findings: (1) that petitioner had a duty to both plaintiffs to "obey the law," and that through his role in obtaining the alcohol, he had violated two statutes (2) that by virtue of his violation of these statutes, he was *prima facie* negligent; (3) that by refusing to pick the girls up later in the evening at their request, he was guilty of common law negligence; (4) that his negligence was a proximate cause of the accident; (5) that Misty's actions in stealing the vehicle, driving without a license, and driving intoxicated were not intervening causes . . . [and] as a result of the foregoing, petitioner was liable to respondent. It is from this finding that petitioner appeals. . . .

[The questions of negligence per se and common law breach are for the jury. We turn to the question of proximate cause.]

Petitioner [Marcus] argues that the illegal consumption of alcohol by the minors, the theft of the vehicle, and Misty's reckless operation of the vehicle without a license and while intoxicated, all constitute intervening causes. . . .

[Marcus] essentially argues that criminal acts are *per se* intervening causes. In support, petitioner cites to *Yourtee v. Hubbard,* 196 W. Va. 683, 690, 474 S.E.2d 613, 620 (1996), wherein the Court stated that "[g]enerally, a willful, malicious, or criminal act breaks the chain of causation." Once again, however, petitioner relies on a generality expressed in *dicta* in *Yourtee,* with little regard for the exception discussed therein . . . which states:

> A tortfeasor whose negligence is a substantial factor in bringing about injuries is not relieved from liability by the intervening acts of third persons if those acts were reasonably foreseeable by the original tortfeasor at the time of his negligent conduct.

[Marcus] nevertheless argues that the criminal acts in this case were not reasonably foreseeable by him and therefore, break the chain of causation. . . .

Reasoning

H/O

In the instant case, we find that it is properly within the province of the jury, under proper legal instruction, to determine the measure of petitioner's knowledge of and participation in the procurement of the alcohol, whether the alcohol was "furnished" to the minors, and then, if so, whether given the facts and circumstances leading up to those events, the subsequent acts of the minors and their friends were reasonably foreseeable to petitioner. Therefore, we find the trial court's award of summary judgment improperly invaded the province of the fact-finder in determining whether petitioner's alleged actions were the proximate cause of the accident at issue and whether the subsequent criminal actions constituted intervening causes and, as such, was error.

COLLINS V. SCENIC HOMES, INC., 38 So.3d 28 (Ala. 2009). Scenic Homes constructed an apartment development. It is undisputed that it did not use a licensed architect to design the plan and to draft the building specifications. Discovery indicated that Scenic Homes did not comply with the applicable fire-safety codes. Inadequate fire-retardant building materials were used, the sprinkler system was inadequate, and the windows in the units were too small to provide a viable exit route for persons living in the apartment complex. Twenty years after the complex was built, a fire started there. April Collins died and several others were injured. After an investigation, Henry Rice was arrested for setting the fire, and he ultimately pleaded guilty to arson. The plaintiffs brought suit against Scenic Homes and Russell, the building owner. The trial court granted summary judgment based on the intervening criminal act. *Held*, summary judgment was improper. "The question is whether the injuries allegedly caused by the inability to escape from the fire were the foreseeable result of the alleged failure of Scenic Homes to build and Russell to maintain a reasonably safe building with regard to fire safety. Indeed, it is a foreseeable risk that a fire at an apartment complex, however started, will cause harm to the inhabitants of the complex if the premises owner fails to provide adequate fire-suppression safeguards and an adequate means of escape from the fire. . . . Because the evidence before us indicates that a genuine issue of material fact exists as to whether Scenic Homes constructed and Russell maintained and operated a reasonably safe apartment building with regard to fire safety, the summary judgment for Scenic Homes and Russell is reversed."

NOTES

1.   **History of intervening criminal acts.** In *Watson v. Kentucky & Indiana Bridge & Railroad*, 126 S.W. 146 (Ky. 1910), defendant railroad negligently derailed a gasoline tank car and it sprung a leak. A man named Duerr threw a match into the area; an explosion resulted, causing the plaintiff

injury. The court held that if Duerr acted "for the purpose of causing the explosion," the railroad would not be liable. The railroad "is not bound to anticipate the criminal acts of others by which damage is inflicted." A view common in the 19th and early 20th centuries was that the deliberate infliction of harm by a "moral being," who was adequately informed, free to act, and able to choose, would "supersede" the negligence of the first actor. *See* H.L.A. HART & A.M. HONORE, CAUSATION IN THE LAW 129 (1962); Patrick J. Kelley, *Proximate Cause in Negligence Law: History, Theory, and the Present Darkness*, 69 WASH. U. L.Q. 49, 78–81 (1991). This reasoning sometimes pops up in contemporary cases. *See, e.g., Alston v. Advanced Brands & Importing Co.*, 494 F.3d 562 (6th Cir. 2007) (holding that parents of minor children who were harmed by drinking alcohol lacked standing to sue the beverage manufacturer and importer because "the causal connection between the defendants' [acts] and the plaintiff's alleged injuries is broken by the intervening criminal acts of the third-party sellers and the third-party underage purchasers. . . . A crime is an independent action."); *cf. Mitchell Crane Services, Inc. v. Page*, 126 So.3d 29 (Miss. 2013) (one who negligently leaves a vehicle in a position to be stolen is not liable to a person injured by the thief's negligent operation of the stolen vehicle; "the act of a thief is an intervening and superseding cause" as a matter of law).

2.   **A modern view.** *Watson* was repudiated in *Britton v. Wooten*, 817 S.W.2d 443 (Ky. 1991), where the court said that if the defendant negligently created the increased risk of fire or its spread, the defendant could be held responsible. Today, most courts, in line with *Marcus* and *Collins*, say that criminal acts may be foreseeable, and so within the scope of the created risk. Where reasonable people can differ on foreseeability, this issue is for the jury. *See, e.g., Mitchell v. Cedar Rapids Community School Dist.*, 832 N.W.2d 689 (Iowa 2013) (whether school district's negligence increased the risk that a special-education student would be raped off-campus was a jury question). *Ecker v. E & A Consulting Group, Inc.*, 924 N.W.2d 671 (Neb. 2019) (homeowners sued defendants after their homes were flooded by a "100-year flood," claiming negligence in the design and building of a drainage system; court assumed without deciding that defendants breached a duty of care, but held that "regardless of breach of duty . . . the proximate cause of the homeowners' damages was the magnitude of the storm").

3.   **Framing the foreseeability question.** Look carefully at the way the foreseeability issue is phrased in *Marcus* and the way it is phrased in *Collins*. Do you see a difference? The Restatement Third section on "Intervening Acts and Superseding Causes" states that "When a force of nature or an independent act is also a factual cause of harm, an actor's liability is limited to those harms that result from the risks that made the actor's conduct tortious." RESTATEMENT (THIRD) OF TORTS: LIABILITY FOR PHYSICAL AND EMOTIONAL HARM § 34 (2010). Is that just the ordinary risk rule? Does it make a difference if the court asks if the injuries allegedly caused by the defendant were the foreseeable result of the defendant's alleged negligence or instead if the court asks if the intervening acts of the third persons were reasonably

foreseeable by the defendant? How might the framing of that question matter in *Collins?*

4. **Foreseeability of intervening criminal acts.** Many courts focus on the foreseeability of the intervening criminal act itself. In *Snell v. Norwalk Yellow Cab, Inc.*, 212 A.3d 646 (Conn. 2019), a taxicab driver left the taxi unattended with keys in the ignition. Teenagers stole it and collided with a pedestrian, who sued the cab company for his injuries. In reversing a superseding cause verdict in favor of the cab company, the court wrote, citing Restatement Second § 442B, "tortious or criminal acts may in themselves be foreseeable, and so within the scope of the created risk, in which case the actor may still be liable for the harm." Foreseeability in this context can involve fact questions, as in *Marcus.* What result when a high school football player was battered during a hazing ritual in the high school locker room? *See C.H. v. Los Lunas Schools Bd. of Educ.*, 852 F.Supp.2d 1344 (D.N.M. 2012) ("Loose-running high school students, like loose-running dogs or roaming prison gangs, are capable of violence, and all three situations present a foreseeable danger."). Should prior incidents of hazing by the members of the school's football team make a difference to the determination? What about prior incidents of hazing by another New Mexico high school football team?

5. **A heightened burden?** Courts may be more inclined to hold that criminal intervening acts are unforeseeable as a matter of law, as compared to negligent intervening acts. *See, e.g., Double Quick, Inc. v. Moore*, 73 So.3d 1162 (Miss. 2011) (granting summary judgment in premises liability action against convenience store sued for failing to protect a victim from a fatal shooting). On occasion courts expressly state that the plaintiff's burden to show foreseeability is "heightened" or that the "the foreseeability of the risk be more precisely shown." In *Board of Trustees of Univ. of Dist. of Columbia v. DiSalvo*, 974 A.2d 868 (D.C. 2009), a student at the University of the District of Columbia who was attacked in an unattended underground campus garage failed to show that previous, unrelated criminal activities on the campus provided the heightened foreseeability required for intervening criminal acts. In the opposite direction, a few courts place the burden on the defendant to prove a superseding cause, regarding it as an affirmative defense. *See, e.g., Mengswater v. Anthony Kempler Trucking Inc.*, 312 S.W.3d 368 (Mo. Ct. App. 2010).

6. **Applying a risk rule.** In *Hines v. Garrett*, 108 S.E. 690 (Va. 1921), the defendant railroad went past the plaintiff's station without stopping. The plaintiff was required to get off and walk back through an area which, as the railroad knew, was especially dangerous. Criminals in the dangerous area did in fact attack the plaintiff. She sued the railroad. The court imposed liability. Here is what was said: "We do not wish to be understood as questioning the general proposition that no responsibility for a wrong attaches whenever an independent act of a third person intervenes. . . . [But] this proposition does not apply where the very negligence alleged consists of exposing the injured party to the act causing the injury."

Another case took a similar tack. A landlord leasing apartments failed to control access to the landlord's copy of keys. Someone used the landlord's keys to gain entrance to the plaintiff's apartment. The intruder raped the plaintiff. In the plaintiff's suit against the landlord, the defendant argued that the intruder was a superseding cause. The court said, "[t]he happening of the very event the likelihood of which makes the actor's conduct negligent and so subjects the actor to liability cannot relieve him from liability." *Tenney v. Atlantic Assocs.*, 594 N.W.2d 11 (Iowa 1999). *But see Doe v. Linder Construction Co.*, 845 S.W.2d 173 (Tenn. 1992) (on similar facts, criminal acts were unforeseeable; summary judgment for defendant affirmed).

7.   **Police chases.** In *Gonzalez v. Johnson*, 581 S.W.3d 529 (Ky. 2019), a deputy sheriff initiated a high-speed chase of a suspected drug dealer. The road was slippery and the officer's siren was not working. The fleeing suspect ran into the plaintiff's car, killing the plaintiff. Abandoning its per se rule that officers could not be the proximate cause of collisions that resulted from high-speed chases, the court held instead that an "officer can be the cause-in-fact and legal cause of damages inflicted upon a third party as a result of a negligent pursuit."

8.   **The "very duty" rule.** The Restatement Third provides that "When an actor is found liable precisely because of the failure to adopt adequate precaution against the risk of harm of another's acts or omissions, or by an extraordinary force of nature, there is no scope-of-liability limitation on the actor's liability." RESTATEMENT (THIRD) OF TORTS: LIABILITY FOR PHYSICAL AND EMOTIONAL HARM § 34 cmt. d (2010). Try applying the logic: If the defendant airplane manufacturer negligently designs airplane cockpit doors so that terrorists can take over and crash the plane, could the designer who is found to be negligent possibly claim that the terrorism was an unforeseeable and therefore superseding cause? *See In re Sept. 11 Litigation*, 280 F.Supp.2d 279 (S.D.N.Y. 2003).

9.   **The role of time.** The negligence in *Collins* took place twenty years before the harm came about. Should that fact have barred the claim? In *Williams v. State*, 969 N.E.2d 197 (N.Y. 2012), a state office of mental health negligently allowed a committed patient, required to be under supervision at all times, to use a restroom out of sight. He escaped, which the office did not report to police. Two years later he attacked a woman, causing serious injuries to her leg. He had originally been committed for a documented history of violence towards women. The New York court felt the proximate cause analysis incorporated a "temporal dimension." No liability.

DELANEY V. REYNOLDS, 825 N.E.2d 554 (Mass. App. Ct. 2005). Plaintiff Delaney began to live with Defendant Reynolds, a police officer, at Reynolds' house. Reynolds routinely stored his gun, loaded and unlocked, in the bedroom. Reynolds knew that Delaney knew where he kept his gun. He also knew that Delaney was depressed and had substance abuse problems. One night Delaney smoked crack cocaine and was drinking heavily. Reynolds ordered her to move out of his house. While packing her belongings, Delaney took Reynolds' loaded gun from the bedroom. She went down the stairway towards the living room in which Reynolds was sitting, aimed the gun at the window, and pulled the trigger twice. The gun did not fire. Delaney then ran back up the stairs, pursued by Reynolds. When they reached the bedroom Delaney put the gun under her chin and pulled the trigger. This time the gun went off, seriously injuring her. In Delaney's suit against Reynolds for negligence, Reynolds claimed that Delaney's intentional act of attempting suicide was a superseding cause of her injuries. The trial judge agreed and granted Reynolds' motion for summary judgment. *Held*, summary judgment reversed.

"[I]t appears to be the historical view that a purposeful act of suicide, rather than any antecedent negligence, will be deemed the legal cause of a decedent's injury unless the defendant's negligence rendered the decedent unable to appreciate the self-destructive nature of the suicidal act or, even if able to appreciate the nature of the act, unable to resist the suicidal impulse. . . . Cases from other jurisdictions discussing the policies underlying this traditional rule cite to (1) the historic notion that suicide is an immoral or culpable act; (2) the reluctance to impose a duty to protect others from harm; (3) the inordinate burden of being one's brother's keeper and the too-great magnitude of imposing a burden to foresee and prevent a suicide; or (4) the unforeseeability of an intentionally self-destructive act. Other jurisdictions have more recently. . . . [W]ere the jury to find that Delaney intended to commit suicide when she turned Reynolds's gun on herself with an intentional suicidal or self-injurious purpose, we think it should also be open to Delaney to show and the jury to find that the risk that she would handle or use Reynolds's gun in a manner so as to cause intentional injury to herself was foreseeable and that his failure to secure his gun was a proximate cause of her injury." See *Sarna v. American Bosch Magneto Corp.*, 195 N.E. 328 (Mass. 1935) (jury could properly find causation where decedent's act of meddling with tank containing poisonous gas could be expected when defendant abandoned tank in location where people came to salvage metal)."

NOTES

1. **Suicide as a superseding cause of harm.** A number of states continue to follow the traditional rule—where a plaintiff intentionally attempts to commit or commits suicide, that act is a superseding cause of plaintiff's harm, freeing the defendant from any liability for negligence. *See Johnson v. Wal-Mart Stores, Inc.*, 588 F.3d 439 (7th Cir. 2009) (widower whose wife shot and killed herself sued the store that sold the bullets and negligently failed to ask her for ID; wife's act of committing suicide is "an unforeseeable act that breaks the chain of causation required by proximate cause"). Some courts have recognized two main exceptions to this traditional rule: (1) where

the defendant's tortious conduct induces a mental illness or an "uncontrollable impulse" in the plaintiff (or decedent) from which the suicide attempt (or suicide) results; and (2) where there is a special relationship between the two parties, that presumes or includes knowledge by the defendant of plaintiff's risk of committing suicide. *Johnstone v. City of Albuquerque*, 145 P.3d 76 (N.M. Ct. App. 2006). Also, suicide may not be a superseding cause to a defendant's intentional tort. *See Rondini v. Bunn*, ___ So.3d ___, 2021 WL 1939171 (Ala. 2021) ("[I]t is unnecessary to analyze whether the decedent's suicide was a foreseeable consequence of the sexual assault; liability may attach without regard to whether the defendant intended or could have reasonably foreseen that result. . . . [S]uicide of a person who is the victim of one specific intentional tort—sexual assault—is not a superseding cause that will absolve the alleged assailant of liability as a matter of law.").

2. **Foreseeability of suicide.** A growing number of states follow the approach adopted in *Delaney* and use a foreseeability test on a case-by-case basis. Recent development are carefully reviewed in *Cotten v. Wilson*, 576 S.W.3d 626 (Tenn. 2019). The *Cotten* court concluded that "the crucial inquiry is whether the defendant's negligent conduct led to or made it reasonably foreseeable that the deceased would commit suicide. If so, the suicide is not an independent intervening cause breaking the chain of legal causation." A case that applied a similar test is *Kivland v. Columbia Orthopaedic Group, LLP*, 331 S.W.3d 299 (Mo. 2011), in which the plaintiff's husband committed suicide after the defendant surgeon performed surgery on him, allegedly negligently, in a way that left him in a great deal of pain. The court held that the widow was required to show that her husband's suicide was a natural and probable result of the pain caused by the negligently performed surgery, and that contested issues of fact on this issue precluded summary judgment on her wrongful death claim. *See also Wickersham v. Ford Motor Co.*, 853 S.E.2d 329 (S.C. 2020), ("[W]hether a suicide is a foreseeable consequence of tortious conduct is first a question of law for a court to decide. If a court determines a particular suicide is not unforeseeable as a matter of law, legal cause—foreseeability—becomes a question for the jury."). Is it preferable to bar any negligence claims brought by a person who attempts suicide, or to consider the foreseeability of the suicide attempt?

3. **Scope of duty and scope of risk.** Do the suicide cases turn as much on the scope of the defendant's duty to the plaintiff as on the scope of risks created? A doctor who cares for a suicidal patient may well owe a duty that encompasses protecting that patient from self-harm. *See, e.g., P.W. v. Children's Hosp. Colo.*, 364 P.3d 891 (Colo. 2016). Does that mean that a doctor's negligence in treatment, followed by the patient's act of self-destruction, is a proximate cause of that harm? *See Komlodi v. Picciano*, 89 A.3d 1234 (N.J. 2014) (for the jury to determine whether patient's oral ingestion of a narcotic patch was reasonably foreseeable, given patient's known propensity to abuse alcohol and drugs).

4. **Liability to plaintiff.** Would it be clearer that Reynolds was a proximate cause of the harm if Delaney had fired a bullet through the

downstairs window and hit a bystander walking down the street? If so, is that because in *Delaney* harm to others is more foreseeable than is harm to plaintiff, or because a desire to deny liability has more to do with plaintiff fault than defendant as a proximate cause? Should comparative fault by percentages rather than all-or-nothing contributory fault affect the superseding cause decision?

B. NEGLIGENT INTERVENING ACTS

DERDIARIAN v. FELIX CONTRACTING CORP.
414 N.E.2d 666 (N.Y. 1980)

COOKE, CHIEF JUDGE.

[Defendant Felix Contracting Corp. was installing an underground gas main, and for this purpose had excavated most of the eastbound lane of traffic. Felix engaged Bayside Pipe Coaters to seal the mains. Bayside had a kettle of liquid enamel, boiling to 400 degrees at the job site. Derdiarian worked for Bayside and was in charge of the kettle. Against Derdiarian's wishes, Felix insisted that he set up the kettle on the west side of the excavation facing the oncoming, eastbound traffic. Felix protected against this oncoming traffic by a single wooden horse barricade and by use of a single flagman.

[James Dickens was driving eastbound on Oak Street when he suffered a seizure and lost consciousness. Dickens was under treatment for epilepsy and had neglected to take his medication at the proper time. His car crashed through a single wooden horse-type barricade and struck the plaintiff, throwing him into the air. He was "splattered over his face, head and body with 400 degree boiling hot liquid enamel from a kettle struck by the automobile. . . . Although plaintiff's body ignited into a fire ball, he miraculously survived the incident."

[The jury found in favor of the plaintiff against Dickens, Felix, and Consolidated Edison. The Appellate Division affirmed. Only the claim against Felix is involved here.]

To support his claim of an unsafe work site, plaintiff called as a witness Lawrence Lawton, an expert in traffic safety. According to Lawton, the usual and accepted method of safeguarding the workers is to erect a barrier around the excavation. Such a barrier, consisting of a truck, a piece of heavy equipment or a pile of dirt, would keep a car out of the excavation and protect workers from oncoming traffic. The expert testified that the barrier should cover the entire width of the excavation. He also stated that there should have been two flagmen present, rather than one, and that warning signs should have been posted advising motorists that there was only one lane of traffic and that there was a flagman ahead.

Following receipt of the evidence, the trial court charged the jury, among other things, that it could consider, as some evidence of negligence, the violation of a Mount Vernon ordinance. The ordinance imposed upon a construction "permittee" certain safety duties. Defendant Felix now argues that plaintiff was injured in a freakish accident, brought about solely by defendant Dickens' negligence, and therefore there was no causal link, as a matter of law, between Felix' breach of duty and plaintiff's injuries.

The concept of proximate cause, or more appropriately legal cause, has proven to be an elusive one, incapable of being precisely defined to cover all situations. This is, in part, because the concept stems from policy considerations that serve to place manageable limits upon the liability that flows from negligent conduct. Depending upon the nature of the case, a variety of factors may be relevant in assessing legal cause. Given the unique nature of the inquiry in each case, it is for the finder of fact to determine legal cause, once the court has been satisfied that a prima facie case has been established. To carry the burden of proving a prima facie case, the plaintiff must generally show that the defendant's negligence was a substantial cause of the events which produced the injury. Plaintiff need not demonstrate, however, that the precise manner in which the accident happened, or the extent of injuries, was foreseeable (Restatement, Torts 2d, § 435, subd. 2).

Where the acts of a third person intervene between the defendant's conduct and the plaintiff's injury, the causal connection is not automatically severed. In such a case, liability turns upon whether the intervening act is a normal or foreseeable consequence of the situation created by the defendant's negligence. If the intervening act is extraordinary under the circumstances, not foreseeable in the normal course of events, or independent of or far removed from the defendant's conduct, it may well be a superseding act which breaks the causal nexus. Because questions concerning what is foreseeable and what is normal may be the subject of varying inferences, as is the question of negligence itself, these issues generally are for the fact finder to resolve.

There are certain instances, to be sure, where only one conclusion may be drawn from the established facts and where the question of legal cause may be decided as a matter of law. Those cases generally involve independent intervening acts which operate upon but do not flow from the original negligence. Thus, for instance, we have held that where an automobile lessor negligently supplies a car with a defective trunk lid, it is not liable to the lessee who, while stopped to repair the trunk, was injured by the negligent driving of a third party. (Ventricelli v. Kinney System Rent A Car), [45 N.Y.2d 950, 411 N.Y.S.2d 555, 383 N.E.2d 1149 (1978)]. Although the renter's negligence undoubtedly served to place the injured party at the site of the accident, the intervening act was divorced from and not the foreseeable risk associated with the original negligence. And the injuries were different in kind than those which would have normally been expected from a defective trunk. In short, the negligence of the renter merely furnished the occasion for an unrelated act to cause injuries not ordinarily anticipated.

By contrast, in the present case, we cannot say as a matter of law that defendant Dickens' negligence was a superseding cause which interrupted the link between Felix's negligence and plaintiff's injuries. From the evidence in the record, the jury could have found that Felix negligently failed to safeguard the excavation site. A prime hazard associated with such dereliction is the possibility that a driver will negligently enter the work site and cause injury to a worker. That the driver was negligent, or even reckless, does not insulate Felix from liability. Nor is it decisive that the driver lost control of the vehicle through a negligent failure to take medication, rather than a driving mistake. The precise manner of the event need not be anticipated. The finder of fact could have concluded that the foreseeable, normal and natural result of the risk created by Felix was the injury of a worker by a car entering the improperly protected work area. An intervening act may not serve as a superseding cause, and relieve an actor of responsibility, where the risk of the intervening act occurring is the very same risk which renders the actor negligent.

[Affirmed].

NOTES

1. **Does manner of harm *ever* matter?** Is *Derdiarian* consistent with the scope-of-risk principle? The defendant could foresee some kind of harm from a motor vehicle entering the excavation and that is what happened. The precise manner in which the injury came about, as we know from *Hughes,* does not necessarily matter. Think about whether the manner in which the injury came about ever matters to the analysis of reasonable foreseeability. Where the harm occurs in some bizarre, unforeseeable manner, is that irrelevant to judging whether the type of harm was foreseeable? Suppose on facts like *Derdiarian* the injury occurs because an airplane crashes into the excavation. Try working that out under a scope-of-risk analysis.

2. **Foreseeability of risk or result?** Many, many cases use foreseeability in some fashion when there are intervening causes, and like *Derdiarian*, often speak of foreseeability of the intervening cause itself rather than foreseeability of the general result. *See Puckett v. Mt. Carmel Reg'l Med. Ctr.*, 228 P.3d 1048 (Kan. 2010) ("If the intervening cause is foreseen or might have been foreseen by the first actor, his negligence may be considered the proximate cause, notwithstanding the intervening cause."). *See also Summy v. City of Des Moines*, 708 N.W.2d 333 (Iowa 2006). Is this the risk rule coupled with a tendency to describe the risk by describing the mechanism that brings the risk about?

3. **Foreseeable negligence of others.** What negligence can a defendant foresee on the part of others? The defendant negligently turned off decedent's electricity for nonpayment of bills. Two days later, with the electricity still off, a resident left a lit candle in the bathroom overnight on a shelf where towels and toilet paper were located. During the night the candle fell, resulting in the death of four people. Could the defendant have foreseen such conduct by the resident? *Eckroth v. Pennsylvania Elec. Inc.*, 12 A.3d 422 (Pa. 2010) (No; 48 hours was enough time to have expected the homeowner to purchase a flashlight with batteries). In *Simler v. Dubuque Paint Equip. Servs., Inc.*, 942 F.3d 448 (8th Cir. 2019), an employee crashed his employer's truck into the rear of another vehicle, causing a severe backup of traffic half-a-mile long across a stretch of the Interstate. Many cars stopped. But between eight and sixteen minutes after the accident, Kim Ross, who was exceeding the speed limit at the time, did not see the traffic stoppage and struck the rear of plaintiff's vehicle with his cargo van. Plaintiff sued the employee who caused the traffic backup among others. "Is a driver who causes an accident on a highway liable for a second one occurring in the traffic backup that follows? Applying Missouri law, we conclude that the answer is no[t] based on the time and distance separating the two accidents." It was not foreseeable that another accident would occur "eight-or-more minutes later in a spot nearly half a mile back—when every driver before Ross had managed to stop."

4. **Obviousness of the original risk.** Does it matter to the analysis if the risks created by the first negligent actor are (or should be) "obvious" to the second actor? Why might that matter? In *Latzel v. Bartek*, 846 N.W.2d 153 (Neb. 2014), a landowner negligently allowed corn to grow seven feet high, up to a ditch near a rural intersection. This obscured drivers' vision of the cross-road. Drivers of two cars crossed the blind intersection simultaneously, and in the ensuing crash a passenger was killed. In the passenger's estate's suit against the landowner, the trial court granted summary judgment on proximate cause grounds. *Held*, affirmed. "There was no evidence that the landowners could have reasonably foreseen the drivers' conduct. . . . [A]lthough the landowners anticipated speeding, they were not bound to anticipate that drivers would disregard the obvious danger of traversing a visually obstructed unmarked intersection without being able to see what they needed to see to do so safely." The court cited other cases where the second actor's disregard of an "obvious danger" broke the causal chain. Most involved drivers who entered obstructed intersections, often at high speed. Should a jury decide whether this is a foreseeable risk created by allowing corn to grow up in such a way as to become a visual obstruction, or is it better policy to hold the drivers solely responsible as a matter of law?

5. **Scope of the original risk.** "[I]f the intervening act of the third person constitutes negligence, that negligence does not constitute a superseding cause if the actor at the time of his negligent conduct should have realized that a third person might so act. In fact, if the likelihood that a person may act in a particular manner is . . . one of the hazards which makes the actor negligent, such an act whether innocent, negligent, intentionally tortious or

criminal does not prevent the actor from being liable for harm cause thereby." *Michaels v. CH2M Hill, Inc.*, 257 P.3d 532 (Wash. 2011). If it is negligent to leave your unlocked loaded gun in a shoebox on a closet shelf, is your child's act of taking the gun out, playing with it, and accidentally shooting his friend a superseding cause of that other child's death? *Adames v. Sheahan*, 909 N.E.2d 742 (Ill. 2009). Have we seen this rule before?

TORRES V. JAI DINING SERVICES (PHOENIX) INC.

497 P.3d 481 (Ariz. 2021)

VICE CHIEF JUSTICE TIMMER, opinion of the Court:

After spending an evening drinking and socializing at Jaguars Club in Phoenix, Cesar Aguilera Villanueva drove his truck from the club while intoxicated. He eventually returned home and fell asleep for a short time before getting up to take a friend home. Tragically, Villanueva was still intoxicated, and he smashed his truck into a car that was stopped at a red light, killing Guadalupe Gastelum Suarez and Jesus O. Torres Guillen. The issue here is whether Villanueva's decision to resume driving after reaching home constituted an intervening and superseding cause of Suarez's and Guillen's deaths as a matter of law, thereby relieving the club's owner from liability for overserving alcohol to Villanueva. We hold it was not, and the trial court therefore properly submitted this issue for a jury to decide. . . .

We granted review to answer a recurring question of statewide importance in dram shop liability cases: Does an overserved patron's decision to drive while intoxicated after safely reaching home or a similar resting place constitute an intervening and superseding cause that breaks the chain of causation as a matter of law, thus relieving the defendant liquor licensee of liability? . . .

Resolution of this issue depends on the scope of the risk in dram shop cases. The risk created by overserving alcohol to a patron is that the patron will drive while intoxicated and cause an accident that results in injury or death to members of the traveling public. The injury-producing conduct by the intoxicated patron—driving a vehicle while impaired by alcohol—is one of the very hazards which makes the tavern owner's act negligent. Consequently, we have stated it is foreseeable to a liquor licensee that an overserved patron will drive while intoxicated and cause an accident that injures or kills another person. . . .

The foreseeable risk that an intoxicated patron might drive and cause an accident that injures or kills someone does not vanish solely because the patron initially returns home with the intent to sleep, eat, change clothes, or do myriad other things before deciding to leave home and resume driving. Intoxicated people frequently make foolhardy decisions, including refusing to stay put and sober up before getting behind the wheel. We agree with Plaintiffs that the risk created by a liquor licensee overserving a patron exists as long as the patron drives while intoxicated, regardless of when or where the patron travels and even with a short stop at home. *See* Restatement (Second) of Torts § 449 (1965) ("If the likelihood that a third person may act in a particular manner is the hazard or one of the hazards which makes the actor negligent, such an act whether innocent, negligent, intentionally tortious, or criminal does not prevent the actor from being liable for harm caused thereby.").

Refusing to adopt JAI's narrower view of the scope of risk in dram shop cases does not impose "potentially never-ending liability" on liquor licensees, as JAI asserts. First, in all cases the risk of liability ends when the patron sobers up. Thus, the risk of liability correlates directly to the degree in which the liquor licensee overserves the patron. Second, there are cases in which the patron's decision to resume driving after reaching home is unforeseeable and extraordinary in hindsight, making the patron's act a superseding cause that relieves the liquor licensee from liability. In most cases, a jury as factfinder must decide that issue. In other cases, however, the issue may be a legal one.

Turning to the case here, the trial court properly declined to enter judgment as a matter of law for JAI. A reasonable person in the club's position could have foreseen that Villanueva would drive while intoxicated, cause an accident, and injure someone, so long as he remained intoxicated. . . . [A] jury could have reasonably concluded that Villanueva's act in driving while intoxicated, even after he reached home, although an intervening cause of the accident, was nevertheless foreseeable by someone in the club's position and not extraordinary in hindsight. The trial court properly submitted this issue to the jury. . . .

MARSHALL v. NUGENT

222 F.2d 604 (1st Cir. 1955)

MAGRUDER, J.

[Plaintiff Marshall was a passenger in Harriman's car. There was ice and hard-packed snow on the highway. As Harriman topped a hill, he saw a truck coming toward him, partly in his lane. Harriman went off the road. The truck driver, Warren Prince, stopped to help pull Harriman's car back on the road. This effort partly blocked the road again, so the plaintiff walked toward the top of the hill to flag any approaching motorists. Before he could reach the top, Nugent drove over the hill, saw the Socony-Vacuum Oil Co. truck blocking the road, and attempted to avoid it. He skidded into the plaintiff, Marshall. Marshall sued both Nugent and the truck driver. The jury found against the truck driver, who appeals urging that he was not a proximate cause.]

To say that the situation created by the defendant's culpable acts constituted "merely a condition," not a cause of plaintiff's harm, is to indulge in mere verbiage, which does not solve the question at issue, but is simply a way of stating the conclusion, arrived at from other considerations, that the causal relation between the defendant's act and the plaintiff's injury is not strong enough to warrant holding the defendant legally responsible for the injury.

The adjective "proximate," as commonly used in this connection, is perhaps misleading, since to establish liability it is not necessarily true that the defendant's culpable act must be shown to have been the next or immediate cause of the plaintiff's injury. . . .

[S]peaking in general terms, the effort of the courts has been, in the development of this doctrine of proximate causation, to confine the liability of a negligent actor to those harmful consequences which result from the operation of the risk, or of a risk, the foreseeability of which rendered the defendant's conduct negligent.

Of course, putting the inquiry in these terms does not furnish a formula which automatically decides each of an infinite variety of cases. Flexibility is still preserved by the further need of defining the risk, or risks, either narrowly, or more broadly, as seems appropriate and just in the special type of case.

Regarding motor vehicle accidents in particular, one should contemplate a variety of risks which are created by negligent driving. There may be injuries resulting from a direct collision between the carelessly driven car and another vehicle. But such direct collision may be avoided, yet the plaintiff may fall and injure himself in frantically racing out of the way of the errant car. . . . Or the plaintiff may faint from intense excitement stimulated by the near collision, and in falling sustain a fractured skull. . . . This bundle of risks could be enlarged indefinitely with a little imagination. In a traffic mix-up due to negligence, before the disturbed waters have become placid and normal again, the unfolding of events between the culpable act and the plaintiff's eventual injury may be bizarre indeed; yet the defendant may be liable for the result. In such a situation, it would be impossible for a person in the defendant's position to predict in advance just how his negligent act would work out to another's injury. Yet this in itself is no bar to recovery.

When an issue of proximate cause arises in a borderline case, as not infrequently happens, we leave it to the jury with appropriate instructions. . . .

Exercising that judgment on the facts in the case at bar, we have to conclude that the district court committed no error in refusing to direct a verdict for the defendant Socony on the issue of proximate cause. . . .

Plaintiff Marshall was a passenger in the oncoming Chevrolet car, and thus was one of the persons whose bodily safety was primarily endangered by the negligence of Prince, as might have been found by the jury, in "cutting the corner" with the Socony truck in the circumstances above related. In that view, Prince's negligence constituted an irretrievable breach of duty to the plaintiff. Though this particular act of negligence was over and done with when the truck pulled up alongside of the stalled Chevrolet without having actually collided with it, still the consequences of such past negligence were in the bosom of time, as yet unrevealed.

If the Chevrolet had been pulled back onto the highway, and Harriman and Marshall, having got in it again, had resumed their journey and had had a collision with another car five miles down the road in which Marshall suffered bodily injuries, it could truly be said that such subsequent injury to Marshall was a consequence in fact of the earlier delay caused by the defendant's negligence, in the sense that but for such delay the Chevrolet car would not have been at the fatal intersection at the moment the other car ran into it. But on such assumed state of facts, the courts would no doubt conclude, "as a matter of law," that Prince's earlier negligence in cutting the corner was not the "proximate cause" of this later injury received by the plaintiff. That would be because the extra risks to which such negligence by Prince had subjected the passengers in the Chevrolet car were obviously entirely over; the situation had been stabilized and become normal, and, so far as one could foresee, whatever subsequent risks the Chevrolet might have to encounter in its resumed journey were simply the inseparable risks, no more and no less, that were incident to the Chevrolet's being out on the highway at all. But in the case at bar, the circumstances under which Marshall received the personal injuries complained of presented no such clear-cut situation. . . .

NOTES

1.   **Termination of risk.** A phrase once used was "termination of the risk." In *Pittsburg Reduction Co. v. Horton*, 113 S.W. 647 (Ark. 1908), a boy named Copple found explosive dynamite caps that the defendant had negligently left in a place where children could be expected to pick them up. Copple kept them at home and his mother knew of them. A week later he traded them to a 13-year-old boy, Jack Horton. Horton lost a hand while playing with them. The court thought that Mrs. Copple's knowing tolerance of the shells "broke the causal connection" and that the defendant which had negligently scattered them around for the children to find would not be liable. "Charlie Copple's parents having permitted him to retain possession of the caps, his further acts in regard to them must be attributable to their permission and were wholly independent of the original negligence of appellants." Commentators have suggested that this is an example of a "terminated risk." Defendant's conduct created a risk but the risk so created

was no longer existent. How do you have to describe the risk if this view is taken? Is the termination of the risk idea consistent with the risk principle?

2.   **The passage of time.** In *Baumann v. Zhukov*, 802 F.3d 950 (8th Cir. 2015), two truck drivers negligently crashed, blocking an interstate highway; the traffic backup was almost a mile long. Vehicles activated hazard lights, and police, fire and ambulance vehicles had overhead lights flashing. The Schmidts were in a car at the back of the long line. Some forty minutes after the original accident, Slezak drove his tractor-trailer into the Schmidts' car at about 75 miles per hour, killing the entire family. In a suit by the Schmidts' estates against the two drivers who caused the original accident, the trial court granted summary judgment for the defense on the ground that the "unanticipated negligence of Slezak was an 'efficient intervening cause.' " The appeals court affirmed, pointing to the length of time between the two crashes and the "patently obvious hazard" that faced Slezak, concluding that "no reasonable jury could conclude otherwise." The dissenting judge argued that in this case, "where to draw the line on proximate cause is an issue for the finder of fact" given that Slezak's negligence was not "so extraordinary" that it severed the causal connection as a matter of law.

3.   **Reaching apparent safety.** The termination of the risk idea emphasizes that the plaintiff had reached a position of "apparent safety." In *Marshall* and in *Torres* why did the courts say that the plaintiffs were not in a position of apparent safety?

4.   **Liability for subsequent medical negligence.** Defendant negligently injures Plaintiff, who is then taken to a hospital for treatment. Is the Defendant liable for any subsequent negligence in medical treatment? While you might see this as a "position of safety" for the plaintiff, virtually all courts agree that when a defendant causes harm to a person, that defendant will also be liable for any "enhanced harm" caused by the later negligent provision of aid, including negligent medical treatment. *See* RESTATEMENT (THIRD) OF TORTS: LIABILITY FOR PHYSICAL AND EMOTIONAL HARM § 35 (2010); *Sloan ex rel. Estate of Sloan v. Providence Health Sys.-Oregon*, 437 P.3d 1097 (Or. 2019) ("[A]n original tortfeasor is liable for the reasonably foreseeable consequences of his initial injuries to a plaintiff, and those consequences can include, but are not limited to, additional injuries caused by a physician's conduct in diagnosing or treating the initial injuries."). Courts have extended the medical-treatment rule to other risks resulting from efforts to assist an injured person. *See, e.g.*, *Anaya v. Superior Court*, 93 Cal. Rptr.2d 228 (Ct. App. 2000) ("Obviously, if the original tortfeasor is liable for injuries or death suffered during course of the treatment of injuries suffered in the accident, the original tortfeasor is liable for injuries or death suffered during transportation of the victim to a medical facility for treatment of the injuries resulting from the accident."). Is this rule consistent with the more general scope-of-risk rule?

5.   **Condition vs. cause.** Sometimes courts resolve scope-of-risk issues involving intervening causes by saying that if the defendant's negligence "merely furnished a condition by which the injury was possible and a

subsequent independent act caused the injury, the existence of such condition is not the proximate cause of injury." *Sturdevant v. Kent*, 322 P.2d 408 (Okla. 1958). Statements like this seem to add nothing to a sound analysis of scope of risk, and indeed courts that use such verbiage seldom pursue any analysis of foreseeability. In *Sheehan v. City of New York*, 354 N.E.2d 832 (N.Y. 1976), a transit authority bus stopped illegally in the driving lane to allow passengers to board or alight. At that point a city sanitation truck crashed into the bus, injuring the plaintiff, a bus passenger. Holding in favor of the bus company, the court concluded that the admitted negligence of the sanitation truck driver was "the sole proximate cause of the injuries, and that the continued presence of the bus in the traveling lane at the time it was struck merely furnished the condition or occasion for the occurrence of the event rather than one of its causes." Is this, as the *Marshall* court said, "mere verbiage," or is there something more to this "condition, not a cause" concept?

NOTE: THE LAWYER'S ROLE

The cases mostly embrace the scope of risk principle by emphasizing foreseeability, yet often employ the diction of intervening cause and "causal" significance. Within a single state you can find wide variation in language and perhaps conception. The courts' use of causal language to apply a scope of risk principle that has little to do with causation makes the lawyer's task difficult but serves to emphasize the importance of advocacy in these cases.

Consider the following general kinds of argumentation in the legal cause situation:

1. *Argumentation from Principle or Policy.*

A lawyer can argue that the risk principle is, or should be, accepted, and that, once it is, the injury to the plaintiff is (or is not) within the risk. The lawyer can argue in terms of policy rather than principle—defendants should be liable for all the harms, the foreseeability of which made their conduct negligent, and by the same token should be liable for no more. What do the countering arguments look like?

2. *Argumentation from Fact-Pattern Rules.*

Lawyers can often describe what courts actually do with a given set of facts, as a kind of "rule" for that set of facts. For instance, courts are pretty well agreed about the rescue situation. In this sense there is a "rule" for rescue cases that does not depend on whether the court uses the language of foreseeability, the language of risk, or the language of remote causation. Since these rules do not seem closely related to any general principle, it is possible that the decisions in such cases are motivated by factors we cannot readily grasp and that the supposed rules will change when a new fact is injected. Perhaps the rescue cases really only apply to certain kinds of rescue or certain kinds of rescuers, for example. In this sense the "rules" in rescue cases may be more uncertain than we might like, but, descriptively speaking, they are still "rules" in the sense that they predict what courts will do in most of the cases. A lawyer can thus argue the "rule" in rescue cases without adopting any position at all about the risk principle.

Fact patterns are not pre-ordained. The lawyer gathers facts by asking questions. Asking different questions will result in gathering facts differently. Additionally, once the lawyer "has" the facts, the lawyer may ethically characterize and categorize those facts in a number of different ways. You could review the cases in this chapter and find many descriptions and groupings. Some fact patterns leap to the eye—fire cases, automobile cases, or thin skull cases, for example. But these categories of fact may not be the most relevant. Might there be a factual category like this: *"Cases in which plaintiff is injured attempting to minimize or escape from a risk negligently caused by the defendant?"* The lawyer adept at finding and describing cases often can find "rules" in his or her favor, not in the language of the courts but in their composite results. A lawyer might write an argument in a brief like this:

> "The courts of this state have consistently held that, when the plaintiff is injured in an attempt to rescue a person injured by the defendant's negligence, the defendant is liable. [citations.] Our courts have also held without dissent that when the plaintiff is injured attempting to avoid a risk of harm created by the defendant's negligence, the defendant is equally liable."

3. *Argumentation from Comparison and Contrast.*

Grouping of cases in more or less factual categories involves sophisticated lawyer skill in argument. Another use of the facts in cases that requires skill is the argument from analogy or disanalogy. Using this technique, the lawyer relies less on groupings of cases to suggest a "rule" for "rescue" or "car theft" or "suicide" cases. Instead, the lawyer attempts to identify special elements for comparison or contrast.

Scope of liability is not easy to understand, much less easy to master. Working out the arguments in particular cases is perhaps the best method of working on the topic. In working out arguments for each side in the following problem what additional facts do you need, if any? If you wish to know more facts, be sure you can state why they are relevant.

———————

PROBLEM

Wolfe v. Gramlich, Inc.

Your client, Gramlich Inc., is being sued by Louis Wolfe on a negligence theory. The following facts are not disputed. Gramlich, as part of its business, maintained a large tank for storing tar. It negligently allowed the tar to spill over, so that the tar flowed from its premises onto an area where plaintiff, a 9-year-old boy, and other children often played.

One day, plaintiff walked into the tar to such depth that his feet were covered up to his ankles. When he returned to his house, his parents saw the tar on his feet and began to remove it by taking the child into the middle of the back yard and using a solvent which is regarded as a safe product for removing tar from skin. While the parents were so engaged, a second child ran into their yard and unexpectedly exploded a cap from a cap-pistol which created a spark that ignited the fumes from the solvent and resulted in serious burns to plaintiff's legs.

Gramlich's general counsel believes that it might be able to move for summary judgment on the ground that even if its actions were negligent, Wolfe's injuries were not within the scope of liability. She has asked you, as outside counsel, to advise her on the strengths and weaknesses of such a motion.

NOTE: THE FUTURE OF SCOPE-OF-RISK ANALYSIS

Proximate cause rules arose before the full development of the joint and several liability system coupled with contribution. Those rules also arose before the development of comparative fault systems. As we will begin to see in the next chapter, comparative fault systems are capable of apportioning liability among many tortfeasors, imposing greater liability upon those who are more at fault. Scope of liability rules, on the other hand, are all-or-nothing. In the intervening cause situation, the first actor may escape liability altogether, while the second bears the whole burden. That is surely as appropriate as it ever was when it is clear that the second defendant created an entirely new and different risk. When the judge merely feels that the second actor is much more at fault, it may be that proximate cause/superseding cause analyses are counterproductive and that comparative fault rules, with each tortfeasor liable for some portion of the damages, may provide the best solution.

Several courts have now said that superseding cause analyses are to be abandoned as confusing and duplicating the basic foreseeability/scope-of-risk rules. *See Barry v. Quality Steel Prods., Inc.*, 820 A.2d 258 (Conn. 2003); *Control Techniques, Inc. v. Johnson*, 762 N.E.2d 104 (Ind. 2002). Do you regard this as a step toward resolving more cases by allocating liability according to fault rather than on an all-or-nothing basis? This is a point to bear in mind as we look at comparative fault apportionment of responsibility in the next chapter.

REFERENCES: DOBBS, HAYDEN & BUBLICK, HORNBOOK ON TORTS §§ 15.1–15.21 (2d ed. 2016); 1 DOBBS, HAYDEN & BUBLICK, THE LAW OF TORTS §§ 198–217 (2d ed. 2011); JOSEPH A. PAGE, TORTS: PROXIMATE CAUSE (2002).

PART 4

DEFENSES TO THE NEGLIGENCE CASE

■ ■ ■

About Defenses

A plaintiff who proves every element of a prima facie case for negligence will survive a directed verdict and get her claim to the jury. Nevertheless, her recovery may be defeated or reduced if the defendant mounts a successful affirmative defense. The defendant has the burden of proving affirmative defenses. This chapter and the two that follow examine the major affirmative defenses. The defenses covered in the next three chapters are the traditional ones. Legislatures may create other defenses for particular cases.

Many other impediments to the plaintiff's recovery exist but are not necessarily affirmative defenses. Among these are rules that reduce or eliminate a defendant's duty of care and those that provide for complete immunity from tort liability. In addition, procedural impediments applied to particular claims like medical malpractice may vastly reduce the number of successful suits. Finally, among the partial defenses enacted by some legislatures are damages caps, limiting liability in particular cases. All of these appear in later chapters.

CHAPTER 9

FAULT OF THE PLAINTIFF

■ ■ ■

§ 1. CONTRIBUTORY NEGLIGENCE: THE COMMON LAW RULE

BUTTERFIELD V. FORRESTER

11 East. 60, 103 Eng. Rep. 926 (1809)

This was an action on the case for obstructing a highway, by means of which obstruction the plaintiff, who was riding along the road, was thrown down with his horse, and injured, & c. At the trial before Bayley J. at Derby, it appeared that the defendant, for the purpose of making some repairs to his house, which was close by the road side at one end of the town, had put up a pole across this part of the road, a free passage being left by another branch or street in the same direction. That the plaintiff left a public house not far distant from the place in question at 8 o'clock in the evening in August, when they were just beginning to light candles, but while there was light enough left to discern the obstruction at 100 yards distance: and the witness, who proved this, said that if the plaintiff had not been riding very hard he might have observed and avoided it: the plaintiff however, who was riding violently, did not observe it, but rode against it, and fell with his horse and was much hurt in consequence of the accident; and there was no evidence of his being intoxicated at the time. On this evidence Bayley J. directed the jury, that if a person riding with reasonable and ordinary care could have seen and avoided the obstruction; and if they were satisfied that the plaintiff was riding along the street extremely hard, and without ordinary care, they should find a verdict for the defendant: which they accordingly did. [The plaintiff sought a "rule" which would have granted him a new trial.]

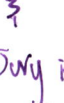

BAYLEY J. The plaintiff was proved to be riding as fast as his horse could go, and this was through the streets of Derby. If he had used ordinary care he must have seen the obstruction; so that the accident appeared to happen entirely from his own fault.

LORD ELLENBOROUGH C.J. A party is not to cast himself upon an obstruction which has been made by the fault of another, and avail himself of it, if he do not himself use common and ordinary caution to be in the right. In cases of persons riding upon what is considered to be the wrong side of the road, that would not authorize another purposely to ride up against them. One person being in fault will not dispense with another's using ordinary care for himself. Two things must concur to support this action, an obstruction in the road by the fault of the defendant, and no want of ordinary care to avoid it on the part of the plaintiff. [The new trial was refused.]

NOTES

1. **Contributory negligence.** After *Butterfield v. Forrester*, the courts developed the rule of contributory negligence as a complete, all-or-nothing defense. Even relatively minor failure of the plaintiff to exercise ordinary care for her own safety would completely bar recovery. This remained true even if the defendant's negligence was extreme, so long as it fell short of a reckless or wanton act.

2. **Justifying *Butterfield*.** It is important, for reasons that will later become apparent, to identify the several grounds on which the result in *Butterfield v. Forrester* might be justified.

    (a) *The fault principle.* If liability is to be based upon fault and the defendant fined because his fault causes harm, should the same fault principle compel the faulty plaintiff to lose his case entirely?

    (b) *Proximate cause.* Could *Butterfield v. Forrester* be understood as applying some view of proximate cause in which the plaintiff is treated as a superseding cause? Test this idea. Imagine that a child, standing near the obstruction, had been injured when the horse fell. Would the defendant, if negligent, have been liable for that?

    (c) *Negligence.* Granted that the defendant owed the plaintiff a duty of care, was that duty breached? Formulate an argument that the defendant's conduct was not negligent at all. Try to draw on specific cases or hypotheticals for a principle or general idea that furthers the defendant's argument.

3. **Origin of the rule.** Why do you think the contributory negligence rule developed in such a stringent fashion? Rules often develop from social and economic needs or assumptions. But sometimes a rule develops from a conceptual failure, that is, because legal professionals are unable at the moment to put together a coherent or logical idea about what a rule ought to be. Does the contributory negligence rule reflect social or economic standards or merely a conceptual failure?

4. **Avoiding the bar to recovery.** In several situations courts found reasons not to apply the contributory negligence defense. When an exception applied, the plaintiff made a full recovery in spite of her own fault. It was still an all-or-nothing system, but when an exception applied it was "all" rather than "nothing" for the plaintiff. We will look at these exceptions and how they fare under modern comparative negligence law in §§ 4–6 below.

§ 2. ADOPTING COMPARATIVE FAULT RULES

NEW YORK MCKINNEY'S CIV. PRAC. LAW § 1411 *pure*

In any action to recover damages for personal injury, injury to property, or wrongful death, the culpable conduct attributable to the claimant or to the decedent, including contributory negligence or assumption of risk, shall not bar recovery, but the amount of damages otherwise recoverable shall be diminished in the proportion which the culpable conduct attributable to the claimant or decedent bears to the culpable conduct which caused the damages.

WISCONSIN STAT. ANN. § 895.045 *modified*

Contributory negligence does not bar recovery in an action by any person or the person's legal representative to recover damages for negligence resulting in death or in injury to person or property, if that negligence was not greater than the negligence of the person against whom recovery is sought, but any damages allowed shall be diminished in the proportion to the amount of negligence attributed to the person recovering. . . .

NOTES

1. **Adoption of comparative fault rules.** The Federal Employers' Liability Act (FELA), 45 U.S.C. § 53, was promulgated in 1906 to facilitate claims against interstate railroads by workers injured on the job. It adopted a comparative negligence system as one of its major provisions. The plaintiff's negligence still reduces, but does not bar, a worker's recovery under this statute. *See CSX Transp., Inc. v. Begley,* 313 S.W.3d 52 (Ky. 2010). Another federal statute, the Jones Act, applied the FELA rules to seafaring workers.

Only a handful of states adopted comparative fault systems until a wave of change occurred after the late 1960s that eventually swept most of the nation. As of the early 21st century, only Alabama, North Carolina, Maryland, Virginia, and the District of Columbia have failed to adopt comparative fault rules. In those jurisdictions, the plaintiff's contributory fault remains a complete bar. *See Coleman v. Soccer Ass'n of Columbia*, 69 A.3d 1149 (Md. 2013) (court would not abrogate common law contributory negligence rule in light of legislative policy to retain the rule, evidenced by the failure of numerous bills that would have abolished or modified it). The traditional *Butterfield* rule has vestigial life in some other jurisdictions. *See, e.g., Murray v. Indianapolis Public Schools*, 128 N.E.3d 450 (Ind. 2019) (state Comparative Fault Act does not apply to governmental entities, thus in suit against a public school district, "Indiana's common law contributory negligence doctrine applies" to bar a plaintiff from all recovery "when he or she is negligent and this negligence is even slightly the cause of the alleged damages").

2.   **Terminology.** Although the New York and Wisconsin statutes are both comparative fault statutes, notice the terminology. Each notes that "contributory negligence" diminishes the plaintiff's proportion of damages. The term "contributory negligence" can still be properly used to describe the negligence of the plaintiff even when the effect of that negligence is no longer to bar the plaintiff's claim. But use of the term "contributory negligence" can be confusing because of its historic association with the older all-or-nothing effect. In court cases, judges may use the term contributory negligence to mean fault of the plaintiff with or without the all-or-nothing effect. However, to be clear, in the notes we will use "contributory negligence" when we refer to the all-or-nothing effect and "comparative negligence" or "comparative fault" when we refer to proportionate liability. The term "comparative fault" is similar to the term "comparative negligence" but can sometimes be construed more broadly to include causes of action other than negligence.

3.   **Pure vs. modified comparative fault.** The approach represented by the New York statute, *supra*, is called pure comparative fault. The approach represented by the Wisconsin statute is called modified comparative fault. Under modified comparative fault, a plaintiff who is assigned more than a 50% fault share recovers nothing whatever; the negligence of the plaintiff bars all recovery because her negligence is greater than the defendant's. *Lake v. D & L Langley Trucking, Inc.*, 233 P.3d 589 (Wyo. 2010).

4.   **Multiple responsible defendants in modified comparative states.** In modified comparative states, where the plaintiff and multiple defendants are found to be legally responsible for the plaintiff's injury, is the plaintiff barred from recovery based on a comparison of the plaintiff's percentage and the combined percentage of all defendants? Or is the comparison done with each individual defendant? The states have not agreed on this. Statutes often provide an answer, and most have adopted a "combined comparison" or "unit" rule, under which the plaintiff is not barred from recovery as long as the plaintiff's percentage is not greater than (or equal to, depending on the state) the combined percentages of all defendants. *See, e.g.*, CONN. GEN. STATS. ANN. § 52–572h. Some states achieve the same result by saying that a plaintiff is barred from recovery only if the plaintiff's percentage is 50% or greater. *See, e.g.*, ARK. CODE ANN. § 16–55–216. Some states, however, require a comparison of the plaintiff's percentage to each defendant's. Look at Wisconsin's statute reprinted above. How would you interpret it on this point? *See Reiter v. Dyken*, 290 N.W.2d 510 (Wis. 1980).

Which is the better rule, and why?

5.   **Jury role in attributing fault percentages.** How much fault is attributable to each party? If the evidence permits reasonable people to differ, this is a "fact" question, not a question of law. *Gonzalez v. Union Pac. R.R. Co.*, 872 N.W.2d 579 (Neb. 2015) (it was for the trier of fact to determine whether the negligence of a child who crossed a train track equaled or exceeded that of Union Pacific, which failed to blow its horn at an obscured intersection); *Bitgood v. Greene*, 108 A.3d 1023 (R.I. 2015). Attribution of fault percentages

is necessarily a rough approximation even though it is expressed in mathematical terms. The jury is usually told, in effect, to treat the total fault in the case as 100%, and to then find the percentage of fault attributable to each person.

6. **Applying the rules.** (a) Suppose four cars, driven by P, B, C, and D all collide. The jury finds that P is 5% responsible, B 10%, C 40% and D 45%. P has damages of $100,000. What does P recover?

(b) Suppose three cars, driving by P, E, and F all collide. The jury finds that P has 30% of the responsibility, E 20%, and D 50%. P has damages of $100,000. What does P recover?

7. **Information for the jury.** Should the jury be told how its comparative fault findings will impact an award of damages? In *Sollin v. Wangler,* 627 N.W.2d 159 (N.D. 2001), Dale Wangler, who was attempting to load a 1200-pound bale of straw into a grinder, dropped it on Richard Sollin, causing serious injuries. The jury assigned 50% of the fault to Sollin, the plaintiff, and 50% to Wangler, the defendant. It then awarded Sollin $100,000 in damages and Wangler $8,000. The trial judge did not answer the jury's question—"is the % of fault going to determine damage awards?" The North Dakota comparative fault statute barred plaintiffs from recovering if their fault was "as great as the combined fault of all other persons." Because plaintiff's fault was as great as defendant's fault, the trial court dismissed with prejudice the plaintiff's claim. The North Dakota Supreme Court rejected "the blindfold rule" and held that the jury should have been informed of the legal consequences of its verdict. The court wrote, "The jury's lack of knowledge does not eliminate sympathy and bias, but merely insures that the jury makes its decision in greater ignorance." Most states, some by statute, require that the jury be informed of the consequences of its assignment of percentages. Some, however, leave it to the judge's discretion whether or not to so inform the jury. *See Baudanza v. Comcast of Massachusetts I, Inc.,* 912 N.E.2d 458 (Mass. 2009).

§ 3. APPLYING COMPARATIVE FAULT RULES

A. APPORTIONING FAULT

POHL V. COUNTY OF FURNAS
682 F.3d 745 (8th Cir. 2012)

MURPHY, CIRCUIT JUDGE. . . .

[Juston Pohl, a resident of Michigan, was returning to a friend's farmhouse. It was 9 p.m. Light snow was falling. Pohl mistakenly turned onto Drive 719 instead of Road 719.] Drive 719 is a gravel road that does not have a posted speed limit but is subject to a general statutory limit of 50 miles per hour. Unlike Road 719 which continues in a straight line . . .

Drive 719 has a ninety degree curve one mile after its intersection with Highway 47. . . .

After turning onto Drive 719, Pohl accelerated to 63 mph, traveling with his high beam headlights on. When Pohl neared the warning sign, he braked too late to prevent the car from missing the curve and going off the road. The car hit an embankment, rolled, and came to rest upside down in a culvert. Pohl lost consciousness. When he came to, he realized he could not move his legs. Since he was unable to walk, he remained in the car all night hoping to be rescued. No help had arrived by daybreak, and Pohl managed to drag himself to a nearby farmhouse where the residents called an ambulance. It was later determined that he had a fracture and cord compression in his thoracic spine as well as frostbite in his feet. . . .

Pohl sued the county for common law negligence under the district court's diversity jurisdiction. He alleged that his injuries were the result of the county's negligent placement of the sign warning about the curve and its negligent failure to maintain it. . . .

At trial Pohl offered his own testimony and that of a traffic engineer and other lay witnesses. . . . Ronald Hensen, a traffic engineer, . . . testified that the sign did not comply with the standards set by the United States Department of Transportation's Manual on Uniform Traffic Control Devices (the Manual), which governs traffic control signs in Nebraska. The sign was deficient, he said, because it was heavily scratched and thus not retroreflective. . . . Hensen explained that because the sign lacked retroreflectivity, the 110 foot distance between the sign and the curve was not enough to provide drivers adequate notice of the curve ahead. He testified that a distance of at least 300 feet would have been needed to comply with the Manual and that "I don't know that I've ever seen in place a sign that defective." In discussing the accident, he explained that had Pohl been traveling at the speed limit of 50 mph, he would have entered the curve at a speed of 45 mph and would have still left the roadway.

The county's case consisted of two expert witnesses and hundreds of photographs of the accident scene. Gregory Vandenberg, a Nebraska state trooper who specializes in accident reconstruction, testified that following the crash he had analyzed data from the car's airbag control module which is also referred to as the black box. The black box records the vehicle's speed and braking pattern for the five seconds prior to deployment of the airbag. Based on these data he determined that the car had been traveling at 63 mph on Drive 719 and that Pohl had applied the brakes when he was closely aligned with the sign, slowing the car to 48 mph at the time it left the roadway. . . . If Pohl had been traveling at the speed limit and had braked when his car was aligned with the sign, the trooper's opinion was that the car would have slowed to a speed where Pohl could have safely negotiated the curve. He also explained that had Pohl been traveling at the speed limit but failed to steer, he would have left the roadway at 15 mph and had a less severe accident because the car likely would have stopped before colliding with the embankment. . . .

The district court found that the county was negligent because of the "combination of the sign's lack of retroreflectivity and its placement. . . . It further found that this negligence and Pohl's negligence in driving 13 miles over the speed limit were the proximate causes of his accident and injuries. In assessing the responsibility for the accident and Pohl's injuries the court allocated 60% of the negligence to the county and 40% to Pohl. The district court then calculated that Pohl was entitled to $678,606.14 in damages for medical expenses and pain and suffering, and awarded him $407,163.38 following a reduction for his comparative negligence.

PH

The county appeals. . . . Pohl cross appeals. . . .

When reviewing a district court's decision following a bench trial in a diversity action, "we look to state law for the standard of review on each issue." . . . Under Nebraska law, the question of whether a defendant is negligent by breaching a duty of care is a question of fact which is reviewed for clear error. . . .

The [district court's] determination that the sign was not retroreflective was supported by Hensen's testimony that the sign was scratched and did not reflect adequate light to meet the Manual's requirement that a sign reflect "a large portion of the light coming from a point source to be returned directly back to a point near its origin." It was also supported by some of the nighttime flash photographs in evidence on which the warning sign for the curve was not visible, but a distant retroreflective sign was. . . .

Because the record supports the district court's findings that the sign was neither retroreflective nor adequately placed to warn nighttime drivers, the court did not err in finding the county negligent. . . .

MD

The county also argues that Pohl cannot show proximate cause because his speeding was an efficient intervening cause. "[A]n efficient intervening cause is new and independent conduct of a third person, which itself is a proximate cause of the injury in question and breaks the causal connection between original conduct and the injury." Nebraska law makes clear however that an intervening cause cuts off a tortfeasor's liability only when it is not foreseeable. Testimony at trial indicated that traffic engineers assume that drivers will exceed the speed limit by 10 to 15 mph on a 50 mph road, and thus Pohl's travel 13 mph in excess of the speed limit was readily foreseeable.

DA

We finally address the county's argument that . . . the district court erred by undervaluing Pohl's contributory negligence. Contributory negligence occurs where the plaintiff breaches a duty of care and his breach "concur[s] and cooperat[es]" with the defendant's negligence to form a proximate cause of the injury. Under Nebraska law, a plaintiff is barred from recovery if his negligence is equal to or greater than that of the defendant. Contributory negligence is an affirmative defense that must be proved by the party asserting it. Since the existence of such negligence is a question of fact, our review is again for clear error.

The county . . . contends that the trial court erred in its assessment of contributory negligence because it should have found that Pohl's contributory negligence in speeding exceeded the county's negligence, thus barring recovery. In support of this argument, it points to Vandenberg's testimony indicating that had Pohl been traveling at the speed limit, he would have been able to negotiate the curve successfully if he had braked when aligned with the sign. This testimony was contradicted, however, by Hensen's testimony that had Pohl been traveling at the speed limit, his speed at the curve would have still been too great to negotiate it successfully. Given this conflicting testimony, we cannot say that the district court clearly erred by not finding that Pohl's negligence exceeded that of the county. *Cf. Anderson v. City of Bessemer,* 470 U.S. 564, 574, 105 S. Ct. 1504, 84 L.Ed.2d 518 (1985) ("Where there are two permissible views of the evidence, the factfinder's choice between them cannot be clearly erroneous."). . . .

On cross appeal, Pohl . . . contends that the district court erred in finding that his injuries would have been less severe had he not been speeding. He essentially argues that because no evidence was introduced from a biomedical expert indicating how he would have suffered fewer injuries had he been traveling at a slower speed, the district court's finding of proximate cause was clearly erroneous. Pohl cites no authority indicating that such evidence is required where the record contains evidence that the accident would have been less severe had the plaintiff not been speeding. Vandenberg's testimony suggested that had Pohl been traveling at the speed limit when he braked and still gone off the road, he would have been traveling at only 15 mph on leaving the road as opposed to 48 mph. There would then have been a "less severe collision," and the car "likely . . . would have stopped short of the . . . embankment." Given this evidence, it was reasonable to find that the accident would have been less severe and Pohl would have sustained less serious injuries had he not been speeding. Accordingly, the district court did not clearly err by finding that his negligence at the time of the crash was a proximate cause of his injuries.

We finally address Pohl's contention that even if the district court's determinations regarding negligence and proximate cause were correct, it should have apportioned less negligence to Pohl. The apportionment of negligence "is solely a matter for the fact finder, and its action will not be disturbed on appeal if it is supported by credible evidence and bears a reasonable relationship to the respective elements of negligence proved at trial." *Tadros v. City of Omaha,* 269 Neb. 528, 694 N.W.2d 180, 187 (2005). As discussed above, the evidence supported the district court's finding that the negligence of both parties contributed to Pohl's injuries. Attributing 40% of the negligence to Pohl was reasonable considering the evidence that the accident would still have happened at a lower speed but with less severe injuries.

Accordingly, we affirm the judgment of the district court.

NOTES

1. **Splitting.** Is this pretty much a modern-day disposition of *Butterfield v. Forrester?* Does a 40%–60% split of the costs by the two negligent parties seem more just than an all-or-nothing outcome, or preferable from the point of view of deterrence and compensation? *See* Guido Calabresi & Jeffrey O. Cooper, *New Directions in Tort Law*, 30 VAL. U. L. REV. 859, 868 (1996) (noting modern tort law's rejection of all-or-nothing rules and trend toward splitting); Robert Cooter & Thomas Ulen, *An Economic Case for Comparative Negligence*, 61 N.Y.U. L. REV. 1067 (1996) ("[T]he rule of comparative negligence is more efficient than its alternatives when it is desirable to give moderate incentives for precaution to both parties rather than strong incentives to one party and weak incentives to the other. Such a situation occurs when the parties are symmetrically situated with respect to the ability of each to take precaution."). Traffic accidents are the quintessential case in which both parties may share responsibility if they fail to use reasonable care. *See Stephens v. CSX Transp., Inc.*, 781 S.E.2d 534 (S.C. 2015); *Samson v. Nahulu*, 363 P.3d 263 (Haw. 2015) (pedestrian's fault for walking outside crosswalk should be compared with driver's duty to exercise due care to avoid colliding with pedestrians).

2. **Methods of comparing negligence.** What conduct was alleged to have been negligent on the part of the State? On the part of Pohl? If a reasonable factfinder, here the trial court judge, could find that both parties failed to use reasonable care, how should the parties' negligence be compared? In *Purvis v. Grant Parish Sch. Bd.*, 144 So.3d 922 (La. 2014), the court said that an allocation of fault to parties in negligence actions considers the following factors: (1) whether the conduct was inadvertent, or involved an awareness of the danger; (2) how great a risk was created by the conduct; (3) the significance of what was sought by the conduct; (4) the actors' capacities; and (5) any extenuating factors that might require the actor to proceed with haste. Should the factfinder give each party a *Carroll Towing* "score" measuring the extent of breach and then compare the scores?

In *Wassell v. Adams,* 865 F.2d 849 (7th Cir. 1989), Judge Posner suggested a different approach: "one way to make sense of comparative negligence is to assume that the required comparison is between the respective costs to the plaintiff and to the defendant of avoiding the injury." Suppose Pohl could have avoided the risk to himself by conduct that "costs" time or effort equivalent to one dollar and the county could have avoided the same risk to the plaintiff only by conduct that cost the equivalent of $99. Should the apportionment in that case be 99% and 1%? It might be easy to calculate the cost of replacing the defective sign in *Pohl*. Could the plaintiff's cost in time or effort to avoid the injury have been quantified in monetary terms as well? Does this method of apportionment seem fair? Is it relevant that the county had specific knowledge of the dangerous curve whereas Pohl only had the general knowledge that speeding can be dangerous? Even if Pohl's effort to avoid the risk only cost one dollar, is that the right item of comparison? What about all the other people who also needed to expend the time and effort to avoid a risk the county could have avoided with a single action?

3. **The process of comparing negligence.** In most cases the court does not discuss the method of comparing the parties' fault at all. Instead, as in *Pohl*, courts typically suggest that apportionment percentages are "a matter for the fact finder," and look to see whether the finding "is supported by credible evidence and bears a reasonable relationship to the respective elements of negligence proved at trial." *See Thompson v. Winn-Dixie*, 181 So.3d 656 (La. 2015) (allocation of fault is a factual determination); *Del Lago Partners, Inc. v. Smith*, 307 S.W.3d 762 (Tex. 2010) (discussing the importance of leaving the comparative negligence issue to the jury). The trial judge in *Pohl* examined evidence that suggested negligence by both parties. Would that evidence also have been sufficient to support an apportionment of 30–70 or 70–30? Why not have an apportionment of 50–50?

4. **Avoiding the jury.** In particular cases, a court may conclude that reasonable people would necessarily find contributory negligence or that the plaintiff's comparative negligence is so great that as a matter of law a directed verdict or summary judgment for the defendant is appropriate. *E.g.*, *Phillips v. Fujitec Am., Inc.*, 3 A.3d 324 (D.C. 2010) (summary judgment on issue of contributory negligence when plaintiff who was stuck in an elevator tried to get out between floors although she was told she should stay put and that help was on the way). If on appeal, a court finds a "clearly wrong" apportionment of fault, it has been held that the appellate court should adjust the award, but only to the extent of lowering or raising it to the highest or lowest point which is reasonably within the trier of fact's discretion. *Johnson v. Morehouse Gen. Hosp.*, 63 So.3d 87 (La. 2011) (adjusting fault among the parties). How might this result support judicial efficiency?

5. **The relationship between care by the parties.** At times, reasonable care by one party eliminates the need for care by the other. In a fraud and misrepresentation case against a lawyer, Judge Posner had this to say about fault of the plaintiff:

> Due care is the care that is optimal given that the other party is exercising due care. It is not the higher level of care that would be optimal if potential tort victims were required to assume that the rest of the world was negligent. A pedestrian is not required to exercise a level of care (e.g., wearing a helmet or a shin guard) that would be optimal if there were no sanctions against reckless driving.

Otherwise drivers would be encouraged to drive recklessly, and knowing this, pedestrians would be encouraged to wear helmets and shin guards. The result would be a shift from a superior method of accident avoidance (not driving recklessly) to an inferior one (pedestrian armor). . . . The law normally does not require duplicative precautions unless one is likely to fail or the consequences of failure . . . would be catastrophic.

Greycas, Inc. v. Proud, 826 F.2d 1560, 1566 (7th Cir. 1987). How does this kind of analysis work, if at all, in a case like *Pohl*?

6. **Comparative negligence vs. all-or-nothing results.** Despite evidence of its negligence, the county sought a completely favorable result based on two all-or-nothing arguments. Can you see them? Why were those arguments rejected?

7. **Harm to self and harm to others.** Should the plaintiff's fault be considered at all in a case in which that fault poses no risk to the defendant? The risks involved in a negligence action are often risks to others' safety. However, in comparative fault, the risks may be only to the plaintiff and not to others. Because of this difference in risk, some scholars have argued that the concepts of negligence and contributory negligence should be kept separate. *See* Gary T. Schwartz, *Contributory and Comparative Negligence: A Reappraisal,* 87 YALE L.J. 697 (1978). In addition, some courts have suggested that plaintiff fault be judged by a different, subjective standard. *See Dodson v. S.D. Dep't of Human Servs.,* 703 N.W.2d 353 (S.D. 2005) (jury should have been instructed to evaluate plaintiff's comparative negligence in light of her own mental capacity). However, the Restatement (Third) of Torts treats risks to self and others in the same way. *See* RESTATEMENT (THIRD) OF TORTS: LIABILITY FOR PHYSICAL AND EMOTIONAL HARM § 3 cmt. b (2010). Did Pohl's negligence risk harm to himself alone?

8. **Apportioning fault by an "equitable and just" approach.** Maine has a comparative negligence rule radically different from most. Instead of requiring the jury to reduce the plaintiff's damages in proportion to the plaintiff's relative fault, the statute requires the jury to make a reduction it considers to be equitable and just. In *Pelletier v. Fort Kent Golf Club,* 662 A.2d 220 (Me. 1995), the jury found that the defendant was more negligent than the plaintiff and that the plaintiff suffered $250,000 in damages. Yet the award was only $40,000. The court held that this was within the jury's discretion. It is obvious that the jury could not have made its reduction on the basis of proportional fault, since on that basis the plaintiff would have recovered something more than $125,000. If the verdict was not based on any legal rule, what might have motivated the jury? Do you think the *Pohl* factfinder would have brought in a different verdict under the Maine statute?

B. APPORTIONING RESPONSIBILITY

RESTATEMENT (THIRD) OF TORTS: APPORTIONMENT OF LIABILITY
(2000)

§ 8. Factors for assigning shares of responsibility

Factors for assigning percentages of responsibility to each person whose legal responsibility has been established include

(a) the nature of the person's risk-creating conduct, including any awareness or indifference with respect to the risks created by the conduct and any intent with respect to the harm created by the conduct; and

(b) the strength of the causal connection between the person's risk-creating conduct and the harm.

Comment:

a. *Assigning shares of responsibility.* The factfinder assigns comparative percentages of "responsibility" to parties and other relevant persons whose negligence or other legally culpable conduct was a legal cause of the plaintiff's injury. The factfinder does not assign percentages of "fault," "negligence," or "causation."

"Responsibility" is a general and neutral term. Assigning shares of "fault" or "negligence" can be misleading because some causes of action are not based on negligence or fault. Assigning shares of "causation" wrongly suggests that indivisible injuries jointly caused by two or more actors can be divided on the basis of causation. Assigning shares of "culpability" could be misleading if it were not made clear that "culpability" refers to "legal culpability," which may include strict liability.

Of course, it is not possible to precisely compare conduct that falls into different categories, such as intentional conduct, negligent conduct, and conduct governed by strict liability, because the various theories of recovery are incommensurate. However, courts routinely compare seemingly incommensurate values, such as when they balance safety and productivity in negligence or products liability law. "Assigning shares of responsibility" may be a less confusing phrase because it suggests that the factfinder, after considering the relevant factors, assigns shares of responsibility rather than compares incommensurate quantities. Nevertheless, the term "comparative responsibility" is used pervasively by courts and legislatures to describe percentage-allocation systems.

b. *Causation and scope of liability.* Conduct is relevant for determining percentage shares of responsibility only when it caused the harm and when the harm is within the scope of the person's liability.

c. Factors in assigning shares of responsibility. The relevant factors for assigning percentages of responsibility include the nature of each person's risk-creating conduct and the comparative strength of the causal connection between each person's risk-creating conduct and the harm. The nature of each person's risk-creating conduct includes such things as how unreasonable the conduct was under the circumstances, the extent to which the conduct failed to meet the applicable legal standard, the circumstances surrounding the conduct, each person's abilities and disabilities, and each person's awareness, intent, or indifference with respect to the risks. The comparative strength of the causal connection between the conduct and the harm depends on how attenuated the causal connection is, the timing of each person's conduct in causing the harm, and a comparison of the risks created by the conduct and the actual harm suffered by the plaintiff.

One or more of these factors may be relevant for assigning percentages of responsibility, even though they may not be a necessary element proving a particular claim or defense. However, these factors are irrelevant even to apportionment if there is no causal connection between the referenced conduct and the plaintiff's injuries. See Comment b. It should be noted that the mental-state factors in this Section may be considered for apportioning responsibility even if they are not themselves causally connected to the plaintiff's injury, as long as the risk-creating conduct to which they refer is causally connected to the injury.

NOTES

1. **The Restatement factors.** Is the Restatement correct in inviting the fact-finder to consider mental states of the parties and the strength of causal connections as well as the unjustified risks they created? Is this just an elaborate version of Maine's "equitable and just" apportionment? A long series of California decisions has said that "comparative negligence does not lend itself to the exact measurements of a micrometer-caliper," and that "the comparative fault doctrine is designed to permit the trier of fact to consider all relevant criteria in apportioning liability" in an "equitable" way. *Phipps v. Copeland Corp.*, 64 Cal.App.5th 319 (2021).

2. **Apportioning responsibility outside negligence.** The Restatement provision contemplates a comparison beyond simply negligence-to-negligence, with its listing of "awareness or indifference" to risk and "intent with respect to harm" as factors in determining percentages. States vary on what can be compared. Some allow only a negligence-to-negligence comparison. Others allow for a comparison of plaintiff negligence to misconduct short of intent. *See, e.g., B.B. v. County of Los Angeles,* 471 P.3d 329 (Cal. 2020) ("California principles of comparative fault have never required or authorized the reduction of an intentional tortfeasor's liability based on the acts of others."); *Berberich v. Jack,* 709 S.E.2d 607 (S.C. 2011) ("Comparative negligence encompasses the comparison of ordinary negligence with

heightened forms of misconduct such as recklessness, willfulness, and wantonness."). Some states not only allow but require a comparison of negligence to even intentional tort. *See Graves v. North Eastern Servs., Inc.*, 345 P.3d 619 (Utah 2015) (interpreting statutory definition of "fault" to include "intentionally tortious activity," thus mandating apportionment of a percentage of fault attributable to one defendant's sexual assault along with a percentage of fault attributable to that defendant's employer's negligence in failing to prevent the attack). Statutory language is often the starting point in the analysis, and sometimes statutes explicitly say what can be compared. Could a plaintiff's negligence reduce or bar recovery in a case brought against the defendant on a strict liability theory? *See Maupin v. Tankersly*, 540 S.W.3d 357 (Ky. 2018) (allowing a comparative negligence defense in a strict-liability dog-bite case, based on state comparative fault statute).

3.   **Terminology.** Under the Restatement view, what would be the term used for the apportioned percentages—it wouldn't be percentages of "negligence" or "fault," would it? The term "comparative responsibility" is sometimes used for systems that include more than just negligence in the apportionment. Can you imagine why?

4.   **Where the parties are under different standards of care.** Similar to the recklessness-negligence comparison, consider the difficulties that would arise if the plaintiff and the defendant were operating under different duties or standards of care, a possibility we'll see in Chapter 12. If both plaintiff and defendant are negligent, how would you compare the fault of the defendant who owed the highest degree of care with the fault of the plaintiff who owed only ordinary care? In *Aguallo v. City of Scottsbluff,* 678 N.W.2d 82 (Neb. 2004), the court seemed to say that the trier should estimate the deviation of the plaintiff from her ordinary care standard, then estimate the deviation of the defendant from his special standard of care, then compare the two deviations. How would the trier do that?

5.   **Comparing fault and causation.** Think back to *Landers* from Chapter 7. In that case, salt water from an oil company and salt water from a disposal company killed the fish in the lake. Imagine that the oil company dumped twice as much salt water as the disposal company, and that the salt water was twice as concentrated, and therefore harmful. However, suppose also that an expert testified that it was somewhat more likely that the salt water from the disposal company reached the lake first. In addition, there was testimony that the disposal company knew with substantial certainty that the salt water would enter the lake, while the oil company should have known of the unreasonable risk. Is the Restatement formula helpful here? The Restatement was careful to separate scope of liability from factual cause in most of its text. In § 8, however, isn't the term "causal connection" somewhat ambiguous?

§ 4. ALL-OR-NOTHING JUDGMENTS AFTER COMPARATIVE FAULT

1. *No plaintiff negligence.* Comparison of plaintiff and defendant fault is only at issue when both parties are negligent. If the plaintiff is not negligent, or if her negligence is not the factual or proximate cause of the harm, no comparison is necessary. *See RGR, LLC v. Settle*, 764 S.E.2d 8 (Va. 2014) (plaintiff not negligent as a matter of law where alleged alternative conduct—stopping on railroad tracks to look and listen for trains—would have placed him in even greater peril). Common features of the negligence analysis, such as the emergency doctrine, apply to the comparative negligence issue just as they do to the negligence question. *Henson v. Klein*, 319 S.W.3d 413 (Ky. 2010).

2. *Plaintiff negligence that is not a factual cause of injury.* Suppose the plaintiff is negligent because she is walking a dog she can't control. She then trips on the sidewalk. However, there is no evidence that she tripped on the sidewalk because she couldn't control the dog. Her negligence does not reduce her damages any more than it would make her liable for someone's injuries that were not caused by her negligence. *See Townsend v. Legere*, 688 A.2d 77 (N.H. 1997). *See also Pavlou v. City of New York*, 868 N.E.2d 186 (N.Y. 2007) (worker operated a crane with an excess load, but a crack in the crane made it unsafe to operate with any load).

3. *Plaintiff injury that is not within the scope of the risk created by the plaintiff's negligence.* It is also possible that the plaintiff's fault will be disregarded because the injury suffered was not within the risk created by that fault. Consider: a house guest negligently blunders onto a dark patio. He is negligent because he is unfamiliar with the place and he might easily trip or fall into the swimming pool. Instead he is struck by his host's runaway car which crashes through the back gate. *See* Dan B. Dobbs, *Accountability and Comparative Fault*, 47 LA. L. REV. (1987). *See also Estate of Moses ex rel. Moses v. Sw. Va. Transit Mgmt. Co.*, 643 S.E.2d 156 (Va. 2007) (reinstating a jury verdict for the plaintiff on the ground that it was within the province of the jury to decide whether the pedestrian's negligence—crossing in the middle of the street when the street looked clear—was a proximate cause of the accident in which he was hit by a bus).

4. *No defendant negligence.* The same all-or-nothing result will obtain if the defendant is not negligent, or if the defendant's negligence is not the factual or proximate cause of the plaintiff's harm. When an element of the plaintiff's prima facie case against the defendant fails, comparative fault is irrelevant and the plaintiff recovers nothing.

5. *Sorting claims into all-or-nothing or comparative elements.* Under the old regime of contributory negligence, a court could say the plaintiff was at fault, or that the defendant's conduct was not a factual or legal cause of the plaintiff's harm, and the result would be the same whichever view

the court took—no recovery for the plaintiff, as was the case in *Butterfield*. With the adoption of comparative fault, you really need to know whether you are talking about plaintiff fault or defendant factual or proximate cause because the effects can now be quite different.

6. *Reasonable care by the defendant in light of plaintiff fault?* What if the defendant doctor fails to diagnose a medical-expert patient who failed to give the doctor the information needed to make an accurate diagnosis? Is this a case of the plaintiff's comparative fault or a case of the defendant's non-negligence as in *Stinnett*? On similar facts, see *Juchniewcz v. Bridgeport Hosp.*, 914 A.2d 511 (Conn. 2007).

7. *Plaintiff's fault as a superseding cause of the harm.* Typically, when both plaintiff and defendant are at fault, the court will leave the apportionment of responsibility to the jury. However, in some cases, courts disclaim plaintiff's recovery altogether on superseding cause grounds, sometimes labeling the plaintiff's unforeseeable negligence as the "sole proximate cause" of the plaintiff's own harm. *See, e.g., Sanchez v. City of New York*, 141 N.Y.S.3d 66 (App. Div. 2021). In *Exxon Co., U.S.A. v. Sofec, Inc.*, 517 U.S. 830 (1996), an Exxon tanker broke away from moorings owned by one defendant and operated by another. The captain managed to get the tanker safely past a number of perils nearby and safely out to sea. But once he reached safety, he neglected to get a fix on his position and he ran aground. The ship was substantially destroyed. Exxon claimed that the owner and operator of the moorings were responsible for the breakaway. The Court held that even if that were so, the captain's negligence in failing to fix his position once he had reached a position of relative safety was a superseding cause. So Exxon could recover nothing, even though admiralty law, which governed the case, uses pure comparative fault to divide damages.

On the superseding cause topic, compare Michael D. Green, *The Unanticipated Ripples of Comparative Negligence: Superseding Cause in Products Liability and Beyond*, 53 S.C. L. REV. 1103 (2002) (criticizing *Sofec* unless it is construed quite narrowly), with Paul T. Hayden, *Butterfield Rides Again: Plaintiff's Negligence as Superseding or Sole Proximate Cause in Systems of Pure Comparative Responsibility*, 33 LOYOLA L.A. L. REV. 887 (2000) (arguing that use of superseding cause to bar overwhelmingly negligent plaintiffs from recovery does not undercut systems of pure comparative responsibility; "rather, these doctrines serve as useful ameliorating doctrines or safety valves that help preserve these 'pure' systems").

8. *Causal apportionment of separate injuries.* Comparative fault reductions may also be inappropriate when the plaintiff and the defendant cause separate injuries which are capable of causal apportionment. Suppose the plaintiff negligently crashes her car into a tree, sustaining

multiple injuries. Dr. Dann's negligent treatment causes paralysis of her legs, which appropriate medical treatment could have avoided. The physician in such a case is not liable for the initial injury itself, but may be liable for enhancement of the plaintiff's injury—some or all of the damages for the plaintiff's leg paralysis.

9. *The mitigation of damages rule.* The avoidable consequences or mitigation of damages rule requires the plaintiff to make reasonable efforts to minimize damages. *See, e.g., Sun Val, LLC v. Com'r of Transp.*, 193 A.3d 1192 (Conn. 2018). As with other defenses, the burden is on the defendant to prove that the plaintiff failed to mitigate damages. *Tibbetts v. Dairyland Ins. Co.*, 999 A.2d 930 (Me. 2010); *Ramkumar v. Grand Style Transp. Enters., Inc.*, 998 N.E.2d 801 (N.Y. 2013) (plaintiff offered a reasonable explanation for the cessation of physical therapy when he stated in his deposition that his insurance benefits were cut off five months previously). If a plaintiff whose foot was bruised by the defendant's negligence could avoid loss of the foot by taking antibiotics, the plaintiff might be expected to do so. If the plaintiff unreasonably refused and lost the foot as a result, recovery for the lost foot would not be allowed.

This is not a rule of comparative fault. Instead, it simply excludes all recovery for a particular item of harm when the court concludes either that the defendant was not a but-for cause of that harm or that the harm was outside the scope of the risk negligently created by the defendant because the plaintiff could have averted some of the damage. When the plaintiff failed to take the prescribed antibiotics, some courts might treat the loss of her foot as if it were caused entirely by the plaintiff's fault. Such courts would not compare fault of the plaintiff in failing to take antibiotics with fault of the defendant in causing the injury in the first place. Instead, they would simply exclude liability for loss of the foot. *See Willis v. Westerfield*, 839 N.E.2d 1179 (Ind. 2006) (defendant "must prove that the plaintiff's failure to exercise reasonable care caused the plaintiff to suffer an identifiable item of harm not attributable to the defendant's negligence"); *see also Langlois v. Town of Proctor*, 113 A.3d 44 (Vt. 2014) (in this case, there are "no discrete damages allegedly attributable solely to plaintiff. Thus, we agree with the Town that the court should have instructed the jury on comparative negligence rather than on damages mitigation.").

Automatic exclusion of all recovery in the foot example looks like an attempt to make a causal apportionment. If so, it seems wrong, because the defendant in that case is clearly a but-for cause of the foot's loss and because the foot's loss also seems to be within the scope of the risk the defendant created. Perhaps with cases like this in mind, the Third Restatement specifically follows some statutes by converting avoidable consequences or minimizing damages cases to comparative fault cases. The plaintiff in the foot case would probably be at fault in failing to take prescribed antibiotics, and thus her fault would be compared with the defendant's fault. RESTATEMENT (THIRD) OF TORTS, APPORTIONMENT OF LIABILITY § 3 cmt. b (2000). *See also Oakly Enterprises, LLC v. NPI, LLC*, 354 P.3d 1073 (Alaska 2015) (distinguishing avoidable consequences from an apportionment of damages).

§ 5. ALLOCATING FULL RESPONSIBILITY TO THE DEFENDANT IN THE INTERESTS OF POLICY OR JUSTICE

BEXIGA V. HAVIR MANUFACTURING CORP.

290 A.2d 281 (N.J. 1972)

PROCTOR, J.

This is a products liability case. Plaintiff John Bexiga, Jr., a minor, was operating a power punch press for his employer, Regina Corporation (Regina), when his right hand was crushed by the ram of the machine, resulting in the loss of fingers and deformity of his hand. His father, John Bexiga, Sr., brought this suit against Havir Manufacturing Corporation (Havir), the manufacturer of the machine. . . . The trial court dismissed the action at the close of the plaintiffs' case. The Appellate Division affirmed. . . .

The particular operation John, Jr. was directed to do required him to place round metal discs, about three inches in diameter, one at a time by hand on top of the die. Once the disc was placed on the die it was held there by the machine itself. He would then depress the foot pedal activating the machine and causing the ram to descend about five inches and punch two holes in the disc. After this operation the ram would ascend and the equipment on the press would remove the metal disc and blow the trimmings away so that the die would be clean for the next cycle. It was estimated by John, Jr. that one cycle as described above would take approximately 10 seconds and that he had completed about 270 cycles during the 40 minutes he operated the machine. He described the accident as follows:

> Well, I put the round piece of metal on the die and the metal didn't go right to the place. I was taking my hand off the machine and I noticed that a piece of metal wasn't in place so I went right back to correct it, but at the same time, my foot had gone to the pedal, so I tried to take my hand off and jerk my foot off too and it was too late. My hand had gotten cut on the punch, the ram.

Plaintiffs' expert, Andrew Gass, a mechanical engineer, testified the punch press amounted to a "booby trap" because there were no safety devices in its basic design and none were installed prior to the accident. . . .

Gass described two "basic types" of protective safety devices both of which were known in the industry at the time of the manufacture and sale. One was a push-button device with the buttons so spaced as to require the operator to place both hands on them away from the die areas to set the machine in motion. The other device was a guardrail or gate to prevent the operator's hands from entering the area between the ram and die when the machine was activated. These and other safety devices were available from companies specializing in safety equipment. . . .

Because of our disposition of the case it is necessary to consider defendant's contention that John, Jr. was contributorily negligent as a matter of law. Neither court below decided this issue. . . . [I]n negligence cases the defense has been held to be unavailable where considerations of policy and justice dictate. . . . We think this case presents a situation where the interests of justice dictate that contributory negligence be unavailable as a defense to either the negligence or strict liability claims.

The asserted negligence of plaintiff—placing his hand under the ram while at the same time depressing the foot pedal—was the very eventuality the safety devices were designed to guard against. It would be anomalous to hold that defendant has a duty to install safety devices but a breach of that duty results in no liability for the very injury the duty was meant to protect against. We hold that under the facts presented to us in this case the defense of contributory negligence is unavailable.

[Reversed and remanded.]

NOTES

1. **Bexiga and comparative fault.** Should the principle in *Bexiga* apply after adoption of comparative fault? On the problem of allocating risks entirely to the defendant or the defendant's special duty to protect even a negligent plaintiff, see 1 DOBBS, HAYDEN & BUBLICK, THE LAW OF TORTS § 224 (2d ed. 2011). Although *Bexiga* found that the defendant's duty encompassed the plaintiff's negligence, it could be said in the alternative that the plaintiff was not negligent in light of his working conditions. *See Fernandes v. DAR Dev. Corp.*, 119 A.3d 878 (N.J. 2015) (worker's "behavior must be evaluated against that of a reasonably prudent person in his exact circumstances, and that evaluation includes whether he had a meaningful choice in the manner in which he performed his assigned task").

2. **Defendant's undertaking to protect the plaintiff.** In *McNamara v. Honeyman*, 546 N.E.2d 139 (Mass. 1989), decedent, who was mentally ill, hanged herself while confined in a state hospital. In a suit for her death, the trial judge rendered a judgment in favor of the plaintiffs against the Commonwealth. Although the court held that mentally ill people "can be comparatively negligent in some circumstances," it nevertheless held that "there can be no comparative negligence where the defendant's duty of care includes preventing the self-abusive or self-destructive acts that caused the

injury." *See also Gregoire v. City of Oak Harbor*, 244 P.3d 924 (Wash. 2010) (jail inmate's suicide was not a basis for comparative fault defense where city and jail official's duty was to protect the health, safety, and welfare of the inmate). Would a non-custodial patient's suicide change the analysis? *See Mulhern v. Catholic Health Initiatives*, 799 N.W.2d 104 (Iowa 2011) (yes; the jury, allowed to assess a percentage of negligence of the plaintiff, set that percentage at 90, and the court entered a judgment for defendants in accord with Iowa's modified comparative scheme); *Gardner v. Oregon Health Sciences Univ.*, 450 P.3d 558 (Or. App. 2019) (comparative fault properly allowed as a defense in action against mental-health providers arising from outpatient's suicide). However, even for custodial patients, the rule against assessment of plaintiff fault is not universal. *See, e.g., Joseph v. State,* 26 P.3d 459 (Alaska 2001) (a jailer owes a duty of care to one in custody to prevent foreseeable suicide, but the jury will be permitted to consider the fault of the person committing suicide and allocate damages accordingly). Should the defendant's responsibility include protecting a plaintiff not only when she is exercising care, but also from her own negligence?

3.   **Plaintiff negligence that occasioned the need for treatment.** What if a plaintiff's negligence occasions the need for defendant's services? In *Mercer v. Vanderbilt Univ.,* 134 S.W.3d 121 (Tenn. 2004), the plaintiff was driving with an estimated blood alcohol level of .20% when he caused a car accident. Several days later, to facilitate a CT scan, he was given a paralytic drug that made him temporarily ventilator dependent. Three portable oxygen tanks were attached to the ventilator. No one checked the ventilator, and the plaintiff stopped breathing. The patient was resuscitated after a code was called, but suffered severe and permanent brain damage. The trial court allowed the jury to compare plaintiff's and defendant's fault. The Tennessee Supreme Court held, however, that the plaintiff's antecedent negligence could not be considered. "[M]ost jurisdictions have held that a patient's negligence that provides only the occasion for medical treatment may not be compared to that of a negligent physician." Quoting another court for the rationale, the court stated, "It would be anomalous to posit, on the one hand, that a health care provider is required to meet a uniform standard of care in its delivery of medical services to all patients, but permit, on the other hand, the conclusion that, where a breach of that duty is established, no liability may exist if the patient's own pre-injury conduct caused the illness or injury which necessitated the medical care." The court agreed that "patients who may have negligently injured themselves are nevertheless entitled to subsequent non-negligent medical treatment and to an undiminished recovery if such subsequent non-negligent treatment is not afforded." *See also Harb v. City of Bakersfield*, 183 Cal.Rptr.3d 59 (Ct. App. 2015) (in plaintiff's negligence action against city and ambulance company whose alleged delay in responding made consequences of stroke much worse, comparative fault could not apply to plaintiff's failure to take blood pressure medicine prior to stroke; comparative fault should apply only when the fault took place concurrently with or after delivery of care and treatment).

The Restatement approves of the result in cases like *Mercer* and *Harb,* but argues that the result cannot be explained on foreseeability/scope of risk grounds. RESTATEMENT (THIRD) OF TORTS: APPORTIONMENT OF LIABILITY § 7 cmt. m (2000). Can you see a basis for the Restatement's position?

4. **Statutes to protect vulnerable plaintiffs.** Statutes sometimes impose a duty upon the defendant to protect plaintiffs who are vulnerable or disabled. Minor workers in dangerous occupations may be so protected by statutes. Similarly, a statute that requires school buses to remain stopped until school children have crossed the road is a recognition that the children may not exercise care to protect themselves when they cross. The school bus driver who violates such a statute may be denied the right to raise contributory negligence of the child as a defense. *See Van Gaasbeck v. Webatuck Cent. Sch. Dist. No. 1,* 234 N.E.2d 243 (N.Y. 1967). Would these be situations in which to impose a *Bexiga* duty upon the defendant?

5. **Other statutes.** Some statutes bar comparative fault claims even when plaintiffs can presumably care for themselves. With pervasive seatbelt use and many state statutes that now require it, failure to wear a seatbelt could count as comparative fault. *Barnes v. Paulin,* 900 N.Y.S.2d 886 (App. Div. 2010) (damages reduction based on seat belt nonuse); *Nabors Well Servs., Ltd. v. Romero,* 456 S.W.3d 553 (Tex. 2015) (evidence of use or non-use of seatbelts admissible for the purpose of allocating responsibility under statute, overruling prior precedent to the contrary). However, a large number of jurisdictions statutorily limit these comparative fault claims. Should they?

6. **Nonreciprocal risks and known disability.** One characteristic that unites many of these cases is that the defendant imposes a risk upon the plaintiff but the plaintiff's fault imposes no similar risk upon the defendant. In other words, the risks are not reciprocal or mutual. Contrast the ordinary automobile collision case in which each driver is acting negligently, thus creating risks to others as well as to self.

Maybe *Bexiga* and similar cases suggest that the plaintiff's vulnerability rightly plays a part in determining responsibility, but only in certain cases. The plaintiff's disability or vulnerability might be especially important if (1) the defendant knows of the plaintiff's disability which prevents or inhibits the plaintiff's care for himself; and (2) the plaintiff's risky conduct endangers himself but not others. Consider the following cases:

Case 1. A mentally disabled adult, Clay, works for a farmer, Johnson. Johnson took Clay in as a foster child, an arrangement made with the welfare department. Johnson put him to work with machinery on the farm, and explained his duties, but did not explain the dangers. Clay put his hand in a grinder and it was severely injured. A reasonable person would have perceived the risk and would not have put a hand in the grinder. Clay did not adequately perceive the risk because of his mental limitations. In Clay's suit against Johnson, the defense was contributory negligence.

Case 2. Kincheloe, a child of 12, is driving a car on a rural road. His neighbor, Davis, was driving in excess of the speed limit in the opposite direction, approaching Kincheloe. He recognized Kincheloe and knew he was inclined to take his father's car and pull dangerous stunts. Nevertheless, Davis did not slow down. Kincheloe pulled over in Davis' lane, and Davis was unable to avoid collision because of his speed. Both Davis and Kincheloe were injured. In Kincheloe's claim against Davis, contributory negligence of Kincheloe was pleaded as a defense.

Case 3. Paulin, a mentally disabled adult, walked down a rural road in the pre-dawn hours. He walked on the right side and wore dark clothes. Dalrymple was driving in the same direction. As he neared Paulin, a car came from the opposite direction and Dalrymple dimmed his lights. He never saw Paulin until the last minute. He struck Paulin, who was seriously injured. Contributory negligence was the defense in Paulin's claim against Dalrymple.

Case 4. Perez and Dittman were both speeding as they traveled south on a public highway. Perez, who was 13, attempted to pass Dittman on a curve. At the same time Dittman lost control and began to skid over to his left. The two cars collided at this point. Each driver was injured. Contributory negligence is pleaded.

These examples might suggest that you agree with the principle in *Bexiga*, but might think that application of the principle to more concrete cases is debatable.

7. **Policy factors in allocation of risks to the defendant.** One article that examines cases in which courts bar plaintiff fault defenses after the shift from contributory negligence to comparative fault concludes that court-created limits are grounded in identifiable and consistent issues of principle or policy. The policies involved when judges limit comparative fault defenses include: plaintiff incapacity (plaintiff lacks total or partial capacity for self-care); structural safety (due to systemic differentials in knowledge, experience or control, the defendant can be expected to take better care of plaintiff's safety than can the plaintiff herself); role definition (defendant's obligation is to care for even a negligent plaintiff because of defendant's responsibilities as a professional rescuer); process values (litigating the comparative fault defense would harm litigants, create unmanageable litigation, or produce statements of relative fault where such statements are problematic); fundamental values (a determination of comparative fault would encroach on fundamental, sometimes constitutional values); and autonomy and self-risk (plaintiff's conduct risked only harm to self and as such receives more latitude for plaintiff choice). *See* Ellen M. Bublick, *Comparative Fault to the Limits,* 56 VAND. L. REV. 977 (2003). Are any of these policies at issue in the cases here?

CHRISTENSEN V. ROYAL SCHOOL DISTRICT NO. 160
124 P.3d 283 (Wash. 2005)

ALEXANDER, C.J. . . .

[Steven Diaz, a 26-year-old teacher engaged in sexual activity with his 13-year-old middle-school student Leslie Christensen. The sexual activity occurred in Diaz's classroom. Diaz claimed that Leslie voluntarily participated in the relationship.]

Leslie and her parents brought suit against Diaz, the Royal School District (the District), and Principal Andersen in federal district court. . . . In their complaint, they claimed that Diaz sexually abused Leslie. Damages were also sought against the District and Andersen based on the allegation that the District and its principal, Andersen, were negligent in hiring and supervising Diaz.

In a responsive pleading, the District and Andersen asserted an affirmative defense that Leslie's voluntary participation in the sexual relationship with Diaz constituted contributory fault . . . . Leslie moved for partial summary judgment on this issue, seeking to strike the affirmative defense. The trial court deferred ruling on the motion pending an answer from this court to the certified question [can contributory fault be assessed against a 13-year-old victim of sexual abuse for her participation in the relationship]. . . .

The existence of a legal duty is a question of law and "depends on mixed considerations of logic, common sense, justice, policy, and precedent."

The District and Andersen argue that contributory fault applies in this case because Leslie had a duty to protect herself against sexual abuse by an adult, a duty she allegedly ignored by voluntarily engaging in a sexual relationship with Diaz. . . .

The District and Andersen contend that contributory fault applies because "Washington has a long history of holding children responsible for their comparative negligence" and that Leslie had a duty to protect herself against sexual abuse but failed to do so. In support of this contention, they cite several cases where contributory fault has been applied against a child. Although the District and Andersen correctly pointed out that Washington does apply contributory fault and the duty of protecting oneself to children in some instances, the cases that they cite are not germane to our inquiry, as none involve sexual abuse. The act of sexual abuse is key here. As indicated above, our public policy is directed to protecting children from such abuse. . . .

[At issue in this case is the idea that a claim of contributory negligence is barred because the acts of sexual molestation were intentional, even though the contributory negligence defense itself is raised by a negligent rather than an intentional tortfeasor.]

Our conclusion that the defense of contributory negligence should not be available to the Royal School District and Principal Anderson is in accord with the established Washington rule that a school has a "special relationship" with the students in its custody and a duty to protect them "from reasonably anticipated dangers." The rationale for imposing this duty is on the placement of the student in the care of the school with the resulting loss of the student's ability to protect himself or herself. . . .

[B]ecause we recognize the vulnerability of children in the school setting, we hold, as a matter of public policy, that children do not have a duty to protect themselves from sexual abuse by their teachers. Moreover, we conclude that contributory fault may not be assessed against a 13-year-old child based on the failure to protect herself from being sexually abused when the defendant or defendants stand in a special relationship to the child and have a duty to protect the child. *See* Ellen M. Bublick, *Comparative Fault to the Limits,* 56 VAND. L. REV. 977, 1004 (2003). Andersen and the District had a clear duty to protect students in their custody, and this duty encompassed the obligation to supervise and control Diaz. . . .

[The defendant alleged that when asked about the sexual relationship by the principal, Leslie did not disclose it]. We have not said in this opinion that the school district should be precluded from defending on the basis that it was not negligent. The fact that it may not, under Washington law, assert that the 13-year-old child was contributorily negligent should not bar it from claiming at trial that it was careful in hiring and supervising the child's teacher and, thus, was without negligence. If, indeed, the District was thwarted in its efforts to ascertain if Leslie Christensen was abused by her teacher, that fact would likely be relevant on the issue of its alleged negligence. . . .

The child, in our view, lacks the capacity to consent to the sexual abuse and is under no duty to protect himself or herself from being abused. An opposite holding would, in our judgment, frustrate the overarching goals of prevention and deterrence of child sexual abuse. . . .

SANDERS, J., dissenting. . . .

Washington law holds minors responsible for contributory negligence in many contexts. The majority dismisses these cases because they do not involve sexual conduct. I fail to see why a minor can be contributorily negligent for driving a snowmobile but cannot be contributorily negligent in a negligence action relating to sexual misconduct. Generally contributory negligence is a question of fact for the jury.

But under the majority's rule, a 15-year-old girl can seduce a male teacher, and then sue the school district for damages knowing she cannot be found contributorily negligent in the school district suit as a matter of law.... [T]his provides a powerful incentive to engage in sexual misconduct. We are deceiving ourselves if we think children are unable to understand the risks and potential rewards. Perhaps some are not, but that is why a jury determines this question as a matter of fact in each case.... I see no reason to deviate from our standard rule on contributory negligence for minors in negligence cases involving sexual activity.

The majority appeals to a school's duty to protect students. Well and good. However, merely because a school must protect the children in its care does not relieve the students of any personal responsibility for their own conduct. Children should not be allowed to take advantage of the school's duty by forcing it to pay damages for injuries invited by the student or injuries which the district could have prevented *but for* obstruction by the student. Such a rule is inequitable and excuses all manner of mischief....

This school district *did* take steps to protect the female student. School officials met with the girl and her parents to determine if anything untoward was occurring with the teacher. The girl, however, allegedly lied about her involvement with the teacher, thwarting the school district's efforts to protect her. She may be below the age of consent, but not below the age of honesty. Yes, school districts must protect their students, but students must cooperate. If a student undermines school officials' actions to protect her, she must bear at least some of the fault for resulting injury. If the girl lied, this is contributory negligence on her part and a proper defense for the school district....

[A separate dissent is omitted.]

NOTES

1. **The plaintiff's "no duty" expression.** The Restatement provides that, in light of principle or policy, plaintiffs, like defendants, might sometimes have "no duty" to act reasonably in self-protection. RESTATEMENT (THIRD) OF TORTS: APPORTIONMENT OF LIABILITY § 3 cmt. d (2000). If a plaintiff has no duty to protect herself by the use of reasonable care, she cannot be charged with comparative fault for failing to do so. The no duty language is misapplied in one respect, since "duty" refers to an obligation enforceable by suit. The point of using no-duty language, however, is to draw attention to a parallel set of rules that relieve defendants of liability for negligent conduct. For instance, we will see in Chapter 12 that landowners frequently do not owe a duty of reasonable care to trespassers. That means the landowner is free to be negligent toward trespassers. The idea of a plaintiff no-duty rule is that the same approach should be taken to protect the interests of the plaintiff.

2. **No duty of a child to guard against sexual abuse by an adult.** What policy interests might be served by the Washington Supreme Court's plaintiff no-duty rule? Child sexual activity with an adult could be treated like any other potential comparative fault by a child. When immature plaintiffs are confronted with involvement in adult activity, might child safety be promoted by placing greater responsibility on the more mature and experienced party? *See Bjerke v. Johnson,* 742 N.W.2d 660 (Minn. 2007) ("Beyond the strong public interest in protecting children from sexual abuse, it seems to us unlikely that children can be expected to comprehend the multitude of long-term effects of sexual abuse by an adult."); *C.C.H. v. Philadelphia Phillies, Inc.,* 940 A.2d 336 (Pa. 2008) ("children as a class . . . due to their youth or inexperience, lack the judgment necessary to protect themselves from sexual aggressors"). Or as the dissent argues, will a no-duty rule encourage young plaintiffs to engage in sexual misconduct? In some ways, the no-duty rule in *Christensen* parallels the doctrine that requires children to use extra care when engaged in adult activities that pose risk to others. When engaged in adult activities that risk the children's own safety, others may owe extra care to them. Ellen M. Bublick, *Comparative Fault to the Limits,* 56 Vand. L. Rev. 977 (2003).

3. **Failure to disclose sexual contact.** The dissent makes much of a contested fact that the plaintiff, when asked by school officials if she was being sexually abused, did not reveal the truth. Would it be relevant, either to a no-duty rule or to a reasonable care analysis, if research shows that fewer than 50% of adolescents ever reveal sexual abuse to anyone at all, and that those who reveal abuse usually reveal it only to a best friend or parent? *See* R.J.R. Levesque, *Sex Differences in the Experience of Child Sexual Victimization,* 9 J. of Fam. Violence 357–69 (1994).

4. **Effect of no-duty rules.** The *Christensen* court struck the defendant's comparative fault defense. As the court made clear, the plaintiff still may not win her claim. Why would the plaintiff want a situation in which she either recovers fully or not at all—are there process considerations? What if victim blame is associated with increased psychological difficulties such as post-traumatic stress disorder? *See* Bonnie L. Katz & Martha R. Burt, *Self Blame in Recovery from Rape,* in Rape & Sexual Assault II 162 (Ann Wolbert Burgess ed., 1988). Might an attorney for the child plaintiff ever want a court to permit a comparative negligence defense in a case like *Christensen* nevertheless?

5. **Plaintiff's rights.** Some of the discourse on this topic is framed in terms of the plaintiff's rights or entitlements. In a quite different context, in *LeRoy Fibre Co. v. Chicago, Milwaukee & St. Paul Ry. Co.,* 232 U.S. 340 (1914), the plaintiff owned land abutting the defendant's railroad. He stacked flax on the land for use in his manufacturing business. He alleged that the railroad negligently emitted sparks and coals that set fire to and destroyed the flax. The defendant argued that the plaintiff was contributorily negligent in stacking the combustible flax so near the railroad. The jury, charged on the contributory negligence defense, found for the defendant. The Supreme Court held that the contributory negligence defense presented no question for the

jury. The Court held that a contrary decision casts upon the plaintiff a duty to use his property not only to avoid injury to another, but also "to use his own property that it may not be injured by the wrongs of another." However, the "legal conception of property is of rights." One way to look at this problem is to recognize that property law, emphasizing the owner's right to use property as she pleases, is sometimes at odds with negligence law, which emphasizes the safety of conduct and evaluates safety case-by-case after the event has occurred. Both approaches represent important values in our culture. How should we determine which prevails? *See* William Powers, Jr., *Border Wars*, 72 TEX. L. REV. 1209 (1994). *See also* RESTATEMENT (THIRD) OF TORTS: APPORTIONMENT OF LIABILITY § 3 cmt. d (2000).

6. **Rights or entitlements not based on rights to possession of tangible property.** The plaintiff may be entitled to use her property even if in doing so she is in danger of harm by the defendant's negligence. Similarly, the plaintiff might have entitlements not grounded in tangible property. She might be entitled to, say, use the public streets although they are dangerous or shop for groceries at night although rape or robbery is an ever-present possibility. If she had such an entitlement, then she could not be charged with comparative negligence merely because she shopped at night.

7. **Determining plaintiff entitlements.** How should courts decide what entitlements a plaintiff has beyond those arising from ownership of tangible property? Can we identify any principle? Consider *Brandon v. Cty. of Richardson*, 624 N.W.2d 604 (Neb. 2001), where a transgendered rape victim reported a rape to the sheriff, who also knew that the rapists were dangerous and might murder Brandon if there were no police protection. The sheriff did not protect Brandon and the rapists did in fact murder Brandon. Should the estate's recovery against the sheriff be reduced on the ground that the victim was negligent in reporting the rape after the rapists warned not to do so? Does Brandon have an entitlement to report crime to the police even if it is risky to do so?

Is a plaintiff guilty of comparative negligence for wearing expensive jewelry in a neighborhood that has a high crime rate? In *Isik Jewelry v. Mars Media, Inc.*, 418 F.Supp.2d 112 (E.D.N.Y. 2005), the music artist Albert Johnson, known as "Prodigy," left a video shoot wearing jewelry valued at over $100,000. He was robbed at gunpoint as he walked across the street to get some water from a convenience store. In a bailment action, the court examined whether Johnson failed to use reasonable care. The court found that Johnson was not negligent as a matter of law. Could the conclusion be said to reflect an entitlement by the plaintiff?

What of a comparative fault instruction based on the argument that the plaintiffs were unreasonable in refusing to immediately give their money and possessions to the three assailants who broke into their room, rather than insisting that they did not have money? *See InTown Lessee Assocs., LLC v. Howard*, 67 So.3d 711 (Miss. 2011) ("To penalize a crime victim for his failure to cooperate with his assailant would constitute a bizarre and perverse misapplication of the doctrine of comparative fault. The trial court did not abuse its discretion in denying InTown's request for a comparative negligence instruction.").

8. **Concern about assignments of relative fault.** Might a plaintiff have an entitlement even outside the context of crime or abuse? What of a comparative fault defense alleging that a plaintiff, hit by a defendant who ran a light, is negligent to some degree for going on green. Can you see why a court might suggest that the plaintiff with the right of way has an entitlement? *See Hayes v. Price*, 313 S.W.3d 645 (Mo. 2010) ("a driver is entitled to assume a car going in the opposite direction will yield the right of way to oncoming traffic before turning," reversing 20% assignment of fault to plaintiff). Or could a front seat passenger in a car be said to have no duty to the passengers in the back? *See Siruta v. Siruta*, 348 P.3d 549 (Kan. 2015) ("If there is no duty, 'a person cannot be at fault and therefore cannot be made a party subject to having his negligence compared.' ")

9. **Autonomy: helmets and 5-inch heels.** Comparative fault claims often involve plaintiffs' risk of harm to self rather than others. Should greater latitude be given for conduct that risks harm only to the plaintiff? In *McKinley v. Casson*, 80 A.3d 618 (Del. 2013), the court held that failure to wear a motorcycle helmet may not be grounds for a comparative fault claim: "In Delaware, motorcyclists over 19 years of age may ride without wearing a helmet. Thus, by statute, an adult does not violate a duty to exercise reasonable care by failing to wear a helmet. There being no statutory requirement to wear a helmet, the remaining question is whether there is a common law duty. We are aware of none, and we follow the numerous other jurisdictions that have declined to adopt a common law duty to wear a helmet." *See also Webber v. Butner*, 923 F.3d 479 (7th Cir. 2019) (failure of plaintiff to wear a hardhat was not admissible for purpose of apportioning fault to him; "The fact that Webber was not wearing a hardhat did not cause the branch to fall and hit him on the head.").

What if a plaintiff risks her safety by wearing 5-inch heels? In *Bongiorno v. Americorp, Inc.*, 159 So.3d 1027 (Fla. Dist. Ct. App. 2015), a worker brought a tort action against a property owner after she slipped on the bathroom floor. At a bench trial, the court found that the defendant was negligent and assigned 50% comparative fault to the plaintiff for wearing 4–5" heels to work. The plaintiff argued that she was not negligent for wearing high heels to work. The appellate court agreed. "Americorp failed to sustain its burden of proving that Bongiorno created a foreseeable zone of risk by wearing high-heeled shoes to work and, therefore, the trial court erred in finding her comparatively negligent for her injuries." Isn't it foreseeable that people wearing 4–5" heels might fall? Could the court justify its decision on grounds of policy rather than foreseeability?

10. **Entitlements vs. case-by-case adjudication of plaintiff fault.** Do we need entitlements decided by a judge like those in *Mercer, Christensen, LeRoy Fibre*, or *Brandon*? Do you think it would suffice instead to judge

comparative fault case-by-case in light of the plaintiff's rights and legitimate interests? For example, couldn't we rely upon juries to hold as a matter of ordinary analysis of comparative fault that a woman is definitely not guilty of comparative fault merely because she shops late at night? If you think juries might be unreliable when it comes to deciding issues of comparative fault, would you expect entitlements formulated by judges in advance to be more trustworthy?

§ 6. TRADITIONAL EXCEPTIONS TO THE CONTRIBUTORY NEGLIGENCE BAR

Cases that allocate full responsibility to the defendant even after a shift to comparative fault may draw on traditional exceptions to the contributory negligence bar. To what extent are these doctrines still necessary?

A. THE RESCUE DOCTRINE

"The rescue doctrine is a rule of law holding that one who sees a person in imminent danger caused by the negligence of another cannot be charged with contributory negligence" when the actor attempts a rescue, unless the rescuer acted recklessly. *Ouellette v. Carde*, 612 A.2d 687 (R.I. 1992). In *Ouellette*, the defendant was pinned in a closed garage under a car the defendant had been fixing. There was gasoline all over the floor. The defendant called a friend for help but when the friend activated the electric garage door opener to rescue him, the gas ignited and the rescuer was badly burned. The rescuer sued the defendant, who asked for a comparative negligence instruction. The trial court denied the instruction and the jury found for the plaintiff-rescuer without reduction in damages. The award was upheld on appeal under the rescue doctrine.

After the advent of comparative fault, some courts leave the allocation of fault between the defendant and the rescuer-plaintiff to the jury. *See Govich v. North American Systems, Inc.*, 814 P.2d 94 (N.M. 1991).

B. LAST CLEAR CHANCE OR DISCOVERED PERIL

In the traditional system that barred all recovery for contributory negligence, courts allowed the negligent plaintiff a full recovery when the plaintiff was left in a helpless position by his own negligence and the defendant, who had the last clear chance to avoid injury, negligently inflicted it anyway. *See* RESTATEMENT (SECOND) OF TORTS §§ 479 & 480 (1965).

The doctrine first appeared in *Davies v. Mann*, 10 M. & W. 546, 152 Eng. Rep. 588 (Exch. 1842). In that case, the plaintiff had left his donkey tied in the road eating grass. The defendant negligently drove a team and wagon down the hill and ran over the animal, which, being fettered, was unable to move. The court held that the plaintiff's contributory negligence was no defense. Baron Parke said that the plaintiff "is entitled to recover," stressing that if the rule were otherwise, "a man might justify the driving over goods left on a public highway, or even a man lying asleep there."

The last clear chance doctrine held that if the defendant discovered or should have discovered the plaintiff's peril, and could reasonably have avoided it, the plaintiff's earlier negligence would neither bar nor reduce the plaintiff's recovery. A slightly less generous version, called the discovered peril doctrine, applied these rules only if the defendant actually did discover the plaintiff's peril. The plaintiff could not invoke these doctrines unless the plaintiff was helpless; if he could extricate himself from danger at any time, the defendant did not have the last chance to avoid injury and the negligent plaintiff's claim would be barred entirely.

In states that have adopted comparative fault systems, the last clear chance and discovered peril doctrines have been discarded, mostly on the ground that they were attempts to aid the plaintiff in a harsh system and not needed once comparative fault rules apply. *See Del Lago Partners, Inc. v. Smith*, 307 S.W.3d 762 (Tex. 2010). Occasionally, courts still face last clear chance arguments. Where the cases still involve contributory negligence, as with a claim against a governmental entity in Indiana, the doctrine might still apply. *See Penn Harris Madison Sch. Corp. v. Howard*, 861 N.E.2d 1190 (Ind. 2007).

Should the last clear chance doctrine be retained in a modified comparative fault system? Would the fact that the defendant had the last chance still be relevant in determining relative fault? On both points, see 1 DOBBS, HAYDEN & BUBLICK, THE LAW OF TORTS § 226 (2d ed. 2011).

C. DEFENDANT'S RECKLESS OR INTENTIONAL MISCONDUCT

Contributory negligence was historically no defense to an intentional tort. By extension of this idea, courts also held that contributory negligence was no defense to willful, wanton, or reckless torts, defined as involving "utter indifference to or conscious disregard for the safety of others." Such torts border on intentional wrongdoing because they involve a bad state of mind as well as risky conduct. Under this rule, the plaintiff charged with contributory negligence was allowed a full recovery against a reckless or wanton defendant.

Once comparative negligence rules are adopted, should courts discard the old rule and simply let the jury apportion fault between plaintiff and defendant, even when the defendant is guilty of reckless conduct? Should comparative negligence rules apply when the defendant is guilty of an intentional tort? Consider these cases:

Case 1. Defendant strikes the plaintiff. When sued, he argues that the plaintiff was guilty of negligence because she provoked the attack.

Case 2. A negligently provides B with keys to A's car, knowing that B is dangerous, in a rage at P, and might attack her. B intentionally runs down P. After P recovers fully against A, A seeks contribution from B.

The Restatement of Apportionment takes "no position" on the first case, whether a plaintiff's comparative fault reduces recovery against an intentional tortfeasor. RESTATEMENT (THIRD) OF TORTS: APPORTIONMENT OF LIABILITY § 1 cmt. c (2000). Some statutes explicitly disallow such a reduction. *See Smith v. R.J. Reynolds Tobacco Co.*, 880 F.3d 1272 (11th Cir. 2018) (applying FLA. STAT. ANN. § 768.81(4)); *Martinez v. Wilson*, 287 So.3d 27 (La. Ct. App. 2019) (applying LA. CIV. CODE art. 2323(C).

On the second case, the Restatement calls for contribution between negligent and intentional tortfeasors. RESTATEMENT (THIRD) OF TORTS: APPORTIONMENT OF LIABILITY § 23 cmt. l (2000). What is your position with respect to both cases?

D. PLAINTIFF'S ILLEGAL ACTIVITY

DUGGER V. ARREDONDO

408 S.W.3d 825 (Tex. 2013)

GREEN, JUSTICE.

[Friends Geoffrey Dugger and Joel Martinez drank tequila, snorted lines of black-tar heroin, and smoked marijuana. Martinez fell asleep, made a choking sound, and subsequently began vomiting. Dugger delayed in calling 911. When he did, police arrived about five minutes later, and paramedics ten minutes after that. Dugger did not tell the police or paramedics that Martinez had ingested heroin, only that he had drunk tequila and smoked marijuana. The paramedics treated Martinez for alcohol poisoning, but could not save him. Martinez died less than two hours later. Martinez's mother, Mary Ann Arredondo, brought a wrongful death action against Dugger. Arredondo alleged that Duggar was negligent in delaying to call emergency services and in failing to advise paramedics who arrived on the scene that Martinez had used heroin. Dugger asserted an affirmative defense based on the common law unlawful acts doctrine, which completely barred a plaintiff from recovery if, at the time of injury, the plaintiff was engaged in an unlawful act that was "inextricably intertwined with the claim and the alleged damages would not have occurred but for the illegal act." The trial court granted Dugger's motion for summary judgment based on the unlawful acts doctrine. Martinez's mother appealed, arguing that section of the Civil Practice and Remedies Code, which allows for comparative fault, replaced the common law unlawful acts doctrine. The court of appeals reversed.]

We hold that the Legislature's adoption of the proportionate responsibility scheme in Chapter 33 of the Civil Practice and Remedies Code evidenced its clear intention that a plaintiff's illegal conduct not falling within a statutorily-recognized affirmative defense be apportioned rather than barring recovery completely. . . .

More than 120 years ago, this Court recognized the common law unlawful acts doctrine as barring a plaintiff from recovering damages if it could be shown that, at the time of injury, the plaintiff was engaged in an illegal act that contributed to the injury. The doctrine originated with the principle of in pari delicto or "unclean hands" in the contract context, but was extended to tort causes of action. The doctrine is based on the public policy that wrongdoers should not be compensated for their immoral acts.

As early as 1888, we recognized that "no action will lie to recover a claim for damages, if to establish it the plaintiff requires aid from an illegal transaction, or is under the necessity of showing or in any manner depending upon an illegal act to which he is a party." Since then, "[c]ourts throughout Texas . . . have used this rule, along with public policy principles, to prevent a plaintiff from recovering damages that arose out of his or her own illegal conduct." . . .

Recently, scholars and courts have disagreed over the viability of the unlawful acts doctrine in modern jurisprudence. The Restatement (Second) of Torts and respected legal scholars reject the principle that tortious or criminal conduct can completely bar recovery. Several courts and legislatures, on the other hand, have approved of the unlawful acts doctrine in statutes and case law.

Since Texas's shift to the proportionate responsibility scheme, . . . most Texas courts have used a plaintiff's unlawful act to measure proportionate responsibility and reduce recovery, rather than completely bar the plaintiff from recovering damages. . . .

Dugger and the dissent argue that if we do not uphold the unlawful acts doctrine, it will be easier for criminals to bring suits and recover. On the other hand, Arredondo argues that recognizing the unlawful acts doctrine could lead to a slippery slope where it would be impossible for many people to access the judicial system and try their claims because they were engaged in an unlawful act while sustaining injuries. Additionally, the Texas Civil Rights Project, as amicus curiae, contends that a broad unlawful acts doctrine could allow people who commit serious tortious conduct against others to have civil immunity merely because the claimant was not in compliance with every law at the time of the tortious conduct. . . .

We hold that the common law unlawful acts doctrine is not available as an affirmative defense in personal injury and wrongful death cases. Like other common law assumption-of-the-risk defenses, it was abrogated by

Chapter 33's proportionate responsibility scheme. Unless the requirements of the affirmative defense in section 93.001 are satisfied [when assumption of the risk is recognized for "a felony, for which plaintiff has been finally convicted" or certain cases involving "committing or attempting to commit suicide"], a plaintiff's share of responsibility for his or her injuries should be compared against the defendant's. We therefore affirm the judgment of the court of appeals, which reversed the summary judgment and remanded the case to the trial court.

HECHT, J. (dissenting). . . .

The Court seems to think that because Chapter 33 abrogated other common law doctrines that barred recovery based on the plaintiff's conduct, like assumption of the risk, imminent peril, and last clear chance, it also abrogated the unlawful acts doctrine. But comparative responsibility determines the amount of recovery based on an allocation of fault contributing to injury. The unlawful acts doctrine holds that the allocation should not be made because any recovery rewards criminal conduct. This case is a good example. Assuming, as we must, that Dugger should have called 9–1–1 a few minutes earlier and should have disclosed Martinez's ingestion of heroin, what is his percentage of responsibility? How much should Dugger pay Arredondo for not acting promptly and not being forthcoming when Martinez was prohibited by law from ingesting the drug that killed him? The point is not simply that the question is hard, though it is, and assigning it to a jury makes it no easier. The point is that to award any damages lessens the law's prohibition against the use of heroin.

Now, if a robber slips in a puddle on the bank floor and breaks his leg, he can sue the bank. A rapist who falls in a hole in the victim's backyard can sue for damages. Lest these examples be thought extreme or unlikely, consider this: can a teenager sue a boy who sold him fireworks from which he extracted gunpowder to make a pipe bomb that exploded in his hands? No, in New York, said the New York Court of Appeals in Barker v. Kallash. In Texas, after today, the answer is yes.

One criticism of the unlawful acts doctrine, a criticism with substance, is that it does not have sufficient limiting principles. The doctrine has proven especially difficult to apply against undocumented aliens[24]. . . . No one argues that a motorist broadsided by a drunk driver should be

---

[24] Compare *Carcamo-Lopez v. Doe*, 865 F.Supp.2d 736, 766–767 (W.D.Tex.2011) (citing the court of appeals' opinion in the present case to conclude that Texas' unlawful acts doctrine does not bar suit by an undocumented alien accidentally struck by a border patrol vehicle while crouching in the dark in vegetation near the bank of the Rio Grande River), with *Rico v. Flores*, 481 F.3d 234, 243–244 (5th Cir.2007) (concluding that it was uncertain whether the Texas unlawful acts doctrine would bar suit for the wrongful death of undocumented aliens who died in a railcar while entering the country illegally against the person hired to help them or the railway), and *Fuentes v. Alecio*, Civil Action No. C-06-425, 2006 U.S. Dist. LEXIS 93013, 2006 WL 3813780 (S.D.Tex. Dec. 26, 2006) (dismissing action for the wrongful death of an undocumented alien who expired from heat exhaustion while entering the country illegally as barred by the unlawful acts doctrine).

prohibited from recovering because he was driving five miles an hour over the speed limit. Nor should the doctrine be used to resurrect outlawry for undocumented aliens. It is true that in the nineteenth century, the doctrine was used to deny recovery to persons injured while violating Blue Laws.[1] But if we were to discard every claim and defense that has been misused, there would be nothing left of the law. Properly applied, the doctrine serves the valuable purpose of promoting compliance with the law and should be retained. . . .

NOTES

1. **After comparative fault.** The bar on recovery of a plaintiff who was involved in illegal activity was created at a time when contributory negligence was an all-or-nothing rule. Should the illegal activity defense survive the transition to comparative apportionment? While *Dugger* would apportion fault, *Greenwald v. Van Handel*, 88 A.3d 467 (Conn. 2014), retained the bar. The issue is both important and current. *See Rodriguez v. Williams*, 355 P.3d 25 (N.M. App. 2015) (plaintiff's own intoxication did not bar recovery in suit for injuries suffered in car accident, but must be taken into account in a comparative fault analysis); *Tug Valley Pharmacy, LLC v. All Plaintiffs Below in Mingo Cty.*, 773 S.E.2d 627 (W. Va. 2015) (rejecting complete bar rule). *Cf. JBS Carriers, Inc., v. Washington*, 564 S.W.3d 830 (Tex. 2018) (error to exclude evidence that jaywalking plaintiff was under the influence of alcohol and illegal drugs when she was struck by defendant's truck; such evidence was relevant to the issue of her comparative negligence).

2. **Illegal activity.** Does any illegal activity whatsoever by the plaintiff bar a claim? In *Winschel v. Brown*, 171 P.3d 142 (Alaska 2007), the trial court granted summary judgment for defendant because the plaintiff was illegally riding his ATV on a bicycle path when he was injured. The Alaska Supreme Court disagreed. This illegal activity did not preclude recovery because the crime was not "serious." However, the crime could be given "significant weight" in fixing the percentage of comparative fault. Does it matter to the availability of the defense if the illegal activity is violating the state's Blue Laws, driving above the speed limit, entering the country illegally, engaging in prostitution, or using heroin? *See Barker v. Kallish*, 468 N.E.2d 39 (N.Y. 1984) (15-year-old making a pipe bomb from firecrackers sold by a 9-year-old); *Price v. Purdue Pharma Co.*, 920 So.2d 479 (Miss. 2006) (defrauding various doctors to obtain Oxycontin). Should the matter be resolved by how wrongful the plaintiff's conduct was? How closely the unlawful conduct was related to the harm? How wrongful plaintiff's conduct was when compared to the defendant's conduct? Does that latter question have to be a jury issue?

3. **Statutory bar.** Statutes in some states bar plaintiffs from all recovery in tort cases if they have engaged in particular forms of misconduct relating to the claim. For example, New Jersey has a statute that bars an

---

[1]   Laws prohibiting certain activities, such as selling alcoholic beverages on Sundays.—Eds.

uninsured motorist from maintaining a personal injury action for damages suffered in an auto accident. The statute was applied in *Aronberg v. Tolbert*, 25 A.3d 1121 (N.J. 2011), to bar a mother's wrongful death action where her son was uninsured.

4. **Commentary.** Joseph H. King, Jr., *Outlaws and Outlier Doctrines: The Serious Misconduct Bar in Tort Law,* 43 WM. & MARY L. REV. 1011 (2002), attacks the serious-misconduct bar as a frustration of tort law goals and the comparative negligence structure, as a doctrine unpredictable and selective in application, and as an invitation to judges to apply the moral flavor of the month. Should plaintiffs guilty of serious misconduct be allowed to present their cases to the jury and see what percentages of responsibility juries assign?

REFERENCES: 1 DOBBS, HAYDEN & BUBLICK, THE LAW OF TORTS §§ 218–231 (2d ed. 2011); DOBBS, HAYDEN & BUBLICK, HORNBOOK ON TORTS, CHAPTER 16 (2d ed. 2016); VICTOR E. SCHWARTZ & KATHRYN KELLY, COMPARATIVE NEGLIGENCE (6th ed. 2020); HENRY WOODS & BETH DEERE, COMPARATIVE FAULT (3d ed. 1996 & 2021 Supp.).

CHAPTER 10

ASSUMPTION OF THE RISK

■ ■ ■

§ 1. EXPRESS ASSUMPTION OF THE RISK (CONTRACTUAL)

STELLUTI V. CASAPENN ENTERPRISES, LLC, 1 A.3d 678 (N.J. 2010). On the day that she joined the Powerhouse gym, Gina Stelluti participated in a "spinning" class. She advised the instructor of her inexperience and the instructor helped her adjust the stationary spin bike. During the class, the handlebars dislodged from the bike, causing Stelluti to fall and suffer injuries. Expert testimony suggested that the locking pin on the bike's handlebars was difficult to engage and had not been fully engaged at the time of the accident. Stelluti sued the gym for negligence in failing to properly maintain and set up the bike and in failing to properly instruct her about to how to use it. The lower court granted summary judgment based on a waiver and release Stelluti had signed, which said that she expressly agreed to discharge all claims against the health club "from any and all claims or causes of action." The appellate division affirmed, except to the extent that the agreement purported to insulate the defendant from reckless acts.

On appeal to the New Jersey Supreme Court, *held*, affirmed. Exculpatory clauses have been historically disfavored and subject to close judicial scrutiny. Although the agreement is a take-it-or-leave-it standardized preprinted form, and therefore a contract of adhesion, it is nevertheless enforceable in this context because Stelluti was not in a position of unequal bargaining power. "Stelluti could have taken her business to another fitness club, could have found another means of exercise aside from joining a private gym, or could have thought about it and even sought advice before signing up and using the facility's equipment." Contracting parties have a long-standing liberty to bind themselves as they see fit. The agreement itself is clear about the waiver of legal rights. It expressly covers "the sudden and unforeseen malfunctioning of any equipment," and prominently disclaims liability for "negligence on the part of the Club, its agents and employees." Looking at the public interest in this context, "Assumption of risk associated with physical-exertion-involving discretionary activities is sensible and has been applied in many other settings." There remains a standard for protection of adults in the context of gyms, and "had Powerhouse's management or employees been aware of a piece of defective exercise equipment and failed to remedy the condition or to warn adequately of the dangerous condition, or if it had dangerously or improperly maintained equipment, Powerhouse could not exculpate itself from such reckless or gross negligence. That showing was not made on this record."

TUNKL V. REGENTS OF UNIVERSITY OF CALIFORNIA, 383 P.2d 441 (Cal. 1963). Tunkl brought this action for injuries received allegedly as a result of the negligence of the hospital operated by defendant. Tunkl was admitted to the hospital on condition that he execute a release, absolving the defendants "from any and all liability for the negligent or wrongful acts or omissions of its employees. . . ." The validity of this release was submitted to the jury, which found it to be valid and the trial court entered judgment for the defendants. *Held*, reversed. "While obviously no public policy opposes private, voluntary transactions in which one party, for a consideration, agrees to shoulder a risk which the law would otherwise have placed upon the other party, the above circumstances pose a different situation. In this situation the releasing party does not really acquiesce voluntarily in the contractual shifting of the risk, nor can we be reasonably certain that he receives an adequate consideration for the transfer. Since the service is one which each member of the public, presently or potentially, may find essential to him, he faces, despite his economic inability to do so, the prospect of a compulsory assumption of the risk of another's negligence. . . . From the observance of simple standards of due care in the driving of a car to the performance of the high standards of hospital practice, the individual citizen must be completely dependent upon the responsibility of others. . . . We cannot lightly accept a sought immunity from careless failure to provide the hospital service upon which many must depend."

NOTES

1. **Contractual agreement to release liability for negligence.** The theory of assumption of the risk is that the parties have voluntarily consented to have one party bear the risk of injury. Contractual or express assumptions of risk are also referred to as exculpatory clauses, releases, disclaimers or limitations on liability. If an exculpatory clause is enforceable, it will entirely bar the plaintiff's claim. People may contractually waive their right to sue for damages caused by the ordinary negligence of others. However, such pre-injury releases are unenforceable 1) if the waiver offends public policy or 2) if the rules of contract limit the waiver. *See* 1 DOBBS, HAYDEN & BUBLICK, THE LAW OF TORTS §§ 232–34 (2d ed. 2011). *See also* RESTATEMENT (THIRD) OF TORTS: APPORTIONMENT OF LIABILITY § 2 cmt. b (2000).

2. **Public policy: the *Tunkl* factors.** Many, many courts look at public policy in assumption of risk cases in light of the *Tunkl* factors. According to

Tunkl, 383 P.2d at 445-46, exculpatory provisions will be held invalid when a transaction exhibits some or all of the following characteristics:

> It concerns a business of a type generally thought suitable for public regulation. The party seeking exculpation is engaged in performing a service of great importance to the public, which is often a matter of practical necessity for some members of the public. The party holds himself out as willing to perform this service for any member of the public who seeks it. . . . As a result of the essential nature of the service, in the economic setting of the transaction, the party invoking exculpation possesses a decisive advantage of bargaining strength against any member of the public who seeks his services. In exercising a superior bargaining power the party confronts the public with a standardized adhesion contract of exculpation, and makes no provision whereby a purchaser may pay additional reasonable fees and obtain protection against negligence. Finally, as a result of the transaction, the person or property of the purchaser is placed under the control of the seller, subject to the risk of carelessness by the seller or his agents.

On the strength of *Stelluti*, would the New Jersey court reject California's *Tunkl* decision? Quite to the contrary; the New Jersey court quoted *Tunkl* with approval in its analysis. How can you reconcile the two cases?

3. **Services dependent on release.** What if *every* business demands a release before it will sell its goods or services? In what settings other than hospital care should exculpatory clauses be unenforceable? What about exculpatory clauses in employment? *Brown v. Soh*, 909 A.2d 43 (Conn. 2006) (exculpatory agreements in the employment context offend public policy). Is day-care an essential service? *Gavin W. v. YMCA of Metro. Los Angeles*, 131 Cal.Rptr.2d 168 (Ct. App. 2003). Should courts enforce an exculpatory agreement as a condition of living in a nursing home? *Marmet Health Care Center, Inc. v. Brown*, 565 U.S. 530 (2012). Would a waiver in an apartment rental agreement be valid with respect to basic common areas or a health facility? *See Lewis Operating Corp. v. Superior Court*, 132 Cal.Rptr.3d 849 (Ct. App. 2011). A houseboat? *See, e.g., Yang v. Voyagaire Houseboats, Inc.*, 701 N.W.2d 783 (Minn. 2005) (likening a houseboat rental company to an innkeeper providing a "public service," thus rendering release invalid).

4. **Recreational activities.** As in *Stelluti,* pre-injury releases of ordinary negligence claims for adults in recreational activities are often upheld, as long as the releases are conspicuous, clear and unambiguous. *See Donahue v. Ledgends, Inc.*, 331 P.3d 342 (Alaska 2014) ("To hold otherwise would impose unreasonable burdens on businesses whose patrons want to engage in high-risk physical activities."); *Penunuri v. Sundance Partners, Ltd.*, 301 P.3d 984 (Utah 2013) (pre-injury release of claims for horse-riding injury did not violate public policy under Equine Act).

However, even in the recreational activity context, courts sometimes strike down the releases based on the public policy of preventing injury. *See*

Bagley v. Mt. Bachelor, Inc., 340 P.3d 27 (Or. 2014) (enforcement of anticipatory release of ski area operator for its own negligence would be unconscionable, where safety of operator's patrons was a matter of broad societal concern and operators would lack the legal incentive to avoid creating unreasonable risks to business invitees if freed from potential negligence liability); *Rothstein v. Snowbird Corp.*, 175 P.3d 560 (Utah 2007) (invalidating skier's waiver of right to sue ski resort for negligence in light of state statute immunizing ski resorts from suits based only on inherent risks of skiing).

5. **The tension between consent to negligence and preventing harm.** When the defendant is the only person who can provide reasonable care for safety, should defendant be permitted to shift the responsibility to another by contract? A vigorous dissent in *Stelluti* thought not: "[T]he Court says, a health club patron has the *right* to contract not only for unsafe conditions at a health club, but also for careless conduct by its employees. . . . This court has recognized that sophisticated commercial entities, exercising equal bargaining power, are capable of protecting their own interests. . . . Never before in the modern era has this Court upheld an exculpatory clause in which a commercial enterprise protects itself against its own negligence, at the expense of a consumer, who had no bargaining power to alter the terms of the contract. . . . Tort law is not just about compensating victims but about preventing accidents. . . . The exculpatory clause in this case unfairly allocates the risk from the commercial operator, who is in the best position to remove and prevent the dangers on the premises, to the unwary patron [and thus] encourages lack of due care." *See also Degliomini v. ESM Prods., Inc.*, 253 A.3d 226 (Pa. 2021) (enforcing of pre-injury exculpatory release in case of bicyclist who was injured when he rode into unmarked sinkhole would jeopardize the public's health, safety, and welfare by removing the city's incentive to maintain public streets in reasonably safe condition).

If waivers for recreational activities shield entities from "potentially crushing liability," *Bukowski v. Clarkson Univ.*, 971 N.E.2d 849 (N.Y. 2012), could their *non*-enforcement have any positive effect? *See Reardon v. Windswept Farm, LLC*, 905 A.2d 1156 (Conn. 2006). Should a court confine express assumption of the risk to negotiated transactions between sophisticated parties? Could there be concern about exculpatory clauses even in that context?

6. **Statutory guidance.** State statutes have weighed in both to endorse exculpatory clauses and to reject them. The Utah Supreme Court's decision in *Rothstein* was invalidated by statute in UTAH CODE ANN. § 78B–4–405 (West 2020) (a skier may "waive a claim that the skier is permitted to bring against a ski area operator"). However, the Utah statute provides that "If the skier is a minor, the skier, or the skier's parent or guardian on behalf of the minor, may not enter into an [exculpatory] agreement." *See also* MINN. STAT. ANN. § 184B.20 (West 2021) ("A waiver of liability signed by or on behalf of a minor for injuries arising out of the negligence of the owner or the owner's employee or designee [with respect to inflatable amusement equipment] is void."). Another statute that limits the ability of parties to limit liability by contract is

applied in *Kawasaki Kisen Kaisha Ltd. v. Regal-Beloit Corp.*, 561 U.S. 89 (2010) (transit of goods by rail carrier).

7. **Parental waivers of care for children.** As reflected in the Utah statute, exculpatory clauses are particularly suspect when they purport to allow failures to take reasonable care for children. In *Galloway v. State*, 790 N.W.2d 252 (Iowa 2010), a parent signed a release for her 14-year-old daughter to attend an educational field trip organized by Upward Bound, a youth outreach program organized by the University of Northern Iowa. On the field trip, the child was struck by a car as she attempted to cross the street. Because a child "may or may not have the knowledge and experience to assess and avoid risks of injury created by the activity," the court joined the majority of courts in deciding that a parent's pre-injury release of a child's rights is invalid. *See also Rutherford v. Talisker Canyons Fin. Co.*, 445 P.3d 474 (Utah 2018) ("a parent cannot release his or her minor child's prospective claims for negligence"); *Woodman v. Kera, LLC*, 785 N.W.2d 1 (Mich. 2010) (pre-injury waiver of liability of commercial children's play facility unenforceable); *Hojnowski v. Vans Skate Park*, 901 A.2d 381 (N.J. 2006) (invalidating exculpatory clause executed by a parent on behalf of a minor seeking to use a skateboard facility). A small number of courts have disagreed, and allowed waivers on a case-by-case basis. *See, e.g., BJ's Wholesale Club, Inc. v. Rosen*, 80 A.3d 345 (Md. 2013) (exculpatory clause signed by parent releasing membership store from liability to child for negligence in children's play area was enforceable where it did not represent "a transaction affecting the public interest"). What concerns might courts have about allowing parents to disclaim the duty of reasonable care owed by others to their children?

8. **Waivers of liability for reckless or intentional torts.** Another area of broad agreement, as articulated in *Stelluti*, is that contractual assumption of the risk clauses that bar recovery for recklessly or intentionally caused injury would offend public policy. *See, e.g., City of Santa Barbara v. Superior Court*, 161 P.3d 1095 (Cal. 2007) (majority of states hold that public policy precludes enforcement of a release that would shelter aggravated misconduct).

MOORE V. HARTLEY MOTORS

36 P.3d 628 (Alaska 2001)

FABE, CHIEF JUSTICE. . . .

Gayle Moore and her husband bought a Suzuki four-wheel ATV in May 1993 from Suzuki, Arctic Cat Motor Sports. At the time of the sale, the salesperson offered the Moores a $50 rebate upon completion of an ATV rider safety class. On October 23, 1993, the Moores attended an ATV rider safety class held on the property of Hartley Motors, Inc. James Croak instructed the class using the curriculum of the ATV Safety Institute. Before starting instruction, Croak requested that all participants sign a consent form and release. Moore signed the consent form and release.

[During the class, Moore was thrown from her ATV when it struck a rock obscured by high grass.]

Moore brought suit in July 1995 against Hartley Motors, the dealer that sold the Moores their ATV, ATV Safety Institute, and Jim Croak. She alleged that the defendants negligently failed to provide a safe ATV rider training course and location, and negligently concealed the fact that the course was unsafe. . . . The superior court granted summary judgment to the defendants.

In *Municipality of Anchorage v. Locker,* we evaluated whether an exculpatory release should be invalidated as against public policy. In *Locker,* we concluded that a limited liability clause in a contract for an advertisement in the yellow pages was unconscionable and void as against public policy. We relied upon *Tunkl v. Regents of the University of California* in identifying the factors for review in invalidating an exculpatory provision on public policy grounds. . . .

Of particular relevance to this case is the type of service performed and whether the party seeking exculpation has a decisive advantage in bargaining strength because of the essential nature of the service. Here, the ATV safety course, although perhaps providing a desirable opportunity for an ATV driver, is not an essential service, and therefore the class providers did not have a "decisive advantage of bargaining strength" in requiring the release for participation in the class. Moore had a choice whether to take the class or not, and chose to sign the release in order to participate. The release in this circumstance does not present a violation of public policy.

Other courts have upheld exculpatory releases for activities similar to ATV riding where the activities themselves were not regulated by statute. . . .

Even if there was no genuine issue of material fact regarding a misrepresentation [as to safety of the course], the trial court erred in failing to consider the scope of the release signed by Moore. Moore agreed to release the ATV Safety Institute and all other organizations and individuals affiliated with the ATV safety class from liability, loss, and damages "including but not limited to all bodily injuries and property damage arising out of participation in the ATV RiderCourse." But the release does not discuss or even mention liability for general negligence. Its opening sentences refer only to unavoidable and inherent risks of ATV riding, and nothing in its ensuing language suggests an intent to release ATVSI or Hartley Motors from liability for acts of negligence unrelated to those inherent risks. Based on this language, we conclude that Moore released ATVSI and Hartley Motors only from liability arising from the inherent risks of ATV riding and ordinary negligence associated with those inherent risks. As we noted in *Kissick v. Schmierer,* an exculpatory release can be enforced if "the intent to release a party from liability for future negligence" is "conspicuously and unequivocally expressed." However, underlying the ATV course release signed by Moore was an implied and reasonable presumption that the course is not unreasonably dangerous.

Moore claims that she was injured when she fell off her ATV after riding over a rock obscured by tall grass. We assume the truth of this assertion for purposes of reviewing the superior court's summary judgment order. Moore asserts that the course on which the class operated was set up in such a way that she had to ride into the grass and that this posed an unnecessary danger.

The allegedly improper course layout may be actionable if the course posed a risk beyond ordinary negligence related to the inherent risks of off-road ATV riding assumed by the release. As we have explained in the context of skiing, "[i]f a given danger could be eliminated or mitigated through the exercise of reasonable care, it is not a necessary danger" and is therefore not an inherent risk of the sport.

We have described an "unreasonable risk" as one for which "the likelihood and gravity of the harm threatened outweighed the utility of the . . . conduct and the burden on the [defendant] for removing the danger." If the course was designed or maintained in such a manner that it increased the likelihood of a rider encountering a hidden rock, then the course layout may have presented an unnecessary danger; holding an ATV safety class on an unnecessarily dangerous course is beyond the ordinary negligence released by the waiver. Holding a safety class on an unreasonably risky course may give rise to liability even if encountering rocks is generally an inherent risk of ATV riding. Moreover, the fact that the course was geared towards novice ATV riders may also affect the level of care required of ATVSI and Hartley Motors to reduce unnecessary dangers and unreasonable risk.

. . . Here, Moore presented facts that could support a finding that the ATV safety course was laid out in an unnecessarily dangerous manner that was not obvious to novice ATV riders and therefore not within the scope of the release. Thus, it was error to grant summary judgment.

[Reversed and remanded.]

NOTES

1. **Contractual limits.** An express assumption of risk is a contract, subject to ordinary contract rules of interpretation and enforcement. For example, a pre-injury release will not be upheld if it is unclear or ambiguous. *See, e.g., Sanislo v. Give Kids the World, Inc.,* 157 So.3d 256 (Fla. 2015); *Hillerson v. Bismarck Public Schools,* 840 N.W.2d 65 (N.D. 2013). And an exculpatory contract must meet "higher standards for clarity than other agreements." *Provoncha v. Vermont Motocross Ass'n,* 974 A.2d 1261 (Vt. 2009).

Moreover, a waiver must be conspicuous, not buried in a mass of print or reduced to a miniscule font size. The 10th Circuit Court of Appeals discerned five factors from Colorado Supreme Court decisions to determine if a release is unambiguous: (1) "whether the agreement is written in simple and clear terms that are free from legal jargon"; (2) "whether the agreement is inordinately long or complicated"; (3) "whether the release specifically addresses the risk that caused the plaintiff's injury"; (4) "whether the contract contains any emphasis to highlight the importance of the information it contains"; and (5) "whether the plaintiff was experienced in the activity making risk of that particular injury reasonably foreseeable." *Hamric v. Wilderness Expeditions, Inc.*, 6 F.4th 1108 (10th Cir. 2021) (not every factor need be satisfied; plaintiff's inexperience at rappelling was insufficient to defeat the release as a whole).

2. **The scope of contractual limitations.** As in *Moore*, courts often differentiate between waivers of inherent risks and waives of negligent risks. Even if a release is clear, unambiguous and conspicuous, the court must determine whether the *scope* of the release covers the claim being asserted by the injured plaintiff. *See, e.g., Donahue v. Ledgends, Inc.*, 331 P.3d 342 (Alaska 2014) (release did cover the risk of defendant rock gym's negligent hiring and supervision of employees); *Thompson v. Hi Tech Motor Sports, Inc.*, 945 A.2d 368 (Vt. 2008) (waiver of liability for injuries on test drive on one of dealership's motorcycles, while not facially invalid, covered only injuries caused by inherent risks of riding, not those caused by dealer's negligence). Many states view releases with disfavor, construe them strictly against the party seeking to enforce them, and require a great degree of specificity about what exactly is being waived. *See. e.g., Horne v. Electric Eel Mfg. Co.* 987 F.3d 704 (7th Cir. 2021) (refusing to enforce clause in rental agreement against customer whose finger was severed by a defective rented drain rodding machine; "Such clauses must spell out the intention of the parties with great particularity and will not be construed to defeat a claim which is not explicitly covered by their terms.").

What if a person hired to be a civilian police officer in Afghanistan is told that he will "be exposed to dangers due to the nature of the mission," including death, and agrees to waive "any claims." Does that agreement waive even the employee's negligence claims? *Deuley v. Dyncorp Int'l, Inc.*, 8 A.3d 1156 (Del. 2010).

3 **Oral contracts.** Although contractual assumption of risk is typically based on a written contract, in some circumstances an express oral agreement will be equally valid. *See Boyle v. Revici*, 961 F.2d 1060 (2d Cir. 1992) (nonstandard cancer treatment); *Amezcua v. Los Angeles Harley-Davidson*, 200 Cal.App.4th 217 (2011) (annual Toy Drive motorcycle procession).

§ 2. PRIMARY IMPLIED ASSUMPTION OF THE RISK

ROUNTREE V. BOISE BASEBALL, LLC, 296 P.3d 373 (Idaho 2013). Boise Hawks season ticket holder Bud Rountree took his wife and two grandchildren to a baseball game at Memorial Stadium in the summer of

2008. During the game, Rountree and his family went to a dining area behind the third base line known as the Executive Club. Although the stadium had mesh netting throughout the seating areas to protect fans from baseballs—and the Executive Club had horizontal netting—the dining area was one of the few areas of the stadium without vertical netting. While in the Executive Club area, Rountree started a conversation with someone and lost track of the game. Then he heard the crowd make noise and returned his gaze to the infield. A foul ball struck Rountree and he lost his eye. Rountree sued several defendants for negligence. The district court denied Boise Baseball's motions for summary judgment, declining to adopt the Baseball Rule, which limits the duty of stadium operators in the event of errant foul balls. The district court also rejected Boise Baseball's argument that Rountree had impliedly consented to the foul ball risk. On appeal to the Idaho Supreme Court, *held*, affirmed.

"Generally speaking, the implied assumption of risk doctrine is divided into two subcategories: 'primary' and 'secondary.' . . . Primary implied assumption of risk arises when the plaintiff impliedly assumes those risks that are *inherent* in a particular activity. In contrasting the two subcategories, some courts have held that primary implied assumption of the risk, because it is 'treat[ed] as part of the initial duty analysis, rather than as an affirmative defense,' is compatible with comparative negligence schemes. . . . [T]his Court held in *Salinas v. Vierstra*, 695 P.2d 369 (Idaho 1985), that, 'the use of assumption of risk as a defense shall have no legal effect in this state.'. . . We reaffirm our holding in *Salinas:* the use of assumption of risk as a defense shall have no legal effect. Furthermore, we . . . hold that the general rule from *Salinas* applies to both primary and secondary assumption of the risk. Thus, primary implied assumption of the risk is not a valid defense. As this Court explained in *Salinas,* 'Section 6–801's intent is clear: Contributory negligence is not to be a complete bar to recovery; instead, liability is to be apportioned between the parties based on the degree of fault for which each is responsible.'

Accordingly, the *Salinas* Court warned of the 'gross legal inconsistency [of] prohibiting the use of contributory negligence as an absolute bar,' while allowing its effect to continue through assumption of risk defenses. . . . Allowing assumption of risk as an absolute bar is inconsistent with our comparative negligence system, whether the risks are inherent in an activity, or not. Moreover, cases involving primary implied assumption of the risk are 'readily handled' by comparative negligence principles; as in any case, fault will be assessed, and liability apportioned, based on the actions of the parties. Whether a party participated in something inherently dangerous will simply inform the comparison, rather than wholly preclude it. Here, whether watching baseball is inherently dangerous, and the degrees of fault to be apportioned to Rountree and Boise Baseball, are questions for the jury. Because comparative negligence can adroitly resolve these questions, there is no need for this Court to disturb its holding in *Salinas:* assumption of the risk—whether primary or secondary—shall not act as a defense."

NOTES

1. **The Baseball Rule.** A large number of states have adopted some version of a limited-duty rule for stadium owners and operators; some have done so by legislation, others by judicial decision. The *Rountree* court described "the Baseball Rule" as one requiring stadium owners and operators to "provide screened seats for as many spectators as may be reasonably expected to call for them on any ordinary occasion." The court also noted some jurisdictional variations to the rule. But the court declined to adopt such a rule, saying that "drawing lines as to where a stadium owner's duty begins, where netting should be placed, and so on . . . [is] appropriate for the Legislature because it has the resources for the research, study and proper formulation of broad public policy." Was the *Rountree* court correct in leaving the Baseball Rule to legislative action in Idaho, or should it have adopted such a rule in this case? *See South Shore Baseball, LLC v. DeJesus*, 11 N.E.3d 903 (Ind. 2014) (also declining to adopt a Baseball Rule, saying, "we are not convinced that any sport, even our national pastime, merits its own special rule of liability," and that any such decision should be left to the legislature). Would the Baseball Rule simplify the analysis in the spectator-injury cases?

2. **Assumption of risk and duty of care.** By declining to adopt a Baseball Rule, and by holding that primary assumption of risk should play no role in the analysis of the case, is the *Rountree* court simply deciding that the stadium owner/operator owed the plaintiff a duty of reasonable care? Do you see, then, how the case will proceed? How might the plaintiff show a breach of duty? And how might the defendant claim that the spectator was comparatively negligent?

COOMER V. KANSAS CITY ROYALS BASEBALL CORP.

437 S.W.3d 184 (Mo. 2014)

PAUL C. WILSON, JUDGE.

John Coomer claims he was injured when he was hit in the eye with a hotdog thrown by Sluggerrr, the Kansas City Royals mascot. [Evidence showed that every Royals home game since 2000 has featured a "Hotdog Launch" between innings, in which Sluggerrr stands on top of the visitor's dugout and either fires hotdogs into the crowd using an air gun, or tosses hotdogs by hand to fans seated nearby.] Coomer sued the Kansas City Royals Baseball Corporation, claiming the team is responsible for Sluggerrr's negligence and the damages it caused. A jury found in favor of the Royals, and Coomer appeals. Among the jury instructions was one asking the jury to decide whether the risk of being injured by Sluggerrr's hotdog toss is one of the inherent risks of watching a Royals home game that Coomer assumed merely by attending. Whether a particular risk is inherent in watching a sporting event is a question of law for the court, not a question of fact for the jury. . . .

It is safe to say that judicial analysis and application of assumption of the risk doctrine has not always achieved high marks for clarity and precision. Historically, courts often failed to draw or maintain important distinctions between this doctrine and defenses such as contributory negligence, which, though they may have seemed similar to assumption of the risk, were quite different. Simons, *Reflections on Assumption of Risk,* 50 UCLA L.Rev. 481, 486 (2002) (*"Reflections"*). Admittedly, those distinctions seldom made any difference as a practical matter because any of these often-overlapping defenses was sufficient to bar completely all recovery by the plaintiff. At least this was so before the advent of comparative fault. . . .

The version of comparative fault adopted by this Court in *Gustafson v. Benda,* 661 S.W.2d 11 (Mo. Banc 1983), fundamentally altered this landscape. Section 1(a) of the Uniform Comparative Fault Act (the "UCFA") provides that "any contributory fault chargeable to the claimant diminishes proportionately the amount awarded as compensatory damages for an injury attributable to the claimant's contributory fault, but does not bar recovery." *Gustafson,* 661 S.W.2d at 18 (quoting from the UCFA). Section 1(b) of the UCFA defines "fault" for purposes of section 1(a) to include "unreasonable assumption of risk not constituting an enforceable express consent." *Id.* . . .

Accordingly, when the plaintiff is injured by the defendant's negligence, this Court holds that the adoption of comparative fault in *Gustafson* precludes any consideration of the plaintiff's conduct in assuming that risk (i.e., implied secondary assumption of the risk) except as a partial defense under a proper comparative fault instruction. Conversely, because the "express" and "implied primary" applications of assumption of the risk result in determinations that the defendant has no duty to protect the plaintiff, the form of comparative fault adopted in *Gustafson* does not preclude these applications as a complete—not merely a partial—bar to the plaintiff's recovery. . . .

[T]he proper application of implied primary assumption of the risk in this case—unaffected by *Gustafson*—is this: if Coomer was injured by a risk that is an inherent part of watching the Royals play baseball, the team had no duty to protect him and cannot be liable for his injuries. But, if Coomer's injury resulted from a risk that is not an inherent part of watching baseball in person—or if the negligence of the Royals altered or increased one of these inherent risks and caused Coomer's injury—the jury is entitled to hold the Royals liable for such negligence and, to the extent the reasonableness of Coomer's actions are in dispute, the jury must apportion fault between the parties using comparative fault principles. . . .

According to the Royals, the risk to a spectator of being injured by Sluggerrr's hotdog toss shares the same essential characteristics as the other risks that this Court (and many others) determined long ago were inherent in watching a baseball game in person, i.e., risks that a spectator will be injured by a flying ball or bat. The Court disagrees.

The rationale for barring recovery for injuries from risks that are inherent in watching a particular sport under implied primary assumption of the risk is that the defendant team owner cannot remove such risks without materially altering either the sport that the spectators come to see or the spectator's enjoyment of it. No such argument applies to Sluggerrr's hotdog toss. Millions of fans have watched the Royals (and its forebears in professional baseball) play the National Pastime for the better part of a century before Sluggerrr began tossing hotdogs, and millions more people watch professional baseball every year in stadiums all across this country without the benefit of such antics. . . .

Accordingly, the Court holds as a matter of law that the risk of injury from Sluggerrr's hotdog toss is not one of the risks inherent in watching the Royals play baseball that Coomer assumed merely by attending a game at Kauffman Stadium. This risk can be increased, decreased or eliminated altogether with no impact on the game or the spectators' enjoyment of it. As a result, Sluggerrr (and, therefore, the Royals) owe the fans a duty to use reasonable care in conducting the Hotdog Launch and can be held liable for damages caused by a breach of that duty. . . .

[T]his Court vacates the judgment and remands the case.

NOTES

1. **Primary and secondary implied assumption of the risk.** As you can see, not all states agree with the *Rountree* court (and others) who have opted for wholesale abolition of the implied assumption of risk defense. A number currently use the approach articulated in *Coomer,* and subdivide the traditional defense into two parts: "primary" (which equates to no duty, or no breach), and "secondary" (which equates to comparative fault).

2. **Spectators and primary assumption of risk.** Primary assumption of risk or limited-duty rules (such as the Baseball Rule discussed in Note 1 after *Rountree*) are often applied to bar claims by spectators injured by risks inherent in the game. Could the *concept* behind this approach be captured by saying that stadium owners and operators simply have no duty to protect spectators (who are, after all, business invitees) against the ordinary hazards of the sports activity, or, perhaps more accurately, to protect against whatever inherent risks remain after due care is exercised? If so, then is the continued use of a "primary assumption of risk defense" still needed?

3. **Determining inherent risks.** How does a court determine which risks are inherent in an activity? What does the *Coomer* court say? Few would argue that the risk of being hit by a hockey puck at a hockey match, or by a foul ball at a baseball game, are not inherent risks. *See, e.g., Hurst v. East Coast Hockey League, Inc.*, 637 S.E.2d 560 (S.C. 2006); *Sciarrotta v. Global Spectrum*, 944 A.2d 630 (N.J. 2008).

As baseball fans know, it is common for players on the field to casually toss baseballs into the stands at times. What if a spectator, not paying attention, is hit by a ball under those circumstances? Is that an "inherent risk," thus barring the claim entirely, or should it be seen as a case for the jury to decide, both on the breach of duty by the defendant and the plaintiff's comparative negligence? *See Loughran v. The Phillies*, 888 A.2d 872 (Pa. Super. Ct. 2005). Is being hit by another spectator who dives for a thrown souvenir tossed into the crowd by a promotional actor in a sports bar an inherent risk of watching a sporting event on television? *FCH1, LLC v. Rodriguez*, 335 P.3d 183 (Nev. 2014).

4. **Increasing inherent risks.** A spectator may recover if the defendant has *increased* the inherent risks of watching the sport. *See* DOBBS, HAYDEN & BUBLICK, HORNBOOK ON TORTS § 17.8, at 422 (2d ed. 2016). Was that the situation in *Coomer*? Might that be the situation in the Nevada thrown-souvenir case in Note 3 above?

5. **Inherent risks: contexts.** Rountree and Coomer are baseball cases, but implied assumption of the risk, in its primary form, is an issue in a number of contexts. In *Gregory v. Cott*, 331 P.3d 179 (Cal. 2014), plaintiff was hired to provide in home care for an 85-year-old woman who suffered from Alzheimer's disease. While plaintiff was washing dishes, the 85-year-old approached her from behind and bumped into her. Plaintiff dropped the knife, which cut her wrist and resulted in injury. The court held that "risk of violent injury is inherent in the occupation of caring for Alzheimer's patients." Because defendant did nothing to unreasonably increase the risk of injury beyond those that were inherent, defendant owed plaintiff no duty to protect her from the ordinary risks that arose in the course of employment."

6. **Applying the ordinary duty of care.** Is it clear that the California court was correct to hold that the plaintiff impliedly agreed to accept the risks of being struck by the person in her care? What if the plaintiff, hired as a housekeeper, trips on stairs because the children of the house have left some items there. The plaintiff had picked up things off the stairs before, so she knew about that risk. In *Betts v. Crawford*, 965 P.2d 680 (Wyo. 1998), the court held that the employer had a duty to provide a safe place to work, and that implied assumption of risk had nothing to do with the case. Affirming a jury verdict for plaintiff, albeit one that reduced her recovery by 15% for her own fault, the court said, "there is no distinction between contributory negligence and assumption of risk when raised as a defense to an established breach of duty." Are *Betts* and *Gregory* (in note 5) distinguishable? Or do they simply expose that duty is a policy decision on which judges will differ?

In *Henson v. Uptown Drink, LLC*, 922 N.W.2d 185, 191 (Minn. 2019) a customer was fatally injured trying to help an employee of a bar to eject an aggressive patron. The defendant argued primary assumption of risk. However, the court wrote: "We see no good reason to extend the doctrine to preclude liability for injuries arising out of the operation and patronage of bars. Although the service and consumption of alcohol can most certainly lead to incidents such as the one here, we have never considered operating and patronizing bars to be inherently dangerous activities. . . . [O]ur precedent is clear that bar owners, as do all innkeepers, have a duty of care." Do you see how the existence of a duty of care is an answer to the primary implied assumption of risk question?

7. **Judge and jury.** The *Coomer* court holds that giving the jury instruction on implied assumption of risk constituted prejudicial error. What did the Supreme Court say was wrong with that instruction? Most of the states that follow the "primary" and "secondary" approach to implied assumption of risk say that in determining whether primary assumption of risk should bar the claim, the court, and not the jury, should determine what risks are "inherent" in a particular activity. *See, e.g., Turner v. Mandalay Sports Entertainment, LLC*, 180 P.3d 1172 (Nev. 2008) (on the ground that primary assumption of risk is a duty issue, thus solely for the court to decide). Yet what risks are "inherent" in an activity is quite fact-sensitive. Is the judge being asked to perform an essential jury function, then? Is this a problem? *See* Dilan A. Esper & Gregory C. Keating, *Putting "Duty" in Its Place: A Reply to Professors Goldberg and Zipursky*, 41 LOY. L.A. L. REV. 1225 (2008).

NOTE: SPORTS PARTICIPANTS

1. *General rules.* Participants in sports activities are governed by rules similar to those that apply to spectators. In the language of primary assumption of risk, sports participants impliedly assume the risk of the dangers inherent in the sport, and thus have no claims for negligence if injury results from those inherent risks. In the newer terminology, we might say that the defendant either owes no duty to reduce inherent risks, or does not breach a duty by failing to protect a participant from such risks. See 1 DOBBS, HAYDEN & BUBLICK, THE LAW OF TORTS § 240 (2d ed. 2011).

2. *Inherent risks.* It is probably safe to say that in general, participating in a sporting activity—skiing, or playing baseball, for example—exposes you to risks that go beyond those of mere spectating. In some settings, these inherent risks do not include the risks created by defendant's negligence. For example, for a skier, falling and being hurt is an inherent risk of the sport, but hitting a hidden bush left on the beginner's slope because of the operator's negligence is not. *See Sunday v. Stratton Corp.*, 390 A.2d 398 (Vt. 1978). A co-participant's violation of the rules of the sport may even be an inherent risk, leaving the injured player

without a negligence claim. *See, e.g., Turcotte v. Fell*, 502 N.E.2d 964 (N.Y. 1986) (professional jockey, injured by another jockey's illegal jostling); *Avila v. Citrus Cmty. Coll. Dist.*, 131 P.3d 383 (Cal. 2006) (batter in college baseball game injured by intentionally thrown "bean ball").

3.   *Limited-duty rules.* A number of courts, and some legislatures, have adopted a limited duty of care in this setting, providing that co-participants owe only a duty to avoid intentionally or recklessly injuring each other. *See, e.g., Angland v. Mountain Creek Resort, Inc.*, 66 A.3d 1252 (N.J. 2013) (common-law recklessness standard applied to suit by a snowboarder against another snowboarder who collided with him); *Feld v. Borkowski*, 790 N.W.2d 72 (Iowa 2010) (recklessness standard applied to claim by first baseman hit by a bat that flew out of batter's hands); *Karas v. Strevell*, 884 N.E.2d 122 (Ill. 2008) (applying "willful or wanton" standard to amateur hockey); *Gauvin v. Clark*, 537 N.E.2d 94 (Mass. 1989) (recklessness standard applied to college ice hockey players).

4.   *Expectations of the parties.* Rather than distinguishing between inherent and non-inherent risks, does it make more sense to focus on the reasonable expectations of the parties? In a case involving a collision of skiers, allegedly the result of negligence, one court thought that the duty of care should turn on the parties' reasonable expectations. As to skiing, the court thought "skiers will expect that other skiers will follow the rules and generally accepted practices of the sport of skiing." *Jagger v. Mohawk Mountain Ski Area, Inc.*, 849 A.2d 813 (Conn. 2004). Sometimes courts focus on player expectations that conduct will be unsafe. In *Bukowski v. Clarkson Univ.*, 971 N.E.2d 849 (N.Y. 2012), a college pitcher pitched to a live batter indoors without a protective L-screen in front of him, which all experienced players know is dangerous. Should the player's expectation that the situation is unsafe excuse the defendant University from its duty of reasonable care? Does the tort policy of limiting preventable harm suggest a result? Does the legal rule itself shape the parties' reasonable expectations? Is that also true of which risks are inherent?

§ 3. SECONDARY IMPLIED ASSUMPTION OF THE RISK

SIMMONS V. PORTER
312 P.3d 345 (Kan. 2013)

The opinion of the court was delivered by BILES, J.:

[Adam Simmons was working for the Porters, doing business as Porter Farms, as a farm truck and machinery mechanic. Simmons was removing a leaky fuel tank from a Ford pickup truck, and noticed that the tank was not secured with proper fastenings. When he attempted to loosen the tank, it fell to one side and doused him with gasoline. He quickly pushed himself out from under the truck, but when he did so he kicked a shop light, which broke and ignited the gasoline, burning him seriously.]

He sued his employer for negligently failing to provide him with a reasonably safe workplace. The district court denied his claim based on the common-law assumption of risk doctrine, which can bar recovery when an employee who knows of a dangerous situation voluntarily exposes himself or herself to that danger. The Court of Appeals affirmed based on existing precedent. . . .

The assumption of risk doctrine is a common-law affirmative defense to negligence. . . . The doctrine is premised on a view that there is an express or implied agreement within the employer-employee relationship that an employee accepts the risk of known dangers to which the employee is exposed as a part of the work and takes responsibility for any resulting injury. . . . In other words, assumption of risk bars recovery when two conditions are present: (1) the employee knew and understood the risk being incurred; and (2) the choice to incur the risk was entirely free and voluntary.

Kansas courts discussed assumption of risk as early as 1898. But in those early cases it was viewed as a "species of contributory negligence." . . . Over time, however, this court recognized distinctions between the two doctrines. . . . Under comparative fault [as set forth in K.S.A. § 60–258a], a plaintiff may recover damages so long as the plaintiff's negligence is less than the collective causal negligence of the other parties to the occurrence; but those damages are diminished in proportion to the plaintiff's own negligence. . . . In adopting comparative fault, the legislature intended to impose individual liability for damages based on the proportionate fault of all parties to the occurrence giving rise to the injuries. . . . The comparative fault statute expressly abolished contributory negligence, but is silent regarding assumption of risk. The question before us is whether the legislature's adoption of comparative fault should abrogate the assumption of risk doctrine. . . .

[W]e severely constricted the assumption of risk doctrine in *Smith v. Massey-Ferguson, Inc.*, 883 P.2d 1120 (Kan. 1994). In that case, a farm employee sued his employer, his supervisor, and a combine manufacturer after seriously injuring his hand in a combine's moving parts. There was conflicting evidence on whether the employee intentionally reached into the moving parts or whether he accidentally came into contact with them. . . . On appeal, the *Smith* court considered whether the district court should have decided as a matter of law whether assumption of risk barred recovery, rather than submitting the issue to the jury. After reviewing our caselaw, the *Smith* court defined its task as considering "whether the danger posed . . . was so obvious that Smith (or an ordinarily prudent person) must have known of it and whether he (or the ordinarily prudent person) must have appreciated the danger attending its use." The court held the evidence did not conclusively show the employee knew or ought to have known of the danger and its consequences, so the district court properly submitted the issue to the jury.

Smith's holding illustrates assumption of risk's more recent and limited utility as an employer's vehicle for securing a judgment as a matter of law. *Smith* essentially recognizes that determining when assumption of risk might apply as a matter of law actually requires the district court to analyze facts in the same way a jury would scrutinize them in assessing a plaintiff's comparative fault—a function that, if performed by the court, is inconsistent with our long-standing caselaw requiring such facts to be determined by a jury. . . . And *Smith* still understood that as a matter of tort law, an employer has a duty to provide a safe workplace and equipment.

[Many state high courts have abandoned] assumption of risk because of comparative fault's enactment in their states. We find the rationale in these cases compelling and are now clearly convinced preserving assumption of risk as a complete bar to recovery is no longer sound and should be of no practical effect given the statutory scheme of comparative fault. . . .

[Reversed and remanded.]

NOTES

1. **Traditional implied assumption of risk.** The traditional formulation of the implied assumption of risk defense was that a plaintiff's claim was completely barred when the plaintiff knew and understood the risk being incurred, and made a free and voluntary choice to incur it. Only a few states continue to follow such a broad all-or-nothing rule today. *See, e.g., S&S Oil, Inc. v. Jackson*, 53 A.3d 1125 (Md. 2012) (assumption of risk differs from contributory negligence and separate jury instruction was required in slip-and-fall case); *Crews v. Hollenbach*, 751 A.2d 481 (Md. 2000) (barring negligence claim by gas company foreman against defendants who caused a gas leak); *Rickey v. Boden*, 421 A.2d 539 (R.I. 1980) (barring negligence claim by elevator operator injured when she fell on a narrow stairway in defendant's building while walking to a coffee-break area). Is an all-or-nothing assumption of the risk rule more compatible with and all-or-nothing contributory negligence rule that still applies in a state like Maryland?

2. **Is knowing risk-taking really "consent"? Prosser's jaywalker.** The traditional complete-bar rule seems to equate a voluntary encounter with known risk with consent to accept all risks of a defendant's negligence. Does that reasoning seem sound? Prosser did not think so. A plaintiff who knows of a risk, understands it, and decides to take it anyway may be negligent in some cases, but a defendant could seldom reasonably understand the plaintiff's conduct to mean that she agreed to accept all risks of the defendant's

negligence. Prosser gave the example of the jaywalking plaintiff. The driver of an automobile cannot reasonably believe that the jaywalking plaintiff is consenting to the driver's negligence. The jaywalker assuredly confronts a known risk and does so voluntarily, but voluntary confrontation of the risk does not communicate any release of the driver from the duties of ordinary care. Instead, the jaywalker is simply negligent. The jaywalker's negligence is to be judged under comparative fault rules. *See* 1 DOBBS, HAYDEN & BUBLICK, THE LAW OF TORTS § 236 (2d ed. 2011) (citing PROSSER & KEETON ON TORTS § 68, at 490 (5th ed. 1984)).

3.   **Abolishing the implied assumption of risk defense.** Many courts have now abandoned the implied defense entirely, often on the ground that the traditional approach is simply inconsistent with comparative fault. The American Law Institute takes this position, pointing out that if the plaintiff is reasonable in facing a risk, she is not negligent, but that when she unreasonably confronts a known risk, her negligence in doing so reduces her recovery of damages. RESTATEMENT (THIRD) OF TORTS: APPORTIONMENT OF LIABILITY § 3 cmt. c (2000). The Restatement's position is subject to two important explanations. First, if the defendant reasonably believes that the plaintiff has accepted the risk, the defendant may not be negligent (and thus not liable at all) in relying on the plaintiff to achieve safety. *See Stinnett,* Chapter 6. Second, as noted in § 1 of this chapter, the Restatement recognizes a complete defense based on *express* assumption of the risk.

4.   **Effect of abolition.** What happens when the defense of implied assumption of the risk is abolished? "Cases formerly resolved under assumption of risk rationales can now be resolved by (1) applying the comparative fault rules, (2) holding that the defendant had no duty of care, or (3) holding that the defendant did not breach a duty. Which resolution is appropriate depends upon the facts of the case." 1 DOBBS, HAYDEN & BUBLICK, THE LAW OF TORTS § 237 (2d ed. 2011). Suppose plaintiff and defendant are rural neighbors, far from medical help. Plaintiff's spouse or partner is injured and needs immediate medical attention, but plaintiff's car is not available. Defendant's car could be used, but it is in a mechanical condition dangerous to the driver. Should defendant refuse permission to use the car? If defendant explains the risks and permits its use, but the car's bad condition causes an injury to the plaintiff, would the plaintiff be entitled to recover, with a reduction for comparative fault? Or would the plaintiff be denied all recovery on no-duty or no-breach grounds?

5.   **Preference for risk.** Many people would no doubt agree that genuine consent to, or preference for, the risk created by the defendant should bar the plaintiff's claim entirely. In *Assumption of Risk and Consent in the Law of Torts: A Theory of Full Preference,* 67 B.U. L. REV. 213 (1987), Professor Ken Simons describes three choices a plaintiff might face: (1) not engage in an activity, (2) engage in the activity and encounter a tortiously created risk, or (3) engage in an activity and not encounter the risk. The fact that a person prefers option 2 to option 1, the typical comparison made in assumption of risk cases, doesn't reflect a preference for risk. A person only has a full preference

for risk if the person would prefer option 2—engaging in the activity the tortious risk—to option 3—engaging in the activity without it. While praising this theory, the Restatement (Third) of Torts felt the category of cases in which plaintiffs had a full preference for risk was sufficiently small, and the room for judicial error sufficiently great, that the better rule was simply to abandon implied assumption of risk. RESTATEMENT (THIRD) OF TORTS: APPORTIONMENT OF LIABILITY § 2 cmt. i (2000) (Reporters' note). Did Prosser's jaywalker (see Note 2) have a full preference for risk?

6. **Action despite risk while retaining the duty of care.** Suppose that plaintiff knows an area has a lot of crime, but ventures there anyway? In *Fraenkel v. Islamic Republic of Iran,* 892 F.3d 348 (D.C. Cir. 2018), the district court suggested that a 16-year-old student with Israeli and United States citizenship, who was kidnapped and murdered by members of terrorist organization, had assumed the risk of harm by hailing a ride home from school on a public street in an area that was fraught with longstanding political tension and a history of terrorism. Rebuking the claim, the Court of Appeals wrote: "[O]ne does not assume the risk that he will be the victim of an intentional tort. Thus, the driver who voluntarily chooses to go out at night does not assume the risk of being hit by an inebriated motorist. The college student who consumes alcohol at a party does not assume the risk of being sexually assaulted by another guest. The employee who enters a hostile crowd of customers does not assume the risk that one of them will physically batter him. And we add that the family of a boy hailing a ride home from school on a public street and engaging in no unlawful conduct does not assume the risk of the boy being kidnapped and killed by terrorists. The District Court's suggestion to the contrary was error." If a court says that the plaintiff assumes the risk of an intentional tort, is it condoning lack of care by the intentional tortfeasor? *Lu v. United States*, 921 F.3d 850 (9th Cir. 2019) (government engaged in bad faith by arguing that asylum-seeker had assumed the risk of federal immigration officer's sexual touching). Might we say that a plaintiff has a right or privilege to walk into a crime-ridden neighborhood despite risk (as in the plaintiff no-duty rules in Chapter 9)?

REFERENCES: DOBBS, HAYDEN & BUBLICK, HORNBOOK ON TORTS §§ 17.1–17.8 (2d ed. 2016); 1 DOBBS, HAYDEN & BUBLICK, THE LAW OF TORTS §§ 232–240 (2d ed. 2011).

CHAPTER 11

DEFENSES NOT ON THE MERITS

■ ■ ■

§ 1. STATUTES OF LIMITATION AND REPOSE

Statutes of limitation are not peculiar to tort law. Almost every kind of claim must be brought within a period of time specified by statutes of limitation. If the claim is brought later, it is barred by the statute, even though it is otherwise a legitimate claim. This is an affirmative defense, so a failure to plead it in a timely manner results in its waiver.

The traditional statute of limitations serves at least two distinct purposes. One is to bar "stale" claims, the presentation of which might be unfair or costly because evidence is lost or subtly altered with time. A second is to permit both personal and business planning and to avoid the economic burden that would be involved if defendants and their insurance companies had to carry indefinitely a reserve for liability that might never be imposed.

The statutory time limit for tort claims varies from state to state and from tort to tort. Often a legislature specifies a different limitations period for intentional torts and for negligence, although this is not always true. State statutes frequently specify a limitations period for particular claims and then have a "catch-all" limitations period for claims not listed specifically. A plaintiff is usually given two or three years in which to bring a negligence claim. Once the action is properly brought, the statute of limitations has no other function. It does not, for example, require *trial* by any certain time, only the commencement of the action.

The traditional analysis of statutes requires the action to be brought within the statutory period after the claim "accrues." When the claim accrues, starting the ticking of the limitations period clock, is often a contested issue. Statutes of repose, discussed at the end of this section, are similar, but serve some different purposes.

A. STATUTES OF LIMITATION

CRUMPTON V. HUMANA, INC.

661 P.2d 54 (N.M. 1983)

H. VERN PAYNE, C.J.

This is a frivolous appeal. We also note that there is a strong indication in the record that counsel for the appellant ineptly and perhaps negligently handled his client's case. Counsel for the appellant failed to file suit before the applicable statute of limitations had run. We are disappointed when members of our State Bar betray the trust and confidence of their clients by engaging in careless and unprofessional practice.

On February 8, 1979, Wanda Crumpton underwent surgery at Llano Estacado Medical Center in Hobbs. She alleged that she sustained injuries to her neck and legs when an attending nurse attempted to lower her hospital bed on February 11, 1979. Her suit was filed more than three years later on February 15, 1982. The trial court granted a motion for summary judgment on the ground that the suit was barred by the three-year statute of limitations. . . .

Crumpton argues that her injury was not ascertainable until some time after the accident occurred. Further, she contends that the statute of limitations should have been tolled during the time the parties were negotiating.

These arguments are entirely without merit. In her deposition, Crumpton plainly testified that her injuries occurred on February 11, 1979. She also testified that she is still having problems in her shoulders, legs and sides which she attributed to the February 11, 1979 incident. Crumpton offers no evidence to contradict the fact that the alleged negligent act and injury occurred simultaneously on February 11, 1979. In our view, the fact that she had continuing treatments and hospitalizations after the injury does not necessarily make the date of the injury unascertainable.

. . . [T]he statute of limitations commences running from the date of injury or the date of the alleged malpractice. . . .

Crumpton cites no authority for her argument that the statute of limitations should be tolled during the time when the parties were negotiating a settlement. The record indicates that defendants did not fraudulently lead Crumpton to believe that the case would be settled at some future date. In fact, the record indicates that in May 1981, defendants sent Crumpton a letter wherein defendants made a final offer for a compromise settlement of the case.

Accordingly, we affirm the trial court's grant of summary judgment against Crumpton. Because we determine this appeal to be frivolous and entirely without merit, costs and attorneys fees are to be borne by appellants.

NOTES

1. **Accrual of a claim.** The *Crumpton* court says the limitations period begins to run "from the date of injury or the date of the alleged malpractice." This reflects a traditional rule, still followed in some states, and in some particular contexts (especially medical malpractice), that the clock begins to run on a plaintiff's claim on a date certain—the date of the injury or the date of the defendant's misconduct (which are often, but not always, the same date)—even if the plaintiff was *unaware* of the negligent act, or even of the fact of injury. *See, e.g., Libby v. Eighth Jud. Dist. Ct.,* 325 P.3d 1276 (Nev. 2014) (applying statute that fixes "date of injury" as the accrual date for medical malpractice cases, barring plaintiff's claim despite her lack of awareness of the cause of her infection until much later); *Shearin v. Lloyd,* 98 S.E.2d 508 (N.C. 1957) (surgeon left a sponge in patient during operation; claim accrued on the date of the operation, even where plaintiff did not know about the sponge problem until much later). Such a result is obviously harsh, and beginning in the 1960s a number of states changed it, adopting instead the "discovery rule," discussed in the next case and its notes below.

2. **Continuous treatment or continuous representation.** A growing number of states have adopted a special rule in medical malpractice cases that delays the start of the statute of limitations until the treatment for which the patient consulted the physician has been concluded. *See, e.g., Lohnas v. Luzi,* 94 N.E.3d 892 (N.Y. 2018); *Chalifoux v. Radiology Associates of Richmond, Inc.,* 708 S.E.2d 834 (Va. 2011); *Harrison v. Valentini,* 184 S.W.3d 521 (Ky. 2006). A similar concept has been widely applied to legal malpractice claims. *See, e.g., Shumsky v. Eisenstein,* 750 N.E.2d 67 (N.Y. 2001). In that setting, a legal malpractice claim does not accrue until the lawyer's representation of the client on the "same subject matter" as the allegedly negligent act has ended. *See* DOBBS, HAYDEN & BUBLICK, LAW OF TORTS § 728, at 54–55 (2d ed. 2011).

3. **Continuous tort.** A similar rule has been applied where there is a "continuous tort," or "continuous conduct," where a plaintiff has been subjected to a series of wrongful acts over time by the defendant. In such a case the plaintiff's claim does not accrue until the most recent act has ceased. *See, e.g., John Doe 1 v. Archdiocese of Milwaukee,* 734 N.W.2d 827 (Wis. 2007) (where child was abused over a long period of time, statute of limitations began to run at the time of the last incident of molestation); *Feltmeier v. Feltmeier,* 798 N.E.2d 75 (Ill. 2003) (husband's continued abuse of wife). The "continuing tort" doctrine does not apply where there is a "one-time act or omission" resulting in continuing harm results. *Jourdan River Estates, LLC v. Favre,* 278 So.3d 1135 (Miss. 2019) ("A continuing tort sufficient to toll a statute of limitations is

occasioned by continual unlawful acts, not by continual ill effects from an original violation.").

4. **Preventing legal malpractice.** Attorneys responsible for failure to file a meritorious suit (or a defense) in time are subject to liability to the client for malpractice. *See* KATHLEEN MARIE ERWINS & JASON T. VAIL, PROFILE OF LEGAL MALPRACTICE CLAIMS 2008–2011 (2012). What would you do to be sure you never filed a late claim, answer, or motion? Why might the attorney have delayed filing suit? Sometimes the client is late in consulting an attorney. Why might a client delay?

SCHMITZ V. NATIONAL COLLEGIATE ATHLETIC ASS'N
122 N.E.3d 80 (Ohio 2018)

FRENCH, J.

... From 1974 through 1978, [Steven] Schmitz played football for Notre Dame, a member institution of the NCAA—the governing body of collegiate athletics. Schmitz participated in full-contact tackling drills, practices, scrimmages, and games during his college football career, and he sustained "repetitive subconcussive and concussive brain impacts." On "many occasions," he "experienced concussion symptoms, including but not limited to being substantially disoriented as to time and place." Yet, neither Schmitz nor Notre Dame's coaching staff recognized that Schmitz suffered from any injury that required monitoring, treatment, therapy or rest. Notre Dame's coaching staff praised tackling and blocking techniques that involved a player's use of his helmeted head and aggravated the risk of head injuries, and the coaching staff ordered players to continue participating in practices and games following a head impact. Schmitz was neither tested nor examined for concussive symptoms, nor was he advised or educated about concussions while playing football for Notre Dame.

Schmitz alleged that until December 2012, he did not know, and had no grounds to believe, that he had suffered a latent brain injury. Rather, he alleged that his December 2012 diagnosis of CTE at the Cleveland Clinic was the first time a "competent medical authority" informed him that he "had suffered a brain injury related to playing football." Schmitz described CTE as a "latent disease" that "involves the slow build-up of the Tau protein within the brain tissue that causes diminished brain function, progressive cognitive decline," and other neurological symptoms.

In October 2014, Schmitz and his wife filed this action against appellants [the University of Notre Dame and the NCAA]; their amended complaint, filed in January 2015, alleged claims of negligence, fraudulent concealment, constructive fraud, breach of express and implied contract, and loss of consortium against appellants. The amended complaint alleges that appellants knew or should have known that college football players are at greater risk for chronic brain injury, both during their football careers and later in life, and that appellants "ignored the medical risks," acted so as to "aggravate[ ] and enhance[ ] the medical risks," "failed to educate" players about the links between football head impacts and chronic neurological damage, and "failed to implement or enforce any system that would reasonably have mitigated, prevented, or addressed concussive and sub-concussive impacts."

Appellants filed motions to dismiss appellees' claims pursuant to Civ.R. 12(B)(6) as time-barred. . . . The trial court granted the motions to dismiss without opinion, and appellees appealed.

[The Eighth District Court of Appeals reversed the trial court's dismissal of the negligence, fraud and fraudulent concealment claims ("the remaining claims"), holding that the amended complaint does not allege facts that would allow the court to conclude as a matter of law that the remaining claims accrued prior to December 2012, when Schmitz was diagnosed with CTE.] The court characterized the amended complaint as alleging a "latent injury" that "did not manifest until decades after Schmitz stopped playing football." . . . This court accepted appellants' discretionary appeal. . . .

Application of a statute of limitations presents a mixed question of law and fact; when a cause of action accrues is a question of fact, but in the absence of a factual issue, application of the limitations period is a question of law. . . .

[Appellees' claims] are subject to the limitations period contained in R.C. 2305.10(A), which states, "[A]n action for bodily injury * * * shall be brought within two years after the cause of action accrues." The dispositive question, then, becomes when appellees' causes of action accrued. If, as appellants contend, the claims accrued by 1978 when Schmitz concluded his college football career, then the claims were time-barred long before 2014, when the Schmitzes filed this action. But if, as appellees contend, the claims accrued when Schmitz was diagnosed with CTE in December 2012, then the Schmitzes timely filed their claims within two years.

Subject to certain exceptions not applicable here, a cause of action for bodily injury accrues and the limitations period begins to run "when the injury * * * occurs." R.C. 2305.10(A). Prior to the General Assembly's enactment of statutory language to define when a cause of action accrues, this court held that a cause of action for bodily injury existed "from the time the wrongful act was committed." Often the wrongful act and injury occur simultaneously. But other times, a tortious act may not result in immediate or immediately apparent injury.

In *O'Stricker [v. Jim Walter Corp.*, 447 N.E.2d 727 (Ohio 1983)], this court recognized that application of the general rule could mean that the statute of limitations bars an injured party's right to recovery before he is even aware that it exists. To alleviate that concern, the court formulated a discovery rule to postpone the accrual of a cause of action for the infliction of bodily injury that does not manifest itself until a point subsequent to the defendant's alleged misconduct. With respect to a latent injury, a claim accrues under the discovery rule on either "the date on which the plaintiff is informed by competent medical authority that he has been injured, or upon the date on which, by the exercise of reasonable diligence, he should have become aware that he had been injured, whichever date occurs first." Accrual of a cause of action for bodily injury requires that the plaintiff "knows or, by the exercise of reasonable diligence should have known, that he had been injured by the conduct of the defendant." Essentially, the statute of limitations begins to run when the plaintiff knows or, in the exercise of reasonable diligence, should know that he has suffered a cognizable injury. . . .

To justify dismissal of this action as untimely . . . the amended complaint must conclusively show that the claims accrued before October 20, 2012, two years before Schmitz and his wife commenced this action. The amended complaint does not make that conclusive showing. . . .

Here, Schmitz sought recovery for severe memory loss, cognitive decline, Alzheimer's disease, CTE, and dementia. The amended complaint contains no allegations that any of those neurological impairments manifested prior to December 2012. But even if Schmitz experienced some neurological impairment prior to his CTE diagnosis in December 2012, the amended complaint alleges that prior to that diagnosis, Schmitz did not know and had no reason to know that he had suffered a latent brain injury while playing football. . . . For purposes of Civ.R. 12(B)(6), we must accept those factual allegations as true. And doing so, we cannot conclusively say that appellees' claims accrued by the time Schmitz finished playing football for Notre Dame in 1978.

Appellants alternatively argue that appellees' remaining claims are time-barred because, in the exercise of reasonable diligence, Schmitz should have known of his claims against appellants by October 2012, two years before he and his wife filed this action. . . .

Ultimately, it may be true—as appellants argue—that appellees' claims accrued before October 2012. But while appellants might be able to prove with facts uncovered during discovery that Schmitz knew or, with reasonable diligence, should have known prior to October 2012 of his neurological impairments and their connection to appellants' alleged conduct, that conclusion does not follow solely from the allegations made in the amended complaint. The amended complaint does not allege whether Schmitz suffered symptoms of neurological impairment between the end of his college football career and his diagnosis with CTE in 2012 or, if so, when those symptoms appeared. And neither the allegation that CTE involves progressive cognitive decline nor the allegation that Schmitz suffered symptoms prior to filing his complaint (almost two years *after* his diagnosis) conclusively demonstrates that Schmitz should have been aware prior to October 2012 that he had been injured as a result of appellants' conduct. The determination of those factual questions will require discovery. . . .

For these reasons, we affirm the Eighth District's judgment reversing the dismissal of appellees' claims for negligence, fraudulent concealment, and constructive fraud. The discovery rule applies to those claims, and after accepting the amended complaint's factual allegations as true and making all reasonable inferences in favor of appellees, we conclude that the amended complaint does not conclusively show that those claims are time-barred. Civ.R. 12(B)(6) therefore does not warrant the dismissal of those claims. . . .

Judgment affirmed.

NOTES

1. **What counts as "discovery."** Exactly what "discovery" ought to count for purposes of the discovery rule? Statutes and case law create some divergence.

(a) One approach, exemplified by *Schmitz*, focuses solely on "the injury." Under this approach, the plaintiff's claim accrues even where a reasonable person would not have discovered either the cause of the injury or that defendant had a role in it. *See Lincoln Elec. Co. v. McLemore*, 54 So.3d 833 (Miss. 2010) (construing statutory language, barring plaintiff's claim on limitations grounds, holding that the claim accrued "upon discovery of the injury, not discovery of its injury and its cause").

(b) A more common approach says that "the statute of limitations begins to run once a plaintiff knows or reasonably should know that she had been injured and her injury was proximately caused by the conduct of the defendant." *Petition of New Hampshire Division for Children, Youth and Families*, 244 A.3d 260 (N.H. 2020) (applying statute). Many cases have said that under this approach the plaintiff must have known or should have known that the defendant's act was wrongful. *See Schlumberger Technology Corp. v. Pasko*, 544 S.W.3d 830 (Tex. 2018) ("The discovery rule delays accrual until the plaintiff knew or in the exercise of reasonable diligence should have known of the wrongful act and resulting injury."); *Walk v. Ring*, 44 P.3d 990 (Ariz. 2002) (dental malpractice claim accrued only when plaintiff discovered that other dentists thought her dentist was at fault).

(c) A third approach is similar to the second, but fixes accrual on the date "when all elements of the claim or cause exist." *See, e.g.*, MONT. CODE ANN. § 27–2–102(1)(a). Under this approach, "the period of limitation does not begin to run until the injured party discovers the facts constituting the claim or, in the exercise of due diligence, should have discovered the facts constituting the claim." *Norbeck v. Flathead County*, 438 P.3d 811 (Mont. 2019). The focus is on the *factual* basis for the claim, not its *legal* basis. *See, e.g., Behroozi v. Kirshenbaum*, 128 A.3d 869 (R.I. 2016) (discovery rule "requires only that the plaintiff be aware of facts that would place a reasonable person on notice that a potential claim exists"); *Oulette v. Beaupre*, 977 F.3d 127 (1st Cir. 2020) (distinguishing between "ignorance of the facts, including an injury and its cause, and ignorance of the law"; "a plaintiff cannot plead ignorance of his or her legal rights to delay accrual"). States adopting this rule often say that a negligence claim accrues when the plaintiff knows or should know "(1) that the plaintiff has been injured, (2) the identity of the entity who owed the plaintiff a duty to act with due care, and who may have been engaged in conduct that breached that duty, and (3) that the conduct of that entity has a causal relation to the injury." *Coffield v. Robinson*, 857 S.E.2d 395 (W.Va. 2021).

2. **Identity of the defendant.** As you may be able to glean from Note 1, courts have not agreed on whether the identity of the defendant must be known or reasonably knowable before a claim accrues. *Compare Harrington v. Costello*, 7 N.E.3d 449 (Mass. 2014) ("Knowledge of the responsible person's identity seems implicit in the requirement that a plaintiff know that the defendant's conduct caused him harm; without such knowledge, the plaintiff does not know whom to sue."), *with Fox v. Ethicon Endo-Surgery, Inc.*, 110 P.3d 914 (Cal. 2005) (that plaintiff neither knows nor suspects the identity of the defendant "does not delay accrual . . . because the identity of the defendant is not an element of a cause of action"); *Nowotny v. L & B Contract Indus., Inc.*, 933 P.3d 452 (Wyo. 1997). The rationale for the latter approach appears to be that a plaintiff who knows of the existence of a cause of action has time to discover the defendant's identity, often by filing a "Doe" complaint and using the tools of discovery to gain the required knowledge in order to serve the proper defendant. Where a tortfeasor intentionally conceals his identity from the plaintiff, however, he may be estopped from asserting the statute of limitations. *See Bernson v. Browning-Farris Indus.*, 873 P.2d 613 (Cal. 1994).

3. **Duty to investigate.** Most courts applying a discovery rule stress that plaintiffs are under a duty to investigate once they have notice of certain facts. *See, e.g., Arnoult v. Webster*, 480 P.3d 592 (Alaska 2020); *McLeod v. Millette*, 301 So.3d 568 (Miss. 2020) ("To benefit from the discovery rule, a plaintiff must be reasonably diligent in investigating her injuries."); *Norgart v. Upjohn Co.*, 981 P.2d 79 (Cal. 1999) (discovery rule requires plaintiff to "seek to learn the facts necessary to bring the cause of action in the first place—he cannot wait for them to find him").

4. **The jury's role.** The discovery rule avoids the harsh result of the traditional rule we saw in *Crumpton*, but it substitutes a good deal of uncertainty, since discovery will depend on the individualized facts of each

case. It also injects a normative issue—when plaintiff *should* have discovered the requisite thing or things. As in *Schmitz*, questions often arise about when the plaintiff discovered sufficient facts to start the limitations clock, or a reasonable person would have done so. These questions are for the jury, if reasonable people can differ. *See, e.g., Ridgway Lane & Associates, Inc. v. Watson*, 189 So.3d 626 (Miss. 2016) (fact issue about when plaintiff homeowner knew or should have known of his breathing problems, in action against defendants who failed to repair a ceiling leak that caused mold to grow inside his home); *Doe 1 v. Lake Oswego School Dist.*, 297 P.3d 1287 (Or. 2013) (claim of offensive battery; fact issue on when plaintiffs should have recognized teacher's conduct was "offensive"). Does the individualized inquiry under the discovery rule undercut the purposes of having statutes of limitation in the first place?

5. **Statutory provisions.** Statutes themselves may specify when a claim accrues. For example, the National Childhood Vaccine Injury Act, 42 U.S.C.A. § 300aa–16(a), provides on its face that the statute of limitations runs from the date of occurrence of the first symptom or manifestation of the onset of the vaccine-related injury recognized as such by the medical profession at large. In *Cloer v. Secretary of Health & Human Services*, 654 F.3d 1322 (Fed. Cir. 2011), the court held that that provision precluded the addition by the court of a discovery rule. State legislatures have adopted some statutes that provide special protections for health care professions, including the elimination of the discovery rule entirely; some of these have been struck down as unconstitutional. *See, e.g., Martin v. Richey*, 711 N.E.2d 1273 (Ind. 1999).

Other state statutes may adopt the discovery rule, but only for certain kinds of claims. For example, an Idaho statute adopts a discovery rule only in cases of foreign objects left in a patient's body after surgery. In *Stuard v. Jorgenson*, 249 P.3d 1156 (Idaho 2011), the Idaho court held that in a case in which the statute did not apply, the statute of limitations began to run on the date that the surgeon performed surgery and caused some damage that was objectively ascertainable, even though the patient had no symptoms or knowledge of the doctor's negligence until over two years later.

The discovery rule is especially appealing for victims of toxic torts, the effects of which may not appear for many, many years or even for generations. A federal statute creates certain liabilities in connection with disposal or release of hazardous substances, and adds that in cases brought under *state* law for personal injury or property damage, the state must give the plaintiff the benefit of the discovery rule. 42 U.S.C.A. § 9658.

NOTE: LATENT POTENTIAL HARM

Partial Injury, Latent Potential

Accrual of a claim under the discovery rule is not delayed simply because the plaintiff does not know of the full extent of her injury or damages. *See, e.g., Bonness v. Armitage,* 942 N.W.2d 238 (Neb. 2020); *Podrygula v. Bray,* 856 N.W.2d 791 (N.D. 2014); *Larson & Larson, P.A. v. TSA Indus., Inc.,* 22 So.3d 36 (Fla. 2009). But suppose a tort occurs and the plaintiff knows it, yet the plaintiff believes damages may later become much worse than they are at present. While it is perfectly possible to claim and recover damages that will occur in the future, under traditional rules this can be done only if the proof shows that such damages will more likely than not occur. If the plaintiff sues now to stay within the statute of limitations, he will avoid that problem, but he will be limited to damages he can presently prove. The *res judicata* rules will prevent a second suit later on. If he waits to see whether damages will become much worse, he will eventually face the statute of limitations bar.

In *Hagerty v. L. & L. Marine Services, Inc.,* 788 F.2d 315 (5th Cir. 1986), Hagerty was drenched with dripolene, a carcinogen. He had some dizziness and leg cramps, and stinging in the extremities, all of which disappeared after showers. He undergoes regular medical checkups because of the cancer threat, but he does not presently have cancer and cancer is not "more likely than not." But his present fear of future cancer is real. Consider the options for the court:

(1) Adopt a view similar to that under the lost chance of recovery cases, Chapter 7. This would allow the plaintiff to recover now for any actual injury, plus all possible future injuries that might result from it, but future injuries would be reduced to reflect their probability. For example, if future cancer appearing in ten years is a 40% probability and would, if it occurs, impose damages of $100,000, the plaintiff would recover $40,000. This is the "enhanced-risk" or reduced-chance recovery.

(2) Reject the enhanced-risk recovery, allow present actual damages only, but with present damages, including the mental anguish or suffering resulting from the plaintiff's fear of future cancer.

(3) Reject the enhanced-risk and fear claims, allow the plaintiff to recover what he can prove in actual damages, and bar any future claims under *res judicata* rules.

(4) Reject enhanced-risk recovery, but allow present damages and leave open the possibility for a second suit if substantially different kinds of damage occur. This would allow recovery for cancer if it later develops.

The *Hagerty* court adopted the fourth option. This eliminates the dilemma created by the statute of limitations on the one hand and the *res judicata* rules on the other. A growing number of cases support allowing a second suit for damages if a different kind of injury occurs later, caused by the same exposure. The California Supreme Court adopted this approach in *Pooshs v. Philip Morris USA, Inc.,* 250 P.3d 181 (Cal. 2011). The court held that an earlier-discovered disease, COPD, does not trigger the statute of limitations on a suit based on a later-discovered separate latent disease, lung cancer, caused by the same tobacco use.

Similarly, in *Daley v. A.W. Chesterton, Inc.,* 37 A.3d 1175 (Pa. 2012), the court extended Pennsylvania's separate-disease rule. It affirmed a trial court decision allowing a claim for malignant mesothelioma when the plaintiff had previously recovered for pulmonary asbestosis and lung cancer from the same asbestos exposure. The court reasoned that allowing a second claim for a separate malignant disease related to a single asbestos exposure would avoid "anticipatory lawsuits, protracted litigation, evidentiary hurdles, speculative damages, and excessive or inadequate compensation." *Accord, Pustejovsky v. Rapid-American Corp.,* 35 S.W.3d 643 (Tex. 2000); *Sopha v. Owens-Corning Fiberglas Corp.,* 601 N.W.2d 627 (Wis. 1999).

Is this the best solution? In *Kiser v. A.W. Chesterton Co.,* 736 S.E.2d 910 (Va. 2013), the court's majority did not think so, rejecting the *Hagerty* rule based on a longstanding common-law rule that "a single wrongful act may not give rise to two independent causes of action." Dissenters argued that "when, as in the case of asbestosis and mesothelioma, there are two distinct and unrelated harms that accrue at different times, the plaintiff may have two separate causes of action. . . . The relatively short latency period for asbestosis, the applicable two-year statute of limitations for personal injury, and substantially longer latency period for mesothelioma virtually guarantees that individuals who have asbestosis will be barred from recovering damages should they subsequently develop mesothelioma."

Exposure Without Symptoms

Suppose the plaintiff is exposed to a toxin in sufficient quantities to raise the possibility of future harm that could occur in ten, twenty or thirty years. But suppose also that the plaintiff has no present symptoms at all. You might think that in this kind of case there is no problem. There is no statute of limitations to confront because the plaintiff merely waits until injury occurs and then sues. However, the plaintiff exposed to chemical poisons in her water or gases in the air she breathes may have two present "injuries" without symptoms. First, the plaintiff may have fear of future harm and that fear may itself poison her life. Second, the plaintiff may have medical expense because continuous medical monitoring is important to minimize future harm by early detection.

Some decisions have treated the non-symptomatic exposure as a tort and have said, with *Hagerty*, that the plaintiff could recover now for the costs of medical monitoring and that an additional suit could be brought later if cancer or other serious disease actually occurs. A landmark case is *Ayers v. Jackson Twp.*, 525 A.2d 287 (N.J. 1987). *See also Meyer ex rel. Coplin v. Fluor Corp.*, 220 S.W.3d 712 (Mo. 2007) (citing cases from a dozen other jurisdictions supporting such a theory). Other courts have rejected claims for medical monitoring damages in the absence of proven physical injury. *See, e.g., Paz v. Brush Engineered Materials, Inc.*, 949 So.2d 1 (Miss. 2007); *Henry v. Dow Chemical Co.*, 701 N.W.2d 684 (Mich. 2005).

Are you willing to say that any exposure, even though not accompanied by symptoms, is a tort for which damages can be recovered?

NOTE: TOLLING AND GRACE PERIODS

1. *The tolling concept.* The discovery rule is not the only avenue of relief for the late-suing plaintiff. Statutes of limitation may be tolled (a term of art, meaning *paused*) so that the clock is not running at all until some impediment to suing has been removed. This may occur before the limitations period ever begins, or after it has begun. For example, the statute of limitations may be tolled while the plaintiff is under a disability such as minority (that is, young age) or mental incompetence.

2. *Tolling for minority.* State laws generally toll the statute of limitations on a child's injury claim until the child has reached the age of majority, usually 18. Thus if the statutory period is two years and the injured child sued within two years after reaching the age of majority, the suit would be timely. Some state courts have held that legislation to the contrary violates their constitution. *See Kordus v. Montes*, 337 P.3d 1138 (Wyo. 2014); *Piselli v. 75th Street Med.*, 808 A.2d 508 (Md. 2002); *Sands ex rel. Sands v. Green*, 156 P.3d 1130 (Alaska 2007). Other courts have upheld legislative restrictions on minority tolling against constitutional attack. *See, e.g., Christiansen v. Providence Health System of Oregon Corp.*, 184 P.3d 1121 (Or. 2008). In some states, minority tolling is available only where a parent or guardian could not sue on the minor's behalf. *See R.R. v. New Life Community Church of CMA, Inc.*, 303 So.3d 916 (Fla. 2020) (relying on state statute).

3. *Tolling for unsound mind.* Minority is a type of legal disability, but the law recognizes other types as well for tolling purposes. For purposes of commitment to an institution, an individual might be deemed of unsound mind if he is a danger to himself or others. In the statute of limitations

context, however, unsound mind usually means that the individual is unable to manage his or her business affairs or estate, or to comprehend his or her legal rights or liabilities. *Ellis v. Estate of Ellis*, 169 P.3d 441 (Utah 2007); *Doe v. Roe*, 955 P.2d 951 (Ariz. 1998). Thus no matter what the psychological impediments to suit, the victim cannot have the benefits of tolling for unsound mind if he can manage his daily affairs by working, buying food, writing checks or the like. *See In re: Mirapex Products Liab. Litigation*, 912 F.3d 1129 (8th Cir. 2019) (applying Cal. law). Whether the patient cannot manage day-to-day affairs such that tolling would apply is often a question of fact. In some jurisdictions, this issue may be resolved by the court in a pre-trial evidentiary hearing. *See Timothy G. v. State, Dept. of Health & Social Services*, 372 P.3d 235 (Alaska 2016).

4. *Repressed memory.* Victims of childhood sexual abuse who have sued their abusers years afterwards may be able to take advantage of the minority-tolling rules, but sometimes too much time has passed for that to work. Some such plaintiffs have claimed that there is another reason for their failure to sue within the limitations period—repressed memory. Scientists and therapists differ about the existence of repression and the accuracy of "recovered" memory. States have disagreed as well, leading to divergent holdings on whether repressed memory is a reason to toll the statute of limitations on tort claims. Most courts that have addressed the issue have admitted repressed memory evidence, at least when supported by expert testimony and the facts of the particular case. *See Maness v. Gordon*, 325 P.3d 522 (Alaska 2014) (collecting cases). But some courts have flatly rejected such evidence. *See, e.g., Doe v. Archdiocese of St. Paul*, 817 N.W.2d 150 (Minn. 2012) ("Because . . . the theory of repressed and recovered memory lacks foundational reliability when offered for the purpose of proving that Doe had a disability delaying the accrual of his causes of action, the district court did not abuse its discretion when it excluded Doe's expert testimony."). A number of states have now extended the statute of limitations for sexual abuse claims, which may make reliance on repressed memory less crucial for many plaintiffs. *E.g.,* IOWA CODE ANN. § 614.8A; OHIO REV. CODE § 2305.111; UTAH CODE ANN. § 78–12–25.1; WASH. REV. CODE § 4.16.340.

5. *Other forms of tolling.* A statute of limitations also may be tolled for other reasons. For example, the statute of limitations may be tolled during the pendency of a suit seeking class action certification, or because the plaintiff is in prison or in the armed forces. *See* DOBBS, HAYDEN & BUBLICK, HORNBOOK ON TORTS § 18.6 (2d ed. 2016).

6. *Grace periods.* Tolling is a true time-out, time not counted on the statute of limitations period. A number of legislatures have now replaced time-out tolling with a grace period. A grace period merely extends the statute of limitations; it does not stop the clock. Some statutes provide hardly any grace at all. For example, Michigan provides that if a child

under thirteen suffers injury to reproductive organs, she must sue before her fifteenth birthday. MICH. COMP. L. ANN. § 600.5851(8). Any foreseeable unfairness with such a rule?

––––––––––

DASHA V. MAINE MEDICAL CENTER, 665 A.2d 993 (Me. 1995). Defendant erroneously diagnosed the plaintiff as having a fatal brain tumor. On that diagnosis, surgery plus radiation to the brain would prolong life for a short time and the plaintiff opted for that treatment. The treatment itself allegedly caused severe brain damage and the plaintiff became incompetent. Two years after the misdiagnosis and treatments, another physician reviewed the diagnosis and discovered that it was erroneous. The plaintiff's original problem had been a relatively benign tumor not calling for such treatments. His guardian sued, but by this time it was more than three years after the original misdiagnosis. Under Maine's legislation, the discovery rule did not apply because, by statute, it was unavailable in most medical malpractice cases. Nor did tolling for mental incapacity work because the plaintiff was mentally sound at the time of the misdiagnosis. The plaintiff argued that, nonetheless, the defendant should be equitably estopped from pleading the statute of limitations, since the defendant's own fault had caused the incapacity as well as the injury. *Held,* no equitable estoppel applies. "[E]stoppel may be used to prevent the affirmative defense of the statute of limitations if the elements of estoppel are present. . . . The gist of an estoppel barring the defendant from invoking the defense of the statute of limitations is that the defendant has conducted himself in a manner which actually induces the plaintiff not to take timely legal action on a claim. The plaintiff thus relies to his detriment on the conduct of the defendant by failing to seek legal redress while the doors to the courthouse remain open to him."

"The stipulated facts of this case do not meet the elements of equitable estoppel. . . . MMC made no affirmative misrepresentation, as required to support the application of equitable estoppel. Although a claim of equitable estoppel can be supported by an act of negligence that is the equivalent of fraud, the misdiagnosis by MMC is not the equivalent of fraud sufficient to support the assertion of equitable estoppel. Dasha relied on the misdiagnosis to seek radiation treatments, but he did not rely on a representation of MMC to decide to forego seeking legal redress."

NOTES

1.   **Elements of equitable estoppel.** Was the estoppel decision in *Dasha* correct? Was the outcome of the case correct? "The elements of an equitable estoppel claim are (1) a delay in filing an action that is induced by the defendant; (2) the defendant misled the plaintiff; and (3) the plaintiff must have acted on the information in good faith to the extent that he failed to

pursue his action in a timely manner." *Archuleta v. City of Rawlins*, 942 P.2d 404 (Wyo. 1997). Equitable estoppel is "employed to ensure fairness, prevent injustice, and do equity." *Rustico v. Intuitive Surgical, Inc.*, 993 F.3d 1085 (9th Cir. 2021) (quoting *Spray, Gould & Bowers v. Associated Int'l Ins. Co.*, 71 Cal.App.4th 1260 (1999)).

2. **Force or threat.** If a defendant prevented suit by physical force or threats, he might be estopped from pleading the statute of limitations as a defense. *See John R. v. Oakland Unified School Dist.*, 769 P.2d 948 (Cal. 1989) (child molester); *Ortega v. Pajaro Valley Unified Sch. Dist.*, 75 Cal. Rptr.2d 777 (Ct. App. 1998) (same).

3. **Fraudulent concealment.** A statute of limitations will be tolled if a defendant fraudulently conceals a cause of action from the plaintiff. This tolling may last until the plaintiff discovers, or should have discovered, either the fraudulent concealment itself, *see Gallant v. MacDowell*, 759 S.E.2d 818 (Ga. 2014), or the facts that establish a cause of action, *see Estate of Brice v. Toyota Motor Corp.*, 373 P.3d 977 (N.M. 2016) (outlining the elements of fraudulent concealment as follows: plaintiff must prove that (1) defendant knew of the alleged wrongful act and concealed it from plaintiff, or had material information that he failed to disclose, and (2) plaintiff did not know, or could not have known through reasonable diligence, of the cause of action within the statutory period). Thus the plaintiff who actually discovers the relevant facts within the limitations period "even if the potential defendant tried unsuccessfully to conceal the offense" cannot take advantage of this doctrine." *Greenhill v. Vartanian*, 917 F.3d 984 (7th Cir. 2019) (applying Ill. law). A number of courts have emphasized that in order to invoke fraudulent concealment to toll the statute of limitations, a plaintiff "must use reasonable diligence to investigate her claims." *Rice v. Diocese of Altoona-Johnstown*, 255 A.3d 237 (Pa. 2021) (citing cases from other states, barring plaintiff's claims of childhood sexual abuse where she "did not exercise any due diligence").

Many courts require that the act of concealment be "active," such as by making an actual misrepresentation of fact as opposed to simply remaining silent. *Embarton v. GMRI, Inc.*, 299 S.W.3d 565 (Ky. 2009); *Polanco v. Lombardi*, 231 A.3d 139 (R.I. 2020); *Burton v. Twin Commander Aircraft LLC*, 254 P.3d 778 (Wash. 2011). A number of courts have said that the concealment need not be active if the parties are in a fiduciary relationship, meaning one of trust and confidence, that places the defendant under a duty of disclosure. *Henderson Square Condominium Ass'n v. LAB Townhomes, LLC*, 46 N.E.3d 706 (Ill. 2015); *Anderson ex rel. Herren v. Iowa Dermatology Clinic, PLC*, 819 N.W.2d 408 (Iowa 2012).

4. **Equitable tolling.** Courts have distinguished equitable estoppel, fraudulent concealment, and equitable tolling, on the ground that the first two involve some misconduct by the defendant while the latter does not. *See, e.g., Williams v. Hawkins*, 594 S.W.3d 189 (Ky. 2020). With equitable tolling, a court may decide to toll the statute "when a litigant has pursued his rights diligently but some extraordinary circumstance prevents him from bringing a

timely action." *Lozano v. Montoya Alvarez*, 572 U.S. 1 (2014); *see also Valdez v. United States*, 518 F.3d 173 (2d Cir. 2008) (equitable tolling may be used when "despite all due diligence [the plaintiff] is unable to obtain vital information bearing on his claim"). Does this give the court more flexibility than would a simple application of the discovery rule?

B. STATUTES OF REPOSE

DURRE v. WILKINSON DEVELOPMENT, INC.
560 N.W.2d 72 (Neb. 2013)

WILKINS, J.:

On April 3, 2009, Durre and his wife were sitting in their pickup truck, which was parked at a gas station/fast-food restaurant in North Platte, Nebraska. About 1 p.m., the restaurant's sign fell onto the cab of the truck, injuring Durre and killing his wife.

The restaurant's sign and the pole structure to which the sign was attached were designed, built, and installed by Tri-City [Sign Company] employees. Tri-City obtained a building permit for the installation of the sign from the city of North Platte, designating 65 feet as the height of the sign. Installation of the sign was completed on or about May 15, 1999. There was no evidence that any of the defendants measured the height of the sign after its construction was completed. [The sign was, in fact, 75 feet high.] The sign collapsed as a result of the shearing of a section of the steel pole which held the sign. . . .

[On November 13, 2009, Durre sued Wilkinson Development, the owner of the restaurant's parking lot, for negligently maintaining the pole and sign. On March 10, 2011, Durre filed an amended complaint naming other defendants, including Tri-City, alleging that it negligently designed and constructed the pole and sign, and failed to warn of the sign's dangerous condition. In a second amended complaint, Durre alleged that Tri-City concealed the height of the sign from the public. The district court granted Tri-City's motion for summary judgment, concluding that Durre's actions were barred by the 10-year statute of repose in NEB. REV. ST. § 25–223. Durre appealed.]

The applicable statute, § 25–223, provides in part:

> In no event may any action be commenced to recover damages for an alleged breach of warranty on improvements to real property or deficiency in the design, planning, supervision, or observation of construction, or construction of an improvement to real property more than ten years beyond the time of the act giving rise to the cause of action.

Durre has alleged a claim to recover for personal injury caused by Tri-City's negligence. He argues that § 25–223 does not apply to personal injuries resulting from an inherently dangerous condition or latent defect of the property caused by a contractor's negligence. We disagree.

Our resolution of this claim is controlled by our decision in *Williams v. Kingery Constr. Co.*, 404 N.W.2d 32 (Neb. 1987). Henry Williams, a school janitor, fell 30 feet backward inside a pipe chase. His fall was caused by a missing section of concrete wall and occurred more than 10 years after construction of the school was completed in 1968. Williams argued that § 25–223 applied only to causes of action for damage to property and not to actions for personal injury. We determined that § 25–223 applied to an action in tort for personal injuries caused by the negligent construction of a building. We held the 10-year period of repose began to run when construction of the building was completed. Thus, Williams' cause of action was time barred before it accrued. . . .

Durre's action against Wilkinson was filed in November 2009, which was more than 10 years after the May 1999 completion and installation of the sign. His action against Tri-City was not commenced until March 10, 2011. The 10-year statute of repose in § 25–223 barred Durre's claim for damages against Tri-City.

Durre argues that if § 25–223 applies to claims for personal injury, Tri-City's fraudulent concealment of the dangerous condition of the sign estopped it from asserting a statute of repose defense. . . . From our review of the pleadings and the evidence offered at the hearing on the motions for summary judgment, we conclude that Durre has failed to provide any evidence that created a material issue of fact whether Tri-City fraudulently concealed any material fact, either with the intention that Durre would act or refrain from acting, or which prevented Durre from timely filing his action against Tri-City. . . .

AFFIRMED.

NOTES

1.   **Statutes of repose.** As the U.S. Supreme Court has explained, a statute of repose "puts an outer limit on the right to bring a civil action. That limit is measured not from the date on which the claim accrues but instead from the date of the last culpable act or omission of the defendant. . . . [T]he injury need not have occurred, much less have been discovered." *CTS Corp. v. Waldburger*, 573 U.S. 1 (2014).

In the last several years, a number of states have enacted statutes of this kind, usually aimed at providing protection for some special group, such as product manufacturers, doctors, architects, engineers, and construction contractors. Statutes in some states are more general in scope. *See, e.g.*, ALASKA STAT. § 09.10.055 (barring "an action for personal injury, death, or property damage unless commenced within 10 years of . . . the last act alleged to have caused the personal injury, death, or property damage," with exceptions for "an intentional act or gross negligence" or "breach of trust or fiduciary duty"). A North Carolina statute provides that claims for personal injury and physical damage to property "shall not accrue until bodily harm to the claimant or physical damage to his property becomes apparent or ought reasonably to have become apparent. . . . Provided that no cause of action shall accrue more than 10 years from the last act or omission of the defendant giving rise to the cause of action." N.C. GEN. STAT. § 1–52(16). The first part of this statute embodies a discovery rule, but the proviso could obviously bar a claim before it accrues. For example, if a doctor negligently administers a drug which causes no harm for 15 years, the cause of action would not accrue until harm was done, but the statute would have run 10 years after the doctor's "last act."

2. **Purpose and policy.** In *CTS v. Waldburger, supra* Note 1, the Court recognized that while "there is substantial overlap between the policies" of statutes of limitation and statutes of repose, "each has a distinct purpose and each is targeted at a different actor." Statutes of limitation encourage plaintiffs to bring actions in a timely manner, as do statutes of repose. But statutes of repose "effect a legislative judgment that a defendant should be free from liability after the legislatively determined time. Like a discharge in bankruptcy, a statute of repose can be said to provide a fresh start or freedom from liability." *Id. See also Wilson v. Durrani*, 173 N.E.3d 448 (Ohio 2020) (comparing purposes of statutes of limitations and statutes of repose).

3. **Equitable tolling, the discovery rule, and fraudulent concealment.** Statutes of repose are not generally subject to equitable tolling, even in cases of extraordinary circumstances beyond the plaintiff's control. *Lozano v. Montoya Alvarez*, 572 U.S. 1 (2014); *Stearns v. Metropolitan Life Ins. Co.,* 117 N.E.3d 694 (Mass. 2019) ("In stark contrast to statutes of limitation, statutes of repose may not be 'tolled' for *any* reason.") (emphasis in original). The court in *Ambers-Phillips v. SSM DePaul Health Center*, 459 S.W.3d 901 (Mo. 2015), said that statutes of repose are "incompatible with equitable tolling." Why would that be?

What about the discovery rule? Given the purposes of statutes of repose, should a plaintiff be able to argue successfully—at least if the statute itself is not clear on the point—that the statute of repose does not bar the claim because the plaintiff neither knew nor should have known of the existence of facts that would allow a suit to be brought? Courts have said no. *See, e.g., Marshall v. Dodds*, 827 S.E.2d 570 (S.C. 2019) (six-year statute of repose for medical malpractice claims constitutes "an outer limit . . . regardless of whether it has or should have been discovered"); *Ex parte Hodge*, 153 So.3d 734 (Ala. 2014) (four-year statute of repose barred claim by patient against doctor who left clamp in her body after hysterectomy, "regardless of when or to what extent the complications from the negligent act would be discovered"); *Lamprey v. Britton Const., Inc.*, 37 A.3d 359 (N.H. 2012) (construction-defect case).

Is fraudulent concealment different? The *Durre* court concludes that the plaintiff failed to prove any act of fraudulent concealment by Tri-City. If the plaintiff had made such proof, should *that* have tolled the statute of repose? Compare *Ingram v. Drouin*, 111 A.3d 1104 (N.H. 2015), with *Snyder v. Love*, 153 P.3d 571 (Mont. 2006).

4. **Constitutionality.** One line of attack on this sort of statute questions its constitutionality, usually on the basis of state constitutional provisions. Some courts have held such statutes unconstitutional. *See, e.g., Yanakos v. UPMC*, 218 A.3d 1214 (Pa. 2019) (statute of repose in Medical Care Act violates state constitutional right to a remedy because is not substantially related to the state's interest in controlling malpractice insurance premiums); *Myers v. Crouse-Hinds Div. of Cooper Industries, Inc.*, 53 N.E.3d 1160 (Ind. 2016) (10-year statute of repose in Product Liability Act unconstitutional as applied, under the state constitution's Equal Privileges and Immunities Clause). Others have been upheld against constitutional attack. *See, e.g., Dapo v. State*, 454 P.3d 171 (Alaska 2019) (rejecting as-applied challenge under constitutional access-to-courts provision).

5. **Arguing inapplicability.** Statutes of repose are often targeted to particular defendants and particular situations, so a plaintiff may be able to argue that the statute does not apply in the particular case. For instance, the statute may protect a contractor who builds a defective building that causes harm more than a decade after it is completed, but may not protect the current owner who fails to repair or maintain the building, *see Davenport v. Comstock Hills-Reno,* 46 P.3d 62 (Nev. 2002), or the manufacturer of a defective hot-water system installed in the building, *State v. Perini Corp.*, 113 A.3d 1199 (N.J. 2015).

REFERENCES: DOBBS, HAYDEN & BUBLICK, HORNBOOK ON TORTS §§ 18.1.7 (2d ed. 2016); 1 DOBBS, HAYDEN & BUBLICK, THE LAW OF TORTS §§ 241–250 (2d ed. 2011).

§ 2. FEDERAL PREEMPTION

VREELAND V. FERRER
71 So.3d 70 (Fla. 2012)

LEWIS, J. . . .

Danny Ferrer entered into an agreement to lease an airplane from Aerolease of America, Inc. (Aerolease) for a period of one year. . . . [After takeoff,] the plane crashed. The pilot, Donald Palas, and his passenger, Jose Martinez, were killed in the crash. John Vreeland, in his capacity as administrator ad litem and personal representative of the Martinez estate, filed a wrongful death action against Aerolease. [Vreeland asserted a number of Florida state law tort claims including a "dangerous instrumentality doctrine" claim that Aerolease, as owner of the aircraft, was liable and responsible for the negligence of the pilot in the operation and inspection of the aircraft.]

Aerolease moved for summary final judgment, contending that a provision of federal law, 49 U.S.C. § 44112 (1994), preempted Florida law. Section 44112, titled "Limitation of Liability," provides, in pertinent part:

> (b) Liability.—A lessor, owner, or secured party is liable for personal injury, death, or property loss or damage on land or water only when a civil aircraft, aircraft engine, or propeller is in the actual possession or control of the lessor, owner, or secured party, and the personal injury, death, or property loss or damage occurs because of—
>
>> (1) the aircraft, engine, or propeller; or
>>
>> (2) the flight of, or an object falling from, the aircraft, engine, or propeller.

The trial court . . . entered a summary final judgment in favor of Aerolease. The trial court noted that under Florida's "dangerous instrumentality" doctrine, the owner or lessor of an aircraft is vicariously liable for the negligent conduct of a pilot. However, the court concluded that 49 U.S.C. § 44112 preempted Florida law and, because Aerolease was not in actual possession or control of the aircraft at the time of the crash, the company was not responsible under the provisions of the federal statute. . . . [The Second District Appellate Court affirmed in part and reversed in part.]

Vreeland filed a petition with this Court seeking review of the Second District's decision. . . .

The dangerous instrumentality doctrine has been a part of Florida common law for almost one hundred years. In 1920, the Florida Supreme Court considered whether a corporation could be held responsible for the negligence of an operator who injured another while driving an automobile owned by the corporation. In its analysis, the Court articulated what is now known as the dangerous instrumentality doctrine and concluded that the doctrine is applicable to motor vehicles: . . .

> An automobile being a dangerous machine, its owner should be responsible for the manner in which it is used; and his liability should extend to its use by any one with his consent. He may not deliver it over to any one he pleases and not be responsible for the consequences.

In a subsequent decision, this Court held that an individual who rented vehicles as part of a business was responsible for the negligence of the driver who rented the vehicle. . . . Recently, the Fifth District Court of

Appeal reiterated the concept and framework of the dangerous instrumentality doctrine and the purpose behind it:

> The doctrine imposes strict liability upon the owner of a motor vehicle by requiring that an owner who "gives authority to another to operate the owner's vehicle, by either express or implied consent, has a nondelegable obligation to ensure that the vehicle is operated safely." The doctrine is intended to foster greater financial responsibility to pay for injuries caused by motor vehicles because the owner is in the best position to ensure that there are adequate resources to pay for damages caused by its misuse. The doctrine also serves to deter vehicle owners from entrusting their vehicles to drivers who are not responsible by making the owners strictly liable for any resulting loss. . . .

It was a federal court in 1951 that first applied Florida's dangerous instrumentality doctrine to aircraft. . . .

Our examination of these authorities and the reasoning underlying their pronouncements leave no room for doubt that, [ ] Florida law, by which we are here governed, . . . imposes liability upon the defendant for the acts and omissions of the pilot of its airplane which the jury was authorized to, and did, find constituted negligence. . . .

With regard to federal preemption, the United States Supreme Court has stated:

> Preemption may be either express or implied, and "is compelled whether Congress' command is explicitly stated in the statute's language or implicitly contained in its structure and purpose.". . . We "begin with the language employed by Congress and the assumption that the ordinary meaning of that language accurately expresses the legislative purpose."

Where a federal law does not expressly preempt state law, preemption may be inferred only where the scheme of federal regulation is sufficiently comprehensive to make reasonable the inference that Congress "left no room" for supplementary state regulation. Preemption of a whole field also will be inferred where the field is one in which "the federal interest is so dominant that the federal system will be assumed to preclude enforcement of state laws on the same subject."

Even where Congress has not completely displaced state regulation in a specific area, state law is nullified to the extent that it actually conflicts with federal law. Such a conflict arises when "compliance with both federal and state regulations is a physical impossibility," or when state law "stands as an obstacle to the accomplishment and execution of the full purposes and objectives of Congress."

The United States Supreme Court has further explained that preemption is very carefully scrutinized when it touches upon areas traditionally governed by state law.... Tort law is one area that is clearly and traditionally regulated by the states....

At issue in this case is whether the federal law currently codified at 49 U.S.C. § 44112 preempts Florida state law with regard to the liability of aircraft owners under the dangerous instrumentality doctrine and, if it does, how broadly the scope of that preemption covers.

There is no express preemption language within [the federal statute.] Therefore, if Florida law with regard to aircraft owner/lessor liability is preempted by section 44112, that preemption can only be implied... To determine whether and to what extent section 44112 may impliedly preempt Florida law, it is necessary to review and understand the legislative history behind this provision....

Every version of the owner/lessor liability federal statute since its enactment in 1948 has referenced injury, death, or property damage that has occurred on land or water, or on the surface of the earth.... The words "on land or water" or "on the surface of the earth" may be read to specify that the limitation on liability only applies to death, injury, or damage that is caused to people or property that are physically on the ground or in the water. Specifically, the limitation on liability would apply only to individuals and property that are underneath the aircraft during its flight, ascent, or descent....

We conclude that by adopting a federal law that specifically referenced damages or injuries that occur on the surface of the earth, the 1948 Congress did not intend to preempt state law with regard to injuries to passengers or aircraft crew....

Decisions with regard to how section 44112/1404 should be interpreted are varied.... [We agree with an interpretation adopted by a Michigan court that the federal statute shields a lessor of an airplane from tort liability for any injury or loss suffered "on the surface of the earth" but not for an injury that occurred "inside the aircraft."]

Florida's dangerous instrumentality doctrine imposes vicarious liability upon owners and lessors of aircraft, even where the aircraft is not within their immediate control or possession at the time of the loss. To the extent that the doctrine applies to injuries, damages, or deaths that occur on the surface of the earth, the doctrine conflicts with, and is therefore preempted by, section 44112. However, because the death of Martinez occurred while he was a passenger in a plane that crashed—not on the ground beneath the plane—the wrongful death action filed by Vreeland is not preempted by section 44112. Rather, Florida's dangerous instrumentality doctrine applies, and the Second District erroneously affirmed the summary final judgment entered by the trial court in favor of Aerolease on the basis of federal preemption. . . .

POLSTON, J., dissenting. . . .

I believe federal law preempts Florida's dangerous instrumentality doctrine here. . . . The majority's assertion that the federal statute does not apply because "Martinez was not 'on land or water' at the time of the crash—he was a passenger inside the aircraft" defies reality. Even though Martinez was in the aircraft when it hit land, his death occurred "on land," not in the aircraft prior to contact with land. The majority's view is inconsistent with the plain meaning of the statute, specifically the plain meaning of "on land."

NOTES

1.　**Supremacy of federal laws.** The Supremacy Clause of Article VI of the U.S. Constitution provides that the federal constitution and laws "shall be the supreme Law of the Land." Congress has the power to override state law as long as it acts within the limits of its own constitutional powers. According to the *Vreeland* court, under what circumstances might federal regulation preempt state tort law?

2.　**Scope of preemption.** If the intent to preempt state law is the "clear and manifest purpose of Congress" in enacting a particular law or regulation, *CSX Transportation, Inc. v. Easterwood*, 507 U.S. 658 (1993), then state laws that conflict with those federal provisions simply cannot be enforced. The effect is to displace tort law and leave the plaintiff without a remedy where the defendant has complied with federal regulations. Congress might preempt state tort law by (1) expressly preempting state tort law by statute; (2) occupying the field with heavy regulation so there is no room for state tort law; or (3) by passing laws that actually conflict with state law.

A federal statute may be found to preempt some of the plaintiff's state tort claims, but not others. *See, e.g., Elam v. Kansas City Southern Ry. Co.*, 635 F.3d 796 (5th Cir. 2011) (Interstate Commerce Commission Termination Act preempts plaintiffs' negligence per se claim based on a state statute, but not their ordinary negligence claim in which they alleged that the railroad negligently failed to provide adequate warning of a train's presence at a crossing). A statute may also be found, as in *Vreeland*, to preempt claims by certain plaintiffs but not others.

3.　**Effect of preemption.** Preemption is a complicated subject of particular importance in the products liability field, as discussed in greater detail in Chapter 24. However, as in *Vreeland*, preemption remains a powerful defense in many cases, including those outside the products sphere. In *Vreeland,* would preemption have defeated the State of Florida's tort policy? Is that a concern? Is there any practical way in which preemption is different from saying that compliance with statute is a defense?

4.   **Express preemption.** The simplest preemption cases are those in which Congress has expressly preempted state tort claims, although even in those cases courts must engage in interpretation. For example, in *Roth v. Norfalco LLC*, 651 F.3d 367 (3d Cir. 2011), the Hazardous Materials Transportation Act expressly preempted plaintiff's state-law claims of negligence, strict liability, products liability and breach of warranty against a shipper of sulfuric acid. The Act itself stated that it preempted all non-federal requirements that were not substantively the same as corresponding federal regulations, and plaintiff's claims, if successful, would require the shipper to install an additional safety valve and pressure gauge on each of its tank cars. And in *Tobin v. Federal Express Corp.*, 775 F.3d 448 (1st Cir. 2014), the Airline Deregulation Act (ADA) expressly preempted the plaintiff's claims of negligence, invasion of privacy, and infliction of emotional distress that were based on FedEx's mistaken delivery of a large package of marijuana to her home, resulting in, among other things, a scary visit from the sender or intended recipient. The ADA provides that a state "may not enact or enforce a law, regulation, or other provision having the force and effect of law related to a price, route, or service of an air carrier." State common-law causes of action "are provisions that have the force and effect of law," the court said, and here, plaintiff's claims are "about FedEx's package handling, address verification, and delivery procedures," which clearly implicate FedEx's "services."

5.   **Railroads.** The federal government regulates many aspects of railroad operations. For example, federal regulations specify the kind of headlights required on railroad trains. This regulation has been held to preempt the field, so that state regulation is not permitted. The plaintiff is struck by a railroad train, the engine of which complies with the federal headlight regulation. The plaintiff attempts to prove, in his state tort law suit, that better lights were available, that a prudent person would have used them on the engine, and that had they been used, the collision could have been avoided. If state tort law permitted this proof, would that be the same as "regulating" the railroad as to a federally-preempted matter? The court so held in *Marshall v. Burlington Northern, Inc.*, 720 F.2d 1149 (9th Cir. 1983). In *Missouri Pacific R.R. Co. v. Limmer*, 299 S.W.3d 78 (Tex. 2009), a plaintiff was hit by a train at a railroad crossing and claimed that the railroad was negligent for failing to install adequate warning signs. *Held,* the claim is preempted if federal regulations specified the kinds of warnings that should be installed, at least where federal funds were used as well, and the defendant did install such warnings. *See also Norfolk Southern Railway Co. v. Shanklin,* 529 U.S. 344 (2000) (where railroad crossing warnings are constructed with federal funds, no state tort action permitted). *Cf. Ryder v. Union Pacific R.R. Co.*, 945 F.3d 194 (5th Cir. 2019) (claim that train engineer negligently sounded horn was preempted by Federal Railroad Safety Act).

REFERENCES: DOBBS, HAYDEN & BUBLICK, HORNBOOK ON TORTS § 18.8 (2d ed. 2016); 1 DOBBS, HAYDEN & BUBLICK, THE LAW OF TORTS § 250 (2d ed. 2011).

PART 5

LIMITING OR EXPANDING THE DUTY OF CARE ACCORDING TO CONTEXT OR RELATIONSHIP

■ ■ ■

"Duty" can be a confusing word in tort cases. Courts often use the term to describe both an obligation to use care *and* the standard or measure of that obligation. For instance, courts may say that the normal duty is the duty to use the care of the reasonable, prudent person under the same or similar circumstances. However, at times it is important to separate the obligation owed from the standard of care by which the obligation is measured, because other standards can be used. For example, in some cases the standard of care requires a high degree of care, or even a strict obligation to protect the plaintiff, meaning that defendant is liable even if not at fault. At the other end of the spectrum, there are cases in which the defendant owes no duty at all. In between there are several possible standards of care that demand more or less than ordinary care under the reasonable person standard. In many cases landowners owe people on the land only the duty to avoid willful or wanton injury. So the term duty often refers to both an *obligation* and a *standard*. In both senses, a duty provides a general principle that measures the defendant's obligations to the plaintiff. This general principle can be applied beyond the facts of the particular case.

As already observed, however, courts sometimes use the term duty as a way of talking about what particular acts are required by the exercise of ordinary care. For instance, a court might say that defendant had "a duty to stop, look, and listen before crossing a railroad track." When a court uses the term duty in this way it is not setting a *standard* for cases generally; it is reaching a conclusion about the *particular case* or stating a very specific rule that cannot be generalized beyond the facts. You will see courts using the term duty in both ways. The aim of this Part, however, is to talk about duty in the first sense, as a standard. In this sense, duties (or standards) range from the very demanding to the very lenient.

CHAPTER 12

CARRIERS, HOST-DRIVERS AND LANDOWNERS

∎ ∎ ∎

§ 1. CARRIERS AND HOST-DRIVERS

DOSER V. INTERSTATE POWER CO., 173 N.W.2d 556 (Iowa 1970). Defendant's bus was involved in an automobile accident and a bus passenger was injured. The evidence was that the automobile turned left in front of the bus and the defendant argued that the plaintiff had not shown negligence. " 'A carrier of passengers for hire must exercise more than ordinary diligence for their protection. Its duty stops just short of insuring their safety. It is bound to protect its passengers as far as human care and foresight will go and is liable for slight negligence.' . . . [T]he high degree of care must be exercised in *foreseeing*, as well as in *guarding against*, danger. Plaintiff made a prima facie case by showing she was injured while a passenger on the bus by a collision between the bus and the automobile. This cast upon defendants the burden to show their freedom from negligence in causing the collision. . . . Given the high degree of care demanded of common carriers and the factual situation presented, we hold the court was correct in submitting the various specifications of negligence to the jury."

NOTES

1. **The "heightened standard" for common carriers.** The traditional "heightened standard" of care owed by common carriers to passengers is often stated as "the highest degree of care," *see, e.g., Davis v. Dionne*, 26 A.3d 801 (Me. 2011); *Todd v. Mass Transit Admin.*, 816 A.2d 930 (Md. 2003), or "the utmost care," *see* CAL. CIV. CODE § 2100. *See also Maison v. New Jersey Transit Corp.*, 245 A.3d 536 (N.J. 2021) (standard requires the carrier to exercise "the utmost caution characteristic of very careful prudent men, or the highest possible care consistent with the nature of the undertaking"). The traditional rule dates at least to the 19th century. *See, e.g., Derwort v. Loomer*, 21 Conn. 245 (1851) (describing the rule as "fully established, in our own courts and elsewhere").

2. **Who is a common carrier?** Many states that apply a heightened standard for common carriers see the category as "narrowly tailored" to include only those in the business of carrying "everyone who asks." *Chavez v. Cedar Fair, LP*, 450 S.W.3d 291 (Mo. 2014); *see also VIA Metropolitan Transit v.*

Meck, 620 S.W.3d 356 (Tex. 2020) (to qualify as a common carrier, the entity must "provide transportation services to the general public, as opposed to providing such services only for particular individuals or groups," and the "primary purpose" of such a business must be "transporting people or goods"). States with such formulations usually include taxis, buses, railroads, airplanes, ferries, and other modes of commercial transportation within that definition. However, some courts have taken a more expansive view. *See, e.g., Gomez v. Superior Court*, 113 P.3d 41 (Cal. 2005) (amusement park ride); *Cash v. Otis Elevator Co.*, 684 P.2d 1041 (Mont. 1984) (elevator).

State statutes may specify which entities fit within the category, although statutes do not always answer all questions. For example, is a ride-sharing company a common carrier, where the statute is silent on that? *See Murray v. Uber Technologies, Inc.*, 486 F.Supp.3d 468 (D. Mass. 2020) ("plaintiff has stated a plausible claim" that Uber is a common carrier "because it operates in substantially the same manner as taxi cab companies," which have been held to fit within Massachusetts' statute, which says a common carrier is one who affords "a means of transportation similar to that afforded by a railway company"); *see also Doe v. Uber Technologies, Inc.*, 2019 WL 6251189 (N.D. Cal. 2019) (unreported) ("Uber's status as an app-based transportation network does not preclude it as a matter of law from being held liable as a common carrier" under Cal. law).

3. **Scope of heightened duty owed to passengers.** A common carrier owes a heightened duty only to passengers. Who qualifies as a passenger? What if the plaintiff paid his fare and entered the train platform intending to board, but after waiting 30 minutes and letting 11 trains pass by, tripped on a container he had dropped and fell to his death from the platform onto an electrified rail. Does the heightened duty apply? *See Anderson v. Chicago Transit Authority*, 131 N.E.3d 1245 (Ill. App. 2019) (no; he was not a passenger at the time of injury because he was "not at all engaged in the act of boarding the train"; mere presence on a platform with intention to board is not enough). Even if the plaintiff in *Anderson* had been deemed a "passenger," would the defendant owe a higher duty with respect to what happened, or merely the duty of reasonable care? *See, e.g., Churchman v. Bay Area Rapid Transit Dist.*, 39 Cal.App.5th 246 (2019) (on similar facts, common carrier does not owe heightened duty with respect to "minor, commonplace hazards in a train station").

4. **The rationale for a higher standard.** What is the rationale for a higher duty? Older cases often stressed the hazardous nature of travel, especially train travel. *See, e.g., Galveston City Ry. Co. v. Hewitt*, 3 S.W. 705 (Tex. 1887) (common carrier duty springs from "the hazardous character of the business, and the fact that human life is imperiled by it"); *see also Katamay v. Chicago Transit Authority*, 289 N.E.2d 623 (Ill. 1972) (degree of care "should be commensurate with the danger to which the passenger is subjected, and the degree of care required to be exercised increases as the danger increases"); In *Speed Boat Leasing, Inc. v. Elmer*, 124 S.W.3d 210 (Tex. 2003), the court said, "The rationale for holding common carriers to a higher standard is that

passengers should feel safe when traveling." Other modern courts have stressed that passengers on common carriers are being "passively carried or transported" and "surrender their freedom of movement and actions" to the carrier. *Nalwa v. Cedar Fair, L.P.*, 290 P.3d 1158 (Cal. 2012). Do any of these rationales really support a standard beyond reasonable care?

5. **What does a "high degree of care" even mean?** Do you think a jury would understand how to apply a "heightened" standard of care, as opposed to the reasonable person standard? In a concurring opinion in *VIA Metropolitan Transit, supra* Note 2, Chief Justice Hecht said that "the rule's analytical problems are the principal reason to abandon it." The standard of a reasonable person *under the circumstances* adequately takes account of the relationship between common carrier and passenger. He continued,

> Unquestionably, a common carrier's duty of reasonable care to its passengers is not the same as that of a private driver taking a friend on an errand. The risks that arise in a common carrier's operation inform its duty. A public transit operator must act with the reasonable care such operators observe. But to say that the reasonable care required of a common carrier is "higher" than the reasonable care required of others transporting passengers is a useless and potentially misleading abstraction.

620 S.W.3d at 372–73 (Hecht, C.J., concurring).

6. **Contemporary rejection of a heightened standard.** Many courts and the Restatement have rejected the traditional higher standard of care in favor of the general negligence standard of reasonable care under the circumstances. For example, in *Nunez v. Professional Transit Management of Tucson*, 271 P.3d 1104 (Ariz. 2012), the court held that although common carriers have a special relationship with their passengers such that they owe a duty both to avoid creating dangers to passengers and to act affirmatively to aid passengers, this duty requires only the exercise of ordinary reasonable care. The court stressed the flexibility of the reasonable care standard and its ability to accommodate a wide range of situations involving risk. "[P]eople entrust their safety to others in many different contexts, such as undergoing surgery. In the medical context, however, the common law imposed upon the surgeon only the duty to act as a reasonable surgeon would under the circumstance." The court rejected the idea that a heightened degree of care made sense for this area of law alone, and addressed practical problems with applying the doctrine. *See also Bethel v. New York City Transit Auth.*, 703 N.E.2d 1214 (N.Y. 1998). Do you agree?

ALA. CODE § 32–1–2

The owner, operator or person responsible for the operation of a motor vehicle shall not be liable for loss or damage arising from injuries to or death of a guest while being transported without payment therefor in or upon said motor vehicle, resulting from the operation thereof, unless such injuries or death are caused by the willful or wanton misconduct of such operator, owner or person responsible for the operation of said motor vehicle.

NOTES

1. **Lower standards.** Some guest statutes state the standard as "gross negligence," others as "willful or wanton misconduct." There are variations of these two basic forms. The willful, wanton standard may be construed to require not merely extremely negligent conduct, but also a bad state of mind. Litigation under guest statutes often examined whether a jury case had been made on the statutory gross negligence or willful misconduct standard.

2. **Who is a guest?** The guest statutes raised some less obvious issues, notably those associated with the question, "Who is a guest?" Problems arise if the "guest" is injured in entering or leaving the car, for example, and also if the "guest" is paying a part of the cost of travel, or is providing non-monetary assistance to the driver.

3. **Constitutionality of guest statutes.** Guest statutes were the product of a specific time, the late 1920s and the 1930s, and began to decline in the 1970s. In *Brown v. Merlo*, 506 P.2d 212 (Cal. 1973), the court held that the California guest statute was unconstitutional as a denial of equal protection under state law, partly because it treated guests and non-guests differently without any rational reason for doing so. The guest statute does not prevent collusion between host and guest because if they wish to collude they can testify that the passenger paid for the ride. The statute is not explicable as a means of encouraging hospitality because hospitality is extended to others who are not barred, and because in any event it is difficult to see why a "hospitable" host should be free to be negligent toward a guest. After *Brown* a good many other courts adopted similar reasoning under their own state constitutions. Legislatures too, repealed many guest statutes. In 1985, the Texas Supreme Court offered this count: "of the twenty-nine states which originally enacted guest statutes, only Texas and four other states still have such statutes." It then promptly reduced the number by holding the Texas statute unconstitutional. *Whitworth v. Bynum*, 699 S.W.2d 194 (Tex. 1985). Nebraska narrowly upheld its guest statute against constitutional attack by a 4–3 vote in *Le v. Lautrup*, 716 N.W.2d 713 (Neb. 2006).

4. **Limited duties—past and present.** The era of the guest statutes is largely over. Why bother to consider them? One reason is that guest statutes set up a limited legal duty that closely resembles some others we will see in this chapter. Consider as you proceed whether your evaluation of the guest statutes should reflect your evaluation of other limited duty cases. Consider also whether the constitutional considerations would be the same when we come to other cases of limited duties, starting with the landowners' rules.

§ 2. LANDOWNERS' DUTIES TO ENTRANTS

A. TRADITIONAL COMMON-LAW DUTIES

CATHOLIC DIOCESE OF EL PASO V. PORTER
622 S.W.3d 824 (Tex. 2021)

CHIEF JUSTICE HECHT delivered the opinion of the Court.

The principal issue in this premises-liability case is whether volunteers working in a third-party vendor's booth at a festival were invitees of the landowner or only licensees. . . .

[For over a century, the San Lorenzo Church has held an annual festival on its grounds called the Fiesta de San Lorenzo. The three-day event features carnival rides, games, music, food and drink, arts and crafts, and vendors selling various items.] The Church profits from the festival in a variety of ways—it receives 30 percent of the carnival's gross proceeds, sells drinks and ice, runs a number of food and activities booths, and rents space to 60 or so vendors who set up their own booths.

At one festival, the El Paso 4-H Leaders Association (4-H) rented a booth, which it used to sell funnel cakes, gorditas, and snow cones. . . . The interior of the booth was off-limits to all but 4-H staffers. 4-H paid the Church $650 to rent the booth. The Church received no part of 4-H's sales.

On Sunday, the third day of the festival, a fire broke out in the 4-H booth. Five volunteers—four teenagers and one adult—were working in the booth at the time, and all suffered injuries from the flames. The parents of the four teenage volunteers (the Families) sued the Church and Heritage Operating, L.P., which had allegedly filled 4-H's propane tank. . . .

In a premises-liability action, the duty an owner or occupier of property owes someone on the property depends on that person's status. The duty owed an invitee is "to exercise reasonable care to protect against danger from a condition on the land that creates an unreasonable risk of harm of which the owner or occupier knew or by the exercise of reasonable care would discover." A lesser duty is owed a licensee: to "use ordinary care either to warn a licensee of, or to make reasonably safe, a dangerous condition of which the owner is aware and the licensee is not." Generally, a premises-liability plaintiff's status is a question of law, though it can be a question for the jury when facts relevant to the legal standard are in dispute. . . .

An invitee is one who enters the property of another with the owner's knowledge and for the mutual benefit of both. . . . We long ago held that the requisite "mutual benefit" to an invitee and an owner or occupier of property is a shared business or economic interest. . . .

We need not decide here whether invitee status always requires that the business benefit shared by the property visitor and the owner/occupier be economic in nature. The Families do not argue to the contrary. Following the *Texas Pattern Jury Charge*, the trial court charged the jury:

> "An invitee" is a person who is on the premises at the express or implied invitation of the possessor of the premises and who has entered thereon either as a member of the public or for a purpose for which the premises are held open to the public or for a purpose connected with the business of the possessor that does or may result in their mutual economic benefit. One who is an invitee cannot be a licensee at the same time.

The Families . . . have not argued at any stage of this case that the charge incorrectly stated the law.

The court of appeals held that the volunteers were invitees because "the El Paso 4-H Club itself was an invitee" and there existed "no legally significant distinction between the status of the Club itself and that of the Club's volunteers." 4-H had "signed a contract with the [Church] in which both parties would benefit economically from food and drink sales", and it "provided these services by using the labor of volunteer staff." Because "[t]he Club and the [Church] both benefitted from the volunteer's [sic] labor," the court reasoned, the "distinction between the Club and its volunteers from the perspective of the [Church] is illusory." Moreover, the court continued, the Church "knew that the Club would use volunteer labor to generate revenue for the mutual benefit of the Club and the [Church]." Since the volunteers "entered the [C]hurch's premises both with the knowledge and for the benefit of the [Church] at the [Church's] implied invitation", the court concluded that the "standard for invitee status is met."

But the volunteers' presence in the 4-H booth did not offer the Church any economic benefit—or any benefit at all. 4-H paid a flat fee to rent the booth, and none of the proceeds from the volunteers' sales of gorditas, funnel cakes, and snow cones went to the Church. The volunteers' presence in 4-H's booth benefitted 4-H but not the Church. . . .

The Families argue that the volunteers could participate in the festival while not working in the 4-H booth, potentially benefitting the Church by spending money on beer, soda, water, and ice (which the Church had the exclusive right to sell at the festival), and in doing so would have been invitees like all the other public attendees. But "[a] person may be an invitee as to certain parts of the premises but not as to others", and a visitor's status is determined at the time of injury. The volunteers were injured inside the 4-H booth, which was off-limits to festival-goers. There they were licensees of the Church.

We conclude that the volunteers were licensees as a matter of law. We hold that absent unusual circumstances not present in this case, a person on property to perform volunteer work for a third party benefits the third party rather than the property owner and therefore is not the owner's invitee. . . . [W]hen a visitor does not economically benefit the landowner, the law imposes on the owner the lesser duty associated with licensees. . . .

We must sustain the jury's finding that the Church did not breach the duty it owed to the volunteers as licensees. . . . Because the evidence does not conclusively establish that the Church actually knew of some condition that created an unreasonable risk of harm to the volunteers, we have no basis on which to reject the jury's finding. Accordingly, we hold that the Families cannot recover against the Church on their premises-liability claim. . . .

NOTES

1. **The traditional classifications of entrants on land.** Under the traditional common-law approach as the Kentucky court recently explained it,

> Visitors to property are classified according to one's purpose in entering the property and whether such entry is with the consent of the property's possessor. The standard of care the possessor must exercise depends on whether the visitor is present without the possessor's consent, *i.e.*, a trespasser; with the possessor's consent, *i.e.*, a licensee; or with the possessor's consent as a member of the public for whom the property is held open or for the possessor's business, *i.e.*, an invitee.

Smith v. Smith, 563 S.W.3d 14 (Ky. 2018). Notice that the traditional definition of invitee would classify social guests as licensees, not invitees, because while they are on the land with the consent of the landowner or occupier, they are neither on land "open to the public" nor present for the pecuniary benefit of the landowner or occupier. A very small number of states broaden the definition of invitee to include social guests on the idea that such guests are "invited." *See Burrell v. Meads*, 569 N.E.2d 637 (Ind. 1991).

2. **The various duties in summary.** About half of the states continue to follow the traditional common-law rules, in which the normal duty of reasonable care is owed only to invitees and a lesser duty—the duty not to willfully or wantonly harm—is owed to licensees and trespassers. As we will see in more detail shortly, the other half of the states depart from this traditional scheme either by holding that (a) the duty of reasonable care is owed to both invitees and licensees, with the lesser willful-wanton duty owed to trespassers, or (b) that a duty of reasonable care is owed to all entrants, regardless of status.

3. **When the special landowner-entrant rules apply.** The classifications apply only when the plaintiff has been injured on land owned or legally occupied by the defendant. Most states require that the injury be caused

by a *condition* on the land, as opposed to an *activity* being conducted on the land; in the latter case, a duty of reasonable care is owed regardless of the entrant's status. *See, e.g., Piech v. Layendecker*, 194 A.3d 543 (N.J. Super. A.D. 2018); *Janis v. Nash Finch Co.*, 780 N.W.2d 497 (S.D. 2010). Some courts have held to the contrary and apply premises-liability rules to conditions and activities being conducted on the land by the landowner-occupier. *See Bjerk v. Anderson*, 911 N.W.2d 343 (N.D. 2018) (but holding those rules inapplicable where activity on defendant's land was done by someone else); *Gladon v. Greater Cleveland Regional Transit Authority,* 662 N.E.2d 287 (Ohio 1996) (traditional landowner-entrant rules applied to case alleging defendant's negligent operation of a rapid transit train). Statutes in some states address this issue directly. *See, e.g.,* COLO. REV. STAT. ANN. § 13–21–115 (retaining categories of entrants, with some modifications to common-law duties, and making statutory rules applicable not only to "conditions" but also to "activities conducted on the property").

4. **Classifying entrants.** Most states say that the entrant's classification as an invitee, licensee or trespasser is for the jury, where reasonable people can differ. Those distinctions can be outcome-determinative. Perhaps the hardest cases are those where the plaintiff is either an invitee or a licensee, as in *Catholic Diocese v. Porter*. How was the distinction drawn in that case? Do you agree that the plaintiffs, who were volunteers for an organization that paid to be on the defendant's land, should be classified as licensees? Would it have made a difference if the plaintiffs were *paid employees* of the vendor? *Cf. Packer v. Riverbend Communications, LLC*, 468 P.3d 1283 (Idaho 2020) (vendor at Christmas festival was invitee of defendant that had rented the land for the festival; vendor paid fee to defendant to rent the booth, and was thus on the land for a purpose directly related to defendant's business and conferred a benefit on defendant).

5. **Potential customers.** Many courts have said that a customer in a store, even where the customer has not bought anything, is an invitee, apparently on the reasoning that even a prospective customer's presence represents a pecuniary benefits to the defendant. Do you think the Texas court in the primary case was correct in rejecting the argument that each of the plaintiffs was a potential customer at the festival, and thus were invitees on that basis? Alternatively, why were they not "public invitees?" If the grounds were open to anyone during the festival, why don't they fit within that category?

6. **Difficult distinctions in other cases.** What's the status category of a person visiting a patient in his hospital room? *Shelton v. Kentucky Easter Seals Soc., Inc.*, 413 S.W.3d 901 (Ky. 2013). How about a plaintiff who tripped on steps as she was going to a free religious course at a church of which she was not a member? Would it matter that the stated reason the church was offering classes was "to increase participation and expand its congregation?" *Turner v. Cathedral Ministries*, 27 N.E.3d 586 (Ohio Ct. App. 2015). Would a prisoner assigned to remodel the warden's home count as an invitee? *Georgia Dept. of Corrections v. Couch*, 718 S.E.2d 875 (Ga. Ct. App. 2011). How about

because of their youth, would not realize the potential danger." The trial court granted the Stanleys' motion for summary judgment, finding that because the decedents were trespassers, the only duty owed to them was "to refrain from wanton and willful misconduct." Because the complaint alleged only a violation of ordinary care, the trial court found for the Stanleys as a matter of law. The appeals court affirmed.]

Ohio has long recognized a range of duties for property owners vis-a-vis persons entering their property. A recent discussion of Ohio's classification system can be found in *Gladon v. Greater Cleveland Regional Transit Auth.* . . . Today, we face the issue of whether child trespassers should become another class of users who are owed a different duty of care.

This court has consistently held that children have a special status in tort law and that duties of care owed to children are different from duties owed to adults:

"[T]he amount of care required to discharge a duty owed to a child of tender years is necessarily greater than that required to discharge a duty owed to an adult under the same circumstances. This is the approach long followed by this court and we see no reason to abandon it. 'Children of tender years, and youthful persons generally, are entitled to a degree of care proportioned to their inability to foresee and avoid the perils that they may encounter. * * * The same discernment and foresight in discovering defects and dangers cannot be reasonably expected of them, that older and experienced persons habitually employ; and therefore the greater precaution should be taken, where children are exposed to them.'" *Di Gildo v. Caponi* (1969), 18 Ohio St.2d 125, 127, 47 O.O.2d 282, 283, 247 N.E.2d 732, 734.

Recognizing the special status of children in the law, this court has even accorded special protection to child trespassers by adopting the "dangerous instrumentality" doctrine [which] imposes upon the owner or occupier of a premises a higher duty of care to a child trespasser when such owner or occupier actively and negligently operates hazardous machinery or other apparatus, the dangerousness of which is not readily apparent to children. . . .

Despite the fact that in premises liability cases a landowner's duty is defined by the status of the plaintiff, and that children, even child trespassers, are accorded special protection in Ohio tort law, this court has never adopted the attractive nuisance doctrine. The doctrine as adopted by numerous states is set forth in Restatement of the Law 2d, Torts (1965), Section 339:

"A possessor of land is subject to liability for physical harm to children trespassing thereon caused by an artificial condition upon land if:

new
rule
adopted

"(a) the place where the condition exists is one upon which the possessor knows or has reason to know that children are likely to trespass, and

"(b) the condition is one of which the possessor knows or has reason to know and which he realizes or should realize will involve an unreasonable risk of death or serious bodily harm to such children, and

"(c) the children because of their youth do not discover the condition or realize the risk involved in intermeddling with it or in coming within the area made dangerous by it, and

"(d) the utility to the possessor of maintaining the condition and the burden of eliminating the danger are slight as compared with the risk to children involved, and

"(e) the possessor fails to exercise reasonable care to eliminate the danger or otherwise to protect the children."

This court has never explicitly rejected the Restatement version of the doctrine, which was adopted in 1965. Instead, Ohio's tradition in this area of the law is based upon this court's rejection in 1907 of the "turntable doctrine" in *Wheeling & Lake Erie RR. Co. v. Harvey* (1907), 77 Ohio St. 235, 83 N.E. 66. In *Harvey,* this court held . . . that "[i]t is not the duty of an occupier of land to exercise care to make it safe for infant children who come upon it without invitation but merely by sufferance."

The "turntable doctrine" was a somewhat controversial doctrine wherein railroads could be liable to children for injuries suffered on unguarded railroad turntables. The theory of liability was established in *Sioux City & Pacific RR. Co. v. Stout* (1873), 84 U.S. (17 Wall.) 657, 21 L.Ed. 745, and had been adopted by many states as of 1907. The burning question for many years was whether to apply the doctrine to non-turntable cases. Many of the states that adopted the turntable doctrine refused to apply it to cases not involving turntables.

However, the theory of liability has evolved since 1907. The Restatement of the Law, Torts (1934) and Restatement of the Law 2d, Torts (1965) removed legal fictions and imposed balancing factors to consider on behalf of landowners. Ohio's refusal to recognize the turntable doctrine in 1907 was not a serious anomaly at the time; today, our failure to adopt the attractive nuisance doctrine is. Ohio is one of only three states that have not either created a special duty for trespassing children or done away with distinctions of duty based upon a person's status as an invitee, licensee, or trespasser. . . .

Adopting the attractive nuisance doctrine would be merely an incremental change in Ohio law, not out of line with the law that has developed over time. It is an appropriate evolution of the common law.

While the present case is by no means a guaranteed winner for the plaintiff, it does present a factual scenario that would allow a jury to consider whether the elements of the cause of action have been fulfilled.

We therefore use this case to adopt the attractive nuisance doctrine contained in Restatement of the Law 2d, Torts (1965), Section 339. In doing so, we do not abandon the differences in duty a landowner owes to the different classes of users. In this case we simply further recognize that children are entitled to a greater level of protection than adults are. We remove the "distinctions without differences" between the dangerous instrumentality doctrine and the attractive nuisance doctrine. Whether an apparatus or a condition of property is involved, the key element should be whether there is a foreseeable, "unreasonable risk of death or serious bodily harm to * * * children." Restatement, Section 339(b).

The Restatement's version of the attractive nuisance doctrine balances society's interest in protecting children with the rights of landowners to enjoy their property. Even when a landowner is found to have an attractive nuisance on his or her land, the landowner is left merely with the burden of acting with ordinary care. A landowner does not automatically become liable for any injury a child trespasser may suffer on that land.

The requirement of foreseeability is built into the doctrine. The landowner must know or have reason to know that children are likely to trespass upon the part of the property that contains the dangerous condition. Moreover, the landowner's duty "does not extend to those conditions the existence of which is obvious even to children and the risk of which should be fully realized by them." *Id.* at Comment *i*. Also, if the condition of the property that poses the risk is essential to the landowner, the doctrine would not apply:

> "The public interest in the possessor's free use of his land for his own purposes is of great significance. A particular condition is, therefore, regarded as not involving unreasonable risk to trespassing children unless it involves a grave risk to them which could be obviated without any serious interference with the possessor's legitimate use of his land."

We are satisfied that the Restatement view effectively harmonizes the competing societal interests of protecting children and preserving property rights. In adopting the attractive nuisance doctrine, we acknowledge that the way we live now is different from the way we lived in 1907, when *Harvey* was decided. We are not a rural society any longer, our neighbors live closer, and our use of our own property affects others more than it once did.

Despite our societal changes, children are still children. They still learn through their curiosity. They still have developing senses of judgment. They still do not always appreciate danger. They still need protection by adults. Protecting children in a changing world requires the common law to adapt. Today, we make that change. . . .

[Reversed and remanded. Concurring and dissenting opinions omitted.]

NOTES

1. **The "attractive nuisance" rule.** As *Bennett* explains, the so-called "attractive nuisance" doctrine, with its special rules for child trespassers, is widely accepted in the states today. *Hill v. National Grid,* 11 A.3d 110 (R.I. 2011) (fact issues with respect to attractive nuisance prevented summary judgment in case of child injured by a protruding metal pole while playing football on a utility company's vacant field). Are you convinced that the policy rationales behind the attractive nuisance doctrine are sound?

2. **Tender years.** The special child trespasser rules apply only to children who, because of their tender years, are foreseeably unlikely to appreciate dangers and to avoid them. *See, e.g., Hayes v. D.C.I. Properties-DKY, LLC,* 563 S.W.3d 619 (Ky. 2018) (child trespasser rules inapplicable where plaintiff was almost 17 and "not only was capable of appreciating but did appreciate the risk" he created to himself); *Burton v. State,* 80 A.3d 856 (R.I. 2013) ("It strains credulity to think that plaintiff, a seventeen-year-old who was about to complete his G.E.D., did not realize the risk involved in climbing a pipe to an upper-story window and entering a dark, abandoned building."). Thus the "attractive nuisance" doctrine applies mainly to children of grade school age or younger, and only rarely to teenagers. *See, e.g., Racine v. Moon's Towing,* 817 So.2d 21 (La. 2002) (doctrine inapplicable to two trespassers, one 14 and one 15, because they were "clearly old enough to know what they were doing was wrong"). If a young child of 10 appreciates the danger of walking along the railroad track but does not avoid the danger, what result under the Restatement test? *See Laster v. Norfolk Southern Ry. Co.,* 13 So.3d 922 (Ala. 2009).

3. **Injury caused by something other than the "attractive nuisance."** What if the young child is injured by something on the property that is different from the "nuisance" that attracted the child in the first place? Can you formulate arguments based on policy that would support liability nonetheless? *See Henson ex rel. Hunt v. International Paper Co.,* 650 S.E.2d 74 (S.C. 2007).

4. **Identifying attractive nuisances.** Some courts have said that "common hazards," such as fire and pools of water cannot be considered attractive nuisances and the trespassing child who drowns in a stock pond is entitled to no protection from the landowner. The better explanation for many of these cases may be that there is a duty of care owed, but that given the importance of stock ponds and the difficulty of fencing them, the duty is not breached, which is to say the defendant is not negligent. This explanation is supported by the fact that even in states that announce a "common hazard" rule, recovery is sometimes allowed for swimming pool deaths and for injuries

by hidden burning embers. Can a defendant's dog be an attractive nuisance? *Clea v. Odom*, 714 S.E.2d 542 (S.C. 2011) (no, not a condition on land).

C. MODIFYING THE TRADITIONAL COMMON-LAW DUTIES OWED TO ENTRANTS

ROWLAND V. CHRISTIAN
443 P.2d 561 (Cal. 1968)

PETERS, JUSTICE.

[Plaintiff was a social guest in Miss Christian's apartment. The porcelain handle of a bathroom faucet broke in his hand and severed tendons and nerves. Miss Christian had known the handle was cracked and had in fact reported it to her lessors, but, though she knew plaintiff was going to the bathroom, she gave him no warning. These facts were established by affidavit and the trial judge gave summary judgment for the defendant.]

Section 1714 of the Civil Code provides: "Everyone is responsible, not only for the result of his willful acts, but also for an injury occasioned to another by his want of ordinary care or skill in the management of his property or person, except so far as the latter has, willfully or by want of ordinary care, brought the injury upon himself. . . ." This code section, which has been unchanged in our law since 1872, states a civil law and not a common law principle. . . .

One of the areas where this court and other courts have departed from the fundamental concept that a man is liable for injuries caused by his carelessness is with regard to the liability of a possessor of land for injuries to persons who have entered upon that land. It has been suggested that the special rules regarding liability of the possessor of land are due to historical considerations stemming from the high place which land has traditionally held in English and American thought, the dominance and prestige of the landowning class in England during the formative period of the rules governing the possessor's liability, and the heritage of feudalism. (2 Harper and James, The Law of Torts, supra, p. 1432.)

The departure from the fundamental rule of liability for negligence has been accomplished by classifying the plaintiff either as a trespasser, licensee, or invitee and then adopting special rules as to the duty owed by the possessor to each of the classifications. . . .

[The court here reviewed the trespasser-licensee-invitee rules and a number of cases which it said created exceptions, complexity and confusion.]

Complexity can be borne and confusion remedied where the underlying principles governing liability are based upon proper considerations. Whatever may have been the historical justifications for the common law distinctions, it is clear that those distinctions are not justified in the light of our modern society and the complexity and confusion which has arisen is not due to difficulty in applying the original common law rules—they are all too easy to apply in their original formulation—but is due to the attempts to apply just rules in our modern society within the ancient terminology.

Without attempting to labor all of the rules relating to the possessor's liability, it is apparent that the classifications of trespasser, licensee, and invitee, the immunities from liability predicated upon those circumstances, and the exceptions to those immunities, often do not reflect the major factors which should determine whether immunity should be conferred upon the possessor of land. Some of those factors, including the closeness of the connection between the injury and the defendant's conduct, the moral blame attached to the defendant's conduct, the policy of preventing future harm, and the prevalence and availability of insurance bear little, if any relationship to the classification of trespasser, licensee and invitee and the existing rules conferring immunity.

Although in general there may be a relationship between the remaining factors and the classifications of trespasser, licensee, and invitee, there are many cases in which no such relationship may exist. Thus, although the foreseeability of harm to an invitee would ordinarily seem greater than the foreseeability of harm to a trespasser, in a particular case the opposite may be true. The same may be said of the issue of certainty of injury. The burden to the defendant and consequences to the community of imposing a duty to exercise care with resulting liability for breach may often be greater with respect to trespassers than with respect to invitees, but it by no means follows that this is true in every case. In many situations, the burden will be the same, i.e., the conduct necessary upon the defendant's part to meet the burden of exercising due care as to the invitees will also meet his burden with respect to licensees and trespassers. The last of the major factors, the cost of insurance, will, of course, vary depending upon the rules of liability adopted, but there is no persuasive evidence that applying ordinary principles of negligence law to the land occupier's liability will materially reduce the prevalence of insurance due to increased cost or even substantially increase the cost. . . .

A man's life or limb does not become less worthy of protection by the law nor a loss less worthy of compensation under the law because he has come upon the land of another without permission or with permission but without a business purpose. Reasonable people do not ordinarily vary their conduct depending upon such matters, and to focus upon the status of the injured party as a trespasser, licensee or invitee in order to determine the question whether the landowner has a duty of care, is contrary to our modern social mores and humanitarian values. The common law rules obscure rather than illuminate the proper consideration which should govern determination of the question of duty. . . .

It may be noted that by carving further exceptions out of the traditional rules relating to the liability to licensees or social guests, other jurisdictions reach the same result. . . .

The Judgment is Reversed.

TRAYNOR, C. J., and TOBRINER, MOSK and SULLIVAN, J. J., concur.

BURKE, Justice (dissenting).

I dissent. In determining the liability of the occupier or owner of land for injuries, the distinctions between trespassers, licensees and invitees have been developed and applied by the courts over a period of many years. They supply a reasonable and workable approach to the problems involved, and one which provides the degree of stability and predictability so highly prized in law. The unfortunate alternative, it appears to me, is the route taken by the majority in their opinion in this case; that such issues are to be decided on a case by case basis under the application of the basic law of negligence, bereft of the guiding principles and precedent which the law has heretofore attached by virtue of the relationship of the parties to one another.

Liability for negligence turns upon whether a duty of care is owed, and if so, the extent thereof. Who can doubt that the corner grocery, the large department store, or the financial institution owes a greater duty of care to one whom it has invited to enter its premises as a prospective customer of its wares or services than it owes to a trespasser seeking to enter after the close of business hours and for a nonbusiness or even an antagonistic purpose? I do not think it unreasonable or unfair that a social guest (classified by the law as a licensee, as was plaintiff here) should be obliged to take the premises in the same condition as his host finds them or permits them to be. Surely a homeowner should not be obliged to hover over his guests with warnings of possible dangers to be found in the condition of the home (e.g., waxed floors, slipping rugs, toys in unexpected places, etc., etc.). . . .

McCOMB, J., concurs.

NOTES

1. **Guest statutes connection?** This is the first decision to abolish the categories and substitute the general duty of reasonable care. California was also the first state to hold guest statutes unconstitutional. *Brown v. Merlo*, 506 P.2d 212 (Cal. 1973). Is there any logical relation between the two decisions?

2. **Abolition of entrant-status categories.** After *Rowland*, some expected a tidal wave of decisions abolishing the traditional common-law entrant categories, but the complete-abolition trend rather quickly "lost its

steam." *Baldwin v. Mosley*, 748 146 (Ark. 1988). Fewer than ten states now say a duty of reasonable care is owed to every entrant on land. In many of those states, the duty of general care has been applied to child trespassers as well, thus eliminating those special rules. *See, e.g., Morse v. Goduti*, 777 A.2d 292 (N.H. 2001).

3.   **Retaining categories, but extending reasonable-care duty to licensees.** A larger number of states (approaching 20) have retained the invitee-licensee-trespasser categories, but extend a duty of reasonable care to both invitees and licensees. This, rather than the move towards complete abolition of categories, appears to be the most current trend. *See, e.g., Koenig v. Koenig*, 766 N.W.2d 635 (Iowa 2009); *Saltsman v. Sharp,* 803 N.W.2d 553 (N.D. 2011); *Demag v. Better Power Equipment*, 102 A.3d 1101 (Vt. 2014). These states retain the limited-duty-to-trespassers rules even though they have dropped the licensee-invitee distinction. *See, e.g., Bennett v. Napolitano,* 746 A.2d 138 (R.I. 2000); *Gable v. Gable*, 858 S.E.2d 838 (W.Va. 2021).

4.   **Further nuances.** The Restatement Third takes the position that all entrants, whether invitees, licensees or trespassers, are owed a duty of reasonable care. However, landowners owe "flagrant trespassers" only a duty not to intentionally, willfully or wantonly injure them. RESTATEMENT (THIRD) OF TORTS: LIABILITY FOR PHYSICAL AND EMOTIONAL HARM § 52 (2010). Similarly, the California legislature enacted a statute which excludes from the ordinary duty of reasonable care those trespassers who are injured "during the course of, or after the commission of, any felonies [specified in the statute]." CAL. CIV. CODE § 847 (2012).

SCURTI V. CITY OF NEW YORK, 354 N.E.2d 794 (N.Y. 1976). A 14-year-old boy was electrocuted in a railroad yard after crawling through a hole in the fence. There was evidence that the fence was part of a city park and the city and others were joined as defendants. New York had previously abolished the trespasser-licensee-invitee distinctions and had adopted the standard of reasonable care for all entrants.

"Under the standard of reasonable care . . . the factors which sustained the landowner's immunity and inspired the exceptions under prior law will no longer be considered decisive. But, as indicated, most of them have some probative value. . . . The fact that the injury occurred on the defendant's property is certainly a relevant circumstance in assessing the reasonableness of defendant's conduct. The defendant has a right to use his property and to develop it for his profit and enjoyment. That often means that he must conduct dangerous activities or permit dangerous instruments and conditions to exist on the premises. However under those circumstances he must take reasonable measures to prevent injury to those whose presence on the property can reasonably be foreseen. Whether the threat is posed by a dangerous condition or a dangerous activity is of little significance in itself. It may have some bearing on the effort required to prevent the injury, but that depends on the facts of the particular case. In this connection it is important to note that the elimination of the immunity conferred by prior law should not pose an unreasonable burden on the use of the property since all that is now required is the exercise of reasonable care under the circumstances. The defendant can always show that it would have been unduly burdensome to have done more. . . . The fact that the plaintiff entered without permission is also a relevant circumstance. It may well demonstrate that the plaintiff's presence was not foreseeable at the time and place of the injury. . . . This does not mean that every case involving injury on private property raises a factual question for the jury's consideration. In any negligence case the court must always determine as a threshold matter whether the facts will support an inference of negligence. . . . However, in this particular case the question of reasonableness of the parties' conduct cannot be resolved as a matter of law."

NOTES

1. **The negligence standard.** When the categories have been abolished, the landowner is still not liable unless he is negligent. Do you believe there are any situations that cannot be justly resolved by applying the prudent person standard? Can you give an example?

2. **Status category as one factor.** How would you characterize what the *Scurti* court is doing with the plaintiff's trespasser status? What do you think of its reasoning? In *Louis v. Louis*, 636 N.W.2d 314 (Minn. 2001), the court said that after the abolition of the common-law distinctions, an entrant's status as an invitee or a licensee was no longer controlling, but that it remained "one element among many to be considered in assessing the landowner's duty to use reasonable care for the safety of persons invited on the premises." Do you agree with that approach?

D. OPEN AND OBVIOUS HAZARDS

KENTUCKY RIVER MEDICAL CENTER V. MCINTOSH

319 S.W.3d 385 (Ky. 2010)

NOBLE, J. . . .

On May 27, 2004, McIntosh, a trained and licensed paramedic, was transporting a critically ill patient to the Hospital. She and two Emergency Medical Technicians (EMTs) arrived at the ambulance dock, and began guiding the patient to the emergency room entrance.

Immediately outside the emergency room entrance there is a flat surface which is eleven feet wide to allow stretchers to be wheeled directly from the ambulance dock into the emergency room. This flat area rises on both sides to form a curb. This curb is unmarked and unprotected.

Essentially, the area looks like a wide curb ramp used for wheelchair access, except that the "ramp" part is flat rather than at an incline.

McIntosh had helped transport about 400 patients to this emergency room entrance before, and she had always navigated past the protruding curb without incident. However, this time she tripped and fell over it, suffering a fractured hip and sprained wrist. McIntosh sued the Hospital, arguing that the curb was an unreasonably dangerous condition which caused her injuries.

While moving towards the entrance, McIntosh's attention was not focused on the curb; rather, she remained focused on attending to the critically ill patient. She testified that when transporting patients from the ambulance dock to the emergency room doors, it is the duty of a paramedic to remain focused on the patient's health and to make sure his intravenous lines do not get caught in the wheels of the stretcher, among other things. (In contrast, EMTs have the duty to physically push the patient from the ambulance to the doors.) One of the patient's family members testified that McIntosh was completely focused on the patient as he was pushed to the entrance.

In addition, evidence was introduced showing that having such a tripping hazard at an emergency room entrance is very rare, if not unique in Breathitt County and the counties adjoining it. In particular, McIntosh testified that she transports patients to several nearby hospitals and that none of them have any uneven surface between the ambulance dock and the doors. An EMT working for McIntosh also testified that among the eight to ten other entrances he had used, the Hospital was the only one that had a ledge or curb near the emergency room entrance. . . .

The Hospital moved the trial court for summary judgment, claiming that the open and obvious doctrine barred McIntosh's recovery as a matter of law. After considering the parties' briefs, the trial court summarily denied this motion.

Ultimately, the jury found the Hospital liable. It awarded McIntosh $40,409.70 for medical expenses, $65,000 for impairment of her earning capacity, and $50,000 for pain and suffering, for a total of $155,409.70. . . . The Hospital appealed to the Court of Appeals, which affirmed because "the Hospital could reasonably expect that a paramedic treating a critically-ill patient could be distracted, could forget (if she had ever observed it) that the curb was uneven, and could fail to protect herself against it." This Court granted discretionary review to determine whether the open and obvious doctrine should have completely barred McIntosh's cause of action. . . .

As a general rule, land possessors owe a duty to invitees to discover unreasonably dangerous conditions on the land and to either correct them or warn of them. However, the open and obvious doctrine states that land possessors cannot be held liable to invitees who are injured by open and obvious dangers. . . . [Defendant contends that open and obvious danger is a matter of duty; plaintiff responds that the existence of an open and obvious danger goes to the factual issue of fault].

Which of these two views is correct is not clear from the history of the doctrine because it arose in the era of contributory negligence. Under contributory negligence, any negligence on the part of the plaintiff completely barred recovery. Thus, it was irrelevant whether an open and obvious danger "excused a land possessor's duty to an invitee, or simply insulated the possessor from liability" by virtue of the plaintiff's contributory negligence in avoiding his own injury. "In either event, the injured invitee could not recover. . . ."

However, almost all states now have comparative fault—including Kentucky. Under comparative fault, whether the doctrine concerns duty or fault becomes very important. If duty is not excused by a known or obvious danger, the injured invitee might recover, albeit in a diminished amount, [by virtue of his own comparative fault]. In contrast, if the invitee's voluntary encounter with a known or obvious danger were deemed to excuse the land owner's duty, then there would be no negligence to compare—and, therefore, no recovery. This distinction is the principal issue of this case.

Our sister states do not unanimously agree about the correct answer. However, "[t]he manifest trend of the courts in this country is away from the traditional rule absolving, ipso facto, owners and occupiers of land from liability for injuries resulting from known or obvious conditions." Instead, these courts allow the jury to evaluate the comparative fault of the parties, typical in modern negligence cases.

The courts following this trend typically adopt the position of the Restatement (Second) of Torts with respect to open and obvious conditions, which states:

> A possessor of land is not liable to his invitees for physical harm caused to them by any activity or condition on the land whose danger is known or obvious to them, unless the possessor should anticipate the harm despite such knowledge or obviousness. Restatement (Second) of Torts § 343A(1) (1965). . . .

The current, tentative draft of the Restatement (Third) takes a position consistent with the Restatement (Second), except that it "amplifie[s]" duties on land possessors in certain situations. See Restatement (Third) of Torts: Liab. Physical Harm § 51 cmt. k (T.D. No. 6, 2009). . . .

[T]his Court concludes that the modern trend, as embodied in the Restatement (Second) of Torts, is the better position. . . .

Whether the danger was known and appreciated by the plaintiff, whether the risk was obvious to a person exercising reasonable perception, intelligence, and judgment, and whether there was some other reason for the defendant to foresee the harm, are all relevant considerations that provide more balance and insight to the analysis than merely labeling a particular risk "open and obvious." In sum, the analysis recognizes that a risk of harm may be foreseeable and unreasonable, thereby imposing a duty on the defendant, despite its potentially open and obvious nature. . . .

For many open and obvious dangers, the land possessor would have no reason to anticipate the harm, and so he would not be liable. However, sometimes "the possessor has reason to expect that the invitee's attention may be distracted, so that he will not discover what is obvious, or will forget what he has discovered, or fail to protect himself against it." In these situations, the injury is still foreseeable, and so liability should still be imposed. . . .

Further, the modern approach is more consistent with Kentucky's rule of comparative fault. By concluding that a danger was open and obvious, we can conclude that the invitee was negligent for falling victim to it, unless for some reason "to a reasonable man in his position the advantages of [encountering the danger] would outweigh the apparent risk. But this does not necessarily mean that the land possessor was not also negligent for failing to fix an unreasonable danger in the first place. Under our rule of comparative fault, the defendant should be held responsible for his own negligence, if any. . . .

The incompatibility between the open and obvious doctrine as an absolute, automatic bar to recovery and comparative fault is great. So great, in fact, that a few states have held that their comparative negligence statutes abolished the open and obvious doctrine outright. The incompatibility between the traditional open and obvious rule and comparative fault . . . should be resolved in favor of comparative fault.

This makes good policy sense. As the Supreme Court of Mississippi aptly stated:

> This Court should discourage unreasonably dangerous conditions rather than fostering them in their obvious forms. It is anomalous to find that a defendant has a duty to provide reasonably safe premises and at the same time deny a plaintiff recovery from a breach of that same duty. The party in the best position to eliminate a dangerous condition should be burdened with that responsibility. If a dangerous condition is obvious to the plaintiff, then surely it is obvious to the defendant as well. The defendant, accordingly, should alleviate the danger. . . .

If the land possessor can foresee the injury, but nevertheless fails to take reasonable precautions to prevent the injury, he can be held liable. . . .

A land possessor's duties are not based only on his superior knowledge. These duties are also based on the land possessor's unique position as the only person who can fix the dangers. . . .

Turning to this case, this Court concludes that the Hospital owed a duty to McIntosh. . . . The Hospital had good reason to expect that a paramedic, such as McIntosh, would be distracted as she approached the emergency room entrance. . . . Thus, even though the curb may have been open and noticeable to some extent, in this case "the possessor has reason to expect that the invitee's attention may be distracted" from it. . . .

[Paramedics] are required to think and act quickly in the most time-sensitive and stressful of circumstances. It is likely that in such a situation, a paramedic such as McIntosh may forget that this particular entrance has a unique danger that she must avoid. . . . [T]he extent to which her absentmindedness comes into play should bear only on her comparative fault rather than as an absolute bar to her recovery.

It is important to stress the context in which McIntosh sustained her injury: she was rushing a critically ill patient into a hospital, in an effort to save his life. Even if we assume that she was neither distracted nor forgetful about the curb, we would still have to conclude that the benefits of her rushing to the door (at the risk of tripping over the curb) outweighed the costs of her failing to do so (at the risk of the patient's condition worsening, perhaps to the point of death, on the Hospital doorstep). . . .

In the present case, the Hospital owed a duty to McIntosh, given that her injury was foreseeable. McIntosh, in turn, had a duty to act reasonably to ensure her own safety, heightened by her familiarity with the location and the arguably open and obvious nature of the danger. Thus, there were genuine issues of material fact that were properly submitted to the jury. . . .

SCHRODER, J., dissenting:

Because I believe the open and obvious doctrine concerns a question of duty, I respectfully dissent. The other hospitals McIntosh served had no curbs to trip over. Appellants had a curb, which contained no building code or OSHA violations, and was open and obvious. It appears the Appellants are being held liable for a breach of a duty: a duty to build its emergency entrance like other hospitals in an undefined area. Until this decision, there was no such duty. Until today, a landowner or possessor of land could not be held liable to invitees who were injured by open and obvious dangers. Now, even though the alleged danger is open and obvious (like snow or ice on a sidewalk), if the possessor can anticipate the harm to an invitee, the possessor has a duty to fix the condition, or to somehow give additional warnings. In this case, to avoid future liability, the hospital will need to build the same type of entrance ramp as some unknown group of hospitals. This is an unwise and unnecessary change in the law in the Commonwealth.

NOTES

1. **"Open and obvious" defined.** A "condition is *obvious* when, objectively, 'both the condition and the risk are apparent to and would be recognized by a reasonable man, in the position of the visitor, exercising ordinary perception, intelligence and judgment.'" *Dick's Sporting Goods, Inc. v. Webb*, 413 S.W.3d 891 (Ky. 2013) (quoting Restatement (Second) of Torts § 343A(1) cmt. b (1965), holding that a wet tile that appeared dry was not an open and obvious hazard; a reasonable person may not have noticed the moisture "because of the inherent difficulty of detecting moisture on a tile floor"). Whether a hazard is open and obvious is typically a question of fact for the jury, where reasonable people can differ.

2. **The no-duty rule.** At one time, courts routinely held that the landowner was not liable even to an invitee for injuries which were caused by an open and obvious danger. Some courts still say this. *See, e.g., General Motors Corp. v. Hill*, 752 So.2d 1186 (Ala. 1999) (parked 25-foot flatbed trailer, even if obscured by darkness, was an open and obvious danger to independent contractor driving a buggy around facility at night to fill vending machines). The idea is frequently expressed by saying the landowner simply owes no duty to protect an entrant from obvious dangers, *see Roy v. State*, 139 A.3d 480 (R.I. 2016) (diving into man-made pond), often because an obvious danger does not create an unreasonable danger in the first place, *see Bufkin v. Felipe's Louisiana, LLC*, 171 So.3d 851 (La. 2014) (pedestrian crossing street next to defendant contractor's dumpster, which obscured his vision, was struck by oncoming bicyclist; no duty to warn of a clearly visible obstruction). As the court put it in *Sundermann v. Hy-Vee, Inc.*, 947 N.W.2d 492 (Neb. 2020), "The rationale behind this general rule is that the open and obvious nature of the condition gives caution so that the risk of harm is considered slight, since reasonable people will avoid open and obvious risks."

3. **Obvious dangers and foreseeable risk.** Under the Restatement Second approach adopted by the *Kentucky River* court, when can we conclude that the defendant should have foreseen a plaintiff's encounter with an admittedly open and obvious hazard? Remember that most states adopting this view leave the issue to the jury, if reasonable people could differ. *See, e.g., Wotzka v. Minndakota Ltd. Parnership*, 831 N.W.2d 722 (N.D. 2013) (plaintiff slipped and fell when getting out of shower in defendant's hotel, where shower was not equipped with a non-skid strip, a bathmat, or a handrail). The cases addressing this issue tend to fall into two general groups. Can you see common themes in each of these categories?

Group 1: A landowner is constructing his own house and has not yet put a railing on a second-floor balcony. A painter (an invitee) accidentally steps off the balcony while stepping back to better see the area he has just painted. *Hale v. Beckstead*, 116 P.3d 263 (Utah 2005). Or suppose a customer trips over a pallet in the aisle of a drug store. *Gilmore v. Walgreen Co.*, 759 N.W.2d 433 (Minn. Ct. App. 2009).

Group 2: An employee of a catering company reported for a catering job at a Mercedes dealership. She could see that ice covered the entire area, and made it inside without slipping. But she slipped and fell soon thereafter, as she was walking from the building to her car to get her cell phone so she could contact her absent supervisor. Is her encounter with the ice foreseeable? *Wood v. Mercedes-Benz of Oklahoma City*, 336 P.3d 457 (Okla. 2014). Or suppose a worker must cross a snow-and-ice-covered parking lot to get to her job. Does it matter whether there is an alternative path that a reasonable person would have used? *See Estate of Livings v. Sage's Investment Group, LLC*, 968 N.W.2d 397 (Mich. 2021).

4. **Open and obvious danger and comparative negligence.** A number of courts, as in *Kentucky River*, see the blanket rule against liability for open and obvious dangers as one that resurrects the all-or-nothing character of contributory negligence or implied assumption of the risk. *See, e.g., Hersh v. E-T Enterprises, Ltd. Partnership*, 752 S.E.2d 336 (W.Va. 2013) (abolishing "open and obvious doctrine" on that basis), *superseded by statute*, W. VA. ANN. CODE § 55–7–28 (2015) (expressly reversing *Hersh* and reinstating no-duty rule for open and obvious hazards).

Suppose a motel builds steps that are steeper than permitted by the state building code and not accompanied by a railing. When the plaintiff climbs the stairs to his room, he trips and breaks his hip. Is it fair to preclude the action on the ground that "the plaintiff is responsible for his or her own decision to proceed through a known danger" as the majority did in *Lang v. Holly Hill Motel, Inc.*, 909 N.E.2d 120 (Ohio 2009)? In dissent, Judge Pfeifer argued that the open and obvious danger doctrine "is a holdover from the days of contributory negligence," and under comparative negligence the jury should be permitted to determine both the defendant and the plaintiff's negligence.

5. **Duty to warn vs. duty to remedy the hazard.** In those states that look to whether the foreseeability of the plaintiff's encounter with an obvious hazard creates a duty of care, it may well matter whether the plaintiff argues that the defendant was under a duty to *warn* or a duty to *remedy. See, e.g., Dos Santos v. Coleta*, 987 N.E.2d 1187 (Mass. 2013) (no duty to warn of an obvious hazard, but duty to remedy the danger presented by a trampoline set up next to a shallow wading pool on defendant's property); *Roy v. State*, 139 A.3d 480 (R.I. 2016) (no duty to warn of the danger of diving into a shallow pond).

6. **Abandoning open and obvious danger.** In light of the tension between comparative fault and open and obvious danger, some courts have not only limited the open and obvious danger doctrine, but have abolished it altogether. *Shelton v. Kentucky Easter Seals Soc., Inc.*, 413 S.W.3d 901 (Ky. 2013); *Steigman v. Outrigger Enterprises, Inc.*, 267 P.3d 1238 (Haw. 2011). Is the "open and obvious" character of the mechanism of plaintiff's injury thus irrelevant? The *Shelton* court said abolishing the no-duty rule "should not be viewed as a major change in our law. The questions are not changing, their locations are." What do you think the court meant by that?

7. **The Restatement Third.** According to the Restatement Third, "Known or obvious dangers pose a reduced risk compared to comparable latent danger because those exposed can take precautions to protect themselves. Nevertheless, in some circumstances a residual risk will remain. . . . Land possessors have a duty of reasonable care with regard to those residual risks." RESTATEMENT (THIRD) OF TORTS: LIABILITY FOR PHYSICAL AND EMOTIONAL HARM § 51 cmt. k (2010). Is this similar to the Second Restatement standard? *See Coburn v. Whitaker Constr. Co.*, 445 P.3d 446 (Utah 2019) (reaffirming adherence to the Second Restatement and expressly declining to adopt the Third Restatement). Was there residual risk in *Kentucky River*?

8. **Barring recovery.** When the plaintiff's fault is great, courts may be particularly inclined to use open and obvious danger as an absolute bar to recovery. In *O'Sullivan v. Shaw*, 726 N.E.2d 951 (Mass. 2000), the plaintiff was injured when he dived into the shallow end of an unmarked swimming pool while attempting to clear the shallow end and emerge at the deep end. The court held that the open and obvious danger doctrine barred his recovery. In a case like *O'Sullivan*, would there be a way to bar the claim without the use of open and obvious danger?

9. **Children and "open and obvious" hazards.** Should it matter whether a person injured by what looks to an *adult* like an obvious hazard is a child of tender years? *See Qureshi v. Ahmed*, 916 N.E.2d 1153 (Ill. App. Ct. 2009) (child playing on a treadmill). Recall the special standard of care for children, and the attractive nuisance doctrine. Do the policies behind those doctrines suggest an answer? *See Bragan v. Symanzik*, 687 N.W.2d 881 (Mich. Ct. App. 2004); *Grant v. South Roxana Dad's Club*, 886 N.E.2d 543 (Ill. App. Ct. 2008).

E. RECREATIONAL-USE STATUTES

1. *Recreational-use statutes.* Most states have now passed statutes dealing with "recreational users" on private land and waters. The gist of these is to retain the landowners' special immunities as to any non-paying recreational user. What "non-paying" means may be specified in the statute. *See, e.g.,* ARIZ. REV. STAT. § 33–1551 ("A nominal fee that is charged by a public entity or a nonprofit corporation to offset the cost of providing the educational or recreational premises and associated services does not constitute an admission fee or any other consideration as prescribed by this section.").

The Michigan statute, MICH. COMP. L. ANN. § 324.73301, imposes liability only for "gross negligence or willful and wanton misconduct of the owner, tenant or lessee." It applies to "a person who is on the lands of another without paying . . . a valuable consideration for the purpose of fishing, hunting, trapping, camping, hiking, sightseeing, motorcycling, snowmobiling, or any other outdoor recreational use, with or without permission." The original statute has been expanded to similarly restrict the redress available to invitees on a farm to buy produce.

California's recreational-use statute provides:

> An owner of any estate in real property . . . owes no duty of care to keep the premises safe for entry or use by others for any recreational purpose or to give any warning of hazardous conditions, uses of, structures, or activities on such premises to persons entering for such purpose, except as provided in this section.

CAL. CIV. CODE § 846. A duty of due care is owed under this section to those who have paid to enter and also those who are "expressly invited rather than merely permitted." Courts have held that the invitation need not have been for a "recreational purpose." *See Hoffman v. Young*, 56 Cal.App.5th 1021 (2020) (express invitation to enter property, even if not specifically to engage in recreational activity, is sufficient to remove protection of statute). Otherwise liability is only for "willful or malicious failure to guard or warn against a dangerous condition, use, structure or activity." Recreational purpose is defined to include many of the activities mentioned in the Michigan statute and others, such as sport parachuting, spelunking, and even "viewing or enjoying historical, natural, archaeological, natural, or scientific sites."

2.   *Theory and coverage of the statutes.* Although the motives for the statutes were undoubtedly associated with a desire to protect private landowners from suits and judgments, the *theory* erected for these statutes was that they were being enacted to limit liability in order to encourage landowners to make land available for recreation in a world becoming increasingly crowded.

Most courts have held that the recreational use statutes do not abrogate a landowner's duty of care to private guests, as opposed to members of the general public who are on the land for recreational purposes. *Estate of Gordon-Couture v. Brown*, 876 A.2d 196 (N.H. 2005) (guest of landowner drowned at private birthday party). Similarly, when a landowner accepts a fee for the plaintiff's use of the land, recreational statutes generally do not provide any protection to the landowner. *See Coleman v. Oregon Parks and Recreation Dept.*, 217 P.3d 651 (Or. 2009) (even when state did not charge a fee to campers who entered park, state's imposition of fees to use particular facilities removed the immunity). What if the landowner charged entry fees to some recreational users but did not charge any fee to the injured party who used the property for such purposes? *See Mayor of City of Garden City v. Harris*, 809 S.E.2d 806 (Ga. 2018) (defendant protected by recreational use statute against negligence suit by non-paying person).

A number of state recreational statutes apply expressly to both private and public landowners. In the absence of specific statutory language to the contrary, however, most courts have refused to extend protection to governmental entities on the ground that a public entity "needs no incentive" to open its lands for recreational purposes. *Bronsen v. Dawes County*, 722 N.W.2d 17 (Neb. 2006) (citing cases from other jurisdictions); *see also Wilkins v. City of Haverhill*, 8 N.E.3d 753 (Mass. 2014) (broader "public use" statute inapplicable to city, given statute's purpose to encourage private landowners to open land to the public).

The effect of granting the protections of a recreational use statute to a governmental entity is to bar most plaintiffs from recovery where they have been injured by negligently maintained facilities in public parks. Does that represent good policy? *See Yattaw v. City of East Providence*, 203 A.3d 1167 (R.I. 2019) ("[N]o matter the age of the child nor the severity of the injury, in light of the protections afforded by the Recreational Use Statute, . . . there is no recourse in our courts, because users of most public parks are treated as trespassers under the law."); *Univ. of Texas v. Garner*, 559 S.W.3d 645 (Tex. 2019) (applying statute that treats users of governmental property as trespassers: "We may not judicially revise statutes because we believe they are bad policy.").

3. *Effect of the statutes.* By lowering the standard of care, recreational-use statutes prevent liability when a defendant's failure to use reasonable care has caused injury, at times deadly injury. For example, in *Coan v. New Hampshire Dep't of Envtl. Servs.*, 8 A.3d 109 (N.H. 2010), the court described the factual situation as follows: "Local residents use Silver Lake for swimming. The boys frequently swam in the lake and had just done so the day before. Despite their familiarity with the lake, the boys did not know that on the afternoon of June 11, 2005, defendant [Department of Environmental Services] added 375 cubic feet per second to the flow coming out of Lochmere dam into the lake, which made the currents in the north end of the lake deadly. Although the defendants knew that people swam downstream from the dam and that swimming there could become dangerous when flow from the dam was increased, neither posted any warnings about the dangers of swimming in the north end of the lake, downstream from the dam. Nor did either defendant place any safety devices on the lakeshore." Nevertheless, parents of boys who died in the currents were denied recovery under a New Hampshire statute which provides that a landowner who permits land to be used for recreational purposes "shall not be liable for personal injury or property damage in the absence of intentionally caused injury or damage." *See also Waco v. Kirwan*, 298 S.W.3d 618 (Tex. 2009) (fatal accident in city park in which cliff crumbled and gave way while young visitor was sitting on cliff's edge; city did not owe duty to warn under recreational-use statute). However, in some cases liability has been found despite the high standard required by

the recreational-use statutes. *See Berman v. Sitrin*, 991 A.2d 1038 (R.I. 2010) (willful and malicious failure in case in which tourist was severely injured when a public walkway along an oceanside cliff crumbled and there had been multiple incidents of death and grievous injury along that walkway before).

4. *Constitutionality.* Could recreational-use statutes be upheld in states that have already ruled guest statutes to be unconstitutional? Remember that one reason given for automobile guest statutes was that they would encourage hospitality. That sounds a great deal like the encouragement supposedly offered by recreational-use statutes. We have seen that the California court found the guest statute to be unconstitutional and that the hospitality purpose did not save it, since not all non-paying persons were treated alike. Interestingly enough, recreational-use statutes have been upheld against constitutional attack. *E.g., Olson v. Bismarck Parks & Recreation Dist.*, 642 N.W.2d 864 (N.D. 2002).

5. *Interpreting the statutes.* Many statutes leave much to be interpreted and fail to provide solutions for some obvious problems. Court interpretations of similar statutes are often quite diverse.

(a) Sometimes the interpretive difficulty relates to the place where the injury takes place. For example, in *Liberty v. State, Dept. of Transp.*, 148 P.3d 909 (Or. 2006), the statute was held not to apply to property owners that permitted members of the public to use their property as a means of access to another property that was used for a recreational purpose. In *Kappenman v. Klipfel*, 765 N.W.2d 716 (N.D. 2009), the statute was held not to apply to a public road "primarily opened for purposes of travel, not recreation." But in *Wilson v. Kansas State University*, 44 P.3d 454 (Kan. 2002), the statute was applied to a case in which the plaintiff was going to the bathroom in a football stadium, on the reasoning that the stadium itself fit the broad definition of open areas for recreational use. What about injury on a dam that created a recreational-use lake? *See Stone v. York Haven Power Co.*, 749 A.2d 452 (Pa. 2000) (statutory immunity covers lake but not dam).

(b) At other times the interpretive difficulty relates to what the plaintiff was doing at the time of the injury, that is, whether the use was truly "recreational." *See, e.g., Crichfield v. Grand Wailea Co.*, 6 P.3d 349 (Haw. 2000) (plaintiff injured on hotel land both for recreational purposes and to eat lunch at the hotel as a business invitee; statute did not protect hotel where plaintiff had business as one of her purposes); *Lawson v. City of Diboll*, 472 S.W.3d 667 (Tex. 2015) (spectating at softball game in park was not "recreation" under statute); *Sallee v. Stewart*, 827 N.W.2d 128 (Iowa 2013) (chaperone was injured when she fell through hole in barn's hayloft while accompanying students on field trip to dairy farm; any activities in the hayloft did not constitute recreational uses under statute). By contrast, in *Ali v. City of Boston*, 804 N.E.2d 927 (Mass. 2004), the plaintiff was injured while riding his bike across a park merely to get home. He sued the city for negligently maintaining a gate in the park. The defendant raised the recreational use statute as a defense. The plaintiff argued that he was injured while using the park for a "nonrecreational purpose." The court held that the plaintiff's subjective intent was irrelevant, and that liability should not turn on precisely what someone was doing in a recreational area: "It matters not that the plaintiff's purpose was transportation, or that the student's purpose is to learn, or that the financial analyst's purpose is to work. What matters is that they are engaging in recreational pursuits permitted in the park."

(c)   Some jurisdictions interpret recreational use statutes to protect against negligence liability for conditions on the land, but not against liability for active negligence on the property. *See Combs v. Ohio Dept. of Natural Resources, Div. of Parks & Recreation*, 55 N.E.3d 1073 (Ohio 2016) (negligent operation of a boom mower); *Klein v. United States*, 235 P.3d 42 (Cal. 2010) (negligent driving of a vehicle).

§ 3. LANDLORDS' DUTY TO TENANTS

PAGELSDORF V. SAFECO INSURANCE CO.
284 N.W.2d 55 (Wis. 1979)

CALLOW, JUSTICE.

[Mahnke owned a two-story, two-family duplex. The upper unit was rented to the Blattners and had two balconies. The railing on one had been replaced, but the one in question was the original wooden railing, composed of 2 x 4s parallel to the floor and 2 x 2 spacers perpendicular to the floor. This was secured by nails to upright 4 x 4s at each end. Mr. Blattner left his family and thereafter Mrs. Blattner moved her children out and made arrangements for her brothers to remove her furniture. The brothers secured the aid of Pagelsdorf in moving heavier items. Pagelsdorf lowered a box spring down over the side of the balcony. When he placed his hands on the railing to straighten up afterwards, the railing gave way and he fell to the ground. He claims for the injuries he suffered in the fall. Inspection showed that the railing assembly had dry rot and would not hold well, but this had not been apparent to the eye. There was evidence that the defendant-lessor had contracted to keep the premises in repair, but also evidence, seemingly accepted by the jury, that this was limited to repair of known or reported defects. The trial judge charged the jury that Mahnke owed no duty to discover dangers of which he was unaware, and the jury found for the defendant.]

[W]ith certain exceptions, a landlord is not liable for injuries to his tenants and their visitors resulting from defects in the premises. The general rule of nonliability was based on the concept of a lease as a conveyance of property and the consequent transfer of possession and control of the premises to the tenant.

There are exceptions to this general rule of nonliability. The landlord is liable for injuries to the tenant or his visitor caused by a dangerous condition if he contracts to repair defects, or if, knowing of a defect existing at the time the tenant took possession, he conceals it from a tenant who could not reasonably be expected to discover it. Additionally, the general rule is not applicable where the premises are leased for public use, or are retained in the landlord's control, or where the landlord negligently makes repairs. The rule of nonliability persists despite a decided trend away from application of the general rule and toward expansion of its exceptions.

None of the exceptions to the general rule are applicable to the facts of this case. The premises were not leased for public use, nor was the porch within Mahnke's control, nor did he negligently repair the railing. The plaintiffs argue that Mahnke contracted to repair defects; but according to Mrs. Blattner's testimony, Mahnke's promise extended only to items the Blattners reported as being in disrepair. . . Finally, the concealed-defect exception does not apply because there was no evidence that the dry rot existed in 1969 when the Blattners moved in. . .

Therefore, if we were to follow the traditional rule, Pagelsdorf was not entitled to an instruction that Mahnke owed him a duty of ordinary care. We believe, however, that the better public policy lies in the abandonment of the general rule of nonliability and the adoption of a rule that a landlord is under a duty to exercise ordinary care in the maintenance of the premises.

. . . Issues of notice of the defect, its obviousness, control of the premises, and so forth are all relevant only insofar as they bear on the ultimate question: Did the landlord exercise ordinary care in the maintenance of the premises under all the circumstances?

Judgment reversed and cause remanded for proceedings consistent with this opinion.

NOTES

1. **Applying the rule.** Will the plaintiff in *Pagelsdorf* necessarily prevail under the new rule adopted by the court?

2. **The traditional rule: lease as conveyance.** The traditional view is that a lease is a conveyance of land. The lessee is the "owner" of the land in question for the period of the lease, and the lessor has no more responsibility for the upkeep of the land than any other person who conveys land. *See, e.g.,*

Benham v. Morton & Furbish Agency, 929 A.2d 471 (Me. 2007). A corollary rule is that the landlord owes no more to the tenant's guests than he owes to the tenant himself. Note that even under the traditional rule, a landlord might be liable on a contract theory for failure to repair defects, or on a tort theory for such things as failing to repair latent defects the landlord knows about, or doing repairs negligently.

3.   **Changing concepts of leases.** *Pagelsdorf* and several other decisions have departed from the traditional rules by imposing upon the landlord the duty to exercise ordinary care to the tenant or those on the premises by virtue of the tenant's rights. *See, e.g., Saunders v. Smothers,* 454 P.3d 746 (Okla. 2019) (reaffirming a "general duty of care upon landlords to maintain the leased premises, including areas under the tenant's exclusive control or use, in a reasonably safe condition"); *Childs v. Purll,* 882 A.2d 227 (D.C. 2005); *Favreau v. Miller,* 591 A.2d 68 (Vt. 1991). For example, where a tenant's infant fell into a bathtub containing scalding hot water, there was a fact issue with respect to whether the landlord and building management company negligently failed to maintain the apartment's hot water system in reasonably safe condition. *Simmons ex rel. Simmons v. Sacchetti,* 934 N.E.2d 877 (N.Y. 2010).

If the landlord's duty is merely to warn of a danger rather than repair it, the tenants may be barred from recovery by the "open and obvious" rule or something like it. *See, e.g., Daniels v. Wiley,* 314 So.3d 1212 (Ala. 2020) (landlord had no duty to mark sidewalk where mud was an open and obvious hazard); *White v. Many Rivers West Ltd. Partnership,* 797 N.W.2d 739 (Minn. Ct. App. 2011) (landlord had no duty to enhance window screens to prevent a child from falling, and no duty to repair screens to a more secure strength than law would otherwise impose, where tenants were fully aware of the hazards the screens presented and had been warned about those dangers by the landlord).

4.   **The Restatement rule.** The Restatement Third provides that lessors have a duty of reasonable care for (a) the portions of the leased premises over which the lessor retains control, (b) conduct of the lessor creating risks to others, and (c) disclosure of certain dangerous conditions. A landlord also has a duty based on applicable statutes, contractual or voluntary undertakings, and compliance with an implied warranty of habitability. RESTATEMENT (THIRD) OF TORTS: LIABILITY FOR PHYSICAL AND EMOTIONAL HARMS § 53 (2010). Some states abrogate the common law rule only for residential leases, *Lucier v. Impact Recreation, Ltd.,* 864 A.2d 635 (R.I. 2005), while others extend obligations to commercial landlords as well. *See Bishop v. TES Realty Trust,* 942 N.E.2d 173 (Mass. 2011).

5.   **Lease terms.** Lease terms can be key in determining liability. *See Henry v. Hamilton Equities, Inc.,* 137 N.E.3d 476 (N.Y. 2019) (where landlord covenants in the lease to make repairs, a duty to make such repairs arises, but a regulatory agreement between the landlord and the federal Department of Housing and Urban Development was not such a "covenant"); *Morrell v.*

Hardin Creek, Inc., 821 S.E.2d 360 (N.C. 2018) (waiver of liability in commercial lease enforced to bar tenants' negligence claims against landlord).

6.   **Statutory duties of landlords.** Many statutes now set standards or impose liability for specific defects, such as the knowing use of lead-based paint that poisons a tenant's child, *see Gore v. People's Savings Bank,* 665 A.2d 1341 (Conn. 1995), or a failure to disclose lead-based paint the lessor should have discovered on reasonable inspection, *Benik v. Hatcher,* 750 A.2d 10 (Md. 2000). Some state statutes require landlords to keep common areas in safe condition, and may be given negligence per se effect. *See, e.g., Mann v. Northgate Investors, L.L.C.,* 5 N.E.3d 594 (Ohio 2014). But statutes may also be interpreted to limit a landlord's duties. *See, e.g., J.H. v. R&M Tagliareni, LLC,* 216 A.3d 169 (N.J. 2019) (declining to adopt a common-law duty requiring landlords to cover radiators with insulation, pointing to statute that specifies certain duties, but not that one).

§ 4. THE FIREFIGHTER'S RULE

MINNICH v. MED-WASTE, INC.
564 S.E.2d 98 (S.C. 2002)

JUSTICE PLEICONES.

[A federal District Court certified a question to the Supreme Court of South Carolina, asking whether the firefighter's rule barred a claim for injury to emergency professionals.] The District Court made the following factual findings:

Jeffrey Minnich ("Plaintiff") was employed by the Medical University of South Carolina ("MUSC") as a public safety officer. While working in this capacity, Plaintiff assisted in loading medical waste from the premises of MUSC onto a tractor-trailer truck owned by Defendant Med-Waste, Inc. Plaintiff noticed the unoccupied truck begin to roll forward, toward a public street. Plaintiff ran to the truck, jumped inside, and stopped the truck.

Plaintiff alleges he suffered serious injuries, proximately caused by the acts or omissions of the defendants' employees, for which he seeks to recover damages. The defendants assert that Plaintiff's claims are barred by the firefighter's rule. The firefighter's rule is a common law doctrine that precludes a firefighter (and certain other public employees, including police officers) from recovering against a defendant whose negligence caused the firefighter's on-the-job injury. . . .

Finding no definitive answer to the certified question in the case law of this state, we examine the various rationales advanced in support of the rule, and its applications and limitations in other states.

The common law firefighter's rule originated in the case of *Gibson v. Leonard,* 143 Ill. 182, 32 N.E. 182 (Ill.1892). There, the Illinois Supreme

Court held that a firefighter who entered private property in the performance of his job duties was a licensee, and as such, the property owner owed the firefighter a duty only to "refrain from willful or affirmative acts which are injurious." Practically, this meant that a firefighter, injured while fighting a blaze on private property, could not recover tort damages from the property owner whose ordinary negligence caused the fire.

A number of courts reason that police officers and firefighters, aware of the risks inherent in their chosen profession, have assumed those risks. As such, the firefighter or police officer should not be allowed to recover when injured as a result of confronting these known and accepted risks.

A third rationale advanced is public policy. . . . First, injuries to firemen and policemen are compensable through workers' compensation. It follows that liability for their on-the-job injuries is properly borne by the public rather than by individual property owners. Second, firemen and policemen, unlike invitees or licensees, enter at unforeseeable times and at areas not open to the public. In such situations, it is not reasonable to require the level of care that is owed to invitees or licensees.

Still other courts reason that the public fisc pays to train firefighters and police officers on the ways to confront dangerous situations, and compensates them for doing so. If these public employees were permitted to bring suit against the taxpayers whose negligence proximately caused injury, the negligent taxpayer would incur multiple penalties in exchange for the protection provided by firefighters and police officers.

Not only have courts been unable to agree on a consistent rationale for the rule, they have not been able to agree on the proper parameters for the rule. A number of courts which recognize the firefighter's rule as a viable defense to negligence claims allow recovery for willful and wanton conduct resulting in injury. As one court observed, "a tortfeasor who acts willfully and wantonly is so culpable that the fireman's rule ought not to preclude the injured officer from suing the egregiously culpable wrongdoer." *Miller v. Inglis*, 223 Mich.App. 159, 567 N.W.2d 253 (1997).

Courts have allowed police officers and firefighters to recover for injuries resulting from an act of negligence unrelated to the specific reason for which the officer or firefighter was originally summoned. As stated by the Supreme Court of New Jersey:

> The core of the "fireman's rule" is that a citizen's ordinary negligence that occasioned the presence of the public safety officer shall not give rise to liability in damages for the injuries sustained by the officer in the course of the response to duty. . . The corollary of the rule is that independent and intervening negligent acts that injure the safety officer on duty are not insulated. . . .

More recently, a number of state legislatures have acted to limit or abolish the firefighter's rule. For instance . . . the Virginia legislature passed a statute providing that:

> An owner or occupant of real property containing premises normally open to the public shall, with respect to such premises, owe to firefighters . . . and law-enforcement officers who in the performance of their duties come upon that portion of the premises normally open to the public the duty to maintain the same in a reasonably safe condition or to warn of dangers thereon of which he knows or has reason to know, whether or not such premises are at the time open to the public.

> An owner or occupant of real property containing premises not normally open to the public shall, with respect to such premises, owe the same duty to firefighters . . . and law-enforcement officers who he knows or has reason to know are upon, about to come upon or imminently likely to come upon that portion of the premises not normally open to the public. . . .

Va.Code Ann. § 8.01–226 (Michie 2001). [The court also discussed statutes from California, Florida, Minnesota, New Jersey, New York and Nevada, some of which effectively abolished the rule altogether.]

. . . [T]hose jurisdictions which have adopted the firefighter's rule offer no uniform justification therefor, nor do they agree on a consistent application of the rule. The legislatures in many jurisdictions which adhere to the rule have found it necessary to modify or abolish the rule. The rule is riddled with exceptions, and criticism of the rule abounds.

Against this backdrop, we answer the certified question in the negative. South Carolina has never recognized the firefighter's rule, and we find it is not part of this state's common law. In our view, the tort law of this state adequately addresses negligence claims brought against non-employer tortfeasors arising out of injuries incurred by firefighters and police officers during the discharge of their duties. We are not persuaded by any of the various rationales advanced by those courts that recognize the firefighter's rule. The more sound public policy—and the one we adopt—is to decline to promulgate a rule singling out police officers and firefighters for discriminatory treatment.

CERTIFIED QUESTION ANSWERED.

NOTES

1.   **The firefighter's rule.** As *Minnich* indicates, the states disagree on the merits of the firefighter's rule. Some legislatures have abolished the rule. *Lazenby v. Mark's Const., Inc.*, 923 N.E.2d 735 (Ill. 2010); *Rowe v. Mazel Thirty, LLC*, 34 A.2d 1248 (N.J. 2012). Most states continue to apply the rule in some

form, and some have adopted or reaffirmed it recently. *Higgins v. Rhode Island Hosp.*, 35 A.3d 919 (R.I. 2012); *Fordham v. Oldroyd*, 171 P.3d 411 (Utah 2007); *Espinoza v. Schulenburg*, 129 P.3d 937 (Ariz. 2006); *Farmer v. B & G Food Enters., Inc.*, 818 So.2d 1154 (Miss. 2002). In a number of states, the rule is applied as modified by legislation. New York courts apply the firefighter's rule, as limited by statute, to actions against a "police officer's or firefighter's employer or co-employee." *Wadler v. City of New York*, 925 N.E.2d 875 (N.Y. 2010) (barring claim brought by police officer who was injured when the car he was driving was thrust four feet into the air after a retractable, concrete security barrier at police headquarters' parking lot entrance was accidentally raised while he was driving across it). Most states continue to hold that a firefighter who is injured in fighting a fire has no claim against the negligent fire-setter.

2. **Assumed risk/no duty.** In those states which still adhere to the firefighter's rule, the exclusion of firefighters from the negligence system is often explained by saying that the firefighter assumed the risk. This could hardly be assumed risk in the sense of contributory fault; it is not negligent to fight fires in a professional way. So the firefighter's rule, though explained in terms of assumed risk, is merely another way of saying "it is appropriate to find that the defendant owes no duty of care." *Neighbarger v. Irwin Industries, Inc.*, 882 P.2d 347 (Cal. 1994).

3. **No duty/public policy.** "No duty" in turn reflects judicial notions of appropriate policy. The *Minnich* court finds the policy rationales for the firefighter's rule unconvincing. Other courts have reached the opposite conclusion. In *Babes Showclub, Jaba, Inc. v. Lair*, 918 N.E.2d 308 (Ind. 2009), a case in which a police officer was attacked by an unruly underage patron after responding to a bar's complaint about that patron, the Indiana Supreme Court wrote: "Many emergencies are caused by the negligence of some party. The public employs firefighters, police officers, and others to respond to emergencies, and these responders knowingly combat the effects of others' negligence." *See also Moody v. Delta W., Inc.*, 38 P.3d 1139 (Alaska 2002) ("The Firefighter's Rule reflects sound public policy."). What do you think?

4. **Expansions.** The earliest cases applying the firefighter's rule were anchored in premises liability law, and applied only to firefighters in suits against landowners and occupiers. But in many states it has been vastly expanded. First, the rule has been applied beyond its original landowner moorings, applying when the injury occurs outside the defendant's land and even where the defendant is not a landowner at all. *See, e.g., White v. State*, 19 A.3d 369 (Md. 2011) (firefighter's rule barred police officer's claim against the state for the negligence of a police dispatcher in reporting a shoplifting incident as an armed robbery, causing the officer to engage in a high-speed chase during which he was injured); *Pinter v. American Family Mut. Ins. Co.*, 613 N.W.2d 110 (Wis. 2000) (applying rule to bar a negligence action by an emergency medical technician injured during a car-crash rescue). Likewise, in most states the rule is no longer limited to firefighters; it has been applied to police officers, EMTs, and even lifeguards. Perhaps the operative category is not firefighters

but publicly employed professional risk-takers or public safety officers. What will courts do with public building inspectors injured in buildings they inspect? *See* 2 DOBBS, HAYDEN & BUBLICK, THE LAW OF TORTS § 365 (2d ed. 2011).

5. **Scope of risks covered by the rule.** Many courts (and a number of statutes) say that the firefighter's rule prohibits recovery by the professional rescuer for injuries from "the negligently created risk that was the very reason for his presence on the scene." *White v. State*, 19 A.3d 369 (Md. 2011). Other courts do not circumscribe the risks as narrowly, and have protected defendants from negligence suits where the rescuer was harmed by risks that are inherent, or reasonably foreseeable, in the situation the rescuer was compelled to confront. See, e.g., *Ellinwood v. Cohen*, 87 A.3d 1054 (R.I. 2014).

Whether a court takes a broader or narrower view of the covered risks may well be outcome-determinative. For example, if a police officer pulls over a car to make a traffic stop, and is then hit by a second, negligently driven vehicle, is the officer's negligence claim against the second driver barred by the rule? *Compare Ellinwood, supra* (broader approach: risk of being hit by second automobile was one that officer would foreseeably encounter, so rule applies), *with Harris-Fields v. Syze,* 600 N.W.2d 611 (Mich. 1999) (narrower approach: act of second driver was not what brought officer to the scene, so rule does not apply). *See also, e.g., Lee v. Luigi, Inc.,* 696 A.2d 1371 (D.C. 1997) (broader approach: risk of slipping on oil while investigating a burglary was covered by rule); *Lipson v. Superior Court of Orange County,* 644 P.2d 822 (Cal. 1982) (narrower approach: rule did not bar negligence claim for injuries caused by explosion of a gasoline tank on the premises, when firefighter was summoned to fight an electrical fire).

6. **Other wrongdoing not covered by the rule.** (1) Most courts hold that the firefighter's rule does not foreclose suit against an intentional or willful wrongdoer. *Ipsen v. Diamond Tree Experts, Inc.*, 466 P.3d 190 (Utah 2020); *Baldonado v. El Paso Natural Gas Co.*, 176 P.3d 277 (N.M. 2008). (2) At least in some jurisdictions, it does not foreclose suit for injuries arising from violation of a fire-safety statute or ordinance. *See, e.g., Mullen v. Zoebe, Inc.,* 654 N.E.2d 90 (N.Y. 1995).

7. **Private rescuers.** The firefighter's rule has no application to private individuals who may undertake assistance at a fire. On the contrary, private persons are considered heroic and it is said under one branch of the "rescue doctrine" that it is not contributory negligence or assumed risk to render assistance in a physical emergency. "The extent of the risk which the volunteer is justified in assuming under the circumstances increases in proportion to the imminence of the danger. . . ." *Moravec v. Moravec,* 343 N.W.2d 762 (Neb. 1984) (plaintiff injured in fighting a fire could recover from homeowner who negligently set it). Some courts have said expressly that the firefighter's rule is an exception to the rescue doctrine.

PROBLEMS

Paton v. Missouri & Atlantic Railway

Paton lived in a small rural house adjacent to a railroad track. A friend of his, Talbot, lived on the other side of the track. The two men sometimes met at or near the track and drank together in the evenings. One evening in July they met at the track and began drinking. Sometime later Talbot awoke and realized that a train was approaching. He did not see Paton in the dark and the train's light was not bright. After the train passed, however, he found Paton near the track. The lower part of his right leg had been severed by the passing train. Paton's lawyer showed: (1) the engineer of the train said he kept a lookout but never saw Paton or anyone on the track, (2) the train was moving slowly and could have stopped within a very short distance, and (3) the headlight was out of repair and fell short of standards prescribed by a regulatory agency. Although all states would recognize a duty on the part of railroads to keep a reasonable lookout at public crossings, only a few states impose a duty of lookout for trespassers along the track. *If Paton's injury did not occur in a state requiring a lookout for trespassers, did the railroad owe him any duty?*

Christie v. Embry Corp.

Christie, a girl of 11 years, entered a garbage dump maintained by the Embry Corporation on its own land. She was looking for any kind of old toys or comic books. Walking on what appeared to be a solid surface, she suddenly sank through and was burned on hot embers below. In her action against Embry Corp., she proved that in past times Embry had had to call the fire department to put out fires that spontaneously flared in the dump. She also proved that other children often went there looking for comics and toys, that there was no fence, and that there were many houses nearby. This was all the proof. *Can she get to the jury?*

Paget v. Owen

Paget asked Owen for permission to enter Owen's large farm to fish in one of the ponds. Owen agreed to this. Owen believed from the location involved, that Paget intended to take the north road on Owen's property. The north road had been undermined by flooding of a creek, though Owen did not know this. The south road had also been undermined by flooding of a different creek, and Owen was well aware of this. Paget drove into the farm land to fish the next day. Although the road appeared to be safe, it caved in where it had been undermined by the flooding. Paget's car overturned and he was injured. *Did Owen breach any duty? Does it matter which road Paget took?*

In re Claims of Picklesimer, Patrick and Plangent

The facts our law firm has after an initial interview with our client, Herman Picklesimer, are as follows:

Picklesimer was driving in a generally southerly direction on highway 101 in an area with which he was only vaguely familiar. It was about 7:30 at night and dark. The road bends slightly to the right about a mile south of the town of Roan. The road also is rising slightly at this point, with the result that headlights are aimed slightly upward. At the point where the road bends to the right, a private unpaved road on the property of James P. Dalzell continues straight ahead. There are no markers, signs, reflectors or other indicators of the curve. Mr. Picklesimer says that there was not even any center stripe and that the road was black. The result of all this was that with his lights forced slightly upward by the road grade, he did not appreciate the fact that it bent to the right. He continued straight until he dropped off the highway and headed downhill on the Dalzell private road. At this point he realized his error, and tried to steer back onto the road, but this compounded the problem and he turned his car over.

According to the police report a car driven by James Patrick was proceeding northerly on the same road at the same time and place. Patrick became confused or at least he tried to react when—according to him—Mr. Picklesimer crossed the road in his path as he proceeded straight onto the Dalzell property. Patrick steered to his left, lost control in the gravel on his left side (the west side) of the road and crashed into a tree some distance from the road. His passenger, Blanche Plangent, suffered head wounds when she hit the windshield. Patrick himself was also injured.

Picklesimer was not aware of any of this. He apparently suffered a concussion and certainly he was confused. He wandered away from the highway on Dalzell's land. He has no recollection of this, but the police report and emergency room report indicate that in the dark he fell into an excavation on Dalzell's land. This was not lighted or marked in any way. In this he broke his hip. He is 68 years old and there were complications in the hospital when a nurse, misreading the doctor's drug order, gave the wrong drug, which in turn created complications when Mr. Picklesimer was under anesthetic. He has emerged with a slight speech impairment, though at this stage we are not sure whether this is psychological or whether it is a result of the hospital mishap. The doctor is Dr. Daniel Doubs and the nurse is Mr. Paul Hadini. The hospital was the Murphy Medical Center in the town of Roan.

We should outline our basic claims and the probable defenses and prepare to investigate as needed.

REFERENCES: DOBBS, HAYDEN & BUBLICK, HORNBOOK ON TORTS §§ 19.1–.3 (common carriers), §§ 20.1–.15 (landowners), and §§ 24.1–.4 (firefighter's rule) (2d ed. 2016); 2 DOBBS, HAYDEN & BUBLICK, THE LAW OF TORTS §§ 271–79 (landowners) and §§ 362–65 (firefighter's rule) (2d ed. 2011); GLEN WEISSENBERGER & BARBARA MCFARLAND, THE LAW OF PREMISES LIABILITY (2021).

CHAPTER 13

DUTIES OF HEALTH-CARE PROVIDERS

■ ■ ■

§ 1. THE STANDARD OF CARE IN MEDICAL MALPRACTICE ACTIONS

Medical malpractice suits are negligence suits, meaning that the plaintiff must prove duty and breach, actual harm, factual cause, and "proximate" cause. *See, e.g., Ruiz v. Tenet Hialeah Healthsystem, Inc.*, 260 So.3d 977 (Fla. 2018); *Glenn v. Peoples*, 185 So.3d 981 (Miss. 2015). But there are some special rules for medical malpractice cases, deriving in part from the professional setting of the doctor-patient relationship.

With some exceptions, a medical doctor owes a duty of care only to patients, and only a patient can bring a medical malpractice suit. *See* DOBBS, HAYDEN & BUBLICK, HORNBOOK ON TORTS § 21.3 (2d ed. 2016); *Levin v. State*, 189 A.3d 572 (Conn. 2018). When a patient sues his or her doctor, there is no doubt that a duty of care is owed; the doctor's acceptance of the patient represents an undertaking of care by the doctor. *See, e.g., Cromer v. Children's Hosp. Med. Ctr.*, 29 N.E.3d 921 (Ohio 2015). In a patient vs. doctor suit, it is also beyond argument that on the scope of liability issue, the patient is a "foreseeable plaintiff."

But what standard of care applies? And how does a plaintiff prove the standard, and that it was breached, and that the doctor's negligence was a factual cause of the harm? Those questions may be analyzed differently than they would be in most negligence cases.

WALSKI V. TIESENGA
381 N.E.2d 279 (Ill. 1978)

KLUCZYNSKI, JUSTICE.

[Defendants operated to remove plaintiff's thyroid. A well-recognized risk of a thyroidectomy is that the recurrent laryngeal nerves, which run through the thyroid, may be damaged, with resulting loss of voice. One solution to the problem is to locate the nerves and segregate them before removal of the thyroid. In this case, however, there was a great deal of scar tissue present as a result of earlier operations and treatments and the defendants, instead of locating the nerve, made a wide cut so as to avoid the area where the nerve was thought to be. In fact they cut the nerve and

445

plaintiff's vocal chords are paralyzed. The trial court directed a verdict for the defendants and the intermediate appellate court affirmed.]

Dr. David M. Berger testified as an expert witness on plaintiff's behalf. . . . His direct testimony concerning acceptable procedures for thyroid surgery was that "in my feeling the standards by which I feel are acceptable practice, one must identify and preserve the recurrent laryngeal nerves on all occasions." On cross-examination Dr. Berger testified that there are always options available in surgery but that in his own mind it was not a proper option to skirt the left recurrent laryngeal nerve. He stated he could not testify generally but only "on the basis of my own opinion as to what I consider a proper option." When asked on cross-examination if there existed a contemporary school of surgeons that will skirt the nerve when they encounter a host of adhesions, Dr. Berger responded that "in the institutions in which I trained that is not the teaching. And I can't speak for other institutions or other areas of training. I can only speak for my own." Defense counsel read a quotation to Dr. Berger from a medical textbook which indicated that there existed a certain amount of controversy in the medical community concerning deliberate exposure of the laryngeal nerve. The quotation concluded with the remark that the situation remained one in which each surgeon will find the approach which suits him best. Dr. Berger indicated that he did not fully agree with that statement, but indicated the decision whether or not to expose the nerve depends on the surgeon and the technique and care he uses. Dr. Berger stated that "[e]verybody who is a certified surgeon doesn't use the same methods, obviously."

One element of a cause of action for medical malpractice is proof of the standard of care by which the defendant physician's conduct is to be measured. . . . [T]he appellate decisions in this State have held that the plaintiff in a medical malpractice action generally must establish the standard of care through expert testimony. The plaintiff must then prove that, judged in the light of these standards, the doctor was unskillful or negligent and that his want of skill or care caused the injury to the plaintiff. Generally, expert testimony is needed to support a charge of malpractice because jurors are not skilled in the practice of medicine and would find it difficult without the help of medical evidence to determine any lack of necessary scientific skill on the part of the physician. However, in those situations where the physician's conduct is so grossly negligent or the treatment so common that a layman could readily appraise it, the appellate decisions indicate that no expert testimony is necessary. . . . A requirement that the standard of care be established through expert testimony except where the common knowledge of laymen is sufficient to recognize or infer negligence is broadly recognized throughout the country. . . .

Plaintiff here had the burden of establishing that the defendant doctors were guilty of malpractice. She failed, however, to introduce evidence of the standard of care to which the defendants were bound to adhere, Plaintiff's expert, Dr. Berger, testified only concerning his own personal preference for isolating the laryngeal nerve under the facts presented to him in the hypothetical question. He at no time testified that there was a generally accepted medical standard of care or skill which required the identification of the laryngeal nerve under the circumstances. . . .

The appellate courts have held that the testimony of the defendant doctor may be sufficient to establish the standard of care, but it is apparent that the defendants' testimony here did not indicate a standard at variance with their actual conduct. Dr. Tiesenga testified that because of prior surgery on and treatment of plaintiff's thyroid, it would have been unwise to attempt to isolate her laryngeal nerve. The better practice, according to Dr. Tiesenga's testimony, was to skirt the area where the nerve might possibly be. Dr. Walsh concurred. When confronted with a statement from a recognized treatise that the first step in performing a thyroidectomy is to expose and identify the recurrent laryngeal nerve, Dr. Tiesenga agreed with the statement only as a general proposition. He testified that where there has been prior surgery and treatment, it is not always good practice to follow the procedure indicated in the treatise. . . .

It is insufficient for plaintiff to establish a prima facie case merely to present testimony of another physician that he would have acted differently from the defendant, since medicine is not an exact science. It is rather a profession which involves the exercise of individual judgment within the framework of established procedures. Differences in opinion are consistent with the exercise of due care. . . .

For the above reasons the judgment of the appellate court is affirmed.

NOTES

1. **The traditional medical standard.** The medical standard of care discussed in the malpractice opinions seldom sounds like a "standard" comparable to the standard of the reasonable and prudent person. The term "standard" suggests a measure or benchmark of some generality. The "medical standard," however, almost always reflects particular customs or procedures used under very particular circumstances, like the "wide-cut" procedure in *Walski*. In other words, the medical "standard" is understood as a rule for the very circumstances involved in the plaintiff's case. *See, e.g., Mody v. Center for Women's Health, P.C.*, 998 A.2d 327 (D.C. 2010) (standard of care required surgeon to reexamine patient's uterine wall after certain medical procedures, but only if perforations were suspected).

2. **Determining the standard.** "The standard of care is determined by the care customarily provided by other physicians, it need not be scientifically tested or proven effective: what the average qualified physician would do in a particular situation *is* the standard of care." *Palandjian v. Foster*, 842 N.E.2d

916 (Mass. 2006) (appropriate question was whether other doctors would have ordered an endoscopy for the patient given the patient's family history of gastric cancer, not whether the patient's risk of gastric cancer was in fact increased). The standard is not what the doctor *himself* would do. *See Murray v. UNMC Physicians,* 806 N.W.2d 118 (Neb. 2011). Nor is it necessarily enough to show that the care used was not good care. *Braswell v. Stinnett,* 99 So.3d 175 (Miss. 2012) ("Dentists are not required to do what is generally done, or what the average dentist would do. And our law certainly does not require dentists to conform to a vague, subjective standard such as good dental practice. Instead, our law requires a plaintiff to establish—through a qualified expert—what is required of a minimally competent dentist.").

3. **Jury instructions.** If the proof is sufficient to get the plaintiff to the jury, the instructions must reflect the medical, not the ordinary care, standard. Instructions often state that the physician must possess the learning, skill and ability of other physicians, must exercise reasonable care in the use of this knowledge and skill and must use his or her best judgment in the care of the patient.

Trial judges sometimes tell the jury that the physician is not liable for an honest mistake or bona fide error in judgment, that the physician is not expected to be infallible, or that he does not guarantee results. These instructions have come under attack by plaintiffs' lawyers as unduly emphasizing the defendant's side of the case, and as misleading to the jury. The "honest mistake" and "error in judgment" instructions have been disapproved in a number of cases. *See Passarello v. Grumbine,* 87 A.3d 285 (Pa. 2014) (such instructions should not be given at all, because they pose substantial risks of confusing juries on the standard of care); *Nestorowich v. Ricotta,* 767 N.E.2d 125 (N.Y. 2002) (error in judgment instruction proper only when physician is choosing among medically acceptable procedures); *McKinnis v. Women & Infants Hosp. of R.I.,* 749 A.2d 574 (R.I. 2000) (vacating judgment where jury instruction came "too close to implying that 'good faith judgment' or 'good faith error' constitutes a complete defense to a claim of medical malpractice," when such terms "have no place in jury instructions").

4. **Expert medical testimony.** In general, expert testimony is required whenever the issue presented is beyond the comprehension of a lay jury, and such testimony will assist the jury in understanding the deciding the issue. The medical standard of care is a classic example, given its very nature. If the plaintiff fails to adduce expert testimony on the medical standard of care, or if the testimony is inadequate to show the standard, the judge will direct a verdict for the defendant. *See, e.g., Toogood v. Rogal,* 824 A.2d 1140 (Pa. 2003). Whether the particular doctor's conduct fell below the standard is also a matter that generally requires expert testimony, *see Love v. Walker,* 423 S.W.3d 751 (Ky. 2014), although not where the doctor's negligence would be obvious to a lay person, *see Ex parte HealthSouth Corp.,* 851 So.2d 33 (Ala. 2002) (giving examples: leaving a sponge in after an operation, operating on the wrong leg, or ignoring a call for assistance). And expert testimony may be needed to prove that the doctor's negligence factually caused the plaintiff's harm. *See, e.g., Ruiz*

v. Killebrew, 459 P.3d 1005 (Utah 2020) (affirming summary judgment for doctor where no expert testified that child's injury could have been avoided had medical personnel not breached duty of care); *Rodriguez v. Clark*, 926 A.2d 736 (Md. 2007) (expert testimony required on whether a doctor's failure to notice an abnormal electrocardiogram more likely than not caused a patient's heart attack).

When expert testimony is required, not just any testimony will do. In *Daubert v. Merrell Dow Pharmaceuticals, Inc.*, 509 U.S. 579 (1993), the Supreme Court requires federal trial courts to review expert testimony for reliability. *See also* FED. R. EVID. 702. Many states have followed suit. *See, e.g., Norman v. Anderson Regional Med. Center*, 262 So.3d 520 (Miss. 2019). Admissibility of expert testimony has become a critical issue in many negligence cases.

5.   **More than one medical "standard" or practice.** Suppose that most doctors in the relevant medical community believe that human bite wounds should not be closed with stitches, but that some disagree and believe that the wound should be stitched and treated with antibiotics. A patient suffers serious infection when his doctor closes the wound. What is the relevant medical standard? "Where competent medical authority is divided, a physician will not be held responsible if in the exercise of his judgment he followed a course of treatment advocated by a considerable number of recognized and respected professionals in his given area of expertise." *Sinclair v. Block*, 633 A.2d 1137 (Pa. 1993); *see also Butts v. United States*, 930 F.3d 234 (4th Cir. 2019) (under W. Va. law, "if there is more than one acceptable method of treatment, the physician need not choose the best one"). What if the defendant says his practices represent a medical standard or school of thought even though no one else in the profession agrees? *See Yates v. University of W.Va. Bd. of Trustees*, 549 S.E.2d 681 (W.Va. 2001).

6.   **Rejecting *T.J. Hooper*.** Medical standards are not to be found in an authoritative book. For the most part, the medical standard of care is the practice of the relevant medical community. Does the medical standard rule reject the rule about custom in *T.J. Hooper*?

7.   **Rejecting reasonable care.** Medical standards will often reflect reasonable care. Notice that under the reasonable person standard, a professional practitioner would be obliged to exercise all the skill and knowledge he actually has, even if that is more skill or knowledge than other people have. So the medical care standard is not different from the reasonable person standard in this respect. *See American Radiology Services, LLC v. Reiss,* 236 A.3d 518 (Md. 2020) ("Where a member of a profession has special training and expertise, their conduct is measured against the standard of a hypothetical reasonable person with similar training and expertise."); *Sloan ex rel. Estate of Sloan v. Providence Health System-Oregon*, 437 P.3d 1097 (Or. 2019) (doctor owes patient "the level of care that a reasonably prudent, careful, and skillful practitioner of the physician's discipline would have provided under the same or similar circumstances and within the same community")

But the medical standard might require *less* care than the reasonable person standard. To see why, suppose Dr. Berger had testified that, as a matter of scientific fact, the risk of severing the nerve is doubled when the wide-cut procedure is used as compared to the nerve identification procedure and that there are no corresponding advantages to the wide-cut procedure. That testimony seems to be important under a *Carroll Towing* or reasonable care standard because it shows an increase of risk. But it does not seem relevant at all, much less determinative, under the medical standard, because it does not address what doctors actually do.

Is it fair to say that a customary standard can also require *more* care than the reasonable person standard in some instances? What result if the medical standard of care is to perform a procedure despite a lack of scientific evidence suggesting that the procedure is generally beneficial? *See Palandjian v. Foster*, 842 N.E.2d 916 (Mass. 2006).

8.   **Accepting reasonable care standards.** A few decisions have indicated that in extreme cases, the reasonable person standard might be used. *See United Blood Serv's, Div. of Blood Sys., Inc. v. Quintana*, 827 P.2d 509 (Colo. 1992); *Helling v. Carey*, 519 P.2d 981 (Wash. 1974) (cheap, efficient test for glaucoma should be given with ophthalmic exam even if that was not the practice of the medical community). Professor Peters' study concludes that 12 cases have shifted to the reasonable care standard and that a number of others have implicitly done so. *See* Philip G. Peters, Jr., *The Quiet Demise of Deference to Custom: Malpractice Law at the Millennium*, 57 WASH. & LEE L. REV. 163 (2000). Logically, the shift implies that testimony about medical custom would no longer be necessary. Some cases like *Helling v. Carey*, in this note, are in accord with that, but it remains to be seen whether all those courts adopting reasonable care will go that far against long-standing tradition.

9.   **Non-medical negligence of health-care providers.** Suppose that you, as a hospital patient, slip and fall because the hospital left a slippery substance on the floor. Would you be required to prove the standard of care for hospitals by expert testimony? *See Self v. Executive Comm. of Ga. Baptist Convention*, 266 S.E.2d 168 (Ga. 1980) (not a claim of medical malpractice, no requirement of expert testimony); *see also Sullo v. Greenberg*, 68 A.3d 404 (R.I. 2013) (doctor owed no "medical" duty of care to patient with respect to her fall on the entrance ramp to his office); *Salerno v. Spectrum Med. Group, P.A.*, 215 A.3d 804 (Me. 2019) (slip and fall in locker room of physical-therapy facility owed and run by hospital was an ordinary negligence claim not within the ambit of state malpractice act).

Do you need expert testimony in this case: a doctor knows a patient is dangerous but fails to warn his coworkers? *Powell v. Catholic Med. Ctr.*, 749 A.2d 301 (N.H. 2000). What about this: a patient's girlfriend becomes infected with herpes and sues the doctor for negligently advising the boyfriend that he had tested negative for herpes? *Doe v. Cochran*, 210 A.3d 469 (Conn. 2019). If a court sees the plaintiff's claim as one for "ordinary" negligence as opposed to medical malpractice, not only will the plaintiff not need to adduce medical expert testimony—the point made in these notes—but the plaintiff will not have to comply with whatever special rules the jurisdiction has adopted for medical malpractice cases—a point made in § 4B of this chapter. *See Southeastern Pain Specialists, P.C. v. Brown*, 811 S.E.2d 360 (Ga. 2018) ("Medical providers owe certain duties of ordinary care to their patients, and a breach of one of those duties is ordinary negligence, not medical malpractice.").

Note that a court may see some of a plaintiff's claims as medical malpractice and some as ordinary negligence in the same case. *See, e.g., Davis v. Frostburg Facility Operations, LLC*, 177 A.3d 709 (Md. 2018) (claim alleging that patient was injured when mattress detached was ordinary negligence claim; claim that clinic negligently provided the mechanical lift that malfunctioned was a medical claim subject to malpractice claims statute); *Trowell v. Providence Hosp. & Med. Centers, Inc.*, 918 N.W.2d 645 (Mich. 2018) (claim that hospital aide dropped patient while trying to move her was ordinary negligence claim; claim that hospital aide failed to properly assist patient while she was in intensive care unit was medical malpractice claim).

10. **Apology.** The defendant might conceivably admit before trial that he violated the appropriate standard of care. If he does so, evidence of this admission can be introduced to show the standard and its breach. Suppose the defendant, after an operation turns out badly, says "I made a mistake, that should not have happened." Would that suffice to show the standard? *Fossett v. Board of Regents of Univ. of Neb.*, 605 N.W.2d 465 (Neb. 2000). Some state statutes permit physicians to apologize to patients for mistakes without risk that the apology will be used in court. *See* Marilyn Wei, *Doctors, Apologies, and the Law: An Analysis and Critique of Apology Laws,* 40 J. HEALTH L. 107 (2007) (listing a dozen such laws). Is this a help to injured patients? To doctors? *Compare* Aaron Lazare, *The Healing Forces of Apology in Medical Practice and Beyond,* 57 DEPAUL L. REV. 251 (2008), *with* Lee Taft, *Apology Subverted: The Commodification of Apology*, 109 YALE. L. J. 1135 (2000). Is it preferable if the apology is accompanied by some form of compensation? Some states have adopted "Disclosure and offer" programs—institutional programs in which clinicians disclose unanticipated outcomes to patients and apologize, sometimes followed by a modest compensation offer. Michelle M. Mello & Allen Kachalia, *Evaluation of Options for Medical Malpractice System Reform: A Report to the Medicare Payment Advisory Commission* 2, 36–42 (2010).

VERGARA V. DOAN

593 N.E.2d 185 (Ind. 1992)

SHEPARD, CHIEF JUSTICE.

Javier Vergara was born on May 31, 1979, at the Adams Memorial Hospital in Decatur, Indiana. His parents, Jose and Concepcion, claimed that negligence on the part of Dr. John Doan during Javier's delivery caused him severe and permanent injuries. A jury returned a verdict for Dr. Doan and the plaintiffs appealed. The Court of Appeals affirmed.

Plaintiffs seek transfer, asking us to abandon Indiana's modified locality rule. We grant transfer to examine the standard of care appropriate for medical malpractice cases.

In most negligence cases, the defendant's conduct is tested against the hypothetical reasonable and prudent person acting under the same or similar circumstances. In medical malpractice cases, however, Indiana has applied a more specific articulation of this standard. It has become known as the modified locality rule: "The standard of care . . . is that degree of care, skill, and proficiency which is commonly exercised by ordinarily careful, skillful, and prudent [physicians], at the time of the operation and in similar localities." Appellants have urged us to abandon this standard, arguing that the reasons for the modified locality rule are no longer applicable in today's society. We agree.

The modified locality rule is a less stringent version of the strict locality rule, which measured the defendant's conduct against that of other doctors in the same community. When the strict locality rule originated in the late 19th century, there was great disparity between the medical opportunities, equipment, facilities, and training in rural and urban communities. Travel and communication between rural and urban communities were difficult. The locality rule was intended to prevent the inequity that would result from holding rural doctors to the same standards as doctors in large cities.

With advances in communication, travel, and medical education, the disparity between rural and urban health care diminished and justification for the locality rule waned. The strict locality rule also had two major drawbacks, especially as applied to smaller communities. First, there was a scarcity of local doctors to serve as expert witnesses against other local doctors. Second, there was the possibility that practices among a small group of doctors would establish a local standard of care below that which the law required. In response to these changes and criticisms, many courts adopted a modified locality rule, expanding the area of comparison to similar localities. . . .

Use of a modified locality rule has not quelled the criticism. Many of the common criticisms seem valid. The modified locality rule still permits a lower standard of care to be exercised in smaller communities because other similar communities are likely to have the same care. We also spend time and money on the difficulty of defining what is a similar community. The rule also seems inconsistent with the reality of modern medical practice. The disparity between small town and urban medicine continues to lessen with advances in communication, transportation, and education. In addition, widespread insurance coverage has provided patients with more choice of doctors and hospitals by reducing the financial constraints on the consumer in selecting caregivers. . . . Many states describe the care a physician owes without emphasizing the locality of practice. Today we join these states and adopt the following: a physician must exercise that degree of care, skill, and proficiency exercised by reasonably careful, skillful, and prudent practitioners in the same class to which he belongs, acting under the same or similar circumstances. Rather than focusing on different standards for different communities, this standard uses locality as but one of the factors to be considered in determining whether the doctor acted reasonably. Other relevant considerations would include advances in the profession, availability of facilities, and whether the doctor is a specialist or general practitioner.

. . . Plaintiff was permitted to present his expert witness, Dr. Harlan Giles, even though he was from Pittsburgh, Pennsylvania (not Decatur or a similar locality). Dr. Giles testified regarding his experience and knowledge of the standard of care in communities similar to Decatur and in hospitals similar in size to Adams County Memorial Hospital. He testified that in his opinion, considering all the factors incident to the pregnancy and birth of Javier Vergara, the standard of care required Dr. Doan to have delivered the baby by cesarean section. He stated that this opinion was based on the standard of care as it existed in 1979 in Decatur or similar communities. He also testified that the failure to have either an anesthesiologist or a qualified nurse anesthetist present at the delivery was a breach of the national standard of care for hospitals the size of Adams County Memorial and smaller. Evidently the jury disagreed with Dr. Giles and found Dr. Doan's conduct reasonable under the circumstances.

what was required by Dr. Doan

We regard our new formulation of a doctor's duty as a relatively modest alteration of existing law. It is unlikely to have changed the way this case was tried. We are satisfied that an instruction without the locality language would not lead a new jury to a different conclusion.

Therefore, we hold that giving instruction 23 was harmless and does not require reversal. . . .

NOTES

1. **The local medical standard and problems of testimony.** Adoption of a local standard means that only a local physician, or one who has actual knowledge of the local standard, can testify against the defendant-doctor. *See, e.g., Dlouhy v. Kootenai Hosp. Dist.,* 474 P.3d 711 (Idaho 2020). What problems does this raise for the plaintiff? In *Robinson v. LeCorps,* 83 S.W.3d 718 (Tenn. 2002), the defendant practiced in Nashville, Tennessee, and the plaintiff's expert was from Johnson City, Tennessee. The expert testified that the defendant violated the national standard, and that the national standard was "the same as the recognized standard of acceptable professional practice as it would be in Nashville, Tennessee." The court, bound by a statutory locality rule, affirmed a dismissal of the claim because the testimony did not meet that rule. A statement that the standard "would be" the same was

not good enough, perhaps meaning that the testimony should have been "is the same." *See also Shipley v. Williams*, 350 S.W.3d 527 (Tenn. 2011) ("a medical expert must demonstrate a modicum of familiarity" with the community in which a defendant practices by knowing statistical information about the community's size and practices, speaking with other local medical providers, or visiting the community); *Navo v. Bingham Memorial Hosp.*, 373 P.3d 681 (Idaho 2016) (no abuse of discretion to exclude testimony of out-of-locality expert who failed to establish he had "actual knowledge of what the standard of care is in Blackfoot as it existed" at the time of the alleged malpractice, where the local standard "had not been replaced by a national or statewide standard of care with which [the expert] was familiar").

Other courts have been less strict in their application of a "same or similar locality" standard. For example, in *Bank v. Mickels*, 926 N.W.2d 97 (Neb. 2019), the court affirmed a jury verdict for a doctor whose expert witness practiced in Kearney, Neb., and "did not specifically testify that he was familiar with the standard of care in Omaha," because the doctor "was trained at the national level, and at the time of trial, served on the faculty of the University of Nebraska." Thus, said the court, "we can assume the jury reasonably found that the locality standard had been satisfied when it returned a general verdict for [the doctor]."

2. **A national medical standard.** It is sometimes argued that adoption of a standard like *Vergara's* would be unfair to doctors in small towns, who might not have the latest equipment. Would a national medical standard be likely to require a small-town doctor to own CT scan technology? What about the reasonable person standard? In *Hall v. Hilbun*, 466 So.2d 856 (Miss. 1985), the Mississippi court adopted a national standard which governs the physician's care and skill, but not the particular resources available to that physician. If you were a small-town doctor without equipment, what would you do about a patient who needed a CT scan?

3. **The standard for specialists.** The medical profession is organized to a large extent around recognized specialties, such as orthopedics, internal medicine, and obstetrics. Medical specialization usually entails several years of study following medical school and success in an examination administered by the "board" which certifies specialists. Specialists are held to the standard of their specialties; thus an orthopedic surgeon is held to a higher standard in setting a fracture than is a family practitioner. It is often assumed or held that the relevant medical community for them is the community of specialists, not a geographical community. *Wall v. Stout,* 311 S.E.2d 571 (N.C. 1984).

States have disagreed on whether an expert witness can testify against a doctor who is a specialist in a different field. A number of state statutes now require that the only experts who can competently testify are those who actually practice within the same specialty. *See, e.g.,* ALA. CODE 1975, § 6–5–548(c)(2) (expert must be "trained and experienced in the same specialty"). Other states more liberally permit an expert to testify if she establishes her knowledge of the standards of the defendant's specialty. *See* DOBBS, HAYDEN & BUBLICK, HORNBOOK ON TORTS § 21.8 (2d ed. 2016).

4.   **The standard for non-physician practitioners.** Practitioners such as chiropractors and podiatrists are permitted to practice according to their schools of belief. They are subject to the standards of the school they profess, not to medical standards. What if a naturopath diagnoses tonsillitis in a child and prescribes orange juice, but in fact the child has diphtheria and dies of it? Should a Christian Scientist practitioner, whose religion opposes medical treatment, be liable for treating a child with prayer when known and readily available medical treatment can save the child's life? In *Lundman v. McKown,* 530 N.W.2d 807 (Minn. Ct. App. 1995), a child whose mother was a Christian Scientist died when the mother called in a Christian Science practitioner instead of a medical doctor. The practitioner would be held to the standard he professes—healing by prayer—in the case of an adult. Would it be different with a child? Is there a limit? *Guerrero v. Smith,* 864 S.W.2d 797 (Tex. App. 1993) (homeopath gave outrageous advice with horrible consequences).

5.   **A duty to refer.** Medical practitioners must refer their patients to specialists when the standard of care so requires. To prevail on a claim alleging negligence in not referring, the plaintiff must not only show that a referral was required, but also that the referral would have been reasonably likely to lead to a better outcome, or at least to improve the patient's chances. *Goldberg v. Horowitz,* 901 N.Y.S.2d 95 (App. Div. 2010) (improved chance or better outcome, evidence sufficient). When a *non*-medical practitioner recognizes or should recognize that a patient has a medical problem, some courts hold that they must refer the patient to a medical doctor. *Kerkman v. Hintz,* 418 N.W.2d 795 (Wis. 1988), however, held that referral is not required or even logically permissible. It is enough, the *Kerkman* court said, that the chiropractor cease treating a condition that lies outside his school of work. What about a church counselor who believes that the word of God is the only counseling anyone requires and for that reason does not refer a suicidal young man to different professional help? *Nally v. Grace Community Church of the Valley,* 763 P.2d 948 (Cal. 1988).

NOTE: OTHER MEDICAL PROFESSIONALS

1.   *Nurses.* Courts now seem to assume that nurses are held to the standard of nurses in a similar practice. *Massey v. Mercy Med. Ctr. Redding,* 103 Cal.Rptr.3d 209 (Ct. App. 2009) (standard of care for nurses is "the level of skill, knowledge and care that a reasonably careful nurse would use in similar circumstances").

2.   *Pharmacists.* The rule in most states is that pharmacists owe their clients no duty to warn of side effects, that the physician has prescribed an excessive dosage, or that a drug is contraindicated, even though the patient may be seriously injured if the prescription is filled. *See,*

e.g., Kowalski v. Rose Drugs of Dardanelle, Inc., 378 S.W.3d 109 (Ark. 2011) (only the doctor has a duty to warn). In these jurisdictions, the pharmacist is liable only if he voluntarily undertakes to give appropriate warnings and negligently fails to do so. *Cottam v. CVS Pharmacy,* 764 N.E.2d 814 (Mass. 2002).

However, states continue to disagree about this issue and some courts have held that a pharmacist owes a duty to warn when serious contraindications are present or the drugs prescribed carry inherent risk. *See Klasch v. Walgreen Co.,* 264 P.3d 1155 (Nev. 2011) (when pharmacist knows that a particular customer has an allergy to a prescribed drug, the pharmacist has a duty either to warn the customer or to notify the prescribing doctor); *Happel v. Wal-Mart Stores, Inc.,* 766 N.E.2d 1118 (Ill. 2002) (pharmacist has a duty to warn when she knows that a prescription is dangerous due to the patient's particular allergies).

3.   *Hospitals.* The present view seems to be that, in performing their own duties, hospitals owe a duty of reasonable care under national standards fixed by the Joint Commission on Accreditation of Hospitals. *See* 2 DOBBS, HAYDEN & BUBLICK, THE LAW OF TORTS § 316 (2d ed. 2011). Hospitals can be subject to liability if they fail to provide appropriate facilities, equipment, and staff support, or where non-medical personnel act negligently in a way that harms a patient. *See Steed v. Rezin Orthopedics and Sports Medicine, S.C.,* 182 N.E.2d 109 (Ill. 2021) ("institutional negligence" claim against medical facility where receptionist allegedly failed to schedule a follow-up appointment).

HIRPA V. IHC HOSPITALS, INC., 948 P.2d 785 (Utah 1997). A patient in active labor at a hospital became unresponsive and her hands began to spasm. Her physician broadcast a "Code Blue" over the hospital intercom. Dr. Daines responded, entering the delivery room and taking over. Seventeen minutes later, the patient was dead. The surviving spouse sued Daines and others involved in a federal court. Daines moved for summary judgment. He invoked a statute covering medical providers: "No person licensed under this chapter . . . who in good faith renders emergency care at the scene of the emergency, shall be liable for any civil damages as a result of any acts or omissions by such person in rendering the emergency care." The federal court certified questions to the state court. One question asked whether the statute applied. *Held*, the statute applies. This was an emergency. The statute is intended to encourage aid without fear of liability, so the location of the emergency in a hospital instead of a roadside is irrelevant, so long as the physician had no preexisting duty to aid. It has no application, however, when the physician already had a duty to aid the patient, for in that case he needs no encouragement. Whether the doctor was under a preexisting duty to the patient could depend upon the doctor-patient relationship, his contractual duty to respond, hospital rules or other factors.

NOTES

1. **Good Samaritan statutes.** The type of statute applied in *Hirpa* is called a Good Samaritan statute, after the Biblical story of the Samaritan who assists a man who had been attacked by robbers and left for dead on the road, after other passers-by had done nothing. Luke 10:25–37. All states have some form of a Good Samaritan statute, but the scope of immunity granted by such statutes varies from state to state. As the court wrote in *Velazquez v. Jiminez*, 798 A.2d 51 (N.J. 2002), "The country's Good Samaritan statutes broadly can be classified as falling into one of three categories: those that expressly exclude hospital care; those that expressly include hospital care; and those, like New Jersey's, that contain no explicit provision one way or the other." The *Velazquez* court said that its statute was designed "to encourage the rendering of medical care to those who would not otherwise receive it, by physicians who come upon such patients by chance, without the benefit of the expertise, assistance, equipment or sanitation that is available in a hospital or medical setting." Thus it did not extend immunity to physicians in the hospital setting. According to the court, in the hospital context "physicians' contracts, hospital protocols, ethical rules, regulatory standards and physicians' personal relationships" make it unlikely that, without immunity, physicians would stand by and allow patients to die. The court believed that the roadside accident is the kind of case for which the immunity is designed. Was there ever any need for immunity in such a case or would ordinary negligence rules protect the physician unless the physician imposes unreasonable risks even in the light of the emergency?

2. **Liability for gross negligence.** The Utah statute applied in *Hirpa* provides for complete immunity. A milder version of the Good Samaritan statute leaves open the possibility of liability for gross negligence, or for wanton conduct or intentional wrongdoing. *See, e.g.,* N.C. GEN STAT. § 20–166(d) (applying to any person, not merely to health care providers); ARIZ. REV. STAT. § 32–1471 (gross negligence standard applies to licensed health care providers who act in an emergency, or any person who gratuitously offers help at the scene of an emergency). "Gross negligence" has been defined as "the absence of even slight diligence," *See Abdel-Samed v. Dailey*, 755 S.E.2d 805 (Ga. 2014) (fact issue whether actions taken by hospital emergency room staff in delaying treatment for plaintiff's hand injury constituted gross negligence), or "a thoughtless disregard of the consequences without the exertion of any effort to avoid them." *Barbre v. Pope*, 935 A.2d 699 (Md. 2007).

3. **Special emergency-care statutes.** Some states have other special statutes protecting physicians who act in an emergency. See, e.g., GA. CODE ANN. § 51–1–29.5 (applicable to emergency medical care provided in a hospital emergency department, requiring proof of gross negligence by clear and convincing evidence); ARIZ. REV. STAT. §§ 12–563 & 573 (allowing negligence claim in connection with medical care during labor and delivery, but requiring

proof by clear and convincing evidence). A major study of preventable medical errors found that "High error rates with serious consequences are most likely to occur in intensive care units, operating rooms, and emergency departments." INSTITUTE OF MEDICINE, TO ERR IS HUMAN: BUILDING A SAFER HEALTHY SYSTEM (2000). Does that fact make legislation protecting doctors more necessary, or more troubling?

> REFERENCES: DOBBS, HAYDEN & BUBLICK, HORNBOOK ON TORTS §§ 21.1–21.8 (medical malpractice duty) & 21.13 (Good Samaritan statutes) (2d ed. 2016); 2 DOBBS, HAYDEN & BUBLICK, THE LAW OF TORTS §§ 292–304 (2d ed. 2011).

§ 2. INFORMED CONSENT

HARNISH v. CHILDREN'S HOSPITAL MEDICAL CENTER
439 N.E.2d 240 (Mass. 1982)

O'CONNOR, JUSTICE.

The plaintiff underwent an operation to remove a tumor in her neck. During the procedure, her hypoglossal nerve was severed, allegedly resulting in a permanent and almost total loss of tongue function.

The plaintiff's complaint charges the defendant physicians and hospital with misrepresentation and negligence in failing to inform her before surgery of the risk of loss of tongue function. The complaint alleges that the purpose of the operation was cosmetic, that the loss of tongue function was a material and foreseeable risk of the operation, and that, had the plaintiff been informed of this risk, she would not have consented to the operation. There is no claim that the operation was negligently performed.

[A medical malpractice tribunal, which functions to screen malpractice claims against physicians, held that the plaintiff's proof was inadequate and on this basis the trial judge dismissed the action.]

. . . "There is implicit recognition in the law of the Commonwealth, as elsewhere, that a person has a strong interest in being free from nonconsensual invasion of his bodily integrity. . . . In short, the law recognizes the individual interest in preserving 'the inviolability of his person.' One means by which the law has developed in a manner consistent with the protection of this interest is through the development of the doctrine of informed consent." "[I]t is the prerogative of the patient, not the physician, to determine . . . the direction in which . . . his interest lie." Every competent adult has a right "to forego treatment, or even cure, if it entails what for him are intolerable consequences or risks however unwise his sense of value may be in the eyes of the medical profession." Knowing exercise of this right requires knowledge of the available options and the risks attendant on each. We hold, therefore, that a physician's failure to divulge in a reasonable manner to a competent adult patient sufficient information to enable the patient to make an informed judgment whether to give or withhold consent to a medical or surgical procedure constitutes professional misconduct and comes within the ambit of G.L. c. 231, § 60B.

. . . Communication of scientific information by the trained physician to the untrained patient may be difficult. The remotely possible risks of a proposed treatment may be almost without limit. The patient's right to know must be harmonized with the recognition that an undue burden should not be placed on the physician. These interests are accommodated by the rule that we adopt today, that a physician owes to his patient the duty to disclose in a reasonable manner all significant medical information that the physician possesses or reasonably should possess that is material to an intelligent decision by the patient whether to undergo a proposed procedure. The information a physician reasonably should possess is that information possessed by the average qualified physician or, in the case of a specialty, by the average qualified physician practicing that specialty. What the physician should know involves professional expertise and can ordinarily be proved only through the testimony of experts. However, the extent to which he must share that information with his patient depends upon what information he should reasonably recognize is material to the plaintiff's decision. "Materiality may be said to be the significance a reasonable person, in what the physician knows or should know is his patient's position, would attach to the disclosed risk or risks in deciding whether to submit or not to submit to surgery or treatment." The materiality determination is one that lay persons are qualified to make without the aid of an expert. Appropriate information may include the nature of the patient's condition, the nature and probability of risks involved, the benefits to be reasonably expected, the inability of the physician to predict results, if that is the situation, the irreversibility of the procedure, if that be the case, the likely result of no treatment, and the available alternatives, including their risks and benefits. The obligation to give adequate information does not require the disclosure of all risks of a proposed therapy, or of information the physician reasonably believes the patient already has, such as the risks, like infection, inherent in any operation.

Many jurisdictions have adopted the rule that a physician must disclose to his patient only such information as is customarily disclosed in similar circumstances. We think that the better is the one we adopt today. The customary practice standard overlooks the purpose of requiring disclosure, which is protection of the patient's right to decide for himself.

We recognize that despite the importance of the patient's right to know, there may be situations that call for a privilege of nondisclosure. For instance, sound medical judgment might indicate that disclosure would

Cope when you don't have to disclose

complicate the patient's medical condition or render him unfit for treatment. Where that it is so, the cases have generally held that the physician is armed with a privilege to keep the information from the patient. . . . The physician's privilege to withhold information for therapeutic reasons must be carefully circumscribed, however, for otherwise it might devour the disclosure rule itself. "The privilege does not accept the paternalistic notion that the physician may remain silent simply because divulgence might prompt the patient to forego therapy the physician feels the patient really needs" (footnotes omitted). *Canterbury v. Spence*, supra at 789. A full discussion of the privilege is neither required nor attempted here, because the burden of proving it must rest with the physician, and thus the question of privilege is inappropriate to the directed verdict standard. . . .

We turn to the question of causation. "An unrevealed risk that should have been made known must materialize, for otherwise the omission, however unpardonable, is legally without consequence." Whether the alleged undisclosed risk materialized is a medical question appropriate to the tribunal's inquiry. At trial, the plaintiff must also show that had the proper information been provided neither he nor a reasonable person in similar circumstances would have undergone the procedure. Such proof, not relating to medical questions, is not appropriate to the tribunal's inquiry.

[The court found that one of the defendants was only an assistant in the operation and had no duty to give the plaintiff information, and that the hospital itself was not liable.]

The judgment as to the defendants Muliken and Holmes is reversed. The judgment as to defendants Gilman and Children's Hospital Medical Center is affirmed.

So Ordered.

WOOLLEY V. HENDERSON, 418 A.2d 1123 (Me. 1980). Defendant operated on the plaintiff's back but because of an abnormality in the spine, he got the wrong interspace between the vertebrae. He also inadvertently tore part of the tissue encasing the spinal cord, which resulted in a number of medical problems for the plaintiff. A tear of this kind is a normal risk of this procedure, but the doctor had not informed the plaintiff. The trial court instructed the jury that the plaintiff was entitled only to disclosures of risks that would be made by a reasonable medical practitioner. The jury found in favor of the defendant. *Held*, affirmed. The standard of disclosure is that of the reasonable medical practitioner and this will ordinarily require expert medical testimony. This rule is justified (1) because this is professional malpractice and the professional standard must be used, (2) because there might be therapeutic reasons for withholding information, and (3) because since the plaintiff must produce medical testimony on other issues, this will add very little burden. The plaintiff in informed consent cases must also prove causation by the objective test, that is, that a reasonable person would have refused the treatment had full information been given, and that the plaintiff herself would have refused it.

NOTES

1. **Negligence vs. battery theory.** Courts recognize a medical battery claim against a doctor who operates when the plaintiff has not consented at all to that procedure. *See Shuler v. Garrett*, 743 F.3d 170 (6th Cir. 2014) (applying Tenn. law; patient was injected with drug over her objections). Some courts also treat cases of consent without appropriate information as battery cases. *See Montgomery v. Bazaz-Sehgal*, 798 A.2d 742 (Pa. 2002). The usual approach, however, is to treat informed consent claims under negligence, not battery rules. *See White v. Beeks*, 469 S.W.3d 517 (Tenn. 2015) (reciting history of informed consent); *Mole v. Jutton*, 846 A.2d 1035 (Md. 2004) (collecting cases).

2. **Practical consequences of the theory.** Use of a negligence approach is important for a number of reasons. The defendant doctor's liability insurance might not cover battery, an intentional tort. Also, negligence rules might make the doctor's duty to disclose depend upon the disclosure the medical community would make, which might require expert testimony. Many courts, like the *Woolley* court, have so held. Further, an informed consent claim may be subject to special statutory limits or conditions for recovery. *See Felton v. Lovett*, 388 S.W.3d 656 (Tex. 2012).

3. **Professional standard or the "patient rule"?** Beginning in the early 1970s, a series of major decisions retained the negligence theory of informed consent but rejected the requirement of proof from the medical community. These cases held that the standard was "materiality" of the information. In the absence of statutory directive otherwise, most of the recent major decisions have taken this view. *See, e.g., Cuc Thi Ngo v. Queen's Medical Center*, 358 P.3d 26 (Haw. 2015) (once patient adduces expert testimony to show that a risk was material, whether the physician was required to supply that information to the patient is for the jury, applying a patient-oriented standard, and no expert is needed to answer that question); *Largey v. Rothman*, 540 A.2d 504 (N.J. 1988) (scope of duty to disclose is "measured by the patient's need, and that need is the information material to the decision"). However, some courts still endorse a reasonable doctor standard. *See Orphan v. Pilnik*, 940 N.E.2d 555 (N.Y. 2010). How different is a standard that requires disclosure of information that would be material to the patient's treatment decision versus information that a reasonable doctor would provide? In *Marsingill v. O'Malley*, 128 P.3d 151 (Alaska 2006), the court thought these two standards were basically indistinguishable. *See also Spar v. Cha*, 907 N.E.2d 974 (Ind. 2009) ("A physician must disclose the facts and risks of a treatment which a reasonably prudent physician would be expected to disclose

under like circumstances, and which a reasonable person would want to know.").

4. **Causation.** Should it matter if the patient consented to prior similar surgeries, which may indicate that she did not consent because of lack of knowledge of the associated risks? *Spar v. Cha,* 907 N.E.2d 974 (Ind. 2009). Most courts have required proof of factual cause. *See White v. Lembach,* 959 N.E.2d 1033 (Ohio 2011). In addition, they have required an "objective" test of causation. This means that the plaintiff cannot recover merely by showing that she herself would have refused the injury-causing operation had she been fully informed. She will have to go further and show that a reasonable person would also have refused it. Is this requirement because the courts are reluctant to permit a jury to believe the plaintiff's testimony on this point? If so, what about the usual rule that the jury is the sole judge of credibility? Or is the "objective" test of causation intended to limit protection to reasonable patients? Is that what autonomy is about—matching other people's expectations of reasonableness? Several courts have sought a compromise, saying that the issue is to be judged by the reasonable person standard in the light of the plaintiff's personal fears and religious beliefs. *Ashe v. Radiation Oncology Assocs.,* 9 S.W.3d 119 (Tenn. 1999).

5. **Incompetent patients and life-saving treatment.** The informed consent rules imply that the patient may refuse treatment. May a physician treat a competent patient over her objection if the treatment is required to save her life? *Shine v. Vega,* 709 N.E.2d 58 (Mass. 1999) (no); *Harvey v. Strickland,* 566 S.E.2d 529 (S.C. 2002) (no). Can a dying patient refuse treatment that would save her fetus? "[E]very person has the right, under the common law and the Constitution, to accept or refuse medical treatment. This right of bodily integrity belongs equally to persons who are competent and persons who are not. . . . Further, it matters not what the quality of a patient's life may be; the right of bodily integrity is not extinguished simply because someone is ill, or even at death's door. To protect that right against intrusion by others—family members, doctors, hospitals, or anyone else, however well-intentioned—we hold that a court must determine the patient's wishes by any means available, and must abide by those wishes unless there are truly extraordinary or compelling reasons to override them." *In re A.C.,* 573 A.2d 1235 (D.C. 1990). When a patient is incompetent, a court must make a substituted judgment determination—determine as best it can what choice that individual, if competent, would make with respect to medical procedures. *Id.* Does the right to refuse life-saving treatment mean that the patient would also have a right to assistance in committing suicide? *Krischer v. McIver,* 697 So.2d 97 (Fla. 1997) ("Forty-five states that recognize the right to refuse treatment or unwanted life-support have expressed disapproval of assisted suicide.").

WLOSINSKI V. COHN, 713 N.W.2d 16 (Mich. Ct. App. 2005). Michael Wrobel suffered kidney failure during his senior year in high school. After researching various medical facilities and their kidney transplant success rates, Michael and his family selected William Beaumont Hospital for treatment. In pre-operative consultations, Dr. Steven Cohn allegedly represented his kidney transplant success rate as "good." The plaintiff, Michael's mother, donated a kidney in an effort to save her son, and Dr. Cohn performed the transplant surgery. Michael experienced severe post-operative complications, resulting in the removal of his new kidney, which ultimately led to his death. Plaintiff's expert inferred medical incompetence by testifying that five out of seven kidney transplants that Dr. Cohn had performed in the months leading up to Michael's surgery had failed. The plaintiff contends that Dr. Cohn owed a duty to Michael to disclose his failure rate before obtaining consent to the procedure. *Held,* "[t]he doctrine of informed consent requires a physician to warn a patient of the risks and consequences of a medical procedure. By itself, Dr. Cohn's success rate was not a risk related to the medical procedure. . . . [W]e simply hold that defendants, as a matter of law, did not have a duty to disclose Dr. Cohn's statistical history of transplant failures to obtain the decedent's informed consent."

NOTES

1. **Physician success rates.** Suppose a surgeon has little experience with the proposed brain surgery or a record of bad results. Must he inform his patient? *Johnson v. Kokemoor*, 545 N.W.2d 495 (Wis. 1996), held that the patient was entitled to information from her surgeon that more experienced brain surgeons were available and had substantially better success rates than inexperienced surgeons. Can the *Wlosinski* court's holding be justified on the ground that a reasonable patient would not have cared about the five out of seven failure rate, or is there some other issue at work? If doctors must disclose success rates, will doctors fudge their records? Reject high-risk patients to establish a better set of statistics? Even if doctors need not disclose information, can they lie about it? In *Willis v. Bender*, 596 F.3d 1244 (10th Cir. 2010), the court said that an informed consent claim is stated when a physician lies to a patient "in direct response to a patient's questions . . . in the course of obtaining the patient's consent and the [patient's] questions seek concrete verifiable facts . . . as to the quality of his performance or abilities."

2. **Procedure success rates.** What if the procedure itself is generally unsuccessful? *See Williamson v. Amrani*, 152 P.3d 60 (Kan. 2007) (holding that expert testimony was necessary to determine whether the lack-of-success rate of recommended back surgery was something a reasonable medical practitioner would have disclosed to the patient).

3. **Jury decisions.** Whether information would be material to an intelligent decision by the patient is usually a jury question. Would a doctor be required to disclose to the patient that he might minimize the risk of an AIDS infection from a blood transfusion by donating his own blood in advance of the operation? *See Doe v. Johnston*, 476 N.W.2d 28 (Iowa 1991). Suppose the doctor for an 81-year-old woman with a broken hip thinks surgery with screws to hold

it together is a bad idea because of her age. He never informs her that without surgery she will probably never walk again. He prescribes bed rest only and in fact she is never able to walk thereafter. Did the doctor breach a duty of providing information? *Matthies v. Mastromonaco*, 733 A.2d 456 (N.J. 1999).

4. **Physician experience.** What if the surgeon represents that the surgeon has extensive experience in performing a highly risky operation when in fact the doctor has much more limited experience? *See Howard v. University of Med. & Dentistry of N.J.*, 800 A.2d 73 (N.J. 2002). What if the doctor simply fails to tell the patient that the doctor lacks training and experience in performing a specific heart-surgery procedure? Is that material information that the patient is entitled to know before consenting to that procedure? *See Andersen v. Khanna*, 913 N.W.2d 526 (Iowa 2018) (reversing partial summary judgment for doctor, holding that fact issues remained as to its materiality). Some states apply to physicians state consumer protection acts which forbid unfair and deceptive practices. After the Kansas Supreme Court held that a doctor's false representation could count as an unfair and deceptive act, the state amended the consumer protection act to exclude medical professionals. *Kelly v. VinZant*, 197 P.3d 803 (Kan. 2008).

5. **Physician impairment.** Georgia says that a physician owes no duty to inform a patient of the physician's own cocaine use, *Albany Urology Clinic, P.C. v. Cleveland*, 528 S.E.2d 777 (Ga. 2000); *see also Williams v. Booker*, 712 S.E.2d 617 (Ga. Ct. App. 2011) (hospital owed no duty to inform the patient that the surgeon suffered a relapse in alcoholism; nor was the surgeon's alcohol addiction at the time he treated patient an independent basis for a medical malpractice claim). A little authority goes the other way on such matters as chronic alcohol abuse or AIDS infection. *See* 2 DOBBS, HAYDEN & BUBLICK, THE LAW OF TORTS §§ 309–310 (2d ed. 2011).

6. **Lack of insurance.** What if the doctor fails to disclose that he does not have statutorily required medical malpractice insurance? *See Jarrell v. Kaul*, 123 A.3d 1022 (N.J. 2015) (any such failure does not vitiate informed consent; the inability to cover a judgment is not the kind of injury contemplated by the informed consent doctrine).

7. **Financial interests.** What about disclosure of the doctor's financial interest in a patient's procedure? In *Moore v. Regents of the University of California*, 793 P.2d 479 (Cal. 1990), the patient claimed that the physicians and hospital withdrew blood ostensibly in the course of treatment. They developed a "cell line" that could be used efficiently to produce a commercial product of great value. None of this was mentioned to the patient. The court refused to permit the plaintiff to pursue a conversion claim, but it said that the physician was under a fiduciary duty to disclose some of the facts to the patient. Is this an informed consent case or something different? Is the standard lower when the issue is not patient treatment but donated tissues? *See Greenberg v. Miami Children's Hospital Research Institute, Inc.*, 264 F.Supp.2d 1064 (S.D. Fla. 2003) (no duty to disclose that doctor planned to patent the gene).

ARATO V. AVEDON, 858 P.2d 598 (Cal. 1993). Mr. Arato was diagnosed with cancer. Doctors performed surgery, but the cancer was a kind that was overwhelmingly likely to cause death in a short time. Although Arato had indicated to his doctor that he wanted to know the truth, his doctor did not tell him that death in a short time was statistically almost certain. Instead, the doctor recommended some post-operative treatments that had been experimentally successful with some other forms of cancer and that the doctors hoped would help Mr. Arato. The treatments were not successful. Mr. Arato's survivors claimed against the doctor. They said he should have told Mr. Arato that his chances were slim to none because that information would have been relevant to his decision to accept the treatments and that, living in a false hope, Mr. Arato had failed to arrange his economic affairs, a failure that led to business and tax losses. The jury found for the defendants. The Court of Appeal reversed for error in instructions. *Held*, the Court of Appeal is reversed. "Patient sovereignty" or autonomy is an extreme. It was not error to leave to the jury the question whether all material information about risks had been given. Furthermore, the doctor had no duty to disclose statistical life expectancy information because it was not information about risks of the procedures. As to relevant information that is not about risks, the standard of disclosure is the "standard of practice within the medical community." Since expert physicians testified that the standard was NOT to reveal this kind of information voluntarily, there could be no liability for failure to give informed consent. As to Mr. Arato's written request to be told the truth, "a patient may validly waive the right to be informed, [but] we do not see how a request to be told the 'truth' in itself heightens the duty of disclosure imposed on physicians as a matter of law."

NOTES

1. **Statistical information.** Why not require doctors to disclose statistical life expectancy information? Would a reasonable person want to know this information?

2. **Emergencies.** In an emergency, would failure to obtain informed consent be a breach of duty? The common law emergency exception has been said to apply when: (1) a medical emergency exists; (2) treatment is required to protect the patient's health; (3) it is impossible or impractical to obtain consent from either the patient or someone authorized to consent for the patient; and (4) there is no reason to believe that the patient would decline the treatment, given the opportunity to consent. *Sekerez v. Rush Univ. Med. Ctr.*, 954 N.E.2d 383 (Ill. App. Ct. 2011) (exception did not apply where decedent, who suffered from terminal cancer, expressly refused blood thinners that physicians continued to administer). If an infant without a heartbeat needs immediate resuscitation, what result when the child is revived 24 minutes

later with severe and permanent disabilities? *Stewart-Graves v. Vaughn,* 170 P.3d 1151 (Wash. 2007) (consent in such a case would be implied). Should the result be different if the state recognizes a parent's right to discontinue extraordinary measures?

3. **Research on healthy children.** Suppose no treatment is involved—a researcher wishes to perform experiments upon healthy human beings. Would you expect informed consent rules to be more demanding or less? *See Grimes v. Kennedy Krieger Inst., Inc.,* 782 A.2d 807 (Md. 2001). If the rules of informed consent are more demanding, you may have to distinguish between experiment ("research") and therapy or medical practice.

4. **Damages.** Knowledge about risks and choices is necessary if patients are to participate in decisions about their bodies. Maybe courts should allow some kind of dignitary damages if the patient is deprived of the right to "vote" on the operation with appropriate knowledge, even if the patient would have given consent if she had been fully informed. What do you think? *See Lugenbuhl v. Dowling,* 701 So.2d 447 (La. 1997) (permitting damages for deprivation of self-determination).

TRUMAN V. THOMAS, 611 P.2d 902 (Cal. 1980). Rena Truman consulted Dr. Thomas as her doctor over a six-year period. She died of cervical cancer, which could have been discovered and successfully treated by a pap smear given early enough. Dr. Thomas did repeatedly advise her to have the pap smear, but never warned her of the purpose or of the dangers of not having one. In an action for her death, the trial judge refused to instruct the jury on the failure to disclose the dangers of refusing the pap smear and the jury found for the defendant doctor. On appeal, *held,* reversed. "If a patient indicates that he or she is going to *decline* the risk-free test or treatment, then the doctor has the additional duty of advising of all material risks of which a reasonable person would want to be informed. . . . [A] jury could reasonably conclude that Dr. Thomas had a duty to inform Mrs. Truman of the danger of refusing the test because it was not reasonable for Dr. Thomas to assume that Mrs. Truman appreciated the potentially fatal consequences of her conduct."

BROWN V. DIBBELL, 595 N.W.2d 358 (Wis. 1999). After conference with the defendant doctors, Mrs. Brown underwent a double mastectomy with some unfortunate results. She sued on an informed consent theory. The jury found that Dr. Dibbell was not negligent in performing surgery but that he was negligent in obtaining Ms. Brown's consent to surgery. The jury also found that a reasonable patient in Ms. Brown's circumstances, if adequately informed, would have refused to undergo the surgery that was performed. Finally, the jury found that Mrs. Brown was chargeable with 50% of the negligence for failing to exercise care for her own health. The plaintiff argued on appeal that it was error for the trial judge to submit the issue of contributory negligence. *Held,* affirming the Court of Appeals, a new trial is required to correct various errors in instruction. As to the plaintiff's comparative fault, the defense may be invoked in an informed consent action. Specifically, a patient may be chargeable with comparative fault for failing to give truthful and complete family history when it is material. But a patient may ordinarily trust the doctor's information and except in a most unusual case could not be charged with fault for failure to ascertain the truth or completeness of the information presented by the doctor or to seek independent advice.

REFERENCES: DOBBS, HAYDEN & BUBLICK, HORNBOOK ON TORTS §§ 21.9–21.12 (2d ed. 2016); 2 DOBBS, HAYDEN & BUBLICK, THE LAW OF TORTS §§ 307–311 (2d ed. 2011).

§ 3. RES IPSA LOQUITUR IN MEDICAL MALPRACTICE CASES

YBARRA V. SPANGARD
154 P.2d 687 (Cal. 1944)

GIBSON, CHIEF JUSTICE.

This is an action for damages for personal injuries alleged to have been inflicted on plaintiff by defendants during the course of a surgical operation. The trial court entered judgments of nonsuit as to all defendants and plaintiff appealed.

On October 28, 1939, plaintiff consulted from Dr. Tilley, who diagnosed his ailment as appendicitis, and made arrangements for an appendectomy to be performed by defendant Dr. Spangard at a hospital owned and managed by defendant Dr. Swift. Plaintiff entered the hospital, was given a hypodermic injection, slept, and later was awakened by Drs. Tilley and Spangard and wheeled into the operating room by a nurse whom he believed to be defendant Gisler, an employee of Dr. Swift. Defendant Dr. Reser, the anesthetist, also an employee of Dr. Swift, adjusted plaintiff for the operation, pulling his body to the head of the operating table and, according to plaintiff's testimony, laying him back against two hard objects at the top of his shoulders, about an inch below his neck. Dr. Reser then administered the anesthetic and plaintiff lost consciousness. When he awoke early the following morning he was in his hospital room attended by defendant Thompson, the special nurse, and another nurse who was not made a defendant.

Plaintiff testified that prior to the operation he had never had any pain in, or injury to, his right arm or shoulder, but that when he awakened he felt a sharp pain about half way between the neck and the point of the right shoulder. He complained to the nurse, and then to Dr. Tilley, who gave him diathermy treatments while he remained in the hospital. The pain did not cease but spread down to the lower part of his arm, and after his release from the hospital the condition grew worse. He was unable to rotate or lift his arm, and developed paralysis and atrophy of the muscles around the shoulder. He received further treatments from Dr. Tilley until March, 1940, and then returned to work, wearing his arm in a splint on the advice of Dr. Spangard.

[Medical evidence for the plaintiff established that his problem resulted from some trauma, pressure or strain applied between his shoulder and neck.]

Plaintiff's theory is that the foregoing evidence presents a proper case for the application of the doctrine of *res ipsa loquitur*, and that the inference of negligence arising therefrom makes the granting of a nonsuit improper. Defendants take the position that, assuming that plaintiff's condition was in fact the result of an injury, there is no showing that the act of any particular defendant, nor any particular instrumentality, was the cause thereof. . . .

The present case is of a type which comes within the reason and spirit of the doctrine more fully perhaps than any other. The passenger sitting awake in a railroad car at the time of a collision, the pedestrian walking along the street and struck by a falling object or the debris of an explosion, are surely not more entitled to an explanation than the unconscious patient on the operating table. Viewed from this aspect, it is difficult to see how the doctrine can, with any justification, be so restricted in its statement as to become inapplicable to a patient who submits himself to the care and custody of doctors and nurses, is rendered unconscious, and receives some injury from instrumentalities used in his treatment. Without the aid of the doctrine a patient who received permanent injuries of a serious character, obviously the result of someone's negligence, would be entirely unable to recover unless the doctors and nurses in attendance voluntarily chose to disclose the identity of the negligent person and the facts establishing liability. If this were the state of the law of negligence, the courts, to avoid gross injustice, would be forced to invoke the principles of absolute liability, irrespective of negligence, in actions by persons suffering injuries during the course of treatment under anesthesia. But we think this juncture has not yet been reached, and that the doctrine of *res ipsa loquitur* is properly applicable to the case before us. . . .

The argument of defendants is simply that plaintiff has not shown an injury caused by an instrumentality under a defendant's control, because he has not shown which of the several instrumentalities that he came in contact with while in the hospital caused the injury; and he has not shown that any one defendant or his servants had exclusive control over any particular instrumentality. Defendants assert that some of them were not the employees of other defendants, that some did not stand in any permanent relationship from which liability in tort would follow, and that in view of the nature of the injury, the number of defendants and the different functions performed by each, they could not all be liable for the wrong, if any.

We have no doubt that in a modern hospital a patient is likely to come under the care of a number of persons in different types of contractual and other relationships with each other. For example, in the present case it appears that Drs. Swift, Spangard and Tilley were physicians or surgeons commonly placed in the legal category of independent contractors; and Dr. Reser, the anesthetist, and defendant Thompson, the special nurse, were employees of Dr. Swift and not of the other doctors. But we do not believe that either the number or relationship of the defendants alone determines whether the doctrine of *res ipsa loquitur* applies. Every defendant in whose custody the plaintiff was placed for any period was bound to exercise ordinary care to see that no unnecessary harm came to him and each would be liable for failure in this regard. Any defendant who negligently injured him, and any defendant charged with his care who so neglected him as to allow injury to occur, would be liable. The defendant employers would be liable for the neglect of their employees; and the doctor in charge of the operation would be liable for the negligence of those who became his temporary servants for the purpose of assisting in the operation.

In this connection, it should be noted that while the assisting physicians and nurses may be employed by the hospital, or engaged by the patient, they normally become the temporary servants or agents of the surgeon in charge while the operation is in progress, and liability may be imposed upon him for their negligent acts under the doctrine of respondeat superior. Thus a surgeon has been held liable for the negligence of an assisting nurse who leaves a sponge or other object inside a patient, and the fact that the duty of seeing that such mistakes do not occur is delegated to others does not absolve the doctor from responsibility for their negligence.

It may appear at the trial that, consistent with the principles outlined above, one or more defendants will be found liable and others absolved, but this should not preclude the application of the rule of *res ipsa loquitur*. The control at one time or another, of one or more of the various agencies or instrumentalities which might have harmed the plaintiff was in the hands of every defendant or of his employees or temporary servants. This, we think, places upon them the burden of initial explanation. Plaintiff was rendered unconscious for the purpose of undergoing surgical treatment by the defendants; it is manifestly unreasonable for them to insist that he identify any one of them as the person who did the alleged negligent act.

The other aspect of the case which defendants so strongly emphasize is that plaintiff has not identified the instrumentality any more than he has the particular guilty defendant. Here, again, there is a misconception which, if carried to the extreme for which defendants contend, would unreasonably limit the application of the *res ipsa loquitur* rule. It should be enough that the plaintiff can show an injury resulting from an external force applied while he lay unconscious in the hospital; this is as clear a case of identification of the instrumentality as the plaintiff may ever be able to make.

An examination of the recent cases, particularly in this state, discloses that the test of actual exclusive control of an instrumentality has not been strictly followed, but exceptions have been recognized where the purpose of the doctrine of *res ipsa loquitur* would otherwise be defeated. Thus, the test has become one of right of control rather than actual control. In the bursting bottle cases where the bottler has delivered the instrumentality to a retailer and thus has given up actual control, he will nevertheless be subject to the doctrine where it is shown that no change in the condition of the bottle occurred after it left the bottler's possession, and it can accordingly be said that he was in constructive control. Escola v. Coca Cola Bottling Co., 24 Cal.2d [453], 150 P.2d 436. . . .

In the face of these examples of liberalization of the tests for *res ipsa loquitur*, there can be no justification for the rejection of the doctrine in the instant case. . . .

We do not at this time undertake to state the extent to which the reasoning of this case may be applied to other situations in which the doctrine of *res ipsa loquitur* is invoked. We merely hold that where a plaintiff receives unusual injuries while unconscious and in the course of medical treatment, all those defendants who had any control over his body or the instrumentalities which might have caused the injuries may properly be called upon to meet the inference of negligence by giving an explanation of their conduct.

The judgment is reversed.

NOTES

1.   **Exclusive control.** A few courts continue to apply the "exclusive control" test of res ipsa loquitur stringently. *See, e.g., James v. Wormuth*, 997 N.E.2d 133 (N.Y. 2013) (res ipsa requirements not met where surgeon was not in exclusive control of a wire that dislodged in patient's body during surgery, "because several other individuals participated to an extent in the medical procedure," and plaintiff produced insufficient evidence to eliminate all explanations for the injury, other than defendant's negligence). However, a greater number of courts, in accord with *Ybarra* and both the Second and Third Restatements, have held that "exclusive control" is no longer a strict

requirement in res ipsa cases, no matter the context. *See, e.g., Kelly v. Hartford Cas. Ins. Co.*, 271 N.W.2d 676 (Wis. 1978); *Giles v. City of New Haven*, 636 A.2d 1335 (Conn. 1994).

2. **Likelihood that defendant caused the harm.** Courts sometimes hold that during the course of a medical operation, the surgeon is "captain of the ship" and becomes responsible for the negligence of all those who are under his immediate control, typically hospital employees such as nurses. *O'Connell v. Biomet, Inc.*, 250 P.3d 1278 (Colo. App. 2010) (captain of the ship doctrine "includes nonmedical persons present in the operating room upon the request and authorization of the physician, where the physician has the right to control and supervise the activities of the nonmedical persons;" sales agent for manufacturer of medical device, in the operating room to supply information about the device being used on a patient, was agent of the physician and consequently released when physician and his agents were released). Can it be said in *Ybarra* that any particular defendant is more likely than not the person whose negligence caused the harm? Then how can res ipsa loquitur apply at all? A number of courts have declined to follow the *Ybarra* approach for that reason.

STATES V. LOURDES HOSPITAL
792 N.E.2d 151 (N.Y. 2003)

CIPARICK, J.

[States underwent surgery for removal of an ovarian cyst. In this medical malpractice suit, she claims that during the operation the anesthesiologist negligently hyperabducted her right arm beyond a 90-degree angle for an extended period of time, causing right thoracic outlet syndrome and reflex sympathetic dystrophy. This court has previously determined that res ipsa loquitur is available in simple medical malpractice cases which require no expert. In this case, we are called upon to answer "whether expert testimony can be used to educate the jury as to the likelihood that the occurrence would take place without negligence where a basis of common knowledge is lacking."]

At the close of discovery, defendant moved for summary judgment on the ground that there was no direct evidence that the plaintiff's arm was hyperabducted during surgery and no evidence of any other negligence. Conceding the absence of direct evidence of negligence, plaintiff opposed the motion, submitting expert medical opinion that her injuries would not have occurred in the absence of negligence. Plaintiff claimed this testimony could be used by a jury in support of a res ipsa loquitur theory.

[The trial court denied defendant's motion for summary judgment and permitted plaintiff to rely on the expert medical opinion to support the conclusion that the injury would not have occurred in the absence of negligence. A divided Appellate Division reversed, and this appeal followed.]

Under appropriate circumstances, the evidentiary doctrine of res ipsa loquitur may be invoked to allow the factfinder to infer negligence from the mere happening of an event. Res ipsa loquitur, a doctrine of ancient origin (*see Byrne v. Boadle,* 2 H & C 722, 159 Eng. Rep. 299 [1863]), derives from the understanding that some events ordinarily do not occur in the absence of negligence. . . .

Defendant contends that res ipsa loquitur cannot apply here because, in order to establish the first prerequisite—that the occurrence would not take place in the absence of negligence—plaintiff must rely on expert medical opinion, and the doctrinal foundation of res ipsa loquitur can only lie in everyday experience. Therefore, when expert testimony is necessary to provide the basis for concluding that the event would not occur in the absence of negligence, the matter is outside the ken of a layperson and res ipsa loquitur is inapplicable.

In the circumstances presented, we conclude that expert testimony may be properly used to help the jury "bridge the gap" between its own common knowledge, which does not encompass the specialized knowledge and experience necessary to reach a conclusion that the occurrence would not normally take place in the absence of negligence, and the common knowledge of physicians, which does. . . .

In an increasingly sophisticated and specialized society such as ours, it is not at all surprising that matters entirely foreign to the general population are commonplace within a particular profession or specially trained segment of society. . . .

Notwithstanding the availability of expert testimony to aid a jury in determining whether an event would normally occur in the absence of negligence, expert opinion of course does not negate the jury's ultimate responsibility as finder of fact to draw that necessary conclusion. The purpose of expert opinion in this context is to educate the jury, enlarging its understanding of the fact issues it must decide. However, the jury remains free to determine whether its newly-enlarged understanding supports the conclusion it is asked to accept. . . .

Applying the foregoing principles to the facts of this case, we conclude that defendant's motion for summary judgment was properly denied by Supreme Court. The jury should be allowed to hear from plaintiff's experts in order to determine whether this injury would normally occur in the absence of negligence. Likewise, defendant must be given an opportunity to rebut the assertion with competent expert evidence to show, for example, that the injury complained of is an inherent risk of the procedure and not totally preventable with the exercise of reasonable care. . . .

NOTES

1. **Common knowledge.** The normal basis for medical res ipsa loquitur is that, as a matter of common knowledge, the plaintiff's injury is more likely than not to have resulted from negligence. The clearest cases are those in which instruments or towels are left in the patient's abdomen after surgery and those in which injury is inflicted upon a part of the body not being treated. *See, e.g., Cummings v. Barber*, 460 P.3d 963 (Nev. 2020) (res ipsa applies where foreign object is left in patient's body). But the instruction is given in other medical contexts as well. "It is within the common knowledge and experience of a layperson to determine that an individual does not enter the hospital for gallbladder surgery and come out of surgery with an ulnar nerve injury to the left arm." *Wick v. Henderson*, 485 N.W.2d 645 (Iowa 1992). Another case decided along similar lines is *Szydel v. Markman*, 117 P.3d 200 (Nev. 2005). There the plaintiff sued on a res ipsa theory over a needle left inside her left breast after a breast lift. The court found that the allegations fit within the common-knowledge exception and thus no expert was required. Similarly, in *Quinby v. Plumsteadville Family Practice, Inc.*, 907 A.2d 1061 (Pa. 2006), a quadriplegic patient who was left unattended on an examining table fell and sustained injuries which ultimately lead to his death. The court held that the res ipsa question did not require expert testimony because "Defendants' positioning and securing of Decedent, a quadriplegic, on an examination table," was "a non-complex medical scenario."

2. **Expert testimony.** Yet expert testimony is "frequently necessary" in a medical malpractice case brought on a res ipsa theory. RESTATEMENT (THIRD) OF TORTS: LIABILITY FOR PHYSICAL AND EMOTIONAL HARM § 17 cmt. c (2010); *see also St. Mary's Ohio Valley Heart Care, LLC v. Smith*, 112 N.E.3d 1144 (Ind. Ct. App. 2018) (patient could not establish res ipsa against surgeon without expert testimony because jury lacked the expertise to understand the procedures at issue). As indicated in *States*, expert testimony can be used in most jurisdictions to fill the role of common knowledge. *See Lageman ex rel. Lageman v. Zepp*, 237 A.3d 1098 (Pa. Super. 2020) (plaintiff entitled to jury instruction on res ipsa even where expert testifies about specific negligence). An expert who cannot pinpoint negligence can nevertheless testify that the injury is one that, in the common knowledge of experts, is likely to occur only because of negligence. *See Seavers v. Methodist Med. Ctr. of Oak Ridge*, 9 S.W.3d 86 (Tenn. 1999). In medical malpractice res ipsa loquitur cases, New Jersey requires the expert to testify, not to his opinion of probability, but that the medical community itself recognizes the probability of negligence under the given facts. *See Khan v. Singh*, 975 A.2d 389 (N.J. 2009) (applying the rule to hold that experts had not laid a foundation for testifying on that issue).

REFERENCES: DOBBS, HAYDEN & BUBLICK, HORNBOOK ON TORTS §§ 13.3–13.7 (res ipsa loquitur generally) (2d ed. 2016); 2 DOBBS, HAYDEN & BUBLICK, THE LAW OF TORTS §§ 305–306 (2d ed. 2011).

§ 4. STATUTORY REFORMS

A. THE MEDICAL MALPRACTICE "CRISIS"

The Institute of Medicine (IOM), in a respected and comprehensive study of medical errors, estimated that at least 44,000 and perhaps as many as 98,000 people die each year in hospitals as a result of preventable medical errors. The IOM concluded that more people die from medical errors than from motor vehicle accidents, breast cancer or AIDS. Common errors include adverse drug events, wrong-site surgery, and mistaken patient identities. To illustrate these problems, the study mentioned a patient who died of a chemotherapy overdose, another who had the wrong leg amputated, and another, a child, who died during minor surgery because of a drug mix-up. The IOM estimated the total cost of preventable medical errors (including the expense of additional care necessitated by the errors, lost income and household productivity, and disability) at between $17 billion and $29 billion per year. According to the IOM, the know-how already exists to prevent many of these mistakes. Consequently, it set a strategy to significantly reduce these errors. *See* INSTITUTE OF MEDICINE, TO ERR IS HUMAN: BUILDING A SAFER HEALTHY SYSTEM (2000). In a follow-up article, *Five Years After To Err is Human: What Have We Learned?*, the authors noted that there have been some narrow improvements in safety, but the progress is marginal and has not impacted the national statistics. However, there may be a recent trend towards voluntary disclosure of medical errors by health-care providers themselves. *See* Joanna C. Schwartz, *A Dose of Reality for Medical Malpractice Reform*, 88 N.Y.U. L. REV. 1224 (2013).

Despite the large number of medical errors, there has been a public outcry against medical malpractice litigation. Medical costs have increased enormously in the last generation. The cost of insurance for doctors has also increased. In some instances and in some years it has been difficult for doctors to procure liability insurance. *Five Years After To Err is Human* suggested insurance policies typically do not subsidize newer, safer equipment. However, if insurance is already unaffordable for some, will anyone be willing to pay the extra cost to reduce medical errors?

On the increased insurance costs, some people have pointed the finger at lawyers: costs go up and insurance becomes expensive or impossible to get because greedy lawyers bring too many malpractice suits (and courts permit judgments against doctors). This kind of talk can be misleading for several reasons:

(1) Existing empirical evidence does not support claims that medical malpractice payouts are increasing significantly, let alone increasing at a staggering rate. For example, several studies looked at all settled and litigated medical malpractice claims in Texas during a time of "crisis."

Although insurance premium costs had gone up dramatically during the time period, the costs of paid and settled malpractice claims remained largely stable. Bernard Black, Charles Silver, David A. Hyman & William M. Sage, *Stability, Not Crisis: Medical Malpractice Claims Outcomes in Texas, 1998–2002*, 2 J. EMPIRICAL LEGAL STUD. 207, 210 (2005). Moreover, headlines about large jury awards may be misleading because the vast majority of verdicts are not paid at their full value. In Texas, 75% of plaintiffs who received jury awards over $25,000 received payouts of less than their full award, with mean reductions of 29%. As the value of the award increased, so did the percentage reduction. For plaintiffs whose award was valued at over 2.5 million dollars, 98% received a reduced award with an average cut of 56%. *See* David A. Hyman, et al., *Do Defendants Pay What Juries Award? Post-Verdict Haircuts in Texas Medical Malpractice Cases, 1988–2003*, 4 J. EMPIRICAL. LEG. STUD. 3 (2007). Insurance policy limits act as an effective cap on recovery. In a study of 9,389 closed claims, 98.5% were resolved with payments at or below policy limits. In the few instances in which doctors did draw on their own assets, their personal contributions were relatively small, with only 10 of those contributions exceeding $300,000. For more comprehensive analysis, *see* Kathryn Zeiler, et al., *Physicians' Insurance Limits and Malpractice Payments: Evidence from Texas Closed Claims, 1990–2003*, 36 J. LEGAL STUD. 9 (2007).

(2) The concern that doctors are particularly vulnerable defendants has not been borne out by empirical data. At least in some locales, plaintiffs prevail against medical doctors in only about one in five claims submitted to a jury. *See* Deborah Jones Merritt & Kathryn Ann Barry, *Is the Tort System in Crisis? New Empirical Evidence*, 60 OHIO ST. L.J. 315, 358 (1999). Also, a study of medical malpractice claims suggests that weak claims are not being paid. A study of over 1400 closed claims concluded that medical errors in fact existed in about 60% of the claims. Most of the claims that did *not* involve medical error by the investigators were *not* paid. David M. Studdert, et al., *Claims, Errors, and Compensation Payments in Medical Malpractice Litigation*, 354 NEW ENG. J. MED. 2024 (2006). Reviewing a large number of studies, one scholar concluded, "Plaintiffs who received substandard care generally obtained compensation; plaintiffs who received proper care generally did not; and plaintiffs whose care quality was uncertain wound up in between." *See* David A. Hyman & Charles Silver, *Medical Malpractice Litigation and Tort Reform: It's the Incentives Stupid*, 59 VAND. L. REV. 1085, 1097 (2006).

(3) As to increases in insurance costs, this has been partly a result of investment cycles. Insurers invest premium monies until they are needed to make payouts under the policy. These investments produce large incomes that help make the payments required by the policy. When investment income is down, premium income must go up if the insurer is to pay. So to some extent, the insurer and the insured are subject to the

fluctuations of the market, and increased costs to the doctors reflect this as well as other factors. But premium increases were less than the increase of doctors' incomes. *See* BARRY R. FURROW, THOMAS L. GREANEY, SANDRA H. JOHNSON, TIMOTHY S. JOST & ROBERT L. SCHWARTZ, HEALTH LAW (3d ed. 2014).

(4) Costs of medical treatment have gone up for a number of reasons not associated with lawsuits. These include the costs of new equipment, buildings, and increased technology and an increase in the pool of elderly. In addition, an increase in the pool of patients who do not pay for services may add to costs, which must be borne by other patients or public funds.

B. LEGISLATIVE RESPONSES

The medical profession had sought favorable legislation before the insurance crisis—the Good Samaritan statutes, for example—but the insurance problem prompted even more demands for special rules. In at least two different crises, many states passed statutes attempting to relieve the insurance problem for health care providers, either directly or indirectly. Indirectly, some provisions attempt to facilitate insurance coverage. The exact package of provisions directly impacting tort law varies from state to state, but most states have adopted one or more of the kinds of provisions listed below.

(1) *Substantive Changes:*

(a) The plaintiff must prove actual negligence, or, more explicitly, res ipsa loquitur may not be used against a health care provider, or may not be used in traditional cases.

(b) The standard of care must be local or statewide, not national.

(c) Statutes of repose and statutes of limitation have an absolute outside limit even when the patient cannot discover the negligence for many years.

(d) No malpractice claim may be based on a contract unless the contract is in writing.

(e) Informed consent claims are limited or discouraged.

(2) *Remedial Changes:*

(a) State statutes limit damages and many include absolute caps on noneconomic damages or total recovery.

(b) Joint and several liability is limited.

(c) Amounts received from other collateral sources such as health and disability insurance may be deducted from the defendant's award.

(d) Periodic payment plans are provided for large damage awards.

(e) Limits on the attorney's fees that can be collected in a successful suit.

(3) *Procedural Changes:*

(a) Statutes strictly limit experts who can testify.

(b) The plaintiff is required to get a certificate of merit—an affidavit at the beginning of the suit certifying that a qualified medical expert believes there are reasonable grounds for the suit.

(c) Statutes of limitation are shortened and statutes of repose are initiated.

(d) Plaintiff is required to submit her claims to pretrial arbitration or screening panels before suing.

(e) Contracts between patient and medical provider may be permitted to require arbitration in lieu of tort claims.

(f) Plaintiff must give notice of intent to sue and then cannot bring suit for a waiting period after that, with complex effects on the statute of limitations.

A particularly thoughtful article discussing some of these reforms is Michelle M. Mello & Allen Kachalia, *Evaluation of Options for Medical Malpractice System Reform: A Report to the Medicare Payment Advisory Commission* (2010). The article also outlines more "innovative reforms" which have not necessarily been adopted yet by any state. These reforms include a schedule of noneconomic damages, health courts, disclosure-and-offer programs, safe harbors for adherence to evidence-based practice guidelines, subsidized, conditional reinsurance, and enterprise medical liability.

What injuries fall under the statutes? Not all claims that occur in a health care setting are medical malpractice claims that garner the special statutory protections. A failure of a hospital's life support systems resulting from a power outage in the aftermath of Hurricane Katrina was not a medical malpractice claim, and thus not subject to the statutory restrictions. *LaCoste v. Pendleton Methodist Hosp., LLC*, 966 So.2d 519 (La. 2007). Nor was a lab's wrongful disclosure of plaintiff's HIV test results. *Doe 163 v. Quest Diagnostics, Inc.*, 395 S.W.3d 8 (Mo. 2013). Nor was a failure to protect the patient from fire. *Cf. Taylor v. Vencor, Inc.*, 525 S.E.2d 201 (N.C. 2000).

Determining whether a particular claim falls within special statutes depends upon the wording of the statute and the court's own conception of policy. In *Rome v. Flower Memorial Hospital*, 635 N.E.2d 1239 (Ohio 1994), the court found injuries covered by the medical malpractice statute when the plaintiff, allegedly improperly secured to a tilting radiology table, slipped off and injured her head when the table was tipped up. This was medical malpractice because it was "ancillary" to an X-ray procedure that was medical in nature. The same result obtained in *Marks v. St. Luke's Episcopal Hosp.*, 319 S.W.3d 658 (Tex. 2010). In that case, plaintiff was injured after falling from his hospital bed after its footboard allegedly collapsed when he stepped on it. On review, the Texas Supreme Court held plaintiff's suit was properly labeled as a health care liability claim because the bed can be considered "medical equipment" and thus is "an integral and inseparable part of the health care services provided." In *Coming Attractions Bridal & Formal, Inc. v. Texas Health Resources*, 595 S.W.3d 659 (Tex. 2020), the same court held that a claim by the owner of a bridal shop, alleging that a hospital negligently failed to prevent the transmission of the Ebola virus and caused the shop to close due to health concern, fell within the state medical malpractice statute because the claim had a "nexus to health care." And in *Dupuy v. NMC Operating Co.*, 187 So.3d 436 (La. 2016), a patient's claim that the hospital failed to maintain and service equipment used to sterilize surgical instruments was held to fall within the special statutes requiring pre-suit presentation to a medical review panel because the claim was "treatment related."

C. STATE CONSTITUTIONAL CHALLENGES TO STATUTORY REFORM

Plaintiffs can challenge medical malpractice statutes, like other tort reform legislation, under state constitutional guarantees. Statutes impeding medical malpractice claims have been challenged under state constitutional "open access to courts" provisions. In *Zeier v. Zimmer, Inc.*, 152 P.3d 861 (Okla. 2006), the Oklahoma Supreme Court examined a state statute which required plaintiffs filing medical malpractice actions to file a certificate of merit—an affidavit attesting that a qualified expert had been consulted and had issued an opinion sufficient to deem the claim meritorious. The court held that the affidavit requirement, which front-loaded litigation costs and disproportionately reduced claims by low-income litigants, was a monetary barrier to suit that violated state constitutional guarantees of open access to the courts. The affidavit requirement also violated the state constitutional prohibition against special laws. In this case the unlawful differential treatment was between victims alleging negligence generally and victims alleging medical negligence. The Oklahoma legislature amended the law, but it was struck down as unconstitutional again, on the same grounds, in *Wall v. Marouk*, 302 P.3d 775 (Okla. 2013). Four years later the pattern repeated, with the court striking down the legislature's third attempt to amend the law. *John v. St. Francis Hosp., Inc.*, 405 P.3d 681 (Okla. 2017). *See also Poutman v. Wenatchee Valley Medical Center, P.S.*, 216 P.3d 374 (Wash. 2009) (striking down on constitutional grounds a statutory requirement that a patient obtain a certificate of merit from a panel before filing suit).

Under another state constitutional clause, the "right to a remedy" clause, the Oregon Supreme Court struck down a statutory cap on damage awards. In *Clarke v. Oregon Health Sciences University*, 175 P.3d 418 (Or. 2007), the plaintiff, a minor patient who was deprived of oxygen after heart surgery, challenged two statutes that together greatly diminished her recovery. One statute capped recovery from a public entity and the other required substitution of the public entity, not its employees, as the sole defendant. Estimates of the economic damages for plaintiff's lifetime exceeded $12 million. Yet under the statutes, the maximum award available was $200,000. The court held that the statute confining claims against the public entity to $200,000 was constitutional with respect to the public entity, which would have been entitled to sovereign immunity at common law. However, the elimination of a cause of action against public employees or agents violates the remedy clause because the substituted remedy against the public body "is an emasculated version of the remedy that was available at common law."

However, some courts have been more cautious about striking down state statutes. For example, a number of courts have upheld caps on noneconomic damages in medical malpractice cases. *See, e.g., Ordinola v. University Physician Assocs.*, 625 S.W.3d 445 (Mo. 2021). In another case, *Ledbetter v. Hunter,* 842 N.E.2d 810 (Ind. 2006), the plaintiff raised a statutory challenge under the state constitution's privileges and immunities clause. Under this provision, the state legislature could not "grant to any citizen, or class of citizens, privileges or immunities, which, upon the same terms, shall not equally belong to all citizens." The statute challenged in *Ledbetter* required minors injured by medical malpractice before age six to file suit within two years of an injury or by their eighth birthday at the latest. Plaintiff contended that the legislation unconstitutionally subjected to differential treatment two classes of minors—those injured by medical negligence and those injured by other types of negligence.

However, the *Ledbetter* court held that the differentiation could be justified based on the legislature's rationale for the legislation—that it *could* prevent a reduction in health care services. This rationale was valid even though "neither the insurance carriers nor the health care associations could produce a single document showing that a change in the disability provision for minors in medical malpractice cases would have any adverse effect on the cost of insurance, the availability of health care services, or the ability to defend malpractice claims." The court left the matter to the legislature, suggesting that the lack of evidence "may well provide powerful support for legislative reconsideration of the challenged minor limitation period." *But cf. Schroeder v. Weighall*, 316 P.3d 482

(Wash. 2014) (striking down statute eliminating general tolling of minor's claims in medical malpractice cases, on the ground that it violated state constitutional prohibition against special privileges and immunities; defendant's assertion that medical malpractice claims by minors raised malpractice insurance rates was "speculative," and thus not a reasonable ground to support the statute).

D. EMTALA CLAIMS: MANDATORY EMERGENCY TREATMENT AND SCREENING

42 U.S.C.A. § 1395dd

§ 1395dd. Examination and treatment for emergency medical conditions and women in labor.

(a) Medical screening requirement

In the case of a hospital that has a hospital emergency department, if any individual (whether or not eligible for benefits under this subchapter) comes to the emergency department and a request is made on the individual's behalf for examination or treatment for a medical condition, the hospital must provide for an appropriate medical screening examination within the capability of the hospital's emergency department, including ancillary services routinely available to the emergency department, to determine whether or not an emergency medical condition . . . exists.

(b) Necessary stabilizing treatment for emergency medical conditions and labor

    (1) In general

If any individual (whether or not eligible for benefits under this subchapter) comes to a hospital and the hospital determines that the individual has an emergency medical condition, the hospital must provide either—

    (A) within the staff and facilities available at the hospital, for such further medical examination and such treatment as may be required to stabilize the medical condition, or

    (B) for transfer of the individual to another medical facility in accordance with subsection (c) of this section. . . .

(c) Restricting transfers until individual stabilized

    (1) Rule

If an individual at a hospital has an emergency medical condition which has not been stabilized . . . the hospital may not transfer the individual unless—

(A)(i) the individual (or a legally responsible person acting on the individual's behalf) after being informed of the hospital's obligations under this section and of the risk of transfer, in writing requests transfer to another medical facility,

(ii) a physician (within the meaning of section 1395x(r)(1) of this title) has signed a certification that based upon the information available at the time of transfer, the medical benefits reasonably expected from the provision of appropriate medical treatment at another medical facility outweigh the increased risks to the individual and, in the case of labor, to the unborn child from effecting the transfer . . . and

(B) the transfer is an appropriate transfer (within the meaning of paragraph (2)) to that facility. . . .

NOTES

1.   **Physician liability?** Note that the statute provides for liability of hospitals only, not physicians. *See Moses v. Providence Hosp. & Med. Ctrs., Inc.*, 561 F.3d 573 (6th Cir. 2009). Physicians are, however, subject to civil money penalties for negligently violating the statute.

2.   **Private right of action.** Must the violation of the statute be a cause of the plaintiff's harm? Subsection (d) of the statute provides that "Any individual who suffers personal harm as a direct result of a participating hospital's violation of a requirement of this section may, in a civil action against the participating hospital, obtain those damages available for personal injury under the law of the State in which the hospital is located, and such equitable relief as is appropriate."

3.   **Labor.** The statute treats childbirth and labor as an emergency. An earlier version of the statute used the phrase "active labor" instead of "labor," which gave rise to its popular name, the Emergency Medical Treatment and Active Labor Act (EMTALA).

4.   **Screening and treatment duties.** Notice the curious shift in the statutory "comes to" language. In subsection (a), which sets up the screening requirement, the statute speaks of an individual who "comes to the emergency department." But in subsection (b), which sets up the treatment and stabilization requirement, the statute speaks of an individual who "comes to a hospital." The Ninth Circuit examined the "comes to the hospital" requirement in *Arrington v. Wong*, 237 F.3d 1066 (9th Cir. 2001). In that case, an ambulance transporting a heart attack patient received direction from the hospital to take the patient to a different hospital, five miles away. On an appeal that considered the EMTALA claim, the court grappled with the ambiguous statutory language. In considering at which point a hospital becomes obligated to screen and stabilize a patient, the court ultimately deferred to the Department of Health and Human Services, which interprets the statute to include all hospital property. In addition, the non-hospital owned ambulance

was covered by EMTALA because of a regulation that a hospital may not deny emergency vehicles hospital access unless the hospital "is in diversionary status." Next step: suppose that the plaintiff comes to the hospital for an emergency that requires screening, which the hospital provides. It then admits the patient to the hospital as a regular in-patient. Would the hospital's duty to stabilize be terminated once the patient has been admitted?

LEWELLEN V. SCHNECK MEDICAL CENTER, 2007 WL 2363384 (S.D. Ind. 2007). Plaintiff Kevin Lewellen is a registered nurse anesthetist in Paris, Tennessee, who drank while driving on a roughly 350 mile journey. His car left the road, rolled once, and ended up in a ditch. Lewellen was assessed at the hospital and x-rays of his lumbar and cervical spine were taken to determine whether Lewellen had fractured his back in the accident. The quality of the x-rays was poor. More were taken. Before the last of Lewellen's x-rays had even printed, at 4:07 p.m., the doctor discharged him. Lewellen refused to sign the consent to discharge, pleaded with the nurse that he was in tremendous pain and begged to talk to the doctor. Trooper Drew, who accompanied Lewellen at the hospital, asked Nurse Davis if the hospital was really done examining him. Nurse Davis responded that Lewellen was fine, he was just drunk. Lewellen was in too much pain to stand or walk. Drew explained to Lewellen that once the hospital had discharged him he had no choice but to transport Lewellen to jail. His second x-rays were read as he was being discharged, and the doctor concluded they were fine. A second reading of the x-rays two hours later states that a fracture "cannot be completely excluded" because the lateral view of the lumber spine was not clear enough to be useful. The doctor who reread the x-ray contacted no one.

It turned out that Lewellen had a burst fracture in his spine that was damaging his spinal nerves while he was being held in the Jackson County Jail. An officer who saw Lewellen crying in pain called the hospital, whose employees repeatedly told the officer not to bring Lewellen back to the hospital. However, the officer persisted and had an ambulance bring Lewellen back.

At 1:00 a.m., a repeat CT scan of his spine revealed that during the night Lewellen spent in jail, a fragment of bone from the burst fracture had displaced and was impinging on his spinal column. Despite an operation, Lewellen suffered from permanent neurological defects including incontinence and sexual dysfunction as a result of this injury. Dr. Schwartz [the surgeon] believes that had Lewellen been properly treated on June 8, 2003, instead of discharged, he "more likely than not would have remained neurologically intact."

Plaintiff sued Schneck under the Emergency Medical Treatment and Active Labor Act ("EMTALA"). Schneck argues that it should receive summary judgment. *Held,* summary judgment denied. "[A] hospital satisfies EMTALA's 'appropriate medical screening' requirement if it provides a patient with an examination comparable to the one offered to other patients presenting similar symptoms, unless the examination is so cursory that it is not 'designed to identify acute and severe symptoms that alert the physician of the need for immediate medical attention to prevent serious bodily injury.'. . .

"Plaintiff presented no evidence that the screen performed on him differed from any other patient's screen. However, a reasonable jury could conclude that the screen performed was so cursory that it was not designed to identify acute and severe symptoms and thus did not meet the requirements of EMTALA. . . . A jury could conclude that either Dr. Reisert did not even bother to look at [the x-rays] or looked at them so casually that he missed what two other physicians said was obvious: that the x-rays demonstrate that Lewellen had a burst fraction in his spine. . . . Lewellen's stay at the hospital was alarmingly brief considering he was in a motor vehicle accident and complaining of severe back pain so bad he could not stand or sit in a chair correctly. Lewellen still had a bleeding gash in his arm with grass and dirt in it when he arrived at prison. . . . [T]his scenario is so grave that a jury could conclude that . . . the screening requirement was simply not met."

NOTES

1. **Screening.** *Lewellen* notes that "EMTALA is not a national medical malpractice statute imposing a standard of care on hospital emergency rooms." However, the case in effect imposes some standard of care, doesn't it? What screening is "appropriate?" The statute itself does not say. Federal courts fear that tests based upon negligence would turn the statute into a federal medical malpractice statute. *See, e.g., Smith v. Crisp Regional Hosp., Inc.,* 985 F.3d 1306 (11th Cir. 2021). Consequently, many have held that "appropriate" screening means "evenhanded" screening—that "there be some screening procedure," and "that level of screening [is provided] uniformly to all those who present substantially similar complaints." *Cruz-Vazquez v. Mennonite General Hosp., Inc.,* 717 F.3d 63 (1st Cir. 2013).

2. **Treatment and stabilization.** In *Roberts v. Galen of Virginia, Inc.,* 525 U.S. 249 (1999), the Supreme Court said that liability may be imposed under the stabilization requirement even if the hospital had no bad motive, such as a motive to dump patients who had no insurance. The Court did not decide whether motive played a part in liability for screening failures. In *Estate of Lacko ex rel. Griswatch v. Mercy Hosp., Cadillac,* 829 F.Supp.2d 543 (E.D. Mich. 2011), a screening case, the court dismissed plaintiff's claim under EMTALA because plaintiff did not allege defendant had an improper motive.

3. **Coordinating with or trumping state law.** Could state-law limits on healthcare claims also limit EMTALA claims? In *Smith v. Richmond*

Memorial Hospital, 416 S.E.2d 689 (Va. 1992), the court said that the state law pre-suit notice of claim requirement had no application to suits brought under the federal EMTALA statute. But in *Hardy v. New York City Health & Hospitals Corp.*, 164 F.3d 789 (2d Cir. 1999), the court asserted that by authorizing damages measured by state law damages rules, EMTALA meant to exclude claims that would be barred altogether under state law because of the plaintiff's failure to give notice of claim within 90 days of the occurrence.

Would you distinguish the pre-suit notice requirement in *Hardy* from a state's statutory cap on damages for health care injury? In *Barris v. County of Los Angeles*, 972 P.2d 966 (Cal. 1999), the court applied the state's damages cap to an EMTALA claim.

Suppose that, under state law, a hospital is completely immune from all tort liability and therefore liable for zero damages. Would an EMTALA claim be barred? *Root v. New Liberty Hosp. Dist.*, 209 F.3d 1068 (8th Cir. 2000).

4. **Unpublished opinions.** The opinion in *Schneck* is an unpublished decision. Unpublished decisions are controlling authority to the parties in the litigation. However, in many jurisdictions they are of no precedential value to other cases. The rules about citing unpublished opinions are in flux and vary by jurisdiction. Most jurisdictions do not permit attorneys to cite these decisions as precedent in later cases. Some jurisdictions allow citation as long as a copy of the opinion is attached to the party's brief. A relatively new federal rule of appellate procedure—FED. R. APP. P. 32.1(a)—allows for citation to unpublished opinions issued on or after January 1, 2007. Why might a court issue an unpublished opinion? According to a standard note inserted in the *Schneck* case, the decision is unpublished because "the discussion [in the case] is not sufficiently novel to justify commercial publication." Should the *Schneck* decision have been published to be used as precedent in later suits alleging EMTALA violations based on inadequate screening? Over 75% of federal appellate court decisions are not published. Commentators have taken different views about whether the large volume of unpublished opinions is necessary for the smooth functioning of courts, or a worrisome problem of unaccountable precedent either on the whole or in particular cases which seem not to fit within the formal criteria for an unpublished decision. For an overview, see Stephen Wasby, *Publication (or Not) of Appellate Court Rulings: An Evaluation of Guidelines*, 2 SETON HALL CIR. REV. 41 (2005).

REFERENCE: DOBBS, HAYDEN & BUBLICK, HORNBOOK ON TORTS §§ 21.14 & 21.17 (2d ed. 2016).

§ 5. ELDER ABUSE IN NURSING HOMES AND OTHER CARE FACILITIES

HORIZON/CMS HEALTHCARE CORP. V. AULD, 985 S.W.2d 216 (Tex. App. 1999). Martha Hary, age 76, became a resident at the nursing home in August 1994. The complaint against the nursing home alleged that its care was substandard. Hary (referred to as "Martha" by the court) developed pressure sores, some described as Stage IV, where the tissue overlying a person's bone rots away and leaves the bone exposed. She also suffered contractures in all extremities. In August 1995, she was taken from the nursing home to Fort Worth's Osteopathic Hospital where she was treated for 10 days. After her discharge, she spent the remaining year of her life at a facility that is not a party to this suit. After hearing testimony about her care, the jury found that the nursing home's negligence proximately caused Martha's injury and awarded $1,750,000 for physical pain and mental anguish, $150,000 for disfigurement, $250,000 for impairment, and $221,000 for medical care. The jury also found gross negligence and awarded $90,000,000 as exemplary damages. On appeal, by statute, the court limited actual damages of $2,371,000 to $1,541,203.13 and capped punitive damages at four times the uncapped actual damages for a total of $9,483,766.92. Evidence of written investigation reports made by investigators for the Texas Department of Human Services were properly admitted at trial as certified copies of a record of a public agency which were relevant to defendant's subjective knowledge of the peril relevant to gross negligence.

On defendant's appeal from the compensatory damages award, *held,* affirmed. "From mid-December 1994 until she was taken from the nursing home on August 6, 1995. . . . Martha's body was not turned or repositioned during approximately 210 eight-hour shifts, totaling 1,680 hours. . . during the same period of months, Martha was not fed regularly and missed 238 meals . . . during the same period of months, Martha was not given incontinent care during approximately 216 eight-hour shifts, totaling 1,728 hours. . . . [T]he nursing home's current and past employees admitted that its records . . . accurately reflected these deficiencies. . . . [H]ospital personnel considered her condition to be terminal due to the pressure sores, contractures, infection, and malnutrition; that those conditions caused her to have to undergo painful treatments at the hospital; and the injuries she suffered while at the nursing home caused her severe physical pain, mental anguish, physical impairment, and physical disfigurement, which lasted until her death nearly a year after she left the nursing home. . . . The evidence is both legally and factually sufficient to support the jury's findings of damages for physical pain and mental anguish, disfigurement, and impairment."

NOTES

1. **Subsequent case history.** This case was affirmed in the Texas Supreme Court except on the issue of prejudgment interest, which the court held was capped by a statute. Horizon/CMS, the defendant in *Auld,* showed total operating revenues of $1,753,084,000 ($1.75 billion) in its 1996 annual report filed with the Securities and Exchange Commission. The punitive damages award was allowed to stand. *Horizon/CMS Healthcare Corp. v. Auld,*

34 S.W.3d 887 (Tex. 2000). Most nursing home claims are like other tort claims; nursing homes may be sued for negligence in the same way as hospitals. *Wilson v. Americare Systems, Inc.*, 397 S.W.3d 552 (Tenn. 2013) (failure to provide adequate nursing staffing at assisted-living facility was actionable as negligence).

2. **Abuse cases.** Elder abuse is distressingly common. A federally funded study indicates that around half a million elders are abused every year in their own homes, usually by their adult children or spouses. Abuse and neglect is hard to document because residents are often incompetent or too afraid to report it. Even when a resident or outsider reports deficiencies in care and injury, a tort action is often impractical. In the *Horizon/Auld* case, actual physical harm was discovered and Horizon's own records helped document its neglect. But in most cases, family members (if any) may not discover the harm or its cause. If a suit is brought, the patient may make a poor witness. Actual damages may be quite limited in many cases: the nursing home may have inflicted pain and misery, but its neglect does not deprive the resident of an active life; if the nursing home hastens death, it does not hasten it by very much. Lawyers can hardly afford to take cases that will require enormous investments of time to recover small damages, so many of these claims may be rejected by lawyers or possibly settled cheaply without suit. *See* 1 BARRY R. FURROW, ET AL., HEALTH LAW §§ 1–2 (2000). Independent claims by family members for emotional distress might help make up for these problems, but such claims are likely to be rejected under special rules that tend to limit emotional distress claims. *See Ess v. Eskaton Properties, Inc.*, 118 Cal.Rptr.2d 240 (Ct. App. 2002) (sister of nursing home victim was not "present" when victim was sexually attacked, no emotional distress claim). These circumstances make punitive damages especially important in nursing home cases—first to provide an appropriate level of deterrence, since ordinary damages may be small, and second to encourage lawyers to bring suits they could not afford to try without a fee based on punitive recoveries.

3. **Access to courts.** Nursing homes may include arbitration agreements in admission papers, requiring residents to forgo their right to seek redress through the courts. Some of these provisions have been held to be unenforceable on public policy grounds. *See, e.g., Shotts v. OP Winter Haven, Inc.*, 86 So.3d 456 (Fla. 2011). However, the Federal Arbitration Act may validate such agreements if the nursing home participates in interstate commerce. *See Marmet Health Care Center, Inc. v. Brown*, 565 U.S. 530 (2012) (reviewing and overturning a West Virginia Supreme Court ruling that had held mandatory arbitration clause unenforceable).

4. **Medical malpractice statutes.** If a victim's survivors manage to identify abuse and bring suit, does the medical standard of care control and do the medical malpractice reform statutes apply to present further obstacles to suit? At times that will be true. *See, e.g., Estate of Curtis v. South Las Vegas Medical Investors, LLC*, 466 P.3d 1263 (Nev. 2020) (allegation that nursing home staff failed to monitor resident after administering morphine was a professional negligence claim that required expert testimony); *Omaha*

Healthcare Center, LLC v. Johnson, 344 S.W.3d 392 (Tex. 2011) (claim of negligence when patient was bitten by a brown recluse spider and died in nursing home care should have been brought as a health care liability claim— "part of the fundamental patient care required of a nursing home is to protect the health and safety of the residents"). But not always. Suppose the nursing home does not provide adequate nutrition, doesn't provide the patient the pain medication prescribed by a doctor, or doesn't wash or clean a helpless patient. Is that a matter of health care as distinct from ordinary negligence? To answer that question the court must look to the relevant statute. *See, e.g., State ex rel. West Virginia Univ. Hospitals, Inc. v. Scott,* 866 S.E.2d 350 (W.Va. 2021) (applying new statutory provision that broadened the definition of "health care" to include claims relating to staffing and hospital policies).

5. **Res ipsa loquitur.** Since the nursing home has a large measure of control over the relatively helpless (sometimes totally helpless) resident, would res ipsa loquitur apply to establish negligence when the resident has bedsores? What if the resident suffers injury because she ingests the wrong medicine? *Harder v. F.C. Clinton, Inc.,* 948 P.2d 298 (Okla. 1997) (doctrine applied though defendant denied providing the medicine, which was not prescribed for the resident at all).

6. **Using regulations to prove a standard of care and/or breach.** Long-term care facilities like nursing homes are regulated both by state and federal law. CMS regulations can conceivably be put in evidence as standards to which the facility must conform. For example, one regulation provides that "Each resident must receive and the facility must provide the necessary care and services to attain or maintain the highest practicable physical, mental, and psychosocial well-being, in accordance with the comprehensive assessment and plan of care." Other regulations provide many more specific standards. For example, the facility must ensure that "(1) A resident who enters the facility without pressure sores does not develop pressure sores unless the individual's clinical condition demonstrates that they were unavoidable; and (2) A resident having pressure sores receives necessary treatment and services to promote healing, prevent infection and prevent new sores from developing." 42 C.F.R. § 483.25. In *In re Conservatorship of Gregory,* 95 Cal.Rptr.2d 336 (Ct. App. 2000), understaffing of a nursing home led to injuries. Although suit was brought under state law, the trial court instructed the jury on federal regulatory standards. This was upheld on appeal.

7. **Inspection or survey reports.** In *Horizon/CMS v. Auld,* the court admitted into evidence the reports of state inspections. These reflect annual surveys made by the states pursuant to federal standards. Failures to meet federal standards (deficiencies) are noted in standardized ways. In the *Auld* case, admission of the survey evidence showed that Horizon knew of its own violations. This might create a basis for punitive damages. Conversely, if the trial judge does not admit such evidence in the case, the plaintiff will have no claim for punitive damages unless she can show the nursing home's malice or recklessness by some other means.

8. **Elder abuse statutes.** A number of states have created statutory tort claims for elders against caregivers under specified circumstances. *See, e.g.*, IOWA CODE § 235F (enacted 2014; allows expedited relief for a "vulnerable elder" who alleges abuse).

California's statute, the Elder Abuse and Dependent Adult Civil Protection Act, CAL. WELF. & INST. CODE §§ 15600 *et seq.*, in effect says that neglect such as failure to provide nourishment, or abuse such as sexual assault, is actionable. Does this add anything to ordinary tort law? *See Winn v. Pioneer Medical Group, Inc.*, 370 P.3d 1011 (Cal. 2016) (interpreting statute).

The statutes may advance the rights of patients in other ways. The Washington statute, the Abuse of Vulnerable Adults Act, has been held to create an implied cause of action against mandated reporters who fail to report abuse. *Kim v. Lakeside Adult Family Home*, 374 P.3d 121 (Wash. 2016). The same statute permits the prevailing victim to recover attorneys' fees. REV. CODE WASH. § 74.34.200. The California statute also permits the victim to recover attorneys' fees, although only if the plaintiff proves oppression, recklessness, or malice by clear and convincing evidence as well as the abuse or neglect itself. *See* CAL. WELF. & INST. CODE § 15657. Such proof then permits the plaintiff to avoid limitations that would apply to medical malpractice claims. *See Delaney v. Baker*, 971 P.2d 986 (Cal. 1999). This includes avoiding the special medical malpractice procedural requirements for an award of punitive damages. *Covenant Care, Inc. v. Superior Court*, 86 P.3d 290 (Cal. 2004).

A different statutory scheme may apply where the elder's claim is against a long-term care provider. California's Long-Term Care Act, CAL. HEALTH & SAFETY CODE § 1430(b), gives a current or former nursing home resident the right to bring a private right of action against the facility for violating certain regulations. Available remedies include injunctive relief, costs and attorneys' fees, and "up to $500" in statutory damages. In *Jarman v. HCR Manorcare, Inc.*, 471 P.3d 1001 (Cal. 2020), the court held that the $500 limit applied per action, not per regulatory violation. The court reasoned that, "Even if a plaintiff's recovery is limited to injunctive relief or includes little to no monetary relief, the potential for attorney fees and costs could still serve as a strong deterrent." Justice Cuellar dissented, saying that the majority's holding "deprives nursing home residents of an important tool to deter and vindicate violations of their rights."

REFERENCE: DOBBS, HAYDEN & BUBLICK, HORNBOOK ON TORTS §§ 21.19–21.22 (2d ed. 2016).

CHAPTER 14

FAMILY MEMBERS AND CHARITIES

■ ■ ■

NOTE: IMMUNITIES

Landowners and health-care professionals—the types of defendants encountered in Chapters 12 and 13—usually obtain special protections from liability because courts limit the duties they owe to something less than the duty of reasonable care. Defendants such as family members, charities, and governmental entities—those we see in the next two chapters—are granted similar protections, but the locution is slightly different. Here courts say that these defendants are *immune* from tort suits or from tort liability.

The difference between a no-duty rule and an immunity rule is miniscule, especially where the immunity is merely from *liability*. But an immunity from *suit*—and many immunities are so construed—is distinct from a no-duty rule, albeit subtly. The term *immunity from suit* means that the defendant cannot properly be sued at all. *Davis Nursing Ass'n v. Neal*, 570 S.W.3d 457 (Ark. 2019) ("Charitable immunity is immunity from *suit*, not simply immunity from liability. Immunity from suit is an entitlement not to stand trial or face the other burdens of litigation."). Thus a defense based on immunity from suit will be asserted in a pre-trial motion, the denial of which is immediately appealable. *See, e.g., Lynch v. Crawford*, 135 N.E.3d 1037 (Mass. 2019) (discussing the difference between immunity from suit and from liability, holding that charitable immunity is an immunity from suit, thus allowing an interlocutory appeal of a ruling denying the immunity); *Ex parte Kelley*, 296 So.3d 822 (Ala. 2019) ("Because one of the purposes of immunity is to spare the defendant from the demands associated with defending a drawn-out lawsuit, a defendant wrongfully denied immunity protection has no adequate remedy if the case is erroneously permitted to go to trial.").

---

§ 1. FAMILY MEMBERS

A. THE TRADITIONAL FAMILY IMMUNITIES

Spouses. The common law took the view that upon marriage the wife lost her legal identity, which was merged with that of the husband. The logical result of this conception was, of course, that the spouses could not sue each other. See Carl W. Tobias, *Interspousal Tort Immunity in America*, 23 GA. L. REV. 359 (1989) (giving complete history of immunity).

Parent and child. There was no such conceptual reason to bar suits between parents and children. The parent-child immunity was introduced rather casually in *Hewellette v. George*, 9 So. 885 (Miss. 1891), with the unadorned argument that family harmony would not permit such actions. "[S]o long as the parent is under obligation to care for, guide, and control, and the child is under reciprocal obligation to aid and comfort and obey, no such action as this can be maintained." Other states followed this decision and it became mainstream law.

Scope and exceptions. (1) *Property interests.* Children were allowed, however, to sue parents to protect property, and after the Married Women's Property Acts spouses were also allowed to sue for such property torts as conversion.

(2) *Relationship terminated.* The parental immunity terminated when the child reached the age of majority, or when the child was emancipated (that is, recognized as self-supporting, or married). Some states have held that the parent-child relationship might also be terminated when the parent dies—with the result that the parent's estate could be sued though the parent could not be. Missouri once held that the immunity did not protect the non-custodial parent. *Fugate v. Fugate*, 582 S.W.2d 663 (Mo. 1979). By contrast, Connecticut—which retains parental immunity—has held that a divorced father who had visitation rights without physical custody retained the parental immunity. *Ascuitto v. Farricielli,* 711 A.2d 708 (Conn. 1998).

(3) *Intentional torts.* Even in states that held a spouse or parents immune from negligent torts, liability was often imposed for intentional torts; this remains the rule in a number immunity-retaining states today. *See, e.g., Doe v. Holt*, 418 S.E.2d 511 (N.C. 1992) (father's sexual molestation and rape of children over several years); *Lusby v. Lusby*, 390 A.2d 77 (Md. 1978) (husband allegedly raped wife at gunpoint); *Hurst v. Capitell*, 539 So.2d 264 (Ala. 1989) (no immunity for sexual abuse of child). This means that the key issue in such states may be whether the parent acted intentionally, or perhaps willfully or with malice; if he did not, then the parent-child immunity applies. *See Needham v. Price*, 780 S.E.2d 549 (N.C. 2015).

(4) *Family injury from violation of duty owed to larger class.* Nor did the immunity apply where family members were involved only fortuitously in an injury-causing event; that is, the injury and the family relationship in no way intersected. For example, if a teenage daughter negligently drives a car and strikes a pedestrian in the crosswalk, the fact that he turns out to be her father would not bar recovery. *Schenk v. Schenk*, 241 N.E.2d

12 (Ill. App. Ct. 1968). Put differently, the immunity may be limited to cases in which the parental conduct involves discretion in discipline or supervision, and does not apply to ordinary negligent accidents. *See Cates v. Cates,* 619 N.E.2d 715 (Ill. 1993); *see also Nolasco v. Malcom*, 949 N.W.2d 201 (Neb. 2020) (children's claims against mother for negligently causing an auto accident were not barred by parental immunity because claims did not allege "ordinary negligence in the exercise of parental authority, discretion, or decisionmaking in the supervision, care, [or] treatment of a child").

Rationale. Two reasons predominate as justifications for the family immunities: (1) To permit suits between family members would be to encourage fraud and collusion; and (2) to permit suits of this kind would be to interfere with the family, and disrupt family harmony or unity.

Can these reasons be fleshed out? If liability insurance covers the defendant spouse, there is, no doubt, a tendency of the insured spouse, with the approval of the other, to assert fault. What may be an ordinary home accident, with no witnesses, may become a case of "negligence" quite readily. And even if it is negligence, there is the probability that both spouses will share in some sense in the recovery. This obviously does not square with ordinary notions of accountability, because the faulty party, far from paying, would share in payment by his insurer.

In the case of parent-child actions, there was obviously some notion at one time that these would interfere with "discipline," and that if the child could sue, the parent's appropriate authority would be disrupted by judicial interference. This argument perhaps has little appeal today, especially if, as is often the case, the parent encourages the child's tort action in order to tap insurance funds. If there is no insurance, the danger is not fraud but misallocation of family funds. If a child recovers $100,000 from a parent, the parent may be unable to meet other obligations within the family, so that one child may enjoy relative riches while others are unable to receive any of the ordinary benefits of childhood. As these comments suggest, the two arguments of fraud and harmony can be expanded quite a bit. Is further elaboration of these arguments possible? When the arguments are fully developed, do you find them convincing?

Rejection of the immunities. By the end of the 1970s a majority of courts had abolished the spousal immunity, though sometimes only as to motor vehicle collisions. *See, e.g., Ellis v. Estate of Ellis*, 169 P.3d 441 (Utah 2007) (holding that Married Women's Act abrogates immunity for all claims); *Waite v. Waite,* 618 So.2d 1360 (Fla. 1993) (complete abrogation of immunity). South Carolina has not only rejected spousal immunity but has said that the immunity would be contrary to natural justice and public policy. For this reason, if one South Carolina spouse negligently injured the other in a state that retained the immunity, the injured spouse would be permitted to sue in South Carolina. *Boone v. Boone,* 546 S.E.2d 191 (S.C. 2001).

What, besides a legal immunity, might deter an abused spouse from suing and what should be done about it? *See* Jennifer Wriggins, *Domestic Violence Torts,* 75 S. CAL. L. REV. 121 (2001).

Parents and children. The courts have been a bit slower in abolishing the parent-child immunity, but it appears that a majority have now done so. *See, e.g., Broadbent v. Broadbent,* 907 P.2d 43 (Ariz. 1995) (abolishing immunity and applying ordinary duty of reasonable care). Some states have abolished the immunity only for special groups of cases, such as those arising out of intentional torts, sexual abuse, motor vehicle accidents, or the conduct of a family business. *E.g., Henderson v. Woolley,* 644 A.2d 1303 (Conn. 1994) (immunity does not bar child's claim for sexual abuse).

Siblings. Generally, state courts have rejected immunity in the context of lawsuits between siblings. In *Lickteig v. Kolar,* 782 N.W.2d 810 (Minn. 2010), a sister sued her brother for sexual abuse that occurred while both were minors. The Minnesota Supreme Court examined the many state cases that follow the general rule that "intrafamilial immunity does not apply to suits between siblings." The court then followed that rule—permitting the sister, an adult at the time of the action, to sue.

B. THE CONTOURS OF PARENTAL IMMUNITY

NEEL V. SEWELL

834 F.Supp. 2d 648 (E.D. Mich. 2011)

ROSEN, CHIEF JUDGE.

On March 8, 2009, Plaintiff Brandon Neel, along with his father, Defendant David Edward Evans, and his aunt, Tina McLean, was helping his step-grandmother, Defendant Beverly Sewell, clean out her house in Monroe County, Michigan. To dispose of excess garbage that had accumulated during this process, a fire was started in the backyard. While Plaintiff was placing crushed plastic milk jugs on the fire, a bag containing an aerosol can exploded in the fire. Plaintiff, who was 17 years old at the time, sustained severe burns to his face and arms, and received treatment at the University of Michigan Hospital. . . . Plaintiff seeks to recover from his father, Defendant Evans, under the theory that his father negligently supervised him by failing to institute and maintain adequate standards for the safe disposal of flammable materials, and by failing to warn and instruct him regarding appropriate procedures to ensure his safety as he assisted in the disposal of hazardous materials. . . .

[Defendant Evans moved for summary judgment.] As the sole argument advanced in the present motion, Defendant Evans contends that, as Plaintiff's father, he is immune from liability under Michigan law for the claims of negligent supervision asserted against him. . . .

The Michigan courts . . . recogniz[e] as a general matter that parents do not enjoy across-the-board immunity from suits brought against them by their minor children. Most notably, in the seminal case of *Plumley v. Klein*, the Michigan Supreme Court abrogated the common-law doctrine of parental immunity, holding that "[a] child may maintain a lawsuit against his parent for injuries suffered as a result of the alleged ordinary negligence of the parent." The court then adopted two exceptions to this rule, however, stating that the Michigan courts would continue to recognize parental immunity "(1) where the alleged negligent act involves an exercise of reasonable parental authority over the child; and (2) where the alleged negligent act involves an exercise of reasonable parental discretion with respect to the provision of food, clothing, housing, medical and dental services, and other care." Whether conduct falls within one of these two *Plumley* exceptions where parental immunity remains available is a question of law for the court.

In his present motion, Defendant Evans appeals exclusively to the first of these two exceptions. . . . This first *Plumley* exception has been the subject of a number of decisions by the Michigan Court of Appeals. In *Paige v. Bing Construction Co.*, a two-year-old child died as a result of falling into a hole made by the defendant, Bing Construction. The defendant construction company brought a third-party complaint against the child's parents for negligent supervision, but the Court of Appeals upheld the trial court's dismissal of this third-party complaint. In so ruling, the court . . . concluded that this exception "does apply so as to bar a claim of negligent parental supervision," reasoning that the "parental authority" referred to in *Plumley* extends beyond discipline and "includes the providing of instruction and education so that a child may be aware of dangers to his or her well being. . . ."

Any remaining uncertainty as to the proper scope of the first *Plumley* exception was resolved in the most recent Michigan Court of Appeals decision on this subject, *Mickel v. Wilson*. In *Mickel*, the defendant father was attending a party with his three-year-old daughter, Jordyn, when she drowned in an inland lake. At the time of Jordyn's drowning, the father had left the beach area to use the restroom without specifically asking anyone to watch his daughter, believing that she was not left unattended because several other adults remained in the area. In addition, while the father was aware that Jordyn could not swim without a life preserver and the host of the party announced that life preservers were available, the father did not make his daughter wear one. Against this backdrop, the court found it undisputed that the plaintiff's claims rested upon the theory that the defendant father had "failed to properly supervise Jordyn."

Accordingly, the Court of Appeals affirmed the trial court's dismissal of the claims against the father on grounds of parental immunity. . . .

Returning to the present case . . . [i]t is clear that [plaintiff's] allegations are intended to support a theory of negligent parental supervision. The conduct that the complaint identifies as negligent is a father's conduct in failing to properly watch over, warn, and instruct his minor son as he engaged in the hazardous activity of burning trash in a fire. The present facts, therefore, are precisely analogous to the man-made hole in Paige . . . and the drowning in *Mickel*. . . . As uniformly established through the above-cited rulings of the Michigan courts, such claims of negligent supervision are properly viewed as involving the "exercise of reasonable parental authority over [a] child," and thus are barred by parental immunity. . . .

[T]o the extent Plaintiff suggests that the particular conduct engaged in by his father cannot qualify as the exercise of "reasonable parental authority.". . . Michigan courts have emphasized that the [first exception] "requires a determination, not of the reasonableness of defendant's conduct, but rather of the scope of 'reasonable parental authority.'". . . [B]ecause the Court has determined that the type of conduct allegedly engaged in by Defendant Evans qualifies as the "exercise of reasonable parental authority," . . . there is no need to inquire whether this conduct was reasonable. . . .

For the reasons set forth above . . . IT IS HEREBY ORDERED that Defendant David Edward Evans' March 30, 2011 motion for summary judgment is GRANTED.

COMMERCE BANK V. AUGSBURGER, 680 N.E.2d 822 (Ill. App. Ct. 1997). The Illinois Department of Children and Family Services arranged for placement of a three-year-old with foster parents, the defendants here. The defendants allegedly confined the child "in an enclosed space described as the 'upper half of a divided shelf of a wooden cabinet inside a bedroom closet at [their] home with the door closed' and did not supervise or monitor her; as a result, she died of asphyxia and hyperthermia." *Held*, dismissal affirmed. The plaintiff did not allege an intentional tort. Illinois has limited the immunity to cases of parental discretion but "parental discretion in the provision of care includes maintenance of the family home, medical treatment, and supervision of the child." The defendant's conduct, though severe, was the very kind to be protected under this standard.

NOTES

1.   **Parental authority and discretion.** Many states follow the limited-immunity formula applied in *Neel* and *Augsburger*. The rule, which

originated in *Goller v. White*, 122 N.W.2d 193 (Wis. 1963), effectively bars most children's claims of negligent parental supervision. The Restatement Second of Torts § 895F approved of this rule but phrased it in terms of a parental privilege for exercising discipline and parental discretion. Are you happy with the application of the formula in *Neel*? In *Augsburger*?

2. **Limits on parental authority?** If the purpose of the parental authority and discretionary immunity is to "remove as a matter of policy or prudence, certain parenting decisions from the judicially created regulatory regime that is the negligence tort," what result when the parent's alleged negligence is the failure to provide a residential smoke detector required by city ordinance? *See Sepaugh v. LaGrone*, 300 S.W.3d 328 (Tex. App. 2009).

3. **The reasonable person standard.** Some states have questioned whether a limited-immunity rule is ultimately akin to a full immunity rule. As the Arizona Supreme Court wrote, "Almost everything a parent does in relation to his child involves 'care, custody, and control.'" Those states have also questioned the wisdom of parental immunity, noting the "paradox of parental immunity can be seen if we assume that a neighbor child from across the street was a guest and was injured at the same time and under the same circumstances as [the parent's own child]." In one case due care would have been owed and in the other it would not. Accordingly, a few courts have said that parents may be liable to children under a reasonable person (or "reasonable parent") standard. *See Broadbent v. Broadbent,* 907 P.2d 43 (Ariz. 1995); *Anderson v. Stream*, 295 N.W.2d 595 (Minn. 1980). Under this standard, the test of the reasonableness of the parent's conduct is "what would an ordinarily reasonable and prudent parent have done in similar circumstances?" *Gibson v. Gibson*, 479 P.2d 648 (Cal. 1971). Does this demand too much of parents, or fail to recognize their important role in making decisions about care of children?

4. **Immunity in negligent-supervision cases.** Other courts have moved in the opposite direction, holding parents owe no legally enforceable duty to supervise their children. As New York's court explained, "Each child is different, as is each parent; as to the former, some are to be pampered while some thrive on independence; as to the latter, some trust in their children to use care, others are very cautious. Considering the different economic, educational, cultural, ethnic and religious backgrounds which must prevail, there are so many combinations and permutations of parent-child relationships that may result that the search for a standard would necessarily be in vain—and properly so. . . . [P]arents have always had the right to determine how much independence, supervision and control a child should have, and to best judge the character and extent of development of their child." *Holodook v. Spencer*, 350 N.Y.S.2d 199 (App. Div. 1973), *quoted with approval on appeal*, 324 N.E.2d 338 (N.Y. 1974). *See also Shoemake v. Fogel, Ltd.*, 826 S.W.2d 933 (Tex. 1992). Thus in *Holodook* there was no liability when a parent failed to control a small child who ran into the street and was struck by a car. New York has at times carried the "inadequate supervision" category to great lengths. In *Nolechek v. Gesuale*, 385 N.E.2d 1268 (N.Y. 1978), the court held

that when a father provided a motorcycle to his teenage son, who was blind in one eye and had impaired vision in the other, it was only a case of "parental supervision," in the same way that decision to monitor a child's play is.

———————

HOPPE V. HOPPE, 724 N.Y.S.2d 65 (App. Div. 2001). "The infant plaintiff was entrusted by his father, the defendant herein, with a hammer and a container of nails which contained an 'explosive nail gun cartridge.' He was injured when he struck the cartridge with the hammer, causing the cartridge to explode. [T]he Supreme Court correctly denied his motion for summary judgment dismissing the complaint. While a child may not sue a parent for negligent supervision, the infant plaintiff possesses a cognizable claim that his injuries were proximately caused by the defendant's alleged breach of a duty of care owed to the world at large, one that exists outside of, and apart from, a family relationship. 'The duty not to negligently maintain explosives is a duty owed to all and is not simply a duty emanating from the parent-child relationship.'"

NOTES

1. **Applications.** A father, knowing his child cannot swim, leaves him alone in the swimming pool. The child is found at the bottom of the pool and rescued, but he suffers brain damage from lack of oxygen. In a suit by the child's guardian against the father, what results (a) under a limited-immunity formula as in *Neel*; (b) under a reasonable-parent standard; or (c) under New York's rule? Which rule is preferable?

2. **Asserting parental immunity against other parties.** Although the issue of parental immunity is often raised in a direct suit in which the child sues the parent, the issue of immunity can also arise in suits in which the child sues another defendant and that defendant seeks to apportion fault to the parent, or seeks contribution from the parent, based on negligent supervision of the child. *See, e.g., Landis v. Hearthmark, LLC*, 750 S.E.2d 280 (W.Va. 2013) (parental immunity held to preclude defendants from asserting contribution claim against parents, but not to preclude their naming of parents as third-party defendants for fault allocation, where young child was burned while attempting to start a fire in the fireplace using fire starter gel left within reach of the child). A third party was the one who raised the issue of parental liability in the *Paige* case mentioned in *Neel*. Does this context affect whether immunity enhances or hinders a child's ability to recover for harm? For example, in *Paige*, would parental immunity aid the child's recovery against the third party? Would parental immunity aid the child's overall recovery? Might the availability of parents' and third parties' insurance to cover a claim affect the answer?

3. **Foster parents, step-parents, and those standing *in loco parentis*.** Notice that the defendants in *Augsburger* were foster parents. Courts are somewhat divided as to whether foster parents are entitled to

parental immunity. *See, e.g., Nichol v. Stass,* 735 N.E.2d 582 (Ill. 2000) (granting immunity to foster parents except for acts in violation of regulations, criminal acts, or child neglect); *Spurgeon v. Alabama Dep't of Human Resources,* 82 So.3d 663 (Ala. 2011) (noting that the absence of a "relationship by blood, marriage, or adoption" warrants lesser rights and granting foster parents immunity with respect to simple negligence claims only). Some courts have given step-parents the same immunity as parents. *See, e.g., Zellmer v. Zellmer,* 188 P.3d 497 (Wash. 2008). Still others suggest that anyone who stands *in loco parentis* (in the parent's shoes) should share the parental immunity. *See, e.g., Smith v. Smith,* 922 So.2d 94 (Ala. 2005) (saying that a non-parent stands in such a role when he or she "assumes the obligations incident to parental status" and "voluntarily performs the parental duties to generally provide for the child"). Are such extensions in line with the policies behind the parental immunity in the first place?

4. **Parent-child relationship.** If parental immunity is granted because of the special relationship between parent and child, should the immunity disappear in situations in which the parent-child relationship is minimal? In *Greenwood v. Anderson,* 324 S.W.3d 324 (Ark. 2009), the grandparents of a deceased five-year-old brought a negligence action against the child's father, who had been the driver in the automobile accident that killed the child. Because the suit was not based on the parent's intentional tort, Arkansas' parental immunity rules barred suit. The grandparents argued that Michael's father was a parent "in only the loosest sense" because he "failed to provide significant financial support to the child" and "spent little of his available time with the child." The court determined that the parental immunity defense did not depend on a significant relationship between parent and child and that inquiries into particular parent-child relationships would be a "highly subjective and ultimately undesirable" approach. Do categorical determinations promote administrative ease? Fairness in individual cases? Both?

§ 2. CHARITIES

Traditional rule. Beginning in the mid-nineteenth century, in response to an English decision, most American states adopted the view that charities were not liable in tort. This included virtually all "non-profit" organizations, such as hospitals, the Boy Scouts, the YWCA and many others; hospitals were by far the most important. The idea initially was that tort liability would divert trust funds from their intended charitable purpose.

Exceptions. This rule followed a development that is by now familiar. First a number of exceptions were developed, with varying emphasis and acceptance in each state:

(1) The charity was not exempt from liability as to non-trust funds. Charities would be liable to the extent that insurance or other free funds were available to pay the judgment.

(2) Some jurisdictions had phrased the rule by saying that the charity would not be liable for the negligence of its servants. Thus the hospital would not be liable for the negligence of the orderly who left a slippery substance on the floor. However, the view was developed that the charity could somehow act "itself" rather than through agents or servants if it acted through its top administrators. In this view, if the hospital administrator had been negligent in hiring a dangerous orderly who was likely to and did attack patients, the hospital would not enjoy an immunity. This is sometimes called "administrative negligence."

(3) The charity could not claim the immunity against those who paid for its services. So, for example, a hospital could not claim an immunity as to a paying patient, but could as to a "charity" patient. This was often expressed as a rule that beneficiaries of the charity's work were barred by the immunity, but others were not.

(4) The charity could not claim an immunity as to its collateral commercial activities. Thus the YMCA ski trip, for which fees were charged, would not be protected by an immunity.

(5) Intentional or "reckless" torts were not protected by the immunity in some states.

General abolition of immunity, with some dissenters. The Restatement (Second) of Torts § 895E (1979), states the rule that there is no charitable immunity, and most states have abolished it entirely, some by statute and some by judicial decision. However, some states retain the immunity, causing litigation over exceptions or over factors in a complicated analysis to determine whether the immunity applies in a particular case. *See, e.g., Byrd Theatre Foundation v. Barnett,* 754 S.E.2d 299 (Va. 2014); *O'Connell v. State,* 795 A.2d 857 (N.J. 2002); *George v. Jefferson Hosp. Ass'n,* 987 S.W.2d 710 (Ark. 1999). For example, New Jersey courts have held that the immunity must be determined on a case-by-case basis, with its application turning on whether at the time of the injury-causing event the charity was "engaged in performing the [charitable] objectives it was organized to promote and whether [the plaintiff] was a direct recipient of those good works" at the time of injury. *Green v. Monmouth Univ.,* 206 A.3d 394 (N.J. 2019) (university entitled to immunity in suit by plaintiff who fell on unsafe stairs at university's activity center while attending a country-music concert that was open to the public). A few states have retained the charitable immunity for negligent torts, but not for intentional torts or willful or wanton acts. *See, e.g., Picher v. Roman Catholic Bishop of Portland,* 974 A.2d 286 (Maine 2009); *Cowan v. Hospice Support Care, Inc.,* 603 S.E.2d 916 (Va. 2004).

Hospitals. The statutes of some states abolish the immunity only as to particular charities such as hospitals. *See, e.g.,* S.C. CODE § 44–7–50 (abolishing immunity as it relates "to hospitals and other medical facilities"). But distinguishing between charitable hospitals and other providers of medical goods and services was held to violate the equal protection clause of the state's constitution. *Bergstrom v. Palmetto Health Alliance,* 596 S.E.2d 42 (S.C. 2004) (determining that the statute was void from the date of its enactment). And given the modern functioning of hospitals, which may offer various services to the community beyond the mere provision of medical care, questions may arise whether the hospital should be granted absolute immunity retained for institutions organized for *charitable or educational* services, despite a statute allowing for limited liability for institutions organized for *hospital* services. *See, e.g., Kuchera v. Jersey Shore Family Health Center,* 111 A.3d 84 (N.J. 2015) (hospital not absolutely immune in suit by plaintiff who slipped and fell while attending a free eye screening; the purpose of the institution, not the use to which the facility is put to any given day, is determinative).

Damages caps. Other statutes abolish charitable immunity but cap damages in cases in which the tort involved activities in furtherance of charitable purposes. *See, e.g.,* MASS. GEN. LAWS ANN. 231 § 85K ($20,000 cap). Does that kind of statute raise concerns? *See English v. New England Medical Center, Inc.,* 541 N.E.2d 329 (Mass. 1989).

Individuals engaged in charitable activities. The traditional charitable immunity protected the charity itself in its form as a trust or corporation, but did not protect individuals who were engaged in its activities. A number of contemporary statutes provide some kind of limitation on the duty of various individuals associated with charities or even with individual charitable acts; the medical Good Samaritan statutes (Chapter 13) may be seen as an example. Some others are quite specific in identifying the specially privileged or protected group. For example, volunteers in various community sports programs may be singled out for protection. *See, e.g.,* 745 ILL. COMP. STAT. § 80/1 (liability may be imposed against volunteer coaches and umpires in non-profit sports programs only if their conduct falls "substantially" below mere negligence); *Welch v. Sudbury Youth Soccer Ass'n,* 901 N.E.2d 1222 (Mass. 2009) (child injured when a soccer goal post flipped over and fractured his leg was barred from suit by statute protecting a "nonprofit association conducting a sports . . . program"). Statutes may immunize donors of food to non-profit organizations. *E.g.,* CAL. CIV. CODE § 1714.25.

Broader yet, some states have enacted statutes protecting all volunteers who assist non-profit corporations. *See, e.g., Ex parte Dixon Mills Volunteer Fire Dept., Inc.,* 181 So.3d 325 (Ala. 2015) (applying Volunteer Service Act; assistant fire chief of volunteer fire department was immune from negligence suit and was not liable where he did not act willfully or wantonly in causing a traffic accident). A federal statute provides absolute immunity for volunteers who work for non-profit corporations, then recognizes some exceptions. *See* 42 U.S.C.A. § 14503(a)(3). An interesting twist on this statute is that it protects volunteers working for any non-profit organization that escapes income taxes under the Internal Revenue Code, 26 U.S.C.A. § 501(c). That includes a number of organizations you might not think of as charities, such as the Chamber of Commerce.

———

PICHER V. ROMAN CATHOLIC BISHOP OF PORTLAND, 974 A.2d 286 (Me. 2009). Picher brought suit against a former priest, Raymond Melville, and the Bishop, based on sexual abuse of Picher by Melville when Picher was a minor in the late 1980s. Melville defaulted on the claims against him. Picher asserts claims against the Bishop for both negligent supervision and fraudulent concealment of facts. Picher alleges that the Bishop was on notice that Melville had abused a child before he was ordained, but the Bishop failed to report Melville to law enforcement officials and concealed Melville's propensities from parishioners and the public. The Bishop was insured by Lloyd's of London under two policies which specifically excluded coverage for "[s]exual or physical abuse or molestation of any person by the Assured, any employee of the Assured or any volunteer worker." The Bishop moved for summary judgment based on its affirmative defense of charitable immunity. The trial court granted the Bishop's motion. *Held,* summary judgment affirmed with respect to all claims of negligence but reversed with respect to claims of fraudulent concealment. "[T]he rationale for charitable immunity has been severely criticized. This criticism has been explained in the Restatement (Second) of Torts:

> [T]here has been resort to ideas of "public policy" for the encouragement of charities and mention of the fear that they may be stifled if donors are discouraged from making gifts because their money may go to pay tort claims. The development of liability insurance has made it quite unlikely that donors would fail to recognize it as a legitimate expense of operation. In fact, all of the supposed reasons for the immunity fail when the charity can insure against liability. . . .

> Except for one significant restriction imposed by statute, [charitable immunity's] applicability in Maine is controlled entirely by the precedents of this Court. . . . We have previously held that we would maintain, but neither expand nor eliminate, the doctrine of charitable immunity. . . . For [these] reasons, we do not recognize the defense of charitable immunity in claims involving intentional torts."

Dissent: "The existence of charitable immunity and the protection it creates is important to the planning and continued existence of many community-based organizations including local granges, arts organizations, fraternal groups, youth programs, churches, and some schools and health care providers. . . . [W]ithout charitable immunity, resources could be sacrificed to feed the hungry maw of litigation, and charitable institutions of all kinds would ultimately cease or become greatly impaired in their usefulness. . . . What the public policy of this State in such an important area of life and action should be may necessitate the conduct of a general investigation which this Court in litigated cases is ill-equipped to undertake. . . . A claim of fraud, fraudulent misrepresentation, or fraudulent concealment . . . is a tort easily pled, but difficult to prove."

NOTES

1. **A policy question.** If it is true that charitable organizations could not exist if they had to bear liability for their own negligent and intentional torts, should the people harmed by these torts subsidize the public benefits these organizations provide?

2. **Subsequent case history.** The dissent in *Picher* worried that the claim of fraudulent concealment is "easily pled, but difficult to prove." The later proceedings suggest that might not be the case. After remand, the Maine Supreme Judicial Court affirmed the trial court's grant of the Bishop's motion for summary judgment on Picher's claim of fraudulent concealment. *Picher v. Roman Catholic Bishop of Portland*, 82 A.3d 101 (Me. 2013). The court wrote, "The summary judgment record before us does not include any evidence, direct or circumstantial, that the Diocese had knowledge, before or during the time when Picher was abused, that Melville was a sexual abuser of minors. The information of which the Diocese may have been aware, which disclosed no prior sexual abuse by Melville, is not the type of material information that triggers a duty to disclose."

REFERENCES: DOBBS, HAYDEN & BUBLICK, HORNBOOK ON TORTS §§ 23.1–23.2 (family members) & §§ 23.3–23.4 (charities) (2d ed. 2016); 2 DOBBS, HAYDEN & BUBLICK, THE LAW OF TORTS §§ 357–359 (family immunities); §§ 360–361 (charitable immunity) (2d ed. 2010).

CHAPTER 15

GOVERNMENTAL IMMUNITY

. . .

§ 1. TRADITIONAL IMMUNITIES AND THEIR PASSING: AN OVERVIEW

1. *Governmental tort immunity.* The English common law said "The King can do no wrong," an ambiguous statement that ultimately was taken to mean that one could not sue government in tort. This idea was carried over to America and perpetuated even after the American Revolution, with the result that the federal government and the states were immune from tort actions. This immunity extends to all their agencies unless statutes provide otherwise. In addition to this general "sovereign immunity" of the federal and state governments, the Eleventh Amendment of the United States Constitution has been construed to immunize states from being sued in federal court.

2. *Taking of property.* One important qualification to the governmental immunity is that under the Due Process clauses of the Fifth and Fourteenth Amendments of the United States Constitution, neither state nor federal governments may "take" private property for public purposes without just compensation.

3. *Tribal sovereign immunity.* "Indian tribes are domestic dependent nations that exercise sovereign authority over their members and territories. Suits against Indian tribes are thus barred by sovereign immunity absent a clear waiver by the tribe or congressional abrogation." *Okla. Tax Comm'n v. Citizen Band Potawatomi Indian Tribe of Oklahoma*, 498 U.S. 505 (1991); *see also Kiowa Tribe of Oklahoma v. Mfg. Techs., Inc.*, 523 U.S. 751 (1998) ("As a matter of federal law, an Indian tribe is subject to suit only where Congress has authorized the suit or the tribe has waived its immunity."). In *Kiowa Tribe*, the Court recognized that tribal enterprises now include a number of commercial activities in which goods and services are provided to non-Indians, and that in that "economic context, immunity can harm those who are unaware that they are dealing with a tribe, who do not know of tribal immunity, or who have no choice in the matter, as in the case of tort victims." 523 U.S. at 758. But the Court itself has deferred to Congress to narrow the immunity if it chooses. The lower courts have applied sovereign immunity to bar almost all tort claims against Indian tribes. *See, e.g., Furry v. Miccosukee Tribe of Indians of Florida*, 685 F.3d 1224 (11th Cir. 2012) (barring tort claim against tribe that owned and operated gambling and resort facility and allegedly, in

violation of state liquor laws, knowingly sold excessive amounts of alcohol to a woman who died in an auto accident after leaving the facility).

4. *Municipal immunity.* Municipalities and other local entities are not "sovereigns." Rather, they are corporations chartered by the sovereign. They were traditionally accorded immunity nonetheless, but over the years, courts freely created various exceptions. Municipalities were and are of course liable for takings of property. But additionally, courts made them liable for nuisances such as unsanitary garbage dumps, and for torts committed in the course of proprietary activities, as distinct from governmental activities. For example, a city might be liable for negligence in the operation of a city-owned electrical company. Cities were also held liable in many states for negligent failure to maintain streets properly. Most states have now substantially limited municipal liability by statute.

5. *State government immunity.* New York State waived its sovereign immunity in 1929. Most states lagged behind for many years, but in the 1960s and 1970s, a number state courts and legislatures moved to limit or abolish state government immunity. Today most states have enacted broad waivers of immunity by statute, although many have retained some significant areas of immunity.

6. *Federal government immunity.* The federal government's immunity from tort suit was waived by Congress just after World War II with the passage of the Federal Tort Claims Act, or FTCA. But as we will see in the next section, the waiver is limited and has significant conditions.

§ 2. THE FEDERAL TORT CLAIMS ACT

A. BASIC SCOPE AND LIMITS

BROWNBACK V. KING, 141 S.Ct. 740 (2021). "In 1946, Congress passed the FTCA, which waived the sovereign immunity of the United States for certain torts committed by federal employees acting within the scope of their employment. *FDIC v. Meyer*, 510 U.S. 471 (1994). The Act in effect ended the private bill system by transferring most tort claims to the federal courts. Plaintiffs were (and are) required to bring claims under the FTCA in federal district court. Federal courts have jurisdiction over these claims if they are actionable under 28 U.S.C.A. § 1346(b). A claim is actionable if it alleges the six elements of § 1346(b), which are that the claim be:

> [1] against the United States, [2] for money damages, . . . [3] for injury or loss of property, or personal injury or death [4] caused by the negligent or wrongful act or omission of any employee of the Government [5] while acting within the scope of his office or employment, [6] under circumstances where the United States, if a private person, would be liable to the claimant in accordance with the law of the place where the act or omission occurred.

Ibid. (quoting § 1346(b)). While waiving sovereign immunity so parties can sue the United States directly for harms caused by its employees, the FTCA made it more difficult to sue the employees themselves by adding a judgment bar provision. That provision states: 'The judgment in an action under section 1346(b) of this title shall constitute a complete bar to any action by the claimant, by reason of the same subject matter, against the employee of the government whose act or omission gave rise to the claim.' § 2676. '[O]nce a plaintiff receives a judgment (favorable or not) in an FTCA suit,' the bar is triggered, and 'he generally cannot proceed with a suit against an individual employee based on the same underlying facts.' *Simmons* v. *Himmelreich*, 578 U.S. 621 (2016). The Act thus opened a new path to relief (suits against the United States) while narrowing the earlier one (suits against employees). . . ."

NOTES

1. **Governing law.** Although FTCA claims against the government must be brought in federal court, the substantive law that governs claims under the FTCA is *not* federal law. Instead, the FTCA itself requires the court to follow the law of the state in which the alleged tort occurred. 28 U.S.C.A. § 1346(b)(1). Thus the outcome of a particular FTCA case may vary depending on the state in which the tort occurred. *See, e.g., Nelson* v. *United States*, 915 F.3d 1243 (10th Cir. 2019) (U.S. government immune from suit by bicyclist who fell into sinkhole, where Colorado Recreational Use Act would provide an immunity if a private person were sued for the same conduct).

2. **"Within the scope of his office or employment."** Under § 1346(b)(1) of the FTCA, the federal government waives immunity only where the government employee's wrongful act is "within the scope of his office or employment." This issue is also governed by the law of the state in which the tort occurred. Thus, if under applicable state law the federal employee's act would *not* be considered "within the scope of employment" for purposes of an employer's vicarious liability (see Chapter 22), the federal government is not liable for harm caused by that act. *See, e.g., Magee* v. *United States*, 9 F.4th 675 (8th Cir. 2021) (mail carrier who accidentally struck friend with mail truck while running errands was not acting within scope of employment at the time under Missouri law, thus U.S. government was not liable to friend under FTCA). This will result in governmental immunity for many intentional torts, since under state law most such acts will not be considered within the scope of employment. *See M.D.C.G.* v. *United States*, 956 F.3d 762 (5th Cir. 2020) (Border Patrol agent's kidnaping, rape and torture of migrants was not "in furtherance of his authorized duties," thus trial court was correct in dismissing claims against federal government for assault, false imprisonment and intentional infliction of emotional distress).

UNITED STATES V. OLSON, 546 U.S. 43 (2005). Injured mine workers sued the United States under the FTCA, claiming that the negligence of federal mine inspectors helped bring about a serious accident in an Arizona mine. The FTCA authorizes private tort actions against the United States only "under circumstances where the United States, if a private person, would be liable to the claimant in accordance with the law of the place where the act or omission occurred." 28 U.S.C. § 1346(b)(1). The trial court dismissed the suit on the ground that Arizona law would not impose liability on a private person in similar circumstances. The Ninth circuit reversed, reasoning that where "unique governmental functions" such a mine inspections are involved, courts must look to the state-law liability of *public entities* for an analogue, and that because Arizona law would make state or municipal entities liable for negligent mine inspections, the FTCA waives the federal government immunity in this case. *Held*, reversed and remanded.

"In *Indian Towing Co. v. United States,* 350 U.S. 61, 64 (1955), this Court rejected the Government's contention that there was no liability for negligent performance of 'uniquely governmental functions.' It held that the Act requires a court to look to the state-law liability of private entities, not to that of public entities, when assessing the Government's liability under the FTCA 'in the performance of activities which private persons do not perform.'" And the FTCA "makes the United States liable 'to the same extent as a private individual under *like circumstances.*' . . . [T]he words 'like circumstances' do not restrict a court's inquiry to the *same circumstances,* but require it to look further afield. . . . The Government in effect concedes that . . . there are private persons in 'like circumstances' to federal mine inspectors, namely 'private persons who conduct safety inspections.' [As we said in *Indian Towing,*] private individuals, who do not operate lighthouses, nonetheless may create a relationship with third parties that is similar to the relationship between a lighthouse operator and a ship dependent on the lighthouse's beacon. The Ninth Circuit should have looked for a similar analogy in this case."

NOTE

Analogous private liability. *Olson* clarifies that in order for FTCA liability to be imposed, the conduct of the federal employee at issue in the case must be analogous to a private person's conduct that could give rise to liability under applicable state law.

The inquiry may be broken down into two components. First, the plaintiff's cause of action against the government must be comparable to a cause of action against a private citizen that is recognized in the state in which the tort occurred. If there is no comparable cause of action, then the federal government cannot be liable under the FTCA. *See, e.g., McGowan v. United States*, 825 F.3d 118 (2d Cir. 2016) (under New York law, private citizens could not be held liable for the kind of wrongful confinement alleged by plaintiff; "[p]rivate persons cannot establish facilities to detain other persons"). Second, even where there *is* a private analog, if a private person would not be liable under state law for engaging in the analogous activity, then the federal government is not liable, either. *See, e.g., In re FEMA Trailer Formaldehyde Products Liability Litigation (Mississippi Plaintiffs)*, 668 F.3d 281 (5th Cir. 2012) (because state statutes abrogate the liability of a private person who allows his property to be used without compensation in a natural disaster, the government's provision of trailers to hurricane victims is also immunized under the FTCA).

NOTE: SPECIFIC STATUTORY CONDITIONS AND LIMITATIONS

1. *Key conditions of the waiver.* The FTCA is a broad waiver of sovereign immunity, but the statute itself contains a number of conditions. For example, before filing a suit in court the plaintiff must submit the claim to the government agency involved; suit is not permitted until the agency has refused payment or has delayed over six months in making a decision on it. Courts lack jurisdiction over suits filed prematurely. *See, e.g., Rollo-Carlson ex rel. Flackus-Carlson v. United States*, 971 F.3d 768 (8th Cir. 2020). The statute also specifies that cases may be brought only in federal court, not state court. Neither side may have a jury; all FTCA trials are bench trials. Strict liability, even when a private individual would be strictly liable, is not permitted, because the FTCA itself says immunity may be waived only for a "negligent or wrongful act or omission." *See Laird v. Nelms*, 406 U.S. 797 (1972).

2. *Specific statutory exceptions for particular activities.* The FTCA itself lays out a number of specific instances in which the government is not liable, that is, in which the immunity is retained. One set of exceptions retains the immunity for specific governmental activities (combatant activities of the military and delivery of mail, for example) and for all claims arising in foreign countries. These exceptions have typically been read broadly, in favor of immunity. *See, e.g., Sosa v. Alvarez-Machain*, 542 U.S. 692 (2004) (holding that the "foreign country" exception bars all claims against the federal government based on any injury suffered in a foreign country, no matter where the alleged tortious act or omission giving rise to that injury occurred).

3. *Specific statutory exceptions for particular torts.* Another set of provisions in the statute retains the government's immunity for a number of specific torts, mostly those of a dignitary or economic kind. These include those "arising out of" assault, battery, false imprisonment, malicious prosecution, abuse of process, libel, slander, misrepresentation and interference with contract. Suppose the government negligently hires a man who has a propensity to commit sexual assaults or to molest children. The man uses his government job to take advantage of a child. The government usually escapes liability in such cases because the claim "arises out of" assault or battery, even though the legal basis of the claim is that the government is negligent in hiring without adequate investigation, or negligent in supervision. *See, e.g., LM v. United States*, 344 F.3d 695 (7th Cir. 2003). And the government may be immune simply because the employee's intentional tort was not "within the scope of employment" under state law, as noted above in Note 2 after *Brownback.*

However, the FTCA expressly provides that the government may be liable for an assault, battery, or false imprisonment if it is committed by "investigative or law enforcement officers" who are acting within the scope of employment. *See, e.g., Iverson v. United States*, 973 F.3d 843 (8th Cir. 2020) (TSA officers fall under this exception, thus government not immune from suit for battery relating to security screening at airport). And if an *off-duty* employee commits a battery, the government might be liable for its negligence in fostering the risk. For example, it might be liable for its negligence in permitting an intoxicated off-duty employee to take a government rifle off-premises. *Sheridan v. United States*, 487 U.S. 392 (1988).

4. *Discretionary immunity.* The most significant statutory exception to the waiver of immunity is for claims that are based on "the exercise or performance or the failure to exercise or perform a discretionary duty," 28 U.S.C.A. § 2680(a). That exception is explored in greater detail in section B below.

NOTE: SUITS AGAINST INDIVIDUAL FEDERAL EMPLOYEES

1. *Immunity under the FTCA.* As referenced briefly in the excerpt from *Brownback*, where the plaintiff's suit alleges harm from a wrongful act of an employee of the federal government, the FTCA places liability on the government itself and immunizes the employee. An amendment to the FTCA called the Westfall Act, 28 U.S.C.A. § 2671, explicitly provides that when the plaintiff sues a federal employee, the Attorney General of the United States may certify that the acts of the employee were within the scope of his federal employment. When such a certificate is presented to the court, the burden falls on the plaintiff to show that the employee's conduct was not within the scope of his or her employment. *See Bolton v. United States*, 946 F.3d 256 (5th Cir. 2019). If the plaintiff fails to meet this burden, the court must dismiss the suit against the employee, leaving the United States as the lone defendant, subject to all of the conditions and limitations of the FTCA. *See Osborn v. Haley*, 549 U.S. 225 (2007). In *Brownback*, the Court held that once the plaintiff receives a judgment (favorable or not) in an FTCA case against the government, the plaintiff cannot proceed with a suit against an individual employee based on the same underlying facts.

2. *Bivens suits against federal executive branch officers.* Because federal employees are not "state actors" for civil rights claims purposes (see Chapter 3 § 5) they cannot be sued under § 1983 for violating a plaintiff's federal rights. However, in *Bivens v. Six Unknown Named Agents of Federal Bureau of Narcotics*, 403 U.S. 388 (1971), the Court held that federal officers could be sued for constitutional violations directly under the Constitution. This is an exceedingly difficult claim to win. The Court has said that "the Constitution's separation of powers requires us to exercise caution in extending *Bivens* to a new 'context.'" This caution dramatically restricts the claim's availability. *Hernandez v. Mesa*, 140 S.Ct. 735 (2020) (refusing to extend *Bivens* to recognize a claim against a Border Patrol Agent who shot a Mexican child across the

U.S.-Mexico border). Lower courts have recognized just three circumstances in which a claim would be recognized because the context was not new: (1) manacling the plaintiff in front of his family and strip-searching him; (2) gender discrimination by a congressman against a staff member; and (3) failure to provide medical attention to an asthmatic prisoner in federal custody. *Oliva v. Nivar*, 973 F.3d 438 (5th Cir. 2020).

And while there is no general absolute immunity in such cases, the officer can assert the same federal qualified immunity we saw in Chapter 3 § 5 for § 1983 cases. *See, e.g., Bryan v. United States*, 913 F.3d 356 (3d Cir. 2019). That means that a federal executive branch officer cannot be sued under *Bivens* unless the officer's actions violate the plaintiff's clearly established constitutional rights. *Ashcroft v. Iqbal,* 556 U.S. 662 (2009). Particular statutes may also immunize federal officers from *Bivens* suits. *Hui v. Castaneda*, 559 U.S. 799 (2010) (officers and employees of the Public Health Service could not be sued directly; the Public Health Service Act precludes *Bivens* actions against them for constitutional violations arising out of their official duties).

3. *Absolute immunity for judicial and legislative officers.* Judicial and legislative officers, both federal and state, are traditionally given absolute immunity under the common law, so long as they are acting with jurisdiction and in their judicial or legislative capacity. Thus both state and federal judges are absolutely immune in their judicial work. The immunity also applies whether the claim is based on ordinary state tort law or on federal civil rights claims. This absolute immunity may extend to people who are not actually "judicial officers" if they were performing functions sufficiently comparable to officials who have traditionally been afforded absolute immunity at common law. *See Butz v. Economou*, 438 U.S. 478 (1978). The core question in extending immunity to non-judicial officers may be whether the person performing "essential judicial functions." *Hornibrook v. Richard*, 171 N.E.3d 725 (Mass. 2021) (court-appointed conservator whose actions were expressly authorized by probate court was entitled to absolute immunity).

B. DISCRETIONARY IMMUNITY

HAJDUSEK V. UNITED STATES
895 F.3d 146 (1st Cir. 2018)

KAYATTA, CIRCUIT JUDGE. . . .

I.

[In August 2010, Joseph Hajdusek signed up for] the Marine Corps Delayed Entry Program ("DEP"), a program through which individuals can sign up to join the Marine Corps but delay entry in order to better prepare for basic training. . . . The DEP is a program that allows individuals to enlist in the Marine Corps Reserve up to one year prior to enlisting in the regular Marine Corps. Individuals participating in the program are known as "poolees." While enrolled in the program, poolees prepare physically and mentally for their enlistment into the active-duty Marine Corps. The program aims to assist in training and reduce attrition. One important aspect of the pool program is particularly relevant here: Poolees, though affiliated with a Marine recruiting station, are not active-duty Marines and are not entitled to Department of Defense type benefits. As guidance documents from the Marine Corps state, poolees "are not Marines yet."

[After participating in the program for several months, Hajdusek was preparing to ship to basic training. While on vacation with his family prior to this final stage,] Hajdusek received a phone call from Staff Sergeant Mikelo, the newly installed manager of his recruiting station, asking why he had not shown up for a pool event. Dissatisfied with Hajdusek's answer, Mikelo ordered him to appear for a physical training session on March 1. Hajdusek did as he was told. When he arrived for the training session, Mikelo put him through a workout that Hajdusek describes in a declaration as "much longer and much more strenuous than any other workout I had ever been given." . . . Near the end of the session he showed signs of overexertion, collapsing several times but nonetheless able to leave under his own power.

After spending the ensuing several days essentially bedridden due to pain, Hajdusek began to experience blurred vision and nausea. He was diagnosed with various ailments, including rhabdomyolysis, a condition caused when muscle tissue dies from extreme overuse and the dead tissue enters the bloodstream. This has left him permanently disabled.

Hajdusek sued the United States in the District of New Hampshire, alleging that Mikelo's actions had caused his physical injuries and disabilities, that these actions were negligent, and that pursuant to the Federal Tort Claims Act, 28 U.S.C. § 1346(b)(1), he was entitled to damages. The United States moved to dismiss on the ground that Hajdusek's claim stemmed from "the performance of a discretionary function," and since the United States has not waived sovereign immunity for such claims, the district court lacked subject matter jurisdiction. The district court agreed with the government and dismissed the case. This appeal followed.

II.

The FTCA serves as a limited waiver of sovereign immunity. . . . 28 U.S.C. § 1346(b)(1). Central to this appeal is an exception to this provision, removing from the district courts' jurisdiction "[a]ny claim . . . based upon the exercise or performance or the failure to exercise or perform a discretionary function or duty on the part of a federal agency or an employee of the Government, whether or not the discretion involved be abused." Id. § 2680(a). In evaluating a claim under the FTCA, a court must therefore determine whether the claim is based on a discretionary function as contemplated by section 2680; if so, the case must be dismissed for want of jurisdiction. We review such dismissals de novo.

In conducting the discretionary function inquiry, we use a "familiar analytic framework." *Shansky v. United States*, 164 F.3d 688, 690 (1st Cir. 1999). First, we "must identify the conduct that allegedly caused the harm. Second, we must ask whether this conduct is of the nature and quality that Congress, in crafting the discretionary function exception, sought to shelter from tort liability. The latter analysis encompasses two questions: Is the conduct itself discretionary? If so, is the discretion susceptible to policy-related judgments? The word "susceptible" is critical here; we do not ask whether the alleged federal tortfeasor was in fact motivated by a policy concern, but only whether the decision in question was of the type that policy analysis could inform. *See United States v. Gaubert*, 499 U.S. 315, 325 (1991) ("The focus of the inquiry is not on the agent's subjective intent in exercising the discretion conferred by statute or regulation, but on the nature of the actions taken and on whether they are susceptible to policy analysis."). In addition, the fact that a government official exercises discretion pursuant to regulatory authority creates a presumption that this discretion was susceptible to policy analysis and thus protected.

Here, the parties are in agreement that the conduct that allegedly caused the harm was Mikelo's decision to subject Hajdusek to the especially arduous workout on the day in question. We therefore turn to the analysis of whether that decision was in fact discretionary, and whether the discretion involved was susceptible to policy analysis.

We have little trouble answering the first question in the affirmative. Guidance from the Marine Corps gives Marines in charge of the DEP only general instructions concerning how physical training programs should run. For example, Marines are instructed that they should concentrate training activities on "upper body strength," "abdominal strength," and "aerobic training," and the guidance suggests running and hikes, among other things, as activities that work toward these goals. The Marine Corps does not dictate such details as how often physical training should occur, of what exercises it should consist, how long it should last, and how intense it should be. These decisions are left to the judgment of the individual Marines in charge of administering the DEP. In short, Mikelo exercised discretion in his choice of an exercise regimen for Hajdusek.

That brings us to the second, and in this matter, more complicated, phase of the analysis: We must decide whether the discretion Mikelo exercised was susceptible to policy analysis. As we have previously recognized, answering this question requires a case-by-case approach, which has, admittedly, "led to some disarray." Both Hajdusek and the government proffer case law ostensibly supporting their respective points of view, often relying on the same cases. For example, both parties rely on

Shansky. In that case, we noted that there was a distinction between "a professional assessment undertaken pursuant to a policy of settled priorities," which is not shielded by the discretionary function exception, and "a fully discretionary judgment that balances incommensurable values in order to establish those priorities," which is. We held that the National Park Service's decision not to place a handrail and warning signs at a particular facility was shielded by the discretionary function exception, because it required a balancing of safety and aesthetic considerations. We also noted, however, that "[w]e do not suggest that any conceivable policy justification will suffice to prime the discretionary function pump."

Hajdusek invokes *Shansky* in arguing that Mikelo's decision was nothing more than a professional judgment done negligently. In his view, the Marine Corps itself settled all policy priorities, and Mikelo's actions were mere implementation. He contends that "no policy was served or implicated in ruining a potential recruit, let alone disciplining someone who policy declared was not to be subjected to military-type discipline." By contrast, the government argues that Mikelo's decision was informed by the need to balance a variety of policy priorities, such as preparing poolees for the daunting mental and physical challenges of basic training, preventing attrition, and using existing poolees to generate new recruits. . . .

As *Shansky* makes clear, deciding whether a government agent's action is susceptible to policy analysis is often challenging, and this case is no exception. However, based upon the record as a whole, we conclude that the government has the better of the argument. Determining just how hard a potential Marine should exercise, and whether, for example, he should do so for 120 or 90 minutes, calls for weighing the policy goals that are furthered by strenuous, even exhaustive exercise against the goals of avoiding attrition through injury or otherwise. Work the poolees too much, and the Corps loses potential new members; work them too little, and preparedness and discipline might suffer. We doubt that Congress intended judges to dictate this balance, especially given that judges would only be reviewing claims of error in one direction. . . .

Threaded throughout Hajdusek's arguments is a concern that if the government prevails, the military will have a license to behave unreasonably in its interactions with individuals who, although military-adjacent, are not active-duty members of the military able to access Department of Defense or Veterans Affairs care when injured. In Hajdusek's view, a ruling for the government has the practical effect of creating a world where individuals can be injured by negligent military actors and have no recourse, and the military will have no incentive to give due weight to the risk of serious injury. In the face of this concern, we emphasize that our decision today is, as all FTCA discretionary function exception cases must be, cabined to the record before us. As the government conceded at oral argument, certain decisions by government actors, though nominally discretionary, may pass a threshold of objective unreasonableness such that no reasonable observer would see them as susceptible to policy analysis. We do not rule out the possibility that a Marine running a pool program could make some decision falling into this category. For example, if a Marine decided that the only way to toughen up poolees was to have them jump off a twenty-foot-high cliff onto concrete, we would have no qualms holding that even though a desire to serve Marine Corps goals of preparing poolees for basic training may have animated the decision, it was simply not a decision that in any objectively reasonable sense could be said to be informed by policy analysis. In that case, the unreasonableness of the activity would be clearly apparent ex ante to any reasonable observer. And such a decision would not constitute a weighing of safety concerns versus intensity concerns; it would amount to a complete rejection of the former in favor of the latter, contrary to guidance from the Marines.

Returning from the hypothetical to the actual, however, we recognize that Hajdusek does not allege anything close to the situation described above. The complaint itself only alleges that Mikelo exercised Hajdusek unreasonably hard. It does not allege facts plausibly supporting an inference that a Marine supervising the activity would have reason to know ex ante that the exercise was sufficiently likely to cause serious injury as to deem it the product of a rejection of a policy goal rather than a balancing of such goals. The additional materials submitted by Hajdusek offer little more. At most, they support a theory that Mikelo's motivation was to discipline Hajdusek. But even assuming this to be true, the use of arduous physical exercise to discipline an individual for a perceived failing would seem to be an appropriate tool of boot camp preparation, which is a primary goal of the DEP. . . .

The facts alleged in this case paint a picture of a workout that was unusually intense, perhaps even unreasonably so, but not so objectively beyond the pale that it could not have been informed by policy analysis. Accordingly, though we acknowledge that there may be a line beyond which discretionary decisions lose protection due to their patent unreasonableness, the allegations here fall short of that line.

III.

Hajdusek's case is a sympathetic one. He attempted to serve his country, was injured in that attempt, and now, due to the quirk of his not-quite-Marine status, the services normally available to injured servicemen and women are unavailable to him. Nonetheless, Congress has decreed that the federal courts cannot use tort claims to second-guess the discretionary choices of federal agents who implement the government's policy choices. In this specific instance, Congress's command means that we cannot second-guess the decision of a Marine about how hard to work out a potential recruit at the end of a training program, at least in the absence of a patent abandonment of any effort to balance Marine Corps policy goals. We therefore *affirm* the judgment of dismissal.

NOTES

1. **Purposes of the discretionary immunity.** Why did Congress retain federal immunity for discretionary functions? In *United States v. Varig Airlines*, 467 U.S. 797 (1984), the Court explained that the discretionary immunity "marks the boundary between Congress' willingness to impose tort liability on the United States and its desire to protect certain governmental activities from exposure to suit by private individuals." Discretionary immunity is designed "to prevent judicial 'second-guessing' of legislative and administrative decisions grounded in social, economic, and political policy through the medium of an action in tort." Other courts have said that the immunity's purpose is in "keeping the judiciary out of the business of reviewing policy judgments by government employees." *Shuler v. United States*, 531 F.3d 930 (D.C. Cir. 2008). Why prevent the judiciary from passing on the legality of the policy-based actions of the other branches of government? Would the balance of power be disturbed by a holding that the drill instructor in *Hajdusek* negligently caused the plaintiff's injuries?

2. **Avoiding "second guessing."** Notice that in *Hajdusek* the court avoids analyzing whether the drill instructor was negligent at all. This is typical of the "discretionary immunity" decisions—the focus is solely on whether the requirements of the immunity are met. Indeed, *avoiding* a judicial analysis of the propriety of the government actor's conduct is the point. *See, e.g., Foster Logging v. United States*, 973 F.3d 1152 (11th Cir. 2020) (courts "should look to the nature of the challenged decision in an objective, or general sense," rather than engaging in "a fact-based inquiry into the circumstances surrounding the government actor's exercise of a particular discretionary function"); *Lam v. United States*, 979 F.3d 665 (9th Cir. 2020) ("[C]ourts should put the negligence issue aside on a [discretionary function immunity]-based motion to dismiss and focus its inquiry on whether the employee's acts were discretionary."). Notice also that the FTCA itself immunizes the government even if the exercise of discretion is "abused."

Does the *Hajdusek* court suggest, however, that where the conduct of the government actor is particularly extreme, the government might not be protected by discretionary immunity? *Cf. Shivers v. United States*, 1 F.4th 924 (11th Cir. 2021) ("[T]here is nothing in the statutory language that limits application of this exception based on the 'degree' of the abuse of discretion or the egregiousness of the employee's performance. Congress could have adopted language that carved out certain behavior from this exception—for example, grossly negligent behavior, or behavior that rises to the level of a constitutional violation. But Congress did not do so. . . ."). Is the line between discretionary immunity and liability sufficiently clear for courts to reach reasoned conclusions?

3. **Where the government makes no conscious decision.** In some cases, the government pursues a course of action without having made any conscious decision, either about policy or anything else. As the *Hajdusek* court points out, the Supreme Court has said that "[t]he focus of the inquiry is not on the agent's subjective intent in exercising the discretion conferred by statute or regulation, but on the nature of the actions taken and on whether they are susceptible to policy analysis." *United States v. Gaubert*, 499 U.S. 315 (1991). Based on this language, many courts have held that whether government employees actually took policy objectives into account is irrelevant. *See, e.g., Ball v. United States*, 967 F.3d 1072 (10th Cir. 2020) ("[T]he absence of record evidence reflecting a policy analysis is immaterial.").

To invoke the discretionary immunity, the government needs only to point to some support in the record that the decisions they made *could have been* subjected to a policy analysis. *See, e.g., Croyle ex rel. Croyle v. United States*, 908 F.3d 377 (8th Cir. 2018) (decision not to warn of a government-employed priest's sexual propensities was susceptible to policy analysis; "supervising employees typically involves policy considerations"); *Chadd v. United States*, 794 F.3d 1104 (9th Cir. 2015) (decision not to destroy a hostile mountain goat in Olympic National Park was susceptible to policy analysis); *Mahon v. United States*, 742 F.3d 11 (1st Cir. 2014) (decision whether to alter height of railing on second story of Commandant's house at Navy Yard was discretionary; the question is whether the exercise or non-exercise of discretion was "actually or potentially" affected by policy-related judgments). Is the "susceptible to policy analysis" approach too protective of the government? A dissenting judge in *Chadd, supra*, criticized the approach as "bad law"; a concurring judge felt bound by precedent, but complained that the Circuit's interpretation of the approach "has gone off the rails."

4. **Planning-level vs. operational-level decisions.** Federal courts once routinely drew immunity lines according to whether government decisions were made at the "planning level," in which case they immune, or at the "operational level," in which case they were not. But in *Gaubert, supra* Note 3, the Court said, "It is the nature of the conduct, rather than the status of the actor, that governs whether the discretionary function exception applies in a given case." Thus a low-level government employee might select a course of action that would be considered discretionary, or a higher-level official might merely implement a policy, which would not be immunized from liability. But where higher-ups are exercising "judgment," the discretionary function immunity is likely to be found.

5. **Implementation vs. design of a course of action.** Some courts have distinguished between designing (or deciding whether to adopt) a particular course of action and merely implementing that course of action. *See, e.g., Whisnant v. United States*, 400 F.3d 1177 (9th Cir. 2005) (holding that the former is protected by discretionary immunity, while the latter is not); *Kim v.*

United States, 940 F.3d 484 (9th Cir. 2019) ("Regardless of the policy considerations that went into the choice to adopt the system [of evaluating the risks posed by trees in Yosemite National Park], the implementation of such system cannot be said to turn on those same considerations."). Is this distinction helpful in making a reasoned decisions?

6. **Property maintenance.** Decisions about routine property maintenance, even if they involve some element of choice, are usually not susceptible to policy analysis. *See, e.g., Gibson v. United States*, 809 F.3d 807 (5th Cir. 2016); *Young v. United States*, 769 F.3d 1047 (9th Cir. 2014). But does this mean that the government's failure to maintain property or buildings would never be protected by discretionary immunity? In *Terbush v. United States*, 516 F.3d 1125 (9th Cir. 2008), the court agreed that "matters of routine maintenance are not protected . . . because they generally do not involve policy-weighing decisions or actions." But the court added that "sometimes 'maintenance' is far from routine and may involve considerable discretion that invokes policy judgment." Especially where maintenance decisions require a federal agency "to prioritize among its repairs," or choose between maintenance and doing something else entirely, such decisions may implicate policy concerns. *Id.*

7. **Funding decisions.** Is it relevant to a determination of the scope of discretionary immunity that a challenged governmental decision was based partially on fiscal concerns? In *Reyes-Colon v. United States*, 974 F.3d 56 (1st Cir. 2020), a Postal Service contractor's truck rear-ended a school bus, causing injuries. Plaintiffs sued under the FTCA, claiming the Postal Service was negligent in failing to do a safety inspection of its contractors' vehicles. The court held that the Postal Service's decision "to contract out mail transportation services required a balancing of factors (cost and safety among them)—making it a policy choice that judges cannot second-guess." Judge Posner, in *Collins v. United States*, 564 F.3d 833 (7th Cir. 2009), said that the "prioritization of demands for government money is quintessentially a discretionary function." Does that cut too broadly?

LOGE V. UNITED STATES, 662 F.2d 1268 (8th Cir. 1981). A federal agency licensed a drug company to manufacture a live-virus oral polio vaccine. A risk of such vaccines is that either a recipient or a person who comes in contact with "shed" virus could develop polio. Recognizing that risk, the agency promulgated regulations pertaining to the safety and potency of these strains, and required drug manufacturers to prove their product's conformity to these regulations before getting a license to manufacture. Mrs. Loge was exposed to the virus and rendered a paraplegic after a doctor inoculated her infant son. She filed an FTCA action alleging that the government was negligent (1) in not requiring the drug manufacturer to comply with the government's own regulations and (2) in licensing at all, or in licensing without additional safety regulations.

Held, the first set of allegations state a claim under applicable state law and are not barred by the discretionary function immunity. The government "has no discretion to disregard the mandatory regulatory commands pertaining to criteria a vaccine must meet before licensing its manufacture or releasing a particular lot of vaccine for distribution to the public." However, "[i]nsofar as the Loges' amended complaint alleged that the government was negligent in promulgating or failing to promulgate regulations that would ensure the safety of live, oral poliovirus vaccines and properly protect susceptible persons such as Mrs. Loge, the district court correctly found that such actions by the government were discretionary functions and therefore immune from suit under FTCA."

NOTES

1.   **Immunity for legislative inaction.** If a court could impose liability when Congress fails to enact safety legislation, courts, not elected members of the political branch, would have ultimate legislative control. Why would this be a problem?

2.   **Violating mandatory regulations.** *Loge* says that the discretionary immunity does not extend to the violation of a "mandatory regulation." Do you see why that is so? *See Myers v. United States*, 652 F.3d 1021 (9th Cir. 2011). In *Sanders v. United States*, 937 F.3d 316 (4th Cir. 2019), surviving victims and estates of Mother Emanuel A.M.E. Church shooting victims sued the federal government for negligently performing a background check that would have prevented the shooter from purchasing the semi-automatic pistol used in the shooting. The court held that the government was not immune on discretionary function grounds because the FBI's National Instant Criminal Background Check System examiner violated mandatory standard operating procedure directives in conducting the background check.

3.   **Violating nonmandatory regulations.** If a regulation exists and imposes duties, is it enough for the plaintiff to claim that the government official breached those duties? The focus is on whether the duties imposed are truly mandatory. If a regulation itself allows discretion in how it is to be complied with, then the government is likely entitled to assert the discretionary immunity even in the face of a regulation. *See, e.g., Spotts v. United States*, 613 F.3d 559 (5th Cir. 2010) (prison official's decision not to evacuate federal prisoners during and after a hurricane was protected by discretionary immunity; Bureau of Prisons standards and regulations allegedly violated were not mandatory); *Indemnity Ins. Co. v. United States*, 569 F.3d 175 (4th Cir. 2009) (immunizing Coast Guard's alleged violations of provisions in Marine Safety Manual); *A. O. Smith Corp. v. United States*, 774 F.3d 359 (6th Cir. 2014) (immunizing Army Corps of Engineers decisions on how to deal with thousand-year flood event in Tennessee). Indeed, the existence of a law, regulation, or policy that allows a government employee the discretion to decide how to act creates a strong presumption that the challenged conduct qualifies as a discretionary function. *See In re Katrina*

Canal Breaches Litigation, 696 F.3d 436 (5th Cir. 2012); *Mahon v. United States*, 742 F.3d 11 (1st Cir. 2014).

4.   **A case example.** A camper falls off an unmarked and unfenced cliff in a campground on government property managed by the Army Corps of Engineers. A federal regulation requires the government to manage its resources so as to "provide the public with safe and healthful recreational opportunities." The Army Corps' written safety plan for the area includes an instruction that "dangerous terrain conditions, such as drop-offs, etc., will be properly marked or fenced." What is the relevance of the safety plan and regulation, and on what basis could the government be held liable in such a case? *Navarette v. United States*, 500 F.3d 914 (9th Cir. 2007).

NOTE: GOVERNMENT CONTRACTORS

1.   *Suit against the government.* The FTCA expressly retains the government's immunity for claims arising out of the acts or omissions of private independent contractors working pursuant to government contracts. *See, e.g., Carroll v. United States,* 661 F.3d 87 (1st Cir. 2011) (FTCA immunizes government from liability for alleged negligence of a childcare facility on property owned by government, and of a landscaping business hired by the government to maintain that property). However, the government is not immune *simply because* it contracted with a private party to perform some task. The key factor is whether the government exerts significant supervision over the contractor's day-to-day operations; if not, then the government may not be held responsible for the independent contractor's negligence. *See United States v. Orleans,* 425 U.S. 807 (1976).

2.   *Suit against the contractor.* Whether the government contractor itself can assert the governmental immunity to escape liability is an entirely separate question. This is often called the "government contractor defense." In *Yearsley v. W.A. Ross Constr. Co.,* 309 U.S. 18 (1940), the Court held that when "authority to carry out the project was validly conferred" by the government, "there is no liability on the part of the contractor for executing its will." That is, where the government has contracted with a private person or entity to perform some task, and the contractor performs that task in conformity with the terms of the contract, the contractor cannot be liable at all. *See, e.g., Ackerson v. Bean Dredging LLC,* 589 F.3d 196 (5th Cir. 2009) (government contracted with defendants to dredge the Mississippi River; contractors immune).

Contractors have also been held to share the government's immunity for injuries arising out of combat activities, where the contractor has been "integrated" into those activities and is supervised by military commanders. *See, e.g., Saleh v. Titan Corp.,* 580 F.3d 1 (D.C. Cir. 2009) (contractors that provided interrogators to the military were immune from suit by Iraqi prisoners who claimed to have been tortured); *In re KBR, Inc., Burn Pit Litigation*, 744 F.3d 326 (4th Cir. 2014) (vacating trial court's grant of contractors' motion to dismiss, holding triable issues remained on whether contractors hired to provide waste disposal and water treatment services at military bases in Iraq and Afghanistan were integrated into the military chain of command); *see also Badilla v. Midwest Air Traffic Control Service, Inc.*, 8 F.4th 105 (2d Cir. 2021) (key question on immunity is "whether the government made the contractor do it"; thus where military did not authorize or direct air traffic controller's decisions in Afghanistan, contractor was not immune from tort suit by estates of pilots and crew members of civilian flight that crashed into a mountain near the Kabul airport).

C. THE *FERES* DOCTRINE

PURCELL V. UNITED STATES
656 F.3d 463 (7th Cir. 2011)

FLAUM, CIRCUIT JUDGE.

Christopher Lee Purcell ("Purcell") committed suicide in his barracks at the Brunswick Naval Air Station, where he was serving on active duty in the Navy. Navy and Department of Defense ("DOD") personnel were called to the scene after being informed that Purcell planned to kill himself. They arrived at his residence before he attempted suicide, but did not find the gun they were told he had. Later, they permitted Purcell to go to the bathroom accompanied by his friend. Upon entering, he pulled a gun from his waistband and committed suicide by shooting himself in the chest.

After attempting unsuccessfully to recover for Purcell's death from the Navy through administrative procedures, his family sought relief in federal court on a wrongful death claim under the Federal Tort Claims Act ("FTCA"). [The family's complaint alleged "that the United States failed to calm Purcell, to search him in accordance with Navy regulations, to maintain proper custody of him after removing his handcuffs, and to transport him to the Brunswick Naval Air Station security precinct in accordance with the Air Station's standard operating procedures." The complaint also alleged "that the responding officers irritated Purcell with profane, derogatory, and threatening comments that were contrary to standard operating procedures."] The district court found the case barred by the *Feres* doctrine, which provides that "the Government is not liable under the [FTCA] for injuries to servicemen where the injuries arise out of or are in the course of activity incident to service." . . .

The FTCA provides that "[t]he United States shall be liable, respecting the provisions of this title relating to tort claims, in the same manner and to the same extent as a private individual under like circumstances." Excepted from this waiver of sovereign immunity, however, are claims "arising out of the combatant activities of the military or naval forces, or the Coast Guard, during time of war." 28 U.S.C. § 2680(j). In *Feres v. United States,* 340 U.S. 135 (1950), the Supreme Court further held that "the Government is not liable under the [FTCA] for injuries to servicemen where the injuries arise out of or are in the course of activity incident to service."

The *Feres* doctrine, while currently viable, is certainly not without controversy. It has been interpreted increasingly broadly over time, and has also been widely criticized. In *United States v. Johnson,* 481 U.S. 681 (1987), in a dissent signed by three other Justices, Justice Scalia wrote that "*Feres* was wrongly decided and heartily deserves the widespread, almost universal criticism it has received." But the majority in *Johnson* reaffirmed *Feres,* and the Court has not squarely addressed the doctrine since then. *Feres* thus remains the law until Congress or the Supreme Court decides otherwise.

When the Court reaffirmed *Feres,* it discussed three rationales that support the doctrine: (1) the need to protect the distinctively federal relationship between the government and the armed forces, which could be adversely affected by applying differing tort laws; (2) the existence of statutory compensatory schemes; and (3) the need to avoid interference with military discipline and effectiveness. . . . "The dispositive inquiry [is] whether the service-member stand[s] in the type of relationship to the military at the time of his or her injury that the occurrences causing the injury arose out of activity incident to military service." *Smith v. United States,* 196 F.3d 774 (7th Cir. 1999).

Applying that test, we conclude that the district court correctly dismissed Michael Purcell's suit based on *Feres.* At the time he committed suicide, which occurred in his on-base residential building, Purcell was on active duty; living in the barracks on a military base, experiencing, according to Michael Purcell, various social and emotional problems that developed shortly after he enlisted; and deliberately avoiding Navy and DOD personnel sent to Purcell's barracks to help him, whom Michael Purcell claims failed to follow their own military regulations, and some of whom, he explains, faced courts-martial and were punished via an extrajudicial proceeding for failing to adequately search and supervise Purcell. Together, these facts demonstrate that Purcell stood "in the type of relationship to the military at the time of his . . . injury that the occurrences causing the injury arose out of activity incident to military service," and thus that *Feres* bars his suit. . . .

Michael Purcell's counsel ably, although ultimately unpersuasively, opposes applying *Feres.* Primarily, he argues that Purcell's death had nothing to do with his military status, and that the military connections to the case are irrelevant because Purcell was effectively acting as and treated like a civilian during the relevant events. We disagree. As explained above, *Feres* is read broadly, and Michael Purcell cannot avoid its reach on the facts of this case. Michael Purcell also points out that neither Purcell nor his estate have received benefits related to his suicide. But that alone does not warrant reversal in this case. *See Maas v. United States,* 94 F.3d 291, 295 (7th Cir.1996) ("[T]his and other courts have applied *Feres* to bar claims that are incident to service even if a serviceman is not entitled to military benefits relating to those claims.").

Like many courts and commentators, we recognize the challenges presented by the *Feres* doctrine. In light of its enormous breadth, however, we AFFIRM the judgment of the district court.

NOTES

1. **Broad constructions of *Feres*.** As the *Purcell* court says, the *Feres* doctrine has been broadly construed to bar claims by active military personnel. *See, e.g., Kitowski v. United States,* 931 F.2d 1526 (11th Cir. 1991) (military trainer brutally held a recruit under water until he died); *United States v. Stanley,* 483 U.S. 669 (1987) (government conducted LSD experiments upon serviceman without informing him of risks; held to be "incident to service"). It also applies to bar claims brought for violation of Constitutional rights rather than for violation of state tort law. *Chappell v. Wallace,* 462 U.S. 296 (1983). It has even been extended to a college ROTC student, *see Lovely v. United States,* 570 F.3d 778 (6th Cir. 2009) (reasoning that the plaintiff's emotional injuries, resulting from his ROTC commander's actions in connection with a school disciplinary proceeding, "arose because of his military relationship with the Government").

2. **"Incident to service."** *Feres* formally covers only those injuries that are "incident to service," seemingly on the assumption that the policy reasons advanced for rejecting liability more or less automatically apply when injury is incident to service and do not apply otherwise. *See Taber v. Maine,* 67 F.3d 1029 (2d Cir. 1995). Exactly what "incident to service" means is not clear. For example, sometimes a service member injured while on furlough will be found to have not been injured incident to service, *see, e.g., Schoenfeld v. Quamme,* 492 F.3d 1016 (9th Cir. 2007), whereas sometimes a soldier injured on furlough will be barred by *Feres* on exactly that ground, *see United States v. Shearer,* 473 U.S. 52 (1985). A soldier injured while on leave but still on active duty, however, is usually injured incident to service. *See, e.g., McConnell v. United States,* 478 F.2d 1092 (9th Cir. 2007) (*Feres* barred claim for death of Air Force pilot killed while waterskiing on Air Force base). Perhaps our best overall doctrinal summary is that *Feres* will not protect the government "if government negligence occurs when the plaintiff has no active connection with the military," with the caveat that "courts have usually interpreted 'incident

to service' quite broadly." 2 DOBBS, HAYDEN & BUBLICK, THE LAW OF TORTS § 338 (2d ed. 2011).

3.   **The breadth of the "military discipline" rationale.** The term "military discipline" has been also given an extremely broad reading in *Feres* doctrine cases. In *United States v. Johnson*, 481 U.S. 681 (1987), a Coast Guard pilot, flying under the control of a civilian FAA controller, was killed in a crash. The surviving spouse asserted that the FAA was negligent in causing the death. The Court applied the *Feres* immunity, partly because "a suit based upon service-related activity necessarily implicates the military judgment and decisions" and "military discipline involves not only obedience to orders, but more generally duty and loyalty to one's service and to one's country. Suits brought by service members against the Government for service-related injuries could undermine the commitment essential to effective service and thus have the potential to disrupt military discipline in the broadest sense of the word."

4.   **Criticisms of *Feres*.** The *Purcell* court notes that the *Feres* doctrine has been criticized, most famously in Justice Scalia's dissent in *Johnson*, *supra* Note 3. More recently, Justice Thomas, dissenting from the Court's denial of certiorari in *Lanus v. United States*, 570 U.S. 932 (2013), expressed his agreement with Justice Scalia's view. *Feres* should be "reconsidered," he wrote, because it lacks support in the text of the FTCA and "has the unfortunate consequence of depriving servicemen of any remedy when they are injured by the negligence of the Government or its employees." In *Daniel v. United States*, 889 F.3d 978 (9th Cir. 2018), the court held that the *Feres* doctrine barred an FTCA suit seeking damages for the death of a female Navy officer due to a complication following childbirth, allegedly caused by medical malpractice in a Naval hospital. The panel lamented that it was "regretfully" bound by precedent, even though the case had nothing to do with "military discipline," commenting, "If ever there were a case to carve out an exception to the *Feres* doctrine, this is it. But only the Supreme Court has the tools to do so." Does the *Feres* doctrine reflect good public policy?

5.   **Spouses and children.** *Feres* does not usually bar a recovery by a spouse or child of a person in the armed forces if the spouse or child is directly injured. Common examples of recovery by spouses or children are those involving medical malpractice in military hospitals. But even in this setting, *Feres* may bar the claim if the family member's injury had its "genesis" in an incident-to-service injury to the service person. *Ritchie v. United States*, 733 F.3d 871 (9th Cir. 2013). For example, where a newborn suffered brain injuries from lack of oxygen during childbirth, which was caused by an allegedly negligent administration of medication to her mother, an active-duty Air Force officer, the child's injury had its genesis in the mother's injury, which was "incident to service," thus barring the child's claim under *Feres*. *Ortiz v. United States*, 786 F.3d 817 (10th Cir. 2015).

Suppose that the Army subjects a service member to inoculations or exposure to radioactive materials that result in birth defects in his or her children. Can the children recover from the government for the harms done to them? *See Minns v. United States*, 155 F.3d 445 (4th Cir. 1998) (Gulf War inoculation causing birth defects, *Feres* bars children's claim because it had its genesis in injury to service members and would implicate military discipline); *Hinkie v. United States*, 715 F.2d 96 (3d Cir. 1983) (exposure of service personnel to radioactive materials, children injured by genetic damage to parent are barred by *Feres*). There are a number of similar cases.

§ 3. IMMUNITY OF STATES AND MUNICIPALITIES

A. UNDER STATE LAW

In our system of government, the states are sovereigns, too, subject only to the limitations of the United States Constitution. At one time the states claimed sovereign immunity on the same basis as did the federal government. Most states now have now enacted tort claims statutes that provide for at least a partial waiver of sovereign immunity. As a matter of structure, most states follow the federal model (often copying from the FTCA) and waive the tort immunity generally, retaining it in particular, specified situations. A smaller, but still significant number work in reverse, retaining the immunity generally but abolishing it in particular, specified situations. Both kinds of statutes do retain substantial blocks of immunity for the states. A small number retain virtually complete immunity. Most states have special procedural rules and remedial restrictions on tort claims against the state. *See* 2 DOBBS, HAYDEN & BUBLICK, THE LAW OF TORTS § 342 (2d ed. 2011).

Municipalities within the states are sometimes covered under state tort claims statutes, so that municipal immunity parallels state government immunity. Other states have separate immunity rules for municipalities.

While generalization is difficult, a number of important issues recur in tort litigation against state and local entities under state law. Some of these issues parallel those faced in FTCA actions against the federal government; others are more or less unique to the non-federal setting—in part because of the different functions for which different levels of government are typically responsible.

RISS V. CITY OF NEW YORK
240 N.E.2d 860 (N.Y. 1968)

[Linda Riss was terrorized for months by a rejected suitor, Burton Pugach. He threatened to kill or maim her if she did not yield to him. She repeatedly sought protection from law enforcement officers. Eventually she became engaged to another man. At a party celebrating the event, she received a phone call warning her that it was her "last chance." She again called police, but nothing seems to have been done. The next day Pugach carried out his threat by having a person hired for the purpose to throw lye in Linda's face. She was blinded in one eye, lost a good portion of her vision in the other and suffered permanent scarring of her face. This is her action against the City of New York for failure to provide police protection. The trial court dismissed the complaint at the end of all the evidence and the Appellate Division affirmed.]

BREITEL, JUDGE.

This appeal presents, in a very sympathetic framework, the issue of the liability of a municipality for failure to provide special protection to a member of the public who was repeatedly threatened with personal harm and eventually suffered dire personal injuries for lack of such protection. . . .

It is necessary immediately to distinguish those liabilities attendant upon governmental activities which have displaced or supplemented traditionally private enterprises, such as are involved in the operation of rapid transit systems, hospitals, and places of public assembly. Once sovereign immunity was abolished by statute the extension of liability on ordinary principles of tort law logically followed. To be equally distinguished are certain activities of government which provide services and facilities for the use of the public, such as highways, public buildings and the like, in the performance of which the municipality or the State may be liable under ordinary principles of tort law. The ground for liability is the provision of the services or facilities for the direct use of members of the public. In contrast, this case involves the provision of a governmental service to protect the public generally from external hazards and particularly to control the activities of criminal wrongdoers.

The amount of protection that may be provided is limited by the resources of the community and by a considered legislative-executive decision as to how those resources may be deployed. For the courts to proclaim a new and general duty of protection in the law of tort, even to those who may be the particular seekers of protection based on specific hazards, could and would inevitably determine how the limited police resources of the community should be allocated and without predictable limits. This is quite different from the predictable allocation of resources and liabilities when public hospitals, rapid transit systems, or even highways are provided.

Before such extension of responsibilities should be dictated by the indirect imposition of tort liabilities, there should be a legislative determination that that should be the scope of public responsibility.

It is notable that the removal of sovereign immunity for tort liability was accomplished after legislative enactment and not by any judicial arrogation of power. It is equally notable that for many years, since as far back as 1909, in this State, there was by statute municipal liability for losses sustained as a result of riot. Yet even this class of liability has for some years been suspended by legislative action, a factor of considerable significance. When one considers the greatly increased amount of crime committed throughout the cities, but especially in certain portions of them, with a repetitive and predictable pattern, it is easy to see the consequences of fixing municipal liability upon a showing of probable need for and request for protection. To be sure these are grave problems at the present time, exciting high priority activity on the part of the national, State and local governments, to which the answers are neither simple, known, or presently within reasonable controls. To foist a presumed cure for these problems by judicial innovation of a new kind of liability in tort would be foolhardy indeed and an assumption of judicial wisdom and power not possessed by the courts.

Nor is the analysis progressed by the analogy to compensation for losses sustained. It is instructive that the Crime Victims Compensation and "Good Samaritan" statutes, compensating limited classes of victims of crime, were enacted only after the most careful study of conditions and the impact of such a scheme upon governmental operations and the public fisc. And then the limitations were particular and narrow.

For all of these reasons, there is no warrant in judicial tradition or in the proper allocation of the powers of government for the courts, in the absence of legislation, to carve out an area of tort liability for police protection to members of the public. Quite distinguishable, of course, is the situation where the police authorities undertake responsibilities to particular members of the public and expose them, without adequate protection, to the risks which then materialize into actual losses (Schuster v. City of New York, 5 N.Y.2d 75,180 N.Y.S.2d 265,154 N.E.2d 534).

Accordingly, the order of the Appellate Division affirming the judgment of dismissal should be affirmed.

DE LONG V. COUNTY OF ERIE, 457 N.E.2d 717 (N.Y. 1983). At 9:29 Mrs. De Long called the 911 emergency number covering all cities and towns in Erie County, New York. She reported that someone was attempting to break in and gave her address. The "complaint writer" assured her someone would come right away. Since her own local police station in the town of Kenmore was only a block and a half away, assistance might have been readily available except for the fact that the complaint writer sent officers to an address in Buffalo instead of Kenmore. When the officers found "no such address," the complaint writer dropped the call as a "fake." In the meantime the burglar gained entrance and at 9:42 Mrs. De Long was seen running from the house bleeding. She collapsed and died of stab wounds. A jury found for the plaintiff in a wrongful death action. *Held*, affirmed. Where police refuse assistance, there is an issue of how to allocate public resources and it should be left to the executive and legislative branches. But in this case "the decision had been made by the municipalities to provide a special emergency service. . . ." There is, as defendants argue, a "familiar rule," that public entities are not liable for "negligence in the performance of a governmental function, including police and fire protection, unless a special relationship existed between the municipality and the injured party. . . ." But here there is a special relationship between the city and the caller. The "victim's plea for assistance was not refused." The special relationship between the defendants and the caller required the defendants "to exercise ordinary care in the performance of a duty it has voluntarily assumed."

NOTES

1.   **Policy concerns over resource allocation.** In considering *Riss*, remember that New York had earlier abolished the state's sovereign immunity. Judge Breitel was obviously concerned about allocation of public resources by way of tort judgments. *See also University of the Incarnate Word v. Redus*, 602 S.W.3d 398 (Tex. 2020) ("Immunity preserves separation-of-powers principles by preventing the judiciary from interfering with the Legislature's prerogative to allocate tax dollars. And immunity protects the public treasury by shielding the public from the costs and consequences of improvident actions of their governments."). But *any* tort judgment against the city would allocate resources, including a judgment based on a city bus driver's negligence. Does the distinction between tort suits against the police department and those against the bus authority hold up?

2.   **Relevance of why assistance was refused.** Judge Breitel did not really say why the police in *Riss* refused assistance. He seemed to assume, however, that there was a professional reason bearing on resource allocation. Suppose that was not the case; suppose the police simply did not follow sound procedure, or made a clerical mistake and failed to record Miss Riss' call. Would the result be different?

3.   **Special relationships and reliance.** More recent cases from New York are clear in requiring that a plaintiff must show four things to establish that "special relationship" that would give rise to a duty on the part of a municipality to protect an individual plaintiff: (1) promises or actions that represent an assumption of an affirmative duty to act on the plaintiff's behalf; (2) knowledge by the municipality's agents "that inaction could lead to harm; (3) some form of direct contact between the municipality's agents and the injured party; and (4) that party's justifiable reliance on the municipality's affirmative undertaking." *Valdez v. City of New York*, 960 N.E.2d 356 (N.Y. 2011) (quoting *Cuffy v. City of New York*, 505 N.E.2d 937 (N.Y. 1987)).

New York courts have explained that the fourth requirement—justifiable reliance—is " 'critical' because it provides the essential causative link between the 'special duty' assumed by the municipality and the alleged injury." *Id.* In

Valdez, the plaintiff claimed that she called the police and told them that her former boyfriend, Perez, had threatened to kill her, and that she was assured by the police that they would arrest him "immediately." After staying in her apartment for many hours, plaintiff left and was shot by Perez. The court held that it was not reasonable for the plaintiff to conclude that "she could relax her vigilance" based simply on a police promise that they were going to arrest Perez. Because she failed to prove justifiable reliance, the police owed her no duty of care. *See also McLean v. City of New York*, 905 N.E.2d 1167 (N.Y. 2009) (contact between city and plaintiff did not constitute any "promise" at all; therefore no special relationship arose and no duty was owed).

4.   **Duty of care and immunity.** Notice that the question of whether the plaintiff can prove a duty of care is distinct from the issue of whether the defendant can assert an immunity, such as discretionary immunity. Can *DeLong* be seen as resting not on a "special relationship," but rather on the fact that no professional judgment at all was involved, only an operational mistake?

5.   **Resource allocation, redux.** Does a "resource allocation" rationale for retaining immunity sweep too broadly? In *Zelig v. County of Los Angeles*, 45 P.3d 1171 (Cal. 2002), the court held that the county was not liable to the estate of a woman who was killed by her husband in the county courthouse despite the county's knowledge that she was coming to court, that her husband had threatened her, and that he was under a court order not to bring guns into her presence. The court stressed that its holding, whether "expressed as a limitation on duty or as a form of governmental immunity," rested on the notion that "the level of police protection is an allocative question best left to the political branches." In *Barillari v. City of Milwaukee*, 533 N.W.2d 759 (Wis. 1995), the city was held immune from liability for the killing of a woman by her estranged boyfriend even though he had earlier sexually assaulted her and police had promised to protect her and to arrest him at a specific time when he was expected to come to her house. They failed to arrest him and did not tell her that he was still at large. Days later he murdered her and killed himself. The police "decisions" were discretionary, said the court: "The nature of law enforcement requires moment-to-moment decision making and crises management, which, in turn, requires that the police department have the latitude to decide how to best utilize law enforcement resources."

HARRY STOLLER AND CO. V. CITY OF LOWELL
587 N.E.2d 780 (Mass. 1992)

[The plaintiff's five brick buildings were destroyed by a fire which started on the sixth floor of one of them. A sprinkler system was in place and had been tested two days earlier. Firefighters, in violation of accepted practice, chose not to use it, fighting the fire with hoses instead. All five buildings and their contents were destroyed. After a jury awarded the plaintiff $785,000, the trial judge granted judgment NOV for the defendant under the state's statutory discretionary immunity. *Held*, reversed.]

WILKINS, J.

This court has declined to apply the discretionary function exception to a variety of governmental acts. A police officer deciding whether to remove from the roadways a motorist, known to be intoxicated, is not making a policy or planning judgment. A physician employed by a city is not engaged in a discretionary function, within the meaning of § 10(b), in her treatment of a patient in a hospital emergency room. . . . The failure to provide sufficient information to enable a person to protect his property against the conduct of a client of the Department of Mental Health does not involve the exercise of choice regarding public policy and planning but rather the carrying out of previously established policies or plans. . . .

There are aspects of firefighting that can have an obvious planning or policy basis. The number and location of fire stations, the amount of equipment to purchase, the size of the fire department, the number and location of hydrants, and the quantity of the water supply involve policy considerations, especially the allocation of financial resources. In certain situations, firefighting involves determinations of what property to attempt to save because the resources available to combat a conflagration are or seem to be insufficient to save all threatened property. In such cases, policy determinations might be involved, and application of the discretionary function exception would be required.

The case before us is different. The negligent conduct that caused the fire to engulf all the plaintiff's buildings was not founded on planning or policy considerations. The question whether to put higher water pressure in the sprinkler systems involved no policy choice or planning decision. There was a dispute on the evidence whether it was negligent to fail to fight the fire through the buildings' sprinkler systems. The firefighters may have thought that they had a discretionary choice whether to pour water on the buildings through hoses or to put water inside the buildings through their sprinkler systems. They certainly had discretion in the sense that no statute, regulation, or established municipal practice required the firefighters to use the sprinklers (or, for that matter, to use hoses exclusively). But whatever discretion they had was not based on a policy or planning judgment. The jury decided that, in exercising their discretion not to use the buildings' sprinkler systems, the Lowell firefighters were negligent because they failed to conform to generally accepted firefighting practices. When the firefighters exercised that discretion, policy and planning considerations were not involved. Therefore, the discretionary function exception does not shield the city from liability. . . .

NOTES

1. **Suing police and fire departments.** As you can see from all of the cases in this section, courts are reluctant to second-guess fire and police

departments in their decisions not to act. Some state statutes contain explicit provisions immunizing police and fire departments from suits alleging a failure to provide, or the method of providing, protection. *See, e.g.,* KAN. STAT. ANN. 2015 Supp. § 75–6104(n); MISS. CODE ANN. § 11–46–9(1)(c) (unless employee acted in "reckless disregard" of a person's safety). In line with *Riss*, New York has held that the fire department's failure to enforce a fire safety rule was not actionable on behalf of someone who suffered a fire loss that could have been avoided, and this was true even though the city had actual notice of the danger. *Motyka v. City of Amsterdam*, 204 N.E.2d 635 (N.Y. 1965). *Cf. Massenburg v. City of Petersburg*, 836 S.E.2d 391 (Va. 2019) (city's provision and maintenance of fire hydrants was a governmental function, protected by sovereign immunity). How then can we explain *Harry Stoller and Co.*? A few courts have imposed liability for failure to provide enforcement of fire safety laws. *Adams v. State*, 555 P.2d 235 (Alaska 1976). And statutes may impose a duty to enforce criminal law for the protection of potential victims, such as those subject to domestic violence. *See Roy v. City of Everett*, 823 P.2d 1084 (Wash. 1992).

2. **Discretionary immunity.** Many state statutes contain discretionary immunity provisions, although state-court interpretations are not always identical those seen in the FTCA case law. For example, some states require that the government must in fact make a policy decision for the immunity to attach; it is not enough that a challenged decision be merely "susceptible" to policy analysis. *See, e.g., Andrews v. Metropolitan Water Reclamation Dist. of Greater Chicago*, 160 N.E.3d 895 (Ill. 2019); *Veolia Water Indianapolis, LLC v. National Trust Ins. Co.*, 3 N.E.3d 1 (Ind. 2014).

Terminology also sometimes diverges from the federal usage, even where the analysis is quite similar to what we see in FTCA discretionary immunity cases. A number of states draw a distinction between "discretionary" and "ministerial" acts, saying that immunity attaches to the former but not the latter. *See, e.g., Commonwealth v. Sexton*, 256 S.W.3d 29 (Ky. 2008). Others distinguish between "planning" and "operational" decisions, with immunity for only the first, not the second. *See, e.g., Haight v. City & Borough of Juneau*, 448 P.3d 254 (Alaska 2019); *Schroeder v. St. Louis County*, 708 N.W.2d 497 (Minn. 2006). A few draw the line between "governmental" and "proprietary" functions, with immunity for the former but not the latter. *See, e.g., Connolly v. Long Island Power Auth.*, 94 N.E.3d 471 (N.Y. 2018); *Meinck v. City of Gastonia*, 819 S.E.2d 353 (N.C. 2018); *Civetti v. Turner*, 233 A.3d 1056 (Vt. 2020).

As with the FTCA, state-law discretionary immunity will shield many governmental units from liability in order to "permit governance without undue inhibition from the threat of tort liability and to limit judicial examination of policy decision entrusted to other government branches." *Lamont Bair Enterprises, Inc. v. City of Idaho Falls*, 454 P.3d 572 (Idaho 2019) (immunizing city decision to adopt water facility plan in suit by landowner whose property was damaged by broken water main). The reported cases are many, and varied. Governments have been protected by this immunity for conduct ranging from the administration of security at the World Trade

Center, *In re World Trade Center Bombing Litigation*, 957 N.E.2d 733 (N.Y. 2011), to the conduct of a child-abuse investigation, *Georgia Dept. of Human Services v. Spruill,* 751 S.E.2d 315 (Ga. 2013), to a decision not to install seatbelts in an inmate transport van, *Maryea v. Velardi,* 135 A.3d 121 (N.H. 2016), to decisions made by state prison officials during a prison riot, *Wizinsky v. State*, 957 N.W.2d 466 (Neb. 2021).

3.   **Suits over defects in government property.** A number of state statutes allow governmental entities to be sued when harm results from a defect in government property. For example, state and local governments are often under a duty to maintain roadways in a safe condition, a duty that may extend "beyond the asphalt" to adjacent roadside vegetation, *Wuthrich v. King County*, 366 P.3d 926 (Wash. 2016), a culvert under the road, *Barneck v. Utah Dept. of Transp.*, 353 P.3d 140 (Utah 2015), a guardrail, *Cagey v. Commonwealth*, 179 A.3d 458 (Pa. 2018), and the median strip, *Cordova v. City of Los Angeles*, 353 P.3d 773 (Cal. 2015).

But the government may be immune if the claim is that the roadway or intersection was negligently *designed. See, e.g., Hampton v. County of San Diego*, 362 P.3d 417 (Cal. 2015) (applying statutory "design immunity"). What if the government becomes aware of a design feature that has created a dangerous condition? Should the state retain its "design" immunity, or at that point is the allegedly negligent conduct about something other than the design? Compare *Martinez v. New Mexico Dept. of Transp.*, 296 P.3d 468 (N.M. 2013), with *Turner v. State*, 375 P.3d 508 (Or. 2016). Statutes and regulations often specify that governments remain potentially liable for defects in sidewalks and public buildings. *See Wise v. Huntingdon County Housing Development Corp.*, 249 A3d 506 (Pa. 2021) (extending statutory liability to insufficient outdoor lighting adjacent to sidewalk). Some states retain immunity where injuries were caused by natural conditions on unimproved property. *See, e.g., Burnett v. State Dept. of Natural Resources*, 346 P.3d 1005 (Colo. 2015).

4.   **Traffic lights and signage.** The defective-property basis for government liability often extends to negligently maintained traffic lights and signage. The government will face liability for failure to correct the problem where that failure is a cause of harm. *See, e.g., Twomey v. Commonwealth*, 825 N.E.2d 989 (Mass. 2005) (traffic sign obscured by bushes); *Hensley v. Jackson County*, 227 S.W.3d 491 (Mo. 2007) (downed stop sign); *Fickle v. State*, 735 N.W.2d 754 (Neb. 2007) (malfunctioning traffic light). Would you expect liability, though, where the suit alleged a negligent failure to install a traffic signal at an intersection? *See Risner v. Ohio Dept. of Transp.*, 46 N.E.3d 687 (Ohio 2015). Or if the claim was negligent placement of a warning sign at an intersection? *Truman v. Griese*, 762 N.W.2d 75 (S.D. 2009). Or if the claim was about the location of a bus stop? *Bonanno v. Central Contra Costa Transit Auth.*, 65 P.3d 807 (Cal. 2003).

5.   **Suits over high-speed chases.** High-speed police chases produce a good deal of litigation, especially when innocent bystanders are injured. *See 2 DOBBS, HAYDEN & BUBLICK, THE LAW OF TORTS § 348 (2d ed. 2011). What is the

best way to handle such cases? Some states provide a specific complete immunity, often by statute. *See, e.g., Colvin v. City of Gardena*, 15 Cal. Rptr.2d 234 (Ct. App. 1992). Conversely, some statutes specifically waive immunity for injuries to innocent people caused by vehicular pursuits. *See Williams v. City of Omaha*, 865 N.W.2d 779 (Neb. 2015) (construing "pursuit" term in statute that imposes strict liability on the government entity). Still other states judge the case according to an ordinary negligence analysis, taking into account the importance of the particular arrest attempt and the degree of risk the chase imposes or does not impose upon others. *See, e.g., Gonzalez v. Johnson*, 581 S.W.3d 529 (Ky. 2019); *Gooden v. City of Talladega*, 966 So.2d 232 (Ala. 2007). Some lower the standard of care so that liability is permitted only when the police officer has acted recklessly or worse. *See, e.g., City of Jackson v. Lewis*, 153 So.3d 689 (Miss. 2014); *Frezzell v. City of New York*, 21 N.E.3d 1028 (N.Y. 2014). Note that states are more likely to allow claims by innocent bystanders, as opposed to the offenders themselves. *See, e.g., Smith v. City of Stillwater*, 328 P.3d 1192 (Okla. 2014) (police owe no duty owed to fleeing felon injured in high-speed chase). What about a passenger in the fleeing vehicle? *See Sellers v. Township of Abington*, 106 A.3d 679 (Pa. 2014) (no duty, distinguishing "innocent bystanders").

In some of the police-chase cases, courts employ a discretionary immunity analysis. *See, e.g., Cole v. City of New Haven*, 253 A.3d 476 (Conn. 2020) (finding genuine issues of fact as to whether policy officer had a "ministerial" duty not to engage in a particular roadblock maneuver during a pursuit). What constitutes "discretion" in this context is a often a contested issue. In *McBride v. Bennett*, 764 S.E.2d 44 (Va. 2014), the court said that discretionary immunity applies where the officer's driving "requires a degree of judgment and discretion beyond ordinary driving situations." Doesn't that just set up a blanket immunity in high-speed chase cases? In *Pletan v. Gaines*, 494 N.W.2d 38 (Minn. 1992), the court found "official immunity," which "involves the kind of discretion which is exercised on an operational rather than a policymaking level. . . . The decision to engage in a car chase and to continue the chase involves the weighing of many factors. . . . It is difficult to think of a situation where the exercise of significant, independent judgment and discretion would be more required." But in *Clark v. South Carolina Dept. of Public Safety*, 608 S.E.2d 573 (S.C. 2005), the court held that a law enforcement officer may not invoke discretionary immunity "for the decision on whether to begin or continue the immediate pursuit of a subject." For the discretionary immunity to attach, the *Clark* court said, the "governmental entity must prove its employees, faced with alternatives, actually weighed competing considerations and made a conscious choice," utilizing "accepted professional standards appropriate to resolve the issue."

6.   **Suits over releasing dangerous prisoners.** The decision to release a dangerous person from custody, such as a violent mental patient or a violent criminal, is typically regarded as "discretionary," both in state and federal cases. *E.g., Payton v. United States*, 679 F.2d 475 (5th Cir. 1982); *Kruger v. Nebraska*, 820 F.3d 295 (8th Cir. 2016) (applying Neb. law). Some

states provide specific statutory immunity. *See, e.g.,* CAL. GOV. CODE § 845.8 (no liability for "parole or release of a prisoner"); *but see* CAL. WELF. & INST. CODE §§ 6600 *et seq.* (the Sexually Violent Predators Act, imposing mandatory duties to evaluate certain inmates before they are released). A few courts impose liability for a negligent or reckless release. *See Faile v. S.C. Dep't of Juvenile Justice,* 566 S.E.2d 536 (S.C. 2002) (no discretionary immunity if officer who placed violent juvenile back with his parents did so with gross negligence); *Grimm v. Ariz. Bd. of Pardons & Paroles,* 564 P.2d 1227 (Ariz. 1977).

However, even where the *decision to release* is immunized, a number of cases impose a duty of reasonable care on government officials to *supervise* parolees. *See, e.g., Starkenburg v. State,* 934 P.2d 1018 (Mont. 1997). Other states limit such a duty to those situations where officials knew or should have known that the parolee posed a danger to a particular individual or identifiable group. *State Dept. of Corrections v. Cowles,* 151 P.3d 353 (Alaska 2006). *Cf. Osborn v. Mason County,* 134 P.3d 197 (Wash. 2006) (no duty to warn of offender's release where victim was not "foreseeable" and there was no reliance); *Thompson v. County of Alameda,* 614 P.2d 728 (Cal. 1980) (no duty to warn of the release of an inmate "who has made nonspecific threats of harm directed at nonspecific victims").

NOTE: THE PUBLIC DUTY DOCTRINE

1. *Scope.* The public duty doctrine is formally different from discretionary immunity. The public duty doctrine holds that public entities and officers are not liable to individuals for failure to carry out a duty, even a statutory duty, owed to the public at large rather than to particular individuals or groups. *See, e.g., Mancini v. City of Tacoma,* 479 P.3d 656 (Wash. 2021). For example, some courts hold that a public entity is not liable for a police officer's failure to arrest a drunk driver who, left free, drunkenly injures or kills others. *Ezell v. Cockrell,* 902 S.W.2d 394 (Tenn. 1995). Perhaps the most important effect of the doctrine is that statutes commanding action by public entities or officers are frequently construed to impose public duties only, so that no private person can recover for a public officer's failure to enforce the statute. *See, e.g., Pace v. State,* 38 A.3d 418 (Md. 2012) (National School Lunch Act and implementing regulations did not create duty to child with food allergy).

2. *Special relationships and non-action.* The public duty doctrine can differ from the discretionary immunity not only in adopting the language of duty but also in recognizing that the duty may be narrowed and liability imposed if the officer or entity takes affirmative action that endangers the plaintiff or if the duty becomes individualized because of a special relationship with the plaintiff. *See, e.g., Breese v. City of Burlington,* 945

N.W.2d 12 (Iowa 2020) (public duty doctrine inapplicable where city was affirmatively negligent in connecting a sewer box to a public pathway without providing guardrails or warning signs); *Eklund v. Trost*, 151 P.3d 870 (Mont. 2006) (special duty owed to pedestrian injured in high-speed chase). This is essentially a specific application of rules about non-action. *See* Chapter 16. A number of courts have held that the public duty doctrine does not shield a defendant from liability where the public entity's agent has acted affirmatively, or has made a promise upon which the plaintiff justifiably relied. *See, e.g., Estate of Graves v. City of Circleville*, 922 N.E.2d 201 (Ohio 2010); *Bassett v. Lamantia*, 471 P.3d 299 (Mont. 2018); *Cope v. Utah Valley State College*, 342 P.3d 243 (Utah 2014).

3. *Statutes creating special duties.* In addition, a statute might create a special duty to a particular group rather than to the public at large. In that case, the court may conclude that the statutory duty is not merely a duty owed to the public at large. For example, a statute creating a specific duty to protect victims of domestic violence may be construed to impose a duty to a special group, so that a failure to provide the protection required will be actionable. *See Washburn v. City of Federal Way*, 310 Wash.2d 732 (Wash. 2013). Or a statute governing operation of emergency vehicles can create a specific duty of care owed to occupants of a vehicle injured in a collision with a fleeing suspect's vehicle during a high-speed police chase. *See Montgomery v. Saleh*, 466 P.3d 902 (Kan. 2020).

4. *Overlaps with discretionary immunity.* In spite of what has been said above, a number of courts have verbally identified the public duty doctrine with discretionary immunity. For instance, Rhode Island expresses the doctrine in terms of discretionary immunity by saying that it "shields the state and its political subdivisions from tort liability arising out of discretionary governmental actions that by their nature are not ordinarily performed by private persons." *Georges v. State*, 249 A.3d 1261 (R.I. 2021). Stated this way, the doctrine sounds like a discretionary immunity that could protect affirmative action as well as a failure to act. Yet Rhode Island also recognizes that a special relationship between public officer and individual plaintiff may eliminate the immunity. *See Schultz v. Foster-Glocester Reg'l Sch. Dist.*, 755 A.2d 153 (R.I. 2000).

5. *Abolition of the doctrine in some states.* The public duty doctrine is a common-law rule of long standing. *See South v. Maryland*, 59 U.S. 396 (1855). While most states continue to follow the rule, a growing number have abolished it, either by court decision or by legislation. *See Coleman v. East Joliet Fire Protection Dist.*, 46 N.E.3d 741 (Ill. 2016) ("[T]he underlying purposes of the public duty rule are better served by application of traditional tort principles and the immunity afforded by statutes than by a rule that precludes a finding of a duty on the basis of the defendant's status as a public entity."). Does the public-duty doctrine add anything to

a normal duty analysis, or to immunity statutes, or is it "obsolete," as the *Coleman* court concluded?

NOTE: STATE-LAW SUITS AGAINST STATE OR LOCAL OFFICIALS

What if a state or local executive branch officer is sued under state law? Under the common law, state or local officers did not share the sovereign immunity of the states themselves. If their conduct is characterized by the court as ministerial, something about which they have no choice or discretion, they may be held liable for torts. *E.g., Morway v. Trombly*, 789 A.2d 965 (Vt. 2001) (operating a snow plow is ministerial and operator is personally liable if he is negligent). If their acts are characterized as discretionary, they are usually protected by a *state-law* qualified immunity, that is, by an immunity destructible by improper purpose or "malice." *See, e.g., Rice v. Collins Communication, Inc.*, 236 P.3d 1009 (Wyo. 2010); *Baptie v. Bruno,* 88 A.3d 1212 (Vt. 2013). These tests leave much room for litigation.

Instead of a discretionary immunity, some states now (a) remove some or all of the immunity but provide indemnity to the officer for cost of defense and amount of any judgment against him; *see, e.g.,* N.J. STAT. ANN. § 59:10–1; or (b) grant a very broad immunity and leave the plaintiff a direct claim against the state for the officer's torts. *See Vaughn v. First Transit, Inc.*, 206 P.3d 181 (Ore. 2009); *Martin v. Brady,* 802 A.2d 814 (Conn. 2002). In a number of states, employees whose act was "within the scope of their duties" are granted an immunity, but such immunity is lost where it is not. *See, e.g., Justice v. Lombardo*, 208 A.3d 1057 (Pa. 2019) (trooper's use of excessive force during traffic stop was not within scope of employment). In some states, where the officer acts with malice or gross negligence, the state is immune from suit, but the officer is not. *See Cooper v. Rodriguez*, 118 A.3d 829 (Md. 2015); *see also West Virginia Regional Jail & Correctional Facility Authority v. A.B.*, 766 S.E.2d 751 (W.Va. 2014) (where officer's actions are outside the scope of employment, which is true when the officer's acts violate clearly established law, state is not vicariously liable).

PROBLEM

In re Claims of Picklesimer, et al.

[Memo from partner in charge of the case.]

Since the initial memo [p. 443 *supra*], I have talked with an engineer who says that the highway design at the point of the accident was dangerous. He is quite specific. The highway appears to be a state highway rather than a local road. Can we sue the state for this, assuming the testimony really does support the claim of negligence? Would it matter whether we claimed (1) failure to mark the road, (2) failure to provide warning signs, (3) the design of the curve or the slope? Also, would our claim against Dalzell prejudice a claim against the state or vice versa?

B. UNDER FEDERAL LAW: § 1983

Although state and municipal immunities have been widely abrogated or limited, considerable immunity remains, as the cases in preceding sections show. These immunities lead plaintiffs to assert federal civil rights claims against states and municipalities in hopes of avoiding any immunity.

Individual state officers' liability under 1983. Where a person acting under color of state law violates a plaintiff's federal rights, the plaintiff can sue the individual state official under 28 U.S.C.A § 1983. But defendants in those cases—often state or local officials—are given the benefit of a powerful federal qualified immunity. Once that immunity is invoked by the defendant, the burden shifts to the plaintiff to prove that the federal right allegedly violated was "clearly established" at the time of the defendant's act. This has proven to be a high hurdle for plaintiffs to overcome in recent years. *See, e.g., Tobias v. Arteaga*, 996 F.3d 571 (9th Cir. 2021) (teenage detainee induced to falsely confess to murder sued police detectives, claiming Fourteenth Amendment substantive due process violation; right not clearly established); *Echols v. Lawton*, 913 F.3d 1313 ((11th Cir. 2019) (alleged defamation of former prisoner by district attorney; First Amendment right not clearly established). *See generally* Chapter 3 § 5.

State liability under § 1983. The Eleventh Amendment, as construed, provides that citizens cannot subject states to federal court suits against their will. In addition, the Supreme Court has held that states are not "persons" who can be sued under § 1983. *Will v. Mich. Dep't of State Police*, 491 U.S. 58 (1989). Although state officers may be sued for acts done in the course of their official duties, a judgment against the officer cannot serve as a basis for reaching the state's funds. *See Hafer v. Melo*, 502 U.S. 21 (1991).

Municipal liability under § 1983. It is now settled that municipalities are "persons" who may be liable under § 1983. There are two peculiarities about this, however. First, the plaintiff can prevail only by proving that some "policy" or custom of the municipality that demonstrates the municipality's "fault" was the "moving force" behind the violation of the plaintiff's federal rights. *Monell v. Dep't of Social Services*, 436 U.S. 658 (1978); *Board of County Com'rs v. Brown*, 520 U.S. 397 (1997). Second, the municipality, unlike the officer, is not entitled to assert the qualified immunity we saw in Chapter 3 § 5.

NAVARRO V. BLOCK
72 F.3d 712 (9th Cir. 1995)

PREGERSON, CIRCUIT JUDGE. . . .

At 10:30 p.m. on August 27, 1989, Maria Navarro was celebrating her birthday with her relatives and friends in her home in East Los Angeles when she received a telephone call from the brother of her estranged husband, Raymond Navarro, warning her that Raymond was on his way to her house to kill her and any others present.

Maria immediately dialed 911 to request emergency assistance. She told the 911 dispatcher that she had just received a warning that her estranged husband was on his way to kill her, that she believed that he was in fact on his way to kill her, and that he was under a restraining order.

When Maria stated that her estranged husband had not yet arrived, but that she believed he would definitely come to her house, the dispatcher responded, "O.K., well, the only thing to do is just call us if he comes over there. . . . I mean, what can we do? We can't have a unit sit there to wait and see if he comes over."

Fifteen minutes after the 911 call, Raymond Navarro entered through the rear of Maria Navarro's house, shot and killed Maria Navarro and four other people, and injured two others.

[The Navarros filed suit against Los Angeles County and the Sheriff, who handled 911 calls. The trial court granted summary judgment for the defendants on all claims.]

Under Monell v. Dept. of Social Services, 436 U.S. 658, 691 (1978), municipalities may not be held liable under 42 U.S.C. § 1983 "unless action pursuant to official municipal policy of some nature caused a constitutional tort." The Supreme Court made clear that in addition to an official policy, a municipality may be sued for "constitutional deprivations visited pursuant to governmental 'custom' even though such custom has not received formal approval through the [governmental] body's official decisionmaking channels."

Proof of random acts or isolated events is insufficient to establish custom. But a plaintiff may prove "the existence of a custom or informal policy with evidence of repeated constitutional violations for which the errant municipal officials were not discharged or reprimanded." Once such a showing is made, a municipality may be liable for its custom "irrespective of whether official policy-makers had actual knowledge of the practice at issue."

The Navarros claim that the County carried out a policy and practice of not treating 911 requests for assistance relating to domestic violence as "emergency" calls. The Navarros rely primarily on the deposition of Helen Pena, the 911 dispatcher who answered Maria Navarro's call. In her deposition, Helen Pena testified that it was the practice of the Sheriff's Department not to classify domestic violence 911 calls as Code 2 or "emergency procedure" calls. Ms. Pena also testified that dispatchers were not instructed to treat domestic violence calls as emergencies, that there were no clearly delineated guidelines for responding to domestic violence calls, and that as such, the dispatchers were allowed to exercise unbridled discretion.

. . . Because there was no conclusive evidence that the Sheriff's Department has a policy of refusing to send a squad car to non-domestic crimes not yet in progress, or of only treating crimes in progress as emergencies, a practice of not treating domestic crimes as emergencies may have been the cause of the failure to send a squad car to assist Navarro.

. . . [T]he district court erred in concluding that there were no genuine issues of material fact as to whether the County had a policy or custom of not classifying domestic violence calls as an "emergency."

The County argues that even assuming that it had a policy of affording victims of domestic violence less police protection than other crime victims, there was no evidence that discrimination against women was a motivating factor behind the administration of the alleged policy.

The Equal Protection Clause of the Fourteenth Amendment states: "No State shall . . . deny to any person within its jurisdiction the equal protection of the laws." Gender-based classifications must pass the "intermediate scrutiny" test, i.e., the classification "must serve important governmental objectives and must be substantially related to achievement of those objectives."

The Navarros contend that the County's custom of treating domestic violence 911 calls differently from non-domestic violence calls impermissibly discriminates against abused women. The custom of according different treatment to victims of domestic violence is gender-neutral on its face. However, it is well established that discriminatory application of a facially neutral law also offends the Constitution.

Nevertheless, a long line of Supreme Court cases make clear that the Equal Protection Clause requires proof of discriminatory intent or motive.

. . . In the present case . . . aside from the conclusory allegation that the County's custom of not classifying domestic violence calls as an emergency discriminates against abused women, the Navarros have failed to offer any evidence of such invidious intent or motive.

Nevertheless, even absent evidence of gender discrimination, the Navarros' equal protection claim still survives because they could prove that the domestic violence/non-domestic violence classification fails even the rationality test. Unless a statute employs a classification that is inherently invidious (such as race or gender), or that impinges on fundamental rights, we exercise only limited review. At a minimum, however, the Supreme Court "consistently has required that legislation classify the persons it affects in a manner rationally related to legitimate governmental objectives." Although we may not substitute our personal notions of good public policy for those of the legislature, the rational-basis standard is "not a toothless one."

Because the district court did not review the rationality of the County's domestic violence/non-domestic violence classification, we remand for a proper determination.

The Navarros also contend that the Sheriff's failure to train dispatchers on how to handle 911 domestic violence calls, and to instruct dispatchers to treat such calls in the same manner as they treat non-domestic violence calls, amounts to deliberate indifference to the equal protection rights of abused women. However, the Navarros fail to offer any evidence to support these claims. . . . Accordingly, we affirm the district court's conclusion that the Navarros' deliberate indifference claim fails to survive summary judgment.

For the foregoing reasons, we (1) affirm the district court's conclusion that the Navarros have failed to provide sufficient evidence to defeat summary judgment on their claim of deliberate indifference to constitutional rights arising from a failure to train 911 dispatchers; and (2) reverse the district court's grant of summary judgment on the Navarros' equal protection claim because genuine issues of material fact remain as to whether the County had a custom of not classifying domestic violence 911 calls as "emergencies." On remand, if the Navarros prove the existence of a discriminatory custom against victims of domestic violence, the district court must review the rationality of such a custom.

AFFIRMED in part, and REVERSED and REMANDED in part.

NOTES

1.   **Failure to train.** A city's failure to train can constitute a "deliberate indifference to the rights of persons with whom the police come into contact," that amounts to a city policy so that the *Monell* rule is satisfied. *City of Canton v. Harris*, 489 U.S. 378 (1989). However, the city is still not liable unless its

policy is one that violates an identifiable constitutional right, *Collins v. City of Harker Heights*, 503 U.S. 115 (1992), and the plaintiff proves that the municipal actor disregarded a known or obvious consequence of his action, *Connick v. Thompson*, 563 U.S. 51 (2011).

2. **Subsequent history of *Navarro*.** On remand of the *Navarro* case, the trial judge concluded that the sheriff's policy excluded domestic violence cases because they were usually cases of violence-not-in-progress and that it was rational to give not-in-progress cases a lower priority than cases in which violence had already begun. On second appeal, however, the Ninth Circuit held that, at the pleading stage, domestic violence calls could not be equated with not-in-progress calls because some domestic violence calls could involve violence in progress. "Nothing in the pleadings suggests that victims of domestic violence are less likely to suffer severe injury or death than are victims of other 9–1–1 emergency crimes." The case was remanded again "for a hearing to determine first, whether the city had a policy or custom of giving lower priority to domestic violence calls than to non-domestic violence calls, and second, if such a policy or custom exists, whether that policy or custom has a rational basis." *Fajardo v. City of Los Angeles*, 179 F.3d 698 (9th Cir. 1999).

3. **Other domestic violence cases.** In *Okin v. Village of Cornwall-on-Hudson Police Dep't*, 577 F.3d 415 (2d Cir. 2009), the court reversed a summary judgment for the defendant city in a case in which the plaintiff, a victim of domestic abuse, alleged that the city failed to train its police officers in how to handle such complaints, and even had a "custom whereby it acquiesced in unconstitutional conduct by its officers." Plaintiff, who had complained more than a dozen times to city police officers about domestic violence, was found to have raised triable issues of fact on her *Monell* claim.

Other domestic violence claims have not fared so well. In *Town of Castle Rock v. Gonzales*, 545 U.S. 748 (2005), a wife sued the city and police officers under § 1983 for failing to enforce a domestic abuse restraining order against her husband, claiming violation of Fourteenth Amendment Due Process rights. The court held that she did not show a protected property interest in the enforcement of the restraining order, in part because state law did not make such enforcement mandatory: "[A] benefit is not a protected entitlement if government officials may grant or deny it in their discretion."

REFERENCES: DOBBS, HAYDEN & BUBLICK, HORNBOOK ON TORTS §§ 22.1–22.16 (2d ed. 2016); 2 DOBBS, HAYDEN & BUBLICK, THE LAW OF TORTS §§ 334–356 (2d ed. 2011); LESTER S. JAYSON & ROBERT C. LONGSTRETH, HANDLING FEDERAL TORT CLAIMS: ADMINISTRATIVE AND JUDICIAL REMEDIES (3 looseleaf volumes, updated continuously).

PART 6

LIMITING THE DUTY OF CARE BASED ON RELATIONSHIPS OR THEIR ABSENCE

■ ■ ■

CHAPTER 16

MISFEASANCE AND NONFEASANCE

■ ■ ■

In the early chapters of this book, we began with the typical situation in which actors owe each other a duty of care, which is measured by the ordinary standard of reasonable care under the circumstances. We also saw that duty is a question for courts to decide. Indeed, duty may be the most important decision that courts are charged with making in common law negligence cases. When and whether a duty is owed defines whether people are required to exercise care to avoid harm to each other or not.

But how do courts determine whether a duty exists? Perhaps the most frequently invoked phrase in duty analysis in courts across the country is Dean Prosser's famous statement that "duty is not sacrosanct in itself, but is only an expression of the sum total of those considerations of policy which lead the law to say that the plaintiff is entitled to protection." KEETON, DOBBS, KEETON & OWEN, PROSSER & KEETON ON TORTS § 54, at 358 (5th ed. 1984).

The policy considerations that courts rely upon in tort law have been traditionally articulated in particular ways. Perhaps the most important policy consideration courts employ in duty analysis in negligence cases is the policy of preventing physical harm. The most important doctrinal consideration in duty cases has been the distinction between acts and omissions, or misfeasance and nonfeasance.

§ 1. THE MISFEASANCE-NONFEASANCE DISTINCTION

Dawson was standing at the window of his third-floor apartment when he saw a woman on the sidewalk below. The woman later proved to be Mrs. Perrera. A man approached her, took out a knife, and appeared to demand her purse. She resisted somewhat, and the man grabbed the purse. Dawson's telephone was within reach but he did not use it. The man did not depart after taking the woman's purse, but began some kind of verbal altercation. She tried to run, but he grabbed her and began to beat her. Dawson continued to watch as he beat her to death, perhaps as long as ten minutes. This is a wrongful death action brought by Perrera's family against Dawson. The allegation is that he could have prevented her death without danger to himself by calling 911.

Taking this allegation to be true, the trial judge upheld Dawson's motion to dismiss the claim. We must affirm.

NOTES

1. **Traditional rules.** The "case" above is fictional but true to life and to legal traditions. Under the general common law rule, one person owes another no duty to take active or affirmative steps for the other's protection. A defendant is not generally subject to liability for nonfeasance (omitting to act). By contrast, a defendant is liable for misfeasance (negligence in doing something active). *See* 2 DOBBS, HAYDEN & BUBLICK, THE LAW OF TORTS § 405 (2d ed. 2011).

2. **Definitions.** Definitions of misfeasance and nonfeasance have stayed very stable for hundreds of years. In *Bell v. Josselyn*, 69 Mass. 309 (1855), the Massachusetts Supreme Judicial Court wrote: "Nonfeasance is the omission of an act which a person ought to do; misfeasance is the improper doing of an act which a person might lawfully do; and malfeasance is the doing of an act which a person ought not to do at all." Today those same definitions pervade. *See e.g.*, NEB. REV. STAT. ANN. § 43–4311 ("Misfeasance means the improper performance of some act that a person may lawfully do.").

3. **Restatement Second rule.** The Restatement Second of Torts articulates the common law misfeasance rule this way: "anyone who does an affirmative act is under a duty to others to exercise the care of a reasonable man to protect them against an unreasonable risk of harm to them arising out of the act." § 302 cmt. a (1965). By contrast, "The duties of one who merely omits to act are more restricted, and in general are confined to situations where there is a special relation between the actor and the other which gives rise to the duty." *Id.*

4. **The Restatement Third's risk-creation standard.** The Third Restatement captures the misfeasance-nonfeasance idea in slightly different language. Instead of focusing on whether the defendant's *affirmative act* created a risk, the Restatement asks whether the actor "*created a risk.*" The risk-creation standard is meant to emphasize the principal concern of the traditional rule, which is not acting but risking. *Brown v. USA Taekwondo*, 483 P.3d 159 (Cal. 2021), ("Although our precedents have sometimes referred to the distinction between 'misfeasance' and 'nonfeasance,' we now understand this terminology to be imprecise and prone to misinterpretation. The proper question is not whether an actor's failure to exercise reasonable care entails the commission or omission of a specific act. Rather, it is whether the actor's entire conduct created a risk of harm.").

Under the Restatement Third when a defendant "creates a risk of physical harm," the defendant ordinarily has a duty to exercise reasonable care. RESTATEMENT (THIRD) OF TORTS: LIABILITY FOR PHYSICAL AND EMOTIONAL HARM § 7 (2010). When a defendant "does not create a risk of physical harm," the default rule is no duty. *Id.* at § 37 (2012).

In either category of cases, courts can craft exceptions based on "principle or policy." RESTATEMENT (THIRD) OF TORTS: LIABILITY FOR PHYSICAL AND EMOTIONAL HARM § 7(b) ("In exceptional cases, when an articulated countervailing principle or policy warrants denying or limiting liability in a particular class of cases, a court may decide that the defendant has no duty or that the ordinary duty of reasonable care requires modification."). Exceptions to § 37's no-duty rule are frequently called "affirmative duties."

5. **Line drawing.** Does the traditional misfeasance-nonfeasance distinction make sense? How can we tell whether a case involves one or the other? *Newton v. Ellis*, 119 Eng. Rep. 424 (K.B. 1855), is the classic case attempting to draw this distinction. The Local Board of Health contracted with Ellis to dig certain wells in the road. Ellis did so, leaving unlighted excavations at night. Newton's carriage was drawn into the unlighted hole and he was injured. Newton sued the contractor, Ellis, who argued this was "nonfeasance" and thus no duty was owed. Lord Campbell reasoned, "The action is brought for an improper mode of performing the work. How can that be called a nonfeasance? It is doing unlawfully what might be done lawfully: digging improperly without taking the proper steps for protecting from injury. . . . Cases where the action has been for a mere nonfeasance are inapplicable: the action here is for doing what was positively wrong."

This reasoning can apply in many situations. Suppose a hotel manager and its engineering staff fail to repair a dangerous wall or ceiling and the plaintiffs are struck by falling debris? *Aldorasi v. Crossroads Hosp. & Mgmt. Co.*, 344 F.Supp.3d 814 (E.D. Pa. 2018). Or suppose the defendant drives a car. When a bicycle appears in front of the car, defendant does nothing. In particular, defendant does not move her foot to the brake pedal. As a result she strikes the cyclist. Are these cases of nonfeasance? Is a distinction between action and inaction necessary to reach the right result with respect to duty in these cases?

BOYNTON V. KENNECOTT UTAH COPPER, LLC

500 P.3d 847 (Utah 2021)

JUSTICE HIMONAS, opinion of the Court:

Larry Boynton was exposed to asbestos while working at several job sites during the 1960s and 1970s. His wife, Barbara Boynton, was later diagnosed with mesothelioma. . . . Larry alleges—and for the purposes of summary judgment and this appeal, we assume—that Barbara was exposed to asbestos dust he carried home from work and that this exposure brought on her mesothelioma and resulting death. More specifically, Larry alleges that he would drive home from work, incidentally leaving asbestos dust in the Boyntons' car. Upon arrival, he would enter the home wearing his work clothes, spreading asbestos dust in the process. Barbara would then launder Larry's clothes, shaking the dust out before washing. Afterwards, she would sweep the laundry room to clean the accumulated asbestos dust. Through this process, Barbara was exposed to asbestos dust in "great quantities." After nearly fifty-four years of marriage, Barbara was diagnosed with malignant mesothelioma on February 4, 2016, and she died from it on February 27, 2016.

[Larry worked at several job sites during the 1960s and 1970s, including those operated by Kennecott, PacifCorp, and Conoco, and was exposed to asbestos dust that settled on his clothing. None of these companies warned Larry about the dangers of asbestos and none provided laundry services that would have prevented him from bringing his contaminated clothing home.]

Following Barbara's death, Larry sought legal relief against the premises operators, among others. . . . On summary judgment before the district court, Kennecott and Conoco argued they owed no duty of care to Barbara. Conoco was successful in its argument; Kennecott wasn't. With respect to these two defendants, the sole issue before us in this interlocutory appeal is whether they owed Barbara a duty of care. . . .

DUTY OF CARE

A. Asbestos Litigation

We are asked to decide in this case whether premises operators owe a duty to employees' co-habitants for "take-home exposure" to asbestos. . . . With respect to these take-home exposure lawsuits, courts have split, often because of how they have analyzed the question of whether the premises operators owed a duty of care to the injured party. Courts that have focused on the relationship between parties when defining duties of care have rejected liability for exposure beyond the workplace. For those courts, the "relationship" is, essentially, too attenuated for a legal duty—someone like Barbara has little, if any, direct relationship with the premises operators. Conversely, courts that have focused on the foreseeability of injury in the duty sphere have often found liability for take-home exposure. But filing a claim in a foreseeability-focused jurisdiction doesn't guarantee relief; indeed, some of these jurisdictions have rejected liability when the suit involves exposure prior to when the employers might reasonably have foreseen the risks from take-home exposure to asbestos. And finally, some jurisdictions, such as Delaware, determine duty largely according to the act-omission distinction and have found liability for take-home exposure whenever employers engaged in misfeasance.

B. Utah Standard for Establishing a Duty of Care

. . . To establish a duty of care, Utah courts ask (1) whether the defendant's allegedly tortious conduct consists of an affirmative act or merely an omission; (2) the legal relationship of the parties; (3) the foreseeability or likelihood of injury; (4) public policy as to which party can best bear the loss occasioned by the injury; and (5) other general policy considerations. The determination of whether a legal duty exists . . . is a purely legal question. . . .

[We have previously] suggested that not all factors were created equal, with our analysis focusing primarily on whether the defendant made an affirmative act. To this end, we noted that the long-recognized distinction between acts and omissions—or misfeasance and nonfeasance—makes a critical difference and is perhaps the most fundamental factor courts consider when evaluating duty. We further noted that a special relationship is not typically required to sustain a duty of care to those who could foreseeably be injured by the defendant's affirmative acts. And we also provided that, once we determine that a party has engaged in affirmative conduct, we will typically only carve out an exception that eliminates the duty in categories of cases implicating unique policy concerns. . . .

C.   Analysis of Duties of Care at a Categorical Level

We consider whether a duty exists for a general category of cases versus on a case-by-case basis: Duty . . . should [also] be articulated in relatively clear, categorical, bright-line rules of law applicable to a general class of cases. . . .

[W]e do not decide in this case whether Kennecott, PacifiCorp, and Conoco specifically owe a duty to Barbara for take-home exposure to asbestos that allegedly caused her mesothelioma. Instead, to determine whether a duty exists, we consider premises operators, take-home exposure to asbestos,[6] all the resulting injuries, and—because in this case, it matters for the general foreseeability analysis—the relevant time period at issue (from 1961 onwards). The litigants will have the opportunity to address the facts of their specific cases when they argue about whether a breach of duty occurred and whether it caused the injury. . . .

But we do not assess this case entirely at the categorical level. . . . [W]e first must consider whether a duty of care exists for that category of cases. . . . [I]f we determine that a duty exists, we must also determine— after allowing for all reasonable inferences in favor of the nonmoving party—whether this case falls within the ambit of the duty of care. That is the second question.

In our duty of care cases, we have not always clearly distinguished between these two questions. For that reason, it may seem confusing why we sometimes analyze case-specific facts in cases about whether a categorical duty of care exists. But a careful reading of our cases shows that

---

[6]   It is certainly an art, not a science, to define the exact scope of generality at which to assess the allegedly tortious activity. The idea is to create a rule that will cover an occurrence of the same general nature. . . . Here, we analyze only asbestos exposure because some parts of the analysis may differ from other toxic materials that can be carried on clothes, in vehicles, or otherwise from a job site to a home. . . .

we only analyze case-specific facts when we ask whether a case falls within the relevant category.

D. Duty Analysis

1. Affirmative Act or Omission

The first factor turns on the common distinction between acts and omissions: Acts of misfeasance, or active misconduct working positive injury to others, typically carry a duty of care. Nonfeasance—passive inaction, a failure to take positive steps to benefit others, or to protect them from harm not created by any wrongful act of the defendant—by contrast, generally implicates a duty only in cases of special legal relationships. We have found that people make "affirmative acts" when they prescribe medication, provide therapy, place inmates in a work-release program, or supply someone with a gun. We have not found an affirmative act when a party *fails* to perform a background check or *fails* to train and supervise employees. . . . The line between acts and omissions is sometimes subtle. Ultimately, however, we follow the lead of Justice Cardozo in asking "whether the putative wrongdoer has advanced to such a point as to have launched a force or instrument of harm, or has stopped where inaction is at most a refusal to become an instrument for good." *Jeffs*, 275 P.3d 228 (quoting *H.R. Moch Co. v. Rensselaer Water Co.*, 159 N.E. 896, 898 (N.Y. 1928) (Cardozo, C.J)).

For the purposes of determining whether a duty of care exists in take-home exposure cases, we conclude that premises operators act affirmatively whenever they have "launched [the] instrument of harm" by directing, requiring, or otherwise causing workers to come in contact with asbestos. Though we cannot predict every situation that will fall within this domain, we are comfortable saying that a premises operator will have engaged in "misfeasance" (as that term is understood in the duty analysis) at least when they (1) instruct workers to handle asbestos, (2) have nearby workers handle asbestos, (3) place asbestos on the premises, (4) send employees to a workspace containing asbestos, or (5) purchase a workspace containing asbestos and invite workers onto it. These categories do not include instances where a premises operator merely fails to prevent an employee from coming into contact with asbestos, like if an employer fails to prevent the spread of asbestos from an adjacent worksite.

For the purpose of resolving the motion for summary judgment, we find that Larry has sufficiently established misfeasance by Kennecott and Conoco, which triggers a duty of care. Larry came into contact with asbestos dust because he and those around him cut, chipped, mixed, sanded, sawed, scrapped, and swept products containing asbestos . . . allegedly contaminating Larry's clothing. And when Larry worked at Conoco, he was allegedly exposed to asbestos when other employees removed asbestos pipe insulation, let it fall to the ground, and then swept it up, again allegedly contaminating his work clothes. Both Kennecott and Conoco therefore allegedly directed Larry and/or nearby employees to handle asbestos. In doing so, each defendant affirmatively "launched [the] instrument of harm" by exposing Larry to the asbestos dust. Larry doesn't merely allege that the defendants failed to protect him and "refus[ed] to become an instrument for good." . . .

2.   Legal Relationship of the Parties

Special relationships arise when one party assumes responsibility for the safety of another or their opportunities for self-protection. For example, innkeepers, guardians, and common carriers typically have special relationships with those in their care. But a special relationship is not typically required to sustain a duty of care to those who could foreseeably be injured by the defendant's affirmative acts. Rather, an omission or failure to act can generally give rise to liability only in the presence of some external circumstance—a special relationship.

Larry alleges that the defendants' actions caused an injury to a third party—Barbara. He doesn't argue that a special legal relationship exists between the defendants and Barbara. But because the defendants engaged in affirmative "misfeasance," Larry doesn't need to establish a special legal relationship in order to establish a duty of care.

3.   Foreseeability of the Injury

Foreseeability relates to the general relationship between the alleged tortfeasor and the victim and the general foreseeability' of harm. We have found certain injuries foreseeable when the defendant acts affirmatively towards one party and thereby injures another. . . . [I]n *Herland*, we found it foreseeable that giving a weapon to an intoxicated individual might create a "risk of harm to others."

The relevant category here is premises operators who direct, require, or otherwise cause workers to come in contact with asbestos. . . . Foreseeability will counsel in favor of finding a duty of care if any circumstances within that category would have included a foreseeable harm. The more specific question—whether the asbestos exposure here could have foreseeably caused harm to Barbara—may be addressed when the lower court considers proximate cause.

There are circumstances in which premises operators would foresee injury from take-home exposure to asbestos during the relevant time period. Larry . . . submitted an expert affidavit from Dr. Richard Lemen explaining the "well-recognized" concerns about asbestos based on publications from that time. . . . At least one study that he listed, from 1965, explicitly described the risks from take-home exposure to asbestos. For that reason, the risk from asbestos was unambiguously foreseeable at least as early as 1965—prior to the time that Larry worked at the Conoco and PacifiCorp locations, and during the end of Larry's time working at Kennecott's smelter. . . .

4.   Who Can Best Prevent the Loss

We have next asked "who can best bear the loss" occasioned by the injury. This factor doesn't refer to who has the financial resources to pay for the resulting damages. Rather, this factor considers whether the defendant is best situated to take reasonable precautions to avoid injury. . . . [T]his factor would cut against the imposition of a duty where a victim or some other third party is in a superior position of knowledge or control to avoid the loss in question. So, going forward, we will more appropriately refer to this factor as "who can best prevent the loss."

Within the category at issue here—exposure to asbestos brought home from the workplace—premises operators have the greater "control" and "knowledge" that would allow them to prevent injury from take-home exposure. Premises operators will typically have greater control of workplace activities than employees. Most significantly, the premises operators may often choose not to introduce asbestos in the first place. In this case, for example, one defendant instructed workers to mix asbestos cement. The defendant—not the workers—had the capacity to choose another cement mix; the workers simply had to follow the directions dictated by the contract their bosses made. We can hardly imagine "a superior position of . . . control" than the ability to choose not to use asbestos at all.

Further, premises operators can institute policies that reduce the likelihood of take-home exposure to asbestos. The premises operators respond that workers can also take steps to reduce take-home exposure to asbestos. True. But even if workers could take some remedial steps, the premises operators do not explain why they could not have implemented the same safety measures through workplace policies. Workers can only adopt a limited number of personal safety measures; the premises operators can require those same safety measures and also institute other workplace policies.

The premises operators also have the "knowledge" that would allow them to prevent danger from take-home exposure to asbestos. At least some employers who use asbestos presumably have expertise when choosing those materials: For example, they might employ research and development teams to research materials and make qualified decisions about how to safely use them. And because companies using asbestos often employ many workers, they can more efficiently make decisions on behalf of the many people who might be exposed to the asbestos. Conversely, workers often lack any significant medical or industrial "knowledge" about workplace materials like asbestos, and they cannot efficiently acquire that knowledge. Even if they could, it makes little sense to require every employee to individually implement personal safety practices, rather than require the employer to make a single determination that protects all employees and their families.

For these reasons, premises operators have both greater "control" and "knowledge" necessary to prevent harm from take-home exposure to asbestos. This factor therefore doesn't caution against the imposition of a duty.

5.   Other Public Policy Considerations

Finally, we ask whether general policy considerations require a categorical decision removing duty from a class of cases. We have carved out common law exceptions from duty, for example, when people assume the risk of competitive sports. But, typically, public policy considerations don't endorse the wholesale rejection of a duty even if they may warrant limiting such a duty.

The premises operators argue that allowing for the existence of a duty here would create an overlarge, indeterminate class of plaintiffs. Indeed, other courts, including those ultimately finding a duty for take-home asbestos exposure, have expressed concerns about exposing asbestos product manufacturers to uncabined liability to myriad plaintiffs in take-home asbestos exposure cases. We understand these concerns. But we do not think these concerns justify rejecting a duty wholesale, especially because we have only addressed a duty to prevent take-home exposure. Premises owners might cause other injuries, such as when a worker visits a friend after work in their work uniform. In future cases we can determine whether those injuries were foreseeable and whether liability would create an unduly indeterminate class of potential plaintiffs. For now, we have addressed liability only for a relatively narrow class of people.

Further, we doubt that this case will have far-reaching public policy implications. We only hold that premises operators have a duty of care when they introduce asbestos into the workplace. The defendants will still have an opportunity to address other elements of tort law. And given those other legal requirements, plaintiffs may find it difficult to ultimately prevail in a negligence action. Other disincentives, like attorney fees and sanctions, will likewise prevent an onslaught of cases from unknown plaintiffs.

We therefore hold that premises operators like Kennecott and Conoco have a duty to exercise reasonable care to prevent take-home exposure to asbestos. When premises operators engage in affirmative acts that cause employees to come into contact with asbestos, they create a foreseeable risk that employees will carry asbestos into their homes. This risk was foreseeable as early as 1961, and no reason counsels against imposing a duty for creating this risk. . . . As such, we affirm the district court's denial of Kennecott's motion for summary judgment, reverse the district court's grants of summary judgment for PacifiCorp and Conoco, and remand for further proceedings not inconsistent with this opinion.

NOTES

1. **Duty analysis.** How does the *Boynton* court determine whether defendants owe a duty in this case? As the Utah Supreme Court notes, many but not all courts have reached the same conclusion. Do you agree with the court that the premises operators owed a duty to the plaintiff?

2. **Affirmative acts and instrument of harm.** Courts often invoke Justice Cardozo's famous question: "whether the putative wrongdoer has advanced to such a point as to have launched a force or instrument of harm, or has stopped where inaction is at most a refusal to become an instrument for good." Do you agree that the defendants' conduct met this test? Could a compressed-gas computer dusting spray that is inhaled by a driver, leading to a car accident, count as an instrument of harm? *McDougall v. CRC Indus., Inc.*, 523 F.Supp.3d 1061 (D. Minn. 2021) (yes, where defendant was aware of the risk of the product and knew that many of its customers intended to abuse the product, evidenced by defendant's inclusion in the spray of a bittering agent, known to be ineffective).

3. **Special relationships.** Where misfeasance is concerned, the actor's affirmative act itself creates the duty. There is no need to establish a special relationship. In nonfeasance, however, there is no duty unless some additional factors such as a special relationship are present. "In almost every instance, an act carries with it a potential duty and resulting legal accountability for that act. By contrast, an omission or failure to act can generally give rise to liability only in the presence of some external circumstance—a special relationship." *B.R. ex rel. Jeffs v. West*, 275 P.3d 228 (Utah 2012).

4. **Creating a risk.** The *Boynton* court cites the *Herland* case for the idea that placing a gun on a countertop within reach of an intoxicated individual top creates a risk, and therefore a duty. In the *Jeffs* case, also cited in *Boynton*, a healthcare provider put a man on at least six prescription medications including testosterone and a number of psychiatric medications. Under the influence of these medications, he shot his wife, a harm for which the children sued the healthcare provider. Defendants argued that the provider owed no duty to the children, who were not patients. Citing an earlier case, the Utah Supreme Court contrasted a doctor's failure to diagnose an existing problem and a doctor's creation of risk: while a physician evaluating an officer's fitness for employment might not owe a duty of care to the examinee (who the court considered was not the doctor's patient), "that does not mean that the physician lacked a duty to avoid affirmatively causing physical injury to the officer. If the physician had used a scalpel instead of a tongue depressor to facilitate a throat examination, presumably the duty would be as obvious as the ensuing injuries." Can you apply the scalpel analogy to *Boynton*?

5. **Policy analysis.** Courts spend a lot of time and thought working through policy issues that support (or don't support) recognition of a duty or

no-duty rule. Another thoughtful example is *Kesner v. Superior Court*, 384 P.3d 283 (Cal. 2016), in which the court recognized that "a duty to take ordinary care in the conduct of one's activities" applies to the use of asbestos on an owner's premises or in an employer's manufacturing processes. The policies that the *Kesner* court examined included the foreseeability during the 1970s of asbestos fibers coming home on clothes, the policy of preventing future harm by imposing costs on the negligent party, the issue of moral blame particularly when some parties are powerless or unsophisticated and others exercise control of hazards, the availability of insurance, the cost of "upholding, not violating" the duty of reasonable care, and the risk of unlimited liability. Yet other courts, by focusing on different factors, have reached a different conclusion. *See, e.g., Quiroz v. ALCOA Inc.*, 416 P.3d 824 (Ariz. 2018) (focusing on special relationship and statutory public policy, employer had no duty that required father's employer to protect son from secondary exposure to asbestos fibers). Would you expect state courts to have different common law tort rules, or different modes of analyzing the duty issue?

6. **Duty and other elements of the negligence case.** Does the fact that the plaintiff has established duty mean that plaintiff will prevail in the negligence case? *Boynton* mentions both breach of duty and proximate cause as issues that must be addressed before liability can be imposed. If issues of breach, factual cause and proximate cause must still be addressed, why not have the court deal with those issues on the question of duty? Can you see how asking the duty question particularized to case specific facts, rather than on a categorical basis, could permit the court to decide all issues?

§ 2. NONFEASANCE AND EXCEPTIONS: AFFIRMATIVE DUTIES

The nonfeasance rule has deep roots in Anglo-American jurisprudence. At the same time, it has come under withering criticism for decades. Many European countries impose an affirmative duty to rescue, often making a failure to rescue a criminal offense. *See* JULIE A. DAVIES & PAUL T. HAYDEN, GLOBAL ISSUES IN TORT LAW 120–29 (2008). A comment in the Second Restatement of Torts remarked that American decisions upholding the nonliability of those who declined an easy chance to rescue another from drowning "have been condemned by legal writers as revolting to any moral sense, but thus far they remain the law." RESTATEMENT (SECOND) OF TORTS § 314 cmt. c (1965).

Not surprisingly, then, courts have developed a number of exceptions to the no-duty rule. First, where a statutory provision imposes an obligation to protect another, a court may rely on the statute to determine that a common law duty exists. RESTATEMENT (THIRD) OF TORTS: LIABILITY FOR PHYSICAL AND EMOTIONAL HARM § 38 (2012); *Brock v. Watts Realty Co.*, 582 So.2d 438 (Ala. 1991) (municipal ordinance that required landlords to maintain door locks created a duty to protect tenants from intruders).

Second, if an actor's prior conduct, whether tortious or innocent, has caused harm to another person, the actor has a duty to render assistance to prevent further harm. *South v. Nat'l R.R. Passenger Corp.*, 290 N.W.2d 819 (N.D. 1980) (without fault, train struck plaintiff; train personnel then had duty to assist reasonably). Also, if a person has created a continuing risk of harm, even innocently, a duty arises to employ reasonable care to prevent or minimize that risk from coming to fruition. RESTATEMENT (THIRD) OF TORTS: LIABILITY FOR PHYSICAL AND EMOTIONAL HARM § 39 (2012). For example, in *Pacht v. Morris*, 489 P.2d 29 (Ariz. 1971), the defendant innocently collided with a horse on the highway, killing it. If the driver did not exercise reasonable care to remove the horse or to provide some kind of effective warning, the driver would be subject to liability if a second driver was injured by hitting the horse or in trying to avoid hitting it.

In addition, nonfeasance may be actionable when the defendant had a special relationship with the plaintiff or the tortfeasor, when the defendant took charge of an imperiled and helpless person, or based on contractual or other undertakings related to safety. Some of these exceptions will be explored in this section, and some in the next two chapters.

––––––––––

ESTATE OF CILLEY V. LANE, 985 A.2d 481 (Me. 2009). Jennifer Lane and Joshua Cilley were in a romantic relationship, and had broken up and gotten back together again several times. Shortly after the last breakup, Cilley entered Lane's trailer, and Lane asked him immediately to leave; she also called a neighbor to help get Cilley to leave. Cilley either left and got a rifle, or picked up a rifle that was already in Lane's trailer. Lane herself left at that point, and immediately heard a loud pop. She looked back and saw Cilley fall to the floor. Lane heard Cilley say "it was an accident." Lane did not see any blood, and "did not investigate or attempt to assess whether Cilley was injured." She went to another friend's trailer and told two friends that "Cilley had pretended to shoot himself inside her trailer." Lane's friend went over to Cilley, and noted that Cilley was turning white, and had difficulty breathing. Another friend went to a neighboring trailer and called 911. Ciley died as a result of a gunshot wound to his abdomen. According to the physician who treated him, Cilley could have been resuscitated if he had arrived at the hospital five to ten minutes earlier. Cilley's estate sued Lane, who moved for summary judgment on the Estate's claim of negligent failure to assist. The trial court granted Lane's motion, and the Estate appealed. *Held*, affirmed.

"Maine law does not impose a 'general obligation to protect others from harm not created by the actor. The fact that the actor realizes or should realize that action on his part is necessary for another's aid or protection does not of itself impose upon him a duty to take such action.' *Bryan R. v.*

Watchtower Bible & Tract Soc'y of N.Y., Inc., 738 A.2d 839 (Me. 1999) (quoting Restatement (Second) of Torts § 314 (1965)). . . .

[T]he Estate urges us to recognize a new common law duty: the duty to seek affirmative emergency assistance through reasonable means. The Estate contends that the mores of the community and the abundance of technology mandate recognition of this duty in order to enhance public safety. . . . [S]ome state legislatures have enacted laws imposing criminal or civil liability for failing to render reasonable assistance to a person in danger or to immediately report a crime that has been committed. . . . [We, like the Maine legislature] also must decline the Estate's request that we recognize a new common law duty.

First . . . the law imposes a duty to aid or protect on established, legal relationships, such as employer-employee or parent-child, because one party has control over another or, in the case of a landowner, control over a location. These duties are widely known and largely accepted, and the affected parties are able to plan and prepare according to known rights and responsibilities. . . . In contrast, the duty the Estate urges us to recognize has none of these features: the duty arises not from any relationship between the parties, but simply from presence at the opportune moment.

Second, we are hesitant to create a duty that would impose liability for the failure to act, or nonfeasance. . . . One of the primary reasons for limiting duties in cases of nonfeasance is the potential for boundless liability. . . . If we were to adopt the duty requested by the Estate, each person would be obligated to contact emergency assistance *any* time she witnessed another's injury, which would indeed be a duty without any practical limit. The Estate contends that liability for breaches of this new duty would be constrained by principles of causation and by the fact that this is a limited duty that requires a telephone call but not any actual aid. Those constraints, however, would not protect an individual from the necessity of defending a lawsuit, even if she were ultimately found not to have breached the duty.

We adhere to our established precedent and conclude that absent a special relationship or conduct that has endangered another, a person owes no duty to call aid for an injured person. . . . Judgment affirmed.

NOTES

1. **Rationales for the rule.** What are the rationales behind the traditional nonfeasance rule? In *Stockberger v. United States,* 332 F.3d 479 (7th Cir. 2003), Judge Posner said this:

> Various rationales have been offered for the seemingly hardhearted common law rule: people should not count on nonprofessionals for rescue; the circle of potentially liable nonrescuers would be difficult to draw (suppose a person is drowning and no one on the crowded

beach makes an effort to save him—should all be liable?); altruism makes the problem a small one and liability might actually reduce the number of altruistic responses by depriving people of credit for altruism (how would they prove they hadn't acted under threat of legal liability?); people would be deterred by threat of liability from putting themselves in a position where they might be called upon to attempt a rescue, especially since a failed rescue might under settled common law principles give rise to liability, on the theory that a clumsy rescue attempt may have interfered with a competent rescue by someone else.

Does *Estate of Cilley* suggest further rationales?

2. **Changing times.** Should the advent of easy ways to come to the aid of others, such as the cell phone, change the no-duty rule? In Philadelphia in October 2021, while a woman was raped on a subway, bystanders on the train took videos of the rape on their cellphones but no one called for help for the victim. *See* Eduardo Medina, *As a Woman Was Raped, Train Riders Failed to Intervene, Police Say*, N. Y. TIMES, Oct. 17, 2021. Should there be a rule that requires a phone call but no further assistance? Under tort common law? *Compare* Jeremy Waldron, *On the Road: Good Samaritans and Compelling Duties*, 40 SANTA CLARA L. REV. 1053 (2000) (using the parable of the Good Samaritan to reprove "the conviction of many self-confident theorists that the category 'human' is too abstract to serve as a focus for what we owe to one another"), with Joshua Dressler, *Some Brief Thoughts (Mostly Negative) About "Bad Samaritan" Laws*, 40 SANTA CLARA L. REV. 971 (2000) ("[T]here are special problems with punishing people for not-doings, particularly in the absence of traditional, objective duty-triggering criteria. There are legality concerns, retributive reasons to worry about punishing innocent persons, and substantial utilitarian objections to such laws. Finally, there are reasons founded on the concept of individual freedom that counsel against expanding the law").

3. **Bad Samaritan statutes.** The *Estate of Cilley* court notes that some states have enacted statutes that impose criminal or civil liability for failure to rescue; the court cited, in a footnote, statutes from eight states, although some of them are limited to helping victims of crime. *See Hudson v. GEICO Ins. Agency, Inc.*, 161 A.3d 1150 (R.I. 2017) § ("Good Samaritan statutes immunize from negligence liability those defendants who do assist a plaintiff in distress . . . [whereas Bad Samaritan statutes] place a defendant under some form of legal duty to assist and provide for criminal or civil liability for non-assistance.") (quoting DOBBS, HAYDEN & BUBLICK, THE LAW OF TORTS § 405, at 656 n.25 (2d ed. 2016)).

Vermont's statute, VT. STAT. ANN. tit. 12, § 519, is a "pure" Bad Samaritan statute. It provides that a "person who knows that another is exposed to grave physical harm shall, to the extent that the same can be rendered without danger or peril to himself or without interference with important duties owed to others, give reasonable assistance to the exposed person unless that assistance or care is being provided by others." Minnesota and Rhode Island have similar statutes. Should more states adopt such a statute? Would such a statute have made a difference in the actual situations or case outcome in *Cilley*?

4.   **Aiding people who have imperiled themselves.** Suppose a business associate or friend tells the plaintiff to jump into water below, and the plaintiff does so, only to drown. Is there a duty of the encouraging party to aid in the rescue? *See Yania v. Bigan*, 155 A.2d 343 (Pa. 1959) (no; strip miner "by cajolery and inveiglement" convinced neighboring miner to jump into a large trench filled with water 8 to 10 feet deep, with side walls 16 to 18 feet high; no duty to rescue unless associate was legally responsible for placing plaintiff in perilous position). Similarly, see *Rocha v. Faltys*, 69 S.W.3d 315 (Tex. App. 2002), in which plaintiff dove off a cliff overlooking the river at the encouragement of a fraternity brother, although he could not swim. When plaintiff drowned, his parents sued the fraternity brother and others for negligence. Summary judgment for defendant fraternity brother; "individuals should be responsible for their own actions and should not be liable for others' independent misconduct." Simply taking an "adult man" to the top of a cliff does not create a dangerous situation giving rise to a duty.

5   **Duties to trespassers.** In a separate part of the opinion, the *Estate of Cilley* court concludes that as a trespasser, the decedent was not owed a duty of reasonable care to assist him. The Third Restatement places a possessor of land under "a duty to flagrant trespassers to exercise reasonable care if the trespasser reasonably appears to be imperiled and (1) helpless or (2) unable to protect him- or herself." RESTATEMENT (THIRD) OF TORTS: LIABILITY FOR PHYSICAL AND EMOTIONAL HARM § 52(b) (2012). Even earlier rules provide that when a trespasser or licensee is discovered in a position of peril, a landowner is required to use ordinary care to avoid injuring him. *See Gladon v. Greater Cleveland Reg'l Transit Auth.*, 662 N.E.2d 287 (Ohio 1996). If the court had followed either of these rules, would the whole case have come out differently? Should it have?

WAKULICH V. MRAZ

751 N.E.2d 1 (Ill. App. Ct. 2001)

JUSTICE MCBRIDE delivered the opinion of the court. . . .

[Suit for the death of 16-year-old Elizabeth Wakulich. The plaintiff alleged that Michael and Brian Mraz, then 21 and 18 years old, provided a quart of Goldschlager alcohol and offered Elizabeth money as a prize if she could drink the entire bottle without losing consciousness or vomiting. Dennis Mraz, the father of the young men, was allegedly in the house and should have known these events.]

In the early morning hours of June 16, decedent, after drinking the Goldschlager, lost consciousness. According to the complaint, Michael and Brian then placed her in the downstairs family room, where they observed her vomiting profusely and making "gurgling" sounds. They later checked on her again, at which time they removed her vomit-saturated blouse and placed a pillow under her head to prevent aspiration. According to the complaint, Michael and Brian did not seek medical attention for decedent and actually prevented others present in the home from calling 911 or seeking other medical intervention. Later in the morning, Dennis ordered Michael and Brian to remove decedent from the home. They then took her to a friend's home. Later, decedent was taken to a hospital where she was pronounced dead.

[The complaint was dismissed for failure to state a cause of action on the ground that Illinois case law eliminated any liability of social hosts for providing alcohol. On appeal the plaintiff argues first that her allegations that her daughter felt compelled to "fit in" with the social host's older sons, and that they offered her money to drink a quart bottle of alcohol, state a claim for negligence against the social host and her sons. We reject that argument.]

Plaintiff next maintains that she has pleaded sufficient facts to establish a cause of action based upon defendants' failure to exercise due care in voluntarily undertaking to care for plaintiff's decedent after she became unconscious. We agree.

"One who voluntarily undertakes to render services to another is liable for bodily harm caused by his failure to perform such services with due care or with such competence and skill as he possesses." . . .

Here, plaintiff has alleged that Michael and Brian voluntarily undertook affirmative steps to care for decedent and did so in a negligent manner. . . .

The viability of the voluntary undertaking counts . . . is not dependent on a duty created through the defendants' provision of alcohol to decedent but, rather, on the defendants having voluntarily undertaken to care for decedent after she became unconscious and having allegedly failed to exercise due care in the performance of that undertaking. . . .

Defendants maintain that none of their alleged acts indicate a voluntary assumption of any responsibility for decedent's health or well-being. We disagree. Specifically, it was alleged that after decedent became unconscious, Michael and Brian carried her downstairs, placed her on a couch, observed her vomiting profusely and making gurgling noises, checked on her later, changed her vomit-saturated shirt, and placed a pillow underneath her head to prevent aspiration. The actions of Michael and Brian . . . clearly demonstrated an undertaking concerning decedent's well-being. . . . We find therefore, that plaintiff has sufficiently pled that defendants Michael and Brian voluntarily assumed a duty to care for decedent.

Defendants maintain that they were not negligent in discharging any responsibility they did undertake, that a finding that there was a duty in this case creates uncertainty as to how that duty may be adequately discharged, and that decedent's death was not the proximate result of any voluntary undertaking on their part. We are confident that a jury or other trier of fact is capable of determining whether defendants, having voluntarily undertaken to care for the decedent after she became unconscious and began to vomit and gurgle, performed that undertaking with due care. We also find that the complaint alleges various acts, including allegations that defendants Michael and Brian prevented other individuals from calling for emergency medical intervention, from which a jury could find the defendants acted negligently in discharging their voluntarily assumed duty, proximately leading to decedent's death.

[The trial court erred in dismissing the counts based on voluntary undertaking.]

NOTES

1.   **Beginning to assist.** The Third Restatement recognizes that an actor who undertakes to render services to another, when the actor knows or should know that those services will reduce the risk of harm to the other, has a duty to use reasonable care in rendering those services if the failure to exercise care would increase the risk of harm beyond what would have existed without the undertaking; or if the other person relies on the actor's using reasonable care in the undertaking. RESTATEMENT (THIRD) OF TORTS: LIABILITY FOR PHYSICAL AND EMOTIONAL HARM § 42 (2012).

2.   **Rendering a person vulnerable.** Could the father in *Wakulich* have been said to have a duty of care in his capacity as a landowner? Could the sons have had a duty based on their creation of a risk or their reason to know that by their conduct, whether tortious or innocent, they have caused such bodily harm to another as to make her helpless and in danger of further harm? A recent Hawaii case suggests that these could have been alternative reasons for the court's ruling. *See Ah Mook Sang v. Clark*, 308 P.3d 911 (Haw. 2013) (social host who invites minor onto his property and serves alcohol owes duty to minor as long as minor is on the property; under such circumstances, if minor is injured, host has inflicted injury directly on the minor).

3.   **Voluntary undertakings vs. positive misconduct.** Distinguish liability for positive acts—preventing others from calling for help in *Wakulich*, for example—from liability for voluntary undertakings, that is, for breach of duties voluntarily assumed where no duty would otherwise exist. For example, most states thankfully place no duty on a passenger in a car to give the driver advice. But if the driver tells the passenger that he cannot see behind him while backing up, and the passenger affirmatively tells the driver that it is clear to back up, the passenger has a legal duty to use reasonable care in giving that advice. *See, e.g., Roos v. Morrison*, 913 So.2d 59 (Fla. Dist. Ct. App. 2005).

What if hosts at a party volunteer to check guests for weapons, but then someone is shot? *See Rice v. White*, 874 N.E.2d 132 (Ill. App. Ct. 2007).

4. **Making matters worse.** Where the defendant discontinues aid, the Third Restatement § 44(b) imposes liability if the defendant, by acting unreasonably, has left the victim in a "worse position than existed before" the defendant took charge. Section 324(b) of the Second Restatement said virtually the same thing, reflecting the vast majority of case law. *See, e.g., Mita v. Guardsmark, LLC*, 328 P.3d 962 (Wash. Ct. App. 2014). How does this stack up with the *Wakulich* case? Could it be said that Elizabeth Wakulich would have been better off if the men had not put a pillow under her head? Is this the right test? See *K.H. v. Morgan*, 914 F.2d 846 (7th Cir. 1990) (Posner, J.) ("If the fire department rescues you from a fire that would have killed you, this does not give the department a constitutional license to kill you, on the ground that you will be no worse off than if there were no fire department. The state, having saved a man from a lynch mob, cannot then lynch him, on the ground that he will be no worse off than if he had not been saved. The Illinois Department of Children and Family Services could not have subjected K.H. to sexual abuse and then defended on the ground that by doing this it did not make her any worse off than she would have been had she been left with her parents. . . . Once the state assumes custody of a person, it owes him a rudimentary duty of safekeeping no matter how perilous his circumstances when he was free. The distinction follows the lines of tort law.").

5. **Duty to take charge reasonably.** Section 44(a) of the Third Restatement says that when a person voluntarily takes charge of an imperiled and helpless person, he has assumed a duty to take charge in a reasonable manner. Does that also explain the reasoning in *Wakulich*? What counts as taking charge? *See Millea v. Erickson*, 849 N.W.2d 272 (S.D. 2014) (man who merely "stopped by" while babysitter was babysitting ten-month-old child did not gratuitously undertake a duty to care for that child, where he never agreed to supervise the child and babysitter never expressly or impliedly relinquished her duty to care for the child). What if a helicopter rescue crew locates an injured woman stranded in a dangerous ice gorge from which, without such a rescue, she could not escape. The crew lowers a sling, and begins to haul her aboard. It then negligently reverses the ratchet and the sling drops into the gorge again, causing a further injury to the woman. Is the crew liable to the woman for the second injury? Why?

6. **Special relationship.** In cases of nonfeasance, special relationships can create a duty of care. Section 40 of the Third Restatement recognizes seven kinds of formal relationships that place a defendant under a duty of reasonable care for the plaintiff's safety. The relationships are those of (1) a common carrier with its passengers; (2) an innkeeper with its guests; (3) a business or possessor of land that holds its land open to the public with those lawfully on the land; (4) an employer with its employees, who while at work are either in imminent danger or are injured or ill and thereby rendered helpless; (5) a school with its students; (6) a landlord with its tenants; and (7) a custodian with those in custody, if the custodian "has a superior ability to protect" the

plaintiff. This represents a slight expansion of a similar list in the Second Restatement. The Third Restatement also explicitly states in a comment that the list is not exclusive and that courts may identify additional relationships that give rise to a duty to assist.

7. **Other determinate relationships.** What other preexisting relationships might generate a duty to act affirmatively when one party is in danger? What if a parent sees a child in danger? What if a sheriff takes no steps to protect a crime witness who is in terrible danger for reporting the crime? What if two people are unmarried, but both parents of a particular child? *See* MERLE H. WEINER, A PARENT-PARTNER STATUS FOR AMERICAN FAMILY LAW (2015) (arguing for this category to be recognized as a special-relationship in a range of contexts, including tort law).

8. **Indeterminate or ad hoc relationships.** In some cases, the parties were not in any preexisting, recognized status with respect to each other. But they did have a relationship that was, for the evening, special. Is this enough to impose a duty? *See Farwell v. Keaton*, 240 N.W.2d 217 (Mich. 1976), in which friends who went out drinking together and were later attacked were "companions on a social venture." The court created a duty, saying: "Implicit in such a common undertaking is the understanding that one will render assistance to the other when he is in peril if he can do so without endangering himself. [Friend] knew or should have known when he left [other friend], who was badly beaten and unconscious, in the back seat of his car that no one would find him before morning." Recall that in *Rocha v. Faltys*, 69 S.W.3d 315 (Tex. App. 2002), Rocha and Faltys were fellow fraternity members who drank at a party and went to a swimming hole where Rocha drowned. What about *Estate of Cilley*? Should an ad hoc special relationship be recognized in these cases?

9. **Scope of special relationships.** Where the plaintiff and defendant are in a special relationship, the defendant will have a duty of reasonable care whether or not the defendant had anything to do with creating or increasing the risk of harm to the plaintiff. RESTATEMENT (THIRD) OF TORTS: LIABILITY FOR PHYSICAL AND EMOTIONAL HARM § 40 cmt. c (2012). However, the duty only applies within the relationship. *See Bell ex rel. Bell v. Dawson*, 82 A.3d 827 (Me. 2013) (defendants who had created custodial relationship with minor plaintiff by allowing him to stay overnight in their home did not owe a duty of supervision to him the next morning, when he skateboarded out of the defendants' driveway and was struck by a car; when plaintiff left defendants' house and returned to his parents' home before the accident, the custodial relationship was severed).

PODIAS V. MAIRS

926 A.2d 859 (N.J. Super. Ct. App. Div. 2007)

PARRILLO, J.A.D.

. . . In the evening of September 27, 2002 and early morning hours of September 28, eighteen-year old Michael Mairs was drinking beer at the home of a friend Thomas Chomko. He eventually left with two other friends, defendants Swanson and Newell, both also eighteen years of age, to return to Monmouth University where all three were students. Mairs was driving. Swanson was in the front passenger seat and Newell was seated in the rear of the vehicle where he apparently fell asleep. It was raining and the road was wet.

At approximately 2:00 a.m., while traveling southbound in the center lane of the Garden State Parkway, Mairs lost control of the car, struck a motorcycle driven by Antonios Podias, and went over the guardrail. All three exited the vehicle and "huddled" around the car. Swanson saw Podias lying in the roadway and because he saw no movement and heard no sound, told Mairs and Newell that he thought Mairs had killed the cyclist. At that time, there were no other cars on the road, or witnesses for that matter.

Even though all three had cell phones, no one called for assistance. Instead they argued about whether the car had collided with the motorcycle. And, within minutes of the accident, Mairs called his girlfriend on Newell's cell phone since his was lost when he got out of the car. Swanson also used his cell phone, placing seventeen calls in the next one-and-one-half hours. Twenty-six additional calls were made from Newell's cell phone in the two-and-one-half hours after the accident, the first just three minutes post-accident and to Matawan, where Chomko resides. None of these, however, were emergency assistance calls. As Swanson later explained: "I didn't feel responsible to call the police." And Newell just "didn't want to get in trouble."

After about five or ten minutes, the trio all decided to get back in the car and leave the scene. Swanson directed, "we have to get to an exit." Upon their return to the car, Swanson instructed Mairs "not to bring up his name or involve him in what occurred" and "don't get us [Swanson and Newell] involved, we weren't there." The three then drove south on the parkway for a short distance until Mairs' car broke down. Mairs pulled over and waited in the bushes for his girlfriend to arrive, while Swanson and Newell ran off into the woods, where Newell eventually lost sight of Swanson. Before they deserted him, Swanson again reminded Mairs that "there was no need to get [Swanson and Newell] in trouble. . ." Mairs thought Swanson was "just scared" and that both defendants were concerned about Mairs "drinking and driving." Meanwhile, a motor vehicle operated by Patricia Uribe ran over Podias, who died as a result of injuries sustained in these accidents. . . . [The Administratrix of Podias' estate sued Mairs, Swanson and Newell. Plaintiff appeals from the trial court's grant of summary judgment in favor of Swanson and Newell.] . . .

Ordinarily, mere presence at the commission of the wrong, or failure to object to it, is not enough to charge one with responsibility inasmuch as there is no duty to take affirmative steps to interfere. Because of this reluctance to countenance "inaction" as a basis of liability, the common law "has persistently refused to impose on a stranger the moral obligation of common humanity to go to the aid of another human being who is in danger, even if the other is in danger of losing his life." . . .

Of course, exceptions are as longstanding as the rule. [Even those under no pre-existing duty may be liable if they voluntarily begin to assist and do so negligently.] . . . Over the years, liability for inaction has been gradually extended still further to a limited group of relations, in which custom, public sentiment, and views of social policy have led courts to find a duty of affirmative action. Thus, a duty to render assistance may either be "contractual, relational or transactional." In New Jersey, courts have recognized that the existence of a relationship between the victim and one in a position to provide aid may create a duty to render assistance. . . .

To establish liability, however, such relationships need not be limited to those where a pre-existing duty exists, or involving economic ties, or dependent on the actor's status as, for instance, a landowner or business owner. Rather, it may only be necessary "to find some definite relation between the parties [ ] of such a character that social policy justifies the imposition of a duty to act." [Keeton, et al, *Prosser and Keeton on Torts* § 56 at 374 (5th ed.)]. . . .

So too, even though the defendant may be under no obligation to render assistance himself, he is at least required to take reasonable care that he does not prevent others from giving it. In other words, there may be liability for interfering with the plaintiff's opportunity of obtaining assistance. And even where the original danger was created by innocent conduct, involving no fault on the part of the defendant, there may be a duty to make a reasonable effort to give assistance and avoid further harm where the prior innocent conduct has created an unreasonable risk of harm to the plaintiff. Indeed, one commentator has suggested that "the mere knowledge of serious peril, threatening death or great bodily harm to another, which an identified defendant might avoid with little inconvenience, creates a sufficient relation to impose a duty of action." *Prosser, supra,* § 56 at 377.

Actually, the extension of liability based on these and other "relational" features mirrors evolving notions of duty, which are no longer tethered to rigid formalisms or static historical classifications. This progression is not surprising. The assessment of duty necessarily includes an examination of the relationships between and among the parties. The fundamental question is whether the plaintiff's interests are entitled to legal protection against the defendant's conduct. In this regard, the determination of the existence of duty is ultimately a question of fairness and public policy, which in turn draws upon notions of fairness, common sense, and morality. . . .

[W]e are satisfied that the summary judgment record admits of sufficient facts from which a reasonable jury could find defendants breached a duty which proximately caused the victim's death. In the first place, the risk of harm, even death, to the injured victim lying helpless in the middle of a roadway, from the failure of defendants to summon help or take other precautionary measures was readily and clearly foreseeable. Not only were defendants aware of the risk of harm created by their own inaction, but were in a unique position to know of the risk of harm posed by Mairs' own omission in that regard, as well as Mairs' earlier precipatory conduct in driving after having consumed alcohol. Even absent any encouragement on their part, defendants had special reason to know that Mairs would not himself summon help, but instead illegally depart the scene of a hit-and-run accident, *N.J.S.A.* 39:4–129; *see also N.J.S.A.* 39:4–130, either intentionally or because of an inability to fulfill a duty directly owed the victim, thereby further endangering the decedent's safety.

Juxtaposed against the obvious foreseeability of harm is the relative ease with which it could have been prevented. All three individuals had cell phones and in fact used them immediately before and after the accident for their own purposes, rather than to call for emergency assistance for another in need. The ultimate consequence wrought by the harm in this case—death—came at the expense of failing to take simple precautions at little if any cost or inconvenience to defendants. Indeed, in contrast to Mairs' questionable ability to appreciate the seriousness of the situation, defendants appeared lucid enough to comprehend the severity of the risk and sufficiently in control to help avoid further harm to the victim. In other words, defendants had both the opportunity and ability to help prevent an obviously foreseeable risk of severe and potentially fatal consequence.

In our view, given the circumstances, the imposition of a duty upon defendants does not offend notions of fairness and common decency and is in accord with public policy, [which] encourages gratuitous assistance by those who have no legal obligation to render it. Simply and obviously, defendants here were far more than innocent bystanders or strangers to the event. On the contrary, the instrumentality of injury in this case was operated for a common purpose and the mutual benefit of defendants, and driven by someone they knew to be exhibiting signs of intoxication. Although Mairs clearly created the initial risk, at the very least the evidence reasonably suggests defendants acquiesced in the conditions that may have helped create it and subsequently in those conditions that further endangered the victim's safety. Defendants therefore bear some relationship not only to the primary wrongdoer but to the incident itself. It is this nexus which distinguishes this case from those defined by mere presence on the scene without more, and therefore implicates policy considerations simply not pertinent to the latter.

Even assuming no independent duty to take affirmative action, at the very least defendants were obligated, in our view, not to prevent Mairs from exercising his direct duty of care. . . . [A]t the very least defendants collaborated in, verbally supported, or approved his decision to leave the scene, and at most actively convinced Mairs to flee as a means of not getting caught. . . . The entire aftermath of the incident betrays an orchestrated scheme among the three to avoid detection not only by taking no action to prevent further harm to the victim, but by affirmatively abandoning the scene, practically guaranteeing his death. . . .

We formulate today no rule of general application since the question of duty remains one of judicial balancing of the mix of factors peculiar to each case. We also stress the narrowness of the issue before us. . . . It is the degree of defendants' involvement, coupled with the serious peril threatening imminent death to another that might have been avoided with little effort and inconvenience, suggested by the evidence, that in our view creates a sufficient relation to impose a duty of action. Of course, it still remains a question of fact whether the primary wrongdoer was able to exercise reasonable care to summon emergency assistance or was prevented from doing so by defendants; whether, on the other hand, defendants knew or had reason to know that Mairs was unable or unwilling to do so, and thereafter were in a position to have influenced the outcome; whether the decision to abandon the victim was otherwise Mairs' alone or the result of encouragement, cooperation or interference from defendants; and finally, if the latter, whether the assistance was substantial enough to support a finding of liability. The facts here are certainly not such that all reasonable persons must draw the same conclusion. We cannot say that upon any version of the facts there is no duty.

Reversed and remanded.

NOTES

1. **Examining the disclaimer.** Why did the court insist it was "formulating no rule of general application?" Did it not articulate a rule about when a duty to assist will arise that could be applied in other cases?

2. **The ad hoc relationship in *Podias*.** The ad hoc relationship in *Podias* is similar to the one found "special" in *Farwell v. Keaton* (Note 8 after *Wakulich*): two "companions on a social venture," where one needed the other's help. But the facts of the two cases are not identical. What facts does the *Podias* court recite in support of its decision, and what role to do those facts seem to play in duty creation?

3. **Moral vs. legal duties.** In *Yania v. Bigan* (Note 4 after *Estate of Cilley*), the Pennsylvania court said that the defendant had a moral duty, but not a legal duty, to rescue a drowning man. In *Farwell v. Keaton*, the Michigan court, after finding a special relationship, said that to conclude that one friend owed the other "no duty to obtain medical assistance or at least to notify

someone of [his] condition and whereabouts would be shocking to human considerations and fly in the face of the commonly accepted code of social conduct." Look again at *Estate of Cilley*, and at *Podias*, to see what the judges said about the difference (or not) between a legal duty and a moral duty. How might one's view of the distinction between the two things influence an opinion about a duty to assist someone in need?

REFERENCES: 2 DOBBS, HAYDEN & BUBLICK, THE LAW OF TORTS §§ 405–412 (2d ed. 2011); DOBBS, HAYDEN & BUBLICK, HORNBOOK ON TORTS ch. 25 (2016).

CHAPTER 17

CONTRACT AND DUTY

■ ■ ■

In many instances, particularly in the case of contracts related to physical safety, the contract or undertaking itself creates, modifies, or limits a tort duty. For example, I might have no duty whatsoever to feed your dogs while you are away, and my failure to do so would ordinarily be nonfeasance. However, suppose I agree to come to your house to feed your dogs every day while you are gone, but fail to do so despite your reliance. You return to find your dog has died of starvation. I will surely be liable for breach of contract, but perhaps also for negligence—misfeasance in light of my bargained-for undertaking. *See* RESTATEMENT (THIRD) OF TORTS: LIABILITY FOR PHYSICAL AND EMOTIONAL HARM § 42 illus. 3 (2010).

Saying that a contract, undertaking, or relationship may create tort duties means that liability will be determined under the rules of tort law and that tort damages will be appropriate if the plaintiff prevails. These damages can include recovery for emotional distress as well as punitive damages.

§ 1. MISFEASANCE IN THE PERFORMANCE OF A CONTRACT: LIABILITY FOR PHYSICAL AND ECONOMIC HARM

TINGLER v. GREYSTONE HOMES, INC.
834 S.E.2d 244 (Va. 2019)

JUSTICE ARTHUR D. KELSEY. . . .

[In 2009, Graystone entered into a construction contract with George and Crystal Tingler]to build a new home with a purchase price of $495,000. During the 30-day inspection of the Home, the Tinglers discovered leaks. Greystone made repairs. The next year additional leaks were found and Greystone made further repairs.] On neither occasion did Graystone specifically look for mold.

After experiencing medical symptoms in early 2014, the Tinglers hired an inspector who discovered mold in the basement underneath the dining room where the leaks had occurred, elevated levels of airborne mold spores throughout the home, and elevated levels of moisture in the dining and kitchen areas [Graystone made substantial further repairs. On its second set of repairs in 2014, a Greystone employee cut wet drywall and took out large moldy pieces of insulation without barriers to contain the mold, in a way that a remediation contractor found inappropriate].

A little over a week later, the Tingler family vacated the home because of continued physical symptoms that they attributed to mold exposure. [The Tinglers sued Graystone for breach of contract, breach of warranty and negligence, including negligent construction, negligent repair, and negligence per se by violating building codes.] The Tinglers and two of their children, the complaints assert, have been "diagnosed with mold toxin syndrome as a result of [their] exposure to the conditions in the Home," and the entire Tingler family remains under continuing medical care for their symptoms.

[The circuit court sustained Graystone's demurrers, and dismissed all claims. The Tingler family appealed, contending that their personal-injury and property-damage claims should have survived demurrer.]

NEGLIGENCE TORT CLAIMS ARISING OUT OF A CONTRACTUAL RELATIONSHIP

1. *General Principles* . . .

We ask. . . whether, under our common-law precedents, tort liability may be imposed upon a home builder who negligently fails to weatherproof the home as required by a construction contract. . . . [I]n order to recover in tort, the duty tortiously or negligently breached must be a common law duty, not one existing between the parties solely by virtue of the contract. . . . Th[is] source-of-duty rule finds its most secure roots in the historical distinction between the escalating degrees of blameworthiness recognized by the common-law doctrines of "omission or non-feasance" on the one hand, and "misfeasance" or malfeasance on the other. . . . Put another way, a fundamental difference exists between lack of performance of something that would have prevented harm and defective performance that caused harm either from a dangerous force or a dangerous condition of something. . . . Our judicial role is . . . modest—to apply the ancient distinction [between nonfeasance and misfeasance] in a pragmatic and sensible way. . . .

2. *Tort Claims Against Home Builders*

. . . Whether viable tort claims arose under the facts pleaded in this case depends both upon the nature of the alleged torts and the types of the alleged damages. Under traditional principles, negligent acts of misfeasance during the construction process that cause reasonably foreseeable personal injuries could implicate tort liability irrespective of a contractual duty to prudently avoid injuring others during the performance of the contract. A home builder, for example, could be sued in tort if he negligently dropped a beam on a bystander or if he negligently left an inconspicuous hole in an unfinished floor into which a visitor fell. *See generally* Restatement (Second) of Torts § 384 (1965).

In this case, the gist of the [negligence claims in the construction process]is that Graystone breached its contractual promise to weatherproof the home. . . . Viewing the claims against Graystone in this manner, the circuit court concluded that the gravamen of the case is simply that Graystone had failed to do what the contract had required. We agree with the court's common-sense approach because it heeds the common law's caution against "turning every breach of contract into a tort," and because it protects the historic distinction between nonfeasance and misfeasance. . . . Applying the source-of-duty rule, we hold that the claims of nonfeasance asserted against Graystone sound only in contract, and thus, the circuit court did not err in sustaining Graystone's demurrers to these claims.

[3.] *Personal-Injury Tort Claims Arising Out of Post-Delivery Repairs*

The Tingler family's complaints also assert that, even if no tort duties arose during Graystone's performance of the original-construction contract, such duties did arise when Graystone later attempted unsuccessfully to repair the leaks and to remediate the mold. We agree in theory that these allegations could support a tort claim, but only to the extent that the complaints allege that the failed repairs made the original condition worse and, by doing so, caused new personal injuries or aggravated preexisting injuries.

a. *Negligent-Repair Allegations . . .*

[In this case], the complaints allege that a Graystone employee cut into the drywall, removed the mold-laden insulation, laid the insulation on the floor, vacuumed it up with the Tinglers' vacuum cleaner, covered up the hole with a black garbage bag, and improperly placed (a later inspector concluded) containment sheeting in the work area. "As a result of the deficiencies . . . in the remediation and repair efforts," the personal-injury complaints assert, "mold growth continued to occur, and harmful and dangerous mold was spread throughout the Home," exposing the Tingler family "to this harmful and dangerous mold" and causing "personal injuries and property damage as a result. The Tingler family's complaints imply that, within a month after Graystone's allegedly negligent remediation efforts, their symptoms worsened enough that they had to move out of the home entirely.

These allegations of misfeasance, along with the reasonable inferences therefrom, assert viable claims for negligent repairs because they reasonably suggest that Graystone either increased the level of mold exposure to the home's inhabitants or extended the duration of the mold's presence and, by doing either, aggravated preexisting mold-exposure injuries suffered by the Tingler family. Graystone could be liable, if the evidence substantiates these inferences, for this aggravation—but not for any preexisting injuries resulting from conditions created by Graystone's nonfeasance during the construction phase of the contract. To this extent, therefore, the circuit court erred in dismissing the negligent-repair tort claims in the Tingler family's personal-injury complaints.

[4.] *Property-Damage & Economic-Loss Claims Against Graystone*

Because all of the complaints at issue in this appeal seek tort remedies for either property damage or economic losses, we must address the "economic loss doctrine." . . . The economic-loss doctrine precludes recovery in tort for any economic loss attributable to the alleged breach of contract or for any property damage specifically involving the home itself, which was the object of the contract. . . . [H]owever, damage to personal property caused by Graystone's misfeasance during *post-construction repairs* can be recovered in tort. Such damage could consist of new damage caused entirely by the negligent repairs or any worsening of preexisting damage (if the evidence can competently prove the degree of aggravation). . . .

[We affirm the dismissal of claims for negligence during the initial construction period and negligent-repair claims seeking recovery for economic loss or damage to the home. We reverse with respect to claims that negligent repairs worsened mold conditions and aggravated personal injuries, and claims that negligent repairs caused damage to personal property that was not the subject of the contract].

NOTES

1. **Independent tort duty.** When a tort suit is brought against a party to a contract, a number of courts ask, as in *Tingler*, whether the alleged injury arises from a tort duty independent of the terms of the contract. *See, e.g., David v. Hett*, 270 P.3d 1102 (Kan. 2011); *Chapman Custom Homes, Inc. v. Dallas Plumbing Co.*, 445 S.W.3d 716 (Tex. 2014). What does that language seem to mean in *Tingler*? The court provided this analogy: "When a home builder swings a hammer and hits someone visiting the site [that] act would be malfeasance if the home builder had intended to strike the visitor and misfeasance if he had merely been reckless. In either scenario, it would be no defense to a tort action against the builder to point out that the construction contract required him to carefully swing his hammer and that he simply had failed to do so." Do you see how the hammer swing could be tort, even if it was also a failure to comply with the contract? Is the analogy useful here?

2. **The Restatement view.** The Third Restatement avoids the independent duty language. The default presumption of a duty of reasonable care applies when the defendant has created a risk. RESTATEMENT (THIRD) OF TORTS: LIABILITY FOR PHYSICAL AND EMOTIONAL HARM § 7 (2010). If defendant hasn't created a risk, the default rule is that the defendant has no duty of care.

Id. § 37. Applying an older standard, at times cases ask whether the defendant "launched an instrument of harm." *In re Lake George Tort Claims*, 461 F. App'x 39 (2d Cir. 2012) (boat canopy, which later collapsed). Here, could it be said that Greystone created a risk or launched an instrument of harm?

3. **Misfeasance.** Many cases in which contracting parties create risks of physical harm look just like cases in which non-contracting parties create risks of physical harm. Although the court talks about duty independent of the contract, it also talks about misfeasance and nonfeasance. Could this case be resolved on that basis? In *Affiliated FM Ins. Co. v. LTK Consulting Servs., Inc.*, 243 P.3d 521 (Wash. 2010), an engineering firm had contracted for repairs to Seattle's monorail system, on which rails a train with passengers later caught fire. The court found the engineering firm's undertaking created a duty of reasonable care independent of the contractual obligations because of the safety interests to people and persons involved.

4. **Nonfeasance.** For claims that the contractor failed to adequately weatherproof the house during the construction period, the plaintiffs might have breach of contract claims, but not tort claims. As the Court noted, some courts would allow tort claims when the breach resulted in physical injury to persons or other property. How might you argue for either the Virginia Supreme Court's view, or for a broader claim for personal injuries, resulting from the original waterproofing problems and not only the faulty repairs?

5. **The economic loss rule.** The district court barred claims for economic loss or damage to property that is the subject of the agreement based on the "economic loss rule," a doctrine that frequently arises when both tort and contract claims exist. *See S K Peightal Eng'rs, LTD v. Mid Valley Real Estate Solutions V, LLC*, 342 P.3d 868 (Colo. 2015) ("The economic loss rule was adopted 'to maintain the boundary between contract law and tort law.'"). Courts have many different iterations of this rule or rules. According to Professor Dobbs, "Two distinct rules tend to limit recovery of economic loss: (1) Subject to qualifications, one not in a special or contractual relationship owes no duty of care to protect strangers against stand-alone economic harm; and (2) again subject to qualifications, those in a special relationship arising out of contract or undertaking may not owe a duty of care to each other; rather, each party is limited to the contract. . . ." Dan B. Dobbs, *An Introduction to Non-Statutory Economic Loss Claims*, 48 ARIZ. L. REV. 713 (2006). The second rule would seem to be the one at issue here. To the extent that defendant's negligence caused physical damage to people or property, rules about economic loss would not apply. Here, the court seems to treat the newly-constructed home as a product and apply a rule that a product that physically injures itself is subject only to contract and not tort liability.

§ 2. NONFEASANCE IN THE PERFORMANCE OF A CONTRACT AND LIABILITY FOR PHYSICAL HARM

What if the defendant does not create a risk of physical harm to the plaintiff's property but instead agrees to render services that should reduce the plaintiff's risk of physical harm yet fails to follow through?

LANGLOIS V. TOWN OF PROCTOR
113 A.3d 44 (Vt. 2014)

DOOLEY, J.

This is an unusual dispute that arose from the failure of plaintiff Kathleen Langlois, owner of a building with commercial space on the first floor and an apartment on the second floor, to pay her water bill for the property to defendant Town of Proctor, and from the Town's alleged failure to turn the water off pursuant to the parties' agreement. Plaintiff alleged, in pertinent part, that she arranged with a representative of the Town that it would disconnect the water service so she would not incur further water expenses, but that the Town failed to do so. She further alleged that in reliance on the Town's promised undertaking she discontinued heating the building, causing the pipes containing water to freeze and split under the first floor of the building, which, in turn, flooded the first floor and basement, causing extensive damage to the building. The jury found the Town negligent and awarded plaintiff damages of $64,918.44. We reverse and remand because of the trial court's failure to instruct on comparative negligence, but affirm in all other respects. . . .

The main count involved in this appeal alleged that the Town was negligent for failure to turn off the water and that its negligence was the proximate cause of plaintiff's damages. Another count alleged that the parties had a contract with respect to the supply of water and that the Town breached the contract by sending a false notice that it had disconnected the water and by failing to remediate its inaction once it was discovered. . . .

[On the claims for negligence and breach of contract, the trial court] concluded:

Plaintiff's claims are rooted in the Town's ordinance governing the relationship between the Town as water supplier and Plaintiff as ratepayer. The ordinance describes itself as "a contract between each ratepayer and the Town." This contractual relationship contained in the ordinance, coupled with Town's alleged misrepresentations in informing Plaintiff that her water had in fact been disconnected when it had not, provides a sufficient legal basis for Plaintiff's claims. . . .

The case was then tried before a jury, which rendered a verdict for plaintiff. . . . [T]he jury found that there was a contract between plaintiff and the Town "regarding the turning off of her water service," . . . [and] that the Town was negligent, that its negligence was a proximate cause of harm to plaintiff, and that plaintiff's damages were $64,918.44.

On appeal, the Town argues that it had no tort duty to properly turn off plaintiff's water service. . . .

We begin with the question of duty. As we held recently, . . . an action for negligence fails in the absence of a duty of care. Whether a duty was present, as well as the scope of any duty, is primarily a question of law. The Town argues that it had no duty to turn off the water, or to turn the service off in a particular way, for nonpayment of water charges. It further argues that the tort duty plaintiff asserted arose out of the contractual relationship between plaintiff and the Town, but that plaintiff's assertion is invalid because a tort duty must arise independent of any contractual obligations.

In response, plaintiff argues that the Town's tort duty arose from its undertaking to disconnect the water service and plaintiff's reliance upon that undertaking. She bases this argument on the Restatement (Second) of Torts § 323 (1965). . . . Section 323 provides:

> . . . One who undertakes, gratuitously or for consideration, to render services to another which he should recognize as necessary for the protection of the other's person or things, is subject to liability to the other for physical harm resulting from his failure to exercise reasonable care to perform his undertaking, if
>
> > (a) his failure to exercise such care increases the risk of such harm, or
> >
> > (b) the harm is suffered because of the other's reliance upon the undertaking. . . .

Without saying so directly, the Town challenges the application of § 323 by claiming that its underlying obligation is contractual. The Town relies on a sentence from *Springfield Hydroelectric Co. v. Copp,* in which this Court stated that a tort duty of care must be " 'independent of any contractual obligations.' " . . . The Town argues that there is no recognizable tort duty because plaintiff is basing the Town's duty on the breach of a contract to turn off the water. . . .

We conclude that the Town reads too much into *Springfield Hydroelectric.* The issue in that case was whether the plaintiff could obtain a tort recovery for purely economic losses in the absence of physical damage. . . . We did not hold that the duty on which plaintiff relies for a tort action can never be contractual.

In fact, many of our duty cases are based on undertakings involving contractually assumed duties. For example, in *Perry v. Green Mountain Mall,* the defendant had a contract with a mall owner to maintain the parking lot and roads around the mall. The plaintiff was an employee of a mall store who was injured when her car skidded on ice in the parking lot, and she sued defendant for negligent failure to remove the ice. We found that the plaintiff's complaint alleged a duty recognized under § 324A of the Restatement. Neither § 323 nor § 324A suggest that the duty stemming from the undertaking cannot be contractually based. Both apply to an undertaking "for consideration," which is one way to describe a contract. . . .

The evidence in this case was sufficient for a factfinder to find that the elements of § 323 were established. Plaintiff testified that the agent of the Town responsible for utility disconnections promised to disconnect the water service to the building. The Town's witnesses established that a Town worker went to the site in May 2009 and believed he had turned off the water at the "curbstop," a valve in the right of way. Thus, there was adequate evidence of an undertaking, whether gratuitous or contractual. . . .

Further, there was evidence that Town workers were aware of the consequences if water was not disconnected and went into an unheated building. In fact, there was testimony that this had happened to another customer about a year before the events of this case. Thus, there was evidence that Town workers recognized that turning off the water was necessary to protect plaintiff's property. Finally, plaintiff testified that she relied upon the Town employee's promise to have the water disconnected when she discontinued heat to the building, meeting the requirement of § 323(b).

[Although the Town had a duty to turn off plaintiff's water due to her reliance on the Town's promise to do so, the trial court's refusal to instruct the jury on comparative negligence constitutes reversible error. Accordingly, the case is reversed and remanded for a new trial.]

NOTES

1.   **Gratuitously or for consideration.** Recall *Wakulich* from Chapter 16. There, the court found that the defendants had voluntarily undertaken to care for the plaintiff's decedent after she drank a quart of Goldschlager and became unconscious. The *Langlois* court says that the Restatement recognizes undertakings that arise "gratuitously or for consideration," and that therefore a contract itself may form the basis for the undertaking.

2. **The nature of the contract.** The jury in *Langlois* had found a contract based on the language of the ordinance and the statement by the Town's representative that the water would be turned off. Do you think that courts are more likely to find a tort duty arising from an undertaking when the contract is an informal one, as in *Langlois*, in contrast with a formal written agreement?

3. **Judge and jury.** The *Langlois* court says that "[w]hether a duty was present, as well as the scope of any duty, is primarily a question of law." Why, then, does the court rely on the jury's findings to uphold the conclusion that the Town had a duty to Langlois?

4. **Hypothetical.** What if the employee sent to turn off Langlois' water had broken the pipe while turning the water off? Would the Town be liable for the damage caused by the broken pipe? Would the basis for the duty be different from what it would be here?

Suppose that in *Affiliated FM Ins. Co. v. LTK, supra* Note 3 after *Tingler*, LTK engineers were hired to investigate whether the monorail's grounding system needed repairs but failed to notice an important safety issue. Would that situation produce the same outcome as in *Langlois*? In *LeBlanc v. Logan Hilton Joint Venture*, 974 N.E.2d 34 (Mass. 2012), the court held that the defendant architects could be liable for negligence in the inspection of electrical equipment that later caused electrocution. Although the contract limited the team to the design and regular inspection of the equipment, and imposed no duty to act, there was a professional duty of care to the third-person electrician, sounding in tort, when the team failed to report problems.

5. **Contracts to provide security.** Peter enters into a contract with a security company for a portable call button for his mother. When his mother pushes the button, the company directs emergency services to the wrong address. Due to the delay Peter's mother dies. Should Peter have a negligence claim against the security company? *See Spengler v. ADT Security Servs., Inc.*, 505 F.3d 456 (6th Cir. 2007) ("ADT's obligation to promptly and correctly dispatch EMS emanated only from the contract, not Michigan common law, and thus no tort claim is available."). There are many other cases to the same effect. *Frost v. ADT, LLC*, 947 F.3d 1261 (10th Cir. 2020) (child and homeowner died in house fire when ADT received several alerts through its monitoring system yet failed to notify emergency services; contract barred tort claim); *Abacus Fed. Sav. Bank v. ADT Security Servs., Inc.*, 967 N.E.2d 666 (N.Y. 2012) (ADT not liable under tort theory for failure to monitor alarm system on bank vault, despite potential gross negligence); *Valenzuela v. ADT Security Servs., Inc.*, 475 F. App'x 115 (9th Cir. 2012) (ADT's legal obligation to provide service arose solely from its contractual relationship with jewelers, not from any independent duty and therefore even gross negligence claim was inappropriate).

Are these cases correctly decided? *See Shakeri v. ADT Security Servs., Inc.*, 816 F.3d 283 (5th Cir. 2016) ("While Plaintiffs assert a duty that sounds similar to the one covered by contract, the nature of Plaintiffs' injury is noneconomic. Plaintiff alleged that he suffered severe and permanent physical injuries when [the jewelry store where worked] was robbed" and the alarm button he pressed didn't work; because injury involved physical harm, the negligence action should not have been dismissed). To the same effect, see 2 DOBBS, HAYDEN & BUBLICK, THE LAW OF TORTS § 412 (2d ed. 2011). How would the cases come out if the courts applied Restatement (Second) of Torts § 323 quoted in *Langlois*?

6.   **The Restatement Third: services designed to reduce risk of physical harm.** The Third Restatement's view is that an actor who undertakes to render services to another, which the actor knows or should know will reduce the risk of physical harm to the other, owes a duty of reasonable care in carrying out that undertaking if (a) the failure to exercise care increases the risk of harm beyond that which would have existed without the undertaking, or (b) the other person relies on the undertaking. RESTATEMENT (THIRD) OF TORTS: LIABILITY FOR PHYSICAL AND EMOTIONAL HARM § 42 (2012). How might the Third Restatement provision have helped the plaintiffs in the *ADT* cases in Note 5?

§ 3. SCOPE OF DUTY BASED ON UNDERTAKING

DIAZ V. PHOENIX LUBRICATION SERVICE, INC., 230 P.3d 718 (Ariz. Ct. App. 2010). On October 30, 2004, Plaintiff Joseph Bryant Diaz ("Bryant") took the Volvo owned by his parents . . . to a Jiffy Lube for an oil change. The oil change service included a check of the Volvo's tire pressure. Bryant did not purchase Jiffy Lube's separate tire rotation and inspection service, which was offered for an additional fee. A few weeks later, when Bryant was driving the Volvo on a wet portion of the road, the car went off the road and rolled over, causing Bryant serious injuries, including paralysis. . . . Bryant filed suit against numerous defendants including Discount Tire which had replaced tires in July 2004, and Volvo North Scottsdale, which serviced the Volvo on September 29, 2004, and November 5, 2004. Volvo North Scottsdale named Jiffy Lube as a non-party at fault, after which Plaintiffs amended their complaint to add Jiffy Lube as a defendant. Plaintiffs claim Jiffy Lube was negligent because the service it performed should have included an examination of the tires and notification of the dangerous wear patterns on the rear tires. All of the Defendants except Jiffy Lube were dismissed from the action. Jiffy Lube then filed a motion for summary judgment asserting that it did not owe Plaintiffs a duty to inspect the inside tread of the Volvo's tires. Defendant's motion for summary judgment was granted.

Held: affirmed. "Jiffy Lube did not owe Plaintiffs a legal duty that would permit a recovery in this case. . . . The oil change agreement between Jiffy Lube and Plaintiffs included only a check of the air pressure in the Volvo's tires, not an overall tire inspection. . . . [In a prior case an Arizona court agreed] that '[w]hen a mechanic contracts to repair a defect in an automobile he does not impliedly contract to inspect and repair the neighboring parts.' ... [W]e derive guidance from the proposed Restatement regarding the importance of the scope of the undertaking by the defendant and the distinction between creating a risk and failing to discover a risk. In contrast to § 7 of the proposed Restatement, § 37 ... provides that "[a]n actor whose conduct has not created a risk of physical harm to another has no duty of care to the other unless a court determines that one of the affirmative duties in §§ 38–44 is applicable." ...

Illustration 4 in comment g to § 42 of the Restatement underscores that courts should usually limit the existence of a duty to the scope of the actual undertaking:

> Lindsay hires Margaret to fix a leaking plumbing fixture in a second-floor apartment. Margaret repairs the leak in a nonnegligent manner. After completing the repairs, Margaret realizes that water that had leaked earlier from the fixture continued to leak from the apartment onto an adjacent alley. When returning home that evening, Lindsay slips and falls on ice that had formed in the alley from the water that continued to leak. Lindsay sues Margaret claiming that she had a duty of reasonable care with regard to the water that leaked out of the fixture. *The risks posed by the water that had previously escaped from the fixture are beyond the scope of Margaret's undertaking to repair the fixture as a matter of law, and Margaret is not subject to liability for Lindsay's harm....*

Similar to the illustration found in § 42 of the proposed Restatement, the risk posed by the Volvo's worn tires was beyond the scope of Jiffy Lube's undertaking, which involved merely checking each tire's air pressure, adjusting the pressure as necessary, and performing other non-tire-related services. ...

NOTES

1. **Risk creation.** What if, while checking the tire pressure, the mechanic in *Diaz* had carelessly nicked the tire with a sharp instrument, contributing to the tire's dangerous condition? Does the *Diaz* court suggest that would be the same case?

2. **Alternative protections.** The Restatement (Third) of Torts says that reliance is a specific manner of increasing the harm. A person who relies on the defendant's performance of a contract may decline "to pursue alternative means for protection." For example, in the case in which a neighbor agrees to make daily visits to care for a pet while the owner is away, a duty of care is owed because the pet owner relies on the neighbor's promise. Why would

reliance make the neighbor's agreement not just a valid contract, but also a valid basis for imposing a tort duty?

3. **Defining the scope of the undertaking.** *Diaz* employs the Restatement rule both to define when an undertaking to make something safer creates a duty and to limit the scope of the duty to the scope of the actual undertaking. *See also Hutchison v. Fitzgerald Equip. Co.*, 910 F.3d 1016 (7th Cir. 2018) (undertaking was limited to the scope of the contract—"to perform the lubrication and operational maintenance inspection[s]"); *Hill v. Superior Prop. Mgmt. Servs., Inc.*, 321 P.3d 1054 (Utah 2013) (maintenance company under contract to mow lawn not liable to resident who tripped over an exposed tree root in a grassy area because its duty "was limited to the extent of its undertaking").

Is the scope of the duty always defined by the written terms of the contract? The *Diaz* plaintiffs alleged that the industry custom during an oil change and tire pressure check was to check the tires for wear. What if the plaintiff had gone further and provided testimony that he relied on the fact that Jiffy Lube followed that custom and would have paid for an additional service or taken the car elsewhere if he had believed the defendant was not going to check the tires?

4. **Known risk.** If the facts showed that the mechanic in *Diaz* saw the problem and realized the tread was too worn, but decided not to comment about it, would that be the same case? Is this the no-duty-to-act rule? *See Hill v. Sears, Roebuck & Co.*, 822 N.W.2d 190 (Mich. 2012) (electrical appliance installers had no duty to report an uncapped gas line; beyond the scope of contract for the installation of the appliances).

5. **Limited contracts.** Suppose that a retailer permits third parties to put animals up for adoption on its premises. One of the adopted animals injures its owner. What is the scope of the retailer's undertaking? Might the result depend on whether the injury occurs in the store or off the premises? In *PetSmart, Inc. v. Eighth Jud. Dist. Ct.*, 499 P.3d 1182 (Nev. 2021), the court wrote: "Nothing in the record suggests that PetSmart knew about Chip's aggressive tendencies, much less undertook affirmative steps to prevent the type of harm that ensued. PetSmart did not vet the individual dogs, watch for dogs that are repeatedly placed for adoption, or investigate the animals prior to adoption. Far from undertaking to share [the third-party agency] AH4S's duty, PetSmart expressly affirmed in its agreement with AH4S that the agency partner alone had control of which pets to present for adoption and was fully responsible for those animals. . . . And although PetSmart took steps to ensure the safety of its store patrons by requiring AH4S to follow guidelines during its adoption fairs, those ordinary safety precautions do not suggest that PetSmart assumed the role of an insurer of adopters' safety after they left the store."

6. **Scope of the agreement and public policy.** Should the parties' agreement always define the scope of the undertaking? What if a defendant had volunteered to drive his drunken friend for most of the night and then drop

him off at his car—limited agreement defining the scope of the obligation? *See Gushlaw v. Milner*, 42 A.3d 1245 (R.I. 2012). How would you argue for and against a duty, based on doctrine and policy?

§ 4. DUTY TO THIRD PARTIES BASED ON UNDERTAKING TO ANOTHER

A. THE MODERN RULE

PALKA V. SERVICEMASTER MANAGEMENT SERVICES CORP., 634 N.E.2d 189 (N.Y. 1994). Palka was a nurse employed by Ellis Hospital. Ellis had contracted with Servicemaster to manage maintenance operations at the hospital. Before that, the hospital had conducted its own safety inspections of such things as fans mounted on walls. After Servicemaster took over, the hospital left all such programs to Servicemaster. Servicemaster did not exercise reasonable care with respect to wall-mounted fans and one of them fell on the plaintiff. She sued Servicemaster. *Held:* (1) safety of such items as wall-mounted fans was within the scope of the contract obligation; and (2) Servicemaster was under a duty to the plaintiff, a non-contracting party. Palka "proved not only that Servicemaster undertook to provide a service to Ellis Hospital and did so negligently, but also that its conduct in undertaking that particular service placed Palka in an unreasonably risky setting greater than that, had Servicemaster never ventured into its hospital servicing role at all." "[U]nlike our decisions in *Moch Co. v. Rensselaer Water Co.* and *Strauss v. Belle Realty Co.*, the instant case presents this array of factors: reasonably interconnected and anticipated relationships; particularity of assumed responsibility under the contract and evidence adduced at trial; displacement and substitution of a particular safety function designed to protect persons like this plaintiff; and a set of reasonable expectations of all the parties. These factors, taken together, support imposition of liability against this defendant in favor of this plaintiff."

NOTES

1. **Duty to third persons.** The Restatement provides that an actor who undertakes to render services the actor knows or should know reduce the risk of harm to which a third person is exposed, has a duty of reasonable care if (a) the failure to exercise care increases the risk of harm beyond that which would have existed without the undertaking, (b) the actor has undertaken to perform a duty owed by another to a third person, or (c) the person to whom services are provided, the third person or another person relies on the undertaking. RESTATEMENT (THIRD) OF TORTS: LIABILITY FOR PHYSICAL AND EMOTIONAL HARM § 43 (2012). How would that standard apply in *Palka*?

2. **Examples.** When is a duty owed to a third party?

(a) An employer's workers' compensation insurer conducted medical monitoring and implemented an industrial-hygiene plan for the employer. The employee developed an incurable respiratory disease in the workplace. Did the insurer's undertaking with respect to the employer create a duty to the employee? *See Maryland Cas. Co. v. Asbestos Claims Ct.*, 460 P.3d 882 (Mont. 2020).

(b) The parent of a 14-year-old girl who plans to sleep over at a friend's house, says to the friend's parent that "his daughter was not to be in a car with any young, male drivers . . . no boys with cars." The friend's parent agrees that she will not allow the girls to ride in a car driven by an inexperienced young male. Hours later, the parent permits just that, with tragic consequences—wildly reckless driving, an accident and the death of the 14-year-old. Was the friend's parent's promise enough to create a duty?

3. **Increased risk over what?** Did Servicemaster's failure to exercise reasonable care truly increase the risk of harm beyond that which would have existed without its undertaking? How would you prove that Palka would have been at less risk if Servicemaster had never ventured into its hospital servicing role? *See Herrington v. Gaulden*, 751 S.E.2d 813 (Ga. 2013) (medical director of hospital emergency department not liable on undertaking theory where he did nothing to escalate risk to patient; liability does not attach for failing to decrease risk of harm).

4. **Baselines.** In *Paz v. State of California*, 994 P.2d 975 (Cal. 2000), a developer delayed in installing traffic signals which led to an accident. The court rejected the negligent undertaking theory on the ground that the delayed installation of the traffic signals was not an increased risk. Instead, "defendants simply did not succeed in completing—before plaintiff's collision—a project that might have reduced the preexisting hazard at the intersection." To which baseline risk should the defendant's conduct be compared—the level of risk at the intersection before installation of the signal or the level of risk at the intersection if the sign had been installed on time? Could you say that the developer created a risk of harm by failing to promptly address the situation? What if the developer had delayed for years beyond the agreed date for signal installation—is there ever a point at which this would be creation of risk? Is this just another instance of nonfeasance-misfeasance reasoning?

5. **Increased risk and reliance.** A 14-year-old boy walking to the bus stop in pre-dawn hours was struck and killed by a truck. The streetlight near which the boy was struck was not operative. His mother sued the streetlight company for negligence. The trial court found no duty. But the court in *Clay Elec. Coop., Inc. v. Johnson*, 873 So.2d 1182 (Fla. 2003), reversed and remanded on both the "increased risk" and "reliance" issues. When the company undertook to maintain the streetlights, the court said, it should have foreseen that proper maintenance was necessary for the protection of children who walked to the bus in the early morning hours before school.

Contrast *Stocker v. State*, 264 A.3d 435 (Vt. 2021). In *Stocker*, plaintiffs, who were abused as children, and their grandparents, brought a tort action claiming that the Department for Children and Families failed to accept or respond to dozens of reports of physical and sexual abuse of the children. The Vermont Supreme Court dismissed their negligent undertaking claim on the ground that they failed to show DCF's alleged negligence increased the risk of harm. "The standard of comparison is not the risk of harm created if defendant exercised reasonable care, but the risk of harm that would be present if defendant had never undertaken to render services. . . . In this case, plaintiffs may be able to show that, had DCF acted with reasonable care, they would not have suffered as much, but they have not presented evidence that DCF's undertaking to protect them put them at greater risk than if DCF had taken no steps at all."

6. **"Third party beneficiaries."** Some courts use the language of contract law in explaining the imposition of a tort duty. For example, in *Doe ex rel. Doe v. Wright Security Servs., Inc.*, 950 So.2d 1076 (Miss. Ct. App. 2007), a student named Jim was sexually assaulted by another student in a restaurant restroom near a school bus stop. Jim sued Wright, the security company hired by the school district, claiming negligence. Reversing a summary judgment for Wright, the court said a tort duty may extend to "third party beneficiaries of a contract," and that here, "one purpose of Wright's contract with [the District] was to prevent violence or altercations among the alternative school students." This "shows as a matter of law that Wright owed a duty to minimize risks to Jim's safety."

7. **Leases.** At one time, most courts held that a tenant could not file a tort action against a lessor based on breach of an agreement to make repairs to the premises, even when personal injury resulted. *See, e.g., Leavitt v. Twin County Rental Co.*, 21 S.E.2d 890 (N.C. 1942) (damages for personal injury are "too remote" and "not within the contemplation of the parties"). Many states have now abrogated this rule by statute with respect to residential leases, and many courts have changed the rule for commercial leases as well. *See Mobil Oil Corp. v. Thorn*, 258 N.W.2d 30 (Mich. 1977). The Restatement (Second) § 357 provides that a lessor is subject to liability for physical harm to a lessee and others on the land with the lessee's permission caused by a condition of disrepair, if (1) the lessor has contracted to repair, (2) the disrepair creates an unreasonable risk, and (3) the lessor fails to exercise reasonable care to perform his contract. The Third Restatement says that a person in a "special relationship with another owes the other a duty of reasonable care with regard to risks that arise within the scope of the relationship." The relationship between a landlord and tenants is specifically listed. RESTATEMENT (THIRD) OF TORTS: LIABILITY FOR PHYSICAL AND EMOTIONAL HARM § 40 (2012). Could this broad provision support the recognition of a tort duty to fulfill a contractual obligation to repair if a tenant is injured by non-repair?

B. AN HISTORICAL PERSPECTIVE

Contemporary rules of tort liability regarding breach of a contract to make something safer contrast with older rules under which lack of privity in contract barred a duty even to foreseeably injured third parties.

WINTERBOTTOM V. WRIGHT, 152 Eng. Rep. 402 (Exch. Pl. 1842). Defendant was under contract with the Postmaster-General to supply coaches for use in delivering mail. The contract also called for the defendant to keep them in good repair. Plaintiff was the coachman on one of the coaches supplied by the defendant and was allegedly lamed for life when the coach broke down and he was thrown from his seat. He alleged that it broke down because the defendant neglected to perform the repair portion of his contract. *Held*, for the defendant. LORD ABINGER, C.B.: "Here the action is brought simply because the defendant was a contractor with a third person; and it is contended that thereupon he became liable to everybody who might use the carriage. If there had been any ground for such an action, there certainly would have been some precedent of it; but with the exception of actions against innkeepers, and some few other persons, no case of a similar nature has occurred in practice. That is a strong circumstance, and is of itself a great authority against its maintenance.

It is however contended that this contract being made on the behalf of the public by the Postmaster-General, no action could be maintained against him, and therefore the plaintiff must have a remedy against the defendant. But that is by no means a necessary consequence—he may be remediless altogether. There is no privity of contract between these parties; and if the plaintiff can sue, every passenger, or even any person passing along the road, who was injured by the upsetting of the coach, might bring a similar action. Unless we confine the operation of such contracts as this to the parties who entered into them, the most absurd and outrageous consequences, to which I can see no limit, would ensue. Where a party becomes responsible to the public, by undertaking a public duty, he is liable, though the injury may have arisen from the negligence of his servant or agent. So, in cases of public nuisances, whether the act was done by the party as a servant, or in any other capacity, you are liable to an action at the suit of any person who suffers. Those, however, are cases where the real ground of the liability is the public duty, or the commission of the public nuisance. There is also a class of cases in which the law permits a contract to be turned into a tort; but unless there has been some public duty undertaken, or public nuisance committed, they are all cases in which an action might have been maintained upon the contract. Thus, a carrier may be sued either in assumpsit or case; but there is no instance in which a party, who was not privy to the contract entered into with him, can maintain any such action. The plaintiff in this case could not have brought an action on the contract; if he could have done so, what would have been his situation, supposing the Postmaster General had released the defendant? That would, at all events, have defeated his claim altogether. By permitting this action, we would be working this injustice, that after the defendant had done everything to the satisfaction of his employer, and after all matters between them had been adjusted, and all accounts settled on the footing of their contract, we should subject them to be ripped open by this action of tort being brought against him."

ALDERSON, B.: "The only safe rule is to confine the right to recover to those who enter into the contract: if we go one step beyond that, there is no reason why we should not go fifty."

H.R. MOCH CO. V. RENSSELAER WATER CO., 159 N.E. 896 (N.Y. 1928). The defendant, a waterworks company, made a made a contract with the City of Rensselear for the supply of water to public and private users. While the contract was in force, a building caught fire. The defendant was notified of the fire but neglected to furnish an adequate supply of water, so that the fire damaged the plaintiff's warehouse. The plaintiff sued in contract and in tort. Motion to dismiss the complaint was denied in the trial court, but reversed on appeal. *Held,* the action is not maintainable in contract or in tort. "The plaintiff would have us hold that the defendant, when once it entered upon the performance of its contract with the city, was brought into such a relation with everyone who might potentially be benefitted through the supply of water at the hydrants as to give to negligent performance . . . the quality of a tort. . . . We are satisfied that liability would be unduly and indeed indefinitely extended by this enlargement of the zone of duty. The dealer in coal who is to supply fuel for a shop must then answer to the customers if fuel is lacking. The manufacturer of goods, who enters upon the performance of his contract, must answer, in that view, not only to the buyer, but to those who to his knowledge are looking to the buyer for their own sources of supply. Everyone making a promise having the quality of a contract will be under a duty to the promisee by virtue of the promise, but under another duty, apart from contract, to an indefinite number of potential beneficiaries when performance has begun. . . .

NOTES

1. **Liability to third persons.** It was once thought that *Winterbottom v. Wright* established a rule about privity. The result was that even if the defendant was guilty of affirmative negligence in performance of a contract, he would not be liable to third persons who were not parties to the contract. This was attacked, not only on grounds of injustice, but on the ground that *Winterbottom v. Wright* was really only a nonfeasance case and that its rule

should be applied only to cases of nonfeasance in the performance of a contract. Do you agree that it was a nonfeasance case?

2. **A modern view.** Given the recent cases we have studied, how might *Winterbottom* be analyzed today?

3. **Scope of duty.** What is the issue in *Moch*? Isn't this misfeasance—operating a water company and doing it badly? Consider this: *Moch* was decided the same year as *Palsgraf*. Is it plausible to treat *Moch* as a scope-of-duty problem? You could ask (a) what persons are within the defendant's promised protection? and (b) what risks are within the promised protection? Such an approach would delineate the duty by asking about the scope of the promise or undertaking rather than by asking about foreseeability, but otherwise it would sound pretty much like a basic proximate cause approach.

4. **Unlimited liability.** Another possibility is that the court is simply afraid of potentially unlimited liability and will arbitrarily mark a limit to that liability. That is the view taken by the Restatement (Third) of Torts. "The better explanation for limitations on the duty of public utilities is concern about the huge magnitude of liability to which a utility might be exposed from a single failure to provide service that affects hundreds, thousands, or, in the case of an electrical blackout, millions." RESTATEMENT (THIRD) OF TORTS: LIABILITY FOR PHYSICAL AND EMOTIONAL HARM § 42 cmt. i (2010). *See also Rice v. Collins Communication, Inc.*, 236 P.3d 1009 (Wyo. 2010) (negligent failure in a communications system caused a half-hour delay in response to a fire; although the negligence increased risks of harm, court was concerned about effect of liability if "a private corporation doing business with a government entity would owe a duty to a private citizen").

5. **Extended liability and physical injury.** A breach of contract may cause financial loss but not physical injury. Most of Cardozo's examples in *Moch* were like this. But suppose a contract promise is intended to protect against physical injury. Would there be any need to worry about extended liability in the examples Cardozo gives? Did Cardozo overlook the fact that *Moch* was a physical harm case and that his concerns about extensive liability were based on economic harms?

6. **Intent of the parties.** Is it possible to interpret the "intent of the parties" without resorting to an automatic rule based on privity? In *Libbey v. Hampton Water Works Co.*, 389 A.2d 434 (N.H. 1978), the court in a *Moch*-type case observed: "Water companies are in business to supply water, not to extinguish fires. Their rates reflect this assumption; they are uniform, not varying with the greater or lesser inherent danger in given areas." This kind of reasoning suggests that even one in privity might be denied recovery for some consequential damages if those damages did not represent harms against which the parties were contracting. Compare the contemplation-of-the-parties rule of *Hadley v. Baxendale*, as to which see DAN B. DOBBS & CAPRICE L. ROBERTS, LAW OF REMEDIES § 12.4 (3d ed. 2018).

§ 5. ACTION AS A PROMISE OR UNDERTAKING

FLORENCE V. GOLDBERG
375 N.E.2d 763 (N.Y. 1978)

JASEN, JUDGE.

[A mother took her 6-year-old child to school each day for two weeks, during which time the city police had stationed a guard at a street crossing. The mother, having observed this protection, ceased to take the child to school. On the day in question the crossing guard regularly assigned there called in sick. Departmental regulations called for sending a substitute if possible and, if not, to cover the most dangerous crossings. No substitute was sent and the principal of the school was not notified. The child was struck at the unguarded crossing and suffered severe brain damage. The plaintiffs recovered against the city and those responsible for operation of the car. The city appeals.]

[A] municipality cannot be held liable for failure to furnish adequate police protection. This duty, like the duty to provide protection against fire, flows only to the general public. (Riss v. City of New York, 22 N.Y. 2d 579. . . .)

[T]here is little question that the police department voluntarily assumed a particular duty to supervise school crossings. . . .

Significantly, the duty assumed by the police department was a limited one: a duty intended to benefit a special class of persons—viz., children crossing designated intersections while traveling to and from school at scheduled times. Thus, the duty assumed constituted more than a general duty to provide police protection to the public at large. Having witnessed the regular performance of this special duty for a two-week period, the plaintiff infant's mother relied upon its continued performance. To borrow once more from Chief Judge Cardozo, "[i]f conduct has gone forward to such a state that inaction would commonly result, not negatively merely in withholding a benefit, but positively or actively in working an injury, there exists a relation out of which arises a duty to go forward." (Moch Co. v. Rensselaer Water Co., 247 N.Y. at p. 167). Application of this principle to the present case leads unmistakably to the conclusion that the police department, having assumed a duty to a special class of persons, and having gone forward with performance of that duty in the past, had an obligation to continue its performance. Had the police department not assumed a duty to supervise school crossings, plaintiff infant's mother would not have permitted her child to travel to and from school alone. The department's failure to perform this duty placed the infant plaintiff in greater danger than he would have been had the duty not been assumed, since the infant's mother would not have had reason to rely on the protection afforded her child and would have been required, in her absence, to arrange for someone to accompany her child to and from school.

[There was also proof that the city was negligent in failing to provide a guard.]

The order of the Appellate Division should be affirmed, with costs.

––––––––––

KIRCHER V. CITY OF JAMESTOWN, 543 N.E.2d 443 (N.Y. 1989). The plaintiff was entering her car in a drug store parking lot when a man, Blanco, accosted her. She screamed. Karen Allen and Richard Skinner heard the screams and saw Blanco force her into the car. Allen and Skinner gave chase, but lost sight of the car in heavy traffic. While trying to catch up to the car, they saw a police officer, Carlson. They explained what they had seen and gave him the car's description and license number. He promised to "call in," but in fact Carlson never even reported the incident. Meanwhile, Blanco repeatedly raped and beat the plaintiff, fracturing her larynx and inflicting other brutal injuries. In the Court of Appeals, *held*, the plaintiff cannot recover.

(1) A city is not held liable for negligent exercise of government functions unless it is in a special relationship with the claimant. "Nevertheless, where a municipality voluntarily undertakes to act on behalf of a particular citizen who detrimentally relies on an illusory promise of protection offered by the municipality, we have permitted liability because in such cases the municipality has by its conduct determined how its resources are to be allocated in respect to that circumstance and has thereby created a 'special relationship' with the individual seeking protection."

(2) Liability on this ground requires the municipality to be in "direct contact" with the claimant and requires justifiable reliance by the claimant upon the municipality's affirmative undertaking. Although Allen and Skinner were in direct contact with police, the plaintiff was not, so the direct contact requirement is not fulfilled.

(3) The reliance requirement is not fulfilled, either. "[T]he helpless and isolated plaintiff could not even communicate with the police, much less rely on any promise of protection the police might have offered. Yet, although plaintiff's failure to rely can be directly attributed to her dire circumstances, this does not, as the dissenters urge, provide a justification for ignoring the reliance requirement altogether."

NOTES

1.   **Action as undertaking.** The issue in many cases is whether the defendant's conduct counted as an undertaking at all. In *Florence*, is it clear

that the city's actions counted as undertakings because they seemed to promise continued protection for the children?

2. **Unreasonable reliance.** Although action may sometimes invite reliance, reliance may not be reasonable at times when the party undertaking the service explicitly warned that reliance was inappropriate. Thus where a repairman attempted to repair a car's parking brake but instructed the car owner that he was unable to do so, the repair shop had satisfied its duty not to induce reasonable reliance. It could not be held liable to employee injured when the truck rolled backwards and injured him. *Lindsey v. E & E Auto. & Tire Serv., Inc.*, 241 P.3d 880 (Alaska 2010).

3. **Why is undertaking relevant?** Turn to a different problem with "undertakings." The idea that "undertaking" may create a duty that did not otherwise exist is generally recognized but profoundly uncertain. First consider why an undertaking might be relevant to the question of the defendant's duty. Would it show: (a) a special relationship, established by the undertaking itself; (b) affirmative action, not mere nonfeasance; (c) the equivalent of a promise from which a tort duty might arise if there is consideration or reliance? *See, e.g., State Auto Ins. Cos. v. B.N.C.*, 702 N.W.2d 379 (S.D. 2005) (discussing duty of care owed by daughter who undertook to watch her father's home while he was on vacation).

4. **Reliance and discriminatory enforcement.** If *Florence* requires reliance in order to justify recovery, is that desirable? What about a child whose parents never knew of the presence of a guard? Or a child both of whose parents knew there was no guard but neither of whom could take the child to school because they both worked? Is there anything wrong with permitting a recovery for the Florence boy but not for the child of non-relying parents?

5. **Why is reliance necessary?** The requirement of reliance works even more dramatically to deny a recovery in *Kircher*. In addition, that case reflects New York's more recent additional "direct contact" requirement. Why require either on the facts of *Kircher*? Can you have no special relationship without reliance? Was the city making some careful calculation about its limited resources when the officer failed even to report as he promised?

6. **Scope of undertaking.** Think back to *Diaz*. Many courts would agree that "the scope of any duty assumed depends upon the nature of the undertaking." *Delgado v. Trax Bar & Grill*, 113 P.3d 1159 (Cal. 2005). What is undertaken in the following case? A mother, seeing the crossing guards in the afternoon, assumes that the school has undertaken to provide crossing safety before and after school and thus allows her child to walk to school unaccompanied the next morning. There are no crossing guards and the child is struck in a crosswalk by a motorist. The school has never provided guards in the morning. Did it (a) undertake to provide crossing safety and do it negligently? or (b) undertake to provide afternoon guards only? In *Jefferson County Sch. Dist. R-1 v. Gilbert*, 725 P.2d 774 (Colo. 1986), the court took the narrower view, that the school had assumed the duty to provide afternoon guards only.

REFERENCE: 2 DOBBS, HAYDEN & BUBLICK, THE LAW OF TORTS §§ 410–12 (2d ed. 2011); DOBBS, HAYDEN & BUBLICK, HORNBOOK ON TORTS §§ 25.6–25.7 (2d ed. 2016).

CHAPTER 18

THE DUTY TO PROTECT FROM THIRD PERSONS

■ ■ ■

§ 1. THE GENERAL RULE AND ITS EXCEPTIONS

BROWN v. USA TAEKWONDO
483 P.3d 159 (Cal. 2021)

Opinion of the Court by KRUGER, J. . . .

The issue before us concerns how courts should decide whether a defendant has a legal duty to take action to protect the plaintiff from injuries caused by a third party. . . . Distilling the principles articulated in prior cases, we now clarify that whether to recognize a duty to protect is governed by a two-step inquiry. First, the court must determine whether there exists a special relationship between the parties or some other set of circumstances giving rise to an affirmative duty to protect. Second, if so, the court must consult the factors described in *Rowland v. Christian*, 443 P.2d 561 (1968), to determine whether relevant policy considerations counsel limiting that duty.* . . .

This case comes to us at the demurrer stage, so for present purposes we assume the truth of the allegations in the complaint. As teenagers, plaintiffs [ ] trained in the Olympic sport of taekwondo. They traveled to compete at various events in California and throughout the country with their coach, Marc Gitelman. Gitelman took advantage of these opportunities to sexually abuse the young athletes. This went on for years until the sponsor of these competitions, USA Taekwondo (USAT), banned Gitelman from coaching. Gitelman was ultimately convicted of multiple felonies for the sexual abuse of the minor athletes he trained.

Plaintiffs (to whom we will generally refer as Brown) filed this civil suit against Gitelman and several others, including respondents USAT and the United States Olympic Committee (USOC). USOC is a federally

---

* [The *Rowland* factors include "the foreseeability of harm to the plaintiff, the degree of certainty that the plaintiff suffered injury, the closeness of the connection between the defendant's conduct and the injury suffered, the moral blame attached to the defendant's conduct, the policy of preventing future harm, the extent of the burden to the defendant, and consequences to the community of imposing a duty to exercise care with resulting liability for breach, and the availability, cost, and prevalence of insurance for the risk involved."—Eds.]

chartered nonprofit corporation whose central function is to coordinate amateur sports throughout the country for athletes hoping to one day compete in the Olympics. In this role, USOC certifies and oversees each sport's national governing body, the entity responsible for conducting and administering the sport in the United States. USAT is the national governing body for the sport of taekwondo. If an athlete wishes to compete in taekwondo at the Olympics or in any other USAT-sponsored competition (as Brown and the other plaintiffs did), the athlete must become a member of USAT and train under a USAT-registered coach (as Gitelman was before USAT banned him).

As relevant here, Brown alleged that USOC and USAT were negligent in failing to protect her from Gitelman's abuse. Brown emphasized that the sexual abuse of young athletes was a known problem; Gitelman's abuse came on the heels of a series of similar instances of abuse of minors by their coaches dating back to the 1980's. In the wake of these incidents, USOC mandated that national governing bodies adopt a Safe Sport Program to protect athletes from such abuse. Brown alleged that USAT failed to implement the program in a timely fashion—a fact known to USOC, which placed USAT on probation as a result. Brown further alleged that USAT took insufficient steps to protect Gitelman's victims once it was made aware of her allegations: USAT temporarily suspended Gitelman, but nevertheless permitted him to continue coaching at USAT competitions for several months before ultimately placing him on its list of banned coaches.

USOC and USAT . . . argued Brown had not adequately alleged they had an affirmative duty to take action to protect her and the other plaintiffs from Gitelman's abuse. The trial court . . . entered judgments of dismissal.

Brown appealed. The Court of Appeal reversed the judgment dismissing USAT but affirmed as to USOC. The court first concluded Brown had sufficiently alleged a special relationship between USAT and Gitelman that enabled USAT to control Gitelman's actions, as demonstrated by the fact that USAT had registered him as a coach, took disciplinary action against him, and ultimately barred him from coaching.

By contrast, the Court of Appeal concluded that USOC, unlike USAT, had no special relationship with either the plaintiffs or Gitelman. . . . The court explained that Brown's case for imposing an affirmative duty on USOC rested largely on allegations that USOC had the ability to regulate USAT's conduct. . . .

The "general rule" governing duty is set forth in [California] Civil Code section 1714 (section 1714). First enacted in 1872, section 1714 provides: "Everyone is responsible . . . for an injury occasioned to another by his or her want of ordinary care or skill in the management of his or her property or person. . . ." This statute establishes the default rule that each person has a duty "to exercise, in his or her activities, reasonable care for the safety of others."

Section 1714 states a broad rule, but it has limits. We have explained that the law imposes a general duty of care on a defendant only when it is the defendant who has "created a risk" of harm to the plaintiff, including when "the defendant is responsible for making the plaintiff's position worse." The law does not impose the same duty on a defendant who did not contribute to the risk that the plaintiff would suffer the harm alleged. Generally, the person who has not created a peril is not liable in tort merely for failure to take affirmative action to assist or protect another from that peril. See Rest.3d Torts, Liability for Physical and Emotional Harm (2012) § 37. For example, a person who stumbles upon someone drowning generally has no legal duty to help the victim. The same rule applies to a person who stumbles upon a mugging, for as a general matter, there is no duty to act to protect others from the conduct of third parties.

This general rule, we have explained, derives from the common law's distinction between misfeasance and nonfeasance, and its reluctance to impose liability for the latter. And although it may sometimes produce outcomes that appear morally questionable, there are several reasons the no-duty-to-protect rule has endured. The most commonly cited reason for the rule is rooted in the liberal tradition of individual freedom and autonomy—the idea that a person should be able to freely choose whether to come to the aid of a stranger, without fear of incurring legal liability for the choice. But our cases have recognized other reasons as well, including the difficulties of setting any standards of unselfish service to fellow men, and the challenge of making any workable rule to cover possible situations where fifty people might fail to rescue.

The no-duty-to-protect rule is not absolute, however; this court has recognized a number of exceptions. Under some circumstances, a defendant may have an affirmative duty to protect the plaintiff from harm at the hands of a third party, even though the risk of harm is not of the defendant's own making. For example, if a person does choose to "undertake to come to the aid of another," she may then have an affirmative duty to exercise reasonable care in that undertaking. Rest.3d Torts, *supra*, § 42. We here focus, along with the parties, on [one] basis for finding an affirmative duty: In a case involving harm caused by a third party, a person may have an affirmative duty to protect the victim of another's harm if that person is in what the law calls a "special relationship" with either the victim or the person who created the harm. See generally Rest.3d Torts, *supra*, §§ 40, 41.

A special relationship between the defendant and the victim is one that gives the victim a right to expect protection from the defendant, while a special relationship between the defendant and the dangerous third party is one that entails an ability to control the third party's conduct. Relationships between parents and children, colleges and students, employers and employees, common carriers and passengers, and innkeepers and guests, are all examples of special relationships that give rise to an affirmative duty to protect. The existence of such a special relationship puts the defendant in a unique position to protect the plaintiff from injury. The law requires the defendant to use this position accordingly.

Where the defendant has neither performed an act that increases the risk of injury to the plaintiff nor sits in a relation to the parties that creates an affirmative duty to protect the plaintiff from harm, however, our cases have uniformly held the defendant owes no legal duty to the plaintiff. . . .

Brown argues . . . that even if the defendant lacks any special relationship with the parties and there are no other circumstances that would give rise to an affirmative duty to protect, such a duty may nonetheless arise after considering the policy factors set out in the landmark decision in *Rowland*. We reject the argument. . . .

The requirement of an affirmative duty to protect . . . reflects a long-standing balance between several competing interests. . . . Where [ ] a special relationship exists between the defendant and a minor, the obligation to provide such protection and assistance may include a duty to protect the minor from third party abuse. And there may be other circumstances that give rise to a comparable affirmative duty to protect. But where no such circumstances exist, the *Rowland* factors do not serve as an alternative basis for imposing duties to protect. . . .

A court considers whether the parties have a special relationship by considering the particular facts and circumstances of their association with one another. The *Rowland* factors, by contrast, consider, "at a relatively broad level of factual generality," whether policy considerations justify limiting any resulting duty of protection. Our opinion in *Castaneda v. Olsher*, 162 P.3d 610 (Cal. 2007), is illustrative of the difference between the two inquiries. In that case, the plaintiff was injured as a bystander to a gang-related shooting at the mobile home park where he lived. He sued his landlord for negligence. Although the parties were in a special relationship, we concluded that the landlord did not have a duty to "withhold rental units from those they believe to be gang members" in order to protect his other tenants. We reasoned that requiring as much would, as a general proposition, result in "arbitrary discrimination on the basis of race, ethnicity, family composition, dress and appearance, or reputation"— all in service of a tenant screening process that was unlikely to effectively prevent injuries like those the plaintiff had suffered. Thus, despite the existence of a special relationship, imposing such a duty on landlords would not be "fair or workable," nor would it be "consistent with our state's public policy as a whole."

. . . [E]ven when a special relationship gives rise to an affirmative duty to protect, a court must still consider whether the policy considerations set out in *Rowland* warrant a departure from that duty in the relevant category of cases.

Brown alleged that USAT and USOC acted negligently by failing to take steps to protect her from her coach's abuse. To evaluate her claim, the Court of Appeal first asked whether a duty existed based on a special relationship. Concluding that USOC had no such relationship with Brown, the court ended its analysis with respect to that defendant. This approach was sound. And after concluding that USAT *did* have a special relationship with plaintiffs, the court went on to apply *Rowland* to determine whether to limit that potential duty—deciding the answer to that question was no. This, too, was the correct approach.

The Court of Appeal's judgment does not mark the end of the case. It affirms the trial court's decision to dismiss one of several named defendants, USOC, for failure to adequately allege a special relationship giving rise to an affirmative duty to protect. . . .

Concurring Opinion by JUSTICE CUÉLLAR. . . .

I write separately to explain how [the opinion's] presumptions and exceptions realize a fundamental substantive principle: In California, tort law—the law of when and how individuals who have suffered harm may seek compensation for their injuries through private actions—serves society's interest in allocating risks and costs to those who can better prevent them, and it provides aggrieved parties with just compensation. . . .

[W]e generally start by presuming everyone has a duty of reasonable care in the management of his or her property or person; we limit it based on policy considerations like those in *Rowland* only in a particular *category* of cases and only if *clearly* supported by *public* policy. Second, in some cases, a defendant may argue that he or she was nothing more than a disengaged bystander—someone society recognizes as categorically outside the scope of any responsibility, having no material role in creating the risk of plaintiff's harm and so no duty of reasonable care. . . .

Whether someone is a "bystander" to a particular risk is shorthand for whether we as a society are willing to say, based on reasonable inferences about the benefits and burdens of potential liability, that a particular defendant should bear no responsibility for the risk. Though the question isn't before us in this case, it bears emphasis, given the all-too-common fact pattern, that USOC is hardly a bystander to plaintiffs' harm. USOC is the organizer of the activity where the harm occurred. Between the organizer of an activity where someone is wronged and a mere bystander there is generally a world of difference: one at least sets the stage for what ends up becoming a tragedy; the other at most stumbles into the theater in the last act, when the story has unfolded and its casualties are known. The person who sets the stage owes the players a general duty to exercise reasonable care. The organizer, by bringing people together, may "create the risk" even if less directly than a criminal or intentional tortfeasor. Considering the benefits and burdens of imposing some responsibility on that person, a court may decide that an organizer—even one lacking either awareness of a material risk or full control of every administrative nuance—is no bystander at all. . . .

"Special relationship" is merely a label for those policy considerations that our shared experience has taught us to treat as especially relevant. . . . As the Restatement explains, "The term 'special relationship' has no independent significance. . . . Whether a relationship is deemed special is a conclusion based on reasons of principle or policy." (Rest.3d, *supra*, § 40, com. h.) Among reasons of principle or policy, our precedents place special emphasis on two reasons in particular: defendant's ability to control the environment, to predict and prevent the risk, and plaintiff's reasonable dependency. A college or university may be well suited to foresee and control risks to students in the campus environment, and students reasonably expect such protection and are especially vulnerable without it. Or a proprietor should be aware of a danger of assault; customers are at the mercy of the proprietor; and so the proprietor has a duty of reasonable care to reduce such risks. In some cases, we have also emphasized the burden on defendant of avoiding certain risks. . . .

Properly understood, the special relationship question plays a limited but important role under our law. If plaintiffs don't want to wade into whether defendants "created the risk" of the harm plaintiffs experienced, they can argue that defendant owed a duty of reasonable care, based on a "special relationship." To do so, plaintiffs have to show why specific policy factors under the "special relationship" rubric supported such a duty. We don't address whether plaintiffs in this case did in fact make such a showing. And we don't address the possibility, because it was not presented to us, that USOC had a general duty to exercise reasonable care in the management of its property or person. It presumptively would if it were not a "bystander," and we certainly don't decide public policy clearly supports exempting a category of organizations including USOC from that general duty.

While we don't address those claims today, we reaffirm that courts should assess such claims with the ultimate aim of deciding whether requiring reasonable care serves the goals tort law embodies: to achieve appropriate deterrence and compensate victims.

Tort law relies heavily on the concept of duty to render tractable a reality where lives are at risk in the very world that sustains them, and people are bound by intricate and far-reaching ties of responsibility and norms of reciprocity. . . . The two-step procedure we endorse is grounded in long-established principles, emphasizing not only the importance of offering civil recourse and compensation to those harmed but also the value of allocating responsibility for losses to minimize future harm. . . . Implicit in this arrangement is the latitude for courts to minimize harms through the proper allocation of losses, and to compensate victims for their uncommon injuries—including in cases where the facts are not only tragic, but tragically all-too-common. Which is why I concur.

NOTES

1. **The general rule.** Courts frequently begin the analysis of third-party harm cases with the general rule that a defendant has no legal duty to protect the plaintiff from injuries caused by another. What does the California Supreme Court say are the reasons for such a rule?

2. **Exceptions: affirmative duty.** The main exception through which a defendant might be found to have a duty to use reasonable care to protect from third-party harm is when the defendant has a special relationship with plaintiff or defendant. What is the majority's view about the importance of special relationships? What function does the concurrence think this category serves?

3. **Establishing special relationships.** The Restatement Third's list of special relationships in § 40, cited in *Brown,* notes categories that have already been recognized by precedent. However, courts can create additional categories. In *Grimes v. Kennedy Krieger Institute, Inc.*, 782 A.2d 807 (Md. 2001), researchers partially abated lead in homes and then arranged for landlords to get public funding to lease the apartments to families with children. Finding a duty of the researchers to the children in the experiment, the court recognized that special relationships and concomitant tort duties might arise from a contract between the parties, from statute regulating their dealings, from the superior knowledge of one of them, and even, perhaps, from international law (the Nuremberg Code). What did Justice Cuellar mean when he said that the court didn't address in this case whether plaintiffs had made such a showing? If you represented the plaintiffs, how might you try to establish a special relationship with the USOC that required its care?

4. **Creating the danger.** According to the concurrence, could the plaintiffs have claim that the defendant USOC created a risk? In *Bell v. Grow With Me Childcare & Preschool LLC*, 907 N.W.2d 705 (Neb. 2018), plaintiffs hired an in-home nanny who had worked at a daycare center. The center fired her for abusive conduct but never reported her to authorities, as required by statute. Plaintiffs argued that the preschool had created the risk because the nanny's employment with childcare centers facilitated her ability to get in-house jobs and abuse other children. The Court reversed a $5 million jury

verdict for plaintiff on the ground that center had not created a risk and no special relationship applied so that center had no duty to plaintiff.

5.   **Shipbreaking.** How far reaching are ties of responsibility and norms of responsibility? The issue is a question of principle and policy. Suppose the defendant sold an oil tanker for $16 million that defendant knew would be broken apart in Bangladesh in a shipyard with negligible safety standards (at best). If defendant had sold the tanker to a yard with better safety standards, defendant would have made $6 million less. Did the seller create the danger to a worker who was killed when demolishing the ship at the yard? See *Begum v. Maran*, [2021] EWCA Civ. 326 ("Whilst I do not underestimate the hurdles that [the attorney's claim] will face at trial, I consider this way of putting the claim is arguable and not fanciful."). *See also* Ellen M. Bublick, *Tort Common Law Future: Preventing Harm and Providing Redress to the Uncounted Injured*, J. OF TORT L. (2022).

6.   **Necessary, but not sufficient?** Is it enough to trigger a duty that the plaintiff and defendant are in a special relationship, or is more required? *See, e.g., Bjerke v. Johnson*, 742 N.W.2d 660 (Minn. 2007) (duty to protect another person from harm will be found if there is a special relationship and the risk is foreseeable); *Commonwealth v. Peterson*, 749 S.E.2d 307 (Va. 2013) (assuming that a special relationship existed between state and students at Virginia Tech, state owed no duty to warn students about a possible shooter on campus where the danger was neither known nor foreseeable); *Mattox v. State, Dept. of Corrections*, 323 P.3d 23 (Alaska 2014) (state owed duty to protect inmate from foreseeable harms, such as attacks by other inmates who had threatened him); *but see Rodriguez v. Del Sol Shopping Center Assocs., L.P.*, 326 P.3d 465 (N.M. 2014) (business invitees were owed duty of reasonable care because of special relationship; foreseeability of harm goes to breach of duty, not to existence of duty itself).

7.   **Duty to protect plaintiffs against negligent acts by third parties.** In this section of the book, we focus mainly on whether a duty exists to protect a plaintiff from a criminal act by a third person. However, the special relationship rules apply much the same way in cases where the plaintiff alleges that the defendant failed to protect from the *negligence* of a third party. *See, e.g., Marshall v. Burger King Corp.*, 856 N.E.2d 1048 (Ill. 2006). Both the Second and Third Restatements are in accord. *See* RESTATEMENT (SECOND) OF TORTS §§ 314A & 344 (1965); RESTATEMENT (THIRD) OF TORTS: LIABILITY FOR PHYSICAL AND EMOTIONAL HARM §§ 19 (2010) & 40 (2012).

8.   **Nonfeasance.** Is a special relationship required only where the plaintiff alleges that the defendant failed to act, or does it apply even when the defendant has acted and created a risk of harm?

§ 2. DEFENDANT'S RELATIONSHIP WITH THE PLAINTIFF

POSECAI v. WAL-MART STORES, INC.
752 So.2d 762 (La. 1999)

MARCUS, JUSTICE. . . .

[On July 20, 1995, Mrs. Posecai shopped at Sam's Club, then returned to her car in Sam's parking lot. It was not dark, but a man hiding under her car grabbed her ankle and pointed a gun at her. He robbed her of jewels worth about $19,000 and released her. Mrs. Posecai sued Sam's, claiming it was negligent in failing to provide security guards in the parking lot. The courts below assessed almost $30,000 in damages against Sam's. Evidence showed that Sam's was adjacent to but was not in a high-crime area. From 1989 to 1995, there were three robberies on Sam's premises. But during the same period, there were 83 predatory offenses at 13 businesses in the same block as Sam's.]

A threshold issue in any negligence action is whether the defendant owed the plaintiff a duty. Whether a duty is owed is a question of law. In deciding whether to impose a duty in a particular case, the court must make a policy decision in light of the unique facts and circumstances presented. The court may consider various moral, social, and economic factors, including the fairness of imposing liability; the economic impact on the defendant and on similarly situated parties; the need for an incentive to prevent future harm; the nature of defendant's activity; the potential for an unmanageable flow of litigation; the historical development of precedent; and the direction in which society and its institutions are evolving. . . .

Other jurisdictions have resolved the foreseeability issue in a variety of ways, but four basic approaches have emerged. The first approach, although somewhat outdated, is known as the specific harm rule. According to this rule, a landowner does not owe a duty to protect patrons from the violent acts of third parties unless he is aware of specific, imminent harm about to befall them. Courts have generally agreed that this rule is too restrictive in limiting the duty of protection that business owners owe their invitees.

More recently, some courts have adopted a prior similar incidents test. Under this test, foreseeability is established by evidence of previous crimes on or near the premises. The idea is that a past history of criminal conduct will put the landowner on notice of a future risk. Therefore, courts consider the nature and extent of the previous crimes, as well as their recency, frequency, and similarity to the crime in question. This approach can lead to arbitrary results because it is applied with different standards regarding the number of previous crimes and the degree of similarity required to give rise to a duty.

The third and most common approach used in other jurisdictions is known as the totality of the circumstances test. This test takes additional factors into account, such as the nature, condition, and location of the land, as well as any other relevant factual circumstances bearing on foreseeability. As the Indiana Supreme Court explained, "[a] substantial factor in the determination of duty is the number, nature, and location of prior similar incidents, but the lack of prior similar incidents will not preclude a claim where the landowner knew or should have known that the criminal act was foreseeable." The application of this test often focuses on the level of crime in the surrounding area and courts that apply this test are more willing to see property crimes or minor offenses as precursors to more violent crimes. In general, the totality of the circumstances test tends to place a greater duty on business owners to foresee the risk of criminal attacks on their property and has been criticized "as being too broad a standard, effectively imposing an unqualified duty to protect customers in areas experiencing any significant level of criminal activity."

The final standard that has been used to determine foreseeability is a balancing test, an approach which has been adopted in California and Tennessee. This approach was originally formulated by the California Supreme Court in *Ann M. v. Pacific Plaza Shopping Center* in response to the perceived unfairness of the totality test. The balancing test seeks to address the interests of both business proprietors and their customers by balancing the foreseeability of harm against the burden of imposing a duty to protect against the criminal acts of third persons. The Tennessee Supreme Court formulated the test as follows: "In determining the duty that exists, the foreseeability of harm and the gravity of harm must be balanced against the commensurate burden imposed on the business to protect against that harm. In cases in which there is a high degree of foreseeability of harm and the probable harm is great, the burden imposed upon defendant may be substantial. Alternatively, in cases in which a lesser degree of foreseeability is present or the potential harm is slight, less onerous burdens may be imposed." Under this test, the high degree of foreseeability necessary to impose a duty to provide security, will rarely, if ever, be proven in the absence of prior similar incidents of crime on the property.

We agree that a balancing test is the best method for determining when business owners owe a duty to provide security for their patrons. The economic and social impact of requiring businesses to provide security on their premises is an important factor. Security is a significant monetary expense for any business and further increases the cost of doing business in high crime areas that are already economically depressed. Moreover, businesses are generally not responsible for the endemic crime that plagues our communities, a societal problem that even our law enforcement and other government agencies have been unable to solve. At the same time, business owners are in the best position to appreciate the crime risks that are posed on their premises and to take reasonable precautions to counteract those risks.

. . . The greater the foreseeability and gravity of the harm, the greater the duty of care that will be imposed on the business. A very high degree of foreseeability is required to give rise to a duty to post security guards, but a lower degree of foreseeability may support a duty to implement lesser security measures such as using surveillance cameras, installing improved lighting or fencing, or trimming shrubbery. . . .

In the instant case, there were only three predatory offenses on Sam's premises in the six and a half years prior to the robbery of Mrs. Posecai. The first of these offenses occurred well after store hours, at almost one o'clock in the morning. . . . Two years later, an employee of the store was attacked in the parking lot and her purse was taken, apparently by her husband. . . . It is also relevant that Sam's only operates during daylight hours and must provide an accessible parking lot to the multitude of customers that shop at its store each year. . . .

We conclude that Sam's did not possess the requisite degree of foreseeability for the imposition of a duty to provide security patrols in its parking lot. . . .

NOTES

1.   **Applying *Posecai*.** How does the balancing test in *Posecai* work in these cases: (a) The plaintiff is attacked in a mall parking lot and claims the mall owners should have provided better lighting; (b) The plaintiff is attacked in a mall which had security guards but scheduled the guards' rounds negligently so they were not covering the attack area appropriately; (c) The plaintiff leases space in an underground parking garage. She is sexually attacked at her car. The garage's surveillance cameras do not work; some of the lights are out; the place is deteriorating; there is a smell of urine. No crimes of personal violence have been committed in the garage though plenty of other crimes have been committed nearby. *Sharon P. v. Arman,* 989 P.2d 121 (Cal. 1999).

2.   **Business creating or enhancing risks.** Suppose a business creates or enhances risks that third persons will attack customers. *Cf. Brown v. Delta Tau Delta,* 118 A.3d 789 (Me. 2015) (national fraternity had duty to exercise reasonable care for the safety of local chapter's invitees, including plaintiff, who was sexually assaulted by a fraternity member, where national fraternity "had effectively handed over a residential building to a group of college students" and was aware of alcohol abuse in frat house). Or suppose a business sells items or brands that are especially coveted by violent people, so that the business itself attracts violence. What if it merely maintains a large,

unguarded parking garage? In *Stewart v. Federated Department Stores, Inc.*, 662 A.2d 753 (Conn. 1995), the court imposed liability on a retail store for the murder of a customer in the store's parking garage. The court thought that the unguarded garage, constantly filled with customers laden with packages, was an "invitation" to violence. What if the business is merely located in a remote setting and stays open late? Might that make a violent attack actionable?

3. **Imminent harm known.** Early cases involved landowners who were present when their invitees were subjected to some imminent threat of harm from others. For instance, in *Greco v. Sumner Tavern, Inc.*, 128 N.E.2d 788 (Mass. 1955), the defendant knew that a man had been drinking in the defendant's tavern all day and causing "trouble." About 10:00 that night he attacked and seriously injured another customer. The tavern owner was held liable for negligence in failing to deal with the situation. Some more recent cases also find a duty owed to invitees where harm is either imminent or when some physical altercation has already begun on the premises. *See, e.g., Del Lago Partners, Inc. v. Smith*, 307 S.W.3d 762 (Tex. 2010); *Morris v. De La Torre*, 113 P.3d 1182 (Cal. 2005); *see also Bailey v. Schaff*, 835 N.W.2d 413 (Mich. 2013) (duty owed to guest of tenant where imminent harm to guest became apparent from known presence of shooter in common area of unit).

Would knowledge of imminent harm, without a special relationship between plaintiff and defendant, suffice to trigger a duty? For example, suppose a bar patron leaves the premises, thus losing her invitee status, but is followed out of the bar by other patrons who had been observed getting her drunk, allegedly for the purpose of sexually exploiting her. Does the bar owe her a duty to protect her from an attack off-premises on those facts? *See Reynolds v. CB Sports Bar, Inc.*, 623 F.3d 1143 (7th Cir. 2010). Or suppose a bar patron is beaten outside the bar in an adjacent alley after leaving the club, when evidence showed that there were fights in the club every week and two fights a month outside the alley entrance. Does the bar owner owe a duty of reasonable care to the patron on those facts? *See Novak v. Capital Mgmt. & Dev. Corp.*, 570 F.3d 305 (D.C. Cir. 2009).

4. **Prior similar incidents approach.** Gradually, a number of courts began to impose liability when attacks by third persons were foreseeable and the business failed to take reasonable steps to protect those on its premises. The usual basis for finding foreseeability in these cases is that there were previous crimes on the premises or nearby. *See, e.g., Nallan v. Helmsley-Spear, Inc.*, 407 N.E.2d 451 (N.Y. 1980). Predictably, what looks like a simple matter of evidence about foreseeability became something of a rule of law for some judges, so that if no similar incidents had occurred on or near the premises, crime was deemed unforeseeable and the business would not be under any duty to take reasonable steps to protect its visitors. *See, e.g., McKown v. Simon Prop. Group, Inc.*, 344 P.3d 661 (Wash. 2015); *Liszewski v. Target Corp.*, 374 F.3d 597 (8th Cir. 2004) (Missouri law). You can expect litigation over what counts as a similar incident. *See, e.g., Surles ex rel. Johnson v. Greyhound Lines, Inc.*, 474 F.3d 288 (6th Cir. 2007) (evidence of prior incidents involving passengers assaulting drivers or attempting to grab the driver or the steering wheel on a

moving bus was properly admitted in case involving a passenger's armed attack on a bus driver); *Jenkins v. C.R.E.S. Mgmt., L.L.C.*, 811 F.3d 753 (5th Cir. 2016) (applying Texas law, error for trial judge to exclude evidence of prior residential burglaries on the premises in case brought by plaintiff who was shot in her apartment); *L.A.C. v. Ward Parkway Shopping Center Co.*, 75 S.W.3d 247 (Mo. 2002) ("Foreseeability does not require identical crimes in identical locations."); *Sturbridge Partners, Ltd. V. Walker*, 482 S.E.2d 339 (Ga. 1997) (knowledge of burglaries might mean that rape is foreseeable).

5.   **Totality of circumstances approach.** Many courts in answering the duty question now treat the foreseeability issue more holistically. *See, e.g., Bray v. St. John Health System, Inc.*, 187 P.3d 721 (Okla. 2008); *Monk v. Temple George Assocs., LLC*, 869 A.2d 179 (Conn. 2005). As *Posecai* explains, this so-called "totality of circumstances" approach takes into account a number of factors, including the existence of prior criminal acts, but the existence of prior crimes is not determinative. See, e.g., *Clohesy v. Food Circus Supermarkets, Inc.*, 694 A.2d 1017 (N.J.1997) ("Generally, our tort law . . . does not require the first victim to lose while subsequent victims are permitted to at least submit their cases to a jury."). Some courts follow this approach without labeling it anything but "ad hoc." *See, e.g., Ouch v. Khea*, 963 A.2d 630 (R.I. 2009) ("[T]here is no clear-cut formula to determine whether a duty exists in a specific case. Instead, the court will employ an *ad hoc* approach that turns on the particular facts and circumstances of a given case, taking into consideration all relevant factors.").

6.   **Balancing approach.** The balancing test is attracting more adherents. *See, e.g., Collum v. McCool*, 432 S.W.3d 829 (Tenn. 2013); *Bass v. Gopal, Inc.*, 716 S.E.2d 910 (S.C. 2011). It is not always favorable to plaintiffs, because under this approach the defendant may have no duty to deal with even foreseeable harm. *See, e.g., Sakiyama v. AMF Bowling Ctrs., Inc.*, 1 Cal. Rptr. 3d 762 (Ct. App. 2003) (no duty owed to an attendee at an all-night "rave" at defendant's facility, despite foreseeability that attendees would use illegal drugs and drive home in fatigued state). The idea got its impetus from *Ann M. v. Pacific Plaza Shopping Center*, 863 P.2d 207 (Cal. 1993), cited in *Posecai*. In that case, the plaintiff, working in a store at a strip mall, was accosted by a man in her place of work, held at knife point, and raped. She sued the mall, claiming it should have had security guards. The court said: "Foreseeability, when analyzed to determine the existence or scope of a duty, is a question of law to be decided by the court. . . . [T]he social costs of imposing a duty on landowners to hire private police forces are also not insignificant. For these reasons, we conclude that a high degree of foreseeability is required in order to find that the scope of a landlord's duty of care includes the hiring of security guards." Given this test, the court held that the shopping mall was not liable in that case for failing to have security guards.

7.   **Duty vs. breach.** As summarized by the Tennessee court, the balancing test works this way: "In determining the duty that exists, the foreseeability of harm and the gravity of harm must be balanced against the commensurate burden imposed on the business to protect against that harm."

McClung v. Delta Square Ltd. P'ship, 937 S.W.2d 891 (Tenn. 1996). This sounds like the risk-utility balance for determining negligence, doesn't it? Does it matter that many courts have used this balancing test in determining *duty* rather than *breach* of duty? Should the risk-utility test be conducted at a different level of generality of it is a part of the duty inquiry?

8. **Foreseeability.** Foreseeability is a part of the breach and proximate cause inquires for the jury. If the court delves into a fact-specific foreseeability inquiry, could it usurp the jury's role? In *Staples v. CBL & Assocs.*, 15 S.W.3d 83 (Tenn. 2000), Justice Holder argued in a concurring opinion that unless the question was so clear that reasonable people could not differ, the balancing should be done by the jury as part of its decision on the negligence issue, not by judges. *See also A.W. v. Lancaster Cty. Sch. Dist. 0001*, 784 N.W.2d 907 (Neb. 2010) (foreseeability is a fact question for the jury on the breach issue, and is not part of a duty analysis); *Gipson v. Kasey*, 150 P.3d 228 (Ariz. 2007) (foreseeability is a fact issue for the jury on the breach and causation elements; "foreseeability is not a factor to be considered by courts when making determinations of duty"); *Rodriguez v. Del Sol Shopping Center Assocs., L.P.*, 326 P.3d 465 (N.M. 2014) (foreseeability is a fact issue for the jury to consider on breach and proximate cause; "courts must articulate specific policy reasons, unrelated to foreseeability considerations, when deciding whether a defendant does or does not have a duty or that an existing duty should be limited").

9. **The Restatement Third on foreseeability.** The Restatement Third observes in a comment that judicial use of foreseeability in duty determinations "occurs more frequently and aggressively in cases involving an affirmative duty than in other cases," and that this tendency is "even more pronounced in cases in which the alleged duty involves protecting the plaintiff from third parties, especially the criminal acts of third persons." RESTATEMENT (THIRD) OF TORTS: LIABILITY FOR PHYSICAL AND EMOTIONAL HARM § 37, cmt. f (2010). The comment goes on to opine that this approach—which may involve the formulation of the kinds of tests the court discussed in *Posecai*— "constitutes an incursion on the role of the jury as factfinder." Do you agree with this critical assessment?

10. **Negligence and causation.** To hold the defendant liable in all these cases, the plaintiff must prove not only a duty but also negligence causation. Would better lighting avoid nighttime attacks? Always, never, or sometimes? In *Shadday v. Omni Hotels Management Corp.*, 477 F.3d 511 (7th Cir. 2007), a guest in a luxury hotel in Washington, D.C., was raped in the elevator by another guest. Should the plaintiff prevail in a negligence suit alleging inadequate security by offering evidence that there had been 637 criminal acts in the surrounding neighborhood in the three years preceding the attack, none involving guest-on-guest violence? What problems do you see for such a claim?

MARQUAY V. ENO

662 A.2d 272 (N.H. 1995)

HORTON, JUSTICE. . . .

The plaintiffs are three women who were students in the Mascoma Valley Regional School District. In separate complaints filed in the district court, each plaintiff alleges that she was exploited, harassed, assaulted, and sexually abused by one or more employees of the school district. According to the complaints, Lisa Burns was sexually abused by Brian Erskine, a high school teacher, beginning in her sophomore year and continuing beyond graduation. . . . [Other plaintiffs made similar allegations about Michael Eno, a sports coach, and Brian Adams, a teacher.] Each plaintiff also alleges that a host of school employees, including other teachers, coaches, superintendents, principals and secretaries either were aware or should have been aware of the sexual abuse. . . .

[The plaintiffs sued the district and its allegedly abusing employees. The federal district court certified a number of questions to this Court.]

I.   RELATIONSHIP OF STATUTORY VIOLATION TO CIVIL LIABILITY

The first certified question asks whether RSA 169–C:29, which, under penalty as a misdemeanor, requires that any person "having reason to suspect that a child has been abused or neglected shall report the same [to the State]," creates a private right of action in favor of abused children against those who have violated the statute's reporting requirement. . . .

At first glance, our cases appear to be inconsistent on this issue. Everett v. Littleton Construction Co., 94 N.H. 43, 46 A.2d 317 (1946), instructs that "the violation of a penal statute is an actionable wrong only when the Legislature expressly so provides . . . , or when the purpose and language of the statute compel such inference. . . ." We have also held, however, that " [t]he breach of a statutory duty results in liability . . . when the plaintiff is in a class the statute is designed to protect and the injury is of the type that the statute is intended to prevent."

The apparent inconsistency in our jurisprudence arises from a failure to distinguish two distinct bases of civil liability: (1) statutorily expressed or implied causes of action; and (2) negligence per se. The former, recognized in Everett, is the principle that whether or not the common law recognizes a cause of action, the plaintiff may maintain an action under an applicable statute where the legislature intended violation of that statute to give rise to civil liability. The doctrine of negligence per se, on the other hand, provides that where a cause of action does exist at common law, the standard of conduct to which a defendant will be held may be defined as that required by statute, rather than as the usual reasonable person standard. The doctrine of negligence per se, however, plays no role in the creation of common law causes of action. Thus, in many cases, the common law may fail to recognize liability for failure to perform affirmative duties that are imposed by statute. . . .

We hold that the reporting statute does not support a private right of action for its violation because we find no express or implied legislative intent to create such civil liability. First, we note that where the legislature has intended that civil liability flow from the violation of a statute, it has often so provided. Where, as here, civil liability for a statutory violation would represent an abrupt and sweeping departure from a general common law rule of nonliability, we would expect that if the legislature, which is presumed to recognize the common law, intended to impose civil liability it would expressly so provide. Here there was no expressed intent. Nor can we divine any implied intent.

We now turn to the negligence per se question. . . . [U]se of a statute to establish the standard of care is limited to situations where a common law cause of action exists, and then, only if the statute is "applicable." Whether a statutory standard is applicable depends, in part, on whether the type of duty to which the statute speaks is similar to the type of duty on which the cause of action is based. Because the duty to which the statute speaks—reporting of abuse—is considerably different from the duty on which the cause of action is based—supervision of students—we hold that a violation of the reporting statute does not constitute negligence per se in an action based on inadequate supervision of a student.

II. COMMON LAW CAUSES OF ACTION

The plaintiffs argue that all school district employees have a common law duty to protect students whom they know or should know are being sexually abused by another school employee. We hold that some employees owe such a duty while others do not. The duty owed by some defendants is based on their relationship to the students; for other defendants the duty derives from their relationship to the alleged abusers.

As a general rule, a person has no affirmative duty to aid or protect another. Such a duty may arise, however, if a special relationship exists. The plaintiffs argue that a special relationship exists between educators and school children, imposing a duty upon educators to protect students whom they know or should know are being sexually abused by another school employee.

"One who is required by law to take or who voluntarily takes the custody of another under circumstances such as to deprive the other of his normal opportunities for protection is under a . . . duty to the other." Restatement (Second) of Torts § 314A at 118 (1965). "[A] child while in school is deprived of the protection of his parents or guardian. Therefore, the actor who takes custody . . . of a child is properly required to give him the protection which the custody or the manner in which it is taken has deprived him." Id. § 320 comment b at 131. We agree with the majority of courts from other jurisdictions that schools share a special relationship with students entrusted to their care, which imposes upon them certain duties of reasonable supervision. The scope of the duty imposed is limited by what risks are reasonably foreseeable. . . .

Major factors influencing our conclusion that a special relationship exists between schools and students include the compulsory character of school attendance, the expectation of parents and students for and their reliance on a safe school environment, and the importance to society of the learning activity which is to take place in public schools. For these reasons, we conclude that "the social importance of protecting the plaintiff[s'] interest outweighs the importance of immunizing the defendant from extended liability."

School attendance impairs both the ability of students to protect themselves and the ability of their parents to protect them. It is this impairment of protection from which the special relationship between school and student arises and from which the duty of supervision flows. We decline, however, to accept the plaintiffs' argument that every school employee shoulders a personal duty simply by virtue of receiving a paycheck from the school district. Instead, the duty falls upon those school employees who have supervisory responsibility over students and who thus have stepped into the role of parental proxy. Those employees who share such a relationship with a student and who acquire actual knowledge of abuse or who learn of facts which would lead a reasonable person to conclude a student is being abused are subject to liability if their level of supervision is unreasonable and is a proximate cause of a student's injury.

While the impairment of protection creates an affirmative duty, it also circumscribes the limits of that duty. Thus the existence of a duty is limited to those periods when parental protection is compromised. That is not to say that employees with a special relationship to a student may not be liable for injuries that occurred off school premises or after school hours, if the student can show that the employee's negligent acts or omissions, within the scope of his or her duty, proximately caused injury to the student. This is a question for the jury.

We note that the principal or superintendent rarely has primary supervisory authority over a student. Because, however, it is the school to which parents turn over custody of their children and from which they expect safety and because the superintendent and principal are charged with overseeing all aspects of the school's operation, we hold that a duty of supervision is owed to each student. Where the principal or superintendent knows or should know that a particular school employee poses a threat to a student, entrustment of the student to the care of that employee will not satisfy the duty of reasonable supervision.

[Employees with supervisory powers of hiring and firing might be liable for negligent hiring or retention of a person they knew or should have known was an abuser.] While we held in section I that the reporting statute is not applicable in an action based on negligent supervision, we hold that it is applicable in a negligent hiring or retention action. Accordingly, under these circumstances, failure to report abuse in accordance with the statute could give rise to liability, provided the plaintiff can show that reporting would have prevented the subsequent abuse.

Remanded.

NOTES

1. **Liability of the abusers.** In *Marquay*, the plaintiffs claimed at-school sexual abuse by employees of the school. The actual abusers are no doubt liable. In fact, if the coach is a public-school employee, his molestation of a student might even count as a violation of § 1983, on the ground that molestation is an infringement of a liberty interest protected by the Due Process Clause. *Doe v. Taylor Indep. Sch. Dist.,* 15 F.3d 443 (5th Cir. 1994).

2. **Vicarious liability.** Employers (including school districts) are normally liable for the torts of their employees, provided the torts are committed within the scope of their employment. Thus a school district could be vicariously liable for the negligence of school personnel in negligently hiring, retaining or supervising teachers and counselors who abuse students. *C.A. v. William S. Hart Union High Sch. Dist.,* 270 P.3d 699 (Cal. 2012). In the case of vicarious liability for intentional torts, courts employ a range of tests. *See* Chapter 22.

3. **Primary liability of schools.** When the school officials know or should know of abuse or harassment by teachers or coaches, the officials seem to be in violation of their duty of care if they do nothing about the abuse. *Doe v. Logan County Bd. of Educ.,* 829 S.E.2d 45 (W. Va. 2019) (reversing dismissal of negligence claim in which 17 year old student alleges that other "educators" observed inappropriate interactions between teacher and student but failed to act). *Marquay* seems to support that rule. *See also Rapuano v. Trustees of Dartmouth Coll.,* 334 F.R.D. 637 (D.N.H. 2020) (plaintiffs need to show that the school owed a duty "not to hire or retain employees that it knew or should have known have a propensity to sexually harass students;" approving $14 million class settlement). School administrators can have a duty to protect students from sexual abuse by school employees, even if the school does not have actual knowledge of a particular employee's history of committing, or propensity to commit, such abuse. *See Doe v. Lawndale Elementary Sch. Dist.,* 72 Cal.App.5th 113 (2021). In addition, the United States Supreme Court has held that a student states a civil rights claim if school officials do nothing about sexual harassment by a sports coach. *Franklin v. Gwinnett Cty. Pub. Sch.,* 503 U.S. 60 (1992). *See also Gebser v. Lago Vista Indep. Sch. Dist.,* 524 U.S. 274 (1998) (setting forth requirements for claim based on teacher's sexual harassment of student). In some of civil rights cases, the more stringent

requirement of "actual notice" of the abuse may apply. *KD v. Douglas Cty. Sch. Dist. No. 001*, 1 F.4th 591 (8th Cir. 2021).

4. **Immunity of teachers.** The federal Coverdell Teacher Protection Act of 2001, 20 U.S.C.A. § 6736, immunizes teachers and administrators from liability for "harm caused by an act or omission of the teacher on behalf of the school," but applies only to states that accept federal funds for particular programs, and states are allowed to opt out of its provisions. State statutes may also immunize public-school teachers from liability for acts or omissions relating to supervision, care or discipline of students. *See, e.g.,* VA. CODE ANN. § 8.01–220.1:2. This immunity may not extend, however, to administrators. *See Burns v. Gagnon*, 727 S.E.2d 634 (Va. 2012) (vice principal not protected by statute).

5. **Child-abuse reporting statutes.** Every state has some kind of child-abuse reporting statute. Some courts have held that a statutory reporting requirement does not affect tort law. *See, e.g., Becker v. Mayo Found.,* 737 N.W.2d 200 (Minn. 2007); *Perry v. S.N.,* 973 S.W.2d 301 (Tex. 1998). However, a court applying Texas law suggested that the breadth of the reporting statute relied upon may have been the reason a failure to report abuse was not negligence per se. Moreover reliance on a "more narrowly tailored" statute that "imposes a duty to report not on any person, but rather only on certain professionals, and limits that duty to those having cause to believe a child has been abused or neglected" may be able to found a negligence per se claim against a teacher. *See also Yates v. Mansfield Bd. of Educ.,* 808 N.E.2d 861 (Ohio 2004); *Landeros v. Flood,* 551 P.2d 389 (Cal. 1976) (statutory violation is negligence per se). A few courts have held that a mandatory-reporter statute implies a private right of action. *See Beggs v. State, Dep't of Social & Health Services,* 247 P.3d 421 (Wash. 2011).

6. **Student-on-student violence.** Could school officials be held liable for failing to protect one student from another? Many courts have said yes. In *Mirand v. City of New York*, 637 N.E.2d 263 (N.Y. 1994), one student threatened to kill another after a perceived slight. The victim of this threat told teachers about it and tried to report it to security officers, but could not find one. As school was ending, a group of students attacked the threatened student with a hammer and knives. She prevailed in her suit against the school. "Schools are under a duty to adequately supervise the students in their charge and they will be held liable for foreseeable injuries proximately related to the absence of adequate supervision." The care owed is that which " 'a parent of ordinary prudence would observe in comparable circumstances.' The duty owed derives from the simple fact that a school, in assuming physical custody and control over its students, effectively takes the place of parents and guardians." The school knew of the threat and also knew that security was needed. Yet no security was present and no steps had been taken to deal with the death threat. *Query:* Did the duty in *Mirand* arise because of the school's relationship to the injured student, or its relationship to the attackers? Does it matter?

In Massachusetts, the state governmental immunity statute was read to preclude school liability when one student pushed another down the stairs, causing permanent paralysis. The immunity statute bars "any claim based on an act or failure to act to prevent or diminish the harmful consequences of a condition or situation, including the violent or tortious conduct of a third person, which is not originally caused by the public employer or any other person acting on behalf of the public employer." *Cormier v. City of Lynn*, 91 N.E.3d 662 (Mass. 2018).

7. **Attacks by third parties against students.** If an intruder on the school grounds attacks a student, the existence of a duty on the school's part does not seem particularly difficult; the school, after all, is the guardian of the students while they are at school. *See* RESTATEMENT (THIRD) OF TORTS: LIABILITY FOR PHYSICAL AND EMOTIONAL HARM § 40, cmt. l (2010). Whether that duty was breached, however, may well raise difficult questions of fact for the jury to resolve. *See, e.g., A.W. v. Lancaster County Sch. Dist. 0001*, 784 N.W.2d 907 (Neb. 2010).

YOUNG V. SALT LAKE CITY SCHOOL DISTRICT, 52 P.3d 1230 (Utah 2002). Eric Young, an elementary school student, was riding his bike to a mandatory after-school Parent-Teacher-Student meeting at the school. He reached the crosswalk leading directly to the school. A parked car allegedly obscured the vision of approaching drivers and those using the cross walk. Young was struck in the crosswalk. He sued the school after settling with the driver. He claimed that the school should have informed the city of dangerous parking conditions, supplied a crossing guard, or provided flashing warning lights. *Held*, the school owed its student no duty of protection. "[W]hen a school district lacks custody, it has no protective obligation and no special relationship exists." The school did not have custody here. "First, Young's elementary school had adjourned for the day, and he had been released into the care of his parents. . . . Second, Young's injury did not occur on premises within the District's control. . . . Lastly, at the time he sustained his injury, Young was not participating in a curricular, or extra-curricular, school-sponsored event; he was simply *in the process of traveling* to such an event."

NOTES

1. **Time and space considerations.** The *Young* court stressed that the injury took place off school grounds and after the school day had ended. Similarly, in *Dinsmoor v. City of Phoenix*, 492 P.3d 313 (Ariz. 2021), a student was murdered by another student after school. Affirming summary judgment for the school, the Court wrote: "Because the school's roles forming the basis for the duty—custodian, land possessor, and quasi-parental figure—apply when the school supervises and controls students and their environment, enabling it to identify and eliminate risks, we are convinced the duty to protect

students exists only while the school is fulfilling these roles. But once students safely leave the school's control, the special relationship ends, and students are simultaneously released to their parents' or guardians' full custodial care. At that point, the school is relieved of any duty to affirmatively protect students from any hazards they encounter." *Cf. Moss Point Sch. Dist. v. Stennis*, 132 So.3d 1047 (Miss. 2014) (no duty of ordinary care to protect students who are injured off campus after dismissal, but fact question on whether student handbook imposed a duty on school officials to report a text message from student's mother to the student that might have prevented the attack).

2. **Care before or after school.** In *Fazzaroli v. Portland School District No. 1J*, 734 P.2d 1326 (Or. 1987), Judge Linde wrote that "the school's duty is not based on ownership of property but on its relation to the student," and that this duty exists "apart from any general responsibility not unreasonably to expose people to a foreseeable risk of harm." The plaintiff in *Fazzaroli*, a 15-year-old student, was attacked by an assailant long before school started, after having been dropped off by her mother at 6:50 a.m. The school argued that whatever duty it owed to its students was limited to the school day. To that argument, Judge Linde said that no such bright-line rule existed; testimony indicated that custodians opened the school before that time, and that some teachers and students were present for other activities. A fact-finder could conclude that "a sensible school administration would take some precautions, if not to provide supervision, then at least to warn students and their parents about its absence before a designated hour." *But see Williams v. Weatherstone*, 15 N.E.3d 384 (N.Y. 2014) (school district owed no duty to a student who was hit by a vehicle while waiting for the school bus near her home, before school started).

3. **Custody and reliance.** What role does "custody" play in establishing a duty? Might it imply a kind of reliance? *See Gniadek v. Camp Sunshine at Sebago Lake, Inc.*, 11 A.3d 308 (Me. 2011) (camp owed no duty to camper who was attacked by a camp volunteer off camp property and two months after camp had ended; camp was no longer in a custodial relationship with the camper "such as to deprive [her of her] normal opportunities for protection").

4. **Breach of duty.** Even if a school owed a duty of reasonable care to a student, would that duty be breached if the injury was unforeseeable? *See Edson v. Barre Supervisory Union # 61*, 933 A.2d 200 (Vt. 2007) (high school student left school secretly and without authorization and was murdered off campus).

NOTE: DUTIES OF COLLEGES

1. *College temptations and stress.* Courts have generally refused to impose upon universities any duty to protect or guide new students with respect to the pleasures and dangers of sex, alcohol, drugs, or even

overstudy. *See Beach v. Univ. of Utah*, 726 P.2d 413 (Utah 1986); *Wilson v. Continental Ins. Cos.*, 274 N.W.2d 679 (Wis. 1979).

2. *Risks of attacks.* Consider whether the college owes a duty of care to its students in these cases.

A. One evening an underage sorority member attended a number of parties hosted by other Greek houses at her college. The college provided employees to supervise at some of the fraternity parties. The young woman became so intoxicated that she fell from a fire escape. *Coghlan v. Beta Theta Pi Fraternity*, 987 P.2d 300 (Idaho 1999). Or suppose a college has rules against drinking parties in dorms, but does not enforce them. A college woman is sexually assaulted by several college football players after she and some of the players attend a drinking party in their dorm. *Tanja H. v. Regents of Univ. of Calif.*, 278 Cal. Rptr. 918 (Ct. App. 1991).

B. A prisoner applied for admission to a state university and was admitted upon his release. The university knew he was a prisoner when he applied but not much else. The new student, with a ten-year history of heroin addiction and a string of arrests, made friends with three other students and shared an apartment with them. He then seriously injured one of his roommates, raped another, and murdered the third. *Eiseman v. State*, 511 N.E.2d 1128 (N.Y. 1987).

C. A college assigns a student to practicum work at a dangerous location. The college knows the danger but it neither warns the student, arranges a different practicum, nor provides protection. The student—an adult—is abducted from the practicum site, robbed, and sexually assaulted. *Nova Southeast Univ., Inc. v. Gross,* 758 So.2d 86 (Fla. 2000). What if the student knows of the danger before she is attacked?

WRIGHT V. PRG REAL ESTATE MANAGEMENT, INC.
826 S.E.2d 285 (S.C. 2019)

JUSTICE JAMES.

[Denise Wright testified that when she chose her apartment, security was an important factor in her decision-making process. At the time she signed her lease she was told that security officers were on duty. The apartment complex also published a "security pager" number in a monthly tenant newsletter. However, the only security provided was a courtesy officer program allowing residents affiliated with law enforcement to receive reduced rent in exchange for occasional service as courtesy officers for the apartment complex. One night on her way home Wright was abducted from a common area of the apartment complex and robbed at gunpoint by two unknown assailants. Wright filed an action against the landlord and apartment managers. The circuit court granted summary judgment for defendants and a divided appellate court affirmed.]

It is well-settled in South Carolina that a landlord generally does not owe an affirmative duty to a tenant to provide security in and around leased premises to protect the tenant from the criminal activity of third parties. . . . In *Cooke v. Allstate Management Corp.*, 741 F.Supp. 1205 (D.S.C. 1990), the United States District Court for the District of South Carolina enumerated four exceptions to the general rule: (1) the affirmative acts exception, (2) the concealed danger exception, (3) the common area exception, and (4) the undertaking exception. . . .

The affirmative acts exception is limited to situations where the landlord's direct action increases a tenant's risk of harm from criminal activities. Examples of such direct action may include a landlord giving out a master key to someone who should not have one, a landlord leaving an apartment door or window unlocked, or a landlord failing to secure a ladder that is used by a criminal to commit a crime. Such affirmative acts by the landlord may impose liability for criminal acts of third parties. On the other hand, the voluntary undertaking exception invokes section 323. . . . See Restatement (Second) of Torts § 323 (1965) ("One who undertakes, gratuitously or for consideration, to render services to another which he should recognize as necessary for the protection of the other's person or things, is subject to liability to the other for physical harm resulting from his failure to exercise reasonable care to perform his undertaking, if (a) his failure to exercise such care increases the risk of such harm, or (b) the harm is suffered because of the other's reliance upon the undertaking."). . . . Here, Wright's argument that Respondents were negligent in failing to provide security invokes the undertaking exception. . . .

The court of appeals concluded, "Under the facts of this case, the duty [R]espondents assumed was limited to exercising reasonable care in maintaining the courtesy officer program, and [there is] no evidence they failed to exercise reasonable care in fulfilling that duty."

The court of appeals' focus was too narrow. . . . Since Wright had no knowledge of the true limitations upon the program, we must examine the question of the existence of a duty of care with a focus upon the undertaking as it was described to Wright. . . . Wright must establish that (a) Respondents' failure to exercise due care in performing the undertaking increased the risk of harm to Wright or that (b) Wright suffered harm because of her reliance upon the undertaking. We conclude there are questions of fact that a jury must resolve to ascertain whether a duty of care arose in this case. . . .

[T]o the dissent's contention that our holding will disincentivize apartment complexes from offering security officer programs at all, our holding does nothing of the sort. If anything, our holding should incentivize the apartment complex that has voluntarily undertaken to offer security officer programs to recognize it has undertaken a duty to administer the programs with due care. The complex would have the right to impose limitations upon the program or even discontinue the program; however, the complex would be incentivized to simply let its tenants know. . . .

[Reversed and remanded.]

JUSTICE KITTREDGE, dissenting:

Today, the majority takes the common existence of an apartment complex's security officer program and morphs that limited undertaking into a sweeping duty to protect tenants from the unforeseen criminal acts of third parties. . . . [T]he record is devoid of any evidence of reliance by Petitioner. . . . [W]hen Petitioner confronted Respondents' representative the day after her ordeal, she "exclaimed that she had not seen any security on the premises since she moved in five years prior." I cannot fathom how, after not seeing any evidence of a security officer for five years, Petitioner could have possibly relied on the existence of a security officer program. . . . I am concerned the majority's decision disincentivizes apartment complexes from offering a security officer program at all. I dissent.

NOTES

1. **Affirmative duties of landlords.** Landlords clearly owe a number of duties to tenants. Many courts have held that a landlord owes a duty of reasonable care to tenants with respect to common areas under the landlord's control, although not all have done so. *See* RESTATEMENT (THIRD) OF TORTS: LIABILITY FOR PHYSICAL AND EMOTIONAL HARM § 40, cmt. m (2010). With respect to a duty to protect tenants from criminal attacks by others, many courts hold that the landlord-tenant relationship alone does not trigger that duty, *see, e.g., Ward v. Inishmaan Assocs. Ltd. P'ship*, 931 A.2d 1235 (N.H. 2007); *Funchess v. Cecil Newman Corp.*, 632 N.W.2d 666 (Minn. 2001), although some disagree, see *Peterson v. Kings Gate Partners-Omaha I, L.P.*, 861 N.W.2d 444 (Neb. 2015) (landlord-tenant relationship alone triggered duty of reasonable care; whether that duty was breached is a question of fact). Which approach is preferable?

2. **Landlord's provision of security standards.** If a tenant relies on promises of security at the time the tenant moves in, for how long can the tenant rely on that promised security In a leading case, *Kline v. 1500 Mass. Ave. Apartment Corp.*, 439 F.2d 477 (D.C. Cir. 1970), the plaintiff leased one of 585 apartments in the defendant's building. At that time, there were several forms of protection against intrusion, including a doorman. Seven years later, there was no doorman and other forms of protection had also been withdrawn, although assaults, larcenies and robberies against tenants in the common

hallways had increased. Plaintiff was attacked and injured by an intruder in the hallway. The court held that the landlord was under a duty to protect tenants against attacks by third persons. Among other things, the court emphasized (a) the control of the landlord over common passageways and the tenant's lack of power to control them or to protect themselves there; (b) the special character of the modern urban multiple-unit lease; and (c) the notice of the landlord that the tenants were being subjected to crimes against their persons. The court added: "[T]he applicable standard of care in providing protection for the tenant is that standard which this landlord himself was employing . . . when the appellant became a resident. . . ." The court said that the precise protections need not be kept, but that the same relative degree of security had to be maintained. *Wright* suggested plaintiff only needed to be informed of the changes. Should that be enough to avoid duty by undertaking?

3. **Physical defects on the premises increasing the risk.** Many courts have agreed that a landlord owes a duty to maintain the physical premises so as not to increase the risk of third-party attacks on tenants. Poor lighting and non-working locks are common problems. *See, e.g., Hemmings v. Pelham Wood Ltd. Liability P'ship*, 826 A.2d 443 (Md. 2003).

4. **Duties owed to guests of tenants.** Suppose the plaintiff is not the tenant but a guest of the tenant. Does the landlord owe the plaintiff a duty of care while the guest is rightfully in the parking lot provided by the landlord or in other portions of the premises in the possession and control of the landlord? *Martinez v. Woodmar IV Condo. Homeowners Assoc., Inc.*, 941 P.2d 218 (Ariz. 1997) (duty of care owed to tenant's guest to protect from attacks in common areas); *cf. Bailey v. Schaff*, 835 N.W.2d 413 (Mich 2013) (apartment owner/manager owed tenant's guest a duty to notify police that a man was in a common area threatening to shoot someone, once owner/manager had been informed of the threat).

5. **Tenant-on-tenant violence.** What if the landlord knows that one tenant, especially a roommate of another tenant, has shown violent tendencies in the past and has threatened previous roommates—does that create a duty to warn? *See Galanis v. CMA Mgt. Co.*, 175 So.3d 1213 (Miss. 2015). Should a landlord owe a duty to protect one tenant from another, even if the landlord does not owe a duty to protect a tenant from a stranger? *See* 2 DOBBS, HAYDEN & BUBLICK, THE LAW OF TORTS § 417 (2d ed. 2011); *see also* § 3 below.

6. **Allocation of responsibility.** Suppose a landlord negligently creates or enhances a risk that someone will criminally attack the plaintiff. Someone does attack the plaintiff but he cannot be found or has no funds. Recall that in states that have abolished joint and several liability, the rule is that each tortfeasor is liable only for his own proportionate fault share. What do you think the landlord's share would be as compared to the criminal? Should several liability states return to the joint and several liability rule for this kind of case? This point is considered in more detail in Chapter 25, but you may wish to have the problem in mind as you review the preceding cases and examine those that follow.

§ 3. DEFENDANT'S RELATIONSHIP
WITH DANGEROUS PERSONS

DUDLEY V. OFFENDER AID & RESTORATION OF RICHMOND, INC., 401
S.E.2d 878 (Va. 1991). Spencer was a convicted felon with a long, active
career in crime. In prison he engaged in vicious beatings of new inmates
and set fires; psychologists warned that he was a potential security
problem. Because of his violence and for other reasons, he was not eligible
to serve any part of his term in a halfway house. Nevertheless, he was
permitted to live in one, operated by a private organization. He repeatedly
violated rules there, including rules about prompt return from outside
work. Security was "practically nonexistent" and Spencer was permitted to
leave without much control. He was unaccounted for at 7:00 p.m. During
that night he broke into an apartment nearby, bound Davis, beat and raped
her, then strangled her to death. In an action against the operator of the
halfway house, the trial court sustained the defendant's demurrer.

Held, reversed and remanded. Under the general rule one owes no
duty to control the conduct of a third person for the benefit of the plaintiff.
However, if the defendant is in a special relationship to either the plaintiff
or the third person, the defendant is under a duty of care. The halfway
house, upon receiving Spencer, became a custodian in charge. The
defendant's duty ran not only to victims that might be identified in advance
but to all those who are "directly and foreseeably exposed to risk of bodily
harm" from the defendant's negligence. The decedent was within the area
of danger.

NOTES

1. **Duty of custodians.** Most states impose a duty of reasonable care
on custodians of dangerous individuals to prevent those individuals from
harming members of the public. *See Scott v. Universal Sales, Inc.*, 356 P.3d
1172 (Utah 2015) (adopting § 319 of the Second Restatement of Torts); *see also*
RESTATEMENT (THIRD) OF TORTS: LIABILITY FOR PHYSICAL AND EMOTIONAL
HARM § 41 (2012). Is there a relationship between custody and foreseeability
of harm? The *Scott* court said that custody provides the custodian "with a
wealth of information about the inmates' physical and mental capacities to
which no one else has comparable access." The court also stressed that the
custodial relationship "involves the legal authority to control the person's
movement and interactions with the public." Why would "control" matter in
imposing a duty of care?

2. **Awareness of a threat to a specific individual.** A few states
require, in order to impose a duty, that the custodian be aware of threats to a
specific victim or to a group of which the victim is a member. The vast majority,
however, do not. Does it make sense for courts to limit a custodian's duty in
this manner, or do other elements of the negligence case more appropriately
apply?

3. **Custody and "control."** Prisons and hospitals are clearly covered by the custodian rules. But is strict "custody" required to invoke the duty of care imposed in *Dudley*? In *Scott, supra* Note 1, the plaintiff's attacker was an inmate with a long record and violent tendencies who had been placed in a "jail industries" work-release program in the community from which inmates could easily escape. The defendant argued that the custodian's duty should not attach, because there was no "actual, physical control over the individual." The Utah court said that accepting the argument "would create perverse incentives," and that focusing instead on "legal control . . . properly encourages all custodians to be careful about which individuals they expose to the general public through rehabilitative programs." Thus it was not necessary for the imposition of a duty that the defendant had the attacker under its "direct supervision" when he escaped.

4. **A duty to control tenants?** A landlord leases an apartment to a man who, after moving in, sometimes fires a gun from the back yard. The landlord does nothing about it. Subsequently the tenant kills a 10-year-old girl, who, while standing in her own yard, was struck by a bullet fired from the apartment building's yard. Did the landlord owe the victim a duty? In *Rosales v. Stewart*, 169 Cal.Rptr. 660 (Ct. App. 1980), the court said where the lessor has control over a danger from the tenant, he is under a duty of care, though he is not liable if there is no control. "In effect . . . the landlord is under a duty to third persons to do all that he legally can to get rid of a dangerous condition *on the leased premises*, even if it means getting rid of the tenant."

Or suppose a prospective tenant tells a prospective landlord that he has a vicious dog. Should the landlord refuse to lease the premises to him? *Strunk v. Zoltanski*, 468 N.E.2d 13 (N.Y. 1984), holds that the landlord is under a duty to take reasonable precautions to protect others from injury by the dog. But what if the court decides that the landlord lacks the ability to control the dog? *See Fields v. Hayden*, 81 A.3d 367 (Me. 2013) (no duty); *Smaxwell v. Bayard*, 682 N.W.2d 923 (Wis. 2004) (landlords owe duty to protect from a tenant's dogs only where the landlord was also the owner or keeper of the dog); *contra, Tracey v. Solesky*, 50 A.3d 1075 (Md. 2012) (landlord with knowledge that a tenant harbored a pit bull was strictly liable for injuries caused by the dog).

5. **A duty to control a spouse or family members?** Consider: A wife knows her husband has a history of sexual misconduct with young children and might invite neighborhood girls to go swimming in the family pool while she is away. Has she any duty to warn anyone? What if she told neighbors it would be safe for the girls to swim? On similar facts, *see Pamela L. v. Farmer*, 169 Cal.Rptr. 282 (Ct. App. 1980). *Compare J.S. v. R.T.II.*, 714 A.2d 924 (N.J. 1998) (duty of care exists) *with D.W. v. Bliss*, 112 P.3d 232 (Kan. 2005) (no duty). In *Eric J. v. Betty M.*, 90 Cal.Rptr. 549 (Ct. App. 1999), the court held that parents and brothers of a repeated offender, paroled on child molesting charges, had no duty to warn the molester's new woman friend that her son might be in danger even though the boy was taken to the home of some of them and molested there. What if an adult man, known by his family to be a habitual drunk driver, crashes his car into the plaintiff. Would an action lie against his

parents or his brother for failing to control him? *Bebry v. Zanauskas*, 841 A.2d 282 (Conn. App. Ct. 2004).

NOTE: A DUTY TO CONTROL CHILDREN?

1. *Basic limits.* Remember that parents are not vicariously liable for a child's torts merely on the basis of the parental relationship. That is not to say, however, that parents may not be liable if they themselves are at fault. But in many states this potential liability has rather strict limits. A number of states have simply not recognized a cause of action for negligent supervision of a child. *See Beddingfield v. Linam*, 127 So.3d 1178 (Ala. 2013). Even in those states that recognize potential parental liability, parents are not liable for failure to control a child merely because the child is known to be rough. Instead, parents are liable only for failing to control some specific dangerous habit of a child of which the parent knows or should know in the exercise of reasonable care. *See Sinsel v. Olsen*, 777 N.W.2d 54 (Neb. 2009) (child threw fireworks into a crowd, no parental liability).

2. *"Ordinary" children.* Are parents responsible if they leave a teenager alone at home while they are out of town and the teen has irresponsible sex with another teenager? *McNamee v. A.J.W.*, 519 S.E.2d 298 (Ga. Ct. App.1999). Would a parent have a duty of reasonable care to control a child riding a bike in a crowd? *Compare Crisafulli v. Bass,* 38 P.3d 842 (Mont. 2001) (overruling an earlier no-duty decision) *with Buono v. Scalia*, 843 A.2d 1120 (N.J. 2004) (father's decision was a valid exercise of parental authority, thus he was immune from suit).

3. *Children known to be violent.* In *Dinsmore-Poff v. Alvord,* 972 P.2d 978 (Alaska 1999), plaintiffs' decedent was murdered by defendants' 17-year-old son. The son had a long history of emotional disturbance and violence. In fact, he had been arrested once for shooting a boy. The parents did not impose curfews or search his belongings. The son used a gun to kill his victim. The court absolved the parents. It said: "plaintiff must show more than a parent's general notice of a child's dangerous propensity. A plaintiff must show that the parent had reason to know with some specificity of a present opportunity and need to restrain the child to prevent some imminently foreseeable harm."

Williamson v. Daniels, 748 So.2d 754 (Miss. 1999), absolved the mother of a 15-year-old boy who shot the plaintiff in the chest. Since the mother was not aware of this specific kind of misconduct in the past, she was not responsible. The court thought liability "would pose the risk of transforming parents from care givers and disciplinarians into the jailors and insurers of their minor children," and that "this is a role most parents are ill equipped to take on."

In one astonishing case the "child"—a teenager with a history of aggressive, anti-social behavior—began beating a woman with a hammer. He demanded she remove her clothes. A daughter ran for the phone; he began beating her with a hammer, then began to saw off an ear of his original victim. His parents were well aware of a long history of serious behavior. Psychiatrists had recommended that the boy be treated. The parents were not liable. Apparently the theory was that they could not have foreseen the particular type of violence. *Parsons v. Smithey*, 504 P.2d 1272 (Ariz.1973).

What if the parent or the parent's domestic partner knows that a ten-year-old child has a propensity for sexually abusing younger females and knows also that a four-year-old girl is playing in the home? *Gritzner v. Michael R.*, 611 N.W.2d 906 (Wis. 2000).

4. *Control.* Some courts stress a parent's inability to control their children's behavior as a reason not to impose a duty of reasonable care. This may be simply because the child is older. *See, e.g., Grover v. Stechel*, 45 P.3d 80 (N.M. Ct. App. 2002) (mother's only "control" over adult son who stabbed the plaintiff was financial); *Moore v. Crumpton*, 295 S.E.2d 436 (N.C. 1982) ("The opportunity to control a young man of [17 years] obviously is not as great as with a younger child."). A non-custodial parent may also lack the ability to control. *See K.H. v. J.R.*, 826 A.2d 863 (Pa. 2003) (child shot another with a BB gun given to him by non-custodial parent).

NOTE: A DUTY TO CONTROL EMPLOYEES

1. *Scope of duty.* Employers are generally vicariously liable for the torts of their employees committed within the scope of employment. *See* Chapter 22. But an employer may also owe a duty of reasonable care to protect others from intentional harm by employees, even where the employee acts outside the scope of employment. *See* RESTATEMENT (SECOND) OF TORTS § 317 (1965) (special relationship between employer and employee places the employer under such a duty, if the employee is either on the employer's premises or is using the employer's chattel); RESTATEMENT (THIRD) OF TORTS: LIABILITY FOR PHYSICAL AND EMOTIONAL HARM § 41 (2012) (such a duty is imposed "when the employment facilitates the employee's causing harm" to another person).

2. *Negligent hiring or retention.* Many courts recognize that an employer may be directly liable for negligently hiring or retaining a dangerous person who later harms the plaintiff. *See, e.g., Spencer v. Health Force, Inc.*, 107 P.3d 504 (N.M. 2005); *Munroe v. Universal Health Serv.,*

Inc., 596 S.E.2d 604 (Ga. 2004). Liability often turns on whether the employer knew or should have known that the employee's conduct would subject others to an unreasonable risk of harm. *See Saine v. Comcast Cablevision of Ark., Inc.*, 126 S.W.3d 339 (Ark. 2003); *Cannizaro v. Marinyak,* 93 A.3d 584 (Conn. 2014). The theory might be applied in some unusual settings. In *Redwing v. Catholic Bishop for the Diocese of Memphis*, 363 S.W.3d 436 (Tenn. 2012), the court held that a church diocese could be held liable on such a theory where a victim of childhood sexual abuse alleged that the diocese was aware or should have been aware that a priest in its employ presented a danger to children but nonetheless placed him in a position where it was foreseeable that he would abuse children on church property. *See also Schelling v. Humphrey*, 916 N.E.2d 1029 (Ohio 2009) (recognizing a claim for "negligent credentialing" against a hospital for granting staff privileges to a surgeon who committed malpractice).

3.   *Negligent supervision or training.* Negligent supervision or training of an employee may also lead to liability. *See, e.g., McGuire v. Curry*, 766 N.W.2d 501 (S.D. 2009) (racetrack owed duty to supervise underage employee to prevent him from becoming intoxicated at work, where employee was given unrestricted access to alcohol as part of his job); *Graves v. N. E. Servs., Inc.*, 345 P.3d 619 (Utah 2015) (provider of services to the disabled owed duty to supervise employee who sexually assaulted a child on the premises); *Doe v. Hartford Roman Catholic Diocesan Corp.*, 119 A.3d 462 (Conn. 2015) (diocese liable for negligent supervision of priest who sexually abused victim over many years; diocese knew that priest's prior acts of sexual molestation were tied to his alcoholism but did not take reasonable actions to monitor his alcohol problem).

Liability often turns on what the employer actually knew about the employee, and what act the employee committed. *See, e.g., Keller v. Koca*, 111 P.3d 445 (Colo. 2005) (male employee known to have fondled and made suggestive remarks to female co-employees brought female child into workplace and sexually assaulted her). The duty of reasonable care may require the employer to conduct an investigation of an employee where there have been complaints about him. *See, e.g., Hall v. City of Newport*, 138 A.3d 814 (R.I. 2016) (family claimed bus driver harassed them). Where the allegation is one of negligent *training* rather than *supervision*, expert testimony on the standard of care may be required. *See Alcala v. Marriott Intern., Inc.*, 880 N.W.2d 699 (Iowa 2016) (because lay persons would not otherwise understand the specific training that would be required for a particular job, in this case de-icing a hotel's outdoor sidewalks).

4.   *Injury caused to others by excessive work demands of employer.* What if an employer requires an employee to work an unreasonably long shift, and the exhausted employee causes an accident while driving home? There is some support in case law for liability, although in those cases the

facts are rather extreme. *See, e.g., Robertson v. LeMaster,* 301 S.E.2d 563 (W.Va. 1983) (employee forced to work for 27 hours straight, and had told employer many times he was tired and wanted to go home). A greater number of cases would agree that even where injury to others is a foreseeable risk from employee fatigue, "a duty to protect the public from fatigued employees would impose a substantial burden on employers, which we do not believe can be reasonably justified." *Nabors Drilling, U.S.A. Inc. v. Escoto,* 288 S.W.3d 401 (Tex. 2009). *Accord Barclay v. Briscoe,* 47 A.3d 560 (Md. 2012); *Black v. William Insulation Co.,* 141 P.3d 123 (Wyo. 2006).

TARASOFF V. REGENTS OF UNIVERSITY OF CALIFORNIA
551 P.2d 334 (Cal. 1976)

TOBRINER, JUSTICE.

On October 27, 1969, Prosenjit Poddar killed Tatiana Tarasoff. Plaintiffs, Tatiana's parents, allege that two months earlier Poddar confided his intention to kill Tatiana to Dr. Lawrence Moore, a psychologist employed by the Cowell Memorial Hospital at the University of California at Berkeley. They allege that on Moore's request, the campus police briefly detained Poddar, but released him when he appeared rational. They further claim that Dr. Harvey Powelson, Moore's superior, then directed that no further action be taken to detain Poddar. No one warned plaintiffs of Tatiana's peril.

Concluding that these facts set forth causes of action against neither therapists and police involved, nor against the Regents of the University of California as their employer, the superior court sustained defendant's demurrers to plaintiffs' second amended complaints without leave to amend. This appeal ensued.

Plaintiffs' complaints predicate liability on two grounds: defendants' failure to warn plaintiffs of the impending danger and their failure to bring about Poddar's confinement. . . . Defendants, in turn, assert that they owed no duty of reasonable care to Tatiana and that they are immune from suit. . . .

In analyzing this issue, we bear in mind that legal duties are not discoverable facts of nature, but merely conclusory expressions that, in cases of a particular type, liability should be imposed for damage done. As stated in Dillon v. Legg (1968) 68 Cal. 2d 728, 734, 69 Cal. Rptr. 72, 76, 441 P.2d 912, 916: "The assertion that liability must . . . be denied because defendant bears no 'duty' to plaintiff 'begs the essential question whether the plaintiff's interests are entitled to legal protection against the defendant's conduct. . . . [Duty] is not sacrosanct in itself, but only an expression of the sum total of those considerations of policy which lead the law to say that the particular plaintiff is entitled to protection.' (Prosser, Law of Torts [3d ed. 1964] at pp. 332–333.)"

In the landmark case of Rowland v. Christian (1968) 69 Cal. 2d 108, 70 Cal. Rptr. 97, 443 P.2d 561, Justice Peters recognized that liability should be imposed "for an injury occasioned to another by his want of ordinary care or skill" as expressed in Section 1714 of the Civil Code. Thus, Justice Peters, quoting from Heaven v. Pender (1883) 11 Q.B.D. 503, 509 stated: " 'whenever one person is by circumstances placed in such a position with regard to another . . . that if he did not use ordinary care and skill in his own conduct . . . he would cause danger of injury to the person or property of the other, a duty arises to use ordinary care and skill to avoid such danger.' "

We depart from "this fundamental principle" only upon the "balancing of a number of considerations"; major ones "are the foreseeability of harm to the plaintiff, the degree of certainty that the plaintiff suffered injury, the closeness of the connection between the defendant's conduct and the injury suffered, the moral blame attached to the defendant's conduct, the policy of preventing future harm, the extent of the burden to the defendant and consequences to the community of imposing a duty to exercise care with resulting liability for breach, and the availability, cost and prevalence of insurance for the risk involved."

The most important of these considerations in establishing duty is foreseeability. As a general principle, a "defendant owes a duty of care to all persons who are foreseeably endangered by his conduct, with respect to all risks which make the conduct unreasonably dangerous." As we shall explain, however, when the avoidance of foreseeable harm requires a defendant to control the conduct of another person, or to warn of such conduct, the common law has traditionally imposed liability only if the defendant bears some special relationship to the dangerous person or to the potential victim. Since the relationship between a therapist and his patient satisfies this requirement, we need not here decide whether foreseeability alone is sufficient to create a duty to exercise reasonable care to protect a potential victim of another's conduct. . . .

Although plaintiffs' pleadings assert no special relation between Tatiana and defendant therapists, they establish as between Poddar and defendant therapists the special relation that arises between a patient and his doctor or psychotherapist. Such a relationship may support affirmative duties for the benefit of third persons. Thus, for example, a hospital must exercise reasonable care to control the behavior of a patient which may endanger other persons. A doctor must also warn a patient if the patient's condition of medication renders certain conduct, such as driving a car, dangerous to others. . . .

Defendants contend, however, that imposition of a duty to exercise reasonable care to protect third persons is unworkable because therapists cannot accurately predict whether or not a patient will resort to violence. In support of the argument amicus representing the American Psychiatric Association and other professional societies cites numerous articles which indicate that therapists, in the present state of the art, are unable reliably to predict violent acts; their forecasts, amicus claims, tend consistently to overpredict violence, and indeed are more often wrong than right. Since predictions of violence are often erroneous, amicus concludes, the courts should not render rulings that predicate the liability of therapists upon the validity of such predictions. . . .

We recognize the difficulty that a therapist encounters in attempting to forecast whether a patient presents a serious danger of violence. Obviously we do not require that the therapist in making that determination, render a perfect performance; the therapist need only exercise "that reasonable degree of skill, knowledge, and care ordinarily possessed and exercised by members of [that professional specialty] under similar circumstances." Within the broad range of reasonable practice and treatment in which professional opinion and judgment may differ, the therapist is free to exercise his or her own best judgment without liability; proof, aided by hindsight, that he or she judged wrongly is insufficient to establish negligence. . . .

Amicus contends, however, that even when a therapist does in fact predict that a patient poses a serious danger of violence to others, the therapist should be absolved of any responsibility for failing to act to protect the potential victim. In our view, however, once a therapist does in fact determine, or under applicable professional standards reasonably should have determined, that a patient poses a serious danger of violence to others, he bears a duty to exercise reasonable care to protect the foreseeable victim of that danger. While the discharge of this duty of due care will necessarily vary with the facts of each case, in each instance the adequacy of the therapist's conduct must be measured against the traditional negligence standard of the rendition of reasonable care under the circumstances. As explained in Fleming and Maximov, The Patient or His Victim: The Therapist's Dilemma (1974), 62 CAL. L. REV. 1025, 1067: ". . . The ultimate question of resolving the tension between the conflicting interest of patient and potential victim is one of social policy, not professional expertise. . . In sum, the therapist owes a legal duty not only to his patient, but also to his patient's would-be victim and is subject in both respects to scrutiny by judge and jury." . . .

The risk that unnecessary warnings may be given is a reasonable price to pay for the lives of possible victims that may be saved. We would hesitate to hold that the therapist who is aware that his patient expects to attempt to assassinate the President of the United States would not be obligated to warn the authorities because the therapist cannot predict with accuracy that his patient will commit the crime.

Defendants further argue that free and open communication is essential to psychotherapy; that "Unless a patient . . . is assured that . . . information [revealed by him] can and will be held in utmost confidence, he will be reluctant to make the full disclosure upon which diagnosis and treatment . . . depends." The giving of a warning, defendants contend, constitutes a breach of trust which entails the revelation of confidential communications.

We recognize the public interest in supporting effective treatment of mental illness and in protecting the rights of patients to privacy, and the consequent public importance of safeguarding the confidential character of psychotherapeutic communication. Against this interest, however, we must weigh the public interest in safety from violent assault. The Legislature has undertaken the difficult task of balancing the countervailing concerns. In Evidence Code section 1014, it established a broad rule of privilege to protect confidential communications between patient and psychotherapist. In Evidence Code section 1024, the Legislature created a specific and limited exception to the psychotherapist-patient privilege: "There is no privilege . . . if the psychotherapist has reasonable cause to believe that the patient is in such mental or emotional condition as to be dangerous to himself or to the person or property of another and that disclosure of the communication is necessary to prevent the threatened danger."[13]

We realize that the open and confidential character of psychotherapeutic dialogue encourages patients to express threats of violence, few of which are ever executed. Certainly a therapist should not be encouraged routinely to reveal such threats; such disclosures could seriously disrupt the patient's relationship with his therapist and with the persons threatened. To the contrary, the therapist's obligations to his patient require that he not disclose a confidence unless such disclosure is necessary to avert danger to others, and even then that he do so discreetly, and in a fashion that would preserve the privacy of his patient to the fullest extent compatible with the prevention of the threatened danger. (See

---

[13] Fleming and Maximov note that "White [section 1024] supports the therapist's less controversial *right* to make a disclosure, it admittedly does not impose on him a *duty* to do so. But the argument does not have to be pressed that far. For if it is once conceded . . . that a duty in favor of the patient's foreseeable victims would accord with general principles of tort liability, we need no longer look to the statute for a source of duty. It is sufficient if the statute can be relied upon . . . for the purposes of countering the claim that the needs of confidentiality are paramount and must therefore defeat any such hypothetical duty. In this more modest perspective, the Evidence Code's 'dangerous patient' exception may be invoked with some confidence as a clear expression of legislative policy concerning the balance between the confidentiality values of the patient and the safety values of his foreseeable victim." (Emphasis in original.) Fleming & Maximov, *The Patient or His Victim: The Therapist's Dilemma* (1974), 62 CAL. L. REV. 1025, 1063.

Fleming & Maximov, *The Patient or His Victim: The Therapist's Dilemma* (1974), 62 CAL. L. REV. 1025, 1065–1066.)

The revelation of a communication under the above circumstances is not a breach of trust or a violation of professional ethics; as stated in the Principles of Medical Ethics of the American Medical Association (1957), section 9: "A physician may not reveal the confidence entrusted to him in the course of medical attendance . . . *unless he is required to do so by law or unless it becomes necessary in order to protect the welfare of the individual or of the community.*" (Emphasis added.) We conclude that the public policy favoring protection of the confidential character of patient-psychotherapist communications must yield to the extent to which disclosure is essential to avert danger to others. The protective privilege ends where the public peril begins.

Our current crowded and computerized society compels the interdependence of its members. In this risk-infested society we can hardly tolerate the future exposure to danger that would result from a concealed knowledge of the therapist that his patient was lethal. If the exercise of reasonable care to protect the threatened victim requires the therapist to warn the endangered party or those who can reasonably be expected to notify him, we see no sufficient societal interest that would protect and justify concealment. The containment of such risks lies in the public interest. For the foregoing reasons, we find that plaintiffs' complaints can be amended to state a cause of action against defendants Moore, Powelson, Gold, and Yandell and against the Regents as their employer, for breach of a duty to exercise reasonable care to protect Tatiana. . . .

Turning now to the police defendants, we conclude that they do not have any such special relationship to either Tatiana or to Poddar sufficient to impose upon such defendants a duty to warn respecting Poddar's violent intentions. Plaintiffs suggest no theory, and plead no facts that give rise to any duty to warn on the part of the police defendants absent such a special relationship. . . .

[Dissenting opinions omitted.]

NOTES

1.   **Scope.** Consider whether, given a *Tarasoff* duty, therapists will be liable in every case in which a patient causes harm after making a threat. On what facts would a therapist be counted as reasonably prudent even if he fails to warn after a threat is made?

2.   ***Tarasoff* and *Thompson*.** Four years after issuing *Tarasoff*, the California court decided *Thompson v. County of Alameda*, 614 P.2d 728 (Cal. 1980). In that case, the court refused to impose liability upon a county which had released a dangerous criminal who was threatening to kill some unnamed child. When released on furlough, he did in fact kill a 5-year-old child. Can

Thompson and *Tarasoff* be squared? The *Thompson* court suggested a possibility: "In those instances in which the released offender poses a predictable threat of harm to a named or readily identifiable victim . . . a releasing agent may well be liable for failure to warn such persons." *See also State Dep't of Corrections v. Cowles*, 151 P.3d 353 (Alaska 2006) (state owed duty to exercise care in supervising parolees only where officials knew or should know that the parolee posed a danger to a particular person or identifiable group of persons); *Osborn v. Mason County*, 134 P.3d 197 (Wash. 2006) (citing *Thompson*, holding county owed no duty to warn of sex offender's presence where victim was "unforeseeable"). Does this reasoning suggest that if Poddar had shown a clear and strong probability that he would kill a number of small children, or old women, the psychiatrist would not owe any duty to later victims? Is the *Thompson* reasoning sound? The Wisconsin court thought there was "no legitimate policy" for the *Thompson* limitation on the duty of care, *Schuster v. Altenberg*, 424 N.W.2d 159 (Wis. 1988), and most jurisdictions have rejected it, at least in its narrowest form. *See Scott v. Universal Sales, Inc.*, 356 P.3d 1172 (Utah 2015) (reversing its own prior precedent that required an "identifiable victim," and collecting cases).

3. **Accepting the *Tarasoff* duty.** The Restatement Third recognizes the special relationship of "mental health professional with patients" as one giving rise to a duty of reasonable care to act for the protection of others. RESTATEMENT (THIRD) OF TORTS: LIABILITY FOR PHYSICAL AND EMOTIONAL HARM § 41 (2012). Many states have adopted some sort of *Tarasoff* duty by statute. In addition, the vast majority of courts that have considered the issue have accepted such a duty. *See Kuligoski v. Brattleboro Retreat*, 156 A.3d 436 (Vt. 2016) (extensively reviewing *Tarasoff*'s acceptance in other states, including variations).

4. **Rejecting or modifying *Tarasoff*.** A few courts have rejected *Tarasoff*. *See, e.g., Tedrick v. Community Res. Ctr., Inc.*, 920 N.E.2d 220 (Ill. 2009) (largely on the ground that a mental health provider owes no duty to a non-patient); *Nasser v. Parker,* 455 S.E.2d 502 (Va. 1995). A duty to warn may be created, however, by a promise made to the victim. *See* 2 DOBBS, HAYDEN & BUBLICK, THE LAW OF TORTS § 423 (2d ed. 2011). Some courts have rejected a duty when the patient is not in the mental health provider's "custody" (as Poddar was not in *Tarasoff*). *See, e.g., Adams v. Board of Sedgwick Cty. Comm'rs,* 214 P.3d 1173 (Kan. 2009); *Santana v. Rainbow Cleaners,* 969 A.2d 653 (R.I. 2009).

5. **Extending *Tarasoff*.** California expanded the *Tarasoff* duty in *Hedlund v. Superior Court*, 669 P.2d 41 (Cal. 1983), holding that the defendant owed a duty not only to the direct victim of a threatened beating but also to her son, who was emotionally upset at seeing his mother attacked. In *Coleman v. Martinez*, 254 A.3d 632 (N.J. 2021), a social worker, Martinez, told her client who was experiencing hallucinations that Martinez had been told about the hallucinations by a child protection employee, Coleman. Believing the disclosure to be detrimental to her goal of regaining custody of her children, T.E. brutally stabbed Coleman at the child protection offices ten days later.

Coleman sued Martinez. The Court held that in light of Martinez's knowledge of her client—prior acts of stabbing, current hallucinations (some of which she had witnessed), and need to see a psychiatrist for medication, harm was foreseeable from disclosing Coleman as the source of the information. Moreover, imposition of a duty was "fair based on the relationship of the parties, nature of the risk, opportunity and ability to exercise care, and the public interest."

6. **Doctors' warnings to patients.** Should a doctor owe a duty to warn a patient of the effects of a drug or treatment the doctor has administered? For example, what if a doctor knows that a patient's driving might be impaired, but does not tell the patient that? The patient then causes a wreck, injuring the plaintiff. *See Davis v. South Nassau Cmtys. Hosp.*, 46 N.E.3d 614 (N.Y. 2015) ("[W]here a medical provider has administered to a patient medication that impairs or could impair the patient's ability to safely operate an automobile, the medical provider has a duty to third parties to warn the patient of that danger."). *Accord, Taylor v. Smith*, 892 So.2d 887 (Ala. 2004); *McKenzie v. Hawai'i Permanente Med. Group, Inc.*, 47 P.3d 1209 (Haw. 2002); *Cf. Hardee v. Bio-Medical Applications of S.C., Inc.*, 636 S.E.2d 629 (S.C. 2006) (dialysis center owed duty to motorists to warn patient that dialysis treatment could make it dangerous for him to drive). *Contra, Schmidt v. Mahoney*, 659 N.W.2d 552 (Iowa 2003); *Medina v. Hochberg*, 987 N.E.2d 1206 (Mass. 2013). Or what if the patient has a communicable disease? Is there a duty to tell the patient how to avoid infecting others? *See DiMarco v. Lynch Homes-Chester Cty., Inc.*, 583 A.2d 422 (Pa. 1990) (yes; duty exists to protect persons other than the patient). Would there be a similar duty to tell a patient not to drive because her eyesight is poor? *See Witthoeft v. Kiskaddon*, 733 A.2d 623 (Pa. 1999). Are these cases easier than *Tarasoff*?

7. **Doctors' warnings to non-patients.** Should a doctor owe a duty to warn a non-patient of a risk posed by the patient's health condition? Suppose T has AIDS or is at risk for AIDS because he received a blood transfusion from a contaminated batch and D knows it. D also knows that T is about to marry P or has regular sexual relations with P. Should D advise P? Legislatures have enacted strong medicine for that kind of case: Doctors, health care providers, blood suppliers may be prohibited from revealing that a person has AIDS or even that he is at risk. *See Santa Rosa Health Care Corp. v. Garcia*, 964 S.W.2d 940 (Tex. 1998).

BRIGANCE V. VELVET DOVE RESTAURANT, INC.
725 P.2d 300 (Okla. 1986)

HODGES, JUDGE.

[The defendant, the Velvet Dove Restaurant, served alcohol to a group of minors, including one Jeff Johnson. Defendant's employees knew Jeff Johnson drove the group to the restaurant. The plaintiffs alleged that alcohol served by the defendant caused Johnson to become intoxicated or increased his earlier intoxication and that this in turn caused a one-car accident in which the plaintiff Shawn was injured. The trial court dismissed the claim.]

At common law a tavern owner who furnishes alcoholic beverages to another is not civilly liable for a third person's injuries that are caused by the acts of an intoxicated patron. Such rule is principally based upon concepts of causation that, as a matter of law, it is not the sale of liquor by the tavern owner, but the voluntary consumption by the intoxicated person, which is the proximate cause of resulting injuries, so that the tavern owner is therefore not liable for negligence in selling the liquor.

In recent years, many states have retreated from the common law rule of nonliability for a liquor vendor regarding it as antiquated and illogical. Several states with dram shop laws have also recognized a new common law right of action against a vendor of liquor. Many of the jurisdictions which now recognize a civil right of action do so on the theory enunciated in Rappaport v. Nichols, 31 N.J. 188, 156 A.2d 1 (1959):

> "When alcoholic beverages are sold by a tavern keeper to a minor or to an intoxicated person, the unreasonable risk of harm . . . to members of the traveling public may readily be recognized and foreseen; this is particularly evident in current times when traveling by car to and from the tavern is so commonplace and accidents resulting from drinking are so frequent."

As shown by the modern trend, the old common law rule of nonliability has been changed by judicial opinion: "Inherent in the common law is a dynamic principle which allows it to grow and to tailor itself to meet changing needs. . . ."

. . . The development of the law of torts is peculiarly a function of the judiciary. Because duty and liability are matters of public policy they are subject to the changing attitudes and needs of society. . . .

Appellees assert that we are not free to change the common law because the Legislature has expressly spoken in this area by its 1959 repeal of Oklahoma's dram shop act and its failure to reenact such provision since that time. We are not persuaded by this argument. The dram shop act was not selectively repealed for it was repealed when intoxicants were legalized in 1959. Because the Legislature has failed to act to impose civil liability, for reasons unknown, does not unequivocally demonstrate legislative intent. To hold otherwise, would be indulging in a type of psychoanalysis of the Legislature. We simply cannot conclude that statutory silence is here indicative of legislative intent to bar the cause of action before us.

We also cannot accede to the view urged by appellees that this area of law is better dealt with by the Legislature. We find that on the basis of the clear trend in this area we are free to establish a civil cause of action by an injured third person against a commercial vendor of liquor for on the premises consumption. In rendering the opinion of Vanderpool v. State, 672 P.2d 1153, 1157 (Okla.1983), which modified the common law doctrine of governmental immunity, this Court stated in response to the oft-expressed view that if the doctrine is to be abrogated such should be done by the Legislature and not the courts of this State: "But having come to the conclusions that the judicially recognized doctrine of governmental immunity in its present state under the case law is no longer supportable in reason, justice or in light of the overwhelming trend against its recognition, our duty is clear. Where the reason for the rule no longer exists, that alone should toll its death knell."

We believe the application of the old common law rule of a tavern owner's nonliability in today's automotive society is unrealistic, inconsistent with modern tort theories and is a complete anachronism within today's society.

The automobile is a constant reminder of a changed and changing America. It has made a tremendous impact on every segment of society, including the field of jurisprudence. In the "horse and buggy" days the common law may not have been significantly affected by the sale of liquor to an intoxicated person. The common law of nonliability was satisfactory. With today's car of steel and speed it becomes a lethal weapon in the hands of a drunken imbiber. The frequency of accidents involving drunk drivers are commonplace. Its affliction of bodily injury to an unsuspecting public is also of common knowledge. Under such circumstances we are compelled to widen the scope of the common law.

We, thus, hold that one who sells intoxicating beverages for on the premises consumption has a duty to exercise reasonable care not to sell liquor to a noticeably intoxicated person. It is not unreasonable to expect a commercial vendor who sells alcoholic beverages for on the premises consumption to a person he knows or should know from the circumstances is already intoxicated, to foresee the unreasonable risk of harm to others who may be injured by such person's impaired ability to operate an automobile.

. . . A commercial vendor for on the premises consumption is under a common law duty to exercise ordinary care under the circumstances. We reach our conclusion in accordance with other courts finding a common law duty, relying on the general rule expressed in Restatement (Second) of Torts § 308 (1965):

> "It is negligence to permit a third person to use a thing or to engage in an activity which is under the control of the actor, if the actor knows or should know that such person intends or is likely to use the thing or to conduct himself in the activity in such a manner as to create an unreasonable risk of harm to others."

And, Restatement (Second) of Torts § 390 (1965):

> "One who supplies . . . a chattel for the use of another whom the supplier knows or has reason to know to be likely because of his youth, inexperience or otherwise to use it in a manner involving unreasonable risk of physical harm to himself and others . . . is subject to liability for physical harm resulting to them."

Even if a commercial vendor for on the premises consumption is found to have breached its duty, a plaintiff must still show the illegal sale of alcohol led to the impairment of the ability of the driver which was the proximate cause of the injury and there was a causal connection between the sale and a foreseeable ensuing injury. . . .

Ordinarily the question of causation in a negligent tort case is one of fact for the jury and becomes one of law only when there is no evidence from which the jury could reasonably find a causal nexus between the negligent act and the resulting injuries. . . .

In adopting a new rule of liability which creates a civil cause of action, we specifically hold that the law hereby established will be applied prospectively to all causes of action occurring from and after the date the mandate issues herein [except that the rule of liability also applies to the parties in this case. Reversed and remanded.]

NOTES

1. **The traditional approach to alcohol-sales cases.** Courts traditionally denied the kind of liability imposed in *Brigance* on the ground that the alcohol provider was not a proximate cause of harm done by the drinker. Some courts or legislatures still reject liability even for providing alcohol to minors or intoxicated persons. *Kudlacik v. Johnny's Shawnee, Inc.*, 440 P.3d 576 (Kan. 2019) (continuing to hold that the decision to impose liability upon the suppliers of alcohol for the torts of their intoxicated patrons or guests is a matter of public policy which the legislature is best equipped to handle); *Warr v. JMGM Group, LLC*, 70 A.3d 347 (Md. 2013); *Wegleitner v. Sattler*, 582 N.W.2d 688 (S.D. 1998) (legislative no-liability rule).

2. **Rulings as a matter of law.** Scope of liability (proximate cause) is usually decided case by case, often by the jury but in any event on the facts peculiar to the case. In the older alcohol-provider cases, however, judges often made a rule of law for all cases: the provider's fault was *never* a proximate cause. Would it make more sense to say that this was a no-duty rule? Are there any policy bases for exculpating the seller of alcohol? What if the server cannot be sure whether a customer is intoxicated?

3. **Reversing the common-law rule.** The *Brigance* case is one of many that have reversed the traditional rules, and have imposed a common-law duty on the part of a licensed seller of alcohol to use reasonable care. Liability is often imposed when the defendant negligently sells alcohol to a

minor or an intoxicated person who, as a result, injures the plaintiff. *See* DOBBS, HAYDEN & BUBLICK, HORNBOOK ON TORTS § 26.12 (2d ed. 2016). Statutes often determine who is liable, and under what circumstances; they sometimes provide an exclusive remedy, sometimes not. *See* NOTE: DRAM SHOP STATUTES, below.

4. **Fixing responsibility.** The common law has expressed in many ways a strong belief that each individual should be responsible for his or her own actions. Not only does this imply, for some judges, that one is not responsible for the acts of others, but it implies that responsibility should not be shared. Thus courts had some difficulty in imposing joint and several liability upon multiple wrongdoers. If the last actor was an intentional wrongdoer, the feeling at one time apparently was that he and only he should be liable. To impose joint liability would lighten his burden and thus diminish his accountability. What arguments can you mount against this kind of outlook? Relatedly, you'll want to remember why the plaintiff is suing the alcohol provider.

5. **Suits by the drinker.** In a state that allows for some alcohol-provider liability, does the provider owe a duty of care to the drinker himself, or only to third persons who may be injured? Some courts have said the duty runs to the drinker as well as to others. *See, e.g., Mann v. Shusteric Enterp., Inc.*, 683 N.W.2d 573 (Mich. 2004) (allowing premises liability action by patron who fell in bar's parking lot after being served liquor illegally by bar). However, most appear to hold that the adult drinker is responsible for his own injury and the provider owes him nothing. *See, e.g., Rodriguez v. Primadonna Co.*, 216 P.3d 793 (Nev. 2009); *Bridges v. Park Place Entertainment*, 860 So.2d 811 (Miss. 2003); *cf. Lydia v. Horton*, 583 S.E.2d 750 (S.C. 2003) (intoxicated entrustee cannot sue for negligent entrustment, both on grounds of public policy and because the intoxicated plaintiff's fault is greater than that of the entruster as a matter of law). If a duty of care is owed to the drinker himself, why is this not a *Bexiga* situation?

6. **Liability of social hosts: basic rules.** Not surprisingly, some courts willing to impose liability upon sellers of alcohol are not willing to impose liability upon social hosts who provide alcohol with the same results. *Reynolds v. Hicks*, 951 P.2d 761 (Wash.1998). Nevertheless, a growing number of courts have approved of such liability, especially where the host has knowingly provided alcohol to minors. *See, e.g., Nichols v. Progressive Northern Ins. Co.*, 746 N.W.2d 220 (Wis. 2008); *Marcum v. Bowden*, 643 S.E.2d 85 (S.C. 2007); *Martin v. Marciano*, 871 A.2d 911 (R.I. 2005) (underage drinker who was served alcohol at high school graduation party). Some states allow social host liability, but require a showing of recklessness rather than negligence in serving alcohol. *See, e.g., Hickingbotham v. Burke*, 662 A.2d 297 (N.H.1995); *Delfino v. Griffo*, 257 P.3d 917 (N.M. 2011) (applying statute). Oregon allows for social host liability, but only where the plaintiff proves by clear and convincing evidence that the social host served a visibly intoxicated guest. *See Deckard v. Bunch*, 370 P.3d 478 (Or. 2016) (construing OR. REV. STAT. § 471.565). Other statutes may make it illegal for an adult to allow underage

persons to consume alcohol on the adult's property. In *Kiriakos v. Phillips*, 139 A.3d 1006 (Md. 2016), the court held that such a statute supported the imposition of a tort duty on social hosts in two consolidated cases, one brought by the mother of a minor who died in an auto accident after leaving a party, and the other by a pedestrian struck by a car driven by an intoxicated minor after leaving a party.

7. **Liability of social hosts: extensions.** California maintains an immunity for social hosts who merely furnish or give drinks away. But by statute, a person not licensed to sell alcohol who sells to an obviously intoxicated minor loses that immunity and can be liable in tort. Suppose a social host charges a fee to enter a party, and payment of that fee entitles guests to drink the provided alcoholic beverages. Does that host face tort liability? *See Ennabe v. Manosa*, 319 P.3d 201 (Cal. 2014) (yes, this can be considered a "sale").

Arizona law also specifically exempts social hosts from liability for harm caused by a drinker of legal age. But in *Gipson v. Kasey*, 150 P.3d 228 (Ariz. 2007), the court held that a man who gave prescription drugs to a female coworker at a company party, who in turn gave the drugs to her boyfriend, who died after taking them, owed a duty of care based largely on statutes criminalizing the distribution of prescription drugs. The court said that "Holding social hosts liable for harm caused by guests to whom they serve alcohol might curb desirable social exchanges. In contrast, no recognized social benefit flows from the illegal distribution of prescription drugs."

8. **Scope of risk, redux.** Even where a duty is owed by an alcohol provider, the defendant might still avoid liability in some cases because the injury is outside the scope of the risk created by the provision of alcohol—or, if you prefer, is not a proximate result of the breach. Suppose the provider supplies alcohol to an obviously intoxicated person, who drives safely to a friend's house where he falls asleep smoking a cigarette. The cigarette causes a fire and the friend's house burns down. Liability? Or what if a bowling alley sells excessive amounts of alcohol to a patron, who drives away and, when chased by police, leaves his car and jumps off a bridge into a river and drowns? Liability? *See Osborn v. Twin Town Bowl, Inc.*, 749 N.W.2d 367 (Minn. 2008). Or what if a bar serves alcohol to a visibly intoxicated patron, who leaves the bar and, without any apparent motive, fires a gun through the doorway of a nearby business, injuring the plaintiff? *See Chapman v. Mayfield*, 361 P.3d 566 (Or. 2015). Determining scope of risk (proximate cause) is for a jury, remember, where reasonable people can differ. *See, e.g., Hoyt v. Gutterz Bowl & Lounge L.L.C.*, 829 N.W.2d 772 (Iowa 2013) (bar owed duty of reasonable care to patron assaulted by another patron in parking lot, but genuine issues of fact on whether bar breached that duty and whether harm was within scope of risks created by bar).

9. **Creating risks without providing the alcohol.** What if a person does not furnish the alcohol at all, but transports an intoxicated person to his car, with terrible consequences for those injured in a later crash? Does the

transporter owe a duty of care to those injured? In *Commerce Ins. Co. v. Ultimate Livery Service, Inc.*, 897 N.E.2d 50 (Mass. 2008), the court said yes; the defendant owed a duty of reasonable care to avoid discharging a passenger who they knew or should have known was intoxicated and would be driving a car. But in *Gushlaw v. Milner*, 42 A.3d 1245 (R.I. 2012), the court rejected any such duty on quite similar facts. Foreseeability alone was not sufficient to trigger a duty, the *Gushlaw* court said, and defining the scope of any such duty was for the legislature, not for the courts. Would it be an easier case for liability if the defendant, who did not furnish the alcohol but only the glasses, ice, mixers and venue, not only ejected a drunk patron but ordered the parking attendant to bring his car to the front door, assisted him into his car, and ordered him to drive away, with tragic results for innocent victims shortly thereafter? *See Simmons v. Homatas*, 925 N.E.2d 1089 (Ill. 2010).

NOTE: DRAM SHOP STATUTES

1.   *Variations.* The traditional view is a statute regulating sales of alcohol—for example, a statute prohibiting sales to minors or intoxicated persons—does not create a private cause of action. *Robinson v. Matt Mary Moran, Inc.*, 525 S.E.2d 559 (Va. 2000). Now, however, many states have adopted statutes called dram shop statutes or civil damage acts that do not merely impose criminal penalties; instead, they expressly impose civil liability upon the dispenser of alcohol. There are many variations. Some statutes impose liability only for certain kinds of sales, such as sales to minors or intoxicated persons. *See, e.g., Kalenka v. Jadon, Inc.*, 305 P.3d 346 (Alaska 2013) (prohibiting sale to a "drunken person"). Others require a higher showing than mere negligence. *See, e.g., Nunez v. Carrabba's Italian Grill, Inc.*, 859 N.E.2d 801 (Mass. 2007) (dram shop statute, which requires proof of the seller's "willful, wanton or reckless" conduct, does not apply when alcohol is furnished to a minor). Some statutes apply only to those who sell alcohol for consumption on the premises, as opposed to stores selling packaged liquor. *See, e.g., Snodgras v. Martin & Bayley, Inc.*, 204 S.W.3d 638 (Mo. 2006) (upholding such a statute against constitutional attack). Others allow suits against those who sell closed or packaged liquor for off-site consumption, if the buyer is noticeably intoxicated and the seller knows he will soon be driving. *See Flores v. Exprezit! Stores 98-Georgia, LLC*, 713 S.E.2d 368 (Ga. 2011).

2.   *Safety effects of statutes.* Dram shop liability has deterred alcohol providers from engaging in certain specific practices that lead to intoxication and drunk driving, such as serving multiple drinks at one time, and has reduced motor vehicle fatalities. *See* Ellen M. Bublick, *China's New Tort Law: The Promise of Reasonable Care*, 13 ASIAN-PAC. L. & POL'Y J. 36, 53 (2011).

3. *Exclusive remedy.* The dram shop statute may be the exclusive remedy against an alcohol provider, barring all common law claims relating to injuries caused by the defendant's sales. *See, e.g., Bauer v. Nesbitt,* 969 A.2d 1122 (N.J. 2009); *Delta Airlines, Inc. v. Townsend,* 614 S.E.2d 745 (Ga. 2005). Some dram shop statutes seem to impose a kind of strict liability upon the provider of alcohol. *See, e.g.,* 235 ILL. COMP. STAT. 5/6–21 (granting civil cause of action to any person injured by an intoxicated person against any person licensed to sell liquor who caused such intoxication, with no proof of fault required).

4. *Immunities.* At the other extreme, legislators in some states have immunized alcohol providers for negligence, even where they have served drunken customers who are likely to drive. *See, e.g.,* TENN. CODE ANN. §§ 57–10–101 *et seq.;* WIS. STAT. ANN. § 125.035. Idaho's statute bars claims by passengers injured in cars being driven by intoxicated drivers. *See McLean v. Maverik Country Stores, Inc.,* 135 P.3d 756 (Idaho 2006) (rejecting constitutional attack). Some dram shop acts give the alcohol seller a "safe harbor" provision, immunizing the employer from liability when the employee has violated the statute, if the employer can show that it required its employees to attend certain training classes. *See 20801, Inc. v. Parker,* 249 S.W.3d 392 (Tex. 2008).

5. *Judicial inactivity in the absence of a statute.* Some states have refused to impose civil liability on alcohol providers in the *absence* of a dram shop statute, saying that such a decision should be for the legislature alone. *See, e.g., Shea v. Matassa,* 918 A.2d 1090 (Del. 2007). Does that represent good policy in this area of law?

NOTE: NEGLIGENT ENTRUSTMENT

1. *Basic contours.* The *Brigance* court cited with approval two sections of the Restatement Second that deal with what is commonly called "negligent entrustment." The thrust of this body of law is that a person in control of a chattel owes a responsibility not to entrust that chattel to a person whom the entruster knows or should know, at the time of the entrustment, is likely to use it in a dangerous way. *See, e.g., Sheffer v. Carolina Forge Co.,* 306 P.3d 544 (Okla. 2013). Many courts have adopted the rules from section 390 of the Restatement Second, and hold that a plaintiff must prove (1) that the defendant entrusted a chattel, (2) to an incompetent entrustee, (3) with knowledge or reason to know of the entrustee's incompetence, and (4) the entrustee's incompetence while using the chattel caused the injury. *Martell v. Driscoll,* 302 P.3d 375 (Kan. 2013). In essence, this is a specific application of general principles of negligence law, and thus other regular negligence rules apply. *See* 2 DOBBS, HAYDEN & BUBLICK, THE LAW OF TORTS § 422 (2d ed. 2011); RESTATEMENT (THIRD)

OF TORTS: LIABILITY FOR PHYSICAL AND EMOTIONAL HARM § 19, cmt. e. (2010).

2.   *Theft of chattel.* Note that if a chattel is stolen from a defendant, the defendant has not "entrusted" the chattel to the thief and is thus not liable on this theory. *See, e.g., Estate of Kim ex rel. Alexander v. Coxe*, 295 P.3d 380 (Alaska 2013). Liability might be found on a general negligence theory in extreme cases, however, where the defendant left a chattel in a place where it was easily accessible to a dangerous person, with full knowledge of impending harm. *Cf. Dorsey v. Reider*, 139 So.3d 860 (Fla. 2014) (defendant left his tomahawk in his truck, easily accessible to man known to be drunk and angry; man took weapon and used it on plaintiff, in defendant's presence; defendant liable because he had control over not just the tomahawk but over "the premises" and could have prevented the attack).

3.   *Kinds of chattels covered.* Most cases involve products that could be operated by the entrustee, such as cars, guns, or cigarette lighters. *See, e.g., Morin v. Moore*, 309 F.3d 316 (5th Cir. 2002) (making an AK-47 automatic rifle accessible to a dangerous person invested in Nazi ideology); *Shirley v. Glass*, 308 P.3d 1 (Kan. 2013) (entrusting shotgun to man known to have been convicted of attempted rape and attempted kidnapping, and "tended to lose control of himself when he was angry"); *Ardinger v. Hummell*, 982 P.2d 727 (Alaska 1999) (furnishing automobile to 15-year-old).

4.   *First-party negligent entrustment.* A negligent entruster may be liable not only to third persons injured by the entrustee, but also to the entrustee himself. *See Herland v. Izatt*, 345 P.3d 661 (Utah 2015) (entrustment of gun to intoxicated party guest, who accidentally shot herself in the head); *Martell v. Driscoll*, 302 P.3d 375 (Kan. 2013) (entrustment of car to person known to have a suspended license, a history of DUI's, and a history of alcohol abuse); *DeWester v. Watkins*, 745 N.W.2d 330 (Neb. 2008) (14-year-old entrustee died in car accident). Some courts characterize the negligent entrustment claim as a form of vicarious liability. *See, e.g., Rippy v. Shepard*, 80 So.3d 305 (Fla. 2012) (liability for entrusting farm tractor to person whose negligent operation injured the plaintiff). Note that some statutes forbid first-party negligent entrustment recoveries, at least in certain situations, and a few judicial decisions reject such claims on public-policy grounds. *See Lydia v. Horton*, 583 S.E.2d 750 (S.C. 2003).

5.   *Testing the limits.* Some courts have been willing to test the boundaries of negligent entrustment. For example, in *Vince v. Wilson*, 561 A.2d 103 (Vt. 1989), the court held that the plaintiff, injured in an accident with an incompetent driver, stated a claim against the driver's great aunt who provided money to buy the car knowing that her grand-nephew was a

substance abuser who had failed the driver's test many times. In *West v. East Tennessee Pioneer Oil Co.*, 172 S.W.3d 545 (Tenn. 2005), the court held that a convenience store could be held liable on a negligent entrustment theory when its clerk sold gasoline to a clearly intoxicated motorist and helped him pump the gas. And in *Morris v. Giant Four Corners, Inc.*, 498 P.3d 238 (N.M. 2021), the court opined that "New Mexico courts have recognized that entrustors owe a duty to refrain from voluntarily supplying a vehicle to an entrustee who is intoxicated. The same logic supports a duty to refrain from supplying the gasoline for a vehicle to an entrustee who the entrustor knows or has reason to know is intoxicated." Do these extensions represent good policy?

PROBLEMS

1.   A railroad, trying to clear its track after a derailment, works an employee more than 24 hours with no substantial rest. When the employee finally heads home, he falls asleep at the wheel and crashes into the plaintiff's car. Since the employee is not "on the job," the employer is not vicariously liable. Is the employer liable for negligence?

2.   The defendant, a physician, prescribed anabolic steroids for a patient. The patient's reaction to the drug or its dosage was to become extremely aggressive and hostile to those around him. After his behavior led his wife to leave the house out of fear, the physician talked to him and concluded he was safe and so advised the wife. The wife then went back to the house to get her clothes, taking a friend with her. The patient shot the friend, causing injury. In prescribing for the patient, did the physician owe any duty to protect third persons? Assume you are in a jurisdiction that recognizes the rule in *Brigance*.

3.   Defendant owned a pistol, which he left in his bedroom. He had a safe on the premises but did not keep the pistol there. While defendant was out of town, his daughter invited guests to the house. One of them stole the pistol and used it later in a robbery, killing decedent in the process. The estate sues the defendant alleging that he negligently failed to secure the pistol.

REFERENCES: DOBBS, HAYDEN & BUBLICK, HORNBOOK ON TORTS §§ 26.1–26.12 (2d ed. 2016); 2 DOBBS, HAYDEN & BUBLICK, THE LAW OF TORTS §§ 413–424 (2d ed. 2011).

PART 7

SPECIAL TYPES OF HARM

■ ■ ■

Judicial attitudes about tort liability depend in part upon the relationships of the parties, as we saw in the last few chapters, but also in part upon the kind of harm the plaintiff claims she suffered.

In the absence of special relationships, courts are most receptive to tort claims when the defendant has risked, and the plaintiff has suffered, physical harm to self or property.

What tort cases do *not* involve physical harms? First, cases of stand-alone economic harm. For example, suppose a defendant negligently provides the plaintiff with information that leads the plaintiff to purchase a piece of property. The information proves erroneous, and the plaintiff loses money on the deal. No one or nothing is physically injured; the loss is purely economic. Second, cases of stand-alone emotional distress. For example, suppose the defendant negligently provides the plaintiff information leading the plaintiff to believe that plaintiff's child has been seriously injured. Before the plaintiff discovers that the information is false, plaintiff suffers serious emotional, but not physical, harm.

Several different torts besides the tort of negligence address emotional interests. Physical torts like battery, assault and false imprisonment obviously have the protection of emotional interests as one component. Defamation (libel and slander), malicious prosecution, the right to privacy and the nuisance tort also protect emotional interests tied to reputation, seclusion, and the enjoyment of land.

The three chapters that follow consider how courts treat negligence claims for emotional harm, prenatal injury and wrongful death.

CHAPTER 19

EMOTIONAL HARM

■ ■ ■

This chapter focuses on stand-alone claims for emotional distress. Such a claim can be for intentional infliction of emotional distress (IIED), or negligent infliction of emotional distress (NIED). As we will see, both claims are subject to significant restrictions.

Courts have long recognized that tortfeasors should be responsible for causing pain, anxiety, emotional distress, and similar intangible harms. But courts approach emotional distress damages in two quite different ways, depending on whether the emotional harm is considered a stand-alone claim—our focus here—or simply as a category of damages "parasitic" to another tort. When emotional distress damages are sought in connection with a tort claim such as negligence (as "pain and suffering") or assault (where the damages are for the mental distress resulting from being aware of an imminent battery), none of the limiting rules discussed in this chapter will apply. That is, the restrictions we see in this chapter have arisen to limit stand-alone emotional distress claims, not to limit the recovery of damages for pain or distress caused by the commission of some other tort. *See* DOBBS, HAYDEN & BUBLICK, HORNBOOK ON TORTS § 29.1 (2d ed. 2016).

§ 1. INTENTIONAL INFLICTION OF EMOTIONAL DISTRESS

CHANKO V. AMERICAN BROADCASTING COMPANIES, INC.

49 N.E.3d 1171 (N.Y. 2016)

STEIN, J. . . .

Mark Chanko (decedent) was brought into the emergency room of defendant The New York and Presbyterian Hospital (the Hospital). He had been hit by a vehicle, but was alert and responding to questions. Defendant Sebastian Schubl was the Hospital's chief surgical resident and was responsible for decedent's treatment. While decedent was being treated, employees of ABC News, a division of defendant American Broadcasting Companies, Inc. (ABC), were in the Hospital—with the Hospital's knowledge and permission—filming a documentary series (N.Y. Med) about medical trauma and the professionals who attend to the patients suffering from such trauma. No one informed decedent or any of the individual plaintiffs—most of whom were at the Hospital—that a camera crew was present and filming, nor was their consent obtained for filming or for the crew's presence.

Less than an hour after decedent arrived at the Hospital, Schubl declared him dead. That declaration was filmed by ABC, and decedent's prior treatment was apparently filmed as well. Schubl then informed the family of decedent's death, with that moment also being recorded without their knowledge.

Sixteen months later, decedent's widow, plaintiff Anita Chanko, watched an episode of N.Y. Med on her television at home. She recognized the scene, heard decedent's voice asking about her, saw him on a stretcher, heard him moaning, and watched him die. In addition, she saw, and relived, Schubl telling the family of his death. She then told the other plaintiffs, who also watched the episode. This was the first time plaintiffs became aware of the recording of decedent's medical treatment and death.

Plaintiffs commenced this action against, among others, ABC, the Hospital and Schubl. Defendants separately moved to dismiss the complaint. [The trial court partially granted the motions, dismissing the causes of action against all defendants for intentional infliction of emotional distress. The Appellate Division affirmed the dismissal of these claims, and plaintiffs appealed.]

This Court has enumerated four elements of a cause of action for intentional infliction of emotional distress: (i) extreme and outrageous conduct; (ii) intent to cause, or disregard of a substantial probability of causing, severe emotional distress; (iii) a causal connection between the conduct and injury; and (iv) severe emotional distress. Liability has been found only where the conduct has been so outrageous in character, and so extreme in degree, as to go beyond all possible bounds of decency, and to be regarded as atrocious, and utterly intolerable in a civilized community. Here, the complaint . . . alleges that the Hospital and Schubl allowed ABC to broadcast and disseminate the footage of the final moments of decedent's life, without the knowledge or consent of decedent or plaintiffs. The complaint alleges that plaintiffs watched the episode and were shocked and upset, that "[d]efendants acted intentionally, recklessly, willfully, maliciously and deliberately," and that it was foreseeable that plaintiffs would be caused to suffer emotional distress. Alternatively, the complaint alleges that "defendants acted with reckless disregard for the probability that they would cause plaintiffs to suffer emotional distress," and that defendants knew or should have known that emotional distress was a likely result of their actions. The complaint further alleges that plaintiffs experienced emotional distress due to defendants' conduct, and that "[d]efendants' conduct was extreme and outrageous, beyond all possible bounds of decency, utterly intolerable in a civilized community, and without privilege."

Although these allegations facially address all of the required elements, they are not sufficient to support this cause of action because they do not rise to the level necessary to satisfy the outrageousness element—the element most susceptible to a determination as a matter of law—which is designed to filter out petty complaints and assure that the emotional distress is genuine. Noting that "the requirements . . . are rigorous, and difficult to satisfy," we have commented that, "of the intentional infliction of emotional distress claims considered by this Court, *every one* has failed because the alleged conduct was not sufficiently outrageous".

The conduct at issue here . . .—the broadcasting of a recording of a patient's last moments of life without consent—would likely be considered reprehensible by most people, and we do not condone it. Nevertheless, it was not so extreme and outrageous as to satisfy our exceedingly high legal standard. The footage aired by ABC was edited so that it did not include decedent's name, his image was blurred, and the episode included less than three minutes devoted to decedent and his circumstances. We cannot conclude that defendants' conduct in allowing the broadcasting of that brief, edited segment is more outrageous than other conduct that this Court and the Appellate Division Departments have determined did not rise to the level required to establish "extreme and outrageous conduct" sufficient to state a cause of action for intentional infliction of emotional distress. For example, we did not deem a newspaper's conduct sufficiently outrageous when it published a picture of a person in a psychiatric facility—thereby informing the world that the photographed person was a patient at such a facility—even though the residents were photographed by someone trespassing on facility grounds and the facility had expressly requested that the newspaper not publish pictures of residents. Similarly, the conduct of a television station has been deemed insufficiently outrageous when the station displayed recognizable images of rape victims after repeatedly assuring them that they would not be identifiable.

We conclude that defendants' conduct here, while offensive, was not so atrocious and utterly intolerable as to support a cause of action in the context of this tort. Hence, there is no need to address whether the newsworthiness privilege is applicable.

[The order dismissing plaintiffs' claims for intentional infliction of emotional distress is affirmed.]

GTE SOUTHWEST, INC. v. BRUCE, 998 S.W.2d 605 (Tex. 1999). Several employees of GTE working under Morris Shields alleged that over a period of years, Shields engaged in a pattern of grossly abusive, threatening, and degrading conduct, regularly using the harshest vulgarity, verbally threatening and terrorizing them. He would physically charge at the employees, put his head down, ball his hands into fists, and walk quickly toward or lunge at the employees, stopping very close to their faces. A number of witnesses testified that Shields frequently yelled and screamed at the top of his voice, and pounded his fists when requesting the employees to do things. There was testimony that he often called one employee into his office and kept her standing there up to thirty minutes while he simply started at her. He required employees to vacuum their own offices daily despite the availability of regular janitorial services. A jury found for plaintiffs in their suit for intentional infliction of emotional distress. *Held,* affirmed.

"Generally, insensitive or even rude behavior does not constitute extreme and outrageous conduct. Similarly, mere insults, indignities, threats, annoyances, petty oppressions, or other trivialities do not rise to the level of extreme and outrageous conduct. In determining whether certain conduct is extreme and outrageous, courts consider the context and the relationship between the parties. . . . Shields's ongoing acts of harassment, intimidation, and humiliation and his daily obscene and vulgar behavior, which GTE defends as his 'management style,' went beyond the bounds of tolerable workplace conduct. . . . Occasional malicious and abusive incidents should not be condoned, but must often be tolerated in our society. But once conduct such as that shown here becomes a regular pattern of behavior and continues despite the victim's objection and attempts to remedy the situation, it can no longer be tolerated. It is the severity and regularity of Shields's abusive and threatening conduct that brings his behavior into the realm of extreme and outrageous conduct."

NOTES

1. **History of the tort.** The American Law Institute recognized the tort of intentional infliction of mental distress in the Restatement of Torts in 1948. The Second Restatement § 46 first employed the "extreme and outrageous conduct" standard and courts widely adopted it. To determine whether conduct is extreme and outrageous courts often ask "whether the recitation of the facts to an average member of the community would arouse her resentment against the defendant so that she would exclaim 'Outrageous!'" *Howerton v. Harbin Clinic, LLC,* 776 S.E.2d 288 (Ga. Ct. App. 2015) (using a test from the Second Restatement and holding that surgeon's lewd actions met the outrageousness threshold).

2. **The Restatement Third of Torts.** The elements under the Third Restatement are slightly different from those in *Chanko.* According to the Restatement, "[a]n actor who by extreme and outrageous conduct intentionally or recklessly causes severe emotional harm to another is subject to liability for

that emotional harm and, if the emotional harm causes bodily harm, also for the bodily harm." RESTATEMENT (THIRD) OF TORTS: LIABILITY FOR PHYSICAL AND EMOTIONAL HARM § 46 cmt. m (2012). In what way does the standard in *Chanko* seem easier to satisfy than the standard in the Restatement? *See Hill v. Cundiff*, 797 F.3d 948 (11th Cir. 2015) (Alabama requires that the actor either intended to inflict emotional distress, "or knew or should have known that emotional distress was likely to result from his conduct"; reasonable jury could conclude that a teacher's aide should have known that emotional distress was likely to result from her decision to talk a female middle school student into subjecting herself to a male student's sexual advances in a "sting" operation that went horribly wrong when the male student took the plaintiff alone into a bathroom and raped her).

3. **Judging extreme and outrageous conduct.** *(a) What the term means.* The outcome of many cases turns on whether the defendant's conduct was extreme and outrageous. The question is often framed as whether conduct is "so outrageous in character, and so extreme in degree, as to go beyond all possible bounds of decency, and to be regarded as atrocious, and utterly intolerable in civilized society," *Tiller v. McLure*, 121 S.W.3d 709 (Tex. 2003), or whether, by contrast, the conduct is only "unfortunate" or engenders "the mere disapproval" of the community. *See Mik v. Federal Home Loan Mortgage Corp.*, 743 F.3d 149 (6th Cir. 2014); *see also Ortberg v. Goldman Sachs Group*, 64 A.3d 158 (D.C. 2013) (anti-Goldman Sachs protestors protesting outside employee's home and chanting "we know where you sleep at night," was not extreme and outrageous). According to the Restatement, the terms extreme and outrageous serve distinct roles. "Some conduct that may be outrageous— for example, marital infidelity—is sufficiently common that it could not be characterized as extreme." Moreover, "some extreme conduct—climbing Mt. Everest, for example—is not outrageous." RESTATEMENT (THIRD) OF TORTS: LIABILITY FOR PHYSICAL AND EMOTIONAL HARM § 46 cmt. d (2012). Could the conduct in *Chanko* and *GTE* be considered both "extreme" and "outrageous?"

(b) Role of judge and jury. The court plays a significant gatekeeping role in the adjudication of this tort. *See* RESTATEMENT (THIRD) OF TORTS: LIABILITY FOR PHYSICAL AND EMOTIONAL HARM § 46 cmt. g (2012) ("the court plays a more substantial screening role on the questions of extreme and outrageous conduct" than it normally does on questions of fact). As the West Virginia court explained, "the role of the trial court is to first determine whether the defendant's conduct may reasonably be regarded as so extreme and outrageous as to constitute the intentional or reckless infliction of emotional distress. Whether conduct may reasonably be considered outrageous is a legal question, and whether conduct is in fact outrageous is a question for jury determination." *Zsigray v. Langman*, 842 S.E.2d 716 (W.Va. 2020). *See also Neppel v. Development Homes, Inc.*, 953 N.W.2d 642 (N.D. 2021) ("The district court must act as a gate-keeper and initially decide, as a matter of law, whether the conduct in question can reasonably be considered 'extreme and outrageous.' If the district court determines that reasonable people could differ, the question . . . is left to the trier-of-fact.").

Given the stringent nature of the substantive test, it is not surprising that appellate courts routinely affirm trial courts' grants of dismissal or summary judgment, based on a finding that the defendant's conduct could not reasonably be considered extreme and outrageous. *See, e.g., Goodwin v. City of Shepherdstown*, 825 S.E.2d 263 (W.Va. 2019) (alleged suppression of alibi evidence in a criminal case); *Harvey v. Regional Health Network, Inc.*, 906 N.W.2d 382 (S.D. 2018) (employer's allegedly inadequate investigation of employee wrongdoing) health care worker's alleged sexual abuse of by health care worker). As the Iowa court concluded in a recent case, affirming a defense summary judgment, "A jury could find certain aspects of the defendants' actions as petty, wrong, or even malicious. But this would not lead an average member of the community to arouse resentment against the defendants and to exclaim, 'Outrageous!'" *Hedlund v. State*, 930 N.W.2d 707 (Iowa 2019). Should the jury in *Chanko* have had an opportunity to evaluate whether the conduct was extreme or outrageous?

4. **Markers of outrage.** Perhaps the most common fact patterns involve conduct that is (a) repeated or carried out over a period of time, (b) an abuse of power by a person with some authority over the plaintiff, or (c) directed at a person known to be especially vulnerable. Which, if any, pattern does *Chanko* fit? Which pattern does *GTE* fit?

5. **Repeated conduct.** A single request for sexual contact, or a single use of an offensive epithet, might be offensive but is usually not found to be sufficiently outrageous. *See Jones v. Clinton,* 990 F.Supp. 657 (E.D. Ark. 1998); *John v. Philadelphia Pizza Team, Inc.*, 209 A.3d 380 (Pa. Super. 2019). On the other hand, repeated conduct of such type can be outrageous. *See Boyle v. Wenk*, 392 N.E.2d 1053 (Mass. 1979) ("Repeated harassment . . . may compound the outrageousness of incidents which, taken individually, might not be sufficiently extreme to warrant liability for infliction of emotional distress."). Conduct that takes place over a long time can be actionable as well. *See Sindi v. El-Moslimany*, 896 F.3d 1 (1st Cir. 2018) (affirming jury verdict for plaintiff on IIED claim, where defendant engaged in a "more than four year war of vituperation" against plaintiff); *Bratton v. McDonough*, 91 A.3d 1050 (Me. 2014) (landlord allowed tenants with young children to live for four years in a house containing toxic levels of lead, and delayed the tenants' relocation for four months after the State had declared the house a lead hazard; jury question). In *Turley v. ISG Lackawanna, Inc.*, 774 F.3d 140 (2d Cir. 2014), the plaintiff adduced sufficient evidence to establish that his supervisor's actions were outrageous, where the supervisor continuously failed over a period of three years to respond to repeated and severe instances of racially motivated harassment of the plaintiff, blocked others to investigate the harassment, and even encouraged the harassment.

6. **Abuse of power.** Abuse of power by the defendant takes many forms. It might involve employers and employees, or public officials and those in a subordinate position. *See, e.g., Brandon v. County of Richardson*, 624 N.W.2d 604 (Neb. 2001) (sheriff crudely questioning rape victim soon after rape); *Hysjulien v. Hill Top Home of Comfort, Inc.*, 827 N.W.2d 533 (N.D. 2013)

(employee who, at a work conference, had fallen asleep after an evening of drinking with the boss and co-workers and awoke shortly after everyone else had left the room to find the boss naked on top of her trying to remove her clothes, stated a claim for outrageous conduct). In *Hayward v. Cleveland Clinic Found.*, 759 F.3d 601 (6th Cir. 2014), parents of a man arrested by police officers for a minor traffic infraction sued the officers for IIED. Plaintiffs alleged that the defendants, without announcing a reason for their actions, arrested the son in front of his parents, at 4 a.m. in their home, using excessive force and using profanity and racial epithets, then dragged him from the home where they beat him severely and tased him numerous times. The officers also threatened the "innocent, elderly couple with physical violence." The trial court dismissed the IIED claim, but the Sixth Circuit reversed, holding that the allegations stated a claim. The alleged conduct could be found to be extreme and outrageous, and plaintiffs alleged severe distress—the elderly father was hospitalized as a result of the incident.

A number of courts have expressed caution about allowing IIED claims in the employment setting to go to juries. One recent case broadly declared that IIED claims "will not ordinarily lie for mere employment disputes," while recognizing that where there is "a pattern of deliberate, repeated harassment over a period of time," a claim may be viable. *Collins v. City of Newton*, 240 So.3d 1211 (Miss. 2018). But clearly more than "typical bad boss behavior" must be shown. *Hedlund, supra* Note 3 ("When evaluating claims of outrageous conduct arising out of employer-employee relationships, we have required a reasonable level of tolerance. . . . Despite our caselaw that indicates an employer 'has a duty to refrain from abusive behavior toward employees,' we have often found that conduct by employers and coworkers did not rise to the level of outrageous conduct."). Is such caution well-founded, or does this view result in a failure to deter bad conduct by abusive bosses?

7. **Knowledge of plaintiff's vulnerability.** This pattern may be seen as a subset of the abuse-of-power pattern. *See, e.g., Liberty Mut. Ins. Co. v. Steadman*, 968 So.2d 592 (Fla. Dist. Ct. App. 2007) (insurance company's conduct was outrageous where it denied and delayed paying for treatment, knowing claimant had limited life expectancy); *Doe v. Corp. of President of Church of Jesus Christ of Latter-Day Saints*, 167 P.3d 1193 (Wash. Ct. App. 2007) (affirming jury verdict for plaintiff where church bishop acted with knowledge of teenaged church member's peculiar susceptibility to emotional distress).

8. **Exercising legal rights.** Cases and the Restatement emphasize that a person cannot be held liable for this tort merely for exercising a legal right, even where he is substantially certain that it will cause emotional distress—such as filing for a divorce, or firing an at-will employee, or seeking to collect a debt. RESTATEMENT (THIRD) OF TORTS: LIABILITY FOR PHYSICAL AND EMOTIONAL HARM § 46 cmt. e (2012). But a person is "not immunized from liability if the conduct goes so far beyond what is necessary to exercise the right that it is extreme and outrageous." *Id.* Thus a creditor would not be acting outrageously simply by demanding payment of an overdue debt, but might be

liable for making harsh threats to a plaintiff known to be mentally fragile. *See MacDermid v. Discover Fin. Servs.*, 488 F.3d 731 (6th Cir. 2007).

9. **Causation.** A plaintiff must prove a sufficient causal link between the defendant's conduct and the plaintiff's distress. This is usually thought to mean factual causation, meaning that the plaintiff must show that but for the defendant's outrageous conduct, the severe distress would not have occurred. *See* RESTATEMENT (THIRD) OF TORTS: LIABILITY FOR PHYSICAL AND EMOTIONAL HARM § 46 cmt. k (2012). *See Turcios v. Debruler Co.*, 32 N.E.3d 1117 (Ill. 2015) (where plaintiff seeks to recover based on decedent's suicide as a result of the intentional infliction of emotional distress, plaintiff must plead facts demonstrating that the suicide was a likely result of defendant's conduct).

10. **Severity of emotional distress.** Although severe distress can be proved without showing physical symptoms, courts insist that the distress must be severe or even debilitating. See, e.g., *Argereow v. Weisberg*, 195 A.3d 1210 (Me. 2018) (affirming dismissal of IIED claim where plaintiff's allegations of distress were "akin to the general feelings of upset and defeat that are insufficient to establish a claim"); *Lyman v. Huber*, 10 A.3d 707 (Me. 2010) (outrageous behavior of defendant left plaintiff feeling "inadequate and withdrawn, socially paralyzed, and fearful and intimated," but that was an insufficient showing of severity of distress). Proof of this element may involve consideration of the same facts that were relevant to the issue of outrageousness. *See, e.g., Rogers v. Louisville Land Co.*, 367 S.W.3d 196 (Tenn. 2012) (listing nonexclusive factors that are relevant to a determination that a plaintiff has suffered severe distress, including physiological manifestations; psychological manifestations such as depression, nightmares and anxiety; evidence of medical treatment and diagnosis; evidence of the duration and intensity of the distress; proof that the distress caused significant impairment of day-to-day functioning; and the extreme and outrageous nature of the defendant's conduct itself); *see also Sindi, supra* Note 5 ("[T]he length of time that plaintiff is forced to endure emotional distress is a highly relevant datum in determining whether that distress is sufficiently severe to be compensable.").

Is severe distress a useful requirement, or should a plaintiff be allowed to recover damages for lesser distress provably caused by a defendant's "extreme and outrageous" behavior?

11. **Overlap with other tort claims.** The tort of intentional infliction of emotional distress "originated as a catchall to permit recovery in the narrow instance when an actor's conduct exceeded all permissible bounds of a civilized society but an existing tort claim was unavailable." RESTATEMENT (THIRD) OF TORTS: LIABILITY FOR PHYSICAL AND EMOTIONAL HARM § 46 cmt. a (2012). Does the fact that the defendants in *Chanko* breached their fiduciary duty to the patient, and that that claim was permitted to proceed, make an intentional infliction of emotional distress claim on the part of the family members more or less essential? Would it matter if the two torts differed in terms of elements or measures of damage? Did some of the supervisor's actions in *GTE* constitute

other intentional torts? Should a plaintiff be allowed to bring a claim for intentional infliction of emotional distress if a claim for battery or assault is stated as well? Some courts have said no. *See, e.g., State ex rel. Halsey v. Phillips*, 576 S.W.3d 177 (Mo. 2019).

12. **Constitutional limitations.** The First Amendment to the United States Constitution guarantees free speech and the free exercise of religion. These clauses may limit a variety of tort claims, including claims for intentional infliction of emotional distress, that are based on communicative or religiously motivated conduct. *See Snyder v. Phelps*, 562 U.S. 443 (2011) (barring claim of intentional infliction of emotional distress against defendant church members who picketed near military service member's funeral; anti-homosexual theme of the demonstration was a matter of public concern and therefore protected by the First Amendment although picketing caused father great distress); *Hustler Magazine v. Falwell*, 485 U.S. 46 (1998) (barring intentional infliction claim by a public figure on First Amendment free speech grounds); *In re Diocese of Lubbock*, 624 S.W.3d 506 (Tex. 2021) ("ecclesiastical abstention" doctrine precluded civil court jurisdiction over IIED and defamation claims brought by church deacon against diocese). Could the *Chanko* court have said the conduct in that case was sufficient to establish extreme or outrageous conduct, but the media defendants had a privilege to publish it anyway because the story was newsworthy?

ROTH V. ISLAMIC REPUBLIC OF IRAN, 78 F.Supp.3d 379 (D.D.C. 2015). American family members of 15-year-old Malka Roth, who died in a Hamas terrorist bombing at a Sbarro restaurant in Jerusalem, Israel, filed suit against the Islamic Republic of Iran and the Iranian Ministry of Information and Security, which played a role in supporting the terrorists. Family members sought damages pursuant to the Foreign Sovereign Immunities Act (FSIA). The family moved for a default judgment as to liability and damages. The district court held that the court had jurisdiction under the state-sponsored terrorism exception to the FSIA and awarded economic loss damages over $1 million, solatium damages (a form of damages intended to compensate persons for mental anguish, bereavement and grief that those with a close personal relationship to a decedent experience) of $5 million to each parent, and $2.5 million to each sibling (except for blind and intellectually disabled sibling for whom there was no evidence of mental anguish), and punitive damages of $112.5 million.

With respect to the claim for intentional infliction of emotional distress, the court wrote: "Plaintiffs seek to recover solatium damages for defendants' intentional infliction of emotional distress. Relying principally on the Restatement (Second) of Torts, this Court has set out the following standard for recovery on a theory of IIED in section 1605A(c) cases: One who by extreme and outrageous conduct intentionally or recklessly causes severe emotional distress to another is subject to liability for such emotional distress, and if bodily harm to the other results from it, for such bodily harm. An actor may also be liable for IIED to a party against whom the extreme and outrageous conduct was not directed if that party is (1) a member of the victim's immediate family and (2) was present at the time of the extreme and outrageous conduct. The 'immediate family' requirement is strictly construed . . .; generally, only spouses, parents, siblings, and children are entitled to recover. As to the issue of presence, this Court has previously held that one need not be present at the time of a terrorist attack upon a third person to recover for severe emotional injuries suffered as a result. This is because terrorism is sufficiently extreme and outrageous to demonstrate that it is intended to inflict severe emotional harm on even those not present at the site of the act. The plaintiffs have stated a valid theory of recovery as to their IIED claims. . . . [A]lthough the family member plaintiffs do not allege that they were present at the site of the attack, this requirement is not imposed when the extreme and outrageous conduct is a terrorist attack such as this."

an exception

Reasoning

NOTES

1.   **Liability to plaintiff when conduct is directed at another person.** As the *Roth* court noted, the Second Restatement (and the Third) limit recovery for intentional infliction of emotional distress when the defendant's extreme and outrageous conduct is directed at someone other than the plaintiff; in that situation, only immediate family members who are present at the time of the conduct, and who suffer severe distress, can recover. *See* RESTATEMENT (THIRD) OF TORTS: LIABILITY FOR PHYSICAL AND EMOTIONAL HARM § 46 cmt. m (2012) (emotional harm caused by harm to a third person). Why impose these limitations? The Third Restatement suggests they "might be justified by the practical necessity of drawing a line, since the number of persons who suffer emotional harm at the news of a homicide or other outrageous attack may be virtually unlimited." *Id.*; *see also Homer v. Long,* 599 A.2d 1193 (Md. Ct. Spec. App. 1992) (husband whose hospitalized wife's therapist seduced her, could not recover for his own emotional distress; therapist's outrageous conduct was not directed at husband and husband was not present at the time of the outrageous conduct).

2.   **Terrorism.** One recognized exception to the usual "presence" requirement occurs in cases of terrorism. *See Owens v. Republic of Sudan*, 924 F.3d 1256 (D.C. Cir. 2019) (family members of victims of terrorist bombings of U.S. embassies could prove IIED claims without having being present at those bombings); *Bettis v. Islamic Republic of Iran*, 315 F.3d 325 (D.C. Cir. 2003) (plaintiffs did not have to be present while their family member was kidnapped and tortured in order to state a claim); *Hatch v. Davis*, 147 P.3d 383 (Utah 2006) ("a plaintiff must establish that the conduct was undertaken, in whole or in part, with the intention of inflicting injury to the absent plaintiff"). Why not preclude families of a terror victim not present at the abuse from recovering

for intentional infliction of emotional distress as well? Is emotional distress substantially certain to occur in terrorism cases? The *Roth* court wrote "acts of terrorism are by their very definition extreme and outrageous and intended to cause the highest degree of emotional distress." If a terrorist intended to cause widespread distress, should there be widespread recovery rather than recovery limited to family members? Absent evidence of mental distress, was the court right to limit recovery to the profoundly disabled sister?

3. **The FSIA.** The FSIA is the "sole basis for obtaining jurisdiction over a foreign state in our courts." *Argentine Republic v. Amerada Hess Shipping Corp.,* 488 U.S. 428, 434 (1989). It provides that federal district courts have original jurisdiction over (1) nonjury civil actions (2) for claims seeking relief *in personam* (3) against a foreign state (4) when the foreign state is not entitled to immunity. One exception to foreign sovereign immunity is the state-sponsored terrorism exception. Under that section, a foreign state has no immunity in any case "in which money damages are sought against a foreign state for personal injury or death that was caused by an act of torture, extrajudicial killing, aircraft sabotage, hostage taking, or the provision of material support or resources for such an act. . . ." 28 U.S.C. § 1605A. After considering these elements, the court found the defendants in *Roth* were state sponsors of terrorism and could be held liable.

4. **Other exceptions to the presence requirement.** The Third Restatement notes that some courts have created an exception to the presence requirement in order to permit parents to recover for their emotional distress at the sexual abuse of their children. RESTATEMENT (THIRD) OF TORTS: LIABILITY FOR PHYSICAL AND EMOTIONAL HARM § 46 cmt. m (2012). Why create such an exception? Is there a principle that should be broader than these two specific types of cases? Some courts have broadened the definition of presence rather than creating an exception. *See, e.g., Bevan v. Fix,* 42 P.3d 1013 (Wyo. 2002) (children who did not actually witness attacks on their mother were "present" if they could show "sensory and contemporaneous" awareness). Does the presence requirement generally represent good policy? *See, e.g., Reid v. Pierce County,* 961 P.2d 333 (Wash. 1998) (barring claim where plaintiffs were not present while defendants used autopsy photos of their relatives for their own purposes).

§ 2. NEGLIGENT INFLICTION OF EMOTIONAL DISTRESS

A. EMOTIONAL DISTRESS FROM DIRECT RISKS OF PHYSICAL HARM

STACY V. REDERIET OTTO DANIELSEN, A.S., 609 F.3d 1033 (9th Cir. 2010). In dense fog, a small group of vessels fished for salmon. Stacy owned and operated a small vessel, the *Marja.* At 5 p.m., the *Marja's* radar picked up a signal from a large freighter a mile away that was on a collision course directly toward the *Marja.* When Stacy realized that the freighter was heading straight for him, he feared for his life and felt sick to his stomach. He signaled the danger to the freighter, which passed by so close to the *Marja* that Stacy could hear its engines and feel its wake. Shortly thereafter, just out of Stacy's sight, the freighter collided with another small fishing vessel, causing the death of that ship's captain. Stacy sued the owner and operator of the freighter for negligent infliction of emotional distress. The trial court dismissed.

Held, reversed and remanded. Under applicable maritime law, "a tort is committed by a defendant subjecting a plaintiff to emotional harm within 'the zone of danger' created by the conduct of the defendant." The zone of danger test allows recovery for those plaintiffs who . . . are placed in "immediate risk of physical harm" by defendant's negligence conduct. As a law review author put it, "those within the zone of danger of physical impact can recover for fright, and those outside of it cannot." Stacy alleged that he was within the zone of danger and that he suffered emotional distress from the fright caused by the negligent action of the defendants. Nothing more was required to assert a cause of action.

MITCHELL V. ROCHESTER RAILWAY CO., 45 N.E. 354 (N.Y. 1896). In the spring of 1891, in Rochester, New York, the plaintiff was in the street about to board a street railway car when the defendant drove a team of horses at her. By the time the horses were stopped, the plaintiff found herself standing between the team, although never touched by them. The plaintiff suffered shock and a miscarriage as a result. The New York Court of Appeals held (1) there could be no recovery for fright alone and (2) as a corollary there could be no recovery for consequences of fright, even physical consequences like the miscarriage. Without a "physical injury," the negligence of the defendant would not be a proximate cause.

NOTES

1. **Recovery for direct stand-alone emotional harm.** The *Stacy* and *Mitchell* cases illustrate the distance the common law has travelled over the last century in permitting recovery for the defendant's negligent conduct that directly inflicts emotional harm on the plaintiff. Although *Mitchell* rejected plaintiff's claim, many courts, as in *Stacy*, would now permit a cause of action on the facts of *Mitchell*. The Third Restatement would also recognize a cause of action on facts like those in *Mitchell*. Under the Restatement: "An actor whose negligent conduct causes serious emotional harm to another is subject to liability to the other if the conduct: places the other in danger of immediate bodily harm and the emotional harm results from the danger." RESTATEMENT (THIRD) OF TORTS: LIABILITY FOR PHYSICAL AND EMOTIONAL HARM § 47 (2012). A small number of courts still do not recognize the tort. *See Dowty v. Riggs*, 385 S.W.3d 117 (Ark. 2010) (on the ground that mental distress without a preceding physical injury is "too remote, uncertain and difficult of

ascertainment"). And, as discussed in the note on development of a stand-alone claim below, some courts add restrictions to the Restatement limits.

2. **Stand-alone harm vs. parasitic damages.** Stand-alone emotional harm is to be distinguished from cases in which a plaintiff suffers both physical and emotional harm. Even under the traditional rule, if the defendant negligently causes physical injury to the plaintiff, the plaintiff can recover all damages that result, including damages for pain, suffering, and emotional harm. *See, e.g., Hagen Ins., Inc. v. Roller*, 139 P.3d 1216 (Alaska 2006) (distinguishing parasitic or "derivative" damages from stand-alone emotional harm claim). So if horses had actually run into Mitchell, causing some small physical harm, even under the older legal rules, she would ordinarily recover not only for that harm but for any immediately ensuing emotional harm as well.

3. **The fright or shock pattern.** Notice that *Stacy* and *Mitchell* involve a very definite pattern: (a) the defendant's negligent acts put the plaintiff at immediate risk of a personal injury at a very definite time and place and (b) the plaintiff's reaction to that risk was fright and shock.

4. **The zone of danger test.** The zone of danger test usually requires the plaintiff to prove that he was immediately threatened with physical injury, as the *Stacy* court says. The damages in negligent infliction of emotional distress cases are for the severe emotional distress suffered as a result of that situation. *See, e.g., Hedgepeth v. Whitman Walker Clinic*, 22 A.3d 789 (D.C. 2011) (recovery allowed for serious and verifiable mental distress "if the defendant's actions caused the plaintiff to be in danger of physical injury and if, as a result, the plaintiff feared for his own safety"); *Grube v. Union Pac. R.R.*, 886 P.2d 845 (Kan. 1994) (FELA case under federal law; the "essential elements for recovery under the zone of danger test are that plaintiff be within the zone of danger and suffer imminent apprehension of physical harm which causes or contributes to the emotional injury").

NOTE: DEVELOPMENT OF A STAND-ALONE CLAIM

1. *Impact.* The first step away from *Mitchell* and towards allowing a stand-alone negligent infliction claim was a small one. Courts began to drop the requirement of a preceding physical injury and substituting a requirement of "physical impact," even if it caused no physical injury at all. (Notice that *Mitchell* also required an "impact.") Most states have abandoned the impact rule. In *Battalla v. State,* 176 N.E.2d 729 (N.Y. 1961), the New York Court of Appeals overruled *Mitchell* entirely, observing that although some claims might be fraudulent, that would also be the case if the plaintiff could claim emotional harm after showing a slight impact. Some speculative claims might be brought, the court said,

but the solution to that is to deny those claims and not to exclude the entire class.

A handful of states retain the impact requirement today, with variations. *See, e.g., Atlantic Coast Airlines v. Cook*, 857 N.E.2d 989 (Ind. 2006); *Lee v. State Farm Mut. Ins. Co.*, 533 S.E.2d 82 (Ga. 2000).

2.   *Physical manifestation of objective symptoms or medically diagnosable emotional disorder.* Other states adopted a different condition: The plaintiff can recover only if she produces evidence of some objective physical manifestation of the shock or fright occurring after the events in question. This approach, too, retains some currency today. *See Berian v. Berberian*, 483 P.3d 937 (Idaho 2020); *Brueckner v. Norwich Univ.*, 730 A.2d 1086 (Vt. 1999). However, many states have abolished this requirement altogether. *See, e.g., Molien v. Kaiser Foundation Hospitals*, 616 P.2d 813 (Cal. 1980) (reasoning that the genuineness of emotional injury can be found in the facts of each case without such a rule). Other states have abolished the requirement in particular situations, *see Clark v. Estate of Rice*, 653 N.W.2d 166 (Iowa 2002), or when facts provide some special guarantee that the harm is genuine. *Doe Parents No. 1 v. State, Dep't of Educ.*, 58 P.3d 545 (Haw. 2002); *Johnson v. State,* 334 N.E.2d 590 (N.Y. 1975).

Some courts have modified or diluted this requirement rather than rejecting it completely. A number have said that the emotional injury must be medically diagnosable as an emotional disorder, but not necessarily reflected in observable physical manifestations. *Paz v. Brush Engineered Materials, Inc.*, 949 So.2d 1 (Miss. 2007); *Hamilton v. Nestor*, 659 N.W.2d 321 (Neb. 2003). *See also Sullivan v. Boston Gas Co.*, 605 N.E.2d 805 (Mass. 1993) (requiring "objective corroboration of the emotional distress alleged").

3.   *Zone of danger.* Other states developed a different rule that allows recovery only where the defendant's negligence placed the plaintiff in danger of physical injury, and because of that danger the plaintiff suffered emotional harm. *See, e.g., AALAR, Ltd. v. Francis*, 716 So.2d 1141 (Ala. 1998). In NIED cases brought under federal maritime law, there must be proof that the plaintiff was in the zone of danger; those cases often involve "plaintiffs on board vessels that experience near misses." *Sawyer Brothers, Inc. v. Island Transporter, LLC*, 887 F.3d 23 (1st Cir. 2018). The zone of danger rule reappears in the *Catron* case below.

4.   *Combinations.* States may combine the rules described above (and others) in myriad ways. *See, e.g., Willis v. Gami Golden Glades, LLC*, 967 So.2d 846 (Fla. 2007) (plaintiff may recover either by showing impact or by proving that emotional distress is manifested in physical injury); *Catron v. Lewis*, 712 N.W.2d 245 (Neb. 2006) (plaintiff who fails to show impact or physical injury must be in zone of danger); *Atlantic Coast Airlines v. Cook,*

857 N.E.2d 989 (Ind. 2006) (plaintiff must show impact, and if the impact is "slight," must also show that the emotional distress is not "speculative, exaggerated, fictitious, or unforeseeable"); *Perrotti v. Gonicberg*, 877 A.2d 631 (R.I. 2005) (plaintiff must be in zone of danger, and must also suffer emotional harm "accompanied by physical symptomatology"); *Siegel v. Ridgewells, Inc.*, 511 F.Supp.2d 188 (D.D.C. 2007) (plaintiff must suffer impact or be within zone of danger, and must prove "verifiable" emotional distress) (D.C. law). There is much state variation in this area of law.

5. *Examples.* What result in the following cases, if you are in an "impact" state, a "physical manifestations" state, a "zone of danger" state, or a state that chooses to adopt the new Restatement rule?

(a) Defendant negligently performed surgery upon the plaintiff in such a way that the plaintiff lost the use or her right hand. She suffers periodic depression and a deep sense of loss, especially on bowling nights, but has no physical symptoms of the depression.

(b) Defendant, angry with a domestic partner, fired a pistol at random in an upscale restaurant. No one was hit, but one shot narrowly missed the plaintiff, breaking the back of his chair. The plaintiff was not touched and suffered no physical injury but wakes up with nightmares every night and has been unable to complete his college courses.

(c) Defendant negligently drove his car into the plaintiff's car, scratching the car but not physically touching or harming the plaintiff. Shortly thereafter, the plaintiff broke out in sweats and rashes, then fainted, all provably a result of the fright or shock.

B. EMOTIONAL DISTRESS RESULTING FROM INJURY TO ANOTHER

CATRON V. LEWIS
712 N.W.2d 245 (Neb. 2006)

McCORMACK, J.

[On July 5, 2002, Gaylen L. Catron took his boat out on Center Lake at a state recreation area, pulling two tubes ridden by two of his daughter's friends, Samantha Rader and Aimee Stuart. The towropes which attached the tubes that Rader and Stuart were riding to Catron's boat were approximately 61 feet long. After going around the lake twice, Catron decided to head for shore. Catron stated that as he was traveling straight east toward the shore, he noticed two jet skis heading north toward the right side of his boat. One of the jet skis was being ridden by 14-year-old Skylar Panek. The jet ski was owned by Marvin Lewis.]

Catron estimated that when he first saw them, the jet skis were 75 yards away going approximately 35 to 40 miles per hour. Catron then looked back behind his boat to confirm that the tubes were traveling straight behind his boat. Stuart confirmed in her deposition testimony that right before the accident, the ropes pulling the tubes were taut and that the tubes were traveling directly behind the boat, inside the wake.

In his deposition, Catron indicated that he feared for his safety "[j]ust when [the jet skis were] aiming at my boat." He subsequently explained during a psychiatric examination that he was not really afraid that the jet skis were going to hit his boat; he just did not know for sure what they were going to do. He was able to make eye contact with Panek and the other boy riding the jet skis before they turned, and he assumed they would either shut down or turn to avoid hitting his boat. Catron did not make any evasive maneuvers. When the jet skis turned, Catron became afraid they were going to hit the tubes Rader and Stuart were on.

Panek did in fact run into Rader, killing her. [Panek and Catron both testified that the accident occurred at least 61 feet from the rear of Catron's boat.] Catron testified that he saw Panek's jet ski hit the tube Rader was on and then saw Rader lying face down in the water "in a pool of blood." Catron jumped in, swam over to her, and floated her back to the boat. Rader was nonresponsive. With assistance, Catron was able to get Rader to shore.

[After the accident, a psychiatrist diagnosed Catron with major depression and anxiety disorder, and Catron was unable to work for three months. He was eventually diagnosed with post-traumatic stress disorder and continues to take antidepressants. He sued Panek, Lewis and the State.]

Catron's action sought damages for emotional distress stemming from his witnessing the accident and his unsuccessful attempt to rescue Rader. Catron alleged that such distress was a proximate result of the negligent acts or omission of the defendants, specifically, the negligent operation of the jet ski by the then 14-year-old Panek, the negligent entrustment of the jet ski to Panek by Lewis, and the failure of the State to operate the Bridgeport State Recreation Area in a manner reasonably safe for foreseeable users under foreseeable conditions.

The district court granted summary judgment in favor of the defendants, and Catron appeals. . . .

In Nebraska, where there is no impact or physical injury to the plaintiff, the plaintiff seeking to bring an action for negligent infliction of emotional distress must show either (1) that he or she is a reasonably foreseeable "bystander" victim based upon an intimate familial relationship with a seriously injured victim of the defendant's negligence or (2) that the plaintiff was a "direct victim" of the defendant's negligence because the plaintiff was within the zone of danger of the negligence in question." . . .

The zone of danger has been described as a complement to the basic requirement that persons exercise reasonable care to protect others from injury. "Those who breach their basic duty of care to others will be required to compensate those who are injured, even when the injuries are not caused by direct impact, but by the operation of foreseeable emotional distress." Hansen v. Sea Ray Boats, Inc., 830 P.2d 236 (Utah 1992). Persons in the zone of danger are clearly foreseeable plaintiffs to the negligent actor insofar as they have been placed at unreasonable risk of immediate bodily harm by the actor's negligence. The fact that the harm results solely through emotional distress should not protect the actor from liability for such conduct. . . .

Here, it is clear that Catron was not immediately threatened with physical injury as a result of the alleged negligence which resulted in Rader's death. While Catron described the jet skis at one point as coming directly toward him at a rapid speed, Catron admitted he was not in immediate danger. Rather, at that point, the jet skis were approximately 75 yards away, and Catron assumed the jet skis would either stop or turn in order to avoid a collision with the boat. This is what apparently happened, resulting in the collision with Rader, who was riding in the tube some 61 feet away from the rear of Catron's boat. . . .

NOTE

Direct victim or bystander? The *Catron* court notes that in Nebraska, plaintiffs can recover either under a "direct victim" rule or a "bystander" rule. Why isn't the father in *Catron* considered a direct victim and able to recover under the zone of danger test? Why can't the father recover as a bystander either?

DILLON V. LEGG, 441 P.2d 912 (Cal. 1968). A mother and infant sister saw a vehicle strike Erin Lee Dillon, a young child, as she crossed the road, causing her death. The mother and sister sued the driver for negligent infliction of emotional distress. The trial court granted defendant's motion for judgment on the mother's claim because she was not in the zone of danger, but denied the motion as it pertained to the sister, because she might have been. *Held*, reversed. "The instant case exposes the hopeless artificiality of the zone-of-danger rule. . . . [T]o rest upon the zone-of-danger rule when we have rejected the impact rule becomes even less defensible." The only reason for the zone-of-danger rule "lies in the fact that one within it will feel the danger of impact." While dropping this requirement may invite some fraudulent claims, this does not "justify a wholesale rejection of the entire class of claims." A defendant might owe a duty to protect not only the injured person but those who might foreseeably suffer emotional harm because of the injury.

Courts should henceforth take into account three factors in determining foreseeability: "(1) Whether plaintiff was located near the scene of the accident as contrasted with one who was a distance away from it. (2) Whether the shock resulted from a direct emotional impact upon the plaintiff from the sensory and contemporaneous observance of the accident, as contrasted with learning of the accident from others after its occurrence. (3) Whether plaintiff and the victim were "closely related." In this case, "the presence of all the above factors indicates that plaintiff has alleged a sufficient prima facie case."

NOTES

1. **Original denial of "bystander" claims.** *Dillon is* the classic case of emotional harm resulting from injury to another. A mother watches in horror as a car strikes her child. The mother's fear and shock is much like the fear and shock in *Mitchell*, but it is fear for her child rather than for herself. Courts originally denied these claims altogether.

2. **Bystander recoveries.** Today, most states allow plaintiffs who are not in the zone of danger to recover damages for the emotional distress of seeing another person injured or killed by a negligent defendant. These states have typically followed either the *Dillon* "factors" approach, or the more rigid "elements" approach of a later California case, *Thing v. LaChusa*, 771 P.2d 814 (Cal. 1989). The *Thing* court criticized the *Dillon* case-by-case approach, saying it "has not only produced inconsistent rulings in the lower courts, but has provoked considerable critical comment by scholars who attempt to reconcile the cases." It replaced the *Dillon* factors with three required elements: the plaintiff *must* be "(1) closely related to the injury victim; (2) present at the scene of the injury producing event at the time it occurs and is then aware that it is causing injury to the victim; and (3) as a result suffers serious emotional distress." The Restatement Third now states the bystander rule this way: A person who negligently causes "serious bodily injury" to a victim is liable for "serious emotional harm caused thereby to a person who: (a) perceives the event contemporaneously, and (b) is a close family member of the person suffering the bodily injury." RESTATEMENT (THIRD) OF TORTS: LIABILITY FOR PHYSICAL AND EMOTIONAL HARM § 48 (2012). Not all courts allow bystander recoveries and a court that retains the impact rule might bar the mother's claim. *See Lee v. State Farm Mut. Ins. Co.,* 533 S.E.2d 82 (Ga. 2000) (no recovery unless mother is herself impacted at the same time). In a state that discards special rules for "direct" victims, are there still reasons to retain special rules for bystanders?

3. **Sensory perception.** Proof of the plaintiff's sensory perception of some sudden, injury-producing event when it happens or at least shortly thereafter is often crucial to a recovery. New York courts have said that a person must either see the incident or be immediately aware of the incident at

the time it occurred. *Coleson v. City of New York*, 24 N.E.3d 1074 (N.Y. 2014) (a boy saw his father with a knife and hid in a broom closet as his father attacked his mother; he heard her screams; "the child was not in the zone of danger because he was in a broom closet while his mother was stabbed, and thus neither saw the incident nor was immediately aware of the incident at the time it occurred"). What is it that a plaintiff has to perceive—that the victim is injured, or that the defendant's negligence caused it? *See Doan v. Banner Health, Inc.*, 442 P.3d 706 (Alaska 2019) ("The test contains no requirement that the plaintiff contemporaneously comprehend that the loved one's injuries were negligently caused.").

4. **"Virtual" contemporaneous awareness.** What if the plaintiff is not physically present at the scene of a family member's injury, but sees it live on a video camera? Does that satisfy the "contemporaneous sensory perception" requirement for bystander NIED recovery? In *Ko v. Maxim Healthcare Services, Inc.*, 58 Cal.App.5th 1144 (2021), parents were attending a sporting event miles from home and observed in real time a caregiver violently hitting, slapping, pinching and shaking their two-year-old child when they accessed an app on their cell phone that allowed them to watch a livestream video recorded on a "nanny cam." The trial court dismissed the NIED claim on the authority of *Thing v. LaChusa, supra* Note 2, because the parents were not "present at the injury-producing event." The appeals court reversed and remanded, holding that "virtual presence without physical presence" satisfied the *Thing* standard. The court noted that "[i]n various areas of the law affecting traditional conceptions of physical presence, the courts have been called upon to interpret longstanding precedent in light of new technologies."

5. **Delayed perception.** The clear case for recovery is one in which the plaintiff actually sees a serious bodily injury to a family member as it occurs. A parent who does not see the event itself but only sees the injured child later, in the hospital, is likely to be denied recovery. *Roitz v. Kidman*, 913 P.2d 431 (Wyo. 1996). What about all the times in between? Isn't it true, as the court said in *Gates v. Richardson*, 719 P.2d 193 (Wyo. 1986), that "the immediate aftermath may be more shocking than the actual impact"? So imagine that a family member arrives at the scene of the injury immediately afterwards. That would not suffice under a rigid application of the rules. *See, e.g., Entergy Miss., Inc. v. Acey*, 153 So.3d 670 (Miss. 2014) (mother who learned that her daughter had been seriously injured from a 911 dispatcher, drove to the accident scene, and saw her daughter, who had been severely burned by electrocution, failed to meet the requirement that she must have contemporaneously observed the accident); *Ra v. Superior Court*, 64 Cal.Rptr.3d 539 (Ct. App. 2007) (woman heard loud noise and turned around to see husband holding his head; not "contemporaneous awareness" of his injury). Some courts, however, allow recovery where the plaintiff arrived at the scene of injury shortly thereafter, before there is a material change in the situation. *See Eskin v. Bartee*, 262 S.W.3d 727 (Tenn. 2008) (allowing claim by mother who saw her young child "lying in a pool of blood in his school's driveway minutes after he had been

struck by an automobile"); *Smith v. Toney*, 862 N.E.2d 656 (Ind. 2007); *Colbert v. Moomba Sports, Inc.*, 176 P.3d 497 (Wash. 2008).

6. **Close relationship.** Whether courts use the rules as guidelines or as elements, they usually insist upon a close relationship—usually a close family relationship, in accord with the Restatement Third—between the plaintiff and the injured person. *See, e.g., Greene v. Esplanade Venture Partnership*, 168 N.E.3d 827 (N.Y. 2021) (holding that grandchild is in the "immediate family" of a grandparent for purposes of a bystander NIED claim, since such relationships enjoy a "special status"). Should a fiancée who witnesses fatal injury to her partner be allowed to recover? *Grotts v. Zahner*, 989 P.2d 415 (Nev. 1999) (no); *Graves v. Estabrook*, 818 A.2d 1255 (N.H. 2003) (yes; unmarried cohabitants who have a "relationship that is stable, enduring, substantial, and mutually supportive . . . cemented by strong emotional bonds and provid[ing] a deep and pervasive emotional security" are "closely related" for this purpose). Is it problematic to make a right to recover turn on the particular "subjective emotional connection of the parties" as the *Graves* dissenters charged? *See also Smith v. Toney*, 862 N.E.2d 656 (Ind. 2007) (discussing problems with not having a bright-line rule). Or does the case-by-case approach better reflect the importance of the specific relationship? *See St. Onge v. MacDonald*, 917 A.2d 233 (N.H. 2007) (noting that the determination had to be made on a case-by-case basis, affirming judgment that a non-cohabitating girlfriend of six months was not in a close relationship with plaintiff). What about using a test like the one the California Supreme Court used in a take-home asbestos case which allowed for recovery of household members rather than family members? *Kesner v. Superior Court*, 384 P.3d 283 (Cal. 2016) ("Being a household member refers not only to the relationships among members of a family, but also to the bonds which may be found among unrelated persons adopting nontraditional and quasi-familial living arrangements.").

7. **Beyond the family?** What about a "bystander" who is really a participant in the events, say a co-worker who attempts to rescue the primary victim but is forced to watch his horrible death instead? In *Michaud v. Great Northern Nekoosa Corp.*, 715 A.2d 955 (Me. 1998), the plaintiff, a diver, attempted to rescue another diver whose leg was trapped deep underwater and who watched as surface chains pulled him up, tearing his body apart. Similarly, in *Hislop v. Salt River Project Agric. Improvement & Power Dist.*, 5 P.3d 267 (Ariz. Ct. App. 2000), the primary victim was burned alive allegedly as a result of the defendant's negligence; the plaintiff pulled the burning man from the trench where he was engulfed with flames. And in *State ex rel. Maxxim Shared Services, LLC v. McGraw*, 835 S.E.2d 590 (W.Va. 2019), the plaintiff was working alongside a co-worker when a methane explosion killed the co-worker. All three courts denied recovery. However, English law may be more generous. *See* M.H. Matthews, *Negligent Infliction of Emotional Distress: A View of the Proposed Restatement (Third) Provisions from England*, 44 WAKE FOREST L. REV. 1177 (2009) (describing the case of *Dooley v. Cammell Laird & Co.*, in which the claimant was operating a crane when a piece of rope snapped

and the load being carried fell into the hold of a ship where people were working; the claimant recovered damages for "nervous shock" that was suffered as a result of fear for the safety of his fellow workmen, whom he could not actually see from his position on the crane).

8. **A bystander who unwittingly causes the harm.** What about a plaintiff who, because of the defendant's negligence, becomes the unwilling trigger of harm to another? In *Kallstrom v. United States,* 43 P.3d 162 (Alaska 2002), the defendant negligently placed a pitcher that appeared to be fruit juice on a kitchen counter; the pitcher actually contained caustic lye. The plaintiff poured a glass for a child, who suffered horrible injuries. The court rejected the plaintiff's claim for emotional harm. Is that approach correct, or is such a person truly a "bystander" at all? *See Miles v. Burcham*, 127 So.3d 213 (Miss. 2013) (when a plaintiff is a participant in the accident, his emotional distress claims are analyzed like any other damage claims, not under special bystander rules; affirming verdict for truck driver who suffered minor back injuries and major emotional distress following an accident in which his vehicle killed someone); *Ridings v. Maze*, 414 P.3d 835 (Okla. 2018) (same; a plaintiff "who was involved in the same accident that gave rise to their emotional suffering" is considered a "direct victim"). Does it make sense to apply ordinary negligence rules, as opposed to special bystander rules, to such cases? England apparently allows recovery in a case like *Kallstrom*.

9. **When the victim is the tortfeasor.** What if the plaintiff sees a family member injured in a car accident that was caused by the same family member? Can such a plaintiff recover for NIED? The court in *Schack v. Schack*, 414 P.3d 639 (Alaska 2018), said no, citing the Third Restatement, which formulates its bystander test as applying when "an actor negligently causes sudden serious bodily injury to a third person." Why would this be a limitation on recovery?

10. **Combining the rules.** States that have adopted special "bystander rules" apply them only to bystanders, of course—only to those claiming to have suffered emotional distress from witnessing an injury to someone else. That means that if the plaintiff is not a "bystander" at all—what some states would call a "direct victim"—a separate set of rules (as seen above in Part A of this Section) would apply. *See, e.g., Jarrett v. Jones*, 258 S.W.3d 442 (Mo. 2008) (bystander limitations not applicable to truck driver who was direct victim of car driver's negligence). Which "separate rules" apply depend, of course, on the state. *See, e.g., Helsel v. Hoosier Ins. Co.*, 827 N.E.2d 155 (Ind. Ct. App. 2005) (impact rule applies to direct victims, special bystander rules to bystanders); *Jablonowska v. Suther*, 948 A.2d 610 (N.J. 2008) (zone of danger rule applies to direct victims, special bystander rules to bystanders). The possible variations, while not endless, are certainly large.

BOUCHER v. DIXIE MEDICAL CENTER
850 P.2d 1179 (Utah 1992)

HALL, CHIEF JUSTICE. . . .

Daniel Boucher, the eighteen-year-old son of James and Torla Boucher, was admitted into Dixie Medical Center with a severely injured right hand. He underwent surgery and lapsed into a coma during the post-operative recovery period. He remained in a coma for ten days before awakening as a severely brain-damaged quadriplegic who will need extensive care for the rest of his life. The Bouchers were present at the hospital and observed their son's condition both before and after he awoke from the coma.

[The Boucher parents claimed damages for (1) negligent infliction of emotional distress and (2) loss of their child's consortium or society, in addition to the claim of Daniel Boucher himself. The trial court dismissed the complaint.]

[The parents' claim for negligent infliction of emotional distress fails because they were not in the zone of danger.] The Bouchers' second claim presents an issue of first impression in this court: Should Utah judicially adopt a cause of action that allows the parents of a tortiously injured adult child to recover for loss of the child's consortium?

Loss of consortium claims are based on the recognition of a legally protected interest in personal relationships. Accordingly, if one member of the relationship is tortiously injured the noninjured party has a cause of action to recover for damage to their relational interest, i.e., the loss of the injured party's " 'company, society, co-operation, [and] affection.' " In the instant case, we are asked to recognize a right of recovery based on the relationship between parents and their adult son. For the reasons set forth below, we decline to adopt such an approach.

A review of the case law reveals little support for the adoption of a cause of action for the loss of filial consortium. At common law, the father of a tortiously injured child did have a cause of action to recover the value of the child's loss of services and the medical expenses incurred on the child's behalf. However, this action was based on a father's right to his minor children's services and a father's obligation to pay his minor children's medical expenses. This right of recovery, therefore, did not extend beyond these two elements of damages, nor did it extend to injuries involving adult or emancipated children.

These common law principles have undergone some modification. However, no widely accepted development has occurred that allows recovery in cases involving adult children, nor has any widely accepted development occurred that allows recovery for the loss of a child's society and affection.

Indeed, the majority of jurisdictions that have addressed the issue have declined to recognize a cause of action for loss of filial consortium. . . . Furthermore, our research reveals only one jurisdiction that has expressly recognized the specific right the Bouchers urge this court to adopt: a judicially created right to recover for the loss of an adult child's consortium.

[Utah's Married Woman's Act has been construed to abolish the claim of spousal consortium.] [A]llowing recovery for the loss of an adult child's consortium and denying recovery for the loss of a spouse's consortium would lead to anomalous results. In many instances, the marital relationship is closer and more involved than the relationship between parents and their adult children and therefore should be granted greater or equal protection. However, . . . we cannot recognize a filial consortium claim and extend the same right of recovery to a plaintiff who suffers a loss of consortium because his or her spouse has been tortiously injured. The adoption of the Bouchers' claim, therefore, would invite inequitable applications of the consortium doctrine. . . .

[C]onsortium claims have the potential for greatly expanding the liability that can flow from one negligent act, and courts that have adopted consortium claims have been unable to develop rational limits on this liability. . . . [T]he recognition of consortium claims may [also impact] the cost and availability of insurance. Finally, given these concerns and the fact that the legislature has previously acted in this area, . . . the legislature is the appropriate body to determine if Utah should recognize consortium claims. . . .

Furthermore, we do not find the Bouchers' arguments persuasive. They claim that because they have reorganized their lives in order to undertake the care of their son, they should be able to recover personally from the parties responsible for their son's condition. However, the expense incurred for Daniel Boucher's nursing care is recoverable as part of the damages in Daniel Bouchers' own suit. Even the jurisdictions that allow recovery for loss of consortium would not allow the Bouchers to recover for the nursing care they have provided, because to do so would be to allow a double recovery. . . .

We decline to adopt a cause of action that allows the parents of a tortiously injured adult child to recover for the loss of consortium. The trial court, therefore, did not err in dismissing the Bouchers' claims of negligent infliction of emotional distress and loss of filial consortium.

Affirmed.

[Concurring and dissenting opinion omitted.]

NOTES

1. **Origins of the loss of consortium claim.** The loss of consortium claim is quite different from the emotional harm claim in its origin. In the earlier common law, the master of an apprentice had a claim against the tortfeasor when the apprentice was injured, since the master would lose the services of the apprentice and might still be bound to provide him with food and housing. The claim had a firm economic basis in such cases. By the 17th century, the idea was carried over to permit a husband to recover from the tortfeasor when the wife was injured, on analogy, then all too true, to the master-servant relationship. Originally the claim was for loss of services, but it gradually expanded to take in non-economic losses such as loss of society and sexual relations.

2. **Scope of consortium.** "The concept of consortium includes not only loss of support or services, it also embraces such elements as love, companionship, affection, society, sexual relations, solace and more." *Millington v. Southeastern Elevator Co.,* 239 N.E.2d 897 (N.Y. 1968). After 1950, courts began to permit the wife to recover for loss of consortium when the husband was injured, thus putting the marital partners on an equal footing in this respect. In doing so, they often emphasized the non-financial side of the claim.

3. **Bystander emotional distress claims compared.** Emphasis on the intangible losses inflicted upon one person when another person is injured brings up the latent comparison to the bystander mental distress claim. Is the claim not one for a species of mental distress or emotional losses? The difference may lie in judicial attitudes. In the emotional distress claim, courts traditionally emphasized an acute moment—shock or fright. With the consortium claim, they recognize legal harm in a chronic, ongoing sense of loss. If emotional distress is the emotional equivalent of a stab wound, then loss of consortium is the emotional equivalent of carrying a large pack all day or living all your life in a cramped room. But both involve intangible and real losses in quality of life.

4. **Spousal consortium claims.** When one spouse is injured in a way that tends to diminish the ability of the partners to take pleasure in each other's company—in conversation, sports, travel, sexual relations, or any other pleasures of life—the other spouse has a loss of consortium claim. "[P]rior to the accident, the Alexanders spent most of their time together, enjoying walking, gardening, and fishing." As a result of injury to one spouse, "they no longer engage in their outdoor activities, and instead spend much of their time watching television." That was evidence of lost consortium. *Wal-Mart Stores, Inc. v. Alexander,* 868 S.W.2d 322 (Tex. 1993). Courts have split on whether a plaintiff must have been married to the spouse at the time of the alleged negligent conduct in order to bring a loss of consortium claim. *Compare Mueller v. Tepler*, 95 A.3d 1011 (Conn. 2014) (no, same-sex domestic partner) *with Conner v. Hodges*, 333 P.3d 130 (Idaho 2014) (yes; patient's husband could not assert a claim because he was not married to his wife yet).

5. **Derivative nature of spousal consortium claims.** Consortium claims are traditionally said to derive from the claim of the physically injured spouse. This means that if the predicate injury claim of the loved one is extinguished, then the derivative claim for loss of consortium is also extinguished. *See, e.g., Voris v. Molinaro*, 31 A.3d 363 (Conn. 2011). It also means that a loss of consortium claim can rise no higher than the claim from which it is derived. *E.g., Wine-Settergren v. Lamey,* 716 N.E.2d 381 (Ind. 1999); *see also Ashmore v. Hartford Hosp.*, 208 A.3d 256 (Conn. 2019) (damages for loss of consortium ordinarily cannot exceed the damages awarded to the directly injured spouse). For example, the contributory negligence of the injured spouse will bar or reduce the consortium claim just as it will bar or reduce the injured spouse's claim.

6. **A child's claim for loss of parental consortium.** In 1980, Massachusetts permitted a claim by a child for loss of parental consortium following a serious injury to a father. *Ferriter v. Daniel O'Connell's Sons, Inc.,* 413 N.E.2d 690 (Mass. 1980) (later modified by statute). A good number of other courts have accepted the idea. *E.g., United States v. Dempsey,* 635 So.2d 961 (Fla. 1994). Most recently, the court in Campos v. Coleman, 123 A.3d 854 (Conn. 2015), reversed prior precedent to recognize such a claim brought on behalf of minor children, finding that the "vast majority" of states now recognize a minor child's cause of action for loss of parental consortium where the parent is either injured or killed. Some states also allow a claim to be brought by adult children. *See Rolf v. Tri State Motor Transit Co.,* 745 N.E.2d 424 (Ohio 2001) (court upheld a claim in favor of adult children living apart from a father whose cognitive and basic bodily functions were seriously impaired); *North Pac. Ins. Co. v. Stucky*, 338 P.3d 56 (Mont. 2014) (allowing an adult child's claim but limiting it to those situations where the parent's injury was so serious, permanent, and severe that it has caused the parent-child relationship to be "destroyed or nearly destroyed"). A number of other cases, however, continue to reject any such extension of liability. *E.g., Harrington v. Brooks Drugs, Inc.*, 808 A.2d 532 (N.H. 2002).

7. **Basis of the general rule for loss of parental consortium.** Grounds for denying a child's recovery for loss of parental consortium have included the points made in *Boucher*. It has also been argued that if children can recover such losses, then there is no principled basis for excluding recovery by siblings, grandparents, and others. In addition, some judges have professed great deference to the legislative branch on this claim. They have also said that damages could readily be magnified by the number of children in a family, with resulting high costs in liability insurance, and that the return for the increased insurance costs would be quite low since a child might become rich on the award, but would remain nonetheless a child deprived of parental guidance.

8. **The parents' claim for loss of a child's society and companionship.** Earlier common law gave the father a claim for loss of a child's services under some circumstances, but this was usually a reflection of the fact that the father was entitled to a child's earnings and to actual work around the house. Otherwise, parents of an injured child have not generally

been allowed a recovery for intangible harm such as loss of society or companionship. *E.g., Vitro v. Mihelcic*, 806 N.E.2d 632 (Ill. 2004). *Roberts v. Williamson*, 111 S.W.3d 113 (Tex. 2003). A few courts, however, have allowed the parents' claim. In most of these, the child was severely injured or comatose and some of the courts emphasized that the injury was total and permanent, or even that it was closely similar to death. *E.g., United States v. Dempsey,* 635 So.2d 961 (Fla. 1994). There are a few statutes on point as well.

9. **Injuries to companion animals.** Might a pet owner have a claim for negligent infliction of emotional distress, or loss of consortium, against a defendant who negligently injures or kills the pet? Courts have been reluctant to allow such claims, on a variety of bases. *See, e.g., Strickland v. Medlen*, 397 S.W.3d 184 (Tenn. 2013) (dog owners cannot state claim for emotional, non-economic damages in case where shelter employee negligently euthanized their dog); *McDougall v. Lamm*, 48 A.3d 312 (N.J. 2012) (reviewing many other cases, citing difficulties in line drawing and the possibility of inconsistent results); *Goodby v. Vetpharm, Inc.*, 974 A.2d 1269 (Vt. 2009) (pet owners could not recover for wrongful death of pet, and could not recover for negligent infliction of emotional distress because they were not in the zone of danger); *Kaufman v. Langhofer*, 222 P.3d 272 (Ariz. Ct. App. 2009) (animals are personal property, thus no loss of consortium claim, which is limited to spouses, parents and children; no recovery for emotional distress claim because plaintiff was not in the zone of danger); *Facler v. Genetzky*, 595 N.W.2d 884 (Neb. 1999) (because animals are personal property, "damages for mental suffering or emotional distress may not be recovered" if the animal is negligently killed). What about the argument that a veterinarian has undertaken an obligation that creates a likely risk that negligent performance of that obligation will cause the plaintiff serious emotional distress? *See McMahon v. Craig*, 97 Cal. Rptr. 3d 555 (Ct. App. 2009) (rejecting such an argument).

C. DUTIES OF CARE TO PROTECT EMOTIONAL WELL-BEING INDEPENDENT OF PHYSICAL RISKS

BURGESS V. SUPERIOR COURT, 831 P.2d 1197 (Cal. 1992). The plaintiff, Julia Burgess, was given prenatal care by her obstetrician, Gupta, who also delivered her child, Joseph. During Burgess' labor, Gupta diagnosed a prolapsed cord, which meant that the child would receive insufficient oxygen. Burgess was aware of this and of the urgent comings and goings thereafter. She knew when she was sedated for the cesarean that followed that something was wrong with the child. By the time the child was taken by cesarean, he had been deprived of oxygen for a lengthy period. He suffered permanent brain damage. Joseph brought suit against Gupta and the hospital. Julia asserted a separate claim for her own emotional distress. *Held*, the *Dillon* rule does not apply. California recognizes two classes of emotional harm cases: In the first, the plaintiff is a bystander; in the second, the plaintiff is a "direct victim." A plaintiff who was in some kind of preexisting relationship with the defendant is a "direct victim," and the bystander rules are inapplicable to such a plaintiff. A "direct victim's" case is based on a breach of duty "assumed by the defendant or imposed on the defendant as a matter of law, or that arises out of a relationship between the two." Liability in this class of cases is not unlimited; it is limited by the relationship established by the parties themselves. Both parties here understood that the physician owes a duty to the pregnant woman, not merely to the fetus alone. If the mother were treated as a bystander, the physician would have an incentive to sedate her, so that she would not see or hear injury and thus would be defeated by the *Dillon* rule.

NOTES

1. **Duty by undertaking.** The fright and shock cases normally involve strangers, that is, persons who had no particular relationship that might affect duties. Any number of people might be frightened by runaway horses and, if you add the possibility of liability to bystanders, even more. *Burgess* is important because it recognizes that some claims are asserted against a defendant who has at least implicitly undertaken to protect the plaintiff and that such cases might call for quite different rules. *See* Dan B. Dobbs, *Undertakings and Special Relationships in Claims for Negligent Infliction of Emotional Distress*, 50 ARIZ. L. REV. 49 (2008).

2. **The growing impact of *Burgess*.** A number of courts have agreed that a defendant owes a general duty to avoid inflicting emotional distress where the defendant has undertaken some obligation to benefit the plaintiff, and that undertaking by its nature "creates not only a foreseeable, but an especially likely, risk that the defendant's negligent performance of the obligation will cause serious emotional distress." *Hedgepeth v. Whitman Walker Clinic*, 22 A.3d 789 (D.C. 2011) (expressly disapproving an earlier case, *Washington v. John T. Rhines Co.*, 646 A.2d 345 (D.C. 1994), that had barred a negligent infliction claim for the negligent handling of a dead body on the ground that the plaintiff was not in the zone of danger); *see also SCI Texas Funeral Services, Inc. v. Nelson*, 540 S.W.3d 539 (Tex. 2017) (emotional distress damages available for negligent mishandling of father's corpse). There is growing support for the concept that "justification exists to extend NIED liability to a subset of cases involving preexisting relationships . . . involving duties that obviously and objectively hold the potential of deep emotional harm in the event of breach." *Toney v. Chester County Hosp.*, 36 A.3d 83 (Pa. 2011).

3. **The Third Restatement approach.** The Third Restatement provides that a person whose negligent conduct causes "serious emotional harm" to another is liable if (a) the defendant's negligence places plaintiff in "danger of immediate bodily harm and the emotional harm results from the danger," [which we saw in section A] *or* (b) the negligence occurs "in the course of specified categories of activities, undertakings or relationships in which negligent conduct is especially likely to cause serious emotional harm." RESTATEMENT (THIRD) OF TORTS: LIABILITY FOR PHYSICAL AND EMOTIONAL HARM § 47 (2012). Comment f gives some examples of the kinds of activities,

undertakings or relationships that might give rise to liability, including the erroneous delivery of a message that someone has died and the mishandling of dead bodies, while admitting that "courts have not provided clear guidance" in identifying guidelines for such categories.

4.   **Undertakings that increase risk of emotional harm.** Wyoming has recognized a negligent emotional distress claim in a case involving two sisters who were negligently separated at birth by a hospital in 1954. In *Larsen v. Banner Health System*, 81 P.3d 196 (Wyo. 2003), the court said that "in the limited circumstances where a contractual relationship exists for services that carry with them deeply emotional responses in the event of breach," and that breach causes severe emotional distress, an action will lie. *See also Miranda v. Said*, 836 N.W.2d 8 (Iowa 2013) (immigration attorney recommended a course of action so flawed that it barred the clients from reentering the United States for ten years, and separated them from their children for that entire time; "when parties to a transaction should reasonably have contemplated that emotional distress will naturally flow from a breach of the contract, the foreseeable consequential damages the plaintiff could recover should include damages for emotional distress"). Could this rule be a parallel to the rule that actors who undertake services to reduce risks of physical harm might have liability for increasing risks to persons relying on the actors? RESTATEMENT (THIRD) OF TORTS: LIABILITY FOR PHYSICAL AND EMOTIONAL HARM § 46 cmt. m (2012).

5.   **Undertakings that do not create a duty.** In *Guerra v. State*, 348 P.3d 423 (Ariz. 2015), public safety officers erroneously informed a family that their daughter had been killed in a car accident, when in fact she had survived. The question in the Arizona Supreme Court was whether the Department of Public Safety (DPS), by undertaking to provide a next-of-kin notification, assumed a duty of care to the family—at least as to the accuracy of the information conveyed. The majority held that it did not, in part based on policy concerns that such a duty might cause officers to delay or limit providing prompt information to family members. A dissent would have recognized the duty under the Third Restatement's category for duty in the course of undertakings especially likely to cause serious emotional harm. As with other undertakings cases, the scope of the defendant's undertaking determines the scope of its duty. *See, e.g., Destefano v. Children's Nat'l Med. Ctr.*, 121 A.3d 59 (D.C. 2015) (6-year-old patient fell down an air shaft in hospital's parking garage, and mother sued for negligent infliction of emotional distress; rejecting mother's argument that she was in a "special relationship" with the hospital because the hospital was treating her son, the court said "the hospital would have had (at most) a duty to avoid causing [the mother] emotional distress in matters relating to the medical care of her child").

HEINER V. MORETUZZO, 652 N.E.2d 664 (Ohio 1995). Defendants tested the plaintiff for AIDS, but, according to allegations accepted as true, negligently and erroneously reported to the plaintiff that she was infected with that disease. They then did a re-test and erroneously confirmed the diagnosis and recommended a specialist in that disease. In fact the plaintiff later discovered that the diagnosis was wrong. She sued for negligent infliction of distress. *Held,* the plaintiff has no claim. "[T]he claimed negligent diagnosis never placed appellant or any other person in real physical peril, since appellant was, in fact, HIV negative. . . . [W]e hold that Ohio does not recognize a claim for negligent infliction of serious emotional distress where the distress is caused by the plaintiff's fear of a nonexistent physical peril."

NOTES

1. **Extending *Heiner.*** Ohio reaffirmed and extended *Heiner* in *Dobran v. Franciscan Medical Center,* 806 N.E.2d 537 (Ohio 2004). The defendant gathered an irreplaceable tissue sample for a cancer test on the plaintiff and then lost it. The plaintiff feared that his cancer would metastasize, and that this fear was caused by the defendant's negligent act. The court, affirming a defense summary judgment, stressed that the plaintiff never faced an actual physical peril since his cancer has not, in fact, ever metastasized.

2. **An analogy: the mishandling of dead bodies.** When a defendant (often a mortuary) mishandles a dead body, causing severe distress to relatives of the deceased, most modern courts have little trouble allowing recovery for the negligently inflicted emotional distress. As suggested in Note 2 after *Burgess,* this may be a logical application of the rule in that case, that no special rules constrain recovery when the defendant has undertaken an obligation that is likely to cause serious emotional distress to the plaintiff if the obligation is not fulfilled. *See, e.g., Guth v. Freeland,* 28 P.3d 982 (Haw. 2001) ("those who are entrusted with the care and preparation for burial of a decedent's body have a duty to exercise reasonable care"—a duty owed to immediate family members who are aware of, and for whose benefit, the funeral or similar services are being performed); *Christensen v. Superior Court,* 820 P.2d 181 (Cal. 1991) (plaintiffs could recover where defendants, who had contracted to provide dignified burials or cremations, instead harvested various human organs from the remains of deceased persons and sold them; defendants had "assumed a duty to the close relatives . . . for whose benefit they were to provide funeral and/or related services"). Distress in this context has long been actionable. *See Shipley v. City of New York,* 37 N.E.3d 58 (N.Y. 2015) (applying common-law "right of sepulcher," which affords deceased's next-of-kin the right to immediate possession of a decedent's body and allows an award of damages against any person who interferes with that right or improperly deals with the decedent's body). Do those cases, and that reasoning, undercut the result and reasoning in *Heiner?*

3. **Negligent misdiagnosis.** Some courts have upheld a right to recover in misdiagnosis cases. *Baker v. Dorfman,* 239 F.3d 415 (2d Cir. 2000); *Chizmar v. Mackie,* 896 P.2d 196 (Alaska 1995); *Bramer v. Dotson,* 437 S.E.2d 773 (W.Va.1993); *cf. Molien v. Kaiser Found. Hosps.,* 616 P.2d 813 (Cal. 1980)

(wife misdiagnosed as having venereal disease, leading to emotional distress of husband).

4. **Death messages.** One kind of misinformation is treated as special in some courts. This is the message, usually carried by telegraph, erroneously announcing the death of a close relative. One group of cases has long permitted the plaintiff to recover for emotional harm in such cases. *E.g., Johnson v. State,* 334 N.E.2d 590 (N.Y. 1975).

———————

BOYLES V. KERR, 855 S.W.2d 593 (Tex. 1993). Dan Boyles, then 17, secretly videotaped his sexual intercourse with 19-year-old Susan Kerr. The tape also included comments made by Boyles' friends. Boyles then showed the tape on several occasions to various friends. Kerr claimed negligent infliction of emotional distress resulting from the tape, its showing, and the gossip that ensued. *Held,* there is no general duty to avoid negligent infliction of distress. Texas will not recognize a cause of action for emotional distress except where the defendant creates a risk of physical harm. Thus bystander recovery is permissible under the rules of *Dillon v. Legg.* Some courts recognize a claim for serious or severe distress, but that standard is inadequate. "It is difficult to imagine how a set of rules could be developed and applied on a case-by-case basis to distinguish severe from nonsevere emotional harm. Severity is not an either/or proposition; it is rather a matter of degree. Thus, any attempt to formulate a general rule would almost inevitably result in a threshold requirement of severity so high that only a handful would meet it, or so low that it would be an ineffective screen. A middle-ground rule would be doomed, for it would call upon courts to distinguish between large numbers of cases factually too similar to warrant different treatment. Such a rule would, of course, be arbitrary in its application." [Quoting Richard N. Pearson, *Liability to Bystanders for Negligently Inflicted Emotional Harm—A Comment on the Nature of Arbitrary Rules,* 34 U. FLA. L. REV. 477, 511 (1982).]

NOTES

1. **Relationships.** The *Kerr* majority said it would recognize a duty based upon special relationships of the parties, and cited the telegraphic death message cases and dead body cases as examples. But it went on to say, without much discussion, that there was no such relationship in this case. Is that right? If the phrase "betrayal of confidence" comes to mind, it surely suggests an important relationship was involved. Even if so, however, it does not necessarily suggest that negligence is the proper basis for liability.

2. **Privacy.** Mental distress is often part of the harm associated with a number of torts that do not entail physical harms, or even risks of physical harms. For example, invasion of privacy, under some circumstances, can be a tort. Some invasions of privacy produce mental distress damages. *Boyles* might

have been brought as a privacy invasion claim in some jurisdictions. *See Fontaine v. Roman Catholic Church of Archdiocese of New Orleans*, 625 So.2d 548 (La. Ct. App. 1993) (allegation: a priest sexually abused a 17-year-old and later published photographs in a magazine and circulated video tapes; a privacy invasion claim is stated). But the privacy claim would be undesirable to the plaintiff if the defendant's liability insurance did not cover privacy claims.

D. NEGLIGENT INFLICTION OF EMOTIONAL DISTRESS AS AN ORDINARY NEGLIGENCE CLAIM?

CAMPER V. MINOR, 915 S.W.2d 437 (Tenn. 1996). Camper was driving a cement truck. Jennifer Taylor, 16, had been stopped at a stop sign, but suddenly pulled out in front of the plaintiff. "The vehicles collided, and Ms. Taylor was killed instantly. Camper exited his truck moments after the crash, walked around the front of his vehicle, and viewed Ms. Taylor's body in the wreckage from close range." Camper sued her estate, claiming negligent infliction of emotional distress, in the form of a post-traumatic stress syndrome. *Held:* (1) The physical manifestation or injury rule will no longer be followed; (2) Negligent infliction of emotional distress claims should be analyzed under the general negligence approach, that is, no differently from any other negligence case. "[T]he plaintiff must present material evidence as to each of the five elements of general negligence—duty, breach of duty, injury or loss, causation in fact, and proximate, or legal, cause—in order to avoid summary judgment. [T]o guard against trivial or fraudulent actions, the law ought to provide a recovery only for serious or severe emotional injury. A serious or severe emotional injury occurs where a reasonable person, normally constituted, would be unable to adequately cope with the mental stress engendered by the circumstances of the case. Finally, we conclude that the claimed injury or impairment must be supported by expert medical or scientific proof."

NOTES

1. **End of the evolutionary line?** *Camper* appears to discard all the constraining rules for negligent infliction of emotional distress cases. Some other courts have also moved in this direction. *See, e.g., Carrol v. Allstate Ins. Co.*, 815 A.2d 119 (Conn. 2003); *Sacco v. High Country Indep. Press, Inc.*, 896 P.2d 411 (Mont. 1995); *Johnson v. Ruark Obstetrics & Gynecology Assocs., P.A.*, 395 S.E.2d 85 (N.C. 1990). The Connecticut court in *Carrol* explained that a plaintiff must prove "that the defendant should have realized that its conduct involved an unreasonable risk of causing emotional distress." An appellate court interpreting *Carrol* affirmed a plaintiff's verdict in *Murphy v. Lord Thompson's Manor, Inc.*, 938 A.2d 1269 (Conn. App. Ct. 2008), where a wedding business negligently cancelled a bride's wedding date reservation. The court held that defendant's actions created an unreasonable risk of causing the bride emotional distress. Does such a case go too far?

2. **New constraints.** In discarding the older constraining rules, the *Camper* court substituted some new requirements—a severe emotional injury and expert medical proof. *See Rye v. Women's Care Ctr. of Memphis, MPLLC,* 477 S.W.3d 235 (Tenn. 2015) (NIED claim failed for lack of evidence of severe distress where there was no "expert proof" establishing it). *See also Sacco, supra* Note 1 (requiring "serious or severe" emotional harm and suggesting that expert testimony would often be helpful to prove that); *Squeo v. Norwalk Hosp. Ass'n,* 113 A.3d 932 (Conn. 2015) (parents who sued hospital for negligent infliction of emotional distress in connection with son-patient's suicide after he was discharged from the hospital did not produce sufficient evidence that their distress was "severe and debilitating"). Do such requirements fulfill the purposes of the earlier constraints we've seen in this Chapter? Is a requirement of expert testimony in all cases too formalistic? *See Thornton v. Garcini,* 928 N.E.2d 804 (Ill. 2010) (rejecting an expert witness requirement).

E. TOXIC EXPOSURES: FEAR OF FUTURE HARM

POTTER V. FIRESTONE TIRE & RUBBER CO.

563 P.2d 795 (Cal. 1993)

BAXTER, JUSTICE. . . .

[Firestone operated a tire manufacturing plant near Salinas. It contracted with Salinas Disposal Service and another company for disposal of industrial wastes in a class II sanitary landfill operated by the City. Class II landfills prohibit disposal of toxic substances because of the danger that they will leach into the groundwater. In addition, the disposal service prohibited solvents, oils and other substances. Firestone assured the service that no such waste would be sent to the landfill. For a while official plant policy required proper disposal of hazardous wastes in a Class I landfill, but that program was costly. A production manager, sent to California from Firestone's Akron, Ohio to make the plant more profitable, became angered over the costs of the hazardous waste disposal program. As a consequence, Firestone's hazardous waste materials were once again deposited and these materials included serious toxins.]

[The plaintiffs, including the Potters, lived near the landfill. They discovered that toxic chemicals had contaminated their domestic water wells. At least two of the chemicals, benzene and vinyl chloride, are known human carcinogens and others are strong suspects. The plaintiffs sued Firestone on theories that included negligent infliction of emotional distress. The trial court awarded $269,500 for psychiatric illnesses and the cost of treating them, $142,975 for the cost of medical monitoring of the plaintiffs, and punitive damages of $2.6 million. The court of appeal modified the judgment in some respects, but affirmed the main elements.]

[The Supreme Court of California raised the possibility that if the plaintiffs had suffered harm to their cells or their immune systems, that might constitute physical injury and that if so, emotional distress damages could be recovered as parasitic to a recovery for that harm. But it concluded that there was not enough evidence in the record to pass on that question.]

We next determine whether the absence of a present physical injury precludes recovery for emotional distress engendered by fear of cancer. . . .

Our reasons for discarding the physical injury requirement in Molien remain valid today and are equally applicable in a toxic exposure case. That is, the physical injury requirement is a hopelessly imprecise screening device. . . .

We next consider whether recovery of damages for emotional distress caused by fear of cancer should depend upon a showing that the plaintiff's fears stem from a knowledge that there is a probable likelihood of developing cancer in the future due to the toxic exposure. This is a matter of hot debate among the parties and amici curiae. . . .

A carcinogenic or other toxic ingestion or exposure, without more, does not provide a basis for fearing future physical injury or illness which the law is prepared to recognize as reasonable. The fact that one is aware that he or she has ingested or been otherwise exposed to a carcinogen or other toxin, without any regard to the nature, magnitude and proportion of the exposure or its likely consequences, provides no meaningful basis upon which to evaluate the reasonableness of one's fear. For example, nearly everybody is exposed to carcinogens which appear naturally in all types of foods. . . .

[W]e would be very hard pressed to find that, as a matter of law, a plaintiff faced with a 20 percent or 30 percent chance of developing cancer cannot genuinely, seriously and reasonably fear the prospect of cancer. Nonetheless, we conclude, for the public policy reasons identified below, that emotional distress caused by the fear of a cancer that is not probable should generally not be compensable in a negligence action. . . .

[A]ll of us are potential fear of cancer plaintiffs, provided we are sufficiently aware of and worried about the possibility of developing cancer from exposure to or ingestion of a carcinogenic substance. The enormity of the class of potential plaintiffs cannot be overstated; indeed, a single class action may easily involve hundreds, if not thousands, of fear of cancer claims.

With this consideration in mind, we believe the tremendous societal cost of otherwise allowing emotional distress compensation to a potentially unrestricted plaintiff class demonstrates the necessity of imposing some limit on the class. Proliferation of fear of cancer claims in California in the absence of meaningful restrictions might compromise the availability and affordability of liability insurance for toxic liability risks.

A second policy concern that weighs in favor of a more likely than not threshold is the unduly detrimental impact that unrestricted fear liability would have in the health care field. As amicus curiae California Medical Association points out, access to prescription drugs is likely to be impeded by allowing recovery of fear of cancer damages in negligence cases without the imposition of a heightened threshold. To wit, thousands of drugs having no known harmful effects are currently being prescribed and utilized. New data about potentially harmful effects may not develop for years. If and when negative data are discovered and made public, however, one can expect numerous lawsuits to be filed by patients who currently have no physical injury or illness but who nonetheless fear the risk of adverse effects from the drugs they used. Unless meaningful restrictions are placed on this potential plaintiff class, the threat of numerous large, adverse monetary awards, coupled with the added cost of insuring against such liability (assuming insurance would be available), could diminish the availability of new, beneficial prescription drugs or increase their price beyond the reach of those who need them most. . . .

A third policy concern to consider is that allowing recovery to all victims who have a fear of cancer may work to the detriment of those who sustain actual physical injury and those who ultimately develop cancer as a result of toxic exposure. That is, to allow compensation to all plaintiffs with objectively reasonable cancer fears, even where the threatened cancer is not probable, raises the very significant concern that defendants and their insurers will be unable to ensure adequate compensation for those victims who actually develop cancer or other physical injuries. . . .

A fourth reason supporting the imposition of a more likely than not limitation is to establish a sufficiently definite and predictable threshold for recovery to permit consistent application from case to case. . . .

Finally, while a more likely than not limitation may foreclose compensation to many persons with genuine and objectively reasonable fears, it is sometimes necessary to "limit the class of potential plaintiffs if emotional injury absent physical harm is to continue to be a recoverable item of damages in a negligence action." . . .

Unless an express exception to this general rule is recognized: in the absence of a present physical injury or illness, damages for fear of cancer may be recovered only if the plaintiff pleads and proves that (1) as a result of the defendant's negligent breach of a duty owed to the plaintiff, the plaintiff is exposed to a toxic substance which threatens cancer; and (2) the plaintiff's fear stems from a knowledge, corroborated by reliable medical or scientific opinion, that it is more likely than not that the plaintiff will develop the cancer in the future due to the toxic exposure. Under this rule, a plaintiff must do more than simply establish knowledge of a toxic ingestion or exposure and a significant increased risk of cancer. The plaintiff must further show that based upon reliable medical or scientific opinion, the plaintiff harbors a serious fear that the toxic ingestion or exposure was of such magnitude and proportion as to likely result in the feared cancer.

[But] we hold that a toxic exposure plaintiff need not meet the more likely than not threshold for fear of cancer recovery in a negligence action if the plaintiff pleads and proves that the defendant's conduct in causing the exposure amounts to "oppression, fraud, or malice" as defined in Civil Code section 3294, which authorizes the imposition of punitive damages. Thus, for instance, fear of cancer damages may be recovered without demonstrating that cancer is probable where it is shown that the defendant is guilty of "despicable conduct which is carried on by the defendant with a willful and conscious disregard of the rights or safety of others." . . .

In our view, Firestone's conduct brings this case within the "oppression, fraud or malice" exception for recovery of fear of cancer damages. . . .

[Remanded. Concurring and dissenting opinions omitted.]

NOTES

1. **Concern over mass torts.** The court emphasizes that "all of us are potential fear of cancer plaintiffs," and that "the enormity of the class of potential plaintiffs cannot be overstated." Clearly the court is concerned with mass torts. Given the mass tort element, would the *Potter* court impose any special limiting rule when the threat of mass exposure is not present?

2. **An exception for oppression, fraud or malice.** In cases of oppression, fraud and malice, why make an exception to the general requirement that plaintiff must show fear of cancer is probable? Even if defendant acted very badly, isn't there a need to show that the bad conduct was the actual cause and proximate cause of some harm? Could the rule be like the extended liability rule in intentional torts? Perhaps in this case, uncertainties should be borne by the culpable actor.

3. **Fear of disease.** Courts can have somewhat different rules. In *Exxon Mobil Corp. v. Albright*, 71 A.3d 30 (Md. 2013), the court held that to recover emotional distress damages for fear of contracting a latent disease because of exposure to some toxic substance, the plaintiff must show (1) actual exposure due to defendant's tortious conduct (2) which led him to objectively and reasonably fear that he would contact a disease, (3) and that as a result of that fear, he manifested some "physical injury" capable of objective determination. The second and third requirements of the fear-of future harm emotional distress case are closely related; unless the plaintiff suffers some physical injury as a result of the fear, the court may believe that the fear itself

is not reasonable. *See also Caronia v. Philip Morris USA, Inc.*, 5 N.E.3d 11 (N.Y. 2013) (no independent cause of action for medical monitoring where there is only a threat of future harm as opposed to some present harm; plaintiffs did not show they had been diagnosed with any smoking-related disease or are under medical investigation for any such suspected disease).

4.   **Medical monitoring.** The *Exxon Mobil* court set up a different test for the recovery of medical monitoring costs resulting from toxic exposure. In that case, the plaintiff must show (1) exposure to a "proven hazardous substance" due to defendant's tortious conduct; (2) that, as a "proximate result of significant exposure, the plaintiff suffers a significantly increased risk of contracting a latent disease"; (3) that this increased risk makes periodic medical diagnoses "reasonably necessary"; and (4) that medical processes exist which make early diagnosis and treatment of the disease "possible and beneficial."

NORFOLK & WESTERN RAILWAY V. AYERS, 538 U.S. 135 (2003). The plaintiffs brought a Federal Employers Liability Act suit against the railroad, their employer, alleging that the employer had negligently exposed them to asbestos and that they contracted asbestosis as a result. Asbestosis is a non-cancerous scarring of the lungs which causes shortness of breath and fatigue. The plaintiffs also claimed mental anguish based on their fear of developing cancer. The trial court permitted the plaintiffs to introduce evidence that, given their medical histories as smokers, the asbestosis significantly increased their risk of developing cancer and instructed the jury that although the plaintiffs could not recover for the possibility of cancer, they could recover for fear of developing it. The jury awarded damages to the plaintiffs, which, because damages were not specified for each item of harm, might have included awards for fear of developing cancer. *Held,* affirmed.

Ginsburg, J.: "[O]ur decisions . . . describe two categories: Stand-alone emotional distress claims not provoked by any physical injury, for which recovery is sharply circumscribed by the zone-of-danger test; and emotional distress claims brought on by a physical injury, for which pain and suffering recovery is permitted. . . . A plaintiff suffering bodily harm need not allege physical manifestations of her mental anguish. [Restatement Second of Torts § 456, cmt. c.] 'The plaintiff must of course present evidence that she has suffered, but otherwise her emotional distress claims, in whatever form, are fully recoverable.' D. Dobbs, Law of Torts 822 (2000). . . . Once found liable for 'any bodily harm,' a negligent actor is answerable in damages for emotional disturbance 'resulting from the bodily harm *or from the conduct which causes it.*' Restatement § 456(a)" The physically harmed plaintiff need not prove physical symptoms of his emotional distress, only that the emotional distress is both genuine and serious.

Kennedy, J., joined by three other Justices, dissenting: (1) Many companies have been bankrupted by asbestos litigation; awards of emotional harm damages like these will exhaust funds of asbestos defendants so that nothing will be available to compensate those who later suffer actual cancers resulting from asbestos exposures. (2) In any event "I do not think the brooding, contemplative fear the respondents allege can be called a direct result of their asbestosis. Unlike shortness of breath or other discomfort asbestosis may cause, their fear does not arise from the presence of disease in their lungs. Instead, the respondents' fear is the product of learning from a doctor about their asbestosis, receiving information (perhaps at a much later time) about the conditions that correlate with this disease, and then contemplating how these possible conditions might affect their lives."

NOTES

1. **Genuine and serious fear.** The majority in *Ayers* also held that an asbestosis sufferer could recover compensation for fear of cancer as an element of his pain and suffering damages, but only upon proof "that his alleged fear is genuine and serious." *CSX Transp., Inc. v. Hensley*, 556 U.S. 838 (2009).

2. **The incentive to plead physical injury.** Plaintiffs in almost all states who seek substantial damages for emotional harm for fear of contracting some disease have an incentive to plead their cases as involving actual physical injury, with the emotional distress as a parasitic element of damages. What if a plaintiff is stuck with a needle, suffering "minimal physical injury," and then suffers "anxiety and mental suffering occasioned by his or her fear of testing HIV positive and contracting AIDS, absent a showing of actual exposure to blood or body fluid infected with HIV?" In *Hartwig v. Oregon Trail Eye Clinic*, 580 N.W.2d 86 (Neb. 1998), the court concluded that this was a "simple negligence" case, not involving any separate claim of negligent infliction of emotional distress and thus not subject to any of its special rules.

3. **Actual exposure without physical harm.** When the plaintiff is actually exposed to HIV, recovery for the resulting distress does not seem to be a problem even if the plaintiff suffers no physical harm. *See John & Jane Roes, 1–100 v. FHP, Inc.*, 985 P.2d 661 (Haw. 1999). Recovery is limited to harms inflicted in the window of anxiety, that is, to the time before testing indicates to a high probability that HIV infection is unlikely. *See Ornstein v. New York City Health & Hosp. Corp.*, 881 N.E.2d 1187 (N.Y. 2008). However, emotional harm in this period might conceivably cause permanent emotional harm for which damages should be assessed.

4. **The actual exposure requirement.** Many courts have required "actual exposure," meaning that there must be a channel of exposure and also a virus or toxin must be shown to exist. *See, e.g., Laurel v. Prince*, 154 So.3d 95 (Ala. 2014) (denial of summary judgment for defendant was error where plaintiff failed to present any evidence "that she had any risk of developing HIV, hepatitis C, or any other illness or infection" from the syringe; merely

being advised "of the need for future testing" for such diseases is not enough); *Majca v. Beekil,* 701 N.E.2d 1084 (Ill. 1998); *Carroll v. Sisters of Saint Francis,* 868 S.W.2d 585 (Tenn. 1993). But several state high courts have permitted recovery in no-exposure cases. *See, e.g., Chizmar v. Mackie,* 896 P.2d 196 (Alaska 1995) (misdiagnosis of AIDS); *Faya v. Almaraz,* 620 A.2d 327 (Md. 1993) (doctor with AIDS infection); *S. Cent. Reg'l Med. Ctr. v. Pickering,* 749 So.2d 95 (Miss. 1999) (unsafe disposal of instruments); *Williamson v. Waldman,* 696 A.2d 14 (N.J. 1997). Some judges in the former camp fear that ignorant people would flood the courts with claims based upon unfounded fears unless the exposure rules were adopted. Why not simply require reasonable fear?

> REFERENCES: 2 DOBBS, HAYDEN & BUBLICK, THE LAW OF TORTS §§ 381–397 (2d ed. 2011); DOBBS, HAYDEN & BUBLICK, HORNBOOK ON TORTS ch. 29 (2d ed. 2016).

CHAPTER 20

PRENATAL HARMS

■ ■ ■

§ 1. PRENATAL AND PRECONCEPTION INJURY

REMY v. MACDONALD

801 N.E.2d 260 (Mass. 2004)

GREANEY, J.

This case presents the issue whether a child, born alive, can maintain a cause of action in tort against her mother for personal injuries incurred before birth because of the mother's negligence. The plaintiff seeks to recover damages based on the alleged negligence of her mother, the defendant Christine MacDonald, in connection with a two-car automobile accident that occurred when the plaintiff was in utero. [At the time of the accident in 1999, MacDonald was 32 weeks pregnant with the plaintiff. The plaintiff was born by emergency caesarian section four days later. She continues to suffer from multiple breathing difficulties associated with her premature birth. The plaintiff claims that her mother's negligent driving caused the accident that led to the plaintiff's premature birth and subsequent related injuries. The trial court granted summary judgment for the defendant.]

In order to succeed on a claim of negligence, a plaintiff first must establish that the defendant owed a legal duty of care. We must decide whether a pregnant woman owes a legal duty of care to her unborn child to refrain from negligent conduct that may result in physical harm to that child. If no such duty exists, a claim of negligence cannot be brought.

Whether a duty exists is a question of common law, to be determined by "reference to existing social values and customs and appropriate social policy." As a general principle of tort law, every actor has a duty to exercise reasonable care to avoid physical harm to others. There are a limited number of situations, however, in which the other legal requirements of negligence may be satisfied, but the imposition of a precautionary duty is deemed to be either inadvisable or unworkable. This is such a case.

The [trial] judge ruled that the defendant did not owe a duty of care to the unborn plaintiff. In his memorandum of decision, the judge noted that no Massachusetts appellate court has recognized the existence of such a duty. Guiding himself by cases in other jurisdictions, the judge reasoned that, due to a "unique symbiotic relationship" between a mother and her unborn child, the judicial creation of such a duty, in this case, could raise a multitude of problematic issues, as well as potentially invade the personal choice of pregnant women. We, essentially, agree.

We begin by taking judicial notice of the fact that, during the period of gestation, almost all aspects of a woman's life may have an impact, for better or for worse, on her developing fetus. A fetus can be injured not only by physical force, but by the mother's exposure, unwitting or intentional, to chemicals and other substances, both dangerous and nondangerous, at home or in the workplace, or by the mother's voluntary ingestion of drugs, alcohol, or tobacco. A pregnant woman may place her fetus in danger by engaging in activities involving a risk of physical harm or by engaging in activities, such as most sports, that are generally not considered to be perilous. A pregnant woman may jeopardize the health of her fetus by taking medication (prescription or over-the-counter) or, in other cases, by not taking medication. She also may endanger the well-being of her fetus by not following her physician's advice with respect to prenatal care or by exercising her constitutional right not to receive medical treatment.

Recognizing a pregnant woman's legal duty of care in negligence to her unborn child would present an almost unlimited number of circumstances that would likely give rise to litigation. Courts would be challenged to refine the scope of such a duty, including the degree of knowledge expected of a mother in order to pinpoint when such a duty would arise (e.g., at the point of pregnancy; at the point of awareness of pregnancy; or at the point of awareness that pregnancy is a possibility) or the particular standard of conduct to which a reasonably careful pregnant woman, in a single case, should be held. There is no consensus on if and when a duty such as the one sought by the plaintiff should be imposed, and there is considerable debate with respect to a mother's civil liability for injuries to her unborn fetus, including disagreement over whether the rights of the child should supersede the legal rights of the mother. No set of clear existing social values and customs exist, and no settled social policy can be identified, to justify the maintenance of the present lawsuit. . . .

There are three appellate decisions in jurisdictions that have allowed a claim brought against one's mother for negligently inflicted prenatal injuries. See *National Cas. Co. v. Northern Trust Bank*, 807 So.2d 86, 87 (Fla. App. 2002) (permitting claims only in context of motor vehicle accidents, up to limit of insurance); *Grodin v. Grodin*, 301 N.W.2d 869 (Mich. App. 1980) (permitting claim based on mother's ingestion of drug that caused child, when born, to develop discolored teeth); *Bonte v. Bonte*, 616 A.2d 464 (N.H. 1992) (permitting claim based on mother's failure to use reasonable care in crossing street). These decisions uniformly were premised on the assumption that, because an unborn child, after birth, may recover for prenatal injuries negligently inflicted by another, and because parental immunity had been abolished in those jurisdictions, logic demands that a child's mother should bear the same liability for injurious, negligent conduct to a fetus as would any third party. The courts undertook no serious analysis of the unique relationship between a pregnant woman and the fetus she carries. The courts also failed to address the collateral social and other impacts of the imposition of a legal (as opposed to a moral) obligation that would hold a pregnant woman to a standard of care towards her unborn child. Because it is on these considerations that our decision rests, we find these cases unpersuasive.

The plaintiff contends that her mother, as the operator of a motor vehicle, had an existing duty of care that extended to all other persons to operate her automobile in a reasonably careful and prudent manner, and argues that, based on this existing duty, there is no legal reason, particularly in the context of motor vehicle negligence, to distinguish between an unborn fetus and a child already born. We do not agree.

This court has recognized the right of a plaintiff to maintain an independent cause of action for prenatal injuries sustained as the result of the negligence of another. See *Payton v. Abbott Labs,* 437 N.E.2d 171 (Mass. 1982) (allowing claim against drug manufacturer for prenatal injuries caused by mother's ingestion of drug). "If the tortious conduct and the legal causation of the harm can be satisfactorily established, there may be recovery for any injury occurring at any time after conception." *Id.,* quoting Restatement (Second) of Torts, § 869 comment d (1979). . . .

It is true that, had the plaintiff been injured while MacDonald was a passenger in an automobile negligently operated by another, the plaintiff (whether or not she survived) would have been able to recover damages against the operator of the vehicle. There is also no question that, had the plaintiff been born at the time of the accident, even if only one hour of age, she would have been able to recover against MacDonald for injuries sustained as a result of her mother's negligence. See *Stamboulis v. Stamboulis,* 519 N.E.2d 1299 (Mass. 1988) ("no absolute curtain of immunity protects a parent who negligently causes injury to his or her minor child"). . . . There is nothing in our statutes or case law, however, that addresses the situation before us.

We reject the plaintiff's argument that a rule permitting a child to recover for negligent injuries inflicted before birth by the child's mother could be restricted solely to a viable fetus claiming negligence in an automobile accident. Massachusetts law provides that there is nothing special about injuries incurred in automobile accidents that sets them apart from other negligently caused injuries, and the limitation sought by the plaintiff would be inconsistent with that law. The presence of automobile liability insurance does not create liability where none previously existed. Further, and more importantly, there is no meaningful way to limit such a rule to automobile accidents cases. It would be only a matter of time before the rule could be extended to a myriad of situations that would make pregnant women liable to their viable fetuses for all manner of allegedly negligent conduct.

We agree with the general principle expressed in Restatement (Second) of Torts § 869 (1979), that "[o]ne who tortiously causes harm to an unborn child is subject to liability to the child for the harm if the child is born alive." The quoted language emphasizes that it is not just a pregnant woman alone who may be harmed by the tortious act of a third party, but also the fetus, whose injuries become apparent at its birth. There is nothing in the Restatement text, or in comments to the text, to indicate that the drafters of § 869 intended to suggest a legal right, never before recognized in law, for a fetus to bring a claim of negligence against its own mother. . . . We have said that "[t]he evolution of the law of negligence has always required courts to make hard (and often fine) distinctions, and to assess and determine, in considering the existence of a duty, contemporary attitudes and public policy." *Cyran v. Ware*, 597 N.E.2d 1352 (Mass. 1992). We conclude that there are inherent and important differences between a fetus, in utero, and a child already born, that permits a bright line to be drawn around the zone of potential tort liability of one who is still biologically joined to an injured plaintiff.

Judgment affirmed.

NOTES

1. **Traditional rule.** A pregnant woman is injured by defendant's negligence. She herself may have a claim for her injury. If the fetus is also injured is there an additional claim? Suppose, for example, a physician negligently prescribes a drug to the mother and the child is born with serious defects. In *Dietrich v. Northhampton*, 138 Mass. 14 (1884), Justice Oliver Wendell Holmes took the view that there could be no action. The opinion suggested the absence of precedent, "remoteness," and the logical problem of injuring a being "before he became a person," but gave little justice or policy reasoning.

In *Klutschkowski v. PeaceHealth*, 311 P.3d 461 (Or. 2013), the Oregon Supreme Court distinguished Dietrich as a case that involved harm to the fetus through negligent injury to the mother, rather than injury to the fetus directly. In *Klutschkowski*, the fetus was injured during labor as a result of medical negligence. The jury awarded $1.3 million in noneconomic damages, which the lower court reduced to $500,000 under a statutory cap. Whether the cap was permissible hinged on the availability of a malpractice claim in 1857. The Court wrote "we are not aware of any nineteenth-century case that discusses one way or the other whether a child could maintain a cause of action for medical malpractice for independent physical injuries that the child sustains during delivery as a direct consequence of the defendant's acts or omissions. Whatever the reason for that absence of authority, our precedents require us to decide whether a cause of action for the injuries Braedon sustained was recognized in 1857. Faced with that question, we follow the general principle that actions for medical malpractice and negligence were recognized in 1857 unless we are persuaded that an action comes within an exception to that rule." Accordingly, applying the cap to limit damages was unconstitutional.

2. **Contemporary rules: child born alive.** The *Dietrich* decision held sway for many years. Judicial reversals began shortly after the end of World War II and today most courts allow a tort claim by the child if the child is born alive. Some courts have insisted that the child must also be viable—capable of living independent of the mother—at the time of the injury. But that requirement seems strikingly unrelated to the reality of suffering after a live birth and most have rejected it. *See, e.g., Gonzales v. Mascarenas*, 190 P.3d 826 (Colo. Ct. App. 2008) (listing states); *Leighton v. City of New York*, 830 N.Y.S.2d 749 (App. Div. 2007).

3. **Child born alive as the physician's patient.** Is the child who is injured before viability and subsequently born alive the physician's patient for the purpose of medical malpractice act limitations? In *Simpson v. Roberts*, 752 S.E.2d 801 (Va. 2014), the court said: "The evidence presented at trial was that the amniocentesis was performed, at least in part, for Simpson's [the fetus's] benefit to determine whether her lungs were developed enough that she could be safely delivered. When Dr. Roberts performed this procedure, he was providing health care to Simpson and her mother. If Simpson had never been born alive, her mother would have been able to recover for the physical and emotional injuries associated with a stillbirth. However, once Simpson was born alive, she became a natural person under the Act. Upon birth, she became a patient of Dr. Roberts under the Act and had her own claim against Dr. Roberts. Under the Act, her claim for negligence included health care provided in utero consistent with the statutory definition. Our holding in *Castle* is applicable here: Dr. Roberts' negligence in performing the amniocentesis 'caused the child, though born alive, to be seriously impaired. . . . The mother and child were both 'patients' of the defendant, each of whom was entitled to a separate statutory damage cap under the Virginia Medical Malpractice Act.' "

4. **Contemporary rules: child not born alive but viable at injury.** Most courts passing on the question now appear to hold that a wrongful death action is allowable when a fetus is stillborn, at least when the fetus was viable at the time of injury. *See, e.g., Pino v. United States*, 183 P.3d 1001 (Okla. 2008). A few states disagree. *See Shaw v. Jendzejec*, 717 A.2d 367 (Me. 1998).

5. **Contemporary rules: child not born alive and not viable at injury or thereafter.** Most courts reject liability if the fetus was not born alive and was never viable at any time. *See, e.g., Santana v. Zilog, Inc.*, 95 F.3d 780 (9th Cir. 1996); *Crosby v. Glasscock Trucking Co., Inc.*, 532 S.E.2d 856 (S.C. 2000). However, a few cases have supported liability under wrongful death statutes for loss of a fetus that was never viable. *See Mack v. Carmack*, 79

So.3d 597 (Ala. 2011) (noting that six other jurisdictions allow such claims). *Cf. Nealis v. Baird,* 996 P.2d 438 (Okla. 1999) (allowing recovery if fetus had "an instant of life outside the womb"); *66 Fed. Credit Union v. Tucker*, 853 So.2d 104 (Miss. 2003) (allowing recovery if fetus was sufficiently developed to move in the womb); *Saleh v. Damron*, 836 S.E.2d 716 (W.Va. 2019) (a nonviable fetus is a "person" under wrongful death statute, but must be "in the womb"; thus an ectopic embryo or fetus is not a "person").

6. **Emotional distress damages.** States are hardly uniform in their rules about recovery of stand-alone negligently inflicted emotional distress. *See* Chapter 19. Should a mother be allowed to recover emotional distress damages for the negligently caused death of a fetus when she has suffered no physical injury? The court in *Broadnax v. Gonzalez*, 809 N.E.2d 645 (N.Y. 2004), allowed such a claim. In *Sheppard-Mobley v. King*, 830 N.E.2d 301 (N.Y. 2005), the court held that *Broadnax* did not allow emotional distress recovery by the mother if the child was born alive, because in such a case the child herself can bring a medical malpractice action for physical injuries. Even where the fetus is not born alive, is there a risk of duplicative recovery if the mother sues for her own emotional harm and as a beneficiary for damages in a wrongful death suit? *See Smith v. Borello,* 804 A.2d 1151 (Md. 2002).

7. **Parental liability: some hard questions.** Should courts hold a mother liable to her child for ingesting dangerous substances while pregnant? Or for failing to get appropriate prenatal care? *See Stallman v. Youngquist,* 531 N.E.2d 355 (Ill. 1988); *Chenault v. Huie,* 989 S.W.2d 474 (Tex. App. 1999) (child suffering permanent and serious harm because of mother's use of cocaine during pregnancy). Do you agree with the *Remy* court's reasons for refusing to recognize a duty of care on the facts before it? Does a woman's right to decide whether to terminate a pregnancy during the first trimester as established in *Roe v. Wade*, 410 U.S. 113 (1973), bear on tort liability for an injury inflicted during that period?

RENSLOW V. MENNONITE HOSPITAL, 367 N.E.2d 1250 (Ill. 1977). When plaintiff's mother was 13 years of age, defendants negligently transfused her with Rh-positive blood. This was incompatible with her own blood, though she had no knowledge of this at the time. Years later, when she became pregnant, she discovered that her blood had become sensitized by this negligent transfusion. As a result of this her child, the plaintiff, was born jaundiced and suffering from hyperbilirubinemia. She has suffered various damages for which she here sues. The trial judge dismissed the claim because plaintiff had not been conceived at the time of the alleged negligence. *Held*, the plaintiff states a claim for relief. Although foreseeability alone does not establish a duty, a duty of care may be owed to one who may be foreseeably harmed, even if the person is unknown or is remote in time or place. The defendants argue a need for an end of liability somewhere and "raise the specter of successive generations of plaintiffs complaining against a single defendant for harm caused by genetic damage done an ancestor," but the judiciary "will effectively exercise its traditional role of drawing rational distinction, consonant with current perceptions of justice, between harms which are compensable and those which are not."

ALBALA V. CITY OF NEW YORK, 429 N.E.2d 786 (N.Y. 1981). Ruth Albala underwent an abortion at Bellevue Hospital during which her uterus was perforated. The plaintiff Jeffrey Albala was born some four years later. This action on his behalf claims he suffered brain damage as a result of the doctor's negligence in perforating his mother's uterus. *Held*, this does not state a claim. Although harm of this kind was foreseeable, foreseeability alone does not establish a duty to the plaintiff. And although New York recognizes prenatal injury claims, those cases are not controlling here because in those cases "there are two identifiable beings within the zone of danger each of whom is owed a duty independent of the other and each of whom may be directly injured." Were liability established in this case, it would be difficult to preclude liability "where a negligent motorist collides with another vehicle containing a female passenger who sustains a punctured uterus . . . and subsequently gives birth to a deformed child," and the "staggering implications are manifest. . . . [R]ecognition of a cause of action under the circumstances of this case would have the undesirable impact of encouraging the practice of 'defensive medicine.' A physician faced with the alternative of saving a patient's life by administering a treatment involving the possibility of adverse consequences to later conceived off-spring of that patient would, if exposed to liability of the magnitude considered in this case, undoubtedly be inclined to advise against treatment rather than risk the possibility of having to recompense a child born with a handicap." This would place "physicians in a direct conflict between their moral duty to patients and the proposed legal duty to those hypothetical future generations outside the immediate zone of danger."

NOTES

1. **A hypo.** Suppose that, in 1970, D builds a defective building. At the time there is no other building around, though it is foreseeable that others will be built. In 1992 another building is completed adjacent to D's building. D's building, because of its defect, collapses and causes harm to the new building. Should New York allow a recovery if *Albala* is still recognized authority in that state?

2. **The DES cases.** A number of manufacturers once marketed a drug, DES, for use by pregnant women. The drug turned out to cause cancers and a number of other problems for the daughters of the women who ingested the drug. In several ways, New York has recognized that the manufacturer of the drug would be liable to the DES daughter. *E.g., Hymowitz v. Lilly & Co.*, 539

N.E.2d 1069 (N.Y. 1989). Is that inconsistent with *Albala*? What if it is a DES granddaughter rather than a DES daughter who suffers? *See Enright v. Eli Lilly & Co.*, 570 N.E.2d 198 (N.Y. 1991).

3. **Applying *Renslow*.** A number of cases are in accord with *Renslow* on various facts. *E.g., Lynch v. Scheininger,* 744 A.2d 113 (N.J. 2000); *see* 2 DOBBS, HAYDEN & BUBLICK, THE LAW OF TORTS § 368 (2d ed. 2011). In a state that follows *Renslow*, defendant negligently injures Christine Taylor in an auto accident. She requires hospitalization and operations twenty-five times as a result and still suffers some deformity of pelvic bones. Seven years later she gives birth to a child, whose head is damaged because during gestation it was shaped by the deformed pelvic bones. If the court would impose liability under *Renslow*, would it also impose liability on these facts? *Taylor v. Cutler,* 703 A.2d 294 (N.J. Super. Ct. App. Div. 1997), *aff'd*, 724 A.2d 793 (N.J. 1999). What of a claim brought by a woman who, because of malpractice, becomes Rh-sensitized but has not had a subsequent pregnancy? *See Rye v. Women's Care Ctr. of Memphis, MPLLC,* 477 S.W.3d 235 (Tenn. 2015) (even if Rh-sensitization is considered a presently existing physical injury, the undisputed facts demonstrate that Mrs. Rye has not sustained any damages related to this injury and that no such damages are reasonably certain to occur").

§ 2. WRONGFUL BIRTH, CONCEPTION, OR LIFE

SHULL V. REID
258 P.3d 521 (Okla. 2011)

COMBS, J.

On June 8, 2009, the Shulls initiated an action sounding in medical malpractice seeking compensation for the injuries suffered as a result of the Appellees' alleged malpractice in failing to properly diagnose a Cytomegalovirus infection [a common herpes virus], that occurred during Patricia Shull's first trimester of pregnancy, and failing to inform the Shulls of the significant health risk to their unborn child. The Shulls alleged that, as a direct and proximate result of this failure to diagnose and inform, Shull's minor son was born on June 9, 2007, with the CMV infection and suffers significant complications rendering the child permanently and completely helpless. The Shulls do not claim Defendants could have treated CMV or that the Defendants were responsible for Mrs. Shull's exposure to CMV. The Shulls claim that, had they known of the virus, they would have terminated the pregnancy.

[Defendants moved for partial summary judgment, alleging that the Shulls may only recover damages for the medical cost of continuing the pregnancy, offset by the cost of terminating the pregnancy. The district court granted the motion in order to let this issue of first impression come to this Court.]

. . . This Court has previously addressed the question of wrongful conception in three separate cases. The first case was Morris v. Sanchez, 746 P.2d 184 (Okla. 1987), where this Court found the birth of a healthy child does not constitute a legal harm for which damages are recoverable. The next case was *Goforth v. Porter Medical Associates, Inc.,* 755 P.2d 678 (Okla. 1988), where again, this Court found that the birth of a normal, healthy child is not a compensable damage. However, this Court held:

> Morris, however, should not, and must not, be interpreted as precluding a claim for other forms of damages that may arise out of the negligent performance of sterilization operations. Insofar as the petition in this case alleges negligence and actual, ordinary damages arising out of the alleged negligence, to-wit: $2,000.00 in medical expenses incurred as result of the unplanned pregnancy, we are of the opinion that the petition adequately states a claim for which relief may be granted.

To reach that result we relied upon [a] Kansas case. . . . We again turn to another Kansas case for guidance. In Arche v. United States of America, Department of the Army, 798 P.2d 477 (Kan. 1990), the Kansas Supreme Court was requested to answer two questions. First, did Kansas law recognize a cause of action for wrongful birth of a permanently handicapped child, and if so, what is the extent of damages which may be recovered upon proper proof. The Kansas Court held:

> Wrongful birth plaintiffs typically desire a child and plan to support the child. Such support is, of course, the obligation of all parents. It is therefore reasonable to deny those normal and foreseeable costs which accrue to all parents. We hold that those expenses caused by the child's handicaps may be recovered, but not those expenses natural to raising any child.

The Kansas Court then addressed the plaintiff's emotional damages and found that such damages were not allowable in this type of medical malpractice action. They held:

> We have thus far held that visibility of results as opposed to visibility of the tortious act does not give rise to a claim for emotional damages. The child's injury in this case occurred without human fault during development of the fetus; the parents were not aware of the injury at the time. . . . We see no reason why a wrongful birth case should be distinguished. We therefore hold that damages for emotional distress of the parents are not recoverable in a wrongful birth case.

Finally, the Kansas Supreme Court addressed the issue concerning allowable damages, and over what period of time such damages may be recovered. The Kansas Court found that recovery may be had only for the period of time of the child's life expectancy or until the child reaches the age of majority, whichever is the shorter period. . . .

Subsequent to the birth of the child in the instant case, the Oklahoma State Legislature passed [a statute] that recognized wrongful birth actions but does not allow a parent, or other person who is legally required to provide for the support of a child, to seek economic or noneconomic damages because of a condition that existed at the time of the child's birth, based on a claim that a person's act or omission contributed to the mother not terminating the pregnancy. This Statute, however, was passed after the birth of the child in the instant matter, and it does not affect our holding in the instant case. . . .

We . . . hold that in any case arising prior to the enactment of [this statute] in 2008, in a wrongful birth action alleging medical malpractice, the measure of damages allowable is the extraordinary medical expenses and other pecuniary losses proximately caused by the negligence. There is no cause of action for emotional distress as the child's injury in this case occurred without human fault during development of the fetus, and the parents were not aware of the injury at the time. Loss of consortium is also not allowable in the instant matter as Oklahoma law does not provide for this type of damage in the instant case. Finally, recovery may be had only for extraordinary expenses, not the normal and foreseeable costs of raising a normal, healthy child, for the period of time of the child's life expectancy or until the child reaches the age of majority, whichever is the shorter period. [This Court has previously held that a parent has a legal duty to support his or her child until the child reaches the age of majority.]

[Reversed and remanded.]

NOTES

1. **"Wrongful birth" cases.** In a typical "wrongful birth" case, a doctor has negligently failed to diagnose a genetic difficulty, with resulting physical harm to the fetus and economic and emotional harm to the parents. Often, as in *Shull*, the parents argue that but for the doctor's negligence, they would have chosen to abort the fetus. Many courts have now upheld such claims. *See, e.g., Lininger v. Eisenbaum*, 764 P.2d 1202 (Colo. 1988); *Smith v. Cote*, 513 A.2d 341 (N.H. 1986); *Thornhill v. Midwest Physician Ctr.*, 787 N.E.2d 247 (Ill. App. Ct. 2003). Similarly, a physician who learns from genetic screening that any child conceived in the future is at risk may owe a duty to inform the prospective parents. *See Didato v. Strehler*, 554 S.E.2d 42 (Va. 2001). A few courts reject the wrongful birth claim entirely. *E.g., Etkind v. Suarez*, 519 S.E.2d 210 (Ga. 1999). A number of state statutes prohibit wrongful birth claims. *See Sernovitz v. Dershaw*, 127 A.3d 783, 792 (Pa. 2015); *see also Tillman v. Goodpasture*, 485 P.3d 656 (Kan. 2021) (upholding state statute against constitutional attack). Even in states that disallow such claims, courts may have to decide whether the plaintiff's particular claim fits within that

category. *See, e.g., Norman v. Xytex Corp.*, 848 S.E.2d 835 (Ga. 2020) (claim that parents would not have purchased sperm from a particular donor had they known of problems that ultimately caused child to be born with impairments was a wrongful birth claim and thus barred, although parents could maintain a negligent misrepresentation claim against sperm bank).

2. **Possible causal difficulties.** Does a wrongful birth claim present intrinsic causal problems, when the case may rest on the parents testifying that the fetus would have been aborted had they been non-negligently informed of problems? The court in *Wilson v. Kuenzi*, 751 S.W.2d 741 (Mo. 1988), thought so: "The percentage of women who under pressure refuse to consider abortion, whether for reasons of religious belief, strong motherly instincts, or for other reasons, is sometimes astounding. It would seem that testimony either more verifiable based upon experience or more verifiable by some objective standard should be required as the basis for any action for substantial damages." Is the court right about this, or should credibility determinations simply be left to the trier of fact?

3. **Emotional distress damages.** In *Shull*, the court applied Oklahoma "bystander" rules to deny recovery for negligent infliction of emotional distress. Should the state's usual restrictions on the NIED claim be applied in wrongful birth cases, or should the plaintiff be able to state an ordinary negligence claim and recover emotional distress damages as part of a parasitic pain and suffering award? In *Bader v. Johnson,* 732 N.E.2d 1212 (Ind. 2000), the court held that so-called wrongful birth actions were merely medical malpractice actions, that general rules of negligence applied, and that all damages proximately caused by the defendant's negligence would be recoverable. Similarly, in *Clark v. Children's Memorial Hosp.*, 955 N.E.2d 1065 (Ill. 2011) (citing 2 DAN B. DOBBS, LAW OF REMEDIES § 8.2 (2d ed. 1993)), the court said that a prayer for emotional distress damages in a wrongful birth case did not require proof that the parents were in a zone of danger, as would normally be required in a stand-alone NIED claim. Such "special restrictions," said the court "have no logical bearing on a wrongful-birth claim, where a tort has already been committed against the parents. Wrongful-birth plaintiffs do not assert a freestanding emotional distress claim, but merely assert emotional distress as an element of damages for a personal tort."

4. **Damages for child-rearing costs.** Many courts recognizing a wrongful birth claim allow recovery for some of the expenses of rearing the now-impaired child. As the *Shull* court holds, recovery is usually limited to the "extraordinary" expenses over and above ordinary child-rearing expenses. Some states have limited the available damages to the expenses of pregnancy and delivery. *See Schirmer v. Mt. Auburn Obstetrics & Gynecology Assocs., Inc.*, 844 N.E.2d 1160 (Ohio 2006). The *Schirmer* court pointed to the "underlying but critical fact" that in such cases the mother is claiming she would have terminated the pregnancy, making "unimpaired life never a possibility in this situation." Does computing "extraordinary" child-rearing expenses require the trier of fact to assess the relative merits of "being versus nonbeing," as the *Shirmer* court concluded?

5. **Choice of law.** State laws in this area can vary significantly. Because of significant differences in New York's and New Jersey's wrongful birth actions, one court reviewed claims against each defendant based on the law in that defendant's jurisdiction. *Ginsberg v. Quest Diagnostics, Inc.*, 147 A.3d 434 (N.J. 2016) ("New Jersey recognizes damages for 'the emotional injury of the parents' and 'the special medical expenses attributable to raising a child with a congenital impairment' but not damages for 'the birth defect or congenital impairment itself.' New York, in contrast, limits damages in wrongful birth cases to 'the pecuniary expense which [the parents] have borne, and . . . must continue to bear, for the care and treatment of their infants' and New York specifically bars damages for 'psychic or emotional harm' resulting from the birth of the child 'in an impaired state.' ").

6. **"Wrongful conception" cases.** Another kind of case, usually labeled "wrongful conception," often involves an allegation that a defendant physician failed to prevent conception because he negligently performed a sterilization procedure on the father or the mother. The child in such cases is normally healthy, but the parents, who had attempted to avoid pregnancy and childbirth, will now face financial costs because of the defendant's negligence. In addition, if they were emotionally unable to care for children, they will almost certainly have increased emotional difficulties. Some legislatures have forbidden courts to entertain these claims. *See Thibeault v. Larson*, 666 A.2d 112 (Me. 1995).

7. **Damages in wrongful conception cases: the healthy but unwanted child.** In wrongful conception cases, most courts have allowed recovery for the mother's pain in pregnancy, and medical costs of pregnancy, abortion, or birth, as well as any lost wages during this period. *See Dotson v. Bernstein*, 207 P.3d 911 (Colo. App. 2009) (negligent failure to terminate a pregnancy). However, the vast majority of courts have denied recovery for the cost of rearing the healthy child. *See, e.g., Chaffee v. Seslar*, 786 N.E.2d 705 (Ind. 2003) (listing states). "The parents of a normal, healthy child whom they now love have not suffered any injury or damage," the Kentucky Court said bluntly in *Schork v. Huber*, 648 S.W.2d 861 (Ky. 1983). In a small group of states, the parents of a child born after a botched sterilization procedure are allowed to recover all costs incurred in rearing the child, without any offset for the benefits that the child's presence may confer. *See, e.g., Zehr v. Haugen*, 871 P.2d 1006 (Or. 1994). A middle ground is to allow all damages that flow from the negligence, but reduce those damages by the benefits conferred on the parents by the child's birth. *See, e.g., Univ. of Ariz. Health Sciences Ctr. v. Superior Court*, 667 P.2d 1294 (Ariz. 1983). Which approach best fulfills the goals of tort law?

8. **"Wrongful life" cases.** There is no support in the cases for a general wrongful life claim, as distinct from a wrongful birth or wrongful conception claim. The child, in other words, cannot recover for being born. Courts have recognized that such a claim would involve "a comparison between life and nonexistence by asserting at least a partial conception of what nonexistence is like—namely, a state of being in which one experiences no economic or

emotional burdens," and boils down to a claim that "the defendants infringed [plaintiff's] interest in remaining in a state of nonexistence." *Tomlinson v. Metropolitan Pediatrics, LLC*, 412 P.3d 133 (Or. 2018) (rejecting such a claim, concluding that it presents "a fundamental conceptual difficulty"). Statutes may prohibit such a claim. *See, e.g., B.D.H. v. Mickelson*, 792 N.W.2d 169 (N.D. 2010); *Sernovitz v. Dershaw*, 127 A.3d 783 (Pa. 2015) (even if state statute prohibiting wrongful life and wrongful birth claims were unconstitutional, where reliance on that statute "has continued for more than 20 years, a presumption naturally arises that any process challenge is too stale to be cognizable regardless of whether the challengers exercised reasonable diligence"). However, several courts have permitted the child to recover the cost of extraordinary care in his own name.

REFERENCE: DOV FOX, BIRTH RIGHTS AND WRONGS (2019); 2 DOBBS, HAYDEN & BUBLICK, THE LAW OF TORTS §§ 366–371 (2d ed. 2011); DOBBS, HAYDEN & BUBLICK, HORNBOOK ON TORTS ch. 27 (2d ed. 2016).

CHAPTER 21

WRONGFUL DEATH AND
SURVIVAL ACTIONS

■ ■ ■

"In a civil Court, the death of a human being could not be complained of as an injury. . . ."

> —Lord Ellenborough in *Baker v. Bolton*, 1 Camp. 493, 170 Eng. Rep. 1033 (1808).

Lord Ellenborough's statement meant or came to mean three separate things:

(1) If an injured person died before receiving judgment against the defendant, his cause of action died with him; put differently, the cause of action did not survive the death of the plaintiff.

(2) If an injured person remained alive after injury but the defendant died before a judgment was rendered against him, the plaintiff's cause of action died as well; put differently, the plaintiff's cause of action did not survive the death of the defendant.

(3) There was no separate cause of action on behalf of those who were dependent upon the deceased person.

In most states all of these rules have been changed; in all states one or more have been changed.[1] The first two rules have been changed by statutes generally known as "survival" statutes, because they provide that the cause of action survives the death of the plaintiff or the defendant or both. The third rule has been changed by statutes usually called "wrongful death" statutes, or "Lord Campbell's" Acts after the sponsor of the first such legislation.

Subject to a minor exception in federal maritime law, wrongful death and survival claims are entirely statutory. Statutes are amended from time to time and many have idiosyncratic elements. Lawyers must always

---

[1] A number of federal statutes also allow for death recoveries in some form. *See, e.g.,* the Federal Employers' Liability Act, 45 U.S.C.A. § 51 (employees of interstate railroads); the Jones Act, 46 U.S.C.A. § 688 (employees at sea); the Death on the High Seas Act), 46 App. U.S.C.A. § 761 (deaths more than one maritime league from shore); the National Vaccine Compensation Program, 42 U.S.C.A. § 300aa–15(a) (deaths caused by vaccinations). Some cases have permitted recoveries for death under the basic federal civil rights statute, 42 U.S.C.A. § 1983.

consult the governing statute and should expect to find local variations in the general scheme described in this chapter.

§ 1. STATUTORY ACTIONS

WEIGEL V. LEE

752 N.W.2d 618 (N.D. 2008)

CROTHERS, JUSTICE.

[Darlyne Rogers died shortly after being admitted to a "regular" room in a hospital despite being critically ill. Her adult children (collectively "the Weigels") sued Dr. Lane Lee and the hospital (collectively "Lee") pursuant to the North Dakota wrongful death statute. The complaint sought damages for the Weigels' own emotional distress and loss of consortium. After a series of motions, orders, and reconsiderations, the trial court dismissed the Weigels' entire case. Ultimately the trial court reasoned that because under *Butz v. World Wide, Inc.*, 492 N.W.2d 88 (N.D. 1992), children do not have a cause of action for either loss of parental consortium or for their own emotional distress damages. The court further suggested that the Weigels could bring only a claim for the emotional distress suffered by Rogers before her death.]

. . . The district court erred by blending three distinct claims for tortious conduct. At various points in its orders, the district court discussed (1) loss of consortium claims arising out of personal injury actions, (2) survival actions and (3) wrongful death actions. This Court and North Dakota's statutes distinguish between these three claims, as we explain below.

[Historically, a loss of consortium claim was available only to husbands whose wives were injured.] In *Hastings,* this Court acknowledged both spouses' right to recover for loss of consortium, but refused to extend this type of recovery to children who suffer the loss of a parent's consortium. Nonetheless, this is not the basis of the Weigels' action, and as this Court importantly clarified in *Hastings,* the inability of children to recover for loss of consortium arising out of personal injury to a parent "should not be construed to prohibit recovery where a parent dies and recovery is allowed under the Wrongful Death Act."

The distinction between loss of consortium in personal injury and in wrongful death actions is important here because Lee argues this Court's decision in *Butz* indicates a decedent's children are not entitled to damages in a wrongful death action. Lee misapplies *Butz. Butz* was not a claim under the wrongful death act because the tortious conduct resulted in severe injury, not in death. . . . Because *Butz* does not address claims made under the wrongful death statutes, it is not applicable to the Weigels' claim.

Second, N.D.C.C. § 28–01–26.1 provides for survival actions: "No action or claim for relief, except for breach of promise, alienation of affections, libel, and slander, abates by the death of a party or of a person who might have been a party had such death not occurred." For example, in *Nodak Mut. Ins. Co. v. Stegman*, 647 N.W.2d 133 (N.D. 2002), an individual was seriously injured in an automobile accident. He underwent hospital treatment, but died approximately two weeks later. This Court stated, "Clearly a personal injury action existed on behalf of [the injured party] against [the tortfeasor] for various damages, including the medical expenses occasioned by the accident, and that action survived [the injured party's] death." Survival statutes "are remedial in nature, and are intended to permit recovery by the representatives of the deceased for damages the deceased could have recovered had he lived. . . . A survival action merely continues in existence an injured person's claim after death as an asset of his estate." Although they could have, the Weigels' complaint indicates they are not seeking damages on Rogers' behalf as part of a survival action. Instead, the Weigels brought a wrongful death action for their own injuries: "The Plaintiffs have sustained mental and emotional anguish as a result of the Defendants' negligence and their mother's death. Furthermore, the Plaintiffs have been denied the society, comfort, counsel and companionship of Darlyne Rogers, all to their injury and damage."

Third, N.D.C.C. ch. 32–21 provides for wrongful death actions. The Weigels offer the wrongful death act as the legal basis for their claim. We conclude the Weigels are entitled to seek compensation for Rogers' wrongful death for the reasons stated below.

There was no wrongful death claim at common law. Early wrongful death statutes severely limited compensable damages. Generally, only pecuniary losses were awarded, with no compensation available for mental anguish or loss of companionship. Contemporary wrongful death statutes tend to address a broader scope of injuries, including those considered non-pecuniary. Wrongful death actions are intended to compensate the survivors of the deceased for the losses they have sustained as a result of a wrongful killing. Dependent upon the specific statutory language, losses recoverable by survivors in wrongful death actions often include the prospective loss of earnings and contribution; prospective expenses; loss of services; loss of companionship, comfort, and consortium; and mental anguish and grief.

North Dakota's wrongful death act, N.D.C.C. ch. 32–21, provides:

"Whenever the death of a person shall be caused by a wrongful act, neglect, or default, and the act, neglect, or default is such as would have entitled the party injured, if death had not ensued, to maintain an action and recover damages in respect thereof, then and in every such case the person who, or the corporation, limited liability company, or company which, would have been liable if death had not ensued, shall be liable to an action for damages, notwithstanding the death of the person injured or of the tort-feasor, and although the death shall have been caused under such circumstances as amount in law to felony."

This statute is not a survival statute intended to increase the estate of the deceased, but its purpose is to give a measure of protection to those persons within a fixed degree of relationship to and dependency on the deceased because of actual injury sustained by them by reason of the wrongful killing of the deceased. Damages under the wrongful death act are based on the loss suffered by the beneficiaries, and not on the loss sustained by the decedent's estate. A jury determines the quantity of damages and "shall give such damages as it finds proportionate to the injury resulting from the death to the persons entitled to the recovery." N.D.C.C. § 32–21–02.

Compensable damages available in wrongful death actions are enumerated in N.D.C.C. § 32–03.2–04 [and specifically include both economic and non-economic damages. Included in the latter are mental anguish, emotional distress, and loss of consortium.]

Section 32–21–04, N.D.C.C., clarifies that intended recipients of damages under the wrongful death act are "the decedent's heirs at law." This Court has determined "heirs at law" for purposes of this statute are "those persons who by the laws of descent would succeed to the property of the decedent in case of intestacy, but in addition, that if members of a preferred class are precluded from recovery for reasons other than death those next entitled to inherit may be considered beneficiaries." A decedent's descendants are designated by the Uniform Probate Code to share in portions of the intestate estate and are therefore able to seek recovery of damages under the wrongful death act.

Persons entitled to recover damages under the wrongful death act should not be confused with persons statutorily authorized to bring an action. Section 32–21–03, N.D.C.C. [authorizes the following persons to bring an action, in the following order: "(1) The surviving husband or wife, if any; (2) The surviving children, if any; (3) The surviving mother or father; (4) A surviving grandparent; (5) The personal representative; (6) A person who has had primary physical custody of the decedent before the wrongful act."]

The distinction between persons eligible to seek damages from wrongful death actions and those entitled to bring such actions is important because the trial judge is charged with splitting the recovery among eligible heirs. . . . In specific wrongful death actions, overlap will likely exist between plaintiffs bringing the action under N.D.C.C. § 32–21–03 and those entitled to any damages. However, those with authority to bring the action do not have an absolute right to the damages recovered, and, instead, bring the action in a representative capacity for the exclusive benefit of the persons entitled to recover. The wrongful death act thus differentiates between the capacity to bring an action and the right to share in the damages recovered. Surviving children are eligible to bring a wrongful death action under N.D.C.C. § 32–21–03(2) if the decedent had no eligible spouse or if the spouse fails to bring an action for thirty days after the children made a demand. But this issue is separate from the children's ability to recover damages in a wrongful death action.

Because the wrongful death act does not exclude the decedent's children from parties entitled to damages and because the damages requested are permitted under N.D.C.C. § 32–03.2–04, the Weigels' claim should not have been dismissed.

[Reversed and remanded.]

NOTES

1. **Wrongful death and survival actions.** A survival action is the claim the decedent could have brought while alive. A wrongful death action is the claim of the decedent's survivors. This means that a personal representative, say the surviving husband of a deceased wife, may bring one suit for the estate—the survival action; and may also bring a separate death action for the appropriate survivors. *See Spangler v. McQuitty*, 141 A.3d 156 (Md. 2016) (a subsequent wrongful death action brought by a decedent's beneficiaries is not barred by the disposition of a decedent's personal injury claim); *Riggs v. Georgia-Pacific LLC*, 345 P.3d 1219 (Utah 2015) (wrongful death action is independent, thus not barred by the fact that the decedent sued during her lifetime and prevailed against the same defendants; the two causes of action "are aimed at compensating different types of loss" to different people). In *Tembenis v. Sec'y of Health & Human Servs.*, 733 F.3d 1190 (Fed. Cir. 2013), using tort law as a baseline for a vaccine act death claim, the court wrote: "Generally, the estate of a person who dies may seek compensation on two related fronts. First, compensation under a wrongful death statute is designed to compensate the survivors or the estate of the deceased for losses they have sustained. Second, the estate may also pursue, under a survival statute, damages which the decedent could have recovered had he lived. Thus, '[i]n a survival action, a claim for lost earnings embraces only the earnings lost up to the time of death.' Future lost earnings are then recovered under a wrongful death statute." The specific terms of the state wrongful death statute dictate what the action entails, what remedies are available and what procedures must be followed. *See In re Woodley*, 777 S.E.2d 560 (Va. 2015).

2. **Wrongful death: parties and procedure.** A wrongful death action, unlike a survival action, does not involve a claim by the estate. Any recovery does not pass through the estate, but instead goes directly to the survivors. The action is often brought by survivors of the decedent; frequently one of them acts as a kind of informal trustee, suing for all of them. In some states the court appoints a trustee, who formally brings the action on behalf of all appropriate

beneficiaries. Very often statutes provide that this person is to be the personal representative of the estate. But where this is so, the personal representative is a trustee for the survivors entitled to recover, not the representative of the estate generally. Many cases concern the appropriate wrongful death claimants and claims procedures. *See, e.g., Craft v. State ex rel. Wyoming Dep't of Health,* 465 P.3d 395 (Wyo. 2020) (adoptive brother could bring wrongful death claim); *Ceja v. Rudolph & Sletten, Inc.,* 302 P.3d 211 (Cal. 2013) (California statute that allows "putative spouse" to bring a wrongful death claim, defining that status as "the surviving spouse of a void or voidable marriage who is found by the court to have believed in good faith that the marriage to the decedent was valid," contemplates only a subjective, good faith belief, not an objectively reasonable one; fact that husband was still married to first wife on the date he married second wife did not bar second wife from asserting subjective good faith); *In re Estate of Bennett,* 308 P.3d 63 (Mont. 2013) (parents of adult child who died in car accident without a will were not heirs, however, the parents "are entitled to recover wrongful death damages, including damages for grief, sorrow, and mental anguish. Such damages are personal to them as Jeremiah's parents and survivors, but would be pursued by the personal representative of the Estate on the [parents'] behalf in one action, along with all other claims.").

3. **Survival statutes: parties and procedure.** The plaintiff in a survival claim is the personal representative of the decedent's estate. The claim is a debt owed to the estate just as any other claim is, and any recovery is paid to the estate. The estate in turn pays the debts of the deceased person and the costs of administering the estate. If any funds are left, the estate pays those to heirs or the beneficiaries of the deceased's will.

§ 2. DAMAGES

LANEY V. VANCE

112 So.3d 1079 (Miss. 2013)

PIERCE, J.

On July 13, 2005, Mamie Vance Hemphill began treatment at St. Dominic's Hospital. She was admitted with complaints of confusion, decreased appetite, and tremors, and also had end-stage renal disease, respiratory failure, pneumonia, and had been on dialysis. An immediate concern was probable sepsis from the dialysis catheter. This was the only access her doctors had to conduct dialysis. She was treated with Levaquin and Vancomycin, and the catheter was left in place for dialysis. Initially, her body responded well to the antibiotics, and her white blood cell count and temperature lowered. On July 16, 2005, Hemphill's blood pressure dropped unexpectedly, and she began to have abdominal pain. The doctors attempted dialysis, but the pain continued and her blood pressure dropped more. The doctors made plans to remove the catheter and administer additional tests to include a CT scan. Dr. Anne B. Whitehurst, an infectious-disease specialist, was brought in, as well. By 1:45 p.m., on July 16, 2005, Hemphill went into cardiopulmonary arrest and could not be revived.

Martin Vance (individually and on behalf of wrongful-death beneficiaries of Mamie Vance Hemphill) complained (at trial) that Dr. Charles Laney failed to recognize Hemphill's medical problems and failed to move her to intensive care soon enough before she died. . . . The main issue to be resolved by the jury was whether Dr. Laney breached the applicable standard of care by deciding to treat the infection with antibiotics and to leave the allegedly infected catheter in place, since it was the only access for dialysis. The jury returned a verdict for $1,000,000, which included $200,000 in economic damages and $800,000 in noneconomic damages.

Dr. Laney has presented three issues to this Court. They include:

I. Whether the trial court erred in remitting the plaintiff's economic damage award to $103,688 when the substantial weight of the evidence proved that the award should be zero.

II. Whether the trial court erred in instructing the jury when the jury instructions are taken as a whole.

III. Whether Plaintiff's counsel's improper comments and arguments, including that the damages should represent "the value of a human life," when combined with the erroneous jury instructions, mandate reversal and a new trial.

Because we find that Issue Three (3) is dispositive, we will not address Issues One and Two. . . .

Dr. Laney alleges that the trial court erred in instructing the jury that an element of damages in this case is the "loss of the value of life of Ms. Hemphill."[1] Dr. Laney asserts that allowing the "value of life" to be considered as an element of damages is inconsistent with Mississippi Code Section 11–1–69(2), which states, "In any wrongful death action, there shall be no recovery for loss of enjoyment of life caused by death." Rather, damages are limited to: "(1) the present net cash value of the life expectancy of the deceased, (2) the loss of the companionship and society of

---

[1]   The trial judge instructed the jury that if it returned a verdict in favor of Plaintiff, it was to award damages as follows:

1. The value of any physical pain and suffering suffered by Mamie Vance Hemphill;

2. The loss of income suffered by the death of Mamie Vance Hemphill, if any;

3. The value of any loss of companionship, love and society, past, present or future mental anguish and distress suffered by her wrongful death beneficiaries;

4. The value of the life of Mamie Vance Hemphill.

(Emphasis added.)

the decedent, (3) the pain and suffering of the decedent between the time of injury and death, and (4) punitive damages."

This Court, in *Rebelwood Apts. RP, LP v. English,* held that "[i]n providing a framework for determination of lost future income, courts are not determining the 'value' of a person." Additionally, Mississippi Code Section 11–1–69(2) bars hedonic damages, which are:

> The damages for the loss of enjoyment of life, which purportedly compensate an injured person for the loss of quality of life or in the case of a wrongful death action for the value of life itself.

 Vance asserts that the jury instructions were proper, because they were not objected to at trial and are correct under Mississippi law. . . .

The Legislature addressed this issue when it amended Mississippi Code Section 11–1–69(2) to include, "In any wrongful death action, there shall be no recovery for loss of enjoyment of life caused by death." . . . [W]e find that it was reversible error for the trial judge to instruct the jury that it might consider the "value of life" of the deceased in awarding damages.

Additionally, the statements made in Vance's attorney's closing argument were prejudicial to Dr. Laney. . . . During closing arguments, counsel for Vance stated the following to the jury:

> The first thing they do in a communist Nazi Country is destroy the jury system. Why do they want to destroy the jury system? Because you represent the line between tyranny and democracy, right and wrong. You have the power . . . You have more power today than the President of the United States. . . .

> But the question is, will you have courage today? Do you have the God given courage. . . .

> The value of the life of Mamie Hemphill. . . . I had to bring each one of the kids up here and ask them, what did your mother mean to you? What did she do with you? What did she do for you? The value of a loss.

Based on the prejudicial nature of the foregoing statements and other statements by counsel for Vance, which were presented to the jury during closing arguments, we reverse and remand for a new trial.

NOTES

Wrongful Death Statutes

1. **The value of a life.** Why do you think that plaintiff argued for the value of a life to be listed as an item of damages? Although the *Laney* court says the jury should not calculate the value of a life in a wrongful death action, is that, in essence, what a wrongful death action does?

2.   **Measures of damages for wrongful death.** Wrongful death statutes traditionally aimed to replace pecuniary losses that would be suffered by others because of the decedent's death. *See Burnette v. Eubanks*, 425 P.3d 343 (Kan. 2018) (referring to wrongful death economic damages as being subject "to the jury's valuation essentially as a replacement for the loss"). "Apart from relatively minor items such as funeral expense, most states measure economic loss by the loss of support to dependents. Some measure it differently, by the loss of projected lifetime savings of the deceased. The first measure is usually called loss-to-survivors or loss-to-dependents measure, while the second is called the loss-to-the estate measure." DAN B. DOBBS & CAPRICE L. ROBERTS, LAW OF REMEDIES § 8.3(3) (3d ed. 2018). Most of the states which use the loss-to-the estate measure calculate the loss by determining the deceased's probable lifetime earnings and then deducting the expenses the decedent would have had in maintaining himself. The statute in *Laney* is somewhat atypical in potentially allowing punitive damages in the wrongful death action.

3.   **Pecuniary emphasis; loss-to-survivors' measure.** Wrongful death statutes originally limited the recovery to pecuniary losses suffered by dependents or those who would inherit. For example, under the loss to survivors' measure of damages, children of a decedent might recover for loss of support they received in the form of housing, food, and clothing. If the deceased person would not have contributed to any beneficiary during his lifetime, damages would be small or nonexistent. *See Armantrout v. Carlson*, 214 P.3d 914 (Wash. 2009) (in parents' suit for wrongful death of adult child, jury should consider services that have a monetary value when assessing the claimants' dependency on the decedent for support).

4.   **Loss-to-estate measure.** The loss-to-estate measure might allow substantial damages even where the decedent was not contributing to the support of others. This measure would allow recovery for whatever sums the decedent would have earned and saved in her normal lifetime, even if she were supporting no one. This would be helpful if decedent would have earned more than her self-support required. Under some circumstances might it lead to a zero award?

5.   **Combining measures.** Several courts have now permitted death action plaintiffs to recover both the loss of support and a loss of inheritance. The loss of inheritance is essentially like the loss to the estate. The claimant must show that the decedent would have accumulated an estate (or an increase in his estate) and that the claimant would have inherited a share. When the claimants were receiving no support, as is often the case with adult children of the decedent, in such jurisdictions they could still recover for reasonably provable loss of inheritance. *See Schaefer v. American Family Mut. Ins. Co.*, 531 N.W.2d 585 (Wis. 1995).

6.   **Non-earning decedents.** Children, spouses who do not work in the labor market, retired persons, and others whose earnings are small or nonexistent create still another problem under the wrongful death statutes. It

would be difficult to say that wrongful death has reduced their ultimate estate and equally difficult to say that they were supporting other persons. Thus neither measure of wrongful death damages is adequate for non-working decedents. In such cases, non-pecuniary damages become all-important. Does that seem like an issue in *Weigel* and *Laney*?

7. **Non-pecuniary claims generally.** At least three basic kinds of non-pecuniary loss might be claimed in death actions: (1) punitive damages; (2) damages for the mental anguish or grief of the survivors; (3) loss of consortium, which might include (a) loss of society or companionship, (b) loss of services, and (c) loss of guidance and care. As *Weigel* explains, claims like these were excluded under most original wrongful death statutes. The first two elements are generally rejected in wrongful death suits, though a few states permit their recovery. The third, loss of consortium, is usually recoverable. Courts stress that loss of consortium does not include emotional distress of the survivors, but that it does include a broad range of mutual benefits of family membership, including love, affection, care, companionship and the like. *See Reiser v. Coburn*, 587 N.W.2d 336 (Neb. 1998) (a zero award to parents of a young independent adult was inadequate, new trial required).

8. **Future losses.** Both the loss-to-survivors rule and the loss-to-the-estate rule require the court to estimate the earnings the decedent would have had but for the death. How many years would the decedent have lived to save money or make contributions to dependents? What would those earnings have been? These are difficult matters of proof and complicated by possible inflation and taxes. A discount must be made after all this to take into account the fact that the plaintiffs will recover all future losses now and can invest the sum at interest. *See generally* DAN B. DOBBS & CAPRICE L. ROBERTS, LAW OF REMEDIES § 8.4 (3d ed. 2018).

9. **Damages caps.** Many states have a statutory cap on noneconomic damages in some types of cases. Limits on noneconomic damage recovery in wrongful death cases may violate state constitutional provisions. *See Smith v. United States*, 356 P.3d 1249 (Utah 2015) ("The right of action to recover damages for injuries resulting in death, shall never be abrogated, and the amount recoverable shall not be subject to any statutory limitation, except in cases where compensation for injuries resulting in death is provided for by law."). If a doctor's negligence results in a wrongful death, should the med mal damages cap be applied in the wrongful death case? *Compare DRD Pool Serv., Inc. v. Freed*, 5 A.3d 45 (Md. 2010), and *Jenkins v. Patel*, 684 N.W.2d 346 (Mich. 2004) (yes), *with Bartholomew v. Wisconsin Patient's Comp. Fund*, 717 N.W.2d 216 (Wis. 2006) (no).

Survival Statutes

10. **Survival of claim after plaintiff's death.** A tort victim might bring a suit to redress a tort, then die before the suit goes to judgment. In that case, the claim is "revived" and continued in the name of the personal representative. Or, the victim might die without having brought suit, so that

the claim is brought by the personal representative in the first place. Either way, the claim is a survival action. It is a species of property which passes to the estate of the deceased person in the same way a share of stock or a bank account might pass.

11. **Survival of claim after defendant's death.** Survival statutes usually also provide for survival of the victim's claim after the defendant's death. In this setting, the living victim asserts the claim for all damages against the estate of the deceased tortfeasor. The case of the deceased victim is the more common one.

12. **Survival damages.** Since the survival action continues the claim held by the decedent for damages accruing up until his death, it may include any medical expenses, wages lost before death, and pain and suffering resulting from the injury. *See, e.g., Bibbs v. Toyota Motor Co.*, 815 S.E.2d 850 (Ga. 2018). In some states it may also include funeral expenses. Most states allow for the recovery of punitive damages in these cases, on a rationale that "if a wrongdoer may be punished if his victim lives, then surely he should not escape retribution if his wrongful act causes a death." *Smith v. Whitaker*, 734 A.2d 243 (N.J. 1999); *see also Guarantee Trust Life Ins. Co. v. Estate of Casper ex rel. Casper*, 418 P.3d 1163 (Colo. 2018) (reversing prior precedent holding to the contrary; punitive damages are disallowed only where the party *against whom* such damages are sought has died).

13. **Special classes of damages.** Survival statutes can create new kinds of damages. A few states authorize "loss of life" damages, designed "to compensate a decedent for the loss of the value that the decedent would have placed on his or her life." *See Durham v. Marberry*, 156 S.W.3d 242 (Ark. 2004). Such damages are available even if the decedent died instantly, since it is not identical to an award for pain and suffering. *Id.; see also Castro v. Melchor*, 414 P.3d 52 (Hawaii 2018) (affirming $250,000 award for stillborn fetus's "loss of enjoyment of life" under survival statute).

FINAL REPORT OF THE SPECIAL MASTER FOR THE SEPTEMBER 11TH VICTIM COMPENSATION FUND OF 2001

Report of Kenneth R. Feinberg, Esq., to U.S. Dep't of Justice (2004)

. . . The Report provides an extensive accounting of the operation and administration of the Fund and of the final resolution of all claims. The Fund is a unique program created in the aftermath of the tragic events of September 11, 2001. It was conceived, implemented, and concluded within a 33-month period. I am pleased to report that, in my view, the Fund was an unqualified success: 97% of the families of deceased victims who might otherwise have pursued lawsuits for years have received compensation through the Fund. The Fund provided generously for those directly affected by the attack. In total, the Fund distributed over $7.049 billion to survivors of 2,880 persons killed in the September 11th attacks and to over 2,680 individuals who were injured in the attacks or the rescue efforts conducted thereafter. The average award for families of victims killed in the attacks exceeded $2 million. The average award for injured victims was nearly $400,000. . . . Nearly every family of an individual killed in the September 11th attacks chose to participate in the Fund. . . .

Statutory Framework

In the immediate aftermath of the terrorist attacks of September 11, 2001, Congress enacted the Air Transportation Safety and System Stabilization Act (the "Act"). That legislation, signed by the President on September 22, 2001, sought to "preserve the continued viability" of the air transportation industry. . . . As a part of that legislation, Congress also created the "September 11th Victim Compensation Fund of 2001. The stated purpose of the fund was "to provide financial compensation to any individual (or relatives of a deceased individual) who was physically injured or killed as a result of [the September 11th attacks]." In creating this Program, Congress intended, in part, to establish a mechanism that would provide financial security and assistance to the victims of the attacks without the uncertainties, delays and costs of traditional litigation. . . .

The Regulations

In developing the Regulations [for the September 11th Victim Compensation Fund], the Department and the Special Master were guided by the plain language, structure, and evident purpose of the Act. First, Congress had created a hybrid compensation system that encompassed some but not all elements of tort compensation: the Act required the Special Master to consider such traditional elements of tort compensation as economic and non-economic loss but precluded the Special Master from considering issues of liability or punitive damages and obligated the Special Master to reduce any awards by payments that the claimant received from certain collateral sources. Second, Congress wanted a system that would quickly provide fair compensation to the families of the victims of the September 11th attacks. . . . Third, Congress did not intend to extend compensation to all persons affected by the events of September 11. The statute focused on a narrow group of individuals physically harmed or killed at the sites and in the immediate aftermath of the attacks. Finally, the structure and language of the Act and the public nature of the Program demonstrated that, while compensation should vary based on the circumstances of the individual claim, Congress did not intend that claimants should receive widely disparate awards from the Program. The Act charged the Special Master with the obligation to determine an "appropriate" award, taking into account the individual circumstances of the claimant, the facts of the claim and the harm to the claimant.

To achieve these purposes, the Department and the Special Master felt it essential to craft a system that would assure fairness and consistency among claimants. . . . To achieve these objectives, the Regulations established . . . a "presumed award" methodology, providing a uniform set of guidelines for the valuation of economic loss which would be favorable to most victims and yet based on information that claimants should be able to obtain easily. . . .

a)   The Presumed Methodology. . . .

In order to minimize, as much as possible, the speculative nature of computing future economic loss, the presumed methodology relies on a combination of the victim's own objectively verifiable historical experience with assumptions about likely future events based on publicly available national data. . . .

The presumed economic loss methodology computes the victim's future earnings by starting with the victim's earnings history. . . . The selected compensation level is then reduced by applicable state and federal taxes. The formula accounts for the fact that some portion of the victim's income is self-consumed and therefore not a measure of the economic loss to the survivors by incorporating a consumption deduction (derived from available national data).

The methodology assumes that the victim's income would grow over time at an average growth rate and would continue through an average work life. Finally, the methodology takes into account the potential for periods of future unemployment by incorporating an unemployment risk factor (based on national average data). The resulting figures are reduced to present value using age adjusted after-tax rates.

The presumed methodology was designed to provide generous awards to the families and to be simple to administer. Claimants . . . needed only to supply the Fund with easily obtained data: the victim's historical earnings, the victim's age, the age and status of members of the victim's household, the victim's employment benefits and collateral offset data. The presumed methodology assured that the economic loss calculation for similarly situated victims (i.e., same age, number of dependents and income level) would be consistent.

The Regulations provide that the presumed award methodology will be applied only to income levels up to the 99th percentile of individual income in the United States. This limitation was dictated by policy as well as fact. First, the Act was intended to provide fair and appropriate awards based upon families' individual circumstances, needs and resources. (The Special Master is directed to determine an appropriate award, not to calculate the maximum, theoretically possible, future earnings of each victim.) Second, the assumptions applied in the presumed methodology are inappropriate and become extremely speculative and conjectural when applied to incomes above the 98th percentile which are often comprised of a variety of forms of compensation, some of which are variable and volatile and tied to factors other than standard inflation and promotion increases.

For victims whose income exceeded the 98th percentile, the Fund calculated a "presumed" economic loss using $231,000 as the income level (i.e., the 98th percentile income level in the year 2000).

The Special Master and the Department understood that the presumed award methodology might be inadequate for claimants with extraordinary needs or circumstances. . . . In numerous instances, the Fund departed from the presumed methodology when the victim's earnings history revealed consistent earnings in excess of the 98 percentile. . . .

The Regulations establish uniform figures for "presumed" non-economic loss for decedents and dependents because the Department and Special Master could not justifiably conclude that one deceased victim or one victim's family suffered more than another. (Non-economic loss for the decedents was intended to address such intangible factors as pain and suffering and loss of enjoyment of life.) This system was administratively simple: each claim received a uniform non-economic award of $250,000 for the death of the victim and an additional non-economic award of $100,000 for the spouse and each dependent of the victim.

The Regulations allow the Special Master to depart from the "presumed" non-economic loss in extraordinary circumstances. The Fund did, in fact, award extraordinary non-economic loss in some instances: for example, the Fund increased the presumed $250,000 non-economic loss award in situations where a victim ultimately died after surviving for days, weeks or even months after the tragedy. . . .

The Regulations do not include a specific methodology for the calculation of awards for surviving victims who suffered physical injury. . . .

b)   The Assessment and Deduction of Collateral Source Compensation

One of the most controversial aspects of the Act is the requirement that the Special Master deduct "collateral offsets" from the award. The Act defines collateral sources to include a variety of types of payments but does not give detailed definitions or guidance. . . .

The deduction of collateral offsets [like life insurance payments] had a significant effect on the amount paid from the U.S. Treasury to victims and their families: collateral source compensation reduced overall payments from the U.S. Treasury by approximately 29%, saving over $2.9 billion. . . .

NOTES

1.   **Damage calculations.** How did the Fund calculate death damages? In what ways were those calculations similar to or different from the way tort law calculates damages? What factors in the Fund's presumed damages calculations discouraged extremely low awards or extremely high awards? As

many tables attached to the report show, payouts to deceased victims' families varied by the decedent's occupation, gender, race and age. Was that a problem?

2.   **The 9/11 Fund as a model.** The Special Master' report describes this system as "an unqualified success." Would a wrongful death fund have been a better alternative than tort law? What aspects of the system are appealing? What potential concerns would you have about a fund? Would a fund be a better alternative than tort law for all cases? For a thoughtful discussion of the Fund, see Lisa Belkin, *Just Money*, N.Y. TIMES, Dec. 8, 2002 ("Tragedy, particularly American tragedy, is always and inevitably about the money. . . . We do this because cash is the only tangible way to measure infinite loss."). For a brief look at the Fund in the context of other federal compensation schemes, see Chapter 29 § 1.

3.   **Damages awarded.** The average death damages awarded under the Fund were generous. Should they have been even more generous? In Eric A. Posner & Cass R. Sunstein, *Dollars and Death*, 72 U. CHI. L. REV. 537 (2005), the authors compare American regulation, which values life at a uniform number, recently $6 million, with tort law, which affords varied, but on average much lower, recoveries. One of Posner and Sunstein's conclusions is that "courts should move in the direction of administrative regulation by taking account of the welfare loss to the decedent. This change would significantly alter wrongful death cases by producing far higher recoveries in many cases." What could be a benefit of higher recoveries? Would deterrence matter in cases paid by a government fund?

4.   **Individualized damages vs. presumptive awards.** In wrongful death cases, rather than calculate individualized damages in each case, Chinese tort law generally awards the decedent's beneficiaries twenty times the average earnings in the decedent's locality. This presumptive award can be decreased in certain circumstances, as in the case of old age, or increased in other circumstances, for example, when the decedent had been living in a city although registered as living in a rural area. *See* SPC Interpretation on Compensation for Personal Injury, cited in THE CHINA LAW CENTER, YALE LAW SCHOOL, TORT LAW IN CHINA: HISTORICAL DEVELOPMENT AND SELECTED ISSUES (2006). Although the presumptive awards have been criticized in China for creating unequal awards, would this type of system create more equal awards in the United States? Why permit widely-disparate individualized awards rather than more consistent awards?

§ 3. BENEFICIARIES

CHAVEZ V. CARPENTER, 111 Cal.Rptr.2d 534 (Ct. App. 2001). Altie Chavez, 24, was killed by a drunk driver, the defendant here, in August. Though unmarried, Altie was the father of a two-year-old daughter, Jazmyne. Jazmyne died from unrelated causes in September. Altie had lived with and perhaps contributed monetary support to his parents, Jose and Elsa. They brought suit for his death. Maria Garcia, Jazmyne's mother, brought suit on behalf of Jazmyne's estate. Held: (1) the statute permits recovery by heirs, but the parents cannot recover as heirs of Altie because parents cannot be heirs if the decedent's child survived him, which Jazmyne did; (2) the statute now permits recovery by parents who were "dependents"; this is a factual question to be addressed at trial; and (3) Jazmyne, as an heir, had a cause of action for the wrongful death of her father, Altie, and that cause of action survived her and may be pursued by her estate.

NOTES

1. **Stepchildren and children given up for adoption.** Statutes may include "stepchildren" among those entitled to recover. *See, e.g., In re Estate of Blessing*, 273 P.3d 975 (Wash. 2012). Most courts interpreting statutes that allow "heirs" or "children" to recover, however, have held that stepchildren do not qualify. *See, e.g., Steed v. Imperial Airlines*, 524 P.2d 801 (Cal. 1974). The California Legislature responded to *Steed* by amending its Civil Procedure Code § 377 to provide that minors living with the decedent for six months or more and receiving more than half their support from decedent could recover for wrongful death. Biological children who have been given up for adoption may or may not be entitled to recover, depending on statutory language. *See Rismiller v. Gemini Ins. Co.*, 330 So.3d 145 (La. 2021) (biological children given up for adoption had no right to assert survival and wrongful death action, based on plain reading of applicable statutes).

2. **Unmarried cohabitants.** Under statutes that distribute damages to heirs, or to named categories, such as "surviving spouse" or "children," there is obviously no room for compensation to the surviving friend or lover. *See, e.g., Langan v. St. Vincent's Hosp. of New York*, 802 N.Y.S.2d 476 (App. Div. 2005) (surviving partner of same-sex civil union not a "surviving spouse" under statute). Modern statutes may expressly provide for broader coverage, such as to provide for same-sex domestic partners. See, e.g., 15 VT. STAT. §§ 1204(a) & 1204(e)(2); CAL. CIV. PROC. CODE § 377.60.

3. **Jury bias.** Along with distributional defects in the statutory wrongful death schemes, there are problems in jury awards. Studies show that jurors award much larger sums to the female spouse of a male decedent than to the male spouse of a female decedent, even when their earnings are the same. *See* Goodman, Loftus, Miller & Greene, *Money, Sex, and Death: Gender Bias in Wrongful Death Damage Awards*, 25 L. & SOC'Y REV. 263 (1991). Female decedents are worth less? Or female survivors need more? Is the disparity justified under either hypothesis?

4. **Distribution among beneficiaries.** Distribution of wrongful death proceeds is a frequent subject of litigation. *See, e.g., Macke v. Patton*, 591 S.W.3d 865 (Mo. 2019) (affirming apportionment of wrongful-death settlement proceeds 98% to father and 2% to mother as "not against the weight of the evidence"); *In re Estate of Dezotell*, 140 A.3d 797 (Vt. 2016) (court entered distribution order, apportioning the amount between wife and children differently than it had in its previous two orders); *Estate of Eubanks v. Eubanks*, 197 So.3d 861 (Miss. 2015) (Chancery Court was without authority

to unequally divide wrongful-death settlement proceeds between decedent's wrongful death beneficiaries). What of a surviving spouse who was a spouse in name only? In *Force v. American Family Mut. Ins. Co.*, 850 N.W.2d 866 (Wis. 2014), the court allowed dependent minor children to recover under a wrongful death statute for the death of their father even though the deceased's spouse is alive but does not recover any wrongful death damages. In the case, the spouse could not recover because she had no compensable damages under the statute; she and her husband had been estranged for over ten years prior to his death and had "no interaction or affection" for each other. Under these circumstances, reading the statute to disallow claims of children because of the existence of a "surviving spouse" would "contravene [the] fundamental purposes of the wrongful death statutes," which are "to impose liability on the wrongdoer and to protect relational interests, especially the interests of the deceased's minor dependent children." Dissenters said the majority's result, excluding a "surviving spouse" from the statutory definition of that term "because she was estranged from her husband at the time of his death," was "appealing" on the facts, but "will create considerable mischief in the future."

§ 4. DEFENSES

A. CONTRIBUTORY NEGLIGENCE AND ASSUMPTION OF RISK

What if the decedent was contributorily negligent, or assumed the risk (either impliedly or expressly), in connection with the injury-causing event that caused the death? Can the defendant in a wrongful death or survival action assert such defenses against the claimant? Jurisdictions have not agreed on this, but the answer seems to turn most crucially on whether the death or survival action is regarded as *derivative* of the deceased person's claim or *independent* of it.

In a survival action, in which the plaintiff is the representative of the decedent's estate, you would expect that the defendant could assert the defenses that could have been asserted had the decedent been litigating the case while alive—and that is indeed the dominant rule.

Should a wrongful death action be treated the same way? The answer will depend on the wording of relevant statutes (both the wrongful death statute and any comparative fault statute), and thus varies from state to state. See *Horwich v. Superior Court*, 980 P.2d 927 (Cal. 1999) ("[T]he application of some limitations or bars to wrongful death actions will turn on statutory interpretation."). In many states, the wrongful death statute itself provides that the claim is derivative, not independent, of the decedent's own claim. In those jurisdictions the courts have routinely held that the defendant in the wrongful death suit can use all (or most) of the affirmative defenses that could have been used if the suit had been brought by the decedent. *See, e.g., GGNC Administrative Services, LLC v. Schrader,*

140 N.E.2d 397 (Mass. 2020); *In re Labatt Food Service, L.P.*, 279 S.W.3d 640 (Tex. 2009) ("While it is true that damages for a wrongful death action are for the exclusive benefit of the beneficiaries . . ., the cause of action is still entirely derivative of the decedent's rights."). Thus in most states, the defendant can use the decedent's contributory negligence to either reduce or bar the wrongful death claimant's recovery. *See, e.g., Tobin v. Norwood Country Club, Inc.*, 661 N.E.2d 627 (Mass 1996); *Adamy v. Ziriakus*, 704 N.E.2d 396 (N.Y. 1998). Other defenses, such as assumption of risk, have been treated similarly. *See Horwich, supra* ("[S]ome defenses can be asserted equally against the defendant or the heirs, principally comparative negligence, release in the case of primary assumption of the risk, privilege, and collateral estoppel."); *Saenz v. Whitewater Voyages, Inc.*, 226 Cal.App.3d 758 (1990) (decedent's pre-injury release could be asserted as a defense against wrongful death claimants).

A number of other states have interpreted their wrongful death statutes differently, however. Where the wrongful death claim is not seen as "wholly derivative" of the decedent's own claim, then the defendant should not be able to assert all of the defenses that the decedent could have asserted. *See, e.g., Boler v. Security Health Care, LLC*, 336 P.3d 468 (Okla. 2014) (listing different states in each camp, holding that an arbitration agreement signed by decedent's attorney was not binding on claimants in wrongful death action); *Ping v. Beverly Enterprises, Inc.*, 376 S.W.3d 581 (Ky. 2012) (same). If the wrongful death statute truly creates a "new and independent claim," then not allowing the defendant to use the decedent's contributory negligence or assumption of risk makes sense, doesn't it?

B. STATUTE OF LIMITATIONS

Albert Weinberg was exposed to asbestos from 1941 to 1948. In 1975 a mesothelioma, or lung cancer, was discovered. This allegedly resulted from the asbestos exposure. Mr. Weinberg brought no action during his life and he died in 1977. Thereafter an action for his death was brought within two years. The death act prescribes two years from death as the limitation period. Is the claim nevertheless barred on the ground that no action for death can be brought unless the decedent could have maintained an action at the same time had he lived? Some courts have taken this view. *See Russell v. Ingersoll-Rand Co.*, 841 S.W.2d 343 (Tex. 1992); *Deggs v. Asbestos Corp. Ltd.*, 381 P.3d 32 (Wash. 2016); *Edwards v. Fogarty*, 962 P.2d 879 (Wyo. 1998).

However, many cases hold that the statute begins running at the time of death and that the wrongful death claim is not barred even if the decedent would be barred had he lived. *E.g., Chapman v. Cardiac Pacemakers, Inc.*, 673 P.2d 385 (Idaho 1983); *Mummert v. Alizadeh*, 77 A.3d 1049 (Md. 2013) (plaintiffs' right to bring action was not contingent on patient's ability to bring negligence action prior to death).

Discovery rule. Courts are divided and uncertain whether the discovery rule applies in wrongful death actions. *See* 2 DOBBS, HAYDEN & BUBLICK, THE LAW OF TORTS § 379 (2d ed. 2011). Many have done so, however, where the wrongful death statute itself does not disallow it. What if the wrongful-death claimant timely discovered the wrongful conduct that caused decedent's death, but not the identity of the responsible defendant? *See Parillo v. Rhode Island Hosp.*, 202 A.3d 942 (R.I. 2019) (applying discovery rule, affirming summary judgment for defendant on statute of limitations grounds); *see also Palmer ex rel. Palmer v. Walker Jamar Co.*, 945 N.W.2d 844 (Minn. 2020) (wrongful death claim accrued when the decedent "learned that asbestos exposure had caused his mesothelioma," even where neither he nor his spouse knew that defendant had caused such exposure).

Some wrongful death statutes contain their own statute of repose. *See, e.g.*, CONN. GEN. STAT. § 52–555 (five-year statute of repose for wrongful death claims, with accrual on "the date of death"). Where such a statute exists, the claimant cannot take advantage of any delayed discovery or tolling rules. *See Angersola v. Radiologic Assocs. of Middletown, P.C.*, 193 A.3d 520 (Conn. 2018) (continuing course of treatment doctrine could not be used to toll wrongful death statute of repose).

REFERENCES: 2 DOBBS, HAYDEN & BUBLICK, THE LAW OF TORTS §§ 372–380 (2d ed. 2011); DOBBS, HAYDEN & BUBLICK, HANDBOOK ON TORTS ch. 28 (2d ed. 2016).

PART 8

THE EBB AND FLOW OF COMMON LAW STRICT LIABILITY FOR PHYSICAL HARMS

■ ■ ■

In the materials covered so far, fault has been the keynote concept in liability. We now consider three areas involving complete or partial strict liability—liability without proof of the defendant's fault. Strict liability means that liability is imposed even without proof that the defendant acted intentionally or negligently.

In the last chapter in this Part, Chapter 24, the topic is products liability. Products liability law sometimes (but not always) imposes liability without proof of fault upon manufacturers and distributors of defective products.

In Chapter 23 we will see older forms of strict liability, those associated with certain problems of trespassing or dangerous animals, neighboring landowners (often making inconsistent uses of land), and with especially hazardous activities that tend to cause harm even when not carried out negligently.

In the first chapter in this Part, Chapter 22, we renew acquaintance with an idea introduced at the very beginning of the course—vicarious liability, which can be perceived as a form of strict liability in which one person or entity is held legally responsible for the fault-based torts of another.

CHAPTER 22

VICARIOUS LIABILITY

■ ■ ■

§ 1. RESPONDEAT SUPERIOR AND SCOPE OF EMPLOYMENT

We recognized early in the course that employers could be held liable for the torts of certain employees, provided those torts were committed within the scope of employment. This principle of liability is often called vicarious liability or the *respondeat superior* principle.

What is meant by the limitation that torts must be committed within the scope of employment? To a large extent the answer to this question turns on a much larger one—why hold the employer liable at all? The employer is not personally at fault, so that his liability is in a sense a kind of strict liability. One case summarized the goals of vicarious liability succinctly as (a) the prevention of future injuries, (b) the assurance of compensation to victims, and (c) the equitable spreading of losses caused by an enterprise. *See Lisa M. v. Henry Mayo Newhall Mem. Hosp.*, 907 P.2d 358 (Cal. 1995).

RIVIELLO V. WALDRON, 391 N.E.2d 1278 (N.Y. 1979). Waldron, employed as a cook at the Pot Belly Pub, a Bronx bar and grill, was talking to a customer and flipping an open knife. This accidentally struck the customer in the eye, causing a loss of its use. The customer sued the bar owner. *Held*, the bar owner is liable; Waldron was within the scope of employment. The scope of employment was originally defined narrowly "on the theory that the employer could exercise close control over his employees during the period of their service." But "social policy has wrought a measure of relaxation of the traditional confines of the doctrine." Reasons for this are that "the average innocent victim, when relegated to the pursuit of his claim against the employee, most often will face a defendant too impecunious to meet the claim, and that modern economic devices, such as cost accounting and insurance coverage, permit most employers to spread the impact of such costs. So no longer is an employer necessarily excused merely because his employees, acting in furtherance of his interests, exhibit human failings and perform negligently or otherwise than in an authorized manner. Instead, the test has come to be whether the act was done while the servant was doing his master's work, no matter how irregularly, or with what disregard of instructions."

FRUIT V. SCHREINER, 502 P.2d 133 (Alaska 1972). Fruit, a life insurance salesman, was attending a company sales convention where his employer required him to be. Events included morning business meetings and evening dinners and cocktail parties. Employees were encouraged to mix freely with out-of-state attendees to learn as much as possible about sales techniques. On the first night of the convention, Fruit and other sales agents went for dinner and drinks to a restaurant and bar in Homer, about five miles from the convention headquarters. The next evening, having slept through a scheduled dinner, Fruit drove back to the Homer restaurant, believing that out-of-state sales agents would be there. He left when he found no one there. It was 2:00 a.m. when, on his way back to the convention headquarters, Fruit skidded and struck Schreiner, whose legs were crushed. Schreiner sued Fruit and his employer. A jury found both liable; the employer was found liable because Fruit's negligent driving was within the scope of his employment. The employer appealed, claiming that the evidence did not support such a finding.

Held, affirmed. The jury could find that when Fruit made his fateful trip to Homer, "he was at least motivated in part by his desire to meet with the out-of-state guests and thus to benefit from their experience so as to improve his abilities as a salesman. . . . The basis of *respondeat superior* has been correctly stated as the desire to include in the costs of operation inevitable losses to third persons incident to carrying on an enterprise, and thus distribute the burden among those benefitted by the enterprise. . . . Insurance is readily available for the employer so that the risk may be distributed among many like insured paying premiums and the extra cost of doing business may be reflected in the price of the product."

NOTES

1.   **Scope of employment.** In both *Riviello* and *Fruit*, the employees were found to have been acting within the scope of employment when they committed their torts. Whether an employee was acting within the scope of employment is a fact question for the jury, where reasonable people can differ. *See, e.g., Hecksher v. Fairwinds Baptist Church, Inc.*, 15 A.3d 1187 (Del. 2015). Traditionally, an employee's conduct is within the scope of employment if it is of the same general kind as authorized or expected, and the employee was acting within authorized time and space limits. The Agency Restatements, followed by many courts, additionally impose a kind of "purpose" or "motive" test—that the employee's action must have been motivated, at least in part, by a purpose to serve the employer. *See* RESTATEMENT (SECOND) OF AGENCY § 228(1)(c) (1959); RESTATEMENT (THIRD) OF AGENCY § 707(2) (2006). Thus some courts find no vicarious liability where the act is "too little actuated by a

purpose to serve the master." *See Doe v. Newbury Bible Church*, 933 A.2d 196 (Vt. 2007). However, a number of modern courts reject or minimize this "purpose" or "motive" test, and instead adopt a broader formulation. *See, e.g., Gina Chin & Associates v. First Union Bank*, 537 S.E.2d 573 (Va. 2000) (motive not determinative; issue is "whether the service itself, in which the tortious act is done, was within the ordinary course of such business"); *Sheffer v. Carolina Forge Co.*, 306 P.3d 544 (Okla. 2013) ("one acts within the scope of employment if engaged in work assigned, or if doing that which is proper, necessary and useful to accomplish the work assigned, or doing that which is customary within the particular trade or business"). While we will see some other definitions throughout this chapter, it is probably good to keep in mind the words of the Delaware Supreme Court: "The phrase, 'scope of employment' is, at best, indefinite. It is nothing more than a convenient means of defining those tortious acts of the servant not ordered by the master for which the policy of law imposes liability on the master." *Doe v. State*, 76 A.3d 774 (Del. 2013) (quoting *Draper v. Olivere Paving & Constr. Co.*, 181 A.2d 565 (Del. 1962)).

2. **Disregarding the employer's instructions or orders.** The *Riviello* court notes that vicarious liability may be found even where the employee disregards the employer's instructions in committing the injurious act. The general rule is that "the employer's vicarious liability extends to the negligent, willful, malicious, or even criminal acts of its employees when such acts are committed within the scope of the employment." *Adames v. Sheahan*, 909 N.E.2d 724 (Ill. 2009); *see also Farmers Ins. Group v. County of Santa Clara*, 906 P.2d 440 (Cal. 1995). The "true test . . . is whether at the time of the commission of the injury the employee was performing a service in the furtherance of his employer's business, not whether it was done in exact observance of the detail prescribed by the employer." *Ohio Farmers Ins. Co. v. Norman*, 594 P.2d 1026 (Ariz. Ct. App. 1979).

3. **Thinking about the rationales.** Do the New York and Alaska Courts in *Riviello* and *Fruit* give the same reasons for expansive liability of an employer? Is either court simply using the theory that the employer represents a "deep pocket"? What reasons can you give for holding an employer liable for the employee's negligence in causing harm to others?

CAMERON V. OSLER

930 N.W.2d 661 (S.D. 2019)

WILBUR, RETIRED JUSTICE.

After being injured in a car accident, Kimberlynn Cameron brought suit against Jason Osler. She subsequently filed an amended summons and complaint, adding a claim for vicarious liability and naming Osler's employer, Waste Connections of South Dakota, Inc., as a defendant. However, Cameron failed to timely serve Osler, and he was dismissed from the suit, leaving only Waste Connections as a defendant. Waste Connections filed a motion to dismiss, asserting Cameron's failure to timely serve Osler precluded suit against Waste Connections. The circuit court agreed and granted Waste Connections' motion to dismiss. Cameron appeals. . . .

Waste Connections' liability, if any, arises from the doctrine of respondeat superior. The ancient doctrine of *respondeat superior* is well established as holding an employer or principal liable for the employee's or agent's wrongful acts committed within the scope of the employment or agency. The employer's liability is merely a derivative of the employee's. Therefore, we have held that a plaintiff cannot proceed against an employer when the negligent employee has been released via a settlement with the plaintiff. This is because the release of the culpable party extinguishes any liability of the non-guilty principal.

Here, however, there has been no settlement and release of Osler. Rather, Cameron's suit against Osler has been dismissed because the statute of limitations expired on her claim against Osler. We have not before examined whether a plaintiff can proceed against an employer when the plaintiff's suit against the employee has been dismissed as time barred. According to Osler, multiple courts have held that such suit is permissible because the employee is not a necessary party to a vicarious liability claim and the employee's negligence can be determined in the employee's absence. In response, Waste Connections identifies contrary authority and contends that suit against an employer is precluded because the employee has been adjudicated not negligent via a dismissal with prejudice. . . .

[R]elying on principles attendant to the doctrine of respondeat superior, the Delaware Supreme Court emphasized that "the employer's liability hinges upon the employee's *culpability*—as distinguished from the employee's *liability*." *Verrastro v. Bayhospitalists, LLC*, 208 A.3d 720 (Del. 2019). The court further reasoned that treating a dismissal as an adjudication on the merits is "not intended to encompass procedural dismissals that do not adjudicate the wrongfulness of the agent's conduct." Ultimately, the court held that "in a negligence action against a principal based on the doctrine of *respondeat superior*, the dismissal of the agent on a defense personal to the agent does not automatically eliminate the principal's vicarious liability." . . .

Focusing particularly on the lack of an actual adjudication on the merits, the Virginia Supreme Court held that a suit against the employer may proceed even though the suit against the employee is time barred. *Hughes v. Doe*, 639 S.E.2d 302 (Va. 2007). The court observed that "the crux of respondeat superior liability is a finding that the employee was negligent." In the court's view, therefore, there must be an "affirmative finding that [the employee] was not negligent" to preclude suit, rather than a dismissal that merely terminated the plaintiff's ability to hold the employee personally liable. . . .

In contrast to the above authorities, other courts [in Arkansas, Michigan and New York] have held that an employer cannot be held vicariously liable unless a viable cause of action exists against the employee. . . .

Having considered the differing views, we find more reasoned the approach that considers the context of the dismissal before precluding suit against the employer for vicarious liability. Respondeat superior is a legal fiction designed to bypass impecunious individual tortfeasors for the deep pocket of a vicarious tortfeasor. The employer's vicarious liability "is a function of status and stems entirely from the tortious conduct of the [employee], not from any tortious conduct by the [employer.]". Therefore, "[i]t is the negligence of the servant that is imputed to the master, not the *liability.*" *Cohen v. Alliant Enters., Inc.*, 60 S.W.3d 536 (Ky. 2001). . . .

Nevertheless, Waste Connections claims it "cannot be independently held liable on a theory of vicarious liability" because Cameron chose to name Osler as a party and Osler was dismissed. We disagree. . . . [L]iability is imposed because the plaintiff brought suit against the employer and put on evidence that the employee committed a tort within the scope of employment. Therefore, contrary to Waste Connections' view, Osler's culpability can be established even though Osler has no civil liability to Cameron.

Here, the dismissal of Osler was purely procedural and available to Osler because Cameron failed to serve him within the time limit allowed by the statute of limitations. The dismissal did not examine or determine Osler's culpability, and there has been no release of Cameron's claim or an exchange of value. Because Cameron properly initiated suit against Waste Connections prior to the expiration of the statute of limitations, the circuit court erred when it held that the dismissal of Osler terminated Cameron's suit against Waste Connections.

Reversed.

NOTES

1. **Vicarious liability and "fault."** When an employer is sued on a vicarious liability theory, the employer's own fault is irrelevant; in this way, it is accurate to call vicarious liability form of strict liability. But no one can be vicariously liable for another's tort unless that other person commits a tort— and as we have seen in this course, that will typically require the plaintiff to prove that the other person (such as an employee), was negligent or acted intentionally. In other words, where the employee has not committed a tort at all, the employer cannot be vicariously liable for whatever harm the employee may have caused. *See* DOBBS, HAYDEN & BUBLICK, HORNBOOK ON TORTS § 425, at 782 (2d ed. 2011).

2.   **Culpability vs. liability of employee.** As you can see from *Cameron*, whether an employer can be held vicariously liable for the employee's tort if the employee is not or cannot be held legally liable is a more nuanced question than you might think. Many courts have held that if the employee personally was not or could not be held *legally responsible* for an otherwise tortious act, the employer cannot be vicariously liable, either. *See, e.g., Ex Parte Labbe*, 156 So.3d 368 (Ala. 2014) (individual volunteer firefighters have statutory immunity, so their employer cannot be vicariously liable for the firefighters' negligent acts); *Strock v. Pressnell*, 527 N.E.2d 1235 (Ohio 1988) ("It is axiomatic that for the doctrine of respondeat superior to apply, an employee must be liable for a tort committed in the scope of his employment.").

But others have taken the position the *Cameron* court does, which is to focus on whether the non-liability of the employee was based on a finding on the merits that the employee did not act tortiously. Only if so will the vicarious liability of the employer be extinguished. In *Verrastro v. Bayhospitalists, LLC*, 208 A.3d 720 (Del. 2019), cited in *Cameron*, the court quoted the Restatement Second of Agency § 217: "In an action against a principal based on the conduct of a servant in the course of employment . . . [t]he principal has no defense because of the fact that an agent had an immunity from civil liability as to the act." On this reasoning, where the employee has not been or cannot be successfully sued personally because of some defense not going to the merits of the employee's culpability, such as the statute of limitations or an immunity, the employer can still be held vicariously liable. *See, e.g., Methodist Healthcare-Olive Branch Hosp. v. McNutt*, 323 So.3d 1051 (Miss. 2021) (employer could still be found vicariously liable for employee's medical malpractice where employee was dismissed on statute of limitations grounds because the plaintiff failed to serve the necessary pre-suit notice on the employee; "A dismissal on statute of limitations grounds does not reach the merits of the case."). Which approach is better, and why?

3.   **Joinder.** In most states, the plaintiff has an option to sue either the employee or the employer or both. That is, the employee is not a necessary party in a vicarious liability suit. *See Methodist Healthcare, supra* Note 2 (calling this a "well-established rule"). Does this fact tend to support the approach taken in the *Cameron* case? Can the fault of the employee be adjudicated in a suit against the employer without the joinder of the employee as a defendant?

4.   **Effect of release.** The *Cameron* court notes that a vicarious liability claim *is* extinguished where the negligent employee has been released from liability via a settlement with the plaintiff. This appears to be the virtually uniform position of courts. *See* RESTATEMENT (SECOND) OF JUDGMENTS § 51, cmt. a (1982); *Christiana Care Health Care Services Inc. v. Carter*, 223 A.3d 428 (Del. 2019); *J&J Timber Co. v. Broome*, 932 So.2d 1 (Miss. 2006).

5.   **Employer's right of indemnity.** If an employer is held vicariously liable because of an employee's tort, the employer has a theoretical right of

indemnity from the employee—that is, a right to recoup from the employee the damages the employer has paid to the plaintiff. *See* RESTATEMENT (SECOND) OF TORTS § 886B(1)–(2)(a) (1979). That right is seldom asserted, however, partly because the employer's liability insurance is likely to protect both employer and employee.

NOTE: ENTERPRISE LIABILITY

As reflected in *Fruit*, the concept of enterprise liability is often close to the surface of any strict liability analysis. In his groundbreaking book, *The Costs of Accidents* (1970), Professor (now Judge) Guido Calabresi urged that tort law's principal function is to reduce the costs of accidents and the costs of avoiding them. We will see Calabresi's ideas in some more depth in Chapter 24, but some of his central conceptions are worth thinking about here.

One idea is that the price of goods and activities should accurately reflect the accident costs they cause. Holding an enterprise strictly liable for harms it causes facilitates this "internalization of costs," which in turn reduces the costs of accidents. How are accident costs reduced? Consumers are influenced by prices. If the price of a particular product or service actually reflects its total costs, including accident costs, the market will tend to favor the cheaper (safer) product or service. Companies will thus have an incentive to make their products and activities safer to compete in the marketplace. Do these ideas support holding an employer strictly liable for the torts of its employees, committed within the scope of employment?

How well does enterprise liability theory mix with accountability for fault? If there is a good reason to hold an employer strictly liable in these cases, why not hold all employers liable, regardless of employee negligence, when an act within the scope of employment causes harm?

NOTE: SERVING TWO MASTERS

1. *Borrowed servants.* Where one employer "loans" one of its employees to another employer and that employee negligently injures someone, which of the "employers" is vicariously liable? This problem is known as the "borrowed servant" situation. The Restatement (Third) of Agency suggests that liability depends upon which "employer is in the better position to take measures to prevent the injury suffered," looking at which employer "has a right to control" the employee's conduct. RESTATEMENT (THIRD) OF AGENCY § 7.03, cmt. d(2) (2006). The traditional approach is that the first employer is vicariously liable, while the

"borrowing" employer is not, unless evidence leads to a different conclusion based on who has the right to "control" the servant. Some authority holds both employers liable if the employee is acting within the scope of his employment for both masters simultaneously. *See* 2 DOBBS, HAYDEN & BUBLICK, THE LAW OF TORTS § 434 (2d ed. 2011).

2.   *The moonlighting police officer.* Suppose a full-time city police officer works at the D-Mart Discount Store as a security guard when he is off-duty. In the course of his work at D-Mart, he uses his police pistol to shoot the plaintiff after a scuffle. The plaintiff alleges that the shooting was negligent or alternatively that it was intentional and unprivileged. Can the plaintiff state a prima facie case against the city, D-Mart, or both? Be sure to distinguish the borrowed servant scenario. In formulating your answer, do you think it would matter whether police officers are always under an obligation, even when off-duty, to enforce the law as to violations occurring in their presence? *See Lovelace v. Anderson,* 785 A.2d 726 (Md. 2001); *White v. Revco Discount Drug Ctrs., Inc.,* 33 S.W.3d 713 (Tenn. 2000). Does it matter whether, at the time of the shooting, the officer was performing a function directed by the store's management? *See Ambling Management Co. v. Miller,* 764 S.E.2d 127 (Ga. 2014).

NOTE: SERVING GRATUITOUSLY

1.   We've been referring to employers and employees, or in the old language of the law, masters and servants. The relationship of master and servant can be established without payment or promise of payment. RESTATEMENT (THIRD) OF AGENCY §§ 1.01, cmt. d & 7.07(3)(b) (2006). However, that relationship is not established unless the putative servant submits himself to the control of the employer. A church member might accept unpaid duties of delivering cookies to shut-ins for a church program. If the church expects him to act on its behalf and he submits to the church's directions, he is a servant. Absent an immunity, the church is therefore liable if he negligently runs someone down while delivering cookies. *Trinity Lutheran Church, Inc. of Evansville, Ind. v. Miller,* 451 N.E.2d 1099 (Ind. Ct. App. 1983).

2.   What about the person who voluntarily assists another, without such submission? *See Austin v. Kaness,* 950 P.2d 561 (Wyo. 1997) (adult son feeding cats while parents were away does not become an agent, servant or employee of parents).

HINMAN v. WESTINGHOUSE ELECTRIC CO.

471 P.2d 988 (Cal. 1970)

PETERS, JUSTICE.

Plaintiff, a Los Angeles policeman, was standing on the center divider of a freeway inspecting a possible road hazard when he was struck by a car driven by Frank Allen Herman, an employee of defendant Westinghouse. As a result of the accident he received permanent injuries. The city paid his medical expenses and disability pension. [Plaintiff sued Westinghouse on a vicarious liability theory.]

At the time of the accident, Herman was employed by Westinghouse as an elevator constructor's helper and was returning home from work from a job site. He had been working for Westinghouse for about four months. His work was assigned from the Westinghouse office. He did not go to the office before or after work but instead went from home directly to the job site and after work returned home from the job site. The particular job on which Herman was working was not completed at the time of the accident, and he would ordinarily return to the job site until the job was completed or he was told not to return.

The union contracts under which Herman worked provided for the payment of "carfare" and travel time in certain circumstances depending on the location of the job site in relation to the Los Angeles City Hall. As to this job, which was 15 to 20 miles from the city hall, Herman received an hour and a half per day as his roundtrip travel time and $1.30 for his travel expense. The employer had no control over the method or route of transportation used by Herman.

The trial judge refused instructions that Herman was acting within the scope of his employment at the time of the accident and instead instructed the jury that whether he was acting within the scope of his employment depended upon a number of factors including among others "whether his conduct was authorized by his employer, either expressly or impliedly; the nature of the employment, its object and the duties imposed thereby; whether the employee was acting in his discharge thereof; whether his conduct occurred during the performance of services for the benefit of the employer, either directly or indirectly, or of himself; whether his conduct, even though not expressly or impliedly authorized, was an incidental event connected with his assigned work. " [So instructed, the jury found that Herman was not within the scope of his employment and hence gave a verdict for Westinghouse.]

Although earlier authorities sought to justify the *respondeat superior* doctrine on such theories as "control" by the master of the servant, the master's "privilege" in being permitted to employ another, the third party's innocence in comparison to the master's selection of the servant, or the master's "deep pocket" to pay for the loss, "the modern justification for vicarious liability is a rule of policy, a deliberate allocation of a risk. The losses caused by the torts of employees, which as a practical matter are sure to occur in the conduct of the employer's enterprise, are placed upon that enterprise itself, as a required cost of doing business. They are placed upon the employer because, having engaged in an enterprise which will, on the basis of past experience, involve harm to others through the torts of employees, and sought to profit by it, it is just that he, rather than the innocent injured plaintiff, should bear them; and because he is better able to absorb them, and to distribute them, through prices, rates or liability insurance, to the public, and so to shift them to society, to the community at large." . . .

Another leading authority also points out that the modern and proper basis of vicarious liability of the master is not his control or fault but the risks incident to his enterprise. "We are not here looking for the master's fault but rather for risks that may fairly be regarded as typical of or broadly incidental to the enterprise he has undertaken. . . ."

Liability of the employer may not be avoided on the basis of the "going and coming" rule. Under the "going and coming" rule, an employee going to and from work is ordinarily considered outside the scope of employment so that the employer is not liable for his torts. The "going and coming" rule is sometimes ascribed to the theory that the employment relationship is "suspended" from the time the employee leaves until he returns or that in commuting he is not rendering service to his employer. Nevertheless, there are exceptions to the rule.

Thus in Harvey v. D & L Construction Co., the court reversed a nonsuit for the employer where it was shown that because of the remote site of the construction project, the employer had asked the employee to recruit other employees, one such employee was riding at the time of the accident, and the employer was furnishing the gas for the trip to the employee's home. . . .

The above cases indicate that exceptions will be made to the "going and coming" rule where the trip involves an incidental benefit to the employer, not common to commute trips by ordinary members of the work force. The cases also indicate that the fact that the employee receives personal benefits is not determinative when there is also a benefit to the employer.

There is a substantial benefit to an employer in one area to be permitted to reach out to a labor market in another area or to enlarge the available labor market by providing travel expenses and payment for travel time. It cannot be denied that the employer's reaching out to the distant or larger labor market increases the risk of injury in transportation. In other words, the employer, having found it desirable in the interests of his enterprise to pay for travel time and for travel expenses and to go beyond the normal labor market or to have located his enterprise at a place remote from the labor market, should be required to pay for the risks inherent in his decision.

We are satisfied that, where, as here, the employer and employee have made the travel time part of the working day by their contract, the employer should be treated as such during the travel time, and it follows that so long as the employee is using the time for the designated purpose, to return home, the doctrine of *respondeat superior* is applicable. It is unnecessary to determine the appropriate rule to be applied if the employee had used the time for other purposes. We also need not decide now whether the mere payment of travel expenses without additional payment for the travel time of the employee . . . reflects a sufficient benefit to the employer so that he should bear responsibility to innocent third parties for the risks inherent in the travel.

The facts relating to the applicability of the doctrine of *respondeat superior* are undisputed in the instant case, and we conclude that as a matter of law the doctrine is applicable and that the trial court erred in its instructions in leaving the issue as one of fact to the jury. . . .

NOTES

1. **The going and coming rule.** The going and coming rule is widely, perhaps universally, accepted. *See Barclay v. Briscoe*, 47 A.3d 560 (Md. 2012). Does the rule make logical sense when you focus on the factors the *Hinman* court used to determine "scope of employment" more generally? Remember that many injuries will be caused by employees while driving their vehicles to and from work; does that fact give the going and coming rule a strong policy basis? See *Ahlstrom v. Salt Lake City Corp.*, 73 P.3d 315 (Utah 2003) ("The major premise of the 'going and coming' rule is that it is unfair to impose unlimited liability on an employer for conduct of its employees over which it has no control and from which it derives no benefit."); *see also Long v. Houser*, 456 P.3d 549 (Kan. App. 2020) ("The rationale behind the going and coming rule is that when someone is driving to work, he or she is subjected only to the same risks or hazards that the public faces while driving. The risks therefore are not causally related to the employment.").

2. **Exceptions.** Courts (and the Agency Restatements) have crafted some specific exceptions to the going and coming rule: (1) Where the employee is "on call," as long as the particular tortious act was otherwise within the scope of employment. (2) Where the employer requires the employee to drive his or her personal vehicle to work so that the vehicle may be used for work-related tasks. (3) Where the employer, either by general policy or specific directive, instructs the employee to carry out some job-related errand during the commute. (4) Where the commute serves a dual purpose for both the employer and the employee. Any of these may present a jury question where the facts are disputed. *See, e.g., Hinkle Metals & Supply Co. v. Feltman*, 280 So.3d 1031

(Ala. 2019) (fact question precluding summary judgment where employee was driving partially for a personal purpose and partially for the purpose of picking up a piece of equipment from employer's warehouse); *Painter v. Amerimex Drilling I, Ltd.*, 561 S.W.3d 125 (Tex. 2018) (fact question where employee crew leader was driving crew members from worksite to employer's bunkhouse). These "exceptions" may not be entirely separable in a given case, and may be applied in combination as part of a broader analysis of scope of employment. *See Carter v. Reynolds,* 815 A.2d 460 (N.J. 2003).

3. **Which exception is being applied in *Hinman*?** Can you articulate why the *Hinman* court finds an exception to the going and coming rule on the facts of that case? In *Faul v. Jelco, Inc.*, 595 P.2d 1035 (Ariz. Ct. App. 1979), the court rejected the plaintiff's argument that *Hinman* should be applied to a situation where a construction worker was required to work at a distant location and caused a car accident on the drive. One exception to the going and coming rule, the court said, was when the commute involves some "special hazard," but distance alone is not such a special hazard. The "dual purpose" doctrine did not apply. And *Hinman* is not on point because the California court "restricts its holding to cases where the employer compensates the employee for both travel expenses and travel time. In this case, the employee was not directly compensated for either." *See also Jack v. McFarland*, 175 So.3d 1169 (La. Ct. App. 2015) (salesman caused accident on his way home after visiting his last client; employer not vicariously liable because the workday had ended and the salesman was not being compensated for this particular travel, even though he was salaried).

EDGEWATER MOTELS, INC. V. GATZKE

277 N.W.2d 11 (Minn. 1979)

SCOTT, JUSTICE.

[Gatzke, a district manager for Walgreen's, stayed in plaintiff's motel while he was in Duluth, Minnesota supervising the opening of a Walgreen-owned restaurant. The motel was damaged by fire, allegedly the result of Gatzke's negligence while in his motel room. The motel sued both Gatzke and Walgreen's.]

[Gatzke] lived at the Edgewater at the company's expense. While in Duluth, Gatzke normally would arise at 6:00 a.m. and work at the restaurant from about 7:00 a.m. to 12:00 or 1:00 a.m. In addition to working at the restaurant, Gatzke remained on call 24 hours per day to handle problems arising in other Walgreen restaurants located in his district. Gatzke thought of himself as a "24-hour-a-day man." He received calls from other Walgreen restaurants in his district when problems arose. He was allowed to call home at company expense. His laundry, living expenses, and entertainment were items of reimbursement. There were no constraints as to where he would perform his duties or at what time of day they would be performed. . . .

[Around midnight or after, Gatzke left the work with others on the job; some went to their hotel rooms, but Gatzke and Hubbard went to the Bellows restaurant for a drink.]

In about an hour's time Gatzke consumed a total of four brandy Manhattans, three of which were "doubles." While at the Bellows, Gatzke and Hubbard spent part of the time discussing the operation of the newly-opened Walgreen restaurant. Additionally, Gatzke and the Bellows' bartender talked a little about the mixing and pricing of drinks. The testimony showed that Gatzke was interested in learning the bar business because the new Walgreen restaurant served liquor.

Between 1:15 and 1:30 a.m. Gatzke and Hubbard left the Bellows and walked back to the Edgewater. Witnesses testified that Gatzke acted normal and appeared sober. Gatzke went directly to his motel room, and then "probably" sat down at a desk to fill out his expense account because "that was [his] habit from traveling so much." The completion of the expense account had to be done in accordance with detailed instructions, and if the form was not filled out properly it would be returned to the employee unpaid. It took Gatzke no more than five minutes to fill out the expense form.

While Gatzke completed the expense account he "probably" smoked a cigarette. The record indicates Gatzke smoked about two packages of cigarettes per day. A maid testified that the ash trays in Gatzke's room would generally be full of cigarette butts and ashes when she cleaned the room. She also noticed at times that the plastic wastebasket next to the desk contained cigarette butts.

After filling out the expense account Gatzke went to bed, and soon thereafter a fire broke out. Gatzke escaped from the burning room, but the fire spread rapidly and caused extensive damage to the motel. The amount of damages was stipulated by the parties at $330,360.

One of plaintiff's expert witnesses, Dr. Ordean Anderson, a fire reconstruction specialist, testified that the fire started in, or next to, the plastic wastebasket located to the side of the desk in Gatzke's room. He also stated that the fire was caused by a burning cigarette or match. After the fire, the plastic wastebasket was a melted "blob." Dr. Anderson stated that X-ray examination of the remains of the basket disclosed the presence of cigarette filters and paper matches.

[The jury found Gatzke to be guilty of 60% of the negligence and the motel guilty of the remainder. The trial judge concluded, however, that Gatzke was not within the scope of his employment, and rendered judgment N.O.V. for Walgreen's.]

To support a finding that an employee's negligent act occurred within his scope of employment, it must be shown that his conduct was, to some degree, in furtherance of the interests of his employer. This principle is recognized by Restatement, Agency 2d, § 235, which states:

> An act of a servant is not within the scope of employment if it is done with no intention to perform it as a part of or incident to a service on account of which he is employed.

Other factors to be considered in the scope of employment determination are whether the conduct is of the kind that the employee is authorized to perform and whether the act occurs substantially within authorized time and space restrictions. No hard and fast rule can be applied to resolve the "scope of employment" inquiry. Rather, each case must be decided on its own individual facts.

The initial question raised by the instant factual situation is whether an employee's smoking of a cigarette can constitute conduct within his scope of employment. This issue has not been dealt with by this court. The courts which have considered the question have not agreed on its resolution. A number of courts which have dealt with the instant issue have ruled that the act of smoking, even when done simultaneously with work-related activity, is not within the employee's scope of employment because it is a matter personal to the employee which is not done in furtherance of the employer's interest.

Other courts which have considered the question have reasoned that the smoking of a cigarette, if done while engaged in the business of the employer, is within an employee's scope of employment because it is a minor deviation from the employee's work-related activities, and thus merely an act done incidental to general employment.

For example, in Wood v. Saunders, a gas station attendant negligently threw his lighted cigarette across an automobile's fuel tank opening while he was filling the vehicle with gasoline. The court, in finding this act to be within the employee's scope of employment, stated:

> In the case at bar, there was no abandonment by the employee of the master's purposes and business while the employee was smoking and carrying the lighted cigarette. There was merely a combining by the employee, with the carrying out of the master's purposes, of an incidental and contemporaneous carrying out of the employee's private purposes. . . .

The question of whether smoking can be within an employee's scope of employment is a close one, but after careful consideration of the issue we are persuaded by the reasoning of the courts which hold that smoking can be an act within an employee's scope of employment. It seems only logical to conclude that an employee does not abandon his employment as a matter of law while temporarily acting for his personal comfort when such activities involve only slight deviations from work that are reasonable under the circumstances, such as eating, drinking, or smoking. . . .

We . . . hereby hold that an employer can be held vicariously liable for his employee's negligent smoking of a cigarette [if] he was otherwise acting in the scope of his employment at the time of the negligent act. . . . It appears that the district court felt that Gatzke was outside the scope of his employment while he was at the Bellows, and thus was similarly outside his scope of employment when he returned to his room to fill out his expense account. The record, however, contains a reasonable basis from which a jury could find that Gatzke was involved in serving his employer's interests at the time he was at the bar. Gatzke testified that, while at the Bellows, he discussed the operation of the newly-opened Walgreen's restaurant with Hubbard. Also, the bartender stated that on that night "[a] few times we [Gatzke and the bartender] would talk about his business and my business, how to make drinks, prices."

But more importantly, even assuming that Gatzke was outside the scope of his employment while he was at the bar, there is evidence from which a jury could reasonably find that Gatzke resumed his employment activities after he returned to his motel room and filled out his expense account. The expense account was, of course, completed so that Gatzke could be reimbursed by Walgreen's for his work-related expenses. In this sense, Gatzke is performing an act for his own personal benefit. However, the completion of the expense account also furthers the employer's business in that it provides detailed documentation of business expenses so that they are properly deductible for tax purposes. In this light, the filling out of the expense form can be viewed as serving a dual purpose; that of furthering Gatzke's personal interests and promoting his employer's business purposes. Accordingly, it is reasonable for the jury to find that the completion of the expense account is an act done in furtherance of the employer's business purposes.

Additionally, the record indicates that Gatzke was an executive type of employee who had no set working hours. He considered himself a 24-hour-a-day man; his room at the Edgewater Motel was his "office away from home." It was therefore also reasonable for the jury to determine that the filling out of his expense account was done within authorized time and space limits of his employment.

In light of the above, we hold that it was reasonable for the jury to find that Gatzke was acting within the scope of his employment when he completed his expense account. Accordingly, we set aside the trial court's grant of judgment for Walgreen's and reinstate the jury's determination that Gatzke was working within the scope of his employment at the time of his negligent act. . . .

temporary residence as opposed to his usual abode." Should the jury have determined scope of liability in that case?

MONTAGUE v. AMN HEALTHCARE, INC.

223 Cal. App.4th 1515 (2014)

MCINTYRE, J. . . .

AMN Healthcare, Inc., doing business as Nursefinders (Nursefinders) is a staffing company that provides prescreened nurses and medical personnel to hospitals and other facilities. Nursefinders hired Theresa Drummond as a medical assistant. It later assigned Drummond to work at a Kaiser facility as a medical assistant. Plaintiff Sara Montague was also a medical assistant at Kaiser. At some point, Drummond and Montague had a disagreement at work regarding how rooms were to be stocked. At the end of the discussion Montague walked away. Montague did not consider the argument serious enough to report to a supervisor or anyone else. They also had a discussion regarding misplaced lab slips where Drummond raised her voice. A few weeks after that discussion, Montague left her water bottle at work. Montague later drank from her water bottle. Her tongue and throat started to burn and she vomited. Drummond admitted that she poured carbolic acid found in a Kaiser examination room into Montague's water bottle.

[Montague and her husband sued Drummond and Nursefinders, the latter on a vicarious liability theory. The trial court granted Nursefinders' motion for summary judgment, holding as a matter of law that Drummond's act of poisoning Montague was outside the scope of Drummond's employment.]

. . . For the employer to be liable for an intentional tort, the employee's act must have a "causal nexus to the employee's work." Courts have used various terms to describe this causal nexus: the incident leading to the injury must be an "outgrowth" of the employment; the risk of tortious injury must be "inherent in the working environment"; the risk must be "typical" or "broadly incidental" to the employer's business; the tort was "a generally foreseeable consequence" of the employer's business.

One way to determine whether a risk is inherent in, or created by, an enterprise is to ask whether the actual occurrence was a generally foreseeable consequence of the activity. Foreseeability in the context of determining scope of employment merely means that in the context of the particular enterprise an employee's conduct is not so unusual or startling that it would seem unfair to include the loss resulting from it among other costs of the employer's business.

These various terms have been condensed into a two-prong disjunctive test. The conduct of an employee falls within the scope of his or her employment if the conduct either (1) is required by or incidental to the employee's duties, or (2) it is reasonably foreseeable in light of the employer's business. . . .

tort

We first consider whether Montague presented evidence showing that Drummond's acts were required by or incidental to her employment with Nursefinders. In evaluating this factor, occupational duties are broadly defined. The fact that an employee is not engaged in the ultimate object of his employment at the time of his wrongful act does not preclude attribution of liability to an employer. However, that is not to say, that employers are strictly liable for all actions of their employees during working hours. If an employee substantially deviates from his duties for personal purposes, the employer is not vicariously liable for the employee's actions.

Montague [presented] no evidence regarding the scope of Drummond's employment with either Nursefinders or Kaiser. While Drummond testified she generally knew that carbolic acid was used for patients with foot issues, it is unknown what specific job duties Drummond had at Kaiser and whether her duties involved the use of carbolic acid. It is also unknown whether Drummond committed the poisoning during working hours or what motivated Drummond to poison Montague.

We next consider whether Montague presented evidence showing Nursefinders could have reasonably foreseen that Drummond would poison a coworker at Kaiser. . . . An injury arising out of a work-related dispute has such a causal nexus, while an injury inflicted out of the employee's personal malice, not engendered by the employment, does not. Montague asserts summary judgment is not appropriate because the evidence shows the poisoning arose out of a work-related dispute. The evidence shows that a few weeks or months before the incident, Drummond and Montague had a disagreement at work regarding how rooms were to be stocked, but Montague did not consider the dispute to be serious. They also had a discussion regarding misplaced lab slips where Drummond raised her voice. A few weeks after that discussion, Drummond poisoned Montague's water bottle. Although Montague asserts the poisoning took place a day or two after she argued with Drummond about the misplaced paperwork, the evidence she cited does not support this assertion. Montague presented no evidence that these past work-related disputes, rather than Drummond's personal animosity toward Montague unrelated to Drummond's work for Kaiser, motivated her actions. (Cf. *Carr v. Wm. C. Crowell Co.* (1946) 28 Cal.2d 652, 657, 171 P.2d 5 [the fact employee and coworker victim had never conversed before the dispute indicated dispute arose out of employment]; *Yamaguchi v. Harnsmut* (2003) 106 Cal.App.4th 472, 476, 486, 130 Cal.Rptr.2d 706 [trial court committed reversible error in ruling, as a matter of law, that restaurant worker's act of throwing hot oil at police officer there to break-up work-related dispute was within the scope of his

Causal nexus

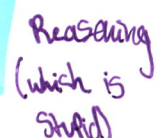

Reasoning (which is stupid)

employment for purposes of respondeat superior liability against restaurant]; *Rodgers v. Kemper Constr. Co.* (1975) 50 Cal.App.3d 608, 615, 621, 124 Cal.Rptr. 143 [when dispute arose, victims were complete strangers to assailants who worked at same job site, thus dispute was within the scope of employment].)

. . . Montague's attempt to establish respondeat superior liability for Nursefinders simply because she and Drummond worked together at Kaiser is misguided. The nexus required for respondeat superior liability—that the tort be engendered by or arise from the work—is to be distinguished from 'but for' causation. That the employment brought tortfeasor and victim together in time and place is not enough. The facts, construed most favorably for Montague, do not support liability against Nursefinders because Drummond's poisoning of Montague was highly unusual and startling.

Finally, the public policy factors underlying the doctrine of respondeat superior do not support the imposition of vicarious liability to Nursefinders under these facts. These public policy factors are: "(1) to prevent recurrence of the tortious conduct; (2) to give greater assurance of compensation for the victim; and (3) to ensure that the victim's losses will be equitably borne by those who benefit from the enterprise that gave rise to the injury." (*Farmers Ins. Group v. County of Santa Clara* (1995) 907 P.2d 440 (Cal. 1995).) Here, the potential for civil and criminal liability provides a deterrent to the type of aberrant conduct that Drummond committed. Additionally, while invoking vicarious liability under these facts would provide greater assurance of compensation to victims, Nursefinders derived no benefit from Drummond's conduct and it would be inequitable to shift the loss to Nursefinders. . . .

The judgment is affirmed. . . .

[handwritten note: do they need to benefit from the tort to be liable?]

NOTES

1. **Intentional torts of employees.** Intentional torts by employees do not usually give rise to vicarious liability of employers. See 2 DOBBS, HAYDEN & BUBLICK, THE LAW OF TORTS § 429 (2d ed. 2011). In a court that regards an employee's motive or purpose to serve the employer's interests as a key or determinative test, as both the Restatement Second and Third of Agency say, this is understandable. *See, e.g., Barnett v. Clark*, 889 N.E.2d 281 (Ind. 2008) (as a matter of law, town employee's false imprisonment and sexual assault of an applicant for public assistance was not within scope of his employment; the act did not "serve any purpose of the employer").

Vicarious liability is possible, however, even where a motive to serve the employer's interests is a highly relevant factor. *See, e.g., Cox v. Evansville Police Dep't*, 107 N.E.3d 453 (Ind. 2018) (reversing summary judgment for defendant employer; two on-duty police officers' sexual assaults on women could give rise to vicarious liability of the department, where duties of officers "may include physically controlling and forcibly touching others without consent"); *Patterson v. Blair*, 172 S.W.3d 361 (Ky. 2005) (affirming jury verdict for plaintiff against a car dealership, held vicariously liable for an employee's act of shooting a pistol at a car's tires in an attempt to repossess it while the plaintiff, a customer, was driving it away; the employee was "acting to further the business interests" of the dealership); *Kirlin v. Halverson*, 758 N.W.2d 436 (S.D. 2008) (issue of fact as to whether employee was motivated by a desire to further the employer's interest when he assaulted a competitor's employee); *cf. Doe v. State*, 76 A.3d 774 (Del. 2013) (jury question on whether officer's sexual assault of arrestee was within scope, suggesting that "a sexual assault can be considered a service to the police on the theory that part of what [the officer] was doing was transporting a prisoner," noting that Delaware has construed the "motive" factor "broadly as a matter for the jury to decide").

What if a person employed as a bouncer in a bar throws an unruly customer out of the door, breaking the customer's arm? Should vicarious liability attach?

2. **Broader tests for vicarious liability.** As we have already seen, many courts use broader (and sometimes looser) tests than one that turns centrally on the employee's motive or purpose. Often the main focus is on the reasonable foreseeability of the employee's act. *See Anderson v. Mandalay Corp.*, 358 P.3d 242 (Nev. 2015) (by statute, "reasonably foreseeable under the facts and circumstances considering the nature and scope of his or her employment"); *Farhrendorff v. North Homes, Inc.*, 597 N.W.2d 905 (Minn. 1999) (counselor in group home made sexual advances to a resident; "inappropriate sexual contact or abuse of power in these situations, although infrequent, is a *well known hazard*" in this kind of enterprise and thus may give rise to vicarious liability). If foreseeability is the ultimate issue for some courts, perhaps the strings of phrases we see in cases like *Montague* are not separate "tests" at all, but rather attempts to articulate relevant factors in the particular case.

3. **Motives connected to employment.** As we saw in *Montague*, it can be difficult to ascertain whether an employee's intentionally tortious acts were sufficiently connected to the employment so as to hold the employer vicariously liable. Not surprisingly, similar cases do not always produce similar outcomes. Compare two cases. In *Davis v. Devereux Foundation*, 37 A.3d 469 (N.J. 2012), the court affirmed a summary judgment for the employer, where the employee intentionally threw a cup of boiling water on a resident of a facility for the developmentally disabled, apparently in retaliation for the resident's aggressiveness towards the employee the previous day. The court regarded the motivation for this act as entirely personal. But in *Rodebush v. Oklahoma Nursing Homes, Ltd.*, 867 P.2d 1241 (Okla. 1993), a nurse's aide in a long-term care facility slapped an elderly Alzheimer's patient. Evidence showed the aide was intoxicated before 7:30 a.m. But the trial judge let the jury decide the case. Affirming the jury verdict for the plaintiff, the court said the jury could find that "the act [was] one which is fairly and naturally incident to the business, and [was] done while the servant was engaged upon the master's business and

[arose] from some impulse of emotion which naturally grew out of or was incident to the attempt to perform the master's business."

In one prominent case, *Lisa M. v. Henry Mayo Newhall Memorial Hosp.*, 907 P.2d 358 (Cal. 1995), an ultrasound technician employed by the defendant hospital committed a sexual battery on an unsuspecting 19-year-old pregnant patient. Rejecting vicarious liability, the court held that the act lacked a sufficient "causal nexus" to the employee's job. For the act to be within the scope of employment, the employment "must be such as predictably to create the risk employees will commit intentional torts of the type for which liability is sought. . . . The flaw in plaintiff's case for Hospital's respondeat superior liability is not so much that [the employee's] actions were personally motivated, but that those personal motivations were not generated by or an outgrowth of workplace responsibilities, conditions or events." *Cf. Our Lady of Peace, Inc. v. Morgan*, 832 S.E.2d 15 (Va. 2019) (whether nursing-home assistant was acting within scope of employment when he raped resident while performing job-related tasks was question of fact; key question is whether employee's "motive produces conduct deviating from the employer's business," and here his rape occurred simultaneously with job-related services such as undressing and bathing residents).

4. **Caregivers.** Caregivers—those who have undertaken, at least implicitly, to care for the plaintiff who is relatively helpless—may be subject to some special rules of liability. Should special obligations of caregivers also affect vicarious liability? Illinois provides by statute that owners and licensees of nursing homes "are liable to a resident for any intentional or negligent act or omission of their agents or employees which injures the resident." 210 ILL. COMP. STAT. 45/3–601. Could courts develop special rules for this kind of setting as well? *See, e.g., Spurlock v. Townes*, 368 P.3d 1213 (N.M. 2016) (adopting the "aided-in-agency theory," under which "an employer may be held liable for the intentional torts of an employee acting outside the scope of his or her employment if the employee was aided in accomplishing the tort by the existence of the agency relation," and holding that it applies only to "cases where an employee has by reason of his employment substantial power or authority to control important elements of a vulnerable tort victim's life or livelihood").

5. **Two cases: scout leaders and priests.** In *Lourim v. Swenson*, 977 P.2d 1157 (Or. 1999), the plaintiff alleged that when the plaintiff was a minor, his Boy Scout leader (Swenson) sexually abused him. *Held*, the Boy Scout organization may be held vicariously liable. A jury could reasonably infer that Swenson's acts "were merely the culmination of a progressive series of actions that involved the ordinary and authorized duties of a Boy Scout leader," that Swenson's performance of his duties "was a necessary precursor to the sexual abuse and that the assaults were a direct outgrowth of and were engendered by conduct that was within the scope of Swensen's employment." Further, it could be inferred that "Swensen's contact with plaintiff was the direct result of the relationship sponsored and encouraged by the Boy Scouts, which invested Swensen with authority to decide how to supervise minor boys under his care."

Accord as to vicarious liability for alleged sexual abuse by a priest who gained the confidence of the minor and his family through pastoral attentions and who was initially focused on carrying out his duties: *Fearing v. Bucher*, 977 P.2d 1163 (Or. 1999) (as alleged, the priest's dutiful acts then led to the acts that injured the plaintiff).

6. **Trust, authority, and incentive.** As recognized in the cases just discussed, an employee's job may provide a "peculiar opportunity and incentive for" misbehavior, which might support vicarious liability. Should vicarious liability be imposed in any of the following cases?

(a) A police officer arrests a woman for shoplifting and offers to take her home instead of to jail if she agrees to have sex with him. Is the department vicariously liable? *Sherman v. State Dep't of Public Safety*, 190 A.3d 148 (Del. 2018).

(b) A church encouraged its priests to engage in marriage counseling. One of the priests engaged in illicit sexual activity with one of the marital partners he was counseling. Is the church itself liable for the harm done? *Destefano v. Grabrian*, 763 P.2d 275 (Colo. 1988); *Byrd v. Faber*, 565 N.E.2d 584 (Ohio 1991).

(c) An employee of a hospital's child-daycare facility becomes upset when a baby under her care will not stop crying. The employee allows the infant to roll of a crib onto the floor then intentionally strikes the child's head against a shelf. Is the hospital vicariously liable? *Baker v. Saint Francis Hosp.*, 126 P.3d 602 (Okla. 2005).

7. **Punitive damages.** Can punitive damages be awarded against an employer who has been held vicariously (not primarily) liable for its employee's reprehensible intentional tort? The Restatements of both Torts and Agency say no, a view shared by most courts. *See* DAN B. DOBBS & CAPRICE L. ROBERTS, LAW OF REMEDIES § 3.11(5), at 336 (3d ed. 2018). In those jurisdictions, punitive damages can be awarded against a vicariously liable defendant only where the defendant authorized, ratified, or participated in the wrongdoing. *See A.H. ex rel. C.H. v. Church of God in Christ, Inc.*, 831 S.E.2d 460 (Va. 2019). Some courts disagree, and have adopted a more liberal view. *See, e.g., Fox v. Mize*, 428 P.3d 314 (Okla. 2018) ("[P]unitive or exemplary damages may be assessed against an employer under the doctrine of respondeat superior if an employee's conduct would serve to justify an exemplary damages award against the employee as an individual tortfeasor.") Which is the better approach?

NOTE: EMPLOYER'S PRIMARY LIABILITY
AS AN ALTERNATIVE THEORY

Where vicarious liability seems doubtful, especially where it appears that the employee's tort may be outside the scope of employment, plaintiffs often plead in the alternative that the employer is liable for its own negligence in hiring, retaining, training, or supervising the employee. *See*

Doe v. Guthrie Clinic, Ltd., 5 N.E.2d 578 (N.Y. 2014); *Doe v. Saint Francis Hosp. & Medical Center*, 72 A.3d 929 (Conn. 2013).

This is not vicarious liability at all, but rather liability based on the employer's own fault. *See, e.g., Dragomir v. Spring Harbor Hosp.*, 970 A.2d 310 (Me. 2009) (no vicarious liability for employee's sexual misbehavior, but plaintiff stated a claim for negligent supervision); *James v. Kelly Trucking Co.*, 661 S.E.2d 329 (S.C. 2008). In these cases, the duty of the employer to the plaintiff is often based on the "special relationship" the employer has with the employee. *See generally* Chapter 18 § 2 (Note: A Duty to Control Employees?). As the court explained in *Doe v. Coe*, 135 N.E.3d 1 (Ill. 2019), "the initiation and existence of an employment relationship imposes a duty upon the employer to exercise reasonable care in employing only competent individuals." A duty to hire and supervise employees reasonably may also be based on a " 'special relationship' between employers and third parties who come into contact with their employees." *Reardon ex rel. Estate of Parsons v. King*, 452 P.3d 849 (Kan. 2019).

What evidence would tend to show that the employer breached this duty? *See, e.g., Synergies3 Tec Services, LLC v. Corvo*, 319 So.3d 1263 (Ala. 2020) (employee who was hired to install home-entertainment equipment in customers' homes, then stole cash and diamonds from those homes, had criminal record of theft that should have been detected in a routine background check). Some courts have held that to make out a claim for negligent hiring or retention, the plaintiff must show that the employer had "actual or constructive knowledge . . . that would make the specific wrongful conduct perpetrated by an employee predictable." *Mueller v. Brannigan Bros. Restaurants & Taverns LLC*, 918 N.W.2d 545 (Mich. Ct. App. 2018) (affirming summary judgment for employer on claim where such knowledge was lacking); *see also Doe ex rel. Doe v. Baker*, 857 S.E.2d 573 (Va. 2021) (requiring that the "specific danger that ultimately manifested itself . . . reasonably could have been foreseen at the time of hiring").

When the claim is for negligent supervision or training, some courts have required the plaintiff to prove that the employer knew or had reason to know that the failure to supervise or train the employee in a certain way would create a risk of harm. *G.A.-H. v. K.G.G.*, 210 A.3d 907 (N.J. 2019); *see also Anderson v. Soap Lake School Dist.*, 423 P.3d 197 (Wash. 2018) (duty of reasonable supervision extends to acts beyond scope of employment when the "employer knew, or in the exercise of reasonable care should have known that the employee presented a risk of danger to others," and that means knowledge "of the dangerous tendencies of the particular employee"). Other courts have not required "prior notice of the [employee's] particular unfitness," instead looking only to a "general foreseeability" that the employee would cause harm if not reasonably supervised. *Doe v. Coe*, supra. The Illinois court in *Doe* said this:

> An employer's duty to supervise . . . is general in nature. An employer has a duty to supervise all employees; the extent to which she must do so depends on many factors, such as the work performed, the employees performing it, the size of the business, the type of work, and the employer's clientele, among others.

135 N.E.3d at 132.

Remember that a claim for negligent hiring, retention, training or supervision is a negligence claim. Thus to succeed the plaintiff must also prove that the risks created by the employer's negligence came to fruition— that is, that the *employer's* negligence was both a factual and proximate cause of the plaintiff's harm.

Claims based on vicarious liability and primary employer negligence are often pursued in the same action. *See MV Transp., Inc. v. Allgeier*, 433 S.W.3d 324 (Ky. 2014). A number of courts have held, however, that where the employer has admitted vicarious liability, the plaintiff cannot proceed on a claim against the employer for negligence in hiring, retaining, training or supervising the employee. *See Bogdanski v. Budzik*, 408 P.3d 1156 (Wyo. 2018) (adopting the rule and asserting that it is the "majority rule" in the states). A significant number of states have disagreed, allowing a plaintiff to pursue a primary negligence claim against an employer even when the employer has admitted vicarious liability. *See Ramon v. Nebo School Dist.*, 493 P.3d 613 (Utah 2021) (listing six other states that take this position, noting that courts can easily prevent "double recoveries," one of the major concerns undergirding the majority rule).

§ 2. INDEPENDENT CONTRACTORS AND OSTENSIBLE AGENTS

MAVRIKIDIS V. PETULLO

707 A.2d 977 (N.J. 1998)

GARIBALDI, J. . . .

This case arose from an automobile accident that resulted in severe injury to plaintiff Alice Mavrikidis, including second-and third-degree burns over twenty-one percent of her body. On September 11, 1990, the intersection collision occurred after defendant Gerald Petullo, operating a dump truck registered to Petullo Brothers, Inc. (Petullo Brothers), drove through a red light, struck plaintiff's car, hit a telephone pole, and then overturned, spilling the truck's contents onto Mavrikidis's car. At the time of the accident, Gerald was transporting 10.99 tons of hot asphalt, which had been loaded onto the truck by Newark Asphalt Corporation (Newark

Asphalt), to his job site at Clar Pine Servicenter (Clar Pine), a retail gasoline and automotive repair shop in Montclair.

[Clar Pine's owner, Karl Pascarello, was renovating the gas station.] Because Pascarello had no experience in the construction or paving business, he hired Gerald's father, Angelo Petullo, and Petullo Brothers to complete the asphalt and concrete work at the Clar Pine job site.] The Petullos supplied the labor, equipment, concrete, and most of the asphalt needed for the job.... Other than general supervision and periodic consultation, Pascarello's limited participation in the asphalt work consisted of payment for three loads of asphalt, including the one involved in this accident, as well as his direction to lay the asphalt in front of the service station's bay doors first to enable him to continue his automotive repairs while the gas station was out of service....

On the morning of the accident, Gerald ordered twenty tons of asphalt from Newark Asphalt's plant. The employees of Newark Asphalt loaded 10.99 tons of asphalt, at a temperature between 300 and 310 degrees Fahrenheit, onto Gerald's truck and 9 tons onto a second truck.... [At trial, an expert testified that the trucks were overloaded and that had Gerald's truck not been overloaded, he would have had better control over the truck.]

[Mavrikidis sued Gerald, Angelo, Petullo Brothers, Newark Asphalt and Clar Pine, among others. In special interrogatories, the jury found that Gerald operated his truck negligently and that his negligence was a proximate cause of the accident; and that Gerald was acting as an employee of Angelo at the time of the accident. The jurors further found that Clar Pine retained control of the "manner and means" of performing the "inherently dangerous" activity of transporting and installing asphalt. The jury also found that Newark Asphalt was negligent in overloading Gerald's truck. The jury awarded the plaintiff $750,000, and fixed percentages of negligence on all liable defendants.] Based on the finding that Clar Pine was vicariously liable for its independent contractor, Angelo, the court entered a judgment against Clar Pine for 89% of the total damages awarded, including the 17% attributed directly to Clar Pine by the jury, the 24% attributed to Angelo, and the 48% attributed to Gerald. The court also entered judgment against Newark Asphalt for 11% of the total damages awarded. Clar Pine and Newark Asphalt appealed. [The Appellate Division reversed the judgment against Clar Pine, holding that there was insufficient evidence to support a finding of vicarious liability.]

The first question is whether Clar Pine is vicariously liable for plaintiff's injuries. As we explained in *Majestic Realty Associates, Inc. v. Toti Contracting Co.,* 153 A.2d 321 (N.J. 1959), the resolution of this issue

must be approached with an awareness of the long settled doctrine that ordinarily where a person engages a contractor, who conducts an independent business by means of his own employees, to do work not in itself a nuisance (as our cases put it), he is not liable for the negligent acts of the contractor in the performance of the contract.

The initial inquiry in our analysis is to examine the status of the Petullos in relation to Clar Pine. Despite plaintiff's alternate theories to the contrary, the Petullos were independent contractors rather than servants of Clar Pine. [As we said in *Baldasarre*, 625 A.2d 458 (N.J. 1993),]

> The important difference between an employee and an independent contractor is that one who hires an independent contractor "has no right of control over the manner in which the work is to be done, it is to be regarded as the contractor's own enterprise, and he, rather than the employer is the proper party to be charged with the responsibility for preventing the risk, and administering and distributing it."

In contrast, a servant is traditionally one who is "employed to perform services in the affairs of another, whose physical conduct in the performance of the service is controlled, or is subject to a right of control, by the other." W. Page Keeton, *Prosser & Keeton on Torts*, § 70 at 501.

In determining whether a contractee maintains the right of control, several factors are to be considered. The *Restatement (Second) of Agency* sets forth these factors, including:

> (a) the extent of control which, by the agreement, the master may exercise over the details of the work; (b) whether or not the one employed is engaged in a distinct occupation or business; * * * (d) the skill required in the particular occupation; (e) whether the employer or the workman supplies the instrumentalities, tools, and the place of work for the person doing the work; (f) the length of time for which the person is employed; (g) the method of payment, whether by the time or by the job; (h) whether or not the work is a part of the regular business of the employer; [and] (i) whether or not the parties believe they are creating the relation of master and servant. . . .

Applying those Restatement factors, it is evident that neither Angelo nor Gerald was a servant of Clar Pine. The masonry work required a skilled individual. Although Pascarello paid for three loads of asphalt, the Petullos provided their own tools and the remainder of the needed materials, other than bolts and plywood supplied by Pascarello to install the canopies. Their work did not involve the regular business of Clar Pine. In addition, the period of employment spanned only the time it took to lay the asphalt and concrete. Following the accident, the Petullos continued the job for which they were hired, which was approved by the Building Inspector of

Montclair. In exchange for their services, the Petullos were not paid by the hour or month. . . .

Based on that threshold determination, we now must determine whether this case falls within any exceptions to the general rule of nonliability of principals/contractees for the negligence of their independent contractors. There are three such exceptions, as delineated by the *Majestic* Court: "(a) where the landowner [or principal] retains control of the manner and means of the doing of the work which is the subject of the contract; (b) where he engages an incompetent contractor; or (c) where . . . the activity contracted for [is inherently dangerous]."

Exceptions

. . . Under the first *Majestic* exception, the reservation of control "of the manner and means" of the contracted work by the principal permits the imposition of vicarious liability. "In such a case the employer is responsible for the negligence of the independent contractor even though the particular control exercised and its manner of exercise had no causal relationship with the hazard that led to the injury, just as in the case of a simple employer-employee situation." Under that test, the reservation of control over the equipment to be used, the manner or method of doing the work, or direction of the employees of the independent contractor may permit vicarious liability.

However, supervisory acts performed by the contractee will not give rise to vicarious liability under that exception. As indicated by the language of the exception, application of principles of *respondeat superior* are not warranted where the contractee's "supervisory interest relates [only] to the result to be accomplished, not to the means of accomplishing it."

Pascarello's actions did not exceed the scope of general supervisory powers so as to subject Clar Pine to vicarious liability for Gerald's negligence. Providing blueprints, paying for some of the asphalt, and directing that a portion of the concrete be completed first are clearly within the scope of a contractee's broad supervisory powers. . . . Pascarello's actions related to the overall renovations of the station and not to the specific work for which the Petullos were engaged. The Petullos were hired to do the paving for the station and were not involved in the renovation other than the paving. . . . When the evidence is viewed in the light most favorable to plaintiffs, Pascarello's actions arose from a general supervisory power over the result to be accomplished rather than the means of that accomplishment.

[Evidence did not support the application of either of the final two *Majestic* exceptions. There was no evidence that the Petrullos were unqualified to perform the masonry work for which they were hired. Further, the "inherently dangerous" exception has no application where the injury was caused merely by negligent driving, which is simply an ordinary risk associated with motor vehicles and the transport of materials.]

[Judgment of the Appellate Division affirmed; remanded for a determination of the liability percentages of the Petullos and Newark Asphalt.]

[Dissenting opinion omitted.]

NOTES

1. **Vicarious liability for the torts of an independent contractor.** The *Mavrikidis* court states the general rule: subject to limited exceptions, a person who hires an independent contractor to perform work is not vicariously liable for the torts committed by that independent contractor. *See* RESTATEMENT (THIRD) OF TORTS: LIABILITY FOR PHYSICAL AND EMOTIONAL HARM § 57 (2012). The setting in *Mavrikidis* is the most common one, where one person (or business) hires another—the independent contractor—to do some particular work.

Do the policy rationales for vicarious liability not apply with the same force when an injury is caused by the negligence of an independent contractor, as opposed to a servant? The California Supreme Court recently explained:

> There is a strong presumption under California law that the hirer of an independent contractor delegates to the contractor all responsibility for workplace safety. . . . [T]he presumption originally stemmed from the following rationales: First, hirers usually have no right to control an independent contractor's work. Second, contractors can factor in the cost of safety precautions and insurance coverage in the contract price. Third, contractors are able to obtain workers' compensation to cover any on-the-job injuries. Finally, contractors are typically hired for their expertise, which enables them to perform the contracted-for work safely and successfully.

Gonzalez v. Mathis, 493 P.3d 212 (Cal. 2021).

2. **Tests for status as independent contractor.** In determining whether an employee is a servant or an independent contractor, courts have often applied the multi-part test from the Restatement (Second) of Agency, as the *Mavrikidis* court did. But in the eyes of many courts, one factor—the right to control the details of the work—is the most important. *See Devore v. American Eagle Energy Corp.*, 937 N.W.2d 503 (N.D. 2020) (liability arises "only when the employer retains the right to control the method, manner, and operative detail of the work; it is not enough that the employer merely retains the right to inspect the work or to make suggestions which need not be followed"). As the West Virginia court said in *France v. Southern Equip. Co.*, 689 S.E.2d 1 (W.Va. 2010), four general factors bear on whether a master-servant relationship exists for purposes of respondeat superior: (1) selection and engagement of the servant; (2) payment of compensation; (3) power of dismissal; and (4) the power of control, and "[t]he first three factors are not

essential to the existence of the relationship; the fourth, the power of control, is determinative." *See also* RESTATEMENT (THIRD) OF AGENCY § 7.07(3)(a) (2006) ("an employee is an agent whose principal controls or has the right to control the manner and means of the agent's performance of work").

To many courts, then, if the employer does have a right of control over the day-to-day operations of the worker, the worker is probably a servant; if not, the worker is probably an independent contractor. *See, e.g., Kuligoski v. Rapoza*, 183 A.3d 1145 (Vt. 2018); *Walderbach v. Archdiocese of Dubuque, Inc.*, 730 N.W.2d 198 (Iowa 2007); *Anderson v. PPCT Management Systems, Inc.*, 145 P.3d 503 (Alaska 2006). Further, for liability to be imposed, the hirer's control over the independent contractor's work "must relate to the condition or activity that caused the injury." *JLB Builders, L.L.C. v. Hernandez*, 622 S.W.3d 860 (Tex. 2021).

However, "control" can be a loose concept, and sometimes it is not at all determinative. The medical group or hospital that employs a physician may have no right to control details of his treatment of patients—that would interfere with the doctor-patient relationship—yet it remains vicariously responsible for his malpractice. *See Dias v. Brigham Med. Assocs., Inc.*, 780 N.E.2d 447 (Mass. 2002). In addition, regardless of its importance, control is only one factor of many. If the person being employed runs his own business and works for others as well as for the contractee, he is not likely to be a servant. If he provides his own tools or uses special skills, that is also likely to indicate that he is an independent contractor.

In many cases these rules are easy to apply. Suppose you have hired a professional painter to paint your house. You are paying him a set price for the job. He is supplying his own paint, brushes and other equipment (although you are paying for them as part of the price of the job). He decides when to come and go from the job. After the house is painted he will paint somewhere else. Is he your servant, so that any torts he commits will leave you vicariously liable?

3.   **Structuring relationships by contract.** Employers often attempt to structure relationships with employees so that employees will be considered independent contractors. A newspaper may contract with scores or hundreds of home delivery drivers and describe the drivers in the contract as independent contractors. If the newspaper has the right to terminate their services for no reason at all, should the contractual label "independent contractor" determine a driver's status? *See Zirkle v. Winkler*, 585 S.E.2d 19 (W.Va. 2003); *see also Hill v. City of Horn Lake*, 160 So.3d 671 (Miss. 2015) (employer may not escape liability to third persons simply by drafting a contract that labels an employee an independent contractor).

4.   **Retained control.** The *Mavrikidis* court applies an important rule (which it sees as an "exception" to the usual rule for independent contractors): employees who are ordinarily independent contractors—general building contractors and their subcontractors, for example—may become "servants" if sufficient control is retained by the employer. *See, e.g., Merit Energy Co. v.*

Horr, 366 P.3d 489 (Wyo. 2016); *Gaytan v. Wal-Mart*, 853 N.W.2d 181 (Neb. 2014). What facts did the New Jersey court look at in determining that there was insufficient evidence of retained control to send the issue to the jury? Retained control may also show that the employer himself was negligent in not exercising the control he has to obtain appropriate safety. *See* RESTATEMENT (THIRD) OF TORTS: LIABILITY FOR PHYSICAL AND EMOTIONAL HARM § 56(b) (2012).

5. **The incompetent independent contractor.** *Mavrikidis* noted a second exception to the no-vicarious-liability rule: knowingly hiring an incompetent independent contractor. It has long been true in virtually all states that a defendant cannot insulate itself from liability by selecting or retaining an incompetent independent contractor. *See* RESTATEMENT (THIRD) OF AGENCY § 7.05(1) (2006). The incompetence can take many forms—for example, the contractor does not know how to do the job, or is known to be an alcohol abuser or someone with anger management problems.

Most courts appear to characterize this not as a vicarious liability theory at all, but rather a claim based on the employer's own negligence. *See, e.g., Puckrein v. ATI Transport, Inc.*, 897 A.2d 1034 (N.J. 2006) (framing the issue as whether the employer "violated its duty to use reasonable care in selecting a trucker and whether it knew or should have known of [the trucker's] incompetence"); *Basic Energy Services, L.P. v. Petroleum Resource Mgmt. Corp.*, 343 P.3d 783 (Wyo. 2015) (reviewing cases from many states, concluding that the claim for negligently hiring an incompetent independent contractor "has gained broad acceptance").

6. **The non-delegable duty rule: inherently dangerous activities.** The third exception to the general no-vicarious-liability rule for the torts of independent contractors mentioned in *Mavrikidis* is that principal cannot discharge a non-delegable duty to exercise reasonable care by hiring an independent contractor to undertake the activity. *See France v. Southern Equipment Co.*, 1 S.E.2d 1 (W.Va. 2010). That final exception is explored below.

PUSEY V. BATOR

762 N.E.2d 968 (Ohio 2002)

DOUGLAS, J. . . .

In April 1987, Wilson, on behalf of Greif Brothers, entered into a contract with Youngstown Security Patrol, Inc. ("YSP") to supply a uniformed security guard to "deter theft [and] vandalism" on Greif Brothers' property during specified hours. Wilson told YSP's owner and president, Carl Testa, that he wanted the security guard to periodically check the parking lot and the inside of the building. Other than those instructions, Wilson did not instruct Testa in the manner that YSP was to protect Greif Brothers' property.

The written security contract did not specify whether the guard was to be armed or unarmed, and Wilson and Testa both later testified that they never discussed the subject. [Wilson became aware later, however, that some guards were armed but never asked for unarmed guards.]

Bator was the guard assigned to Greif Brothers' property from 11:00 p.m., August 11 to 7:00 a.m., August 12, 1991. [He was not certified to carry a gun, but he kept one in his briefcase.] At approximately 1:00 a.m., Bator looked out through a window in the guard office and saw two individuals, later identified as Derrell Pusey and Charles Thomas, walking through Greif Brothers' parking lot. Bator used the radio in the office to inform a YSP guard on duty at another location that two people were on Greif Brothers' property.

[Bator first went outside without the gun, but when the men were first evasive and then became angry and called Bator a "mother fucker," Bator then went in and got the gun. When he revealed it to the men, Pusey made a quick movement. Bator thought he was reaching for a gun and Bator fired. The bullet struck Pusey in the back of his head. Another guard arrived, then the police.]

Derrell was transported to the hospital, where he died from his wound. Thereafter, plaintiff-appellant, Ethel Pusey, Derrell's mother, individually and as executor of Derrell's estate, filed a wrongful death and survivorship action against Bator, YSP, and Greif Brothers. YSP and Bator settled with Pusey soon after the jury trial began, leaving Greif Brothers as the only defendant.

[The trial court granted a directed verdict in favor of Greif Brothers. The Court of Appeals affirmed in a divided opinion.]

We find that, even when viewed in the light most favorable to Pusey, the evidence clearly established YSP's status as an independent contractor. Greif Brothers specified the result to be accomplished, i.e., to deter vandals and thieves, but the details of how this task should be accomplished, with the exception noted above regarding periodic patrolling of the property, were left to YSP. . . .

[A]n employer is generally not liable for the negligent acts of an independent contractor. There are, however, exceptions to this general rule, several of which stem from the nondelegable duty doctrine. Nondelegable duties arise in various situations [including] duties imposed on the employer that arise out of the work itself because its performance creates dangers to others, i.e., inherently dangerous work. [In such cases the] employer may delegate the *work* to an independent contractor, but he cannot delegate the *duty*. In other words, the employer is not insulated from liability if the independent contractor's negligence results in a breach of the duty. . . .

Work is inherently dangerous when it creates a peculiar risk of harm to others unless special precautions are taken. . . .

To fall within the inherently-dangerous-work exception, it is not necessary that the work be such that it cannot be done without a risk of harm to others, or even that it be such that it involves a high risk of such harm. It is sufficient that the work involves a risk, recognizable in advance, of physical harm to others, which is inherent in the work itself.

The exception does not apply, however, where the employer would reasonably have only a general anticipation of the possibility that the contractor may be negligent in some way and thereby cause harm to a third party. For example, one who hires a trucker to transport his goods should realize that if the truck is driven at an excessive speed, or with defective brakes, some harm to persons on the highway is likely to occur. An employer of an independent contractor may assume that a careful contractor will take routine precautions against all of the ordinary and customary dangers that may arise in the course of the contemplated work.

The inherently-dangerous-work exception does apply, however, when special risks are associated with the work such that a reasonable man would recognize the necessity of taking special precautions. The work must create a risk that is not a normal, routine matter of customary human activity, such as driving an automobile, but is rather a special danger to those in the vicinity arising out of the particular situation created, and calling for special precautions. . . .

We find that work such as YSP was hired to perform does create a peculiar risk of harm to others. When armed guards are hired to deter vandals and thieves it is foreseeable that someone might be injured by the inappropriate use of the weapon if proper precautions are not taken. Thus, such an injury is one that might have been anticipated as a direct or probable consequence of the performance of the work contracted for, if reasonable care is not taken in its performance. Also, the risk created is not a normal, routine matter of customary human activity, such as driving an automobile, but is instead a special danger arising out of the particular situation created and calling for special precautions. We therefore hold that when an employer hires an independent contractor to provide armed security guards to protect property, the inherently-dangerous-work exception is triggered such that if someone is injured by the weapon as a result of a guard's negligence, the employer is vicariously liable even though the guard responsible is an employee of the independent contractor.

We do not mean to suggest by the foregoing that we have determined that Derrell's death resulted from YSP's negligence. That issue is to be determined by a finder of fact. If the fact finder so finds, however, then, pursuant to our holding herein, Greif Brothers is liable for the damages even though the negligence was that of an employee of an independent contractor. . . .

Judgment reversed and cause remanded.

[COOK, J., joined by Judges Moyer and Stratton, concurred in the judgment only. Those judges thought that the inherent danger question could be answered as a matter of law in some cases, but that in others it would be a question of fact or a mixed question of fact and law.]

NOTES

1. **"Non-delegable" terminology.** When courts say a duty is non-delegable, they mean only that the person who hires an independent contractor does not escape liability under the independent contractor rules. The independent contractor himself is also liable for his own negligence. *See Rodriguez v. Kroger Co.*, 422 P.3d 815 (Utah 2018).

2. **Inherent danger and peculiar risk.** Courts have widely adopted provisions of the Restatement Second of Torts on non-delegable duties. *See* RESTATEMENT (THIRD) OF AGENCY § 7.06, cmt. a (2006). The Restatement Second of Torts applies the non-delegable duty rule to inherently dangerous activities in its § 427 and also, in § 416, to cases of "peculiar risk." The two classes of cases are similar. Peculiar risk must be different in some way from ordinary risks. For example, transporting asphalt in *Mavrikidis* was held to be an ordinary, not a peculiar, risk. *See also King v. Lens Creek Ltd. Partnership*, 483 S.E.2d 265 (W.Va. 1996) (operation of empty logging trucks is not inherently dangerous). The Restatement Third of Torts reiterates that an actor who hires an independent contractor for an activity the actor knows or should know poses a "peculiar risk" may be vicariously liable where the contractor's negligence causes harm, RESTATEMENT (THIRD) OF TORTS: LIABILITY FOR PHYSICAL AND EMOTIONAL HARM § 59 (2012). The same Restatement would impose vicarious liability on an actor who hires an independent contractor to construct or maintain instrumentalities used in highly dangerous activities and the contractor's negligence in connection with those instrumentalities causes harm. ID., § 60.

The cases do not apply these exceptions consistently. Courts have held the duty non-delegable when poisons are sprayed and when explosives and strong acids are used—in other words, in cases of instrumentalities dangerous by nature. *See, e.g., Brandenburg v. Briarwood Forestry Services, LLC*, 847 N.W.2d 395 (Wis. 2014) (landowner vicariously liable for contractor's negligence in spraying herbicide, an "inherently dangerous activity"). But courts have also applied the inherently dangerous rule in many fairly ordinary cases. A contractor sprays paint, and some of it splatters on the plaintiff's property next door; an independent distributor hires door-to-door salesmen to sell the manufacturer's vacuum cleaners, and one of them had a criminal record and assaulted a woman once in her home; a worker for an independent contractor turns over a tractor on a grassy slope. All these cases and others have been held to count as inherent danger or peculiar risk. *See* 2 DOBBS, HAYDEN & BUBLICK, THE LAW OF TORTS § 432 (2d ed. 2011).

3. **Duties imposed by statutory instruments.** Vicarious liability may also be imposed when a statute or administrative regulation imposes obligations on the actor concerning the work that the independent contractor is hired to do, and the contractor's failure to comply with that obligation causes harm. RESTATEMENT (THIRD) OF TORTS: LIABILITY FOR PHYSICAL AND EMOTIONAL HARM § 63 (2012); RESTATEMENT (SECOND) OF TORTS § 424 (1965); *see, e.g., Vargas v. Inland Washington, LLC*, 452 P.3d 1205 (Wash. 2019) (non-delegable duty under state Industrial Safety and Health Act); *Sanatass v. Consolidated Investing Co.*, 887 N.E.2d 1125 (N.Y. 2008) (non-delegable duty under state "scaffold law").

4. **Landowners and construction contractors.** Owners of even non-commercial property frequently hire independent contractors to perform construction, repair or other work. What if someone is injured on the property (a private home, for example) after the work is done and the owner resumes possession? Would be owner be liable? Most courts would say yes. If the landowner owes a duty to the injured person to maintain the property in a safe condition, that duty cannot be delegated to someone else. *See Otero v. Jordon Restaurant Enterprises*, 895 P.2d 243 (N.M. Ct. App. 1995) (relying on RESTATEMENT (SECOND) OF TORTS § 422). There is an exception for situations in which the contractor has done some work improperly and has negligently created a temporarily risky condition during construction. In that situation, the landowner is not liable unless he himself is at fault. *Id.*

5. **Accepted-work doctrine.** At one time, most courts followed the "accepted-work doctrine" (also called the "completed and accepted rule") under which the contractor would not be liable for injuries caused to third persons after completion of the work and acceptance by the owner. Most courts have now abrogated that rule—leaving the contractor potentially liable along with the owner. *See Dorrell v. South Carolina Dept. of Transp.*, 605 S.E.2d 12 (S.C. 2004); *Peters v. Forster*, 804 N.E.2d 736 (Ind. 2004). Even where the accepted-work doctrine has been abandoned, a landowner may not be liable where he lacked either actual or constructive notice of a latent defective condition created by the independent contractor's negligence. *See Parker v. Holiday Hospitality Franchising, Inc.*, 446 S.W.3d 341 (Tenn. 2014). That is, many courts that have rejected the accepted-work doctrine have replaced it with a "foreseeability rule." *Sumsion v. J. Lyne Roberts & Sons, Inc.*, 443 P.3d 1199 (Utah 2019) (discussing contours and uncertainties of the modern rule).

O'BANNER v. MCDONALD'S CORP.

670 N.E.2d 632 (Ill. 1996)

JUSTICE HARRISON delivered the opinion of the court:

Reginald O'Banner brought an action in the circuit court of Cook County to recover damages for personal injuries he allegedly sustained when he slipped and fell in the bathroom of a McDonald's restaurant. In his complaint, O'Banner named as defendants McDonald's Corporation (McDonald's) and certain "unknown owners." McDonald's promptly moved for summary judgment on the grounds that the restaurant was actually owned by one of its franchisees and that it neither owned, operated, maintained, nor controlled the facility. . . .

The circuit court here entered summary judgment in favor of McDonald's based on the company's argument that it was merely the franchisor of the restaurant where O'Banner was injured and, as such, had no responsibility for the conditions that caused his accident. O'Banner challenged this conclusion in the appellate court by theorizing that even though McDonald's was a franchisor, it could nevertheless be held liable for the franchisee's negligence under principles of respondeat superior because there was sufficient evidence in the record to establish that the franchisee served as McDonald's actual agent. In the alternative, O'Banner contended that McDonald's could be vicariously liable for the acts and omissions of the franchisee based on the doctrine of apparent agency.

The appellate court rejected the actual agency theory based on the documentary evidence, but held that there remained genuine issues of material fact with respect to O'Banner's alternative theory of apparent agency. Accordingly, it reversed and remanded for further proceedings. . . .

In the appeal before this court, the issue of actual agency has not been pursued. The sole question before us is whether the appellate court erred in reversing and remanding based on the theory of apparent agency. . . .

Apparent agency, also known in Illinois as apparent authority, . . . is based on principles of estoppel. The idea is that if a principal creates the appearance that someone is his agent, he should not then be permitted to deny the agency if an innocent third party reasonably relies on the apparent agency and is harmed as a result.

Under the doctrine, a principal can be held vicariously liable in tort for injury caused by the negligent acts of his apparent agent if the injury would not have occurred but for the injured party's justifiable reliance on the apparent agency. The fundamental obstacle to O'Banner's recovery in this case concerns this element of reliance. Even if one concedes that McDonald's advertising and other conduct could entice a person to enter a McDonald's restaurant in the belief it was dealing with an agent of the corporation itself, that is not sufficient. In order to recover on an apparent agency theory, O'Banner would have to show that he actually did rely on the apparent agency in going to the restaurant where he was allegedly injured.

No amount of liberal construction can alter the fact that the record before us is devoid of anything remotely suggesting that the necessary reliance was present here. The pleadings and affidavit submitted by

O'Banner in the circuit court state only that he slipped and fell in the restroom of a McDonald's restaurant. They give no indication as to why he went to the restaurant in the first place. The fact that this was a McDonald's may have been completely irrelevant to his decision. For all we know, O'Banner went there simply because it provided the closest bathroom when he needed one or because some friend asked to meet him there.

If O'Banner had any basis to support his position, he was obliged to present it to the circuit court. He did not do so, and the time for substantiating any claim of reliance has passed. The appellate court was therefore wrong to reverse the circuit court's entry of summary judgment in McDonald's favor based on the apparent agency doctrine.

For the foregoing reasons, the judgment of the appellate court is reversed, the judgment of the circuit court is affirmed, and the cause is remanded to the circuit court for further proceedings consistent with this opinion.

[Dissenting opinion omitted.]

NOTES

1. **Meaning of reliance.** What does "reliance" mean in *O'Banner*— (a) the plaintiff in fact believed and believed reasonably that the restaurant was operated by McDonald's, *or* (b) that the plaintiff reasonably so believed *and* that he would not have used the restroom had he known that it was operated by a franchisee? Courts have not always taken the same approach. In a case involving a claim that doctors working in a hospital were apparent agents of the hospital, the court, quoting other authority, said that the reliance issue "simply focuses on the patient's belief that the hospital or its employees were rendering health care." *Burless v. W. Va. Univ. Hospitals, Inc.*, 601 S.E.2d 85 (W.Va. 2004).

Other courts have also focused simply on whether the patient was looking to the institution rather than the doctor for care. *Dewald v. HCA Health Services of Tennessee*, 251 S.W.3d 423 (Tenn. 2008); *see also Popovich v. Allina Health System*, 946 N.W.2d 885 (Minn. 2020) (reliance is shown where "the plaintiff looked to the hospital for care and relied on the hospital to select the personnel to provide services to the plaintiff"). But in *Cefaratti v. Aranow*, 141 A.3d 752 (Conn. 2016), another medical malpractice case, the court held that detrimental reliance in this context means "the plaintiff would not have dealt with the tortfeasor if the plaintiff had known that the tortfeasor was not the principal's agent or employee."

Some courts do not require reliance at all, but look instead to whether the principal manifested to the plaintiff that an independent contractor was in fact an agent, and the agent reasonably believed that fact. *See Green v. Pennsylvania Hosp.*, 123 A.3d 310 (Pa. 2015); *Jones v. Healthsouth Treasure Valley Hosp.*, 206 P.3d 473 (Idaho 2009). And some courts have flatly refused to hold a hospital liable on the apparent or ostensible agency theory. *See Sanchez v. Medicorp Health System*, 618 S.E.2d 331 (Va. 2005).

2. **Managed health care or HMOs.** Health maintenance organizations, usually corporations, are not physicians. Instead they are contractors who manage health care programs. In one type of HMO, the HMO hires its own doctors and they are its employees. In a second type, the HMO contracts with independent physicians to provide the services needed. Suppose you go to work for a law firm which has a health care program through an HMO of the second type. You select a physician from the approved list and he negligently injures you. Is the HMO vicariously liable? In *Petrovich v. Share Health Plan of Illinois, Inc.*, 719 N.E.2d 756 (Ill. 1999), the Illinois court held that the HMO was subject to vicarious liability on the same apparent agency theory it rejected in *O'Banner*. The court said the patient would be relying upon the HMO if the patient is not selecting a specific physician for some reason such as a prior relationship with that physician but merely because some physicians had to be selected from the list furnished. Is the court's concept of reliance the same as it was three years earlier in *O'Banner*?

§ 3. OTHER FORMS OF VICARIOUS RESPONSIBILITY

1. *Partnership.* L and N form a partnership to sell groceries. They agree to, and do, acquire a truck for deliveries. N negligently drives the truck while delivering groceries and Grogan is injured. N is liable personally. Is L also liable? If there were a distinct business entity known as the partnership, the partnership could be viewed as the employer. If that were the case, both N and the partnership would be liable, as in any other master-servant relationship. But a partnership is not a separate entity in the way a corporation is—and both partners are personally liable. Each partner can be seen as a general agent for the other partner or partners.

2. *Joint enterprise.* D, E and F, three salespersons who are selling for three different companies but who are not servants, discover they all intend to drive from Buffalo to Chicago at the same time. They decide to rent a single car, share expenses and share driving. While one of them, D, is driving, there is a collision with Grogan's car. D may have been negligent. Grogan is injured. If D is negligent, he is personally liable. Are E and F also liable?

Courts have imposed liability upon all members of a joint enterprise when persons outside the enterprise are injured. This is said to exist where there is (1) an agreement, express or implied, (2) a common purpose, (3) a community of interest and (4) an equal right of control. These terms are sometimes interpreted liberally. The agreement need not be spelled out in words and it is enough if the parties had a tacit understanding. In some cases, however, courts have held or stated that a social venture will qualify if all the elements are present. Under this view three friends sharing expenses, having a common purpose and equal right to control, might all be liable if one of them drives negligently on a fishing trip. Is this sound or not?

When members of the enterprise itself are injured, the rule is different, and there is no imputation of negligence among the enterprisers themselves. Thus if A, B, and C are on a joint enterprise, and A drives negligently, causing an injury to B, B will have a claim against A for his negligence, but no claim against C based on imputation of A's fault to C.

3. *Concert of action and civil conspiracy.* In most states, "civil conspiracy is a vicarious liability theory that imparts joint-and-several liability to a co-conspirator who may not be liable for the underlying tort. Liability depends on injury from the underlying tort, not the conspiracy itself." *Agar Corp. v. Electro Circuits Int'l, LLC*, 580 S.W.3d 136 (Tex. 2019). The "concert of action" theory makes a defendant vicariously liable for the torts of another where "the defendant (1) knew that the other person's conduct constituted a breach of duty and (2) gave substantial assistance or encouragement to the other person in conducting himself that way." *Bowyer ex rel. Eskra v. Adono*, 156 N.E.3d 594 (Ill. Ct. App. 2020) (citing Restatement (Second) of Torts § 876(b) (1979)).

In some states, civil conspiracy and "concert of action" have been combined into a single theory of vicarious liability. As one court explained recently, civil conspiracy "requires an underlying tort and the conspiracy consists in agreeing to, or assisting in, this underlying tort. . . . To prove a 'concerted action' conspiracy, a plaintiff must show that defendants either (1) acted in concert with or pursuant to a common design with the tortfeasor or (2) gave substantial assistance to the tortfeasor's conduct." *Thomas v. Harrington*, 909 F.3d 483 (1st Cir. 2018) (summarizing Mass. law).

An early basis for joint and several liability was much like the idea behind liability of one partner or joint enterpriser for the acts of another. Conspirators or those who act in concert to commit a tort are partners, as it were, in a tortious enterprise. *See, e.g., Reilly v. Anderson*, 727 N.W.2d 102 (Iowa 2007) (front-seat passenger who attempted to steer and driver who was attempting to light a marijuana pipe were acting in concert when they wrecked the car, causing injuries to plaintiff).

4. *Aiding and abetting.* Aiders and abettors are in much the same position, in that they too are acting in concert with a principal tortfeasor. In *Courtney v. Courtney*, 413 S.E.2d 418 (W.Va. 1991), the complaint alleged Maud supplied her son with alcohol and drugs even though she knew that when he used them he beat his wife. The court held the complaint stated a claim on behalf of the family victims. Suppose that, as A begins to beat the plaintiff, A's uncle B shouts "Kill him, kill him!" *Rael v. Cadena*, 604 P.2d 822 (N.M. 1979). Is B subject to liability?

Aiding and abetting is not identical to civil conspiracy, however. As a recent decision explains, "The two doctrines are conceptually different, with the former involving an agreement and the latter focusing on assistance in committing the underlying tort." *Meridian Medical Systems, LLC v. Epix Therapeutics, Inc.*, 250 A.3d 122 (Me. 2021) (recognizing a cause of action for aiding and abetting another's commission of a tort, after having rejected civil liability for conspiracy). Aiding and abetting liability requires the defendant's actual knowledge that the principal tortfeasor is engaged in tortious conduct, and the defendant's commission of acts that constitute substantial assistance in the commission of the underlying tort. *Id.* (citing Restatement (Second) of Torts § 876(b)).

5.   *Tacit agreement to participate in a tort.* Drag racing is a classic example of action in concert. Two teenagers driving two different cars are stopped at a light. One guns his engine. The other does the same. When the light changes, they take off and rapidly gain speed. One of them loses control and crashes into the plaintiff, but the other drives safely by. Is the other liable because he was acting in concert by tacitly agreed to the illegal activity? In *Nelson v. Nason,* 177 N.E.2d 887 (Mass. 1961), the court commented: "Direct testimony of an agreement to race was not required. . . . There was evidence of challenge and response in the speed and relative positions of the two automobiles." But in *Canavan v. Galuski,* 769 N.Y.S.2d 629 (App. Div. 2003), the court was unwilling to find a tacit agreement where a group of defendants, insulted online, gathered together to go to the Lewis house to "resolve" the matter. They found the plaintiff in the driveway. Someone, unidentified, hit the plaintiff from behind. The court thought "parallel activity" by the defendants did not permit an inference of concert of action. It relied on authority holding that parallel *economic* activity by corporations in marketing their products was not evidence of a conspiracy.

6.   *Entrustment of a vehicle.* Defendant, owner of a car, permits T to drive it. T is not a servant, partner, or joint enterpriser. If T drives negligently, will defendant be liable? There are at least five distinct situations:

(a)   *Negligent entrustment.* Defendant may be liable for his own negligent entrustment of the car to one who is incompetent to drive. This is not vicarious liability, but instead requires proof that the entrustor-defendant knew or should have known of the entrustee's incompetence, and that the plaintiff's injury resulted from that incompetence. *See* Chapter 18 § 2 (Note: Negligent Entrustment). The entrustor is thus assigned a percentage of the responsibility under comparative fault rules, and his liability calculated according to that percentage. *See Ali v. Fisher,* 145 S.W.3d 557 (Tenn. 2004).

(b) *Owner in the car with right of control.* When the defendant permits another to drive, but himself remains in the car, as owner he retains some degree of legal control and he may be liable for failing to exercise that control. Again, this may reflect not vicarious liability but ordinary negligence. In some cases courts have emphasized the legal right of control even if he is not actually negligent. This view is probably on its way out. Thus "the mere presence of the owner in an automobile driven by another does not create any presumption of a master-servant relationship or joint enterprise." *Reed* v. *Hinderland,* 660 P.2d 464 (Ariz.1983).

(c) *Ordinary bailment.* If the owner-defendant simply lends the car to a competent driver, so that there is a bailment, with neither actual nor legal right of control, there is no agency and no liability. This is the common law rule.

(d) *Owner-consent statutes.* Statutes of several states make the individual owner liable for the negligence of the driver even in the case of a pure bailment, provided only that the owner consented to the use of the car. This kind of statute may give rise to litigation over whether the defendant actually consented to the use of the car and if so whether the driver went beyond the consent. Commercial lessors of vehicles may be subject to further regulation in many states. In *Murdza v. Zimmerman,* 786 N.E.2d 440 (N.Y. 2003), A leased to B who consented to C's use but not the use by others; C permitted D to drive in violation of B's restriction. The court held that the restriction avoids B's liability, but A as lessor cannot take advantage of B's restriction on use. What if the lease requires the driver to have a valid contract and the lessee does not have one? *See Fojtik v. Hunter,* 828 A.2d 589 (Conn. 2003).

(e) *Family-purpose doctrine.* This doctrine, invented by the courts, was that if a car was maintained for general family use, the legal owner would be liable for its negligent use by a member of the family. The effect was that the driver was treated as the servant of the owner. At the time the doctrine originated, it was typically applied to hold a husband or father liable for the negligent driving of a wife or child. About a dozen states have such a rule. *See, e.g., Young v. Beck,* 251 P.3d 380 (Ariz. 2011) (explaining that the primary purpose of the rule is "to provide for an injured party's recovery from the financially responsible person—the family head— deemed most able to control to whom the car is made available").

7. *Imputed negligence and the "both ways" rule.* O, the owner of a car, is a passenger in the vehicle and has allowed another person, B, to drive. If B negligently causes an accident that injures C, is B's negligence imputed to O, making O vicariously liable to the C? Under a doctrine called "imputed negligence," the answer was yes. Under the same rule, if O wanted to sue C for damages, the contributory negligence of B was attributed to O, which would have the effect of either barring or reducing

O's damages against C. It was "based on the presumption that the owner, although not at the wheel, is in control of the vehicle, or at least has the right to exert control." *Seaborne-Worsley v. Mintiens*, 183 A.3d 141 (Md. 2018). This rule has largely fallen out of favor as "divorced from reality" insofar as it imputes the negligence of the driver to the car's owner simply because the owner also happened to be a passenger. *Id.; see Weber v. Stokely-Van Camp, Inc.*, 144 N.W.2d 540 (Minn. 1966) (partially rejecting the rule).

The Restatement of Apportionment takes the position that "the negligence of another person is not imputed to a plaintiff solely because of the plaintiff's ownership of a motor vehicle or permission for its use by the other person." RESTATEMENT (THIRD) OF TORTS: APPORTIONMENT § 5 (2000). However, the same section says that "The negligence of another person is imputed to a plaintiff whenever the negligence of the other person would have been imputed had the plaintiff been a defendant." This is called the "both ways" rule. Here's how it works: imagine that O, the owner of the car, was the employer of B, who was driving the car within the scope of B's employment. B and C are involved in a car accident, and O sues C for negligence. Under this "both ways" rule, any negligence of B would be imputed to C as a plaintiff. *See id.*, cmt. b. That is, where O would be held vicariously liable for B's negligence if O was a defendant, B's negligence will also be imputed to O when O is a plaintiff—in other words, the rule works "both ways." But the imputation of B's negligence to O as a plaintiff in the case against C is not due to O's ownership of the car—it is due to the fact that B was O's employee, acting within the scope of employment.

REFERENCES: DOBBS, HAYDEN & BUBLICK, HORNBOOK ON TORTS §§ 31.1–31.8 (2d ed. 2016); 2 DOBBS, HAYDEN & BUBLICK, THE LAW OF TORTS §§ 425–436 (2d ed. 2011).

CHAPTER 23

COMMON LAW STRICT LIABILITY

■ ■ ■

§ 1. HISTORICAL STRICT LIABILITY FOR TRESPASSORY TORTS AND THE ADVENT OF FAULT THEORY

The Trespass form of action. In medieval England, lawsuits in the King's courts were initiated by obtaining a "writ," a highly formal document giving jurisdiction to the King's court. The earliest, apart from cases involving rights in property and the like, was the writ called *Trespass.* This writ or form of action could be obtained whenever the plaintiff claimed an injury that was both (a) direct and (b) forcible. This form of action became the basis for torts we know today as battery, assault, false imprisonment, trespass to land and trespass to chattels. The judges in such cases asked only if a direct and forcible injury was inflicted. They did not ask whether the defendant acted with any particular intent or with negligence. Thus the *Trespass* writ imposed strict liability—liability without proof of fault.

The Case form of action. Eventually, plaintiffs were able to obtain a second kind of writ when the injury was indirect. This second writ (or form of action) was called *Trespass on the Case,* or more commonly, simply *Case.* When the plaintiff suffered indirect injury, *Case* and only *Case* would be the appropriate writ. When the writ of *Case* was used, one applicable rule was that the plaintiff was required to prove some kind of negligence or, later, "unlawful" act. So negligence came into the law of tort, but only when the writ of *Case* was used and injury was indirect.

Weaver v. Ward. In a famous case decided in 1616, the plaintiff and defendant were in bands of men practicing military exercises. The plaintiff was wounded when the defendant discharged his musket. The defendant argued that he did not intentionally cause the musket ball to strike the plaintiff. But the court held that this was no defense. The claim was based on the writ of *Trespass* (because injury was direct) and in *Trespass* the law awards damages for hurt or loss, that is, without requiring intent or negligence. The court did, however, recognize that if the plaintiff had run in front of the defendant's weapon as he fired, the defendant might not be liable. *Weaver v. Ward,* 80 Eng. Rep. 284 (K.B. 1616).

The shift to fault-based liability: Brown v. Kendall. In the next 200 years, for various reasons, plaintiffs brought more suits in *Case* for negligence. In 1850, in a blockbuster case, the Massachusetts high court finally held that negligence was required even in cases that fit the old *Trespass* form of action. In that case, *Brown v. Kendall*, 60 Mass. 292 (1850), a man was using a stick to separate two fighting dogs. Raising it over his head, he struck the plaintiff, who was behind him. This fit the *Trespass* pattern of direct injury. But the court held that proof of negligence would be *required* to establish liability for unintended harms and that the plaintiff had the burden of proving it. It defined negligence in terms we understand today: the care that would be used by persons of ordinary prudence in the circumstances. The "correct rule," said the court, is "that the plaintiff must come prepared with evidence to show either that the intention was unlawful, or that the defendant was in fault; for if the injury was unavoidable, and the conduct of the defendant was free from blame, he will not be liable." Rejecting the application of strict liability, the court concluded, "unless it also appears to the satisfaction of the jury, that the defendant is chargeable with some fault, negligence, carelessness, or want [of] prudence, the plaintiff fails to sustain the burden of proof, and is not entitled to recover."

Pockets of strict liability. After *Brown v. Kendall*, negligence, not strict liability, became the normal basis for liability for unintended harms. Despite this fundamental change in tort law to a fault-based system, particular pockets of strict liability survived *Brown v. Kendall,* and some other kinds of strict liability advanced. We explore some of the major areas in the remainder of this chapter. In the next, we will see the rise and partial fall of strict liability as a dominant theory in a purely modern area of law, products liability.

REFERENCE: 1 DOBBS, HAYDEN & BUBLICK, THE LAW OF TORTS § 17 (2d ed. 2011).

§ 2. STRICT LIABILITY TODAY

Liability without proof of fault remains the exception, not the rule. Some of the remaining areas of strict liability today predate *Brown v. Kendall's* revolutionary fault-based conception of tort law; others have developed more recently. In each area, the history of how and why they developed, while not always crystal clear, is important to understanding their scope today.

A. INJURIES CAUSED BY ANIMALS

1. Trespassing Animals

The Restatement Third provides that an owner of livestock or other animals (other than dogs and cats) that intrude on another person's land, "is subject to strict liability for physical harm caused by the intrusion." RESTATEMENT (THIRD) OF TORTS: LIABILITY FOR PHYSICAL AND EMOTIONAL HARM § 21 (2010). How did this become the rule?

Under the writ of *Trespass*, the plaintiff could redress all direct harms, even if the defendant was not at fault; and under the writ of *Case*, he would redress indirect harms, provided the defendant was at fault. But there was a period in which the only writ, or the dominant one, was *Trespass*. As an English legal historian has pointed out, a lawyer writing a book about torts in the late 14th century would have called the book "*Trespass*," because at the time tort law was embodied in *Trespass*; *Case* developed later. S. MILSOM, HISTORICAL FOUNDATIONS OF THE COMMON LAW 261 (1969). What was done with claims for indirect injury before the writ of *Case* was developed?

As it happened, some of them were treated as *Trespass* cases and strict liability seems to have been imposed. If the defendant owned cattle and drove them onto the plaintiff's land, the writ of *Trespass* would be proper, or at least it could be argued. Such an entry would be reasonably "direct," and it might also meet the later test of "unlawfulness." However, suppose that the defendant's cattle merely strayed, or broke loose from an enclosure, and that they then entered the plaintiff's land and did harm such as crop damage. In such an instance, there seems to be no "direct" connection between the defendant's conduct and the harm—he did not "act"—and consequently the writ of *Trespass* would be inappropriate. But *Case* had not been developed, so the choice was to dismiss the claim or to entertain it under the writ of *Trespass*. The courts seem to have chosen the latter course, and since *Trespass* carried with it the rule of strict liability, cattle trespass became a strict liability tort. This rule, having gained its foothold in *Trespass*, remained the same even after *Case* was developed. As another English historian has said, if the claims had arisen later in time, *Case* would have been available and would have been used, with the result, presumably, that liability would have been based on negligence. G. WILLIAMS, LIABILITY FOR ANIMALS 133 (1939).

The cattle cases were apparently thought of as a special category of liability. Not only did the rule of strict liability for cattle trespass survive the advent of *Case*, to some degree it also survived the shift toward fault-based liability ushered in by *Brown v. Kendall*. That is, the "universal" fault formula in *Brown v. Kendall* found an exception in the trespassing cattle cases.

The rule for cattle included the barnyard beasts in general—cows, horses, sheep and others. It did not include pets, such as dogs, even though dogs might have important functions on a farm. There was also a special exception even as to cattle: if they strayed from a highway on which they were being driven, there was no strict liability for their trespass.

Under some cases and the earlier Restatement, strict liability for these barnyard animals would not apply to personal injury, only to "trespass" damage. *Cf. Hastings v. Sauve*, 989 N.E.2d 940 (N.Y. 2013) (negligence liability only for defendant whose cow strayed from property onto highway, where plaintiff collided with it and was injured). But the Restatement Third extends strict liability to any injury resulting from animal intrusion upon land that is a characteristic of such intrusion, which may include personal injuries. Thus being hurt trying to chase a bull off your property might give you a strict liability claim, but tripping over a goat sleeping on your land at night would not. *See* RESTATEMENT (THIRD) OF TORTS: LIABILITY FOR PHYSICAL AND EMOTIONAL HARM § 21 cmt. g (2010). Many states—especially those where large open grazing is feasible and desirable—have adopted different rules, often by statute; many of these statutes provide for a local option or a fencing district, giving counties or other districts the power to develop their own rules.

2.   Abnormally Dangerous Animals

The Restatement Third provides for a form of strict but limited liability for the owner or possessor of an animal that has "dangerous tendencies abnormal for the animal's category." RESTATEMENT (THIRD) OF TORTS: LIABILITY FOR PHYSICAL AND EMOTIONAL HARM § 23 (2010). Strict liability is imposed if, but only if, the owner knows or has reason to know of the animal's abnormally dangerous tendencies (to attack without warning, for example), and liability attaches only "if the harm ensues from that dangerous tendency." *Id.* The Restatement recognizes that apart from wild animals, most animals are normally safe, but that particular animals might in fact present both "significant and abnormal dangers" to others. *Id.*, cmt. b. The rationale for strict liability is that it "gives the owner an incentive to consider whether the animal should be retained." *Id.* Thus this form of strict liability does not apply to a veterinary clinic, where the owner's dog attacked another patron in the waiting room. *Hewitt v. Palmer Veterinary Clinic, PC*, 159 N.E.3d 228 (N.Y. 2020). This strict-liability rule seems to apply to any kind of animal—that is, there is no strict liability where the owner does not know of the *particular* animal's abnormally dangerous propensities. *See, e.g., Bard v. Jahnke*, 848 N.E.2d 463 (N.Y. 2006) (bull); *Olier v. Bailey*, 164 So.3d 982 (Miss. 2015) (goose); *Knapton v. Monk*, 347 P.3d 1257 (Mont. 2015) (purebred pit bull).

Some states have rejected strict liability for harms caused by domestic animals, requiring proof of the owner's or keeper's negligent conduct. *See*

Vendrella v. Astriab Family Ltd. Parnership, 87 A.3d 546 (Conn. 2014) (factual issue found as to whether bite injury was reasonably foreseeable to defendant who kept horse on farm; owner owes duty of reasonable care to prevent foreseeable injuries where animal belongs to a class that is naturally inclined to cause such injuries, without regard to whether the particular animal had previously caused an injury). Does the "strict liability" requirement that the owner knew or should have known of an animal's propensity to harm others actually create a negligence standard? *See Martin v. Christman*, 99 A.3d 1008 (Vt. 2014) (rejecting strict liability for dog bites, suggesting that an owner may be negligent where he knows of the dog's vicious tendencies and does not take reasonable steps to protect others).

Statutes and ordinances often impose additional liabilities on dog owners, through leash laws or otherwise. *See, e.g., Pawlowski v. American Family Mut. Ins. Co.*, 777 N.W.2d 67 (Wis. 2009) (applying statute to impose strict liability on homeowner who "harbored" a dog that did not belong to her). Note that if the plaintiff cannot prove the elements of a strict-liability claim based on a dog bite statute, a negligence claim may still succeed against the dog owner. *See, e.g., Goldhagen v. Pasmowitz*, 255 A.3d 1191 (N.J. 2021); *Smith v. Meyring Cattle Co., L.L.C.*, 921 N.W.2d 820 (Neb. 2019).

3. Wild Animals

With respect to animals said to be "wild by nature," strict liability is usually imposed for injuries connected with the wild characteristics of the animal, so that the person in charge will be held liable in spite of all possible care. Animals in this "wild" category" include lions and tigers and bears that people have seen fit to import and exhibit. RESTATEMENT (THIRD) OF TORTS: LIABILITY FOR PHYSICAL AND EMOTIONAL HARM § 22 (2010).

B. IMPOUNDMENTS, NUISANCES AND BEYOND

RYLANDS V. FLETCHER
Exchequer: 3 Hurl & C. 774 (1865)
Exchequer Chamber: L.R. 1 Exch. 265 (1866)
House of Lords: L.R. 3 H.L. 330 (1868)

[Plaintiff operated a mine in the county of Lancaster. Defendants operated a mill in the vicinity, and had contractors build a reservoir or pond to supply water. The contractors did build such a pond, though in fact it was located immediately over some vertical shafts once used in mining. The shafts had been filled rather inadequately, but gave the appearance of solid earth. When the pond was filled with water, its weight caused the material in the shafts to give way, and the water flooded down the vertical shafts. From there it flowed through horizontal mine shafts of an intervening mine into the plaintiff's mine. This is an action by the plaintiff for damages caused by this flooding. A procedure was used in which an arbitrator stated a special case or found facts. The case was then considered in the Court of Exchequer, followed by review in the Exchequer Chamber and finally in the House of Lords. The style of the case is that used in the House of Lords.]

[IN THE COURT OF EXCHEQUER]

BRAMWELL, B. . . .

The plaintiff's right then has been infringed; the defendants in causing water to flow to the plaintiff have done that which they had no right to do; what difference in point of law does it make that they have done it unwittingly? I think none, and consequently that the action is maintainable. . . .

It is said there must be a trespass, a nuisance, or negligence. . . . But why is not this a trespass? Wilfulness is not material: Leame v. Bray (3 East, 593). Why is it not a nuisance? The nuisance is not in the reservoir, but in the water escaping. As in Backhouse v. Bonomi the act was lawful, the mischievous consequence is a wrong. . . .

MARTIN, B. . . .

First, I think there was no trespass. . . . I think the true criterion of trespass is laid down in the judgments in the former case, viz., that to constitute trespass the act doing the damage must be immediate, and that if the damage be mediate or consequential (which I think the present was), it is not a trespass. Secondly, I think there was no nuisance in the ordinary and generally understood meaning of that word, that is to say, something hurtful or injurious to the senses. The making a pond for holding water is a nuisance to no one. The digging a reservoir in a man's own land is a lawful act. . . . To hold the defendants liable would therefore make them insurers against the consequence of a lawful act upon their own land when they had no reason to believe or suspect that any damage was likely to ensue. . . .

[Pollock, C. B., agreed with Martin, B., that the facts found by the arbitrator were not a sufficient basis for relief.]

[IN THE EXCHEQUER CHAMBER]

May 14, 1866. BLACKBURN, J., read the following judgment of the court. . . .

We have come to the conclusion that the opinion of Bramwell, B., was right, and that the answer to the question should be that the plaintiff was entitled to recover damages from the defendants by reason of the matters stated in the Case. . . .

What is the liability which the law casts upon a person who, like the defendants, lawfully brings on his land something which, though harmless while it remains there, will naturally do mischief if it escapes out of his land? It is agreed on all hands that he must take care to keep in that which he has brought on the land, and keep it there in order that it may not escape and damage his neighbor's, but the question arises whether the duty which the law casts upon him under such circumstances is an absolute duty to keep it in at his peril, or is, as the majority of the Court of Exchequer have thought, merely a duty to take all reasonable and prudent precautions in order to keep it in, but no more. . . .

We think that the true rule of law is that the person who, for his own purposes, brings on his land, and collects and keeps there anything likely to do mischief if it escapes, must keep it in at his peril, and, if he does not do so, he is prima facie answerable for all the damage which is the natural consequence of its escape. He can excuse himself by showing that the escape was owing to the plaintiff's default, or, perhaps, that the escape was the consequence of vis major, or the act of God; but, as nothing of this sort exists here, it is unnecessary to inquire what excuse would be sufficient. . . .

The case that has most commonly occurred, and which is most frequently to be found in the books, is as to the obligation of the owner of cattle which he has brought on his land to prevent their escaping and doing mischief. The law as to them seems to be perfectly settled from early times; the owner must keep them in at his peril, or he will be answerable for the natural consequences of their escape, that is, with regard to tame beasts, for the grass they eat and trample upon, although not for any injury to the person of others, for our ancestors have settled that it is not the general nature of horses to kick or bulls to gore, but if the owner knows that the beast has a vicious propensity to attack man he will be answerable for that too. . . . So in May v. Burdett, the court, after an elaborate examination of the old precedents and authorities, came to the conclusion that a person keeping a mischievous animal is bound to keep it secure at his peril. . . .

As has been already said, there does not appear to be any difference in principle between the extent of the duty cast on him who brings cattle on his land to keep them in, and the extent of the duty imposed on him who brings on his land water, filth, or stenches, or any other thing which will, if it escape, naturally do damage, to prevent their escaping and injuring his neighbor. Tenant v. Goldwin [a case decided in 1704 and reported in a number of places, including 1 Salk. 21 and 360, 91 Eng. Rep. 20 and 314, 2 Ld. Raym, 1089, 92 Eng. Rep. 222, and 6 Mod. Rep. 311, 87 Eng. Rep. 1051] is an express authority that the duty is the same, and is to keep them in at his peril. [In that case the defendant had a privy on his land and formerly had it enclosed by a wall. By reason of the defendant's failure to repair the wall, the filth of the privy flowed into the plaintiff's cellar.]

In the report in 6 Mod. Rep. at p. 314, it is stated:

> "And at another day per totam curiam the declaration is good, for there is a sufficient cause of action appearing in it, but not upon the word solebat. If the defendant has a house or office enclosed with a wall which is his, he is, of common right, bound to use it so as not to annoy another. . . . The reason here is, that one must use his own so as thereby not to hurt another, and as of common right one is bound to keep his cattle from trespassing on his neighbor, so he is bound to use anything that is his so as not to hurt another by such use. . . ."

No case has been found in which the question of the liability for noxious vapours escaping from a man's works by inevitable accident has been discussed, but the following case will illustrate it. Some years ago several actions were brought against the occupiers of some alkali works at Liverpool for the damage alleged to be caused by the chlorine fumes of their works. The defendants proved that they had, at great expense, erected a contrivance by which the fumes of chlorine were condensed, and sold as muriatic acid, and they called a great body of scientific evidence to prove that this apparatus was so perfect that no fumes possible could escape from the defendant's chimneys. On this evidence it was pressed upon the juries that the plaintiff's damage must have been due to some of the numerous other chimneys in the neighborhood. The juries, however, being satisfied that the mischief was occasioned by chlorine, drew the conclusion that it had escaped from the defendant's works somehow, and in each case found for the plaintiff. No attempt was made to disturb these verdicts on the ground that the defendants had taken every precaution which prudence or skill could suggest to keep those fumes in, and that they could not be responsible unless negligence were shown, yet if the law be as laid down by the majority of the Court of Exchequer it would have been a very obvious defense. [T]he uniform course of pleading in actions for such nuisances is to say that the defendant caused the noisome vapours to arise on his premises and suffered them to come on the plaintiff's without stating that there was any want of care or skill on the defendant's part; and that Tenant v. Goldwin showed that this was founded on the general rule of law that he whose stuff it is must keep it so that it may not trespass. There is no difference in this respect between chlorine and water; both will, if they escape, do damage, the one by scorching and the other by drowning, and he who brings them on his land must at his peril see that they do not escape and do that mischief.

. . . But it was further said by Martin, B., that when damage is done to personal property, or even to the person by collision, either upon land or at sea, there must be negligence in the party doing the damage to render him legally responsible. This is no doubt true. . . . but we think these cases distinguishable from the present. Traffic on the highways, whether by land or sea, cannot be conducted without exposing those whose persons or property are near it to some inevitable risk; and, that being so, those who go on the highway, or have their property adjacent to it, may well be held to do so subject to their taking upon themselves the risk of injury from that inevitable danger . . . and it is believed that all the cases in which inevitable accident has been held an excuse for what prima facie was a trespass can be explained on the same principle, namely that the circumstances were such as to show that the plaintiff had taken the risk upon himself. But there is no ground for saying that the plaintiff here took upon himself any risk arising from the uses to which the defendants should choose to apply their land. He neither knew what there might be, nor could he in any way control the defendants. . . .

The view which we take of the first point renders it unnecessary to consider whether the defendants would or would not be responsible for the want of care and skill in the persons employed by them. We are of opinion that the plaintiff is entitled to recover. . . .

[IN THE HOUSE OF LORDS]

LORD CAIRNS, L.C. . . .

The principles on which this case must be determined appear to me to be extremely simple. The defendants, . . . might lawfully have used that close for any purpose for which it might, in the ordinary course of the enjoyment of land, be used, and if, in what I may term the natural user of that land, there had been any accumulation of water, either on the surface or underground, and if by the operation of the laws of nature that accumulation of water had passed off into the close occupied by the plaintiff, the plaintiff could not have complained that that result had taken place. If he had desired to guard himself against it, it would have lain on him to have done so. . . .

On the other hand, if the defendants, not stopping at the natural use of their close, had desired to use it for any purpose which I may term a non-natural use, for the purpose of introducing into the close that which, in its natural condition, was not in or upon it—for the purpose of introducing water, either above or below ground, in quantities and in a manner not the result of any work or operation on or under the land, and if in consequence of their doing so, or in consequence of any imperfection in the mode of their doing so, the water came to escape and to pass off into the close of the plaintiff, then it appears to me that that which the defendants were doing they were doing at their own peril. . . .

These simple principles, if they are well founded, as it appears to me they are, really dispose of this case. The same result is arrived at on the principles referred to by Blackburn, J., in his judgment in the Court of Exchequer Chamber. . . .

In that opinion, I must say, I entirely concur. Therefore, I have to move your Lordships that the judgment of the Court of Exchequer Chamber be affirmed, and that the present appeal be dismissed with costs.

LORD CRANWORTH.

I concur with my noble and learned friend in thinking that the rule of law was correctly stated by Blackburn, J., in delivering the opinion of the Exchequer chamber. If a person brings or accumulates on his land anything which, if it should escape, may cause damage to his neighbor, he does so at his peril. If it does escape and cause damage, he is responsible, however careful he may have been, and whatever precautions he may have taken to prevent the damage. In considering whether a defendant is liable to a plaintiff for damage which the plaintiff may have sustained, the question in general is, not whether the defendant has acted with due care and caution, but whether his acts have occasioned the damage. This is all well explained in the old case of Lambert and Olliot v. Bessey. The doctrine is founded on good sense, for when one person in managing his own affairs causes, however innocently, damage to another, it is obviously only just that he should be the party to suffer. He is bound sic uti suo ut non laedat alienum. This is the principle of law applicable to cases like the present, and I do not discover in the authorities which were cited anything conflicting with it. . . .

NOTES

1. **Why strict liability in *Rylands*?** What is the scope of strict liability in *Rylands* and why is it imposed?

2. **Special hazards in *Rylands*?** Does *Rylands* require any special hazard as a prerequisite to liability? Substances like dynamite may represent unusual hazards. Is water like that?

3. ***Rylands* as an "escaping impoundments" case.** One central characteristic of *Rylands* is that it involved the escape of something that was held on the land by the defendant (water, in that case) that was likely to do harm to others if it escaped. How might this basis of strict liability apply today? In *Thomalen v. Marriott Corp.*, 845 F.Supp. 33 (D. Mass. 1994), a Marriott Hotel hosted a "Murder Mystery Weekend," in which a troupe of actors staged murder mystery entertainments. One member of the group, attempting to perform a fire-eating act, became engulfed in flames; another member ran to the stage to help but knocked over a can of lighter fluid. This ignited and caused burns to a guest close to the stage. The guest claimed Marriott was strictly liable under *Rylands*. The court disagreed. While Massachusetts has adopted *Rylands v. Fletcher* strict liability, the court said, there was "no escape of a dangerous instrumentality from Marriott's property," so that rule does not apply.

On the precise facts of *Rylands*—the sudden escape of ponded water—very few modern courts would impose strict liability, although some have. *See Covey v. Brishka*, 445 P.3d 785 (Mont. 2019) (4.5 million-gallon man-made fish pond breached its banks and flooded downhill landowners' property; uphill landowner held strictly liable because the pond was an "abornmally dangerous condition"). However, in two variants on the *Rylands* facts, strict liability may be more readily imposed. The first is where the defendant impounds noxious substances that suddenly escape. *See, e.g., Cities Service Co. v. State*, 312 So.2d 799 (Fla. Dist Ct. App. 1975) (escape of billions of gallons of phosphate slimes from a mine); *State Dept. of Envtl. Prot. v. Ventron Corp.*, 468 A.2d 150 (N.J. 1983) (escape of 268 tons of mercury). The second variation involves impounded liquids that do not escape suddenly, but merely percolate through the soil and contaminate a well or otherwise cause harm. These percolation cases almost always involve noxious impoundments, and may be traced to *Tenant v. Goldwin*, discussed in *Rylands*, where the judges appeared willing to impose strict liability for the escape of filth from a privy. *See Yommer* v. *McKenzie*, 257 A.2d 138 (Md. 1969) (gasoline); *Iverson v. Vint*, 54 N.W.2d 494 (Iowa 1952) (molasses dumped in ditch, percolation into farmer's well, strict liability). Some of these cases can be explained on other grounds, for example, that there was *Garratt v. Dailey* intent, or that there was a species of fault in carrying on an activity in an inappropriate place. Can there really be any principle, other than a whimsical one, that distinguishes damage caused by sudden escape from damage caused by percolation?

4.　**Legitimate land uses endangering one another.** In one respect *Rylands* may be easy to understand. Suppose that thousands of acres of land in an agricultural area are devoted to farming Murg, a kind of grain that requires repeated aerial spraying. Into the midst of this great agricultural area move two new businesses: one is a beekeeper and one is a heavy industry. If, without fault, the aerial spraying of the Murg fields injures the bees or prevents them from finding usable pollen, should the beekeeper have a claim? If, without fault, the heavy industry discharges pollution that contaminates 3,000 acres of Murg growing in the fields, should the Murg owners have a claim?

5.　**Does *Rylands* fit the inconsistent land uses pattern?** Cases like *Rylands*, and most nuisance cases today, can be seen as instances of inconsistent land uses. Though there is nothing "wrong" with moving a factory to the country, if it presents dangers to existing investments through its pollution, perhaps the most economical thing to do is to protect those investments without regard to "fault." Does this describe *Rylands*? After all, coal can be mined and that resource exploited only in places where the coal lies, but one could build a millpond almost anywhere in a pluvial country.

6.　**A test case.** To test this idea, imagine that the coal mine in *Rylands* somehow caused damage to the mill owner or to nearby farmers. Would strict liability have been imposed then? Take an actual case: Salt water is used in oil well drilling, and must be stored in ponds. If the oil well driller's salt water pond collapsed without the driller's fault, would the farmer whose fields were ruined have an action based on strict liability? In *Turner v. Big Lake Oil Co.*, 96 S.W.2d 221 (Tex. 1936), the court rejected strict liability on such facts. While the court said it repudiated *Rylands,* is the result one *Rylands* might actually support? How?

7. **Coming to the nuisance.** There are similar ideas in pure nuisance cases. Although one who "comes to the nuisance" is not necessarily barred from recovery, since a number of factors must be weighed in nuisance cases, it seems clear that one who moves a home to a factory district cannot successfully enjoin operation of the factories or even recover damages. Compare the situation of the beekeeper in Note 4. If the factory moves into a residential neighborhood, the situation is reversed and it may well be found to be a nuisance.

NOTE: NUISANCES TODAY

1. *Nuisance in context.* *Rylands* itself has been seen as a kind of "nuisance" case, although today nuisance cases are rarely a matter of truly strict liability. Contemporary cases require the plaintiff prove negligence, or intent to interfere with the plaintiff's interests, or the creation of a nuisance through abnormally dangerous activity, the subject of the next section below. *See, e.g., Crosstex North Texas Pipeline, L.P. v. Gardiner*, 505 S.W.3d 580 (Tex. 2016); *Ross v. Lowitz*, 120 A.3d 178 (N.J. 2015); *see also* 2 DOBBS, HAYDEN & BUBLICK, THE LAW OF TORTS § 400 (2d ed. 2011). Nuisance is an important tort claim when a defendant's acts—often a use by the defendant of his own land—substantially interfere with the plaintiff's use and enjoyment of her land. Often the invasions onto land that constitute nuisances are intangible—tangible invasions are often actionable as trespass to property—and almost always involve incompatible land uses. *See Wilson v. Interlake Steel Co.*, 649 P.2d 922 (Cal. 1982) (drawing this nuisance/trespass distinction). Nuisance cases often arise because the defendant's activity causes some kind of pollution, as by smoke, dust, chemicals, smells or noise. *See, e.g., McKiver v. Murphy-Brown, LLC*, 980 F.3d 937 (4th Cir. 2020) ("odors, pests, and noises" emanating from neighboring hog production facilities); *Sowers v. Forest Hills Subdivision*, 294 P.3d 427 (Nev. 2013) (wind turbine that would generate noise and shadow flicker).

2. *Substantial interference.* To constitute a nuisance, the interference with the plaintiff's use and enjoyment of her land must be substantial. This is a matter of degree, and a plaintiff's success will often turn on effective proof. *See West v. Jewett & Noonan Transp., Inc.*, 189 A.3d 277 (Me. 2018) (plaintiffs did not have to prove a specific depreciation in land value caused by the spilling of 9,000 gallons of oil and kerosene onto their property, where they proved that "interest in the development of their property disappeared after the spill"); *Post and Beam Equities Group, LLC*

v. Sunne Village Development Property Owners Ass'n, 124 A.3d 454 (Vt. 2015) (reviewing plaintiff's evidence proving that defendant's installation of a guardrail blocking access to restaurants over a subdivision's roadway caused substantial interference with plaintiff's use and enjoyment of land). A brief whiff of an unpleasant smell emanating from the yard next door will likely not suffice. What if your neighbor built an "aesthetically displeasing" house with a metallic roof that interfered with your view of a lake? Is that enough to show a nuisance? *See Newton v. MJK/BJK, LLC*, 469 P.3d 23 (Idaho 2020) ("A landowner does not have the right under nuisance law to prohibit an adjoining neighbor from erecting structures that they consider to be displeasing.").

3. *Unreasonable invasion.* The invasion of the plaintiff's use and enjoyment of her land must be unreasonable, not in the sense that the defendant creates an unreasonable risk, but in the sense that given the time, place, and social expectations of the locale, it is unreasonable to expect the plaintiff to put up with the invasion without compensation. An intentional invasion may thus be permissible: defendant burns leaves in the fall, or operates a brick kiln that regularly causes odors, but not for long. Other intended invasions may be actionable as nuisances if it is unreasonable to expect the plaintiff to put up with them. But this raises the question: how would you prove something is "unreasonable" if not by proving unreasonably risky conduct? The widely cited Restatement Second of Torts, in section 826, provides the traditional answer that the invasion is a nuisance if the gravity of the harm to the plaintiff "outweighs" the utility of the defendant's conduct. This would require a balancing of harm (not *risk* of harm) and utility of the conduct causing the invasion. *See, e.g., Lakey v. Puget Sound Energy, Inc.*, 296 P.3d 860 (Wash. 2013) (concluding that electromagnetic fields emanating from power company's substation was not a nuisance, where social utility of company's conduct outweighed interference with homeowners' enjoyment of their property). But the Restatement adds another alternative test: if the defendant could compensate the plaintiff and all others whose interests are invaded by the defendant's conduct, and could still stay in business, then compensation should be made. The idea is that it would be unreasonable to permit the defendant's activity to continue without paying, and the invasion will be regarded as a nuisance.

4. *Coming to the nuisance.* The fact that the plaintiff moved in next door to a nuisance is a significant fact in judging unreasonableness and hence in judging whether there is a nuisance at all. But no enterprise is allowed to create a noisome condition on its own land and insist that forever after anyone who comes into the area must be willing to tolerate such a condition. To permit this would be to allow an enterprise to condemn the land of others and to force a stasis on a dynamic and changing world. The fact that the plaintiff came to the nuisance is therefore only one factor to

be considered in determining whether a nuisance exists. If the natural spread of a city brings it to the edge of the defendant's smelly feed lot, the lot, which was no nuisance at all when the area was devoted to farming, may become one when the area becomes suburban. On the other hand, the plaintiff who moves from Palm Springs to Bakersfield cannot complain about oil wells.

Another possibility when the plaintiff comes to the nuisance is that he has already been compensated for it. This is so because, if the nuisance is open and obvious, the plaintiff will probably have paid the former owner a smaller price because of the nuisance.

5. *Public nuisances.* "A cause of action for public nuisance exists for conduct that amounts to a substantial interference with the exercise of a common right, such as endangering the health or safety of a considerable number of persons." *Benoit v. Saint-Gobain Performance Plastics Corp.*, 959 F.3d 491 (2d Cir. 2020). Suppose the defendant, an industrial enterprise, dumps wastes on its own ground. These percolate through the soil and pollute a river, a lake, and even estuarine waters. All these bodies of water are public property. If the fish are killed or the waters become unusable, does anyone have a claim? Conceivably, landowners adjacent to these waters would have a nuisance claim on the principles stated above if the pollution substantially diminished the use and enjoyment of their land. What about a non-landowner who fishes for sport and can no longer catch fish because they are dead? Or one who fishes commercially and can no longer catch them for the same reason? If the pollution constitutes a public nuisance because it substantially interferes with public health, safety, or convenience, the rule is that any person who has damages different in kind from the public generally may recover damages for the nuisance. *See Hopi Tribe v. Arizona Snowbowl Resort Ltd. Partnership*, 430 P.3d 362 (Ariz. 2018) (special injury means "damage that is different in kind or quality from that suffered from the public in common"); *Baptiste v. Bethlehem Landfill Co.*, 965 F.3d 124 (3d Cir. 2020) (under Pa. law, plaintiff must suffer harm "of a greater magnitude and of a different kind than that which the general public suffered"). The claimant who loses commercial fishing profits may thus have "standing to sue" because the claimant's injury differs from that of the public at large. *Cf. Benoit, supra* (defendant caused public nuisance by contaminating village's drinking water; plaintiffs who used privately owned wells showed special injury where 95% of village residents received their water from village wells). The plaintiff who merely fishes for sport may be denied recovery, since her damages are not so different from those of other persons. In some states, a concern for environmental protection or enhancement may lead to a wider standing on the part of individuals. *See* DOBBS, HAYDEN & BUBLICK, HORNBOOK ON TORTS § 30.7 (2d ed. 2016).

6. *Environmental and zoning laws.* The common law of nuisance leads directly to contemporary legislation and administrative regulations aimed at pollution. It also leads to zoning laws, designed to maximize appropriate land-use. Although it would be theoretically possible to import a great deal of environmental and land-use law into a torts course, those fields have become major specialties of their own. Consequently, the bulk of nuisance law today may be better developed in connection with courses in property, land use, environmental protection, and public health and safety.

C. ABNORMALLY DANGEROUS ACTIVITIES

DYER V. MAINE DRILLING & BLASTING, INC.

984 A.2d 210 (Me. 2009)

SILVER, J.

[Vera Dyer and her sons sued Maine Drilling for damage to their home caused by the blasting of rock nearby in connection with a construction project to replace a bridge and bridge access roads. The Dyers asserted causes of action in strict liability and negligence. Maine Drilling moved for summary judgment on all claims. The court granted the motion. On the strict liability claim, the trial court relied on *Reynolds v. W.H. Hinman Co.,* 145 Me. 343, 75 A.2d 802 (1950), and other Maine precedent. The Dyers filed this appeal.]

DISCUSSION

... We adopt today the Second Restatement's imposition of strict liability for abnormally dangerous activities, and remand to the court to determine if the blasting in this case was an abnormally dangerous activity under the Restatement's six-factor test. *See* Restatement (Second) of Torts §§ 519–520 (1977).[4] In doing so, we overrule our prior opinions requiring proof of negligence in blasting cases.

Strict liability doctrine originated in the English case *Rylands v. Fletcher* (1868) 3 L.R. 330 (H.L.), where the court held that a defendant

---

[4] The Second Restatement states:

§ 519. General Principle

(1) One who carries on an abnormally dangerous activity is subject to liability for harm to the person, land or chattels of another resulting from the activity, although he has exercised the utmost care to prevent the harm.

(2) This strict liability is limited to the kind of harm, the possibility of which makes the activity abnormally dangerous.

§ 520. Abnormally Dangerous Activities

In determining whether an activity is abnormally dangerous, the following factors are to be considered:

(a) existence of a high degree of risk of some harm to the person, land or chattels of others;

was liable regardless of negligence when he used his land in a way that was non-natural and likely to cause injury, and injury in fact resulted. ("If a person brings, or accumulates, on his land anything which, if it should escape, may cause damage to his neighbour, he does so at his peril. If it does escape, and cause damage, he is responsible, however careful he may have been."). This Court rejected *Rylands* in the 1950s, deciding that proof of negligence would be required in blasting cases.

In *Reynolds,* we noted that strict liability was the historic rule, but that the majority of states had switched to a negligence approach in abnormally dangerous activities cases. Additionally, the opinion quoted a law review article arguing against strict liability based in part on the "difficulty of drawing the line between the danger which calls for care and the extra hazard. There are, as yet[,] no unanimously approved rules or criteria as to this subject." Finally, our *Reynolds* decision was supported by the conclusions that blasting is a reasonable and lawful use of land, and that plaintiffs would generally be able to recover under a negligence scheme.

These rationales have been undermined in the last half-century. Policy approaches have shifted nationwide, leading almost every other state to adopt strict liability in blasting and other abnormally dangerous activity cases, and leading Maine to apply strict liability in other contexts. Additionally, the Second Restatement has provided a scheme of clear criteria for delineating which activities require a strict liability approach. In light of these changes, we overturn *Reynolds* and its progeny and adopt strict liability under the Restatement's six factor test.

Reynolds operated on the assumption that negligence liability would allow most plaintiffs to recover in blasting cases. However, we have recognized that blasting is inherently dangerous, and most courts have recognized that this inherent danger cannot be eliminated by the exercise of care. The Dyers' expert testified that blasting may cause damage even when it is within the Bureau of Mines's guidelines. Consequently, although blasting is a lawful and often beneficial activity, the costs should fall on those who benefit from the blasting, rather than on an unfortunate neighbor.

The negligence approach to abnormally dangerous activities initially taken by American courts was rooted in part in the idea that dangerous activities were essential to industrial development, "and it was considered that the interests of those in the vicinity of such enterprises must give way

---

(b) likelihood that the harm that results from it will be great;

(c) inability to eliminate the risk by the exercise of reasonable care;

(d) extent to which the activity is not a matter of common usage;

(e) inappropriateness of the activity to the place where it is carried on; and

(f) extent to which its value to the community is outweighed by its dangerous attributes.

to them, and that too great a burden must not be placed upon them." But today, that attitude has changed, and strict liability seeks to encourage both cost-spreading and incentives for the utmost safety when engaging in dangerous activities. Additionally, blasters are already required by the rules of the Maine Department of Public Safety and by many town ordinances to have liability insurance covering damages that result from blasting. Thus, a strict liability scheme should not greatly increase costs for these businesses.

Policy reasons

At least forty-one states have adopted some form of strict liability for blasting, with only two of those clearly limiting it to damage caused by debris. . . .

Not only has the weight of authority shifted nationally, but we, acting pursuant to our common law authority, have applied forms of strict liability in certain circumstances. For example, we have adopted the Second Restatement approach to injuries caused by wild animals, analogizing those cases to blasting. *See Byram v. Main*, 523 A.2d 1387 (Me. 1987) ("The keeping of wild animals is categorized with such dangerous activities as blasting, pile driving, storing inflammable liquids, and accumulating sewage."). Owners of domestic animals may be held strictly liable as well. . . .

[The Restatement Second's approach] strikes the right balance of policy interests by considering on a case-by-case basis which activities are encompassed by the rule, and by taking account of the social desirability of the activity at issue. . . .

A person who creates a substantial risk of severe harm to others while acting for his own gain should bear the costs of that activity. Most of the courts of the nation have recognized this policy, and we now do as well. For these reasons we adopt strict liability and remand for a determination whether the activity in this case subjected Maine Drilling to liability under the Second Restatement approach.

Under a strict liability analysis, proof of a causal relationship between the blasting and the property damage is still required. . . . [T]he Dyers produced sufficient evidence on the issue of causation to survive Maine Drilling's motion for summary judgment. . . . A fact-finder could reasonably find that the blasting was the . . . cause of damage to the Dyer home, because of: (1) the condition of the home observed before and after blasting commenced; (2) the temporal relationship between when the strongest blasting vibrations occurred and when damage was first observed; (3) evidence that the damage could have been caused by blasting; and (4) the reasonable inference that such damage was unlikely to be caused by other forces that typically cause cracking over longer periods of time. . . .

Judgment vacated. Remanded for further proceedings consistent with this opinion.

[Concurring and dissenting opinions omitted.]

NOTES

1. **The Restatement Third.** The Restatement Third also recognizes that abnormally dangerous activities may subject a defendant to strict liability, but offers a simpler, two-part test for determining when an activity is abnormally dangerous: (1) the activity must create "a foreseeable and highly significant risk of physical harm even when reasonable care is exercised by all actors; and (2) the activity is not one of common usage." RESTATEMENT (THIRD) OF TORTS: LIABILITY FOR PHYSICAL AND EMOTIONAL HARM § 20 (2010).

2. **Justifications for strict liability.** Why impose strict liability? (a) When the defendant engages in abnormally dangerous activities, knowing that he will reap the gains from the activity but that others may be harmed because it cannot be made safe by reasonable care, perhaps there is a moral basis for liability. If a defendant were *certain* that harm would result, you can make a moral case for liability. Is it so clear that the same is true when the defendant is not substantially certain of harm but merely knows of the high risk? Notice that, right or wrong, this idea is not to deter the activity—after all, it is not negligent—but to make it "pay its own way." (b) The Restatement Third suggests in § 20, comment b, that it is difficult to prove that an entire activity (like driving or building dams) is negligent and that some kinds of activity may involve negligence that cannot be detected or proved; strict liability, it suggests, is a good response to such cases.

3. **Risks or harms avoidable by reasonable care.** Notice that if reasonable care would reduce risks to a less-than-significant-level, strict liability does not apply. What if risks would be less than significant only if both the defendant and its potential victims were to exercise reasonable care? The Restatement Third provides in § 20, comment h, that the defendant's activity is not "unavoidably dangerous" and therefore not a matter of strict liability if potential victims can "commonly succeed in avoiding injuries." It is partially for this reason that the operation of a train that crosses a highway is not considered "abnormally dangerous" activity; if both the defendant and the plaintiff exercise reasonable care, the likelihood of injuries is minimal. *Id.*

4. **When plaintiff or others contribute to the activity.** In another comment, the Restatement Third emphasizes an additional matter—that strict liability is appropriate where the activity, such as blasting, causes harm "without meaningful contribution from the conduct of the victim or of any other actors." In most cases, the victim is an uninvolved and innocent party who is doing nothing. *See Id.,* cmt. e. In *Pullen v. West,* 92 P.3d 584 (Kan. 2004), the plaintiff was helping with a fireworks display and suffered injury when struck by a fireworks rocket. The court rejected his strict liability claim because it said he participated in the activity. The court said he might still recover under negligence rules.

5. **Common usage.** If an activity is normal in the community—"a matter of common usage"—strict liability does not apply and liability is limited

to cases in which the plaintiff can prove either negligence or intent. The common-usage rule certainly serves to limit the application of strict liability, but is a principle behind it? The Restatement Third in § 20, comment j, suggests two possibilities—first that the reason for strict liability might to some extent represent a concern for the acceptability of the activity and that when it is common, that concern tends to disappear. Second, when an activity is common, its benefits are likely to be distributed widely in the community and the basis for strict liability is stronger when benefits are concentrated among a few. *Cf.* Mark Geistfeld, *Should Enterprise Liability Replace the Rule of Strict Liability for Abnormally Dangerous Activities?*, 45 U.C.L.A. L. REV. 611 (1998). What do you think? If nuclear energy were not regulated by statutes, would you say that benefits of a nuclear power plant (a high risk activity) were concentrated among a few when electricity is distributed to virtually everyone?

6. **"Common carrier" exception to strict liability.** The Restatement Second § 521 recognizes an exception to strict liability where the defendant engaged in abnormally dangerous activity "pursuant to its duty as a public officer or employee, or a common carrier." A number of courts have adopted this exception. *See In re Hanford Nuclear Reservation Litigation*, 534 F.3d 986 (9th Cir. 2008) (noting that the "vast majority" of jurisdictions have done so). Many of the cases deal with the transportation of hazardous materials through residential areas, and justify applying the exception because "it would be unjust to subject a common carrier to strict liability for any danger done by a material the carrier is required to transport by law." *BNSF Railway Co. v. Eddy*, 459 P.3d 857 (Mont. 2020) (defendant railroad's transportation of vermiculite ore through crowded urban area was abnormally dangerous, but common-carrier exception applied). Even if a defendant is not subject to strict liability under this exception, "it may still be found liable under a theory of ordinary negligence for the manner in which it conducted" the activity. *Id.*

7. **Factual cause.** Can a plaintiff prevail on a strict liability claim simply by proving that the defendant engaged in an abnormally dangerous activity? Of course not. As *Dyer* makes clear, a plaintiff must also prove that the defendant's activity was a factual cause of harm. The rules applied in this context are the same ones we saw in negligence cases in Chapter 7.

8. **Scope-of-liability limitations.** Under the Restatement Second § 519, the defendant is not strictly liable for *all* harms caused by his abnormally dangerous activity, but only those "the possibility of which makes the activity abnormally dangerous." This simply articulates the basic scope of-liability (proximate cause) rule we saw in connection with negligence, doesn't it? *Accord*, RESTATEMENT (THIRD) OF TORTS: LIABILITY FOR PHYSICAL AND EMOTIONAL HARM § 29, cmt. l (2010).

Suppose a defendant engages in blasting, but the harm that results is neither harm from propelled objects, nor harm from vibrations. Instead the loud noises upset mother minks on nearby mink ranches and as a result they killed their kittens, resulting in loss to the breeder. This is not the kind of harm which led courts in the first place to consider blasting as abnormally dangerous, since it involves neither flying debris nor vibrations of the earth, and liability has been denied on facts like these. *See Foster v. Preston Mill Co.*, 268 P.2d 645 (Wash. 1954). *Cf. Indiana Harbor Belt Railroad Co. v. American Cyanamid Co.*, 916 F.2d 1174 (7th Cir. 1990) (toxic material leaked from railroad car, but not as a result of the inherent properties of the toxic material; no strict liability). This of course would not preclude liability for negligence or nuisance. *See Summit View, Inc. v. W. W. Clyde & Co.*, 403 P.2d 919 (Utah 1965).

So what role does foreseeability play? The Restatement Third § 20, comment i, suggests that a case for strict liability is "strengthened when the defendant has actual knowledge of the risky quality of the activity in which the defendant is engaging." In most cases of abnormally dangerous activities, of course, defendants do possess such knowledge. If a defendant "sincerely and reasonably believes" that his activity is not harmful, however, "there is inadequate reason to impose strict liability. *Id.*

9.   **History of strict liability for blasting.** The imposition of strict liability for abnormally dangerous activities may be traced back to *Rylands v. Fletcher*, as the *Dyer* court itself does. With respect to blasting activities in particular, the history is more recent. In a case from 1900, a 19-year-old girl was struck and killed by a stump that had been blasted out of the ground by the defendant. The court affirmed a verdict for her estate, not on the basis of abnormal danger, but on the ground that this was a "trespass to person" because the stump struck her on the fly. *Sullivan v. Dunham*, 55 N.E. 923 (N.Y. 1900). The court suggested that if the blasting had caused damage through a concussion or a shaking of the earth, no liability would be imposed. *Sullivan* seemed to distinguish between two claims that seemed morally indistinguishable—the injury from debris thrown up by a blaster and injury from the same blast but occurring through the medium of vibrations in the ground. In both cases, the defendant's act was the same and the plaintiff's injury equally real.

Some decades later, the Second Circuit faced the kind of alternative situation *Sullivan* had contemplated. In *Exner v. Sherman Power Construction Co.*, 54 F.2d 510 (2d Cir. 1931), defendant's blasting shook the plaintiff's house so violently that she was thrown out of bed. The court affirmed a jury verdict for her on the ground that the case was one of strict liability. Attacking the false distinction of "direct" versus "indirect" harms, the court said, "in every practical sense there can be no difference between a blasting which projects rocks in such a way as to injure persons or property and a blasting which, by creating a sudden vacuum, shatters buildings or knocks down people." The court also stressed the policy rationales behind its ruling:

"The extent to which one man in the lawful conduct of his business is liable for injuries to another involves an adjustment of conflicting interests. The solution of the problem . . . has never been dependent upon any universal criterion of liability (such as 'fault') applicable to all situations. If damage is inflicted, there ordinarily is liability, in the absence of excuse. When, as here, the defendant, though without fault, has engaged in the perilous activity of storing large quantities of a dangerous explosive for use in his business, we think there is no justification for relieving it of liability, and that the owner of the business, rather than a third person who has no relation to the explosion, other than that of injury, should bear the loss."

The first Restatement of Torts, drafted shortly after this decision was rendered, introduced a whole chapter on "Ultrahazardous Activities," which years later became the basis for the rules we have today.

––––––––––

NOTE: STRICT LIABILITY FOR OTHER ABNORMALLY DANGEROUS ACTIVITIES

1. *Other high-energy activities.* The strict liability seen in explosives cases carries over to closely analogous activities where enormous force is involved, including the testing of rockets, *Smith v. Lockheed Propulsion Co.*, 247 Cal.App.2d 774 (1967) (ground vibration damaged water well); the use of pile driving equipment, *Caporale v. C. W. Blakeslee & Sons, Inc.*, 175 A.2d 561 (Conn. 1961) ("intrinsically dangerous," strict liability for vibration damage); and even a "blow out" of an oil well in a populated area, *Green v. Gen. Petroleum Corp.*, 270 P. 952 (Cal. 1928).

2. *Fireworks.* Is conducting a commercial firework display an abnormally dangerous activity, or is it "a matter of common usage?" Perhaps the answer depends on whether the focus is on how many people conduct professional fireworks displays (not many), or how many watch (millions). The court in *Toms v. Calvary Assembly of God, Inc.*, 132 A.3d 866 (Md. 2016), focused on the latter to reject strict liability in a case where the noise from a church-sponsored fireworks display conducted by a professional fireworks company allegedly caused a stampede inside plaintiff's dairy barn, resulting in the death of four cows and other damage. By contrast, in *Klein v. Pyrodyne Corp.*, 810 P.3d 917, *amended by* 817 P.3d 1359 (Wash. 1991), where a misfiring shell injured spectators at a public fireworks show, the court imposed strict liability, concluding that conducting fireworks displays was not a matter of common usage because various regulations prohibit members of the general public from engaging in such activities. Which approach best supports the goals of strict liability, do you think?

3. *Poisons.* In *Loe v. Lenhardt,* 362 P.2d 312 (Or. 1961) strict liability was applied to crop-dusting activities. Might this be justified on a pure *Rylands v. Fletcher* rule, without resort to any "abnormally dangerous activity" rule? Courts have imposed strict liability for abnormally dangerous activity in pest control and fumigation cases. *Luthringer v.*

Moore, 190 P.2d 1 (Cal. 1948); *Old Island Fumigation, Inc. v. Barbee*, 604 So.2d 1246 (Fla. Dist. Ct. App. 1992).

4. *Hazardous wastes.* Activities involving toxic substances are good candidates for strict liability based on abnormal danger. In *T & E Industries, Inc. v. Safety Light Corp.*, 587 A.2d 1249 (N.J. 1991), a plant used radium that left its own ground contaminated. Later it sold the property, which eventually passed to the plaintiff. Upon discovery of the contamination in the property it had purchased, the plaintiff sued. The court held that seller would be strictly liable not only to adjoining landowners who suffered harm, but also to purchasers like the plaintiff. The federal Superfund Act provides a fund, derived in part from taxes on industry, for the government to use to clean up substances released into the environment. Representatives of the fund may sue the responsible industry for reimbursement. Liability is strict and applies not only to one who actually released the substance but also to owners of the contaminated land whether they released the substance or not. *See* 42 U.S.C.A. § 9607(a).

5. *Lateral and subjacent support.* "Between adjacent landowners, the general principle . . . is that each has an absolute property right to have his land laterally supported by the soil of his neighbor, and if either in excavating on his own premises so disturbs the lateral support of his neighbor's land as to cause it, in its natural state, by the pressure of its own weight, to fall away or slide from its position, the one so excavating is liable." *Prete v. Cray*, 141 A. 609 (R.I. 1928). Can this form of strict liability be explained by the Restatement's "abnormally dangerous activity" theory? How does it compare, if at all, with other cases, such as those involving percolation, that appear to regulate property rights of near neighbors? *Cf.* RESTATEMENT (SECOND) OF TORTS § 817 (1979). The same rule is applied to "subjacent" support, that is, where an owner of minerals removes them so that the surface subsides. *See Id.* § 820.

NOTE: CONTRIBUTORY NEGLIGENCE
AND ASSUMPTION OF RISK

1. *Traditional rule.* The traditional rule, still followed by some states and the one adopted by the Restatement Second, is that contributory negligence as such is no defense to a strict liability claim. The defendant, not at fault at all (because liability is strict), is thus held fully liable to a plaintiff who is guilty of negligence causing his own harm. At least a formal reason for this result can be found in the argument that since the defendant's liability is not based on negligence in the first place, his liability is not limited by contributory negligence of the plaintiff. Are you satisfied with this reasoning? The Restatement Second also takes the view that the plaintiff's "assumed risk," and also any contributory negligence in

"knowingly" subjecting himself to risks of harm, *is* a defense. *See* RESTATEMENT (SECOND) OF TORTS § 524 (1977).

2. *Comparative responsibility and the Restatement Third*. The advent of comparative negligence (or "comparative responsibility," as the Restatement of Apportionment calls it) appears to call for a change in the traditional analysis. The Restatement of Apportionment, in § 8, provides that in all cases involving physical injury, the fact finder should assign shares of responsibility to each party, regardless of the legal theory of liability. That is, the Apportionment Restatement says that juries can and should assign percentages of responsibility even where one party is strictly liable and the other negligent. *Accord*, RESTATEMENT (THIRD) OF TORTS: LIABILITY FOR PHYSICAL AND EMOTIONAL HARM § 25 (2010) (if the plaintiff in a strict liability case is contributorily negligent "in failing to take reasonable precautions" his recovery should be reduced by his share of comparative responsibility).

With respect to assumption of risk, recall that in Chapter 10 we saw that that defense is no longer a unified one, and it is not self-evident what the label means without examining its context. Suppose, for example, in a comparative negligence state, that the defendant is blasting near or on a highway. Adequate signs are posted but the plaintiff negligently fails to observe them, drives into the danger area and is hurt by falling rocks from a blast. Should the plaintiff recover without any reduction in damages, or should a jury be allowed to compare the plaintiff's contributory negligence with the defendant's non-negligent activity? The Restatement Third (both of Apportionment and Liability for Physical and Emotional Harms) does not recognize a separate defense of implied assumption of risk at all. However, the Restatement rejects strict liability altogether if the plaintiff seeks contact with the abnormally dangerous activity to secure a benefit of his own, and states that if the risk of the defendant's activity can be reduced to a modest level by reasonable care of the plaintiff (or anyone else), the activity is not "abnormally dangerous" at all. RESTATEMENT (THIRD) OF TORTS: LIABILITY FOR PHYSICAL AND EMOTIONAL HARM §§ 24 & 20, cmt. h (2010).

> REFERENCES: DOBBS, HAYDEN & BUBLICK, HORNBOOK ON TORTS §§ 32.1–32.9 (common law strict liability) & §§ 30.1–30.7 (nuisance) (2d ed. 2016); 2 DOBBS, HAYDEN & BUBLICK, THE LAW OF TORTS §§ 437–446 (common law strict liability) & §§ 398–404 (nuisance) (2d ed. 2011).

CHAPTER 24

TORT LIABILITY FOR
DEFECTIVE PRODUCTS

■ ■ ■

§ 1. HISTORY, RATIONALES, AND SCOPE OF PRODUCTS LIABILITY

A. THE EVOLUTION OF LIABILITY THEORIES

Products liability law deals with the liabilities of manufacturers and distributors of products. Products liability law has undergone sweeping change in the last several decades. Under the law today, those involved in commercial distribution of products are potentially liable for harm caused by those products. Commercial distributors include manufacturers, wholesalers and retailers in the regular business of selling the particular product at issue. "Casual sellers" are not covered by products liability rules; thus if you sell your car to a neighbor, the tort law in this chapter would not apply to you (unless selling cars is your regular business).

The basis and extent of tort liability for injuries caused by faulty products continues to be debated. Indeed, the law of products liability is not limited to tort actions. A plaintiff may claim on a contract theory for breach of warranty, or on tort theories of negligence, strict liability, or even fraud. Tort theories dominate in cases of physical harm to person or property, but they cannot be understood in isolation from the law of contract and warranty.

The "Citadel of Privity" and Its Fall

Negligence action—the privity requirement. The oldest products cases were brought on a negligence theory, some arising before negligence was regarded as a general approach to tort liability. In these earlier cases, courts thought that the manufacturer's liability for an injury-causing product was derived from a contractual undertaking to the purchaser. Since the basis for liability was not the general duty of reasonable care but the duty implicitly undertaken in a contract of sale, the manufacturer could be liable only to buyers who were in privity of contract. Consequently, a manufacturer who did not sell a product directly to the injured plaintiff could not be sued at all for a product-related injury suffered by the plaintiff. The privity rule insulated most manufacturers from liability.

In a leading New York case, *Losee v. Clute*, 51 N.Y. 494 (1873), the defendant Clute allegedly manufactured a boiler in a negligent way and sold it to Saratoga Paper Company. The boiler exploded and damaged, not Saratoga Paper, but the plaintiff's nearby property. The Court of Appeals of New York, following the privity rule, held that the complaint was properly dismissed. Defendants "contracted with the company . . . and when the boiler was accepted they ceased to have any further responsibility. . . ." Thus even active negligence was protected under the privity rule.

Courts did recognize exceptions for extreme cases. In *Thomas v. Winchester*, 6 N.Y. 397 (1852), the defendant mislabeled a jar of "belladonna, which is a deadly poison," and as a result the plaintiff, consuming it, became ill. Had the defendant sold the jar to the plaintiff, there would have been no privity problem. But the defendant had sold the jar to Aspinwall, who sold it to Ford, who sold it to the plaintiff. There was thus no privity between plaintiff and the defendant. Nevertheless, the Court concluded that where death or great bodily harm would be "the natural and almost inevitable consequence of the sale" under a false label, privity would not be required.

Finally, in 1916, the New York Court of Appeals decided the landmark case of *MacPherson v. Buick Motor Co.*, 111 N.E. 1050 (N.Y. 1916). In *MacPherson* the wheel on an automobile collapsed. The plaintiff, who had purchased the car from a retail dealer, was injured. He sued the manufacturer of the car. Since he had purchased from the retailer, not the manufacturer, there was no privity between plaintiff and defendant. Justice Cardozo, writing for the court, said:

> We hold, then, that the principle of *Thomas v. Winchester* is not limited to poisons, explosives, and things of like nature, to things which in their normal operation are implements of destruction. If the nature of a thing is such that it is reasonably certain to place life and limb in peril when negligently made, it is then a thing of danger. . . . If [the manufacturer] is negligent where danger is to be foreseen, a liability will follow.

Cardozo in effect substituted foreseeability for contract or undertaking and thus applied general negligence principles to a case involving a defective product. The landmark case of *Donoghue v. Stevenson* [1932] UKHL 100, in which plaintiff fell ill after drinking a ginger beer which contained a decomposed snail, established a similar principle for common law jurisdictions worldwide.

Misrepresentation. *MacPherson*'s rejection of the privity requirement for a products-liability negligence case came to be accepted everywhere. However, it did not assist every plaintiff. Some plaintiffs were injured by products that were not negligently made, and some simply could not prove negligence. Inventive lawyers attempted other theories to assist injured clients. One result was that it came to be held that a manufacturer would be liable for injuries resulting from conditions of the product that were misrepresented, even without privity. In *Baxter v. Ford Motor Co.*, 12 P.2d 409 (Wash. 1932), the plaintiff lost his eye when his windshield broke on impact from a pebble. The manufacturer had described its windshields as shatterproof. This was sufficient for liability, even though the manufacturer had not sold the car directly to the plaintiff. The misrepresentation approach can still aid plaintiffs and might even produce punitive damages awards. *See Williams v. Philip Morris Inc.*, 176 P.3d 1255 (Or. 2008) (tobacco industry statements about safety of smoking and industry research on safety, upholding $32 million in punitive damages).

Warranty. Another theory that plaintiffs could rely on when they could not prove negligence was *express warranty*. To take *Baxter*'s facts as an example, if Ford had sold the car to Baxter directly and had, as part of the contract, promised or guaranteed that the windshield was "shatterproof," this would be an express warranty, a kind of contract. Contract liability is usually strict liability; that is, proving breach of contract does not require proving that the breaching party is at fault. This contract theory is not often available, however, because manufacturers rarely make express guarantees about their products' safety directly to purchasing consumers.

Thus plaintiffs' lawyers began to argue to courts that the sale of goods gave rise to an *implied warranty*. For example, the act of selling a bottle of milk—whether it is sold by a retailer or by a manufacturer—seems to imply that it is not a bottle of belladonna, and also that it is not contaminated with human toes, dead flies, or unspeakable viruses. In other words, it should meet some kind of normal expectation as to quality and safety. Over the years, courts came to reject the maxim *caveat emptor*—let the buyer beware—and to accept the idea of a warranty implicit in the act of sale. The Uniform Commercial Code (UCC) Art. 2–314, which applies to any seller of goods, recognizes an implied warranty that goods are "fit for the ordinary purposes for which such goods are used"; and that they are as good as the seller claims they are.

The implied-warranty theory carries with it all the advantages and disadvantages of contract law—liability for breach is strict, but privity is required While some courts created exceptions to the privity rule in cases involving such things as bad food and intimate products such as soaps, hair dyes and the like, these cases seemed to lack any underlying principle and they came to an evolutionary dead-end. In the 1960s, however, courts started off in an entirely new direction.

A leading case of the period was *Henningsen v. Bloomfield Motors, Inc.*, 161 A.2d 69 (N.J. 1960). *Henningsen* involved an automobile purchased by

Mr. Henningsen as a present for his wife. The car's steering failed, and the car crashed into a wall. The Henningsens sued the retailer and the manufacturer. In the purchase contract, the manufacturer and dealer had provided that there were no warranties except that defective parts would be replaced within certain time limits. Since Mrs. Henningsen was badly injured, this was not helpful. The New Jersey Court held that there was an implied warranty in addition to this express warranty, that the implied warranty ran to the ultimate purchaser and not merely to the retailer, and that the disclaimer of liability would be ineffective to protect the manufacturer. *Henningsen,* in other words, did for warranty about the same thing that *MacPherson* did for negligence—extend it to the injured party.

Warranty remains a viable theory today in many products cases. However, to a very large extent warranty theory has been displaced by, or at least supplemented with, a theory of strict liability in tort.

The Development of Strict Products Liability

Strict tort liability emerged as a leading theory for products cases in *Greenman v. Yuba Power Products, Inc.,* 377 P.2d 897 (Cal. 1963). In that case, plaintiff's wife bought him a power tool that caused him serious injuries. Claiming the tool was defective, he sued the retailer and manufacturer on the two grounds then available to him: negligence and warranty. Affirming a jury verdict against the manufacturer, the court reasoned that in the case of defective products, "the liability is not one governed by the law of contract warranties but by the law of strict liability in tort." Justice Traynor wrote that the purpose of strict liability "is to insure that the costs of injuries resulting from defective products are borne by the manufacturers that put such products on the market rather than by the injured persons who are powerless to protect themselves."

Greenman was strongly influential in the drafting of the Restatement Second of Torts § 402A, promulgated in 1964. Section 402A quickly gained wide acceptance in the courts. By the mid-1960s, then, the developing law of strict products liability was freed from the older logic of the warranty theory and thus from the privity limitation. Section 402A became the lodestar of products liability discussion and development for a whole generation or more. Its essential provisions were simple: (a) sellers were strictly liable for physical injuries to persons or property other than the product itself; this meant that the injured consumer could recover without proving fault; (b) privity rules were abolished; this meant that the injured consumer could recovery without privity; and (c) strict liability attached to products that were "defective" because they were unreasonably dangerous to the consumer; and (d) the consumer's reasonable expectations defined what counted as a defective product.

The (Partial) Decline of Strict Products Liability

All of the arguments for broad strict products liability have been challenged, and as courts worked out the details of strict liability over a thirty-year period many critics asserted that strict liability for defectively-designed products was wrong in principle. Many states passed statutes in the 1980s limiting products liability cases in one respect or another as the criticisms reached critical mass.

A major turning point was the 1998 publication of the Restatement Third of Torts: Products Liability, which was by its own terms "an almost total overhaul of the Restatement Second as it concerns the liability of commercial sellers of products." RESTATEMENT OF PRODUCTS LIABILITY, Introduction (1998). The Products Restatement itself does not focus on the various theories of liability, but rather on whether products are proven to be "defective." Section 2 of the Products Restatement sets forth when a product is defective in manufacture, design, or because of inadequate instructions or warnings. The Products Restatement essentially retains strict liability only for products flawed in manufacture, and adopts a negligence standard or something very like it for design and warning defects.

The Products Restatement is increasingly influential, but many states continue to use some version of the Second Restatement for many if not all claims. Thus strict products liability may be said to be in decline, but it very much alive in a number of states.

B. RATIONALES FOR STRICT PRODUCTS LIABILITY

Strict products liability may be justified on one or more of the rationales discussed below. What do you think of them?

1. *Consumer expectations*. Manufacturers implicitly represent that the products they make are safe and healthy, and consumers are justified in relying on that implicit representation.

2. *Enterprise liability or "loss spreading."* Manufacturers and commercial sellers of goods can more easily spread the costs that result from injuries caused by defective products, by raising prices or purchasing insurance. Compensation is needed, and the most practical way to secure it is to have all consumers share the cost by paying more for the product. It has also been argued that strict liability justly imposes legal responsibility for injuries that are statistically associated with the enterprise of manufacturing and selling, making liability a cost of doing business that should be borne by someone other than injured individuals.

3. *Practicality*. Since a retailer in privity with the plaintiff may be held liable on warranty, and since if so held the retailer could have indemnity from the manufacturer, it would be cheaper to permit the plaintiff to sue

the manufacturer directly. Another argument from "practicality" is that, since most defective products are that way because of negligence, imposing strict liability saves the legal system the time and expense of proving negligence.

4. *Fairness*. Another set of justifications stresses the basic *fairness* of a strict liability regime. First, because the manufacturer enjoys the advantages of sending its products into commerce, it should also take the disadvantages in the form of injury costs when the risks of such activity come to fruition. (On this argument, compare the reasons for the liability of a master for the torts of a servant.)

A second fairness-based justification is that the manufacturer imposes a special kind of risk—*nonreciprocal risks*—on the consumer. That is, the manufacturer imposes risks on the consumer that are quite different from any risks the consumer imposes on the manufacturer, and this fact justifies strict liability. George P. Fletcher developed the theory of nonreciprocal risks in a very influential article, *Fairness and Utility in Tort Theory*, 85 HARV. L. REV. 537 (1972). One example Fletcher uses of a non-reciprocal risk is the risk an airplane pilot imposes upon those on the ground. He imposes a risk of crashing into them but they impose no comparable risk upon him. To Fletcher, the crashing plane that causes ground damages represents a good case for strict liability in the absence of a defense.

Fletcher's theory attacks the fairness of risk-utility balancing commonly followed in analysis of negligence claims. In part, he does so by pointing to criminal law. No individual human being should suffer criminal sanctions for the sake of the common good. Similarly, no injured person should be required to give up a claim against the defendant merely because the defendant's activities are socially useful. If these activities are socially useful, they need not be prohibited, but they should be "taxed" by tort law to provide compensation for harms they cause. Fletcher recognizes that his theory will not lead inexorably to a predictable result. You would have to ask whether the defendant imposed a risk so excessive that it should be considered non-reciprocal. He doubts, however, whether the risk-utility balancing is any more certain. For some later Fletcherian ideas, see George P. Fletcher, *Corrective Justice for Moderns*, 106 HARV. L. REV. 1658 (1993) (Book Review of Jules Coleman, *Risks and Wrongs* (1992)).

5. *Deterrence*. If strict liability is imposed, manufacturers will tend to make products safer in order to avoid the increased costs resulting from liability. Liability of the manufacturer will drive the manufacturer to increase the price so as to cover the liability costs. As prices rise on unsafe products consumers will seek cheaper substitutes. These substitutes will usually be safer products; they are cheaper because they are not bearing the costs of tort liability. In addition, manufacturers, to avoid this loss of

customers and the liability itself, will seek to find ways to make products more safe.

Guido Calabresi, in his 1970 book *The Cost of Accidents,* offered an economic analysis of the accident cost-reduction effects of strict liability. Much of his book is devoted to an idea he calls primary accident cost reduction or primary accident cost avoidance, focusing on reducing accident costs by reducing the number or severity of accidents themselves. This can be done in his view by using some combination of two major devices:

a. *Specific deterrence.* One way to reduce primary accident costs is to prohibit conduct that is excessively risky. This can be done by legislation or administrative regulation, for example. Specific prohibitions might be made because conduct is either "immoral" or because it does more harm than good. However, it is difficult to decide by political processes what risks are more harmful than useful. Calabresi believes that "the market" can make this judgment in a much better way.

b. *General deterrence.* This is a technical term and an economic notion. The idea is that if a given activity, such as driving, causes accidents, that activity could be made to pay the costs. Calabresi believes that if an activity is made to pay all the costs it really causes, this will in fact reduce accidents or the severity of accidents. Here's how. Suppose that convertibles are riskier than sedans, especially in turnover accidents. If manufacturers of convertibles had to pay all the costs of convertible injuries, they would raise the price of convertibles. Potential buyers will know comparative risks if the price of the convertibles reflect their true costs to society. Purchasers would not have to think about relative risks at all when they considered purchasing a convertible; they would have only to look at its price tag. Some people would buy the more expensive convertible even so. But others would reject it as too expensive. Even if they did not think about risks that were included in the price, their decision would be more informed because they would know the true costs of operating the convertible. Because a number of people would reject the more dangerous convertible, convertible-caused injuries would be reduced.

Athens and Sparta examples. Calabresi offered an example. He supposed that in Athens accident costs of an activity (like driving) were always charged to that activity so that insurance costs for an activity like driving would be higher than they would be otherwise. In Sparta, on the other hand, all injuries were compensated from general public funds raised by taxes. Taney is thinking of buying a second car. The costs of owning the second car would be $200 a year for operating plus another $200 for insurance. The alternative would be to take taxis occasionally, a cost of about $250 a year. In Athens he might reject the second car because its total cost, including the insurance which reflected accident costs, would be much greater than the cost of taxis. In Sparta, however, he would have no insurance costs, since injuries would be taken care of by public assistance. So his cost for the second car would be $200 a year as compared to taxis costing $250. He would buy the second car.

The Athens plan reduces accident costs by showing people like Taney the true cost of activities they are considering. The point is not that everyone would forgo the car, but that some people, getting the risk information through the price, would do so. Calabresi thought there was a second and maybe more important way that general deterrence would help reduce accident costs. He thought that it would encourage us to make activities safer if we knew the real costs of risks associated with them. If cars cause an average of $200 a year in accident costs but a new brake costing the equivalent of $50 a year can reduce those costs to $100, then Taney would install the new brake if he lived in Athens.

Cheapest cost avoider. Ideally, the costs of accidents should be borne by acts or activities that could avoid the accident costs most cheaply. A new car manufacturer might be a good choice, for example, if the manufacturer could add the $50 brake when it produces the car. If it is liable for car accidents, it will have the incentive to add the $50 brake.

C. WHO IS SUBJECT TO STRICT LIABILITY?

LOOMIS V. AMAZON.COM LLC

63 Cal.App.5th 466 (2021)

OHTA, J. . . .

[Plaintiff Kisha Loomis ordered a hoverboard on Amazon's website as a Christmas gift for her son. The listing identified the seller as TurnUpUp, a name used by a China-based company to sell its products on Amazon. The board was shipped to Loomis by Forrinx Technology (USA), Inc. Loomis's son plugged the board into an outlet in Loomis's bedroom to charge. Loomis's boyfriend later discovered a fire burning in her bedroom. Her bed and the hoverboard were on fire. Loomis suffered burns to her hand and foot as a result of fighting the fire. Loomis filed a products liability suit in California court against Forrinx and Doe defendants, later amending her complaint to name Amazon. Amazon moved for summary judgment on a number of grounds, including that it did not fall within the "chain of distribution" for products liability purposes, because it was neither a manufacturer nor a seller of the hoverboard. The trial court granted the motion, and Loomis appealed.]

DISCUSSION

The Doctrine of Strict Liability in California

Greenman v. Yuba Power Products, Inc., 59 Cal.2d 57 (1963), established the doctrine of strict products liability when it held "[a] manufacturer is strictly liable in tort when an article he places on the market, knowing that it is to be used without inspection for defects, proves to have a defect that causes injury to a human being." . . .

The California Supreme Court extended the doctrine to retailers in *Vandermark v. Ford Motor Co.*, 61 Cal.2d 256 (1964), reasoning, "Retailers like manufacturers are engaged in the business of distributing goods to the public. They are an integral part of the overall producing and marketing enterprise that should bear the cost of injuries resulting from defective products. In some cases the retailer may be the only member of that enterprise reasonably available to the injured plaintiff. In other cases the retailer himself may play a substantial part in insuring that the product is safe or may be in a position to exert pressure on the manufacturer to that end; the retailer's strict liability thus serves as an added incentive to safety. Strict liability on the manufacturer and retailer alike affords maximum protection to the injured plaintiff and works no injustice to the defendants, for they can adjust the costs of such protection between them in the course of their continuing business relationship." . . .

[handwritten margin note: Reasoning for the rule]

A consumer injured by a defective product may now sue any business entity in the chain of production and marketing, from the original manufacturer down through the distributor and wholesaler to the retailer; liability of all such defendants is joint and several. The purpose for this approach is to extend liability to all those engaged in the overall producing and marketing enterprise who should bear the social cost of the marketing of defective products.

The strict liability doctrine derives from judicially perceived public policy considerations, i.e., enhancing product safety, maximizing protection to the injured plaintiff, and apportioning costs among the defendants. Where these policy justifications are not applicable, the courts have refused to hold the defendant strictly liable even if that defendant could technically be viewed as a "link in the chain" in getting the product to the consumer market. In other words, the facts must establish a sufficient causative relationship or connection between the defendant and the product so as to satisfy the policies underlying the strict liability doctrine. . . .

Analysis

As technology advances, innovation is paving the way to new business practices. Amazon is on the leading edge of e-commerce. Based on our review of Amazon's third-party business model . . ., we are persuaded that Amazon's own business practices make it a direct link in the vertical chain of distribution under California's strict liability doctrine.

Contrary to Amazon's assertion that it merely provided an online storefront for TurnUpUp and others to sell their wares, it is undisputed Amazon placed itself squarely between TurnUpUp, the seller, and Loomis, the buyer, in the transaction at issue. When Loomis wanted to buy a hoverboard for her son, she perused product listings on Amazon's website. Amazon took Loomis's order and processed her payment. It then transmitted the order to TurnUpUp, who packaged and shipped the product to Loomis.

When Loomis wondered whether the hoverboard would arrive in time for Christmas, she communicated her concerns through Amazon. TurnUpUp was not allowed to communicate with Loomis directly. If Loomis had wanted to return the hoverboard, the return would have been routed through Amazon.

Amazon remitted Loomis's payment to TurnUpUp after deducting its fees, including a 15 percent referral fee based on the total sale price. These facts undermine Amazon's characterization of its marketplace as an online mall providing online storefronts for sellers. Owners of malls typically do not serve as conduits for payment and communication in each transaction between a buyer and a seller. Moreover, they do not typically charge a per-item fee rather than a fixed amount to rent their storefronts. Instead, these actions—1) interacting with the customer, 2) taking the order, 3) processing the order to the third-party seller, 4) collecting the money, and 5) being paid a percentage of the sale—are consistent with a retailer or a distributor of consumer goods.

Although we conclude Amazon is a link in the vertical chain of distribution, we nevertheless recognize e-commerce may not neatly fit into a traditional sales structure. The stream-of-commerce approach or market enterprise theory offers an alternative basis for strict liability.

Under the stream-of-commerce approach to strict liability no precise legal relationship to the member of the enterprise causing the defect to be manufactured or to the member most closely connected with the customer is required before the courts will impose strict liability. It is the defendant's participatory connection, for his personal profit or other benefit, with the injury-producing product and with the enterprise that created consumer demand for and reliance upon the product (and not the defendant's legal relationship (such as agency) with the manufacturer or other entities involved in the manufacturing-marketing system) which calls for imposition of strict liability. Thus, a defendant may be strictly liable under the stream-of-commerce approach if: (1) the defendant received a direct financial benefit from its activities and from the sale of the product; (2) the defendant's role was integral to the business enterprise such that the defendant's conduct was a necessary factor in bringing the product to the initial consumer market; and (3) the defendant had control over, or a substantial ability to influence, the manufacturing or distribution process.

Viewing the evidence in the light most favorable to Loomis, there exists a triable issue of material fact as to each of the three factors identified above. First, Amazon does not dispute it received a direct financial benefit in the form of fees, including a monthly subscription fee and a 15 percent referral fee, from the sale of the product. . . . [T]he evidence shows Amazon received $110,645.92 from its sale of TurnUpUp hoverboards from September 14, 2015, to December 16, 2015. . . .

For the same reason, there exists a triable issue with respect to the second factor—whether Amazon's role was integral to the business enterprise. Amazon has failed to meet its burden to demonstrate this factor cannot be established because it has presented no evidence of its role in bringing TurnUpUp's hoverboards to market.

Third, the record demonstrates Amazon had substantial ability to influence the manufacturing or distribution process through its ability to require safety certification, indemnification, and insurance before it agrees to list any product. . . .

In analyzing whether strict liability is appropriate in new circumstances, courts assess whether relevant public policy goals are furthered by its application. . . . [T]he relevant public policy considerations are: (1) whether Amazon may play a substantial part in insuring that the product is safe or may be in a position to exert pressure on the manufacturer to that end, (2) whether Amazon may be the only member in the distribution chain reasonably available to the injured plaintiff, and (3) whether Amazon is in a position to adjust the costs of compensating the injured plaintiff amongst various members in the distribution chain. We address each in turn.

As to product safety, Amazon contends it has no proactive authority over product design or manufacture because its relationship is typically with the distributor or retailer, not the manufacturer. It asserts it can only reactively address safety issues by removing or suspending sellers after a product has been shown to be unsafe. Thus, imposing strict liability on it will not enhance product safety.

By its very argument, Amazon acknowledges it plays a role in ensuring product safety. Indeed, sellers are required under [the Business Solutions Agreement, the contract between them and Amazon ("BSA")] to comply with all applicable laws, including, presumably, consumer safety laws and regulations. The evidence shows Amazon may require proof that a product complies with recognized safety standards before it is listed. . . .

These steps, which Amazon has taken to ensure product safety in limited circumstances, refute its contention it has no ability to proactively affect product safety. Application of strict liability in this case may incentivize Amazon to expand its safety compliance requirements to more products and thus further the goal of product safety.

Moreover, we agree with [the court in *Bolger v. Amazon.com*, 53 Cal.App.5th 431 (2020),] that "[j]ust like a conventional retailer, Amazon can use its power as a gatekeeper between an upstream supplier and the consumer to exert pressure on those upstream suppliers (here, third party sellers) to enhance safety." Under the BSA, "Amazon sets fees that it would retain for the sale of a third-party product, protects itself by requiring third-party vendors to indemnify Amazon should any 'claim, loss, damage, settlement, cost, expense or other liability' occur, and reserves the right to refuse to provide . . . services for a product that does not comport with Amazon's policies. With the rights retained, Amazon could halt the placement of defective products in the stream of commerce, deterring future injuries."

As to consumer compensation, Amazon may be the only member of the distribution chain reasonably available for an injured consumer to recover damages. Amazon contends there is no evidence to show how frequently an injured plaintiff is truly left without recourse. The record shows, however, that Forrinx, the only other defendant in this matter, failed to appear and a default was taken against it. Indeed, the same issue arose in *Bolger,* where two defendants failed to appear, and a third could only be served in China.

As to loss spreading, Amazon can adjust the costs of consumer protection between it and third-party sellers through its fees, indemnity requirements, and insurance. Amazon does not argue it is unable to spread the costs in these, and other, ways. It instead contends these costs will result in higher prices to be paid by consumers and small businesses will also be required to bear these higher costs. Amazon's argument obfuscates the goal of loss spreading. At issue is whether the loss should be borne solely by the injured consumer who may have no recourse against other defendants, or whether it may be spread among those who profited from the sale of the defective product. In our view, these policy considerations support the application of strict liability to Amazon's third-party seller business model. . . .

The judgment is reversed. The trial court is directed to vacate its order granting summary judgment [and to] conduct further proceedings not inconsistent with this opinion. . . .

WILEY, J., Concurring.

The Amazon is the world's largest river. Amazon.com supposedly chose its trademark because it aimed to create the world's largest river of commerce. Amazon.com can control what it created.

Unbeknownst to Amazon, a manufacturer may use Amazon's site to sell a defective product that will cause future accidents. Perhaps it is a computer battery that can explode. Perhaps it is a hoverboard that ignites fires.

Whatever it is, Amazon is situated swiftly to learn of and to contain the emerging problem, thereby reducing accidental injuries. Amazon can cabin the danger by stopping sales. Amazon can alert past buyers who have yet to experience the lurking hazard: Amazon has information about its customers and their purchases. Other measures are possible.

Once Amazon is convinced it will be holding the bag on these accidents, this motivation will prompt it to engineer effective ways to minimize these accident costs. Tort law will inspire Amazon to align its ingenuity with efficient customer safety. Customers will benefit.

Amazon maintains it already safeguards customer safety. On appeal, Amazon's brief says it "voluntarily implemented a product safety system years ago, independent of the specter of tort liability, and . . . it spends hundreds of millions of dollars annually to ensure that products offered on the website are safe, compliant, and authentic." The cited source of this assertion is not the record, but rather an online press release written by Amazon posted in response to a Wall Street Journal story about the safety of products offered in [the Amazon.com] store.

Amazon's cited post makes the following admissions:

"[W]e [at Amazon.com] have developed, and continuously refine and improve, our tools that prevent suspicious, unsafe, or non-compliant products from being listed in our store. Our proactive measures begin when a seller attempts to open an account. Our new seller account vetting includes a number of verifications and uses proprietary machine learning technology that stops bad actors before they can register or list a single product in our store. All products offered in our stores must comply with applicable laws and regulations, and our own policies. For example, we require toys to be tested to relevant safety standards set by the Consumer Product Safety Commission. We have a dedicated global team of compliance specialists that review submitted safety documentation, and we have additional qualification requirements that sellers must meet to offer products. In 2018, our teams and technologies proactively blocked more than three billion suspect listings for various forms of abuse, including non-compliance, before they were published to our store. Once a product is available in our store, we continuously scan our product listings and updates to find products that might present a concern. Every few minutes, our tools review the hundreds of millions of products, scan the more than five billion attempted daily changes to product detail pages, and analyze the tens of millions of customer reviews that are submitted weekly for signs of a concern and investigate accordingly. Our tools use natural language processing and machine learning, which means new information is fed into our tools daily so they can learn and constantly get better at proactively blocking suspicious products. In addition, we provide a number of ways for regulatory agencies, industry organizations, brands, customers, and our customer service teams to report safety issues. When we receive these reports, we move quickly to protect customers, remove unsafe products from our store, and investigate. For example, if a customer reports a concern with a product, a customer service associate can instantly trigger an investigation. Additionally, because of our direct relationships with customers, we are able to trace and directly notify customers who purchased a particular product online and alert them to a potential safety issue—our systems are far more effective than other online and offline retailers and customers can feel confident they'll have the information they need. We also regularly work with agencies including the Food and Drug Administration and Consumer Product Safety Commission, and the information we share helps them identify trends and develop regulations. We are active in industry working groups and committees that are dedicated to developing new solutions and guidelines that will benefit all retailers and consumers. We invest significant resources to protect our customers and have built robust programs designed to ensure products offered for sale in our store are safe and compliant. We want customers to shop with confidence and if ever a customer has a concern, they can contact our customer service team, and we will investigate."

These words are good. The admissions confirm the obvious: Amazon can control its river. It can undertake cost-effective steps to minimize accidents from defective products sold on its website. Strict tort liability will underline the priority Amazon places on its safety efforts.

Thus we have an easy case that beautifully illustrates the deep structure of modern tort law: a judicial quest to minimize the social costs of accidents—that is, the sum of the cost of accidents and the cost of avoiding accidents. Judges have been applying this social cost-benefit analysis as a felt instinct for a long time. . . . That deep structure makes this case simple to decide. When efforts to minimize accident costs are relatively inexpensive and apt to be effective, courts impose tort duties. Amazon has cost-effective options for minimizing accident costs. Amazon therefore has a duty in strict liability to the buyers from its site, including Kisha Loomis.

NOTES

1. **The chain of distribution.** "Requiring the defendant in a products liability case to be either the manufacturer or seller of the product is the majority rule in this country." *McNair v. Johnson & Johnson*, 818 S.E.2d 852 (W.Va. 2018) (collecting cases). But perhaps it is more accurate to say that the defendant must be a "distributor," that is, one in the chain of commercial distribution of the product. Distributors subject to the products rules centrally include manufacturers, wholesalers, and retailers. Under some circumstances, even an endorser, or a franchisor/trademark licensor might be strictly liable for the product that bears the franchise name. *See Torres v. Goodyear Tire &*

Rubber Co., 786 P.2d 939 (Ariz. 1990). The Restatement of Products Liability provides in § 14 that one who "distributes as its own a product manufactured by another" is liable as if it were the manufacturer. A retailer or wholesaler who is held liable usually has an indemnity claim in its favor against the manufacturer.

2.   **E-commerce.** Whether an internet marketplace such as Amazon can be held liable in a products liability action as a seller or distributor of goods has been hotly litigated in recent years. Not all courts have reached the same conclusion. With the primary case, compare *Erie Ins. Co. v. Amazon.com, Inc.*, 925 F.3d 135 (4th Cir. 2019) (because Amazon did not "transfer title" to the headlamp, Amazon was not a "seller" of a defective headlamp and thus not liable under Maryland products liability law).

Judicial interpretations of different terms in applicable state products liability statutes explain some differences of opinion. *Compare, e.g., Stiner v. Amazon.com, Inc.*, 164 N.E.3d 394 (Ohio 2020) (Amazon not a "supplier" under Ohio statute, thus not liable for the death of a man who ingested a fatal dose of caffeine powder purchased on its site); *Amazon.com, Inc. v. McMillan,* 625 S.W.3d 101 (Tex. 2021) (Amazon not a "seller" under Texas statute because it did not hold then relinquish title to the product, thus not liable for injuries caused by defective remote control purchased on its site); and *Fox v. Amazon.com, Inc.*, 930 F.3d 415 (6th Cir. 2019) (Amazon not a "seller" under Tennessee statute, where it did not exercise sufficient "control" over the product, thus not strictly liable for injuries caused by hoverboard that caught on fire); *with State Farm Fire & Cas. Co. v. Amazon.com, Inc.*, 390 F.Supp.3d 964 (W.D. Wis. 2019) (Amazon a "seller" under Wisconsin statute where it "is an integral part of the chain of distribution, an entity well-positioned to allocate the risks of defective products to participants in the chain").

Based on the policy rationales for strict liability described in *Loomis*, do you think Amazon and similar on-line sellers should be subject to strict products liability for their role in the chain of distribution when a defective product purchased on their site causes an injury?

3.   **Commercial vs. non-commercial providers.** Non-commercial providers of products are not usually considered sellers or distributors. *See, e.g., Burnett v. Covell*, 191 P.3d 985 (Alaska 2008) (law office owner who provided a chair to a visitor was not a distributor of the chair and thus not subject to strict products liability); RESTATEMENT OF PRODUCTS LIABILITY § 1, cmt. c (1998). The commercial-noncommercial distinction may not fully capture the idea, however. As noted at the beginning of the chapter, the seller must be in the regular business of selling the product that is the subject of the lawsuit. For instance, if you are not in the car business, you are not a distributor when you sell your car. *Cf. New Texas Auto Auction Services, L.P. v. Gomez*, 249 S.W.3d 400 (Tex. 2008) (automobile auctioneer could not be held strictly liable for defect in car he sold because he did not actually place the product in the stream of commerce).

4. **"Casual" or "occasional" sellers.** What about a *business* that sells a product outside its usual line, in a so-called "casual sale"? In *Griffin Industries, Inc. v. Jones*, 975 S.W.2d 100 (Ky. 1998), plaintiff brought a products liability case against defendant, which had manufactured and sold to plaintiff's employer a conveyor belt system that caused the injury. The defendant's main business was rendering animal waste. It manufactured the belts for its own use, did not market them, and sold the belts to plaintiff's employer in an isolated transaction. Held, defendant is an "occasional seller," thus not liable in a products suit. *See* RESTATEMENT OF PRODUCTS LIABILITY § 1, cmt. c (1997). *See also Jaramillo v. Weyerhaeuser Co.*, 570 F.3d 487 (2d Cir. 2009) (former owner of used industrial machine who sold it to plaintiff was not a regular seller, and thus not subject to strict products liability rules).

5. **Lessors of goods.** At one time it was supposed that products liability could be triggered only when there was a "sale" of goods. It now seems well accepted that a technical sale is not required, and a plaintiff injured by the explosion of a defective soft drink bottle in the grocery store recovers whether the explosion occurred after the customer paid for it or before. And suppliers who do not sell are also liable for defects, provided they are in the business of supplying goods. This covers lessors of goods, for example. What if a retailer gives away chewing gum to shoppers as part of a promotion and the gum proves to be deleterious?

6. **Sellers of used goods.** An individual who sells her car is not in the business of selling cars and is thus not liable as a distributor. What about a dealer in used cars? It is clear that the dealer in used goods may be held liable for negligence, misrepresentation, or breach of any express warranty. The UCC Art. 2–316(a) permits exclusion of warranty when selling goods "as is" with all faults. For personal injury cases, strict tort liability represents the most interesting possibility. The cases are somewhat divided. *Compare, e.g., Gaumer v. Rossville Truck and Tractor Co.*, 257 P.3d 292 (Kan. 2011) (strict liability action allowed against the commercial seller of a used farm baler), *with Allenberg v. Bentley Hedges Travel Serv., Inc.*, 22 P.3d 223 (Okla. 2001) (commercial seller of used goods exempt from strict liability). Do you expect to have more difficulty in judging defectiveness of a used product? What about a used product sold for a limited purpose, as where an old car is sold for scrap metal?

NOTE: PRODUCTS VS. SERVICES

1. *Products.* For strict products liability to attach, the defendant must be a distributor of a *product.* In most cases, whether a "product" is involved is not an issue because neither party contests it. When it is litigated, it is a pure question of law and courts make the decision based on the same policy considerations we have seen thus far in this chapter. *See, e.g., Schueller v. Ad Art, Inc.*, 472 P.3d 686 (Nev. 2020) (large sign on casino

was a "product;" permitting the manufacturer of the sign to be sued on a strict liability theory would further public policy considerations); *In re Eighth Judicial Dist. Asbestos Litigation*, 129 N.E.3d 891 (N.Y. 2019) (large industrial code oven in decedent's workplace was a "product" for which strict liability could attach); *see also* RESTATEMENT OF PRODUCTS LIABILITY § 19, cmt. a (1998).

2.   *Pure services.* By contrast, defendants are not strictly liable for delivering defective *services*. Thus a surgeon is not strictly liable when an operation goes horribly wrong, nor is a lawyer strictly liable when the lawyer loses an easy case. *See* RESTATEMENT OF PRODUCTS LIABILITY § 19(b) (1998) ("Services, even when provided commercially, are not products.").

3.   *Hybrid transactions.* Many transactions involve both the transfer of tangible items and also the delivery of a service. The leading case on such transactions is *Newmark v. Gimbels, Inc.,* 258 A.2d 697 (N.J. 1969), which held that strict liability on an implied warranty theory could be imposed where a beauty parlor used a permanent solution on a patron, burning her scalp. The court characterized the transaction as "a hybrid partaking of incidents of a sale and a service," and that the use of the permanent solution on the plaintiff as part of a service was indistinguishable from a sale of that solution to the plaintiff for home use.

4.   *Hybrid medical transactions.* What if a doctor selects a medical prosthesis, then surgically implants it. The prosthesis proves to be defective and its manufacturer is bankrupt. Should the doctor be strictly liable as a seller or distributor? *Cafazzo v. Cent. Med. Health Servs., Inc.,* 668 A.2d 521 (Pa. 1995), held not, arguing that first and most simply there was no sale, but that in any event the policy basis of strict products liability had no application. Doctors could not get better safety for products approved by the Food and Drug Administration. The health care system should not bear and spread the costs of bad medical prostheses because that would "further endanger the already beleaguered health care system." *Accord, In re Breast Implant Prod. Liab. Litig.*, 503 S.E.2d 445 (S.C. 1998) (health care providers who implanted breast implants were not "sellers" of medical devices and thus could not be held strictly liable). What about a pharmacist who dispenses prescriptions? In *Madison v. Home Products Corp.*, 595 S.E.2d 493 (S.C. 2004), the plaintiff sued a pharmacy for properly filling a prescription for anti-depressants that allegedly caused her to attack her son and attempt suicide. The court held that strict products liability could not apply because the pharmacy was providing a service, not selling a product.

5.   *Should some providers be strictly liable for pure service defects?* If strict liability is right in principle, why exempt service providers? Suppose a plane from Houston to Atlanta crashes without anyone's fault due to a

bizarre failure of radar. What passengers bought was a service—transport—not a product. Still, wouldn't it serve the purposes of strict liability to impose liability?

D. EXCLUDING STAND-ALONE ECONOMIC HARM: PRODUCTS LIABILITY'S ECONOMIC LOSS RULE

MOORMAN MFG. CO. V. NATIONAL TANK CO.
435 N.E.2d 443 (Ill. 1982)

THOMAS J. MORAN, JUSTICE.

[Plaintiff purchased from defendant a steel grain storage tank for use in plaintiff's feed processing plant. About ten years later, a crack developed in one of the steel plates on the tank. The plaintiff sued on theories of strict tort liability, misrepresentation, negligent design, and express warranty.]

The tort law of products liability stems from the contract cause of action for breach of warranty. In MacPherson v. Buick Motor Co. (1916), 217 N.Y. 382,111 N.E. 1050, liability in negligence was imposed upon a manufacturer to an ultimate consumer without privity of contract. Subsequently, courts began to hold manufacturers liable for personal injuries without negligence; the theory generally utilized to reach the manufacturers was based upon the law of sales warranty. (See Prosser, The Assault Upon The Citadel, 69 Yale L.J. 1099,1126 (1960) (Prosser I).) However, recognition of the difficulties facing consumers with respect to items such as notice and privity led most courts to abandon the privity requirement in implied-warranty actions (see Prosser, The Fall of the Citadel, 50 Minn. L.Rev. 791 (1966) (Prosser II)) and to ultimately abandon the fiction of warranty in favor of strict liability in tort.

This State adopted the tort theory of strict liability in Suvada v. White Motor Co. (1965), 32 I11.2d 612, 210 N.E.2d 182, to allow a plaintiff to recover from a manufacturer for personal injuries. Suvada, however, did not address the question of whether a consumer could recover under a strict liability in tort theory for solely economic loss. That issue was first addressed in Santor v. A & M Karagheusian, Inc. (1965), 44 N.J. 52, 207 A.2d 305. There, the plaintiff purchased, from a third-party seller, carpeting that had been manufactured by the defendant. After several months, unsightly lines began to appear on the surface of the carpeting. The Supreme Court of New Jersey held that the plaintiff could maintain a breach-of-warranty claim directly against the manufacturer despite the lack of privity between them. In dicta, the court went on to declare that although the strict liability in tort doctrine had been applied principally in connection with personal injuries, the responsibility of the manufacturer should be no different where damage to the article sold or to other property is involved. 44 N.J. 52, 66, 207 A.2d 305, 312. Several months later, in Seely

v. White Motor Co. (1965) 63 Cal.2d 9,403 P.2d 145, 45 Cal.Rptr.17, the Supreme Court of California rejected the rationale by which the court in Santor imposed strict liability in tort for economic loss. In Seely, plaintiff purchased a truck manufactured by defendant. After he took possession, Seely discovered that the truck bounced violently. Nine months later, the truck overturned after brake failure, causing damage to the truck but no personal injury to Seely. Plaintiff had the damage repaired and subsequently stopped making his installment payments. Defendant repossessed the truck, at which time plaintiff sued on theories of breach of express warranty and strict tort liability, and sought damages for the repair of the truck, for money paid on the purchase price, and for profits lost by virtue of the truck's unsuitability for normal use. The court affirmed the trial court's award to Seely for money paid on the purchase price and for lost profits on the basis of express warranty. The court, however, went on to state that these economic losses are not recoverable under strict liability in tort. The court also declared, in reference to Santor, "Only if someone had been injured because the rug was unsafe for use would there have been any basis for imposing strict liability in tort." Thus, the court refused to expand the scope of its opinion in Greenman v. Yuba Power Products, Inc. (1963), 59 Cal.2d 57, 62, 377 P.2d 897, 900, 27 Cal. Rptr. 697, 700, which declared that a manufacturer is strictly liable in tort for a product that has a defect that causes injury to a person.

Subsequent to these two seminal cases in the area, some courts have held a manufacturer liable under the theory of strict liability in tort for solely economic losses. Most courts, however, have denied recovery under strict liability in tort for solely economic losses. . . . Contrary to the conclusion reached by the appellate court, we believe the language limiting section 402A to unreasonably dangerous defects resulting in physical harm to the ultimate user or consumer, or to his property, reflects sound policy reasons.

First, the law of sales has been carefully articulated to govern the economic relations between suppliers and consumers of goods. The framework provided by the UCC includes the parol evidence rule, implied warranties, express warranties, rules on disclaimers, notice requirements, limitations on the extent of a manufacturer's liability, and a statute of limitations. Although warranty rules frustrate just compensation for physical injury, they function well in a commercial setting. These rules determine the quality of the product the manufacturer promises and thereby determine the quality he must deliver.

We note, for example, section 2–316 of the UCC, which permits parties to a sales contract to limit warranties in any reasonable manner, or to agree that the buyer possesses no warranty protection at all. The parties may even agree to exclude the implied warranties of merchantability and fitness if they do so in writing, and may modify the implied warranty by clear and conspicuous language. Yet, a manufacturer's strict liability for economic loss cannot be disclaimed because a manufacturer should not be permitted to define the scope of its own responsibility for defective products. Thus, adopting strict liability in tort for economic loss would effectively eviscerate section 2–316 of the UCC.

Further, application of the rules of warranty prevents a manufacturer from being held liable for damages of unknown and unlimited scope. If a defendant were held strictly liable in tort for the commercial loss suffered by a particular purchaser, it would be liable for business losses of other purchasers caused by the failure of the product to meet the specific needs of their business, even though these needs were communicated only to the dealer. Finally, a large purchaser, such as plaintiff in the instant case, can protect itself against the risk of unsatisfactory performance by bargaining for a warranty. Or, it may choose to accept a lower purchase price for the product in lieu of warranty protection. Subsequent purchasers may do likewise in bargaining over the price of the product. We believe it is preferable to relegate the consumer to the comprehensive scheme of remedies fashioned by the UCC, rather than requiring the consuming public to pay more for their products so that a manufacturer can insure against the possibility that some of his products will not meet the business needs of some of his customers. . . .

We do hold, however, that when a product is sold in defective condition that is unreasonably dangerous to the user or consumer or to his property, strict liability in tort is applicable to physical injury to plaintiff's property, as well as to personal injury. When an unreasonably dangerous defect is present, such as the truck's nonfunctioning brakes in Seely, and physical injury does, in fact, result, then "[p]hysical injury to property is so akin to personal injury that there is no reason to distinguish them." This comports with the notion that the essence of a product liability tort case is not that the plaintiff failed to receive the quality of product he expected, but that the plaintiff has been exposed, through a hazardous product, to an unreasonable risk of injury to his person or property. On the other hand, contract law, which protects expectation interests, provides the proper standard when a qualitative defect is involved, i.e., when a product is unfit for its intended uses.

Plaintiff argues that economic loss is not sought in this case. It asserts in its brief that a product defect existed that posed an "extreme threat to life and limb, and to property of plaintiff and others, a defect which resulted in a sudden and violent ripping of plaintiff's tank, and which only fortunately did not extend the full height of the tank." Plaintiff further asserts that, because costs of repairs are not economic losses, consequential damages resulting from the loss of use of the tank during repairs does not constitute economic loss either.

"Economic loss" has been defined as "damages for inadequate value, costs of repair and replacement of the defective product, or consequent loss of profits—without any claim of personal injury or damage to other property . . ." (Note, Economic Loss in Products Liability Jurisprudence, 66 Colum. L. Rev. 917, 918 (1966)) (Economic Loss) as well as "the diminution in the value of the product because it is inferior in quality and does not work for the general purposes for which it was manufactured and sold." (Comment, Manufacturers' Liability to Remote Purchasers for "Economic Loss" Damages—Tort or Contract? 114 U.Pa.L.Rev. 539, 541 (1966).) These definitions are consistent with the policy of warranty law to protect expectations of suitability and quality.

The demarcation between physical harm or property damage on the one hand and economic loss on the other usually depends on the nature of the defect and the manner in which the damage occurred. . . .

We . . . hold that, where only the defective product is damaged, economic losses caused by qualitative defects falling under the ambit of a purchaser's disappointed expectations cannot be recovered under a strict liability theory. Here, count I of the complaint alleged that during the last few months of 1976 and the first few months of 1977, "a crack developed in one of the steel plates on the second ring of [the] tank; such crack was not discovered by plaintiff . . . until such tank was being emptied on or about August 24, 1977." This was not the type of sudden and dangerous occurrence best served by the policy of tort law that the manufacturer should bear the risk of hazardous products. . . .

Our conclusion that qualitative defects are best handled by contract, rather than tort, law applies whether the tort theory involved is strict liability or negligence. Tort theory is appropriately suited for personal injury or property damage resulting from a sudden or dangerous occurrence of the nature described above. The remedy for economic loss, loss relating to a purchaser's disappointed expectations due to deterioration, internal breakdown or nonaccidental cause, on the other hand, lies in contract. . . .

The policy considerations against allowing recovery for solely economic loss in strict liability cases apply to negligence actions as well. When the defect is of a qualitative nature and the harm relates to the consumer's expectation that a product is of a particular quality so that it is fit for ordinary use, contract, rather than tort, law provides the appropriate set of rules for recovery. . . .

NOTES

1. **The economic loss rule.** Most courts, following California Supreme Court Justice Traynor's lead in *Seely v. White Motor Co.*, discussed in *Moorman*, have agreed that stand-alone economic harm is recoverable only on

the basis of contract or warranty. *See, e.g., Brian and Christie, Inc. v. Leishman Elec., Inc.,* 244 P.3d 166 (Idaho 2010) (reviewing history of rule, noting its application beyond the products-liability setting). The effect is to allocate cases of non-physical harms to the law of warranty and cases of physical harms to persons or other property to the law of tort. The basic principle is easy to apply in many cases. For example, where a vacuum cleaner quits working without harming any person or other property, the economic loss rule forbids a tort claim. A few state statutes do allow recovery on a strict products liability theory when a product damages only itself. *See Corvias Military Living, LLC v. Ventamatic, Ltd.,* 450 P.3d 797 (Kan. 2019) (explaining that this is a departure from the common-law rule).

2. **What constitutes "separate property?"** This is not a difficult question in many cases. If the vacuum cleaner shorted out and burned down the house, a tort action would lie for the house-damage. But where the product that fails is arguably a part of something larger, and the entire product is damaged or destroyed, line-drawing is not so simple. Many courts have held that "if a product was purchased as a complete whole, damage to that product caused by one of its component parts is considered damage to the product itself—rather than damage to other property—and limited to recovery in contract by the economic loss rule." *Golden Spread Electric Coop., Inc. v. Emerson Process Management Power & Water Solutions, Inc.,* 954 F.3d 804 (5th Cir. 2020); The Restatement of Products Liability is in accord. RESTATEMENT OF PRODUCTS LIABILITY § 21, cmt. e (1998) (if the component is part of an "integrated whole," then no tort action can lie because the product is deemed to have damaged only itself). Where the defective component part is not characterized as part of an "integrated whole," then strict products liability may be imposed when that part damages other parts. *See Dean v. Barrett Homes, Inc.,* 8 A.3d 766 (N.J. 2010) (applying the rule, holding it did not bar a tort claim where the exterior siding on plaintiffs' home was not an integrated part of the home itself where it was not "integral" to the structure).

The "separate property" concept is widely applied in cases, although the results turn on the specific facts. *Compare, e.g., State Farm Mut. Auto. Ins. Co. v. Ford Motor Co.,* 592 N.W.2d 201 (Wis. 1999) (barring tort claim where a car's faulty ignition caused the car to catch fire, destroying the car), *with Saratoga Fishing Co. v. J.M. Martinac & Co.,* 520 U.S. 875 (1997) (tort claim allowed against boat engine's manufacturer where engine caused fire that damaged other equipment on the boat) *and Gunkel v. Renovations, Inc.,* 822 N.E.2d 150 (Ind. 2005) (tort claim allowed for water damage to home caused by defective installation of separately installed stone façade).

3. **The "calamitous event" exception.** A number of courts, especially in the period of the early development of products liability law, found an exception to the economic loss rule where the event that caused the damage was sudden and calamitous. As the court explained in *Giddings & Lewis, Inc. v. Industrial Risk Insurers,* 348 S.W.3d 729 (Ky. 2011), many of the decisions endorsing this exception "focus on what could have been"; although no person or other property was harmed, the sudden and violent way the event occurred

"could have produced serious injury to people or property." While this idea retains some currency, most courts—including *Giddings & Lewis, supra,* overruling its earlier precedent—have rejected this exception. *See, e.g., Dobrovolny v. Ford Motor Co.,* 793 N.W.2d 445 (Neb. 2011); *Lincoln General Ins. Co. v. Detroit Diesel Corp.,* 293 S.W.3d 487 (Tenn. 2009).

4. **A mini-problem.** Suppose that TankCo manufactures tanks for storing toxic chemicals. ChemCo purchases toxic chemicals for use in its factory and stores them in tanks it has purchased from TankCo. One of the tanks is defective and a leak occurs. The leak contaminated ChemCo's property and also adjoining property that belongs to the plaintiff. Is TankCo strictly liable for the costs of cleaning up the contamination (a) incurred by ChemCo on its property? (b) incurred by the plaintiff for cleaning up its adjoining property?

§ 2. ESTABLISHING A PRIMA FACIE CASE

Courts have recognized three types of product defects that may lead to liability: (1) manufacturing defects (also called production flaws); (2) design defects; and (3) information defects. Perhaps the most crucial questions in products cases—and the focus of the Restatement of Products Liability—concern whether a product is "defective" in the first place, and what a plaintiff has to prove to establish such a defect.

A. MANUFACTURING DEFECTS

LEE V. CROOKSTON COCA-COLA BOTTLING CO.

188 N.W.2d 426 (Minn. 1971)

ROGOSHESKE, JUSTICE.

[Plaintiff, a waitress in the Norman Steak House at Ada, Minnesota, was injured when a Coca-Cola bottle exploded in her hand. The trial judge refused to submit a claim based on strict tort liability, and the jury, apparently finding no negligence and no breach of warranty, returned a defendant's verdict. Plaintiff appeals, arguing that the court should have submitted jury instructions on the strict liability claim.]

[Evidence showed that before exploding, the bottle had not struck anything and had not been mishandled or subjected to temperature extremes.]

The rule of strict liability, as revised and adopted by the American Law Institute in 1964, is embodied in Restatement, Torts (2d) § 402A. It imposes liability, without proof of negligence or privity of contract, upon a manufacturer or seller for injury caused by a dangerously defective product. To recover under the rule, the injured party must present evidence, direct or circumstantial, from which the jury can justifiably find that (1) the product was in fact in a defective condition, unreasonably dangerous for its intended use; (2) such defect existed when the product left defendant's control; and (3) the defect was the proximate cause of the injury sustained.

The greatest difficulty in establishing liability under this rule is in proving that the product was defective and that the defect existed when the product left defendant's control. While in conventional tort terms no proof of negligence is necessary, in many cases proof of a defect may simply be a substitute word for negligence. Thus, strict liability does not mean that the defendant is held liable as an insurer of his product regardless of circumstances. As is true in negligence cases with respect to the mere fact of an accident, the mere fact of injury during use of the product usually is insufficient proof to show existence of a defect at the time defendant relinquished control. . . . Also, liability is not imposed where the injured party has not eliminated the probability that improper handling by intermediate parties might have caused the defect. . . .

The narrow question presented here, however, is whether circumstantial evidence, the core of the res ipsa loquitur doctrine, is sufficient to take the case to the jury on the theory of strict liability as well as on the theory of negligence. . . .

It surely must be conceded that circumstantial evidence of the type present in . . . this case justifies submission of the issue of liability on the theory of res ipsa. . . . As testified to by defendant's expert, there are three fundamental causes of bottle failure: Thermo-shock, internal pressure, and external force. According to the expert's testimony, failure because of thermo-shock could only result from drastic changes in temperature applied to the outside of the bottle, such as would be produced by placing a bottle containing hot liquid in cold water. Failure caused by external force, of course, usually results from an impact, such as striking or dropping the bottle. Failure because of internal pressure due to excessive carbonation is ordinarily unlikely because the bottle is designed to withstand approximately four times the pressure created by the gas introduced, and after the carbonated liquid is added to the syrup mixture, any excessive carbonation is equalized by exposure to atmospheric pressure during the interval between carbonation and capping. The capacity of different bottles to withstand internal pressure varies, however, in part due to bottlers' customary reuse of bottles. Some bottles have been refilled for years and might have been subjected to "rough" handling numerous times, thereby increasing the probability that even though they are designed to withstand such handling, some could develop defects which would escape detection by the most careful bottler. This may be the only plausible explanation for the bottle's failure in this case, since there is uncontradicted evidence dispelling the probability that the failure was attributable to thermo-shock or external force. Absent expert opinion, as in a case of this type, circumstantial evidence may be the only available means of establishing a claim of either negligence or a defective product.

Under the theory of strict liability, the elements of proof as noted above are few and uncomplicated. The significant difference is that under strict liability the jury need not infer from the circumstantial evidence that defendant was negligent in order to impose liability. It is sufficient that the evidence establishes that the manufacturer placed a dangerously defective product on the market, knowing that it is to be used without inspection for defects. . . .

In short, under the theory of strict liability plaintiff should not be required to prove specifically what defect caused the incident, but may rely upon circumstantial evidence from which it can reasonably be inferred that it is more probable than not that the product was defective when it left defendant's control. . . .

The jury could properly have found on the evidence submitted that defendant was not causally negligent. This finding, of course, defeats plaintiffs' claim on the theory of negligence. As has been pointed out above, however, it would not necessarily preclude recovery under the theory of strict liability. Under instructions solely on negligence, a jury might conclude that the bottle was defective when it left defendant's control but that defendant was not liable because the defect did not result from negligence. Under instructions on strict liability, on the other hand, a finding that the bottle was defective when defendant put it on the market would *compel* a verdict *for plaintiffs*, absent the aforementioned defenses and without considering the question of negligence.

Thus, the trial court's refusal to submit plaintiffs' claim upon the theory of strict liability in tort must also be regarded as reversible error. The court's ruling deprived plaintiffs of a legitimate choice of theories on which to submit the case. Plaintiffs are entitled to attempt to prove their case on either or both theories—that defendant was negligent or that it put a dangerously defective product on the market.

It could be argued that the case in effect was submitted to the jury on strict liability, since the jury was instructed on implied warranty. Although strict liability in tort and in warranty are very similar, we cannot view the court's instructions as sufficient to constitute submission of the question of strict liability in tort to the jury. The jury was told that defendant warranted that the bottle of Coca-Cola "was reasonably fit for the ordinary and usual handling as it might reasonably anticipate in the exercise of reasonable care." This language falls short of conveying to the jury that if a defect existed in defendant's product when it left its control, defendant should be found liable for the injuries caused by such defect.

Reversed and new trial granted.

NOTES

1.   **Manufacturing defects.** A manufacturing defect can occur even if there is nothing at all wrong with the product's design—the product simply comes off the production line containing some flaw. Manufacturing defects typically affect only a small percentage of a manufacturer's products in a particular product line.

2.   **The consumer expectations test.** The Restatement Second § 402A in effect imposes strict liability when the product is defective and unreasonably dangerous. It tests defect/unreasonable danger by asking whether the product is "dangerous to an extent beyond that which would be contemplated by the ordinary consumer who purchases it, with the ordinary knowledge common to the community as to its characteristics." RESTATEMENT (SECOND) OF TORTS § 402A, cmt. i (1965). This is usually called the "consumer expectations" test.

3.   **The Products Liability Restatement's test.** The Products Liability Restatement states the test differently. It provides that "a product contains a manufacturing defect when the product departs from its intended design even though all possible care was exercised in the preparation and marketing of the product." RESTATEMENT OF PRODUCTS LIABILITY § 2(a) (1998). How does the newer Restatement's standard relate to the Second Restatement's "consumer expectations" standard?

4.   **Retaining the consumer expectations test.** Many courts today continue to apply the consumer expectations test in manufacturing defect cases, the more recent Products Restatement notwithstanding. *E.g., Potter v. Chicago Pneumatic Tool Co.,* 694 A.2d 1319 (Conn. 1997) (with other tests in some cases). Subject to qualification, the consumer expectations test is also widely used in the products liability law of countries in Europe, Asia, South America and elsewhere. *See* Mathias Reimann, *Liability for Defective Products at the Beginning of the Twenty-first Century: Emergence of a Worldwide Standard?*, 51 AM. J. COMP. LAW. 751, 768 (2003).

5.   **Elements of a strict liability claim.** To prevail on a strict liability claim, the plaintiff must prove not only that the product was defective, and that the defect was a factual and proximate cause of plaintiff's harm, but also that the product was defective when it left the defendant's hands. This latter part may not be easy to prove in a manufacturing defect case, particularly when the product has been in use for a long time before it fails. *See Barnish v. KWI Building Co.,* 980 A.2d 535 (Pa. 2009). Even where a manufacturing defect is proved, a plaintiff's evidence may fall short of proving that the defect actually caused the plaintiff's harm. This may be especially true where the manufacturing defect is only a small deviation from the intended design. *See, e.g., BIC Pen Corp. v. Carter,* 346 S.W.3d 533 (Tex. 2011).

6.   **Inferences from circumstantial evidence.** As *Lee* shows, drawing inferences is often necessary to make the plaintiff's case. The Restatement of Products Liability § 3 provides that it may be inferred that a product defect existing at the time of sale or distribution caused plaintiff's harm when the

event (a) was of a kind that ordinarily occurs as a result of product defect; and (b) was not solely the result of causes other than product defect. As one court recently explained, the thrust of this "malfunction theory" is that in some cases where there is a good deal of "missing evidence" as to what specific defect caused the harm, "the malfunction itself is circumstantial evidence of a defective condition." *Pitts v. Genie Industries, Inc.*, 921 N.W.2d 597 (Neb. 2019). What does the Restatement formulation remind you of?

7. **Applications.** In *Kerr v. Corning Glass Works*, 169 N.W.2d 587 (Minn. 1969), a Pyrex baking dish "exploded" when the plaintiff removed it from the oven. The Minnesota Court held this was not proof of a defect existing when the dish left the manufacturer's hands, since the explosion might have occurred because of subsequent damage. Does the Minnesota Court have a different attitude in *Lee*?

In a 1964 New Jersey case, the plaintiff, working for Ford, operated a grinding machine with a grinding disc produced by the defendant. The same disc had been on the grinder earlier when the machine was used by another employee. When the plaintiff used the machine, the disc snapped and struck him. The court held this did not suffice to prove that the disc was defective. Although a manufacturing flaw was possible, it was equally possible that mishandling would explain the accident. *Jakubowski v. Minn. Mining & Mfg.*, 199 A.2d 826 (N.J. 1964). In a later New Jersey decision, the plaintiff was driving a six-month-old Lincoln Continental. He heard a "gink" in the front and the steering mechanism locked. The car then collided with a tree. The trial judge refused to charge the jury that it could infer a defect, but this time the New Jersey Court held that proof was sufficient to permit a finding of defect. Although other causes were possible, a defect in the car when it left the manufacturer was deemed sufficiently probable. *Moraca v. Ford Motor Co.*, 332 A.2d 599 (N.J. 1975). Although the later cases from New Jersey and Minnesota are probably distinguishable from the earlier cases in those states, it is probably fair to say they represent a more relaxed attitude about the proof problem.

Could a jury could infer a defect caused the harm when the plaintiff's car burst into flames while unattended in her garage, even though the plaintiff cannot show whether the fire was caused by a defective fuel tank, electrical system, or something else? What if the house burned down, and it was not even clear that it was the car that started the fire? *See Metropolitan Property & Casualty Ins. Co. v. Deere & Co.*, 25 A.3d 571 (Conn. 2011) (suit against manufacturer of lawn tractor, alleging that a manufacturing defect caused a fire that burned down the plaintiff's home).

8. **Defect and negligence.** The use of *res ipsa* analogies, as in *Lee*, suggests a similarity between strict liability and negligence, as does the "unreasonable danger" phrase. One difference, however, is that a negligence claim focuses on the defendant's conduct, while a strict products liability claim focuses on the product itself. *See Fasolas v. Bobcat of New York, Inc.*, 128 N.E.3d 627 (N.Y. 2019); *Godoy ex rel. Gramling v. I.E. du Pont de Nemours &*

Co., 768 N.W.2d 674 (Wis. 2009). Thus, as in *Lee,* a jury might find no negligence and still find a product defective. A defendant which has done the best anyone can do to produce a safe product is still liable for the inevitable defects that cause harm. But in the great bulk of cases, it can be inferred that negligence caused the manufacturing defect. Since this will so often be true, this kind of strict liability might be regarded as a "shortcut" to the same result a negligence rule would ordinarily achieve, but without the necessity of long, detailed trials over the fault issue. *See* Gary T. Schwartz, *Understanding Products Liability,* 67 CAL. L. REV. 435, 460–461 (1979). Under this view, strict liability differs from negligence because it is cheaper to use. But as to most defendants most of the time, it will add very little liability. What do you think of this analysis?

MEXICALI ROSE V. SUPERIOR COURT (CLARK V. MEXICALI ROSE), 822 P.2d 1292 (Cal. 1992). Clark ordered a chicken enchilada at the Mexicali Rose restaurant. He swallowed a one-inch chicken bone contained in the enchilada, sustaining a throat injury for which he sues. He claims negligence, breach of implied warranty, and strict tort liability. *Held,* demurrer to the warranty and tort strict liability claims should be sustained. "If the injury-producing substance is natural to the preparation of the food served, it can be said that it was reasonably expected by its very nature and the food cannot be determined unfit or defective. A plaintiff in such a case has no cause of action in strict liability or implied warranty." The "defendants owe no duty to provide a perfect enchilada," but under this rule they may still be liable for negligence in preparing the food if that negligence is proved.

JUSTICE MOSK, dissenting: "The majority hold that processed food containing a sharp, concealed bone is fit for consumption, though no reasonable consumer would anticipate finding the bone. They declare in effect that the bone is natural to the dish, therefore the dish is fit for consumption. The majority never explain why this should be the rule, when it is universally held that in the analogous case of a sharp bit of wire in processed food, liability occurs under both the implied warranty of fitness and the theory of strict liability for defective consumer products."

JACKSON V. NESTLE-BEICH, INC., 589 N.E.2d 547 (Ill. 1992). The plaintiff allegedly broke a tooth on a hard pecan shell embedded in a chocolate-covered pecan-caramel candy purchased in a sealed can and manufactured by Nestle. Nestle moved for summary judgment on the ground that the substance was natural to pecans, not foreign. *Held,* affirming the intermediate appellate court's decision, "the foreign-natural doctrine is unsound and should be abandoned." Instead, the consumer's reasonable expectation is the test of defectiveness under the Second Restatement's § 402A, cmt. i.

NOTES

1. **Food products and consumer expectations.** The Products Restatement provides that a harm-causing ingredient in a food product is a defect "if a reasonable consumer would not expect the food product to contain that ingredient." RESTATEMENT OF PRODUCTS LIABILITY § 7 (1998). Is the consumer expectations test particularly apropos in food cases? If the standard was simply whether the food "departs from its intended design," which is the new Restatement's general standard for manufacturing defects, would that mean that if the seller of chicken enchiladas or nut-candies never even tried to remove bones or shells there would be no strict liability, since in that case there would be no departure from "intended design"? Most courts do not follow the foreign-natural distinction in *Mexicali Rose* but rely on consumer expectations instead. *See Schafer v. JLC Food Systems, Inc.*, 695 N.W.2d 570 (Minn. 2005) (calling the foreign-natural distinction "arbitrary").

2. **Emotional distress damages.** Finding something unpleasant in food may cause emotional distress without any physical harm. Courts have traditionally restricted such "pure emotional" claims. *See* Chapter 19. In *Bylsma v. Burger King Corp.*, 293 P.3d 1168 (Wash. 2013), the court held that the plaintiff, a deputy sheriff, could recover damages for emotional distress from finding phlegm inside his hamburger, as long as he proved that his distress was reasonable and was manifested by objective symptoms. "When a food manufacturer serves a contaminated food product, it is well within the scope of foreseeable harmful consequences that the individual served will suffer emotional distress," the court said. Dissenters thought that rules developed for negligence cases should not be carried over to strict products liability, and that there should be no recovery absent physical harm.

3. **Proof.** Might a plaintiff have proof problems in some food cases? Suppose that a plaintiff purchases packaged food at a store, and later, upon eating it, gets sick. How does the plaintiff prove that the food was "defective," and that it was a defect in the food (as opposed to, say, improper storage or preparation of it) that made her sick? In *Massey v. Conagra Foods, Inc.*, 328 P.3d 46 (Idaho 2014), the plaintiff consumed the defendant's poultry pot pies, purchased frozen from a grocery store. She got violently sick and was diagnosed with salmonellosis. In response to defendant's motion for summary judgment, she testified that she ate at least one if not several of the pot pies, that she "always" followed the cooking instructions, and that the strain of salmonella that infected her had been found in defendant's pot pies. The trial court granted defendant's motion, holding that her evidence on "defect" was insufficient. Reversing, the Idaho Supreme Court held that her testimony alone was sufficient to create a fact issue on whether the pot pie failed to meet the reasonable expectations of the ordinary consumer as to its safety.

B. DESIGN DEFECTS

LEICHTAMER V. AMERICAN MOTORS CO., 424 N.E.2d 568 (Ohio 1981).
Plaintiffs were passengers in a Jeep driven by Paul Vance on an off-road
facility. Vance was negotiating hills and terraces when he overturned the
Jeep in a back-to-front flip over. The rollbar, attached to relatively thin
metal housing, displaced toward the passengers when the housing
collapsed. Vance and his wife were killed. The plaintiff Jeanne
Leichtamer's legs were twisted through the front seat and she is now a
paraplegic. The plaintiffs sued claiming that, though Vance was negligent,
their injuries were enhanced because of the roll-bar's displacement. The
jury found for the plaintiffs, awarding $1 million in compensatory and $1
million in punitive damages to Jeanne and $100,000 compensatory and
$100,000 punitive to Carl Leichtamer. *Held*, affirmed.

"Appellees did not claim that there was any defect in the way the
vehicle was manufactured in the sense of departure by the manufacturer
from design specifications. The vehicle was manufactured precisely in the
manner in which it was designed to be manufactured. It reached Paul
Vance in that condition and was not changed. . . . [T]he vast weight of
authority is in support of allowing an action in strict liability in tort . . . for
design defects. . . . Strict liability in tort has been applied to design defect
'second collision' cases. While a manufacturer is under no obligation to
design a 'crash proof' vehicle, an instruction may be given on the issue of
strict liability in tort if the plaintiff adduces sufficient evidence that an
unreasonably dangerous product design proximately caused or enhanced
plaintiff's injuries in the course of a foreseeable use. . . . [A] product may be
found defective in design if the plaintiff demonstrates that the product
failed to perform as safely as an ordinary consumer would expect when
used in an intended or reasonably foreseeable manner. . . . A product will
be found unreasonably dangerous if it is dangerous to an extent beyond the
expectations of an ordinary consumer when used in an intended or
reasonably foreseeable manner." Since the roll-bar was designed for a side
roll-over only and not a back-to-front roll-over, and since the company knew
it had not provided tests for this kind of hazard when it advertised the Jeep
for off-the-road use, punitive damages were warranted.

NOTES

1. **Design defects.** Notice that the "defect" in *Leichtamer* was in the
design of the product, and was not simply the result of some flaw in
manufacture. Design defects are difficult to define and identify. In addition,
design defect claims threaten manufacturers in ways that manufacturing
defect claims do not. If a product is defective in manufacture, only a few
products with flaws will be in circulation; but if a product is defectively
designed, every one of the products represents a potential lawsuit against the
manufacturer.

2.   **Consumer expectations and unreasonable danger.** As noted in § 2 above, the Restatement Second's § 402A provides that a product would be considered defective if it was more dangerous than the "ordinary consumer" would expect. When applied to design defect cases, this test raises many difficult questions. Cars do not provide roll-bars built into the roof. Does the consumer expectations test help decide whether such cars are defective? Would it be enough to show a defect if you could prove that consumers had a general expectation that cars would be safe? Or would it be necessary to show that consumer experience led to specific design expectations? *See Soule v. Gen. Motors Corp.*, 882 P.2d 298 (Cal. 1994) (requiring specific expectation based on everyday experience). Think about how consumer expectations might be proved in court. Would it be proved by (a) the plaintiff's testimony about her own expectations; (b) the jury's general knowledge about safety expectations; or (c) expert testimony? In *Wilson Sporting Goods Co. v. Hickox*, 59 A.3d 1267 (D.C. 2013), the plaintiff was a professional baseball umpire who was injured during a major league game when a foul-tipped ball struck his mask, which was manufactured by the defendant. The jury, instructed on the consumer expectations test, found for the plaintiff. *Held*, affirmed. The court stressed evidence that the plaintiff had been personally told by a manufacturer's representative that the mask was safer than other similar models; that, said the court, would lead an ordinary consumer to expect the mask to perform safely, which it did not.

3.   **Consumer expectations and obvious dangers.** Many commentators and courts consider the consumer expectations test of section 402A a "pro-plaintiff" test. But what if a product's danger is obvious? Wouldn't a plaintiff always lose such a case, because the product would not be "more dangerous than the ordinary consumer would expect?" *See Bourne v. Marty Gilman, Inc.*, 452 F.3d 632 (7th Cir. 2006); *Blue v. Environmental Engineering, Inc.*, 828 N.E.2d 1128 (Ill. 2005); 2 DOBBS, HAYDEN & BUBLICK, THE LAW OF TORTS § 455 (2d ed. 2011).

4.   **Bystanders or strangers.** Suppose you are not using the product, but you are injured by it. You fall against an exercise machine and, quite surprisingly, a part pierces your thigh, cutting blood vessels and damaging nerves. *See Jones v. Nordictrack, Inc.*, 550 S.E.2d 101 (Ga. 2001). Or a defective lighter as used by one child causes burns to another child. See *Hernandez v. Tokai Corp.*, 2 S.W.3d 251 (Tex. 1999). Or you inhale asbestos fibers unknowingly brought into the house on the clothes of a worker who was exposed to such toxic materials. *See Stegemoller v. ACandS, Inc.*, 767 N.E.2d 974 (Ind. 2002); *Lunsford v. Saberhagen Holdings*, 106 P.3d 808 (Wash. Ct. App. 2005).

Courts impose liability in such cases, but how can a bystander have any expectation about the particular product's safety? In *Gaines-Tabb v. ICI Explosives, USA, Inc.*, 160 F.3d 613 (10th Cir. 1998), victims of the Oklahoma City terrorist bombing sued the manufacturer of the fertilizer used to construct the bomb, claiming a design defect. The court said that under the consumer expectations test used in Oklahoma, they failed to prove that the fertilizer was less safe than ordinary consumers of the product (farmers) would expect. In *Horst v. Deere & Co.*, 769 N.W.2d 536 (Wis. 2009), the court said that the focus remains on the expectations of the actual consumer, but that such a consumer may have safety expectations relating to bystanders, which can be taken into account by the jury in deciding whether the product is unreasonably dangerous in design. When the consumer expectations test is not used at all (see the next section below), there is no barrier to a bystander bringing a design defect claim. *See Berrier v. Simplicity Mfg., Inc.*, 563 F.3d 38 (3d Cir. 2009).

5.   **Crashworthiness.** At one time, a defendant in a case like *Leichtamer* could prevail on an argument that if a product was used in an unintended way—like getting involved in a car crash—then that unintended use, not any defect, was the sole cause of the harm. Such a restrictive view is no longer followed; manufacturers are liable for harms caused by defective products that are put to "foreseeable uses," even if unintended by the manufacturer. This is often called the "crashworthiness doctrine." *See, e.g., Malen v. MTD Products, Inc.*, 628 F.3d 296 (7th Cir. 2010) ("The premise underlying the crashworthiness doctrine is that some products, although not made for certain purposes—such as accidents—should nevertheless be reasonably designed to minimize the injury-producing effect of an accident."); *see also Donze v. General Motors, LLC*, 800 S.E.2d 479 (S.C. 2017) (applying doctrine, holding that defendant cannot use plaintiff's contributory negligence to reduce its liability for a defect that caused enhanced injuries in a drunk-driving case). A few courts have rejected the crashworthiness doctrine. *See Holiday Motor Corp. v. Walters*, 790 S.E.2d 447 (Va. 2016) (requiring plaintiff to prove that a soft-top convertible's roof design was not reasonably safe "for the purpose for which it [was] intended"). *See also § 3, infra.*

6.   **Enhanced injuries.** The crashworthiness doctrine (Note 5 above) allows a plaintiff to sue for the injuries that were enhanced by the product's defective design. For example, suppose the plaintiff is injured when a defectively-designed airbag fails to deploy in an auto accident. The airbag defect, even if proved, did not cause the accident in the first place, right? Rather, what the defect caused was the enhanced injury—the injuries that would not have occurred without the product defect. How is that proved? Compare *Piltch v. Ford Motor Co.*, 778 F.3d 628 (7th Cir. 2015) (burden on plaintiff; plaintiff needed expert testimony on causation in order to separate the injuries caused by collision from those caused by the failure of the air bag) with *Polston v. Boomershine Pontiac-GMC Truck Inc.*, 423 S.E.2d 659 (Ga. 1992) (once plaintiff proves defect, burden shifts to defendant to prove which damages were not caused by the defect). Which approach represents sounder policy? *See* RESTATEMENT (THIRD) OF TORTS: PRODUCTS LIABILITY § 16 & cmt. d (1998) (if "proof does not support a determination . . . of the harm that would have resulted in the absence of the product defect, the product seller is liable for all of the plaintiff's harm"; "The defendant, a wrongdoer who in fact has caused harm to the plaintiff, should not escape liability because the nature of the harm makes such a determination impossible.").

KNITZ V. MINSTER MACHINE CO.
432 N.E.2d 814 (Ohio 1982)

[Defendant manufactured a press which delivered 60 tons of force in pressing die halves together. It was originally activated with a two-hand button tripping device, so that the operator's hands were necessarily outside the danger area. This press, with the button tripping device, was sold by defendant to Toledo Die and Manufacturing Company. Toledo, however, also purchased an optional foot pedal tripping device and it was in use at the time of the injury. Plaintiff, the press operator for Toledo, found it necessary to move the foot pedal with her foot; in doing so, she leaned on the bottom portion of the die with her hand. Her foot accidentally activated the foot pedal and the press descended, amputating two fingers. There was another safety device, intended to physically pull back the operator's hands, but it was not attached. The trial judge granted summary judgment for the manufacturer.]

WILLIAM B. BROWN, JUSTICE.

The case presents us with the question of whether a motion for summary judgment pursuant to Civ. R. 56 should have been granted to appellee. . . .

The focus of the inquiry in *Leichtamer* was what constituted a "defective condition unreasonably dangerous" as formulated by Section 402A of the Restatement of Torts. We adopted a variation of the familiar "consumer expectation test" of Comment *i* to Section 402: "A product is in a defective condition unreasonably dangerous to the user or consumer if it is more dangerous than an ordinary consumer would expect when used in an intended or reasonably foreseeable manner." This standard followed as a logical development from commercial warranty origins of strict liability in tort. It reflected "the commercial reality that '[i]mplicit in . . . [a product's] presence on the market . . . [is] a representation that it [will] safely do the jobs for which it was built.' "

Unlike the factual setting in *Leichtamer*, there are situations in which "the consumer would not know what to expect, because he would have no idea how safe the product could be made." Such is the case *sub judice*. Difficulty could arise, for example, where the injured party is an innocent bystander who is ignorant of the product and has no expectation of its safety, or where a new product is involved and no expectation of safety has developed. Conversely, liability could be barred hypothetically where industrial workmen "gradually learn of the dangers involved in the machinery they must use to make a living and come to 'expect' the dangers." In such cases, the policy underlying strict liability in tort, requires that "a product may be found defective in design, even if it satisfies ordinary consumer expectations, if through hindsight the jury determines that the product's design embodies 'excessive preventable danger,' or, in other words, if the jury finds that the risk of danger inherent in the challenged design outweighs the benefits of such design."

Accordingly, we hold that a product design is in a defective condition to the user or consumer if (1) it is more dangerous than an ordinary consumer would expect when used in an intended or reasonably foreseeable manner, or (2) if the benefits of the challenged design do not outweigh the risk inherent in such design. Factors relevant to the evaluation of the defectiveness of the product design are the likelihood that the product design will cause injury, the gravity of the danger posed, and the mechanical and economic feasibility of an improved design.... [W]e conclude that appellant has made out genuine issues of fact of whether appellee's press design was defective by allowing accidental tripping of the foot pedal control and in failing to provide a point of operation guard when the foot pedal is operative. Specifically, appellant provided an affidavit of James J. McCarthy, a former safety engineer for General Motors Corporation, involved with analysis of machine accident potential. McCarthy's affidavit states, *inter alia*, that in his opinion the press is defective "because of inadequate guarding at the point of operation caused by failure to attach a barrier or interlock gate guard to prevent entry of the operator's hands into the danger area while the ram is descending . . . the press is defective because of inadequate guarding of the foot pedal of the foot switch to prevent inadvertent entry and tripping."

NOTES

1. **Different tests for design defects and manufacturing defects.** The distinction between design defects and manufacturing defects is fundamental in American law. The Restatement Second used the same test—consumer expectations—for both kinds of defects, and some courts continue to do that. *See, e.g., Aubin v. Union Carbide Corp.*, 177 So.3d 489 (Fla. 2015). The products liability laws of many other countries also apply the same rules to each type of defect. *See* Mathias Reimann, *Liability for Defective Products at the Beginning of the Twenty-first Century: Emergence of a Worldwide Standard?*, 51 AM. J. COMP. LAW. 751 (2003); Jane Stapleton, *Bugs in Anglo-American Products Liability*, 53 S.C. L. REV. 1225 (2002).

But a great number of modern American courts utilize a different set of rules for each type of defect—frequently today using some form of strict liability for manufacturing defects (often using the consumer expectations test) and risk-utility balancing for design defects. The Restatement Third expressly "adopts a reasonableness ('risk-utility balancing') test as the standard for judging the defectiveness of product designs," but provides in a comment that consumer expectations, while they "do not constitute an independent standard for judging" design defects, "may substantially influence or even be ultimately determinative on risk-utility balancing," because they relate to foreseeability and frequency of the risks of harm. RESTATEMENT OF PRODUCTS LIABILITY § 2(b), cmts. d & g (1998). Does this preserve a useful role for both tests?

2.   **Using both tests for design defects.** Some jurisdictions use the consumer expectations and risk-utility balancing tests in combination, usually in the alternative, either leaving it to the parties' choice or choosing one or the other based on its suitability to the facts of the case. *See, e.g., Tincher v. Omega Flex, Inc.*, 104 A.3d 328 (Pa. 2014); *Soule v. Gen. Motors Corp.*, 882 P.2d 298 (Cal. 1994). The court in *Mikolajczyk v. Ford Motor Co.*, 901 N.E.2d 329 (Ill. 2008), said that where both parties argue a design-defect case based solely on consumer expectations, the jury should be instructed only on that test. However, "both the consumer-expectation test and the risk-utility test continue to have their place in the law of strict product liability based on design defect. Each party is entitled to choose its own method of proof, to present relevant evidence, and to request a corresponding jury instruction. If the evidence is sufficient to implicate the risk-utility test, the broader test, which incorporates the factor of consumer expectations, is to be applied by the finder of fact."

Would the flip-side work, as well? In other words, would it be possible to amalgamate the two tests by saying that consumer expectations is the test, but what a consumer expects is affected by the balance of risks and utilities? *McCathern v. Toyota Motor Corp.*, 23 P.3d 320 (Or. 2001). *See also Izzarelli v. R.J. Reynolds Tobacco Co.*, 136 A.3d 1232 (Conn. 2016) (applying its "modified consumer expectation test," under which "the jury would weigh the product's risks and utility and then inquire, in light of those factors, whether a reasonable consumer would consider the product design unreasonably dangerous").

3.   **Negligence disguised as "strict liability"?** Where the consumer expectations test is discarded and the risk-utility test is adopted to control liability for design defects, does all this sound like *Carroll Towing* and thus like a regular negligence analysis? Sometimes courts have tried to distinguish risk-utility balancing on a negligence theory from the same balancing in strict liability cases by saying negligence is about conduct of the manufacturer, while strict products liability is about the defectiveness of the product itself. *E.g., Dart v. Wiebe Mfg., Inc.*, 709 P.2d 876 (Ariz. 1985). Yet behind every product's quality or lack of quality is the defendant's conduct. Is the distinction therefore illusory?

4.   **"Negligent design" theory.** A number of states allow a plaintiff to proceed on a "negligent design" theory, which requires proof of the same elements as any other negligence case. In *Reis v. Volvo Cars of North America*, 18 N.E.3d 383 (N.Y. 2014), the court said that in such cases, the reasonable-person standard "has been given more specific form: the question is whether the product is one as to which if the design defect were known at the time of manufacture, a reasonable person would conclude that the utility of the product did not outweigh the risk inherent" in marketing the product with that defect. *See also 5 Star, Inc. v. Ford Motor Co.*, 759 S.E.2d 139 (S.C. 2014) (plaintiff must establish that defendant failed to exercise due care in designing the product, based on what the defendant knew or should have known at the time of manufacture; plaintiff must present evidence of a reasonable

alternative design). Indiana's products liability statute requires the plaintiff in a design defect case to "establish that the manufacturer or seller failed to exercise reasonable care under the circumstances in designing the product." IND. CODE § 34–20–2–2. Judge Posner, commenting on this statutory provision in *Mesman v. Crane Pro Services*, 409 F.3d 846 (7th Cir. 2005), *abrogated on other grounds by Kaiser v. Johnson & Johnson*, 947 F.3d 996 (7th Cir. 2020), said that "*expressly* requiring proof of negligence in a design-defect case, as Indiana law does, though unusual, really isn't much of a legal innovation, since 'defect' always implied something that should not have been allowed into the product—something, in other words, that could have been removed at a reasonable cost in light of the risk that it created."

BARKER V. LULL ENGINEERING CO., 573 P.2d 443 (Cal. 1978). Plaintiff, an inexperienced operator of a high-lift industrial loader, lifted a load of lumber 10–18 feet off the ground. The ground was uneven and the loader began to vibrate as if it were about to tip over. Responding to warning shouts of fellow workers, the plaintiff scrambled out of the loader. He was hit and seriously injured by lumber falling from the load. The loader had no protective canopy and no outriggers to steady it. "We hold . . . that a product is defective in design (1) if the plaintiff demonstrates that the product failed to perform as safely as an ordinary consumer would expect when used in an intended or reasonably foreseeable manner or (2) if the plaintiff proves that the product's design proximately caused his injury and the defendant fails to prove . . . that on balance the benefits of the challenged design outweigh the risk of danger inherent in such design."

NOTES

1. **Burden-shifting.** Notice that *Barker* shifts the burden of proof to the defendant to justify its design by pointing to a suitable risk-utility balance. Only a few courts have embraced this burden-shifting idea. *See Quilez-Velar v. Ox Bodies, Inc.*, 823 F.3d 712 (1st Cir. 2016) (Puerto Rico law); *Shanks v. Upjohn Co.*, 835 P.2d 1189 (Alaska 1992). The shift occurs quite easily; all the plaintiff must do is prove that the design caused the harm. The burden of justifying the product's design then falls on the defendant. *See Mikolajczyk v. Ford Motor Co.*, 901 N.E.2d 329 (Ill. 2008) (expressly adopting *Barker*'s burden shift). If the defendant fails to prove that the benefits of the design outweigh the risks of the design, the plaintiff will prevail. How does *this* differ from the usual negligence case?

2. **Applying *Barker*.** In *Campbell v. General Motors Corp.*, 649 P.2d 224 (Cal. 1982), the plaintiff was a 62-year-old woman who was injured when thrown from her seat while riding on a city bus. She was sitting in the forward-most front-facing seat. The seats immediately behind the plaintiff had grab bars on them, so that if she had sat in one of them, she would have had something to hold onto. There was also a vertical bar in the aisle in front of the

side seat immediately in front of the plaintiff, but she could not reach it from her own seat. After she settled with the city, she sued the manufacturer of the bus. *Held*, it can be fairly inferred that the bus's design "caused" the injury, thus she prevails under the second test in *Barker*. Would this proof suffice in an ordinary negligence case, do you think?

3. **Limiting *Barker*'s application.** Strict liability under the consumer expectations test will not always be available under *Barker*, because California plaintiffs can choose the consumer expectations test only where the ordinary consumer, based on "everyday experience," could determine how safely a product would have performed in the injury-causing event that occurred. *Soule v. General Motors Corp.*, 882 P.2d 298 (Cal. 1994). The key factor is not the product's complexity, but whether "in the context of the facts and circumstances of its failure, the product is one about which the ordinary consumers can form minimum safety expectations." *McCabe v. Am. Honda Motor Co.*, 123 Cal.Rptr.2d 303 (Ct. App. 2002) (plaintiff allowed to proceed on consumer expectations test in case of non-deploying air bag); *see also Romine v. Johnson Controls, Inc.*, 169 Cal.Rptr.3d 208 (Ct. App. 2014) (consumer expectations test used in a case where vehicle driver's seat collapsed rearward in rear-end collision). Illinois, which also follows the *Barker* model, has said that "Nothing in our past decisions, even when we have applied the risk-utility test, has signaled a rejection of the consumer-expectation test merely because a complex product was involved." *Mikolajczyk, supra* Note 1.

Are you troubled by allowing a jury to assess the defectiveness of a complex design using the consumer expectations test? In *Verrazono v. Gehl Co.*, 263 Cal.Rptr.3d 663 (Ct. App. 2020), the court held that it was proper not to instruct the jury on the consumer expectations test where the plaintiff put on no evidence of the "safety expectations of a hypothetical reasonable" user of a rough terrain forklift that tipped over. The court in *Show v. Ford Motor Co.*, 659 F.3d 584 (7th Cir. 2011), held that a plaintiff was required under Illinois law to present expert evidence on the issue of defectiveness even when relying on the consumer expectations test. Does that solve the problem?

GENIE INDUSTRIES, INC. v. MATAK

462 S.W.3d 1 (Tex. 2015)

CHIEF JUSTICE HECHT delivered the opinion of the Court. . . .

A product manufacturer is not liable for a design defect unless a safer alternative design exists and the defect renders the product unreasonably dangerous—that is, its risks outweigh its utility. . . .

[Genie Industries manufactures and sells aerial lifts throughout the world. An aerial lift is used to raise a worker on a platform to reach the ceilings of tall buildings or other high places. One of these lifts is the AWP-40S. The Cathedral in the Pines Church owns an AWP-40S, which it uses to reach the ceilings in its buildings. Matak and Boggan, employees of Gulf Coast Electric, were hired to run fiber optic cable in the ceiling at a church.

They were safely using the church's lift to do the job when a church employee watching them suggested that rather than lowering the platform and having the man on the platform get off each time the lift needed to be moved, that they raise the stabilizing jacks, roll the lift to the new location, and then lower the jacks again, leaving the man at the top of the lift, fully extended, the entire time. One Gulf Coast worker expressed reservations about this method, but the church employee reassured him that it was safe. A sign on the machine itself displays an image of a man pushing the lift while elevated, with the text, "DANGER: Tip-over hazard. Attempting to move the machine with the platform raised will tip the machine over and cause death or serious injury." That is what happened; on the first attempt at moving the lift fully extended, it suddenly tipped over and crashed to the ground.]

Matak died of massive injuries to his head, and this action for wrongful death and survivor damages ensued. [The jury found for the plaintiff, and apportioned responsibility 55% to Genie, 20% to the Church, 20% to Gulf Coast, and 5% to Matak.] The trial court rendered judgment on the verdict, and Genie appealed. The court of appeals affirmed, holding that there was legally sufficient evidence to support the jury's design defect finding. We granted Genie's petition for review. . . .

[Safer alternative design]

. . . The plaintiffs' evidence of a safer alternative design for the AWP-40S came from two sources. Ken Zimmer, an expert on aerial lift design and manufacture, testified to three alternative designs, referred to as the "automatic drop-down" design, the "pothole protection" design, and the "chain and padlock" design. A fourth design—the "block" design—was suggested by Matak's attorney during direct examination of Genie's expert, Rick Curtin. . . .

Zimmer's automatic drop-down design idea is fairly simple. . . . Releasing an outrigger would trigger an alarm and automatically begin lowering the platform at one foot per second, reducing the height from which a worker would fall if the lift still tipped over. Zimmer testified that the design would have saved Matak's life. But nothing in the record indicates that the automatic drop-down design could have stabilized the lift or would have lowered the platform enough to prevent Matak's fall and serious injuries. Zimmer, himself, acknowledged that falls from 10 or 15 feet could be fatal, and the record, read generously, does not indicate that the platform could have reached a lower height. . . . But an even greater problem is the added danger that this design would cause. There was evidence that a sudden, unexpected movement of the platform could startle a worker, creating an even more dangerous situation when working with live electrical wires or leaving the worker hanging onto ceiling rafters as the platform suddenly descended. Even if the design could have prevented some or all of Matak's injuries, it could just as well have increased the risks of injury to himself and others.

Zimmer's pothole protection design would simply incorporate into the AWP-40S a feature on many mobile lifts. When a mobile lift is raised beyond a certain height, small stabilization bars—also called outriggers—automatically deploy from the vehicle, not all the way to the ground, but hovering just above it to reduce the machine's ground clearance. . . . If the modified pothole technology were incorporated to Genie's lift, the existing outriggers would need to be permanently attached to the lift so that they could be mechanized. Permanent attachment and mechanization would presumably add to the lift's weight and size, thereby diminishing one of the lift's key utility factors—its versatility. Furthermore, this design would still require that the user manually lower the leveling jacks for the lift to operate safely. . . . Zimmer's conclusion that the design would have been safer for Matak has little support in the evidence, and there is no evidence the design would be safer in other circumstances.

Zimmer's chain and padlock design was the simplest of all: the leveling jack handles would be chained and padlocked, and the key held by the worker on the platform, preventing the outriggers from being raised while the lift is extended. The obvious flaw in the design is that it would do little to prevent misuse. The key could simply be left with the person on the ground, or even thrown down to him by the worker on the platform. It cannot be imagined that users intent on disregarding multiple, plain, obvious warnings of danger would be stymied by the need for a key. Indeed, it is hard to imagine why users seeking to avoid the inconvenience of lowering the platform to move the lift would accept the inconvenience of chaining and locking the jack handles every time the outriggers were set.

Matak's counsel himself suggested a fourth design during his examination of Genie's expert: two of the lift's four wheels would be replaced by a block so that the lift could not be moved without tilting it back on its two wheels, and off its block, to roll the machine like a loaded dolly or a two-wheeled cart. This design would not directly ensure the proper deployment of the outriggers, but the obvious necessity of tilting the machine to move it would discourage attempts to move the machine while its platform was elevated. . . . While a two-wheel design would make it impossible to move a lift with the platform raised, a two-wheeled lift would also be much harder to move than a machine on four wheels. . . . If every move required putting a machine in that mode, every move would become that much more difficult. The impact of this design would be felt in the utility of the machine.

To impose liability on Genie, the plaintiffs must have presented evidence of an alternative design that (1) would have been safer for Matak and prevented or significantly reduced his risk of injury, (2) would not have been less safe in other circumstances and increased the risks to other users, (3) would not have substantially impaired the lift's utility, and (4) was economically and technologically feasible at the time. Genie argues that there was no evidence to support a design of this kind. We disagree. The evidence of a safer alternative design is weak, but we cannot say that it is less than a scintilla. Accordingly, we turn to Genie's second argument, that there is no evidence the AWP-40S is unreasonably dangerous.

[Risk-utility balancing]

Whether a defective design renders a product unreasonably dangerous depends on whether the product's risks outweigh its utility. . . . This balancing is for the jury unless the evidence allows but one reasonable conclusion. . . .

In the case before us, the evidence of the AWP-40S's utility is undisputed. The lift is designed to be small, lightweight, portable, and relatively inexpensive. To accommodate a wide variety of working environments, the lift uses outriggers with manual leveling jacks to stabilize the lift once it is positioned. This allows the lift to be used on surfaces that are not completely flat, such as the gradually sloped floor in this case, without having to sacrifice stability. Furthermore, the lift is designed so that the outriggers are removable in order to keep the lift as narrow as possible when being moved. This allows the AWP-40S to fit through standard door frames, therein expanding the range of uses for the machine. As previously explained, the lift also incorporates a mechanical interlock to make sure that all four outriggers are installed and the leveling jacks are firmly pressed against a given workspace. Until the outriggers are properly set, the lift cannot be operated. This maximizes the utility of the lift while still ensuring that it is used safely.

The risk is that a user will ignore the instructions in the user manual, the signs on the lift itself, and the danger, obvious to even a casual observer, that the lift will tip if the outriggers are removed when a person is on a fully elevated platform. So obvious is the risk of danger from misuse of the lift that the evidence does not reflect a single other accident involving a fully extended 40' lift. . . . The undisputed evidence is that Genie has sold more than 100,000 AWP model lifts all over the world, which have been used millions of times. But the record does not reflect a single misuse as egregious as that in this case.

The five factors to be considered in determining whether a product's risk outweighs its utility . . . conclusively establish that the AWP-40S is not, on this record, unreasonably dangerous. The first is whether the gravity and likelihood of injury outweighs the lift's utility. While misuse of the lift can result in the most serious injury, as this case illustrates, the likelihood of its occurrence is all but nonexistent. . . . [T]he danger was patent. The second factor asks whether there is a substitute that would meet the same need and not be unsafe or unreasonably expensive. There is no evidence of one. The third factor is whether there is a safer alternative design. As we have already explained at length, there is only slight evidence of such a design. The fourth factor is whether the danger of misuse is obvious and readily avoidable. The risk of tip-over is both. . . . The last factor considers ordinary consumers' expectations. Again, the danger of misuse is obvious, even to someone not trained in handling the AWP-40S. These factors require the conclusion that the AWP-40S is not unreasonably dangerous. . . .

Accordingly, we reverse the judgment of the court of appeals and render judgment for Petitioner.

[Dissenting judges argued that because there was "some evidence" in the record to support the jury verdict, the court should have affirmed.]

NOTES

1. **Reasonable alternative design ("RAD").** "Throughout the 20th century, the great majority of design defect cases have involved proof by the plaintiff of a feasible alternative design—proof of some practicable, cost-effective, untaken design precaution that would have prevented the plaintiff's harm." DAVID G. OWEN & MARY J. DAVIS, OWEN & DAVIS ON PRODUCTS LIABILITY § 8.10 (4th ed. 2021). The Products Restatement says that a product is defective in design when the seller could have reduced or avoided the product's "foreseeable risks of harm" by "the adoption of a reasonable alternative design, and the omission of the alternative design renders the product not reasonably safe." RESTATEMENT OF PRODUCTS LIABILITY § 2 (1998). In other words, the Products Restatement requires RAD proof, with only very narrow exceptions. Does the *Genie Industries* court agree?

2. **Rejecting the RAD requirement.** Some courts have soundly rejected the Restatement Third's approach, and along with it, any requirement of proof of a reasonable alternative design. *See Aubin v. Union Carbide Corp.*, 177 So.3d 489 (Fla. 2015) (expressly rejecting the Third Restatement on the ground that its test improperly "reintroduces principles of negligence into strict liability," and is insufficiently protective of plaintiffs). Logically, the consumer expectations test includes no requirement of RAD proof, so courts that reject risk-utility balancing generally also reject a RAD requirement. *See Delaney v. Deere & Co.*, 999 P.2d 930 (Kan. 2000); *Green v. Smith & Nephew AHP, Inc.* 629 N.W.2d 727 (Wis. 2001) Of course, that such proof is not *required* does not mean that it is not offered in many cases; certainly if the existence of RAD is a factor in a multi-part test, as in a number of states, it remains an important piece of evidence. *See, e.g., Kaiser v. Johnson & Johnson*, 947 F.3d 996 (7th Cir. 2020) (under Indiana law, evidence of RAD is not required, but is relevant to whether the challenged design is unreasonably dangerous). Why would a plaintiff want to introduce evidence of RAD, regardless of the legal test used in the case? *See Tincher v. Omega Flex, Inc.*, 104 A.3d 328 (Pa. 2014).

3.   **What is an "alternative" design?** A most intriguing question arises when you try to figure out what counts as an "alternative" design. Suppose there are three drugs on the market that, by different chemical formulas, help avoid some painful symptom like heartburn or rashes. All do the job, although by different means. The defendant manufactures a fourth drug, based on still a fourth formula. The defendant's drug, however, has serious side effects for a substantial number of people. Should the existing drugs be considered as alternatives, on the ground that they have the same end function? Or should they NOT be considered as alternatives on the ground that, whatever their function, their chemical formulas are widely different?

The Products Restatement poses a different set of facts for this problem. It supposes that the defendant manufactures a toy gun that shoots hard pellets at high velocity, presumably very dangerous to those who might be in close range of a child playing with the toy. The defendant could have manufactured a toy gun that is not harmful, say one that fires soft gelatin pellets or ping pong balls. Would a ping-pong-ball gun be an alternative for the hard-pellet gun? It depends how you characterize the product. If you think the product is "toy guns capable of doing injury," the ping-pong-ball gun will not be an alternative. You might think the pellet gun was defective because it should not be marketed at all, but you would not think it defective because it fails to achieve the safety of a ping-pong-ball gun. *See* RESTATEMENT OF PRODUCTS LIABILITY § 2, cmt. e (1998).

4.   **When is an alternative design "reasonable?"** A number of courts have held that a plaintiff has proved the existence of a reasonable alternative design by adducing expert testimony that a specific improvement is safer and would not impair the product's usefulness or impose unreasonable costs. *See* DOBBS, HAYDEN & BUBLICK, HORNBOOK ON TORTS § 33.11, at 822 (2d ed. 2016). A proposed alternative design may be "reasonable" even where it reduces a product's capacity to perform a function for which it was designed. *In re Depuy Orthopaedics, Inc.*, 888 F.3d 753 (5th Cir. 2018) (under Texas law, metal-on-plastic hip implants were viable alternative design to metal-on-metal hip implants).

5.   **Feasibility.** "Evidence of an alternative design introduces the question of feasibility because a manufacturer's product cannot be faulted when safer alternatives are not feasible." *Gillespie v. Edmier*, 182 N.E.3d 54 (Ill. 2020). Both technological and economic feasibility are thus important components of plaintiff's RAD proof. In *Honda of America Mfg., Inc. v. Norman*, 104 S.W.3d 600 (Tex. Ct. App. 2003), survivors of Karen Norman, a motorist who drowned when the automatic seatbelt in her car malfunctioned and trapped her in her car, sued the car's manufacturer on a design-defect theory. Plaintiffs' experts testified that there were three alternative seatbelt designs that Honda could have used: (a) incorporation of a timer on the seatbelt-release button; (b) relocation of the release button to hip level, as used in Toyota vehicles; and (c) use of two release buttons. Reversing a jury verdict for plaintiff, the court held that this testimony was insufficient to prove RAD. There was no testimony to suggest that the timer—alternative (a)—was

feasible, or that it would be safer than the challenged design. With respect to proposed alternative (b), there was no proof that the design "would have prevented or significantly reduced the risk of Karen's death without imposing an equal or greater risk of harm under all relevant circumstances"; further, the mere fact that Toyota used that design did not prove that it was safer, or that it would be *economically* feasible for Honda to adopt it. And on alternative (c), the court said there was no proof that it was technologically feasible; one of plaintiffs' experts even testified that it was not.

6.   **Applying the RAD test.** Suppose that an automobile passenger was injured when the car in which she was riding was struck from the side by another vehicle traveling at high speed. The passenger sues the manufacturer of the car in which she was riding, claiming that the car was defectively designed, in that the doors should have protected her in the crash. Could the car be made safer for passengers if it was reinforced throughout with steel, and resembled a U.S. Army tank? Of course. But would that be found to be a *reasonable* alternative design? Perhaps it would weigh 30 tons, require super-premium fuel, get laughably awful gas mileage, look ugly, and cost $350,000. How would the *Genie Industries* court analyze whether the "tank-car" design would be a reasonable alternative?

7.   **Already-existing alternatives.** Perhaps the clearest evidence of a reasonable alternative design is that similar products already on the market have *safer* designs. RESTATEMENT OF PRODUCTS LIABILITY § 2, cmt. f (1998). However, mere proof that a competitor uses a *different* design does not by itself establish that the competitor's design is *safer* than the defendant's design, or that it would be economically feasible for the defendant to adopt it. *See Honda, supra* Note 5.

What if a plaintiff shows that the defendant-manufacturer itself uses a safer design in another part of the product that performs the same function as the challenged design? *See Goodner v. Hyundai Motor Co.*, 650 F.3d 1034 (5th Cir. 2011) (plaintiffs challenged the risks presented by front seats in a car that could recline more than 45 degrees, and proved that the manufacturer installed rear seats in its own vehicles that could not recline more than 45 degrees). Even where an alternative design exists, however, it may not be found to be a reasonable substitute in the actual market. *See Evans v. Lorillard Tobacco Co.*, 990 N.E.2d 997 (Mass. 2013) (low-tar, low-nicotine cigarettes were not a reasonable alternative to regular cigarettes for the subclass of consumers who were already addicted).

8.   **Experts and prototypes.** In requiring reasonable alternative design evidence, the Products Restatement specifically asserts that the plaintiff is not required to build a prototype. RESTATEMENT OF PRODUCTS LIABILITY § 2, cmt. f (1998); *accord, General Motors Corp. v. Sanchez*, 997 S.W.2d 584 (Tex. 1999) ("[P]laintiffs did not have to build and test an automobile transmission to prove a safer alternative design. A design need only prove 'capable of being developed.' "). But might the plaintiff run a strong risk of losing a design defect case if she can't afford to design, build, and test an

alternative design? RAD testimony is virtually always offered through an expert witness. Some decisions have discarded the testimony of highly qualified experts on the ground that the expert had not built and tested an alternatively designed product. *See Dhillon v. Crown Controls Corp.*, 269 F.3d 865 (7th Cir. 2001) ("neither expert has actually designed a model of a forklift truck with a rear door. Nor has either performed any tests of such a model to see if it is both economically feasible and just as safe or safer than the model without the door."); *see also Petersen v. Raymond Corp.*, 994 F.3d 1224 (10th Cir. 2021) (expert testimony excludable for failure to commit to any definite feasible design alternative).

9. **Manifestly unreasonable designs.** The Products Restatement provides that in one narrow case, the jury might properly infer that safer and reasonably feasible alternative designs were available without explicit evidence. Section 2, comment e, suggests that the designs of some products are so "manifestly unreasonable" because of their negligible utility and high risk of danger, that defectiveness could be found even without proof of an alternative. It uses the dangerous toy gun (*see* Note 3 above) as an example. Would a trampoline qualify, do you think? *See Parish v. ICON Health and Fitness, Inc.*, 719 N.W.2d 540 (Iowa 2006).

McCarthy v. Olin Corp.

119 F.3d 148 (2d Cir. 1997)

Meskill, Circuit Judge. . . .

On December 7, 1993, Colin Ferguson boarded the Long Island Railroad's 5:33 p.m. commuter train departing from New York City and opened fire on the passengers. Six people, including Dennis McCarthy, were killed and nineteen others, including Kevin McCarthy and Maryanne Phillips, were wounded in the vicious attack. Ferguson was armed with a 9mm semiautomatic handgun, which was loaded with Winchester "Black Talon" bullets (Black Talons). The injuries to Dennis and Kevin McCarthy and Maryanne Phillips were enhanced by the ripping and tearing action of the Black Talons because, unfortunately, the bullets performed as designed. [The plaintiffs sued the manufacturer of the bullets, alleging the negligent manufacture, advertising and marketing of a product that was unreasonably designed and ultrahazardous, the making of an unreasonably dangerous product, and strict liability in tort. The trial judge dismissed the complaint, and plaintiffs appealed].

The Black Talon is a hollowpoint bullet designed to bend upon impact into six ninety-degree angle razor-sharp petals or "talons" that increase the wounding power of the bullet by stretching, cutting and tearing tissue and bone as it travels through the victim. The Black Talon bullet was designed and manufactured by Olin Corporation (Olin) through its Winchester division and went on the market in 1992. Although the bullet was originally developed for law enforcement agencies, it was marketed and available to the general public. In November 1993, following public outcry, Olin pulled the Black Talon from the public market and restricted its sales to law enforcement personnel. Colin Ferguson allegedly purchased the ammunition in 1993, before it was withdrawn from the market. . . .

Appellants' first argument is that Olin should be held strictly liable for their injuries because the Black Talon ammunition was defectively designed and the design and manufacture of the bullets were inherently dangerous.

. . . Appellants argue that the Black Talons were defectively designed because the expansion mechanism of the bullets, which causes ripping and tearing in its victims, results in enhanced injuries beyond ordinary bullets. The district court rejected this argument because the expanding of the bullet was an intentional and functional element of the design of the product. We agree.

To state a cause of action for a design defect, plaintiffs must allege that the bullet was unreasonably dangerous for its intended use. "[A] defectively designed product is one which, at the time it leaves the seller's hands, is in a condition not reasonably contemplated by the ultimate consumer." This rule, however, is tempered by the realization that some products, for example knives, must by their very nature be dangerous in order to be functional. The very purpose of the Black Talon bullet is to kill or cause severe wounding. Here, plaintiffs concede that the Black Talons performed precisely as intended by the manufacturer and Colin Ferguson.

> Sadly it must be acknowledged that: [m]any products, however well-built or well-designed may cause injury or death. Guns may kill; knives may maim; liquor may cause alcoholism; but the mere fact of injury does not entitle the [person injured] to recover . . . there must be something wrong with the product, and if nothing is wrong there will be no liability.

DeRosa v. Remington Arms Co., 509 F.Supp. 762, 769 (E.D.N.Y.1981) (under New York law, shotgun as designed by defendant was not unreasonably dangerous for its foreseeable use).

Appellants have not alleged that the bullets were defective. As a matter of law, a product's defect is related to its condition, not its intrinsic function. The bullets were not in defective condition nor were they unreasonably dangerous for their intended use because the Black Talons were purposely designed to expand on impact and cause severe wounding.

Appellants next argue that under the risk/utility test analysis applied by New York courts, appellee should be held strictly liable because the risk of harm posed by the Black Talons outweighs the ammunition's utility. The district court properly held that the risk/utility test is inapplicable "because the risks arise from the function of the product, not any defect in the product." There must be 'something wrong' with a product before the risk/ utility analysis may be applied in determining whether the product is unreasonably dangerous or defective.

The purpose of risk/utility analysis is to determine whether the risk of injury might have been reduced or avoided if the manufacturer had used a feasible alternative design. However, the risk of injury to be balanced with the utility is a risk not intended as the primary function of the product. Here, the primary function of the Black Talon bullets was to kill or cause serious injury. There is no reason to search for an alternative safer design where the product's sole utility is to kill and maim. Accordingly, we hold that appellants have failed to state a cause of action under New York strict products liability law.

Appellants also argue that Olin should be held strictly liable because the Black Talon ammunition is "unreasonably dangerous per se." According to the appellants' theory, a product is unreasonably dangerous per se if a reasonable person would conclude that the danger of the product, whether foreseeable or not, outweighs its utility. As the district court held, this is essentially a risk/utility analysis, which we have refused to apply. Under New York's strict products liability jurisprudence, there is no cause of action for an unreasonably dangerous per se product. Thus, this claim was properly dismissed.

. . . The crux of appellants' negligence theory is that Olin negligently marketed and placed the Black Talon ammunition for sale to the general public. Appellants argue that because of the severe wounding power of the bullets, Olin should have restricted sales to law enforcement agencies, for whom the bullet was originally designed. They also argue that Olin should have known that their advertising, which highlighted the ripping and tearing characteristics of the bullet, would attract "many types of sadistic, unstable and criminal personalities," such as Ferguson. . . .

New York courts do not impose a legal duty on manufacturers to control the distribution of potentially dangerous products such as ammunition. Accordingly, although it may have been foreseeable by Olin that criminal misuse of the Black Talon bullets could occur, Olin is not legally liable for such misuse. As the district court pointed out, appellants have not alleged that any special relationship existed between Olin and Ferguson. Here, Olin could not control the actions of Ferguson. "[I]t is unreasonable to impose [a] duty where the realities of every day experience show us that, regardless of the measures taken, there is little expectation that the one made responsible could prevent the . . . conduct [of another]."

. . . To impose a duty on ammunition manufacturers to protect against criminal misuse of its product would likely force ammunition products— which legislatures have not proscribed, and which concededly are not defectively designed or manufactured and have some socially valuable uses—off the market due to the threat of limitless liability. Because Olin did not owe a legal duty to plaintiffs to protect against Colin Ferguson's horrible action, appellants' complaint does not state a cause of action for negligence and the claim was properly dismissed. . . .

[Judgment affirmed. Dissenting opinion omitted.]

NOTES

1. **Considering what is defective.** Does the product in *McCarthy* have more than negligible social utility when marketed to the public? Does it present an extremely high danger? Why, then, is it not "defective?" If a product's "sole utility is to kill and maim," does it follow that it is not defective when it inflicts as much pain and possible?

2. **Black Talons under a consumer expectations test.** Would it help the plaintiff in *McCarthy* to show that the Black Talon is "defective" if the court accepted the consumer expectations test? Psychological studies show that consumers, in judging what risks are acceptable, are influenced by factors unlike those entailed in risk-utility assessments. For instance, consumers in general appear to think a risk is high or a benefit is low according to their feelings unrelated to probability or even to actual harm that might be caused. The trustworthiness of the manufacturer might affect consumers' judgment about how risky or useful the product is, for example. This has led one commentator to suggest that since consumers dread some deaths more than others, the Black Talons might be judged defective on a revitalized consumer expectations test, based on expert studies of what risks consumers find unacceptable. Douglas A. Kysar, *The Expectations of Consumers,* 103 COLUM. L. REV. 1700, 1767, 1774 (2003). This idea was criticized in James A. Henderson, Jr. & Aaron D. Twerski, *Consumer Expectations' Last Hope: A Response to Professor Kysar,* 103 COLUM. L. REV. 1791 (2003). What do you think?

3. **Firearms: design defect theories.** Plaintiffs have had limited success in design defect cases against gun manufacturers where properly-working guns were at issue. In *Halliday v. Sturm, Ruger & Co.,* 792 A.2d 1145 (Md. 2002), a three-year-old found a hidden handgun that had no safety lock. The child also found the separately hidden ammunition, loaded the gun, and accidentally killed himself. The highest court of Maryland, though also emphasizing the father's fault, held that the gun was simply not defective—it worked exactly as it was designed and intended to work and as any ordinary consumer would have expected it to work. *Smith v. Bryco Arms,* 33 P.3d 638 (N.M. Ct. App. 2001), marked a different view. A teenager bought a handgun and ammunition for $40. He removed the magazine and then let friends examine the gun. They believed that with the magazine removed, it was impossible to fire the gun. One of them pulled the trigger. In fact there was a bullet in the chamber, the gun fired, and the bullet struck the other teenager in the face. The court held that a jury could find the handgun defective because it lacked both a trigger lock and a visual indication that the chamber was

loaded and because the jury could find that a mistaken belief that the gun was not loaded when the magazine was removed was foreseeable.

4. **Firearms: federal statutory immunity.** In 2005 Congress passed the Protection of Lawful Commerce in Arms Act (PLCAA), 15 U.S.C.A. §§ 7901–7903, and President George W. Bush signed it into law. The PLCAA prohibits legal claims against federally licensed manufacturers, distributors, dealers and importers of guns or ammunition "for the harm solely caused by the criminal or unlawful misuse of firearm products or ammunition products by others when the product functioned as designed and intended." The Act directed that any legal claims pending at the time of enactment "shall be immediately dismissed." The PLCAA has withstood constitutional attack in a number of cases. There are narrow exceptions, most notably where a manufacturer or seller (1) "knowingly violated a State or Federal statute applicable to the sale or marketing of the product, and the violation was a proximate cause of the harm for which relief is sought," or (2) "aided, abetted or conspired with any other person" to sell guns or ammunition "knowing, or having reasonable cause to believe, that the actual buyer . . . was prohibited from possessing or receiving" the product. *See Soto v. Bushmaster Firearms Intern., LLC*, 202 A.3d 262 (Conn. 2019) (estates of Sandy Hook Elementary School students and faculty could maintain claim against the manufacturer of the automatic rifle used in the 2012 massacre, based on a theory that defendant violated a Connecticut statute by marketing its weapon to civilians "for criminal purposes"). In early 2022, the families of nine Sandy Hook victims settled this suit against the gun manufacturer for $73 million, in what is believed to be the largest such settlement in U.S. history. Rick Rojas, Karen Zraick & Troy Closson, *Sandy Hook Families Settle with Gunmaker for $73 Million Over Massacre*, N.Y. TIMES, Feb. 15, 2022.

5. **Firearms: other theories of liability.** Prior to the passage of the PLCAA, a few courts had permitted plaintiffs to proceed on defective or negligent marketing claims, as where the plaintiffs allege that manufacturers deliberately promote sales through channels likely to lead to purchases by criminals and insane persons who are prohibited from buying from regular retailers. *See Ileto v. Glock, Inc.*, 349 F.3d 1191 (9th Cir. 2003); *City of Cincinnati v. Beretta U.S.A. Corp.*, 768 N.E.2d 1136 (Ohio 2002) (multiple theories including design defects and marketing to criminals so as to create a public nuisance).The PLCAA cuts off most tort cases involving firearms and ammunition, *see District of Columbia v. Beretta U.S.A. Corp.*, 940 A.2d 163 (D.C. 2008), but may leave room for some theories. *See, e.g., Smith & Wesson Corp. v. City of Gary*, 875 N.E.2d 422 (Ind. Ct. App. 2007) (allowing public nuisance action under PLCAA exception); *City of New York v. A-1 Jewelry & Pawn, Inc.*, 2007 WL 4462448 (E.D.N.Y. 2007) (same); *contra, City of New York v. Beretta U.S.A. Corp.*, 524 F.3d 384 (2d Cir. 2008) (state criminal nuisance statute could not support a civil claim consistent with the PLCAA).

NOTE: DEFECTIVE DRUGS

1. *Restatement Second.* Section 402A of the Restatement Second, comment k, provided that some products "are quite incapable of being made safe in their intended and ordinary use," saying that this is often true with drugs. The Pasteur rabies vaccine is given as the prime example, a vaccine which "not uncommonly leads to very serious and damaging consequences," but which guards against a disease which "invariably leads to a dreadful death." Thus, according to comment k, such a product is neither defective nor *unreasonably* dangerous. The court in *Cochran v. Brooke*, 409 P.2d 904 (Or. 1966), quoted this comment with approval in affirming a directed verdict for the drug manufacturer in a case in which the plaintiff was rendered almost blind as a result of taking a prescription drug for treatment of arthritis. Some courts still work out their products decisions in terms of the old § 402A, and hence apply comment k in drug and medical product cases. *See, e.g., Burningham v. Wright Medical Technology, Inc.*, 448 P.3d 1283 (Utah 2019).

2. *Restatement of Products Liability § 6.* The Products Restatement, by requiring foreseeable harm in all design defect claims, has made Comment k's special rules obsolete where the new Restatement is fully accepted. The Products Restatement actually goes further than Comment k by providing immunity in any cases where a reasonable health care provider who knows both the benefits and risks would prescribe the drug. RESTATEMENT OF PRODUCTS LIABILITY § 6 (1998). This seems to mean that manufacturers of drugs and related products need not exercise reasonable care under a risk-utility balance to make a safer drug. To get this protection, the drug must provide benefits in excess of harms, but it still need not be as safe as it could be with reasonable cost or effort. Most courts that have considered this provision of the Products Restatement have rejected it. 2 DOBBS, HAYDEN & BUBLICK, THE LAW OF TORTS §§ 456–462 (2d ed. 2011).

3. *Manufacturing defects.* Strict liability may still apply to drugs and medical products if a *manufacturing flaw* is demonstrated. *Transue v. Aesthetech Corp.*, 341 F.3d 911 (9th Cir. 2003) (breast transplants covered by Restatement (Second) § 402A, comment k, which exempts them from strict liability for design defects but does not exempt them from strict liability for manufacturing defects).

C. WARNING OR INFORMATION DEFECTS

LIRIANO V. HOBART CORP.

170 F.3d 264 (2d Cir. 1999)

CALABRESI, CIRCUIT JUDGE:

[Luis Liriano was severely injured on the job when his hand was caught in a meat grinder manufactured by Hobart Corporation and owned by his employer, Super Associated. The meat grinder had been sold to Super with a safety guard, but the safety guard was removed while the machine was in Super's possession and was not on the meat grinder at the time of the accident. The machine bore no warning indicating that the grinder should be operated only with a safety guard attached.

[Liriano sued Hobart, who brought a third-party claim against Super. The only claim that went to the jury was Liriano's failure to warn claim. The jury found for Liriano, attributing a degree responsibility to all three parties. Hobart and Super appealed, arguing (1) that there was no duty to warn, and (2) that even if there had been a duty to warn, the evidence presented was not sufficient to allow the failure-to-warn claim to reach the jury. The federal court certified both questions to the New York Court of Appeals, which rejected appellants' first argument but declined to address the second, leaving it for this court.]

More than a hundred years ago, a Boston woman named Maria Wirth profited from an argument about obviousness as a matter of law that is very similar to the one Hobart urges today. See Lorenzo v. Wirth, 170 Mass. 596, 49 N.E. 1010 (1898). Wirth was the owner of a house on whose property there was a coal hole. The hole abutted the street in front of the house, and casual observers would have no way of knowing that the area around the hole was not part of the public thoroughfare. A pedestrian called Lorenzo fell into the coal hole and sued for her injuries. Writing for a majority of the Supreme Judicial Court of Massachusetts, Oliver Wendell Holmes, Jr., held for the defendant. He noted that, at the time of the accident, there had been a heap of coal on the street next to the coal hole, and he argued that such a pile provided sufficient warning to passers-by that they were in the presence of an open hole. "A heap of coal on a sidewalk in Boston is an indication, according to common experience, that there very possibly may be a coal hole to receive it." And that was that.

It was true, Holmes acknowledged, that "blind men, and foreigners unused to our ways, have a right to walk in the streets," and that such people might not benefit from the warning that piles of coal provided to sighted Bostonians. But Holmes wrote that coal-hole cases were simple, common, and likely to be oft repeated, and he believed it would be better to establish a clear rule than to invite fact-specific inquiries in every such case. "In simple cases of this sort," he explained, "courts have felt able to determine what, in every case, however complex, defendants are bound at their peril to know." With the facts so limited, this was an uncomplicated case in which the defendant could, as a matter of law, rely on the plaintiff's responsibility to know what danger she faced.

Justice Knowlton disagreed. His opinion delved farther into the particular circumstances than did Holmes's opinion for the majority. In so doing, he showed that Lorenzo's failure to appreciate her peril might have been foreseen by Wirth and hence that Wirth's failure to warn might constitute negligence. He noted, for example, that the accident occurred after nightfall, when Lorenzo perhaps could not see, or recognize, the heap of coal for what it was. There was "a throng of persons" on the street, such that it would have been difficult even in daylight to see very far ahead of where one was walking. And the plaintiff was, in fact, a foreigner unused to Boston's ways. "[S]he had just come from Spain, and had never seen coal put into a cellar through a coal hole." In sum, the case was not the "simple" one that Holmes had made it out to be. What is more, none of the facts he recited was either unusual or unforeseeable by Wirth. "What kind of conduct is required under complex conditions, to reach the usual standard of due care, namely, the ordinary care of persons of common prudence, is a question of fact. . . . [and thus] a question for a jury." Even cases involving "obvious" dangers like coal holes, Knowlton believed, might not be resolvable as matters of law when viewed in the fullness of circumstances that rendered the issue less clear than it would be when posed in the abstract.

Holmes commanded the majority of the Supreme Judicial Court in 1898, but Knowlton's position has prevailed in the court of legal history. "'[T]he so-called Holmes view—that standards of conduct ought increasingly to be fixed by the court for the sake of certainty—has been largely rejected. . . . The tendency has been away from fixed standards and towards enlarging the sphere of the jury.'" Fowler V. Harper, Fleming James, Jr., & Oscar S. Gray, The Law of Torts § 15.3, at 358–59 n. 16 (2d ed.1986).

The courts of New York have several times endorsed Knowlton's approach and ruled that judges should be very wary of taking the issue of liability away from juries, even in situations where the relevant dangers might seem obvious. . . . [Even so] there have been situations in which New York state courts have deemed dangers to be sufficiently clear so that warnings were, as a matter of law, not necessary. See, e.g., . . . Caris v. Mele, 134 A.D.2d 475, 476, 521 N.Y.S.2d 260, 261 (1987) (holding that there is no duty to warn of the danger of diving headfirst into an above-ground swimming pool only four feet deep).

. . . Liriano was only seventeen years old at the time of his injury and had only recently immigrated to the United States. He had been on the job at Super for only one week. He had never been given instructions about how to use the meat grinder, and he had used the meat grinder only two or three times. And . . . the mechanism that injured Liriano would not have been visible to someone who was operating the grinder. It could be argued that such a combination of facts was not so unlikely that a court should say, as a matter of law, that the defendant could not have foreseen them or, if aware of them, need not have guarded against them by issuing a warning. . . .

Nevertheless, it remains the fact that meat grinders are widely known to be dangerous. . . . [W]e might well be of two minds as to whether a failure to warn that meat grinders are dangerous would be enough to raise a jury issue.

But to state the issue that way would be to misunderstand the complex functions of warnings. As two distinguished torts scholars have pointed out, a warning can do more than exhort its audience to be careful. It can also affect what activities the people warned choose to engage in. See James A. Henderson, Jr., and Aaron D. Twerski, Doctrinal Collapse in Products Liability: The Empty Shell of Failure to Warn, 65 N.Y.U. L.Rev. 265, 285 (1990). And where the function of a warning is to assist the reader in making choices, the value of the warning can lie as much in making known the existence of alternatives as in communicating the fact that a particular choice is dangerous. It follows that the duty to warn is not necessarily obviated merely because a danger is clear.

To be more concrete, a warning can convey at least two types of messages. One states that a particular place, object, or activity is dangerous. Another explains that people need not risk the danger posed by such a place, object, or activity in order to achieve the purpose for which they might have taken that risk. Thus, a highway sign that says "Danger—Steep Grade" says less than a sign that says "Steep Grade Ahead—Follow Suggested Detour to Avoid Dangerous Areas."

If the hills or mountains responsible for the steep grade are plainly visible, the first sign merely states what a reasonable person would know without having to be warned. The second sign tells drivers what they might not have otherwise known: that there is another road that is flatter and less hazardous. A driver who believes the road through the mountainous area to be the only way to reach her destination might well choose to drive on that road despite the steep grades, but a driver who knows herself to have an alternative might not, even though her understanding of the risks posed by the steep grade is exactly the same as those of the first driver. Accordingly, a certain level of obviousness as to the grade of a road might, in principle, eliminate the reason for posting a sign of the first variety. But no matter how patently steep the road, the second kind of sign might still have a beneficial effect. As a result, the duty to post a sign of the second variety may persist even when the danger of the road is obvious and a sign of the first type would not be warranted.

One who grinds meat, like one who drives on a steep road, can benefit not only from being told that his activity is dangerous but from being told of a safer way. . . . Given that attaching guards is feasible, does reasonable care require that meat workers be informed that they need not accept the risks of using unguarded grinders? Even if most ordinary users may—as a matter of law—know of the risk of using a guardless meat grinder, it does not follow that a sufficient number of them will—as a matter of law—also know that protective guards are available, that using them is a realistic possibility, and that they may ask that such guards be used. It is precisely these last pieces of information that a reasonable manufacturer may have a duty to convey even if the danger of using a grinder were itself deemed obvious.

. . . A jury could reasonably find that there exist people who are employed as meat grinders and who do not know (a) that it is feasible to reduce the risk with safety guards, (b) that such guards are made available with the grinders, and (c) that the grinders should be used only with the guards. Moreover, a jury can also reasonably find that there are enough such people, and that warning them is sufficiently inexpensive, that a reasonable manufacturer would inform them that safety guards exist and that the grinder is meant to be used only with such guards. Thus, even if New York would consider the danger of meat grinders to be obvious as a matter of law, that obviousness does not substitute for the warning. . . .

Hobart [also] raises the issue of causation. It maintains that Liriano "failed to present any evidence that Hobart's failure to place a warning [on the machine] was causally related to his injury." Whether or not there had been a warning, Hobart says, Liriano might well have operated the machine as he did and suffered the injuries that he suffered. Liriano introduced no evidence, Hobart notes, suggesting either that he would have refused to grind meat had the machine borne a warning or that a warning would have persuaded Super not to direct its employees to use the grinder without the safety attachment.

[Hobart's argument] assumes that the burden was on Liriano to introduce additional evidence showing that the failure to warn was a but-for cause of his injury. . . . But Liriano does not bear that burden. When a defendant's negligent act is deemed wrongful precisely because it has a strong propensity to cause the type of injury that ensued, that very causal tendency is evidence enough to establish a prima facie case of cause-in-fact. The burden then shifts to the defendant to come forward with evidence that its negligence was not such a but-for cause.

We know, as a general matter, that the kind of negligence that the jury attributed to the defendant tends to cause exactly the kind of injury that the plaintiff suffered. . . . In such situations, rather than requiring the plaintiff to bring in more evidence to demonstrate that his case is of the ordinary kind, the law presumes normality and requires the defendant to adduce evidence that the case is an exception. Accordingly, in a case like this, it is up to the defendant to bring in evidence tending to rebut the strong inference, arising from the accident, that the defendant's negligence was in fact a but-for cause of the plaintiff's injury.

This shifting of the *onus procedendi* has long been established in New York. Its classic statement was made more than seventy years ago, when the Court of Appeals decided a case in which a car collided with a buggy driving after sundown without lights. See Martin v. Herzog, 228 N.Y. 164, 170, 126 N.E. 814, 816 (1920). The driver of the buggy argued that his negligence in driving without lights had not been shown to be the cause-in-fact of the accident. Writing for the Court, Judge Cardozo reasoned that the legislature deemed driving without lights after sundown to be negligent precisely because not using lights tended to cause accidents of the sort that had occurred in the case. The simple fact of an accident under those conditions, he said, was enough to support the inference of but-for causal connection between the negligence and the particular accident. . . .

The words that Judge Cardozo applied to the buggy's failure to use lights are equally applicable to Hobart's failure to warn: "If nothing else is shown to break the connection, we have a case, prima facie sufficient, of negligence contributing to the result." . . . See Guido Calabresi, Concerning Cause and the Law of Torts: An Essay for Harry Kalven, Jr., 43 U. Chi. L.Rev. 69 (1975).

. . . The district court did not err. We affirm its decision in all respects.

[Concurring opinion omitted.]

NOTES

The Duty to Provide Information

1.   **Information defects.** As indicated in *Liriano*, a manufacturer's failure to provide appropriate information about a product may make an otherwise safe product dangerous and defective. Warnings about dangers represent one important kind of information necessary for some products. Thus, a product becomes defective when the product's foreseeable risks of harm could have been reduced or avoided by the provision of a reasonable warning, and the omission of such a warning renders the product "not reasonably safe." RESTATEMENT OF PRODUCTS LIABILITY § 2(c) (1998).

2.   **Warnings where equipment is initially safe.** The New York Court of Appeals had earlier rejected Hobart's argument that it owed no duty to warn as a matter of law, in *Liriano v. Hobart Corp.*, 700 N.E.2d 303 (N.Y.

1998). How could Hobart have a duty to warn about the dangers of operating its grinder without a guard when Hobart had equipped it with a guard?

3. **Functions of product information.** Necessary information to make a product reasonably safe may include directions for use, warnings, or some combination. Warnings may be needed either to alert users to risks that are not obvious, or to inform users of safer alternatives. *See* 2 DOBBS, HAYDEN & BUBLICK, THE LAW OF TORTS § 464 (2011).

Obvious Dangers

4. **Warning of obvious dangers.** Because the cost of giving a warning is usually rather small, it may be easy to conclude that the risk-utility balance always calls for a warning. Even so, some warnings simply are not needed. Should a manufacturer of safety glasses warn that they will break under the force of a five-pound sledge-hammer dropped from a height of seven feet? *Amer. Optical Co. v. Weidenhamer*, 457 N.E.2d 181 (Ind. 1983). Should a pickup truck manufacturer be required to warn of the risks of riding unrestrained in the open cargo bed? *Josue v. Isuzu Motors Amer., Inc.*, 958 P.2d 535 (Haw. 1998). Should a BB gun manufacturer warn users that the gun could kill someone shot from close range? *Abney v. Crosman Corp.*, 919 So.2d 289 (Ala. 2005). Are consumers more likely to read a few important warnings, or a long list including warnings about trivial risks?

As the Restatement Third has it, "no duty exists" to warn of dangers that are obvious or should be obvious. RESTATEMENT OF PRODUCTS LIABILITY § 2, cmt. j (1998). Is this merely the logical outcome of risk-utility balancing? And isn't it even more clearly dictated by a consumer expectations test? *See Braswell v. Cincinnati Inc.*, 731 F.3d 1081 (10th Cir. 2013). Some states have codified a no-duty rule. Michigan's statute, for example, provides that a "defendant is not liable for failure to warn of a material risk that is or should be obvious to a reasonably prudent product user or a material risk that is or should be a matter of common knowledge to persons in the same or similar position as the person upon whose injury or death the claim is based in a product liability action." MICH. COMP. LAWS § 600.2948(2).

5. **Obvious dangers and comparative fault.** Distinguish the no-duty rule from defenses based upon obvious danger. If the plaintiff is or should be actually aware of the specific danger and its magnitude, the defendant might avoid or limit liability under assumed risk or comparative negligence rules. See § 3, *infra*. Courts sometimes conflate the plaintiff-fault issue with the defendant-duty issue. In addition, courts may throw in proximate cause and "misuse" into the discussion. The straightforward explanation for most obvious danger problems, however, is simply that if the danger is foreseeably obvious in a significant degree, then the product is not defective at all for lack of a warning.

6. **Obvious dangers and design defects.** A product that presents an obvious danger, and thus provides its own warning, may still be defectively designed. Diving into a pool of unknown depth is obviously dangerous, so no

warning for that is required. However, if the manufacturer should foresee that harm will befall users in spite of the obvious danger, the manufacturer may be liable for design defect if it could easily mark the depth and failed to do so. *See Camacho v. Honda Motor Co.*, 741 P.2d 1240 (Colo. 1987) (a product can be unreasonably dangerous under the risk-utility test even if it is not more dangerous than the consumer expected; the consumer expectation test cannot be used to bar the plaintiff in such a case); *Uloth v. City Tank Corp.*, 384 N.E.2d 1188 (Mass. 1978) ("If a slight change in design would prevent serious, perhaps fatal, injury, the designer may not avoid liability by simply warning of the possible injury.").

7. **Obvious dangers and consumer expectations.** If the danger is truly obvious, the product could seldom be defective under the consumer expectations test, since the consumer could not expect safety in the face of obvious danger. What would the plaintiff's attorney argue in such a case? *See also Tabieros v. Clark Equip. Co.*, 944 P.2d 1279 (Haw. 1997) (open and obvious danger may prevent liability for failure to warn under consumer expectations test, but not necessarily under a risk-utility test).

8. **Warnings about defective designs.** Could a defendant escape liability for an injury caused by a defective design by pointing to a warning about that very design defect? *Compare Rivera v. Philip Morris, Inc.*, 209 P.3d 271 (Nev. 2009) ("We strongly adhere to the principle that a manufacturer must make products that are not unreasonably dangerous, no matter what instructions are given in the warning."), *with Hickerson v. Yamaha Motor Corp., U.S.A.*, 882 F.3d 476 (4th Cir. 2018) (under S.C. law, "an adequate warning operates to 'cure' a product's alleged design defects"). Which view seems preferable and why?

Causation

9. **The "heeding presumption."** Suppose the plaintiff proves that the defendant failed to give a warning that was needed to make the product safe and that a safe warning would have been on the label of the product or on instructions accompanying it. Most case law says that a failure to warn cannot be a cause of the plaintiff's harm unless a different warning would have altered the way the plaintiff used the product or would have prompted the plaintiff to take precautions to avoid the injury. *Motor Coach Industries, Inc. v. Khiabani ex rel. Rigaud*, 493 P.3d 1007 (Nev. 2021). But courts usually "presume" that the plaintiff would have read and heeded the warning, a phenomenon known as the "heeding presumption." *See, e.g., Moore v. Ford Motor Co.*, 332 S.W.3d 749 (Mo. 2011). This presumption is rebuttable by the defendant.

What result if the plaintiff admits that he did not read any of a product's accompanying instructions or warnings? *See Kirkbride v. Terex USA, LLC*, 798 F.3d 1343 (10th Cir. 2015) (when asked if he had read the safety manual for the front-loader on which he was injured, plaintiff responded, "Why would you read a manual?"); *see also Karst v. Shur-Co.*, 878 N.W.2d 604 (S.D. 2016). Consider a different scenario: the defendant fails to give a warning, but the plaintiff was already intimately familiar with the danger. Does the plaintiff's knowledge of the danger go to the issue of defendant's duty, the issue of cause in fact, or something else? *See Burke v. Spartanics, Ltd.,* 252 F.3d 131 (2d Cir. 2001) (facts similar to *Liriano* except the plaintiff knew the danger).

10.   **Shifting the burden of proof.** The *Liriano* court placed the burden on the defendant to prove that its negligent failure to warn was not a factual cause of the plaintiff's harm, once the plaintiff proved that such failure "greatly increased the likelihood of the harm that occurred." How, if at all, does this approach differ from the heeding presumption? Can you compare *Liriano*'s burden-shifting approach to that in *Barker v. Lull?*

CARRUTH V. PITTWAY CORP., 643 So.2d 1340 (Ala. 1994). Seven family members were killed in a house fire. Their estates sued Pittway, a smoke-detector manufacturer, claiming that the deaths were caused by its negligence in providing insufficient installation instructions and warnings. Just two days before the fire, the victims' father had installed the smoke detector near a ceiling-wall junction. The device was accompanied by a seven-page pamphlet, set in small type. The pamphlet stated: "Dead air spaces are often . . . in the corners between ceilings and walls. Dead air may prevent smoke from reaching a detector." None of these statements was captioned by the words "warning," "caution," or "danger," as were other cautionary statements. The "dead air" statements were contained in a portion of the pamphlet that included numerous instructions and illustrations that together "could be viewed as confusing at best." A colored and highly visible diagram purported to show effective smoke detector locations, including the area immediately below a wall-ceiling junction. Ultimately, "from the pamphlet's format and print size, and the seemingly sufficient diagram on the box, a fair-minded person could reasonably infer that a user would be induced to only scan the pamphlet and thereby not get from the pamphlet the information about dead-air-space." A jury question was thus presented "as to whether the Pittway pamphlet provided a legally adequate warning about dead-air-space concerns."

NOTES

1.   **Content or expression.** Warnings must be reasonably clear, and of sufficient force and intensity to convey the nature and extent of the risks to a reasonable person. "A manufacturer's techniques in promoting the product, inconsistencies or undue qualifications in stating the warning or directions, and depictions of uses that run counter to warnings may each nullify or dilute the warnings provided in printed literature. . . . When possible harm is severe, quite specific information may be required. A drug warning about possible blood clotting may disguise rather than reveal the possibility of a stroke." 2 DOBBS, HAYDEN & BUBLICK, THE LAW OF TORTS § 465 (2d ed. 2011). But a proposed alternative warning that contains too much detail may well be rejected by the court as unnecessary. *See, e.g., Weigle v. SPX Corp.,* 729 F.3d

724 (7th Cir. 2013) ("SPX was not required to explain the physics of the support stands to satisfy its duty to provide adequate instructions and warnings. Rather, it is enough that SPX instructed users on how to use the stand ('[a]lways use the support pin') and warned users of the inherent dangers of not following those instructions ('personal injury' with a pictogram of a load falling on a person).").

2.   **Form and location.** Placing a warning directly on a product can be effective, but a reasonable warning may be provided even in advertisements, posters or media releases; it is up to the jury to decide whether on the facts presented the warning's placement is reasonable. *See Patch v. Hillerich & Bradsby Co.*, 257 P.3d 383 (Mont. 2011). Can a warning be defective because it is in a form or location where it is not likely to be read? The father in *Carruth* admitted that he did not read the instruction pamphlet "in depth." Why wasn't this enough to support a summary judgment for the defense?

3.   **Nature and seriousness of harm.** Sometimes the warning must not only alert the user to danger and how to avoid it but also to the extent of harm that can result. In *Pavlik v. Lane Ltd./Tobacco Exporters International*, 135 F.3d 876 (3d Cir. 1998), the estate of a man who died from self-administered butane inhalation sued the distributor, claiming that the single warning on the can ("DO NOT BREATHE SPRAY") was inadequate. The court left it to the trier to determine whether a more specific warning would have averted the harm. What might such a warning have said? In *Benjamin v. Wal-Mart Stores, Inc.*, 61 P.3d 257 (Or. Ct. App. 2002), a Coleman heater carried this: "WARNING: FOR OUTDOOR USE ONLY. Never use inside house, camper, tent, vehicle or other unventilated or enclosed areas." Deceased used it in his tent while camping; the heater depleted the oxygen and the user died as a result. Was the warning adequate?

4.   **Duty to provide foreign language warnings.** If the warning must be reasonably clear, should it be presented in any language besides English? See *Farias v. Mr. Heater, Inc.*, 684 F.3d 1231 (11th Cir. 2012) (manufacturer of propane-gas heater had no duty to provide Spanish language warnings in the absence of evidence of specific marketing to Spanish-speaking customers). Should marketing be the deciding factor? Would it matter that the retailer that sold the heater had an internal policy for vendors to provide bilingual English and Spanish packaging?

5.   **Language of the warning.** In which languages should a warning be provided? *Cf. Nam Soon Jeon v. 445 Seaside, Inc.*, 2013 WL 431846 (D. Haw. 2013) (duty to warn in a foreign language "turns on the facts of the specific case. If, for example, a hotel catered exclusively to non-English speaking Korean tourists, a jury might reasonably determine that the absence of signs in both Korean and English was a breach of the duty to warn"). Should product warnings include pictures and symbols to help convey the message to non-readers? If a poison contains verbal warnings but no skull and crossbones or unhappy faces, is that adequate?

NOTE: LEARNED INTERMEDIARIES
AND SOPHISTICATED USERS

1. *Prescription drugs: the learned intermediary rule.* What warnings should accompany a prescription drug and to whom should the warnings be given? Most courts say the manufacturer must provide warnings only to the doctor who might prescribe, not directly to the patient. *See, e.g., Centocor, Inc. v. Hamilton,* 140 S.W.3d 140 (Tex. 2012) (recognizing only one state that has rejected the rule). When the manufacturer does in fact give appropriate warning or information to the physician, it is said that the physician is a "learned intermediary" upon whom the manufacturer can properly rely, and the warning can be couched in terms the physician can understand, not necessarily terms the consumer would grasp. And no warning at all is required if the physician already knows the danger. The rule has been extended "to exempt pharmacies from strict products liability when they properly fill a physician's prescription." *Schaerrer v. Stewart's Plaza Pharmacy, Inc.,* 79 P.3d 922 (Utah 2003).

2. *Direct marketing of drugs.* If a drug manufacturer advertises its prescription drugs directly to consumers, does the learned intermediary doctrine apply to defeat a consumer's failure-to-warn claim? *Perez v. Wyeth Laboratories., Inc.,* 734 A.2d 1245 (N.J. 1999), held that it did not. But few if any states have agreed with this "direct marketing exception." *See Watts v. Medicis Pharmaceutical Corp.,* 365 P.3d 944 (Ariz. 2016) (declining to adopt the *Perez* exception, saying only New Jersey follows it).

3. *The Products Restatement approach.* The Products Restatement provides that warnings about the health risks of prescription drugs and medical devices must be given directly to consumers only when the manufacturer knows or had reason to know that the learned intermediary "will not be in a position to reduce the risks of harm in accordance with the instructions or warnings." RESTATEMENT OF PRODUCTS LIABILITY § 6(d) (1998). When might this occur? Comment e gives as an example the administration of mass inoculation, where health care providers are not in a position to evaluate individualized risks of the vaccine. Patients should be directly warned in that situation, if such warnings are feasible and would be effective.

4. *Sophisticated users.* Similar rules apply to those who supply products to sophisticated users, meaning those users who are already aware or should be aware of the product's dangers, such as members of a trade or profession in which such knowledge is widespread. In such a case, the sophisticated users' knowledge of the product's dangers is the equivalent of prior notice. *See, e.g., Johnson v. American Standard, Inc.,* 179 P.3d 905 (Cal. 2008) (applying rule in case brought by air conditioning technician against air conditioning equipment manufacturer for failure to warn to equipment's dangers). Is the "sophisticated user" rule merely a

variant of the "open and obvious" rule? *See Webb v. Special Electric Co.,* 370 P.3d 1022 (Cal. 2016).

5. *Suppliers of bulk goods.* Similarly, those who supply goods in bulk may be permitted to rely upon their buyers to use the goods properly and to pass on any appropriate warnings. For instance, a supplier of bulk chemicals to a manufacturer ordinarily need not try to warn ultimate users of the manufactured product. This means that the product is not defective for lack of a warning to the ultimate consumer. Although some courts treat this "defense" as a rule of law, others make it turn on the reasonableness of relying upon the particular buyer to pass warnings along to those who might be affected. In the latter view, the trier would consider the risks and utilities and the ease or difficulty of giving a warning directly to the user who might be affected. *See Ritchie v. Glidden Co.,* 242 F.3d 713 (7th Cir. 2001); *cf. Ramsey v. Georgia Southern Univ. Advanced Development Center,* 189 A.3d 1255 (Del. 2018) (manufacturer had no duty to warn wife of industrial plant employee about dangers of laundering his asbestos-covered clothing, but employer could be liable for its failure to warn her and give her safe laundering instructions).

6. *Manufacturers of component parts.* Manufacturers of components used in producing a final, complete product are rarely required to warn ultimate users of dangers that may result from the way their components—or raw materials they have supplied—are integrated into the final product. *See Ramos v. Brenntag Specialties, Inc.,* 372 P.3d 200 (Cal. 2016); *Braaten v. Saberhagen Holdings,* 198 P.3d 493 (Wash. 2008). Nor does the manufacturer of one component part owe any duty to warn about the hazards of some other component part when both have been integrated by someone else into a final product. *See O'Neil v. Crane Co.,* 266 P.3d 987 (Cal. 2012).

A slightly different scenario is presented where a manufacturer knows that its product *must* be used in combination with a third-party product in order to function. In *Air & Liquid Systems Corp. v. DeVries,* 139 S.Ct. 986 (2019), the Court held that under maritime law, a manufacturer has a duty to warn when (1) its product requires incorporation of a part; (2) the manufacturer knows or has reason to know that the integrated product is likely to be dangerous for its intended uses; and (3) the manufacturer has no reason to believe that the product's users will realize that danger. *See also In re New York City Asbestos Litigation,* 59 N.E.3d 458 (N.Y. 2016) (steam-pipe valve manufacturers had duty to warn end users of the dangers arising from integrated product); *cf. Whelan v. Armstrong Intern. Inc.,* 231 A.3d 640 (N.J. 2020) (manufacturer of asbestos-containing component can be strictly liable for failure to warn of foreseeable dangers of third-party's asbestos-containing replacement component later integrated into the product during routine maintenance). *Contra, Coffman v. Armstrong Intern., Inc.,* 615 S.W.3d 888 (Tenn. 2021) (manufacturer had no duty to warn of the dangers associated with post-sale integration of asbestos-containing parts manufactured and sold by others, based on state statutory language that requires proof that a defect existed "at the time it left the control of the manufacturer or seller").

NOTE: POST-SALE WARNINGS

1. *The Products Restatement approach.* The Products Restatement provides that a seller or distributor is obliged to give a post-sale warning when a reasonable person would do so. A reasonable person would give such a warning if (a) he knew or should know that the product poses a substantial risk of harm; (b) those to whom a warning might be given can be identified and assumed to be unaware of the risk; (c) a warning can be effectively communicated; and (d) the risk of harm outweighs the burden of giving a warning. RESTATEMENT OF PRODUCTS LIABILITY § 10 (1998). The reasonable person standard means that a jury instruction on post-sale duty to warn should tell the jury to consider any factors that make it burdensome for the manufacturer to provide a warning. *Lovick v. Wil-Rich*, 588 N.W.2d 688 (Iowa 1999). In *Lewis v. Ariens Co.*, 751 N.E.2d 862 (Mass. 2001), the court reiterated its support for a post-sale duty to warn, but held that, as a matter of law, no duty existed where the manufacturer could not feasibly identify the potential victim because he had purchased the product secondhand sixteen years after it was originally sold, and did not own the product until years after a duty to provide additional warnings arguably arose. "In these circumstances, he is a 'member of a universe too diffuse and too large for manufacturers or sellers of original equipment to identify.'"

2. *Recognizing post-sale duties.* Courts are divided about post-sale duties and unsure how far to take them or where they could stop. On the one hand there is authority that if the danger is sufficient and the cost is limited, the manufacturer might even be obliged to provide a corrective device or make a repair itself. *See Gracyalny v. Westinghouse Elec. Corp.*, 723 F.2d 1311 (7th Cir. 1983). One area where post-sale duties are clear is in the area of drugs. Federal regulations require a drug manufacturer to monitor the effects of the drugs they place on the market and update the warning labels on such drugs. *See In re Accutane Litigation*, 194 A.3d 503 (N.J. 2018) ("Under federal law, the manufacturer is responsible for the adequacy of a drug's warnings not only when it files a [New Drug Application with the Food and Drug Administration], but also during the period when the drug is on the market after FDA approval.") Under the learned intermediary doctrine, these updated warnings are typically provided to prescribing doctors rather than directly to the users, however. *See Wyeth v. Levine*, 555 U.S. 555 (2009).

3. *Rejecting post-sale duties.* On the other hand, some courts have firmly denied that there is any post-sale duty at all, even to give a warning, where the product's defect was not known at the time of sale. *See, e.g., Jablonski v. Ford Motor Co.*, 955 N.E.2d 1138 (Ill. 2011) (manufacturer has no duty "to issue postsale warnings or to retrofit its products to remedy defects first discovered after a product has left its control"); *Bragg v. Hi-Ranger*, Inc., 462 S.E.2d 321 (S.C. Ct. App. 1995) (approving instruction that "[A] manufacturer, ladies and gentlemen, has no duty to notify previous purchasers of its products about later developed safety devices or to retrofit those products if the products were non-defective under standards existing at the time of the manufacture or sale."). Even where a post-sale duty to warn is not categorically rejected, "the seller's inability to identify those for whom warnings would be useful may prevent a post-sale duty to warn from arising." RESTATEMENT OF PRODUCTS LIABILITY § 10, cmt. e (1997); *see Wurster v. Plastics Group, Inc.*, 917 F.3d 608 (8th Cir. 2019) ("Without a direct relationship with users of its gas cans, TPG had no way of determining who purchased the cans and who should have been warned);

4. *Plaintiff's use of a post-sale warning as evidence.* Could a plaintiff introduce evidence of a warning that the manufacturer gave to users *after* the injury to the plaintiff occurred to prove that the earlier lack of a warning made the product defective? *See Giles v. Wyeth, Inc.*, 556 F.3d 596 (7th Cir. 2009) (no). Why such a holding?

5. *Statutory recall/repair duties.* Statutes or regulations may require post-sale warnings or repairs. Some standards for motor vehicles are set by federal regulation. If a manufacturer fails to comply with standards, the Secretary of Transportation may require the manufacturer to (a) give notice of the defect to purchasers and dealers and (b) to remedy the defect. 49 U.S.C.A. § 30118. The Consumer Products Safety Commission has the power to require a recall of dangerous products or to order their replacement. 15 U.S.C.A. § 2064(d). The Products Restatement limits liability for failure to recall or repair to cases in which a recall obligation is imposed by statute or regulation or in which the manufacturer voluntarily undertakes a recall and fails to follow through in a reasonable way. RESTATEMENT OF PRODUCTS LIABILITY § 11 (1998).

D. SPECIAL ISSUES OF PROOF

BITTNER V. AMERICAN HONDA MOTOR CO., 533 N.W.2d 476 (Wis. 1995). The plaintiff, riding a three-wheeled, all-terrain vehicle (ATV), suffered severe injuries when it overturned. The plaintiff sued the manufacturer asserting both negligence and strict product liability claims, in part because of the allegedly dangerous high-center-of-gravity design. The defendant introduced evidence (1) that injury rates associated with use of snowmobiles, mini-bikes and trail bikes were *less* than injury rates associated with ATVs; and (2) that injury rates of many sports, including scuba-diving and football, were much higher than rates associated with ATV use. From the first set of evidence, the defendant argued that because the recreational vehicles in question were similar in purpose to ATVs, the lower rate of injury suggested that ATV accidents were due to operator error. From the second set of evidence, the defendant argued that "if fewer individuals are injured riding ATVs than, for instance, playing football, then the risk of injury associated with ATV riding is reasonable." *Held,* the first set of evidence is admissible as tending to show operator error, but the second set of evidence is not admissible. Evidence of greater risks of activities that are generally acceptable is not relevant. "[T]he comparative risk evidence comparing ATV riding with dissimilar products and activities, such as sky diving, cannot be introduced, as Honda asserts, to demonstrate that ATVs are not unreasonably dangerous."

NOTES

1. **Similar accidents.** In design and information defect cases, evidence that a product either has or has not caused similar accidents is usually admissible as tending to show that the product was or was not defective, and that the defendant did or did not have notice of the danger. *See, e.g., Uniroyal Goodrich Tire Co. v. Martinez,* 977 S.W.2d 328 (Tex. 1998) (no error in admission of evidence of 34 other lawsuits against defendant involving similar product claims); *Spino v. John S. Tilley Ladder Co.,* 696 A.2d 1169 (Pa. 1997) (no abuse of discretion in the admission of testimony of company president that 100,000 of its ladders had been marketed in a 100-year period, without any prior claims against the company). However, when the plaintiff claims only a manufacturing flaw in the particular item, the safety history of the product line generally seems irrelevant. Does any of this sound like a basis for the *Bittner* court's ruling on the first set of evidence?

2. **Comparative risks and risk-utility weighing.** Consider the second set of evidence in *Bittner,* that the risks of injury in, say, football, were greater than the risks of injury in ATVs. If higher risks are acceptable in a variety of life's activities, would *Carroll Towing* or any form of risk-utility analysis suggest that the risk of ATVs would be a reasonable one? *Cf.* David A. Fischer, *Proportional Liability: Statistical Evidence and the Probability Paradox,* 46 VAND. L. REV. 1201 (1993) (arguing that liability limited to a percentage of the plaintiff's damages, based on proportional causation, is undesirable because whenever the environment generally becomes more dangerous, the liability of individuals would be reduced).

NOTE: SUBSEQUENT REMEDIAL MEASURES

Suppose that a plaintiff is injured by the defendant's product or property. After the defendant learns of the injury, he repairs the property or modifies the product to make it safer. The rule in negligence cases is that evidence of the defendant's subsequent remedial measures is not admissible to show negligence. First, subsequent repairs or other safety measures (like warnings) do not say much if anything about whether the defendant should reasonably have perceived danger before the injury or whether a reasonable person would have recognized the need for safety measures. Second, coupled with this low relevance is high risk that the jury would treat subsequent repairs as an admission of negligence. Third, courts have speculated that if evidence of subsequent safety measures were admissible, some defendants might refuse to make needed changes lest their efforts be used against them in court.

Federal Rule of Evidence 407 makes inadmissible evidence of remedial measures "taken after an injury or harm allegedly caused by an event," including such evidence offered to prove "a defect in the product, a defect in the product's design or a need for a warning or instruction." This rule applies only in federal court, and states are free to depart from it.

Some state courts do in fact hold that evidence of subsequent safety measures is admissible in strict liability products cases. A leading case is *Ault v. International Harvester Co.*, 528 P.2d 1148 (Cal. 1974); *see also Caprara v. Chrysler Corporation,* 417 N.E.2d 545 (N.Y. 1981) ("spirit of strict liability" and desire to aid plaintiff in proof make blanket exclusion in strict liability cases inappropriate); *Forma Sci., Inc. v. BioSera, Inc.*, 960 P.2d 108 (Colo. 1998) (such evidence should be admitted in strict liability design-defect cases, since its probative value outweighs any unfair prejudice to the manufacturer). Does the persuasive weight of these cases suffer in a state that adopts the Restatement of Products Liability, with its emphasis on risk-utility analysis and its rejection of strict liability for product defects?

Although in many jurisdictions, evidence of subsequent safety measures cannot be offered to prove negligence (and maybe not a product defect either), those subsequent safety efforts could at least indicate that a safer product is feasible. Such evidence has been admitted for that limited purpose. *Duchess v. Langston Corp.*, 769 A.2d 1131 (Pa. 2001) (where defendant put feasibility in issue, trial judge should admit evidence of subsequent remedial changes to show feasibility unless the evidence will be unduly prejudicial to the defendant).

NOTE: PROVING THAT A DEFECT CAUSED HARM
IN CASES REQUIRING EXPERT TESTIMONY

1. *Expert testimony.* A plaintiff in a products liability suit, just as in any other tort suit, must prove factual cause. In some products liability cases, such proof is not at all simple and is dependent on reliable expert testimony. *See, e.g., Moeller v. Garlock Sealing Technologies, LLC*, 660 F.3d 950 (6th Cir. 2011) (expert testimony was inadequate to prove that defendant's asbestos-containing gaskets caused a pipefitter's death from mesothelioma); *Whirlpool Corp. v. Camacho*, 298 S.W.3d 631 (Tex. 2009) (expert opinion that a design defect in a clothes dryer caused a fire was legally insufficient to support a verdict for plaintiff). And the plaintiff may face an initial hurdle in simply getting the expert testimony admitted into evidence. *See, e.g., Blackwell v. Wyeth*, 971 A.2d 235 (Md. 2009) (trial court did not abuse its discretion in excluding the testimony of plaintiffs' experts due to their lack of qualifications in epidemiology in a case alleging that the defendant's vaccines caused their son's autism).

2. *The Daubert standard.* The Supreme Court considered admissibility of scientific evidence in federal court in *Daubert v. Merrell Dow Pharmaceuticals, Inc.*, 509 U.S. 579 (1993). Under the *Daubert* decision, scientific opinion can be admitted as evidence even though it is not generally accepted. However, the trial judge must decide that it will be "helpful" to the jury and that the opinion offered is "derived by the scientific method," that is, based on "good grounds" in the light of what is known and testable in future scientific studies. The trial judge must make "a preliminary assessment of whether the reasoning or methodology underlying the testimony is scientifically valid" and whether it can be applied in the case. The judge should consider (a) whether the expert's theory or technique has been tested; (b) whether it has been subjected to peer review; (c) whether it has a known potential error rate; and (d) whether it is generally accepted. All these matters, however, are only factors; none is dispositive of the decision.

The trial judge's wide discretion in admitting expert testimony (or not) was reaffirmed in *General Electric Co. v. Joiner*, 522 U.S. 136 (1997) (holding that such rulings were reviewed only for an abuse of discretion). And in *Kumho Tire Co., Ltd. v. Carmichael*, 526 U.S. 137 (1999), the Court extended *Daubert* to all expert testimony, not just "scientific" testimony. Rule 702 of the Federal Rules of Evidence was then amended to state the principles behind these decisions rather than a list of factors. The *Daubert* test has been said to be designed primarily to exclude "junk science," and should not be misused by a judge as a way to make a preliminary inquiry into the merits of the plaintiff's case. *985 Assocs., Ltd. v. Daewoo Electronics America, Inc.*, 945 A.2d 381 (Vt. 2008) (reversing trial judge's decision to exclude expert testimony on causation, finding it met the

Daubert test even if in the judge's view it did not satisfy the plaintiff's burden of proof on the merits of the case). Nor should the court judge the expert's credibility; the court's "gatekeeper" role is to determine that the proffered testimony is both sufficiently reliable and relevant. *Sardis v. Overhead Door Corp.*, 10 F.4th 268 (4th Cir. 2021).

3. *State evidence law.* For trials in state court, federal evidence rules do not control, leaving states free to use their own standards for admissibility of expert testimony. The rule followed in federal courts and most state courts before *Daubert* was based on *Frye v. United States*, 293 F. 1013 (D.C. Cir. 1923). A dwindling minority of states continue to follow the *Frye* test, which requires that an expert's techniques must "generate results accepted as reliable within the scientific community generally, and are "sufficiently established to have gained general acceptance in the particular field in which it belongs." *See, e.g., Walsh v. BASF Corp.*, 234 A.3d 446 (Pa. 2020).

Frye has been characterized as an approach which "emphasizes counting scientists' votes, rather than on verifying the soundness of a scientific conclusion." *Parker v. Mobil Oil Corp.*, 857 N.E.2d 1114 (N.Y. 2006) (reaffirming New York's use of the *Frye* test rather than the *Daubert* test). This means that unless the expert is using a novel and not-generally-accepted methodology, no special analysis is required to determine the admissibility of expert testimony. *See Hayes v. Decker*, 822 A.2d 228 (Conn. 2003); *Castillo v. E.I. Du Pont de Nemours & Co., Inc.*, 854 So.2d 1264 (Fla. 2003).

4. *General and specific causation.* In toxic-tort and many pharmaceutical cases, professionals speak of "general causation" (*i.e.*, that a particular substance or product is capable of causing a given disease, and "specific causation" (*i.e.*, that exposure to the substance or product actually caused the particular plaintiff's harm). *See, e.g., Cornell v. 360 West 51st Street Realty, LLC*, 9 N.E.3d 884 (N.Y. 2014) (applying rules to tenant's case against landlord, alleging harms caused by exposure to dampness and mold). To prove factual cause, a plaintiff may have to produce expert testimony on both general and specific causation. *See, e.g., Merck & Co. v. Garza*, 347 S.W.3d 256 (Tex. 2011). In some cases, proof of general causation will be sufficient to prove specific causation, but this is not always true. *See, e.g., Terry v. Caputo*, 875 N.E.2d 72 (Ohio 2007); *Aventis Pasteur, Inc. v. Skevofilax*, 914 A.2d 113 (Md. 2007); RESTATEMENT (THIRD) OF TORTS: LIABILITY FOR PHYSICAL AND EMOTIONAL HARM § 28, cmt. c (2010). "General causation" seems an odd conception for lawyers. If a product is not capable of causing harm, how could it have caused the harm? And how can such a product be defective at all?

5. *Legal vs. scientific purposes.* The Supreme Court in *Daubert* viewed science as a continuous inquiry, with answers always tentative and

open to revision. More research, a better hypothesis, a different interpretation of data could all yield a different scientific picture. Judicial resolution of particular disputes, however, requires a final decision and a decision now, not one made after many years of further research. Does this difference between the goals and methods of science on the one hand and law on the other suggest anything about what law should do in toxic tort cases when the exact risk of the chemical in question cannot be determined? *See* Heidi Li Feldman, *Science and Uncertainty in Mass Exposure Litigation*, 74 TEX. L. REV. 1 (1995).

§ 3. DEFENSES AND DEFEATS

A. COMPARATIVE FAULT AND ASSUMPTION OF RISK

BOWLING V. HEIL CO.

511 N.E.2d 373 (Ohio 1987)

HERBERT R. BROWN, JUSTICE.

[Heil manufactured a dump hoist system which was installed on a dump truck owned by Rogers. Brashear borrowed the truck for personal use. He and Bowling delivered gravel to Bowling's residence and dumped it, but the truck bed would not return to the down position after the load had been dumped. Bowling leaned underneath over the truck chassis to see what was wrong. This put him underneath the upraised truck bed. In this posture he grabbed the control lever on the pump valve assembly and manipulated it. The truck bed rapidly descended upon him, killing him instantly. Bowling sued Heil and various others involved in the hoist assembly and controls. The jury found that Bowling was guilty of contributory negligence but did not assume the risk of injury. Damages were assessed at $1.75 million. The trial court and the court of appeals treated Bowling's contributory negligence in different ways.]

... Currently, two affirmative defenses based upon a plaintiff's misconduct are recognized. First, an otherwise strictly liable defendant has a complete defense if the plaintiff voluntarily and knowingly assumed the risk occasioned by the defect. Second, such a defendant is also provided with a complete defense if the plaintiff misused the product in an unforeseeable manner. The court of appeals below, construing Comment n to Section 402A, attempted to distinguish between negligent "affirmative action" by a plaintiff and negligent passive conduct by him in failing either to discover a defect or to guard against the possibility of its existence. The court held that although a plaintiff's passive contributory negligence provides no defense to a products liability action, his contributorily negligent "affirmative action" does provide a defense, and that such affirmative negligence should be compared by a jury to the fault of a strictly

liable manufacturer of a defective product, in a manner similar to the
principles of comparative negligence embodied in [the statute].

Comment n to Section 402A provides:

> "Contributory negligence. * * * Contributory negligence of the
> plaintiff is not a defense when such negligence consists merely in
> a failure to discover the defect in the product, or to guard against
> the possibility of its existence. On the other hand the form of
> contributory negligence which consists in voluntarily and
> unreasonably proceeding to encounter a known danger, and
> commonly passes under the name of assumption of risk, is a
> defense under this Section as in other cases of strict liability. If
> the user or consumer discovers the defect and is aware of the
> danger, and nevertheless proceeds unreasonably to make use of
> the product and is injured by it, he is barred from recovery."

The court of appeals has carved out a middle ground, to wit: contributory
negligence consisting of "affirmative action," theoretically located between
a plaintiff's failure to discover or guard against a defect and his voluntary
assumption of a known risk. There is no such middle ground. Comment n
covers the entire spectrum of conduct which can be termed "contributory
negligence," as applicable to products liability actions. That spectrum
begins with a mere failure to discover a defect in a product, continues with
a failure to guard against the existence of a defect, and concludes with an
assumption of the risk of a known defect. "Affirmative action" by the
plaintiff is not left uncovered. Failure to guard against a defect can be
"affirmative action." Indeed such would describe the conduct of David
Bowling in this case.

Under Comment n, either a plaintiff's contributory negligence
amounts to a voluntary assumption of a known risk, or it does not. If it
does, then that conduct provides an otherwise strictly liable defendant with
a complete defense. If it does not, the contributory negligence of the
plaintiff provides no defense.

In the case sub judice, the jury found that Bowling was contributorily
negligent but that he had not assumed a known risk. Therefore, his
contributory negligence did not provide Heil with a defense to appellant's
strict liability claim. . . .

The definitive statement of the policy and goals underlying the
application of strict liability in tort to cases involving defective products is
provided in Comment c to Section 402A, at 349–350:

> "On whatever theory, the justification for the strict liability has
> been said to be that the seller, by marketing his product for use
> and consumption, has undertaken and assumed a special
> responsibility toward any member of the consuming public who

may be injured by it; that the public has the right to and does expect, in the case of products which it needs and for which it is forced to rely upon the seller, that reputable sellers will stand behind their goods; that public policy demands that the burden of accidental injuries caused by products intended for consumption be placed upon those who market them, and be treated as a cost of production against which liability insurance can be obtained; and that the consumer of such products is entitled to the maximum of protection at the hands of someone, and the proper persons to afford it are those who market the products."

Dean Prosser has expressed this idea in slightly different terms:

"The costs of damaging events due to defectively dangerous products can best be borne by the enterprisers who make and sell these products. Those who are merchants and especially those engaged in the manufacturing enterprise have the capacity to distribute the losses of the few among the many who purchase the products. It is not a 'deep pocket' theory but rather a 'risk-bearing economic' theory. The assumption is that the manufacturer can shift the costs of accidents to purchasers for use by charging higher prices for the costs of products."

Prosser & Keeton, Law of Torts (5th Ed.1984) 692–693, Section 98.

Under negligence principles, on the other hand, liability is determined (and, under R.C. 2315.19, apportioned) according to fault. In negligence, we seek to make the person or persons responsible for causing a loss pay for it. In other words, we "blame" the loss on the negligent party or parties because it was they who could have avoided the loss by conforming to due care. Conversely, in strict liability in tort we hold the manufacturer or seller of a defective product responsible, not because it is "blameworthy," but because it is more able than the consumers to spread that loss among those who use and thereby benefit from the product.

We recognize that strict liability cannot be absolutely divorced from traditional concepts of fault. In a sense we "blame" the loss on the manufacturer or seller because it introduced the defective product into the marketplace. However, it must be reemphasized that strict liability is at odds with traditional notions of due care. . . .

Comparative negligence or comparative fault has been applied in products liability cases by a number of courts, both in states that have comparative negligence statutes and in states where comparative negligence was judicially adopted. On the other hand, numerous courts have refused to apply comparative negligence principles to products liability cases.

We believe that the better-reasoned decisions are those that decline to inject a plaintiff's negligence into the law of products liability. We agree with the court's holding in Kinard v. Coats Co., Inc. (1976), 37 Colo. App. 555, 557, 553 P.2d 835, 837, which states:

> ". . . Products liability under § 402A does not rest upon negligence principles, but rather is premised on the concept of enterprise liability for casting a defective product into the stream of commerce. * * * Thus, the focus is upon the nature of the product, and the consumer's reasonable expectations with regard to that product, rather than on the conduct either of the manufacturer or the person injured because of the product."

We agree with Justice Mosk of the California Supreme Court, who stated in his dissent in Daly v. General Motors Corp., supra:

> "The defective product is comparable to a time bomb ready to explode; it maims its victims indiscriminately, the righteous and the evil, the careful and the careless. Thus when a faulty design or otherwise defective product is involved, the litigation should not be diverted to consideration of the negligence of the plaintiff. The liability issues are simple: was the product or its design faulty, did the defendant inject the defective product into the stream of commerce, and did the defect cause the injury? The conduct of the ultimate consumer-victim who used the product in the contemplated or foreseeable manner is wholly irrelevant to those issues."

Therefore, when we search the decisions from other jurisdictions, we find no rationale which persuades us that comparative negligence or comparative fault principles should be applied to products liability actions.

Based upon the foregoing analysis, we hold that principles of comparative negligence or comparative fault have no application to a products liability case based upon strict liability in tort. Strict liability, in focusing on the product rather than the conduct of its manufacturer or seller, does not seek to apportion a loss among all persons who have caused or contributed to it. Rather, it seeks to spread the loss among all users of the product. The concept of comparative fault is fundamentally inapplicable.

We therefore reverse the judgment of the court of appeals with respect to its reduction of appellant's verdict by the thirty percent found by the jury to be attributable to contributory negligence. . . .

[Concurring and dissenting opinions omitted.]

NOTES

1. **Comparative-fault reductions.** *Bowling* applies the traditional rule that some forms of contributory negligence of the plaintiff are not a defense to a strict liability claim. Some courts continue to hold these views. *See, e.g., Jett v. Ford Motor Co.*, 84 P.3d 219 (Or. Ct. App. 2004) ("a plaintiff's incidental carelessness or negligent failure to discover or guard against a product defect is not an appropriate defense" to strict product liability claims); *Fontenot v. Taser Intern., Inc.*, 736 F.3d 318 (4th Cir. 2013) (under N.C. law, contributory negligence cannot be raised as a defense where the plaintiff was not a "user" of the product; the plaintiff was the administratrix of an arrestee who died after a police officer used stun gun, manufactured by defendant, on him). Most courts, however, apply comparative fault rules to strict products liability cases. *Daly v. General Motors Corp.*, 575 P.2d 1162 (Cal. 1978). The Products Restatement provides that whatever comparative responsibility system is used in a given state should apply to products liability claims as well. RESTATEMENT OF PRODUCTS LIABILITY § 17 (1998).

2. **Discovered vs. undiscovered defect.** Many states that do allow a contributory fault defense in products cases restrict that defense at times. In *Hernandez v. Barbo*, 957 P.2d 147 (Or. 1998), the plaintiff was a mechanic whose hand was partially amputated when it contacted a saw blade. He sued the saw's sellers and others, claiming that the product was defective because the on/off switch was inconspicuous. Defendants argued that the plaintiff was contributorily negligent. *Held*, a plaintiff's recovery will not be reduced when his negligence consisted solely of failure to discover or guard against the product's defect. Many courts agree with this rule. Texas has said that "a duty to discover defects, and to take precautions in constant anticipation that a product might have a defect, would defeat the purposes of strict liability." *General Motors Corp. v. Sanchez*, 997 S.W.2d 584 (Tex. 1999). Does this distinction between failing to discover or guard against defects and other kinds of negligence make sense? Would it be better to formulate the rule by saying that a plaintiff is not negligent for trusting the defendant's product until there is some reason to distrust it?

3. **Obvious danger.** We have seen that a product is sometimes considered defective even when its danger is obvious and the plaintiff could be safe by taking the product's characteristics into account. In such a case, would a state adopting the Products Restatement's rule of comparative fault reduce the plaintiff's recovery? And would a court applying the *Bowling* rule allow full recovery?

4. **Assumption of the risk.** Recall that in a growing number of states, implied assumption of risk is subsumed within the comparative responsibility rules, and is not regarded as a separate defense at all. *See* Chapter 10 § 2. Some states continue to agree with the *Bowling* court's view, however, that assumption of risk is a complete defense to a strict products liability suit, even if contributory negligence is not. *See* DOBBS, HAYDEN & BUBLICK, HORNBOOK ON TORTS § 33.17, at 835 (2d ed. 2016). Should courts distinguish between a

plaintiff's negligence and "assumption of the risk," or should all forms of plaintiff "misconduct" enter into the comparison?

5. ***Bexiga.*** If you would apply ordinary comparative negligence in products cases, maybe there are still cases in which you would not want to apply it. How would you feel about applying the comparative fault rule in *Bexiga v. Havir Mfg. Corp.*, 290 A.2d 281 (N.J. 1972), in Chapter 9 § 5—where the defendant was found to owe a duty to protect the plaintiff from his own carelessness? Or an eclectic approach in which you apply comparative fault where you think it would encourage safety by the plaintiff without removing safety incentives of the defendant? *See Cotita v. Pharma-Plast, U.S.A., Inc.,* 974 F.2d 598 (5th Cir. 1992) (nurse exposed to AIDS virus as a result of defectively capped needle, but nurse was himself negligent).

6. **Effect on deterrence.** Does taking a plaintiff's contributory negligence into account in a products liability case remove incentives from manufacturers to make their products safer? Is this a greater problem in those states that follow either modified comparative fault or the old contributory negligence rules, where barring a plaintiff entirely on negligence grounds is a very real possibility? Or is the newer approach of the Products and Apportionment Restatements a sound way to account for a plaintiff's own responsibility for causing injury?

7. **Causal apportionment.** Suppose the plaintiff's fault contributes to his injury and so does the defendant's defective product, but it is possible to say that the product caused a broken arm and the plaintiff's fault caused a broken leg. Would either *Bowling* or *Daly* (Note 1, *supra*) foreclose a causal apportionment? Alternatively, suppose that the injury is indivisible so that no causal apportionment is possible between the plaintiff and the defendant. In *Owens Corning Fiberglass Corp. v. Parrish,* 58 S.W.3d 467 (Ky. 2001), the plaintiff's smoking contributed to a lung disease and the defendant's defective product contributed to a different lung disease, both resulting in a shortness of breath. It was not possible to say how much of the plaintiff's ultimate injury resulted from the asbestosis. Consequently the court permitted the jury to use comparative fault to apportion responsibility. What result under *Bowling*?

B. MISUSE

HUGHES V. MAGIC CHEF, INC.

288 N.W.2d 542 (Iowa 1980)

UHLENHOPP, JUSTICE. . . .

Plaintiff Vincent E. Hughes was severely burned on March 9, 1976, when a stove manufactured by defendant Magic Chef, Inc., exploded in his mobile home. The propane gas tank which fueled the stove had run dry on March 7, 1976. After the propane tank was refilled that evening, two pilot lights on the top of the stove were re-lit but a third pilot light in the oven broiler cavity was not re-ignited. Experts testified that a resultant buildup of propane gas in the stove produced an explosion and fire when Hughes attempted to use the stove on the evening of March 9th. . . .

Hughes and his wife Eileen brought this strict liability action against Magic Chef, alleging the stove was unreasonably dangerous in several respects. Magic Chef raised affirmative defenses of assumption of risk and misuse of product. The jury found for Magic Chef and the trial court overruled the Hugheses' motion for new trial. Hugheses then appealed. . . .

As to Hughes' first argument, this court held in *Rosenau* that in an ordinary negligence case in which the defendant raises the issue of the plaintiff's own negligence, assumption of risk is not to be pled and submitted as a separate defense. Instead, the essential elements of assumed risk, if supported by substantial evidence, are to be included in the contributory negligence instruction. Separate instructions on those defenses might result in the jury's rendering inconsistent verdicts and in the trial court's over-emphasizing a particular aspect of a case.

Hughes' argument that the *Rosenau* reasoning applies equally to the products liability defenses of misuse of product and assumption of risk does not recognize the differing natures of those two issues. Misuse precludes recovery when the plaintiff uses this product "in a manner which defendant could not reasonably foresee." Assumption of risk is a defense to a strict liability action when the plaintiff has "voluntarily and unreasonably proceed[ed] to encounter a known danger. . . ." The misuse of product doctrine has to do with the producer's responsibility in the first place; he has no liability at the outset if the product is misused. The assumption of risk doctrine has to do with the user's culpability; he bars himself from recovering if he voluntarily proceeds in the face of known danger. Although we recognize that in certain cases a plaintiff might have *both* used the product in a manner which the defendant could not reasonably foresee and voluntarily and unreasonably proceeded to encounter a known risk, we reject the idea that a plaintiff cannot do one without doing the other.

Despite our rejection of Hughes' attempt to apply *Rosenau* by analogy to this case, we agree with his basic contention that the trial court should not have given an instruction on misuse as a *defense* in this strict liability action. Misuse is not an affirmative defense but rather has to do with *an element of the plaintiff's own case.*

This conclusion departs somewhat from language in some of our prior products cases. Under that language the misuse issue may arise twice: first in connection with the plaintiff's prima facie case and again in connection with the defendant's affirmative defense. . . . [A]s part of his prima facie case, the plaintiff must establish that the product was unreasonably dangerous in a reasonably foreseeable use.

We have also said, however, that a defendant may defend a section 402A action by pleading and proving that the injured person misused the product, that is, he used it in a manner not reasonably foreseeable. The result of this prior language is that precisely the same issue—whether the product was used in a reasonably foreseeable manner—may be decisive both as to whether the plaintiff made a prima facie case and as to whether the defendant established an affirmative defense.

If we continued to treat misuse as an affirmative defense distinct and additional to the plaintiff's burden of proving that the product was used in reasonably foreseeable manner, we would create the potential for inconsistent jury findings in the same case. In addition we would create the possibility of a shifting burden of proof on the issue. The burden of proof regarding the use made of the product should not shift depending on the subtle distinction of whether the defendant offers evidence of misuse to rebut the plaintiff's evidence or instead offers it "to support an affirmative defense he is attempting to raise." . . .

Misuse of product is no longer to be considered an affirmative defense in products liability actions but is rather to be treated in connection with the plaintiff's burden of proving an unreasonably dangerous condition and legal cause. Regardless of whether a defendant does or does not plead misuse of the product, the burden is on the plaintiff to prove that the legal cause of the injury was a product defect which rendered the product unreasonably dangerous in a reasonably foreseeable use. . . .

Hughes' second challenge to the misuse instruction is that it erroneously held him to a "reasonableness" standard in the use of the product. The instruction directed the jury as follows:

> The Defendant asserts the affirmative defense that the Plaintiff Vincent Hughes misused the stove. The burden of proof is on the Defendant.
>
> The Defendant claims that this Plaintiff knew, or ought reasonably to have known, of the existence of the pilot light in the oven area and that it was not lit after the service call by the Thermogas service man. The Defendant claims further that the Plaintiff took no action to relieve against this situation but instead attempted to utilize the oven or broiler on the second day thereafter and that such constituted a misuse of the stove by this Plaintiff.
>
> If you find the Defendant has proved the above, that such action or failure to act on the part of the Plaintiff was not reasonably foreseeably [sic] by the Defendant, and further that such action or failure to act by the Plaintiff was the proximate cause of the accident, then the Plaintiff may not recover. . . .

If Hughes is correct that this misuse instruction imposes a "reasonableness" standard on his conduct the instruction is indeed erroneous, for in some situations negligent use of a product by a consumer is reasonably foreseeable by the producer and therefore is not "misuse" for liability purposes. To hold otherwise would interpose contributory negligence as a defense under the guise of misuse.

We find no necessity to resolve this issue, however, because the misuse instruction is objectionable on another ground; it gives undue emphasis, in such an instruction, to what Hughes personally knew or should have known.

If the ordinary user would reasonably be aware that use of a product in a certain way is dangerous, use of the product in that manner is less foreseeable by the producer than a use to which danger is not normally ascribed. But the ordinary user's awareness that use of the product in a certain manner is dangerous does not conclusively establish that such use is not reasonably foreseeable, for the defendant may in a given case reasonably foresee that a given product will be used by persons such as children who do not possess the knowledge of the ordinary user. Hence knowledge which can be reasonably attributed to the ordinary user is to be considered as a factor in determining whether the manner in which the plaintiff used the product was reasonably foreseeable.

The problem with the misuse instruction here is that it specifically directed the jury to consider what Hughes knew or ought reasonably to have known. What Hughes knew or should have known about the pilot light has slight relevance to the issue of whether Magic Chef should reasonably have foreseen the use to which the stove was put. The personal characteristics of users or, in this case, knowledge of users, becomes relevant to foreseeability of use only when the characteristics are attributable to a substantial group of users. By including a specific reference to what Hughes knew or should have known, the misuse instruction invited the jury to consider a matter of little relevance to the issue it had to resolve—whether Magic Chef should reasonably have foreseen that users would attempt to operate the stove after an interruption in gas service without first igniting all the pilot lights.

We thus hold that on retrial misuse is not to be treated in the jury instructions as an affirmative defense. Instead, the instructions with respect to the use to which the stove was put must place the burden of proof on Hughes to establish by a preponderance of the evidence that the use made of the stove was reasonably foreseeable by Magic Chef. Reference to knowledge reasonably attributable to the ordinary user may be made, but the instruction must make clear that such knowledge is one factor to be weighed in determining whether Hughes' manner of using the product was reasonably foreseeable by Magic Chef. If on retrial Hughes proves by a preponderance of the evidence that the use made of the stove was reasonably foreseeable and that the stove was unreasonably dangerous when so used, then he will have established the first element of his case; otherwise the case is over.

Reversed.

NOTES

1. **What "misuse" might mean.** What does the *Hughes* court think about unforeseeable misuse of a product that causes harm? (a) Unforeseeable misuse means the plaintiff is guilty of contributory negligence. (b) Unforeseeable misuse means the plaintiff assumed the risk. (c) Unforeseeable misuse means that, with respect to harms caused by the misuse and that would not have been caused by a properly used product, the product simply is not defective at all. *See Matthews v. Remington Arms Co.*, 641 F.3d 635 (5th Cir. 2011) (use of rifle without bolt-assembly pin was not a reasonably anticipated use, thus gun was not defective in design). In *Payne v. Gardner*, 56 So.3d 229 (La. 2011), a 13-year-old boy climbed onto the moving pendulum of an oil well pump and attempted to "ride" it. He was injured—thankfully not killed—and sued the manufacturer of the oil well pump, claiming a design defect. How should that case be analyzed?

2. **Defendant strategy.** Suppose you are in a jurisdiction that considers plaintiff's comparative fault in a products liability action to reduce recovery. If you represent the defendant would you rather establish (a) no defect or (b) plaintiff's fault? Why?

3. **Comparing contributory fault, assumption of risk and no-defect.** How can you determine whether the plaintiff's conduct is "misuse" on the one hand or contributory fault or assumed risk on the other? Is it more important to distinguish one kind of act from another, or foreseeable uses from unforeseeable ones? *Cf. Campbell Hausfeld/Scott Fetzer Co. v. Johnson*, 109 N.E.3d 953 (Ind. 2018) (applying statute, "misuse" is a complete defense, but is proven only where such misuse caused the harm and was "not reasonably expected by the seller").

4. **Comparative apportionment.** Many courts today apply comparative fault principles to products strict liability cases and also treat misuse as merely one form of comparative fault. *Chapman v. Maytag Corp.*, 297 F.3d 682 (7th Cir. 2002).

5. **Misuse as superseding cause.** Remember that regardless of the legal theory being used, the plaintiff must prove that the defect in the product (or, if negligence is the theory, the defendant's conduct) is both a factual and proximate cause of her injury. *See, e.g., Stahlecker v. Ford Motor Co.*, 667 N.W.2d 244 (Neb. 2003) (motorist was murdered after the tires on her car failed, stranding her in a dangerous area; manufacturer not liable because there was no "causal relationship" between any product defect and the murder). Might "misuse" be regarded as a type of superseding cause, thus causing a failure of the prima facie case on scope of liability (proximate cause)

grounds? *See Moyer v. United Dominion Industries, Inc.*, 473 F.3d 532 (3d Cir. 2007) (Pa. law). Could the *Payne* case in Note 1, *supra*, be viewed this way?

In *Hood v. Ryobi America Corp.*, 181 F.3d 608 (4th Cir. 1999), the plaintiff was injured when a blade detached from a miter saw he was using. The plaintiff had removed the saw's guards in contravention of unambiguous warnings. In his suit against the manufacturer, *held*, summary judgment for defendant was proper. The plaintiff's act of alteration was the superseding cause of his harm. If the alteration had been foreseeable to the manufacturer, would the analysis and outcome change?

In *Jeld-Wen, Inc. v. Gamble*, 501 S.E.2d 393 (Va. 1998), parents sued a window and screen manufacturer for negligence and breach of warranty after their infant pushed on the screen and then fell two stories to the ground when it gave way. Could the child's own "misuse" constitute a complete defense? What do you see as the key arguments?

6. **Foreseeability of misuse.** In many states, the manufacturer must ordinarily design a product reasonably in the light of known or foreseeable misuses, not merely for "intended" use. Thus the usual rule of "crashworthiness" (see § 2.B, *supra*) is that if a car will collapse when it is in a foreseeable collision, it may be defective, even though the manufacturer never intended it to be crashed. *Slone v. General Motors Corp.*, 457 S.E.2d 51 (Va. 1995); *see also Collins v. Navistar, Inc.*, 155 Cal.Rptr.3d 137 (Ct. App. 2013) (truck manufacturer could be held liable in products case where windshield was shattered by chunk of concrete thrown from a levee; manner of harm did not matter if chunk of concrete was a reasonably foreseeable road hazard). Foreseeability has also become the test for bystander injury. When misuse is foreseeable and a reasonable alternative design would have prevented harm from the misuse, the manufacturer cannot avoid liability on the ground that the product was not defective or that the defect was not a proximate cause. *See, e.g., Perkins v. Wilkinson Sword, Inc.*, 700 N.E.2d 1247 (Ohio 1998) (rejecting argument by cigarette lighter manufacturer that it did not have to make its lighters childproof, since children are not the intended users). Bear in mind, however, that in some cases a plaintiff's "misuse" might be regarded as a form of contributory fault or assumed risk, with whatever defensive advantage those doctrines might produce.

7. **Well-known dangers.** If a product's danger is well-known and generally understood, should the manufacturer be liable for foreseeable "misuse"? Manufacturers of alcohol can certainly foresee that users of that substance will on occasion, or even very often, become intoxicated and harm themselves or others. Is foreseeability of this misuse enough to make the manufacturer prima facie liable? In *Joseph E. Seagram & Sons, Inc. v. McGuire*, 814 S.W.2d 385 (Tex. 1991), the plaintiffs were alcoholics suing the manufacturers and distributors of the brands they drank. They claimed that the defendants depicted alcohol as safe when in fact it was not and that the defendants should have warned them of the danger and the addictive quality

of alcohol. The court held that the danger of alcohol in causing alcoholism has long been generally known, and that no duty was owed the plaintiffs.

8. **Statutory solutions.** In some states, statutes resulting from "tort reform" initiatives by defense groups have addressed the issue just raised. A California statute provides:

> (a) In a product liability action, a manufacturer or seller shall not be liable if both of the following apply:
>
>> (1) The product is inherently unsafe and the product is known to be unsafe by the ordinary consumer who consumes the product with the ordinary knowledge common to the community.
>>
>> (2) The product is a common consumer product intended for personal consumption, such as sugar, castor oil, alcohol, and butter, as identified in comment i to Section 402A of the Restatement (Second) of Torts.

CAL. CIV. CODE § 1714.45. Similar provisions have been enacted in other states as well. *E.g.,* N.J. STAT. ANN. § 2A:58C–3(a)(2).

9. **Intended users.** Courts used to say that the product was not defective if it was reasonably safe for intended users. In *Phillips v. Cricket Lighters,* 841 A.2d 1000 (Pa. 2003), people died in a fire started by a two-year-old's use of a lighter that lacked available child-proofing. The lead opinion of a divided court held that the manufacturer would not be strictly liable because it intended the lighter to be used only by adults, even though child use was foreseeable. Other courts follow a test of foreseeability rather than intention. One of the claims arising from the September 11 crashes was for death and injury to persons on the ground. The plaintiffs claimed that the Boeing planes had defective cockpit doors that permitted terrorists to take control and ultimately to crash the planes. Boeing argued that "since the terrorists who hijacked the airplanes were not the intended users of the cockpit doors, one cannot say that the doors were unreasonably dangerous or unsafe in relation to the use that terrorists would be expected to make of the doors." *In re Sept. 11 Litig.,* 280 F.Supp.2d 279 (S.D.N.Y. 2003). The court of course rejected that argument. For the most part, "intended user" is no longer the governing test.

NOTE: THIRD-PARTY MODIFICATION OR MISUSE

1. *A third party's "misuse" or modification as superseding cause.* Could a defendant argue that a third party—such as the plaintiff's employer—"misused" the product, for example by modifying it, and that action was a superseding cause of the harm? In *Reid v. Spadone Machine Co.,* 404 A.2d 1094 (N.H. 1979), the defendant, a manufacturer of a "guillotine-type" cutting machine on which the plaintiff was injured, made that very argument. The court said this:

"In the usual case, no reason of the law stands to prevent a defendant in a products liability action from arguing a third person's negligence or misuse of the product as the sole proximate cause of the plaintiff's injury. The availability of this defense depends, however, on the foreseeability of the alleged misuse or negligence and, on the nature of the alleged design defect. In New Hampshire, the manufacturer is under a general duty to design his product reasonably safely for the uses which he can foresee. This duty is necessarily limited to foreseeing the probable results of the normal use of the product or a use that can reasonably be anticipated. Thus, before a defendant may successfully argue a third person's negligence or misuse as a superseding cause, he must prove that the negligence or misuse was not reasonably foreseeable."

2.   *The role of foreseeability.* Is the foreseeability of third-party "misuse" determinative? *Compare Robinson v. Reed-Prentice Division of Package Co.,* 403 N.E.2d 440 (N.Y. 1980) (employer modified machine by removing a safety feature to make it work faster; the manufacturer knew that the employer had modified like machines in the past, but the manufacturer was not strictly liable: "Substantial modifications of a product from its original condition by a third party . . . are not the responsibility of the manufacturer"), *with Tanksley v. ProSoft Automation, Inc.,* 982 So.2d 1046 (Ala. 2007) (manufacturer remains liable for a design defect if the alteration was foreseeable). *Cf. Snyder v. LTG Lufttechnische GmbH,* 955 S.W.2d 252 (Tenn. 1997) (evidence that plaintiff's employer removed a safety device from its cotton press, resulting in plaintiff's injury, was admissible to prove that product was not defective).

In *Hoover v. New Holland North America, Inc.,* 11 N.E.3d 693 (N.Y. 2014), the daughter of a man driving a tractor-driven post-hold digger was injured when her coat became caught in the machine. Evidence showed that the digger's safety shield had been removed, after years of use, by the owner of the digger. In a suit against the digger's manufacturer by the injured plaintiff, the defendant raised the "substantial modification defense" established in *Robinson, supra.* Reversing a summary judgment for defendant, the court held that the reason the owner removed the shield was key: here, he had removed it because it was no longer functional, not because he wanted the machine to operate faster. Thus the gravamen of plaintiff's complaint was that the shield itself was defectively designed; the substantial modification defense simply did not apply.

3.   *Statutes.* Some states deal with the product-modification issue by statute. *See, e.g., Stark v. Ford Motor Co.,* 723 S.E.2d 753 (N.C. 2012) (allowing manufacturer to defend a design defect case under state statute providing for non-liability where someone other than the manufacturer

altered the product after it left the manufacturer's control, unless the manufacturer consented to or directed the modification).

NOTE: WARNINGS AND DISCLAIMERS

1. *Warnings and misuse.* Misuse is intimately related to questions about warnings, instructions, and obvious or generally known dangers. For instance, in *Hughes v. Magic Chef*, if Magic Chef had given no instructions or warnings about the number or location of pilot lights, it might be quite easy to say that the product was defective for lack of a warning or instructions and by the same token that the plaintiff's failure to light the third pilot was entirely foreseeable. Conversely, if the user is fully shielded by instructions and warnings, his violation of instructions or failure to heed warnings may quite easily count as an unforeseeable misuse. In *Halliday v. Sturm, Ruger & Co., Inc.*, 770 A.2d 1072 (Md. Ct. Spec. App. 2001), a father purchased a handgun and kept it under his mattress with shells located elsewhere. His three-year-old son allegedly found the gun there and managed to load the magazine. While playing with the gun he accidently shot himself. He died. The gun could have had a trigger lock to protect against such a discharge, but it did not. Still, the court held that the gun was not defective. One reason was that the father was chargeable with unforeseeable misuse. Was it really unforeseeable? The plaintiff argued that the manufacturer was aware that parents left guns unlocked, but the court thought that the explicit warning that accompanied the gun made the father's action in storing the gun under the mattress unforeseeable as a matter of law.

2. *Disclaimers.* Granted that a manufacturer can exert a degree of control over the misuse issue by providing warnings or instructions about use, can the manufacturer or other supplier of a product simply disclaim liability altogether? Suppose the product were covered with embossed warnings in bright red letters saying "This product is dangerous. Use it at your own risk. The manufacturer is not liable for any injury that may result." Or suppose the manufacturer provided for a limited remedy by saying that it would be liable for any defects in the product, but only for the cost of repair or replacement.

— For tort law claims for personal injury, the usual answer is that the manufacturer cannot avoid liability by disclaimers. *See* RESTATEMENT OF PRODUCTS LIABILITY § 18 (1998).

— For warranty claims under the UCC, a warranty may be effectively disclaimed. UCC Art. 2–316. If it is effectively disclaimed, the plaintiff would have no warranty claim. If it is *not* effectively disclaimed, the seller can still limit remedies for consequential damages, except that, prima facie, it is unconscionable to limit damages for personal injury resulting from the breach of warranty. Unconscionable limitations are not enforceable in the courts. UCC Art. 2–719.

Suppose the manufacturer or supplier sells an automobile that is dangerous if driven but perfectly harmless if used for scrap metal or old parts and tells the buyer, "this is for parts or scrap only, not to be driven." Suppose the buyer is a 16-year-old who actually drives the car and is injured when it cannot be controlled. Is the manufacturer's description and sale for a limited purpose a warning or a disclaimer? If it is a warning, is the buyer's misuse nevertheless foreseeable? And if it is foreseeable, is the risk great enough to justify imposing liability upon the seller?

C. FEDERAL PREEMPTION

DOOMES V. BEST TRANSIT CORP.

958 N.E.2d 1183 (N.Y. 2011)

JONES, J. . . .

On April 23, 1994, a bus carrying approximately 21 passengers was returning from a visit to Adirondack Correctional Facility in Ray Brook, New York. The bus was equipped with a seatbelt for the driver, but not for the passengers. During the trip along the New York State Thruway, the driver, defendant Wagner M. Alcivar, "dozed off" while the bus was traveling approximately 60 miles per hour. The bus veered across the highway from the right-hand lane into the passing lane, and encountered a median strip and a sloping embankment. Alcivar awakened, but his belated attempts to regain control of the bus were futile as the vehicle rolled over several times, injuring many of the passengers.

[Three of the injured passengers, including Gloria Doomes, sued various defendants, including Warrick Industries, Inc., the manufacturer who completed the construction of the bus. Plaintiffs alleged, among other things, that the absence of passenger seatbelts was a cause of the injury. Warrick moved to preclude any evidence that the bus was defective or that it was negligent due to a lack of seatbelts on the ground that Federal Motor Vehicle Safety Standard (FMVSS) 208 (49 CFR § 571.208), which did not require the installation of passenger seatbelts, preempted any claims of liability for failure to install such seatbelts. The trial court declined to rule on the motion, and the jury found Warrick liable. The Appellate Division reversed, holding that plaintiffs' seatbelt claims were preempted, reasoning that these claims conflicted with the federal goal of establishing a uniform regulatory scheme for transit safety. Plaintiffs appealed.]

Under the Supremacy Clause of the United States Constitution (US Const, art VI, cl 2), preemption analysis requires us "to ascertain the intent of Congress." Express preemptive intent is discerned from the plain language of a statutory provision. Implied preemption may be found in two distinct ways when either "the Federal legislation is so comprehensive in its scope that it is inferable that Congress wished fully to occupy the field of its subject matter (field preemption), or because State law conflicts with the Federal law."

Plaintiffs contend that the Appellate Division erred in finding preemption because the relevant portions of FMVSS 208, compelling only the inclusion of a driver seatbelt, neither reflects a pervasive scheme of regulation nor makes compliance with federal and state standards impossible. Moreover, it is argued that the United States Supreme Court's recent decision in *Williamson v Mazda Motor of America, Inc.* (131 S Ct 1131 [2011]) disposes of this appeal in plaintiffs' favor. Warrick claims that the statute affords manufacturers the option to choose among different protective devices for installation at the driver's seat, and this availability of discretion places this appeal squarely within the holding of *Geier v American Honda Motor Co.* (529 US 861 [2000]).

First turning to express preemption, the pertinent statutory clause of the National Traffic and Motor Vehicle Safety Act (Safety Act) provides that

> "[w]hen a motor vehicle safety standard is in effect under this chapter, a State or a political subdivision of a State may prescribe or continue in effect a standard applicable to the same aspect of performance of a motor vehicle or motor vehicle equipment only if the standard is identical to the standard prescribed under this chapter. However, the United State Government, a State, or a political subdivision of a State may prescribe a standard for a motor vehicle or motor vehicle equipment obtained for its own use that imposes a higher performance requirement than that required by the otherwise applicable standard under this chapter" (49 USC § 30103 [b]).

In *Geier*, the Supreme Court considered the preemptive effect of a pre-1994 edition of the above preemption clause that similarly limited the authority of states to prescribe motor vehicle safety standards (*see* former 15 USC § 1392 [d]). However, rather than parsing the precise significance of the plain language of the provision, the Supreme Court concluded that Congress did not intend the preemption clause to be construed so broadly as to preclude state claims because the "saving" clause explicitly reserved a right to assert common-law claims.

As relevant here, the instant saving clause provides that "[c]ompliance with a motor vehicle safety standard prescribed under this chapter does not exempt a person from liability at common law." When read in conjunction with the preemption provision, the saving clause permits the commencement of common-law claims; compliance with applicable federal motor vehicle safety standards is not necessarily a preclusive bar. Accordingly, the presence of the saving clause limits a potentially broad reading of the preemption provision and does not expressly prohibit plaintiffs' seatbelt claims.

With respect to implied "field preemption," it does not appear that the federal statutes were intended to so greatly envelop the field of motor vehicle safety standards as to leave little room for state participation or operation. Certainly, the guidelines, as the Appellate Division noted, are consonant "with the federal goal of establishing uniform standards." And, the preemption clause constrains states from enacting guidelines that deviate from federal standards. However, the goal of uniformity cannot be singularly pursued at the expense of the Safety Act's primary purpose to "reduce traffic accidents and deaths and injuries to persons resulting from traffic accidents." This is evinced by the presence of the saving clause which expressly allows the commencement of state common-law claims. As the Supreme Court has reasoned previously, "the saving clause reflects a congressional determination that occasional nonuniformity is a small price to pay for a system in which juries not only create, but also enforce, safety standards" (*Geier*, 529 US at 871). Further, the saving clause represents a purposeful intent to allow meaningful state participation as a finding of preemption would "treat all such federal standards as if they were *maximum* standards, eliminating the possibility that the federal agency seeks only to set forth a *minimum* standard potentially supplemented through state tort law" (*Williamson*, 131 S Ct at 1139 [emphasis added]). Consequently, there is no implied "field preemption" as the explicit permission of common-law claims indicates that the federal statutes promulgated under the Safety Act are not so pervasive as to encompass the entire scheme of motor vehicle safety guidelines.

The significant point of contention between the parties is whether plaintiffs' seatbelt claims are barred under implied conflict preemption. We conclude they are not.

Implied conflict preemption can arise in two situations: when "it is 'impossible for a private party to comply with both state and federal requirements' ... or where state law 'stands as an obstacle to the accomplishment and execution of the full purposes and objectives of Congress'" (*Freightliner Corp. v Myrick*, 514 US 280, 287 [1995]). The Supreme Court has made clear that a state law will be preempted under the latter form of implied conflict preemption only where it would frustrate "a *significant objective* of the federal regulation" (*Williamson*, 562 US at ___, 131 S Ct at 1136 [emphasis added]).

... A plain reading of [the federal regulations here] shows that they only mandate the inclusion of protective devices at the driver's seat of a bus and are absolutely silent regarding the installation of passenger seatbelts.

This does not make it impossible to comply with both the federal standards and the gravamen of plaintiffs' seatbelt claims, which seek liability for the failure to install such protective devices. Quite simply, Warrick could have installed passenger and driver seatbelts without running afoul of federal motor vehicle safety standards. Hence, plaintiffs' seatbelt claims are not preempted under the first category of implied conflict preemption. . . .

The NHTSA has consistently acknowledged the enhanced safety benefits of seatbelts, but it has neither imposed the installation of passenger seatbelts, nor expressed an intention to provide such an option to manufacturers of the type of bus involved in the instant appeal. . . .

Further, any contention that manufacturers impliedly had an option to install rear passenger seatbelts in buses over 10,000 pounds, because the NHTSA was cognizant of the safety benefits of rear passenger seatbelts, is belied by the plain language of FMVSS 208 and the federal regulations which simply do not consider the inclusion of such protective devices for vehicles of this type. As such, like *Williamson*, there is simply no preemptive intent to be discerned from the regulations with respect to state common-law claims seeking the inclusion of passenger seatbelts in buses of this type.

In sum, we find neither express nor implied preemption of plaintiffs' seatbelt claims. . . .

[Order reversed.]

NOTES

1. **Types of federal preemption.** The Supremacy Clause gives Congress the power to override state law, as long as it acts within the limits of its own constitutional powers. As the New York court explained in *Doomes*, Congress can effectively forbid the enforcement of state law not only when the state law would conflict directly with federal statutes or regulation, but also when Congress wishes to impose a single scheme of regulation or control. Congress might thus "preempt" state law by (1) occupying the field with heavy regulation so that there is no room left for state law; (2) by passing laws that actually conflict with state laws; or (3) by providing for preemption in particular cases, either expressly or by implication. The essence of "conflict" preemption is that is impossible for the defendant to comply with both federal and state requirements. *See Wyeth v. Levine*, 555 U.S. 555 (2009) (no preemption found where such compliance was not impossible); *Sikkelee v. Precision Airmotive Corp.*, 907 F.3d 701 (3d Cir. 2018) (same).

Even when Congress has expressly provided for preemption, courts must construe the statute to determine what was and what was not preempted. In general, the Supreme Court is reluctant to find preemption of state powers unless the Congress has clearly manifested its purpose. *See Medtronic, Inc. v.*

Lohr, 518 U.S. 470 (1996). Congress has exhibited such a preemptive purpose with increasing frequency, however.

2.   **Effect in products cases.** Preemption is particularly important in products liability cases. Suppose a federal statute sets a minimum standard for warnings that must be contained on labels of a dangerous product. A state law that required a better warning or additional information would not actually conflict with the federal statute and would therefore not be preempted under the actual conflict rule. Nevertheless, the federal labeling statute might either expressly or impliedly preempt statute law. If it did, the result would be that the manufacturer who complied with the federal statute would not be liable for failing to comply with the state statute. *See, e.g., In re Tobacco Cases II*, 163 P.3d 106 (Cal. 2007) (Federal Cigarette Labeling and Advertising Act preempts false advertising and unfair competition claims brought under state statutes). Of course, where state laws are found to actually conflict with the federal statute, preemption is also found. *See, e.g., BIC Pen Corp. v. Carter*, 251 S.W.3d 500 (Tex. 2008) (Consumer Product Safety Commission regulations preempt state law design-defect claim over disposable lighter);

3.   **Airbags and seatbelts.** Preemption has played an important role in claims against automobile manufacturers. In *Geier v. American Honda Motor Co.*, 529 U.S. 861 (2000), the plaintiff claimed that Honda was negligent in failing to equip its 1987 Accord with a driver's side airbag. The Court decided, 5–4, that plaintiff's state-law claim was impliedly preempted by federal regulations that had sought a "variety and mix of [restraint] devices" in cars in order to "help develop data on comparative effectiveness," to give "the industry time to overcome the safety problems and the high production costs associated with airbags," and to "facilitate the development of alternative, cheaper, and safer passive restraint systems." To allow the plaintiff to establish that Honda owed a duty under state law to install an airbag in its 1987 Accords would conflict with these federal goals; thus her claim was preempted.

Construing a later version of the same federal regulations, the Court in *Williamson v. Mazda Motor of America, Inc.*, 562 U.S. 323 (2011), held that a state suit claiming that a minivan was defectively designed for having only a simple lap belt in the center rear seat was not preempted. The regulation itself specified that lap-and-shoulder belts must be installed in seats next to a vehicle's doors or frame, but allowed manufacturers to install either lap belts or lap-and-shoulder belts on inside seats. The Court concluded, however, that this "seatbelt choice" was "not a significant objective of the federal regulation," and thus did not have preemptive effect. *See also Lake v. Memphis Landsmen, LLC*, 405 S.W.3d 47 (Tenn. 2013) (relying on *Williamson*, holding that federal regulations did not preempt injured airport-bus passenger's products liability suit alleging that bus was defectively designed because it lacked seatbelts and had tempered-glass instead of laminated-glass side windows).

4.   **The growth of the preemption defense.** Arguments that federal law preempts state law products claims have reached the Supreme Court with

regularity, and most of the decisions favor defendants. In *Riegel v. Medronic, Inc.*, 552 U.S. 312 (2008), the Court held that where the Food and Drug Administration has given premarket approval to a particular medical device, federal law preempts common-law claims challenging the safety or effectiveness of such a device. In *PLIVA v. Mensing*, 564 U.S. 604 (2011), the Court held that federal law preempted state laws requiring generic drug manufacturers to warn of the risks of long-term use of their product, where it was impossible for the manufacturers to comply with both state and federal law on labeling. *See also Mutual Pharmaceutical Co. v. Bartlett*, 570 U.S. 772 (2013) (similar). All design-defect claims against vaccine manufactures claiming injuries from side-effects were held preempted by the federal National Childhood Vaccine Act, in *Bruesewitz v. Wyeth LLC*, 562 U.S. 223 (2011). In *Kurns v. Railroad Friction Prods. Corp.*, 565 U.S. 625 (2012), the Court held that state-law claims of defective design and failure to warn about the dangers of asbestos brake pads used on railroad cars were preempted by the federal Locomotive Inspection Act. Do you see why manufacturers do not always see federal regulation in a negative light?

5. **Federal statutes creating a federal tort right.** The preemption discussed above may effectively destroy the plaintiff's claim. But some federal preemption works differently. Instead of effectively enacting a federal defense, some federal statutes enact a federal claim by granting the plaintiff a cause of action more favorable than he had under state law. The FELA (Federal Employers Liability Act) creates federal tort rights for interstate railroad workers and, when it was enacted, was substantially more favorable to the workers than was state tort law. The FELA claim is still more favorable in certain ways. Other federal statute may enact an alternative system of liability, with different claims, defenses, and procedures.

6. **Federal preemptive statutes not creating a private right of action.** Statutes creating a private federal right are rare, however. (Federal law-making culture is oriented toward official regulation rather than toward private rights.) In most cases, then, the defendant's violation of a federal statute does not give the plaintiff a right of action for the violation, even if that violation harms the plaintiff. In such cases, the plaintiff's state tort claim may be barred by preemption and the plaintiff has no federal claim at all because the preempting statute created no private right of action.

NOTE: NON-PREEMPTIVE ROLES OF
STATUTES AND REGULATIONS

1. *Compliance creating a presumption of non-defectiveness.* State statutes may provide that a manufacturer's or seller's compliance with any federal or state statute or regulation raises a rebuttable presumption that the product is not defective with respect to design or information defects.

See, e.g., TENN. CODE ANN. § 29–28–104; TEX. CIV. PRAC. & REM. CODE § 82.008.

2. *Statutes or regulations setting the standard of care.* In rare cases courts may choose to adopt a regulatory standard as the standard of care in a products case. This occurred in *Ramirez v. Plough, Inc.*, 863 P.2d 167 (Cal. 1993), in which a young child developed Reye's Syndrome (a serious disease causing severe neurological damage) after his mother, not fluent in English, gave him aspirin manufactured by defendant. The aspirin package contained warnings about Reye's, but only in English. FDA regulations required a warning about Reye's syndrome. But, except for Puerto Rico and areas where some other language predominates, the FDA only required a warning in English. California statutes were similar. The court held that the defendant was under no duty to provide a Spanish-language warning. "Given the existence of a statute expressly requiring that package warnings on nonprescription drugs be in English, we think it reasonable to infer that the Legislature has deliberately chosen not to require that manufacturers also include warnings in foreign languages. The same inference is warranted on the federal level. The FDA's regulations abundantly demonstrate its sensitivity to the issue of foreign-language labeling, and yet the FDA regulations do not require it. Presumably, the FDA has concluded that despite the obvious advantages of multilingual package warnings, the associated problems and costs are such that at present warnings should be mandated only in English." The task of specifying language of warnings, said the court, is best left to legislators and administrators.

D. THE GOVERNMENT CONTRACTOR DEFENSE

BOYLE V. UNITED TECHNOLOGIES CORP., 487 U.S. 500 (1988). A U.S. Marine helicopter copilot was killed when his helicopter crashed during a training exercise. His father sued Sikorsky Division of United Technologies Corporation (Sikorsky), which built the helicopter under contract for the United States. Plaintiff alleged two state-law claims: (1) that Sikorsky had defectively repaired a device called the servo in the helicopter's automatic flight control system, which allegedly malfunctioned and caused the crash, and (2) that Sikorsky had defectively designed the copilot's emergency escape system. The jury found for plaintiff and awarded him $725,000. The Court of Appeals reversed and remanded with directions that judgment be entered for Sikorsky, partly because it was protected by what the court called the "military contractor defense."

Held, "Liability for design defects in military equipment cannot be imposed, pursuant to state law, when (1) the United States approved reasonably precise specifications; (2) the equipment conformed to those specifications; and (3) the supplier warned the United States about the dangers in the use of the equipment that were known to the supplier but not to the United States." The governing principle underlying this defense is the FTCA's discretionary immunity clause, which retains immunity for the federal government itself for tort cases "based upon the exercise or performance or the failure to exercise or perform a discretionary function or duty on the part of a federal agency or an employee of the Government, whether or not the discretion involved be abused." The government's selection of the design of military equipment "is assuredly a discretionary function within the meaning of this provision. . . . It makes little sense to insulate the Government against financial liability for the judgment that a particular feature of military equipment is necessary when the Government produces the equipment itself, but not when it contracts for the production. In sum, we are of the view that state law which holds Government contractors liable for design defects in military equipment" must be displaced under the circumstances presented here.

NOTES

1. **Applying _Boyle_.** _Boyle_ has been held to immunize federal government contractors from tort liability in a number of major cases. _See, e.g., In re "Agent Orange" Product Liability Litigation_, 517 F.3d 76 (2d Cir. 2008). Does the rule reflect sound policy?

2. **_Boyle_ as a compliance case.** The general rule is that a defendant's compliance with a statute, while relevant, is not a complete defense either in a negligence case or a case brought on some other products liability theory. _See Doyle v. Volkswagenwerk Aktiengesellschaft_, 481 S.E.2d 518 (Ga. 1997) RESTATEMENT OF PRODUCTS LIABILITY § 4(b) (1998). How does this relate to _Boyle_? _Boyle_ does turn on the defendant's compliance with overriding law affecting product design; if the plaintiff's injury results from the contractor's non-compliance rather than its compliance with specifications, the _Boyle_ defense would not apply. The compliance required to trigger the _Boyle_ defense, however, is not compliance with a legislative enactment, but with specifications used by the government in making a private contract.

3. **Manufacturing defects.** What if the plaintiff is injured by a product made for the government and to government specification, but the injury results because of a manufacturing rather than a design defect? What if the plaintiff claims that the contractor could have supplied a warning to make the product safer? _See Densberger v. United Technologies Corp._, 297 F.3d 66 (2d Cir. 2002).

4. **Is _Boyle_ limited to military contractors or product manufacturers?** Before the Court decided _Boyle_, some Circuits had been much taken with the military aspects in government contractor cases and some had referred to the "military contractor" defense. These cases emphasized the impropriety of judicial interference with military decisions and they grounded the defense partly in those concerns. Does the _Boyle_ rationale make it clear that the defense is much broader than that?

5. ***Feres* and *Boyle*.** Under the *Feres* doctrine (*see* Chapter 15 § 2.C), military service members are barred from suing the federal government for injuries that are "incident to service." The *Boyle* court declined to rest its decision on *Feres*, but also avoided deciding whether *Feres* immunity could ever be applied derivatively to a federal military contractor. In *McMahon v. Presidential Airways, Inc.*, 502 F.3d 1331 (11th Cir. 2007), the issue was joined. Survivors of U.S. soldiers who were killed when the airplane in which they were being flown crashed in Afghanistan filed a negligence suit against the civilian contractors who provided air transportation and support services to the government. The defendant argued "that it is entitled to claim the whole of the government's *Feres* immunity under the doctrine of derivative sovereign immunity." The court held that derivative *Feres* immunity should not be recognized in the case because "it would single out soldiers and would not protect sensitive military judgments in suits brought by anyone else (including journalists or private contractor employees." The court said that "we do not mean to foreclose the possibility" of a government contractor immunity but that "any such immunity must, if it is to have any basis in reason, apply to civilians as well as soldiers: including the employees of private contractors, and other civilians." Does *McMahon* conflict with *Boyle*?

6. **State (not federal) contractors.** *Boyle* was distinguished in *Conner v. Quality Coach, Inc.*, 750 A.2d 823 (Pa. 2000). In that case, a private company had contracted with a state agency to provide modifications on the vehicles of disabled persons. The plaintiff alleged that the defendant contractor utilized a defective design for its brake/throttle control, resulting in an injury-causing accident. The defendant argued that it was immune under *Boyle,* but the state court disagreed. *Boyle* is limited to federal contractors. In Pennsylvania, the courts have abolished common law immunity, leaving only immunities established by the legislature, which has established none here. Contractors are protected when they reasonably rely upon specifications, but only because in that case they are not negligent at all. When they participate in the design decision, as here, they are liable for their negligence. Any general policy to lower government procurement costs by protecting government contractors is "lacking in empirical support," and is "ill-suited to serve as a counterweight to the policies favoring just compensation underlying our tort system."

7. **Private contractors providing products to private customers.** Suppose the local bus company orders a fleet of buses, specifying a gas tank in a dangerous location and in fact the gas tank blows up when the bus is rammed by a car. Would an injured bus passenger have a products liability claim against the manufacturer?

E. STATUTES OF LIMITATION

1. *Choice of statute.* (a) *Negligence and strict liability*. Many states have special products statutes, setting up some rules about products liability and also a special statute of limitations that may be different from

the ordinary negligence/personal injury statute. Suppose the products statute is two years, while the negligence statute is four. The plaintiff sues the manufacturer of a machine for injury resulting when the manufacturer installed it at the plaintiff's employer's business without assuring ventilation needed to make it safe. Suit was filed three years after the injury. Is the suit timely?

(b) *Warranty.* When the plaintiff sues on a warranty theory, or includes a warranty theory among others, the statute of limitations intended to govern "contract" or warranty claims may apply. The UCC in fact specifies in Art. 2–725(1):

> An action for breach of any contract for sale must be commenced within four years after the cause of action has accrued.

A number of courts have held that this provision governs a warranty claim, even where the damage claimed is for personal injury. This is important in a state—Alabama, for instance—in which strict tort liability is not accepted as such and in which most strict liability may be based on a warranty theory.

Other courts, however, seem more interested in determining whether the underlying claim is the kind tort law has sought to protect, and in these courts the fact that "warranty" is the theory might not be determinative if the underlying claim is a claim for physical harm to person or property of the same kind a products tort liability case might cover. The New York Court of Appeals said something like this in *Victorson v. Bock Laundry Machine Co.*, 335 N.E.2d 275 (N.Y. 1975). Quoting Prosser on Torts, the court said that "The fundamental difference between tort and contract lies in the nature of the interests protected." Even if warranty is part of the verbiage used to state the claim, if physical harm is the damage claimed, the warranty statute of limitations is inappropriate, and whatever statute governs torts or personal injury claims would be chosen instead. This view is consistent with the distinction drawn in Section 1, *supra*, between economic harm, for which warranty is especially suited, and physical harm, for which tort doctrine seems to work better.

2. *Accrual of the claim.* (a) *Sales or later date.* If the claim is for personal injury and based solely on tort doctrine, the tort statute, however that may be phrased in a particular state, will govern. When will the statute begin to run? In tort law this ordinarily occurs when injury is inflicted, subject to the discovery rule. Certainly, it does *not* begin to run on the date of sale. If the claim is based on a warranty theory, however, and if the UCC statute is applied, it is quite possible that the statute begins to run from the time the product is sold by the defendant. This is, in fact, the express provision of UCC Art. 2–725(2): "A breach of warranty occurs when tender of delivery is made. . . ." Although the UCC statute is for four years, and although this is longer than most tort statutes, it begins running

before injury. In *Waldrop v. Peabody Galion Corp.*, 423 So.2d 145 (Ala. 1982), the defendants sold (or "tendered delivery" of) a garbage truck in 1974. The plaintiff, a city employee working on the truck was injured, allegedly by a defect, in 1976. At that time the statute had already been running two years. When his suit was actually brought in 1979 it was barred by the four-year statute. If he had been able to sue on a tort theory and a three-year tort statute had applied, his suit would have been timely.

(b) *Injury or later date*. Most states will not force an injured plaintiff to use warranty theory to pursue a products liability claim, but will permit or even require use of a tort theory instead. Under the general statutes of limitation applied to tort claims, the claim does not accrue until injury; and the statute cannot start running before injury. Under the discovery rule seen in Chapter 9, the statute does not begin to run until the harm is or should have been discovered.

3. *Statutes of repose.* (a) *The problem.* The typical statute of limitations in tort cases has run from the time of injury or some later date. After the initial explosive expansion of product liability, manufacturers and others in the commercial world exerted considerable effort to restrict liability. One special problem was the "long tail" of possible liabilities that could occur. A product sold in 1959 might not cause harm until 1999. If the victim sued immediately, he would not be barred by an ordinary statute of limitations, which does not begin to run until injury occurs, or later. But this would mean that a manufacturer would have to plan for potential liabilities 20, 30, 40 years into the future, or even more.

(b) *Statutory response.* With ideas like these in mind, many legislatures have passed statutes of "ultimate repose," under which products claims are barred if injury occurs more than, say, 12 years after the product was initially sold or delivered.

Similar statutes of repose have been passed in some states to protect architects, engineers, real estate developers and doctors. All these are structured like the products statute: the statutory period is a long one, but it begins to run from the time the product was sold, or the work or service completed.

(c) *Constitutionality.* Some of these statutes have been held unconstitutional under the provisions of state constitutions. New Hampshire also held its statute to be in violation of its state constitution partly because it denied equal protection to products plaintiffs and partly because it denied reasonable access to courts. The court commented:

> The unreasonableness inherent in a statute which eliminates a plaintiff's cause of action before the wrong may reasonably be discovered was noted by Judge Frank [who] condemned the 'Alice in Wonderland' effect of such a result:

'Except in topsy-turvy land, you can't die before you are conceived, or be divorced before you marry, or harvest a crop never planted, or burn down a house never built, or miss a train running on a non-existent railroad. For substantially similar reasons, it has always heretofore been accepted, as a sort of logical "axiom," that a statute of limitations does not begin to run against a cause of action before that cause of action exists, i.e., before a judicial remedy is available to a plaintiff.'

Heath v. Sears, Roebuck & Co., 464 A.2d 288 (N.H. 1983).

The quotation from Judge Frank is a beautiful example of effective rhetoric. Is there, however, any rule of state constitutions that requires the legislature to accept logical axioms? Given the difficult problem, can you be sure that the solution of the legislature is not only unjust but a violation of the constitution? Local constitutional provisions are most important in these cases.

(d) *Continuing duty to warn.* Whatever the constitutionally of the statutes of repose in the ordinary case, can they apply at all to the case in which the defendant's liability is based, not upon defect at the time of sale, but upon failure to warn of the defect it discovers after sale? Five years after a car is marketed, the manufacturer discovers a steering defect and does nothing. Unwarned, the plaintiff has a horrible wreck six years after that. Should the statute of repose apply to such a case? *See, e.g., Watkins v. Ford Motor Co.*, 190 F.3d 1213 (11th Cir. 1999). What if liability is based on failure to warn of an unknown defect?

REFERENCE: 2 DOBBS, HAYDEN & BUBLICK, THE LAW OF TORTS § 475 (2d ed. 2011).

PART 9

PRACTICALITIES AND VALUES

∎ ∎ ∎

CHAPTER 25

APPORTIONMENT AND SETTLEMENT

■ ■ ■

§ 1. APPORTIONMENT SYSTEMS

"If two people kill a third, it is not the case that each has half-killed him."

—Tony Weir, *All or Nothing?*, 78 TUL. L. REV. 511 (2004).

When more than one actor's tortious conduct causes harm, how are the damages to be divided among the different tortfeasors? This is the central question in an area of tort law that is sometimes called "apportionment of liability," "comparative apportionment," or "comparative liability." The rules in this area have changed over time, and have become increasingly varied among U.S. jurisdictions, as described below.

DOBBS, HAYDEN & BUBLICK, THE LAW OF TORTS
Vol. 3, § 487 (2d ed. 2011)

§ 487. Apportionment of liability: an overview

Apportionment basics. . . . There are two basic forms of liability apportionment: causal apportionment and fault or responsibility based apportionment.

Causal apportionment. When two or more tortfeasors cause divisible harms to the plaintiff, most authorities agree that causal apportionment should be employed. For example, if tortfeasor A negligently causes the plaintiff to suffer a broken leg and tortfeasor B negligently causes the plaintiff broken arm, each tortfeasor is normally liable for 100% of the damages that the tortfeasor separately caused. Causal apportionment . . . may also be required when the plaintiff suffers a single injury rather than distinct harms but the single injury is capable of being apportioned in some rational way. . . .

Fault apportionment. Causal apportionment is often contrasted with fault apportionment. Fault apportionment takes place when a plaintiff has suffered a single indivisible injury at the hands of two or more tortfeasors and the loss cannot be reasonably allocated by causal measures between the two. Instead, the loss is allocated based on percentages of fault. For example, suppose tortfeasor A, who is speeding, crashes into plaintiff's car. Tortfeasor B, who is sending a text message while driving, fails to keep a lookout and hits the plaintiff's car as well. The plaintiff emerges from the near-simultaneous accidents with a serious back injury. Experts attribute the injury to the combined impact of the crashes but cannot segregate the amount of harm caused by each. Because both defendants are factual causes of the plaintiff's single injury and no causal apportionment of the injury is possible, a jury would be asked to apportion liability by assigning a percentage of fault to each defendant.

Joint and several and several liability. Suppose the jury finds that defendant A is chargeable with 60% of the fault and defendant B with 40% of the fault. The jury also finds that the plaintiff has suffered $100,000 in damages: $50,000 in past and future medical expenses and $50,000 in pain and suffering. If joint and several liability applies, each defendant will be liable to the plaintiff for the full $100,000 in damages, subject to the caveat that the plaintiff can only receive one satisfaction of the judgment. Consequently, if the plaintiff recovers the full $100,000 from defendant B, she can recover nothing at all against defendant B. However, defendant A can call upon defendant B for contribution for the $40,000 owed by B. If on the other hand, several liability applies, the plaintiff can call on defendant A for payment of only $60,000 and defendant B for payment of $40,000. If either of the two negligent defendants cannot pay, it is the plaintiff who will bear the uncompensated loss.

Other ways to apportion liability. Although joint and several liability and several liability are two prominent options for sharing the loss, they are far from the only options. Some jurisdictions retain joint and several liability, but only for certain elements of the damages such as those based on the economic harm done to the plaintiff. In a jurisdiction like this, defendant A would be jointly and severally liable for the $20,000 of defendant B's liability to plaintiff for economic losses (40% of the plaintiff's $50,000 economic loss damages), but not jointly and severally liable for the $20,000 of defendant B's share that was due to pain and suffering. Similarly, some jurisdictions retain joint and several liability only if the defendant's percentage of responsibility exceeds a certain threshold percentage such as 50%. In a jurisdiction with this rule, defendant A, assigned 60% of the liability, would be jointly and severally liable for defendant B's uncollectible share. However, defendant B, assigned 40% of the total liability, would not be jointly and severally liable if defendant A's share were uncollectible. Other possibilities exist. Some jurisdictions have joint and several liability with reallocation. This means that if the plaintiff cannot collect a judgment from one of the parties, that portion of the judgment will be reallocated among the remaining parties on the basis of the remaining parties' fault. In the example with defendant A and B, because the plaintiff was assigned no fault, defendant A would bear the full cost of defendant B's insolvency. However, if instead the plaintiff had been assigned 30% of the fault and defendant A 30% of the fault, defendant B's uncollectible 40% share would be split by defendant A and the plaintiff 1:1—each would bear their assigned shares of the loss plus one-half of B's share.

The varied rules. As the variations in these illustrations suggest, apportionment of liability among multiple actors, once a fairly straightforward topic, has now become increasingly fragmented and complex. In fact, so divided is state law that when the Restatement Third of Torts was published at the start of the millennium, its provisions recognized five alternative "tracks" of liability apportionment that states might employ to address the situation of multiple tortfeasors who create indivisible harms—one for joint and several liability, another for several liability, one for joint and several liability with reallocation, another for hybrid liability based on a threshold percentage of comparative responsibility, and a final chapter on hybrid liability based on the type of damages. One English commentator has called the tracked sections of the Restatement of Apportionment "a trackless morass, Dismal Swamp, and Desolation of Smaug." Tony Weir, *All or Nothing?*, 78 TUL. L. REV. 511, 534 n.63 (2004). . . . [G]iven the varied apportionment-related statutes and case law in existence at the time the Restatement was enacted,[10] no single approach to the issue could have been followed in all jurisdictions. As is the case whenever statutes pervade and state case law varies, reference to the legislation and precedent of particular jurisdictions is essential. Despite jurisdictional differences, the issue of indivisible injury remains significant across the board. In joint and several liability the defendant is liable for that indivisible injury. . . .

Issues within apportionment systems. The jurisdictional differences concerning joint and several liability and other types of liability is a significant divider. . . . However, many additional issues pervade the apportionment landscape. . . . Because several liability systems typically apportion liability into mutually exclusive portions, the key questions in these systems center on (1) which types of conduct and which types of actors can be a part of the apportionment percentages, (2) on what basis percentage apportionments are made, and (3) in what circumstances exceptions to the several liability rule are called for.

Apportionment and policy choices. Courts frequently address apportionment of liability as though the apportionment itself is a neutral issue—the defendant should be accountable for its fair share of responsibility and no more. However, the variation in state answers to the question of what constitutes a fair share of damages for which to hold a defendant to account, highlights just how important a policy question apportionment of liability has become. . . .

---

[10] Restatement (Third) of Torts: Apportionment of Liability § 17 Tables at 151–159 (2000).

§ 2. APPORTIONMENT WITH JOINT AND SEVERAL LIABILITY

HILL V. RHINEHART, 45 N.E.3d 427 (Ind. Ct. App. 2015). Patient John A. Hill was admitted to Parkview Memorial Hospital for a coronary artery bypass surgery. Because of some complications after the surgery, several orders were placed to stop all administration of Heparin. However, on several occasions, plaintiff nevertheless was given heparin. Hill developed life threatening complications and ultimately had three limbs amputated as result of heparin-induced thrombocytopenia with thrombosis (HITT). Hill entered into settlements with Parkview Hospital and Indiana Patient's Compensation Fund for $250,000—the amount of the statutory cap for medical malpractice actions. He then brought a malpractice action against four doctors involved in his care. The physicians moved for summary judgment, arguing that the patient had received the maximum recovery under the Medical Malpractice Act. The trial court denied the motion for summary judgment on the ground that the three amputations might count as distinct injuries, but granted motion for judgment on the evidence for two of the doctors after the close of patient's case-in-chief. The court subsequently entered judgment on a jury verdict in favor of the remaining doctors. Patient contends that the trial court erred by granting Drs. Lloyd and Csicsko's motion for judgment on the evidence because it prejudiced Hill by preventing the jury from "evaluating the liability of the doctors jointly and severally as a team."

Held, in medical malpractice actions in Indiana, common law applies. "At common law, joint tortfeasors are two or more persons jointly or severally liable in tort for the same injury to person or property. Their actions unite to cause a single injury. When more than one unite in the commission of a wrong, each is responsible for the acts of all, and for the whole damage; also, where separate and independent acts of negligence by different persons concur in perpetrating a single injury, each is fully responsible for the trespass. Courts will not undertake to apportion the damage in such cases among the joint wrongdoers. The injured party has at his election his remedy against all, or any number. Thus, to impose joint and several liability on Drs. Lloyd and Csicsko, it is imperative that these doctors contributed to the negligent actions which resulted in Hill's injury. In other words, joint and several liability does not impose liability on a defendant who is otherwise not liable. The fact that Drs. Csicsko and Lloyd contributed and collaborated with the two other doctors to jointly provide treatment to Hill does not equate to a transfer of liability of one doctor to the non-liable physicians simply by virtue of their collaboration."

NOTES

1. **Joint and several liability.** Under rules of joint and several liability, several defendants might be held liable together, jointly and severally, so that the plaintiff might enforce a judgment entirely against any one of them. In *Burg v. Dampier*, 346 S.W.3d 343 (Mo. Ct. App. 2011), the court wrote: "A plaintiff may sue all or any of the joint or concurrent tortfeasors and obtain a judgment against all or any of them." But note, as in *Hill*, that it's not just any defendants who are sued who are jointly and severally liable. What else has to be true before a defendant can be held jointly and severally liable?

2. **Contribution.** What if the plaintiff tried to enforce a judgment against one tortfeasor for the full amount of the judgment? How might that defendant seek to share the costs with other defendants?

3. **One satisfaction.** Why does the total amount of money plaintiff is permitted to recover under the medical malpractice act matter? Recall that even if all four doctors had been negligent, and plaintiff could enforce his judgment against any or all of the tortfeasors, under the "one satisfaction rule," he cannot recover more than the total amount of his damages.

4. **Fairness.** Suppose the jury had found two of the doctors liable to the plaintiff for medical negligence. How could plaintiff argue it would be fair for either doctor to pay plaintiff's full damage award? Would it be more fair for the non-negligent plaintiff to bear the loss?

5. **Applicability.** Joint and several liability was once the dominant rule for fault apportionment. Now it is the main rule in a minority of states, but, as in *Hill*, at times still applies in states with several liability rules. Also, some federal statutes impose joint and several liability for matters within their scope. This is the rule under CERCLA, a statute imposing liabilities for hazardous substances. *See United States v. Stringfellow*, 661 F.Supp. 1053 (C.D.Cal. 1987). The Supreme Court has also retained joint and several liability in FELA cases. *Norfolk & W. Ry. v. Ayers,* 538 U.S. 135 (2003).

NOTE: TRADITIONAL CONTEXTS FOR JOINT AND SEVERAL LIABILITY

The rule of joint and several liability may apply in four distinct situations.

(1) *Concerted action.* Joint and several liability applies to true joint torts, those in which A and B act in concert to commit an unlawful act. This includes intentional torts pursued jointly, as where A and B agree, tacitly or formally, to beat the plaintiff. It also includes intended law violations, as where A and B agree to race on the public highway and in the course of the race A collides with the plaintiff.

(2) *Indivisible injury.* The rule of joint and several liability applies in cases of concurrent torts where there is no concert or agreement, but where the acts of A and B produce a single indivisible injury. For example, recall the *Landers* case, in which both defendants' toxins combined to kill the fish in plaintiff's lake.

(3) *A creates a risk of harm by B.* The rule of joint and several liability applies in part when A's negligence not only creates a harm to the plaintiff, but also creates a risk of further harm by reason of B's negligence. A negligently runs the plaintiff down and leaves him concussed and unconscious, but otherwise unharmed, in the street. B later negligently runs over and breaks the plaintiff's leg. Although B can only be held liable for the separate injury he caused, A is jointly and severally liable for the entire harm under the rules of "proximate cause, since he created a foreseeable risk of harm from B." Thus if B proved to be uninsured and insolvent, the plaintiff would be entitled to recover his entire damages from A. This is the import of the proximate cause rules. Similarly, if A does not directly harm the plaintiff but creates a risk that B will do so, joint and several liability is no doubt proper. For instance, in *Nallan v. Helmsley-Spear, Inc.*, 407 N.E.2d 451 (N.Y. 1980), a building owner failed to protect an invitee from a gunman. The building owner was held fully liable, not limited to its comparative share.

(4) *A defendant is vicariously liable.* An employer is liable for the torts of an employee committed in the scope of employment. The employee is also liable for his own torts. The result is that they are jointly and severally liable.

Which of these four situations would be relevant to *Hill*?

NOTE: TRADITIONAL FORMS OF SETTLEMENT WITH ONE OF SEVERAL TORTFEASORS

Suppose that instead of getting a judgment against all tortfeasors, the plaintiff settles with one of them. Imagine that the plaintiff has damages of $200,000 and A offers to settle A's share for $100,000. Can the plaintiff accept this settlement and then pursue B for the remainder?

1. *Older rules: plaintiff's claim is fully satisfied.* If the plaintiff settles with A, the common law rule was that a release of one tortfeasor was a release of all those who were jointly and severally liable. The idea was that a release extinguished the cause of action itself, so that there was no ground left on which to sue B. Under such a rule, settlement would be unlikely because the plaintiff would be hesitant to not give A a release that might end plaintiff's claim against B. And A would not make a payment unless without assurance that there wouldn't be further liability. To effect

a settlement in this situation, lawyers came up with a new kind of settlement document—a "covenant not to sue." This was not a release of the claim, but merely a contract by the plaintiff not to sue A. Thus if a plaintiff wished to settle with one tortfeasor and still sue the other, this was the settlement paperwork the parties would use.

2. *Modern developments.* In many states, statutes or court decisions have changed all this. The UNIFORM CONTRIBUTION AMONG TORTFEASORS ACT § 4 (1955), provides expressly that a release of one tortfeasor "does not discharge any of the other tortfeasors from liability . . . unless its terms so provide. . . ." As the court wrote in *Bernardi Ortiz v. Cybex Int'l, Inc.,* 345 F.Supp.3d 107 (D.P.R. 2018), "whether a settlement agreement extinguishes a claim depends on the settling parties' intent. The language in the agreement controls. The release or discharge from liability granted by a plaintiff to a joint codebtor does not release the other joint tortfeasors from liability for the damage when the intention of the parties in the settlement and release agreement has acknowledged this fact." Such a view is a more typical of courts today. As always, attorneys must be alert to jurisdictional variations.

———

NOTE: CONTRIBUTION AND INDEMNITY

1. *Contribution.* (a) *General availability.* In Chapter 6, we saw that if one tortfeasor, A, paid more than A's share of damages, A could recover contribution from the other tortfeasors. Although contribution may still be denied to intentional tortfeasors, states generally permit contribution.

(b) *The common liability rule.* The person claiming contribution must show that both tortfeasors were liable to the plaintiff. If one defendant is immune from suit, for example, no contribution could be had from that party. *See, e.g., Crotta v. Home Depot, Inc.,* 732 A.2d 767 (Conn. 1999) (intra-familial immunity).

(c) *Payment in settlement.* In some states A can obtain contribution from B only when A has paid a judgment. If instead A *settles* with P for full compensation, A is usually, but not always entitled to contribution from B.

(d) *Amount of contribution.* The traditional rule for apportionment in contribution was one of "pro rata shares": if there is a single indivisible injury caused by two tortfeasors, each should pay one-half. Thus if A pays the entire $200,000, B would be liable to make contribution to A of $100,000. *See* Robert A. Leflar, *Contribution and Indemnity Between Tortfeasors,* 81 U. PA. L. REV. 130 (1932). Of course, now, most contribution claims are divided by percentages. *See generally* 3 DOBBS, HAYDEN & BUBLICK, THE LAW OF TORTS § 489 (2d ed. 2011).

2. *Indemnity.* While contribution involves a sharing of liability between the tortfeasors, indemnity involves a shifting of that liability. In a few situations, A may be technically liable to the plaintiff, but it may be that B is the only person really at fault. If A, because of a technical liability, pays the entire amount of the plaintiff's damages, A may recover, not merely a share from B, but the entire sum. This is known, traditionally, as indemnity.

There are not many occasions for indemnity in this sense. The chief example involves the negligence of the employee for which the employer is vicariously liable. In such a case the employer has a right of indemnity against the negligent employee, though it is not a right often exercised in practice. There is also a right of indemnity in some products cases, as where the retailer is held strictly liable for a defective product supplied by the manufacturer: the retailer will be entitled to recover indemnity from the manufacturer. *See generally* 3 DOBBS, HAYDEN & BUBLICK, THE LAW OF TORTS § 489 (2d ed. 2011).

§ 3. APPORTIONMENT IN JURISDICTIONS WITH SEVERAL LIABILITY

A. ABOLISHING OR LIMITING JOINT AND SEVERAL LIABILITY

Most states have abolished joint and several liability. Data from the Restatement Third suggests that as of the year 2000, only 15 states retain pure joint and several liability, and 4 more adopted it when the plaintiff was not at fault. RESTATEMENT (THIRD) OF TORTS: APPORTIONMENT OF LIABILITY § 17 Tables at 151–59 (2000). The shift to several liability primarily resulted from statutory changes based on tort reform. However, in a few jurisdictions, judges rejected the traditional joint and several liability rule, setting up a judicially created several liability system. *See, e.g., Volz v. Ledes,* 895 S.W.2d 677 (Tenn. 1995).

CAL. CIV. CODE § 1431.2

(a) In any action for personal injury, property damage, or wrongful death, based upon principles of comparative fault, the liability of each defendant for non-economic damages shall be several only and shall not be joint. Each defendant shall be liable only for the amount of non-economic damages allocated to that defendant in direct proportion to that defendant's percentage of fault, and a separate judgment shall be rendered against that defendant for that amount.

(b)(1) For purposes of this section, the term "economic damages" means objectively verifiable monetary losses including medical expenses, loss of earnings, burial costs, loss of use of property, costs of repair or replacement, cost of obtaining substitute domestic services, loss of employment and loss of business or employment opportunities.

(2) For the purposes of this section, the term "non-economic damages" means subjective, non-monetary losses including, but not limited to, pain, suffering, inconvenience, mental suffering, emotional distress, loss of society and companionship, loss of consortium, injury to reputation and humiliation.

NOTES

1. **Scope.** Remember that with the adoption of a comparative fault system, no defendant was liable to a plaintiff for the *plaintiff's* comparative fault share. Statutes abolishing joint and several liability do not affect that rule. Rather, they change the rule that defendants could be treated as a group so that each was liable for the comparative fault share of all defendants.

2. **Effects.** The most obvious effect of abolishing joint and several liability is that the plaintiff, not the tortfeasor, will bear the risk of a second tortfeasor's inability to pay. If A's share is 60% and B's is 40% but B is insolvent, the plaintiff will recover only 60% of the loss from A and none from B, even though A is an actual and proximate cause of the entire harm. *Vollaro v. Lispi*, 168 Cal.Rptr.3d 323 (Ct. App. 2014) ("Under Proposition 51, an injured plaintiff bears the entire risk of loss for any unpaid noneconomic damages attributable to a tortfeasor who has not been sued or is statutorily immune.").

3. **Constitutionality.** So far, courts have generally upheld statutes of this kind. *E.g., State Farm Ins. Cos. v. Premier Manufactured Sys., Inc.*, 172 P.3d 410 (Ariz. 2007). However, some states have found them violative of various state constitutional provisions. *Best v. Taylor Mach. Works,* 689 N.E.2d 1057 (Ill. 1997); *State v. Sheward,* 715 N.E.2d 1062 (Ohio 1999).

4. **The economic/non-economic distinction.** The California statute is one of a group which *retains* joint and several liability for actual pecuniary ("economic") losses. New York is another such state. *See* N.Y. C.P.L.R. § 1601.

5. **The relative fault distinction.** Another kind of statute retains some joint and several liability when the plaintiff's fault is small or the defendant's is great. New York's statute, for example, limits a defendant's liability for non-economic damages to his comparative fault share but only when defendant's liability is "fifty percent or less of the total liability assigned to all persons liable." N.Y. C.P.L.R. § 1601.

6. **Combination systems.** A number of statutes combine the non-economic loss distinction with the relative fault distinction in some way. For instance, Florida Statutes § 768.81(3), prescribes:

> In cases to which this section applies, the court shall enter judgment against each party liable on the basis of such party's percentage of fault and not on the basis of the doctrine of joint and several liability; provided that with respect to any party whose percentage of fault

equals or exceeds that of a particular claimant, the court shall enter judgment with respect to economic damages against that party on the basis of the doctrine of joint and several liability.

7. **The more severe statutes.** Another group of statutes is more severe, abolishing joint and several liability as to all the plaintiff's damages, both pecuniary and non-pecuniary, and regardless of the plaintiff's lack of fault. *E.g.*, ARIZ. REV. STAT. § 12–2506. As with most other statutes, some of these exempt particular torts, such as those based on hazardous wastes or pollution.

B. TYPES OF ACTIONABLE CONDUCT SUBJECT TO APPORTIONMENT

SAFEWAY STORES, INC. V. NEST-KART, 579 P.2d 441 (Cal. 1978). The plaintiff was injured when a shopping cart in Safeway broke and fell on her foot, requiring surgery. The jury found that the plaintiff was not at fault, that Safeway was strictly liable and also negligent, and that Nest-Kart, the manufacturer of the cart, was strictly liable. The jury also fixed the comparative responsibility of Safeway at 80% and the comparative responsibility of Nest-Kart at 20%. The trial court ordered each defendant ultimately to share payment of the judgment on a 50–50 basis, so that Nest-Kart would owe 50% in spite of the comparative responsibility finding. On appeal, *held*, the traditional contribution rule embodied in existing statutes does not prevent apportionment under "comparative indemnity" principles, even though one of the parties is negligent and the other strictly liable without proof of fault. Juries are competent to apportion between negligence and strict liability. And strictly liable defendants should be entitled to apportionment against negligent tortfeasors.

NOTES

1. **Apportioning contributory negligence and strict liability.** The principle that comparative fault can operate to reduce recovery from a person who is strictly liable is applied in *Safeway* on the contribution issue. If it is a valid principle there, then presumably it is equally valid to reduce the recovery of a faulty plaintiff under contributory negligence/comparative fault rules. *See Daly v. General Motors Corp.*, 575 P.2d 1162 (Cal. 1978).

2. **Apportioning tortfeasor fault and strict liability.** On its facts, *Safeway* operates to deny a negligent party any contribution from a non-negligent party who has paid its "comparative fault" share. But is this the legal significance of the case? Suppose Nest-Kart had paid the entire judgment in favor of the plaintiff and had sought contribution. Does the principle adopted in the case limit Nest-Kart's recovery from Safeway to 80%? If so, is this justified, given the fact that Nest-Kart is not shown to be guilty of any fault and Safeway is?

3. **Restatement of Apportionment.** Recognizing that comparing negligence, intentional wrongdoing, and activities that warrant strict liability requires the trier to compare incommensurable qualities, the Restatement of Apportionment rejects the terms comparative negligence and comparative fault altogether in favor of comparative responsibility. *See* RESTATEMENT (THIRD) OF TORTS: APPORTIONMENT OF LIABILITY § 8 cmt. a (2000). Under this section, the trier considers various factors in assigning responsibility. "The nature of each person's risk-creating conduct includes such things as how unreasonable the conduct was under the circumstances, the extent to which the conduct failed to meet the applicable legal standard, the circumstances surrounding the conduct, each person's abilities and disabilities, and each person's awareness, intent, or indifference with respect to the risks." *Id.*, cmt. c. Is this merely one way of saying the trier considers the *Carroll Towing* factors? If not, then does this approach invite the triers to exercise their biases? How can an appellate court review the sufficiency of evidence for any particular assignment of "responsibility?"

BOARD OF COUNTY COMMISSIONERS OF TETON COUNTY V. BASSETT

8 P.3d 1079 (Wyo. 2000)

GRANT, DISTRICT JUDGE. . . .

The Wyoming Highway Patrol pursued Ortega from Dubois at high speeds. [Ortega was wanted in two jurisdictions and considered to be armed and dangerous.] Ortega repeatedly swerved from his own lane toward oncoming traffic, and otherwise presented a menace to the traveling public in an apparent attempt to cause a crash which would divert the pursuing officers or involve them in a crash. These efforts failed, but the officers were unable to stop Ortega, making the roadblock necessary.

[Sheriff's deputies decided to establish the roadblock] beyond the intersection of U.S. Highway 89 and Antelope Flats Road. At that location, they placed improvised road spikes in the hope that Ortega would turn off of the highway onto the road and be stopped when the spikes disabled his vehicle. Ortega did not turn off of the highway, and continued on until he was stopped by the crash just on the Jackson side of the roadblock.

As these events were unfolding, appellees, Michael Coziah (Coziah) and Rayce Bassett (Bassett), were enroute home from fishing at Coulter Bay. As they approached Moran Junction, where they would turn south toward Jackson, they passed several officers who were at the right of the road. These were Sergeant Wilson of the Wyoming Highway Patrol and park police whom he was briefing. None of these officers made any effort to warn appellees of the hazardous situation developing on U.S. Highway 89 onto which appellees' vehicle turned.

As appellees approached the roadblock, surprised officers began frantically gesturing for them to go through as a deputy sheriff moved his car for their passage. Ortega, approaching at 100 miles per hour or more, went through the same opening, smashing into Coziah's car which was going approximately thirty miles per hour. Coziah and Bassett were injured, and Ortega was arrested.

. . . [Bassett and Coziah sued.] The jury allocated 0% fault to Coziah, 40% fault to the Wyoming Highway Patrol, 20% fault to the Sheriff's officers, and 40% fault to the National Park Service. . . .

Since it is dispositive, we turn first to the question of whether Ortega, whose conduct was willful and wanton or intentional, should have been included among the actors whose fault would be determined and compared with that of the other actors by the jury in apportioning fault among the actors as required by Wyo. Stat. Ann § 1–1–109. Appellees contend, and the district court held, that Ortega's willful and wanton or intentional conduct could not be compared with the conduct of appellants. . . .

Unlike the version before the 1994 amendment to Wyo. Stat. Ann. 1–1–109, which used "negligence," its present iteration introduces the more inclusive term "fault" and defines it as including conduct that is "in any measure negligent" eliminating degrees or varieties of negligence consistent with one of the purposes of the statute, that is to ameliorate the harshness of the doctrine of contributory negligence. The comparative negligence statute remedied the injustice of the doctrine of contributory negligence by stating that a plaintiff's negligence prevents recovery only in proportion as it causes plaintiff's damages.

The use of the word "includes" is significant because "includes" generally signifies an intent to enlarge a statute's application, rather than limit it, and it implies the conclusion that there are other items includable, though not specifically enumerated.

Appellees insist this is not so because the words "reckless," "wanton," "culpable" or "intentional" were stricken from the definition of "fault" in Senate File No. 35 evincing clear intent that they were not included in the definition of "fault" as conduct "in any measure negligent." This argument reads more into the deletion than we think justified. It leaves unexplained the legislature's expansion of "negligence" to "fault" which includes conduct "in any measure negligent." It may be as reasonable to attribute the deletions to a belief that the deleted words are subsumed in the phrase "in any measure negligent" as it would be to attribute them to other motives. . . .

Application of Wyo. Stat. Ann. § 1–1–109 in this case to include Ortega as an actor is also consistent with the other purpose of the statute, the elimination of joint and several liability. Subsection (e) provides that "[e]ach defendant is liable only to the extent of that defendant's proportion of the total fault * * *." To leave an actor such as Ortega out of the apportionment calculation exposes the remaining appellants to the possibility that they will be held to answer for his misconduct. Such a result does act as an incentive to those with a duty to protect against intentional harm, and "[a] number of courts therefore have concluded that persons who negligently fail to protect against the specific risk of an intentional tort should bear the risk that the intentional tortfeasor is insolvent." Restatement (Third) of Torts § 24 cmt. b at 164 (Proposed Final Draft (Revised) 3/22/99). The statutory elimination of joint and several liability, however, forecloses our consideration of the merits of such a policy. . . .

The exclusion of Ortega from the verdict form frustrates the legislature's expressed intent, and the defendants were entitled to have the causation rule of DeWald given as an instruction to the jury. We reverse and remand for a new trial.

NOTES

1. **Comparing negligence with intentional wrongdoing.** Several courts agree with the proposition that negligence of one defendant can be compared with intentional or willful wrongdoing of another. *Slack v. Farmers Ins. Exch.*, 5 P.3d 280 (Colo. 2000) (statute construed to require comparison of intentional wrong and negligence where defendant referred plaintiff to a chiropractor it should have known might sexually assault her); *see Barth v. Coleman*, 878 P.2d 319 (N.M. 1994) (bar owner negligently failed to oust or control a threatening attacker, he attacked plaintiff; fault must be apportioned between bar owner and attacker; held, bar owner liable only for his own percentage of fault); *Rodenburg v. Fargo-Moorhead Young Men's Christian Ass'n*, 632 N.W.2d 407 (N.D. 2001) ("A negligent tortfeasor's conduct is compared with an intentional tortfeasor's conduct."); *Berberich v. Jack*, 709 S.E.2d 607 (S.C. 2011) ("comparative negligence encompasses the comparison of ordinary negligence with heightened forms of misconduct"). For a different view, see the next case.

2. **Attributing less fault to an intentional tortfeasor.** Could a jury ever attribute less fault to an insolvent, intentional tortfeasor? In *Hutcherson v. City of Phoenix*, 961 P.2d 449 (Ariz. 1998), a woman made a 911 call reporting a credible threat that she would be killed in a few minutes. She was, and it could have been prevented if the dispatcher had categorized the call as a priority one call, which would have provided an immediate police response. The jury allocated 75% of the fault to the city based upon the dispatcher's negligence and only 25% to the killer. This was upheld by the court of appeals. The state Supreme Court avoided the issue by declaring that the defendant had no duty to plaintiffs. *See* Ellen M. Bublick, *Upside Down? Terrorists, Proprietors, and Civil Responsibility for Crime Prevention in the Post-9/11 Tort-Reform World*, 41 LOY. L.A. L. REV. 1483, 1521 (2008) (suggesting that these apportionments can be upheld if they are viewed as apportionments of civil responsibility rather than as apportionments of fault).

3. **Plaintiff-defendant comparisons.** Distinguish: plaintiff, chargeable with contributory fault, sues an intentional tortfeasor. Ellen M. Bublick, *The End Game of Tort Reform: Comparative Apportionment and Intentional Torts,* 78 NOTRE DAME L. REV. 355 (2003), notes that courts rarely call for apportionment of responsibility as between a contributorily negligent plaintiff and an intentionally wrongdoing defendant. In *Landry v. Bellanger,* 851 So.2d 943 (La. 2003), the court, governed in part by a statute, held: (1) the plaintiff who negligently provokes an intentional tort will recover full damages against the intentional tortfeasor; (2) the plaintiff who is herself an intentional tortfeasor can recover against an intentional tortfeasor defendant with damages reduced for comparative fault; (3) the plaintiff can recover nothing against a defendant whose intentional attack is privileged, as in the case of self-defense.

TURNER V. JORDAN, 957 S.W.2d 815 (Tenn. 1997). The plaintiff was a nurse and the defendant a psychiatrist at the same facility. One of the defendant's patients had a known history of violence, but the psychiatrist took no steps to protect those who might be attacked. He later said he did not know the patient's history of violence, but he himself had been attacked by the patient, and he had referred to that history in suggesting that the patient be encouraged to leave "against medical advice." The patient beat the plaintiff, causing a severe head injury. The jury attributed all the fault to the psychiatrist and awarded the plaintiff $1,186,000. The trial judge, however, thought the allocation of fault unjustified and ordered a new trial. *Held,* reversed and remanded for reinstatement of the jury verdict. The key issue is "whether the negligent act of a defendant should be compared with the intentional act of another in determining comparative fault. . . . [T]he concern in cases that compare the negligence of a defendant with the intentional act of a third party is not burdening the negligent tortfeasor with liability in excess of his or her fault; conversely, the primary concern in those cases that do not compare is that the plaintiff not be penalized by allowing the negligent party to use the intentional act it had a duty to prevent to reduce its liability. In our view, the conduct of a negligent defendant should not be compared with the intentional conduct of another in determining comparative fault where the intentional conduct is the foreseeable risk created by the negligent tortfeasor." Such a comparison presents practical difficulties in comparing acts that are different in both degree and kind and "reduces the negligent person's incentive to comply with the applicable duty of care." Further, a negligent defendant "should not be permitted to rely upon the foreseeable harm it had a duty to prevent so as to reduce its liability."

NOTES

1. **Rejecting apportionment between intentional and negligent tortfeasors.** A number of cases or statutes side with *Turner* by holding or providing that apportionment between a negligent defendant and an intentional tortfeasor is not permitted, at least not in situations like the one reflected in *Bassett* and *Turner*. *See Bhinder v. Sun Co.*, 819 A.2d 822 (Conn. 2003); *Kansas State Bank & Trust Co. v. Specialized Transp. Servs., Inc.*, 819 P.2d 587 (Kan. 1991); *Veazey v. Elmwood Plantation Assocs., Ltd.*, 650 So.2d 712 (La. 1994). In *Brandon v. County of Richardson*, 624 N.W.2d 604 (Neb. 2001), the court construed its statutes to exclude comparison between negligence and intent, but also observed that "it would be irrational to allow a party who negligently fails to discharge a duty to protect to reduce its liability because there is an intervening intentional tort when the intervening intentional tort is exactly what the negligent party had a duty to protect against."

2. **Intent and negligence under the Restatement of Apportionment.** The Restatement of Apportionment favors comparison of all forms of culpability, so that the trier assigns a percentage of responsibility both to the negligent and to the intentional actor. However, when a negligent defendant specifically risks an intentional tort to the plaintiff, there is no apportionment to reduce the plaintiff's damages—the negligent defendant remains jointly and severally liable to the plaintiff. RESTATEMENT (THIRD) OF TORTS: APPORTIONMENT OF LIABILITY § 14 (2000). And the intentional tortfeasor is always jointly and severally liable for the entire damage. *Id.* § 12; *cf. Woods v. Cole*, 693 N.E.2d 333 (Ill. 1998) (joint and several liability remains for concerted action).

3. **Intentional tortfeasor's indemnity obligation.** If a negligent tortfeasor is held liable for the entire amount of the plaintiff's damages, could he obtain an indemnity judgment against the intentional tortfeasor? *See Degener v. Hall Contracting Corp.*, 27 S.W.3d 775 (Ky. 2000).

4. **Causal apportionment?** In *Welch v. Southland Corp.*, 952 P.2d 162 (Wash. 1998), the court held that apportionment of "fault" under the statute only includes some species of negligence, not intentional wrongdoing, so the defendant who negligently permits an intentional tortfeasor to harm the plaintiff is liable without apportionment. Yet in *Tegman v. Accident & Medical Investigations, Inc.*, 75 P.3d 497 (Wash. 2003), the same court said that while the negligent tortfeasor could not apportion "fault" to the intentional tortfeasor, the negligent tortfeasor would not be liable for damages caused by the intentional tortfeasor. Under standard concepts of causation, how could this work?

5. **Single, indivisible injury; either defendant's act is sufficient to cause harm.** Suppose two defendants negligently set separate fires. Each fire is blown by winds towards the plaintiff's farm. Either would suffice to burn the house down, but by happenstance of the winds, the two fires "combine" before they reach the plaintiff's farm. It is then burned down by the combined

fire. Defendant A is fully insured but B has no insurance and no assets. Should A be liable for only one-half the damages? Notice that (a) his negligence is exactly the same as if B did not exist, and (b) the damage is exactly the same as if B did not exist.

6. **A's negligence creates B's opportunity for harm.** In one kind of traditional joint and several liability case, the first tortfeasor's negligence makes the second tortfeasor's fault possible. In *Hines v. Garrett*, 108 S.E. 690 (Va. 1921), the railroad was responsible for putting the plaintiff at risk of rape by unknown persons. She was in fact raped and the railroad was held liable. The railroad's fault is significant but obviously not in the category with that of the rapists. Does it really make any sense to apportion fault at all in this kind of case, and, if so, to limit the railroad's liability?

7. **A problem.** Suppose that Tenant leases premises from Landlord. The landlord's duty to the tenant is to warn of dangers of which the landlord actually knows and the tenant does not. The landlord knows the floor is flimsy and could collapse and he does warn the tenant. The tenant thereafter invites a social guest to the premises without warning the guest. The floor collapses with the guest, causing her injuries. What liabilities if any should be visited upon Landlord and Tenant in a state that has abolished joint and several liability? *Rittenour v. Gibson*, 656 N.W.2d 691 (N.D. 2003).

C. NON-PARTIES AT FAULT

CRAMER V. STARR

375 P.3d 69 (Ariz. 2016)

PELANDER, VICE CHIEF JUSTICE.

[Defendant Courtney Cramer rear-ended a car in which plaintiff Tammy Munguia was a passenger. Munguia had an MRI that revealed disc protrusions in her lumbar spine. Approximately eight months later, Dr. John Ehteshami performed spinal fusion surgery, which did not cure Munguia's symptoms and might have exacerbated her condition. Munguia filed suit against Cramer. Cramer filed a notice naming Dr. Ehteshami as a non-party at fault. The trial court granted Munguia's motion for partial summary judgment to strike the notice, based on determination that Cramer, as the original tortfeasor, was liable for foreseeable risks, including risk of negligently performed medical treatment. The Court of Appeals declined to exercise jurisdiction. Cramer petitioned for and was granted review in the Arizona Supreme Court.]

Under Arizona's comparative fault regime, "[i]n assessing percentages of fault" in a personal injury action, "the trier of fact shall consider the fault of all persons who contributed to the alleged injury." A.R.S. § 12–2506(B). In allocating fault, the trier may consider a nonparty's negligence or fault if the defendant gives notice that "a nonparty was wholly or partially at fault." *Id.* . . .

Cramer argues that the trial court, by striking her notice, erroneously took the issue of comparative fault from the jury, in violation of A.R.S. § 12–2506. She also asserts that Second Restatement § 457, on which the trial court relied, could never trump that controlling Arizona statute and case law and, in any event, has been superseded by Restatement (Third) of Torts, Liability for Physical and Emotional Harm § 35 (Am. Law Inst. 2009) ("Third Restatement § 35").

Munguia counters that Arizona courts have long embraced the OTR [original tortfeasor rule] embodied in Second Restatement § 457 (as retained and broadened in Third Restatement § 35), a rule she characterizes as one of causation that was not displaced or abrogated by the Uniform Contribution among Tortfeasors Act ("UCATA"). A.R.S. §§ 12–2501 through –2509. Under the OTR, Munguia asserts, Cramer cannot escape or reduce her liability by claiming harm was caused by non-party Dr. Ehteshami, but rather she is independently liable for any and all enhanced harm proximately resulting from her actions and foreseeably caused by a successive tortfeasor.

We agree with Cramer that UCATA applies and controls the outcome here. As first enacted in 1984, the Act allowed a tortfeasor who paid more than the percentage of damages attributed to it by the factfinder to seek contribution from co-tortfeasors. The legislature amended the Act three years later by generally eliminating plaintiffs' ability to recover jointly from any or all liable defendants. With certain exceptions not applicable here, the liability of each defendant for damages is several only. Thus, Arizona's pure comparative fault scheme protects defendants from bearing more than their fair share of liability for a plaintiff's injuries under the harsh common-law rule of joint and several liability.

UCATA requires apportionment of damages based on degrees of fault. Under § 12–2506(A), "[e]ach defendant is liable only for the amount of damages allocated to that defendant in direct proportion to that defendant's percentage of fault." "Fault" is broadly defined as "an actionable breach of legal duty, act or omission proximately causing or contributing to injury or damages sustained by a person seeking recovery." UCATA is thus based on the concept of fault, which necessarily presupposes a duty, breach of duty, and causation.

Under A.R.S. § 12–2506(B), the trier of fact assesses percentages of fault after considering the fault of all persons who contributed to the alleged injury. That mandate applies "regardless of whether the person was, or could have been, named as a party to the suit." UCATA thus contemplates and permits the naming of nonparties whose alleged fault the trier of fact may consider in apportioning liability. . . . We have repeatedly held that under UCATA, the trier of fact must consider the fault of all parties and properly named nonparties in assessing and allocating percentages of fault. . . .

Neither the court's ruling nor Munguia's argument can be reconciled with UCATA's clear directives. Section 12–2506(D) identifies various circumstances under which "a party is responsible for the fault of another person, or for payment of the proportionate share of another person." But those exceptions do not apply here. And the statutes contain no exception to UCATA's several-liability rule when (1) a medical provider's post-accident services, even if medically necessary and foreseeable, are allegedly negligent and cause the claimant to sustain new or enhanced injury, or, more broadly, (2) when a non-party at fault is a medical practitioner.

Having named Dr. Ehteshami as a nonparty at fault, Cramer is entitled to have the trier of fact consider Dr. Ehteshami's alleged negligence in assessing percentages of fault. . . . As Cramer acknowledges, she bears the burden of proving any fault on Dr. Ehteshami's part. . . .

The trial court based its ruling on Second Restatement § 457, entitled "Additional Harm Resulting From Efforts to Mitigate Harm Caused by Negligence," which sets forth the OTR:

> If the negligent actor is liable for another's bodily injury, he is also subject to liability for any additional bodily harm resulting from normal efforts of third persons in rendering aid which the other's injury reasonably requires, irrespective of whether such acts are done in a proper or a negligent manner.

The comments to that section indicate that when a negligent actor causes an injury that may require medical services, it is reasonably foreseeable that such services could be performed negligently, thereby adding to the original injury. In such cases, the original tortfeasor is responsible for any additional injury resulting from the other's exposure to the risk of negligently performed medical services. Our court of appeals has referred to and arguably relied on, but not expressly adopted, Second Restatement § 457. . . .

In Arizona, if there is no statute or case law on a particular subject, we have traditionally followed the Restatement of Laws, and generally will embrace the Restatement if it prescribes a sound and sensible rule. Here, however, UCATA and our case law clearly permit Cramer's notice of nonparty at fault and, assuming evidentiary support exists, require the trier of fact to consider Dr. Ehteshami's alleged negligence in assessing and allocating fault and to determine liability. Thus, to the extent Second Restatement § 457 can be read to preclude those procedures and to support the trial court's ruling, it is directly contrary to Arizona law and we reject it. . . .

The Restatement (Second) of Torts has been updated and revised by the Restatement (Third) of Torts. As it relates to the OTR, the Third Restatement generally reiterates Second Restatement § 457. *See* Third Restatement § 35, cmt. a. Entitled "Enhanced Harm Due to Efforts to Render Medical or Other Aid," Third Restatement § 35 provides:

> An actor whose tortious conduct is a factual cause of harm to another is subject to liability for any enhanced harm the other suffers due to the efforts of third persons to render aid reasonably required by the other's injury, so long as the enhanced harm arises from a risk that inheres in the effort to render aid.

The Third Restatement emphasizes that adoption of several-only liability statutes like UCATA does not require or imply any change to the OTR. As Comment (d) explains, this is because "[m]odern adoption of pure several liability *limits the liability* of each defendant liable for the same harm to that defendant's comparative share of the harm." Several liability, however, does not provide rules about *when* defendants are liable for harm that they caused. Instead, as Comment (d) clarifies, when the state's governing law imposes several liability, each of the defendants is held liable for the amount of damages reflecting the enhanced harm *discounted* by the comparative share of responsibility assigned by the factfinder to that defendant.

Thus, the OTR, now set forth in Third Restatement § 35, can be read in conjunction with the governing law of the state. When the state's law generally provides for several-only liability, as does UCATA, the OTR provides guidelines only regarding *when* a defendant may be subject to liability for future, enhanced harm that stems from the original negligent conduct—e.g., when the original tortfeasor's conduct created a reasonably foreseeable risk that future medical services may be necessary and that those services may be performed negligently. But the Third Restatement makes clear that the OTR yields to a state's law governing the apportionment of fault (and consequently, damages) based on the factfinder's determination of each potential tortfeasor's comparative share of responsibility. . . .

Subject to UCATA, the OTR can serve a useful purpose in cases like this. As stated earlier, the rule cannot be used to automatically impute to the original tortfeasor the subsequent negligence of a medical provider or other person who renders aid reasonably required by the original tortfeasor's act. But because UCATA defines fault as an actionable breach of duty that proximately caused the plaintiff's injury, plaintiffs remain free to argue under Third Restatement § 35 that an original tortfeasor proximately caused subsequent, enhanced injury and shares all or at least some responsibility for that injury. *See* Third Restatement § 35, cmt. d (noting that the "subsequent negligence of one rendering assistance to an injured person is not a superseding cause of any enhanced harm, thereby including such harm within the initial tortfeasor's scope of liability").

UCATA does not immunize or shield Cramer from liability for the enhanced harm allegedly caused by Dr. Ehteshami's negligence. If Munguia shows that the conditions of Third Restatement § 35 are met, Cramer will have proximately caused the enhanced harm, and her liability for such harm will be determined, consistent with UCATA, by the jury's assessment of comparative fault.

The trial court erred in striking Cramer's notice of nonparty at fault. . . .

PRICE V. KITSAP TRANSIT, 886 P.2d 556 (Wash. 1994). The plaintiff, already suffering from a whiplash in an earlier bus accident, was riding the defendant's bus. A four-year-old boy, walking in the aisle and holding his father's hand, suddenly reached into the driver's area and engaged an emergency stop switch, bringing the bus to a sudden halt and causing serious injury to the plaintiff. The jury found that the boy was guilty of 80% of the negligence, his father 10% and the bus company 10%. Tort reform legislation required the jury to apportion fault among "every entity which caused the claimant's damages, including the claimant or person suffering personal injury or incurring property damage, defendants, third-party defendants, entities released by the claimant, entities immune from liability to the claimant and entities with any other individual defense against the claimant. . . ." *Held,* no fault can be apportioned to the boy. Children under six years of age are incapable of negligence. Although fault of an immune entity is to be considered, the boy is not immune; rather, he is not at fault. "This interpretation agrees with the fundamental practice of not assigning fault to animals, inanimate objects, and forces of nature which are not considered 'entities' under the statute."

NOTES

1.   **UCATA.** The Uniform Contribution among Tortfeasors Act was a model act prepared by the National Commissioners on Uniform State Laws. The act was quite influential, and adopted by over 20 state legislatures. The Act shifted away from all-or-nothing contributory fault and provided for the division of responsibility between parties by percentages assigned by the jury. The Act retained joint and several liability. However, most legislatures, as in Arizona, changed the rule to several liability. The Uniform Law Commission replaced the Act with the Uniform Apportionment of Tort Responsibility Act ("The Uniform Apportionment Act"). This subsequent act would reapportion uncollectible shares between the parties. Though many commentators regard the later Act as more fair and coherent, most state legislatures have not changed their rules.

2.   **Apportioning fault to non-parties.** What happens if the jury apportions a large percentage of the fault to the surgeon? Does the driver have to pay it? Does the surgeon have to pay it? Who bears that portion of the loss? Why wouldn't the plaintiff just sue both the driver and the surgeon? If the defendant has to prove the doctor was a non-party at fault, should the defendant have to bring in expert testimony and comport with other burdens of proving medical negligence?

3.   **Effects of eliminating some defendants or non-parties from the calculus.** As *Price* suggests, the effects of abolishing joint and several liability may be mitigated if the negligence of some persons is disregarded in calculating comparative fault. Notice that the result in *Price* does not quite mimic the result of a joint and several liability system. The bus company is not liable for 90% but presumably only 50%.

4.   **Phantom tortfeasors.** Plaintiffs have sometimes argued that the fault of any person who is not joined as a party in the suit should be ignored, so that only the fault of the plaintiff and the actual defendants should be compared. The plaintiff would not join an insolvent tortfeasor and could not join an unknown tortfeasor like a hit and run driver. Some courts have held that the fault of everyone, joined or not joined, is to be considered. However, the Uniform Apportionment Act allocates responsibility among those who are actual parties to the litigation and disregards the fault of all nonparties except released persons. *See* UNIFORM APPORTIONMENT OF TORT RESPONSIBILITY ACT, PREFACE, APPORTIONING TORT RESPONSIBILITY IN THIS ACT (2002).

5.   **Immune tortfeasors.** One major area of current decision in the courts is whether liability should be apportioned to immune parties such as employers. Some cases oppose this apportionment. *See CSX Transp., Inc. v. Miller*, 46 So.3d 434 (Ala. 2010) (FELA). However, others have held that the negligence of immune persons must be considered in determining the fault percentages of other tortfeasors. *E.g., Collins v. Plant Insulation Co.*, 110 Cal. Rptr. 3d 241 (Ct. App. 2010). The inevitable result of including the immune tortfeasors is that the amount of fault attributable to the solvent and non-immune defendant is reduced, and his liability along with it. Sometimes statutes so provides. *See* LA. CIV. CODE § 2324B. This is also the provision of the Uniform Apportionment Act.

6.   **Settlement effects.** Suppose the plaintiff suffers $100,000 damages as a result of the combined negligence of A and B. A settles for $50,000. The plaintiff goes to trial against B and the jury finds her total damages to be $100,000 and B's negligence is 70%, while P's negligence is 10% of the total. If joint and several liability is abolished, isn't it clear that the plaintiff should recover $70,000 from B, even though that gives her a recovery in excess of the total damage? *See Wells v. Tallahassee Mem'l Reg'l Med. Ctr., Inc.*, 659 So.2d 249 (Fla. 1995). The Uniform Apportionment Act considers the fault of and apportions responsibility to only those tortfeasors who are parties, *except* that it considers the fault of (a) immune persons and (b) persons who have settled with the plaintiff. Under this approach, if the plaintiff settles with A, then sues

B, and the jury in the suit against B finds A's fault to be 75% and B's 25%, B owes only 25% of the damages. In contrast, Massachusetts has held that the fault of a settling tortfeasor is ignored in its joint and several liability system; the jury apportions 100% of the fault between the plaintiff and defendant. *Shantigar Found. v. Bear Mountain Builders,* 804 N.E.2d 324 (Mass. 2004).

§ 4. METHODS OF APPORTIONING LIABILITY: SPECIAL CONTEXTS

In Chapter 9, we saw jury allocations of fault between negligent parties, as well as the Restatement (Third) of Torts' idea about factors for assigning shares of responsibility. In certain contexts that we will see in this section, apportioning liability raises special questions.

A. CRASHWORTHINESS CASES: CAUSAL OR FAULT APPORTIONMENT?

D'AMARIO V. FORD MOTOR CO.
806 So.2d 424 (Fla. 2001)

PER CURIAM. . . .

Clifford Harris, a minor, was injured when the car in which he was riding as a passenger collided with a tree and then burst into flames. The car was driven by a friend of Harris who was allegedly intoxicated and speeding at the time of the accident. As described in the opinion below:

> A witness to the crash circled the car twice and noticed a fire in the engine area. Some minutes later, the fire spread and an explosion occurred, engulfing the car in flames. Harris was severely injured, losing three limbs and suffering burns to much of his body.

Harris, and his mother, Karen D'Amario, sued Ford alleging that a defective relay switch in the automobile caused Harris's injuries. The plaintiffs did not seek damages against Ford for the injuries to Harris caused by the initial collision with the tree. Rather, they sought damages for the injuries caused by the alleged defective relay switch only. Ford asserted as an affirmative defense that the injuries were proximately caused by the negligence of a third party, although in its answer to the complaint, Ford did not specifically identify the vehicle's driver as a non-party tortfeasor.

At trial, the two sides advanced conflicting theories as to the cause of the fire and Harris's injuries. The plaintiffs' "theory of liability was that a relay switch failed, thus preventing it from disrupting the flow of power to the fuel pump." Plaintiffs' experts "testified that gasoline continued to be pumped after the impact and caused the fire." On the other hand, Ford's experts countered that the relay switch and fuel pump properly worked and that the original crash caused an oil pan to burst, which resulted in an oil-based fire. . . .

[A]t trial, Ford moved to amend its affirmative defenses to include an allegation that Harris's injuries were caused by the fault of a third party, and proffered evidence of the driver's intoxication and excessive speed. The trial court granted Ford's request and held that an apportionment defense was available and evidence of the driver's actions in causing the initial accident could be admitted in support of such defense. In the face of such ruling, the parties stipulated to the jury that the negligent and excessive speed of the driver caused the initial accident and that at the time the driver had a blood alcohol level of .14 percent.

Following deliberations, the jury returned a verdict for the defense, finding that Ford was not a legal cause of the injuries to Harris. [The trial judge granted a new trial, but the intermediate appellate court reversed, upholding the defense verdict.]

. . . Outside of Florida, courts have wrestled with the comparative fault issue and have adopted conflicting views. Under what has been characterized by *Whitehead v. Toyota Motor Corp.*, 897 S.W.2d 684 (Tenn.1995), as the "majority view," the fault of the plaintiff or a third party in causing the initial accident is recognized as a defense to a crashworthiness case against a product manufacturer. This line of cases reasons that the fault of the person causing the accident that created the circumstances in which the second accident occurred should be compared with the role of the automobile manufacturer's negligence in designing a defective product in assessing total responsibility for the claimant's injuries. [The court cited seven other cases supporting this view.

In contrast to the approach of the "majority" view, the "minority" view, rejecting the application of comparative fault principles, focuses on the underlying rationale for imposing liability against automobile manufacturers for secondary injuries caused by a design defect. . . .

Jimenez pointed out that the rule of damages in crashworthiness cases also effectively acts to apportion fault and responsibility between the first and second collisions and their respective causes:

. . . [T]he concept of "enhanced injury" effectively apportions fault and damages on a comparative basis; defendant is liable only for the increased injury caused by its own conduct, not for the injury resulting from the crash itself. Further, the alleged negligence causing the collision is legally remote from, and thus not the legal cause of, the enhanced injury caused by a defective part that was supposed to be designed to protect in case of a collision.

Under this reasoning, concerns about fairness in apportioning responsibility for damages based upon fault in crashworthiness cases are satisfied by the limitation of liability of a manufacturer to only those damages caused by the defective product.

Hence, the primary reason offered by courts excluding evidence of the driver's fault in causing an accident is that the accident-causing fault is not relevant to whether an automobile manufacturer designed a defective product, and, further, that such evidence, if admitted, may be unduly prejudicial to the plaintiff. . . .

The automobile manufacturers urge us to adopt the "majority" view. . . . They cite section 768.81(3), Fla. Stat. (1997), which provides for the entry of "judgment against each party liable on the basis of such party's percentage of fault" and this Court's interpretation of the statute in *Fabre v. Marin,* 623 So.2d 1182 (Fla.1993).

In *Fabre* . . . [we] interpreted the term "party" to include all persons who contributed to the accident "regardless of whether they have been or could have been joined as defendants." However, it is not entirely clear that our holding in *Fabre* resolves the question presented today since *Fabre* involved a simple automobile accident involving joint and *concurrent* tortfeasors, and did not involve successive tortfeasors or enhanced or secondary injuries allegedly stemming from a manufacturing or design defect. . . .

We have searched for an appropriate analogy to help us resolve the issue. In the context of a medical neglect case, for example, courts in this state have concluded that (1) the cause of an initial injury which may require medical assistance is not ordinarily considered as a legal cause of injuries resulting from the subsequent negligence of the medical-care provider; and (2) an initial wrongdoer who causes an injury is not to be considered a joint tortfeasor with a subsequent medical provider whose negligence enhances or aggravates injuries caused by the initial wrongdoer. In other words, in cases involving medical malpractice, the cause of the underlying condition that brought the patient to the professional, whether a disease or an accident, is not to be compared to the cause of the independent enhanced injury allegedly resulting from medical neglect. . . .

In *Whitehead,* the plaintiff's decedent was brought to the defendant hospital after he attempted to commit suicide. While under the care of the treating doctor, Whitehead died. An expert testified that the care received by Whitehead deviated from the standard practice in the community and that but for the doctor's negligence, Whitehead would have survived. The jury was instructed that it could consider Whitehead's own conduct as a defense to the medical malpractice claim against the doctor and hospital and the jury returned a verdict for the defense.

On appeal, however, the First District reversed, holding that Whitehead's conduct was too remote and could not be considered the proximate legal cause of his injuries from the alleged professional malpractice. . . .

[C]rashworthiness cases involve separate and distinct injuries—those caused by the initial collision, and those subsequently caused by a second collision arising from a defective product. We agree that when viewed in this light, crashworthiness cases may be analogized to medical malpractice cases involving a successive negligent medical provider who is alleged to have either aggravated an existing injury or caused a separate and additional injury. Thus, just as the injury-causing fault of the patient in *Whitehead* was held not relevant in assessing the doctor's subsequent and separate negligence, the accident-causing fault of the driver would not be relevant in crashworthiness cases in assessing a manufacturer's neglect in designing an automobile or its parts. The initial accident merely furnished the occasion for the manufacturer's fault to be tested. . . .

We are not unmindful of the concerns that a manufacturer not end up improperly being held liable for damages caused by the initial collision. Of course, we must remember that in crashworthiness cases the plaintiff not only has the burden of proving the existence of a defect and its causal relationship to her injuries, but she must also prove the existence of additional or enhanced injuries caused by the defect. In this regard, we are impressed with the reasoning of the federal district court in *Jimenez* that the proper application of the crashworthiness doctrine is also consistent with comparative fault principles. The major concern of those courts following the majority rule is in seeing that successive tortfeasors only be held liable for the damages they cause, and not be held liable for damages caused by the initial tortfeasor. We agree with this concern, but see no reason why it cannot be properly addressed, as in *Jimenez,* by a recognition of the crashworthiness doctrine's legal rationale limiting a manufacturer's liability only to those damages caused by the defect. . . .

We also conclude that to inject the issue of the driver's fault in causing the initial accident into the trial of a crashworthiness case tends to unduly confuse the jury by focusing attention on the conduct giving rise to the accident instead of the issues of the existence of a defect and its role in causing the enhanced injuries. . . .

[The decision of the District Court of Appeal upholding the verdict for Ford is quashed.]

NOTES

1.   **Subsequent law.** After *D'Amario,* a Florida Court of Appeal panel considered its scope in *Jackson v. York Hannover Nursing Centers,* 876 So.2d 8 (Fla. Dist. Ct. App. 2004). In that case, the Medical Center transferred a

patient to the defendant nursing home. At time of transfer the patient suffered from pressure sores and was in a state of dehydration; but the Medical Center did not so advise the nursing home. The nursing breached its duty to assess the patient and to provide care for the dehydration and sores, and the patient died three weeks later. In a suit against the nursing home, the nursing home claimed that the Medical Center was negligent and that its negligence should be considered in apportioning fault, even though the Medical Center was not a party. The personal representative argued *D'Amario.* The court held that *D'Amario* had no application because there was no "distinct injury." Consequently, a jury verdict attributing 75% of the fault to the Medical Center and only 25% of the fault to the nursing home was upheld. Is *D'Amario* fundamentally about "distinct" injuries?

2.   **Legislative action.** In an action designed specifically to overrule *D'Amario,* the Florida Legislature passed the following statute: "In a products liability action alleging that injuries received by a claimant in an accident were enhanced by a defective product, the trier of fact shall consider the fault of all persons who contributed to the accident when apportioning fault between or among them. The jury shall be appropriately instructed by the trial judge on the apportionment of fault in products liability actions where there are allegations that the injuries received by the claimant in an accident were enhanced by a defective product." Fla. Stat. Ann. § 768.81. The legislature was concerned that failure to apportion would be unfair to the products liability defendant. What concerns might apportionment itself raise in crashworthiness cases? See Ellen M. Bublick, *The Tort-Proof Plaintiff: The Drunk in the Automobile, Crashworthiness Claims, and the Restatement (Third) of Torts,* 74 BROOK. L. REV. 707 (2009) ("[C]rashworthiness cases involving drunk drivers present one instance of a crucial but newly configured challenge in tort law: how to preserve the structural accountability of negligent and strictly liable tortfeasors within an apportionment system that is not only dominated by several liability, but for the first time in the long history of tort law, apportions responsibility not only to negligent actors but to strictly liable, reckless, and intentional wrongdoers as well.").

3.   **Indivisible injuries.** Do you think that *D'Amario* would control a case in which no one could show how much harm was caused by the second impact? In that case, how should responsibility be apportioned where joint and several liability has been abolished? *See* RESTATEMENT (THIRD) OF TORTS: PRODUCTS LIABILITY § 16 (1998).

B. MARKET SHARE LIABILITY

HYMOWITZ V. ELI LILLY & CO.

539 N.E.2d 1069 (N.Y. 1989)

WACHTLER, CHIEF JUDGE.

[In 1941, the Food and Drug Administration (FDA) approved marketing of a drug known generically as diethylstilbestrol or DES. Over the years the drug was marketed for use by pregnant women. One of its purposes was to prevent miscarriages. The drug was a generic drug, that is, not the patented property of any one company. New companies would market the drug, others would drop out. Some 300 companies in all sold the drug for varying lengths of time to varying numbers of consumers.

[Although the drug first appeared to be safe, it later appeared that female children of mothers who used the drug were at risk for vaginal cancers and terrible complications when they reached adult years. It was often impossible for mothers to know or recall the name of the manufacturer of a drug she had taken twenty years earlier. For this reason, a DES daughter might be unable to show which of the manufacturers produced the particular specimen ingested by her mother.

[The cases before the Court here are suits by DES daughters against one or more DES manufacturers. In the trial court, the defendants moved for summary judgment on the ground, among others, that the defendant which had produced the particular chemical ingested by the plaintiffs' mothers could not be identified. These motions were denied. The Appellate Division affirmed.]

The paradigm of alternative liability is found in the case of Summers v. Tice, (33 Cal.2d 80, 199 P.2d 1). In Summers, plaintiff and the two defendants were hunting, and defendants carried identical shotguns and ammunition. During the hunt, defendants shot simultaneously at the same bird, and plaintiff was struck by bird shot from one of the defendants' guns. The court held that where two defendants breach a duty to the plaintiff, but there is uncertainty regarding which one caused the injury, "the burden is upon each such actor to prove that he has not caused the harm" The central rationale for shifting the burden of proof in such a situation is that without this device both defendants will be silent, and plaintiff will not recover; with alternative liability, however, defendants will be forced to speak, and reveal the culpable party, or else be held jointly and severally liable themselves. Consequently, use of the alternative liability doctrine generally requires that the defendants have better access to information than does the plaintiff, and that all possible tortfeasors be before the court It is also recognized that alternative liability rests on the notion that where there is a small number of possible wrongdoers, all of whom breached a duty to the plaintiff, the likelihood that any one of them injured the plaintiff is relatively high, so that forcing them to exonerate themselves, or be held liable, is not unfair.

In DES cases, however, there is a great number of possible wrongdoers, who entered and left the market at different times, and some of whom no longer exist. Additionally, in DES cases many years elapse between the ingestion of the drug and injury. Consequently, DES defendants are not in any better position than are plaintiffs to identify the manufacturer of the DES ingested in any given case, nor is there any real prospect of having all the possible producers before the court. Finally, while it may be fair to employ alternative liability in cases involving only a small number of potential wrongdoers, that fairness disappears with the decreasing probability that any one of the defendants actually caused the injury. . . .

Nor does the theory of concerted action, in its pure form, supply a basis for recovery. This doctrine, seen in drag racing cases, provides for joint and several liability on the part of all defendants having an understanding, express or tacit, to participate in "a common plan or design to commit a tortious act" (Prosser and Keeton, Torts § 46, at 323 [5th ed.];) As . . . the present record reflects, drug companies were engaged in extensive parallel conduct in developing and marketing DES. There is nothing in the record, however, beyond this similar conduct to show any agreement, tacit or otherwise, to market DES for pregnancy use without taking proper steps to ensure the drug's safety. Parallel activity, without more, is insufficient to establish the agreement element necessary to maintain a concerted action claim. Thus this theory also fails in supporting an action by DES plaintiffs.

In short, extant common-law doctrines, unmodified, provide no relief for the DES plaintiff unable to identify the manufacturer of the drug that injured her. This is not a novel conclusion; in the last decade a number of courts in other jurisdictions also have concluded that present theories do not support a cause of action in DES cases. Some courts, upon reaching this conclusion, have declined to find any judicial remedy for the DES plaintiffs who cannot identify the particular manufacturer of the DES ingested by their mothers. Other courts, however, have found that some modification of existing doctrine is appropriate to allow for relief for those injured by DES of unknown manufacture.

We conclude that the present circumstances call for recognition of a realistic avenue of relief for plaintiffs injured by DES. . . .

Indeed, it would be inconsistent with the reasonable expectations of a modern society to say to these plaintiffs that because of the insidious nature of an injury that long remains dormant, and because so many manufacturers, each behind a curtain, contributed to the devastation, the cost of injury should be borne by the innocent and not the wrongdoers. This is particularly so where the Legislature consciously created these expectations by reviving hundreds of DES cases. Consequently, the ever-evolving dictates of justice and fairness, which are the heart of our common-law system, require formation of a remedy for injuries caused by DES.

We stress, however, that the DES situation is a singular case, with manufacturers acting in a parallel manner to produce an identical, generically marketed product, which causes injury many years later, and which has evoked a legislative response reviving previously barred actions. Given this unusual scenario, it is more appropriate that the loss be borne by those that produced the drug for use during pregnancy, rather than by those who were injured by the use, even where the precise manufacturer of the drug cannot be identified in a particular action. We turn then to the question of how to fairly and equitably apportion the loss occasioned by DES, in a case where the exact manufacturer of the drug that caused the injury is unknown. . . .

In Sindell v. Abbott Labs, [607 P.2d 924 (Cal. 1980)], the court synthesized the market share concept by modifying the Summers v. Tice alternative liability rationale in two ways. It first loosened the requirement that all possible wrongdoers be before the court, and instead made a "substantial share" sufficient. The court then held that each defendant who could not prove that it did not actually injure plaintiff would be liable according to that manufacturer's market share. The court's central justification for adopting this approach was its belief that limiting a defendant's liability to its market share will result, over the run of cases, in liability on the part of a defendant roughly equal to the injuries the defendant actually caused.

In the recent case of Brown v. Superior Ct., 44 Cal.3d 1049, 245 Cal.Rptr. 412, 751 P.2d 470, the California Supreme Court resolved some apparent ambiguity in Sindell v. Abbott Labs., and held that a manufacturer's liability is several only, and, in cases in which all manufacturers in the market are not joined for any reason, liability will still be limited to market share, resulting in a less than 100% recovery for a plaintiff. Finally, it is noteworthy that determining market shares under Sindell v. Abbott Labs. proved difficult and engendered years of litigation. After attempts at using smaller geographical units, it was eventually determined that the national market provided the most feasible and fair solution, and this national market information was compiled.

Four years after Sindell v. Abbott Labs., the Wisconsin Supreme Court followed with Collins v. Eli Lilly & Co., 116 Wis.2d 166, 342 N.W.2d 37. Deciding the identification issue without the benefit of the extensive California litigation over market shares, the Wisconsin court held that it was prevented from following Sindell due to "the practical difficulty of defining and proving market share" (id., at 189, 342 N.W.2d, at 48). Instead of focusing on tying liability closely to the odds of actual causation, as the Sindell court attempted, the Collins court took a broader perspective, and held that each defendant is liable in proportion to the amount of risk it created that the plaintiff would be injured by DES. Under the Collins structure, the "risk" each defendant is liable for is a question of fact in each case, with market shares being relevant to this determination (id., at 191, 200, 342 N.W.2d 37). Defendants are allowed, however, to exculpate themselves by showing that their product could not have caused the injury to the particular plaintiff (id., at 198, 342 N.W.2d 37).

The Washington Supreme Court, writing soon after Collins v. Lilly & Co., took yet another approach (see Martin v. Abbott Labs., 102 Wash.2d 581, 689 P.2d 368). . . .

Under the Washington scheme, defendants are first allowed to exculpate themselves by proving by the preponderance of the evidence that they were not the manufacturer of the DES that injured plaintiff. Unexculpated defendants are presumed to have equal market shares, totaling 100%. Each defendant then has the opportunity to rebut this presumption by showing that its actual market share was less than presumed. If any defendants succeed in rebutting this presumption, the liability shares of the remaining defendants who could not prove their actual market share are inflated, so that the plaintiff received a 100% recovery (id., at 605–606, 689 P.2d 368).[1] The market shares of defendants is a question of fact in each case, and the relevant market can be a particular pharmacy, or county, or State, or even the country, depending upon the circumstances the case presents (George v. Parke-Davis, 107 Wash.2d 584, 733 P.2d 507).

[W]e are led to the conclusion that a market share theory, based upon a national market, provides the best solution. As California discovered, the reliable determination of any market smaller than the national one likely is not practicable. Moreover, even if it were possible, of the hundreds of cases in the New York courts, without a doubt there are many in which the DES that allegedly caused injury was ingested in another State. Among

---

[1] The actual operation of this theory proved more mathematically complex when the court was presented with the question of what to do about unavailable defendants. Recognizing that the possibility of abuse existed when defendants implead unavailable defendants, who would then be assumed to have had an equal share of the market, the court placed the burden upon appearing defendants to prove the market share of the absent ones (George v. Parke-Davis, 107 Wash.2d 584, 733 P.2d 507). If this can be proved, the plaintiff simply cannot recover the amount attributable to the absent defendant, and thus recovery in the case is less than 100%. If the market share of the absent defendant cannot be shown, the remaining defendants who cannot prove their market shares have their shares inflated to provide plaintiff with full recovery. Finally, if all appearing defendants can prove their market shares, their shares are never inflated, regardless of whether the market share of a nonappearing defendant can be proved or not; thus, in this situation, the plaintiff again will not recover her full damages (id.).

the thorny issues this could present, perhaps the most daunting is the spectre that the particular case could require the establishment of a separate market share matrix. We feel that this is an unfair, and perhaps impossible burden to routinely place upon the litigants in individual cases.

Nor do we believe that the Wisconsin approach of assessing the "risk" each defendant caused a particular plaintiff, to be litigated anew as a question of fact in each case, is the best solution for this State. Applied on a limited scale this theory may be feasible, and certainly is the most refined approach by allowing a more thorough consideration of how each defendant's actions threatened the plaintiff. We are wary, however, of setting loose, for application in the hundreds of cases pending in this State, a theory which requires the fact finder's individualized and open-ended assessment of the relative liabilities of scores of defendants in every case. Instead, it is our perception that the injustices arising from delayed recoveries and inconsistent results which this theory may produce in this State outweigh arguments calling for its adoption.

Consequently, for essentially practical reasons, we adopt a market share theory using a national market. We are aware that the adoption of a national market will likely result in a disproportion between the liability of individual manufacturers and the actual injuries each manufacturer caused in this State. Thus our market share theory cannot be founded upon the belief that, over the run of cases, liability will approximate causation in this State. Nor does the use of a national market provide a reasonable link between liability and the risk created by a defendant to a particular plaintiff. Instead, we choose to apportion liability so as to correspond to the over-all culpability of each defendant, measured by the amount of risk of injury each defendant created to the public-at-large. Use of a national market is a fair method, we believe, of apportioning defendants' liabilities according to their total culpability in marketing DES for use during pregnancy. Under the circumstances, this is an equitable way to provide plaintiffs with the relief they deserve, while also rationally distributing the responsibility for plaintiffs' injuries among defendants.

To be sure, a defendant cannot be held liable if it did not participate in the marketing of DES for pregnancy use; if a DES producer satisfies its burden of proof of showing that it was not a member of the market of DES sold for pregnancy use, disallowing exculpation would be unfair and unjust. Nevertheless, because liability here is based on the over-all risk produced, and not causation in a single case, there should be no exculpation of a defendant who, although a member of the market producing DES for pregnancy use, appears not to have caused a particular plaintiff's injury. It is merely a windfall for a producer to escape liability solely because it manufactured a more identifiable pill, or sold only to certain drugstores. These fortuities in no way diminish the culpability of a defendant for marketing the product, which is the basis of liability here.

Finally, we hold that the liability of DES producers is several only, and should not be inflated when all participants in the market are not before the court in a particular case. We understand that, as a practical matter, this will prevent some plaintiffs from recovering 100% of their damages. However, we eschewed exculpation to prevent the fortuitous avoidance of liability, and thus, equitably, we decline to unleash the same forces to increase a defendant's liability beyond its fair share of responsibility. . . .

MOLLEN, JUDGE [concurring in part and dissenting in part].

. . . I respectfully disagree with the majority's conclusion that there should be no exculpation of those defendants who produced and marketed DES for pregnancy purposes, but who can prove, by a preponderance of the evidence, that they did not produce or market the particular pill ingested by the plaintiff's mother. Moreover, in order to ensure that these plaintiffs receive full recovery of their damages, as they are properly entitled to by any fair standard, I would retain the principle of imposing joint and several liability upon those defendants which cannot exculpate themselves. . . .

NOTES

1. **The *Sindell* court's adoption of market-share.** Market-share apportionment is one of those rules that has a specific beginning point. Building on the suggestion of a law review writer, Comment, *DES and a Proposed Theory of Enterprise Liability*, 46 FORDHAM L. REV. 963 (1978), the California Supreme Court initiated market-share liability in *Sindell v. Abbott Laboratories,* 607 P.2d 924 (Cal. 1980).

2. **Several, not joint liability.** The idea was so new that the California Court itself may initially have had some kind of idea that it involved joint and several liability. The California court later made it clear that the market-share idea is not one of joint and several liability. It is several liability apportioned according to the defendant's relative share of the market in the drug that caused injury. Thus it is not (a) liability apportioned according to fault; (b) it is not liability apportioned on the basis of relative causation; and (c) it is not joint and several liability. *See Brown v. Superior Court*, 751 P.2d 470 (Cal. 1988).

3. **Market-share and probabilistic causation.** Is market-share similar to the loss of chance idea we first saw in Chapter 7? Cases recognizing that theory have seemingly approved a recovery for the lost *chance* of good health, even if that chance was not a very large one; and, correspondingly, such cases seem to contemplate that damages would be proportional to the chance, which would be only a fraction of the damage caused by the injury itself. Professor Farber has described "proportional" recovery as one that "spreads compensation over all possible victims, fully compensating no one but paying something even on the weakest claim." Daniel A. Farber, *Toxic Causation*, 71 MINN. L. REV. 1219 (1987). Notice, however, that the market-share solution addresses only the defendants' causal responsibility for *exposure* to the drug.

The connection between exposure and subsequent injury remains an issue of fact.

4. **Acceptance of market-share theories.** Several courts have accepted the central thrust of the market-share idea but have modified some details. *See, e.g., Smith v. Cutter Biological, Inc.*, 823 P.2d 717 (Haw. 1991); *cf. Thomas v. Mallett*, 701 N.W.2d 523 (Wis. 2005) (allowing "risk-contribution theory" against lead carbonate manufacturers, without deciding how damages might be apportioned among liable manufacturers). But several states have expressly rejected the market-share approach. Illinois, for instance, rejected market-share on the ground that the plaintiff's burden of proving causation was a fundamental principle of tort law. *Smith v. Eli Lilly & Co.*, 560 N.E.2d 324 (Ill. 1990). Ohio took a similar line in *Sutowski v. Eli Lilly & Co.*, 696 N.E.2d 187 (Ohio 1998). Rhode Island rejected the whole thing in two conclusory sentences, without giving a single reason pro or con. *Gorman v. Abbott Labs.*, 599 A.2d 1364 (R.I. 1991). Missouri rejected the theory as applied to a lead paint case in *City of St. Louis v. Benjamin Moore & Co.*, 226 S.W.3d 110 (Mo. 2007), saying even if the plaintiff could prove "that a particular defendant held a certain share of the lead paint market in the city at the relevant time or even if it could prove that because of defendant's market share there was a statistical probability that its paint was in a certain percentage of the properties at issue, that would not establish that the particular defendant actually caused the problem."

5. **Alternative causation.** Michigan rejected market share in favor of a *Summers v. Tice* approach, but then hampered practical use of that approach by requiring the plaintiff to bring in all the actors and to prove negligence rather than strict liability. *Abel v. Eli Lilly & Co.*, 343 N.W.2d 164 (Mich. 1984).

6. **Concert of action, enterprise liability.** A theory often raised in these cases but almost never accepted is that all of the manufacturers should be held jointly and severally liable because they acted in concert. The conscious parallel actions in the way they produced or warned of the product might be interpreted as an implicit agreement, just as two drag racers who take off together from a stop light might be regarded as having agreed to race even if no one spoke a word. The concert of action theory appeals to the oldest form of joint and several liability, and it works in the drag racing case. But in the products liability cases it has not been accepted on the basis of parallel business practices alone. A variation on the idea of concerted action is sometimes called "enterprise liability." It is based on common adherence to an industry-wide standard, which only seems to be a different form of proof. Most decisions have refused to apply these theories to products liability cases.

Two unusual cases that found enough on the particular facts to justify potential liability on an "enterprise liability" or concerted action theory are *Hall v. E.I. DuPont de Nemours & Co.*, 345 F.Supp. 353 (E.D.N.Y. 1972) (six manufacturers produced all the dynamite caps, none labeled, followed practices of trade association), and *Nicolet, Inc. v. Nutt*, 525 A.2d 146 (Del. 1987) (actual conspiracy to fraudulently conceal dangers of asbestos alleged).

7. **Cases for excluding market-share liability?** Should market-share liability, if appropriate in DES cases, be used in any of the following: (a) The strict liability claim is not based on the claim of a design defect but only a manufacturing flaw. (b) The defendant's product is one of many using the dangerous substance, but the various products use the substance in different amounts. For example, shipyard workers were once exposed heavily to asbestos in working around insulating materials but they might also be exposed if they had used hair dryers in the same period of time. (c) Only a small number of people are exposed to the dangerous substance in quantities that create a risk of harm.

8. **Blood products.** People whose blood does not readily coagulate (hemophiliacs) sometimes need a blood protein called a "factor" in order to control bleeding. The factor is derived from donated blood and can carry the AIDS virus or HIV. Plaintiff has tested positive for AIDS. The virus was apparently communicated through the Factor VIII administered to the plaintiff. It was produced by one of several manufacturers, but no one can say which one. The blood shield law provided against liability except that each entity "shall remain liable for . . . its own negligence or wilful misconduct." Does "its own negligence" mean that no entity supplying blood can be liable on market-share theories? In any event, notice that the blood factor provided is not uniform, because not all units will contain HIV. Should the producers nevertheless be held on a market share theory? *Smith v. Cutter Biological, Inc.*, 823 P.2d 717 (Haw. 1991).

9. **Useful drugs.** When a plaintiff attempted to apply market-share theories to an injury from a childhood vaccine (DPT), the New Jersey Court drew back. Although the court did not reject market-share generally, it did reject that theory as applied to the vaccine involved. Because the vaccine was "essential to public welfare," and because some manufacturers had withdrawn from the market due to threats of products liability, the court feared market-share liability would either diminish manufacture of the drug or diminish safety research. It might also prevent development of other important drugs, such as a vaccine against AIDS. In addition, the court was persuaded that the right of vaccine-injured plaintiffs to recover compensation under the National Childhood Vaccine Injury Act provided an adequate, non-tort remedy. *Shackil v. Lederle Labs.*, 561 A.2d 511 (N.J. 1989). The Vaccine Injury Act creates a fund for payment of specified vaccine injuries by levying a tax on the vaccines. The fund is then liable for individual injuries covered by the statute. Doesn't this work out to be a form of market-share liability?

10. **Questions for evaluation.** If market-share liability works in practice as its theory predicts, would it impose any liabilities greater than the liability that would be imposed if we knew all the facts about causation? If the concern is that liability may drive manufacturers from the market or from desirable research, is that concern limited to market-share claims, or does it apply to *any* liability? And why do we ordinarily argue that liability will encourage more safety research but think that it would prevent such research in the drug or vaccine case? These or similar ideas are discussed by Justice

O'Hern in his dissent in *Shackil, supra* Note 9. Is it possible to think of the *Shackil* rule as an exemption from liability which amounts to a subsidy paid by the injured persons?

§ 5. AN INTRODUCTION TO SETTLEMENTS

NOTE: BEING AWARE OF INSURANCE

Knowledge of insurance and insurance law is extremely important in personal injury law practice. The subject usually gets a course to itself in law schools. We must omit details, but a few things must be understood.

One kind of insurance is "first party" insurance. You buy the coverage you want in case of harm to you or your property. Fire insurance and automobile collision insurance is like this. A common feature of first-party insurance policies is that the insured is entitled to recover upon proof of loss covered by the policy and it is not necessary to show fault on the part of anyone. Indeed, even the insured's own fault, short of intentional damage to his own property, is irrelevant.

A second general kind of insurance is "liability" insurance. You buy liability insurance in the amount you want or the amount you are legally required to have, but the insurance does not pay you. Instead it pays your *legal liability* to a person who claims you caused harm to him or to his property. Such insurance pays the claimant only if you are legally liable, so your insurance company has a right to your cooperation and a right to defend you. It also has a *duty* to defend you up to the amount of your policy.

The duty to defend carries with it the insurer's right to be involved in, if not to control, the investigation, negotiation and settlement of the case. It imposes upon the insurer the obligation to retain an attorney to defend the insured's interests. The result of all this is that to a very large extent the insurer is the *de facto* defendant, though in most states the named defendant in court is the insured, not the insurer. The lawyer, even if retained by the insurer, continues to owe his primary duty to the insured as the client, but must cooperate with the insurer except where the insurer and the insured's interests conflict.

The liability insurer's exact duties depend primarily on the contract between it and the insured, that is, upon the policy terms. The insurer can argue that under the terms of the policy it has a "policy defense"—some reason under the policy that the particular claim against the insured is excluded from insurance coverage. This creates a complex relationship between insured persons and their insurers, and sometimes serious conflicts. If the liability insurer fails to meet either its duty to defend or to pay on your behalf, it may become liable to you in tort. You can see an example in *State Farm Mut. Auto. Ins. Co. v. Campbell*, 538 U.S. 408 (2003).

An important effect of liability insurance is that it provides a fund available to pay judgments, without which legal liability might be meaningless. Over the years there has been an increased "socialization" of insurance, in which liability insurance is seen as a tool for financing injury loss. The existence of liability insurance encourages the expansion of tort liability, and could at times encourage excessive damages awards. KENNETH S. ABRAHAM, THE LIABILITY CENTURY: INSURANCE AND TORT LAW FROM THE PROGRESSIVE ERA TO 9/11 (2008). Does liability insurance protection undercut the idea of individual accountability and the effects of deterrence?

A. BASIC RULES

Settlement entails a prediction of what would happen if the case were tried. That in turn requires lawyers to know both the substantive tort doctrine and the rules of damages. It also requires lawyers to estimate whether the defendant has assets or insurance that would pay the award. And since most torts involve at least two potential defendants, intelligent settlement also requires lawyers on all sides to know how liability can be apportioned among defendants. The practical concerns in this chapter also raise important questions about values and goals.

The vast majority of tort suits are settled without trial. The plaintiff accepts a sum of money and gives the defendant a document, usually a "release," the effect of which is to absolve the defendant of further liability. Consequently, settlement practice is part of the actual practice of tort law.

In general, settlement negotiations happen behind the scenes. Terms of proposed settlement offers cannot be admitted at trial either as an admission of fault or for any other purpose. Furthermore, statutes in a number of states provide that a defendant may make a written offer to settle a claim for a certain amount (called an "offer of judgment"). If the plaintiff rejects this offer and then fails to obtain a more favorable judgment at trial, the plaintiff must pay all of the defendant's costs, including attorney fees, from the time of the offer. *See, e.g.,* N.Y. C.P.L.R. § 3221; CAL. CIV. PROC. CODE § 998 (also applying, in a limited way, to plaintiffs' offers). What impact do such provisions have on settlement strategy? What goals are served by such laws?

Settlements reflect the lawyers' estimates of how the facts will play out at trial and how legal issues will probably be decided. So the standard of care requires lawyers to prepare for settlement much as they would prepare for trial, with good development of the facts and clear understanding of the legal issues and arguments. Knowing the facts bearing on liability is not enough; lawyers must also know the facts about injury, its probable extent, and possible future effects. Settlement estimates cannot be made with certainty and sometimes settlement law involving multiple parties is itself complex.

The law and ethics rules pertaining to lawyers provides that it is the client's decision, not the lawyer's, whether and on what terms to settle a claim. The lawyer is obligated to explain the ramifications of settlement offers with sufficient clarity to allow the client to reach such a decision. This is both an ethical and a legal obligation. RESTATEMENT OF THE LAW GOVERNING LAWYERS § 22 (2000); ABA MODEL RULES OF PROFESSIONAL CONDUCT 1.2(a) & 1.4. The lawyer who fails fully to inform his client about acceptance of a settlement is subject to liability for malpractice. *Wood v. McGrath, North, Mullin & Kratz, P.C.,* 589 N.W.2d 103 (Neb. 1999). Moreover, a lawyer who negligently advises a client to settle may be subject to a legal malpractice claim as well. *See* PAUL T. HAYDEN & DOUGLAS NEJAIME, ETHICAL LAWYERING 136–44 (4th ed. 2018). In rare cases, a lawyer may be found to have breached a fiduciary duty to the client in connection with settlement recommendations. A rather egregious example is *Johnson v. Nextel Communications, Inc.,* 660 F.3d 131 (2d Cir. 2011), where the court found such a breach of duty when the firm entered into a secret agreement with the clients' employer in which the employer paid money to the lawyers in exchange for the lawyers' persuading the clients to abandon their ongoing legal and administrative actions against the employer, and to instead accept an expedited ADR procedure.

B. IMPROVIDENT SETTLEMENT

GLEASON V. GUZMAN

623 P.2d 378 (Colo. 1981)

QUINN, J.

On September 29, 1970, Darlene Benavidez, then a fourteen-year-old minor, was struck on the head by a vending machine that fell from a truck operated by Irwin Gleason in the course of his employment with Coin Fresh, Inc. (defendants). Darlene Benavidez has since married and is now known as Darlene Guzman (plaintiff). Immediately after the accident she was taken to Denver General Hospital for examination. She complained of headache, vomiting and some disorientation and, after two days of observation and testing, her injury was diagnosed as a left temporal lobe contusion and she was released as improved. On October 13, 1970, the plaintiff was readmitted to the hospital with complaints similar to those previously experienced. Further testing resulted in a diagnosis of left intratemporal lobe hematoma and the plaintiff was discharged as improved on October 20, 1970. Shortly thereafter plaintiff returned to high school and a normal routine. She and her parents, Mr. and Mrs. Benavidez, believed that plaintiff had fully recovered from the injury.

In November 1970 the plaintiff's parents retained an attorney in connection with their daughter's claim. Approximately two years later this attorney initiated settlement negotiations with the defendants' insurance carrier. It was mutually agreed that the case be settled for $6,114.35. The insurance carrier hired an attorney to prepare a petition for the probate court's approval of settlement and the appointment of the plaintiff's father, Mr. Benavidez, as guardian of his minor daughter's estate. The probate court approved the settlement and Mr. Benavidez, as duly appointed guardian, executed a general release of his daughter's claim against the defendant.

In May 1974, approximately forty-four months after the accident, the plaintiff experienced her first epileptic seizure during her senior year in high school. Other seizures followed. Having become emancipated through marriage, she retained her present attorneys and a complaint was filed in November 1975. The complaint sought money damages against the defendants for negligently causing personal injuries to the plaintiff in the accident of September 29, 1970. The defendants in their answer raised as an affirmative defense the release executed by the guardian and endorsed on their answer a demand for a jury trial. Thereafter, the defendants filed a motion for summary judgment on the basis of the guardian's release. The plaintiff countered with a motion to set aside the release on the ground that it was executed under a mistake as to the nature of the injury actually sustained. The court heard both motions in a consolidated hearing on November 14, 1977.

[The trial judge granted the defendants' motion for summary judgment and denied the plaintiff's motion to set aside the release. The court of appeals reversed the entry of summary judgment.]

The defendants urge two reasons why the court of appeals erred in reversing the trial court's entry of summary judgment. First, they argue that the mistake related to a future complication of a known injury, as distinct from a mistake about the nature of the injury actually suffered in the accident. Next, they contend that the release was a general release encompassing both known and unknown injuries and it thereby precluded rescission even for a mistake as to an unknown injury. . . .

Cases addressing the problem of mistake in the settlement of personal injury claims reflect a tension stemming, on the one hand, from the general need for finality in the contractual settlements of actual or potential lawsuits and, on the other hand, from a recognized need to alleviate the distorting and unintended effects which human error can impose on a transaction. See, e.g., II G. Palmer, The Law of Restitution § 11.2, 12.22 (1978); Dobbs, Conclusiveness of Personal Injury Settlements: Basic Problems, 41 N.C.L. Rev. 665 (1963). Although the approaches are not totally discrete, they do lean in different directions. One approach denies rescission even though the injuries were not known or suspected at the time of the settlement. Under this view the releasor assumes the risk that the nature and extent of known injuries might be more severe than was believed at settlement. Another approach allows rescission based on any mistake as to the condition of the injured claimant, whether the mistake relates to the nature of the injuries or to their further consequences. Midway between these approaches is the view that rescission is available for mistakes relating to the nature of known injuries but not for mistakes as to the future course and effects of those injuries. The assumption here is that rescission must be based on mistake, and mistake for legal purposes must relate to a past or present fact rather than an opinion or prophecy about the future.

This latter approach represents the rule in this jurisdiction. [In *McCarthy v. Eddings*] the plaintiff suffered a broken arm but, based on his doctor's representation, believed that the injury was temporary in duration and executed a release. Thereafter, he discovered that the broken bones in the arm had not united and the resulting disability was permanent. We affirmed the jury verdict for the plaintiff and held that a release obtained as the result of a mutual basic mistake could be set aside as ineffective.

The *McCarthy* rule was further refined in *Davis v. Flatiron Materials Co.*, 511 P.2d 28 (Colo. 1973), which upheld the validity of a release. . . . Noting that the injury was correctly diagnosed and that the plaintiff was fully informed about the nature of her condition, we held that to justify rescission the mistake "must relate to a present existing fact or a past fact," rather than as there present, a mistake concerning the future course of recovery from the known injury.

We again addressed this problem in *Scotton v. Landers*, 543 P.2d 64 (Colo. 1975), where the plaintiff, believing that he suffered a fractured rib and bruises in an automobile accident, executed a general release only to discover shortly thereafter that his spleen had been ruptured and had to be surgically removed. We concluded that the mistake was sufficient to avoid the release because it was grounded in the nature of injuries suffered in the accident.

As *McCarthy, Davis* and *Scotton* demonstrate, the distinction between unknown injuries and unknown consequences of known injuries is a useful analytic standard but it does not yield a litmus-type resolution to these problems. The words we use, "though they have a central core of meaning that is relatively fixed, are of doubtful application to a considerable number of marginal cases." Indeed, this is such a marginal case. With respect to post-traumatic epilepsy, the margin of difference between a mistake in diagnosis and a mistake in prognosis, or the difference between that condition as an injury and as a consequence, cannot easily be fitted into predetermined categories of exclusivity.

Judge Learned Hand pointed up the difficulty of conceptual differentiation in these matters:

> "There is indeed no absolute line to be drawn between mistakes as to future, and as to present facts. To tell a layman who has been injured that he will be about again in a short time is to do more than prophesy about his recovery. No doubt it is a forecast, but it is ordinarily more than forecast; it is an assurance as to his present condition, and so understood."

Scheer v. Rockne Motors Corp., 68 F.2d 942 (2d Cir. 1934). . . .

Knowledge of the nature of an injury requires an awareness and some appreciation of its extent, severity and likely duration. Admittedly, line-drawing here is difficult and its direction may well vary with the thrust of evidence. These basic components of knowledge, however, relate primarily to a comprehension of the basic character of the injury as distinct from a prediction or opinion about the future course of recovery when its basic nature is otherwise known. . . .

The record before us provides an adequate basis from which one may reasonably infer the existence of mistake in the execution of the release by the guardian. He had little formal education and was not adept or articulate in the English language. According to the deposition testimony of the attorney who originally represented the plaintiff, the most sophisticated concept used by the guardian in connection with the injury was "concussion."

As noted by the court of appeals, from the date of the accident through the settlement the plaintiff experienced only minor symptoms. It may reasonably be inferred that when the release was executed the guardian believed the injury was minor, that it posed no risk of complication, that it was temporary in duration, and that his daughter had fully recovered. There is no evidence that anyone, including physicians and the original attorney, disabused the guardian of these beliefs. In fact, the attorney's legal preparation and his settlement correspondence to the defendants' insurance carrier belie any awareness that the injury posed any risk of brain dysfunction, much less post-traumatic epilepsy. This attorney's belief that the plaintiff had fully recovered from her injury is clearly discernible in his representations to the probate judge at the settlement hearing. . . .

When the record is examined in its entirety, it is apparent that there exists a genuine factual issue on whether the guardian was mistaken about the nature of his daughter's injury when he executed the release. Under these circumstances, summary judgment was inappropriate. . . .

The defendants argue that the guardian's release constitutes a bar to the plaintiff's claim as a matter of law because its terms are all inclusive and encompass unknown injuries that may later develop or be discovered as well as their effects and consequences.

Although some jurisdictions give effect to the language of a release so as to preclude avoidance even as to unknown injuries, the tendency of the law is to the contrary. Most courts provide for avoidance in appropriate circumstances, such as mistake or lack of intent, despite the presence of language in the release broad enough to cover the claim in question. . . .

Resolution of the intent issue necessarily means going behind the language of the release. If unknown injuries were not within the contemplation of the parties, the release will be set aside. . . .

[Judgment of the Court of Appeals, reversing the trial court's judgment, is affirmed. Concurring and dissenting opinions are omitted.]

NOTES

1. **Applying *Gleason*.** Is it clear how you can apply the rule in *Gleason*? In *Nevue v. Close*, 867 P.2d 635 (Wash. 1994), the plaintiff thought she had a neck sprain and settled for $150, then discovered a back injury. The court said its rule was that "where there are known injuries, here the neck sprain, the release is binding as to those injuries and as to the unknown consequences of the known injury. However, as to an injury unknown to the plaintiff, and not within the contemplation of the parties to the release, the release should not be binding per se. The plaintiff should bear the burden of proving that the injury was reasonably unknown and not within the contemplation of the parties." This rule seems to be about the same as the rule in *Gleason*. Given that rule, how would the court decide the case?

2. **Mutual mistake.** In *Maglin v. Tschannerl,* 800 A.2d 486 (Vt. 2002), the court said: "[P]laintiff has to show, at the very least, that the mistake was mutual. But plaintiff showed only that *she* was mistaken as to her injuries. Without a mutual mistake of fact 'one of the parties can no more rescind the contract without the other's express or implied assent, than he alone could have made it.'" Does this mean releases could never be set aside? After all, the defendants' insurers intend to secure a release for both known and unknown injuries, and releases in fact usually so state. If the insurer knows that it doesn't know all the injuries and doesn't care, because it only wants to shed responsibility, how can you say it is mistaken? Conscious ignorance—an awareness that you do not know—may negate any idea that you are mistaken. *See* 2 DAN B. DOBBS, LAW OF REMEDIES § 11.2 (1993) On this analysis, perhaps no releases should be set aside for "mistake." Or do you think that the mistake rules used in ordinary commercial contract cases are inappropriate in injury release cases?

3. **Release of unknown injuries.** In *Bernstein v. Kapneck*, 430 A.2d 602 (Md. 1981), a child was injured in 1975 in a car crash. Doctors diagnosed her with a laceration on the forehead, fractured nasal bones, a broken shoulder and a "moderately severe traumatic neurosis." Her mother, on advice of

counsel, accepted a settlement of $7,500 and signed a release that covered all claims for "bodily injuries, known and unknown, and which may have resulted or may in the future develop." Much later the child developed epileptic symptoms diagnosed to have resulted from a brain injury sustained in the 1975 accident. The mother went to court to have the release set aside on the ground of mistake. The court said no. Where, as here, there was a "mutually intended release of unknown injuries then the nature and extent of the misfortune is beside the point."

4. **Intent to assume the risk.** If the release itself provides that the injured person assumes the risk of, or releases her claims for unknown injuries, should that prevent a recovery later if the plaintiff can show that she never had any intent to assume the risk? *See Smothers v. Richland Mem'l Hosp.*, 493 S.E.2d 107 (S.C. 1997) (release bars claims for unknown injury); *Williams v. Glash*, 789 S.W.2d 261 (Tex. 1990) (intent governs but cannot be judged by the release language alone; the parties' knowledge and other factors would be considered); 2 DAN B. DOBBS, LAW OF REMEDIES § 11.9 (1993).

5. **The lawyer's role.** Consider what you would do as a lawyer to fulfill your special responsibility to ascertain the client's condition before advising a settlement.

6. **Release payments.** Notice that if the release is set aside, the plaintiff must still prove her case. Suppose that the jury ultimately finds for the defendant. The defendant is out the money paid for the release and didn't get the peace that settlement was supposed to bring either. Would the alternative be to require the plaintiff to restore the consideration paid for the release as a prerequisite to a suit on the merits?

7. **Fraud, coercion and incapacity.** Fraud, coercion, and incapacity are also grounds for avoiding a release. Incapacity represents a serious problem if the injured person is approached for settlement in the hospital, or is under sedation. Some states have enacted statutes designed to provide safeguards. New York makes it unlawful to enter a hospital to negotiate a settlement or obtain a release in most instances. N.Y. JUD. LAW § 480. Maryland provides that any personal injury release signed within five days of the injury is voidable for the next sixty days. MD. CODE ANN. CTS. & JUD. PROC. § 5–401.1.

REFERENCE: 3 DOBBS, HAYDEN & BUBLICK, THE LAW OF TORTS §§ 487–501 (2d ed. 2011); DOBBS, HAYDEN & BUBLICK, HORNBOOK ON TORTS Chapter 35 (2d ed. 2016).

CHAPTER 26

DAMAGES

■ ■ ■

§ 1. COMPENSATORY DAMAGES

Factors affecting settlement are largely factors that also affect the trial and ultimate award. As a plaintiff you don't accept an offer of $100 if you think the jury will award you $100,000. As a defendant you don't offer $100,000 if you think the jury will award nothing at all. Estimating probable jury awards is no easy matter. Lawyers must consider matters having little to do with legal rules—the probable evidence that the jury will hear and the jurors' probable reaction to that evidence, for example. However, lawyers must also know the legal rules that guide, counsel, and constrain jurors' damage awards—rules that may be enforced by the judge's instructions, directed verdict, or reduction in awards for excessiveness.

A. PROVING AND COMPUTING BASIC DAMAGES

The topic of tort damages is a part of two larger fields. One field might be called "trial practice," which concerns itself with strategy, tactics, rules of procedure and evidence for trials. The trial practice side of damages appears in this chapter only incidentally. The other field is that of "remedies," which includes not only the damages remedy but also the remedies of injunction and restitution. All three remedies are available in many tort cases. The field of remedies is a broad one, but some of the key rules are covered here.

Constitutional torts. We have seen that the plaintiff might have a personal injury or property damage claim under § 1983 based on the defendant's violation of plaintiff's constitutional rights. In such cases, courts apply the same damages rules that apply in any personal injury or property damage case. Some constitutional violations, though, cause no obvious physical injury to person or property. For instance, suppose you are denied the right to vote or your right to free speech is infringed in violation of the Constitution. In these cases, the United States Supreme Court has held that nominal damages can provide the necessary redress for a completed violation of a legal right such that courts have Article III standing to hear the case. *Uzuegbunam v. Preczewski*, 141 S. Ct. 792 (2021) ("The award of nominal damages was one way for plaintiffs at common law to 'obtain a form of declaratory relief in a legal system with no general declaratory judgment act.'") (quoting DOUGLAS LAYCOCK & RICHARD HASEN, MODERN AMERICAN REMEDIES 636 (5th ed. 2019)). However, a dissent in *Uzuegbunam* argues that the defendant should be able to moot the case at the outset by paying the dollar sought. However, a plaintiff may also be able to prove actual damages such as pecuniary loss or mental distress. 2 DAN B. DOBBS, THE LAW OF REMEDIES (2d ed. 1993) § 7.4 (hereafter cited as DOBBS, REMEDIES).

Property torts. Quite a few torts involve physical injury to, or dispossession of, tangible property, real or personal. We have already seen that for total dispossession of personalty there is a conversion action, in which damages are measured by the full market value of the thing converted. When there is similar dispossession of real property, there is no analogous damages claim. Instead, the plaintiff recovers the rental value of the property during the time of dispossession. When physical harm is done to tangible property, the measure of damages is very often the diminished value of the property. Thus if A trespasses on Blackacre and damages a house, the owner or possessor will be entitled to recover a sum equal to the difference between the value immediately before and the value immediately after the damage. When the diminished value cannot be measured through this metric, because the property "has no commercial or market equivalent, its value, or plaintiff's damages, must be ascertained in some other rational way." *See U.S. v. CB & I Constructors, Inc.*, 685 F.3d 827 (9th Cir. 2012) (upholding a jury award of $28.2 million for intangible environmental harm to government property after defendants' negligence destroyed 18,000 acres of national forest).

The diminished value rule, based on the market value, is applied in cases of damage to chattels, such as automobiles. However, for a number of reasons, the cost of repair may be substituted as a measure of damages in certain cases, especially where the repair will not likely enhance the damaged property to make it more valuable. *See Brooks v. City of Huntington*, 768 S.E.2d 97 (W.Va. 2014) (plaintiff may recover reasonable repair costs for damage to residential property even if the costs exceed the fair market value of the property before the damage, and may also recover related expenses caused by the inconvenience and loss of use of the property during the repair period).

The injunctive remedy is also important in certain tort cases. If the defendant repeatedly trespasses on the plaintiff's land, or threatens to trespass in some way that will cause irreparable harm, such as by cutting down old oak trees, the plaintiff may be entitled to an injunction prohibiting such a tort. Injunction is also important in many cases involving intangible property, such as a trademark, and in other business tort cases, such as those involving interference with contracts. *See generally* 1 DOBBS, REMEDIES, Chapter 5.

Personal injury torts. Personal injuries may occur through intentional torts, through negligence, or through strict liability torts. But the *compensatory* damages are theoretically the same for any given broken jaw without regard to whether the jaw was broken through intent, negligence, or wholly without fault. "The purpose of compensatory damages is to make the plaintiff whole for [the] injury." *Clausen v. Icicle Seafoods, Inc.*, 272 P.3d 827 (Wash. 2012). "[A]n award of damages to a person injured by the negligence of another is to compensate the victim, not to punish the wrongdoer. The goal is to restore the injured party, to the extent possible, to the position that would have been occupied had the wrong not occurred." *McDougald v. Garber*, 536 N.E.2d 372 (N.Y. 1989). The purpose of punitive damages is quite different. It is "to punish the defendant and deter similar conduct." *Clausen,* 272 P.3d at 832; *see also Opati v. Republic of Sudan,* 140 S. Ct. 1601, 1609 (2020) ("punitive damages aren't merely a form a compensation but a form of punishment"). Punitive damages may be warranted in some cases where the defendant's conduct is "malicious" or wanton.

The main elements of compensatory damages for personal injuries can be stated quite easily:

(1) Damages for reasonably incurred medical expenses resulting from the tort.

(2) Damages for lost earning capacity or wage loss resulting from the tort.

(3) Damages for pain and suffering resulting from the tort, including mental pain and suffering.

(4) In a limited number of cases, an award to pay for the cost of medical monitoring of the plaintiff's condition to intercept a prospective disease, such as cancer, that may develop in the future.

(5) Any other specifically identifiable harm that has resulted from the tort, such as special expenses necessary to travel for medical attention.

In each category, the plaintiff is not only entitled to recover for past and present damage, but is also entitled to recover for future damages if they are reasonably certain to occur. How difficult is it to calculate these elements of damages?

MARTIN V. UNITED STATES

471 F.Supp. 6 (D. Ariz. 1979)

JAMES M. BURNS, DISTRICT JUDGE.

[Federal Tort Claims Act case tried to the judge. The plaintiffs, two school boys, riding a motorbike, struck a sagging power line negligently maintained by the government. Each "suffered tragically severe and permanent injuries" from the burns.

Plaintiff Melvin Burrows II sustained severe burns to his face, head, back, buttocks, arms, and legs. Medical expenses to Burrows to the time of trial came to $48,130.97, and future medical expenses will come to about $49,000 additional. $5,000 for psychological treatments, as recommended by a psychologist, is also appropriate. Loss of earnings evidence and calculations are as follows.]

Clarence Martin is principal of the Florence middle school, owner of a roofing business that employs Melvin Burrows' father, and uncle of the other plaintiff in this case. He testified upon the basis of his observation of Melvin during the seven years he has known him and the month and a half that Melvin had attended the middle school prior to the accident. He believed that Melvin was average or above average in intelligence and probably would have become a skilled worker, perhaps a mechanic or a carpenter. Dr. Glenn Wilt, an associate professor of finance at Arizona State University and an investment counselor stated:

[I]t can be reasonably presumed that, but for their injuries, both Melvin and Jeffrey would have gravitated into positions in one of the construction trades. Clearly, that is exactly what most of their uninjured classmates will do, and considering the general demand in this territory, due to the growth of population and need for attendant services in the construction field, a strong demand can be forecast for these jobs.

Dr. David Yandell, a clinical psychologist and vocational rehabilitation counselor called by the defendant, testified that the intelligence and aptitude tests administered by Dr. Donald [Guinourd] show that Melvin could not have pursued a career in the skilled crafts but instead probably would have become a laborer. Defendant's other witness, Dr. John Buehler, chairman of the department of economics at the University of Arizona, expressed his opinion that neither plaintiff probably would have become a worker in the skilled trades, but rather each would have earned average wages.

Based upon my evaluation of the testimony and the expertise and credibility of the witnesses, I conclude that Melvin Burrows probably would have become a skilled worker. Dr. Wilt stated that a carpenter would, at 1978 wage rates, earn about $9,450 per year during a four-year apprenticeship and during a subsequent 42-year career as a journeyman carpenter would earn about $18,900 annually in wages and $3,900 annually in fringe benefits. I accept these figures as reasonable approximations of Melvin's lifetime earnings had he not experienced this accident.

Dr. Guinourd testified that Melvin might be employable as a night watchman or night diesel mechanic not involved with the public interaction aspect of either business. Dr. Wilt concluded that, because of Melvin's disfigurement and intolerance to sunlight and perspiration, he would probably be unable to find a job suited to his handicap. Dr. Canter testified that Melvin would benefit psychologically from working even at a lowly position.

Based upon the testimony and my own observation of Melvin Burrows, I conclude that he probably will be able to work at an entry-level position for at least half of his normal working life. According to Dr. Wilt, such work would generate an annual income of $3,120 in 1978 dollars. Thus, Melvin is entitled to recover in 1978 dollars $6,330 per year for four years (apprenticeship period), then $19,680 per year for the following 42 years (journeyman period). . . .

I find that the award can presently be invested at very little risk and return 7.5% compounded annually. I find that 5.5% is a reasonable annual rate of wage inflation to be expected during Melvin's working lifetime.

I award an amount for the loss of Melvin's earning capacity sufficient when invested at a 7.5% annual rate of return to generate in 1978 dollars $6,330 per year for the four years 1983–1986 (hypothetical apprenticeship period) and $19,680 per year for the following 42 years 1987–2028 (hypothetical journeyman period). These amounts in 1978 dollars are to be converted to current dollars for each year by application of a 5.5% expected annual rate of wage inflation, then discounted at 7.5% per year back to 1979. By this method of calculation, the award for loss of Melvin's earning capacity amounts to $548,029.

The power line struck Melvin on the face, head and perhaps also on the back, causing severe and extensive burns on those areas and on "blowout holes" on his buttocks, legs, left arm and right hand, where the electric current left his body seeking the ground. More than 80% of his head and face was burned, 70% to the third degree or worse. He also suffered third degree burns on 40% of his back, on his entire left buttocks and on at least six blowout ulcers. Melvin regained consciousness soon after the accident and was found wandering in the desert near the scene. Dr. Williams Clemans, a general practitioner in Florence, treated Melvin briefly in the back of a pickup truck outside the local hospital before having him sent to the burn treatment unit at the Maricopa County Hospital in Phoenix. Dr. Clemans testified that Melvin appeared to be in critical condition. He doubted whether Melvin would survive long enough to reach the burn unit.

At the Maricopa County Hospital where Melvin remained for four months, the surgeons removed the charred layers of skin and tissue from Melvin's face, head, buttocks and other areas of his body. They performed numerous skin grafts and attempted to fashion a functioning right eyelid, which Melvin still cannot close. Melvin lost his right ear entirely and the top third of his left ear. To graft skin onto his left temple, which had been burned down to the skull, the doctors ground the skull down to granulation tissue that would accept a graft. Restoring hair growth to this area would require an additional series of scalp rotation operations. The operations have left Melvin's face and scalp severely scarred, his mouth permanently contorted into a sneer. Because his facial nerves and muscles have been burned away, even additional surgery will never restore to him the ability to smile.

Of the expected eleven future operations, Melvin will undergo eight additional operations to his face. Skin grafts not infrequently dry out, crack, become infected and ulcerated and must be replaced by new grafts. Sunlight darkens grafted skin permanently, highlighting the injured area. Grafted areas are also more susceptible to skin cancer than normal tissue. Melvin testified that the grafted areas hurt and itch constantly. Dr. Sacks testified that additional plastic surgeries and skin grafts will not restore a normal appearance to Melvin.

Melvin has suffered psychologically as well as physically. At the burn unit Dr. Canter treated Melvin by hypnosis to relieve pain, prevent regurgitation of food and restore a will to live. Since emerging from the hospital Melvin has faced teasing and ridicule from his peers and startle reactions and revulsion from strangers.

For several months Melvin wore a mask to protect his healing face from further injury. His schoolmates labeled him "Maskatron." During a school outing children from another school saw him and ran away in horror. Strangers often ask, "What happened to you?" Clarence Martin testified that Melvin has become reclusive, reluctant to attend school. Dr. Canter stated that Melvin has become somewhat detached from life, blames himself for his father's heart trouble and may develop schizophrenic tendencies as a result of his injuries. Nor is it likely that Melvin will have a normal social or sexual life, given the severity of the injuries.

Based upon the testimony and my own observation of Melvin, I award $1,000,000 in compensation for pain and suffering.

[The claims made by plaintiff Martin warrant a similar analysis.]

I find that the plaintiffs are entitled to awards as follows:

	BURROWS	MARTIN
Past Medical	$48,130.97	$15,384.38
Future Medical	53,629.00	30,000.00
Loss of Earning Capacity	548,029.00	453,088.00
Pain and Suffering	1,000,000.00	750,000.00
Total	$1,649,788.97	$1,248,472.38

The foregoing shall constitute findings of fact and conclusions pursuant to Rule 52, Fed. R. Civ. P., together with earlier findings and conclusions set out in my oral opinion on February 14, 1979.

NOTES

1. **Inflation and reduction to present value.** Notice that the judge had to make an upward adjustment in the award for future loss in order to account for expected inflation. The judge also made a downward adjustment to account for the fact that although the loss will take place over many years in the future, all of the money to compensate the plaintiff will be paid now and can be invested. This reduction to present value requires the judge or the trier to determine the amount the plaintiff can earn in safe investments of the award. Any reduction may require expert testimony. *See* 1 DOBBS, REMEDIES §§ 3.7, 8.5; *Indalecio v. Mobil Oil Marianas, Inc.*, 2020 WL 1656217 (N. Mar. I. 2020) (in case of plaintiff injured at Mobil Oil plant, "the defendant has the burden to provide expert testimony to reduce future damages to present cash value").

2. **Periodic payments.** These adjustments would not be necessary if, instead of a lump sum award, future loss were compensated in periodic payments that could be varied as inflation occurred. Some states authorize such payments in a limited class of cases. *See* Roger Henderson, *Designing a Responsible Periodic Payment System for Tort Awards*, 32 ARIZ. L. REV. 21 (1990). At least two courts have held periodic payments statutes unconstitutional under state constitutional provisions against denial of due process and limitation of damages.

3. **Loss of earning capacity.** How should courts evaluate loss of earning capacity for young people who do not yet have actual earnings to guide the analysis? Would it be better not to calculate these damages at all? In *Louisville SW Hotel, LLC v. Lindsey*, 636 S.W.3d 508 (Ky. 2021) a five-year-old died in defendant's swimming pool that had cloudy water and no lifeguard despite being very crowded with children. The evidence at trial included testimony by a vocational economics expert on behalf of the estate that estimated the child's lifetime earning capacity to be between $1,890,874, and $3,770,805. However, the jury awarded $0 for lost earning capacity. The court held this award was within the jury's discretion, and also affirmed the jury's $211,000 award for medical costs and funeral expenses but reduced its $3

million punitive damage award to $1 million. A dissenting judge would have found the lost earnings judgment inadequate on the argument that "[D]amages flow naturally from the wrongful death of a person unless there is evidence from which the jury could reasonably believe that the decedent possessed no power to earn money."

4. **The scope of pain and suffering.** The pain and suffering recovery includes all forms of pain, including mental or emotional distress. *Wald v. Grainger*, 64 So.3d 1201 (Fla. 2011) (pain and suffering includes evidence of sensitivity and discomfort). The pain and suffering recovery includes the negative emotional reactions to pain as well as the pain itself. For example, a disfiguring injury, no longer physically painful, may cause a plaintiff to become self-conscious or even to withdraw from social contact. If so, such reactions count as part of the pain for which damages may be assessed. *See Engquist v. Loyas*, 787 N.W.2d 220 (Minn. Ct. App. 2010) (young girl injured after a dog bit her face, leaving permanent scars; court affirmed $15,000 award for past pain and suffering, disability, disfigurement, and emotional distress); 2 DOBBS, REMEDIES § 8.1(4). In *Martin,* how would you value never being able to smile?

5. **Proving and evaluating pain.** Pain is notoriously difficult to measure or even to talk about meaningfully. In *District of Columbia v. Howell*, 607 A.2d 501 (D.C. 1992), a nine-year-old boy was badly burned in a chemical explosion in school. "The chemicals burned at 5000 degrees Fahrenheit, and Dedrick was burned over 25% of his body including his hands, arms, chest, and face." The jury awarded $8 million in pain and suffering damages. If this award and Martin's had been made in the same year, could you say that one was wrong or even that one was closer to the mark than the other? In *Surette v. Islamic Republic of Iran,* 231 F.Supp.2d 260 (D.D.C. 2002), a group encouraged by the Republic of Iran tortured Buckley for a long period before he died of his mistreatment. In a suit for his death and for his pre-death pain and suffering, the court said: "Subject to adjustment for cases deviating from the more common experience of victims, this Court typically has awarded former hostages or their estates roughly $10,000 for each day of captivity." *See also Estate of Brown v. Islamic Republic of Iran*, 872 F.Supp.2d 37 (D.D.C. 2012) (case on behalf of victims of 1983 terrorist bombing of military barracks in Beirut, Lebanon, calculating pain and suffering among other damages).

6. **Argumentation.** Lawyers have developed some effective jury arguments, one of which is called the per diem or unit-of-time argument. It asks the jury to consider the value of pain by the minute or hour and then to multiply by the number of hours the plaintiff will continue to suffer pain over his lifetime. Federal circuit courts are divided on whether this type of argument is admissible. *Rodriguez v. Señior Frog's de la Isla, Inc.*, 642 F.3d 28 (1st Cir. 2011). In a case against Monsanto by a school district's grounds manager who he developed non-Hodgkin's lymphoma after using the herbicide roundup, plaintiff's attorney stressed that sometimes plaintiff could not leave his bedroom for several days after chemotherapy, and argued for "A million dollars per year. For all that suffering, all that pain, it's a million dollars per year." *Johnson v. Monsanto Co.*, 266 Cal.Rptr.3d 111 (Cal. App. 2020). On

appeal, the court reduced the award of future noneconomic damages from $37 million to $4 million.

7. **Pain and suffering pays attorney's fees.** One important thing to bear in mind when you judge pain and suffering awards is the American Rule that each side pays its own attorney. *See* 1 DOBBS, REMEDIES § 3.10. That rule explains why the contingent percentage fee is so important in personal injury cases. Lawyers for injured people must recover their fee from the damages award, since hardly any individual would be able to pay a guaranteed hourly fee for the lawyer's services. If there were no substantial pain and suffering award, lawyers would often be unable to pursue the claim with the vigor it requires simply because damages equal to the plaintiff's pecuniary loss would not bring enough money to justify the time invested.

B. LOST ENJOYMENT OF LIFE

MCDOUGALD V. GARBER, 536 N.E.2d 372 (N.Y. 1989). Plaintiff Emma McDougald, then 31 years old, underwent a Caesarean section and tubal ligation. During the surgery, Mrs. McDougald suffered oxygen deprivation which resulted in severe brain damage and left her in a permanent coma. This action was brought by Mrs. McDougald and her husband, suing derivatively, alleging that the injuries were caused by the defendant doctors' acts of malpractice. The trial court charged the jury that if Emma McDougald was so neurologically impaired that she was incapable of experiencing painful sensation or any emotional reaction to it, then there could be no recovery for pain and suffering. But the court went on to instruct the jury that the plaintiff could recover for loss of the pleasures and pursuits of life even if she was unaware of any loss. So instructed, the jury awarded Emma McDougald $9,650,102 in damages, including $1,000,000 for conscious pain and suffering and $3,500,000 for loss of the pleasures and pursuits of life. The balance of the damages awarded to her were for pecuniary damages—lost earnings and the cost of custodial and nursing care. On defendants' post-trial motions, the Trial Judge reduced the total award to Emma McDougald to $4,796,728, in part by reducing the separate awards for conscious pain and suffering and loss of the pleasures and pursuits of life to a single award of $2,000,000. The Appellate Division affirmed.

Held, the court erred. Lost enjoyment of life is not separate from but encompassed by pain and suffering, and cannot be awarded to a person who is not aware of her loss. "We accept [the legal fiction that money can compensate for an injury], knowing that although money will neither ease the pain nor restore the victim's abilities, this device is as close as the law can come in its effort to right the wrong.... [However, in these circumstances, an] award for the loss of enjoyment of life 'cannot provide (such a victim) with any consolation or ease any burden resting on him * * * He cannot spend it upon necessities or pleasures. He cannot experience the pleasure of giving it away.' . . . Traditionally, in this State and elsewhere, . . . the plaintiff's inability to enjoy life to its fullest has been considered one type of suffering to be factored into a general award for nonpecuniary damages, commonly known as pain and suffering. . . .

Translating human suffering into dollars and cents involves no mathematical formula; it rests, as we have said, on a legal fiction. . . . Thus, we are not persuaded that any salutary purpose would be served by having the jury make separate awards for pain and suffering and loss of enjoyment of life. We are confident, furthermore, that the trial advocate's art is a sufficient guarantee that none of the plaintiff's losses will be ignored by the jury. *Dissent,* "The capacity to enjoy life—by watching one's children grow, participating in recreational activities, and drinking in the many other pleasures that life has to offer—is unquestionably an attribute of an ordinary healthy individual. . . . As in the case of a lost limb, an essential characteristic of a healthy human life has been wrongfully taken, and, consequently, the injured party is entitled to a monetary award as a substitute. . . . The victim's ability to comprehend the degree to which his or her life has been impaired is irrelevant, since, unlike 'conscious pain and suffering,' the impairment exists independent of the victim's ability to apprehend it. . . .

NOTES

1. **Noneconomic damages.** Compensatory damages are typically divided into two categories—economic or pecuniary, and noneconomic or nonpecuniary damages. The *McDougald* court defined the categories this way: "By nonpecuniary damages, we mean those damages awarded to compensate an injured person for the physical and emotional consequences of the injury, such as pain and suffering and the loss of the ability to engage in certain activities. Pecuniary damages, on the other hand, compensate the victim for the economic consequences of the injury, such as medical expenses, lost earnings and the cost of custodial care." Would modifications to an injured employee's home count as pecuniary damage that plaintiff might be entitled to receive? *Lewis v. MBC Constr. Co.,* 962 N.W.2d 359 (Neb. 2021). Noncompensatory damages are often the more controversial of the two groups. What is the purpose of these damages? Why not just award pecuniary damages?

2. **Physical disfigurement.** Courts may recognize additional categories of damage. *See Averyt v. Wal-Mart,* 265 P.3d 456 (Colo. 2011). "[U]nder Colorado common law, damages for physical impairment and disfigurement have historically been recognized as a separate element of damages. . . . 'If someone tortiously inflicts a permanent injury on another he or she has taken away something valuable which is independent and different from other recognized elements of damages such as pain and suffering and loss of earning capacity. For this invasion the plaintiff should be awarded a separate sum in addition to the compensation for the other elements and such

recovery should be proportional to the severity of the injury.' . . .The principle that a victim is entitled 'to have a sound body and mind throughout his or her life' provides the rationale for this distinction. . . . Physical impairment and disfigurement constitute a permanent injury irrespective of any pain or inconvenience." *Pringle v. Valdez,* 171 P.3d 624 (Colo. 2007). Do you think courts should recognize some intrinsic value of a sound body and mind in *McDougald*? Does Colorado's cap on pain and suffering damages influence whether you approve of a separate category of damage for physical impairment and disfigurement?

3. **Hedonic damages: the terminology.** In the 1980s, plaintiffs' lawyers and some judges began to use the term hedonic damages from the Greek word referring to pleasure or happiness. Courts may award hedonic damages for loss of enjoyment of life—to "compensate a plaintiff for the lost ability to engage in activities that once brought pleasure." *Stachulski v. Apple New England, LLC,* 191 A.3d 1231 (N.H. 2018). Courts sometimes permit expert testimony on the issue, as in *Stachulski.* But in other cases, the court will not allow such testimony *Castro v. Melchor,* 414 P.3d 53 (Haw. 2018) ("A jury may draw upon its own life experiences in attempting to put a monetary figure on the pleasure of living. It is a uniquely human endeavor. . .requiring the trier of fact to draw upon the virtually unlimited factors unique to us as human beings. Testimony of an economist would not aid the jury in making such measurements because an economist is no more expert at valuing the pleasure of life than the average juror.")

The hedonic damages term has acquired ambiguity because those who use it sometimes seem to suggest: (a) a right of recovery for the plaintiff's awareness of lost pleasures; (b) a right of recovery for lost pleasures even when the plaintiff is *not* aware of the loss or, in fact, has died; or (c) a certain type of economic evidence.

4. **Plaintiff's awareness of loss.** When the plaintiff has lost the ability to pursue life's pleasures and knows it, that knowledge or awareness is itself a source of unpleasant feelings, a sense of loss, and even anguish. Recovery is allowed now in most courts without hesitation. *See Foradori v. Harris,* 523 F.3d 477 (5th Cir. 2008) (applying Mississippi law, affirming award of $10 million); *Maldonado v. Sinai Med. Group, Inc.,* 706 F.Supp.2d 882 (N.D. Ill. 2010) ($6.7 million noneconomic award not excessive in light of plaintiff's impaired ability to perform necessary life functions like bathing and dressing as well as pleasures such as walking and dancing); *Kenton v. Hyatt Hotels Corp.,* 693 S.W.2d 83 (Mo. 1985) (reinstating an award of $4 million which included plaintiff's loss of ability to play tennis, ski, jog, and carry on other athletic activities).

5. **Overlap with pain and suffering.** Two categories or one—should a jury be instructed that the plaintiff can recover both for pain and suffering and loss of enjoyment of life as separate sets of damages? Some courts have approved this idea. *See, e.g., Stachulski v. Apple New England, LLC,* 191 A.3d 1231 (2018) (two); *Guillory v. Saucier,* 79 So.3d 1188 (La. Ct. App. 2011)

(upholding separate awards for pain and suffering, and loss of enjoyment of life). Would it be less confusing to the jury to instruct broadly on pain and suffering and to make it clear that consciousness of lost enjoyment is a part of that pain and suffering? That was what the *McDougald* court thought. *See also Gregory v. Carey*, 791 P.2d 1329 (Kan. 1990) (concluding lost enjoyment is inextricably included in damages for pain and suffering).

6. **Plaintiff's lack of awareness of loss.** When the plaintiff is unaware of her loss, as in *McDougald*, there is no tradition of awarding damages for that "loss." However, more recent cases have gone both ways. *Compare Dillingham v. IBP, Inc.*, 219 F.3d 797 (8th Cir. 2000) (reversing judgment for pain and suffering award based on insufficient evidence), *with Flannery v. United States*, 297 S.E.2d 433 (W.Va. 1982) (stating that the underlying function of the loss of enjoyment award may be measured objectively and does not require the plaintiff's subjective awareness). *Holston v. Sisters of Third Order of St. Francis*, 650 N.E.2d 985 (Ill. 1995), may have accomplished the same thing by permitting recovery for the "disability" of a comatose patient who died after a week. Should hedonic damages be recoverable when defendant's negligence causes the still birth of plaintiff's fetus? *Castro v. Melchor*, 414 P.3d 53 (Haw. 2018) (yes; hedonic damages "may be the only way to appropriately compensate [the estate for fetus'] injury").

7. **Considering comparable awards.** You have now seen a number of jury awards in very significant injury cases. Awards can vary. Could the jury consider awards in comparable cases to fix the amount of noneconomic damages? Many courts have disapproved of this kind of evidence at trial. *See, e.g., Richardson v. Chapman*, 676 N.E.2d 621 (Ill. 1997). Where the trial judge is the trier of fact, however, a number of appellate courts approve of, and perhaps even require, the consideration of such information, usually on the ground that the trial judge is required to explain the basis for her decision. *Arpin v. United States*, 521 F.3d 769 (7th Cir. 2008) (reversing trial judge's award of damages where he did not consider awards in similar cases). On appeal, many appellate courts also consider comparable cases when determining whether an award is excessive. *See, e.g., Okraynets v. Metropolitan Transp. Auth.*, 555 F.Supp.2d 420 (S.D.N.Y. 2008) (applying New York law that requires reviewing courts to "compare verdicts sustained by New York courts in similar cases"); *Meals v. Ford Motor Co.*, 417 S.W.3d 414 (Tenn. 2013) (reinstating jury verdict for $43.8 million in favor of six-year-old car passenger who suffered spinal fracture and internal injuries from lap belt in collision with another vehicle; court detailed child's severe injuries and looked at awards in other cases involving paralysis of a young child).

But not all courts employ such evidence. *Allied Concrete Co. v. Lester*, 736 S.E.2d 699 (Va. 2013) ("Although a trial court may grant remittitur on the grounds that the award is disproportionate to the injuries suffered, we have specifically rejected comparing damage awards as a means of measuring excessiveness;" remittitur of $6.22 million jury award for wrongful death of wife in accident with cement truck was an abuse of discretion because it compared award to award in case for same victim brought by her parents). Do you see any problems with allowing a jury to consider awards in prior cases? Do all of those problems disappear when a trial or appellate judge is making the determination? Do you see any problem with not comparing?

8. **Presumptive awards.** What about creating some sort of guidelines with respect to presumptive awards? In setting up the 9/11 Victim's Compensation fund, the special master created a presumptive pain and suffering award that applied to all victims regardless of their particular situation. Would something like that be a good idea? At what amount would you set the award? Would someone with temporary but severe pain receive more or less than someone with moderate chronic pain?

NOTE: THE SPECIAL CASE OF MEDICAL MONITORING DAMAGES

The plaintiffs—sometimes whole neighborhoods or an entire workforce—are exposed to a toxic substance which increases the likelihood of a disease, usually some form of cancer. However, the plaintiffs have no demonstrable physical injury at present. They might conceivably claim either an increased risk of cancer or emotional harm resulting from their fear of future disease. But courts have typically denied both of those claims.

If the plaintiffs suffer from any physical harm because of the toxic exposure, the defendant would be liable for that harm and damages for the costs of periodic medical checks that could detect future cancers in early stages so as to permit early intervention. *See Donovan v. Philip Morris USA, Inc.*, 914 N.E.2d 891 (Mass. 2009) (where plaintiffs alleged that they had sustained present injury resulting in substantially increased risk of cancer, they stated a claim for medical monitoring expenses).

Some courts have gone further by allowing medical monitoring damages even when no physical harm has been done and no emotional harm claim is allowable. *See, e.g., Sadler v. PacifiCare of Nev.*, 340 P.3d 1264 (Nev. 2014) (plaintiff can state a cause of action for negligence with medical monitoring without asserting any present physical injury; negligence on the part of health maintenance organizations in failing to monitor medical providers who used unsafe injection practices, resulting in the plaintiffs being placed at risk of contracting, blood-borne diseases); *Perrine v. E.I. du Pont de Nemours & Co.*, 694 S.E.2d 815 (W. Va. 2010) (permitting medical monitoring claim); *Burns v. Jaquays Mining Corp.*, 752 P.2d 28 (Ariz. Ct. App. 1987) (stating that plaintiffs should be entitled to damages for the costs of regular medical monitoring without present physical symptoms after being exposed to asbestos).

But other courts have insisted that medical monitoring costs are not "actual harm" that supports a claim. Instead, these courts require the plaintiff to prove either actionable physical harm or at least physical changes before medical monitoring costs can be recovered. *See, e.g., Dougan v. Sikorsky Aircraft Corp.*, 251 A.3d 583 (Conn. 2020) (to recover for medical monitoring, plaintiff exposed to asbestos in workplace must "demonstrate that he or she suffers from a subcellular change that substantially increases his or her risk of disease"); *Benoit v. Saint-Gobain Performance Plastics Corp.*, 959 F.3d 491 (2d Cir. 2020) (New York law requires "clinically demonstrable presence of [toxins] in the plaintiff's body, or some indication of [toxin]-induced disease"). Two commentators have suggested that any other rule would be judicial "madness." James A. Henderson, Jr. & Aaron D. Twerski, *Asbestos Litigation Gone Mad: Exposure-based Recovery for Increased Risk, Mental Distress, and Medical Monitoring*, 53 S.C. L. REV. 815 (2002). Do you agree?

C. ADJUSTMENTS IN DAMAGES

NOTE: AVOIDABLE CONSEQUENCES

What if the plaintiff is injured by dental malpractice, but her failure to follow the dentist's postoperative instructions leads to her hospitalization? In *Keans v. Bottiarelli*, 645 A.2d 1029 (Conn. App. Ct. 1994), the trial court held that plaintiff's damages of $20,000, should be reduced by $5034.46, the amount of plaintiff's hospital expense, based on a finding that the plaintiff had failed to mitigate her damages. "[O]ne who is injured by the negligence of another must use reasonable care to promote recovery and prevent any aggravation or increase of the injuries." *Id*. The trial court concluded that the three requirements to establish a failure to mitigate damages were present. The plaintiff's conduct exacerbated her initial injury. The plaintiff failed to take reasonable action to lessen the damages. This failure on the part of the plaintiff caused the need for her hospitalization. The court of appeals affirmed.

The avoidable consequences or "mitigation" rule requires the plaintiff to exercise reasonable care to minimize damages and denies a recovery to the extent that damages should have been but were not reasonably minimized or avoided. *See generally* 1 DOBBS, REMEDIES §§ 3.9 & 8.7. Avoidable consequences rules reduce damages for discrete identifiable items of loss caused by the plaintiff's fault. In other words, avoidable consequences rules are "causal" apportionment rules as we saw in Chapter 7.

The Restatement of Apportionment uses a comparative responsibility approach to avoidable consequences cases. RESTATEMENT (THIRD) OF TORTS: APPORTIONMENT § 3 cmt. b (2000). Thus on the facts of *Keans*, the Restatement's rule does not call for the *Keans* result; rather, the plaintiff's recovery in *Keans* for the hospital expenses would be reduced for the plaintiff's comparative fault. *See id*. § 3 ill. 4. The Restatement view is that the doctor was alone in culpably causing the initial injury and is fully liable for that, but that he and the plaintiff together culpably cause the indivisible component of hospital expense. Since causal apportionment of the hospital expense is not possible because they both caused it, comparative fault apportionment by the jury is required. Today, courts rarely invoke the avoidable consequences doctrine.

NOTE: THE COLLATERAL SOURCE RULE AND ITS COUSINS

1.　*The collateral source rule.* Suppose the injured plaintiff, as a result of injury, collects medical insurance, continues to receive full pay from work while in the hospital, and is a recipient of a donation from sympathetic neighbors. The general rule is that in figuring the defendant's liability, all these "collateral benefits" to the plaintiff must be ignored. *See* 1 Dᴏʙʙꜱ, Rᴇᴍᴇᴅɪᴇꜱ §§ 3.8 & 8.6; *Hairston v. Harward*, 821 S.E.2d 384 (N.C. 2018) (payment of uninsured motorist benefits fell within scope of collateral-source rule and thus could not be credited against money judgment). The defendant pays the full medical expenses of the plaintiff even though they may have been paid already by the medical insurance. The defendant pays full lost earnings or lost earning capacity even though the plaintiff collected full pay as a gift from his employer or as part of his job benefits.

2.　*The windfall effect.* As perceived by many, the collateral source rule sometimes gives the plaintiff a kind of windfall: in effect, plaintiff may collect twice for the medical expenses and the "lost" wages. In *Covington v. George,* 597 S.E.2d 142 (S.C. 2004), the plaintiff's hospital bills came to about $4,000, which were claimed as damages. The defendant offered evidence that the hospital actually accepted payments, apparently from Medicare, of about $700 in full payment. This evidence was excluded, even though it suggested that the reasonable value of the medical services was much less than the nominal value of $4,000. The court said: "While a defendant is permitted to attack the necessity and reasonableness of medical care and costs, he cannot do so using evidence of payments made by a collateral source." Some jurisdictions have a different rule. *Meek v. Montana Eighth Judicial Dist. Court*, 349 P.3d 493 (Mont. 2015) (while payments made by insurers were a collateral source, evidence of the amount Medicare or other insurance paid towards plaintiff's medical expenses were admissible on the issue of the reasonableness of plaintiff's medical bills, to be considered by the court after a verdict).

3.　*The subrogation protection effect.* At other times the collateral source rule merely preserves the subrogation right of the insurer who paid the plaintiff to recover back its loss from the tortfeasor. For instance, suppose that the plaintiff's car is damaged by defendant's negligence. The plaintiff's own collision insurer pays for repairs. In the ordinary case, the collision insurer is subrogated to the plaintiff's claim against the defendant to the extent that it has paid for the car damage. In such a case the plaintiff would be entitled to recover against the defendant for the plaintiff's personal injuries and also for the car damage, but the recovery for car damage goes, by way of subrogation, to the plaintiff's collision insurance company. This can be done only because the collateral source rule allows the plaintiff to recover in spite of the fact that he has been paid. However, if the insurer has paid all of the medical claims in full, the plaintiff may not be able to show any injury at all. See *Lewis v. Lead Indus. Ass'n*, 178 N.E.3d 1046 (2020) (all mandatory lead paint testing of children was paid by Medicaid).

4. *The direct source or direct benefits rule.* The collateral source rule does not apply to payments made by the defendant itself or by a source identified with the defendant, such as the defendant's insurer. For instance, suppose the defendant has "medical pay" insurance—a kind of accident insurance that protects occupants of the defendant's car even when the defendant is not at fault. If the medical payment insurance makes a payment to the injured occupant and that occupant later sues the defendant in tort, the defendant will be entitled to a credit for the payment. The difference between this situation and the collateral source situation is that, here, the payment comes from the defendant himself or from his insurer.

Some courts have credited the defendant with the medical charges waived by a health-care provider. For example, where the plaintiff paid only $5,000 instead of $10,000 for medical care because the provider agreed to accept the lower amount, the defendant would owe only that lower amount. *See, e.g., Howell v. Hamilton Meats & Provisions, Inc.*, 257 P.3d 1130 (Cal. 2011); *Law v. Griffith*, 930 N.E.2d 126 (Mass. 2010) (range of payments provider generally accepted for services was admissible); *Swanson v. Brewster*, 784 N.W.2d 264 (Minn. 2010) (by statute, plaintiff's health insurer's "negotiated discount" must be deducted under MINN. STAT. ANN. § 548.251). Other courts would not credit the health-care provider's reduction to the defendant. *Volunteers of Am. Colo. Branch v. Gardenswartz*, 242 P.3d 1080 (Colo. 2010) (plaintiff could recover damages for full amount of medical expenses, not only the discounted amount paid by third-party insurer).

5. *Criticizing the collateral source rule.*

(a) *Eliminating subrogation to eliminate transaction costs.* The collateral source rule has many critics. In the best case, it protects an insurer's subrogation recovery. But even in this best case, it merely sets up a system where one insurer recovers from another. Since this shift of the loss entails costs, it might be better to abolish the collateral source rule.

This would mean that the collision insurer would bear the loss instead of the liability insurer for the negligent defendant. This might be unfair in some sense, but perhaps the roles of the two insurers would be reversed in the next case, so that the losses might more or less average out. If so, the costs of shifting the loss could be avoided. Even if this were not the case, abolishing the collateral source rule might be a good idea because it would mean that the loss would be paid by collision insurers which operate more efficiently than liability insurers, and hence that the loss would be handled more cheaply.

(b) *Eliminating windfalls to eliminate windfall costs.* When the collateral source rule does not merely protect a subrogation right, it may be seen as a windfall to the plaintiff. This is not entirely so, because, in the case of insurance at least, the plaintiff has paid for the right to the insurance proceeds. Still, if the plaintiff is to recover twice for some elements of damages, the total cost is excessive. The excess is charged against insurers who must reflect it sooner or later in premiums. Eventually, all insurance purchasers would pay more for insurance or goods in order to give random claimants a windfall. Putting the compulsory insurance aspects of tort recoveries together with the collateral source rule, we find that citizens who would prefer lower premiums on their liability insurance must nevertheless pay the higher price entailed to provide the windfalls of double recovery.

6. *Abolishing the collateral source rule.* The tort reform movement of the 1980s sought to limit defendants' liabilities in a number of ways, one of them by abolishing or substantially altering the collateral source rule in selective cases, usually medical malpractice claims, or those against public entities. The collateral source rule has been abolished or limited in many states or more. *E.g.,* N.Y. C.P.L.R. § 4545 (a). Some of the limiting statutes have been upheld against constitutional attack, *see, e.g., Eastin v. Broomfield,* 570 P.2d 744 (Ariz. 1977), while others have been struck down, *see, e.g., Farley v. Engelken,* 740 P.2d 1058 (Kan. 1987).

D. CAPPING AND LIMITING DAMAGES

CAL. CIV. CODE § 3333.2

(a) In any action for injury against a health care provider based on professional negligence, the injured plaintiff shall be entitled to recover noneconomic losses to compensate for pain, suffering, inconvenience, physical impairment, disfigurement and other nonpecuniary damage.

(b) In no action shall the amount of damages for noneconomic losses exceed two hundred fifty thousand dollars ($250,000).

MD. CODE ANN., CTS. & JUD. PROC. § 11–108

(a) In this section: (2)(i)(1) "noneconomic damages" means pain, suffering, inconvenience, physical impairment, disfigurement, loss of consortium, or other nonpecuniary injury; and (2)(ii) "Noneconomic damages" does not include punitive damages.

(b) In any action for damages for personal injury in which the cause of action arises on or after July 1, 1986, an award for noneconomic damages may not exceed $350,000. . . .

(d)(1) In a jury trial, the jury may not be informed of the limitation established under subsection (b) of this section. (2) If the jury awards an amount for noneconomic damages that exceeds the limitation established under subsection (b) of this section, the court shall reduce the amount to conform to the limitation.

NOTES

1. **Caps on pain and suffering awards.** In theory, damages are compensatory. For this reason, customarily, tort damages have been limited only by the evidence, not by any arbitrary dollar amount or by any formula.

2. **Two statutory waves.** Two waves of statutes have been passed changing this common law tradition. The first resulted from the supposed medical malpractice insurance "crisis" of the 1970s. The second resulted from a supposed "crisis" in the 1980s. This second wave, however, was the product of long and persistent efforts by a much wider group of defendants and insurers who felt threatened by tort law. The statutory limits were based on a perception that there was a crisis in the affordability and availability of insurance, especially for target groups like health care providers and public entities, or sometimes simply on the claim that juries had gone wild.

3. **Line-up of the states.** Some kind of cap or limit has been enacted in well over half of the states. As indicated below, however, some have been held unconstitutional, some are applied to only one particular kind of claim, and some are overridden by statutes such as California's Elder Abuse Act, which allows recovery for reckless neglect of the elderly without a cap. As to this last, *see Delaney v. Baker,* 971 P.2d 986 (Cal. 1999) (interpreting Elder Abuse act to allow heightened remedies for professional negligence).

4. **Types of statutes: which defendants are covered.**

(a) *All injury defendants vs. medical defendants.* Notice that the Maryland statute applies by its terms to "any action for damages for personal injury." The California statute, on the other hand, applies only to claims against health care providers and then only for professional negligence—in other words, to medical malpractice claims. Most of the statutes follow one of these two patterns, applying either generally or to some special group. South Carolina has a two-tiered statutory damages cap in its Tort Claims Act, in which claims against government entities are capped at $300,000 per person or $600,000 per occurrence, and claims for medical malpractice are capped at $1.2 million. The statute was upheld against constitutional attack in *Boiter v. South Carolina Dep't of Transp.*, 712 S.E.2d 401 (S.C. 2011).

(b) *Caps partially restoring lost immunities of favored defendants or limiting new statutory claims.* In some states, statutory caps for special defendants reflect traditional protective attitudes that the common law itself shared. For instance, the common law provided immunities to governmental entities and charities. It is not surprising to see that when liability is imposed on these defendants, legislative caps put a ceiling to that liability. *See, e.g.,* ME. REV. STAT. ANN. tit. 14, § 8105 ($400,000 cap on all claims against government entity or employees). The common law's protective attitude toward purveyors of alcohol, like the traditional attitude toward immunities, has been much modified, but again, it is no surprise to see legislative caps on dram shop recoveries. *E.g.,* UTAH CODE ANN. § 32B–15–301(2) ($1,000,000 to any person, and $2,000,000 in the aggregate for all damages arising from one occurrence). Similarly, some new statutory claims may be subjected to a dollar limit, as where parents are subjected to liability for the torts of their children. *E.g.,* W. VA. CODE § 55–7A–2 ($5000). Finally, caps may be indirectly imposed when a new compensation system is substituted for traditional tort law, as with the National Childhood Vaccine Injury Act.

5. **Types of statutes: which damages are covered.** Most of the statutes so far enacted cap nonpecuniary damages but do not cap the recovery for actual pecuniary loss. The cap on nonpecuniary damages, however, is serious to plaintiffs, since it is the nonpecuniary recovery that furnishes a basis for the attorney's fees. Without this award, attorneys often cannot afford to pursue complex and time-consuming claims. A few statutes go beyond the cap on nonpecuniary damages and place a cap that limits damages of any kind. *E.g.,* COLO. REV. STAT. § 13–64–302 (subject to a limited possibility that the plaintiff could recover pecuniary losses in excess of the cap).

6. **Capping plaintiffs vs. capping defendants.** Suppose the cap is $250,000 but the plaintiff has damages of $500,000. If two defendants are liable, could the plaintiff recover up to $250,000 from each? *General Elec. Co. v. Niemet,* 866 P.2d 1361 (Colo. 1994) (yes, as a matter of statutory construction, Colorado's cap applies to individual defendants, not to plaintiffs). A somewhat similar question arises when a person dies and children bring a wrongful death action. Does the cap apply to the children's' claims as a unit, or could each child recover a sum up to the cap's limit? See *THI of Tex. at Lubbock I, LLC v. Perea,* 329 S.W.3d 548 (Tex. App. 2010), in which the decedent's sons sued a nursing facility for wrongful death and survival damages after their father died from a fatal drug dose. According to Texas statute, the four sons and the estate of the decedent were considered one claimant for purposes of the damages cap because they were claiming damages from a single person's death.

7. **Caps and comparative fault.** Suppose the plaintiff has $300,000 in nonpecuniary damages as well as pecuniary loss that can be separately

calculated. The state has a cap on nonpecuniary damages of $250,000 and a pure comparative fault statute. The jury finds the plaintiff to be chargeable with 20% of the negligence. What should the plaintiff recover? Consider:

(a) $300,000 reduced to the cap of $250,000, minus 20% of the $300,000 or $60,000 = a net of $190,000 for nonpecuniary damages.

(b) $300,000 reduced to the cap of $250,000, minus 20% of the damages as capped, or $50,000 = a net recovery of $200,000.

(c) $300,000 minus 20% = $240,000; since this falls below the cap, no further reduction is required.

See McAdory v. Rogers, 264 Cal.Rptr. 71 (Ct. App. 1989) ("There is no legitimate or logical reason for reducing that award to the $250,000 cap prescribed by section 3333.2 before reducing it further due to Ms. McAdory's 22 percent comparative fault.").

8. **Caps unconstitutional.** Several courts have found the capping statutes to be unconstitutional under various provisions of their respective state constitutions. *E.g., Atlanta Oculoplastic Surgery, P.C. v. Nestlehutt*, 691 S.E.2d 218 (Ga. 2010) (noneconomic damages cap in medical malpractice cases); *Lebron v. Gottlieb Mem'l Hosp.*, 930 N.E.2d 895 (Ill. 2010) (same); *Trujillo v. City of Albuquerque*, 965 P.2d 305 (N.M. 1998); *State v. Sheward*, 715 N.E.2d 1062 (Ohio 1999); *Klutschkowski v. PeaceHealth*, 311 P.3d 461 (Or. 2013) (cap on non-economic damages in medical malpractice and negligence actions unconstitutional under jury trial provision of Oregon Constitution because causes of action preexisted adoption of the Oregon Constitution).

9. **Constitutional themes.** The capping statutes, state constitutional provisions, and cases are varied. Some statutes have been condemned as special legislation or in violation of the right to trial by jury. Broad themes discussed, however, include some version of these ideas:

(a) the injured plaintiff cannot be made to bear the burden of reducing insurance costs for others or for society as a whole;

(b) it is arbitrary to select the particular group of defendants for special attention;

(c) no alternative redress or even assistance is provided for the injured plaintiff; the plaintiff shoulders the burden others are feeling without a quid pro quo;

(d) caps are in themselves arbitrary, especially when injuries may be quite different among those affected;

(e) no showing is made that the caps will actually resolve the supposed insurance crisis.

10. **Caps constitutional.** The California statute set out above was upheld in *Fein v. Permanente Medical Group*, 695 P.2d 665 (Cal. 1985). The Ohio Supreme Court, after striking down broad tort reform legislation that included caps in *State v. Sheward*, later upheld a revised statute that caps

noneconomic damages in some but not all cases and contains exceptions for "serious injuries." *Arbino v. Johnson & Johnson*, 880 N.E.2d 420 (Ohio 2007). A number of other decisions have upheld caps against arguments that the caps violated jury trial rights, due process, equal protection, or various analogous state constitutional provisions, or that they contravened the Americans with Disability Act. *See, e.g., Samples v. Florida Birth-Related Neurological Injury Comp. Ass'n*, 114 So.3d 912 (Fla. 2013) (infants found to have birth-related neurological injury; statute provides no-fault compensation via an alternative plan, and lifts the cap where clear and convincing evidence shows bad faith, malice, or willful and wanton disregard of human rights, safety or property); *Espina v. Jackson*, 112 A.3d 442 (Md. 2015) (state cap on damages against public entities, set at $200,000 per individual claim, $500,000 per total claims from the same occurrence); *Dixon v. Ford Motor Co.*, 70 A.3d 328 (Md. 2013) (lump sum statutory maximum on damages from asbestos exposure); *Tam v. Eighth Judicial Dist. Court,* 358 P.3d 234 (Nev. 2015) (cap on non-economic damages in suits against a healthcare provider). *MacDonald v. City Hosp., Inc.*, 715 S.E.2d 405 (W.Va. 2011) (reduction of medical malpractice award of $1.5 million in economic damages to $500,000 based on the state's statutory cap did not violate plaintiff's right to a jury trial, separation of powers, equal protection, special legislation, nor "certain remedy" provisions of the West Virginia Constitution). Will caps on the pain and suffering award shortchange the most seriously-injured plaintiffs or remove just claims from the judicial system?

11. **Discrimination against women and children?** Certain kinds of cases produce noneconomic (but real) harms. Some sexual abuse, for example, may be so harmful that the victim is actually unable to work effectively, but very often the main component of damages is noneconomic. Most, but not all, sexual abuse victims are women. Does this mean that if tort reformers cap pain and suffering damages, they are discriminating against women? *See* Lucinda Finley, *The Hidden Victims of Tort Reform: Women, Children, and the Elderly,* 53 EMORY L. REV. 1263 (2004); Thomas Koenig & Michael Rustad, *His and Her Tort Reform: Gender Injustice in Disguise*, 70 WASH. L. REV. 1 (1995). Similarly, statutory caps on noneconomic damages may dramatically reduce claims of the families of deceased children. For example, in *DRD Pool Service, Inc. v. Freed*, 5 A.3d 45 (Md. 2010), a five-year-old child drowned in a country club swimming pool. In a suit against the pool maintenance service, the jury awarded over $4 million in damages. However, pursuant to state caps on non-economic damages, which the Maryland Court of Appeals found constitutional, the verdict was reduced to approximately $1 million.

12. **Side effects of caps.** Maybe caps will have some unintended side effects. Would judges or juries be more inclined to resolve close questions of *liability* for the plaintiff where caps limit the *damages*? After the 9/11 terrorist attacks, Congress set up a victims' compensation scheme but permitted victims to opt for tort suits instead. If they opted for tort suits, however, damages were capped (except in suits against terrorist-associated defendants) at the total of the defendants' liability insurance. In *In re September 11 Litigation*, 280

F.Supp. 2d 279 (S.D.N.Y. 2003), one question was whether the airlines owed a duty of care to potential victims on the ground. The court held that they did. One factor: there would be no limitless liability because of the caps.

REFERENCE: 3 DOBBS, HAYDEN & BUBLICK, THE LAW OF TORTS §§ 479–81 (2d ed. 2011); DOBBS, HAYDEN & BUBLICK, HORNBOOK ON TORTS §§ 34.1–34.3 (2d ed. 2016).

§ 2. PUNITIVE DAMAGES

A. GENERAL RULES

DAN B. DOBBS, THE LAW OF REMEDIES
§ 3.11(1) (2d ed. 1993)

1. Punitive damages are awarded only for . . . misconduct coupled with a bad state of mind involving malice or at least a reckless disregard for the rights of others.

2. The stated purposes of punitive damages almost always include (a) punishment or retribution and (b) deterrence. Sometimes the purpose also encompasses (c) the desire to assist in financing useful litigation by providing a source from which fees and costs can be paid. The purposes are somewhat conflicting in that they do not necessarily call for the same amount of punitive recovery.

3. If the judge decides that the facts warrant submission of the case to the jury on the punitive damages issue, the jury's discretion determines (a) whether to make the award at all and (b) the amount of the award, as limited by its purposes, subject only to review as other awards are reviewed.

4. Punitive damages are not per se unconstitutional under the double jeopardy, excessive fines, or due process provisions of the United States Constitution. However, extreme awards, given without appropriate guidance to the jury and without adequate review by judges, may violate due process.

5. Statutes in some states now limit the amount of punitive damages that can be awarded, or, alternatively, direct a portion of the award to some public entity. In addition, some double and treble damages statutes may have the effect of precluding ordinary punitive damages.

6. Punitive damages were traditionally proven by the ordinary civil standard of proof, a preponderance of the evidence. Some courts now demand clear and convincing evidence.

7. The jury is normally allowed to hear evidence about the defendant's wealth, income, or profits as a basis for determining an appropriate amount of punitive damages.

8. Under one rule, punitive awards may be levied against defendants who are only vicariously responsible. Under another rule, employers and others can be responsible for punitive damages for torts of agents or servants only if the employer participated in, encouraged, or ratified the tort.

9. Under one view, probably the majority, liability insurers whose policies do not eliminate coverage for punitive damages are liable for punitive damages judgments against the insured. Under another view, the "punishment" will not be effective if the wrongdoer can insure, so insurance coverage for such awards is against public policy.

10. A defendant whose wrongs have caused many harms to different people may be subjected to more than one punitive liability.

11. Courts sometimes say that punitive damages cannot be awarded unless the plaintiff suffers actual harm or recovers actual damages. Some courts now read this rule to mean only that the plaintiff cannot recover punitive damages unless she first establishes a cause of action.

12. Courts sometimes say that the amount of punitive damages must be in some reasonable proportion to actual damages. . . .

NOTES

1. **State of mind.** Punitive or exemplary damages are given partly to punish. They thus share a criminal law purpose. What is the bad state of mind required to trigger punitive damages? It is usually said that the defendant must act with malice or at least wanton or reckless disregard for the rights of others. *See, e.g., Ross v. Louise Wise Servs., Inc.*, 868 N.E.2d 189 (N.Y. 2007) (punitive damages were unavailable where there was no evidence of malicious or vindictive intent, or a high degree of moral turpitude). Reckless disregard of the rights of others includes conscious indifference to the risk. Although the wantonness standard is less demanding than the malice standard, both require some kind of bad state of mind, not merely extremely negligent conduct. *Galaxy Cable, Inc. v. Davis*, 58 So.3d 93 (Ala. 2010) (intent to do a wrongful act with reckless indifference to consequences is enough for wantonness). Notice too that it is not enough that the defendant "act intentionally" if there is no malice or bad state of mind. *See Doe v. Isaacs*, 579 S.E.2d 174 (Va. 2003) (intentional violation of traffic law does not support punitive award, without more).

2. **Serious misconduct.** Punitive damages are typically awarded only when the defendant's conduct and state of mind both depart seriously from ordinary expectations in a civil society. You might think that punitive damages are thus unavailable in a negligence case, but that is not always true. A plaintiff may bring a case founded on a negligence theory, but may be entitled

to punitive damages where he can further prove that the defendant exhibited a conscious indifference to the consequences of his acts, or knew that his conduct was substantially certain to violate the plaintiff's rights. This evidence may allow a jury to infer a defendant's reckless disregard or malicious state of mind. *See McCoy v. Montgomery*, 259 S.W.3d 430 (Ark. 2007) (medical malpractice claim); *Hutchison v. Luddy*, 896 A.2d 1260 (Pa. 2006) (negligent hiring and supervision claim); *Strenke v. Hogner*, 694 N.W.2d 296 (Wis. 2005) (negligent driving claim).

3. **Some settings for punitive damages.** Courts often talk as if the punitive award was created to punish the bully who deliberately beats or sexually abuses the plaintiff, and there are indeed cases like that. *See Mrozka v. Archdiocese of St. Paul & Minneapolis*, 482 N.W.2d 806 (Minn. Ct. App. 1992) (bishops and archbishop knew of priest's long continued sexual molestation of young boys, refused to do anything significant about it; punitive award justified in spite of First Amendment). But punitive damages in contemporary law have been applied to a wide variety of defendants and in a wide variety of circumstances. Very commonly today, punitive damages are imposed upon defendants who have reaped financial profit from tortious activity and are likely to continue to do so unless deterred by punitive awards. *E.g., McLemore ex rel. McLemore v. Elizabeth Med. Investors, Ltd. P'ship*, 389 S.W.3d 764 (Tenn. Ct. App. 2012) (defendants did profit from negligent behavior—taking in high needs patients, but understaffing to increase profits; punitive damages award affirmed).

4. **Exclusions.** Punitive damages are seldom granted for breach of contract unaccompanied by tortious acts. They are almost always denied in suits against public entities as well, in the absence of a statute to the contrary. There are also statutory causes of action which permit only compensatory damages. *See Barnes v. Gorman,* 536 U.S. 181 (2002) (Americans with Disabilities Act does not authorize punitive damages).

OWENS-CORNING FIBERGLAS CORP. V. BALLARD, 749 So.2d 483 (Fla. 1999). Ballard proved that he had developed mesothelioma, a cancer of the chest lining, due to thirty years of exposure to asbestos in the defendant's product, Kaylo. Evidence showed that "for more than thirty (30) years Owens-Corning concealed what it knew about the dangers of asbestos. In fact, Owens-Corning's conduct was even worse than concealment, it also included intentional and knowing misrepresentations concerning the danger of its asbestos-containing product, Kaylo. For instance, in 1956, Owens-Corning, after having been told by the Saranac Laboratory that Kaylo dust was 'toxic,' and that asbestos was a carcinogen, advertised Kaylo as being 'non-toxic.' In 1972, after Owens-Corning developed an asbestos-free version of the Kaylo product, Owens-Corning knowingly and intentionally contaminated the new product with asbestos containing debris from its old Kaylo, and then intentionally and knowingly claimed falsely that the new Kaylo product was asbestos[-]free." The jury awarded compensatory damages of $1.8 million and punitive damages of $31 million. *Held,* affirmed.

NOTES

1. **Deterrence function.** This case represents the tort-for-profit punitive damage case in contrast to the bully case. The defendant in such cases has a motive to continue its tortious activity unless the total expected damages liability will be greater than the profit. Although the courts always focus on the defendant's bad state of mind as a justification for awarding punitive damages, *Ford Motor Co. v. Washington,* 431 S.W.3d 210 (Ark. 2013), deterrence seems to be the major goal in many cases.

2. **Illustration.** Suppose the defendant is making so much money from the sale of the product that compensatory damages awards will never induce the defendant to take it off the market. That might be because, although damages are high, some victims do not discover that the defendant caused their harm. A national products manufacturer which deliberately markets a dangerous product like the Dalkon Shield after its dangers are known may continue to do so (as the Robins company did) unless punitive damages are enough to deny it any profit. See the shocking behavior of the manufacturer as described in *Tetuan v. A.H. Robins Co.,* 738 P.2d 1210 (Kan. 1987). *See also* Thomas Galligan, *Augmented Awards: The Efficient Evolution of Punitive Damages,* 51 LA. L. REV. 3 (1990). Or perhaps the right amount of punitive damages would be to bring the manufacturer's total liability up to the level it would have paid in ordinary compensatory damages if all victims had appropriately recovered. *See* A. Mitchell Polinsky & Steven Shavell, *Punitive Damages: an Economic Analysis,* 111 HARV. L. REV. 869, 888–96 (1998).

3. **Strict liability cases.** Defendants used to argue that punitive awards could not be made in strict liability claims, even if the underlying conduct involved the kind of knowing wrong seen in cases like *Owens-Corning Fiberglas Corp. v. Ballard.* This has now changed, and punitive damages are understood to be warranted by conduct and state of mind, not by the name of the legal theory used. The classic article is David G. Owen, *Punitive Damages in Products Liability Litigation,* 74 MICH. L. REV. 1257 (1976).

B. MEASUREMENT OF PUNITIVE DAMAGES

NOTE: TRADITIONAL FACTORS IN MEASURING PUNITIVE DAMAGES

1. *Reprehensibility of the defendant's misconduct.* If punitive damages are warranted by the defendant's serious misconduct, courts must then identify an appropriate sum. You might think that the most important consideration would be to identify the amount necessary to ensure that the defendant does not repeat the wrong. However, courts have often said that

the degree of reprehensibility of the defendant's conduct is the most important single consideration. *State Farm Mut. Auto. Ins. Co. v. Campbell*, 538 U.S. 408 (2003). At the same time, courts identify other factors, not necessarily consistent.

2. *Wealth.* Courts have traditionally admitted evidence of the defendant's wealth as bearing on punitive damages, on the theory that a person of great wealth might not be deterred by a small award. *See, e.g., Tarr v. Bob Ciasulli's Mack Auto Mall, Inc.*, 943 A.2d 866 (N.J. 2008). If the tort itself is profitable, profits from the wrongdoing would also be highly relevant. *Must* the plaintiff introduce wealth evidence to warrant punitive damages? *See, e.g., Adams v. Murakami*, 813 P.2d 1348 (Cal. 1991). Judge Posner incisively criticized this view in *Kemezy v. Peters,* 79 F.3d 33 (7th Cir. 1996), on the ground that the introduction of wealth evidence risks prejudice to the wealthy defendant. *See also Branham v. Ford Motor Co.,* 701 S.E.2d 5 (S.C. 2010). Partially because of this problem, it is now common to bifurcate the trial so that the punitive damages evidence is excluded until the jury has already found fault.

3. *Ratio rules.* Courts have long said that punitive damages should bear some kind of reasonable comparison to the compensatory damages, or to actual or potential harm done. In its crudest form, this ratio rule suggests limits incompatible with the purposes of punitive damages in the first place. Suppose the defendant malevolently and repeatedly fires his rifle at the plaintiff, but has so far only chipped the plaintiff's $10 sunglasses. If the jury awards $10 compensatory damages, the ratio rule suggests that punitive awards should be some modest multiple of that sum. It is apparent that this cannot be right under either a punitive or deterrence rationale and it is even less right if the defendant's conduct is profitable even after he pays compensatory damages. The more sophisticated form of the rule does not compare punitive awards to compensatory awards. It compares punitive awards to the potential actual harm that could have resulted from the defendant's conduct. This form of the ratio rule is in fact merely a way of measuring the seriousness of the defendant's misconduct.

Some other factors are sketched in discussing the constitutional decisions in the next Note.

————————

NOTE: LIMITING PUNITIVE AWARDS

1. *Moves to limit punitive awards.* There is a perception that punitive damages awards are common, but that perception is incorrect. Recent studies show that punitive damages are awarded in only 2–5% of all cases in which plaintiffs prevail. Remember that most cases do not even

go to trial. "Thus, for every 1,000 tort claims filed, typically only 50 are resolved by trial, only 25 produce trial outcomes favorable to the plaintiff, and only 1.25 have a punitive damages award." Thomas A. Eaton, David B. Mustard & Susette M. Talarico, *The Effects of Seeking Punitive Damages on the Processing of Tort Claims*, 34 J. LEGAL STUD. 343, 344 (2005). Another common misperception is that punitive damages awards are primarily a problem produced by "runaway juries." Studies show that judges award such damages at about the same rate as juries. *See* Theodore Eisenberg, Neil LaFountain, Brian Ostrom, David Rottman & Martin T. Wells, *Juries, Judges, and Punitive Damages: An Empirical Study,* 87 CORNELL L. REV. 743 (2002). However, repeat defendants greatly fear punitive awards. Because punitive damages are not reliably measurable, the trier of fact is free to vent any anger they may feel by inflicting an award that cannot be evaluated against any effective standard. As punitive damages have sometimes run into the millions of dollars, defendant-oriented lobbies have tried to find ways to limit those awards in statutes and by more restrictive judicial decisions.

2.　*Two types of limitations.* Although several means have been used to limit punitive awards, they fall mainly into two large categories. Because the main problem with punitive damages is to find a suitable measure or standard for guiding the award and evaluating it afterward, some legal changes attempt to enhance the methods for measuring the awards. A second and much broader way to limit total damages awarded is to limit the number of cases in which punitive damages may be awarded.

3.　*Increased proof standards.* One way to filter out potential punitive damages claims is to increase the plaintiff's burden of proof. A number of courts and legislatures have done this, usually requiring the plaintiff to prove grounds for punitive damages by clear and convincing evidence rather than by a mere preponderance. *E.g., Hester v. Vision Airlines, Inc.,* 687 F.3d 1162 (9th Cir. 2012).

4.　*Single liability statute.* Georgia enacted a statute that immunized a product liability defendant from all punitive liability for a given product, once the defendant had been vaccinated by a single punitive award. So the first plaintiff to recover was the only one to do so. GA. CODE ANN. § 51–12–5.1(e)(1).

5.　*Specific malice requirement.* Another effort to cut punitive damages off at the pass requires the plaintiff to prove some specific malice or oppressive intent toward the plaintiff, eliminating wanton and reckless misconduct as a basis. *See* NEV. REV. STAT. § 42.005.

6.　*Redirection of awards and the problem of financing tort suits.* A fourth line of legislative attack intended to cut down the number of claims redirects a portion of any punitive award from the plaintiff (or the plaintiff's attorney) to the state or some designated beneficiary. *E.g.,* IOWA

CODE ANN. § 668A.1. These statutes can retain the full capacity for deterring the defendant once the award is made because they do not necessary reduce or cap the award. In *Kirk v. Denver Public Co.*, 818 P.2d 262 (Colo. 1991), the court held one such statute unconstitutional as a taking of property without just compensation. *Cheatham v. Pohle,* 789 N.E.2d 467 (Ind. 2003), disagreed, upholding the statute.

7. *Statutory ratios, multiples, or caps.* With the push for tort reform, some states have enacted ratio cap statutes. For instance, Colorado limited punitive awards to no more than actual damages, with the added possibility of punitive damages up to three times actual damages if the defendant's misconduct continued during the trial. COLO. REV. STAT. ANN. § 13–21–102. In Ohio, the statute caps damages at twice the amount of compensatory damages awarded. *See Sivit v. Village Green of Beachwood*, 143 Ohio 3d 168 (2015). Utah, by court decision, has produced a kind of sliding scale ratio rule that varies according to whether the compensatory damages awarded are low or high. *Crookston v. Fire Ins. Exch.*, 817 P.2d 789 (Utah 1991) (3–1 ratio for punitive awards under $100,000, much closer ratio for higher awards). Georgia enacted a flat cap limiting punitive damages in some cases to $250,000. GA. CODE ANN. § 51–12–5.1. Indiana limits punitive damages to three times compensatory damages or $50,000, requiring that 75% of the amount goes to violent crime victim charities. *State v. Doe*, 987 N.E.2d 1066 (Ind. 2013) (remand for reduction in damages awarded to sexual abuse victim in lawsuit against clergyman). Some limitations on punitive damages have been struck down as unconstitutional. *See, e.g., Bayer Cropscience LP v. Schafer*, 385 S.W.3d 822 (Ark. 2011) (statutory cap on punitive damages unconstitutional under section of Arkansas Constitution prohibiting the legislature from limiting the amount to be recovered for injuries resulting in death or for injuries to persons or property); *Lewellen v. Franklin*, 441 S.W.3d 136 (Mo. 2014) (statute that capped punitive damages to $500,000 or five times the amount of a judgment awarded to the plaintiff violated the state constitutional right to a jury).

8. *Assessing the filters.* What is your assessment of these efforts? Do they help the problem of measurement? Are the filters too fine? Is there a good chance, in your view, that the deterrence or litigation finance function of punitive awards needed in some of the cases will be filtered out by these rules?

STATE FARM MUT. AUTO. INS. CO. V. CAMPBELL
538 U.S. 408 (2003)

JUSTICE KENNEDY delivered the opinion of the Court. . . .

In 1981, Curtis Campbell (Campbell) was driving with his wife, Inez Preece Campbell, in Cache County, Utah. He decided to pass six vans traveling ahead of them on a two-lane highway. Todd Ospital was driving a small car approaching from the opposite direction. To avoid a head-on collision with Campbell, who by then was driving on the wrong side of the highway and toward oncoming traffic, Ospital swerved onto the shoulder, lost control of his automobile, and collided with a vehicle driven by Robert G. Slusher. Ospital was killed, and Slusher was rendered permanently disabled. The Campbells escaped unscathed.

In the ensuing wrongful death and tort action, Campbell insisted he was not at fault. Early investigations did support differing conclusions as to who caused the accident, but "a consensus was reached early on by the investigators and witnesses that Mr. Campbell's unsafe pass had indeed caused the crash." Campbell's insurance company, petitioner State Farm Mutual Automobile Insurance Company (State Farm), nonetheless decided to contest liability and declined offers by Slusher and Ospital's estate (Ospital) to settle the claims for the policy limit of $50,000 ($25,000 per claimant). State Farm also ignored the advice of one of its own investigators and took the case to trial, assuring the Campbells that "their assets were safe, that they had no liability for the accident, that [State Farm] would represent their interests, and that they did not need to procure separate counsel." To the contrary, a jury determined that Campbell was 100 percent at fault, and a judgment was returned for $185,849, far more than the amount offered in settlement.

At first State Farm refused to cover the $135,849 in excess liability. Its counsel made this clear to the Campbells: "You may want to put for sale signs on your property to get things moving." Nor was State Farm willing to post a supersedeas bond to allow Campbell to appeal the judgment against him. Campbell obtained his own counsel to appeal the verdict. During the pendency of the appeal, in late 1984, Slusher, Ospital, and the Campbells reached an agreement whereby Slusher and Ospital agreed not to seek satisfaction of their claims against the Campbells. In exchange the Campbells agreed to pursue a bad faith action against State Farm and to be represented by Slusher's and Ospital's attorneys. The Campbells also agreed that Slusher and Ospital would have a right to play a part in all major decisions concerning the bad faith action. No settlement could be concluded without Slusher's and Ospital's approval, and Slusher and Ospital would receive 90 percent of any verdict against State Farm.

In 1989, the Utah Supreme Court denied Campbell's appeal in the wrongful death and tort actions. State Farm then paid the entire judgment, including the amounts in excess of the policy limits. The Campbells nonetheless filed a complaint against State Farm alleging bad faith, fraud, and intentional infliction of emotional distress. The trial court initially granted State Farm's motion for summary judgment because State Farm had paid the excess verdict, but that ruling was reversed on appeal. On remand State Farm moved *in limine* to exclude evidence of alleged conduct that occurred in unrelated cases outside of Utah, but the trial court denied the motion. At State Farm's request the trial court bifurcated the trial into two phases conducted before different juries. In the first phase the jury determined that State Farm's decision not to settle was unreasonable because there was a substantial likelihood of an excess verdict. . . .

[The Utah Court summarized evidence in phase II:] "State Farm argued during phase II that its decision to take the case to trial was an 'honest mistake' that did not warrant punitive damages. In contrast, the Campbells introduced evidence that State Farm's decision to take the case to trial was a result of a national scheme to meet corporate fiscal goals by capping payouts on claims company wide. This scheme was referred to as State Farm's 'Performance, Planning and Review,' or PP & R, policy. To prove the existence of this scheme, the trial court allowed the Campbells to introduce extensive expert testimony regarding fraudulent practices by State Farm in its nation-wide operations. Although State Farm moved prior to phase II of the trial for the exclusion of such evidence and continued to object to it at trial, the trial court ruled that such evidence was admissible to determine whether State Farm's conduct in the Campbell case was indeed intentional and sufficiently egregious to warrant punitive damages."

Evidence pertaining to the PP & R policy concerned State Farm's business practices for over 20 years in numerous States. Most of these practices bore no relation to third-party automobile insurance claims, the type of claim underlying the Campbells' complaint against the company. The jury awarded the Campbells $2.6 million in compensatory damages and $145 million in punitive damages, which the trial court reduced to $1 million and $25 million respectively. Both parties appealed.

The Utah Supreme Court sought to apply the three guideposts we identified in [*BMW of North America, Inc. v. Gore,* 517 U.S. 559 (1996)] and it reinstated the $145 million punitive damages award. . . .

While States possess discretion over the imposition of punitive damages, it is well established that there are procedural and substantive constitutional limitations on these awards. The Due Process Clause of the Fourteenth Amendment prohibits the imposition of grossly excessive or arbitrary punishments on a tortfeasor. The reason is that "[e]lementary notions of fairness enshrined in our constitutional jurisprudence dictate that a person receive fair notice not only of the conduct that will subject him to punishment, but also of the severity of the penalty that a State may impose."

Although these awards serve the same purposes as criminal penalties, defendants subjected to punitive damages in civil cases have not been accorded the protections applicable in a criminal proceeding. . . . We have admonished that "[p]unitive damages pose an acute danger of arbitrary deprivation of property. Jury instructions typically leave the jury with wide discretion in choosing amounts, and the presentation of evidence of a defendant's net worth creates the potential that juries will use their verdicts to express biases against big businesses, particularly those without strong local presences." . . .

In light of these concerns, in *Gore, supra,* we instructed courts reviewing punitive damages to consider three guideposts: (1) the degree of reprehensibility of the defendant's misconduct; (2) the disparity between the actual or potential harm suffered by the plaintiff and the punitive damages award; and (3) the difference between the punitive damages awarded by the jury and the civil penalties authorized or imposed in comparable cases. We . . . mandated appellate courts to conduct *de novo* review of a trial court's application of them to the jury's award. Exacting appellate review ensures that an award of punitive damages is based upon an " 'application of law, rather than a decisionmaker's caprice.' "

Under the principles outlined in *BMW of North America, Inc. v. Gore,* this case is neither close nor difficult. It was error to reinstate the jury's $145 million punitive damages award. We address each guidepost of *Gore* in some detail.

"[T]he most important indicium of the reasonableness of a punitive damages award is the degree of reprehensibility of the defendant's conduct." We have instructed courts to determine the reprehensibility of a defendant by considering whether: the harm caused was physical as opposed to economic; the tortious conduct evinced an indifference to or a reckless disregard of the health or safety of others; the target of the conduct had financial vulnerability; the conduct involved repeated actions or was an isolated incident; and the harm was the result of intentional malice, trickery, or deceit, or mere accident. The existence of any one of these factors weighing in favor of a plaintiff may not be sufficient to sustain a punitive damages award; and the absence of all of them renders any award suspect. It should be presumed a plaintiff has been made whole for his injuries by compensatory damages, so punitive damages should only be awarded if the defendant's culpability, after having paid compensatory damages, is so reprehensible as to warrant the imposition of further sanctions to achieve punishment or deterrence. . . .

While we do not suggest there was error in awarding punitive damages based upon State Farm's conduct toward the Campbells, a more modest punishment for this reprehensible conduct could have satisfied the State's legitimate objectives, and the Utah courts should have gone no further.

This case, instead, was used as a platform to expose, and punish, the perceived deficiencies of State Farm's operations throughout the country. The Utah Supreme Court's opinion makes explicit that State Farm was being condemned for its nationwide policies rather than for the conduct direct toward the Campbells. . . .

A State cannot punish a defendant for conduct that may have been lawful where it occurred. Nor, as a general rule, does a State have a legitimate concern in imposing punitive damages to punish a defendant for unlawful acts committed outside of the State's jurisdiction. Any proper adjudication of conduct that occurred outside Utah to other persons would require their inclusion, and, to those parties, the Utah courts, in the usual case, would need to apply the laws of their relevant jurisdiction.

Here, the Campbells do not dispute that much of the out-of-state conduct was lawful where it occurred. They argue, however, that such evidence was not the primary basis for the punitive damages award and was relevant to the extent it demonstrated, in a general sense, State Farm's motive against its insured. This argument misses the mark. Lawful out-of-state conduct may be probative when it demonstrates the deliberateness and culpability of the defendant's action in the State where it is tortious, but that conduct must have a nexus to the specific harm suffered by the plaintiff. A jury must be instructed, furthermore, that it may not use evidence of out-of-state conduct to punish a defendant for action that was lawful in the jurisdiction where it occurred. A basic principle of federalism is that each State may make its own reasoned judgment about what conduct is permitted or proscribed within its borders, and each State alone can determine what measure of punishment, if any, to impose on a defendant who acts within its jurisdiction.

For a more fundamental reason, however, the Utah courts erred in relying upon this and other evidence: The courts awarded punitive damages to punish and deter conduct that bore no relation to the Campbells' harm. A defendant's dissimilar acts, independent from the acts upon which liability was premised, may not serve as the basis for punitive damages. A defendant should be punished for the conduct that harmed the plaintiff, not for being an unsavory individual or business. Due process does not permit courts, in the calculation of punitive damages, to adjudicate the merits of other parties' hypothetical claims against a defendant under the guise of the reprehensibility analysis, but we have no doubt the Utah Supreme Court did that here. Punishment on these bases creates the possibility of multiple punitive damages awards for the same conduct; for in the usual case nonparties are not bound by the judgment some other plaintiff obtains. . . .

The Campbells have identified scant evidence of repeated misconduct of the sort that injured them. Nor does our review of the Utah courts' decisions convince us that State Farm was only punished for its actions toward the Campbells. Although evidence of other acts need not be identical to have relevance in the calculation of punitive damages, the Utah court erred here because evidence pertaining to claims that had nothing to do with a third-party lawsuit was introduced at length. . . . The reprehensibility guidepost does not permit courts to expand the scope of the case so that a defendant may be punished for any malfeasance, which in this case extended for a 20-year period. In this case, because the Campbells have shown no conduct by State Farm similar to that which harmed them, the conduct that harmed them is the only conduct relevant to the reprehensibility analysis.

Turning to the second *Gore* guidepost, we have been reluctant to identify concrete constitutional limits on the ratio between harm, or potential harm, to the plaintiff and the punitive damages award. We decline again to impose a bright-line ratio which a punitive damages award cannot exceed. Our jurisprudence and the principles it has now established demonstrate, however, that, in practice, few awards exceeding a single-digit ratio between punitive and compensatory damages, to a significant degree, will satisfy due process. In *Haslip,* in upholding a punitive damages award, we concluded that an award of more than four times the amount of compensatory damages might be close to the line of constitutional impropriety. We cited that 4-to-1 ratio again in *Gore.* The Court further referenced a long legislative history, dating back over 700 years and going forward to today, providing for sanctions of double, treble, or quadruple damages to deter and punish. While these ratios are not binding, they are instructive. They demonstrate what should be obvious: Single-digit multipliers are more likely to comport with due process, while still achieving the State's goals of deterrence and retribution, than awards with ratios in range of 500 to 1, or, in this case, of 145 to 1.

Nonetheless, because there are no rigid benchmarks that a punitive damages award may not surpass, ratios greater than those we have previously upheld may comport with due process where a particularly egregious act has resulted in only a small amount of economic damages. The converse is also true, however. When compensatory damages are substantial, then a lesser ratio, perhaps only equal to compensatory damages, can reach the outermost limit of the due process guarantee. The precise award in any case, of course, must be based upon the facts and circumstances of the defendant's conduct and the harm to the plaintiff. . . .

The compensatory award in this case was substantial; the Campbells were awarded $1 million for a year and a half of emotional distress. This was complete compensation. The harm arose from a transaction in the economic realm, not from some physical assault or trauma; there were no physical injuries; and State Farm paid the excess verdict before the complaint was filed, so the Campbells suffered only minor economic injuries for the 18-month period in which State Farm refused to resolve the claim against them. The compensatory damages for the injury suffered here, moreover, likely were based on a component which was duplicated in the punitive award. Much of the distress was caused by the outrage and humiliation the Campbells suffered at the actions of their insurer; and it is a major role of punitive damages to condemn such conduct. Compensatory damages, however, already contain this punitive element.

The third guidepost in *Gore* is the disparity between the punitive damages award and the "civil penalties authorized or imposed in comparable cases." We note that, in the past, we have also looked to criminal penalties that could be imposed. The existence of a criminal penalty does have bearing on the seriousness with which a State views the wrongful action. When used to determine the dollar amount of the award, however, the criminal penalty has less utility. Great care must be taken to avoid use of the civil process to assess criminal penalties that can be imposed only after the heightened protections of a criminal trial have been observed, including, of course, its higher standards of proof. Punitive damages are not a substitute for the criminal process, and the remote possibility of a criminal sanction does not automatically sustain a punitive damages award.

Here, we need not dwell long on this guidepost. The most relevant civil sanction under Utah state law for the wrong done to the Campbells appears to be a $10,000 fine for an act of fraud an amount dwarfed by the $145 million punitive damages award. The Supreme Court of Utah speculated about the loss of State Farm's business license, the disgorgement of profits, and possible imprisonment, but here again its references were to the broad fraudulent scheme drawn from evidence of out-of-state and dissimilar conduct. This analysis was insufficient to justify the award. . . .

The punitive award of $145 million, therefore, was neither reasonable nor proportionate to the wrong committed, and it was an irrational and arbitrary deprivation of the property of the defendant. The proper calculation of punitive damages under the principles we have discussed should be resolved, in the first instance, by the Utah courts.

The judgment of the Utah Supreme Court is reversed, and the case is remanded for proceedings not inconsistent with this opinion.

It is so ordered.

[Justices Scalia and Thomas dissented, both essentially on the ground that there was no Constitutional, substantive due process constraint on punitive awards.]

JUSTICE GINSBURG, dissenting. . . .

The large size of the award upheld by the Utah Supreme Court in this case indicates why damage-capping legislation may be altogether fitting and proper. Neither the amount of the award nor the trial record, however, justifies this Court's substitution of its judgment for that of Utah's competent decisionmakers. In this regard, I count it significant that, on the key criterion "reprehensibility," there is a good deal more to the story than the Court's abbreviated account tells. . . .

"[T]he Campbells presented considerable evidence," the trial court noted, documenting "that the PP & R program . . . has functioned, and continues to function, as an unlawful scheme . . . to deny benefits owed consumers by paying out less than fair value in order to meet preset, arbitrary payout targets designed to enhance corporate profits." That policy, the trial court observed, was encompassing in scope; it "applied equally to the handling of both third-party and first-party claims."

Evidence the jury could credit demonstrated that the PP & R program regularly and adversely affected Utah residents. Ray Summers, "the adjuster who handled the Campbell case and who was a State Farm employee in Utah for almost twenty years," described several methods used by State Farm to deny claimants fair benefits, for example, "falsifying or withholding of evidence in claim files." A common tactic, Summers recounted, was to "unjustly attac[k] the character, reputation and credibility of a claimant and mak[e] notations to that effect in the claim file to create prejudice in the event the claim ever came before a jury." State Farm manager Bob Noxon, Summers testified, resorted to a tactic of this order in the Campbell case when he "instruct[ed] Summers to write in the file that Todd Ospital (who was killed in the accident) was speeding because he was on his way to see a pregnant girlfriend." In truth, "[t]here was no pregnant girlfriend." . . .

Regarding liability for verdicts in excess of policy limits, the trial court referred to a State Farm document titled the "Excess Liability Handbook"; written before the Campbell accident, the handbook instructed adjusters to pad files with "self-serving" documents, and to leave critical items out of files, for example, evaluations of the insured's exposure. Divisional superintendent Bill Brown used the handbook to train Utah employees. While overseeing the Campbell case, Brown ordered adjuster Summers to change the portions of his report indicating that Mr. Campbell was likely at fault and that the settlement cost was correspondingly high. . . .

The trial court further determined that the jury could find State Farm's policy "deliberately crafted" to prey on consumers who would be unlikely to defend themselves. In this regard, the trial court noted the testimony of several former State Farm employees affirming that they were trained to target "the weakest of the herd"—"the elderly, the poor, and other consumers who are least knowledgeable about their rights and thus most vulnerable to trickery or deceit, or who have little money and hence have no real alternative but to accept an inadequate offer to settle a claim at much less than fair value."

The Campbells themselves could be placed within the "weakest of the herd" category. At the time of State Farm's wrongful conduct, "Mr. Campbell had residuary effects from a stroke and Parkinson's disease."

To further insulate itself from liability, trial evidence indicated, State Farm made "systematic" efforts to destroy internal company documents that might reveal its scheme. . . .

State Farm's inability to produce the manuals, it appeared from the evidence, was not accidental. Documents retained by former State Farm employee Samantha Bird, as well as Bird's testimony, showed that while the Campbells' case was pending, Janet Cammack, "an in-house attorney sent by top State Farm management, conducted a meeting . . . in Utah during which she instructed Utah claims management to search their offices and destroy a wide range of material of the sort that had proved damaging in bad-faith litigation in the past—in particular, old claim-handling manuals, memos, claim school notes, procedure guides and other similar documents." . . .

"As a final, related tactic," the trial court stated, the jury could reasonably find that "in recent years State Farm has gone to extraordinary lengths to stop damaging documents from being created in the first place." . . .

The Court dismisses the evidence describing and documenting State Farm's PP & R policy and practices as essentially irrelevant, bearing "no relation to the Campbells' harm." It is hardly apparent why that should be so. What is infirm about the Campbells' theory that their experience with State Farm exemplifies and reflects an overarching underpayment scheme, one that caused "repeated misconduct of the sort that injured them"? The Court's silence on that score is revealing: Once one recognizes that the Campbells did show "conduct by State Farm similar to that which harmed them," it becomes impossible to shrink the reprehensibility analysis to this sole case, or to maintain, at odds with the determination of the trial court, that "the adverse effect on the State's general population was in fact minor."

Evidence of out-of-state conduct, the Court acknowledges, may be "probative [even if the conduct is lawful in the state where it occurred] when it demonstrates the deliberateness and culpability of the defendant's action in the State where it is tortious. . . ." "Other acts" evidence concerning practices both in and out of State was introduced in this case to show just such "deliberateness" and "culpability." The evidence was admissible, the trial court ruled: (1) to document State Farm's "reprehensible" PP & R program; and (2) to "rebut [State Farm's] assertion that [its] actions toward the Campbells were inadvertent errors or mistakes in judgment." Viewed in this light, there surely was "a nexus" between much of the "other acts" evidence and "the specific harm suffered by [the Campbells]." . . .

No longer content to accord state-court judgments "a strong presumption of validity," *TXO*, 509 U.S. at 457, 113 S.Ct. 2711, the Court announces that "few awards exceeding a single-digit ratio between punitive and compensatory damages, to a significant degree, will satisfy due process." . . .

I remain of the view that this Court has no warrant to reform state law governing awards of punitive damages. Even if I were prepared to accept the flexible guides prescribed in *Gore,* I would not join the Court's swift conversion of those guides into instructions that begin to resemble marching orders.

NOTES

1. **The tort: bad faith failure to settle within policy limits.** States generally hold that (a) an insurer has no obligation to pay more than its policy limit, but (b) when judgment against its insured is likely to be much higher than the limit and the insurer can settle for its policy limit or less, it must use good faith or maybe even reasonable care to do so to protect its insured. If it does not, and an excess judgment is entered against its insured, the insurer may be liable for that judgment and for other damages its misconduct has inflicted upon the insured. Frequently, as in *Campbell*, the insured's right of action is in effect sold in whole or part to the injured persons in exchange for a release, so the injured, not the insured, will be the only or primary beneficiary of any recovery.

2. **Relevance of out-of-state conduct?** Granted that Utah cannot punish out-of-state conduct that has no effect in Utah, does that mean that out-of-state conduct is irrelevant to every issue in the case? In *Campbell*, wouldn't State Farm's pattern of conduct elsewhere tend to rebut its argument that it just made an innocent mistake?

3. **Relevance of out-of-state conduct on the award itself?** Couldn't out-of-state patterns of conduct be relevant to a punitive award and not just as evidence on some other issue? Suppose a state insurance commissioner has power to exclude insurers from selling insurance in the state if their conduct in other states has demonstrated a substantial risk that consumers will be injured. Suppose the insurance commissioner is not merely a creature of the insurance industry and that the federal Congress has not preempted her powers. Would the commissioner be acting unconstitutionally if she concluded that State Farm should be excluded from selling insurance in the state because of its pattern of evil, but legal practices elsewhere?

4. **What is similar conduct?** The Court in *Campbell* seems to recognize that some outside activities are relevant, but insists that they must be similar to those that injured the insured. What is similar, though, depends on characterization and the level of generalization you are prepared to accept.

If you characterize State Farm's misbehavior as lying and cheating its own customers, that covers both the *Campbell* conduct and the out-of-state conduct. Is that a fair description of the conduct?

5. **Ratio-rule limitations.** Is there really any basis for saying that punitive awards should bear some more or less specific ratio to compensatory awards? After *Campbell*, courts have limited claims. *See Kimble v. Land Concepts, Inc.*, 845 N.W.2d 395 (Wis. 2014) (jury awarded plaintiffs $50,000 in compensatory damages and $1 million in punitive damages in claim against insurance company for bad faith and breach of contract; relying on *Campbell*, punitive damages award was excessive and reduced to $210,000). Courts have also struggled to draw a ratio-based constitutional line. *See, e.g., Goddard v. Farmers Ins. Co.*, 179 P.3d 645 (Or. 2008) (as a general rule, the constitution prohibits a punitive award more than four times the compensatory award, at least where the injuries to the plaintiff are economic rather than physical); *Flax v. DaimlerChrysler Corp.*, 272 S.W.3d 521 (Tenn. 2008) (upholding a punitive award 5.35 times greater than the compensatory award in a products liability suit involving a child's death); *Bennett v. Reynolds*, 315 S.W.3d 867 (Tex. 2010) (punitive damages in cattle theft case excessive; remanded to lower court for remittitur consistent with ratio analysis). In *Exxon Shipping Co. v. Baker*, 554 U.S. 471 (2008), the court held that a 1:1 ratio of compensatory to punitive damages was the constitutional limit for admiralty cases. It is not clear how broadly the *Baker* holding might be extended, although the Court itself was careful to limit its holding to the facts and maritime law setting.

MATHIAS V. ACCOR ECONOMY LODGING, INC.
347 F.3d 672 (7th Cir. 2003)

POSNER, CIRCUIT JUDGE.

[The plaintiffs, a brother and sister, were guests at a Motel 6 hotel where they were bitten by bedbugs. Evidence showed that the hotel's exterminating service discovered bedbugs in 1998 and offered to spray every room, for which it would charge only $500. The hotel refused and year by year the bedbug problem grew.]

The infestation continued and began to reach farcical proportions, as when a guest, after complaining of having been bitten repeatedly by insects while asleep in his room in the hotel, was moved to another room only to discover insects there; and within 18 minutes of being moved to a third room he discovered insects in that room as well and had to be moved still again. . . . Desk clerks were instructed to call the "bedbugs" "ticks," apparently on the theory that customers would be less alarmed, though in fact ticks are more dangerous than bedbugs because they spread Lyme Disease and Rocky Mountain Spotted Fever. Rooms that the motel had placed on "Do not rent, bugs in room" status nevertheless were rented.

[The plaintiffs sued the defendant for "willful and wanton conduct." The jury awarded each plaintiff $186,000 in punitive damages though only $5,000 in compensatory damages. The defendant appeals, complaining primarily that the punitive damages award was excessive and that any award in excess of $20,000 to each plaintiff deprives the defendant of its property without due process of law].

Motel 6 could not have rented any rooms at the prices it charged had it informed guests that the risk of being bitten by bedbugs was appreciable. Its failure either to warn guests or to take effective measures to eliminate the bedbugs amounted to fraud and probably to battery as well as in the famous case of *Garratt v. Dailey,* 46 Wash.2d 197, 279 P.2d 1091, 1093–94 (1955), which held that the defendant would be guilty of battery if he knew with substantial certainty that when he moved a chair the plaintiff would try to sit down where the chair had been and would land on the floor instead. There was, in short, sufficient evidence of 'willful and wanton conduct' . . . to permit an award of punitive damages in this case.

But in what amount? In arguing that $20,000 was the maximum amount of punitive damages that a jury could constitutionally have awarded each plaintiff, the defendant points to the U.S. Supreme Court's recent statement that "few awards [of punitive damages] exceeding a single-digit ratio between punitive and compensatory damages, to a significant degree, will satisfy due process." *State Farm Mutual Automobile Ins. Co. v. Campbell,* 538 U.S. 408, 123 S.Ct. 1513, 1524, 155 L.Ed.2d 585 (2003). . . . The ratio of punitive to compensatory damages determined by the jury was, in contrast, 37.2 to 1.

The Supreme Court did not, however, lay down a 4-to-1 or single-digit-ratio rule—it said merely that "there is a presumption against an award that has a 145-to-1 ratio," *State Farm Mutual Automobile Ins. Co. v. Campbell, supra,* 123 S.Ct. at 1524—and it would be unreasonable to do so. We must consider why punitive damages are awarded and why the Court has decided that due process requires that such awards be limited. The second question is easier to answer than the first. The term "punitive damages" implies punishment, and a standard principle of penal theory is that "the punishment should fit the crime" in the sense of being proportional to the wrongfulness of the defendant's action, though the principle is modified when the probability of detection is very low (a familiar example is the heavy fines for littering) or the crime is potentially lucrative (as in the case of trafficking in illegal drugs). Hence, with these qualifications, which in fact will figure in our analysis of this case, punitive damages should be proportional to the wrongfulness of the defendant's actions.

Another penal precept is that a defendant should have reasonable notice of the sanction for unlawful acts, so that he can make a rational determination of how to act; and so there have to be reasonably clear standards for determining the amount of punitive damages for particular wrongs.

And a third precept, the core of the Aristotelian notion of corrective justice, and more broadly of the principle of the rule of law, is that sanctions should be based on the wrong done rather than on the status of the defendant; a person is punished for what he does, not for who he is, even if the who is a huge corporation.

What follows from these principles, however, is that punitive damages should be admeasured by standards or rules rather than in a completely ad hoc manner, and this does not tell us what the maximum ratio of punitive to compensatory damages should be in a particular case. To determine that, we have to consider why punitive damages are awarded in the first place. See *Kemezy v. Peters,* 79 F.3d 33, 34–35 (7th Cir.1996).

England's common law courts first confirmed their authority to award punitive damages in the eighteenth century, see Dorsey D. Ellis, Jr., "Fairness and Efficiency in the Law of Punitive Damages," 56 *S. Cal. L. Rev.* 1, 12–20 (1982), at a time when the institutional structure of criminal law enforcement was primitive and it made sense to leave certain minor crimes to be dealt with by the civil law. And still today one function of punitive-damages awards is to relieve the pressures on an overloaded system of criminal justice by providing a civil alternative to criminal prosecution of minor crimes. An example is deliberately spitting in a person's face, a criminal assault but because minor readily deterrable by the levying of what amounts to a civil fine through a suit for damages for the tort of battery. Compensatory damages would not do the trick in such a case, and this for three reasons: because they are difficult to determine in the case of acts that inflict largely dignitary harms; because in the spitting case they would be too slight to give the victim an incentive to sue, and he might decide instead to respond with violence-and an age-old purpose of the law of torts is to provide a substitute for violent retaliation against wrongful injury-and because to limit the plaintiff to compensatory damages would enable the defendant to commit the offensive act with impunity provided that he was willing to pay, and again there would be a danger that his act would incite a breach of the peace by his victim.

When punitive damages are sought for billion-dollar oil spills and other huge economic injuries, the considerations that we have just canvassed fade. As the Court emphasized in *Campbell,* the fact that the plaintiffs in that case had been awarded very substantial compensatory damages—$1 million for a dispute over insurance coverage—greatly reduced the need for giving them a huge award of punitive damages ($145 million) as well in order to provide an effective remedy. Our case is closer to the spitting case. The defendant's behavior was outrageous but the compensable harm done was slight and at the same time difficult to quantify because a large element of it was emotional. And the defendant may well have profited from its misconduct because by concealing the infestation it was able to keep renting rooms. Refunds were frequent but may have cost less than the cost of closing the hotel for a thorough fumigation. The hotel's attempt to pass off the bedbugs as ticks, which some guests might ignorantly have thought less unhealthful, may have postponed the instituting of litigation to rectify the hotel's misconduct. The award of punitive damages in this case thus serves the additional purpose of limiting the defendant's ability to profit from its fraud by escaping detection and (private) prosecution. If a tortfeasor is "caught" only half the time he commits torts, then when he is caught he should be punished twice as heavily in order to make up for the times he gets away.

Finally, if the total stakes in the case were capped at $50,000 (2 x [$5,000 + $20,000]), the plaintiffs might well have had difficulty financing this lawsuit. It is here that the defendant's aggregate net worth of $1.6 billion becomes relevant. A defendant's wealth is not a sufficient basis for awarding punitive damages. That would be discriminatory and would violate the rule of law, as we explained earlier, by making punishment depend on status rather than conduct. Where wealth in the sense of resources enters is in enabling the defendant to mount an extremely aggressive defense against suits such as this and by doing so to make litigating against it very costly, which in turn may make it difficult for the plaintiffs to find a lawyer willing to handle their case, involving as it does only modest stakes, for the usual 33–40 percent contingent fee.

In other words, the defendant is investing in developing a reputation intended to deter plaintiffs. It is difficult otherwise to explain the great stubbornness with which it has defended this case, making a host of frivolous evidentiary arguments despite the very modest stakes even when the punitive damages awarded by the jury are included. . . .

All things considered, we cannot say that the award of punitive damages was excessive, albeit the precise number chosen by the jury was arbitrary. It is probably not a coincidence that $5,000 + $186,000 = $191,000/191 = $1,000: i.e., $1,000 per room in the hotel. But as there are no punitive-damages guidelines, corresponding to the federal and state sentencing guidelines, it is inevitable that the specific amount of punitive damages awarded whether by a judge or by a jury will be arbitrary. (Which is perhaps why the plaintiffs' lawyer did not suggest a number to the jury.) The judicial function is to police a range, not a point.

But it would have been helpful had the parties presented evidence concerning the regulatory or criminal penalties to which the defendant exposed itself by deliberately exposing its customers to a substantial risk of being bitten by bedbugs. That is an inquiry recommended by the

Supreme Court. But we do not think its omission invalidates the award. We can take judicial notice that deliberate exposure of hotel guests to the health risks created by insect infestations exposes the hotel's owner to sanctions under Illinois and Chicago law that in the aggregate are comparable in severity to the punitive damage award in this case.

"A person who causes bodily harm to or endangers the bodily safety of an individual by any means, commits reckless conduct if he performs recklessly the acts which cause the harm or endanger safety, whether they otherwise are lawful or unlawful." 720 ILCS 5/12–5(a). This is a misdemeanor, punishable by up to a year's imprisonment or a fine of $2,500, or both. Of course a corporation cannot be sent to prison, and $2,500 is obviously much less than the $186,000 awarded to each plaintiff in this case as punitive damages. But this is just the beginning. Other guests of the hotel were endangered besides these two plaintiffs. And, what is much more important, a Chicago hotel that permits unsanitary conditions to exist is subject to revocation of its license, without which it cannot operate. Chi. Munic. Code §§ 4–4–280, 4–208–020, 050, 060, 110. We are sure that the defendant would prefer to pay the punitive damages assessed in this case than to lose its license.

NOTES

1. **Wrongdoing.** Recall *Garratt v. Daily* (Chapter 3), cited by Judge Posner in *Mathias*. What would be the prima facie case for battery here? Fraud is an intentional material misrepresentation of fact that is intended to and does induce justifiable reliance and proximately causes harm. 3 DOBBS, HAYDEN & BUBLICK, THE LAW OF TORTS § 664 (2d ed. 2011). What is the intentional, material misrepresentation that Motel 6 made to its guests and how did they rely on it?

2. **Ratios.** Do you agree with Judge Posner's assessment that high punitive damages to compensatory damage ratios are more acceptable in some types of cases than others? The Texas Supreme Court noted that several significant ratio cases have involved intangible rights, for example concerning discrimination. *See Bennett v. Reynolds*, 315 S.W.3d 867 (Tex. 2010) (discussing cases that had upheld even triple-digit ratios); *see also Goff v. Elmo Greer & Sons Constr. Co.*, 297 S.W.3d 175 (Tenn. 2009) (nuisance case against company that buried waste tires on owners' property). In the billion-dollar oil spill cases, do compensatory awards more fully account for harm such that the incentives function of punitive damages is less relevant?

3. **Institutional profit from harm.** Why didn't the hotel in *Mathias* eradicate the problem? Judge Posner suggests it must have been more profitable for the hotel to operate in that way. Judge Posner frames this case as more of an intentional tort than a significant economic injury. But looking at the defendant's unjust gains, rather than the plaintiffs' losses, isn't it clear that significant economic interests are at stake? The major modern cases

involve the wrongdoer who engages in wrong in order to make a large profit. Shouldn't profit from the wrong be far more relevant than any ratio between compensatory and punitive awards? The point would be to retain full deterrence by eliminating the profits and to retain the capacity of the punitive award to provide appropriate incentives to sue. *See* Dan B. Dobbs, *Ending Punishment in "Punitive" Damages: Deterrence-Measured Remedies*, 40 ALA. L. REV. 831 (1989).

4. **Revisiting *Owens*.** The *Owens-Corning* asbestos case involved significant harm to the plaintiff, who had developed mesothelioma. Yet, as a later court noted, the ratio of punitive damages to compensatory damages in *Owens* is 18:1. *Sun Int'l. Bahamas, Ltd. v. Wagner,* 758 So.2d 1190 (Fla. Dist. Ct. App. 2000). *Owens* justified that award on the on the basis that "it would be difficult to envision a more egregious set of circumstances than those found herein by the trial court to constitute a blatant disregard for human safety involving large numbers of people put at life-threatening risk." Should *Owens* be considered outside constitutional bounds after *Campbell*?

5. **Litigation-finance function.** As Judge Posner's discussion in *Mathias* highlights, punitive damages may serve societal goals, for example by acting as a deterrent to the defendant by providing source for payment of attorney fees. *See Haralson v. Fisher Surveying, Inc.,* 31 P.3d 114 (Ariz. 2001); *Estate of Hoch v. Stifel,* 16 A.3d 137 (Me. 2011). Punitive damages may encourage lawyers to invest the time, effort and expense necessary to prevail in cases that require investigation and evidence. The lawyer will not pursue the case unless there is reason to hope for a large award sufficient to pay her a reasonable fee for her efforts. In some cases the lawyer's investment is so large that she must expect a punitive award to cover her fee and expenses, else give up the case. If punitive damages had not been awarded in *Mathias*, would the case have been worth pursuing?

PHILIP MORRIS USA V. WILLIAMS, 549 U.S. 346 (2007). The widow of a heavy cigarette smoker sued the cigarette manufacturer for negligence and deceit, seeking both compensatory and punitive damages after her husband died of lung cancer. The jury found in her favor and awarded $821,000 in compensatory damages and $79.5 million in punitives. The trial judge reduced the compensatory damages to $500,000 and the punitive award to $32 million. After several interim rulings and decisions after remand, the case came to this Court. Defendant now argues that the trial judge should have instructed the jury that it could not punish the defendant for injury to persons not parties before the court. *Held,* a punitive damages award based in part on a jury's desire to punish a defendant for harming nonparties violates due process. A state may properly impose punitive damages, but it must do so in a way to cabin the jury's discretionary authority, and give the defendant "fair notice . . . of the severity of the penalty." Penalizing a defendant for misconduct towards nonparties who are "strangers to the litigation" adds a nearly standardless dimension to the punitive damages equation, and magnifies this Court's due process concerns in these cases: arbitrariness, uncertainty, and lack of notice. There is no authority at all for using punitive damages awards to punish a defendant for harming persons not before the court. While evidence of harm to nonparties may show that a defendant's conduct was particularly reprehensible, a jury may not go further and use a punitive damages award to punish a defendant directly for harms to such nonparties. States must develop procedures to insure that harm to nonparties is considered only on the reprehensibility issue and does not form the basis of the amount of the punitive award itself.

NOTES

1. ***Williams* results on remand.** The Court did not reach the issue of whether the amount of punitive damages was excessive, but instead remanded for further proceedings. On remand, the Oregon Supreme Court held that the trial court did not err in refusing to give the particular jury instruction the defendant had requested, and remanded for further proceedings. *Williams v. Philip Morris Inc.*, 176 P.3d 1255 (Or. 2008). Subsequently, defendant paid compensatory damages and part of the punitive damages award (which had been reduced to $32 million), but contested the state's statutory share of punitive damages. In *Williams v. RJ Reynolds Tobacco Co.*, 271 P.3d 103 (Or. 2011), the court ruled that the state had a right to pursue its statutory share of punitive damages.

2. **Applying *Williams*.** In *White v. Ford Motor Co.*, 500 F.3d 963 (9th Cir. 2007), the jury in a products liability action involving a child's death awarded $52 million in punitive damages against Ford. The Ninth Circuit reversed on the basis of *Williams*, holding that the trial judge was required by due process to instruct the jury that while it could consider evidence of actual harm to nonparties as part of its reprehensibility determination, it could not use its punitive damages verdict to punish the defendant directly. Can a trial court make that distinction understandable to a jury? *See also Schwarz v. Philip Morris Inc.*, 235 P.3d 668 (Or. 2010): for repeated wrongful conduct: (a) conduct not causing compensatory damages to the plaintiff may not be used as a *basis* for awarding punitive damages, but (b) such conduct may bear on reprehensibility and hence on the *amount* of punitive damages when punitive damages are otherwise authorized. The focus on deterring repeated wrongful actions also has been interpreted to permit argument that a case was important to wider industry practices beyond the case itself. *Weinstein v. Prudential Prop. & Cas. Ins. Co.*, 233 P.3d 1221 (Idaho 2010).

3. **Another view.** Four justices (Stevens, Thomas, Scalia and Ginsburg) dissented in the U.S. Supreme Court's *Williams* decision. Justice Stevens commented on the majority's distinction between using harm to nonparties as evidence of reprehensibility but not to punish the defendant, "This nuance eludes me." He added, "A murderer who kills his victim by

throwing a bomb that injures dozens of bystanders should be punished more severely than one who harms no one other than his intended victim." Thus, in his view, the jury should be free not only to take conduct towards nonparties into account on the reprehensibility issue, but also to punish the defendant on that very basis. Do you agree?

4. **Magnitude of risks to others.** Does it matter that in *Mathias* harm to others was so small that they could not have been reasonably expected to sue about it, while in *Williams* the harm to others may have been significant and the subject of separate suits? This distinction has been important in some class action consumer fraud and civil RICO cases.

REFERENCES: 3 DOBBS, HAYDEN & BUBLICK, THE LAW OF TORTS §§ 479–86 (2d ed. 2011); DOBBS, HAYDEN & BUBLICK, HORNBOOK ON TORTS §§ 34.4–34.7 (2d ed. 2016).

CHAPTER 27

EVALUATING TORT LAW

■ ■ ■

How good are tort systems at coping with the problem of injury in modern American life? Any system used to deal with the injury problem will be severely strained. According to the National Safety Council, https://injuryfacts.nsc.org/all-injuries/overview/, Americans suffer

- about 48.3 million nonfatal injuries per year, of which more than 4.5 million are from motor vehicle accidents.

- 173,040 accidental deaths a year; about 39,100 from motor vehicle accidents alone.

- 4.5 million work-related injuries.

- economic impact of unintended injury of $1,097.9 billion in 2019 (by the measure of "dollars spent and income not received due to injuries and fatalities").

- economic costs of $463 billion from motor vehicles alone equivalent to about $2000 per licensed driver.

Despite this staggering number of injuries, injury rates have declined substantially over the last century. National Safety Council statistics show that "Between 1912 and 2007, unintentional-injury deaths per 100,000 of population were reduced 53% . . . from 82.4 to 38.8. The reduction in the overall rate during a period when the nation's population tripled has resulted in 5,500,000 fewer people being killed due to unintentional injuries than there would have been if the rate had not been reduced." National Safety Council, Injury Facts 2010 and 2012.

§ 1. RULES, PRACTICES AND THEORIES OF TORT LAW

Looking back over the rules of torts, do tort rules promote safety? Fairness? Would you have any major criticisms of the tort rules? In the past, the rule of contributory negligence and the rules of assumed risk and fellow-servant were often the butt of serious criticisms. These rules no longer automatically bar recovery. Do new rules of comparative fault and apportionment resolve all problems? What, in the fault system today would you find that warrants substantial change?

The strict liability system has been confined to a fairly narrow set of cases in recent years. Should it be applied more broadly? Does a more restricted strict liability system mean that tort recoveries will contract? An astute and careful observer argued that the expansion of tort liability that occurred in the latter half of the 20th century was accomplished largely through negligence law, not strict liability, and that tort law had become stabilized by the late 1980s. Gary T. Schwartz, *The Beginning and the Possible End of the Rise of Modern American Tort Law*, 26 GA. L. REV. 601 (1992).

The practical application of tort law in the context of damages and apportionment may give some ground for concern. Are there practical aspects of tort cases that cause serious problems?

What about theoretical problems in tort law? Is there any need to move from a theory based predominantly on fault to a theory based on, say, general deterrence? On compensation? Would changes in tort theory, if they occurred, resolve the practical problems of administering tort law on a massive scale? Might some sort of compensation fund or other injury-response program fare better?

§ 2. TORT WARS

Tort Reform

Major Criticisms Advanced by the Tort Reformers

Critics say the tort system is running amok; liability is everywhere; the American public wants to sue whenever anything goes wrong; and lawyers' greed has brought the country to the brink of disaster. Some of these charges lead to long battles about whether litigation really has increased.

More soberly, tort reformers say that the tort system as presently administered has caused specific problems because of the costs it imposes on defendants and insurers:

(1) liability insurance costs too much, especially for certain defendants like malpractice defendants (the affordability crisis);

(2) insurance has or may become unavailable for some defendants (the availability crisis);

(3) some goods or services of vast importance may become unavailable because the threat of tort liability is driving some producers out of the market.

Evaluating the Criticisms

The data suggest that injured people actually should be claiming redress more often than they do and that juries, far from running amok, award recoveries less often than judges do. Here are some major items of information.

- Most suits filed, around 86 million a year, deal with crimes, divorce, juvenile proceedings, debt claims, and traffic and parking infractions. The number of tort claims is a small percentage of courts' incoming civil litigation—about 5%. See Joe Palazollo, *We Won't See You in Court: The Era of Tort Lawsuits Is Waning*, W.S.J. (in 2015, tort lawsuits accounted for less than 5% of all civil filings in state courts). 69% percent of the state courts' civil litigation claims are contract-based. *See* R. LaFountain, R. Schauffler, S. Strickland, S. Gibson, & A. Mason, *Examining the Work of State Courts: An Analysis of 2009 State Court Caseloads* (National Center for State Courts 2011). An earlier study found that a full 60% of the tort cases filed stem from automobile accidents. *See* B. Ostrom, N. Kauder, N. LaFountain, *Examining the Work of State Courts 2002* (National Center for State Courts 2003). *See also* Deborah Jones Merritt & Kathryn Ann Barry, *Is the Tort System in Crisis? New Empirical Evidence*, 60 OHIO ST. L.J. 315 (1999); Michael J. Saks, *Do We Really Know Anything About the Behavior of the Tort Litigation System— And Why Not?*, 140 U. PA. L. REV. 1147 (1992); Joseph Sanders and Craig Joyce, *"Off to the Races": The 1980s Tort Crisis and the Law Reform Process*, 27 HOUS. L. REV. 207 (1990).

- Only about 10% of injured people make any claim at all; probably many more could justly assert claims. *See* Marc Galanter, *Real World Torts: An Antidote to Anecdote*, 55 MD. L. REV. 1093 (1996).

- Settlements, which constitute the great majority of tort dispositions, on the average probably undercompensate. *See* Deborah L. Rhode, *Frivolous Litigation and Civil Justice Reform: Miscasting the Problem, Recasting the Solution*, 54 DUKE L. J., 447, 460 (2004) (contending that "although excessive litigation is the pathology dominating public discussion and policy agendas, systematic research reveals that the more serious problems are undercompensation of victims").

- A Bureau of Justice Statistics study showed that the median total award in a sample of tort cases was only $24,000, although the National Safety Council estimates that the average economic cost (apart from human cost) of incapacitating injury in automobile cases is much greater—

about $70,200. *See* Bureau of Justice Statistics, Civil Bench and Jury Trials in State Courts, 2005 (October 2008); and National Safety Council, Estimating the Costs of Unintentional Injuries (2012).

- Juries have not run amok; in a Bureau of Justice Statistics sample, juries found for the plaintiff in only 52% of the cases. Judges found for the plaintiff only a little more often. When judges act as triers of fact, their awards resemble those of juries, even with punitive damages. *See* Theodore Eisenberg, Neil LaFountain, Brian Ostrom, David Rottman & Martin T. Wells, *Juries, Judges, and Punitive Damages: an Empirical Study*, 87 CORNELL L. REV. 743 (2002).

- Some torts, with disastrous consequences to human beings, really are being committed. Litigation should be perceived as a problem only if litigation outruns actionable injury. Striking studies show that in fact many more tortious injuries are caused than are sued for. *See* Michael J. Saks, *Do We Really Know Anything About the Behavior of the Tort Litigation System—And Why Not?*, 140 U. PA. L. REV. 1147 (1992); Localio, et al., *Relation between Malpractice Claims and Adverse Events Due to Negligence*, 325 N. ENG. J. MED. 245 (July 25, 1991). The question perhaps should be, not whether the amount of litigation has increased in any given time period, but whether it is too extensive or not enough and whether there are better alternatives. *See* Dan B. Dobbs, *Can You Care for People and Still Count the Costs?*, 46 MD. L. REV. 49 (1986) (commenting on Marc Galanter, *The Day After the Litigation Explosion*, 46 MD. L. REV. 3 (1986)).

Frank Cross, a professor of Business, Law and Government at the University of Texas recently examined whether states that had pro-defendant tort law as judged by Chamber of Commerce indices enjoyed greater economic growth or other benefits. Professor Cross concluded that "Contrary to conventional wisdom, evidence shows no negative economic effects from more pro-plaintiff tort law. . . . More pro-plaintiff law is associated with higher economic growth. . . . The finding [with respect to tort costs and economic growth] is powerful evidence that tort law is at least not harming states' economies." This finding accorded with the theory that tort law should be economically beneficial because it forces firms to internalize costs imposed on others and expands the number of economic transactions. Frank B. Cross, *Tort Law and the American Economy*, 96 MINN. L. REV. 28, 86–89 (2011). In light of the data, why have some people claimed that the courts are giving money away in ridiculous cases?

In part, this may reflect bias against courts—which, after all, are independent and on the whole not subject to political pressure or legislative control. Recent analysis suggests that restrictions on tort actions may also reflect racial bias. *See* Donald G. Gifford & Brian Jones, *Keeping Cases from Black Juries: An Empirical Analysis of How Race, Income Inequality, and Regional History Affect Tort Law*, 73 WASH. & LEE L. REV. 557 (2016) (based on data analysis, concluding: "Even in the twenty-first century, supreme courts in a number of states with substantial percentages of African-Americans in their largest cities, particularly those in the South, continue to follow outmoded substantive doctrines of tort law that make it more difficult for personal injury plaintiffs to have their cases decided by juries. These tort doctrines are but the latest iteration of various means used by courts during the past 150 years to keep African-Americans from participating as jurors in personal injury cases.").

Anti-tort law opinion also has been molded by anecdotes that shamefully distort the cases they purport to report. For example: (1) The story was that a burglar recovered when he fell through a skylight of a building he was trying to burglarize; the fact was that it was a student who fell when he was on the roof of a school to fix a floodlight. (2) The story was that a man who was struck by a car while he was in a telephone booth recovered from the phone company; the fact was that he tried desperately to get out of the booth when he saw the car coming, but the door jammed and he was trapped. Even if anecdotes were correct, they would tell us little about the system as a whole. When they are so terribly misleading, they generate conflict but not information. On the anecdotes, see Joseph Page, *Deforming Tort Reform*, 78 GEO. L. J. 649 (1990) (book review of PETER W. HUBER, LIABILITY: THE LEGAL REVOLUTION AND ITS CONSEQUENCES (1988)); Saks, *supra*. To read about the campaigns to shape public opinion in a misleading way, see Elizabeth G. Thornburg, *Judicial Hellholes, Lawsuit Climates and Bad Social Science: Lessons from West Virginia*, 110 W. VA. L. REV. 1097 (2008). For a thorough review of many empirical studies, see John T. Nockelby, *How to Manufacture a Crisis: Empirical Claims Behind "Tort Reform,"* 86 OR. L. REV. 533 (2007).

§ 3. THE IMPACT OF TORT LAW ON THE INJURY PROBLEM

The Old Tort Reform

The tort reform movement discussed above was and is fueled mainly by industries, insurers and others who wish to see greater protection for defendants. The first tort reformers approached tort law with different questions and a different orientation. They were not focused on liability reduction, but asked in part: How well does the tort system work in the real world? Does it cope adequately with the problem of massive injury?

Does it adequately deter wrongdoing? Compensate the injured? Encourage rehabilitation and otherwise minimize economic loss?

People can bring many viewpoints to the problem of injury. Here are two that may account in part for some of the criticisms we see of injury systems:

(1) Insurance funds, created by premiums to which many of us contribute, might be regarded as community funds, to be used in the interest of those whose contributions make them up. They are, in a sense, a bit like public funds created by tax contributions. The taxpayer or premium payer should have something to say about how they are used. In other words, the premium payer might like to "buy" more or less liability insurance, but what in fact is bought must depend largely on what the law says about the extent of liability. The premium payer might want the law to contract or expand liability so that the insurance funds are distributed differently. Not only might the premium payer be interested in how the insurance pie is cut, one might also be interested in how efficiently it is cut. The premium payer might want to find ways to reduce overhead costs and hence to minimize the premium paid. Since liability insurance is the fuel of the torts system, these concerns, however, cannot be dealt with directly by the insurance market, because the market must reflect the legal liability. If anyone is interested in changing the distribution or efficiency of liability insurance, then that person must first change the law of torts.

(2) Injury on the massive scale we know it in contemporary American society is a social problem. Injury that causes economic loss, at least, has radiating effects that impose losses on others—family members, employers, and society as a whole. The effects are not necessarily only economic in nature, and society also has an interest in seeing to it that uncompensated economic harm to a worker, for example, does not lead to a spiraling disintegration of the family structure itself. This view might result in the feeling that some minimal compensation would be more important than a careful determination of fault.

Nine points involving some of these criticisms are set out below for discussion. To what extent are these points predicated upon one or both of the viewpoints stated above?

Problems with the Tort System?

1. *Undercompensation.* Studies have repeatedly shown that many claimants are not fully compensated. This point has three parts: (a) undercompensation is itself a failure of the tort system to achieve its own goals; (b) undercompensation has social consequences—the hardships on the injured and their families may be translated into welfare claims on society, or into crime and juvenile delinquency; (c) undercompensation of some groups of claimants is part of a larger picture in which some other groups are—according to many thinkers—overcompensated, with the

result that the system not only fails its goals, but also provides a "maldistribution" of the insurance pie and fails to treat people equally.

How does undercompensation come about under the tort systems? Consider these possibilities: (1) The cost of going to court is such that settlement is imperative; in many ranges of injury, lawyers will encourage settlement and, with or without encouragement, plaintiffs will be compelled to accept a fraction of their actual losses. (2) Delay in trial may force the claimant to accept a settlement now. (3) Other factors would encourage a settlement for less-than-loss. These include estimates of liability, and estimates about problems in proof, effectiveness of witnesses and the bias of juries. (4) In spite of compulsory insurance laws, one in five or six drivers is uninsured and often insolvent, so that their victims have little chance of collecting any compensation, much less adequate compensation. This is a very serious problem the states have not dealt with adequately. A California statute provides that a vehicle owner cannot recover pain and suffering damages for injuries he sustains in an accident with his vehicle if that vehicle is uninsured. CAL. CIV. CODE § 3333.4. Do you think this would adequately address the problem of the underinsured motorist?

One of the earliest studies was Conard, Morgan, Pratt, Volz & Bombaugh, Automobile Accident Costs and Payments (1964), hereafter cited as Conard. Of 86,000 persons who suffered economic loss, some 20,000 received no compensation from any source. Of those who were compensated, the majority received compensation from their own insurance, workers' compensation or the like—not from the tort system. More recent figures suggest that more than two-thirds of those injured in vehicle accidents receive at least some compensation, although because of the problem of uninsured motorists, that compensation may be from their own uninsured motorist coverage. *See* Gary T. Schwartz, *Auto No-fault and First-party Insurance: Advantages and Problems*, 73 S. CAL. L. REV. 611, 624 (2000). Recent evidence suggests that post-tort reform, fewer injured people are bringing actions. Stephen Daniels & Joanne Martin, *Where Have All the Cases Gone? The Strange Success of Tort Reform Revisited*, 65 EMORY L.J. 1445 (2016) ("it is not that jury trials are vanishing, it is the cases themselves"). In the area of intentional torts, victims may be particularly likely to go without compensation. In his article, *Uncompensated Torts*, 28 GA. ST. U. L. REV. 721 (2012), Rick Swedloff outlines the reasons that victims of intentional acts, acts causing more than $460 billion of damages each year, have few practical remedies.

Are the individual and social consequences of these facts significant enough to warrant changing the tort system if this is the only objection?

2. *Overcompensation.* Students of accident compensation have repeatedly found that some claimants are grossly overcompensated.

Although one expects that many claimants will recover more than their financial losses—because of pain and suffering recoveries—this does not seem to explain the enormous overcompensation at the lower end of the scale. The Department of Transportation completed an extensive study of the auto accident problem in the early 1970s. This showed, in line with some other studies, that where the economic loss was low, the average recovery might more than double the loss. For instance, if the average economic loss was $330, the average recovery was $829. Westat Research Corp., Economic Consequences of Automobile Accident Injuries 38 (Department of Transportation Automobile Ins. & Compensation Study 1970) (hereafter cited as Economic Consequences). At the upper end of the scale, where pain and suffering would likely be more, the reverse was true, and undercompensation was common.

Knowing what you do about the tort system and how it works, what is your best guess as to the reason for this overcompensation feature?

What impact does this overcompensation have? Is it, standing alone, sufficient to warrant changing the tort system?

3. *Misuse of limited resources.* The DOT study concluded that the personal economic losses from auto accidents in the year 1967 were between $5 and $9 billion. *See* Economic Consequences at 40. That figure did not include either pain and suffering or social losses, such as lost production. The same study concluded that the tort-insurance system paid net compensation of about .8 billion dollars or less than 20% of the actual economic losses. *See id.* at 146. More recent estimates of the total economic cost of motor vehicle crashes placed the cost at $230.6 billion. "Lost market productivity accounted for $61 billion of this total, while property damage accounted for nearly as much-$59 billion. Medical expenses totaled $32.6 billion. . . Each fatality resulted in an average discounted lifetime cost of $977,000. Public revenues paid for roughly 9 percent of all motor vehicle crash costs, costing tax payers $21 billion in 2000." U.S. Department of Transportation, National Highway Traffic Safety Administration, *The Economic Impact of Motor Vehicle Crashes 2000* (2002).

Do figures showing that only a small portion of individual economic losses are compensated by insurance funds reflect any misuse of resources? Some of the division of the "insurance pie" goes for pain and suffering claims. Every dollar paid for pain and suffering is a dollar that cannot be used to pay basic economic loss. The result is that while some claimants recover for pain, other claimants don't even get their medical bills or lost wages paid. There simply is not enough in the premium fund to go around.

Is this, as some critics argue, a misuse of the limited resources available? If it is, would this be ground, standing alone, for changing the tort system in any substantial way? Would you, instead, favor multiplying liability insurance premiums several fold in order to cover all economic losses?

Notice that the misuse of resources argument as it is cast here could be resolved in part by eliminating the pain and suffering recovery in tort. Would that be desirable, neutral, or undesirable?

4. *Inefficiency of the tort-liability insurance system.* Without liability insurance there would be no tort system as we know it in auto accident cases. The liability insurance system is, however, a three-party system, in which you buy insurance from the company, who will pay a third person— the plaintiff. This builds in certain costs and the tort system itself builds in more. The insurer must investigate fault, cause, damage, and, sometimes, complex legal issues as well. Given fault as a trigger of liability, much of the premium dollar must be devoted to administration costs.

In addition to the costs of the parties and the insurer, the tort system imposes costs on the public because it entails the cost of judges, courthouses, juries, clerks and other apparatus of the judicial system. Special problems appear in class actions, which literally involve hundreds of thousands of claims.

A rather different inefficiency comes from the fact that in mixing a liability insurance system with other kinds of insurance, there will be double coverage on some items. Double coverage means more premium charges. If you and your brother each drove a car and each had hospital insurance, you might agree between yourselves that if one of you negligently injured the other, the injured person would not hold the other liable for hospital costs, and the injured person would collect from the hospital insurance instead. (This would utilize the more efficient premium dollar.) The two of you might then approach your insurance agent and ask to have your liability policy amended accordingly and your premium reduced. "I'll never be liable to pay for the hospital costs," you might say, "because my brother will guarantee to rely on his own hospital insurance. So reduce my premium." If you could agree with all persons who might be hurt by your driving to rely on their hospital insurance, this plan might work and the liability insurer might indeed reduce the premium because it would have reduced its risks of liability. But you cannot agree with the whole world, so the scheme won't work. The result is that for practical purposes the law forces you to purchase the same insurance twice.

Would the inefficiencies suggested in these paragraphs be enough, standing alone, to warrant any attempt to find substitutes for the tort system in auto accident cases?

5. *Delay in payment under the tort system.* If a claimant is entitled to recover but cannot be paid for months or even years, a number of harmful consequences come about. This is not a problem peculiar to torts. All law attempts to make a careful investigation into the facts and to give full

opportunity to debate the legal issues. These good points of law, however, carry a heavy price in forcing delay. In tort cases, the substantive rules requiring proof of fault, cause and damage, along with the ambiguities of many rules, require especially intensive investigation and especially intensive trials. Delay seems unavoidable.

Delay is also due to the fact that the claimant must assert all claims for the future in one legal action. This may require a period of waiting to better estimate future losses and it certainly requires extensive proof about the future.

Delay may also be used strategically by defendants. The procedural system, aimed at supporting the law's aim of full investigation and complete opportunity to be heard, is readily manipulated to delay trial. Defendants can, within the ethics of the system, often delay trial and hence delay settlement or payment. This is useful from the defendant's point of view, since the plaintiff, deprived of wages, will feel more and more pressure to accept smaller and smaller settlements as time goes by.

Would these problems of delay warrant making a substantial change in the tort system if they stood alone? Could you eliminate some of the problems of delay without eliminating the tort system?

6. *The failure to deter or compensate.* The tort system begins with a determination to fix fault. It assumes that fault can be determined in a rational way, and that when it is determined, the imposition of liability in accord with fault will accomplish two purposes: (a) it will administer justice by imposing liability upon faulty persons, and (b) it will deter similar faulty conduct in others. To some, the justice argument itself fails. We have all been faulty in driving at one time or another, quite probably very often by today's standards of negligence in auto cases. Since we are all at fault, according to this view, it is largely a matter of fortuity that some of us get involved in an accident because of fault and some escape an accident. It is even more a matter of fortuity that some of us may cause large damages and some may cause quite small damages. *Cf.* Marc Franklin, *Replacing the Negligence Lottery*, 53 VA. L. REV. 774 (1967). Under these circumstances, it is less than clear that imposing liability in accord with fault is truly "just."

Whatever may be said about the justice side of the argument, the deterrent effect of tort liability is undercut by the presence of liability insurance. When a defendant is held liable, that defendant does not ordinarily make payments to the injured plaintiff in the tort system. The liability insurer does so. In many states, punitive as well as compensatory damages are covered by insurance, so that insurance may protect even a reckless defendant from any personal accountability in money. In addition, the court's desire to compensate the plaintiff has led to many cases in which "fault" is found in a defendant who has behaved in a way that, but for insurance, most people would not find faulty at all. In this view, then, the tort system fails to accomplish one of its main purposes—deterrence.

Is it true that the tort system does not accomplish any of its main goals—justice, deterrence, compensation? If it is true, would this criticism standing alone lead you to seek a substitute system?

7. *Participation in the insurance fund—lack of reciprocity.* Although the tort system is fueled on liability insurance, not everyone purchases such insurance. Among those who do purchase it, many have procured only low-limit policies, inadequate to protect a seriously injured plaintiff. A person who purchases only minimal insurance protection or none at all may nevertheless be the beneficiary of a high-limits policy purchased by someone else. Suppose X buys no insurance, but, while driving recklessly, causes serious harm to C. Unless X has extraordinary personal resources, the result will be that C will recover little or nothing from X and will rely instead on public resources or on his own private resources. But X, having failed to provide even minimal compensation for his own negligence, is in no way limited in his own recovery. If X is injured by D's negligence, and D has provided himself with adequate insurance, X will receive full compensation. He can, in short, draw on the insurance others have provided, without providing his share of the protection for others. This is only one of several peculiarities of using liability insurance in which the protection of one rests in the hands of others. Is this justified on the ground that, after all, X may be relatively poor and may find it possible to drive only because he does not purchase liability insurance?

A second problem of reciprocity in the participation in insurance funds can be seen if one imagines that poor people as a class will draw less of the insurance pie than others because for any given injury they will have less wage loss. Yet they will pay the same premiums paid by wealthier persons. Again, this is a result of the fact that injury is compensated through the insurance of others, not through one's own insurance.

Do these observations amount to a criticism of the tort system? If so, would this criticism standing alone warrant an effort to change the tort system?

8. *Is the tort system a lottery?* Some lawyers think so. There are at least three senses in which this may be so.

(a) There is a large element of fortuity from the injured person's point of view. If a woman is injured in an ordinary car collision, she will have to prove negligence to recover. If the collision occurs while she is in the course of employment, she will not be required to prove negligence, though her workers' compensation recovery will be limited to economic losses. If the collision occurs because of a defective steering apparatus, she will be entitled to recover from the manufacturer without proving negligence and she will not be limited to economic losses. From her point of view, her legal rights depend almost wholly on the luck of the case—whether she was working or not, whether her injury was caused by the manufacturer or by another driver. There are a number of these fortuitous elements in the negligence case. Consider: The defendant is negligent, but by luck he causes no harm at all; or the defendant is negligent, but by luck the plaintiff was also guilty of substantial negligence, though the defendant would have caused the same harm to a non-negligent plaintiff. See Franklin, supra.

(b) The torts system may be viewed as a lottery for more quotidian reasons. Consider: the plaintiff is injured, but as luck would have it, the plaintiff herself is not very attractive and does not capture the jury's sympathy; or the only witness is quite truthful, but has an abrasive personality and makes a bad impression; or there is no witness at all; or defendant's witnesses have been packaged and stage managed to create the best impression; or the defendant is a sympathetic local person and the plaintiff is an outsider. Similarly, lawyers' abilities to deal with complex issues vary greatly; some plaintiffs lose because their lawyers were not up to the demands of the particular case, not because the case itself was unworthy.

(c) A final sense in which the tort system may be considered a lottery is rather different. Tort damages range from quite trivial sums to many millions. Suppose a defense attorney, defending a case in which the plaintiff is seriously injured but the defendant does not appear to be at fault, makes a small offer of settlement. The plaintiff's attorney might believe that the plaintiff will in fact lose the case on a directed verdict and that, therefore, a small offer should be accepted. But the lawyer might also believe that there is one chance in a thousand that the trial judge will let the case go to the jury and that there is one chance in ten that the jury, if it gets the case, will bring in a very large judgment indeed. If so, the lawyer may press on to trial. The result is that many weak cases that probably should not win may yet go to trial, and at times they might pay off.

Are any of these "lottery" reasons ground for reconsidering the tort system?

9. *Are the lump-sum award and pain and suffering compensation justifiable?* The instinctive answer of almost everyone is that something should be paid for pain and suffering, at least when that pain is caused by wrongdoing of others. Yet the pain and suffering award does not compensate in the ordinary sense. If wages are lost, money can repay that loss. If one is in pain, the money award cannot relieve the pain. (Pain relievers are covered under medical expense awards.) To the extent these awards are used to pay lawyers' fees, they are explicable in practical terms; but lawyers are needed in the first place chiefly because the tort system requires detailed analysis of fault, cause and damage. If the system were

changed, the role of lawyers would be very different, as it is in workers' compensation systems. Perhaps pain awards are symbolically important and important in deterrence. What do you think?

If you think there is something wrong with pain awards, do you also think that is ground standing alone to reconsider the whole tort system?

New Directions

If either the old or the new tort reformers are right or partly right in their central perceptions, would it be a good idea to find alternatives to some or all parts of the tort system?

Many of the criticisms summarized above are reviewed by Professor Sugarman, who insists that tort law fails in the goal of inducing safety, providing compensation, or doing justice if you look at the system as a whole and consider alternatives. STEPHEN SUGARMAN, DOING AWAY WITH PERSONAL INJURY LAW (1989). Sugarman proposes a comprehensive welfare program that would take care of injuries as well as any other misfortune. Employers would cover short term needs, government the rest. Safety incentives would be provided by regulation, not by threat of liability. But regulation does not always work or work efficiently and we do not know a great deal about how to make it effective as a substitute for liability. *See* Jerry Mashaw & David Harfst, *The Struggle for Auto Safety (1990); Michael J. Trebilcock, Requiem for Regulators: The Passing of a Counter-Culture?*, 8 YALE J. REG. 497 (1991).

Other critics have suggested that society should allocate certain kinds of injury problems to some institutions other than tort law, but that tort law should be retained for at least some kinds of cases. *E.g.,* Richard B. Stewart, *Crisis in Tort Law? The Institutional Perspective*, 54 U. CHI. L. REV. 184 (1987); W. Kip Viscusi, *Toward a Diminished Role for Tort Liability: Social Insurance, Government Regulation, and Contemporary Risks to Health and Safety*, 6 YALE J. REG. 65 (1989). See also the good short discussion as to toxic torts in Robert Rabin, *Book Review*, 98 YALE L. J. 813 (1989) (reviewing Peter Schuck, Tort System on Trial: The Burden of Mass Toxics Litigation (1987)).

One alternative "institution" for dealing with injury might be specific regulation, such as regulation requiring air bags or seat belts. Another institution might be the free market, leaving people to contractual arrangements. Finally, some form of social or private insurance might provide the best institution for dealing with certain injuries not suited to the tort system. In evaluating the tort reform movement, and tort law itself, some of these alternatives must be considered. Some of the major ones other than regulation or contract are considered next.

PART 10

ALTERNATIVES TO TORT LAW

■ ■ ■

For many, including many legislatures, the disadvantages of the tort system have outweighed its advantages, at least in particular settings. As a consequence, legal thinkers and state and federal legislatures have provided several non-tort alternatives to the tort system. All of these, however, have limited application, for example, to employment injuries or automobile accidents.

This Part introduces some of these alternatives. In many ways they are enormously different from tort systems. But this should not obscure the similarities. In considering these alternatives, consider whether the same issues must be resolved in both systems, and whether similar problems arise (perhaps in new language) for the judiciary in deciding claims. More importantly, consider whether any of these alternative systems is better than the tort system. If they are not to wholly supplant the tort system, can they be satisfactorily meshed with tort law?

CHAPTER 28

WORKERS' COMPENSATION

■ ■ ■

§ 1. INTRODUCTION

A. THE EMPLOYER'S TORT LIABILITY AT COMMON LAW

In the pre-industrial period in England, servants injured in the service of a master were often living in the household as apprentices or indentured servants. At least at some times and places, the practice and legal obligation of masters was to take care of the injured servant by furnishing him room and board during the period of the indenture or contract. A similar practice developed in the maritime law, and seamen injured in the service of the ship were entitled to "maintenance and cure"—basic support and medical attention. The assistance received by the servant or seaman in such cases was no doubt minimal compared to a tort remedy, but was available without respect to the employer's fault. In addition, the seaman injured by an "unseaworthy" condition of a ship had a strict liability claim against the owner. *See* THOMAS SCHOENBAUM, ADMIRALTY AND MARITIME LAW § 4–28–4–35 (1994); 5 U.S.C.A. § 8102.

With the development of industrial plants, the picture was very different. The force of machinery was multiplied through levers, pulleys and gears, then through water and steam power. The injuries caused by massive forces in the factory or on the rails were both numerous and horrible. At the very time injury was becoming the formidable problem it remains today, the system of apprentices and indentured servants was becoming obsolete. An injured plant worker could not expect that the employer would provide for him when injury made work impossible.

The common law tort system might have provided a very handsome remedy for the injured worker had it retained or developed the notion that an actor was liable for *trespassory* torts to the person, even without intent or negligence. But that notion largely went underground with the 1850 decision in *Brown v. Kendall (see* Chapter 23). The result was that the injured employee was required to prove employer negligence in all injury cases.

This might not have been an intolerable burden in many instances, but the defenses erected against the employee were effective barriers to many claims. The absolute common law defenses of contributory negligence, assumed risk and fellow servant barred a great many claims. The fellow servant rule in particular was often a hardship. That rule, supposedly grounded in assumed risk, held that the worker could not recover against the employer for negligence of the worker's fellow servant. Even though the master would be liable for the torts of a servant, he would not be liable for the torts of one servant to another.

Injured industrial workers in the 19th century were in difficult straits. They were without insurance or health benefits, without modern social services, and very often without a tort remedy. Piecemeal efforts were made in legislatures to ameliorate this situation. Factory Acts sometimes attempted to provide safer working conditions. One example of safety legislation was the Federal Safety Appliance Act, 45 U.S.C.A. §§ 1 *et seq.*, enacted in 1893 and requiring railroads to use such safety devices as automatic couplers and brakes operable by the engineer. In 1908, the Federal Employers' Liability Act, (FELA) 45 U.S.C.A. §§ 51 *et seq.* was passed. This attacked some major sources of the problem by abolishing the defenses of fellow servant and assumed risk and by adopting a comparative negligence scheme. The statute applied to railroad workers in interstate commerce, and as it stands today, it applies to virtually all railroad workers.

The FELA did not address the problems of factory or other workers. Nor did it address the fundamental problem of delay. The worker who was injured by an employer's negligence could indeed recover once the defenses were abolished. But recovery might take years if litigated in the court system. Since urban workers had little if any support if they were unable to work, even a good tort remedy might in practice be illusory.

This was the situation when workers' compensation provisions were first considered.

B. THE ADOPTION OF WORKERS' COMPENSATION

The first workers' compensation scheme was adopted in Germany in 1884. Although German philosophers had laid down the foundations of the idea in their conception of the state as a protector of the citizens, there were more immediate reasons for the adoption of the scheme, the foundation of which is compulsory insurance. One reason may have been that the German state, united under Prussian leadership in 1870, was a convenient means through which to organize the capital necessary to manage a widespread insurance scheme. An even more immediate reason was Bismarck's fear that, without some such plan, radical Marxist movements would be successful. With Bismarck's support, workers' compensation was adopted to provide a sufficient level of support to undermine Marxism. *See generally* 1–2 LARSON'S WORKERS' COMPENSATION LAW Ch. 2 (2012).

American states began enacting workers' compensation statutes, some quite limited, just after the turn of the century. The first comprehensive act was the 1910 New York statute. It was quickly declared unconstitutional in *Ives v. South Buffalo Railway Co.*, 94 N.E. 431 (N.Y. 1911), on the ground that in imposing liability without fault of the employer, the statute was a taking of property without due process of law. "When our Constitutions were adopted, it was the law of the land that no man who was without fault or negligence could be held liable in damages for injuries sustained by another." The liability of the employer to pay workers' compensation under a compulsory insurance scheme "is a liability unknown to the common law, and we think it plainly constitutes a deprivation of liberty and property. . . ."

New York amended its constitution, however, and a new statute was passed in 1913. Other states began enacting workers' compensation statutes, sometimes avoiding constitutional challenge by making the provisions elective. Most states had enacted a statute by 1920, and all states eventually did so. There is a separate federal statute for federal employees and another for longshoremen and harbor workers.

C. CHARACTERISTICS OF THE STATUTES

Although the statutes are varied in detail, they are alike in these characteristic provisions:

1. *Strict liability.* Employers are made strictly liable for on-the-job injury of employees. Thus a worker injured on the job is entitled to compensation even if the employer is not negligent.

2. *Limited liability.* The employer's liability is limited. The compensation provided is not common-law damages, but relatively fixed amounts, expressed as specific sums for certain injuries like the loss of a thumb, or as a percentage of average wages where there is total disability. Liability includes compensation for medical needs and wage loss, but nothing for pain and suffering. This limited liability is a trade-off for strict liability and sometimes is emphasized as a constitutional justification for the strict liability.

3. *Exclusive remedy and third-party claims.* Most statutes provide that the injured employee's remedy against the employer is workers' compensation, and that this remedy is exclusive of any other remedy. In other words, with few exceptions, there is no tort action against the employer. The exclusive remedy provision, however, is aimed only at preventing suits against the employer. The employee injured by a third person, such as a manufacturer of a machine used on the job, still has a tort suit against that third person.

4. *Most defenses are abolished.* Contributory negligence, assumed risk and fellow servant defenses are abolished completely. Thus even the

employee who is guilty of contributory negligence recovers full compensation. A statute of limitations still applies and may be asserted as a defense.

5. *Immediate and periodic payment.* An injured worker is entitled, after a short waiting period, to immediate periodic payments. This is in contrast to the common law lump-sum method. Payments continue as long as the disability exists, subject to any statutory maximum amounts.

6. *Enforcement and administration.* Where there is no dispute, the employer (or its insurer) pays directly to the worker on a periodic basis. If there is a dispute, the worker reports the claim to an administrative agency, called the Industrial Commission, Workers' Compensation Commission, or something similar. The agency usually sends a hearing officer or referee to the locality to hold an informal hearing and settle the dispute. The statutes contemplated that there would be no need for lawyers, but today lawyers do in fact appear in many of these hearings. However, the procedure is relaxed and informal, and there are no rules of evidence, so it remains true at least in theory that lawyers are not required.

7. *Financing.* The scheme is essentially a compulsory insurance scheme, though in some states the "insurance" fund is managed by the state rather than by private insurers. The employer is required by statute to purchase insurance. The insurance must provide coverage as outlined by the statute.

8. *Courts.* Courts have a most limited role in workers' compensation. They do, however, decide the meaning of the statute and whether evidence is sufficient to warrant the decisions of the administrators who decide disputes under the statute. In other words, one may appeal from an award of the compensation tribunal, but the courts will not overturn the award if there is evidence to support it and it is based on a correct interpretation of the law. There is no jury trial in either the initial hearing or in the appeal to the courts.

D. COVERAGE

No state has enacted workers' compensation benefits for every single worker within the state. Several devices in the statutes operate to limit coverage of workers.

1. *Election of coverage.* At one time, many of the statutes provided that workers' compensation coverage was not compulsory, but was elective only. The employer could elect not to be covered, but if this happened, the employer would be liable in tort and would be deprived of the common law defenses. The employer was thus encouraged to elect workers' compensation. The employee also had an election, but was presumed to elect in favor of compensation in the absence of some active rejection of it. This system has met with much disapproval, and many states now use a

fully compulsory system. In states where an election is possible, an election by either employer or employee may eliminate workers' compensation coverage in particular cases.

2. *Definition of employer.* Several of the critical determinants of compensation are hidden in definitional sections of the statutes. The statute may define "employer" or "employee" or both, and the statutory definitions will necessarily exclude certain persons from coverage. Many statutes exclude from coverage the following groups of workers, usually by definition of terms like "employee":

(A) *"Casual workers."* Example: someone who trims your hedge for you on one occasion. Obviously this category can present line-drawing problems, but it is not a major problem.

(B) *Domestic workers.* Example: a home cleaning person. Notice this is not the same as "janitorial."

(C) *Agricultural workers.*

(D) *Non-business employees.* This seems broader in some ways than "domestic workers."

(E) *Small employers.* Several states exempt employers whose employees are not numerous. The cut-off varies from two to six employees.

Since the definition of employee may take several pages of statutory print, there are a good many details to be assessed under particular statutes. Although many states do not cover agricultural employees, public employees and corporate executives are often covered. Even prisoners may be covered. Obviously the governing statute must be consulted.

3. *Expanding coverage.* In some situations an enterprise that would not normally be considered an employer will be defined as an employer under the compensation statute. Some provisions are quite unusual. For example, § 3366(a) of the California Labor Code provides that where a private citizen engages in "active law enforcement" service at the request of a law enforcement officer and is injured in the process, the private citizen is limited to recovering workers' compensation benefits for that injury. *See Gund v. County of Trinity*, 472 P.3d 435 (Cal. 2020) (applying statute to bar plaintiffs' negligence action against county and deputy sheriff after plaintiff walked into a murder scene after responding to deputy's request to check on a neighbor who had made an emergency call). Material on "statutory employers" and "loaned employees" is considered in § 3.

E. BENEFITS

If an entire section could be devoted to a study of the benefits payable under workers' compensation, quite a few major issues would emerge. Some of the decisions and some of the statutes would be subject to various criticisms. In some cases, benefits are woefully inadequate. In others, courts seem to have moved to a more tort-like assessment of liability. However, the mainstream cases and the principles of workers' compensation benefits are fairly straightforward. In general they look something like this:

1. *Death benefits.* If the worker dies from an on-the-job injury, death benefits based on his or her earnings are paid to certain survivors. Often, these are dependents rather than heirs. In this respect, some workers' compensation statutes differ from many of the wrongful death statutes governing tort liability.

2. *Medical benefits.* Statutes now provide more or less unlimited medical benefits, including all forms of needed care, prosthetic devices, and the like. For the most part, issues over medical care have been extremely narrow and minor. However, a current controversy exists over whether an employer must reimburse a workers' compensation claimant for the cost of medical cannabis purchased to treat pain arising from a work-related injury. *Compare Hager v. M&K Construction*, 247 A.3d 864 (N.J. 2021) (yes), with *Wright's Case*, 156 N.E.3d 161 (Mass. 2020) (no, based on a provision in state Medical Marijuana Act), and *Musta v. Mendota Heights Dental Center*, 965 N.W.2d 312 (Minn. 2021) (no, because federal Controlled Substances Act, which criminalizes cannabis, preempts Minnesota Compensation Act, which mandates reimbursement of medical cannabis purchase).

3. *Disability benefits.* In principle, workers' compensation statutes sought to replace or avoid economic loss suffered from injury. There was no award for pain and suffering. The award was intended instead to replace wages lost due to disability. Thus if a worker was injured and disabled for six months, during which time he or she could earn no wages, the ideal benefit would be equal to six months' wages. And if the worker regains part of her earning capacity, benefits would be reduced accordingly. *See Metropolitan Stevedore Co. v. Rambo,* 515 U.S. 291 (1995).

Limits on benefits. No statute affords 100% wage replacement in providing disability benefits. If a worker collected 100% of wages during disability, there would be an incentive to feign injury or disability. Even if that did not happen, there might be an unconscious tendency to prolong disability. In addition, federal law makes payments for personal injury tax-exempt. Workers' compensation benefits, since they are not taxable, are "worth more" than the wages themselves. For these and similar reasons, compensation is limited to a percentage of average wages. This percentage is often fixed at two-thirds of the average wage, and it is, ordinarily, paid on a weekly or monthly schedule. There are, in some instances, also limits on the total amount in any given week. This might be expressed in terms of a dollar amount, such as $200 per week. Or it might be expressed as a percentage of the average wage for the entire state. In either event, very high-earning employees might be entitled to considerably less than their actual wage loss. Finally, there may be limits on the total number of weeks for which compensation is payable.

Classifications of disability. Disability is typically classified as temporary or permanent on the one hand, and as either partial or total on the other. Most industrial injuries cause some temporary total disability, as where an employee is injured and cannot work at all for two months. Such an employee would ordinarily be entitled to two months' compensation. If the disability is permanent, compensation may run for life, but in some states it may be limited to a specified period, such as 500 weeks or 600 weeks. In the case of partial disability there may be compensation due, but at a reduced level.

Scheduled injuries. Injuries that were painful but caused no wage loss were not originally compensable at all, since there was no claim for pain and suffering. A worker who lost testicles or was sexually disfigured might, therefore, recover medical benefits and wage loss during any healing period, but since these injuries would not prevent work, there would be no compensation after the healing period. Some statutes have now added a small compensatory sum in the case of "disfigurement." More importantly, virtually all states have a "schedule" of benefits for certain injuries. For example, if a worker loses the sight in one eye in an industrial injury, the schedule specifies a fixed amount of compensation. Such a worker might receive 66 2/3% of the average monthly wage for 30 months. This would be awarded even if there was no demonstrable "disability," as reflected in wage loss. An unscheduled injury, in comparison, would be compensable only if it resulted in a disability.

Functional or industrial disability. The principle of computing benefits by schedule and the principle of computing by actual wage loss are obviously at odds. The original idea was to replace wages, or at least a reasonable percentage of wages. Over the years, the principle behind the schedules has moved courts and legislatures toward a "functional" assessment of disability and away from the wage-loss or "industrial" assessment of disability. This may permit courts to say that, though the claimant has not lost work time except for a healing period, nevertheless the body as a whole is impaired in function, and a disability should be found accordingly. Different statutes and different courts may thus get quite different results when a worker is injured in a way that impairs bodily function but does not seriously affect earning capacity. These notes suggest that problems arise in computing benefits. In addition, benefits may tend to under-compensate, as where there is a 500-week limit on compensation for total and permanent disability. And benefits may over-compensate where the principle of the schedule is carried out. All of these problems and others, that could be identified in computing benefits, are problems worthy of attention by those who could improve the law. But, especially for the purpose of comparisons to tort law, the central features of benefits payable under workers' compensation statutes are quite simple. In the great majority of cases, benefits will be paid regularly and without dispute as long as disability continues, but in most cases, benefits will reflect something less than actual wage loss.

On the theoretical side, workers' compensation has been justified on grounds much like those that were advanced later for vicarious liability and strict products liability. The idea is that enterprise ought to bear responsibility for the costs it typically or recurrently imposed and pass those costs along to consumers. Because workers are routinely injured, the costs of their injuries should be treated as a cost of doing business and internalized by the business. *See* George L. Priest, *The Invention of Enterprise Liability: A Critical History of the Intellectual Foundations of Modern Tort Law,* 14 J. LEGAL STUD. 461, 465–67 (1985).

Pragmatic justifications are different. Workers' compensation statutes attempt to provide for some minimum well-being for injured workers. But they also attempt to provide a quick, efficient remedy, one that will not bog down in litigation, and that will provide payments quickly and with relative certainty. *See Burke v. Raven Electric, Inc.,* 429 P.3d 1196 (Alaska 2018) ("The workers' compensation system consists of a trade-off, sometimes called the 'grand bargain,' in which workers give up their right to sue in tort for damages for work-related injury or death in exchange for limited but certain benefits, and employers agree to pay the limited benefits regardless of their own fault in causing the injury or death."). The statutes thus attempt to provide a system that allows only a minimum range of dispute. Benefits, for example, are relatively fixed and certain; there are no long trials devoted to proving extensive pain and suffering. Likewise, by eliminating investigations into fault, grounds for dispute are minimized.

Litigated cases expose an interesting phenomenon with respect to the shifting motivations of the injured worker and the employer. As a Fifth Circuit panel recently noted,

> Workers' compensation laws strike a statutory bargain between labor and management. They all but guarantee that a worker will recover from an employer for workplace injuries. In exchange for that certainty, the worker gives up the right to pursue a potentially larger recovery in a tort suit—employers are immune from such claims.
>
> These tradeoffs mean that questions about whether the statutory scheme covers an injured worker can cause businesses and workers alike to oscillate between seemingly opposed positions. A worker uncertain about the chances of a tort suit will

often seek workers' compensation, prompting the business to argue that the worker does not fall within the statutory protections. If the worker has a strong tort claim, the roles may flip—the business then has an incentive to argue that workers' compensation is the worker's exclusive remedy.

Jorge-Chavelas v. Louisiana Farm Bureau Cas. Ins. Co., 917 F.3d 847 (5th Cir. 2019).

But with fault out of the picture and little ground for litigating over benefit levels, have the workers' compensation statutes provided that Utopia, long sought by citizens the world over, a system that works without lawyers? That was, quite clearly, the statutory drafters' goal. To achieve it, they would have to provide what is missing in some of the torts cases—an efficient trigger for liability. In the workers' compensation statutes, the trigger for liability is only job-relatedness; that is, the injury must be one "arising out of and in the course of employment." The next section explores how efficient this trigger is.

§ 2. JOB-RELATED INJURY

A. ARISING OUT OF AND IN THE COURSE OF EMPLOYMENT

WAIT V. TRAVELERS INDEMNITY CO. OF ILLINOIS
240 S.W.3d 220 (Tenn. 2007)

WILLIAM M. BARKER, C.J.

[Plaintiff Kristina Wait worked as an executive with the American Cancer Society ("ACS"). Due to a lack of office space in its Nashville facility, ACS allowed Wait to work from her East Nashville home. She converted a spare bedroom into an office, and ACS furnished office equipment and a budget to purchase office supplies. She performed all her daily work for ACS at her home office, and her supervisor and co-workers attended meetings at her home office. Her work did not require her to open her house to the public. One day as plaintiff was preparing her lunch she opened her door to a neighbor, Nathaniel Sawyers, who brutally beat her for no apparent reason. Plaintiff sought workers' compensation benefits from Travelers Indemnity, the insurer of ACS. The chancery court granted summary judgment for defendant on the grounds that the injuries did not arise out of or occur in the course of her employment.]

. . . The Workers' Compensation Act ("Act"), codified at Tennessee Code Annotated sections 50–6–101 to –801 (2005), is a legislatively created quid pro quo system where an injured worker forfeits any potential common law rights for recovery against his or her employer in return for a system that provides compensation completely independent of any fault on the part of the employer. The Act should be liberally construed in favor of compensation and any doubts should be resolved in the employee's favor. . . .

This case requires us to apply the Act to a new and growing trend in the labor and employment market: telecommuting. An employee telecommutes when he or she takes advantage of electronic mail, internet, facsimile machines and other technological advancements to work from home or a place other than the traditional work site. In 2006, approximately thirty-four million American workers telecommuted to some degree. . . . [T]his innovative working arrangement has resulted in an issue of first impression: whether the injuries a telecommuter sustains as a result of an assault at her home arise out of and occur in the course of her employment.

It is well settled in Tennessee, and in many other jurisdictions, that for an injury to be compensable under the Act, it must both "arise out of" and occur "in the course of" employment. Tenn. Code Ann. § 50–6–103(a) (2005). Although both of these statutory requirements seek to ensure a connection between the employment and the injuries for which benefits are being sought, they are not synonymous. As such, the "arising out of" requirement refers to cause or origin; whereas, "in the course of" denotes the time, place, and circumstances of the injury. Furthermore, we have consistently abstained from adopting any particular judicial test, doctrine, formula, or label that purports to clearly define the line between accidents and injuries which arise out of and in the course of employment and those which do not.

In this case, we will consider the second requirement first. An injury occurs in the course of employment "when it takes place within the period of the employment, at a place where the employee reasonably may be, and while the employee is fulfilling work duties or engaged in doing something incidental thereto." *Blankenship,* 164 S.W.3d at 354 (quoting 1 Arthur Larson, *Workers' Compensation Law* § 12 (2004)).

Generally, injuries sustained during personal breaks are compensable. *Holder v. Wilson Sporting Goods Co.,* 723 S.W.2d 104, 107 (Tenn.1987). In *Holder,* we affirmed an award of workers' compensation benefits for an employee who slipped and fell in his employer's parking lot while he was putting his lunch box into his vehicle after finishing his meal. We noted that "[t]he remedial policies of the Worker's Compensation Act would be undermined if too severe a line were drawn controlling the compensability of injuries that occur during the normal course of the work day after employees have arrived for work, have started working, and before they have left for the day."

Much like the defendant in *Holder,* the defendant here argues that the plaintiff's injuries are not compensable because the plaintiff was not "fulfilling a work duty" in admitting Sawyers into her kitchen. It is true that the plaintiff suffered her injuries while preparing her lunch in the kitchen of her home; however, the plaintiff's work site was located within her home. Under these circumstances, the plaintiff's kitchen was comparable to the kitchens and break rooms that employers routinely provide at traditional work sites. . . . It is reasonable to conclude that the ACS realized that the plaintiff would take personal breaks during the course of her working day including "such incidental acts as eating, drinking, smoking, seeking toilet facilities, and seeking fresh air, coolness or warmth." *Carter v. Volunteer Apparel, Inc.,* 833 S.W.2d 492, 495 (Tenn.1992) (citing 1A Arthur Larson, *Workmen's Compensation Law* §§ 21.10–21.50 (1990)).

Thus, after careful review, we conclude that the injuries the plaintiff sustained while on her lunch break, like the injuries at issue in *Holder,* occurred during the course of the plaintiff's employment. . . . Unless instructed otherwise by the employer, an employee working from a home office who answers a knock at her door and briefly admits an acquaintance into her home does not necessarily depart so far from her work duties so as to remove her from the course of her employment. This is not to say, however, that situations may never arise where more prolonged or planned social visits might well remove the employee from the course of the employment. . . .

In arguing that the plaintiff's injury did not occur "in the course of" her employment, the defendant maintains that the plaintiff's decision to admit Sawyers into her home was not a work duty. However, this argument misses the mark on this requirement because the Act does not explicitly state that the employee's actions must benefit the employer; it only requires that the injuries occur in "the course of" the employment. . . . The question is not whether the plaintiff's injuries occurred while she was performing a duty owed to the ACS, but rather whether the time, place, and circumstances demonstrate that the injuries occurred while the plaintiff was engaged in an activity incidental to her employment. . . .

Even though the plaintiff's injuries occurred "in the course of" her employment, we nevertheless hold that they did not "arise out of" her job duties with the ACS. The phrase "arising out of" requires that a causal connection exist between the employment conditions and the resulting injury. With respect to whether an assault arises out of employment, we have previously delineated assaults into three general classifications:

> (1) assaults with an "inherent connection" to employment such as disputes over performance, pay or termination; (2) assaults stemming from "inherently private" disputes imported into the

employment setting from the claimant's domestic or private life and not exacerbated by the employment; and (3) assaults resulting from a "neutral force" such as random assaults on employees by individuals outside the employment relationship.

Woods v. Harry B. Woods Plumbing Co., 967 S.W.2d 768, 771 (Tenn. 1998).

When an assault has an "inherent connection" to the employment it is compensable. On the other hand, assaults originating from "inherently private" disputes and imported into the work place are not compensable. However, whether "neutral assaults" are compensable turns on the "facts and circumstances of the employment."

The assault in this case is best described as a "neutral assault." . . . A "neutral force" assault is one that is "neither personal to the claimant nor distinctly associated with the employment." 1 Arthur Larson, *Workers' Compensation Law* § 3.05 (2007). The *Woods* categories focus on what catalyst spurred the assault, i.e., was it a dispute arising from a work-related duty, was it a dispute arising from a personal matter, or was it unexplained or irrational? An assault that is spurred by neither a catalyst inherently connected to the employment nor stemming from an inherently private dispute is most aptly labeled as a "neutral force" assault. Here, the undisputed facts clearly show that the assault had neither an inherent connection with the employment, nor did it stem from a personal dispute between Sawyers and the plaintiff. Therefore, we must focus our attention on the facts and circumstances of the plaintiff's employment and its relationship to the injuries sustained by the plaintiff.

Generally, for an injury to "arise out of" employment, it must emanate from a peculiar danger or risk inherent to the nature of the employment. Thus, "an injury purely coincidental, or contemporaneous, or collateral, with the employment . . . will not cause the injury . . . to be considered as arising out of the employment." *Jackson v. Clark & Fay, Inc.*, 197 Tenn. 135, 270 S.W.2d 389, 390 (1954). However, in limited circumstances, where the employment involves "indiscriminate exposure to the general public," the "street risk" doctrine may supply the required causal connection between the employment and the injury. [We have held that] the "street risk" doctrine applies where an employee's "indiscriminate exposure to the general public is one of the conditions under which her work [is] required to be performed, and the actions of those persons on the premises are reasonably considered hazards of the employment." . . .

The plaintiff argues that had it not been for her employment arrangement, she would not have been at home to suffer these attacks. However, we have never held that any and every assault which occurs at the work site arises out of employment. . . . The "street risk" doctrine is not a limitless means of allowing recovery for every situation. As such, this case presents us with an opportunity to outline the boundaries of the doctrine. When an employee suffers a "neutral assault" within the confines of her employer's premises—whether the premises be a home office or a corporate office—the "street risk" doctrine will not provide the required causal connection between the injury and the employment unless the proof fairly suggests either that the attacker singled out the employee because of his or her association with the employer or that the employment indiscriminately exposed the employee to dangers from the public. The facts of this case clearly illustrate that the "street risk" doctrine does not apply. There is nothing in the record to fairly suggest or provide any weight to the assertion that the plaintiff's injuries were causally connected with the nature of her employment. Therefore, the chancery court's holding that the plaintiff's injuries did not arise out of her employment is affirmed.

In sum, the plaintiff's injuries were suffered during the course of her employment; however, they did not arise out of her employment. . . . We therefore affirm the judgment of the chancery court dismissing the complaint.

NOTES

1. **"Arising out of" employment: increased risk.** Most courts no longer insist that the employment risk be "peculiar" to the employment in the sense that it is different in its nature from risks faced by people in general. *But see Chaney v. Team Technologies, Inc.*, 568 S.W.3d 576 (Tenn. 2019); *Lopez v. Intercept Youth Services, Inc.*, 861 S.E.2d 392 (Va. 2021) (both requiring that the hazard or risk be "peculiar to the work"). Courts very commonly do, however, insist that employment must somehow *increase* these risks. Thus if employment requires a worker to drive a van delivering flowers, injury in a collision on the street will be one arising out of employment, even though everyone is subjected to "street risks." The worker in such a case has increased exposure, though the nature of the risk is the same. *See, e.g., Jivan v. Economy Inn & Suites*, 260 S.W.3d 281 (Ark. 2007) (hotel assistant manager required by employer to live in hotel was put at greater risk of injury by hotel fire than someone who did not live there). Some courts would impose liability for compensation in such a case even if the employment only occasionally puts the employee on the streets, so long as it in fact does so. *See* 1–6 LARSON'S WORKERS' COMPENSATION LAW § 6.02 (2012). Does the *Wait* court's formulation of the "street risk" doctrine as it applies to attacks at the workplace provide a workable test for future cases?

2. **"Arising out of" employment: positional risks.** While the increased-risk test is commonly used, some courts have adopted and use a "positional risk" test. This is basically a rule that liability for compensation is triggered if, but only if, the employment is a but-for cause of injury. *See, e.g., Sedgwick CMS v. Valcourt-Williams*, 271 So.3d 1133 (Fla. Dist Ct. App. 2019) (denying coverage for injury sustained when claimant tripped over her dog while reaching for a coffee cup in her kitchen while working from home because

such "risk exists whether the claimant is at home working or whether she is at home *not* working"); *Johme v. St. John's Mercy Healthcare*, 366 S.W.3d 504 (Mo. 2012) (injury sustained by claimant when she turned, twisted her ankle and fell out of her thick-soled shoe after making coffee in office kitchen did not arise out of a risk related to her employment, since she would have been exposed to a similar risk in her normal non-employment life; she failed to show the requisite causal connection between the injury and her work activity); *Voeller v. HSBC Card Services, Inc.*, 834 N.W.2d 839 (S.D. 2013) (death of employee shot by her estranged husband in employer's parking lot did not arise out of her employment; there was no proof that there was a causal connection between the injury and the employment).

A well-known decision is *Industrial Indemnity Co. v. Industrial Accident Commission*, 214 P.2d 41 (Cal. App. 1950). In that case, an angry wife entered a bar and fired a shot at her husband. The shot ricocheted off the bar and struck a waitress, who had nothing to do with the quarrel but who died as a result. Conceivably, one could say that risk of injury of bar employees as a result of angry customers (or spouses) is somewhat increased by their employment. The court took a much broader line, however, emphasizing that "her employment required her to be in what turned out to be a place of danger." It would be sufficient for liability, the court said, that "injury results from a danger to which [the employee] was exposed as an employee." *See also Kolson v. District of Columbia Dept. of Employment Services*, 699 A.2d 357 (D.C. 1997) (bus driver attacked on the street while walking to a hotel after completing his shift at 4:30 a.m.; injury "grew out of his employment because it resulted from a risk created by his employment—his arrival at odd hours in places away from his home and the necessity of using the public streets to seek lodging"). What about a case in which a supervisor orders an employee to come out to see someone at the place of business, and that person shoots the employee in connection with a personal dispute? *See Kerr-McGee Corp. v. Hutto*, 401 So.2d 1277 (Miss. 1981) (held, "the employee's death was so strongly connected to the directive of his superior that it cannot be completely disassociated from his employment").

3. **"In the course of" employment and the going and coming rule.** Compensation for an injury requires that it occur "in the course of" employment, which emphasizes time and place—injury must occur "at work" and during working hours. *See Clements v. Aramark Corp.*, 261 A.3d 665 (Conn. 2021) ("[T]he requirement that the injury must occur in the course of employment relates to the time, place and circumstance of the accident.").

This means that an injury that occurs while an employee is going to or coming from work is not compensable. *See, e.g., Feiereisen v. Newpage Corp.*, 5 A.3d 669 (Me. 2010); *Harris v. Westin Management Co. East*, 230 S.W.3d 1 (Mo. 2007); *see also Hersh v. County of Morris*, 86 A.3d 140 (N.J. 2014) (by statute, employment commences "when an employee arrives at the employer's place of employment to report for work"; thus when employee was injured before the work day started, as she was walking from a parking garage to her office a few blocks away, her injury did not "arise out of and in the course of" employment).

There are exceptions, however, including where a commuting employee is running a "special errand" for the employer, *see Bob Allyn Masonry v. Murphy*, 183 P.3d 126 (Nev. 2008), or where the employer receives some "incidental benefit" from the employee's commute that were not common to ordinary commutes, *see Salt Lake City Corp. v. Labor Com'n*, 153 P.3d 179 (Utah 2007). In *Leordeaunu v. American Protection Ins. Co.*, 330 S.W.3d 239 (Tex. 2010), the employee was injured on her way home from an employee-sponsored dinner, intending to stop first at a storage facility supplied by her employer to empty her car of business supplies; the court held that was in the course and scope of her employment. What if an employee's commute is made more hazardous by the employer's "extraordinary demands" for overtime work? *See Snowbarger v. Tri-County Elec. Coop.*, 793 S.W.2d 348 (Mo. 1990).

4. **Traveling employees.** Employees who routinely work away from home are known as "traveling employees." Under the traveling employee doctrine, also known as the "commercial traveler rule," or the "continuous coverage rule," such employees are considered to be "in the course of employment continuously during the entire trip, except during a distinct departure on a personal errand." *Ball-Foster Glass Container Co. v. Giovanelli*, 177 P.3d 692 (Wash. 2008). A number of cases hold that traveling employees are "in the course of" employment even when they are injured during recreational or social activities. *See, e.g., McCann v. Hatchett*, 19 S.W.3d 218 (Tenn. 2000) (employee drowned in hotel pool at 10 p.m.); *Giovanelli, supra* (employee was walking to a park near his hotel to listen to music). The traveling employee doctrine may also be seen as an exception to the going and coming rule. *See Labadie v. Norwalk Rehabilitation Services, Inc.*, 875 A.2d 485 (Conn. 2005) (home health care worker injured going to her first assignment of the day). Should the traveling employee rules apply to telecommuters?

5. **Incidental departures from working.** The *Wait* court holds, as most courts do, that an employee who is on a momentary break, or having lunch at the workplace, remains "in the course of" employment. Such "personal comfort missions" are not considered outside the course of employment. *See, e.g., City of Eugene v. McDermed*, 282 P.3d 947 (Or. App. 2012) (employee hit by car crossing the street to get a cup of coffee); *K-Mart Corp. v. Herring*, 188 P.3d 140 (Okla. 2008) (night watchman who was shot during a trip to a fast-food restaurant during a 7-hour shift with no scheduled breaks); *Gooden v. Coors Technical Ceramic Co.*, 236 S.W.3d 151 (Tenn. 2007) (employee had heart attack while playing basketball on company premises during work break) A substantial departure will take the employee out of the course of employment, although "reentry" may occur at some point. This is true even with traveling employees. *See, e.g., Ray Bell Const. Co. v. King*, 642 S.E.2d 841 (Ga. 2007). Does this remind you of a rule we saw in Chapter 22 on the vicarious liability of an employer for the torts of an employee?

CARVALHO V. DECORATIVE FABRICS CO.
366 A.2d 157 (R.I. 1976)

BEVILACQUA, CHIEF JUSTICE.

[The employee worked in a factory handling yarn. At the end of the shift fellow employees customarily assisted removing lint from each other's clothes by using an air hose. On this occasion a fellow worker placed the air hose "in the vicinity of petitioner's rectum," and the petitioner felt his stomach blow up. He was unable to work the next day and later went to the emergency room in pain. He was found to have a perforated rectum. The commission denied compensation on the ground that this involved horseplay and assault and was therefore not arising out of employment.]

In the early workmen's compensation cases involving "horseplay" (sometimes referred to as "sportive assault," "larking" or "skylarking") courts were reluctant to award compensation, even to the innocent, non-participating victim. Reasoning that employees were hired to work and not to play, courts concluded that injuries resulting from "horseplay" did not arise out of and in the course of employment. In addition, courts denied compensation sustaining the defense that the claimant was a "participant" in or "instigator" of "horseplay." However, these decisions are contrary to the scope and intent of the Workmen's Compensation Acts. These Acts were designed to provide compensation to victims of work-connected injuries and to eliminate the tort defenses of negligence and fault. In effect, these early decisions judicially reinstituted common law defenses which had been abolished by statute.

Later courts recognized that the primary purpose of workmen's compensation is to provide economic assistance to an employee who is injured and thereby suffers a loss of earnings; such legislation "... was intended to impose upon the employer the burden of taking care of the casualties occurring in his employment, thus preventing the injured employee from becoming a public charge." Moreover, the worker need no longer be free from fault to receive compensation. . . .

In the case of the victim who does not participate in the "horseplay" and is innocent of any wrongful conduct, we need no extended justification to hold that the injuries received are compensable. In *In re Leonbruno v. Champlain Silk Mills*, 128 N.E. 711 (N.Y. 1920), the late Mr. Justice Cardozo stated:

> "The claimant was injured, not merely while he was in a factory, but because he was in a factory, in touch with associations and conditions inseparable from factory life. The risks of such associations and conditions were risks of the employment."

When people are placed together and are in close association with one another in performing their work there is a natural instinct to fool around and play pranks on one another. Such activity is part of the work environment, an incident of the employment. The claimant need only establish that the injury arose out of and in the course of employment: a nexus or causal connection between the injury and the employment must be shown. . . .

The injured claimant should not be denied compensation merely because of his participation in "horseplay." As the court in *Maltais v. Equitable Life Assur. Soc'y of United States*, 40 A.2d 837 (N.H. 1944) stated:

> ". . . to hold that an injury arises out of the employment if it is inflicted on a workman attentive to duty by the sportive conduct of a fellow-employee, but that it does not so arise if the injured workman participates, however slightly, in the sport is to draw a distinction based on the injured workman's fault, when the only faults specifically named in the statute as precluding recovery are intoxication, violation of law, and serious or wilful misconduct."[4]

Clearly, where horseplay has become customary, a participant can recover since his act is an incident of the work environment. However, where there is no evidence that "horseplay" is customary, the issue is whether the "horseplay" constituted a substantial deviation from the employment. The substantiality of the deviation should be determined not by the seriousness of the resulting injuries but solely by the extent to which the "horseplay" constitutes a departure from the course of the employment. 1 ARTHUR LARSON, WORKMEN'S COMPENSATION LAW, § 23.63 (1972).

Where the use of an air hose to clean off clothes is a daily practice, play with the hose is a risk of the employment and part and parcel of the working environment. Such activity should be regarded as part of the course of employment, particularly where, as in the instant case, the employer places in the hands of the employee the instrumentality which was used in the "horseplay" and caused the injury. . . .

NOTES

1. **Workers' comp vs. a tort claim.** If an injury is not compensable under workers' compensation, then the injured worker might well be able to bring a tort claim against a co-worker for an injury resulting from "horseplay." *Grabowski v. Mangler*, 938 A.2d 637 (Del. 2007). Larsen's treatise points to four important factors in making a coverage determination: "(1) the extent and seriousness of the deviation from work; (2) the completeness of the deviation (i.e., whether it was co-mingled with the performance of duty or involved an abandonment of duty); (3) the extent to which the practice of horseplay had become an accepted part of the employment; and (4) the extent to which the

---

[4]　In *Maltais,* two workers, while cleaning each others' clothes off with an air hose, began fooling around with it, causing claimant's death. Although claimant participated in the "horseplay," compensation was awarded.

nature of the employment may be expected to include some horseplay." 2–23 LARSON'S WORKERS' COMPENSATION LAW § 23.01 (2012). What about a case in which an emergency medical technician with a reputation as a "kid in an adult's body" suddenly picks up a cardiac defibrillator while riding in an ambulance and shocks a co-worker, resulting in her death? What additional facts would you want to know? *See Hilton v. Martin*, 654 S.E.2d 572 (Va. 2008).

2. **Instigators.** Even the instigator of horseplay may claim compensation for horseplay injury, provided that the horseplay is not a substantial deviation from the job. *See Prows v. Indus. Comm'n of Utah*, 610 P.2d 1362 (Utah 1980).

3. **Intended battery.** Even an intended battery by a co-worker, distinct from a playful injury, could be considered to be within the scope of employment if it arises from a job-related dispute. *See, e.g., Ford Motor Co. v. Industrial Commission*, 399 N.E.2d 1280 (Ill. 1980); *PF Chang's v. Industrial Com'n of Arizona*, 166 P.3d 135 (Ariz. Ct. App. 2007).

4. **Company-sponsored recreation.** Sometimes unintended injuries occur during company social or recreational events. Courts often scrutinize the facts of these cases very carefully. If the employer actually sponsors the event, expects employee attendance, and pays the costs, injury during the event is likely to be one that arises from employment. *See, e.g., Sikorski's Case*, 918 N.E.2d 30 (Mass. 2009). If any of these elements is missing, courts may hold that injury is unrelated to employment. *See, e.g., Frost v. Salter Path Fire & Rescue*, 639 S.E.2d 429 (N.C. 2007).

UNION COLLIERY CO. V. INDUSTRIAL COMMISSION, 132 N.E. 200 (Ill. 1921). This is a claim for compensation by a widow and children of a deceased worker. The deceased was employed in the employer's coal mine, working at the top of the "cage" or elevator on which coal was hoisted. He was to dump the coal when the cage arrived at the top, but he also had underground duties. On the night of his death, he rode up on the cage with a load of coal. Circumstantial evidence suggested he was crushed between the cage and a beam. To ride up in a loaded cage or hoist was a violation of the state statutes on mining safety. The Industrial Commission made an award of compensation, but the trial court, reviewing this, set it aside. *Held*, compensation should be awarded. The employer argues that violation of the statute, like violation of an employer's instruction, would show that the injury and death "did not arise out of and in the course of employment." However, violation of the statute would at most show negligence. Nor does violation of an employer's rules automatically place the employee outside the sphere of his employment. In this case, injury arose out of employment.

NOTES

1. **What a violation might show.** Conceivably, some violations of statute or employer rules would show more than negligence. *See Sapko v. State*, 44 A.3d 827 (Conn. 2012) (employee's ingestion of excessive quantities of prescription drugs broke the chain of causation rendering the injury unrelated the employment and thus not compensable).

2. **Older cases: a narrow view.** Early cases sometimes took a narrow view about what injuries arose in employment. On facts similar to those in *Union Colliery*, the Pennsylvania Court barred recovery in *Pokis v. Buck Run Coal Co.*, 132 A. 795 (Pa. 1926). In so doing it relied in part on an earlier decision in which a worker entered a portion of the mine known to contain gas. This was prohibited by law. The court said that "as to this danger zone, he had no employment," and that the injury was not therefore one arising out of employment. *Walcofski v. Lehigh Valley Coal Co.*, 122 A. 238 (Pa. 1923).

3. **Modern cases: a more liberal view.** Narrow decisions of this kind no longer represent the courts' approach to the issue of "arising out of employment," although an employee's willful misconduct may in some instances be a defense. *See, e.g., Brackett v. Focus Hope, Inc.*, 753 N.W.2d 207 (Mich. 2008) (state statute bars compensation where employee has engaged in "intentional and willful misconduct"). The modern approach is and long has been to give a very liberal interpretation to coverage under workers' compensation statutes and to resolve doubts in favor of the employee's coverage. *See, e.g., Griggs v. Bounce N' Around Inflatables, L.L.C.*, 281 So.3d 628 (La. 2019) (exclusive remedy provisions barred tort claim by minors who were injured while illegally employed).

B. ACCIDENT, INJURY AND DISEASE

NOTE: "ACCIDENT" AND "ACCIDENTAL INJURY"

1. *Injury by accident; accidental injury.* Workers are initially covered for compensation only when injury arises out of and in the course of employment and when, in addition, they are injured by "accident" or suffer "accidental injury." These requirements remain today except that workers may recover for disability resulting from certain occupational diseases. Where the employee has suffered a compensable injury, the workers' comp statute routinely applies to limit recovery to that provided in the statute. This will ordinarily include not only the original injury, but subsequent aggravations. *See, e.g., South Coast Framing, Inc. v. Workers' Compensation Appeals Bd.*, 349 P.3d 141 (Cal. 2015) (employee entitled to workers' comp benefits if new or aggravated injury results from medical treatment for a workplace injury; here, claimant's accidental death from a combination of drugs prescribed to him following a fall at work was causally related to his work injury).

2. *Meaning of accident/accidental terminology.* The statutory phrase, "injury by accident," or the more liberal "accidental injury," has been made to bear the weight of a multitude of legal issues. The requirement of accident might mean any one, or some combination, of these three ideas: (a) the injury must not have been intentional on the part of the worker; (b) the injury must have occurred on some definite occasion, or "event"; or (c) the injury must have proceeded from external causes, as distinct from a degenerative breakdown within the body. Actually, analysis reveals even further ambiguities. If the word "accident" refers to something that is not expected, is it the cause, or is it the result? If it refers to a definite occasion or event, is it the cause or the result?

And courts sometimes are called on to decide what constitutes an "injury" for workers' compensation purposes. In *Nakamoto v. Kawauchi*, 418 P.3d 600 (Hawaii 2018), county employees sued their employer (and others) claiming that the defendants defamed them by making false allegations of misconduct that were reprinted in a newspaper article. The trial court granted the county's motion to dismiss on the ground that workers' compensation was the exclusive remedy. The Supreme Court reversed, holding that the torts of defamation and false light invasion of privacy are not within the ambit of the workers' compensation law because harm to reputation is not a "personal injury."

3. *Accident/accidental: suicide.* Statutes frequently exclude from coverage the self-inflicted injury, including suicide and injuries resulting from intoxication. The requirement of "accident" would perhaps have sufficiently covered the self-inflicted injury. When the self-inflicted injury is suicide, complications occur. If injury on the job causes insanity, which in turn leads to suicide, the resulting death may still be considered part of the "accident," and, on reasoning like that used in the tort cases, not the product of a "moral being." The death in such cases is compensable. Thus the legal cause reasoning is imported into the workers' compensation area. *See, e.g., Vredenburg v. Sedgwick CMS*, 188 P.3d 1084 (Nev. 2008). The exact kind of insanity—or "depression"—sufficient to permit this causal analysis in favor of the workers' dependents had been subject to debate and vacillation. It is perhaps fair to say that nothing like "insanity" is really required in many of the cases, and that pain and depression will be sufficient instead. *See Graef v. Continental Indemnity Co.*, 959 N.W.2d 628 (Wis. 2021) (injury from attempted suicide was covered by workers' comp where initial workplace injury was covered and resulted in depression; thus gunshot injury grew out of and was incidental to his original workplace injury).

4. *Accident/accidental: self-inflicted injury.* The term "accident" may exclude cases that "self-inflicted injury" would not exclude. A worker has an unsatisfactory conversation with his superior and kills himself. Is this an accident? *Zach v. Nebraska State Patrol*, 727 N.W.2d 206 (Neb. 2007).

HARRIS V. BOARD OF EDUCATION OF HOWARD COUNTY
825 A.2d 365 (Md. 2003)

ELDRIDGE, JUDGE. . . .

In January 1999, the petitioner, Vernell Harris, was fifty-eight years old and had been employed by the respondent, the Howard County Board of Education, for twelve years at Wilde Lake High School, as a "Food and Nutritional Service Assistant I." Ms. Harris's duties included preparing lunches for the students, tending to the cash register, cleaning the kitchen area, and laundering all linens used throughout the day. It is undisputed that Ms. Harris's regular work involved lifting boxes of frozen food weighing approximately thirty-five pounds from the freezer and carrying them to the appropriate food preparation area.

On the day that she incurred her injury, January 25, 1999, Ms. Harris was doing laundry with a co-worker, as she typically did at the end of her workday. [Ms. Harris had to drag a heavy box of laundry detergent, then lift the inner bag of powder.] After bending down to scoop some soap detergent into a cup, Ms. Harris bent down a second time to tie up the bag of soap powder. At that point, her back "cracked" and she screamed. Ms. Harris was unable to stand upright, and, when a co-worker brought her a chair, she was unable to sit. She appeared to be in excruciating pain. With the aid of another co-worker, Ms. Harris walked to the cafeteria manager's office who gave her an incident form authorizing her to see a doctor at a nearby medical office.

Ms. Harris was seen by Dr. Prudence Jackson at the Concentra Medical Center later that afternoon. Dr. Jackson testified that it was her expert medical opinion, within a reasonable degree of medical certainty, that dragging the heavy box of laundry soap outside caused Ms. Harris's back injury.

[Ms. Harris' claim was allowed by the Workers' Compensation Commission, but on judicial review in the Circuit court, the judge left to the jury the question whether the injury arose out of "unusual activity." The jury returned a verdict in favor of the employer. The intermediate appellate court affirmed.]

The current Maryland Workers' Compensation Act, in § 9–101(b) of the Labor and Employment Article, defines "accidental personal injury" as follows:

§ 9–101. DEFINITIONS.

(a) *In general.*—In this title the following words have the meanings indicated.

(b) *Accidental personal injury.*—"Accidental personal injury" means:

(1) an accidental injury that arises out of and in the course of employment. . . .

The above-quoted language contains no mention of "unusual activity." Under the plain language of the statute, what must be "accidental" is the *injury* and not the activity giving rise to the injury. The activity giving rise to the injury need only "arise[ ] out of and in the course of employment," and not be otherwise excluded by the Act. . . .

The line of cases in this Court requiring that an accidental personal injury arise out of "unusual activity" for there to be coverage obviously adds a requirement not contained in the statutory language. That line of cases requires both (1) that the accidental injury arise out of and in the course of employment and (2) that the accidental injury arise out of "unusual activity." Such cases cannot be reconciled with the often-repeated principle that this Court will "neither add nor delete words in order to give the statute a meaning not otherwise communicated by the language used." . . .

The Court in *Victory Sparkler* concluded as follows (147 Md. at 382, 128 A. at 640):

> "The Maryland act is remedial and should receive a liberal construction so as to give to it the most beneficial operation; and when it contains positive direction that should 'be so interpreted and construed to effectuate its general purpose,' the Court must act under the compulsion of this mandate, and not disappoint an explicit provision, plainly expressed. . . ."

The requirement that an accidental injury, arising out of and in the course of employment, must also arise out of unusual activity for there to be coverage, directly conflicts with this "mandate" set forth in *Victory Sparkler*. Instead of a "liberal construction so as to give to it the most beneficial operation," the respondent's position makes the Maryland Act the most restrictive in the nation. . . .

If the decisions of this Court had uniformly required that an injury, arising out of and in the course of employment, must also result from unusual activity in order to be covered by the Workers' Compensation Act, a not unreasonable argument could be made that our erroneous insertion of language into the statute had become too ingrained to be corrected by judicial decision and that any correction should be made by the Legislature. Our decisions, however, have not been uniform or consistent. We have on numerous occasions held that accidental injuries were compensable even though they did not result from unusual activities. . . .

Under *Schwind,* an injury is an "accidental injury" if it is the result of an "untoward event which [the employee] neither expected nor intended." Applying this principle to the present case clearly mandates coverage. . . .

There is another line of Maryland cases which hold that the "unusual activity" requirement is pertinent only when there is no apparent causal connection between the accidental injury and the employment. In other words, under the opinions, the presence or absence of "unusual activity" is an aspect in the "arising out of the course of employment" analysis. Judge Markell for the Court in the often-cited opinion, *Perdue v. Brittingham,* thus explained (emphasis added):

> "It must always be shown that the injury arose not only 'in the course of [the] employment' but also 'out of the employment.' . . . There must be a 'causal connection between the conditions under which the work is required to be performed and the resulting injury.' . . . The causal connection may relate either (a) to the act or event, *e.g.,* a fall, which produces the injury or (b) to the consequences of the particular act or event. If there is other evidence that the work causes the act or event, *then it is immaterial how usual or trivial the act or event is,* or how unusual or abnormal the consequence. . . . If, however, there is no apparent causal connection between the work and the event, *e.g.,* a cerebral hemorrhage or an epileptic fit, then *unusual or extraordinary conditions* of the employment, constituting a risk peculiar to the work, *may establish the causal connection* between the work and the injury." . . .

In still other cases, purporting to require that an injury arise out of unusual activity, this Court and the Court of Special Appeals have strained to label as "unusual" activities which appear to be entirely normal in the particular employments, and thus have upheld coverage. . . .

In other areas of the law, where a judicially created standard has not been uniformly followed, has been inconsistently applied, and has treated differently persons who were similarly situated, this Court has not hesitated to change or abandon the standard. . . .

Only a small minority of other jurisdictions have adopted the "unusual activity" requirement with regard to continuing conditions in the workplace. . . . With regard to of the type involved in the present case, namely injuries arising out of and in the course of employment and based on specific, sudden, unexpected and unintended events, the line of Maryland cases following *Atlantic Coast Shipping Co. v. Stasiak,* requiring "unusual activity," seems to constitute a minority of one. A review of decisions under the workers' compensation statutes of the other states, as well as the federal workers' compensation acts, indicates that no other jurisdictions presently require that an accidental injury of the type here involved arise out of "unusual activity" for there to be coverage. . . .

[W]e reverse the judgments of both courts below and direct that the decision of the Workers' Compensation Commission be affirmed. In addition, we overrule the holdings in *Slacum v. Jolley, supra,* 153 Md. 343, 138 A. 244; *Miskowiak v. Bethlehem Steel Co., supra,* 156 Md. 690, 145 A. 199; *Atlantic Coast Shipping Co. v. Stasiak, supra,* 158 Md. 349, 148 A. 452, and similar holdings.

NOTES

1.   **Scope and meaning of *Harris*.** A worker, doing nothing unusual at her job, suffers a heart attack and can never work again. Does *Harris* mean that the worker is entitled to compensation? Many courts have said that in such cases, unusual exertion or some kind of sudden or external event is required for various "internal" injuries such as heart attacks, strokes, hernias, and general backache, and statutes sometimes address the problem.

2.   **Alternative tests.** Some heart attacks or strokes are merely part of the worker's genetic heritage or aging rather than a result of the work. The unusual-exertion test might exclude some of those. Consider whether there might be alternative tests. In *Farrington v. Total Petroleum, Inc.,* 501 N.W.2d 76 (Mich. 1993), the court, applying a statutory rule, said: "The heart injury must be significantly caused or aggravated by employment considering the totality of all the occupational factors and the claimant's health circumstances and nonoccupational factors." It went on to say that ordinary everyday work, without unusual exertion, might contribute to a heart attack, but to determine whether work was a significant cause, the "factfinder must also consider the causal effect of every-day work activities in relation to the claimant's other, nonoccupational factors. These factors would include, for example, age, weight, diet, previous cardiac ailments or injuries, genetic predispositions, and the claimant's consumption of alcohol and use of tobacco or other drugs." *See also Harper v. Banks, Finley, White & Co.,* 167 So.3d 1155 (Miss. 2015) (death from stroke was a compensable injury, where employee's dependents "proved that the only source of his stress was his work, that stress was the cause of his high blood pressure, and that high blood pressure caused his stroke"); *Clements v. Aramark Corp.,* 261 A.3d 665 (Conn. 2021) (no workers' comp coverage for an "idiopathic" fall at work brought on by a purely personal condition, unrelated to employment, that could have manifested itself anywhere) .

What would the claimant need to prove if a pre-existing neck injury was aggravated while she was working? *Rakestraw v. General Dynamics Land Sys., Inc.,* 666 N.W.2d 199 (Mich. 2003).

3.   **Statutes.** Although courts may reject the unusual-exertion test in many instances, see 2–43 LARSON'S WORKERS' COMPENSATION LAW § 43.01 (2012), the job must still cause the harm if it is to be compensable. Statutes may add specific proof requirements in heart attack and similar cases. For instance, a statute may enact the unusual-exertion requirement. *E.g.,* KAN. STAT. ANN. § 44–501(e). Or it may go further, requiring not only that the job be a direct cause of the heart condition, but that the "acute symptoms of the cardiac condition are clearly manifested not later than four (4) hours after the alleged causative exertion." WYO. STAT. § 27–14–603(b).

4. **Pre-existing conditions and amount or award.** In tort cases, it is at least theoretically possible that, though the defendant takes the plaintiff as he finds him, the plaintiff's damages will be calculated with the fact in mind that his pre-existing conditions would sooner or later have caused the same kind of harm. Is there room in the workers' compensation statutes for any adjustment of the award to accomplish the same end if the job triggers a heart attack, but the plaintiff would have suffered such an attack sooner or later even without working? *Cf. Tomlinson v. Puget Sound Freight Lines, Inc.*, 206 P.3d 657 (Wash. 2009) (preexisting partial disability is immaterial to workers' compensation award).

SHEALY V. AIKEN COUNTY, 535 S.E.2d 438 (S.C. 2000). Claimant was an undercover officer of the Sheriff's department working deep cover without police backup or identification. As such, he was subjected to continual stress. He eventually became unable to work and claimed compensation. "Mental or nervous disorders are compensable accidental injuries under the statute when 'the emotional stimuli or stressors are incident to or arise from unusual or extraordinary conditions of employment.' [C]ourts should use the 'heart attack standard' to determine when a mental-mental injury is compensable. A heart attack suffered by an employee constitutes a compensable accident if it is induced by unexpected strain or overexertion in the performance of his duties of employment, or by unusual and extraordinary conditions in employment." That standard is met here.

"Over several months in 1992, Shealy experienced death threats, gun incidents with violent drug dealers, high tension confrontations, fear of losing his cover, loss of security as a police officer, and loss of his insurance. Knowing that a specific plot has been developed for one's murder by people who are willing and able to commit such a crime is certainly extraordinary. Furthermore, to have knowledge of an imminent death threat and then be stripped of the protection of the Sheriff's Department constitutes an extraordinary condition of employment." Even so, the claimant cannot recover. "Shealy was suffering from financial problems that led to bankruptcy; marital problems, including a divorce and a custody battle over his son; memories of a gun fight and shooting a man during a previous employment; and the constant stress of fighting alcoholism. Based on these non-job stressors," the trier properly found that the job was not a cause of his disability.

NOTES

1. **Mental or emotional disorders: sudden event in the fright-shock pattern.** When the worker is physically injured on the job and suffers emotional or mental disability as a result, courts can easily conclude that the statutory requirement of accidental injury arising out of and in the course of

employment has been met. *See, e.g., Manchester v. Drivers Management, LLC,* 775 N.W.2d 179 (Neb. 2009). In the "mental-mental" case—when the employee is subjected to some kind of mental or emotional stress causing mental or emotional injury without physical injury—courts may feel less certain.

Overall, the stronger case for compensation with mental injuries resulting from mental stimuli is probably one in which a sudden on-the-job event causes or triggers the emotional reaction, and some states require that. *See, e.g., McGrath v. State Dept. of Public Safety,* 159 P.3d 239 (Nev. 2007). Such a case would be similar to the old fright-shock pattern of tort claims for negligent infliction of emotional distress. An example is *Ivey v. Trans Global Gas & Oil,* 3 S.W.3d 441 (Tenn. 1999), where a robber pointed a gun at the face of an employee of a convenience store and compensation was permitted. What would the same court do if the worker suddenly came in contact with blood of a fellow worker and was disabled by fear of AIDS? *Guess v. Sharp Mfg. Co. of America,* 114 S.W.3d 480 (Tenn. 2003). Or what if a custodian is struck by PTSD after being ordered to clean up the scene of a suicide of a high school student he knew? Is that a compensable injury? *See Rothwell v. Nine Mile Falls School Dist.,* 206 P.3d 347 (Wash. App. 2009).

2. **Mental or emotional disorders: cumulative stress.** Cumulative job stress—meeting deadlines, arguing with co-workers and superiors, for example—is probably overall less likely to yield a compensable mental-mental claim. *See, e.g., Martin v. Rhode Island Public Transit Auth.,* 506 A.2d 1365 (R.I. 1986). Such claims may present serious causation issues. *See, e.g., Verga v. Workers' Comp. Appeals Bd.,* 70 Cal. Rptr.3d 871 (Ct. App. 2008). Still, individual facts count, as does the exact statutory language. If the events triggering disability from emotional distress amount to discrimination of a kind outlawed by statute, courts may feel that the discrimination statutes, rather than workers' compensation statutes, should control.

3. **Occupational disease.** Statutes now provide for some degree of coverage for occupational diseases, although coverage is usually more restrictive than for "injury by accident." First, the disability must count as a "disease." *See Stenrich Group v. Jemmott,* 467 S.E.2d 795 (Va. 1996) (repetitive stress injuries neither a "disease" nor an "injury by accident"). Second, courts may insist that a disease is not compensable unless it is somehow especially related to the job. *See City of Las Vegas v. Evans,* 301 P.3d 844 (Nev. 2013) (firefighter proved that cancer was an occupational disease caused by his work exposure to toxic chemicals and smoke).

What about someone who suffers serious respiratory disability from second-hand smoke on the job? Since one might be subjected to smoke in many places, does that mean the disability is not compensable as a disease? *See Palmer v. Del Webb's High Sierra,* 838 P.2d 435 (Nev. 1992) (environmental smoke in casino where claimant worked was not uniquely incident to employment, bronchitis not compensable); *but see Johannensen v. New York City Dep't of Housing Etc.,* 638 N.E.2d 981 (N.Y. 1994) (injury from second-hand smoke compensable as accidental injury rather than as an occupational disease). What about gradual noise-induced hearing loss as a result of exposure to hazardous levels of noise on the job? *See Arrant v. Graphic Packaging Intern., Inc.*, 169 So.3d 296 (La. 2015). Or what about post-traumatic stress disorder resulting from cumulative stress? That would definitely not sound like an "accident," but could it be an occupational disease in stressful occupations—like police work? *See Brunell v. Wildwood Crest Police Dept.*, 822 A.2d 576 (N.J. 2003).

C. MULTIPLE EXPOSURE OR INJURY

UNION CARBIDE CORP. V. INDUSTRIAL COM'N, 581 P.2d 734 (Colo. 1978). Benally worked as a uranium miner from 1955 to 1970 and died of lung cancer. He worked for Climax Uranium for four years before he was hired on April 28, 1970 by Union Carbide. The Union Carbide hiring was based upon a proviso that he pass a physical examination, but he began work before the test results were in. He worked eight days for Union Carbide before the tests came back and showed lung cancer. He was dismissed under the original proviso of his hiring. He was exposed to radiation during his short tenure at Union Carbide as well as at his earlier employment. *Held*, Union Carbide is liable for the worker's compensation death benefits since Benally's last injurious exposure was there. "[T]his rule makes good sense. . . . If the employee has worked for many different employers, it may well be that no single exposure with any one employer was in fact sufficient, in itself, to cause the disease. . . . [A] test for liability based upon the employee's actual length of exposure with each employer could well deny the employee any recovery for the disease. In contrast, the 'last injurious exposure' rule looks at the concentration of radiation received during the last employment to determine whether the employee was exposed to a harmful quantity. . . . If the rule were otherwise, the employee would be burdened with the almost impossible task of apportioning liability among his several employers."

BRACKE V. BAZA'R, INC., 646 P.2d 1330 (Or. 1982). Bracke worked as a meat wrapper from 1974 until early 1977 for Baza'r. In early 1977, she also worked part time for Albertson's and Thriftway food markets. Her last employment with Baza'r ended March 30, with Albertson's on May 9, and with Thriftway on May 13. Claiming "meat wrapper's asthma," she applied for compensation with all three, and all denied her claim. She did not seek a hearing as to Thriftway's denial within the required 60-day limit. The Worker's Compensation Board found she suffered an occupational disease and that Thriftway would have been responsible because of the last injurious exposure rule, except that no hearing had been requested. Since Thriftway was the last injurious exposure, neither other employer was responsible. The Court of Appeals reversed this order of the board.

In the Supreme Court, *held*, the Court of Appeals judgment is affirmed. Testimony showed that with this disease there is no problem until one becomes sensitized by exposure to the fumes involved in cutting plastic wrap with a hot wire and dealing with price labels. But once one is sensitized, there will always be an allergic reaction thereafter. Sensitization occurred while the plaintiff was working for Baza'r, and later work does not make this "sensitization" any worse. Justification for the several variants of the last injurious exposure rules may be found "not in their achievement of individualized justice, but rather in their utility in spreading liability fairly among employers by the law of averages and in reducing litigation. . . . It is fair to employers only if it is applied consistently so that liability is spread proportionately among employers by operation of the law of averages." Hence the employer may assert the rule as a defense, as Baza'r does here, since this will "assure that they are not assigned disproportionate share of liability relative to other employers. . . ." But in this case Baza'r was properly held liable, because subsequent employment "did not cause or aggravate the underlying disease. Had that occurred, a later employer would be liable. . . . Rather, claimant's subsequent employment only activated the symptoms of a pre-existing disease."

NOTES

1. **Where the last-injurious-exposure rule does not apply.** Several problems must be distinguished. One problem is whether any employer is responsible for injury or disease. In the case of a disease, it must not be merely a disease to which everyone is more or less equally at risk. What is the test of liability for compensation where both work and non-work exposures contribute to the disease? *See Deschenes v. Transco*, 953 A.2d 13 (Conn. 2008) (considering several alternatives, and deciding that a proportional reduction of benefits is appropriate when an employer proves that a disability is caused in part by work-related disease processes and in part by non-work-related processes). Is there any comparable problem in cases of injury by accident?

2. **Where the last-injurious-exposure rule does apply.** A separate problem is to allocate responsibility among employers where several have, or may have, contributed to disease or injury. The last-injurious-exposure rule deals with this problem. What is the test of liability under that rule?

3. **Second-injury funds.** In addition to the two problems just identified, there are two other broad problem areas. The first involves the worker who comes to the job with an existing injury or disability. If he is injured on the job, his pre-existing condition may mean that the job injury will be much more serious than otherwise it would have been. For example, if he comes to the job with one eye, an injury to his good eye may mean total blindness, not merely the partial loss of vision. Total blindness in turn might mean that the employer would be liable for a great deal more compensation than if a worker merely lost one of two good eyes. Given this situation, an

employer might discriminate heavily against workers with an existing disability. To avoid this employer discrimination, most states created a second-injury fund which would pay any added compensation needed in such situations. The result is that the employer in the example given pays for the loss of one eye, not for total blindness; the additional compensation is paid from the fund. The fund itself is created in various ways, sometimes by what amounts to a special tax levied against compensation insurance carriers.

4.　**Compensable injury causing further injury.** The employer may be held liable for compensation not only for the original injury, but for medical aggravation.

§ 3. WORKERS' COMPENSATION AS THE EXCLUSIVE REMEDY

> The liability of an employer under this act shall be exclusive and in place of any and all other liability to such employees, their legal representative, husband or wife, parents, dependents, next of kin or anyone otherwise entitled to damages in any action at law or otherwise on account of any injury or death or occupational disease as defined in this Act.

In one form or another, workers' compensation statutes contain such an exclusive remedy provision, in effect forbidding the employee's tort recovery against the employer. Seamen, interstate railroad workers, and job discrimination victims all have tort claims under federal statutes. These are not barred by the workers' compensation claim. Otherwise, the exclusive remedy provision had broad impact to immunize both employers and co-workers from liability to victims of on-the-job injury. *See, e.g., Folta v. Ferro Engineering*, 43 N.E.3d 108 (Ill. 2015) (barring tort suit of employee who was diagnosed with mesothelioma 41 years after leaving employer; injury was "compensable" under workers' comp statute "even though no compensation is available" because of 25-year statute of repose for workers' comp claims, thus leaving plaintiff without any remedy at all). Co-workers share the employer's immunity on the ground that the statute intended to put the burden on the enterprise as a whole, and most definitely not upon individual workers. Employers enjoy the tort immunity on the ground that it represents the price workers paid to get workers' compensation rights.

The exclusive-remedy provision typically bars derivative claims by the worker's family members for such things as negligent infliction of emotional distress, loss of consortium and wrongful death, as well. *Hesse v. Ashland Oil, Inc.*, 642 N.W.2d 330 (Mich. 2002) (barring NIED claim by parents of worker who was killed on the job); *Pittman v. Western Engineering Co.*, 813 N.W.2d 487 (Neb. 2012) (barring wife's NIED claim where her claim "arose" from husband's fatal on-the-job injury). However, where the plaintiff's tort claim is truly independent of the employee's workers' comp claim, it will not be barred. *See, e.g., Snyder v. Michael's Stores, Inc.,* 945 P.2d 781 (Cal. 1997) (plaintiff exposed in utero to a gas at mother's workplace; claim is for her own injuries, not her mother's, therefore not barred by exclusivity provision); *Collins v. COP Wyoming, LLC,* 366 P.3d 521 (Wyo. 2016) (where father witnessed his son's work-related death, his NIED claim was not derivative and thus not barred by workers' comp).

One well-established exception to the exclusivity of workers' compensation is for the intentional torts of the employer. That is, where the employee is injured by an employer's intentional tort, the employee may sue in tort, rather than merely seeking workers' comp recovery. What does the plaintiff have to prove to fall within this exception?

BOWDEN V. YOUNG
120 So.3d 971 (Miss. 2013)

KITCHENS, JUSTICE, for the Court:

[The two plaintiffs were formerly employed as paralegals by the law firm of Vaughn, Bowden (V & B). They sued V & B (among others) for various intentional torts, alleging they suffered injuries caused by the presence of toxic mold and other harmful substances in the law firm's offices. V & B moved to dismiss on the ground that the Mississippi Workers' Compensation Act (MWCA), Miss. Code Ann. § 71–3–9 (Rev. 2011), is the exclusive remedy. Plaintiffs argued in opposition to the motion that their claims fall within the "intentional tort exception" to the MWCA, as established by Mississippi precedent. The trial court denied V & B's motion, and this interlocutory appeal followed.]

This court repeatedly has held that, in order for a willful tort to be outside the exclusivity of the MWCA, . . . the plaintiff must allege and prove that the employer acted with an actual intent to injure the employee, with full knowledge that the employee would be injured and with the purpose of the action being to cause injury to the employee. . . .

The plaintiffs asserted claims for battery, intentional infliction of emotional distress (IIED), . . . and conspiring and aiding and abetting with the [building owner] in negligently maintaining [the building] as well as committing the above-named torts. We will examine each claim to determine whether it falls outside the exclusivity provision of the MWCA.

[*Battery.*] The plaintiffs allege that they were exposed intentionally to toxic mold, to a toxic Mold Killer Spray designed to get rid of the mold, and to poisonous fumes from a sewage leak. . . . With regard to the toxic mold, the plaintiffs contend that V & B battered the plaintiffs when it failed to remediate the mold conditions, and the plaintiffs thereafter inhaled the toxic mold. However, none of the claims asserts that V & B acted with "actual intent" to batter and injure the plaintiffs. Several of the alleged acts of battery involved the use of the Mold Killer Spray, which was being used to kill the mold that was causing injury to the plaintiffs. It is not possible that the defendants were allowing the mold to exist with the intent of injuring the plaintiffs while at the same time attempting to destroy the mold. Further, the application of the Mold Killer Spray clearly was not done with any "actual intent" to injure the plaintiffs. Rather, it was applied in an attempt to remediate the mold situation. . . .

[*Intentional Infliction of Emotional Distress.*] Under Mississippi law, a plaintiff may recover under a theory of intentional infliction of emotional distress . . . [where defendant's conduct is] "so outrageous in character, and so extreme in degree, as to go beyond all possible bounds of decency, and to be regarded as atrocious, and utterly intolerable in a civilized community." . . .

Taking the allegations of the plaintiffs' complaint as true, they have failed to state a claim upon which relief can be granted. V & B initially denied that there was any mold in the building. Management suggested other potential causes of the plaintiffs' ailments. When it became apparent that mold was in fact present in the building, V & B attempted to remediate the situation by applying the Mold Killer Spray. . . . While the defendants' handling of the mold problem may have been negligent, the allegations do not rise to the level of outrageous and extreme conduct that is necessary to support a claim for intentional infliction of emotional distress. Further, the plaintiffs still must be able to show that the actions of the defendants were conducted with "actual intent" to injure the plaintiffs. The fact that V & B attempted to remediate the mold issue, and ultimately decided to relocate its offices due to the mold, leads to the inevitable conclusion that the actions of V & B were not done with the actual intent to inflict emotional distress upon the plaintiffs. The claim for intentional infliction of emotional dismiss fails as a matter of law and must be dismissed.

[*Conspiracy and Aiding and Abetting.*] . . . The claims for conspiracy and aiding and abetting to commit battery and intentional infliction of emotional distress should be dismissed for failure to make a claim for which relief can be granted, because the underlying substantive claims . . . upon which the claims are based are themselves incapable of achieving relief. . . .

The plaintiffs urge this Court to adopt the reasoning of Justice Graves's concurring opinion in *Franklin Corp. v. Tedford*, 18 So.3d 215 (Miss. 2009). Justice Graves opined that employers' actions that were "substantially certain" to result in injury also should be exempt from workers' compensation immunity. This case presents no compelling reason to change the precedent created in *Franklin*. This Court consistently has rejected that position, and a majority of states are in agreement. . . .

[T]he sole avenue of relief for the plaintiffs lies in a claim under the Mississippi Workers' Compensation Act. Accordingly, we reverse the Circuit Court of the First Judicial District of Harrison County's denial of the defendants' Motion to Dismiss, and render judgment dismissing all claims against the defendants. . . .

NOTES

1. **The employer's intentional torts: tests of intent.** The *Bowden* court requires a plaintiff to prove that the employer's "actual intent" was to injure the employee, in order to apply the exception to workers' comp exclusivity. As the court itself says, most states agree that this means proof that the employer had the purpose to injure. Statutes themselves often specify this standard. *See, e.g., Harris v. State, Dept. of Corrections*, 294 P.3d 382 (Mont. 2013); *Bartholomay v. Plains Grain & Agronomy, LLC*, 881 N.W.2d 249 (N.D. 2016); *see also Pixley v. Pro-Pak Industries, Inc.*, 28 N.E.3d 1249 (Ohio 2014) (statute requires deliberate intent to cause injury, but where employer deliberately removes a safety guard, that act is rebuttably presumed to represent such intent to injure).

The *Bowden* court rejects the plaintiff's invitation to accept *Garratt v. Dailey* "substantial certainty" intent (Chapter 4 § 1) as sufficient to overcome the exclusivity provision. A growing number of states have adopted this standard, thus following the traditional tort law definition of intent. *See, e.g., Lucenti v. Laviero*, 176 A.3d 1 (Conn. 2018); *Bakerman v. The Bombay Co.*, 961 So.2d 259 (Fla. 2007). Some statutes themselves adopt this definition of intent. *See, e.g., Danos v. Boh Bros. Constr. Co.*, 132 So.3d 958 (La. 2014). As we have already learned, even under the "substantial certainty" test, negligence or even recklessness will not suffice. *See, e.g., Berkel & Company Contractors, Inc.*, 612 S.W.3d 280 (Tex. 2020) (applying "substantial certainty" test, stressing that it is not enough to show that the employer believed that its actions were merely "highly likely to increase overall risks to employees"); *Wells v. Oklahoma Roofing & Sheet Metal, L.L.C.*, 457 P.3d 1020 (Okla. 2019) ("Mere carelessness or negligence, however gross, will not suffice."). But some of the cases seem to apply "substantial certainty" for what is no more than a substantial *risk* of harm. *See Helf v. Chevron U.S.A., Inc.*, 203 P.3d 962 (Utah 2009) ("intent to injure" language in statute requires only that the injury resulted from an act that the employer knew or expected would cause injury).

2. **Employer's purposeful conduct.** The cases, including *Bowden*, make clear that the intentional tort exception can be difficult for a plaintiff to overcome; this is especially true if the test is "purpose to injure." In *Franklin Corp. v. Tedford*, 18 So.3d 215 (Miss. 2009), cited in *Bowden*, the outcome was different on quite different facts. As summarized by the *Bowden* court, "The plaintiffs included several employees who had worked in the manufacturing plant owned by the defendant, where a pressurized aerosol adhesive had been used to assemble furniture. Some of the plaintiffs were required to apply the adhesive in small, unventilated wooden booths without respiratory masks or protective equipment. At one point, two employees were made to clean up a

spill of 330 gallons of the toxic adhesive without any protective clothing or respiratory equipment. The defendants were aware that the adhesive was toxic, that prolonged exposure would cause damage to the central nervous system and respiratory system, and that the manufacturer's instructions specifically stated that the spray was to be used only with adequate ventilation. Nevertheless, the defendants repeatedly and consistently ignored entreaties from employees to install adequate ventilation equipment or provide respiratory and protective gear." The trial court denied defendant's motion to dismiss, because taking the plaintiff's allegations to be true, they satisfied the intentional-tort exception because they showed "actual intent to injure" the employees.

Suppose an employer knowingly fails to maintain brakes on a heavily loaded truck and the employee is killed when brakes fail on a steep hill. Is that closer to *Bowden*, or to *Franklin*?

3. **Intentional torts of co-worker.** Co-workers are ordinarily immunized by the exclusive remedy provision as well. *See, e.g., Estate of Gorman ex rel. Gorman v. State*, 307 So.3d 421 (Miss. 2020) (tort claim barred by workers' comp where co-worker accidentally shot decedent during a firearms-training exercise). What if, in the course and scope of employment, a co-worker *intentionally* shoots the plaintiff? *See, e.g., Mayberry v. Dukes*, 742 A.2d 448 (D.C. 1999) (co-worker liable in tort).

4. **Rejecting the exception.** Some states have entirely rejected the intentional tort exception. *See, e.g., Ex parte Rock Wool Mfg. Co.*, 202 So.3d 669 (Ala. 2016) (statute contains no such exception, so legislative intent is to bar civil actions "even if caused by the willful and intentional conduct of the employer"); *Estate of Teague ex rel. Martinosky v. Crossroads Coop. Ass'n*, 834 N.W.2d 236 (Neb. 2013) (and upholding constitutionality of statute that itself does not contain such an exception).

KERANS V. PORTER PAINT CO., 575 N.E.2d 428 (Ohio 1991). Sally Kerans worked as a decorator for Porter Paint. Kerans claimed that she was sexually molested on five occasions by her store manager, Al Levine. Kerans and her husband sued Levine and Porter Paint. Plaintiffs settled with Levine but pursued their claim against Porter Paint for, *inter alia*, intentionally or negligently maintaining a policy of encouraging, permitting, or condoning sexual harassment by Levine, inflicting emotional distress, and negligently hiring and/or retaining Levine. The trial court granted summary judgment for defendant on the basis of the exclusive remedy provisions of the workers' compensation statute. *Held*, reversed. First, this is not an "injury" as defined in the statute; rather, it is a "non-physical injury with purely psychological consequences. . . . If the workers' compensation scheme were adjudged to be the exclusive remedy for claims based upon sexual harassment in the workplace, as appellee urges, victims of sexual harassment would often be left without a remedy." Workers' compensation laws and sexual harassment laws are aimed at vastly different concerns. "Workers' compensation addresses purely economic injury; sexual harassment laws are concerned with a much more intangible injury to personal rights."

Further, there is a material issue of fact concerning whether Levine was acting within the scope of his employment. Even if he was not, "both state and federal courts have held that an employer may be liable for failing to take appropriate action where that employer knows or has reason to know that one of its employees poses an unreasonable risk of harm to other employees. . . . [W]here a plaintiff brings a claim against an employer predicated upon allegations of workplace sexual harassment by a company employee, and where there is evidence in the record suggesting that the employee has a past history of sexually harassing behavior about which the employer knew or should have known, summary judgment may not be granted in favor of the employer, even where the employee's actions in no way further or promote the employer's business. An employer has a duty to provide its employees with a safe work environment and, thus, may be independently liable for failing to take corrective action against an employee who poses a threat of harm to fellow employees, even where the employee's actions do not serve or advance the employer's business goals."

NOTES

1. **Language of the statute.** How much of a difference did it make in *Kerans* that the workers' compensation statute did not at the time define "injury" to include emotional distress? In *Driscoll v. General Nutrition Corp.,* 752 A.2d 1069 (Conn. 2000), the plaintiff, a sales clerk for the defendant, was at work when Gregory Popielarczyk entered, forced her into a back room, and forced her to perform fellatio. The plaintiff sued her employer for emotional distress. The court found it was barred by the exclusive remedy provision, reasoning that the legislature defined personal injury to exclude emotional harm when that harm does not arise from personal injury, but in this case the emotional harm was a direct result of physical injury—the sexual assault perpetrated by Popielarczyk. Hence the harm is a personal injury covered by workers' compensation statute and the exclusive remedy provision applies to bar this tort suit.

2. **Coverage of the statute.** In *Horodyskyj v. Karanian,* 32 P.3d 470 (Colo. 2001), the plaintiff alleged sexual harassment by a fellow employee and sued the company for battery and other torts. The court first classified "assaults:" (a) those inherently employment related, as where they arise out of arguments over work equipment; (b) those inherently private, as where they arise from private relationships unrelated to the job; and (c) those that are neutral. It thought that since private matters are not within the statute's coverage, the exclusive remedy would be no bar to tort claims for such injuries.

3. **Conflict with other statutes.** In *Byrd v. Richardson-Greenshields Securities, Inc.*, 552 So.2d 1099 (Fla. 1989), the Florida court suggested still another rationale for allowing the tort claim that might be independent of the *Kerans'* rationale: the exclusive remedy provision should not be applied to bar sexual harassment claims if that would conflict with policies expressed in anti-discrimination and anti-harassment statutes.

4. **Separating the questions.** Distinguish two questions: (a) Did the employer commit a tort, either vicariously or directly?, and (b) Is there ground for holding a tortious employer liable in spite of the exclusive remedy clause?

5. **Federal statutes.** Several federal statutes provides rights to workers that can potentially overlap or conflict with workers' compensation rights. These include:

(a) *Title VII.* Title VII forbids discrimination against workers on the basis of gender or race, for example, and under some circumstances permits a federal suit if the employer violates the statute. 42 U.S.C.A. § 2000e.

(b) *ADA.* The Americans with Disabilities Act (ADA) and some similar federal legislation forbids employer discrimination against employees with disabilities and provides that employers must make reasonable accommodations to permit the employee to work. This may require adjustments in work schedules, temporary leave, or addition of special features to the worksite. This statute, too, permits a suit by an employee whose rights under the statute are violated.

(c) *FMLA.* The Family and Medical Leave Act requires employers to grant up to twelve weeks unpaid leave to an employee who becomes a parent, adopts a child or becomes a foster parent, or when the employee suffers "a serious health condition that makes the employee unable to perform the functions of the position of such employee." 29 U.S.C.A § 2612. (The FMLA was held unconstitutional as applied to a state government agency, in *Coleman v. Court of Appeals of Maryland*, 566 U.S. 30 (2012).)

(d) *Social Security Disability.* The disability provisions of the social security statutes permit totally disabled persons to receive monthly benefits equivalent to early retirement. If the disability results from injury compensable under workers' compensation, adjustment is made, either in the compensation benefits or in the social security benefits. Social security disability is considered in the next chapter.

Many problems arise when two or more of these statutes could apply in the same case. The interaction of these statutes must be left to courses in employment law. However, it is important to notice here that since state law cannot control federal rights, the exclusive remedy provision of the states' workers' compensation statutes does not prevent a worker from claiming her rights under any of these federal statutes

6. **State discrimination laws.** State statutes may also give the plaintiff rights against an employer who engages in forbidden discrimination. As a matter of construing the statutes, the court may conclude that the exclusive remedy provision does not bar either the discrimination claim or a claim for emotional harm that grows out of the discrimination. *See Murray v. Oceanside Unified Sch. Dist.,* 95 Cal.Rptr.2d 28 (Ct. App. 2000).

7. **Wrongful termination.** What impact, if any, would a workers' compensation statute have on a common law claim for wrongful termination? In *Sutton v. Tomco Machining, Inc.,* 950 N.E.2d 938 (Ohio 2011), the court held that the wrongful termination claim, when the employee was fired in retaliation for threatening to file a workers' compensation claim, was not barred by the exclusivity provision, but that a statute prohibiting such a discharge limited the employee's available remedies.

§ 4. TORT CLAIMS AGAINST THIRD PARTIES

Virtually all states permit the injured worker to sue a third party or outsider who tortiously causes an on-the-job injury. In such a case, the worker may have both a tort claim against the outsider and a compensation claim against the employer, subject only to certain adjustments to prevent "double recovery." This raises a number of questions of practice, procedure and principle.

A. CO-EMPLOYEES

1. *Co-employees in the scope of employment.* In most states a co-employee who, acting within the scope of his employment, negligently causes injury to the worker is not regarded as a third party who can be sued in tort. Instead, as we have seen, the co-employee shares the employer's immunity under the exclusive remedy rule. *See, e.g., Progressive Halcyon Ins. Co. v. Philippi,* 754 N.W.2d 646 (S.D. 2008); *Peters v. Wady Industries, Inc.,* 489 S.W.3d 784 (Mo. 2016) (workers' comp the exclusive remedy unless the co-worker owed a duty to the claimant independent of the employer's duty to provide a safe workplace). The chief reason for this is that the compensation scheme is intended to put the burden of industrial injuries upon the enterprise and to shift them away from the employees. The enterprise itself is thought to be the source of injury, and the products should, in this view, reflect the costs that are inevitable parts of that enterprise.

2. *Co-employees* not *in the scope of employment.* If the injuring co-employee deviates sufficiently from employment, such as by engaging in a personally motivated, intentional tort, he loses the immunity. *See O'Connell v. Chasdi,* 511 N.E.2d 349 (Mass. 1987). Likewise when the co-employee responsible for injury acts in another capacity, then he may be liable for injuries arising from that other capacity, as where the landlord/

co-employee maintains a defective stair. *Sauve v. Winfree,* 907 P.2d 7 (Alaska 1995).

B. THE STATUTORY EMPLOYER AND BORROWED SERVANTS

1. *Statutory employers.* Workers' compensation statutes usually provide that when an employer hires independent contractors to carry out the employer's regular work or business, the employer is to be treated as the "statutory employer" of the independent contractor's employees. A, a general contractor, hires B to do the framing on a building A is building. B hires five workers, one of whom is injured on the job. The statutory employer provision permits B's injured worker to claim worker's compensation benefits from A. This will normally be a significant advantage only if B has not secured his own workers' compensation insurance. So A will usually protect himself by requiring his contractors to have workers' compensation insurance coverage.

2. *Statutory employer's immunity from tort suits.* Can the injured worker sue A in tort? The theory would be that the worker is employed by B, not A, so that A is a third person and does not enjoy the employer's immunity. However, if A is a statutory employer, he presumably gets the protection that all employers obtain when they are liable for workers' compensation—complete immunity from tort suits.

3. *Borrowed servants.* A supplies temporary employees to B, who controls the details of their work in B's business. Suppose such an employee is injured by B's negligence. Does the exclusive remedy provision bar a tort claim against B? *See Waste Management of Texas, Inc. v. Stevenson,* 622 S.W.3d 273 (Tex. 2021) (where temporary worker was injured while on assignment to client company, which controlled details of his work, client was the employer and workers' compensation was his exclusive remedy against client); *Kaiser v. Millard Lumber, Inc.,* 587 N.W.2d 875 (Neb. 1999) (when labor broker who employs worker then provides worker to business that controls his work, the worker is the employee of both and workers' compensation is his only remedy).

C. ADJUSTMENTS AMONG THE PARTIES

1. *The employer's lien rights against tortfeasors who injured the employee.* The employer who pays workers' compensation benefits to an injured employee has a lien on the employee's tort claim against third persons to the extent of the employer's past or future benefits payments. *See, e.g., Sourbier v. State,* 498 N.W.2d 720 (Iowa 1993). If the tort suit is successful, the payments made by the tortfeasor will go in part to the employer (or its workers' compensation insurer). *See, e.g., Hawkins v. Southwest Kansas Co-op Service,* 484 P.3d 236 (Kan. 2021).

2. *The employer's subrogation rights against tortfeasors who injured the employee.* If the injured employee does not bring a tort suit against the third person tortfeasor within a time specified in the statute, the employer is subrogated to the employee's rights against the tortfeasor, to the extent the employer has paid benefits. The employer may thus sue the tortfeasor, recover the damages due to the injured person, repay himself for the workers' compensation benefits, and turn over the balance to the employee.

3. *The third person tortfeasor's claim against the negligent employer in a joint and several liability system.* Frequently both the employer and a third person negligently cause injury to the employee. Because the employee cannot recover in tort against the employer, his tort suit will run against the third person. Traditionally, the third person tortfeasor would be liable for all the employee's damages and would not be entitled to contribution against the immune employer. Thus the third person would bear all the loss and the negligent employer none. A few courts have slightly mitigated this extreme result by permitting limited contribution against the employer up to the amount of it workers' compensation benefits, but most courts have not.

4. *The third person tortfeasor's claim against the negligent employer where joint and several liability is abolished.* Where joint and several liability has been abolished, the employer would still be immune and the third person tortfeasor would pay only his comparative fault share. That would leave the employee with only a percentage of his tort damages even if the employee herself was not at fault and the employer was.

REFERENCES: DOBBS, HAYDEN & BUBLICK, HORNBOOK ON TORTS §§ 36.2–36.5 (2d ed. 2016); 3 DOBBS, HAYDEN & BUBLICK, THE LAW OF TORTS §§ 503–507 (2d ed. 2011).

CHAPTER 29

PUBLIC COMPENSATION SYSTEMS, INCLUDING SOCIAL SECURITY

■ ■ ■

§ 1. COMPENSATION SCHEMES THAT REPLACE TORT LIABILITY

A. TAXING INDUSTRY AND ELIMINATING ITS TORT LIABILITY

Is some kind of public system for compensating injury a good idea, either to supplement or to replace the tort and workers' compensation systems? One approach might be to add a tax on industries that cause harm and use the fund so created to pay for the harms done.

Something like this has been done in the National Childhood Vaccine Injury Act, 42 U.S.C.A. § 300aa–1. Compulsory vaccination is an overall health benefit, but vaccines cause devastating side effects with permanent brain damage to particular infants. A child who is entirely normal at birth may be so damaged by a vaccine that he cannot move, talk, or feed himself. Such a child will require a lifetime of care and may suffer other medical problems, such as repeated seizures. The Vaccine Act addresses this problem and is an important experiment in alternatives to tort law. Judge Breyer (later Justice Breyer) summarized the Vaccine Act this way in *Schafer v. American Cyanamid Co.,* 20 F.3d 1 (1st Cir. 1994):

"The National Childhood Vaccine Injury Act provides a special procedure to compensate those who are injured by certain vaccines. The Act bars those who accept an award under that procedure from later bringing a tort suit to obtain additional compensation. The question before us in this appeal . . . is whether the Act also bars the family of such a person from bringing a tort suit to obtain compensation for their own, related, injuries, in particular, for loss of companionship or consortium. . . .

"The National Childhood Vaccine Injury Act represents an effort to provide compensation to those harmed by childhood vaccines outside the framework of traditional tort law. Congress passed the law after hearing testimony 1) describing the critical need for vaccines to protect children from disease, 2) pointing out that vaccines inevitably harm a very small number of the many millions of people who are vaccinated, and 3) expressing dissatisfaction with traditional tort law as a way of compensating those few victims. Injured persons (potential tort plaintiffs) complained about the tort law system's uncertain recoveries, the high cost of litigation, and delays in obtaining compensation. They argued that government had, for all practical purposes, made vaccination obligatory, and thus it had a responsibility to ensure that those injured by vaccines were compensated. Vaccine manufacturers (potential tort defendants) complained about litigation expenses and occasional large recoveries, which caused insurance premiums and vaccine prices to rise, and which ultimately threatened the stability of the vaccine supply. . .

"The Vaccine Act responds to these complaints by creating a remedial system that tries more quickly to deliver compensation to victims, while also reducing insurance and litigation costs for manufacturers. The Act establishes a special claims procedure involving the Court of Federal Claims and special masters (a system that we shall call the "Vaccine Court"). 42 U.S.C. § 300aa–12. A person injured by a vaccine may file a petition with the Vaccine Court to obtain compensation (from a fund financed by a tax on vaccines). He need not prove fault. Nor, to prove causation, need he show more than that he received the vaccine and then suffered certain symptoms within a defined period of time. The Act specifies amounts of compensation for certain kinds of harm (e.g., $250,000 for death, up to $250,000 for pain and suffering). And, it specifies other types of harm for which compensation may be awarded (e.g., medical expenses, loss of earnings).

"At the same time, the Act modifies, but does not eliminate, the traditional tort system, which Congress understood to provide important incentives for the safe manufacture and distribution of vaccines. The Act requires that a person injured directly by a vaccine first bring a Vaccine Court proceeding. Then, it gives that person the choice either to accept the Court's award and abandon his tort rights (which the Act transfers to the federal government) or to reject the judgment and retain his tort rights. (He can also keep his tort rights by withdrawing his Vaccine Court petition if the Court moves too slowly.)

"The Act additionally helps manufacturers by providing certain federal modifications of state tort law. For example, it forbids the award of compensation for injuries that flow from 'unavoidable side effects'; it frees the manufacturer from liability for not providing direct warnings to an injured person (or his representative); it imposes a presumption that compliance with

Food and Drug Administration requirements means the manufacturer provided proper directions and warnings; it limits punitive damage awards; and it requires that the trial of any tort suit take place in three phases (liability; general damages; punitive damages)."

Data from the Department of Health and Human Services show that between 1989 and 2013, over 12,000 claims had been filed by claimants alleging injuries from vaccines administered after Oct. 1988, the effective date of the Act. About a third of these claims have alleged that vaccines caused autism, although these have virtually stopped since the Federal Court of Claims ruled in *Mead v. Sec'y of Health & Human Services*, 2010 WL 892248 (Ct. Cl. 2010), that there was no epidemiologic evidence supporting such an allegation. In the same period, just over 3,100 claims had been granted, with awards and costs totaling about $2.5 billion.

A claimant who shows he received a vaccination listed in the Vaccine Injury Table and suffered an injury listed in the Table within a prescribed period is afforded a presumption of causation. *See, e.g., Andreu v. Sec'y of Health & Human Services*, 569 F.3d 1367 (Fed. Cir. 2009). But critics of the Act's actual operation have pointed out that factual causation is often a difficult issue. *See* Katherine E. Strong, *Note, Proving Causation Under the Vaccine Injury Act: A New Approach for A New Day*, 75 GEO. WASH. L.REV. 426 (2007). The claims are handled by a handful of special masters who have wide decision-making authority. A special master's findings are reviewed under the arbitrary and capricious standard, and legal determinations are reviewed using a "not in accordance with law" standard. *See W.C. v. Sec'y of Health & Human Services*, 704 F.3d 1352 (Fed. Cir. 2013).

The Vaccine Act includes an "unusual scheme" for compensating lawyers who work on these cases. They are prohibited from charging their clients any fee for services in connection with a vaccine injury petition. *Sebelius v. Cloer*, 569 U.S. 369 (2013) (citing 42 U.S.C.A. § 300aa–15(e)(1)). If the petitioner wins, then reasonable fees and costs are awarded. If the petitioner loses, then the special master or the court "may" award reasonable fees and costs, if it is determined that (1) the petition was brought in good faith, and (2) there was a reasonable basis for the claim. *See Cottingham ex rel. K.C. v. Sec'y of Health & Human Services*, 971 F.3d 1337 (Fed. Cir. 2020) (special master's determination that petitioner was not entitled to attorney fee award based on finding that petitioner provided no evidence of causation for injury was abuse of discretion). By statute, interim fees and costs may be awarded, especially where a final outcome is going to take years. *See Rehn v. Sec'y of Health & Human Services*, 126 Fed. Cl. 86 (Ct. Cl. 2016).

The special-master system has been repeatedly upheld against arguments that it denies fundamental fairness or is arbitrary and capricious. *See, e.g., Cedillo v. Sec'y of Health & Human Services*, 89 Fed. Cl. 158 (Ct. Cl. 2009); *Snyder v. Sec'y of Health & Human Services*, 88 Fed. Cl. 706 (Ct. Cl. 2009). But critics have complained that claimants have a markedly better chance with some special masters than others. *See* Derry Ridgway, *No-fault Vaccine Insurance: Lessons From The National Vaccine Injury Compensation Program,* 24 J. HEALTH POL. POL'Y & L. 59 (1999). And most of those who receive no compensation under the Vaccine Act find none in the tort system either. *See* Elizabeth A. Breen, *A One Shot Deal: the National Childhood Vaccine Injury Act,* 41 WM. & MARY L. REV. 309 (1999).

If the problems raised by critics are fixable, the statute still raises many issues of policy and justice. It uses public powers for the direct benefit of one class of manufacturers. Among the many questions you might consider are these: (1) What happens to safety incentives under the statute and how would you compare it on that point with workers' compensation? (2) Do you think it is harmful to the interests of vaccine-injured plaintiffs as a whole? (3) How do you rate the Act as a solution to the problem of compensation for injury—is it a good model for developing broader solutions?

B. TAXING THE PUBLIC TO PROTECT INDUSTRIES AND PROVIDE COMPENSATION TO VICTIMS— THE 9/11 COMPENSATION SYSTEM

A federal statute, known as the Air Transportation Safety and System Stabilization Act (ATSSSA), 49 U.S.C.A. § 40101, created a unique system for dealing with the injuries and fears arising from the airplane-based terrorist attacks of September 11, 2001. First, the bail-out provisions used public money as direct compensation and as loans for airlines to cover losses incurred from the terrorist attacks. Second, the statute set up an optional administrative compensation scheme. If claimants chose this option, they could not sue the airlines in tort. And payment is from public funds, not the funds of the airlines or their insurers.

The original fund closed in 2004, having paid out more than $7 billion to survivors of 2,880 people who died in the attacks, and 2,680 who were injured in either the attacks or the rescue efforts that followed. A new phase of the program commenced in 2011, to provide medical treatment and monitoring for 9/11-related health conditions. *See* Sheila L. Birnbaum (Special Master), First Annual Status Report of the September 11 Victim Compensation Fund (Oct. 2012).

The compensation fund is administered by a federal administrator called a Special Master. Only those present at the 9/11 sites and their families qualify to assert claims for losses. Although the Act aimed to provide complete recovery of economic losses and limited recovery of non-economic losses, the Special Master promulgated regulations governing amounts of compensation for some losses and guidelines for others. To manage the large numbers of claims expeditiously, he provided calculations on work-life expectancy, on probable wage increases, taxes, and other matters, then promulgated a table of presumed awards for each age/earnings group. There was also a floor in death cases—$500,000 for a victim with a spouse or dependent, for example. Besides calculation of economic losses by way of the table, there was a flat $250,000 for non-economic loss. Collateral source payments were deducted, including some not normally deducted under the state tort reform statutes, such as life insurance. These regulations left room for some individualization of awards. In particular, the Master to some extent took into account the financial needs of the claimant. 28 C.F.R. § 104.41. The point seemed to be to flatten the awards to high earners to minimize the difference between awards for death of low-earning victims and death of those whose earnings were quite modest.

If a claimant pursued the compensation alternative, she could not sue in tort. But she could choose to sue in tort instead of claiming compensation. However, she was required to sue in a federal court in New York and total liability of the airlines was limited by the amount of their insurance coverage. Of course, there could be no guarantee that the tort claimants would win in the tort system, but it has been held that the airlines at least owe a duty of care to victims on the ground. *In re Sept. 11 Litig.*, 280 F.Supp.2d 279 (S.D.N.Y. 2003).

NOTES

1. **Financing features compared.** Compare the financing features of the Vaccine Act with ATSSSA. Could you mount an argument that one financing system is better than the other?

2. **Comparing workers' compensation.** Notice that both the Vaccine Act and ATSSSA give the plaintiff the option of seeking a kind of strict liability (with limited compensation) or suing in tort, although the tort option may be burdened with new disadvantages. Compare the workers' compensation system, which, under the exclusive remedy clause, denies the worker any option to sue in tort.

3. **Suitability for other situations.** Is this public compensation a good model for other injury cases? If so, why wasn't it applied to, say, the victims of Timothy McVeigh's bombing of the federal building in Oklahoma City? Or for that matter, to any victims of injury? *See* John G. Cullhane, *Tort, Compensation, and Two Kinds of Justice*, 55 RUTGERS L. REV. 1027 (2003); Betsy J. Grey, *Homeland Security and Federal Relief: A Proposal for a Permanent Compensation System for Domestic Terrorist Victims*, 9 N.Y.U. J.

LEGIS. & PUB. POL'Y 663 (2006); George W. Conk, *Will the Post-9/11 World Be a Post-Tort World?*, 112 PENN. ST. L. REV. 175 (2007).

4. **Other federal compensation schemes.** There are a number of federal compensation schemes, and/or liability caps for industries. Compensation systems include, for example, no-fault benefits for miners suffering from Black Lung and victims of swine flu vaccines. Liability caps are imposed for the protection of involved industries in certain environmental contamination and the nuclear energy industry.

§ 2. SOCIAL SECURITY DISABILITY BENEFITS

The Social Security Act of 1935 is aimed at increasing economic security by providing, among other things, unemployment compensation, retirement benefits, and survivor's benefits. Later amendments included Medicare and Medicaid provisions. This chapter introduces another feature—benefits paid for serious disabilities that prevent work.

The program has enormous public importance. Although the figures vary from month to month, over 10 million disabled workers are receiving benefits. The annual payout in benefits to the disabled and their families exceeds $20 billion.

At the most immediate professional level, lawyers must be aware that an injured client may be entitled to social security benefits. In some cases, the existence of those benefits will figure in a large way in pursuit or defense of a tort claim. Social security benefits may keep the plaintiff going while the tort claim is developed. Or lawyers may find they can reach a settlement only because the total package of benefits, including those under social security legislation, is high enough to provide adequate care. Tort settlements must also be structured with trusts or otherwise to protect the client's rights to public assistance programs such as Medicaid. More broadly, does the disability benefit system suggest an alternative to, or improvement in, tort law?

42 U.S.C.A. § 423
(as amended 2015)

(a) Disability insurance benefits

(1) Every individual who—

   (A) is insured for disability insurance benefits (as determined under subsection (c)(1) of this section),

   (B) has not attained retirement age . . .,

   (C) [meets certain requirements if non-citizens or non-U.S. nationals,]

   (D) has filed application for disability insurance benefits, and

(E) is under a disability (as defined in subsection (d) of this section), shall be entitled to a disability insurance benefit. . . .

(d) "Disability" defined

(1) The term "disability" means—

(A) inability to engage in any substantial gainful activity by reason of any medically determinable physical or mental impairment which can be expected to result in death or which has lasted or can be expected to last for a continuous period of not less than 12 months; or

(B) in the case of an individual who has attained the age of 55 and is blind . . . inability by reason of such blindness to engage in substantial gainful activity requiring skills or abilities comparable to those of any gainful activity in which he has previously engaged with some regularity and over a substantial period of time.

(2) For purposes of paragraph (1)(A)—

(A) An individual shall be determined to be under a disability only if his physical or mental impairment or impairments are of such severity that he is not only unable to do his previous work but cannot, considering his age, education, and work experience, engage in any other kind of substantial gainful work which exists in the national economy, regardless of whether such work exists in the immediate area in which he lives, or whether a specific job vacancy exists for him, or whether he would be hired if he applied for work. For purposes of the preceding sentence (with respect to any individual), "work which exists in the national economy" means work which exists in significant numbers either in the region where such individual lives or in several regions of the country.

(B) In determining whether an individual's physical or mental impairment or impairments are of a sufficient medical severity that such impairment or impairments could be the basis of eligibility under this section, the Commissioner of Social Security shall consider the combined effect of all of the individual's impairments without regard to whether any such impairment, if considered separately, would be of such severity. If the Commissioner of Social Security does find a medically severe combination of impairments, the combined impact of the impairments shall be considered throughout the disability determination process.

(C) An individual shall not be considered to be disabled for purposes of this subchapter if alcoholism or drug addiction would (but for this subparagraph) be a contributing factor material to the Commissioner's determination that the individual is disabled.

(3) For purposes of this subsection, a "physical or mental impairment" is an impairment that results from anatomical, physiological, or psychological abnormalities which are demonstrable by medically acceptable clinical and laboratory diagnostic techniques. . . .

(5)(A) An individual shall not be considered to be under a disability unless he furnishes such medical and other evidence of the existence thereof as the Commissioner of Social Security may require. An individual's statement as to pain or other symptoms shall not alone be conclusive evidence of disability as defined in this section; there must be medical signs and findings, established by medically acceptable clinical or laboratory diagnostic techniques, which show the existence of a medical impairment that results from anatomical, physiological, or psychological abnormalities which could reasonably be expected to produce the pain or other symptoms alleged and which, when considered with all evidence required to be furnished under this paragraph (including statements of the individual or his physician as to the intensity and persistence of such pain or other symptoms which may reasonably be accepted as consistent with the medical signs and findings), would lead to a conclusion that the individual is under a disability. Objective medical evidence of pain or other symptoms established by medically acceptable clinical or laboratory techniques (for example, deteriorating nerve or muscle tissue) must be considered in reaching a conclusion as to whether the individual is under a disability. . . .

NOTES

1.   **Procedures for claim.** A disability claim is initially administrative, not judicial. The claimant files a claim in the Social Security office, but it is initially determined by a state agency. The claimant may appeal to a federal Administrative Law Judge (ALJ), who holds a hearing. *See* 1 HARVEY L. MCCORMICK, SOCIAL SECURITY CLAIMS AND PROCEDURES § 1:8 (5th ed. 2008). After administrative appeals from his decision have been exhausted, the claimant can seek review in the United States District Court. The District Judge must affirm the ALJ's factual findings if they are supported by substantial evidence, but may reverse or remand for errors in law and may reject factual findings not supported by substantial evidence. 42 U.S.C.A. § 405(g).

2.   **Insured status.** The claimant under § 423 must meet the requirements listed in subsection (a)(1), including insured status. The claimant recovers benefits only because she has worked and paid "premiums" in the form of payroll tax deductions. However, a welfare component of the social security laws provides similar benefits for similar disabilities to persons who have made no contributions or insufficient contributions to the system. This is known as Supplemental Security Income or SSI. The SSI claimant must meet a "needs" test and cannot recover benefits if he or she has assets or income beyond certain levels.

3. **Benefits.** Disability may be viewed as a form of involuntary early retirement, and indeed the benefits provided are calculated as if the claimant were 62 when disability struck. The actual computation is complex, because it takes into account the claimant's monthly wages over a lifetime of employment and also "indexes" the wages so that inflation can be factored out and all wages can be on the same scale. In general you can say that benefits are not generous but that they matter greatly to anyone unable to work and lacking independent income.

4. **Disability.** Subsection (d) defines disability, and it has two main components, one medical and one work-related. There must be a medical "impairment," and that medical condition must render the claimant unable to engage in any substantial gainful employment in the national economy for a period of at least 12 months, given the claimant's age, education and work experience.

MCLAIN V. SCHWEIKER, 715 F.2d 866 (4th Cir. 1983). McLain is 49 years old, has completed high school and two years of college. He has in the past been employed as a traveling sales representative for a cheesecake company and later as a security guard. His testimony is that he can no longer work in these stressful environments, as he cannot tolerate noise, including telephones, and typewriters. Doctors and psychiatrists report a 20 year history of nervous disorders and "inadequate personality." Dr. Katherine Kemp, a psychiatrist, reported a paranoid-like trend in his thoughts and stated he could not "interrelate" with others and would be unable to withstand the pressures of the employment world. The ALJ found an impairment, but concluded that McLain would be able to perform his previous work in "nonstressful environments," noting that this might include telephone sales work and sedentary security guard positions. He therefore denied benefits. The Secretary then denied benefits and the district court affirmed. McLain appeals. *Held*, vacated and remanded. McLain "presented a prima facie case of disability by showing that he was unable to perform his previous work. . . . [T]he medical findings and opinions unanimously support the conclusion that McLain has a serious psychiatric disorder. It is clear that McLain's impairment prevents him from performing the demands of his previous jobs as a salesman and security guard." Once he made that case, the Secretary could prevail only by showing that "could perform an alternative job existing in significant numbers in the national economy."

NOTES

1. **Applying the statute.** (a) Suppose the claimant could do limited work sorting potatoes into bins. The only place where such employment is possible is 1,000 miles from the claimant's life-long residence. Is the claimant disabled? What does the statute say?

(b)   What if the claimant could do limited work sorting potatoes into bins, and such employment actually exists, but there is no job open and long lines of people are on the waiting list? What does the statute say?

2.   **The five-step analysis.** The regulations provide for a five-step process or decision tree that goes something like this: (1) Is the claimant currently engaged in substantial gainful activity? If yes, the claimant is not disabled. If no, then (2) does the claimant have a severe impairment that limits her ability to work? If no, she is not disabled, but if yes, then (3) is the impairment in the listings (Note 4, below)? If yes, disability is proved and benefits computed. If no, then (4) in spite of impairment, can the claimant perform her past work? If yes, she is not disabled. If not, (5) she is presumptively disabled and the burden falls upon the Commissioner to show that there is a job in the national economy that she would be able to perform.

3.   **Burden-shifting and older workers.** Although disability is determined by the claimant's ability to perform jobs rather than on her ability to obtain them, the burden-shifting in the five-step analysis can greatly assist the claimant. In addition, claimants over 60 get a break. If they suffer a severe impairment, the burden not only shifts to the Commissioner under the five-step analysis, but the burden becomes qualitatively more difficult. The Commissioner must show not only that the over-60 claimant has transferrable skills but also that they are "highly marketable." *See, e.g., Kerns v. Apfel,* 160 F.3d 464 (8th Cir. 1998).

4.   **The listings.** At one time each case was decided on the proof adduced in the hearing before the ALJ. This often led to vocational testimony about kinds of jobs the claimant might or might not do. This could be repetitious and wasteful. In some instances, disability was a very likely finding, as in the case of blindness or severe visual impairment. Although some individuals might be able to work with such impairments, most would not. What would you propose? How about a schedule of impairments that would automatically qualify as "disability?" This is what the Secretary provided in the governing administrative regulations, which, like other federal regulations, are codified in the Code of Federal Regulations ("CFR"). In this case the regulations are known as the "listings" and are found in 20 CFR part 404, Subpart P, Appendix I. Although the listings can be used to provide automatic awards, they cannot be used the other way around, to foreclose awards for disabilities that are not listed. Each claimant is entitled to proceed on the evidence if he fails to succeed under the listings. *See Sullivan v. Zebley,* 493 U.S. 521 (1990).

NOTE: THE MEDICAL-VOCATIONAL GUIDELINES (THE GRIDS)

Federal regulations referred to as "the grids" come into play when there is no automatic disability found in the listings of Appendix I. The grids provide a disability profile of the claimant by setting up a table of several factors: (1) degree of medical impairment or Residual Functional

Capacity ("RFC"); (2) age; (3) education; (4) previous work experience. These four factors are in turn broken down into subcategories. One might have an RFC that permits only sedentary work, or an RFC that permits "limited to light work," or "limited to medium work." Age might be "advanced," "approaching advanced," "younger," and so on. Similarly, education and work experience are sub-categorized.

The Code of Federal Regulations reduces these factors to a set of tables or grids. The ALJ may simply determine the RFC, age, education and experience and then automatically come up with a decision. It is, in short, a simple mechanical version of what a computer might do. Reading the combination of factors on the appropriate grid leads the ALJ to a definite conclusion—disability or no disability.

Here is a sample of one of the grids based on 20 CFR Pt. 404, Subpt. P, App. 2. Note that the title of the table sets one of the conditions that determines the outcome, with the column at the far right indicating the outcome of the claim based on the presence of the variables in the preceding columns.

Table No. 1—Residual Functional Capacity: Maximum Sustained Work Capability Limited to Sedentary Work as a Result of Severe Medically Determinable Impairment(s)				
Rule	Age	Education	Previous work experience	Decision
201.01	Advanced	Limited or less	Unskilled or none	Disabled.
201.02	same	same	Skilled or semiskilled-skills not transferable	Disabled.
201.03	same	same	Skilled or semiskilled-skills transferable	Not disabled.

The grids channel decision-making in a very firm way and probably provide a uniformity and simplicity of decision-making that would not otherwise exist. Are they nevertheless unfair?

HECKLER V. CAMPBELL
461 U.S. 458 (1983)

JUSTICE POWELL delivered the opinion of the Court.

The issue is whether the Secretary of Health and Human Services may rely on published medical-vocational guidelines to determine a claimant's right to Social Security disability benefits.

The Social Security Act defines "disability" in terms of the effect a physical or mental impairment has on a person's ability to function in the work place. It provides disability benefits only to persons who are unable "to engage in any substantial gainful activity by reason of any medically determinable physical or mental impairment." And it specifies that a person must "not only [be] unable to do his previous work but [must be unable], considering his age, education, and work experience, [to] engage in any other kind of substantial gainful work which exists in the national economy, regardless of whether such work exists in the immediate area in which he lives, or whether a specific job vacancy exists for him, or whether he would be hired if he applied for work."

Prior to 1978, the Secretary relied on vocational experts to establish the existence of suitable jobs in the national economy. After a claimant's limitations and abilities had been determined at a hearing, a vocational expert ordinarily would testify whether work existed that the claimant could perform. Although this testimony often was based on standardized guides, vocational experts frequently were criticized for their inconsistent treatment of similarly situated claimants.

To improve both the uniformity and efficiency of this determination, the Secretary promulgated medical-vocational guidelines as part of the 1978 regulations. See 20 CFR pt. 404, subpt. P, app. 2 (1982).

These guidelines relieve the Secretary of the need to rely on vocational experts by establishing through rulemaking the types and numbers of jobs that exist in the national economy. They consist of a matrix of the four factors identified by Congress—physical ability, age, education, and work experience—set forth rules that identify whether jobs requiring specific combinations of these factors exist in significant numbers in the national economy. Where a claimant's qualifications correspond to the job requirements identified by a rule, the guidelines direct a conclusion as to whether work exists that the claimant could perform. If such work exists, the claimant is not considered disabled.

In 1979, Carmen Campbell applied for disability benefits because a back condition and hypertension prevented her from continuing her work as a hotel maid. After her application was denied, she requested a hearing *de novo* before an Administrative Law Judge. He determined that her back problem was not severe enough to find her disabled without further inquiry, and accordingly considered whether she retained the ability to perform either her past work or some less strenuous job.

He concluded that even though Campbell's back condition prevented her from returning to her work as a maid, she retained the physical capacity to do light work. . . . Relying on the medical-vocational guidelines, the Administrative Law Judge found that a significant number of jobs existed that a person of Campbell's qualifications could perform. Accordingly, he concluded that she was not disabled. . . .

The Court of Appeals held that "[i]n failing to show suitable available alternative jobs for Ms. Campbell, the Secretary's findings of 'not disabled' is not supported by substantial evidence." It thus rejected the proposition that "the guidelines provide adequate evidence of a claimant's ability to perform a specific alternative occupation," and remanded for the Secretary to put into evidence "particular types of jobs suitable to the capabilities of Ms. Campbell." The court's requirement that additional evidence be introduced on this issue prevents the Secretary from putting the guidelines to their intended use and implicitly calls their validity into question. Accordingly, we think the decision below requires us to consider whether the Secretary may rely on medical-vocational guidelines in appropriate cases.

The Social Security Act directs the Secretary to "adopt reasonable and proper rules and regulations to regulate and provide for the nature and extent of the proofs and evidence and the method of taking and furnishing the same" in disability cases.

We do not think that the Secretary's reliance on medical-vocational guidelines is inconsistent with the Social Security Act. It is true that the statutory scheme contemplates that disability hearings will be individualized determinations based on evidence adduced at a hearing. But this does not bar the Secretary from relying on rulemaking to resolve certain classes of issues. The Court has recognized that even where an agency's enabling statute expressly requires it to hold a hearing, the agency may rely on its rulemaking authority to determine issues that do not require case-by-case consideration. A contrary holding would require the agency continually to relitigate issues that may be established fairly and efficiently in a single rulemaking proceeding.

. . . As noted above, in determining whether a claimant can perform less strenuous work, the Secretary must make two determinations. She must assess each claimant's individual abilities and then determine whether jobs exist that a person having the claimant's qualifications could perform. The first inquiry involves a determination of historic facts, and the regulations properly require the Secretary to make these findings on the basis of evidence adduced at a hearing. We note that the regulations afford claimants ample opportunity both to present evidence relating to their own abilities and to offer evidence that the guidelines do not apply to them. The second inquiry requires the Secretary to determine an issue that is not unique to each claimant—the types and numbers of jobs that exist in the national economy. This type of general factual issue may be resolved as fairly through rulemaking as by introducing the testimony of vocational experts at each disability hearing.

As the Secretary has argued, the use of published guidelines brings with it a uniformity that previously had been perceived as lacking. To require the Secretary to relitigate the existence of jobs in the national economy at each hearing would hinder needlessly an already overburdened agency. We conclude that the Secretary's use of medical-vocational guidelines does not conflict with the statute, nor can we say on the record before us that they are arbitrary and capricious.

We now consider Campbell's argument that the Court of Appeals properly required the Secretary to specify alternative available jobs. . . . Rather the court's reference to notice and an opportunity to respond appears to be based on a principle of administrative law—that when an agency takes official or administrative notice of facts, a litigant must be given an adequate opportunity to respond.

This principle is inapplicable, however, when the agency has promulgated valid regulations. Its purpose is to provide a procedural safeguard: to ensure the accuracy of the facts of which an agency takes notice. But when the accuracy of those facts already has been tested fairly during rulemaking, the rulemaking proceeding itself provides sufficient procedural protection.

The Court of Appeals' decision would require the Secretary to introduce evidence of specific available jobs that respondent could perform. It would limit severely her ability to rely on the medical-vocational guidelines. We think the Secretary reasonably could choose to rely on these guidelines in appropriate cases rather than on the testimony of a vocational expert in each case. Accordingly, the judgment of the Court of Appeals is

Reversed.

[Concurring and dissenting opinions omitted.]

NOTES

1.   **Beating the grids.** Is Campbell's position a reasonable one? Suppose Campbell has diligently searched for work that fits her skills, education and capacity. She or her attorney consults the grids and determines that they will require the ALJ to deny disability. Can she prove there is really *not* a job she can do? Can she effectively dispute the "hidden" premises of the grids—that somewhere there is some undefined job she can somehow find? Just how can the Secretary determine, once and for all, what jobs are available for persons of given impairments?

2.   **Nonexertional limitations.** The grid system does not apply to nonexertional limitations. *E.g., Reddick v. Chater,* 157 F.3d 715 (9th Cir. 1998). For example, limited intellectual capacity is a nonexertional impairment, meaning one that does not vary with exertion. Hence a claimant who is found to have a significant mental impairment must be given benefits unless the ALJ

hears a vocational expert who establishes that there are jobs the claimant can perform. *Foreman v. Callahan,* 122 F.3d 24 (8th Cir. 1997).

3.   **Pain.** Both pain and psychological impairments can count as, or cause, disability. What if the claimant merely testifies to pain, but neither he nor anyone else can find a medical source of the pain? See 42 U.S.C.A. § 423 (d)(5). What if the claimant testifies to his severe pain, and doctors provide objective medical evidence of the underlying impairment that could reasonably be expected to cause pain, but the doctors cannot opine about the severity of that pain? *See Lingenfelter v. Astrue,* 504 F.3d 1028 (9th Cir. 2007) (error for ALJ to rule against claimant on such facts, at least without specific findings about why the claimant was not credible).

4.   **Expanding welfare programs to eliminate tort law?** Professor Sugarman proposed a system of comprehensive coverage for people in need, without regard to whether their need derives from injury or something else. His program would substantially expand the social program we have just glanced at and do away with tort law altogether. The welfare program would provide compensation, and safety and deterrence would be achieved through regulation. *See* STEPHEN SUGARMAN, DOING AWAY WITH PERSONAL INJURY LAW (1989). This program would significantly reduce costs now borne by the tort system, he thought, and could be financed in part by that reduction. What do you think?

REFERENCE: 3 DOBBS, HAYDEN & BUBLICK, THE LAW OF TORTS § 508 (social security); § 510 (government compensation funds); § 511 (taxing industry to create compensation funds) (2d ed. 2011).

CHAPTER 30

PRIVATE INSURANCE SOLUTIONS

■ ■ ■

Can private insurance solve the injury problem? If it is to improve on the tort system, workers' compensation and social security benefits, it would have to provide at least a large portion of the following:

(1) Basic coverage for most injuries causing medical loss or work-disability; (2) efficient return on premiums; (3) coverage for most if not all persons who may be injured; (4) a limit on any public subsidy; and (5) a system of safety incentives. Is it possible that this could be done by private insurance?

NOTE: INSURANCE INSIDE AND OUTSIDE THE TORT SYSTEM

1. *Within the tort system.* The principal insurance schemes that work strictly within the confines of the tort system have been directed at one narrow but severe problem of those systems—the negligent driver who has insufficient liability insurance or none at all. *See* Nora Freeman Engstrom, *When Cars Crash: The Automobile's Tort Law Legacy*, 53 WAKE FOREST L. REV. 293 (2018) (analyzing effect of automobiles on the contours, purposes and limits of tort law, including "our (mostly) ill-fated experiment with no-fault automobile compensation"). Legislatures have enacted financial responsibility laws, under which, after an auto accident, the driver is required to show that he has insurance or the ability to pay damages; but these laws did not require the driver to purchase insurance before an accident occurred and they seldom worked to assure compensation. A few states added a provision for unsatisfied judgment funds, created by assessing an extra fee in licensing. These funds were used to help satisfy claims of injured victims when the defendant could not do so. This might secure a degree of compensation, not by putting responsibility upon negligent drivers but upon drivers as a class, "distributing" the costs of driving in much the way that products liability rules might "distribute" the cost of products to users. A third system simply permits drivers to buy their own insurance against the possibility of injury by uninsured, or underinsured, motorists.

In the last generation, most states have dealt with the uninsured motorist problem by mandating liability insurance for all vehicles. That has proved to be surprisingly ineffective because some drivers leave cars unregistered to avoid insurance, or purchase insurance to register, then cancel it. If you are injured by a negligent driver, chances are about one in five that he won't be insured even under compulsory insurance laws.

2. *Outside the tort system.* Uninsured motorists are not the only problem with the tort way of handling vehicle accidents. The time and expense of shifting loss through adjudication and the consequent premium cost for insurance also represent serious problems. Several kinds of insurance that do not require adjudication of fault are available to help protect against losses from injury. You can buy for yourself collision insurance (to pay for damages to your own car), accident insurance (to pay predetermined sums for specified injuries to yourself), or medical payment insurance (to pay limited sums for medical costs resulting to you or occupants of your car in a collision). These methods of covering costs of injury are limited, but they have some advantages. For instance, you yourself decide whether collision insurance is worth buying, how much coverage to buy, and what deductible to use. If you do buy such insurance, you can be assured that your car will be repaired whether or not you can prove that someone else was at fault, and you can handle the matter more or less expeditiously, without going to court. Could these advantages be generalized to supplant tort law for all cases of relatively small injuries, and thus to guarantee compensation without resort to the courts?

NOTE: NO-FAULT AUTO INSURANCE

No-fault auto insurance plans were first proposed by Robert Keeton and Jeffrey O'Connell in a now-classic book, BASIC PROTECTION FOR THE TRAFFIC VICTIM (1965). Their proposal contains several specific new ideas for reform. It envisions a two-tier system of injury law. Tort law is retained for larger claims, but smaller claims would be handled by insurance similar to medical and disability insurance. The insurer's liability is not based on fault, but on the fact of an auto injury. Yet it is not strict liability in the ordinary sense, because the injured victim merely claims against her own insurer for benefits. Benefits include only a percentage of wage loss and all medical expenses (with a cap) with nothing for pain and suffering. If injury is more serious, the victim may then move to the second tier and "re-enter" the tort system.

Principal features of the Keeton-O'Connell plan are as follows:

1. *Insurance is compulsory.* The no-fault insurance is compulsory. The person registering a car must show proof that such insurance covers the car for injury arising from ownership, maintenance or use.

2. *Insurance is "first-party."* The no-fault insurance covering the car provides, by the insurance contract, benefits for auto injury to driver and all occupants, and in addition, to any injured pedestrian. This contemplates that the injured person claims against her own insurer, not against another's insurer. Even the pedestrian is a kind of third party beneficiary of the insurance purchased by the owner of the car. In other words, the claim is like a claim for medical or disability insurance, not a liability insurance claim.

3. *Tort claims abolished.* In all small claims covered by no-fault, an injured person is deprived of the tort claim altogether and must rely exclusively on no-fault insurance (and any other added insurance that may cover the victim). Correlatively, even a negligent defendant is protected from liability as to these small claims.

4. *Re-entering the tort system.* If injury is severe, the victim will be permitted to sue in tort for injury not compensated by no-fault insurance. One could sue in tort if pain and suffering would exceed $5,000 or economic loss would exceed $10,000 (in 1965 dollars, remember). In such a case, the victim would first collect no-fault benefits and then sue in tort. If the damages exceeded these sums, the defendant would be liable, but liability would be reduced by $5,000 for pain and suffering and $10,000 for other damages. In other words, no-fault insurance superseded tort liability as to the first $10,000 of economic loss and the first $5,000 of pain and suffering.

Since there is potential tort liability for larger injuries, liability insurance is a part of the no-fault insurance package. But since that portion of the insurance is not responsible for the smaller injuries, the premium would be less in no-fault states.

5. *Benefits.* As with all no-fault laws, the Keeton-O'Connell benefits excluded all recoveries for pain and suffering. However, one could purchase added protection for greater benefits (at a higher premium). Added benefits could include coverage for pain and suffering. The limits on benefits might vary from state to state; the plan itself called for a maximum limit of $10,000 and also imposed a $100 work-loss deductible. Wage losses were also subject to a monthly maximum. Property damage was not covered at all.

The plan also adopted a coordination of benefits approach in many respects, in effect rejecting the collateral source rule. This was done by providing that all benefits received or receivable because of injury, from sources other than basic or added no-fault insurance, would be "subtractable." No subtraction would be made, however, for benefits from family members, life insurance, or inheritance.

All the existing no-fault plans follow the Keeton-O'Connell Plan by providing for periodic payments of benefits as the losses accrue. It is interesting to notice that periodic payment—rather than a lump sum payment—is characteristic also of workers' compensation, social security benefits and "structured settlements" of tort claims.

NEW YORK INSURANCE LAW

§ 5103. Entitlement to first party benefits; additional financial security required

(a) Every owner's policy of liability insurance [for automobiles and any other device intended to comply with the compulsory insurance requirements] shall also provide for . . . the payment of first party benefits to:

(1) Persons, other than occupants of another motor vehicle or a motorcycle, for loss arising out of the use or operation in this state of such motor vehicle. . . .

(2) The named insured and members of his household, other than occupants of a motorcycle, for loss arising out of the use or operation of (i) an uninsured motor vehicle or motorcycle, within the United States, its territories or possessions, or Canada; and (ii) an insured motor vehicle or motorcycle outside of this state and within the United States, its territories or possessions, or Canada. . . .

(4) The estate of any covered person, other than an occupant of another motor vehicle or a motorcycle, a death benefit in the amount of two thousand dollars for the death of such person arising out of the use or operation of such motor vehicle which is in addition to any first party benefits for basic economic loss.

(b) An insurer may exclude from coverage required by subsection (a) hereof a person who:

(1) Intentionally causes his own injury.

(2) Is injured as a result of operating a motor vehicle while in an intoxicated condition or while his ability to operate such vehicle is impaired by the use of a drug within the meaning of section eleven hundred ninety-two of the vehicle and traffic law.

(3) Is injured while he is: (i) committing an act which would constitute a felony, or seeking to avoid lawful apprehension or arrest by a law enforcement officer, or (ii) operating a motor vehicle in a race or speed test [or carrying out certain other acts].

NOTES

1. **"First party benefits."** "First party benefits" required by § 5103 "means payments to reimburse a person for basic economic loss on account of

personal injury arising out of the use or operation of a motor vehicle, less: (1) Twenty percent of lost earnings. . . . (2) Amounts recovered or recoverable on account of such injury under state or federal laws providing social security disability benefits, or workers' compensation benefits, [and certain other benefits]." § 5102(b).

2. **"Basic economic loss."** "Basic economic loss" for which the first party benefits are to compensate is capped at $50,000, but, subject to that cap, covers all necessary medical or "remedial" expenses, loss of earnings from work that the injured person otherwise would have performed, substitute services expense, and "all other reasonable and necessary expenses incurred, up to twenty-five dollars per day for not more than one year from the date of the accident causing the injury." § 5102(a).

NEW YORK INSURANCE LAW

§ 5104. Causes of action for personal injury

(a) Notwithstanding any other law, in any action by or on behalf of a covered person against another covered person for personal injuries arising out of negligence in the use or operation of a motor vehicle in this state, there shall be no right of recovery for non-economic loss, except in the case of a serious injury, or for basic economic loss. . . .

(b) In any action by or on behalf of a covered person, against a non-covered person, where damages for personal injuries arising out of the use or operation of a motor vehicle or a motorcycle may be recovered, an insurer which paid or is liable for first party benefits on account of such injuries has a lien against any recovery to the extent of benefits paid or payable by it to the covered person. . . .

NOTES

1. **Economic losses.** This section creates the tort exemption and sets the threshold for reentry into the tort system. There is no right of recovery for "non-economic loss" unless it is "serious," and no right of recovery for economic losses except so far as they exceed "basic economic loss." Thus the first $50,000 of economic loss must come from the no-fault or PIP benefits, not from the tort claim.

2. **Non-economic losses.** Non-economic loss such as pain and suffering is limited to cases involving "serious injury." Serious injury is defined in § 5102(d) to mean "a personal injury which results in death; dismemberment; significant disfigurement; a fracture; loss of a fetus; permanent loss of use of a body organ, member, function or system; permanent consequential limitation of use of a body organ or member; significant limitation of use of a body function or system; or a medically determined injury or impairment of a non-permanent nature which prevents the injured person from performing substantially all of

the material acts which constitute such person's usual and customary daily activities for not less than ninety days during the one hundred eighty days immediately following the occurrence of the injury or impairment."

Is this a better "threshold" than the dollar amount envisioned in the original Keeton-O'Connell proposal?

Statutes, of course, differ in many such details. It will be helpful, however, to apply the statute to a concrete case:

PROBLEM

In re Claims of Picklesimer, et al.

Since obtaining the basic facts (see p. 443), Mr. Picklesimer has furnished us the following information about damages to date:

> Dr. Doubs.. $1,250.00
>
> Murphey Med. Center $3,500.00

Dr. Doubs' bill does not include any charge for treatment following the complications. Mr. Picklesimer says that his medical insurance paid $2,800 of the hospital and doctor's bill. Dr. Doubs and our own consulting physician, Dr. Newton, say that there will be further treatments over Picklesimer's lifetime, probably calling for $7,500 in future medical expenses (for drugs, perhaps prosthetics, and for examination and treatment). They also say that he will have limited motion the rest of his life, though he is mobile.

Please give me a brief memo on the following problems:

(1)   Under the no-fault law, do we have any tort suit at all?

(2)   Are our no-fault claims likely to be prejudiced by claims of Patrick or Plangent? Specifically, might their claims use up the no-fault coverage?

NOTES

1.   **Below the threshold.** Should Picklesimer be permitted to sue the landowner, car manufacturer, medical defendants, and the state responsible for the road design, even if his damages do not reach the tort threshold? Suppose, for example, his pain and suffering is less than $5,000 and his total economic damages are less than $10,000.

2.   **Damage to land.** Could Dalzell claim against Picklesimer's policy for damage to his land if any was done?

3.   **More than one cause of harm.** If Picklesimer's injuries result partly from injury on Dalzell's land after the car came to a stop, and partly from medical negligence, are these injuries covered at all by no-fault? What phrase in the New York statute would be most relevant to resolution of this question? Is there any similar problem in tort law?

4. **PIP and tort recovery.** Suppose Picklesimer recovers several thousand dollars in PIP benefits under his no-fault policy and then recovers in tort from Dalzell, the state agency responsible for road design, the doctor, or the car manufacturer. Should he be compelled to share the tort recovery with his insurer, much as the injured worker must share the tort recovery with the workers' compensation insurer? Does § 5103 cover this situation?

5. **Reentering the tort system.** Legislatures have had difficulty in defining the cut-off point or the "threshold" for reentering the tort system. Keeton and O'Connell used pain and suffering as one of the doorways back into tort, and relatively high economic loss as the other. The New York statute does not use pain and suffering as such, but rather lists a number of injury qualities that might suggest pain. See the Notes following § 5104 above. Economic loss in excess of $50,000 is also a threshold. How serious a problem is this matter of defining the threshold?

LICARI V. ELLIOTT
441 N.E.2d 1088 (N.Y. 1982)

JASEN, JUDGE.

The issue raised on this appeal is whether the plaintiff in this negligence action brought to recover damages for personal injuries has established a prima facie case that he sustained a "serious injury" within the meaning of . . . the "No-Fault" Law.

On February 13, 1979, plaintiff was injured in a motor vehicle accident. After being examined at the hospital, plaintiff was diagnosed as having a concussion, acute cervical sprain, acute dorsal lumbar sprain and a contusion of the chest. He was released two hours later and went home. Later that day, plaintiff consulted his family physician and, after relating the events of the day, was told to rest in bed. On February 15, 1979, plaintiff again consulted his physician and complained that he was coughing up reddish phlegm. Concerned about possible rib damage, his physician had plaintiff admitted to the hospital for tests. The test results showed no rib damage and that plaintiff's lungs were clear. The hospital physician examined plaintiff upon his admission and testified at trial that plaintiff's lungs were clear, reflexes normal, and that he suffered only a "very mild limitation" of movement in the back and neck areas. No further medical testimony was elicited with respect to the extent of plaintiff's limitation of movement. On February 17, 1979, plaintiff stated that he felt better and requested his release from the hospital. He was discharged and returned home. On March 9, 1979, 24 days after the accident, plaintiff returned to his job as a taxi driver. Immediately upon returning to work, plaintiff resumed driving a taxicab 12 hours per day, 6 days a week, as he had prior to the accident. The only proof of limitation with respect to his work performance was plaintiff's own testimony that he was unable to help some of his fares with their luggage "if they happened to have luggage." Plaintiff also testified that he could not help his wife with various household chores as much as he had before the accident. Finally, plaintiff stated he had occasional transitory headaches and dizzy spells which were relieved by aspirin.

After the close of evidence, defendant moved to dismiss the complaint on the ground that plaintiff failed to establish that his injury met any of the threshold requirements of a serious injury. . . . The court reserved decision on the motion and submitted the case to the jury on the theories that, in order to recover, plaintiff had to establish, by a preponderance of the evidence, that he had suffered either a medically determined injury of a nonpermanent nature which prevented him from performing substantially all his daily activities for not less than 90 days during the 180 days immediately following the accident or that as a result of the accident he sustained a significant limitation of use of a body function or system. . . .

[The jury found for plaintiff on both grounds. The Appellate Division reversed, finding that plaintiff failed as a matter of law to prove "serious injury" under either definition.]

In construing the statutory definition of serious injury, it is necessary to examine the policies and purposes underlying this State's no-fault legislation. The so-called No-Fault Law was adopted by the Legislature to correct certain infirmities recognized to exist under the common-law tort system of compensating automobile accident claimants.

The Legislature provided that "there shall be no right of recovery for non-economic loss [i.e., pain and suffering] except in the case of a serious injury, or for basic economic loss." . . . Although the statute sets forth eight specific categories which constitute serious injury, we are only concerned on this appeal with construing two of them, to wit: whether the plaintiff suffered a serious injury which resulted in either (1) a "significant limitation of use of a body function or system"; or (2) "a medically determined injury or impairment of a nonpermanent nature" which endured for 90 days or more and substantially limited the performance of his daily activities. . . .

There can be little doubt that the purpose of enacting an objective verbal definition of serious injury was to "significantly reduce the number of automobile personal injury accident cases litigated in the courts, and thereby help contain the no-fault premium." "The verbal definition provided in the [legislation placed] a reasonable restriction and further limitation on the right to sue, in order to preserve the valuable benefits of no-fault, at an affordable cost." The Governor voiced his support of these policies when he signed the legislation into law. While it is clear that the Legislature intended to allow plaintiffs to recover for noneconomic injuries in appropriate cases, it had also intended that the court first determine whether or not a prima facie case of serious injury has been established which would permit a plaintiff to maintain a common-law cause of action in tort.

In light of this mandate, plaintiff's argument that the question of whether he suffered a serious injury is always a fact question for the jury is without merit. It is incumbent upon the court to decide in the first instance whether plaintiff has a cause of action to assert within the meaning of the statute. By enacting the No-Fault Law, the Legislature modified the common-law rights of persons injured in automobile accidents, to the extent that plaintiffs in automobile accident cases no longer have an unfettered right to sue for injuries sustained. Thus, to the extent that the Legislature has abrogated a cause of action, the issue is one for the court, in the first instance where it is properly raised, to determine whether the plaintiff has established a prima facie case of sustaining serious injury. Since the purpose of the No-Fault Law is to assure prompt and full compensation for economic loss by curtailing costly and time-consuming court trials requiring that every case, regardless of the extent of the injuries, be decided by a jury would subvert the intent of the Legislature and destroy the effectiveness of the statute. The result of requiring a jury trial where the injury is clearly a minor one would perpetuate a system of unnecessary litigation. . . . Thus, we believe the Legislature intended that the court should decide the threshold question of whether the evidence would warrant a jury finding that the injury falls within the class of injuries that, under no-fault, should be excluded from judicial remedy. If it can be said, as a matter of law, that plaintiff suffered no serious injury within the meaning of . . . the Insurance Law, then plaintiff has no claim to assert and there is nothing for the jury to decide.

. . . Since plaintiff was able to maintain his daily routine for most of each day after returning to work, it should be abundantly clear that plaintiff was not prevented from performing substantially all of his daily activities during anything close to 90 days following the occurrence of the injury. Thus, the Appellate Division correctly held, as a matter of law, that plaintiff did not meet the statutory standard of serious injury. . . .

It requires little discussion that plaintiff's subjective complaints of occasional, transitory headaches hardly fulfill the definition of serious injury. Plaintiff offered no proof that his headaches in any way incapacitated him or interfered with his ability to work or engage in activities at home. In fact, plaintiff testified that such headaches occurred only once every two or three weeks and were relieved by aspirin. . . .

To hold that this type of ailment constitutes a serious injury would render the statute meaningless and frustrate the legislative intent in enacting no-fault legislation.

As to plaintiff's contention that he suffered a "significant limitation of use of a body function or system," taken in its most favorable light, the evidence at trial established only that plaintiff suffered a painful sprain which limited the movement of his neck and back. Plaintiff offered no evidence as to the extent of the limitation of movement. . . .

Accordingly, the order of the Appellate Division should be affirmed, with costs.

NOTES

1.   **Proof.** What kind of proof is required to prove "serious injury" under the New York statute? In *Toure v. Avis Rent A Car Systems, Inc.*, 774 N.E.2d 1197 (N.Y. 2002), the court held that there must be "objective proof" by an expert—usually a medical expert, of course—and that "subjective complaints alone are not sufficient. Applying that rule to three consolidated cases, the court found that in two of them, the plaintiff had adduced sufficient proof, through doctors who testified to having performed various tests, including MRI's, to meet the "serious injury" threshold. In the third, however, where the plaintiff relied solely on her own testimony and that of her chiropractor, who did not indicate "what test, if any" he performed to ascertain the nature of her injuries, her proof was insufficient as a matter of law. Whether a claimant has proved "serious injury" will often be a contested issue of fact for a jury to decide. *See Perl v. Meher*, 960 N.E.2d 424 (N.Y. 2011). This may be especially true when, even in the face of objective medical proof of the injury itself, additional contributory factors interrupt the "chain of causation between the accident and claimed injury—such as a gap in treatment, an intervening medical problem or a preexisting condition." *Pommells v. Perez,* 830 N.E.2d 278 (N.Y. 2005).

2.   **Adoption of no-fault.** Existing no-fault plans in the United States are varied in detail. *See* Roger C. Henderson, *No-Fault Insurance for Automobile Accidents: Status and Effect in the United States*, 56 OR. L. REV. 287 (1977). About 15 states have enacted a no-fault system. Another ten permit the driver to buy extra no-fault insurance but these are added-cost systems. All of the statutes are so-called modified or "hybrid" rather than pure statutes—meaning that they envision no-fault only for one tier of accidents, not as a complete replacement of the tort system. A pure system would guarantee very high or unlimited payments for actual economic losses, and no access to the tort system at any time. In a few of those states, notably New York and Michigan, the caps on benefits are fairly high. No-fault in those states comes closer to a pure no-fault system.

3.   **A stalled movement?** No new state has adopted a no-fault system since 1976, and a handful of states that once adopted no-fault have repealed that legislation. Why this is so is a complex question. Perhaps the no-fault systems create unforeseen problems themselves, such as increased fatality rates. Perhaps promised insurance premium adjustments did not occur—although the reasons for that are also not entirely clear. One observer concludes that while all of these reasons may be valid, another may be even

more critical to no-fault's stagnation: "No-fault has become increasingly lawyer driven and adversarial," while "the tort system in the automobile context has become less litigious and has started to deliver broader yet shallower compensation." In other words, the two systems, the tort system and no-fault, "have become progressively more and more alike." Nora Freeman Engstrom, *An Alternative Explanation for No-Fault's "Demise,"* 61 DEPAUL L. REV. 303 (2012).

4. **No-fault outside the vehicle accident setting.** The no-fault idea has generated a second-generation of smaller no-fault plans with different mechanisms for other kinds of injury. We have seen one form in the Childhood Vaccine Injury Act, 42 U.S.C.A. §§ 300aa–1, providing limited but certain compensation in lieu of tort liability for injuries resulting from childhood immunization programs. For a comparison of several no-fault systems, *see* Robert L. Rabin, *The Renaissance of Accident Law Plans Revisited,* 64 MD. L. REV. 699 (2005).

5. **No-fault and deterrence.** Does a no-fault system deter bad behavior? Professor Gary Schwartz argued in *Auto No-fault and First-party Insurance: Advantages and Problems,* 73 S. CAL. L. REV. 611 (2000), that it has about the same deterrent effect as tort law, because if no-fault insurance premiums are left to the market, insurers will tend to raise premiums for bad no-fault drivers, and also for good drivers who are members of a dangerous group like teenagers. Uninsured drivers may have no assets to protect and may not be deterred under either system. J. David Cummins, Richard D. Phillips, & Mary A. Weiss, *The Incentive Effects of No-fault Automobile Insurance,* 44 J.L. & ECON. 427 (2001), presents an empirical study and concludes that no-fault weakens safety by weakening deterrence effects of tort law, but that, as Schwartz suggested, rating systems that increase insurance costs of bad drivers would restore some of the deterrence effect.

6. **Pure vs. hybrid no-fault.** Professor Schwartz also concluded that hybrid no-fault systems, though not losers, are definitely not winners. On the other hand, a pure no-fault systems—one that excludes tort law altogether— is a clear winner. Recall that this would eliminate all pain and suffering damages. On the other hand, it would take care of the most serious injuries as well as minor ones. And it would entail much more efficient use of premium dollars, returning as much as 93% of the premium dollar in compensation to the injured. What do you think? Would you favor pure over hybrid no-fault? Over the tort system?

7. **Pain.** If you think pain and suffering represents real loss for which, in justice, the defendant should compensate the plaintiff, it will be hard for you to approve a pure no-fault system. But there is evidence suggesting that awards may actually reinforce some kinds of pain. *See* Ellen Smith Pryor, *Compensation and the Ineradicable Problems of Pain,* 59 GEO. WASH. L. REV. 239 (1991). If it is true that awards not only don't help get over pain but actually encourage it, are you willing to eliminate all claims for pain?

CHAPTER 31

EVALUATING INJURY SYSTEMS: A DISCUSSION AGENDA

■ ■ ■

This book has explored many facets of tort law. In the last three chapters it has also looked at some prominent alternative systems for dealing with torts that cause physical harm. This chapter poses a few of the many questions that can promote evaluation of the different ways we as a society could deal with accidental injuries.

1. *Judicial process*

You might notice that some critics of tort law distrust the judicial system—judges, juries, and lawyers. Some of them, for example, believe that many fraudulent claims succeed in the "tort system"—meaning in courtrooms where judges and juries actually see and hear each claimant and defendant. What is your guess—that critics know that persons they've never seen are engaging in fraudulent conduct, while judges and juries somehow systematically miss this fact?

The question is important not because it deals with fraud, but because it deals with the judicial process. One salient characteristic of tort law and the judicial process generally is that each claim is judged on its own merits. Judges decide nothing about whether humans are generally fraudulent or whether plaintiffs lie more than defendants. Instead judges and juries look at the particular plaintiff and the particular defendant asserting claims and defenses about their individual facts. Neither is a token in a board game or an icon who stands for a group. To the extent that rules of law eliminate individual characteristics and particular facts from consideration this essential idea of justice is lost.

How do you think alternative systems stack up in this regard? Are any important individual facts—fault or extent of injury, for example—discarded under workers' compensation, social security disability, or no-fault? If so is that good or bad?

2. *Personal accountability and social responsibility—fairness or justice*

If personal responsibility for wrongs done is an ideal, does tort law actually enforce that accountability? If so, is something lost in moving to workers' compensation, social security, or no-fault? If not, should we rate the systems as equal on this score?

3. *Safety and deterrence*

(a) Some risks are desirable, otherwise nothing is accomplished; but too many risks are not. Does tort law promote optimal risk-taking? Does it appropriately deter undesirable risks? Indeed, does it deter any conduct at all? If your answer is that tort law (perhaps along with cultural constraints) does provide some deterrence, would that be lost in any of the other systems considered here?

(b) Even if, by and large, tort theories do not encourage safety in most instances, might some other injury systems have an adverse effect on safety? In a no-fault system, could that depend in part on whether the driver's no-fault insurance premiums are raised when he shows a propensity for numerous accidents?

(c) Before making a final decision, consider whether non-tort systems might have some non-obvious deterrence or safety effects. Maybe workers' compensation insurers inspect factories and encourage safer practices. Maybe no-fault insurers would reduce premiums for insureds who have airbags or other safety devices. Could such devices actually create better conditions for safety? If so, would that judgment apply only to vehicle accidents or would it apply equally to, say, toxic tort cases or medical malpractice cases?

4. *Costs*

Pure (not hybrid) no-fault might lead to a highly efficient use of the premium dollar—returning 90% or more in benefits, compared to something around 50% return of the liability insurance dollar. What is the trade-off for this great efficiency? Is it worth it? What do you think about the probable cost comparisons of a welfare system for injury modeled on social security disability or workers' compensation? Should we as a society seek to get highly reliable data?

5. *Delay in payment*

One criticism of the courts is that they can take a very long time to produce a decision. Due process is expensive and perhaps not every dispute should be subjected to its rigors. An early study indicated that under Massachusetts' no-fault system, medical expenses were paid in about seven days from the time the insurer received the necessary documentation. Will concerns about medical expenses lessen if more people are covered?

6. *The most important questions*

Questions about fairness, efficiency and deterrence are endless. We believe that the most important questions readers should ask are those that trouble them most. What do you see as the most important issues today about injury law?

PART 11

ECONOMIC AND DIGNITARY TORTS

■ ■ ■

CHAPTER 32

COMMUNICATION OF PERSONALLY HARMFUL IMPRESSIONS TO OTHERS

■ ■ ■

§ 1. DEFAMATION—LIBEL AND SLANDER

A. THE COMMON LAW RULES

PENSACOLA MOTOR SALES, INC. v. DAPHNE AUTOMOTIVE, LLC, 155 So.3d 930 (Ala. 2013). Shawn Esfahani, a United States citizen who was born in Iran, opened Daphne Automotive, LLC, d/b/a Eastern Shore Toyota ("EST"), an automobile dealership selling Toyota vehicles. EST is a direct competitor of another Toyota dealership, Pensacola Motor Sales, Inc., d/b/a Bob Tyler Toyota ("BTT"). In an apparent effort to discourage potential customers from purchasing from EST, BTT's salespeople regularly referred to EST as "Taliban Toyota" and told customers who indicated an interest in buying a vehicle from EST that Esfahani and EST were "terrorists," "support the Taliban," and "are actively involved in promoting attacks against the United States and its citizens." As a result of the alleged slanderous remarks by defendant BTT and its agents, Esfahani and EST alleged that they had been "deprived of public confidence" and that their "business reputation has been damaged and the business has lost profits and has otherwise been devalued." A jury found for Esfahani and EST against both BTT and its sales manager and awarded $7.5 million in compensatory and punitive damages.

Held, affirmed. "[W]hen a defamatory statement is slanderous per se, the law infers injury to reputation and the plaintiff is relieved of the requirement of proving actual harm to reputation or any other damage.". . . [G]eneral damages that are presumed to flow from defamation per se include the loss or impairment of reputation and/or standing in the community *and* mental anguish or suffering. The Plaintiff need not prove any mental anguish since it is assumed to flow from the very nature of the defamatory words spoken in a per se case. In light of the applicable standard. . . . Esfahani need not have presented evidence of either damage to his reputation or mental anguish, because both were presumed. Regardless, . . . Esfahani *did* present evidence establishing the fear and worry—for his safety and the safety of his business and his family—that he had experienced after being repeatedly linked to terrorist activity. He further explained the political persecution that led him to leave

Iran and come to the United States as a teenage refugee and the resulting horror he felt on being accused of both funding terrorism and of being an enemy of the country he loves and is proud to call 'home.' [We also agree with the trial court that] BTT's and the sales manager's slanderous attacks on Esfahani's and EST's reputations are deserving of Alabama law's 'most severe condemnation, its highest blameworthiness and its most deserving culpability' . . . and [that the award would] 'serve the dual purposes of (a) making clear that [BTT's and the manager's] conduct was especially reprehensible, and (b) discouraging or deterring [BTT and the manager] and others from conducting themselves similarly in the future.' "

STANTON V. METRO CORP., 438 F.3d 119 (1st Cir. 2006). The teenaged plaintiff's photograph appeared in *Boston* magazine, a monthly general-interest publication, accompanying an article about teenage sexual promiscuity in Massachusetts. The cover refers to the article with the phrase, "Fast Times at Silver Lake High: Teen Sex in the Suburbs." Inside, the plaintiff is one of five teenagers pictured. The photo was taken at a high school dance. Three of the students are smoking cigarettes, but plaintiff is simply looking at the camera, smiling slightly. A "superhead" reads, "They hook up on line. They hook up in real life. . . ." The article describes the frequent, casual and drunken sexual encounters of several teenagers, quoting many by their first names. Small type at the bottom of the first page says that the photographs in the article were taken as part of a "five-year project on teen sexuality," and that "the individuals pictured are unrelated to people or events described in this story." Plaintiff, who lives in New Hampshire, sued the magazine's publisher for defamation. The trial court dismissed the complaint. *Held*, reversed. A reasonable jury could find the publication defamatory, meaning that it had a reasonable tendency to injure her reputation, and could also find that she was one of the teenagers described in the story. There need not be any express connection between the article and the photo to make the communication defamatory. Nor is the disclaimer determinative, because it could be ignored or missed by a reasonable reader. Her complaint also sufficiently alleges that the defendant published the article with negligent disregard for the truth.

NOTES

1. **Common law requirements.** The common law defamation action had three basic elements: 1) defendant's publication to a third person, 2) of defamatory material, 3) of and concerning the plaintiff. Can you see how the statements at issue in *Pensacola Motor Sales* and in *Stanton* would satisfy these elements?

2. **Common law presumptions.** At common law, once the plaintiff proved that the defendant had published defamatory material about the

plaintiff, the law inflicted three presumptions on the defendant. First, the publication was presumed false, so the defendant had the burden of proving truth as an affirmative defense. Second, the publication was presumed to cause damages, so the plaintiff never had to prove any actual loss of reputation, much less pecuniary losses. Third, the publication was presumed to be malicious, so the plaintiff never had to prove fault. Courts still accept these presumptions in a number of cases. *See Bierman v. Weier*, 826 N.W.2d 436 (Iowa 2013) ("The United States Supreme Court has never invalidated the common law libel presumptions as they now apply in Iowa—to private plaintiff/private concern cases against nonmedia defendants.").

3. **Common law evolution.** The common law rarely remains static, and the rules on defamation are no exception. Nowadays, most courts have modified one or more of the common law elements, with the result that the plaintiff may be required to prove additional elements such as falsity, fault, damages, lack of privilege, or some combination of these. *Smith v. Anonymous Joint Enter.*, 793 N.W.2d 533 (Mich. 2010).The Rhode Island Supreme Court's formulation is a common iteration of the elements required in many jurisdictions: "To prevail in a defamation action, a plaintiff must prove: (a) *a false* and defamatory statement concerning another; (b) an *unprivileged* publication to a third party; (c) *fault* amounting at least to negligence on the part of the publisher; and (d) *damages*, unless the statement is actionable irrespective of special harm." *Ferreira v. Child & Family Servs.*, 222 A.3d 69 (R.I. 2019) (emphasis added). Would these additional elements seem to be met in *Pensacola Motor Sales* and *Stanton*? Attention to the rules of the particular jurisdiction and the constitutional dimensions of the case are critical to determining which additional elements might apply and require proof by the plaintiff.

4. **Publication.** "Publication" is a term of art, and does not necessarily mean a media publication. Any communication to a third person is sufficient. Defendant tells his neighbor that the minister at the church is having an affair. This is a publication of the kind called slander, since it is oral. Or defendant writes his cousin that a city council member has taken a bribe. This is also a publication, and since it is in writing it is called libel.

5. **Repeaters as publishers.** A newspaper publishes a libel about the plaintiff. Readers and other newspapers report what the newspaper said, correctly attributing the defamation to the first newspaper. Under the rule that repeaters are publishers, they are also subject to liability unless they have a privilege.

6. **Reference to the plaintiff.** The defendant's publication is not actionable for defamation of the plaintiff unless people can reasonably take it as referring to the plaintiff. As *Stanton* indicates, this rule did not and does not require reference to the plaintiff by name, if in fact some readers would reasonably understand that the plaintiff was referred to. The readers' reasonable understanding, not necessarily intent of the author, controls. Thus, reasonable inferences from the published material, or even from outside facts,

might lead a reader to believe the defamatory material refers to the plaintiff. *Cf. Doe v. Hagar*, 765 F.3d 855 (8th Cir. 2014) (genuine issue of material fact as to whether statements in musician Sammy Hagar's autobiography were of and concerning plaintiff). If a magazine article viewed by over 2 million people alleges that a brutal gang rape took place at a fraternity house of 53 members, do all of the members have a defamation claim? *See Elias v. Rolling Stone LLC*, 872 F.3d 97 (2d Cir. 2017).

7. **Defamatory meaning.** Publications are actionable as defamation only if they carry some negative implication, something that makes the publication "defamatory." A publication that engenders "hatred, ridicule or contempt" for the plaintiff would qualify, but so would publications that merely lower esteem for the plaintiff among some substantial segment of the community. *See Levesque v. Doocy*, 560 F.3d 82 (1st Cir. 2009) (a communication is defamatory when it exposes plaintiff to ridicule tinged with contempt); *Schaecher v. Bouffault*, 772 S.E.2d 589 (Va. 2015) ("Reputation must be affected to a magnitude sufficient to render one odious, infamous, or ridiculous, or subject to disgrace, shame, scorn, or contempt.").

Defamation actions have been permitted to proceed in a range of cases. *See Green v. Cosby*, 138 F.Supp.3d 114 (D. Mass. 2015) (denying defendant's motion to dismiss: public statements that alleged sexual assault victim was lying about her accusations could be found to be defamatory); *Cashion v. Smith*, 749 S.E.2d 526 (Va. 2013) (statements made by trauma surgeon following death of patient that anesthesiologist could have saved him if he tried and that he effectively euthanized the patient are actionable as defamation).

Mere name-calling is not enough. "He's a jerk" with nothing more is not actionable. *Cf. Steinhausen v. HomeServices of Nebraska, Inc.*, 857 N.W.2d 816 (Neb. 2015) (statements in email that plaintiff was a "total idiot" were not actionable; statement was "hyperbolic rhetoric rather than a reference to arrested intellectual development"); *Hogan v. Winder*, 762 F.3d 1096 (10th Cir. 2014) (not defamatory to say that contractor was terminated for "performance issues," or that he exhibited "erratic behavior," or that he had been "accused of extortion"). The defamatory quality of a publication is a core issue in many cases. *See, e.g., Damon v. Moore*, 520 F.3d 98 (1st Cir. 2008) (army reservist's non-consensual placement in Michael Moore's anti-war documentary Fahrenheit 9–11 could not reasonably be viewed as "discrediting the reservist in the minds of any considerable and respectable class of the community to which the statement was addressed"); *Pippen v. NBCUniversal Media, LLC,* 734 F.3d 610 (7th Cir. 2013) (statements in news reports that former NBA star Scottie Pippen was personally bankrupt did not constitute defamation per se under Illinois law).

8. **Judge and jury.** Defamatory meaning is generally a jury question, but where reasonable people could not interpret a publication as defamatory, the judge will properly find against the plaintiff. *See, e.g., Knievel v. ESPN*, 393 F.3d 1068 (9th Cir. 2005) (caption under photo of sports celebrity and his wife on defendant's website that said, "Evel Knievel proves that you're never

too old to be a pimp," could not be construed by a reasonable person to mean that Knievel was a pimp and that his wife was a prostitute, given that the tone of the entire website was "lighthearted and jocular").

9. **Damages.** In many cases, including all cases of libel, the traditional common law presumed that the plaintiff suffered damages. This meant that in most cases the plaintiff could recover without proving any actual losses at all. Recovery might be augmented by proof of pecuniary loss, as where the plaintiff lost a job because of the libel. But the derogatory words would be sufficient to warrant a recovery. The damages thus recovered were not merely nominal but were quite substantial. Under the rule, which can still govern some kinds of cases today, juries can presume that a defamatory publication has caused harm to reputation and then award substantial sums of money even in the absence of evidence as to any particular amount of damages. Is *Pensacola Motor Sales* like this? Even though the court did not require Esfahani to prove damages, Esfahani testified to his own losses and retained an expert to estimate business losses. Why do you think Esfahani's attorney presented evidence of damage in the case even though that evidence was not required? Would you submit this proof in a case in the same jurisdiction even after the *Pensacola Motor Sales* ruling?

10. **Libel and slander.** The traditional common law carefully distinguished libel from slander and made different rules of damages for the two forms of defamation. Libel was originally thought of as written material; slander as oral. Television, movies, and electronic publication have put the libel/slander categories in doubt. However, it is a good guess that media publications will all be treated as libel if the distinction continues to matter, though there may be close cases, such as the use of a loudspeaker system without broadcast or recording. Most communications by computer are no doubt in the category of libel. *Too Much Media, LLC v. Hale*, 993 A.2d 845 (N.J. Super. Ct. App. Div. 2010). What would be the applicable torts in *Pensacola Motor Sales*? In *Stanton*?

11. **Slander per se.** The common law traditionally treated virtually all libel as libel per se, meaning that damages would be presumed. Slander, however, required that the plaintiff prove pecuniary loss, meaning the loss of money or money's worth. This might happen, for example, if the plaintiff were to lose her job because of slanderous statements. Three or four kinds of slander, however, were regarded as being especially serious and to warrant a presumption of damages. In such cases it was said that the slander was per se and it was not necessary for the plaintiff to prove pecuniary loss to sustain a claim. Damages were presumed if the publication imputed that the plaintiff (1) had committed a serious crime; (2) had a loathsome disease, historically leprosy and venereal diseases; (3) had traits or had engaged in conduct incompatible with plaintiff's business, trade or profession, such as saying of a minister that she is drunk while off-duty; or (4) had engaged in serious sexual misconduct. *See Greene v. Tinker*, 332 P.3d 21 (Alaska 2014) (patient's complaint to health clinic operator about the clinic employee's alleged breach of medical confidentiality was defamatory per se because the conduct alleged

by the defendant would adversely affect the plaintiff's fitness to be employed at a medical clinic; upholding verdict for plaintiff). Which slander per se category seems most applicable to *Pensacola Motor Sales*?

12. **Truth or falsity.** If defamatory content was shown, the traditional common law approach was to presume that the statement was untrue. This left the defendant with the entire burden of proving the truth of the statements made. In many situations in many states, the burden of proof on "truth" now rests with the plaintiff, as we will see in subpart B below.

Courts do not focus exclusively on the literal truth or falsity of a statement, but rather on its gist or sting. An inaccurate statement may be substantially true. What if a pro-life advocacy organization's political billboard says that a United States representative who had voted for Affordable Care Act (ACA) had "voted for taxpayer funding of abortion"? *Susan B. Anthony List v. Driehaus*, 779 F.3d 628 (6th Cir. 2015) (not a "false statement" for purposes of defamation; the gist or sting of the statement appeared to have at least some truth or to be subject to differing interpretations). What if a reporter describes exploding rifle targets as basically "a bomb"? *Tannerite Sports, LLC v. NBCUniversal News Grp.*, 864 F.3d 236 (2d Cir. 2017).

The Unites States Supreme Court said that a "materially false statement" is one that would "have a different effect on the mind of the reader or listener from that which the truth would have produced." *Air Wisconsin Airlines Corp. v. Hoeper*, 571 U.S. 237 (2014), In *Air Wisconsin*, an airline's statements to the TSA that the pilot "may be armed," "was terminated today" and that the airline was "concerned about his mental stability" were not materially false, as a matter of law. The "gist" of all statements was accurate.

NOTE: COMMON-LAW PRIVILEGES

1. *Judge-made privileges.* Under the traditional common law rules a publisher might be held in damages not only in cases in which he was not at fault but also in cases in which what he published was strictly accurate. To mitigate this, courts developed a series of privileges—affirmative defenses that could in special cases provide protection, provided the defendant was able to shoulder the burden of proving them. Most of these privileges remain in place today, at least where not displaced by constitutional rules described below in subpart B. The chief privileges include:

A. *Official privileges.* (1) *The litigation privilege.* Judges, lawyers, and witnesses enjoy an absolute privilege to defame when they communicate in the course of and in relation to the subject matter of litigation. *See, e.g., Mahoney & Hagberg v. Newgard*, 729 N.W.2d 302 (Minn. 2007); *Shell Oil Co. v. Writt*, 464 S.W.3d 650 (Tex. 2015) (statements company made in report to Department of Justice regarding possibly criminal activity by contractor were absolutely privileged because they were made preliminarily to a proposed judicial proceeding). This privilege has been expanded to encompass adversary work before administrative agencies and other quasi-judicial adjudicative bodies. *See, e.g., Rosenberg v. MetLife, Inc.*, 866 N.E.2d 439 (N.Y. 2007) (privilege applied to termination notice filed with national stock exchange). The absolute privilege to defame in connection with judicial or quasi-judicial proceedings has been extended to attorney disciplinary proceedings, *see Morgan & Pottinger, Attorneys, P.S.C. v. Botts*, 348 S.W.3d 599 (Ky. 2011), and to protect lawyers who made defamatory statements to a newspaper reporter and gave the reporter a copy of a complaint filed in a case, *see Norman v. Borison*, 17 A.3d 697 (Md. 2011). In *Clark County School Dist. v. Virtual Education Software, Inc.*, 213 P.3d 496 (Nev. 2009), the court held that the absolute litigation privilege extends to a non-lawyer's allegedly defamatory communication in response to threatened litigation. It also can protect witnesses. *Harrison v. Roitman*, 362 P.3d 1138 (Nev. 2015) (in case extending judicial privilege to expert witness in divorce case, deciding whether an absolute privilege protects a defendant should be decided by answering three questions: (1) did the person seeking immunity perform functions sufficiently comparable to those of persons who have traditionally been granted such an immunity; (2) is the likelihood of harassment or intimidation by personal liability sufficiently great to interfere with the person's performance of his or her duties; and (3) do procedural safeguards exist in the system that would adequately protect against illegitimate conduct by the person seeking immunity).

There are limits to the absolute privilege's sweep, however. It does not bar an action for malicious prosecution. *See, e.g., McKinney v. Okoye*, 806 N.W.2d 571 (Neb. 2011). It will also not protect a defendant from liability on a tort claim that arises independently from anything said in connection with judicial proceedings. *See Berman v. Laboratory Corp. of America*, 268 P.3d 68 (Okla. 2011) (absolute privilege did not bar the plaintiff's negligence claim alleging the defendant laboratory had a duty to perform accurate DNA testing for purposes of determining the paternity of the plaintiff's child in an administrative paternity proceeding); *Schanne v. Addis*, 121 A.3d 942 (Pa. 2015) (judicial privilege inapplicable when allegedly defamatory statement made without any intent to initiate judicial proceedings). And as with all qualified privileges, it is lost on a showing of actual malice or excessive publication. Whether this absolute privilege is really necessary to assure vigorous and unfettered advocacy is debatable. *See* Paul T. Hayden, *Reconsidering the Litigator's Absolute Privilege to Defame*, 54 OHIO ST. L. J. 985 (1993); *cf. McKinney, supra* ("absolute privilege does not bar an action for malicious prosecution," because "there is a kind of qualified immunity built into the elements of the tort").

(2) *Legislative privilege.* Federal legislators are given an absolute privilege to utter defamatory statements in the course of their official duties by the U.S. Constitution, Art. I, § 6. State and local legislators usually enjoy a similar privilege.

(3) *Executive privilege.* Executive officers have mostly enjoyed only a qualified privilege, one destroyed if there is actual malice, although there are still some cases in which federal executives still enjoy an absolute privilege as to utterances in the scope of their duties.

B. *The privilege to communicate in one's own interest, the interest of third persons, or in common interest of publisher and recipient.* These vaguely worded privileges permit defendants in some cases to indulge in self-defense ("I didn't do it, he did"), protection of loved ones ("Don't trust him, daughter, he's no good") and sharing of important information within a group ("Our minister is having an affair with the church secretary"). This privilege often applies to protect an employer who sends a negative reference letter to an employee's prospective new employer. *See, e.g., Miron v. University of New Haven Police Dep't*, 931 A.2d 847 (Conn. 2007); *Toler v. Sud-Chermie, Inc.*, 458 S.W.3d 276 (Ky. 2015) (absent evidence of malice by employer, an employer's qualified immunity defeats employee's allegation of defamation). The privilege is destroyed if abused, as where the speaker has an improper purpose or malice, or publishes excessively.

C. *The privilege to report information pertaining to crime or the like to appropriate officers. Cucinotta v. Deloitte Touch, LLP*, 302 P.3d 1099 (Nev. 2013) (absolute privilege protected accounting firm's communications with corporation's audit committee regarding alleged illegal activities by corporate officers; SEC Act required firm to report illegal activity to the appropriate level of corporate management); *Thomas v. Sumner*, 341 P.3d 390 (Wyo. 2015) (child's mother and investigating social worker made comments plaintiff alleged were defamatory; social worker protected by immunity and mother's comments were true or not made in bad faith, and therefore, not defaming). Again, the privilege may be lost if there is malice and perhaps if there is negligence. *See, e.g., Gallo v. Barile*, 935 A.2d 103 (Conn. 2007) (witnesses who made false statements to police lost qualified privilege).

D. *The privilege to report a public document, meeting or activity.* Example: a report of a trial. This privilege is lost only if the report is biased or inaccurate.

E. *Fair comment.* A person is privileged to comment about accurately stated facts concerning some matter of public concern, including political, social, and artistic matters. This is limited to comment about facts that are accurately stated. Comment without statement of facts (and an accurate statement at that) is not protected.

2. *Statutory privileges or immunities.* Statutes may create additional privileges. The advent of the internet has made it possible for almost anyone to post defamatory material on web bulletin boards, in chat rooms, or other sites controlled by a provider. Is the internet provider liable for defamation for failing to remove or prohibit a defamatory message posted by others? A federal statute, the Communications Decency Act, 47 U.S.C.A. § 230(c)(1), gives internet providers or message board operators immunity from liability for allegedly defamatory postings made by third party subscribers. *See, e.g., Universal Communication Systems, Inc. v. Lycos, Inc.*, 478 F.3d 413 (1st Cir. 2007); *Zeran v. America Online, Inc.*, 129 F.3d 327, 333 (4th Cir. 1997); *Jones v. Dirty World Entertainment Recordings LLC*, 755 F.3d 398 (6th Cir. 2014) (holding defendant immune under CDA); *Klayman v. Zuckerberg*, 753 F.3d 1354 (D.C. Cir. 2014) (same). The Act does not appear to protect the person who actually posts a defamatory message on an internet site or sends a defamatory email. *Cf. Too Much Media, LLC v. Hale*, 20 A.3d 364 (N.J. 2011) (without citing the CDA, holding that the state Shield Law which creates a newsperson's privilege does not protect people who post defamatory comments on internet message boards). Also, the CDA was held not to bar a claim by a model against the operator of a social networking site for its negligent failure to warn that rapists were using the website to lure models to fake auditions, where they would be drugged and attacked; the CDA does not declare a general immunity from liability deriving from third-party content. *See Doe No. 14 v. Internet Brands, Inc.*, 824 F.3d 846 (9th Cir. 2016).

REFERENCES: 3 DOBBS, HAYDEN & BUBLICK, THE LAW OF TORTS §§ 519–51 (2d ed. 2011); DOBBS, HAYDEN & BUBLICK, HORNBOOK ON TORTS, ch. 37 (2d ed. 2016); ELLEN BUBLICK, JANE BAMBAUER & DANIEL ARELLANO, DOBBS ON ECONOMIC AND DIGNITARY TORTS: CASES AND MATERIALS, chs. 1 & 2 (2d ed. 2022).

B. THE CONSTITUTIONAL CONSTRAINTS OF FREE SPEECH

NEW YORK TIMES CO. V. SULLIVAN
376 U.S. 254 (1964)

[The New York Times published an advertisement signed by a committee of distinguished persons and asking for donations to help defend Dr. Martin Luther King, Jr. in a perjury indictment against him and for other civil purposes. It said that efforts to enforce civil rights had been met with a "wave of terror," and that "Southern violators" had "bombed his home," and had "arrested him seven times" on various charges. The advertisement referred to the police "ringing" the campus at Alabama State College, and said that "authorities" had padlocked the campus dining hall in an effort to starve the student body into submission.]

[The plaintiff in this case is L.B. Sullivan, elected Commissioner of the City of Montgomery, Alabama. In that capacity he is in charge of the Police Department. He was not named in the advertisement, but he contends that references to the police must be read as implicating him; and similarly that references to "arrests" must be read as accusing him of intimidation and violence. The trial judge charged the jury that the statements were libelous per se, that falsity, malice and damages were presumed. The jury awarded $500,000 and the Supreme Court of Alabama affirmed.]

BRENNAN, J. delivered the opinion of the Court. . . .

We reverse the judgment. We hold that the rule of law applied by the Alabama courts is constitutionally deficient for failure to provide the safeguards for freedom of speech and of the press that are required by the First and Fourteenth Amendments in a libel action brought by a public official against critics of his official conduct. We further hold that under the proper safeguards the evidence presented in this case is constitutionally insufficient to support the judgment for respondent. . . .

Under Alabama law as applied in this case, a publication is "libelous per se" if the words "tend to injure a person in his reputation" or to "bring [him] into public contempt"; the trial court stated that the standard was met if the words are such as to "injure him in his public office, or impute misconduct to him in his office, or want of official integrity, or want of fidelity to a public trust." The jury must find that the words were published "of and concerning" the plaintiff, but where the plaintiff is a public official his place in the governmental hierarchy is sufficient evidence to support a finding that his reputation has been affected by statements that reflect upon the agency of which he is in charge. Once "libel per se" has been established, the defendant has no defense as to stated facts unless he can persuade the jury that they were true in all their particulars.

His privilege of "fair comment" for expressions of opinion depends on the truth of the facts upon which the comment is based. Unless he can discharge the burden of proving truth, general damages are presumed, and may be awarded without proof of pecuniary injury. . . .

The general proposition that freedom of expression upon public questions is secured by the First Amendment has long been settled by our decisions. The constitutional safeguard, we have said, "was fashioned to assure unfettered interchange of ideas for the bringing about of political and social changes desired by the people."

> "The maintenance of the opportunity for free political discussion to the end that government may be responsive to the will of the people and that changes may be obtained by lawful means, an opportunity essential to the security of the Republic, is a fundamental principle of our constitutional system." "[I]t is a prized American privilege to speak one's mind, although not

always with perfect good taste, on all public institutions," and this opportunity is to be afforded for "vigorous advocacy" no less than "abstract discussion."

The First Amendment, said Judge Learned Hand, "presupposes that right conclusions are more likely to be gathered out of a multitude of tongues, than through any kind of authoritative selection. To many this is, and always will be, folly; but we have staked upon it our all."

Mr. Justice Brandeis, in his concurring opinion in Whitney v. California, 274 U.S. 357, 375–376, 47 S.Ct. 641, 648, 71 L.Ed. 1095, gave the principle its classic formulation:

> Those who won our independence believed . . . that public discussion is a political duty; and that this should be a fundamental principle of the American government. They recognized the risks to which all human institutions are subject. But they knew that order cannot be secured merely through fear of punishment for its infraction; that it is hazardous to discourage thought, hope and imagination; that fear breeds repression; that repression breeds hate; that hate menaces stable government; that the path of safety lies in the opportunity to discuss freely supposed grievances and proposed remedies; and that the fitting remedy for evil counsels is good ones. Believing in the power of reason as applied through public discussion, they eschewed silence coerced by law—the argument of force in its worst form. Recognizing the occasional tyrannies of governing majorities, they amended the Constitution so that free speech and assembly should be guaranteed.

Thus we consider this case against the background of a profound national commitment to the principle that debate on public issues should be uninhibited, robust, and wide-open, and that it may well include vehement, caustic, and sometimes unpleasantly sharp attacks on government and public officials.

The present advertisement, as an expression of grievance and protest on one of the major public issues of our time, would seem clearly to qualify for the constitutional protection. The question is whether it forfeits that protection by the falsity of some of its factual statements and by its alleged defamation of respondent.

Authoritative interpretations of the First Amendment guarantees have consistently refused to recognize an exception for any test of truth—whether administered by judges, juries, or administrative officials—and especially one that puts the burden of proving truth on the speaker. . . . That erroneous statement is inevitable in free debate, and that it must be protected if the freedoms of expression are to have the "breathing space" that they "need . . . to survive," was also recognized by the Court of Appeals for the District of Columbia Circuit in Sweeney v. Patterson. . . .

If neither factual error nor defamatory content suffices to remove the constitutional shield from criticism of official conduct, the combination of the two elements is no less inadequate. This is the lesson to be drawn from the great controversy over the Sedition Act of 1798. . . . [The Sedition Act made it a crime to publish "false, scandalous and malicious writing" against the government or its main officers. The Act was attacked by many of the Founders and eventually repealed on a consensus that it was inconsistent with the First Amendment.]

What a State may not constitutionally bring about by means of a criminal statute is likewise beyond the reach of its civil law of libel. The fear of damage awards under a rule such as that invoked by the Alabama courts here may be markedly more inhibiting than the fear of prosecution under a criminal statute. . . .

The state rule of law is not saved by its allowance of the defense of truth. A defense for erroneous statements honestly made is no less essential here than was the requirement of proof of guilty knowledge which, in Smith v. California, 361 U.S. 147, 80 S.Ct. 215, 4 L.Ed.2d 205, we held indispensable to a valid conviction of a bookseller for possessing obscene writings for sale. . . . A rule compelling the critic of official conduct to guarantee the truth of all his factual assertions—and to do so on pain of libel judgments virtually unlimited in amount—leads to a comparable "self-censorship." Allowance of the defense of truth, with the burden of proving it on the defendant, does not mean that only false speech will be deterred. . . . Under such a rule, would-be critics of official conduct may be deterred from voicing their criticism, even though it is believed to be true and even though it is in fact true, because of doubt whether it can be proved in court or fear of the expense of having to do so. They tend to make only statements which "steer far wider of the unlawful zone." The rule thus dampens the vigor and limits the variety of public debate. It is inconsistent with the First and Fourteenth Amendments. The constitutional guarantees require, we think, a federal rule that prohibits a public official from recovering damages for a defamatory falsehood relating to his official conduct unless he proves that the statement was made with "actual malice"—that is, with knowledge that it was false or with reckless disregard of whether it was false or not. . . . Since respondent may seek a new trial, we deem that considerations of effective judicial administration require us to review the evidence in the present record to determine whether it could constitutionally support a judgment for respondent. This Court's duty is not limited to the elaboration of constitutional principles; we must also in proper cases review the evidence to make certain that those principles have been constitutionally applied. . . .

[W]e consider that the proof presented to show actual malice lacks the *Has no Proof of malice* convincing clarity which the constitutional standard demands, and hence that it would not constitutionally sustain the judgment for respondent under the proper rule of law. . . .

[We reject the argument that "actual malice" can be found because the Times did not retract and because it did not check the accuracy against news stories in its own files. The imputed knowledge from its own files was not sufficient to show an actual state of mind necessary to support a finding of knowing or reckless falsehood. The evidence is also constitutionally deficient because the criticisms did not clearly refer to the plaintiff. This is too much like permitting an action for criticism of the government itself.]

[JUSTICES BLACK and DOUGLAS and GOLDBERG, in two concurring opinions, argued for an absolute right to speak, with no liability even for knowing falsehoods.]

NOTES

1. **Public officials and public figures.** The rules in *Times v. Sullivan* originally applied only to public officials, either appointed or elected. In 1967, a much-divided Court extended the same rules to cover "public figures," who were neither candidates for office nor actual public employees. *Curtis Publ'g Co. v. Butts*, 388 U.S. 130 (1967). One rationale for this extension was that many private citizens have a key role in influencing social policy and in "ordering society." The rules apply to protect both public and private comments on matters of public concern. *See Lippincott v. Whisenhunt*, 462 S.W.3d 507 (Tex. 2015) (court reversed the appeals court's interpretation that given its purpose, the statute protects only "public communications," holding that the statute protects both private and public communications as long as they are "made in connection with a matter of public concern").

2. **Actual malice.** In protecting publications about public officials (and later public figures), the *Times v. Sullivan* Court drew on familiar words in holding that "actual malice" was required as a condition of liability, but the words proved confusing in the end because the court was not referring to spite or ill-will. Instead, the plaintiff must prove that the defendant knew the publication was false or, just short of this, that the defendant published "recklessly." It is now established that recklessness in this sense requires a "high degree of awareness of probable falsity," or that the publisher "in fact entertained serious doubts as to the truth of his publication." *St. Amant v. Thompson*, 390 U.S. 727 (1968). A deliberate intent to avoid the truth coupled with knowledge of an allegation's probable inaccuracy may establish actual malice. *Murphy v. Boston Herald, Inc.*, 865 N.E.2d 746 (Mass. 2007); *Gambardella v. Apple Health Care, Inc.*, 969 A.2d 736 (Conn. 2009) (adhering to a demonstrably false and groundless belief and publishing that belief constitutes reckless disregard for the truth; bad motive is not required but may bolster a claim). Mere negligence, as in a failure to investigate, is clearly insufficient. *Levesque v. Doocy*, 560 F.3d 82 (1st Cir. 2009) (news reporters

lacked actual malice despite clearly being "negligent in their failure to question" the accuracy of a source quoted in a news story and in their failure to do further research); *Bertrand v. Mullin*, 846 N.W.2d 884 (Iowa 2014) (failure to investigate information contained in a political attack ad did not constitute reckless disregard for truth or falsity; a "shoddy investigation" does not constitute actual malice).

3.   **Fair comment.** Would the common law fair comment privilege ever protect a publication that would not be protected under *Times v. Sullivan?*

4.   **Truth.** In the early years after *Times v. Sullivan*, libel lawyers continued to think in common law terms and often spoke of the case as erecting a "Constitutional privilege." But common law privileges were affirmative defenses, and it gradually became clear that *Times v. Sullivan* rewrote the elements of the plaintiff's prima facie case in all claims brought by public officials (and later extended to public figures). Thus the plaintiff in such a case must prove that the published statements are false; the burden is no longer on the defendant to prove truth.

5.   **Widespread publication.** Widespread publication, electronic or not, has put new emphasis on interstate and international defamation, raising issues of domestic and foreign jurisdiction, choice of law, and enforcement of foreign judgments that do not recognize what Americans may consider basic free speech rights. On the domestic jurisdiction issues, *see Charlton v. Mond*, 987 A.2d 436 (D.C. 2010) (defamatory telephone calls into District of Columbia and causing harm there were not sufficient for personal jurisdiction over non-resident under the District's long-arm statute, which required additional acts); *Internet Solutions Corp. v. Marshall*, 39 So.3d 1201 (Fla. 2010) (allegedly defamatory material posted on web site by Washington resident about a Florida plaintiff; Florida had jurisdiction under its long-arm statute). Also, injunctions are rarely appropriate even in the context of widely disseminated speech. *See McCarthy v. Fuller*, 810 F.3d 456 (7th Cir. 2015) (" 'Prior restraint' is only a fancy term for censorship"; while there is not an absolute prohibition on an injunction against speech, it "harms not just the speakers but also the listeners") (Posner, J.).

6.   **Foreign defamation judgments.** In terms of foreign jurisdiction, the U.S. Congress has recently addressed by statute the issue of U.S. enforcement of foreign defamation judgments. *See* Securing the Protection of Our Enduring and Established Constitutional Heritage (SPEECH) Act, Pub. L. No. 111–223, 124 Stat. 2381 (2010) (codified at 28 U.S.C. §§ 4101–05). The legislation prevents a domestic court from enforcing a foreign judgment unless the defamation law applied in the foreign court provided at least as much protection for freedom of speech and press as would be provided by the First Amendment to the United States Constitution; or the party opposing recognition or enforcement of that foreign judgment would have been found liable for defamation by a domestic court applying the First Amendment to the United States Constitution.

GERTZ V. ROBERT WELCH, INC.

418 U.S. 323 (1974)

[The plaintiff, Elmer Gertz, is a lawyer. A police officer named Nuccio shot and killed a youth named Nelson and was convicted of second degree murder. Gertz represented the Nelson family in civil claims against Nuccio. The defendant publishes an organ known as American Opinion, representing the views of the John Birch Society. This organization, arguing that the prosecution of Nuccio was a part of the Communist campaign against police, portrayed Gertz as an architect of the "frame-up" of Nuccio, and went on to identify him as a Leninist and Communist-fronter. In fact Gertz had nothing to do with the criminal prosecution and there was no basis for claiming him to be a Leninist or Communist-fronter. Gertz sued. The trial court concluded that Gertz was not a public official or a public figure, but that the *Times v. Sullivan* rules applied anyway. Accordingly, it entered a judgment for the defendant. The Court of Appeals concluded that there was no clear and convincing evidence of "actual malice," and affirmed.]

JUSTICE POWELL delivered the Court's opinion.

The principal issue in this case is whether a newspaper or broadcaster that publishes defamatory falsehoods about an individual who is neither a public official nor a public figure may claim a constitutional privilege against liability for the injury inflicted by those statements. The Court considered this question on the rather different set of facts presented in *Rosenbloom v. Metromedia, Inc.*, 403 U.S. 29, 91 S. Ct. 1811, 29 L. Ed.2d 296 (1971). Rosenbloom, a distributor of nudist magazines, was arrested for selling allegedly obscene material while making a delivery to a retail dealer. The police obtained a warrant and seized his entire inventory of 3,000 books and magazines. He sought and obtained an injunction prohibiting further police interference with his business. He then sued a local radio station for failing to note in two of its newscasts that the 3,000 items seized were only "reportedly" or "allegedly" obscene and for broadcasting references to "the smut literature racket" and to "girlie-book peddlers" in its coverage of the court proceeding for injunctive relief. He obtained a judgment against the radio station, but the Court of Appeals for the Third Circuit held the New York Times privilege applicable to the broadcast and reversed. 415 F.2d 892 (1969).

This Court affirmed the decision below, but no majority could agree on a controlling rationale. The eight Justices who participated in Rosenbloom announced their views in five separate opinions, none of which commanded more than three votes. . . . We begin with the common ground. Under the First Amendment there is no such thing as a false idea. However pernicious an opinion may seem, we depend for its correction not on the conscience of judges and juries but on the competition of other ideas. But there is no constitutional value in false statements of fact. Neither the intentional lie nor the careless error materially advances society's interest in "uninhibited, robust, and wide-open" debate on public issues. . . .

Although the erroneous statement of fact is not worthy of constitutional protection, it is nevertheless inevitable in free debate. . . . The First Amendment requires that we protect some falsehood in order to protect speech that matters.

The need to avoid self-censorship by the news media is, however, not the only societal value at issue. If it were, this Court would have embraced long ago the view that publishers and broadcasters enjoy an unconditional and indefeasible immunity from liability for defamation. . . .

The legitimate state interest underlying the law of libel is the compensation of individuals for the harm inflicted on them by defamatory falsehood. . . .

The *New York Times* standard defines the level of constitutional protection appropriate to the context of defamation of a public person. Those who, by reason of the notoriety of their achievements or the vigor and success with which they seek the public's attention, are properly classed as public figures and those who hold governmental office may recover for injury to reputation only on clear and convincing proof that the defamatory falsehood was made with knowledge of its falsity or with reckless disregard for the truth. . . . We think that these decisions are correct, but we do not find their holdings justified solely by reference to the interest of the press and broadcast media in immunity from liability. Rather, we believe that the *New York Times* rule states an accommodation between this concern and the limited state interest present in the context of libel actions brought by public persons. . . . Because an *ad hoc* resolution of the competing interests at stake in each particular case is not feasible, we must lay down broad rules of general application. Such rules necessarily treat alike various cases involving differences as well as similarities. Thus it is often true that not all of the considerations which justify adoption of a given rule will obtain in each particular case decided under its authority.

With that caveat we have no difficulty in distinguishing among defamation plaintiffs. The first remedy of any victim of defamation is self-help—using available opportunities to contradict the lie or correct the error and thereby to minimize its adverse impact on reputation. Public officials and public figures usually enjoy significantly greater access to the channels of effective communication and hence have a more realistic opportunity to counteract false statements than private individuals normally enjoy. Private individuals are therefore more vulnerable to injury, and the state interest in protecting them is correspondingly greater.

More important than the likelihood that private individuals will lack effective opportunities for rebuttal, there is a compelling normative consideration underlying the distinction between public and private defamation plaintiffs. An individual who decides to seek governmental office must accept certain necessary consequences of that involvement in public affairs. He runs the risk of closer public scrutiny than might otherwise be the case. And society's interest in the officers of government is not strictly limited to the formal discharge of official duties. As the Court pointed out in Garrison v. Louisiana, 379 U.S. at 77, 85 S.Ct., at 217, the public's interest extends to "anything which might touch on an official's fitness for office. . . . Few personal attributes are more germane to fitness for office than dishonesty, malfeasance, or improper motivation, even though these characteristics may also affect the official's private character."

Those classed as public figures stand in a similar position. Hypothetically, it may be possible for someone to become a public figure through no purposeful action of his own, but the instances of truly involuntary public figures must be exceedingly rare. For the most part those who attain this status have assumed roles of especial prominence in the affairs of society. Some occupy positions of such persuasive power and influence that they are deemed public figures for all purposes. More commonly, those classed as public figures have thrust themselves to the forefront of particular public controversies in order to influence the resolution of the issues involved. In either event, they invite attention and comment.

Even if the foregoing generalities do not obtain in every instance, the communications media are entitled to act on the assumption that public officials and public figures have voluntarily exposed themselves to increased risk of injury from defamatory falsehood concerning them. No such assumption is justified with respect to a private individual. He has not accepted public office or assumed an "influential role in ordering society." . . .

Thus, private individuals are not only more vulnerable to injury than public officials and public figures; they are also more deserving of recovery. . . .

We hold that, so long as they do not impose liability without fault, the States may define for themselves the appropriate standard of liability for a publisher or broadcaster of defamatory falsehood injurious to a private individual. This approach provides a more equitable boundary between the competing concerns involved here. It recognizes the strength of the legitimate state interest in compensating private individuals for wrongful injury to reputation, yet shields the press and broadcast media from the rigors of liability for defamation. At least this conclusion obtains where, as here, the substance of the defamatory statement "makes substantial danger to reputation apparent." This phrase places in perspective the conclusion we announce today. Our inquiry would involve consideration somewhat different from those discussed above if a State purported to condition civil liability on a factual misstatement whose content did not warn a reasonably prudent editor or broadcaster of its defamatory potential. . . .

Our accommodation of the competing values at stake in defamation suits by private individuals allows the States to impose liability on the publisher or broadcaster of defamatory falsehood on a less demanding showing than that required by *New York Times*. . . . But this countervailing state interest extends no further than compensation for injury. For the reasons stated below, we hold that the States may not permit recovery of presumed or punitive damages, at least when liability is not based on a showing of knowledge of falsity or reckless disregard for the truth.

. . . Under the traditional rules pertaining to actions for libel, the existence of injury is presumed from the fact of publication. Juries may award substantial sums as compensation for supposed damage to reputation without any proof that such harm actually occurred. The largely uncontrolled discretion of juries to award damages where there is no loss unnecessarily compounds the potential of any system of liability for defamatory falsehood to inhibit the vigorous exercise of First Amendment freedoms. Additionally, the doctrine of presumed damages invites juries to punish unpopular opinion rather than to compensate individuals for injury sustained by the publication of a false fact. More to the point, the States have no substantial interest in securing for plaintiffs such as this petitioner gratuitous awards of money damages far in excess of any actual injury. . . .

We also find no justification for allowing awards of punitive damages against publishers and broadcasters held liable under state-defined standards of liability for defamation. . . . Notwithstanding our refusal to extend the *New York Times* privilege to defamation of private individuals, respondent contends that we should affirm the judgment below on the ground that petitioner is either a public official or a public figure. . . .

Respondent's characterization of petitioner as a public figure raises a different question. That designation may rest on either of two alternative bases. In some instances an individual may achieve such pervasive fame or notoriety that he becomes a public figure for all purposes, and in all contexts. More commonly, an individual voluntarily injects himself or is drawn into a particular public controversy and thereby becomes a public figure for a limited range of issues. In either case such persons assume special prominence in the resolution of public questions.

Petitioner has long been active in community and professional affairs. He has served as an officer of local civic groups and of various professional organizations, and he has published several books and articles on legal subjects. Although petitioner was consequently well known in some circles, he had achieved no general fame or notoriety in the community. None of the prospective jurors called at the trial had ever heard of petitioner prior to this litigation, and respondent offered no proof that this response was atypical of the local population. We would not lightly assume that a citizen's participation in community and professional affairs rendered him a public figure for all purposes. Absent clear evidence of general fame or notoriety in the community, and pervasive involvement in the affairs of society, an individual should not be deemed a public personality for all aspects of his life. It is preferable to reduce the public-figure question to a more meaningful context by looking to the nature and extent of an individual's participation in the particular controversy giving rise to the defamation.

In this context it is plain that petitioner was a not a public figure. . . .

[Remanded for further proceedings. Concurring and dissenting opinions are omitted.]

NOTES

1.   **The *Gertz* fault standard.** For public officials and public figures, the *Times v. Sullivan* standard remains applicable after *Gertz*. For plaintiffs who are private persons, the *Gertz* Court held that there was no need to prove knowing or reckless falsehood. The Court did, however, put a Constitutional surcharge on the common law rules for private persons in *Gertz*-like cases: they can only recover if they prove (a) some kind of fault, to be specified by the states under state tort law, and (b) actual damages.

2.   **The states' fault standard.** Most states, accepting *Gertz'* invitation to apply any fault standard they chose, fell back on the most familiar word—negligence. Thus liability would be imposed in most states on *Gertz*-type claims if the jury found defendant published "negligently." A few states have decided on a tougher standard and have kept the *Times v. Sullivan* standard even for private person cases, or have adopted some other variation, such as "grossly irresponsible," or the professional standards of journalists.

3.   **Types of fault.** Is it really possible to carry over the negligence standard to these cases? What kind of conduct and what kind of risks are entailed in the fault required here? The *Gertz* Court almost certainly had in mind fault as to the truth or falsity of the defamatory statements, as for example, fault in failure to investigate unsubstantiated charges. Would a negligence analysis work just as well when the fault, if any, lies in a reporter's perception of fast-moving events? Suppose a reporter writes that the plaintiff was leading demonstrating trespassers at a nuclear power plant, but plaintiff says he was merely out in front watching? What about fault that does not bear on the truth or falsity at all, for example, spite or ill-will? What about fault in writing an ambiguous sentence, in which one meaning is defamatory but the meaning intended is not?

4. **Actual damages.** Suppose the private-person plaintiff proves the defendant was guilty of a knowing or reckless falsehood, so that the test laid down in *Times v. Sullivan* is met. Would both presumed and punitive damages then be available?

5. **Public figures under *Gertz*.** After the decisions in *Times v. Sullivan* and *Gertz*, one of the central issues has been whether the plaintiff in a libel action is a public figure or whether he is a private person, since this determines the kind of proof required. The common law notion of public figures was rather broad, although not necessarily well defined. *Gertz* limited the concept of public figures quite stringently. Justice Powell seemed to concede that a plaintiff might be "drawn into a particular public controversy and thereby [become] a public figure." But his main emphasis seems to be on the case in which the plaintiff "voluntarily injects himself" into a public issue or has "thrust" himself "to the forefront of particular public controversies." Later cases have emphasized this "thrusting" and also the idea that true public figures have a greater access "to the channels of effective communication." *See, e.g., Hatfill v. New York Times Co.*, 532 F.3d 312 (4th Cir. 2008) (research scientist held to be a public figure); *American Future Systems, Inc. v. Better Business Bureau of Eastern Pennsylvania*, 923 A.2d 389 (Pa. 2007) (telemarketer held to be a public figure); *cf. O'Connor v. Burningham*, 165 P.3d 1214 (Utah 2007) (public high school basketball coach not a public figure because she lacked authority to make policy about public issues such as life, liberty and property).

6. **Development of "public figure" status.** Some Supreme Court cases have taken these stringent tests of public figurehood to extremes. The Court has held a party to a lawsuit, at least if it is a divorce, is not a public figure for that reason alone, with the result that a publisher who inaccurately states the court's opinion may be denied the *Times v. Sullivan* protections. *Time, Inc. v. Firestone*, 424 U.S. 448 (1976). In *Wolston v. Reader's Digest Ass'n*, 443 U.S. 157 (1979), the Court held that a person who is charged with and convicted of crime is not a public figure merely for that reason because he did not "voluntarily thrust" himself into a public controversy.

7. **Public officials.** The decision that some public employees are not public figures puts renewed emphasis on the idea of a public official. The Court has long recognized that not every public employee is a public official for *Times v. Sullivan* purposes. It has so far not clearly delineated its ideas on this subject, but it has said that an employee is not a public official unless "[t]he employee's position [is] one which would invite public scrutiny and discussion of the person holding it, entirely apart from the scrutiny and discussion occasioned by the particular charges in controversy." *Rosenblatt v. Baer*, 383 U.S. 75 (1966). What if there is evidence that a janitor at the local high school is selling heavy drugs to students? Presumably he would not be an "official" under the *Rosenblatt* test. Presumably also he did not thrust himself into a controversy. Might the Court find he is a public figure because he is "drawn into" a public controversy?

8. **Publishers and broadcasters.** The common law of defamation used the term "publication" and "publisher" to refer to any communication to someone other than the plaintiff. Justice Powell in *Gertz* repeatedly refers, however, to "publishers and broadcasters," and even to "news media." Does he mean to limit *Gertz* to cases in which a private citizen sues a media publisher? Suppose an employer or the dean of a college writes a letter about an employee or a college student. If there is reason to require both fault and actual damages in media cases, does it apply equally to private publications as well? There are a few cases saying that it does not and that the common law rules apply in full force to the private letter writer.

9. **Internet posters.** Internet issues have also posed new questions regarding protection of internet anonymity. Under some rules, the trial judge must protect the identity of internet posters and confidential informants unless the judge has first ensured that the plaintiff has provided evidence that would, if uncontradicted, demonstrate a prima facie case on all elements of the plaintiff's claim, or at least those elements that can be presented without knowing the identity of the defendant. *See SaleHoo Group, Ltd. v. ABC Co.*, 722 F.Supp.2d 1210 (W.D. Wash. 2010); *Mortgage Specialists, Inc. v. Implode-Explode Heavy Indus., Inc.*, 999 A.2d 184 (N.H. 2010).

10. **Truth (redux).** We saw above that *Times v. Sullivan* changed the role of truth from an affirmative defense to an element of the plaintiff's prima facie case if the plaintiff is a public figure. In *Philadelphia Newspapers, Inc. v. Hepps*, 475 U.S. 767 (1986), the Court held that a *Gertz*-type plaintiff must similarly prove falsity as part of the prima facie case. The Court has not yet decided, however, whether the states could constitutionally presume falsity when the plaintiff is a private person and the subject matter of the publication is of no public concern.

11. **Constitutional protection for "opinion" statements.** "[T]here is no such thing as a false idea." This statement in *Gertz* seemed to create a new limitation on recovery for defamation. The common law denied recovery for mere name-calling, but at least on occasion could impose liability for statements of opinion and even for unkind satire. *Gertz* seemed to commit the Court to the proposition that the defamation must involve a factual misstatement and that it must be reasonably understood as such. Later, in *Hustler Magazine v. Falwell*, 485 U.S. 46 (1988), the defendant published a nasty parody of an ad that used "first time" as its theme. The parody presented Falwell, a famous evangelist, as having his "first time" with his own mother. No one believed that the publisher intended this parody to be taken as a fact and no one did take it as a fact. The Court held that the defendant could not be liable because the plaintiff could not prove that the defendant knowingly or recklessly published a "fact."

Two years later, the Court said there was no separate constitutional protection for "opinion," but reiterated its holdings that liability depended upon statements or at least implications of something "provably false." *Milkovich v. Lorain Journal*, 497 U.S. 1 (1990). What if protestors at an abortion clinic carry signs saying "This clinic murders babies"? *Cf. Horsley v. Rivera*, 292 F.3d 695 (11th Cir. 2002) ("You are an accomplice to homicide" said of anti-abortion activist who maintained a website listing names of abortion doctors, graying out those who had been wounded and x-ing out those who had been killed). What if a hospital senior executive told a new doctor that the plaintiff doctor was not competent to operate on a dog? *See Lawnwood Med. Ctr., Inc. v. Sadow*, 43 So.3d 710 (Fla. Dist. Ct. App. 2010) (mere conclusion or opinion that the plaintiff is incompetent in her job, without any express or implied assertion of facts, may not be accepted as a sufficient basis for a defamation claim). What if the statement is made attributing the suicide of a former member of the rock band Boston to the founder of the band and pressures over the breakup? *Scholz v. Delp*, 41 N.E.3d 38 (Mass. 2015) (statements were "statements of opinion and not verifiable fact," and could therefore not form the basis of a claim of defamation against the newspaper that reported the allegations).

DUN & BRADSTREET, INC. V. GREENMOSS BUILDERS, INC., 472 U.S. 749 (1985). The defendant, Dun & Bradstreet, supplied a confidential credit rating report about the plaintiff to five subscribers. The report was negligently compiled by a reporter who misinterpreted or mistranscribed some court documents. It erroneously stated that plaintiff, which was a business operation, had filed a petition for bankruptcy. The plaintiff feared the report would seriously affect credit or other business affairs. He asked for correction and for the names of the subscribers who had received the report. The defendant gave a correction, but the plaintiff regarded it as inadequate. The defendant refused altogether to give him the names of subscribers. In the trial court, the plaintiff recovered $50,000 presumed compensatory and $300,000 punitive damages, which the Vermont Supreme Court upheld, saying that *Times v. Sullivan* had no application to non-media defendants. In the Supreme Court of the United States, *held*, presumed and punitive damages are recoverable in this case without proof of *Times v. Sullivan* malice. *Gertz* held that a private individual could obtain only restricted damages from a publisher of a libel that involved a matter of public concern, but did not address the case of a private person libeled on a matter of private concern. In the private-figure/private-concern case, the state's interest in compensation is just as strong as elsewhere, but the First Amendment interest is weak. The speech here is not on a matter of public concern, as determined by "content, form, and context." The interest is of the individual speaker and its specific business audience; no free flow of information is involved, since Dun & Bradstreet prohibited subscribers from passing the information on. The speech is also hardy and unlikely to be deterred by "incidental state regulation," because profit motive is involved.

NOTES

1. **Reaction to *Dun & Bradstreet*.** *Gertz* seemed to focus on the character of the plaintiff rather than the nature of the issue under discussion as the basis for invoking *Times v. Sullivan* or avoiding it. For this reason, *Dun & Bradstreet* was a surprise to many observers.

2. **Subsequent cases.** After *Dun & Bradstreet*, the rules to be applied with respect to proof and damages for defamation appear to be a function of at least two variables: First, is the plaintiff a public figure? And second, was the issue under discussion or the communication involved a matter of public interest? *Dun & Bradstreet* addressed the case in which the answer to both questions was "no," and in that case allowed the plaintiff to recover presumed damages without proof of the knowing or reckless falsehood required by *Times v. Sullivan*.

3. **Effect on other issues.** *Dun & Bradstreet* involved only the question whether the plaintiff could recover common law "presumed" damages. This means that one of the two main rules in *Gertz* has no application in cases of private person plaintiffs and private concern issues. What is your prediction about the other rule in *Gertz*?

4. **State protections.** The Supreme Court's decisions on defamation are constitutional rules which govern the states. But they only prescribe minimum protections for free speech, meaning that states may provide more protection for speakers and less for victims of defamation. *See Wilkow v. Forbes, Inc.,* 241 F.3d 552 (7th Cir. 2001) (subjective opinion statements protected under Illinois law); *Newberry v. Allied Stores, Inc.,* 773 P.2d 1231 (N.M. 1989) (rejecting the new liabilities permitted by *Dun & Bradstreet*).

C. DEFAMATION IN THE INTERNET AGE

BUBLICK, BAMBAUER & ARELLANO, DOBBS ON ECONOMIC AND DIGNITARY TORTS
115–116 (2d. ed. 2022)

"Most of the effects of the Internet on dignitary and economic torts flow from four qualities of the Internet more generally, and its platforms specifically:

(A) *Everybody has a press.* The Internet has greatly reduced the costs of creating and delivering content to an audience (either to a wide audience, or to a narrow-but-particular audience. Both raise special benefits and risks.)

(B) *Everybody has a cloak.* The Internet has allowed individuals to create and post content anonymously without having to take costly precautions that would have been necessary for anonymous books, articles, or leaflets.

(C) *Everybody has a personal curation service.* The Internet has dramatically reduced the costs to users who are searching for particular types of content.

(D) *Everybody has a paparazzi that relentlessly follows them everywhere.* The Internet has enabled and incentivized the collection of detailed data about how individuals browse and interact with content.

Each of these changes independently creates new problems and pressures for many [ ] torts . . . including defamation. . . ."

NOTE

How might the effects of the internet challenge the doctrines and rationales we have seen in this chapter? For a full examination of internet defamation cases, see ELLEN BUBLICK, JANE BAMBAUER & DANIEL ARELLANO, DOBBS ON ECONOMIC AND DIGNITARY TORTS: CASES AND MATERIALS, ch. 5 (2d ed. 2022).

REFERENCES: 3 DOBBS, HAYDEN & BUBLICK, THE LAW OF TORTS §§ 552–72 (2d ed. 2011); DOBBS, HAYDEN & BUBLICK, HORNBOOK ON TORTS §§ 37.15–37.19 (2d ed. 2016); BUBLICK, BAMBAUER & ARELLANO, DOBBS ON ECONOMIC AND DIGNITARY TORTS: CASES AND MATERIALS, chs. 3, 4 & 5 (2d ed. 2022).

§ 2. MALICIOUS PROSECUTION AND OTHER ABUSES OF THE LEGAL SYSTEM

A. MALICIOUS PROSECUTION

Illustration 1

Max Parrillo owned a socket wrench purchased from Lambert's Hardware. He wished to replace a socket used on the wrench, so he took the wrench and socket to Lambert's store. He went directly to the wrench display where he took his own wrench out of his pocket and made some comparisons. Not finding the right size, he put his wrench in his pocket and walked out of the store. Right outside the store, a store detective employed by Lambert's stopped him and accused him of stealing the wrench. The detective called the police and told the officer that Parrillo had stolen the wrench. Up until this time, the detective had refused to listen to Parrillo's side of the story. The detective told the officer that he had watched Parrillo the whole time and that he had stolen the wrench. Parrillo was prosecuted on the basis of this information, but was found not guilty. He then sued Lambert's Hardware. These facts will justify a recovery of any special damages, such as cost of defending the criminal trial, plus "general" damages and punitive damages.

Illustration 2

Penny Pfennig saw an officer in the act of arresting a friend of Pfennig's, Shirley Schilling. Schilling, it appeared, had been driving while intoxicated. Pfennig stopped her car and walked back to the scene of the arrest. She said: "I don't want to interfere, but this is a friend of mine. Can I help her in any way?" At this point another officer, Rex Stebbins, pulled up and strode aggressively over to the scene. Apparently he assumed that Pfennig was also under arrest; he pushed her back and told her to get on the sidewalk. Pfennig's husband, Thaler, then arrived and protested Stebbins' actions, whereupon Stebbins arrested Pfennig and Thaler for obstructing justice and interfering with an arrest. After they were found not guilty, they sued Stebbins and the city for (a) false arrest and (b) malicious prosecution. They are entitled to recover for false arrest for damages from the time of detention until formal prosecution was begun, and for malicious prosecution for damages arising after prosecution was begun.

The malicious prosecution claim is often compared to *false imprisonment*, and there is much resemblance. But false imprisonment is a trespassory tort, involving direct physical detention of the person. Prosecution is indirect interference. In the case of false imprisonment, the plaintiff makes a prima facie case by showing an intended detention of which the plaintiff was aware. Any privilege based on the existence of a warrant or probable cause for arrest must be shown affirmatively by the defendant. In the malicious prosecution case, on the other hand, the plaintiff cannot recover unless he affirmatively shows that the accuser lacked probable cause and was also motivated by malice. Damages in the two torts are different, too. The false arrest or imprisonment damages include any damages from the time of detention to the time of prosecution, but no more. Damages for malicious prosecution include any damages occurring after prosecution has begun. Thus in many cases the plaintiff may have both claims, and may need to assert both to collect full damages.

Defamation and malicious prosecution. In some ways, malicious prosecution more closely resembles a defamation claim. All malicious prosecution claims necessarily involve a defamatory communication—an accusation of crime. Under the law of defamation, there is a privilege to report a crime and other facts to responsible officials, so that under the ordinary law of libel there could be no recovery for a good faith report which resulted in prosecution. *See Williams v. Tharp*, 914 N.E.2d 756 (Ind. 2009) (defendant erroneously told police that a customer in a store had "pulled a gun," held qualifiedly privileged). The law of malicious prosecution is, in a sense, a special case of defamation with special rules. What the common law sought in these rules was a system that would redress genuine grievances of the wrongly-prosecuted plaintiff without discouraging defendants from reporting crimes or suspected crimes. In a very real way, this parallels the *Times v. Sullivan* concern to redress injury while avoiding self-censorship.

The common law rule. The common law solution, like that of *Times v. Sullivan*, is something of a compromise, and one intended to protect similar values. But the common law solution is structured quite differently from that in *Times v. Sullivan*. The common law rule denies the plaintiff any claim unless:

(1) *There is a prosecution.* This is a requirement that the only kind of damage recognized is prosecution itself, and mere report of a crime to an officer is not itself sufficient.

(2) *The defendant in the malicious prosecution suit instigated the prosecution.* Either a private citizen or an officer might instigate the prosecution; indeed, there may be several instigators. The idea is to locate one or more persons who played a significant role in causing prosecution. An honest factual report to an officer, not accompanied by any pressure to prosecute, will ordinarily not be sufficient. On the other hand, it is clear that the store detective in Illustration 1 and the officer in Illustration 2 both are instigators.

(3) *The defendant acted maliciously.* Malice is a specialized term in tort law. It may at times mean spite or ill-will, but is seldom limited to that meaning. Many of the results of cases suggest that any improper purpose will do, and so will abuse of position or authority or denial of ordinary decencies to the accused. Thus in both Illustrations, the defendants refused to hear the plaintiffs' side of the story, and considering they acted from positions of power or authority, this may have justified a finding of malice.

(4) *The defendant acted without probable cause.* The false report of a crime is not by itself enough, even if the defendant acts maliciously. The defendant must also have acted without probable cause, that is, without reasonable cause for believing that the plaintiff has committed the crime charged. *See, e.g., Papa John's Int'l, Inc. v. McCoy*, 244 S.W.3d 44 (Ky. 2008); *Brunson v. Affinity Fed. Credit Union*, 972 A.2d 1112 (N.J. 2009) (lack of probable cause is the "essence" of the malicious prosecution claim; the plaintiff must establish a negative, namely that probable cause did not exist). Where facts are capable of dispute, the accuser may be under some obligation to check the facts where this is reasonably possible. This is one of the grounds on which the store detective could be found to lack probable cause in Illustration 1.

(5) *The criminal action is terminated in favor of the present plaintiff.* The plaintiff cannot recover for malicious prosecution unless the criminal action against him has terminated and terminated in his favor. Thus he cannot sue for the tort while the criminal action is pending. And he cannot

sue after it has terminated if he was convicted. In a third group of cases, the criminal action is terminated by compromise or some other procedure that does not determine guilt or innocence. In many courts this is not considered a termination favorable to the accused. *Cf. Bronowicz v. Allegheny County*, 804 F.3d 338 (3d Cir. 2015) (trial court's order vacating a judgment is a favorable termination, even where the court expressly declined to address the legality of the sentence); *Lemoine v. Wolfe*, 168 So.3d 362 (La. 2015) (answering certified question, *nol pros* will constitute favorable termination unless the charge is dismissed for one of a set of named reasons, including an agreement of compromise, mercy, or the impracticality of bringing the accused to trial).

Defenses. The litigation immunities sketched in connection with defamation claims also apply to malicious prosecution and other torts. Thus the judge and the prosecutor are absolutely immune from malicious prosecution claims, so long as they are acting in their judicial and prosecutorial capacities respectively. The prosecutor who takes on police work, however, risks a loss of the absolute immunity. A second defense is "guilt-in-fact." Even if the accuser lacked probable cause for the accusation and acted with malice, and even if the accused is found not guilty in the criminal trial, the accuser may offer it as a defense in the malicious prosecution action that the plaintiff was in fact guilty. This is analogous to the truth "defense" in libel cases.

Malicious prosecution after Times v. Sullivan. Since malicious prosecution involves communication, and invariably reputation as well, it may be regarded as merely a special case of defamation. Would *Times v. Sullivan* and *Gertz* apply, then, to restrict liability in these cases? Look back at the common law rule. Does it effectively provide the same protections provided by *Times v. Sullivan* and *Gertz*? One element that may give trouble is the "presumed" damages in malicious prosecution cases. These were forbidden under the *Gertz* test.

B. IMPROPER CIVIL LITIGATION

The defendant in malicious prosecution cases has accused the plaintiff of a crime and instigated criminal prosecution. But in "malicious civil prosecution" the defendant has brought a civil action against the person who is now the plaintiff. If it was brought without probable cause, was malicious, and was terminated in favor of the person who is now plaintiff, there may be a cause of action for malicious civil prosecution under that name or under some other descriptive term. The rules in the two actions are much the same. Still, access to courts is a valuable individual right and civil suits often serve social purposes as well by breaking new ground. Consequently, one who complains that he was civilly sued must make a strong showing that the suit was unjustified. In one or two respects some courts have fashioned special limitations on the claim for improper civil litigation.

———————

XCENTRIC VENTURES, LLC V. BORODKIN, 798 F.3d 1201 (9th Cir. 2015). Plaintiff Xcentric Ventures, LLC operates the website www.ripoffreport. com ("Ripoff Report"), an online forum where users can read and post messages about businesses that purportedly have ripped off consumers. Defendants are the Asia Economic Institute, LLC ("AEI"), a company that publishes current news and events online, and AEI's attorney Lisa Jean Borodkin. AEI brought an action against Xcentric for civil racketeering predicated on extortion and wire fraud. The gist of the claim was that Xcentric deliberately manipulated the Ripoff Report so that negative posts about AEI rose to the top of internet searches, and then used its Corporate Advocacy Program ("CAP") to coerce AEI into paying Xcentric money in exchange for giving AEI more favorable treatment. AEI dismissed its claim after it could not get a personal assistant to the manager of Xcentric to agree to come to California for a deposition. Summary judgment was granted on AEI's additional claims. Xcentric then sued AEI and attorney Borodkin for malicious prosecution. The district court dismissed claims against Borodkin and entered summary judgment in AEI's favor.

Held, affirmed. "We agree with the district court that Xcentric cannot prove an element of its malicious prosecution claims, that the underlying claims were brought or continued without factual or legal probable cause. . . . Legal probable cause exists if 'any reasonable attorney would have thought the claim tenable' on the facts known to him. Legal probable cause exists even if the claims are 'extremely unlikely' to win. The standard is an objective question of law to be decided by the court. We agree with the district court that the claims asserted by [AEI] and Borodkin in California were tenable . . . The underlying attempted racketeering extortion claim alleged that Xcentric attempted to extort money by encouraging third parties to post negative reviews, manipulating the posts to highlight negative reviews and to further highlight the negative reviews if the businesses posted rebuttals, and then charging high fees to 'turn the negative into a positive.' The claim was tenable because a district court had previously held that similar allegations stated an extortion claim against Xcentric. *Hy Cite Corp. v. badbusinessbureau.com, L.L.C.*, 418 F.Supp. 2d 1142, 1149–50 (D. Ariz. 2005) (holding that allegations that Xcentric created and solicited false, defamatory complaints against businesses and then charged $50,000 and monthly fee of $1,500 to remove or stop posting the complaints stated an extortion claim). [AEI] sufficiently alleged and proved the requisite injury to business and property and economic loss, including that they paid an expert to mitigate the damaging posts and lost specific business opportunities and contracts because of the negative posts. . . .

NOTES

1. **Probable cause.** Common law is developed through civil actions. Typically, tortious civil litigation cases require the plaintiff to show both subjective bad faith and objective lack of probable cause. *Parrish v. Latham & Watkins*, 400 P.3d 1 (Cal. 2017). Courts find probable cause exists when the plaintiff in the first suit has a plausible ground for believing the litigation might succeed. *See Roop v. Parker Northwest Paving Co.*, 94 P.3d 885 (Or. Ct. App. 2004) ("standard for probable cause to bring a civil action is less stringent than that required to prosecute a criminal action"); 3 DAN B. DOBBS, PAUL T. HAYDEN & ELLEN M. BUBLICK, THE LAW OF TORTS §§ 592 & 588 (2d ed. 2011). Part of the *Xcentric* case was dismissed and the remainder thrown out on summary judgment. Why does the Ninth Circuit find probable cause nonetheless?

2. **Reliance on advice of counsel.** Would a client who retains an attorney to file a claim be liable for malicious prosecution when the claim is defeated? Would reliance on the attorney's advice in filing suit show probable cause? "Non-lawyers may judge appearances by relying in good faith upon advice of fully informed counsel who is admitted to the bar in the state or otherwise appears to be reasonably competent." *See* 3 DOBBS, HAYDEN & BUBLICK, THE LAW OF TORTS § 588 (2d ed. 2011). However, if the client "acted in bad faith or withheld facts from counsel he or she knew or should have known would have defeated the cause of action, probable cause is not established. Counsel's advice must be sought in good faith and not as a mere cloak to protect one against suit for malicious prosecution." *Palmer v. Zaklama*, 1 Cal.Rptr.3d 116 (Ct. App. 2003).

3. **Rules of ethics and procedure.** Note that in *Xcentric*, the attorney was sued alongside the client. Rules of professional responsibility for lawyers provide that it is a disciplinary infraction for a lawyer to bring frivolous claims or make frivolous contentions in litigation. *See* ABA MODEL RULE OF PROFESSIONAL CONDUCT 3.1. Discipline may be severe. *See, e.g., In re Hawkley*, 92 P.3d 1069 (Idaho 2002) (three-year suspension for filing two frivolous lawsuits). A federal court may sanction a lawyer under Federal Rule of Civil Procedure 11 for filing a paper that is either frivolous or presented for an "improper purpose." *See, e.g., Whitehead v. Food Max of Mississippi, Inc.*, 332 F.3d 796 (5th Cir. 2003). A number of other state and federal statutes and rules provide for similar sanctions. Does the existence of these sanctions lessen the need for a civil cause of action?

4. **Tort actions against counsel.** Malicious prosecution suits against counsel are difficult to maintain. "Even if the attorney acts without probable cause to believe the client's claim will succeed, the improper purpose which may subject an attorney to liability to a nonclient must be something other than simply earning a fee. . . . Other factual allegations beyond the customary

aspects of client representation [ ] are necessary to support the improper purpose element." *Seiller Waterman, LLC v. RLB Properties, Ltd.*, 610 S.W.3d 188 (Ky. 2020). Some courts have gone further: under lack of probable cause, "[o]nly those actions that any reasonable attorney would agree are totally and completely without merit may form the basis for a malicious prosecution suit." *Parrish v. Latham & Watkins*, 400 P.3d 1 (Cal. 2017). Should an absolute "litigation privilege" protect attorneys against civil actions which arise as result of their conduct or communications in representation of clients, related to judicial proceedings? *Taylor v. McNichols*, 243 P.3d 642 (Idaho 2010) (yes).

5. **The special-injury rule.** Some courts require civil malicious prosecution plaintiffs to prove special injury. The concern is that lawsuits beget lawsuits which beget more lawsuits. See *Friedman v. Dozorc*, 312 N.W.2d 585 (Mich. 1981). There is a split in authority on whether proof of special injury is required in an improper civil litigation claim. In states that require it, the plaintiff must show that there was a seizure of property, as where property is attached or subjected to an injunction; or seizure of the person, as where one is civilly committed; or, in some cases, where there was repeated re-litigation of the same claim. The injury that may arise to a doctor's reputation from a malpractice claim is not sufficient. *Cf. Havilah Real Property Services, LLC v. VLK, LLC*, 108 A.3d 334 (D.C. 2015) (reaffirming narrow "special injury" rule, holding that the filing of 31 *lis pendens* did not constitute a special injury).

C. ABUSE OF PROCESS

Illustration 1

Purtle broke into Dominic's house with felonious intent. Dominic caught him and turned him over to the police, having probable cause to believe he was guilty, which in fact he was. While Purtle was in jail, Dominic visited him. Dominic said, "I will drop charges if you will work for one year in my guano factory at minimum wage." Dominic is guilty of an abuse of process.

Illustration 2

Cline, a patient of Dr. Tellman, suffered injury in the course of surgery. Cline consulted a lawyer, Dalmar, who brought suit against Tellman. Dalmar concluded that Dr. Puccinni had nothing to do with the injury suffered by Cline, but that, if sued, Puccinni would testify against Tellman in order to protect himself. For this reason, Dalmar made Puccinni a defendant as well. The jury in the malpractice case brought in a verdict for Puccinni. Dalmar is not guilty of an abuse of process.

Elements of abuse of process. Abuse of process involves misuse of legal process for an ulterior or improper purpose. *Jordet v. Jordet*, 861 N.W.2d 147 (N.D. 2015) ("There are two essential elements for an abuse of process claim: (1) an ulterior purpose, and (2) a willful act in the use of the process not proper in the regular conduct of the proceeding."). The defendant may be held liable even if he rightly invoked the process and even if the person against whom it is invoked is in fact guilty of the crime or civilly liable. The reason for this is that the gist of the tort is misuse of the legal system for some personal end. Thus Illustration 1 reflects a typical case in which legal process is properly issued, but the instigator attempts to use it for extortionate purposes. The instigator is thus liable for abuse of process. However, courts have often said that some act, threat or demand must be made *after* process has issued in order to support recovery. Thus the tort is not made out in Illustration 2, since the lawyer there made no demand for favorable testimony from Dr. Puccinni after process was issued. Perhaps not all courts would require this, but a number have done so. *Cf. Weinstein v. Leonard*, 134 A.3d 547 (Vt. 2015) (lawyer's conduct in sending letters to property owners threatening legal process did not constitute an abuse of process because the conduct did not involve any misapplication of court processes; even the filing of a frivolous lawsuit cannot itself be the predicate for a claim of abuse of process, because that would not show that court processes have themselves been used improperly).

What if plaintiff's neighbors filed complaints of (1) code violations at plaintiff's home, (2) nuisance animals, (3) a petition for a mental evaluation, and (4) requests for restraining orders, at least some of which were well-founded? Plaintiff maintains that defendants were trying to drive her from the neighborhood and that this is a classic example of the abuse of legal process to obtain a collateral advantage—ejection of the plaintiff from her home and her neighborhood. See *Pallares v. Seinar,* 756 S.E.2d 128 (S.C. 2014).

Settlement. Does the abuse of process claim chill the prospects of settling a lawsuit? In the criminal case it is arguable that no one should make any kind of bargain whatever with a person charged with crime. But consider civil cases. A brings an action against B, attaching B's car. While the car is attached, so that B has no means of transport, A offers to settle all claims between the parties, including some that have no bearing on the attached car. He offers to release the car if settlement is accepted. Does this offer run a risk that B will sue for abuse of process?

SLAPP suits. In recent years some environmentally concerned citizens have argued that some developers, whose projects might be opposed by environmentalists and others, have used lawsuits to discourage their opponents, for example, by suing critics for defamation, malicious prosecution, or abuse of process. These suits against critics are said to be Strategic Lawsuits Against Public Participation (SLAPP suits), and some states have enacted laws (anti-SLAPP statutes) to deter them. They have since been applied to a number of situations beyond the developer context. *See, e.g., Taus v. Loftus*, 151 P.3d 1185 (Cal. 2007) (suit brought against author of scholarly articles). These statutes may require the plaintiff to prove before trial or discovery that plaintiff will probably win. *See* CAL. CODE CIV. PROC. § 425.16. In effect, it represents a kind of defensive use of the abuse of process idea. Perhaps there is room for caution. The Massachusetts court observed in *Baker v. Parsons,* 750 N.E.2d 953 (Mass. 2001), that in dismissing the plaintiff's complaint before factual development, the statute protects "one party's exercise of its right of petition [but] impinges on the adverse party's exercise of its right to petition." In *Opinion of the Justices (SLAPP Suit Procedure),* 641 A.2d 1012 (N.H. 1994), the court ruled that a proposed statute unconstitutionally infringed on the right to jury trial. *See also Davis v. Cox,* 351 P.3d 862 (Wash. 2015) (anti-SLAPP statute unconstitutionally denies right to jury trial, because of evidentiary burden that requires trial judge to make a factual determination of whether plaintiff has established a probability of prevailing by clear and convincing evidence).

Sham petitioning. Courts have been reluctant to allow sanctions against litigation that is not objectively baseless, even if brought for an improper purpose. *See Boyer v. Health Grades, Inc.,* 359 P.3d 25 (Colo. 2015) (heightened pleading standards for abuse of process claims in cases of public concern, which reflect the sham litigation exception to the Noerr-Pennington doctrine, are inapplicable to a resort to administrative or judicial process implicating purely private disputes).

§ 3. PRIVACY

For many years, courts recognized certain rights that might today be labeled rights of privacy but which were originally protected under some other name. And there are still cases today in which interests in privacy are protected under other theories. For instance, if someone enters your apartment without permission, the law will protect your rights of privacy by imposing liability under a trespass theory. If someone publishes your private papers, the law may offer redress under a theory of copyright or conversion. Recognizing this, "two young Boston lawyers" argued that the law court recognizes a separate tort for any invasion of privacy. In part they were offended by gossip columnists. But they also saw law as a source of protection for the core of human dignity and they wanted a law of privacy to support the individual's self-development and self-conception by guaranteeing privacy. Long before the term "self-image" came into popular use, they wanted to protect the individual's "estimate of himself." Samuel Warren & Louis Brandeis, *The Right to Privacy*, 4 HARV. L. REV. 193 (1890). Gradually the courts accepted the idea and today privacy claims are recognized in some form everywhere.

A wide variety of claims have been brought as privacy claims, although some of them involve privacy only in the most attenuated sense. For instance, non-physical sexual harassment, obnoxious and harassing debt collection methods, even stalking and threats have been characterized as privacy claims. *E.g., Rumbauskas v. Cantor,* 649 A.2d 853 (N.J. 1994). Prosser, attempting to make sense out of the mass of cases, came up with the proposition that modern cases really involved four distinct torts, all using the name "privacy." William Prosser, *Privacy*, 48 CAL. L. REV. 383 (1960). Perhaps not all "privacy" cases fit comfortably within these categories, but they remain the chief modes of privacy analysis. They are:

1. *Intrusive invasions*. If the plaintiff has a reasonable expectation of privacy—meaning here seclusion or solitude—and the defendant intentionally invades that right in a way that would be highly offensive to a reasonable person, a tort action might lie. *See* RESTATEMENT (SECOND) OF TORTS § 652B (1976). The contours of this privacy tort are not clear, but cases have found actionable intrusions by electronic recording devices such as hidden video cameras.

2. *Commercial appropriation*. One might publish the plaintiff's name, face or figure in a commercial advertisement without the plaintiff's permission. This might not libel the plaintiff, but the plaintiff should still control how her face or name is used for commercial purposes. (We address this tort in the next chapter.)

3. *False light*. The plaintiff might be presented in a false light, again without libel. For example, it might be reported that the plaintiff had emotions which were perfectly commendable, but which the plaintiff did not feel or did not wish revealed; or associated with a political cause that was perfectly uplifting but which the plaintiff did not support.

4. *Public revelation of private facts*. The defendant might publish true statements about the plaintiff on matters utterly private. This would not be libelous even if the facts were derogatory since truth could be shown; but it might still be an invasion of privacy.

Although they are only common-law privacy rights, Judge Posner has suggested that those rights may bear some relation to privacy rights protected by the United States Constitution. For a vivid example of the connection, see *Wolfe v. Schaefer*, 619 F.3d 782 (7th Cir. 2010). *Wolfe* suggests that social interests in disclosure and private interests in privacy must be balanced against each other. At times the social interest in information may be dwarfed by great individual interests in privacy. "If Congress required airline passengers to fly nude in order to reduce the risk of a terrorist incident, one imagines that the law might well be held to infringe a constitutional right to privacy even though there is a substantial social interest in airline safety." However, in *Wolfe* itself, the social interest in information from an official investigation of a candidate for public office outweighs the plaintiff's interest in selective concealment of information.

———————

IN RE FACEBOOK, INC. INTERNET TRACKING LITIGATION, 956 F.3d 589 (9th Cir. 2020). Facebook uses plug-ins to track users' browsing histories when they visit third-party websites, and then compiles these browsing histories into personal profiles which are sold to advertisers to generate revenue. Facebook engaged in these tracking practices after its users had logged out of Facebook. Facebook compiled some personal user profile data using "cookies"—small text files stored on the user's device. When a user creates a Facebook account, more than ten Facebook cookies are placed on the user's browser. These cookies store the user's login ID, and they capture, collect, and compile the referer headers from the web pages visited by the user. As most relevant to this appeal, these cookies allegedly continued to capture information after a user logged out of Facebook and visited other websites. Plaintiffs, Facebook users, filed suit for claims including intrusion. Facebook filed a motion to dismiss.

Held, "Plaintiffs have sufficiently pleaded the 'reasonable expectation of privacy' and 'highly offensive' elements necessary to state a claim for intrusion upon seclusion and invasion of privacy to survive a 12(b)(6) motion to dismiss." "We first consider whether a defendant gained unwanted access to data by electronic or other covert means, in violation of the law or social norms. . . . [T]he relevant question here is whether a user would reasonably expect that Facebook would have access to the user's individual data after the user logged out of the application. Facebook's privacy disclosures at the time allegedly failed to acknowledge its tracking of logged-out users, suggesting that users' information would not be tracked. . . . Plaintiffs have plausibly alleged that, upon reading Facebook's statements in the applicable Data Use Policy, a user might assume that only logged-in user data would be collected. Plaintiffs have alleged that the applicable Help Center page affirmatively stated that logged-out user data would not be collected. Thus, Plaintiffs have plausibly alleged that Facebook set an expectation that logged-out user data would not be collected, but then collected it anyway. In light of the privacy interests and Facebook's allegedly surreptitious and unseen data collection, Plaintiffs have adequately alleged a reasonable expectation of privacy. . . . The nature of the allegedly collected data is also important. Plaintiffs allege that Facebook obtained a comprehensive browsing history of an individual, no matter how sensitive the websites visited, and then correlated that history with the time of day and other user actions on the websites visited. This process, according to Plaintiffs, resulted in Facebook's acquiring 'an enormous amount of individualized data' to compile a 'vast repository of personal data. . . . [V]iewing the allegations in the light most favorable to Plaintiffs, as we must at this stage, the allegations that Facebook allegedly compiled highly personalized profiles from sensitive browsing histories and habits prevent us from concluding that the Plaintiffs have no reasonable expectation of privacy."

NOTES

1. **Intrusion on seclusion.** An intentional intrusion upon the solitude or seclusion of another or on her private affairs is subject to liability if the intrusion would be highly offensive to a reasonable person. RESTATEMENT (SECOND) OF TORTS § 652B (1976). Highway patrol officers came upon the scene of an accident and e-mailed photos of an 18-year-old accident victim's decapitated corpse to friends and family members for Halloween. Can the actions support a privacy claim by family members? *Catsouras v. Department of Cal. Highway Patrol*, 104 Cal.Rptr.3d 352 (Ct. App. 2010). What if the picture had been taken by a person passing by the accident site—reasonable expectation of privacy?

2. **Data collection.** The Facebook case was decided on a motion to dismiss. Other cases have found that collecting and sharing browsing data for the purposes of behavioral advertising is not highly offensive, even when the collection violates the website's privacy policies. *In re Google, Inc. Privacy Policy Litigation*, 58 F.Supp.3d 968 (N.D. Cal. 2014). The fact that Facebook users were logged out when data was collected is a highly important fact for sustaining this sort of intrusion case. Do you agree that defendants' data collection was highly offensive, and that plaintiffs had a reasonable expectation of privacy? If you represented each party, what sorts of information would ou seek to gather in discovery in the case?

3. **Violations of privacy policies.** Although plaintiffs have had a hard time surviving motions to dismiss based on firms' violations of their own privacy policies, the Federal Trade Commission has consistently found such conduct to be a "deceptive trade practice" under the FTC Act and has taken enforcement actions against companies that do it. *See* Daniel J. Solove & Woodrow Hartzog, *The FTC and the New Common Law of Privacy*, 114 COLUM. L. REV. 583 (2014).

SNYDER V. PHELPS, 562 U.S. 443 (2011). "A jury held members of the Westboro Baptist Church liable for millions of dollars in damages for picketing near a soldier's funeral service. The picket signs reflected the church's view that the United States is overly tolerant of sin and that God kills American soldiers as punishment. The question presented is whether the First Amendment shields the church members from tort liability for their speech in this case." *Held*, the First Amendment shields picketers from liability under state tort law for intentional infliction of emotional distress and invasion of privacy by intrusion on seclusion. "Westboro's funeral picketing is certainly hurtful and its contribution to public discourse may be negligible. But Westboro addressed matters of public import on public property, in a peaceful manner, in full compliance with the guidance of local officials. The speech was indeed planned to coincide with Matthew Snyder's funeral, but did not itself disrupt that funeral, and Westboro's choice to conduct its picketing at that time and place did not alter the nature of its speech. Speech is powerful. It can stir people to action, move them to tears of both joy and sorrow, and—as it did here—inflict great pain. On the facts before us, we cannot react to that pain by punishing the speaker. As a Nation we have chosen a different course—to protect even hurtful speech on public issues to ensure that we do not stifle public debate."

Alito, J., dissenting: "[S]uppose that A were physically to assault B, knowing that the assault (being newsworthy) would provide A with an opportunity to transmit to the public his views on a matter of public concern. The constitutionally protected nature of the end would not shield A's use of unlawful, unprotected means. And in some circumstances the use of certain words as means would be similarly unprotected.'" (Quoting Justice Breyer's concurring opinion). "This captures what respondents did in this case. Indeed, this is the strategy that they have routinely employed—and that they will now continue to employ—inflicting severe and lasting emotional injury on an ever growing list of innocent victims."

NOTES

1. **Balancing interests.** Is the speech in *Snyder* a tortious assault on a grieving parent, akin to a punch in the stomach? What if evidence in the record shows that the defendant's conduct caused the bereaved parent great suffering, more than would be induced by a punch? Is there any way to protect the parent against this harm?

2. **Means of intrusion.** Short of trespass, one might still intrude in unpermitted ways on solitude, as by using electronic recording devices. *See Koeppel v. Speirs*, 808 N.W.2d 177 (Iowa 2011) (employer placed hidden video camera in employee bathroom; liability if proven); *Polay v. McMahon,* 10 N.E.3d 1122 (Mass. 2014) (homeowners sufficiently alleged an unreasonable intrusion on seclusion by alleging that their neighbor had installed several video cameras directed at their property, that the cameras could see into their windows, and that the cameras recorded them continuously); *but see Hernandez v. Hillsides, Inc.*, 211 P.3d 1063 (Cal. 2009) (employer placed a surveillance camera in employees' office; intrusion was insufficiently offensive or serious to give rise to liability). What about harassing telephone calls made by one person? Made by telemarketers as a group? The cases clearly allow recovery where the defendant commits a virtual trespass, entering the plaintiff's possession or domain by electronic means such as tapping telephones or using other listening devices, or by hacking into the plaintiff's email account. *Garback v. Lossing*, 2010 WL 3733971 (E.D. Mich. 2010); *see also Sheehan v. San Francisco 49ers, Ltd.*, 201 P.3d 472 (Cal. 2009) (pro football season ticket holders alleged a good claim for invasion of privacy where football club implemented a "pat-down" policy at games).

3. **Reasonable expectation of privacy.** For the intrusion claim, the plaintiff must assert a reasonable expectation of privacy. For example, a

woman who attended a comedy performance by Joan Rivers, and sued after footage of her speaking to Rivers backstage was used in a documentary film that was sold nationwide, had no reasonable expectation of privacy in the backstage area in which security personnel and film crew were present. *Bogie v. Rosenberg*, 705 F.3d 603 (7th Cir. 2013). When the conversation is open, the invasion of privacy claim is more difficult to establish. But while the person entering into a conversation may have no expectation of confidentiality with respect to the person she is speaking to, the question is whether she may yet have an expectation that the conversation will not be recorded. Courts have reached different conclusions. *Compare Caro v. Weintraub*, 618 F.3d 94 (2d Cir. 2010) (setting up iPhone and hitting record in conversation to which defendant was a party could be intrusion tort), *with Bradley v. Atlantic City Bd. of Educ.*, 736 F.Supp.2d 891 (D.N.J. 2010) (secretly recording telephone call concerning harassment did not warrant intrusion claim). Individual state laws about the legality of such recordings may affect conclusions.

THE FLORIDA STAR V. B.J.F., 491 U.S. 524 (1989). The plaintiff was a rape victim. A Florida statute makes it unlawful to publish the name of any victim of a sexual offense. A reporter-trainee for the defendant was sent to the police press room to compile material for the paper's "Police Reports" section. He copied the rape report verbatim. The resulting "Police Reports" notation under the heading of "Robberies" reported the rape, the plaintiff's name, and the location. This violated internal policy of the paper as well as Florida law. The plaintiff suffered emotional distress not only from hearing about it from fellow workers but in receiving threatening phone calls. *Held*, to impose liability would violate the First Amendment. In *Cox Broadcasting Corp. v. Cohn*, 420 U.S. 469 (1975), the publisher took the victim's name from court records open to the public. "Significantly, one of the reasons we gave in *Cox Broadcasting* for invalidating the challenged damages award was the important role the press plays in subjecting trials to public scrutiny and thereby helping guarantee their fairness. That role is not directly compromised where, as here, the information in question comes from a police report prepared and disseminated at a time at which not only had no adversarial criminal proceedings begun, but no suspect had been identified. Nor need we accept appellant's invitation to hold broadly that truthful publication may never be punished consistent with the First Amendment." However, where the publisher "lawfully obtains truthful information about a matter of public significance then state officials may not constitutionally punish publication of the information, absent a need to further a state interest of the highest order." That need has not been demonstrated here given the government's power to prevent access to the information in the first place and its failure to prohibit dissemination of the information except by mass media.

NOTE

If there is a state need of the highest order, the state might forbid publication of records that are otherwise open to public access. But the state might instead restrict public access to records. The first instance is hard to imagine in the light of the second. *See Ostergren v. Cuccinelli*, 615 F.3d 263 (4th Cir. 2010) (state could not prevent private party from posting social security numbers from land records when it had not yet redacted social security numbers from records it put on line).

REFERENCE: 3 DOBBS, HAYDEN & BUBLICK, THE LAW OF TORTS §§ 578–84 (2d ed. 2011); DOBBS, HAYDEN & BUBLICK, HORNBOOK ON TORTS, chs. 38 & 39 (2d ed. 2016); BUBLICK, BAMBAUER & ARELLANO, DOBBS ON ECONOMIC AND DIGNITARY TORTS: CASES AND MATERIALS, ch. 6 (2d ed. 2022).

§ 4. INTERFERENCE WITH FAMILY RELATIONSHIPS

In an early period of the common law, a master could have a real interest in his servant's health. If the servant were injured, the master might be obliged to continue support of the servant, but without getting the work he expected in return. It is not surprising, then, that the common law gave the master a tort action against anyone who beat and injured the servant. It later came to be thought that the husband stood in a similar relationship to his wife. Consequently, anyone who tortiously injured a wife was subject to tort liability to her husband, and it is true even today that either spouse may have a consortium claim for the injury to the other.

These earlier lines of cases were expanded to permit three other recoveries by the husband, and then later by the wife:

1. *Abduction.* Defendant carried one spouse away from the other, or "harbored" a spouse who wished to escape the marital bonds. Abduction of children, especially by former spouses, is a major problem, but is outside the scope of this chapter on communicative torts.

2. *Criminal conversation.* Defendant had sexual relations ("conversation") with the plaintiff's spouse. Even if this did not disrupt the marriage or cause other harm, it was regarded as a dishonor to the non-participating spouse. Consent of the participating spouse was no defense.

3. *Alienation of affections.* The defendant secured the affection of the plaintiff's spouse, or at least alienated those affections from the plaintiff. This might or might not be accompanied by sexual attentions; sometimes friends or relations simply persuaded one spouse to leave the other.

These torts required affirmative action by the defendant, and that the act caused harm, though not necessarily financial harm. The only fault required was an intent to interfere in the prohibited way. For example, if a defendant intended to persuade the wife to leave her husband, the defendant would be liable for alienation if he succeeded, unless he could affirmatively prove a privilege. The main privilege was a good faith effort by a relative or disinterested party to persuade the wife to leave her husband for her own good, which in some cases also protected religious advisors. Love and affection were not entitled to any similar protection, however, and the woman who persuaded a man to leave his wife, or the man who induced a woman to leave her husband, would be liable for alienation or criminal conversation, or both.

If parents sued for interference with their relationships with their children, the rights were substantially constricted. One would be liable for enticement of a child, or abduction, or seduction of a minor, but there is scant authority for permitting a claim for alienating the child's affections. A few states allow a cause of action for tortious interference with a parental or custodial relationship, *see Kessel v. Leavitt*, 511 S.E.2d 720 (W. Va. 1998), or interference with child custody and visitation rights, *see Khalifa v. Shannon*, 945 A.2d 1244 (Md. 2008). Children have been given almost no rights when an outsider interferes with parental relationships. If one parent is induced to leave the home and run off with a "home-wrecker," the children may have claims in only a couple of states.

Since the 1930s, about half the states have abolished or severely limited the action for alienation of affections, or for criminal conversation, or both. Sometimes this is accompanied by abolishing the action for breach of a promise to marry as well. Abolition has been accompanied in many instances through legislation, but in some cases courts themselves have abolished the action, and some jurisdictions have never recognized it. Some of the reasons have been that the action leads to blackmail, that interference without violence or other tortious activity probably has little effect on a healthy family relationship, and that recovery in these actions does not accomplish any real good. In addition, it has been suggested that the criminal conversation and alienation of affections actions imply that one spouse has ownership rights in another, and that they interfere with personal autonomy. *See* Dan B. Dobbs, *Tortious Interference with Contractual Relationships,* 34 ARK. L. REV. 335, 358–59 (1980).

However, in a few states, the alienation of affection action or the criminal conversation action or both are alive and kicking. *See, e.g., Cedar v. Johnson,* 921 N.W.2d 178 (S.D. 2018) (permitting alienation of affections action by husband against wife's employer with whom wife had a romantic relationship); *Widenhouse v. Colson,* 747 S.E.2d 188 (S.C. 2013) (enforcing foreign judgment from North Carolina, where alienation of affections and criminal conversations are still viable causes of action, despite elimination of these actions in South Carolina). *See also* William R. Corbett, *A Somewhat Modest Proposal to Prevent Adultery and Save Families: Two Old Torts Looking for a New Career,* 33 ARIZ. ST. L.J. 985 (2001) (supporting a kind of criminal conversation liability to "prevent adultery and save families").

Are there free speech (or privacy) arguments for abolishing liability based on love or sex between two consenting and competent parties? Suppose defendant says, "I love you; leave your wife and come live with me." Given *Times v. Sullivan* and *Gertz*, are the states free to make this a tort? Could first amendment free speech and free association guarantees, constrain the scope of the alienation of affection tort in a similar manner to the constitutional constraints on defamation and privacy torts? *Compare* H. Hunter Bruton, *The Questionable Constitutionality of Curtailing Cuckolding: Alienation-of-Affection and Criminal-Conversation Torts*, 65 DUKE L.J. 755 (2016), *with* Don Corbett, *If Loving You Is Wrong . . . Can First Amendment Protection Be Right? Alienation of Affection, Criminal Conversation, and the Right to Free Speech*, 38 N.C. CENT. L. REV. 93 (2016). What about the Fourteenth Amendment right to sexual autonomy and privacy?

Even after abolition of the alienation of affections tort, some kind of tort claims may still be viable in extreme cases, as where the marriage counselor takes advantage of the therapeutic relationship to alienate the affections of one spouse.

REFERENCE: 3 DOBBS, HAYDEN & BUBLICK, THE LAW OF TORTS §§ 601–04 (2d ed. 2011); DOBBS, HAYDEN & BUBLICK, HORNBOOK ON TORTS, ch. 40 (2d ed. 2016); BUBLICK, BAMBAUER & ARELLANO, DOBBS ON ECONOMIC AND DIGNITARY TORTS: CASES AND MATERIALS, ch. 9 (2d ed. 2022).

CHAPTER 33

COMMUNICATION OF COMMERCIALLY HARMFUL IMPRESSIONS TO OTHERS

■ ■ ■

In Chapter 32, all of the torts involved communication of facts or impressions about the plaintiff to some other person or persons. In each of those cases, the harm caused might have been partly economic. One who is libeled or maliciously prosecuted, for example, might lose a job. However, the torts we studied in that chapter also involved intensely personal elements, mainly reputation and privacy. Even if economic harm is done in those cases, the tort also reaches a highly personal level. Those torts are, preeminently, dignitary torts.

The torts we will study in this chapter also turn on communication to third persons, but in contrast they are preeminently commercial. Some of them at times touch highly personal or dignitary interests as well, but by and large they are important as means of gaining or preserving some commercial interest. They also at times raise questions about political and social values. Since they are communicative torts, there is at least the possibility that First Amendment issues will be implicated.

§ 1. INJURIOUS FALSEHOOD

BRUNSON COMMUNICATIONS, INC. v. ARBITRON, INC.

266 F.Supp. 2d 377 (E.D. Pa. 2003)

BAYLSON, JUDGE. . . .

[The plaintiff alleged: The plaintiff owned a small independent television station. Defendant purported to measure the number of viewers watching each television station in the market area at any given time and purported to measure the entire market, but in fact did not measure the viewers watching the plaintiff's station. This led to biased or erroneous information. Defendant published this erroneous information about the number of viewers to "advertising agencies, advertisers, television stations and other media sources, representing that the data were complete and accurate." Defendant moved to dismiss. That motion is before the court.]

In its commercial disparagement count, Plaintiff asserts that Defendant's false statements as to the accuracy and completeness of its test surveys caused substantial pecuniary loss to Plaintiff, in that prospective advertisers would conclude from the data that WGTW's viewership was "so insignificant as not to warrant either inclusion in the survey or recognition of the exclusion, as was foreseen by the defendant." . . .

The Court of Appeals for the Third Circuit has recently predicted that the Pennsylvania Supreme Court would adopt a Restatement of Torts section regarding commercial disparagement. That Restatement section, § 623A, provides that:

> One who publishes a false statement harmful to the interests of another is subject to liability for pecuniary loss resulting to the other if
>
> (a) he *intends* for publication of the statement to result in harm to interests of the other having a pecuniary value, *or* either recognizes or should *recognize that it is likely* to do so, *and*
>
> (b) he *knows* that the statement is *false* or acts in *reckless disregard* of its truth or falsity.

Restatement (Second) of Torts § 623(A) (1977) (emphasis added). . . .

Thus, to sustain its cause of action for commercial disparagement, Plaintiff must allege, 1.) that Defendant made a false statement, which caused pecuniary loss to Plaintiff, 2.) that Defendant intended for publication of the statement to result in harm to Plaintiff's pecuniary interests, or either recognized or should have recognized that it was likely to do so, and 3.) that Defendant knew that the statement was false or acted in reckless disregard of its truth or falsity. . . .

Under notice pleading, these allegations fulfill the requirement of a "false statement," the requirement that Defendant should have recognized the potential harm the statement could cause, and the requirement that Defendant knew the statement was false or acted in reckless disregard of its truth or falsity. Although Plaintiff does not allege that Defendant made any statements *directly referring to WGTW,* this Court concludes that Plaintiff has made out a disparagement case strong enough to withstand the present motion to dismiss. While Defendant may not have expressly mentioned WGTW in any of its statements, Plaintiff may, nevertheless, be able to prove that the total effect of Defendant's various statements and actions was to disparage Plaintiff's business—and to reduce WGTW's standing in the eyes of the persons and companies it must solicit to buy the station's product.

However, as noted above, Plaintiff has not specifically identified a pecuniary loss resulting from the allegedly false statements. Rule 9(g) [of the Federal Rules of Civil Procedure] provides that "[w]hen items of special damage are claimed, they shall be specifically stated." This Court has previously held that, to successfully plead a cause of action for disparagement, a plaintiff must allege

> facts showing an established business, the amount of sales for a substantial period preceding publication, and amount of sales subsequent to the publication, facts showing that such loss in sale were the natural and probable result of such publication, and the facts showing the plaintiff could not allege the name of particular customers who withdrew or withheld their custom. . . .

In the case at bar, Plaintiff does not allege a general decline in business, much less a specific type of pecuniary loss. However, because the allegedly disparaging statements were made approximately one year ago, Plaintiff should now be able to readily determine and specifically allege the type and extent of its economic damages. *See* Plaintiff's Motion for Leave to Amend at ¶ 4 (suggesting that "now that a year has passed," Plaintiff may be able to "quantitatively assess the actual damage"). Therefore, this Court will dismiss Plaintiff's commercial disparagement claim without prejudice to Plaintiff's right to file a Third Amended Complaint within twenty days, alleging facts showing specific types and amounts of damages, such as alleging the amount of sales for a substantial period preceding Defendant's statements, and the amount of sales subsequent to Defendant's statements, and also alleging specific facts showing that such losses in sales were the natural and probable result of Defendant's statements. . . .

[As to the plaintiff's claim of negligence:] This Court cannot conclude that Defendant owed a legal duty of care to Plaintiff under the circumstances set forth in the Second Amended Complaint. While Plaintiff has cited numerous Pennsylvania negligence cases in its brief, not one of the cases cited establishes the formation of a duty based upon the type of business activity involved in this case.

NOTES

1. **Injurious falsehood defined.** Commercial disparagement is a form of the tort the Second Restatement calls injurious falsehood. Another tort within the "injurious falsehood" umbrella is slander of title, in which the defendant falsely casts aspersions on plaintiff's ownership of real or personal property. Slander of title requires plaintiff to prove (1) some interest in the property, (2) that the words published were false, (3) that the words were published with malice, and (4) that the plaintiff suffered pecuniary loss or injury as a result of the false statement. *See, e.g., Jeffrey v. Cathers*, 104 S.W.3d 424 (Mo. Ct. App. 2003). Some courts have said that injurious falsehood claims require proof of the publication of a false statement of fact. *See, e.g., HipSaver, Inc. v. Kiel*, 984 N.E.2d 755 (Mass. 2013) (doctor's critical comments about hip-protection device were not untrue; no action for commercial disparagement); *see also Seaton v. TripAdvisor LLC*, 728 F.3d 592 (6th Cir. 2013) (affirming

dismissal of complaint where plaintiff hotel sued website for putting its hotel on the "Dirtiest Hotels" list; placement on that list "cannot reasonably be interpreted as stating an actual fact").

2. **Connection to defamation.** The torts in the injurious falsehood family involve assertions that disparage the plaintiff's title or ownership rights (in the case of slander of title) or the plaintiff's product (in the case of commercial disparagement), but do not qualify as ordinary libel or slander. *Cf. In re Lipsky*, 460 S.W.3d 579 (Tex. 2015) (defamation and business disparagement serve different interests: the former "chiefly serves to protect the personal reputation of an injured party" while the latter "protects economic interests"). Some courts nevertheless allow a defamation case based on statements that disparage a plaintiff's business, *see, e.g., Senna v. Florimont*, 958 A.2d 427 (N.J. 2008), but it is not personally libelous to print that the plaintiff does not own Blackacre or that his product is not very good. Notice that the rules for the injurious falsehood tort require proof that is far more demanding than required by common law libel rules. In fact, don't the rules come close to requiring the same proof that would be required in a libel suit by a public figure?

3. **Statutory actions.** The common law tort of injurious falsehood is generally if not universally recognized by the courts, but injurious falsehood or commercial disparagement may also count as a statutory tort under state unfair competition or deceptive trade practices acts. In addition, the plaintiff in such cases may have a cause of action under the now-expanded version of the federal trademark legislation, § 43(a) of the Lanham Act, 15 U.S.C. § 1125(a). *See, e.g., POM Wonderful LLC v. Coca-Cola Co.*, 573 U.S. 102 (2014) (private party may sue competitor under Lanham Act, challenging a food label that is regulated by the FDCA where that label tended to "mislead and trick consumers, all to the injury of competitors"); *Lexmark Int'l, Inc. v. Static Control Components, Inc.*, 572 U.S. 118 (2014) (under Lanham Act, plaintiff must prove it is within the "zone of interests" protected by the Act in order to sue; here, the manufacturer of components necessary for the remanufacture of defendant supplier's toner cartridges alleged sufficient injuries, in the form of lost sales and damage to reputation, to fall within the "zone of interests" test). Statutory actions may carry certain advantages or disadvantages—federal jurisdiction in some cases, perhaps a right to recover attorneys' fees if the plaintiff prevails.

§ 2. INTENTIONAL INTERFERENCE WITH CONTRACT AND EXPECTANCY

LUMLEY V. GYE, 2 El. & Bl. 216, 118 Eng. Rep. 749 (1853). The plaintiff operated an opera theater. He had retained a singer, Wagner, to perform exclusively at his theater. Before the term of her contract was up, the defendant, knowing of the contract, "enticed" or induced Wagner to cease further performance for the plaintiff and to perform at the defendant's theater instead, to the plaintiff's damage. The plaintiff sued the defendant claiming that inducing a breach of contract was a tort. *Held*, for the plaintiff. Erle, J.: "[P]rocurement of the violation of the right is a cause of action. . . ."

NOTES

1. **The basis of liability.** *Lumley* made inducing breach of contract, by itself, a tort. The defendant was liable if he intended to interfere with a known contract, even if he used no wrongful means. The defendant might be able to justify his actions, but that would come in as a defense if it came in at all, and the burden would be on the defendant to persuade judges and juries that his conduct was truly justified. Although most courts now appear to agree that proof of the defendant's intent to interfere with a valid contract is no longer by itself sufficient for liability, such intent is definitely required as one element among others. *See Blondell v. Littlepage*, 991 A.2d 80 (Md. 2010).

2. **Inducing and other forms of interference.** *Lumley* involved only inducing breach, but today other forms of intentional interference with contract are also actionable. This can occur in many ways. One example: Employees of the Pershing Company validly contract to continue work for Pershing for one year and not to work for a competitor during that year. Eloise Empson leaves Pershing after one month and goes to work for the Damich Company. Two weeks later, Damich learns that Empson is breaching her non-competition covenant but Damich continues to employ her. Damich has not induced a breach but nevertheless has intentionally interfered with the contract and is liable to Pershing. *See Fowler v. Printers II, Inc.*, 598 A.2d 794 (Md. Ct. Spec. App. 1991).

3. **Negligent interference with contract.** Intentional interference is normally required to state a claim for interference with contract; negligence is not enough. *See, e.g., Telemundo Network Grp., LLC v. Azteca Int'l Corp.*, 957 So.2d 705 (Fla. Dist. Ct. App. 2007). However, there are certain cases in which negligence will suffice. For example, suppose that A contracts with B to keep B's private road in good repair. D negligently crashes an oil truck into a nearby tree, there is an explosion, and the road is heavily damaged. As a result, A must spend additional money in keeping her contract to repair. A has a claim against D. This pattern of cases is equivalent to the subrogation pattern in which A insures B's car. When D negligently damages B's car, A pays and is then "subrogated" to B's rights against D. The damages claimed are the same damages that could have been claimed by someone even if there were no contract at all. In these cases, then, to permit A's claim is merely to say that A, rather than B, is the plaintiff. Hence, if negligence would warrant a claim by B, it would equally warrant substituting A as the plaintiff. Several cases, however, have gone beyond this pattern and have ostensibly allowed recovery for negligent interference with contract. *J'Aire Corp. v. Gregory*, 598 P.2d 60 (Cal. 1979), is such a case, although it might have been explained on a contract theory with the plaintiff a third party beneficiary. The plaintiff in *J'Aire* operated a restaurant in an airport. Defendant contracted with the airport for

a reasonably expeditious improvement. Operation of the restaurant was impossible while the work was being done and the defendant negligently delayed completing the work, to the restaurant's loss. This was held actionable. A few other cases involving close relationships among landowners, construction contractors, and architects or engineers also allow recovery for negligent interference with contract.

4. **Independent torts causing interference; distinguishing the fact of interference from the tort of interference.** The striking characteristic about interference with contract is that the defendant may be liable without doing anything wrong besides making a business deal. But some interference with contract occurs through the commission of particular torts. For example, if A contracts to sell a supply of vaccines to B for distribution, the defendant might steal the vaccines so that A could not perform his contract with B. Or the defendant might libel B, representing that he represents a terrorist group or foreign power which will misuse the vaccines. When the defendant interferes with contract by converting the goods involved or libeling the promisee, we describe the facts by saying he interfered with the contract. Yet we usually think that the tort involved is conversion or libel, not *the tort* of interference with contract. In those cases, we ordinarily expect that the rules applied are the rules of conversion or libel, although damages may include the loss of the contract.

5. **Interference by disparagement.** But wait. If the defendant in *Lumley* merely offered the singer a better contract, the defendant would have been liable, period. Under such a broad rule the plaintiff need not prove fraud, or libel, or any other wrongdoing. Suppose, however, that the defendant in *Lumley* induced Miss Wagner to breach her contract with plaintiff by telling her that the plaintiff's opera house was losing money and might cease to exist, or that its productions were generally of low quality. That sounds like disparagement. We know that for injurious falsehoods the plaintiff must prove knowing or reckless falsity and pecuniary damages. Would these disparagement rules apply in such a case, or could the plaintiff simply ignore disparagement and claim the interference with contract tort? If the answer is that we can ignore the stringent rules of disparagement, then isn't that tort obsolete? If the answer is that the plaintiff must prove knowing falsity, isn't it strange or even irrational to say that if the defendant merely persuades a contracting party to breach he is automatically liable but that if he does so by disparagement he can shield himself with the rules requiring knowing or reckless falsity? Is it possible that it was a mistake to recognize interference with contract as a tort on such wide-ranging terms?

RESTATEMENT (THIRD) OF TORTS: LIABILITY FOR ECONOMIC HARM

(2020)

§ 17. Interference with Contract

(1) A defendant is subject to liability for interference with contract if:

(a) a valid contract existed between the plaintiff and a third party;

(b) the defendant knew of the contract;

(c) the defendant engaged in wrongful conduct as defined in Subsection (2);

(d) the defendant intended to cause a breach of the contract or disruption of its performance;

(e) the defendant's wrongful conduct caused a breach of the contract or disruption of performance; and

(f) the plaintiff suffered economic loss as a result.

(2) Conduct is wrongful for purposes of this Section if:

(a) the defendant acted for the purpose of appropriating the benefits of the plaintiff's contract;

(b) the defendant's conduct constituted an independent and intentional legal wrong; or

(c) the defendant engaged in the conduct for the sole purpose of causing harm to the plaintiff.

ELDRIDGE V. JOHNDROW

345 P.3d 553 (Utah 2015)

[Joseph and Lindsey Eldridge manage residential property and provide various other services for wealthy homeowners. David Johndrow was a former friend and client of the Eldridges. Lindsey Eldridge accused Johndrow of attacking her at a restaurant, and Johndrow accused the Eldridges of spreading false rumors and stealing his mobile phone. Johndrow hired an "investigative team," which discovered various embarrassing facts about the Eldridges: liens, a foreclosure, an old felony conviction, and unflattering news reports. Johndrow threatened that if the Eldridges refused to retract their accusations and compensate him for the allegedly stolen phone, he would protect his "credibility" by revealing what he had found to the people to whom he had recommended the Eldridges. When the Eldridges did not accede to his demands, he emailed embarrassing information to "at least nine" of the Eldridges' institutional clients and communicated it verbally to a number of their individual clients. The Eldridges sued, asserting several theories of liability including tortious interference with economic relations, tortious interference with prospective economic relations, defamation, false light, and intentional infliction of emotional distress. The tortious interference theories rested on two separate allegations: first, that by defaming the Eldridges, Johndrow had interfered with their economic relations through an improper means; and second, that because Mr. Johndrow's only goal was to hurt the Eldridges' business, he had interfered with their economic relations in pursuit of an improper purpose. The district court concluded that the information Johndrow had disseminated was "at least substantially true" and "not susceptible to a defamatory interpretation." It therefore granted summary judgment on the defamation and false light claims. Further, because the "improper means" basis for tortious interference liability depended on Johndrow's alleged defamation of the Eldridges, the court granted summary judgment on the tortious interference claims insofar as they were based on improper means. However, the district court denied summary judgment on the tortious interference claims insofar as they were based on allegations of improper purpose. Johndrow appealed. *Held*, no tortious interference claim can succeed without evidence of improper means.]

[D]etermining the predominant purpose behind a defendant's actions raises significant evidentiary problems. . . . [O]nce a plaintiff presents evidence of an improper purpose, no legal standard exists to guide fact-finders' determination of whether that purpose or the defendant's legitimate purposes predominated. Juries are required to look into the defendant's soul and discern which of her mixed motives was the real cause of her action. . . .

Because improper-purpose findings are so dependent on fact-finders' personal sympathies, and so insulated from appellate review, the outcome of an improper-purpose suit becomes unpredictable as soon as any evidence of improper purpose is introduced. This is a problem not merely because it may lead to unjust outcomes in individual cases, but because it makes it impossible for private parties to understand their rights and duties under tortious interference law.

Under the improper-purpose prong as it has developed, a business owner could be sued for undercutting his competitor's prices if he held a grudge against her. An investor in a Ponzi scheme might be sued for exposing the scheme if she did so with enough malice towards her swindlers. And a customer leaving angry reviews online might receive a response to her complaints via service of process.

It is of course likely that few juries would find a predominantly improper purpose in any of these cases, but that is beside the point. The mere risk that a jury might find liability, coupled with the low bar the claims need to clear in order to reach a jury in the first place, could become a substantial deterrent to socially beneficial speech and conduct if improper-purpose suits became common. In the First Amendment context, the tendency of a law to deter conduct it does not actually prohibit is known as a chilling effect, and is sometimes sufficient to invalidate the law as an infringement of the freedom of speech even when the object of the law is constitutionally unobjectionable.

We do not hold that the improper-purpose doctrine actually violates the First Amendment—that question is not before us, and we have no need to reach it. But we are persuaded that the improper-purpose doctrine as it currently exists in Utah is in tension with First Amendment principles, and this tension is a further reason to abandon the precedent on which it is based. . . . [T]he improper-purpose prong's emphasis on defendants' motivations, rather than their actions, prevents courts from articulating clear distinctions between appropriate conduct and conduct that ought not to be acceptable under the law. The better approach is to encourage further development of the improper-means prong. . . .

Finally, we observe that we are not alone in determining that improper-purpose liability does more harm than good. In the context of intentional interference with prospective economic relations, one prominent treatise acknowledges "a definite movement toward limiting or even eliminating motive-based liability." 3 DAN B. DOBBS, ET AL., THE LAW OF TORTS § 639 (2d ed. 2011). . . . [I]n recent decades a number of courts have concluded that tortious interference liability should result from wrongful conduct rather than mere malice. *See, e.g., Avilla v. Newport Grand Jai Alai LLC*, 935 A.2d 91 (R.I. 2007).

Although we reject our past doctrine that improper purpose is sufficient grounds for tortious interference liability, this does not mean that defendants' motives and intent are entirely irrelevant to tortious interference claims. . . . First and more obviously, tortious interference remains an intentional tort. . . . [E]vidence of defendants' motives will frequently shed light on their intent. Second, defendants' motivation will often be relevant to the improper means prong of the [ ] test. [Torts such as abuse of process may require showings with respect to purpose].

[A] person who violates no legal duties, infringes no one's rights, and commits no wrongful action can never be held liable for malice alone. . . . In order to win a tortious interference claim under Utah law, a plaintiff must now prove (1) that the defendant intentionally interfered with the plaintiff's existing or potential economic relations, (2) . . . by improper means, (3) causing injury to the plaintiff. The Eldridges' tortious interference claims fail the second prong of this test: they have failed to produce evidence of an improper means.

NOTES

1.   **Wrongful motive.** The Restatement Third takes the view that "if a defendant's *sole purpose* is the infliction of harm on the plaintiff, liability is appropriate." RESTATEMENT (THIRD) OF TORTS: LIAB. FOR ECON. HARM § 17 cmt. f (2020). Would *Eldridge* have come out differently if the court had applied the Restatement Third's "sole purpose" test? Should a jury be permitted to consider bad motive if the defendant's conduct is otherwise permissible? Does the opinion in *Eldridge* persuade you that improper purpose alone should not provide grounds for a tortious interference claim?

2.   **Wrongfulness.** Several recent cases require the plaintiff to prove that the defendant's interference was wrongful in some sense, although they do not necessarily require an independent tort. *See, e.g., Nostrame v. Santiago,* 61 A.3d 893 (N.J. 2013) (affirming dismissal of complaint for tortious interference with prospective contractual relationship where there was no allegation that defendants used improper or unlawful means). *But see Gieseke v. IDCA, Inc.,* 844 N.W.2d 210 (Minn. 2014) (claim for tortious interference with prospective business advantage is limited to interference that is both intentional and independently tortious or unlawful rather than merely "unfair," to avoid chilling fair competition). A number of scholars have urged a focus on conduct rather than motive as grounds for the tort. *See* Harvey Perlman, *Interference with Contract and Other Economic Expectancies: A Clash of Tort and Contract Doctrine,* 49 U. CHI. L. REV. 61 (1982); Dan B. Dobbs, *Tortious Interference with Contractual Relationships,* 34 ARK. L. REV. 335 (1980).

3.   **Interference with contract vs. opportunity.** *Eldridge* involves interference with contracts and expectancies. *Eldridge* does not draw a sharp distinction between the two torts. The case cites the Dobbs treatise about a trend towards limiting liability in interference with expectancy cases. The treatise suggests problems with using motives in contract as well as expectancy cases. 3 DOBBS, HAYDEN & BUBLICK, THE LAW OF TORTS § 634 (2d ed. 2011). Should it matter to the court's outcome and reasoning whether defendant Johndrow gave the adverse information to people who had existing contracts with the Eldridges and not just to people who might have future dealings with them? A defendant who interferes with economic opportunities may have a broader range of privileges—to compete for business, for example, and to offer better prices in doing so. Thus, expectancies tend to be less protected.

4.   **Improper means in cases of improper motive.** Could the plaintiffs in *Eldridge* have argued that threatening to disclose information to clients unless money was paid to the defendant constituted a sort of harassment or extortion? Think about racial discrimination in the sale of housing. That would involve an improper motive too. In *Martin v. Tug & Barge, Inc.,* 271 F.3d 823 (9th Cir. 2001), the court wrote: "where unlawful motive is the basis for sanctioning behavior . . . the forbidden motive is generally a

specific one, proscribed by a particular statute, regulation, or constitutional provision, not one derived from general conceptions of public policy."

5. **Animus.** In *Fikes v. Furst,* 81 P.3d 545 (N.M. 2003), both plaintiff and defendant were anthropologists. They had a contentious relationship for many years. Fikes prepared a book manuscript containing statements about Furst's work, including this: "I discovered what may be the most complicated and fascinating anthropological hoax of the 20th century." Dr. Fikes had a contract with Madison Books to publish the manuscript. "Dr. Furst found out about it and wrote to the publisher threatening to sue for libel if the book was published. Madison Books then canceled the contract with Dr. Fikes to publish the book." Fikes sued on several grounds. On the interference with contract ground Furst argued that he was not motivated by ill-will or a desire to harm but by a desire to protect his own interest—his professional reputation and livelihood. Do you think that the interference with contract was improper? On a sole-motive test, is this a question that should go to the jury? Would you say that protecting one's own economic interests is always enough to negate bad motive?

6. **Damages in contract and tort.** In most interference cases, the contract promisor, like the singer in *Lumley,* has itself breached the contract. The plaintiff may recover either on contract against the promisor or in tort. Should the damages be the same? There are cases permitting recovery in the tort claim that would not be permitted in the contract claim—punitive damages and mental distress damages, for example. *See, e.g., Mooney v. Johnson Cattle Co., Inc.,* 634 P.2d 1333 (Or. 1981).

7. **Traditional privileges.** Under the traditional rules, defendant would be liable both for intentional interference with contract and intentional interference with economic prospects, but in either case might defeat liability by showing a privilege or justification for the interference. Two privileges are fairly well-defined. These are (1) the privilege to interfere with a promise to marry, and (2) the privilege to interfere with economic expectancies (but not actual contracts) by competing for business. Other privileges, such as privileges to act in the interest of self, others, or the public interest, might also apply.

NOTE: INTERFERENCE BY INVADING PUBLIC INTEREST

Boycotts. One form of interference with contract or prospective advantages is the boycott, which is a refusal to deal. Apart from statutes, such as anti-discrimination statutes, any one individual may refuse to deal with any other for any reason whatever. When the individual organizes others or calls upon them to join in this refusal, it is a boycott and analysis becomes more complicated. For example, some boycotting activity, in which people may make speeches and picket in order to make others aware of their grievances, is constitutionally protected. *See NAACP v. Claiborne Hardware Co.,* 458 U.S. 886 (1982) (business boycotts by NAACP).

Anti-competitive boycotts. Some boycotts are illegal because of serious anti-competitive elements in them. Suppose T, who controls the entire supply of a rock star's new recording, agrees with retailers A, B, and C that the recording will not be sold to retailer D. D, unable to obtain this popular recording, may be unable to compete, not only in this item, but on others. This kind of boycott, which usually involves a combination of several actors, will very likely be found to violate federal and state antitrust laws. Frequently, a complaint in cases of this kind may contain both a claim for antitrust violations and also a common law claim for interference with contract.

Secondary boycotts. Suppose T has a dispute with B. T, seeking to induce B to discharge certain employees of B, tells B "I won't buy your products until you fire those people." If B agrees, the discharged employees might have a claim for interference with contract on prospects. Suppose, however, T goes further and tells A: "You must also pressure B to discharge the employees, and if you do not do so, I will also quit buying *your* product." This is called secondary boycott. It draws A into a dispute in which he has no part and holds him hostage for B's good behavior. These boycotts are almost always condemned for this reason. If B loses business because of this kind of boycott, B would have a claim. Conceivably A might also have a claim.

Labor boycotts. Strikes by labor organizations were once considered illegal because they were interferences with contract or with business relations. The union calling a strike was inducing employees not to continue work and it was liable in tort. Over a very long period of time, this has been changed by federal statute. Although certain strikes involving secondary boycotts are impermissible under federal law, most others are entirely legal. And to a very large extent, federal law has preempted the field of labor organizations. This topic is thus a part of advanced courses in labor law.

Free speech and interference with business claims. If the defendant's only "wrong" is to offer the singer a better contract, shouldn't the defendant be protected by First Amendment free speech rights? *See* David A. Anderson, *Torts, Speech, and Contracts,* 75 TEX. L. REV. 1499 (1997); Dan B. Dobbs, *Tortious Interference with Contractual Relationships,* 34 ARK. L. REV. 335 (1980). Should First Amendment protection be afforded for all interferences based on words used rather than conduct that is tortious by some independent standard?

REFERENCE: 3 DOBBS, HAYDEN & BUBLICK, THE LAW OF TORTS §§ 616–43 (2d ed. 2011); DOBBS, HAYDEN & BUBLICK, HORNBOOK ON TORTS §§ 42.1–42.11 (2d ed. 2016).

§ 3. INTELLECTUAL PROPERTY AND UNFAIR COMPETITION—TRADEMARK INFRINGEMENT

NOTE: INTELLECTUAL PROPERTY AND UNFAIR COMPETITION

1. *What is intellectual property?* Intellectual property includes rights in intangibles such as patents, copyrights, marks (such as trademarks) that identify a business or goods it sells, and trade secrets. Personality or "identity" of performers might be included, but we deal with that in the next section. The term "unfair competition," long identified especially with one person's misuse of another's trademark or misappropriation of some intangible commercial value, is now often used to refer to almost any form of competitive misconduct. Each of the fields of intellectual property is large in itself and supports large books and many legal specialists. We sketch a few high points, mainly about trademarks and unfair competition.

2. *Patents.* This chapter concerns commercial communications, but we mention patents briefly as one kind of intellectual property. Only the federal government can grant a patent, which is a monopoly for a limited period of time, meant to encourage inventions. You can have a valid patent for inventing a machine (or even a part or a process) that is novel and inventive and not an extension of prior "art," but only if the knowledge is not already in the public domain. Besides all this, you have to reveal quite precisely all the knowledge necessary to make the machine, which goes on file and is open to the public at the Patent and Trademark Office (a federal agency). The point is to encourage invention by giving the inventor a monopoly, but only for the ultimate purpose of getting the knowledge into the public domain. So your patent will expire in 17 years and after that anyone can use the knowledge to make the machine and even go into competition against you. States cannot offer more protection by making it a tort to copy the useful features of an unpatented article or one in which the patent has expired. All this is explored in *Bonito Boats, Inc. v. Thunder Craft Boats, Inc.,* 489 U.S. 141 (1989). Although the mechanical invention is the prototype or fundamental model for patent, today's patent law now affords the patent monopoly to some surprising other items, such as genes and gene sequences that are by no means invented but have been discovered by scientists.

3. *Copyrights.* Copyright protection is also exclusively federal. If you are the "author" of any original work of tangible expression you are entitled to copyright protection. "Author," includes any creator, such as composers, painters, and photographers. Filing copies with the Library of Congress and filling out a form will enhance your protection but is not necessarily required. The copyright monopoly is now for a very long period—life of the author plus 70 years. You can have a copyright even if your work is not creative; it must be original in the sense that it originated with you and in

the sense that it is something more than a mere alphabetical list like a telephone book. The federal copyright statute allows a plaintiff to elect statutory damages in lieu of actual damages. These statutory damages range from $750 to $30,000 for each work infringed, and the court is given discretion to increase or decrease the award based on the infringer's relative innocence or willfulness. This statutory damages provision was upheld against constitutional attack in *Sony BMG Music Entertainment v. Tenenbaum*, 719 F.3d 67 (1st Cir. 2013), a case in which several recording companies sued a downloader for willfully infringing the copyrights of 30 music recordings by using file-sharing software, then distributing those recordings to others without authorization. The court affirmed a jury award of $22,500 for each infringed recording, which fell within the statutory range established by Congress. The court stated that statutory damages under the Copyright Act are designed not only to provide "reparation for injury" but also "to discourage wrongful conduct."

Since copyright law gives a monopoly over expression, doesn't that impair the freedom of speech? Copyright law provides two protections for free speech. First, only the specific expression you created is copyrighted; anyone can use the ideas and the facts, just not your expression or a close imitation of it. Second, the statute itself permits "fair use" of copyrighted material. Fair use is an affirmative defense on which the defendant has the burden of proof. *Latimer v. Roaring Toyz, Inc.*, 601 F.3d 1224 (11th Cir. 2010) ("fair use of copyrighted work is an affirmative defense and should be pleaded as such," citing U.S. Supreme Court usage).What counts as fair use may not be easy to determine in advance and that fact may dampen free speech. The factors to be considered in determining fair use are vaguely expressed in the statute: "(1) the purpose and character of the use, including whether such use is of a commercial nature or is for nonprofit educational purposes; (2) the nature of the copyrighted work; (3) the amount and substantiality of the portion used in relation to the copyrighted work as a whole; and (4) the effect of the use upon the potential market for or value of the copyrighted work." While each of the four enumerated fair-use factors must be weighed in light of the purposes of copyright, whether the allegedly infringing work is "transformative" is often the central inquiry. *Gaylord v. United States*, 595 F.3d 1364 (Fed. Cir. 2010). That the copyrighted work is used by the defendant for commercial purposes cuts against a finding of fair use. *See Bouchat v. Baltimore Ravens Ltd. P'ship*, 619 F.3d 301 (4th Cir. 2010) (defendant NFL team's use of plaintiff's "Flying B" logo on its highlight films for commercial purpose was not a fair use, but use of the same logo in the lobby of the team's office was fair use, where there was "no clear-cut commercial purpose" to that display). What if an evangelist copies a page of copyrighted material from Hustler Magazine and mails it to many supporters, presumably to show the nature of the enemy. He requests donations and reaps $700,000. Does the copyright owner have a claim or is this fair use? *See Hustler Magazine Inc. v. Moral Majority Inc.,* 796 F.2d 1148 (9th Cir. 1986).

4. *Trade secrets.* Any information that can be used to economic advantage in the operation of an enterprise—such as chemical formulas or production techniques—can qualify as a trade secret. *See* RESTATEMENT (THIRD) OF UNFAIR COMPETITION § 39 (1993). The secret must have economic value in part because it is not generally known and in fact is kept secret. Once trade secrets are generally known, they no longer get legal protection. Typical trade secret cases involve employees or former employees who reveal a business' secret to competitors for a price, or else use the secret to go into business themselves competing with the former employer. The tort is almost always committed by violating the plaintiff's rights of confidentiality. If a stranger simply buys the plaintiff's product on the market, and figures out the secret for himself, he has committed no tort. He can then go into competition with the erstwhile owner of the secret, manufacturing and selling the same product based on the same secret. Would a business ever prefer to use trade secret protections for an important formula rather than patent law?

5. *Trademarks and unfair competition.* The common law of trademarks began with the tort often called "passing off." The customer asks for a brand name item, Mopsy; the seller secretly substitutes his own brand, Flopsy, instead. If you want to protect consumers in their right to choose what they buy, you let the manufacturer of Mopsy sue and recover an injunction or damages (he lost a customer). This is the rudimentary point of traditional unfair competition or "trademark" law.

QUALITEX CO. v. JACOBSON PRODUCTS CO.

514 U.S. 159 (1995)

JUSTICE BREYER delivered the opinion of the Court. . . .

[The plaintiff sells pads to dry cleaners for use with their pressing machines. The pads are a distinctive green-gold color. The defendant, Jacobson, a competitor, started selling pads of the same color. The plaintiff registered its pad color with the Patent and Trademark Office and sued Jacobson under the Federal Lanham Act.]

The Lanham Act gives a seller or producer the exclusive right to "register" a trademark, and to prevent his or her competitors from using that trademark. Both the language of the Act and the basic underlying principles of trademark law would seem to include color within the universe of things that can qualify as a trademark. The language of the Lanham Act describes that universe in the broadest of terms. It says that trademarks "includ[e] any word, name, symbol, or device, or any combination thereof." Since human beings might use as a "symbol" or "device" almost anything at all that is capable of carrying meaning, this language, read literally, is not restrictive. The courts and the Patent and Trademark Office have authorized for use as a mark a particular shape (of a Coca-Cola bottle), a particular sound (of NBC's three chimes), and even a particular scent (of plumeria blossoms on sewing thread). If a shape, a sound, and a fragrance can act as symbols why, one might ask, can a color not do the same?

A color is also capable of satisfying the more important part of the statutory definition of a trademark, which requires that a person "us[e]" or "inten[d] to use" the mark "to identify and distinguish his or her goods, including a unique product, from those manufactured or sold by others and to indicate the source of the goods, even if that source is unknown." True, a product's color is unlike "fanciful," "arbitrary," or "suggestive" words or designs, which almost automatically tell a customer that they refer to a brand. The imaginary word "Suntost," or the words "Suntost Marmalade," on a jar of orange jam immediately would signal a brand or a product "source"; the jam's orange color does not do so. But, over time, customers may come to treat a particular color on a product or its packaging (say, a color that in context seems unusual, such as pink on a firm's insulating material or red on the head of a large industrial bolt) as signifying a brand. And, if so, that color would have come to identify and distinguish the goods—i.e. "to "indicate" their "source"—much in the way that descriptive words on a product (say, "Trim" on nail clippers or "Car-Freshner" on deodorizer) can come to indicate a product's origin. In this circumstance, trademark law says that the word (e.g., "Trim"), although not inherently distinctive, has developed "secondary meaning." . . .

In principle, trademark law, by preventing others from copying a source-identifying mark, "reduce[s] the customer's costs of shopping and making purchasing decisions," 1 J. McCarthy, McCarthy on Trademarks and Unfair Competition § 2.01[2], p. 2–3 (3d ed. 1994) (hereinafter McCarthy), for it quickly and easily assures a potential customer that this item—the item with this mark—is made by the same producer as other similarly marked items that he or she liked (or disliked) in the past. At the same time, the law helps assure a producer that it (and not an imitating competitor) will reap the financial, reputation-related rewards associated with a desirable product. The law thereby "encourage[s] the production of quality products," and simultaneously discourages those who hope to sell inferior products by capitalizing on a consumer's inability quickly to evaluate the quality of an item offered for sale. It is the source-distinguishing ability of a mark—not its ontological status as color, shape, fragrance, word, or sign—that permits it to serve these basic purposes. . . .

Neither can we find a principled objection to the use of color as a mark in the important "functionality" doctrine of trademark law. The functionality doctrine prevents trademark law, which seeks to promote competition by protecting a firm's reputation, from instead inhibiting legitimate competition by allowing a producer to control a useful product feature. It is the province of patent law, not trademark law, to encourage invention by granting inventors a monopoly over new product designs or functions.... If a product's functional features could be used as trademarks, however, a monopoly over such features could be obtained without regard to whether they qualify as patents and could be extended forever (because trademarks may be renewed in perpetuity). Functionality doctrine therefore would require, to take an imaginary example, that even if customers have come to identify the special illumination-enhancing shape of a new patented light bulb with a particular manufacturer, the manufacturer may not use that shape as a trademark, for doing so, after the patent had expired, would impede competition—not by protecting the reputation of the original bulb maker, but by frustrating competitors' legitimate efforts to produce an equivalent illumination-enhancing bulb. This Court consequently has explained that, "[i]n general terms, a product feature is functional," and cannot serve as a trademark, "if it is essential to the use or purpose of the article or if it affects the cost or quality of the article," that is, if exclusive use of the feature would put competitors at a significant non-reputation-related disadvantage. Although sometimes color plays an important role (unrelated to source identification) in making a product more desirable, sometimes it does not. And, this latter fact—the fact that sometimes color is not essential to a product's use or purpose and does not affect cost or quality—indicates that the doctrine of "functionality" does not create an absolute bar to the use of color alone as a mark....

Third, Jacobson points to many older cases—including Supreme Court cases—in support of its position....

These Supreme Court cases, however, interpreted trademark law as it existed before 1946, when Congress enacted the Lanham Act. The Lanham Act significantly changed and liberalized the common law to "dispense with mere technical prohibitions," most notably, by permitting trademark registration of descriptive words (say, "U-Build-It" model airplanes) where they had acquired "secondary meaning." The Lanham Act extended protection to descriptive marks by making clear that (with certain explicit exceptions not relevant here), "nothing . . . shall prevent the registration of a mark used by the applicant which has become distinctive of the applicant's goods in commerce." This language permits an ordinary word, normally used for a nontrademark purpose (e.g., description), to act as a trademark where it has gained "secondary meaning." . . .

[W]e conclude that the Ninth Circuit erred in barring Qualitex's use of color as a trademark. For these reasons, the judgment of the Ninth Circuit is

Reversed.

NOTES

1. **Infringement.** How do you infringe a trademark? You use a symbol or device with enough similarity to create confusion or likelihood of confusion among potential consumers. *See, e.g., Network Automation, Inc. v. Advanced Sys. Concepts, Inc.*, 638 F.3d 1137 (9th Cir. 2011) (insufficient likelihood of consumer confusion; in the Internet context, emerging technologies require a "flexible approach" to the issue); *One Indus., LLC v. Jim O'Neal Dist., Inc.*, 578 F.3d 1154 (9th Cir. 2009) (no likelihood of confusion between two marks used by competitors in motocross clothing market); *North American Med. Corp. v. Axiom Worldwide, Inc.*, 522 F.3d 1211 (11th Cir. 2008) (infringement by using competitor's trademarks within defendant's "meta tags" on its website). *See also Fortres Grand Corp. v. Warner Bros. Entertainment Inc.*, 763 F.3d 696 (7th Cir. 2014) (affirming trial court's grant of motion to dismiss in favor of movie producer in case brought by owner of computer software company that claimed trademark infringement and unfair competition; consumer confusion was unlikely where movie using "the clean slate" to describe a hacking program was shown primarily in theaters and the plaintiff's "Clean Slate" computer software was sold only on plaintiff's own website). Suppose you start manufacturing canned soup sold with red and white labels and call it "Camp's Soup." Some customers would unthinkingly pick up your soup when they meant to pick up Campbell's. Expect to hear from Campbell's.

2. **Dilution.** Notice that traditional trademark law protected the consumer (albeit by giving a cause of action to the trademark holder). State legislatures, followed by Congress, then went beyond that protection and created a cause of action for the trademark owner based on dilution of the trademark value. Suppose you manufacture and market "TIFFANY'S CAT CHOW" or "TIFFANY'S PLASTIC STAINED GLASS." Nobody who buys cat chow is likely to think he is getting an exquisite Fifth Avenue creation, so the requisite consumer confusion is lacking. However, you can see why a jeweler might not want to be identified with cat chow, however much you might love cats. This is an example of dilution by "tarnishment." It would also be possible to dilute by "blurring." Judge Posner gave an illustration in *Ty Inc. v. Perryman*, 306 F.3d 509 (7th Cir. 2002), where he imagined an upscale restaurant calling itself Tiffany. No one is likely to think the jeweler has opened a restaurant, so there is no confusion. But the association of the two tends to blur the unique standing of the Tiffany mark. State and federal statutes now authorize trademark owners to sue for dilution. The federal statute limits this antidilution protection to owners of "famous" marks.

3. **Free speech: trademark cases.** We saw that copyright law withdrew some of its protection for authors in the interest of free speech. Is there anything similar with trademarks? Suppose a group of nutritionists tries to persuade members of Congress that the cold cereal industry should be regulated by federal law. To do this, the group publishes: (1) a booklet reproducing cereal ads in an effort to show that these ads are misleading consumers about the nutritional content of cereals, and (2) posters on which pictures of actual cereal boxes are reproduced, with a stamp across them

saying "Dangerous to Your Health." Suppose in each case the reproductions include reproductions of trademarks or trade names. Is there a free speech issue? *Cf. Jordan v. Jewel Food Stores, Inc.*, 743 F.3d 509 (7th Cir. 2014) (store operator's advertisement in magazine, commemorating plaintiff Michael Jordan's induction into NBA Hall of Fame, was commercial speech for First Amendment purposes, reversing the trial court's ruling that the ad was "fully protected noncommercial speech" in its ruling against Jordan in his Lanham Act and state-law claims; those claims can proceed).

> REFERENCES: RESTATEMENT (THIRD) OF TORTS, UNFAIR COMPETITION, §§ 9–17 (1995); J. THOMAS MCCARTHY, TRADEMARKS AND UNFAIR COMPETITION (4th ed. 2012); 3 DOBBS, HAYDEN & BUBLICK, THE LAW OF TORTS § 734 (2d ed. 2011); DOBBS, HAYDEN & BUBLICK, HORNBOOK ON TORTS §§ 46.1–46.5 (2d ed. 2016).

§ 4. MISAPPROPRIATION OF COMMERCIAL VALUE

CARSON V. HERE'S JOHNNY PORTABLE TOILETS, INC., 698 F.2d 831 (6th Cir. 1983). Plaintiff John W. Carson is a famous entertainer, whose "Tonight Show" on television is introduced with the phrase "Here's Johnny." The phrase is generally associated with Carson and the show by a substantial segment of the television viewing public. Carson has authorized use of the phrase by others, who have used it to identify restaurants, men's clothing and men's toiletries. The defendant is a corporation which rents and sells portable toilets under the name "Here's Johnny." The founder was aware of the television significance of the phrase when he adopted it for the toilets. Carson sued. The trial court dismissed the claim. Held, vacated and remanded for further proceedings. (1) The "Here's Johnny" mark is a relatively "weak" mark, so that its use on other goods should not be entirely foreclosed, and there is insufficient evidence to establish a likelihood of confusion. Consequently the trademark claim fails. (2) Prosser delineated four types of the right of privacy, including intrusion upon solitude, public disclosure of embarrassing private facts, publicity that places one in a false light, and commercial appropriation of one's name for the defendant's advantage. The first three involve the right to be let alone, but the fourth is best referred to, not as a privacy claim, but as a right of publicity. In this case there is no violation of any real right to privacy, even though Carson may be embarrassed to be associated with the defendant's product. However, there is an invasion of the right of publicity, since the plaintiff's identity is valuable in the promotion of products and he has an interest in preventing unauthorized commercial exploitation of that identity.

NOTES

1.   **Privacy/right of publicity.** Prosser's insights in identifying the four kinds of "privacy" have been generally recognized, but, as in *Carson*,

courts and writers now believe that it would be more accurate in this "commercial appropriation" version of privacy to label the right as one of "publicity." "[T]he right of publicity protects the right to control the commercial value of one's identity." *Montgomery v. Montgomery*, 60 S.W.3d 524 (Ky. 2001). Commercial advertising includes ads using the plaintiff's unique vocal sounds, *Midler v. Ford Motor Co.*, 849 F.2d 460 (9th Cir. 1988), or the plaintiff's style of dress as seen on a television game show, *White v. Samsung Elec. Am., Inc.*, 971 F.2d 1395 (9th Cir. 1992) (Vanna White). Products embodying the plaintiff's likeness have been treated the same way. *See In re NCAA Student-Athlete Name & Likeness Licensing Litig.*, 724 F.3d 1268 (9th Cir. 2013) (courts permitted former college players to proceed with several class action lawsuits against video game developers that used players' identities to create digital avatars); *Comedy III Prods., Inc. v. Gary Saderup, Inc.*, 21 P.3d 797 (Cal. 2001) (sweatshirts bearing the likeness of the Three Stooges as sketched and lithographed by the defendant); *Martin Luther King, Jr., Ctr. for Soc. Change, Inc. v. Am. Heritage Prods., Inc.*, 296 S.E.2d 697 (Ga. 1982) (busts of Martin Luther King).

2. **Duration.** Should your right not to have your personality exploited commercially be passed down to your heirs and their heirs in perpetuity? Should descendants of Thomas Jefferson get royalties for the use of his picture? Some states treat the right as "descendible." In that case, should we follow the guide of copyright and patent law and put a time limit on the right? Or should we follow the trademark practice and permit the right to run in perpetuity?

3. **Commercial use.** Commercial use is primarily use associated with sales. An advertisement is a commercial use, but feature stories, biographies, news, and creative works like movies are not considered commercial. Use of the plaintiff's identity in noncommercial works is thus fully permissible, both because the right of publicity does not extend to such uses and because constitutional free speech rights protect against liability. In *Hoffman v. Capital Cities/ABC, Inc.*, 255 F.3d 1180 (9th Cir. 2001), a feature story on fashion, using a computer to graft new fashion designs on famous Hollywood figures, including the actor Dustin Hoffman, was not deemed commercial; in addition, the court thought that *Times v. Sullivan* rules would apply to require a knowing or reckless falsehood. The court entered judgment for the publisher.

4. **Private individuals.** Some cases have involved celebrities who, if given the protection invoked in *Carson*, would be able to sell their names, faces, or endorsements for a price. *See Christoff v. Nestle USA, Inc.*, 213 P.3d 132 (Cal. 2009) (unauthorized commercial use of professional model's likeness held actionable); *Toffoloni v. LPF Publ'g Grp., LLC*, 572 F.3d 1201 (11th Cir. 2009) (estate of professional female wrestler stated claim for violation of right of publicity against publisher of nude photographs taken 20 years prior to her death); *see also Gignilliat v. Gignilliat, Savitz & Bettis, L.L.P.*, 684 S.E.2d 756 (S.C. 2009) (wife's claim that law firm continued to use her husband's name in the firm name; claim defeated because husband had consented to it). But private individuals, whose face or endorsement would sell for little or nothing, also have a protectable interest. The fact that a citizen is unknown does not

permit an advertiser to use her picture to accompany its advertising. *See, e.g.,* *Bullard v. MRA Holding, LLC*, 740 S.E.2d 622 (Ga. 2013) (teenager whose image and video footage of her exposing her breasts were used without her permission in *College Girls Gone Wild* video, in television and internet ads for the video, and on the box of the video, stated a claim for appropriation of likeness and could recover actual damages from defendant video producer). If the picture or name is used to advertise a product the plaintiff finds offensive or demeaning, there is undoubtedly a very personal interest involved and not merely a commercial one. Is there also such an interest in *Carson*? Should the court have recognized a privacy right and not a publicity right? Would there be a First Amendment difference?

REFERENCES: RESTATEMENT (THIRD) OF UNFAIR COMPETITION § 38 (1995); J. THOMAS MCCARTHY, THE RIGHTS OF PUBLICITY AND PRIVACY (2d ed. 2012); 3 DOBBS, HAYDEN & BUBLICK, THE LAW OF TORTS § 579 (2d ed. 2011); BUBLICK, BAMBAUER & ARELLANO, DOBBS ON ECONOMIC AND DIGNITARY TORTS chs. 10–13 (2022); DOBBS, HAYDEN & BUBLICK, HORNBOOK ON TORTS § 46.6 (2d ed. 2016).

CHAPTER 34

MISREPRESENTATION AND OTHER MISDEALINGS

■ ■ ■

§ 1. MISREPRESENTATION CAUSING PHYSICAL HARM

Misrepresentation is a factual element in many, many kinds of tort claims. It is often pled in cases involving economic harm. However, misrepresentations can also inflict emotional distress or cause physical harm.

JOWERS V. BOC GROUP, INC.
2009 WL 995613 (S.D. Miss. 2009)

O'MALLEY, J. . . .

This case has been consolidated with the Multidistrict Litigation known as *In re: Welding Fume Prods. Liab. Litig.,* case no. 03-CV-17000, MDL no. 1535. [Previous proceedings in the litigation include three trials of individual welding fume cases and four other cases that were set for trial but ultimately were not tried. Plaintiff Robert Jowers brings this action against three defendants, Lincoln Electric Company, BOC Group, Inc., and ESAB Group, Inc., who are all manufacturers of welding rods that Jowers used during his career as a welder. Jowers alleges the fumes given off by these welding rods caused him to suffer neurological injury. Jowers brings claims for numerous torts including conscious and negligent misrepresentation involving risk of physical harm.]

The following material facts . . . are not in dispute. For many years, the welding rod manufacturing defendants have shipped their welding consumables with warning labels and Material Safety Data Sheets ("MSDSs"), but Jowers' review of these written materials was extremely limited. Jowers testified that he never read a MSDS. He recalled reading warning labels only a few times in his career. Further, Jowers testified he never read any of the books, magazine articles, medical or scientific studies, or other publications regarding welding fumes that were sponsored or distributed by the manufacturing defendants or the trade organizations to which they belonged (e.g., the American Welding Society). On the other hand, Jowers' employer, Ingalls Shipyard, did receive publications sponsored or distributed by some or all of the defendants that addressed the safety and hazards of welding fumes and the use of welding products. These publications were available to Ingalls supervisory employees, including industrial hygienists and safety supervisors and managers in charge of training welders, and the defendants intended these supervisory employees to rely on the publications for safety information related to welding.

The elements of a claim for negligent misrepresentation under Mississippi law are:

> (1) a misrepresentation or omission of a fact; (2) that the representation or omission is material or significant; (3) that the defendant failed to exercise that degree of diligence and expertise the public is entitled to expect of it; (4) that the plaintiff reasonably relied on the defendant's representations; and (5) that the plaintiff suffered damages as a direct and proximate result of his reasonable reliance.

Skrmetta v. Bayview Yacht Club, Inc., 606 So.2d 1120, 1124 (Miss. 2002). The elements of a claim for conscious misrepresentation—also known as fraud—under Mississippi law are:

> (1) a representation; (2) its falsity; (3) its materiality; (4) the speaker's knowledge; (5) his intent that it should be acted upon by the hearer and in the manner reasonably contemplated; (6) the hearer's ignorance of its falsity; (7) his reliance on its truth; (8) his right to rely thereon; and (9) his consequent and proximate injury.

Levens v. Campbell, 733 So.2d 753, 761–62 (Miss. 1999). The plaintiff must prove the elements of a claim for negligent misrepresentation by a preponderance of the evidence, but must prove the elements of a claim for conscious misrepresentation by clear and convincing evidence.

Among others, the elements that the two claims have in common are that the plaintiff must prove he *relied upon* a material representation. As defendants note, it is undisputed that the only representations or omissions that Jowers could have relied upon *directly* were the warning labels that accompanied the welding consumables he used. Jowers never read any MSDS nor any public literature regarding welding fumes, so there can be no argument that he relied directly upon representations or omissions they contained; and, therefore, there can be no finding of liability premised on those representations or omissions. In contrast, Jowers asserts there were representations and omissions made by the defendants to his employer, Ingalls Shipyard, regarding the hazards (or lack thereof) associated with welding, and that he relied on these representations and omissions *indirectly* because Ingalls conveyed this information to him, as the defendants intended.

Conscious Misrepresentation (Fraud)

. . . "Mississippi courts . . . have consistently held that a claim of fraud may not be based upon an omission or silence, unless there exists a special relationship between the parties." . . . Jowers argues that the "special relationship" need not be a fiduciary relationship: "liability for nondisclosure can arise in situations where there is no fiduciary relationship at all, but rather in the context of an adversarial, arms-length business transaction." As the Court discussed in [a prior case], however, even if the special relationship need not be fiduciary in character, it must still be a "similar relation of trust and confidence." [T]he facts in this case make clear that Jowers does not have the necessary relationship with the defendants. . . .

Jowers asserts that his fraud claim is not based simply upon "an omission or silence," thereby requiring a special relationship. Rather, Jowers argues, his fraud claim is based on assertion of "half-truths"—that is, the defendants allegedly made "partial representations but also suppresse[d] some material facts"—and that, in such circumstances, no "special relationship" is required at all. . . . Although Jowers does a valiant job of identifying principles of Mississippi law . . . , he does not identify any specific, definitive Mississippi case law showing that there is a "half-truth" exception to the rule that a claim of fraud may not be based upon an omission or silence absent a special relationship. . . . [T]his Court must conclude that conscious misrepresentation claims based on omissions or half-truths will fail as a matter of law.

Jowers' third argument is that, even though he cannot point to any affirmative misrepresentations made by the defendants upon which he relied *directly,* the defendants made affirmative misrepresentations to his employer, Ingalls Shipyard, with the expectation that Ingalls would essentially repeat those misrepresentations to him; and, further, that Ingalls supervisors and managers did, in fact, pass on those misrepresentations and Jowers did, in fact, reasonably rely upon them. As an example, Jowers notes that defendant Lincoln provided to Ingalls a 1972 welding handbook stating that welding fumes are "innocuous." Jowers asserts the evidence will show that: this statement is false; Lincoln knew it was false when it made it; Lincoln expected Ingalls to pass this false information on to its welder-employees; Ingalls actually did pass this information on to Jowers; and Jowers reasonably relied upon it, to his detriment. Thus, Jowers argues summary judgment on his fraud claim is inappropriate because he can establish *indirect* reliance upon affirmative misrepresentations made by the defendants. . . .

Having examined Mississippi law, the Court concludes that Jowers must be allowed to pursue a theory of fraud premised upon *indirect* reliance on affirmative misrepresentations made by a defendant to Ingalls.

The *Restatement (Second) of Torts* (1965) addresses indirect reliance in two consecutive, related sections, and each section may be applied to the facts of this case. The Mississippi Supreme Court has adopted § 311 of the *Restatement (Second) of Torts* (1965), which states: "One who negligently gives false information to another is subject to liability for physical harm caused by action taken by the other in reasonable reliance upon such information, where such harm results . . . to such third persons as the actor should expect to be in peril by the taken action." Clark v. St. Dominic-Jackson Memorial Hosp., 660 So.2d 970, 974 (1995). Certainly, Mississippi courts would also find liability if the actor *purposefully* "gives false information to another" in the same circumstances, as Jowers alleges. Jowers asserts the defendants purposefully gave false information regarding welding fume safety to Ingalls, Ingalls reasonably relied upon this false information when instructing Jowers on how to weld safely, this reliance had the effect of placing Jowers in peril—ultimately causing him to suffer physical harm—and defendants could expect that giving this false information to Ingalls would imperil Jowers and other Ingalls welders. Based on the evidence so far presented, all of these assertions have more than a scintilla of evidentiary support.

In addition, *Restatement* § 310 states: "An actor who makes a misrepresentation is subject to liability to another for physical harm which results from an act done by the other or a third person in reliance upon the truth of the representation, if the actor (a) intends his statement to induce or should realize that it is likely to induce action by the other, or a third person, which involves an unreasonable risk of physical harm to the other, and (b) knows (i) that the statement is false, or (ii) that he has not the knowledge which he professes." In this case, Jowers asserts the defendants purposefully gave false information regarding welding fume safety to Ingalls (knowing the information would be passed on to Ingalls welders), the defendants knew or should have known this information would induce Jowers to take insufficient protective measures when welding, Jowers and other Ingalls welders actually relied on the false information provided by the defendants, and Jowers' reliance and actions involved an unreasonable risk of physical harm. Again, all of these assertions have a colorable evidentiary basis.

Given the current state of the evidentiary record, this Court cannot grant summary judgment to defendants on Jowers' claim of fraud as a matter of law, to the extent that his claim is premised on indirect reliance on *affirmative* misrepresentations.

The Court holds, however, that Jowers may prevail on this claim only if he shows at trial that: (a) a defendant made an affirmative misrepresentation to Jowers' employer; (b) the defendant reasonably expected that the employer would convey substantially the same affirmative misrepresentation to Jowers; (c) the employer actually did so;

and (d) Jowers actually and reasonably relied upon the affirmative misrepresentation. Also, the type of showing to support this alleged indirect reliance is exacting, and a fraud claim will only lie against the individual defendant who made the relied-upon affirmative misrepresentation. Finally, given that Jowers admits there were no affirmative misrepresentations contained in the defendants' warnings,[18] the affirmative misrepresentations upon which he allegedly relied *indirectly* must be appear outside of the defendants' warning labels, themselves.

In sum, to the extent that Jowers' fraud claim is premised on omissions or half-truths, summary judgment is granted; however, to the extent Jowers' fraud claim is premised on indirect reliance upon affirmative misrepresentations, summary judgment is denied.

Negligent Misrepresentation.

. . . Jowers asserts he relied upon defendants to tell him everything he reasonably needed to know to weld safely, but the defendants did not fully disclose certain hazards to him (or to his employers)—a failure of omission. To the extent Jowers claims he "relied upon" anything communicated by the defendants to him *directly,* his reliance is only upon the warnings, themselves, and what they did and did not say. In other words, this aspect of Jowers' claim for negligent affirmative misrepresentation is entirely contiguous with his claim for negligent failure to warn. And, the common law claim for negligent failure to warn is duplicative of, if not abrogated by, the [Missouri Products Liability Act] claim for strict liability failure to warn.

In *King,* the plaintiff pointed to affirmative misrepresentations made by the tobacco-industry defendant that were *in addition to and separate from* the cigarette warnings, and upon which she relied *directly. King,* 921 So.2d at 270 (referring to "deceptive advertising"); *cf.* Cipollone v. Liggett Groups, Inc. 683 F. Supp. 1487 (D.N.J. 1988) (discussing various sorts of statements, separate from warnings, made by tobacco companies that could qualify as affirmative misrepresentations). This sort of alleged negligent misrepresentation goes beyond any failure to warn, and so is not simply a "product liability claim," and, thus, is not automatically abrogated by the MPLA. . . . In this case, however, there is simply no communication from the defendants upon which Jowers alleges he relied directly, other than the defendants' warnings, themselves.

Jowers also asserts the defendants engaged in negligent misrepresentation by making affirmative misrepresentations and half-truths to Ingalls, which reasonably relied upon the substance of those

---

[18] For example, there is no affirmative statement in any of defendants' warnings—such as 'this product may be used safely without a respirator,' or 'fumes from this product are known to cause only temporary respiratory problems'—upon which Jowers alleges he relied.

communications and repeated them to him, and upon which he then reasonably relied, himself. In other words, Jowers repeats both of his "indirect reliance" arguments. For the same reasons as were explained above in the context of Jowers' fraud claim, the Court concludes that Jowers must be allowed to pursue a theory of negligent misrepresentation premised upon *indirect* reliance on affirmative misrepresentations made by a defendant to Ingalls. As before, Jowers may prevail on this claim only if he shows that: (a) a defendant made an affirmative misrepresentation to Jowers' employer; (b) the defendant reasonably expected that the employer would convey substantially the same affirmative misrepresentation to Jowers; (c) the employer actually did so; and (d) Jowers actually and reasonably relied upon the affirmative misrepresentation.

In sum, to the extent that Jowers' negligent misrepresentation claim is premised on omissions, summary judgment is granted; however, to the extent Jowers' negligent misrepresentation claim is premised on half-truths or indirect reliance upon affirmative misrepresentations, summary judgment is denied. While Jowers may premise his negligent misrepresentation claim on half-truths, he may not premise his fraud claim on half-truths; this is because, to prevail on a fraud claim using half-truths, the parties must have a "special relationship," but there is no similar requirement under a negligent misrepresentation theory. . . .

[A grant of summary judgment is not warranted on plaintiffs' negligent misrepresentation, fraud, or punitive damages claims. Nor is summary judgment warranted on defendants' defenses of comparative fault and sophisticated user/learned intermediary. The latter defense alleges that "the plaintiff and his employers are sophisticated users of welding electrodes who not only understand the potential fume hazard associated with welding, but the means to reduce it, i.e., ventilation and/or respiratory protection." Furthermore, apportionment of fault to the immune employer is not appropriate under state law.]

IT IS SO ORDERED.

NOTES

1. **Subsequent case history.** The *Jowers* case was tried to a jury, which found in favor of the plaintiff and awarded $1.2 million in compensatory damages and $1.7 million in punitive damages. The jury apportioned 40% of the fault to Jowers, thereby reducing the compensatory award to $720,000. The trial judge upheld the award. The Fifth Circuit reversed in part on the ground that the employer should have been included in the apportionment. *Jowers v. Lincoln Elec. Co.,* 617 F.3d 346 (5th Cir. 2010). On remand from the Court of Appeals, the case settled.

2.   **Causes of action.** The plaintiff in *Jowers* pleaded many claims sounding in negligence and products liability. Why might a plaintiff also plead deliberate or negligent misrepresentation?

3.   **Elements.** The *Jowers* court set out the elements required to prove fraud and for negligent misrepresentation. As you will see in the economic tort cases in the next section, the elements mentioned by the court are typical of the standards in the economic misrepresentation context as well. Is the court right to permit recovery based on indirect reliance?

4.   **Representations creating physical risks.** A number of cases involve misrepresentations that create physical risk of harm. D tells P that his brakes are safe when D should have known better. In reliance, P drives the car and is injured when the brakes don't work. P has a good claim. What if an employer writes a positive letter of recommendation that fails to disclose that the employee had been subject to complaints about sexual improprieties with students? The employee accepts the new job, working with middle-school students, one of whom he allegedly molests. Would the former employer be liable for those physical harms? *See Randi W. v. Muroc Joint Unified Sch. Dist.,* 929 P.2d 582 (Cal. 1997). What if the publisher of a telephone directory creates and publishes a Yellow Pages advertisement that intentionally misrepresents a doctor's qualifications? A patient who relies on the advertisement suffers physical harm from the liposuction surgery performed on him by the doctor. Is the publisher liable for those physical harms? *See Knepper v. Brown,* 195 P.3d 383 (Or. 2008).

What if a patient took generic drugs but sued the brand-name drug manufacturer for misrepresentation? *See Wyeth, Inc. v. Weeks,* 159 So.3d 649 (Ala. 2014) (brand-name drug manufacturer could be held liable to a consumer of a generic version of the drug for fraud and misrepresentation based on statements it made about the drug, because under FDA regulations the generic drug label had to match the brand-name manufacturer's label; the alleged misrepresentations were drafted by the brand-name manufacturer and merely repeated by the generic manufacturer). What if a boyfriend deliberately concealed from the plaintiff-girlfriend that he had herpes? *See Behr v. Richmond,* 123 Cal.Rptr.3d 97 (Ct. App. 2011).

5.   **Emotional harm recovery.** Misrepresentation actions are not confined to physical damage. What if a prospective employer makes misrepresentations in a job interview with the plaintiff about the company's growth prospects? The plaintiff suffers no physical harm, but does allege emotional harm. Liability? *See Brogan v. Mitchell Int'l, Inc.,* 692 N.E.2d 276 (Ill. 1998) (no recovery). What about a misrepresentation by an employer that plaintiff was covered by health insurance when he was not, which causes only emotional and not physical harm? *See Southern Alaska Carpenters Health & Sec. Trust Fund v. Jones,* 177 P.3d 844 (Alaska 2008) (allowing recovery). Are the two cases distinguishable? In addition to the misrepresentation claim, other "economic tort" causes of action may give rise to a claim for emotional distress. *See Miller v. Hartford Life Ins. Co.,* 268 P.3d 418 (Haw. 2011) (an

insured may recover emotional distress damages in a bad faith action without proving any economic or physical harm). Does allowing emotional harm recovery on the basis of misrepresentation present gatekeeping problems like those encountered with stand-alone emotional harm? See *Leining v. Foster Poultry Farms, Inc.*, 275 Cal.Rptr.3d 682, 696 (2021), in which a consumer brought a negligent misrepresentation action for against a poultry producer and animal-welfare certification program for allegedly misleading product labels that certified that producer's chickens had been humanely treated. Claim denied. Information made available to the general public would not be actionable.

§ 2. MISREPRESENTATION IN AN ECONOMIC CONTEXT: THEORIES OF LIABILITY AND THEIR CONSEQUENCES

As you saw in the previous section, misrepresentation can support a claim for physical harm to a person, or one for emotional distress. Although a misrepresentation is important in such cases, they are not the sort of cases we commonly think of when we speak of fraud or deceit. The traditional fraud or deceit claim—or today, negligent misrepresentation claim—is about economic loss in a bargaining transaction.

Illustration 1

DuBois was negotiating to sell his house to Pace. DuBois told Pace that the roof was in good condition and never gave any problems. In fact, as DuBois knew, a tree had fallen on the roof and caused serious damage. This had happened over a year ago and deterioration was now substantial. Pace, relying upon DuBois' statement, purchased the house for $100,000. This would have been its value if the roof had been in good condition, but because of the condition of the roof, the house was worth no more than $90,000. When Pace discovered this, she sued DuBois for fraud. Pace is entitled to recover $10,000.

This illustration typifies many fraud or misrepresentation claims for money damages at common law. The case differs from the kinds of cases involved in the two preceding chapters in that, while there is a communication by the defendant, it is made directly to the plaintiff, not to third persons. The fraud claim usually arises in a bargaining situation. The claim is frequently asserted against the seller, or someone representing the seller. Finally, the claim is very often found in real property cases or the sale of securities, such as corporate stocks or bonds. The reason for this is that the law of warranty, with its strict liability, is likely to govern the liability of chattel sellers, so it is only in other cases that the plaintiff will fall back on the law of tort, attempting to prove "fraud."

DERRY V. PEEK, 14 App. Cas. 337 (H.L. 1889). Defendants, selling shares of stock in a Tramways company, represented that they had the right under an act of Parliament, to use steam or mechanical power as well as horses. In fact, they could use steam power only if the Board of Trade consented, though defendants believed that such consent would be given as a matter of course. They were wrong; the consent was never given, and the corporation failed. In the meantime, relying on the statement that the company was authorized to use steam power, the plaintiff had purchased shares of stock. When the corporation failed, he lost his investment and he sued for fraud. The Court of Appeals held that defendants honestly believed their statements to be true, but that they were nonetheless liable to the plaintiff. In the House of Lords, *held*, reversed. (a) A rescission of the contract may be had where there is an innocent misrepresentation, but (b) damages for fraud may not be recovered unless the defendant made a false representation "(1) knowingly or (2) without belief in its truth, or (3) recklessly, careless whether it be true or false."

NOTES

1.   **Scienter.** The requirement of an intent to deceive—a knowing or reckless falsehood—was called scienter and taken as the common law rule until recent years. It remains the favored ground for recovery. The Restatement Third provides that for fraud liability, "A misrepresentation may result in liability only if: (a) the maker of it knows or believes that it is false; (b) the maker of it knowingly states or implies a false level of confidence in its accuracy; or (c) the maker of it knowingly states or implies a basis for the representation that does not exist." RESTATEMENT (THIRD) OF TORTS: LIAB. FOR ECON. HARM § 10 (2020). Because scienter fraud is an intentional tort, the defendant who commits it may be liable for both compensatory and punitive damages. *McCulley v. U.S. Bank of Montana,* 347 P.3d 247 (Mont. 2015) (bank switched documents at closing and customer ended up with more expensive and more onerous loan; in light of the reprehensibility of the bank's conduct, ratio of punitive to compensatory damages not excessive).

2.   **Elements of fraud.** The Restatement Third defines the full tort of fraud this way: "One who fraudulently makes a material misrepresentation of fact, opinion, intention, or law, for the purpose of inducing another to act or refrain from acting, is subject to liability for economic loss caused by the other's justifiable reliance on the misrepresentation." RESTATEMENT (THIRD) OF TORTS: LIAB. FOR ECON. HARM § 9 (2020). Can you identify whether this rule would be met in *DuBois* or *Derry*?

3.   **Negligence.** It is now generally accepted that negligence can also form a basis of liability for misrepresentations. However, the conditions for imposing liability are more stringent, and the scope and amount of liability are also limited. Typically, arms-length bargainers do not have a duty of

reasonable care for the financial interests of the other party to the transaction. However, a duty of care may be owed by a fiduciary or someone in the business of supplying information for the benefit of the plaintiff. See *Onita Pacific Corp. v. Trustees of Bronson,* 843 P.2d 890 (Or. 1992). The rule of the Third Restatement would impose liability for negligent misrepresentation only when, "An actor who, in the course of his or her business, profession, or employment, or in any transaction in which the actor has a pecuniary interest, supplies false information for the guidance of others is subject to liability for pecuniary loss caused to them by their reliance upon the information, if the actor fails to use reasonable care in obtaining or communicating it." RESTATEMENT (THIRD) OF TORTS: LIAB. FOR ECON. HARM § 5 (2020).

4. **Puffing.** As in other cases, the plaintiff must justifiably rely on the representation in order to have a claim. In *Westby v. Gorsuch,* 50 P.3d 284 (Wash. Ct. App. 2002), the plaintiff had a "ticket" from the Titanic. Needing money immediately, he took it to the defendant, a dealer in antiques. The dealer indicated that it had little value, but eventually paid the plaintiff $1,000 for the ticket. It turned out to be quite valuable. Would the dealer be under a duty of reasonable care so that, even if he did not act fraudulently, he would be liable for negligence? Statements of value and those proclaiming a good buy are often puffing or opinion statements and as such they are not actionable. *See Ward Farms P'ship v. Enerbase Co-op. Resources,* 863 N.W.2d 868 (N.D. 2015) (statements that a tractor was "field ready" and "in good shape" are "puffery because they were expressions or opinions by the seller commending the item being sold").

5. **Representations by non-parties.** Most representations are made by parties to a negotiation that is followed by a contract or sale. However, outsiders could also be held liable for misrepresentations if they were fraudulent. If, in Illustration 1, DuBois' representation is repeated to the plaintiff by a neighbor, who also knows of its falsity, the neighbor would also be liable. This rule applies only to fraud; warranty claims require privity.

Suppose in Illustration 1 that DuBois had represented to A that his roof was sound and that A repeated it later to B, who then bought the house for $100,000 from DuBois. Should B, to whom no representation was made, have a fraud action? Some older cases took a tough line about this, denying liability to plaintiffs who were merely foreseeable. But according to the Second Restatement § 533, the defendant is liable not only to the person to whom the representation is made, but also to third persons if he "intends or has reason to expect that its terms will be repeated. . . ." Sound familiar to *Jowers*? This raises the problem seen in the next case.

ULTRAMARES CORP. V. TOUCHE, NIVEN & CO.

174 N.E. 441 (N.Y. 1931)

CARDOZO, C.J.

[Defendants were public accountants. Pursuant to a contract with Stern they undertook to prepare an independent audit of the business, showing its net worth. As defendants knew, this was to be used by potential lenders, who, relying upon defendants' independent assessment of Stern's financial situation, would lend money to Stern. The audit showed a net worth of over a million dollars, and defendants certified this as accurate and prepared 32 originals for Stern to show potential lenders. In fact, relying on the audit and balance sheet furnished by defendants, the plaintiff loaned $165,000 to Stern. When Stern collapsed, the plaintiff was unable to obtain repayment of the loan. The plaintiff brought this action against the defendants for the damages thus suffered, claiming both scienter fraud and negligent misrepresentation. There was evidence that the defendants did not examine Stern's books with appropriate care, and that had they done so, discrepancies would have been revealed which would have led to a more accurate audit. The trial judge set aside the jury's verdict for the plaintiff. The Appellate Division thought that the fraud action should be dismissed, but not the negligence claim.]

We are brought to the question of duty, its origin and measure.

The defendants owed to their employer a duty imposed by law to make their certificate without fraud, and a duty growing out of contract to make it with the care and caution proper to their calling. Fraud includes the pretense of knowledge when there is none. To creditors and investors to whom the employer exhibited the certificate, the defendants owed a like duty to make it without fraud, since there was notice in the circumstances of its making that the employer did not intend to keep it to himself. A different question develops when we ask whether they owed a duty to these to make it without negligence. If liability for negligence exists, a thoughtless slip or blunder, the failure to detect a theft or forgery beneath the cover of deceptive entries, may expose accountants to a liability in an indeterminate amount for an indeterminate time to an indeterminate class. The hazards of a business conducted on these terms are so extreme as to enkindle doubt whether a flaw may not exist in the implications of a duty that exposes to these consequences. We put aside for the moment any statement in the certificate which involves the representation of a fact as true to the knowledge of the auditors. If such a statement was made, whether believed to be true or not, the defendants are liable for deceit in the event that it was false. The plaintiff does not need the invention of novel doctrine to help it out in such conditions. . . .

The assault upon the citadel of privity is proceeding in these days apace. How far the inroads shall extend is now a favorite subject of juridical discussion. In the field of the law of contract there has been a gradual widening of the doctrine of Lawrence v. Fox, 20 N. Y. 268, until today the beneficiary of a promise, clearly designated as such, is seldom left without a remedy. Even in that field, however, the remedy is narrower where the beneficiaries of the promise are indeterminate or general. Something more must then appear than an intention that the promise shall redound to the benefit of the public or to that of a class of indefinite extension. The promise must be such as to "bespeak the assumption of a duty to make reparation directly to the individual members of the public if the benefit is lost." *Moch Co. v. Rensselaer Water Co.*, 247 N.Y. 160, 164; Restatement of the Law of Contracts, § 145. In the field of the law of torts a manufacturer who is negligent in the manufacture of a chattel in circumstances pointing to an unreasonable risk of serious bodily harm to those using it thereafter may be liable for negligence though privity is lacking between manufacturer and user. *MacPherson v. Buick Motor Co.*, 217 N.Y. 382; Restatement of the Law of Torts, § 262. . . .

Liability for negligence if adjudged in this case will extend to many callings other than an auditor's. Lawyers who certify their opinions as to the validity of municipal or corporate bonds, with knowledge that the opinion will be brought to the notice of the public, will become liable to the investors, if they have overlooked a statute or a decision, to the same extent as if the controversy were one between client and adviser. Title companies insuring titles to a tract of land, with knowledge that at an approaching auction the fact that they have insured will be stated to the bidders, will become liable to purchasers who may wish the benefit of a policy without payment of a premium. These illustrations may seem to be extreme, but they go little, if any, farther than we are invited to go now. Negligence, moreover, will have one standard when viewed in relation to the employer, and another and at times a stricter standard when viewed in relation to the public. Explanations that might seem plausible, omissions that might be reasonable, if the duty is confined to the employer, conducting a business that presumably at least is not a fraud upon his creditors, might wear another aspect if an independent duty to be suspicious even of one's principal is owing to investors. "Every one making a promise having the quality of a contract will be under a duty to the promisee by virtue of the promise, but under another duty, apart from contract, to an indefinite number of potential beneficiaries when performance has begun. The assumption of one relation will mean the involuntary assumption of a series of new relations, inescapably hooked together." Moch Co. v. Rensselaer Water Co., *supra*, at page 168. "The law does not spread its protection so far." Robins Dry Dock & Repair Co. v. Flint, *supra*, at page 309 of 275 U.S.

Our holding does not emancipate accountants from the consequences of fraud. It does not relieve them if their audit has been so negligent as to justify a finding that they had no genuine belief in its adequacy, for this again is fraud. It does no more than say that, if less than this is proved, if there has been neither reckless misstatement nor insincere profession of an opinion, but only honest blunder, the ensuing liability for negligence is one that is bounded by the contract, and is to be enforced between the parties by whom the contract has been made. We doubt whether the average business man receiving a certificate without paying for it, and receiving it merely as one among a multitude of possible investors, would look for anything more. . . .

[Remanded for trial as to the fraud claim and dismissed as to the negligence claim.]

NOTES

1. **A hypothetical.** Suppose Stern had told the accountants to send one copy directly to the plaintiff as quickly as possible, because the plaintiff might make a loan. Would the defendant then be liable for negligence?

2. **Scope of foreseeable reliance.** Suppose the defendant, a jeweler, certifies that a diamond owned by S is genuine. Defendant knows that S will distribute numerous copies of this certificate in an attempt to sell the diamond. S does so and one reader of the certificate buys the diamond in reliance. If the defendant was merely negligent, does *Ultramares* bar recovery against the defendant?

3. **Indeterminate liabilities.** Does *Ultramares* make sense to you? Consider another Cardozo decision, *Moch v. Rensselaer Water Co.* Presumably the water sold there was priced by the unit of water, not according to the value of the houses served by the fire hydrants. Presumably the services of the accountant are priced by the hour or unit of work, not according to the amount of loans that might be made in reliance on the statement. The implication of the price seems to be that indeterminate liabilities to third persons are not part of the bargain. Would it even be possible for a prudent insurer to calculate a premium to insure for accountants' liabilities? After all, we do not know whether any sum will be loaned or how much it will be. Is indeterminate liability a bigger issue in the economic context than in the physical injury context?

4. **The Second Restatement's view.** Whatever sense *Ultramares* might have made, the Second Restatement's § 552 took a more liberal position, extending liability to all those in a "limited group of persons for whose benefit and guidance" the information is supplied, if the transaction is similar to the one he expected to influence. *See Brand Mktg. Grp. LLC v. Intertek Testing Servs., N.A., Inc.*, 801 F.3d 347 (3d Cir. 2015) (Pennsylvania law: product distributor, injured when product found not be conform to safety standards, had negligent representation claim against product testing company who had stated the product conformed to standards); *Audler v. CBC Innovis Inc.*, 519 F.3d 239 (5th Cir. 2008) (Louisiana law). California has adopted a rule similar

to the Restatement's rule, allowing a recovery only by specifically identifiable plaintiffs. *Bily v. Arthur Young & Co.*, 834 P.2d 745 (Cal. 1992). New York extends liability to third persons only when the defendant has a close "bond" with the plaintiff, as by some direct contact or representation. *See Credit All. Corp. v. Arthur Andersen & Co.*, 483 N.E.2d 110 (N.Y. 1985). One or two states go further in negligent misstatement cases, imposing liability for all proximately caused economic harms. *See Touche Ross v. Commercial Union Ins.*, 514 So.2d 315 (Miss. 1987); *Citizens State Bank v. Timm, Schmidt & Co.*, 335 N.W.2d 361 (Wis. 1983). In the latter case, the court added, however, that public policy might preclude liability on the facts of particular cases, emphasizing factors such as highly extraordinary harm, remoteness, and disproportion between negligence and harm.

5. **The Restatement Third's articulation.** According to the Restatement Third, "Liability for fraud requires a showing that the defendant spoke for the purpose of influencing the plaintiff or a class of parties in which the plaintiff was included. The liability, in turn, extends to damage suffered by those whose reliance the defendant intended to induce. It also includes damage suffered by others whom the defendant had reason to expect would rely on a statement. The plaintiff need not have dealt directly with the defendant. It is enough if the defendant had reason to expect that the plaintiff would receive the statement and rely on it." RESTATEMENT (THIRD) OF TORTS: LIAB. FOR ECON. HARM § 12 (2020). How does the "purpose of influencing" or "reason to expect" standard of the Restatement Third compare to the Restatement Second standard and to *Ultramares*?

6. **Unforeseeable types of harm.** Suppose the plaintiff is foreseeable, and even within a limited class for whose guidance the information is purchased, but the plaintiff relies on the information in a wholly unsuspected way: instead of lending money to the business that has been audited, the plaintiff buys its stock. What kind of issue does this raise?

Illustration 2

Durham sells a bull to Bynum, who purchases it in reliance on a knowingly false representation by Durham that the bull is a pedigreed Guernsey. If this had been true, the bull would have been worth $90,000. It was not true and the bull was worth only $5,000. Bynum paid $80,000 for the bull. He is entitled to recover a sum sufficient to give him the benefit of his bargain. Since, if the bull had been as represented, he would have made a gain of $10,000, he is entitled to recover a sum sufficient to put him in that position. This will require $85,000 in damage. This, added to the value of the bull which he has, will give him $90,000—the benefit of his bargain, for which he paid $80,000.

Illustration 3

Danton, an art dealer, negligently inspected a painting and concluded it was a genuine Giaccomo Jones. He represented this to be the case and, relying on this representation, Pierre bought it for $200,000, expecting to resell it for $250,000. He would have been able to do so if it had been a genuine Jones, but it was not. It was worth only $175,000. Pierre's loss of bargain is $50,000, but he can only recover his $25,000 "out-of-pocket" damages.

Illustration 4

The facts are the same as in Illustration 3, except that Pierre incurred $10,000 in brokerage fees to sell the painting, and would have incurred no brokerage fee to sell it if it had been a Jones. He is entitled to recover his out-of-pocket damages of $25,000 plus his consequential or special damages of $10,000.

NOTES

1. **Scienter fraud: "Benefit of the bargain" measure.** If the defendant is guilty of a scienter fraud, the plaintiff may recover the benefit of his bargain in most jurisdictions. This is a sum sufficient to give him the gain in asset value he would have made had the representation been true. *See* RESTATEMENT (SECOND) OF TORTS § 549 (1977); 2 DAN B. DOBBS, THE LAW OF REMEDIES § 9.2 (1) (2d ed. 1993). *Zorilla v. Aypco Constr. II, LLC*, 469 S.W.3d 143 (Tex. 2015) (but benefit-of-bargain measure of damages is available only where there is an enforceable contract). Even in the case of scienter fraud, New York limits recovery to the out-of-pocket measure described below and does not permit the usual loss of bargain damages.

2. **Scienter fraud: optional "out-of-pocket" measure.** The plaintiff who proves scienter fraud also has an option to claim a different measure, the out-of-pocket damages, plus any consequential damages. The out-of-pocket measure can be seen in Illustration 3. This represents the difference between what the plaintiff paid and what he got. In Illustration 3 it is obviously less than the loss of bargain measure, which would have given the plaintiff a recovery of $75,000 (to give him his $50,000 expectancy). The out-of-pocket measure simply puts the plaintiff in the financial position he would have been in had there been no transaction at all. Why would a plaintiff ever choose this measure of damages if he could claim the loss of bargain?

3. **Consequential damages.** If the plaintiff recovers the out-of-pocket measure, he can also recover appropriate consequential or special damages. This would include any special expenses he incurred because of the fraud. *See* Illustration 4. These might be denied in New York in order to make its out-of-pocket rule effective.

4. **Negligent misrepresentation.** When the defendant is guilty of negligence, but not scienter fraud, the damages are limited to the out-of-pocket

plus the consequential damages. *BDO Seidman, LLP v. Mindis Acquisition Corp.,* 578 S.E.2d 400 (Ga. 2003); RESTATEMENT (SECOND) OF TORTS § 552B (1977). Thus in Illustration 3 above, the plaintiff cannot recover the $50,000 loss of bargain.

GAUERKE V. ROZGA
332 N.W.2d 804 (Wis. 1983)

CECI, JUSTICE.

[The Rozgas owned a hotel property, which they listed for sale with Gudim Realty. They told Gudim that, according to former owners, the property was five and one-half acres. Gudim seems to have put this information in a specification sheet. In the meantime, the Gauerkes were looking for hotel property and asked Robert Frost Realty, Inc. to act for them. A Frost agent contacted Gudim, obtained the specification sheet, put a Frost card at the top, and submitted it to the Gauerkes. The Gauerkes eventually purchased the property, but two years later they discovered that the property contained less than three acres. They brought this action against the Rozgas, Robert Frost Realty, and Gudim. Gudim settled and the case was submitted to a jury against Robert Frost and its agent. A jury found for the plaintiff and Frost was held liable on a "theory of strict responsibility for the misrepresentations."]

Frost argues that the theory of strict responsibility should not have been submitted to the jury, because that theory is only applicable where the defendant could normally be expected to know the facts represented to be true without investigation. . . . The court of appeals reasoned that "in strict liability the loss is to fall on the innocent defendant rather than the innocent plaintiff. . . ."

[Wisconsin requires] (1) a representation made as of defendant's own knowledge, concerning a matter about which he purports to have knowledge, so that he may be taken to have assumed responsibility as in the case of warranty, and (2) a defendant with an economic interest in the transaction into which the plaintiff enters so that defendant expects to gain some economic benefit. In other words, strict responsibility applies in those circumstances which 'indicate that the speaker either had particular means of ascertaining the pertinent facts, or his position made possible complete knowledge and the statements fairly implied that he had it.' Therefore, the speaker ought to have known or else ought not to have spoken.

We agree with the court of appeals that the applicability of the doctrine of strict responsibility does not depend upon the actual source of the speaker's knowledge; rather, this element is satisfied if the speaker professes or implies personal knowledge. The other key element is the buyer's justifiable reliance on the statement. If the fact represented is something that one would not expect the speaker to know without an investigation, this might be a factor in determining there was justifiable reliance on the part of the buyer.... [Money award to the plaintiff affirmed.]

NOTES

1.   **Strict liability for physical harm.** When should there be strict liability for misrepresentations?

(a)   A seller of staples honestly and reasonably represents them as safe for use in the buyer's staple gun. In fact they are not safe; a small piece breaks off and puts out the plaintiff's eye. Is there any doubt about strict liability? *See* RESTATEMENT OF PRODUCTS LIABILITY § 9 (1998).

(b)   A homeowner has her roof repaired in May. In June she tells a would-be buyer, "The roof is in excellent shape." She is honest and reasonable, but in fact the roofer has done a poor job and the roof is already developing hidden cracks. Is there to be strict liability?

2.   **Strict liability and consciously ignorant representations.** In some instances a speaker may be guilty of a scienter fraud if he states facts as if he had knowledge of them when in truth he knows that he does not know the facts. Seller says: "The well on this farm will pump enough to water 500 head of cattle." The seller has never tried to pump that much, though he honestly and reasonably believes it is so based on pump specifications. However, it is not in fact the case. If he is consciously aware of his own ignorance is he nevertheless not guilty of a scienter fraud?

3.   **Warranty strict liability.** One basis for strict liability is that the buyer may reasonably believe the seller is warranting the statement to be true. But if the theory is warranty or an analogy to warranty, should the claim then be defeated if there is a disclaimer or a merger clause in the deed? The disclaimer or merger clause would often not suffice to defeat an actual scienter fraud claim.

4.   **Causes of action.** The Restatement Third's view of innocent misrepresentation is that "[I]f a plaintiff was induced to enter into an exchange with the defendant by the defendant's innocent misrepresentation, the plaintiff has recourse under the law of restitution, warranty, and estoppel," not tort. RESTATEMENT (THIRD) OF TORTS: LIAB. FOR ECON. HARM § 3 (2020).

Other Bases for Strict Liability

5.   **Rescission.** Under contract law, a mutual mistake of basic fact may be sufficient to avoid a contract and justify rescission, sometimes on the theory that, given such a mistake, there was no contract at all. The case of an honest misstatement by one party and belief by the other is a special instance of mutual mistake and just as good a ground for rescission. Thus, as recognized in *Derry v. Peek*, neither negligence nor scienter is required when the plaintiff

seeks rescission. Should rescission be granted also for misrepresentation of any material fact? Rescission would be granted for misrepresentation that "this is a Guernsey," when in fact it was a polled Hereford. Should rescission also be granted for a misrepresentation that "this cow won first prize at the fair" when in fact it won second?

6. **Fiduciaries.** Fiduciaries, such as trustees in relationship to the beneficiaries of their trusts and lawyers in relationship to their clients, are obliged to exercise the utmost good faith, and to act in each transaction for the best interest of the other party. For failure to do this, they may be held liable for constructive fraud. The effect is strict liability. *Cf. In re Lemington Home for the Aged*, 777 F.3d 620 (3d Cir. 2015) (affirming jury verdict finding breach of fiduciary duty where director/CFO of mismanaged senior care home failed to monitor financial records of home; corporate officers are required to "devote themselves to the corporate affairs with a view to promote the common interests and not their own"). A similar idea may extend to persons who are not classic fiduciaries, but who have led the plaintiff to place special trust and confidence in them. One who aids and abets a breach of a fiduciary may also be liable to the plaintiff. *See RBC Capital Markets, LLC v. Jervis*, 129 A.3d 816 (Del. 2015) (corporate board financial advisor aided and abetted board's breach of fiduciary duty during process of sale of corporation).

7. **Statutory strict liability.** Federal and state statutes sometimes provide for strict liability for particular misstatements, although the situations in which this is true are limited. More frequently statutes, particularly in the areas of securities and mass sales of real property, require scienter. *See, e.g.,* 15 U.S.C. §§ 77a *et seq.* (securities); §§ 1701 *et seq.* (land).

Scope of Strict Liability and Damages

8. **The *Ultramares* problem.** Reconsider the *Ultramares* problem. To what group of potential plaintiffs should strict liability extend? Only to the very person to whom the representation was made? This is the provision of the RESTATEMENT (SECOND) OF TORTS § 552C, comment d (1977).

9. **The damages problem.** What damages should be available when strict liability is imposed? The Second Restatement would limit damages to the out-of-pocket measure. This eliminates recovery of the benefit of the bargain damages and also consequential damages. *See id.* § 552C(2) & cmt. f.

§ 3. RELIANCE AND RELATED DOCTRINES

1. *Reliance in fact.* If the plaintiff pays no attention to the defendant's misrepresentation, or does not care, or relies on his own investigation instead, then the defendant's representations have in fact caused no harm. That is, the normal requirement of actual cause is met in this context by the rule that the plaintiff must have relied in fact on the false statement (or a false implication of silence). *See Stuart v. Freiberg*, 116 A.3d 1195 (Conn. 2015) ("Without actual reliance, reasonable reliance cannot possibly exist"; plaintiffs' own testimony that they did not read the financial

statements established that they did not rely on those statements in fact, which was fatal to their fraud and negligent misrepresentation claims); *Conroy v. Regents of Univ. of Cal.*, 203 P.3d 1127 (Cal. 2009). Reliance in fact may simply mean that the plaintiff suffered losses caused by the misrepresentation. *See Ironworkers Local Union 68 v. AstraZeneca Pharm., LP*, 634 F.3d 1352 (11th Cir. 2011) (plaintiffs failed to allege any injury arising from pharmaceutical manufacturer's alleged misrepresentations about the safety and effectiveness of their drugs). If the plaintiff did not suffer any losses caused by the misrepresentations, then the plaintiff cannot recover under any of the misrepresentation theories.

In some cases, like *Jowers*, the plaintiff may be permitted to show that she relied indirectly upon the defendant's representation. However, indirect reliance claims are typically limited to a showing that the defendant made the misrepresentation to one person who told it to another. Claims that the defendant made the misrepresentation and the plaintiff relied upon market values that were themselves influenced by the misrepresentation are referred to as the "fraud on the market" theory, presently available only under federal securities laws. Most state courts have rejected the theory in a common law tort context. *See Clark v. Pfizer Inc.*, 990 A.2d 17, 26 (Pa. Super. Ct. 2010) ("Courts have been uniformly hostile to attempts to extend the fraud-on-the-market theory to consumer fraud cases" and "a variety of state cases . . . have similarly rejected . . . a fraud on the market theory to presume reliance and causation in common law fraud or statutory deceit lawsuits."); *see also Mirkin v. Wasserman*, 858 P.2d 568 (Cal. 1993) (rejecting the fraud on the market theory for state law claims); *Kaufman v. i-Stat Corp.*, 754 A.2d 1188 (N.J. 2000) (same).

2. *Contributory negligence/comparative fault.* At a time when all actionable misrepresentations were scienter frauds under *Derry v. Peek*, the tort was necessarily an intentional one. As a result, contributory negligence could not furnish any defense. This remains the ordinary rule today as to scienter frauds. *Erdelyi v. Lott*, 326 P.3d 165 (Wyo. 2014) (comparative fault statute does not apply in actions for fraud). As to negligent misrepresentations, however, contributory negligence is usually taken into account either to bar the claim or, under comparative fault rules, to reduce a plaintiff's damages. *See, e.g., Williams Ford, Inc. v. Hartford Courant Co.*, 657 A.2d 212 (Conn. 1995); RESTATEMENT (THIRD) OF TORTS: LIAB. FOR ECON. HARM § 5 (2020) ("A plaintiff's recovery under this Section is subject to the same principles of comparative responsibility that apply to other claims of negligence.").

3. *Justified reliance.* Somewhat strangely, the law has required that the plaintiff not only rely, but that the reliance be "justified." This rule applies not only to negligent misrepresentations, but also to actual fraud. For example, in *Bonhomme v. St. James*, 945 N.E.2d 1181 (Ill. 2011), the plaintiff alleged that she had been befriended by the defendant, who then

"used various media to communicate with plaintiff while in the guise of these fictional characters, even going so far as to use a device to disguise her voice and make her sound like a man." This "extensive masquerade" allegedly caused the plaintiff emotional distress and the loss of over $10,000, which she gave to the defendant in the guise of several different "characters." One of the key issues in the case was whether the plaintiff's reliance was justified. By the court of appeals, *held*, "a person may rely on a statement without investigation if the party making the statement creates a false sense of security or blocks further inquiry," as appeared to be the case here. However, the Illinois Supreme Court disallowed the claim on the ground that the fraudulent conduct involved a purely personal relationship, not business or transactional dealings. *Bonhomme v. St. James*, 970 N.E.2d 1 (Ill. 2012). To the same effect, see *Yazdianpour v. Safeblood Technologies, Inc.*, 779 F.3d 530 (8th Cir. 2015) (under Arkansas law, plaintiffs had no duty to investigate the veracity of defendant's allegedly fraudulent misrepresentations, even where information could have been checked easily on-line, "unless it was apparent they were being deceived"). *See also* RESTATEMENT (THIRD) OF TORTS: LIAB. FOR ECON. HARM § 11 (2020).

4. *Justified reliance and plaintiff fault.* Is the justified reliance rule distinguishable from a rule of contributory negligence? The Restatement suggests that justified reliance is more subjective and personal to the particular plaintiff and does not impose a community standard of care. *See* RESTATEMENT (SECOND) OF TORTS § 545A cmt. b (1977). Thus perfect fools have been allowed to recover for representations that would not take in the ordinary prudent person. However, in practice, justified reliance can look very much like contributory negligence. *See Dickerson v. Strand*, 904 N.E.2d 711 (Ind. Ct. App. 2009) (purchasers of home could not reasonably rely on representations made by vendors when they had a right to inspect but failed to do so).

On the other hand, the law has developed out of the "justified reliance" requirement a series of rather formalized rules about cases that do not ordinarily justify reliance. These include representations that are not material and representations that are not factual. The latter includes most representations of opinion, representations about law, and representations about the future. For example, reliance on ambiguous remarks may be found to be unreasonable as a matter of law. *See Greenberg, Trager & Herbst, LLP v. HSBC Bank USA*, 958 N.E.2d 77 (N.Y. 2011) (alleged oral statement by bank representative that check had "cleared"); *ACA Fin. Guar. Corp. v. Goldman, Sachs & Co.*, 32 N.E.3d 921 (N.Y. 2015) (jury may find justifiable reliance as alleged, but when a plaintiff senses "hints of falsity" in a representation, a "heightened degree of diligence" is required, and plaintiff "cannot reasonably rely on such representations without making additional inquiry to determine their accuracy").

5. *Reliance on false statements of opinion or value.* Some opinions can be relied upon. The Restatement Third specifies that liability may be imposed for "opinion" statements in some cases. Specifically, "A false statement of opinion may result in liability only if:

> (a) the parties are in a fiduciary or confidential relationship;

or

> (b) the defendant claims to have expertise or other knowledge not accessible to the plaintiff and offers the opinion to provide the plaintiff with a basis for reliance.

RESTATEMENT (THIRD) OF TORTS: LIAB. FOR ECON. HARM § 14 (2020).

6. *Reliance on oral representations contradicted by contract.* Perhaps the justified reliance requirement is an indirect way to determine whether the plaintiff actually relied, and whether the defendant really made the representation and intended to induce reliance. At times when a written contract contradicts defendant's oral claims, plaintiffs are expected to have read the contract. *See also MacDonald v. Thomas M. Cooley Law Sch.*, 724 F.3d 654 (6th Cir. 2013) (law school graduates could not prove reasonable reliance on statements from law school about "average starting salary for all graduates," even if the statement was false; "[u]nreasonable reliance includes relying on an alleged misrepresentation that was expressly contradicted in a written contract that a plaintiff reviewed and signed," and here the allegedly false statements were contradicted by other statements in the very same report that showed the basis for those statements); *National Property Holdings v. Westergren*, 453 S.W.3d 419 (Tex. 2015) (fraud claim failed for want of proof of justifiable reliance, where evidence showed that plaintiff had ample opportunity to read a release that contained the alleged misrepresentation but chose not to).

7. *Materiality.* The representation must be material and reliance on an immaterial statement is not justified. Example: Defendant, attempting to sell a car, says to the plaintiff, "Oh, are you a member of the Elks Club? Me, too." Defendant is not a member and has no reason to think that the plaintiff's decision would hinge on the representation, though he does expect to win the plaintiff's good will by this lie.

PINNACLE PEAK DEVELOPERS V. TRW INVESTMENT CORP., 631 P.2d 540 (Ariz. Ct. App. 1980). TRW purchased 40 acres from Pinnacle Peak for a residential subdivision. The purchase agreement required TRW to make certain off-site improvements, such as roads, and electrical, telephone, and water distribution systems. TRW had a written option to purchase additional acreage, but only if a certain portion of the off-site improvements had been completed by the option deadline. When the option deadline was reached, the improvements had not been made and the seller took the position that the option had therefore expired. TRW took the position that the seller had fraudulently induced TRW to forego the improvements and that for this reason the option should be treated as extant. TRW argues that it was induced to enter into the purchase and option agreement by reliance on Pinnacle Peak's representation that the off-site improvements would be no obstacle to the exercise of the option so long as there was reasonable progress on those improvements, and that this representation was false when made. The trial court granted summary judgment for the seller. *Held,* affirmed. "A promise, when made with a present intention not to perform it, is a misrepresentation which can give rise to an action of fraud. . . . Representations which give rise to an action of fraud must, of course, be of matters of fact which exist in the present, and not merely an agreement or promise to do something in the future, or an expression of opinion or judgment as to something which has happened or is expected to happen. To this there is one exception, that when a promise to perform a future act is made with the present intention on the part of the promisor that he will not perform it, it is such a representation as will give rise to an action of fraud."

However, the trial court properly held that the parol evidence rule bars the introduction of evidence of the allegedly fraudulent representation here, which was made prior to execution of the written option agreement. The parol evidence rule "renders inadmissible any evidence of prior or contemporaneous oral understandings and of prior written understandings, which would contradict, vary or add to a written contract which was intended as the final and complete statement or integration of the parties' agreement." The states are split on "whether to permit parol evidence which contradicts a writing when fraud in the inducement is alleged." Many courts have applied the parol evidence rule even to allegedly fraudulent misrepresentations where the parties have "expertise and business sophistication" and have freely negotiated a formal written contract. Here, the parties were sophisticated and represented by counsel during their negotiations, justifying the trial judge's ruling.

NOTES

1.   **Rule.** It is generally agreed that one's present intention to do some future act is a fact about one's state of mind, and that a misrepresentation about that state of mind is actionable as fraud. According to the Restatement Third, a statement of a speaker's intention to perform a promise "may result in liability only if the intention does not exist at the time the statement is made." RESTATEMENT (THIRD) OF TORTS: LIAB. FOR ECON. HARM § 15 (2020). "Since it is not tortious to break a promise, it may seem surprising that it can be tortious to make a promise while not intending to keep it. But the party to whom a promise is made typically values the promisor's intention to perform, and would not do business as readily, or at all, with a promisor whose intentions were known to be otherwise." *Id.* Scienter is a key to this action. Ian

Ayres & Gregory Klass, *New Rules for Promissory Fraud*, 48 ARIZ. L. REV. 957 (2006) (courts faced with claims of promissory fraud should pay more attention to scienter).

2. **Proof.** What proof would suffice to show that the speaker did not have the intention at the time the statement was made? Since nonperformance of the stated intention might simply result from a change of heart, the plaintiff's proof can be difficult; mere proof that the statement was made and not performed would not suffice. *See Milwaukee Auction Galleries Ltd. v. Chalk*, 13 F.3d 1107 (7th Cir. 1994). What if a mayor represents that he did not know of a competing developer and the city attorney said that so long as the developer showed reasonable progress in negotiations with the National Football League, the city's exclusive agency agreement with the developer would be renewed? *Rand Resources, LLC v. City of Carson*, 433 P.3d 899 (Cal. 2019) (city replaced a developer with a competitor as the representative in negotiations with the National Football League (NFL) regarding a potential football franchise for city).

3. **Contract doctrines.** The statute of frauds, the parol evidence rule, and disclaimers or merger clauses in deeds might each prevent a recovery in the case of oral representation. The view of most courts has been that the statute of frauds does not prevent a recovery for a fraudulent misrepresentation, though it would bar enforcement of a promise. As to the parol evidence rule, it is more likely to prevent recovery in the case of more sophisticated parties; courts also look at the extent of the contradiction between pre-contract representations and the final contract. Disclaimers may appear in several forms. One is the merger clause, which provides that all promises and agreements are contained in the written documents. This is a contractual form of the parol evidence rule. Disclaimers may also state that the vendor has made no representations, or that the buyer does not rely on representations. If the plaintiff is induced to enter the contract, including the disclaimer, by fraud, then the disclaimer may not protect the defendant from liability. But a statement in the written documents that no representations have been made, or that the buyer does not rely upon them, will at least raise the question whether the buyer's reliance was reasonable in light of the notice these documents gave that reliance was not expected. *See Wittenberg v. Robinov*, 173 N.E.2d 868 (N.Y. 1961).

4. **Economic loss rule.** Problems once dealt with by considering disclaimers, merger clauses, or the parol evidence rule may now be addressed through the economic loss rule. Recall that in *Moorman Mfg. Co. v. National Tank Co.*, 435 N.E.2d 443 (Ill. 1982) (Chapter 24), the court held that a product purchaser who claimed stand-alone economic loss rather than physical harm to person or property must sue under contract or warranty and could not sue in tort for strict liability or negligence. The idea of this economic loss rule is to honor the contract and to emphasize the potential role of contracts in resolving disputes between contracting parties. Courts are not always consistent in applying the economic loss rule to misrepresentation cases. *See* Dan B. Dobbs,

An Introduction to Non-Statutory Economic Loss Claims, 48 ARIZ. L. REV. 713, 728–33 (2006).

A number of courts have barred negligent or innocent misrepresentation claims on this ground. *See, e.g., JMB Mfg., Inc. v. Child Craft, LLC,* 799 F.3d 780 (7th Cir. 2015) (economic loss doctrine barred manufacturer's negligent misrepresentation); *LAN/STV v. Martin K. Eby Constr. Co.,* 435 S.W.3d 234 (Tex. 2014) (economic loss rule barred contractor's tort claim for delay damages allegedly caused by the project architect's negligent misrepresentations in the plans and specifications for a construction project); *Terracon Consultants W., Inc. v. Mandalay Resort Grp.,* 206 P.3d 81 (Nev. 2009) (economic loss rule bars tort claim against design professionals for negligently providing design advice in connection with improvements on commercial property); *Stieneke v. Russi,* 190 P.3d 60 (Wash Ct. App. 2008) (barring negligent misrepresentation claim by purchaser of home).

A few courts are now applying a modified version of the economic loss rule to bar fraud claims. *See, e.g., Below v. Norton,* 751 N.W.2d 351 (Wis. 2008) (economic loss rule bars all intentional misrepresentation claims in connection with residential real estate transactions); *Digicorp, Inc. v. Ameritech Corp.,* 662 N.W.2d 652 (Wis. 2003) (a claim of fraud would be barred unless the fraud was "extraneous" to the contract; it actually barred the fraud claim even though the alleged fraud did not actually contradict the contract provisions). This practice has been sharply and persuasively criticized. *See, e.g.,* Jean Braucher, *Deception, Economic Loss and Mass-Market Customers: Consumer Protection Statutes As Persuasive Authority in the Common Law of Fraud,* 48 ARIZ. L. REV. 829 (2006) ("Private ordering is impaired when it is founded on misrepresentation; it is hard to shop for the best deal if one must assume all claims, express or implied, are false.")

§ 4. DUTY TO DISCLOSE

OLLERMAN V. O'ROURKE CO.
288 N.W.2d 95 (Wis. 1980)

ABRAHAMSON, JUSTICE.

[Ollerman purchased a lot from O'Rourke Co. When he excavated to build a house, an underground well was uncovered and uncapped, and water was released. Ollerman alleged he had spent over $2,700 to cap the well and that building changes costing over $10,500 were necessitated by its presence. He alleged that O'Rourke Co. knew of the underground well but did not disclose it. The trial court overruled the defendant's motion to dismiss.]

[Silence where there is a duty to disclose is equivalent to a misrepresentation of fact and a seller obliged to disclose can be held liable for an "intentional" representation.]

We recognize that the traditional rule in Wisconsin is that in an action for intentional misrepresentation the seller of real estate, dealing at arm's length with the buyer, has no duty to disclose information to the buyer and therefore has no liability in an action for intentional misrepresentation for failure to disclose. . . .

Under the doctrine of caveat emptor no person was required to tell all that he or she knew in a business transaction, for in a free market the diligent should not be deprived of the fruits of superior skill and knowledge lawfully acquired. The business world, and the law reflecting business mores and morals, required the parties to a transaction to use their faculties and exercise ordinary business sense, and not to call on the law to stand *in loco parentis* to protect them in their ordinary dealings with other business people.

Over the years society's attitudes toward good faith and fair dealing in business transactions have undergone significant change, and this change has been reflected in the law. Courts have departed from or relaxed the "no duty to disclose" rule by carving out exceptions to the rule and by refusing to adhere to the rule when it works an injustice. Thus courts have held that the rule does not apply where the seller actively conceals a defect or where he prevents investigation; where the seller has told a half-truth or has made an ambiguous statement if the seller's intent is to create a false impression and he does so; where there is a fiduciary relationship between the parties; or where the facts are peculiarly and exclusively within the knowledge of one party to the transaction and the other party is not in a position to discover the facts for himself.

On the basis of the complaint, the case at bar does not appear to fall into one of these well-recognized exceptions to the "no duty to disclose" rule. However, Dean Prosser has found a "rather amorphous tendency on the part of most courts toward finding a duty of disclosure in cases where the defendant has special knowledge or means of knowledge not open to the plaintiff and is aware that the plaintiff is acting under a misapprehension as to facts which could be of importance to him, and would probably affect his decision."

Dean Keeton described these cases abandoning the "no duty to disclose" rule as follows:

"In the present stage of the law, the decisions show a drawing away from this idea [that nondisclosure is not actionable], and there can be seen an attempt by many courts to reach a just result in so far as possible, but yet maintaining the degree of certainty which the law must have. The statement may often be found that if either party to a contract of sale conceals or suppresses a material fact which he is in good faith bound to disclose then his silence is fraudulent.

"The attitude of the courts toward nondisclosure is undergoing a change and . . . it would seem that the object of the law in these cases should be to impose on parties to the transaction a duty to speak whenever justice, equity, and fair dealing demand it. This statement is made only with reference to instances where the party to be charged is an actor in the transaction. This duty to speak does not result from an implied representation by silence, but exists because a refusal to speak constitutes unfair conduct." *Fraud—Concealment and Nondisclosure*, 15 Tex. L. Rev. 1, 31 (1936).

The test Dean Keeton derives from the cases to determine when the rule of nondisclosure should be abandoned—"whenever justice, equity and fair dealing demand it"—present, as one writer states, "a somewhat nebulous standard, praiseworthy as looking toward more stringent business ethics, but possibly difficult of practical application." Case Note, *Silence as Fraudulent Concealment—Vendor & Purchaser—Duty to Disclose*, 36 Wash. L. Rev. 202, 204 (1961). . . .

The draftsmen of the most recent Restatement of Torts (Second) (1977) have attempted to formulate a rule embodying this trend in the cases toward a more frequent recognition of a duty to disclose. Sec. 551(1) of the Restatement sets forth the traditional rule that one who fails to disclose a fact that he knows may induce reliance in a business transaction is subject to the same liability as if he had represented the nonexistence of the matter that he failed to disclose if, and only if, he is under a duty to exercise reasonable care to disclose the matter in question. . . . Sec. 551(2) (e) is the "catch-all" provision setting forth conditions under which a duty to disclose exists; it states that a party to a transaction is under a duty to exercise reasonable care to disclose to the other "facts basic to the transaction, if he knows that the other is about to enter into it under a mistake as to them, and that the other, because of the relationship between them, the customs of the trade or other objective circumstances, would reasonably expect a disclosure of those facts." . . .

Section 551(2) (e) of the Restatement (Second) of Torts limits the duty to disclose to disclosure of those "facts basic" to the transaction. Comment j to sec. 551 differentiates between basic facts and material facts as follows:

"A basic fact is a fact that is assumed by the parties as a basis for the transaction itself. It is a fact that goes to the basis, or essence, of the transaction, and is an important part of the substance of what is bargained for or dealt with. Other facts may serve as important and persuasive inducements to enter into the transaction, but not go to its essence. These facts may be material, but they are not basic."

However, the draftsmen of the Restatement recognized that the law was developing to expand the duty to disclosure beyond the duty described in sec. 551. . . . The seller contends, in its brief, that if this court affirms the circuit court's order overruling the motion to dismiss and allows the buyer to proceed to trial, the court is adopting "what really amounts to a strict policy of 'let the seller beware.' " The seller goes on to state, "Woe indeed to anyone who sells a home, a vacant lot or other piece of real estate and fails to itemize with particularity or give written notice to each prospective buyer of every conceivable condition in and around the property, regardless of whether such a condition is dangerous, defective or could become so by the negligence or recklessness of others. A seller of real estate is not and should not be made an insurer or guarantor of the competence of those with whom the purchaser may later contract." . . .

The seller's arguments are not persuasive in light of the facts alleged in the complaint and our narrow holding in this case.

Where the vendor is in the real estate business and is skilled and knowledgeable and the purchaser is not, the purchaser is in a poor position to discover a condition which is not readily discernible, and the purchaser may justifiably rely on the knowledge and skill of the vendor. Thus, in this instant case a strong argument for imposing a duty on the seller to disclose material facts is this "reliance factor." The buyer portrayed in this complaint had a reasonable expectation of honesty in the marketplace, that is, that the vendor would disclose material facts which it knew and which were not readily discernible. Under these circumstances the law should impose a duty of honesty on the seller.

. . . [W]e hold that a subdivider-vendor of a residential lot has a duty to a "non-commercial" purchaser to disclose facts which are known to the vendor, which are material to the transaction, and which are not readily discernible to the purchaser. A fact is known to the vendor if the vendor has actual knowledge of the fact or if the vendor acted in reckless disregard as to the existence of the fact. This usage of the word "know" is the same as in an action for intentional misrepresentation based on a false statement. A fact is material if a reasonable purchaser would attach importance to its existence or nonexistence in determining the choice of action in the transaction in question; or if the vendor knows or has reason to know that the purchaser regards or is likely to regard the matter as important in determining the choice of action, although a reasonable purchaser would not so regard it.

NOTES

1.   **What must be disclosed?** In *Van Dinter v. Orr*, 138 P.3d 608 (Wash. 2006), a seller did not disclose to a purchaser of unimproved property that a capital facilities rate for sewer construction would be imposed once the land was developed. The buyer sued for negligent misrepresentation, but the court

held there was no duty to disclose. *But see Santiago v. Tanaka*, 366 P.3d 612 (Haw. 2016) (seller had duty to disclose to commercial property purchasers information regarding amount of private sewer fees that she knew may have justifiably induced purchasers to act or refrain from acting in purchase transaction). In *Nei v. Burley,* 446 N.E.2d 674 (Mass. 1983), a seller knew that the water table on his property was high and that there was a seasonal stream which was not apparent in dry season. He revealed neither. The buyer was required to spend more to install a septic tank because of these unrevealed features of the land. The court followed the traditional rule that there was no duty to disclose. Similarly, in *Laybourn v. City of Wasilla*, 362 P.3d 447 (Alaska 2015), the court held that the city had no duty to disclose to property owners that an access road project was subject to public notice and comment as well as further approvals, because the parties had dealt at arm's length, there was no inequality of bargaining power, and the information was of a type that the buyer would be expected to discover by ordinary inquiry. Would the Wisconsin Court, on the basis of *Ollerman*, get a different result in *Van Dinter, Nei,* or *Laybourn?* Notice that the limitation of the duty is to "basic" facts. In *Maybee v. Jacobs Motor Co.,* 519 N.W.2d 341 (S.D. 1994), the seller of a used vehicle did not tell the buyer that the engine had been rebuilt and that it used a gas not now generally available. The court held that there *may be* liability: if these were basic facts, the seller was under a duty to disclose and that it was up to the jury to determine whether the facts were basic.

2. **Partial disclosure.** V, attempting to sell a vacant lot, tells P: "I want to warn you—there is an easement across the edge of this property." P finds this acceptable and purchases the property. She then discovers that there is another easement in the middle and she cannot use the property for her purposes. The cases are agreed that P can recover. What is the principle? What if V honestly and reasonably believes there is only the one easement but later, before any contract for sale is signed, discovers the second one?

3. **Information requests.** Under the traditional rule, the buyer can avoid the problem by asking the right question. For example, if the seller denies the termite damage he knows to exist, he has made a knowingly false representation and is liable. *Cf. Arnesen v. Rivers Edge Golf Club & Plantation, Inc.,* 781 S.E.2d 1 (N.C. 2015) (lender for sales of undeveloped subdivision lots owed no duty to disclose appraisal information to borrowers, where borrowers never requested that information).

4. **Fraud.** S, attempting to sell a car, moves its odometer back from 65,000 miles to 30,000 miles. He says nothing whatever about the mileage and P does not ask. If P buys in reliance on the odometer, has he a claim? On the basis of what rule?

5. **Financial information.** L, a lawyer who represents C, offers to sell C shares of stock in a corporation. He says nothing about the fact that the corporation has manufactured, among other things, asbestos, and may be subject to catastrophic liabilities for injuries. C purchases, then the corporation goes bankrupt over asbestos liabilities. Has C a claim against her lawyer? On

the basis of what rule? Concealment of assets, losses, profits, or other material financial information from a buyer or partner may also subject the defendant to liability for misrepresentation. Concealment of a conflict of interest can operate in the same way. *See Skilling v. United States*, 561 U.S. 358 (2010); *United States v. McGeehan*, 625 F.3d 159 (3d Cir. 2010).

6. **Duty to disclose.** The Restatement Third well summarizes the duty to disclose. According to the Restatement: "A failure to disclose material information may result in liability if the actor has a duty to speak. Such a duty exists when:

(a)   the actor has made a prior statement and knows that it will likely mislead another if not amended, even if it was not misleading when made;

(b)   the actor is in a fiduciary or confidential relationship with another that obliges the actor to make disclosures; or

(c)   the actor knows that the other party to a transaction is mistaken about a basic assumption behind it, and that the other party, because of the relationship between them, the customs of the trade, or other circumstances, would reasonably expect disclosure of what the actor knows."

RESTATEMENT (THIRD) OF TORTS: LIAB. FOR ECON. HARM § 13 (2020).

7. **Statutory disclosure duties.** The securities laws, the Interstate Land Sales Act, and other statutes, including some state statutes, frequently impose affirmative duties to disclose material. In some states, consumer protection acts have been passed which may also require disclosure. A claim for nondisclosure therefore requires a careful study of the statutes.

REFERENCES: DOBBS, HAYDEN & BUBLICK, HORNBOOK ON TORTS §§ 43.2–43.10 (2d ed. 2016); 3 DOBBS, HAYDEN & BUBLICK, THE LAW OF TORTS §§ 662–94 (2d ed. 2011); DAN B. DOBBS, THE LAW OF REMEDIES § 9.2 (6) (2d ed. 1993).

INDEX

Using the Index

This index refers to key words, legal rules or ideas, legal issues, key parties, and important factual settings. It is not a concordance or a computer-generated word list. Hence not every instance of a word is listed. Equally, the referenced page may discuss or exemplify the legal idea indexed without using the indexing word. References are to pages. When indexed material appears in a main case, only the first page of the case is given, unless inclusive references are more practical. Similarly, only the first page is typically given when a broad topic covers many succeeding pages. When indexed material appears in notes, the first page of an inclusive reference is the page on which the note begins.

ABNORMALLY DANGEROUS ACTIVITIES
See Strict Liability

ABUSE OF PROCESS
See Tortious Litigation

ACCIDENT DATA
See also Tort Systems Evaluation
Injury rates and costs, 474–76, 959–63
Insurance inefficiency figures, 475, 966
Rate of recovery, 474–75, 961–62
Rate of suing, 16, 961

ACTUAL CAUSE
See Factual Cause

ACTUAL HARM
Element of negligence claim, 237
Presumed or not required in trespassory tort cases, 55, 69–71
Required in negligence cases, 237

ADMINISTRATIVE AGENCIES
Regulations
construing statutes, regulatory construction, 482, 488
nursing homes, 487
September 11, 2001 compensation system, 1016–17
social security disability determinations under, 1020
violation of
discretionary immunity, none for violation, 517
negligence per se or not, 156, 162

ADMIRALTY
Maintenance and cure of and strict liability to seamen, 975
Unseaworthiness, negligence analogy, 219

AGENCY
See Vicarious Liability

AGGRAVATED INJURY
Causal apportionment
indivisible injury, fault apportionment required, 871–72, 885
preexisting probability of death, 258
Foreseeable aggravation, first tortfeasor liable, 314
Indivisible injury, 871–72, 885–86
Medical aggravation of negligently caused injury, 314
Negligence in causing original injury disregarded, 336–37
Plaintiff's failure to minimize damages as, 337, 926–27

AIDING AND ABETTING
Conversion, 75
Vicarious liability and, 749

AIDS OR HIV
Doctor's duty to warn of another's aids, 625
Emotional distress claims from possible exposure, 673
Negligent diagnosis of, emotional harm, 665
Privacy, 625
Window of anxiety recovery after exposure, 673

Workers' compensation, exposure on the
job, 1000

AIMS OF TORT LAW
See Torts and Tort Law

ALCOHOL
See Intoxicants and Intoxicated Persons

ALIENATION OF AFFECTIONS
See Family Members

ALTERNATIVES TO TORT LAW
See Compensation Systems

ANIMALS
Companion animals, injury to
Emotional harm to owner, 662
Domestic animals, vicious propensity rule,
756–57
Emotional harm from damage to, 662
Strict liability for
domestic, vicious propensity, 756–57
trespassing cattle, 755–56
wild, personal injury, 757

**APPORTIONMENT OF
RESPONSIBILITY**
See also Comparative Fault;
Contribution and
Indemnity; Joint and
Several Liability
Generally, 871
Among defendants or tortfeasors
proportionate or several liability, 878
settlement of one, 876–77
Amounts apportioned, see Contribution
and Indemnity
Avoidable consequences, apportionment by,
337, 926–27
Causal apportionment
Generally, 247–48, 251, 336–37, 871,
885, 892
Comparative causation, 885
Comparative fault
Generally, see Comparative
Fault
intentional misconduct compared to
negligence, 881–85
strict liability compared to
negligence, 774–75, 843–53,
880
Crashworthiness cases, 892
Fault apportionment, 197, 317, 324, 871–
72, 885
Immune tortfeasors, allocating fault of,
199, 891
Insolvent tortfeasors, 199
Intentional and negligent tortfeasors,
between, 881–85
Joint and several liability, 874
Market share apportionment, 897–905
Negligent and intentional tortfeasors,
between, 881–85

Negligent and strictly liable defendants,
between, 880
Nonparties, allocating fault of or not, 891
Proportionate share, see several liability,
this topic
Res ipsa loquitur and, 235
Several liability apportionment
Generally, 197–98, 199, 878
causal apportionment affecting, 892
diagram of, 198
effect on plaintiff's recovery
Generally, 879
indivisible injury predicate, 885–86
proportionate shares for negligent
and intentional tortfeasors,
881–85
Strictly liable tortfeasor and negligent
tortfeasor, 880
Uniform Apportionment of Tort
Responsibility Act, 890–91
Workers' compensation, employer vs. third-
party tortfeasor, 1012

ARREST
See also False Imprisonment
False arrest, 66–67
Fourth Amendment violations, civil rights
claims, 78–79
Police, warrant or probable cause, 79
Privilege to arrest or detain, 100

ASBESTOS
See also Toxic Torts
Conspiracy or enterprise liability, 903
Exposure, fear of cancer, emotional harm,
668, 672–73
Products liability, bystander claims, 807
Punitive damages for concealing toxic
character, 936
Statute of limitations, 387

ASSAULT
Generally, 58
Apprehension of contact
fear distinguished, 61
imminence requirement, 62
reasonableness of, 58–60
Conditional threat, 58, 62
Free Access to Clinics Entrances Act and,
63
Governmental immunity (federal), 507
Imminent, meaning of, 62
Stalking and, 63
Transferred intent and, 62
Words alone, 61–62

ASSUMPTION OF THE RISK
See also Sports
Generally, 357
Baseball Rule and, 364, 366
Caregiver of Alzheimer's patient, 144, 147
Children, parents' release in advance, 361
Comparative fault, assumed risk as, 368,
374

Construction of release-in-advance, 362, 363–64
Contractual assumed risk, 357
Employment, in, 368, 372, 374–75
Express assumption, see contractual assumed risk, this topic
Fellow servant rule, abolished in FELA, 976
Firefighters' rule, 437
Implied assumption of risk generally, 371
Increased risk, 366–68
Insane patient, caregiver's assumed risk of harm by, 144, 147
Knowledge of risk, 373–74
Medical treatment, assumed risk exacted as precondition to, 358
Primary, 368
Products liability, 843–53
Public policy limits on contractual, 358, 364
Reckless or intentional torts, waivers invalid, 361
Recreational activities and, 357, 359–60, 364
Risks inherent in sport, 368–69
Secondary, 368, 374
Sports cases
    Generally, 364
    Baseball Rule, 364, 366
    inherent risks, 368–69
    participants, 368–71
    recklessness standard in, 371
    rule violations and, 370
    spectators, 364–71
    statutes, 371
Strict liability
    abnormally dangerous activity cases, 774–75
    products cases, 843–53
Voluntariness, 373–74

ATTORNEY'S FEES
American rule, 15
Contingent fees, 15
Ethics rules on, 15
Offer of judgment statutes and, 241, 906
Pain and suffering awards and, 921, 931
Parties pay own, effects, 15, 134, 955
Punitive damages and, 955
Statutory recovery, civil rights claims, 79

ATTORNEYS
Clients' rights against, 906–07
Fees, 15
Settlement of claims by, 906–07

ATTRACTIVE NUISANCE
Child trespassers, duty to, 414, 418
Instrumentality of injury, 418
Tender years, 418

AVOIDABLE CONSEQUENCES
Apportioning liability to causes not by fault, 337, 926–27
Comparative fault compared, 337, 926

Wrongful conception cases, argument from, 686

BATTERY
    See also Intent; Sexual Abuse
    Generally, 37
Bodily touching required, 37
Children
    liability of, 8, 46, 50–51
    parental liability for, 51
Contact required, 37, 53
Damages for, 55–56
Dual and single intent, 42–45
Elements, 37
Emotional distress and, 55–56
Federal government immunity for, 507
Indirect contact, 53
Insane persons, by, 42–43, 45
Intent
    children and, 46, 50–51
    dual and single intent, 42–45
    mentally infirm persons and, 42–43, 45
    negligence distinguished, 50
    offensive contact, 40
    purpose, 49
    recklessness distinguished, 50
    single and dual intent, 42–45
    substantial certainty, 46–50
    transferred intent, 56–57, 62
Medical, 44, 117–18
Nominal damages, 55
Offense, 40
On the job, workers' compensation
    horseplay, 900–02
    intended battery, 900–02, 1004
    sexual harassment, 1007–10
Presumed damages, 55
Punitive damages, 56
Purposeful infliction of bodily harm tort, 53
Single and dual intent, 42–45

BLASTING
Strict liability, 767–72

BLOOD OR BODY PARTS OR PRODUCTS
    See also AIDS or HIV
Conversion claims, 74, 464

BONA FIDE PURCHASER
Property purchased from one with voidable title, 75

BOYCOTTS
Interference with contract or prospects by, 1095–96

BURDEN OF PROOF
Defenses, affirmative, defendant's burden, 91, 319
Directed verdict for party having, 208
Elements of case, plaintiff's burden, 37, 133
Preponderance of the evidence, meaning and requirement, 201, 267–69

Prima facie case, 37
Products liability
    design defect, shifting burden, 812–
      13
    warnings defects, presumed cause,
      832

CAPACITY
See Incapacity; Mentally Disabled Persons

CAREGIVERS
    See also Elder Abuse; Medical
        Malpractice; Nursing Homes
Assuming risk of injury by patient, 144,
    147
Daycare center, SIDS, 149
Incapacitated person striking, intent, 42–
    43, 45, 144–48
Limited duty owed by disabled person to,
    144, 147
Nursing homes, 236
Res ipsa loquitur, 487
Vicarious liability for acts of, 732

CARROLL TOWING DOCTRINE
See Risk-Utility Analysis

CAUSE IN FACT
See Factual Cause

CHARITIES
Damages caps, 499
Hospitals, immunity, 498–99
Immunity of, 497
Individuals engaged in charitable
    activities, 499–500

CHILDREN
    See also Family Members; Prenatal
        Harms
Adult standard of care, applicability to,
    149–52
Child abuse
    duty to report, 162–63, 607
Child trespassers, duty to, 414
Consent, capacity to give, 114
Discipline, privilege to, 106
Duty, 149–52, 157, 170, 414, 418
Intent, 46, 50
Intentional torts, liability for, 46, 50
Negligent torts, liability for, 149–52
Parental duty to control, 51, 616
Parental liability statutes, 51
Parental waiver of claims of, 361
Rule of sevens, 152
School crossing guards withdrawn, injury
    or death, 585
Sexual abuse, statute of limitations
    extended, 389
Standard of care of, 149–52
Trespassing, landowner's duty to, 414
Vaccine Act, 904, 1013–16
Willful misconduct of, 46, 51

CIVIL LAW
Common law contrasted, 46

CIVIL RIGHTS
    See also Discrimination; First
        Amendment; Sexual Abuse or
        Harassment
Attorney's fees, recovery of, 79
Common-law torts and, 77–79
Discriminatory non-protection, 536
Domestic violence, 536
Due process, see Fourteenth Amendment,
    this topic
Duty to protect, discrimination as basis for,
    536
Eighth Amendment, cruel punishment, 79
Failure to train officers, 538–39
Federal claims under § 1983 generally, 77
Fees, recovery of, 79
Fourteenth Amendment, test of violation,
    80
Fourth Amendment, test of violation, 79
High-speed chases, police, 530–31
Immunity, qualified, 82–90, 536
Municipal and state liability, 535
Nonaction, racial or sexual discrimination,
    535
Police chases, 530–31
Practical value of § 1983 claims, 78
Prisoners, 80
Qualified immunity, 82–90, 536
Schools, 606
State and municipal liability, 535
Statute, text of § 1983, 78
Taking of property, 503
Trespassory torts, civil rights analogies,
    77–78

CLERGY
See Religious Bodies or Clergy

COMMERCIAL TORTS
See Economic Torts

COMMON CARRIERS
Defined, 404
Duty or standard of care, 403

COMMON LAW WRITS
Originating suit with, 753
Trespass and case, 10, 753

COMPANION ANIMALS
See Animals

**COMPARATIVE FAULT OR
    RESPONSIBILITY**
    See also Apportionment of
        Responsibility;
        Contributory Negligence;
        Joint and Several
        Liability
    Generally, 323
Actual cause required, 336–37
Adoption of, 323

Allocating fault of immune tortfeasor, 199, 891

Apportionment between negligent plaintiff and strictly liable defendant, 774–75, 843–53

Apportionment between strictly liable and negligent defendants, 880

Assessing responsibility of each party
    comparing costs of safety for each party, 325, 330
    equitable or just approach, 331
    factors approach, 342
    rescue by plaintiff, 349
    Restatement of Apportionment, 332
    standards of parties different, 334

Avoidable consequences or minimizing damages
    choice between two approaches, 337, 926–27

Bexiga principle, 338

Causal vs. Fault apportionment of damages, 336–37, 871–72

Causation, non-causal fault disregarded, 336–37

Comparing responsibility, see assessing responsibility of each party, this topic

Computation
    examples, 323, 330
    Maine rule, 331

Consortium claim, reduced by victim's fault or not, 661

Damages caps and, computational issues, 931–32

Defendant under a duty to protect from third persons, 885–86

Defendant's reckless or intentional misconduct, 350–51, 881–85

Disregarding fault on causation or scope of risk grounds, 343–49

Duty to protect plaintiff from plaintiff's own fault, 338

Entitlement to act negates defense, 343–49

Estimating fault of parties, see assessing responsibility of each party, this topic

Expectation of care by others, 338

Factors in assessing responsibility, see assessing responsibility of each party, this topic

FELA, 323

Illegal acts of plaintiff, 351–54

Immune tortfeasors, 199, 891

Informed consent, in, 466

Intentional or reckless misconduct of defendant, 350–51, 881–85

Intentional tort of third person risked by defendant, 885

Jury
    informing jury of effect of modified system, 325
    role in allocating fault, 324

Landowner's use of own land, entitlement, 346

Last clear chance and, 349–50

Medical malpractice, patient's fault, 336

Misrepresentation claims, in, 1124–25

Mitigation of damages and, 337

Modified system
    informing jury of effects, 325
    types of, 324

Negligence compared to intentional wrongs, 350–51, 881–85

No-duty rules, 343–49

Nonparties, comparing fault of or not, 886, 891

Phantom tortfeasors, 891

Plaintiff entitlement to act negates defense of, 343–49

Plaintiff's conduct sole proximate cause, 336

Plaintiff's illegal activity, 351–54

Proximate cause and, 335–36

Proximate cause as apportionment, 317, 335–36

Pure system, modified contrasted, 324

Rape victim's conduct as, 347

Reciprocal and non-reciprocal risks, 338, 341–42

Reckless or intentional torts of the defendant, 343, 350–51, 881–85

Res ipsa loquitur and, 235

Rescue, plaintiff's fault in attempting, 349

Restatement of Apportionment factors in assessing responsibility, 332

Risk of intentional tort by another, 885

Scope of risk, disregarding fault outside of, 335

Settlement effects, 876–77

Several or proportionate share liability systems, effects, 878

Sexual abuse and, 343–49

Standard of care
        Generally, 147
    parties under different standard, 334

Statutes, representative, 323

Statutory duties to the plaintiff, 341

Superseding cause and, 336

Uniform Contribution Among Tortfeasors Act, 890

COMPENSATION SYSTEMS
ATSSA, 1016–17
Evaluating systems, 1041–42
No-fault auto insurance, 1030–39
Private insurance systems, 1029–39
September 11 compensation fund, 1016–17
Social security disability, 1018–27
Vaccine Act, 1013–16
Workers' compensation, 975–1012

COMPENSATORY DAMAGES
See Damages

COMPLIANCE WITH STATUTE
Breach of duty, evidence of lack of, 221–22
Defense or not, 857, 863
Fault, tending to prove lack of, 222

Federal preemption as a compliance
        defense, 395–400, 857–62
Products liability cases, 857, 863

COMPROMISE
        See also Settlement
Offer of judgment, 241

CONCERT OF ACTION
Basis for finding, 749, 903
DES cases, 897, 904
Joint and several liability, ground for, 748,
        875

CONCURRENT TORTS
See Apportionment of Responsibility; Joint
        and Several Liability

CONSENT
        See also Assumed Risk;
                Informed Consent
        Generally, 108
Apparent, 108–10, 111
Battery and, 111
Capacity to give
        adults, 113, 118
        defendant's knowledge of incapacity,
                113
        minors, 118
        substituted consent, 118
        test of, 118
Conditional, 118
Crime, to, 116–17
Duress inducing, 113
Employee's apparent, sexual activity, 118–
        19
False imprisonment and, 113
False representations or fraud inducing,
        115
Incapacity to consent, 113–14, 119
Informed consent (medical), 458
Intoxication, 119
Medical (informed consent), 458
Minors, by, 118
Mistake or ignorance, 119
Power relationships and, 113–14
Presumed, 112
Revocation of, 116
Scope, exceeding, 117–18
Silence as, 110
Single and dual intent and, 111
Substituted consent, 119

CONSORTIUM, LOSS OF
Bystander NIED compared, 660
Companion animals, 662
Death actions, claim in, 698
Defined, 660
Derivative claim or not, 660
Emotional harm, as, 658–62
History of claim for, 660
Parental consortium, 661
Spousal claims, 660

CONSPIRACY
Concealing danger of product or identity of
        manufacturers, 903
Enterprise liability of all producers of a
        product, 903
Vicarious liability, form of, 748

CONTINGENT FEES
See Attorney's Fees

CONTRACT AND TORT
                See also Consent; Assumed
                        Risk; Interference with
                        Contract;
                        Misrepresentation
                Generally, 3, 567
Action as an undertaking, 585
Assuming duty of another, 579
Breach of contract to repair, historic privity
        bar, 582–84
Content of duty imposed by promise or
        undertaking, 587
Contract or undertaking, tort duty and, 567
Contractual limitation of tort duty, 576
                See also Assumption of the Risk
Damages, tort or contract measures, 567
Economic loss rule and, 567, 571
Economic promises vs. Safety promises,
        567, 576
Electrical company's nonperformance,
        personal injury, 584
Increased risk requirement, 580
Lessor's promise to repair, 581
Misfeasance and nonfeasance, 567, 572
Misrepresentation by non-party, 1116
Privity of contract, 582–84
Promise to third persons, effects, 582–84
Reliance on undertaking, requirement of,
        580–81, 585
Scope of duty created by promise or
        undertaking, 567, 587
Shifting duty or responsibility by contract,
        579
Special relationship, contract creating, 567,
        576
Tort duties arising from promise or
        undertaking, 523, 532, 553–54, 567
Undertaking, 523, 532, 553–54, 567
Water company's nonperformance, 583

CONTRIBUTION OR INDEMNITY
                See also Apportionment of
                        Responsibility; Joint and
                        Several Liability; Settlement
Common liability requirement, 877
Contribution
        amount, 877
        availability in joint and several
                liability cases, 198, 875, 877
        diagram, with joint and several
                liability, 198
        immunity of one tortfeasor, effect on,
                199

tortfeasor's claim against workers' compensation employer, 1012
Indemnity
    contribution and, 878
    employer's right to against employee, 716–17
    products liability, retailer's right to, 782
Workers' compensation, tortfeasor's claim against employer, 1012

CONTRIBUTORY NEGLIGENCE
    See also Apportionment of Responsibility; Comparative Fault
Bar to negligence claim, 321
Causation and, 336–37
Duty of others to prevent harm to plaintiff, effect, 338
Entitlement to act negating contributory fault defense, 343–49
Exceptions to the bar, 322, 338, 349
Illegal activity of plaintiff, 351–54
Imputed to employer, 751–52
Intentional misconduct of defendant, 350–51
Last clear chance, 349–50
Misrepresentation claims, 1124–25
Plaintiff's entitlement to act negating defense, 343–49
Products liability, effect, 843–53
Proximate cause and, 335–36
Rationales for bar of, 322
Reckless conduct of defendant, 350–51
Standard of care, 142, 144, 147
Strict liability, abnormally dangerous activity cases, 774–75

CONVERSION
Aiding and abetting, 75
Blood, taking of, 74, 464
Body parts, taking of, 74
Bona fide purchasers, 75
Damages for, 914
Domain names, taking of, 73–74
Dominion required, 73–74
Electronic data, 74–75
Factors determining, 73–74
Intent required, 73
Mistake, 73
Property subject to, 73
Remedies, 73, 914
Serial conversion, 75
Substantial dominion, 73–74
UCC provisions on, 75

COPYRIGHT
Availability, protection and free speech rights, 1097–99

CORRECTIVE JUSTICE
Torts and, 5

CRIME
Duty to protect from, 589–634
September 11 compensation fund, 1016–17
Tort and, 3

CRIMINAL CONVERSATION
See Family Members

CUSTOM
    See also Medical Malpractice; Sports
As a shield, 218–21
As a sword, 217–18
Awareness of custom, relevance, 217
Defendant's non-violation of, 218–21
Defendant's own custom or rules, 215–16
Defendant's violation of, 217–18
Evidence, not standard, 217–18
Medical, conclusive standard of care, 445–55
Non-safety custom, 218
Proof, industry codes or manuals, 218
Proving what, 218
Standard of care, evidence, not standard, 217–18
Statute customarily violated, 217–18

DAMAGES
    See also No-Fault Compensation; Workers' Compensation
Generally, 913
Actual harm
    presumed or not required in trespassory tort cases, 55, 69–71
    required in negligence cases, 237
Adjustments in awards, 14, 919, 926–27
Attorney's fees and, 15, 134, 955
Avoidable consequences, 337, 926–27
Battery, 55–56
Benefits resulting from tort
    collateral benefits, 927–29
    direct benefits, 928
Caps or limits on
    Generally, 929–33
    abolishing or limiting pain awards, 929–33
    computational issues, 931–32
    constitutionality of, 932–33
    damages covered by cap, 931
    defendants covered by cap, 930–31
    effect on liability in close cases, 933
    punitive damages, 938–40
    remittitur, 15
Civil rights cases, 81
Collateral source rule, 927–29
Comatose plaintiff, 921, 924
Comparable awards, 924–25
Compensatory damages generally, 10, 913
Components, personal injury cases, 14, 915
Constitutional torts, 81, 913
Criticisms of, 16, 928–29, 933
Death, measures for, 694–703

Defamation
    presumed at common law, 1049
    proof constitutionally required, when,
        1058, 1066
Direct benefits resulting from tort, 928
Elements, personal injury claims, 14, 915
Emotional harm
        See also Emotional Harm
    battery, 55–56
    pain and suffering, included in, 920
Extended liability, 56–58, 71
False imprisonment, 66–67
Fees, attorney's, 15, 134, 955
Future losses, elements of damages, 915
Goals of tort law and, 11
Hedonic damages, 923
Inflation, 919
Introduction to, 11
Judge and jury, role of, 15
Loss of enjoyment of life, 921–25
McDonald's hot coffee case, 16
Medical monitoring costs where risk is
    future injury, 387, 672, 915, 925–26
Minimizing damages, see avoidable
    consequences, this topic
Misrepresentation, 1121–24
Mitigation of, and comparative fault, 337
Negligence claims, actual harm required,
    237
Nominal
    amounts of, 240
    constitutional torts without physical
        harm, 81, 913
    intentional trespassory torts, 55, 69–
        71
    negligence cases, unavailable without
        actual harm, 240
Pain and suffering
    assault, 55–56
    attorney's fees, relevance to recovery
        for, 921
    battery, 55–56
    comatose patient, 921, 924
    comparable awards, 924–25
    component of recoverable
        damages,14, 15, 915, 921
    dollar value, assessing and arguing,
        14, 920
    element of recoverable damages, 14,
        15, 916–21
    false imprisonment, 55
    limiting damages for, 929–33
    scope of damages for, 920
    social security benefits and, 1020,
        1027
    trespassory torts, 55, 69–70
Parasitic damages, 637, 672–73
Periodic payments, 919
Personal injury, elements of, 14, 239–40,
    915
Physical harm defined, 240
Presumed, trespassory torts, 55, 69–71
Property torts, 914

Punitive damages
        Generally, 934
    actual damages a precondition or not,
        935
    attorney's fees, relevance to recovery
        of, 934, 955
    battery, 55
    caps, 939–40
    civil rights cases, 81
    concealment of danger, 936
    constitutional limits on, 940–57
    deterrence function, 936–37
    employer's respondeat superior
        liability for, 935
    factors in measuring, 934, 937
    judges compared to juries in
        awarding, 939
    limiting punitive awards, 938–40,
        955
    litigation finance function, 955
    McDonald's hot coffee case, 16
    measurement of, 934, 937
    nominal damages as basis for or not,
        240, 935
    ratio, compensatory to punitive, 938,
        940, 950, 951, 954
    redirecting punitive awards to
        another person, 939–40
    statutes limiting, 939–40
    strict liability cases, 937
    trespass to land, 71
    vicarious liability for, 935
    wealth of defendant, relevance to, 938
Purposes, 11–16
Reduction to present value, 919
Remittitur, 15
Survivor actions, 699
Tort duty based upon promise, contract or
    tort damages, 567
Trespass
    Damages presumed, 55, 71
    Extended liability, 71
Wrongful birth, wrongful conception, 682–
    87
Wrongful death, 696–99

DEATH
Common law, not actionable, 689
Consortium claims and, 698
Damages
    jury awards, problems with, 704
    survival action, 699
    wrongful death action, 694–98
Loss of consortium and, 698
Parties and procedure, 693–94
Statutes of limitations for, 706
Stepchildren as heirs, 704
Survival, wrongful death actions
    distinguished, 690–94
Unmarried cohabitant claiming as
    survivor, 704
Wrongful death action, 689

DEFAMATION
Common law rules of, 1045–53
Constitutional free speech limits on claims
 for
  defamation on a non-public issue,
   1066
  limited to publishers and
   broadcasters or not, 1065
  private individuals suing, 1058, 1066
  proof required, 1053–67
  public officials of public figures suing,
   proof required, 1053–58
  states free to enlarge speech
   protections, 1067
  status as public figure or official,
   1064
Damages presumed at common law, 1049
Damages proof constitutionally required,
 when, 1053–67
Defamatory meaning requirement, 1048
Fault requirement under the Constitution,
 1053–67
Foreign judgments, 1058
Free speech and, 1053–67
Ideas or opinions vs. Facts, 1065–66
Injurious falsehood compared, 1088
Internet posters, 1065
Internet publication, privilege, 1053
Libel and slander, 1049
Malicious prosecution compared, 1070
Opinion statements, 1065–66
Privileges, common law, 1050
Public official and public figures, suits by,
 1053–58
Publication requirement, 1047
Reference to the plaintiff requirement,
 1047
Repeaters rule, 1047
Slander per se, 1049–50
Truth
 common law defense, 1050
 constitutional rule, 1058, 1065
Widespread publication, 1058

DEFENSES TO INTENTIONAL TORTS
 See also Consent
 Generally, 91
Arrest or false imprisonment
 mistake, 105
 privilege to arrest or detain, when,
  100
 reporting crime as, 105
 self-defense, assault or imprisonment
  in, 95
 shopkeeper's privilege, 100
 statutes on, 100, 104, 105
 trespassers, detaining, 105
Consent, see the topic Consent
Deadly force, 95
Defense of others, 97
Defense of property, 97–100
Defense of third persons, 97
Discipline, 106

Necessity
 private, 124–28
 public, 120–24
 taking of property, 123
Provocation, 91, 94
Public necessity vs. Taking of property, 123
Reasonableness issues in, 107
Repossession of land and chattels,
 privilege, 99–100
Self-defense
  Generally, 91
 assault or imprisonment as, 95
 deadly force, 95
 elements, 91, 94
 excessive force, 94
 mistake, 95
 provocation, 91, 94
 retreat, 95
 shopkeeper's privilege, 100
 "stand your ground" laws, 96
Third persons, defense of, 97
Threat of force as, 99
Trespass to land, privilege to defend
 against, 97, 105

DEFENSES TO NEGLIGENT TORTS
 See also Immunities; and named
  torts and named defenses such
  as Assumption of the Risk and
  Comparative Fault or
  Responsibility
About defenses, 319
Assumption of the risk, 357–68
Comparative fault or contributory
 negligence, 321–55
Compliance with statute, 862
Preemption, 395–400, 857–62
Statutes of limitation, 378–95, 865–68

DISABLED PERSONS
 See also Incapacity; Discrimination;
  Workers' Compensation; Social
  Security Disability Benefits
Abuse of, vicarious liability for, 732
Contract with state to modify vehicles for,
 immunity rejected, 865
Duty to use care, undertaking a duty, 532
Epilepsy
 foreseeable seizure and proximate
  cause, 306
Genetic harms, wrongful birth cases, 682–
 85
Governmental undertaking of care, public
 duty doctrine, 532
Release, unsuspected injury, 907–12
Standard of care owed by one under
 mental disability, 139–43
 physical disability, 142–44
Standard of care owed to one under
 disability, 147, 341–42
Statute of limitations, tolling for, 388
Workers' compensation second-injury fund,
 1002–03

DISCIPLINE
Privilege to discipline child, 106

DISCRIMINATION
Employment discrimination forbidden, 114
Governmental failure to protect, 536
Sexual harassment or exploitation
    consent and capacity, 113–14
    vicarious liability for, 731–33
    workers' compensation and, 1007–10
Statutes against, effects on common law
    rules, 144–47

DISPARAGEMENT
Injurious falsehood, form of, 1085–87

DRAM SHOP STATUTES
See Intoxicants and Intoxicated Persons

DUE PROCESS
See Civil Rights

DUTY
    See also Contract and Tort;
        Governmental Entities;
        Landowners; Medical
        Malpractice; Nonfeasance;
        Standard of Care; Third
        Persons, Duty to Control or
        Protect From; Third Persons,
        Liability to
Affirmative acts, no duty to take, 543–53
Alcohol providers, to third persons, 625–31
Breach of duty vs. Duty analysis, 177, 179–
    80, 401, 423, 601
Chance of better outcome, duty to
    maximize, 267–68
Children, 149–52, 157, 170, 414, 418
Clergy, see Religious Bodies or Clergy
Concept
    breach of duty vs. duty analysis, 177,
        179–80, 401, 423, 601
    proximate cause alternative, 280
Contract or undertaking affecting, 553–54,
    567–88, 662–64
Death, common law immunity for causing,
    689
Disclosure, duty of, 1130
Element in prima facie case, 133
Guest statutes limiting, 406
Health care providers generally, 445
Landowners generally, 407
Lessors generally, 434
Negligence analysis vs. Duty analysis, 177,
    179–80, 401, 423, 601
Open, obvious danger as a no-duty rule,
    423, 831
Premises liability, see Landowners
Prenatal protections, 675–87
Proximate cause alternative, 280
Reasonable care, duty of generally, 135
Relationship affecting, 560–66, 662–64
Third persons, duty to protect from
    generally, 589

To fetus, 675–82
To preserve plaintiff's chance of life or
    health, 261–70
To protect plaintiff from plaintiff's own
    fault, 338–49
To provide emergency treatment, 480, 481
To recreational users of land, 430

ECONOMIC ANALYSIS OF TORT LAW
    See also Risk-Utility Analysis
    Generally, 7
Accident costs reduction approach, 717,
    783–84
Calabresi's approaches, 717, 783–84
Efficiency, 192–97
In products liability cases, 783–84
Posner's approach, 194

**ECONOMIC TORTS (INDEPENDENT
OF PERSONAL INJURY)**
Copyright, free speech and, 1098
Defamation, see the topic Defamation
Disparagement, commercial, 1085
Economic loss doctrine, 567, 571, 794–99,
    1129–30
Injurious falsehood, 1085
Interference with contract and economic
    values, see the topic Interference
    with Contract and Prospects
Malicious prosecution, see Tortious
    Litigation
Misrepresentation, fraud, or deceit, 1107–
    35
Patent protection, nature of, 1097
Slander of title, 1087
Trade secrets, 1099
Trademarks and unfair competition, 1097–
    1103

ELDER ABUSE
    See also Caregivers
Extent, 486
Nursing homes generally, 484
Res ipsa loquitur, 487
Statutes, 488

EMERGENCY
Emergency medical treatment, duty to
    provide, 480–81
Jury instructions on, 139–42
Standard of care in generally, 139–42

EMOTIONAL HARM
    See also Consortium, Loss of;
        Prenatal Harms; and
        particular topics such as
        Sexual Abuse or
        Harassment
    Generally, 637–74
Abolishing limiting rules, 667
AIDS misdiagnosis of causing anxiety, 665
AIDS possible exposure without infection,
    673
Animal injured, owner's distress, 662

Asbestos, asbestosis and fear of cancer, 672–73
Battery, 55–56, 645
Consortium loss as form of, 658–62
Dead bodies, 665
Death messages, 666
Duty of reasonable care instituted, 667
Employer's abusive and threatening conduct, 639, 642–43
Fear of future harm from toxic exposure, 668–74
Fetus, prenatal injury, mother's emotional distress, 680, 686
First Amendment limitations on claim, 645
Independent of physical risks, 662–67
Information or ideas communicated
    to others about the plaintiff, 665
    to the plaintiff, 645, 664–66
Intentional
    abuse of power pattern, 639, 643
    causation, proof, 644
    elements, Restatement Third statement of, 640
    employer's treatment of employees, 639, 643
    evidence of distress, 644
    markers of outrage, 642
    other tort claims and, 644–45
    outrageous conduct required, 637, 639, 641
    patterns of actionable behavior, 642
    racial epithets, 643
    repeated conduct, 642
    severe distress required, 644
    third person not present, liability or not, 645–46
    vulnerability of plaintiff, 643
    words inflicting distress, 645
Negligent infliction of
    AIDS exposure without disease, 673
    AIDS wrongly diagnosed, 665
    combination of tests for, 657
    dead body, treatment of, 665
    death messages, 666
    fright or shock from physical risks, 647
    impact requirement, 649
    injury to another
        Generally, 653
        close family relationship requirement, 654, 656
        duty undertaken to plaintiff to protect another, 662–64
        presence or sensory perception at the time, 654, 655
        zone of danger rule, 653, 654–55
    legal rights, exercise of, 643–44
    misinformation to others, other torts for, 644, 665
    misinformation to plaintiff, 664–66
    parasitic damages, 637, 672–74

physical manifestations or symptoms required or not, 649
relationship of parties, relevance, 654, 656
Restatement Third on, 654
severe harm must be foreseeable, 668
third person, duty undertaken to, 662–64
toxic exposure without provable physical harm, 668–74
videotapes of plaintiff's sexual acts, 666
zone of danger rule, 653, 654–55
Outrage, 637–43
Parasitic damages, recoverable as, 637, 672–74
Privacy invasion, 666–67
Terrorism, 645–46
Toxic exposures, 668–74
Undertaking or relationship creating duty care for protection of emotional interests, 662–64
Window of anxiety recovery after AIDS exposure, 673
Words, 645
    See also information, this topic
Workers' compensation coverage, 999
Zone of danger rule, 653, 654–55

EMPLOYERS
    See also Vicarious Liability
Common law duties to employees, 560, 975–76
Emotional harm intentionally inflicted, 639, 643
Sexual abuse or harassment
    by, 114
        emotional harm claim, 643
        vicarious liability for, 731–33
        workers' compensation, 1007–10

EMPLOYMENT DISCRIMINATION
See Civil Rights; Discrimination; Employers; Sexual Abuse or Harassment

ENHANCED INJURY
See Aggravated Injury

ESTOPPEL
Statute of limitations and, 390–92, 394

ETHICS RULES
Attorney's fees, 15
Frivolous claims, 1073
Scope of lawyer's authority under, 906–07
Settlement, 906–07

EVIDENCE
    See also Res Ipsa Loquitur; Statistical Evidence
Circumstantial generally, 203, 208
Credibility rule, 207–08
Defendant's safety rules as evidence on standard of care, 215–16

Epidemiological, 896
Expert testimony
    emotional distress, to prove, 667
    medical malpractice cases, 445, 448
    not required, when, 209–10, 448
    permitted or required, when, 209–10,
        448
    product design defect cases, 838–43
    res ipsa loquitur, establishing
        probability, 228–29, 471, 473
Inferences, see circumstantial evidence,
    this topic
Negligence generally, 201
Opinion testimony, 209–10
Presumption
    meanings, 226–27
    product is non-defective, statutory,
        862
    warning would have been heeded if
        given, 832
Scientific testimony, admissibility under
    Daubert standard, 841–43

EXTENDED LIABILITY
    See also Transferred Intent
Limits on, 57, 71
Principle of, transferred intent as, 56–58
Trespass to land cases, 70–71

FACTUAL CAUSE
    See also Apportionment
    Generally, 241
Alternative causation, 258, 260, 903
Apportionment to causes, 247–48, 251, 260,
    871, 892
Burden of proof, 241
But-for test
    alternatives to, 252
    applied, 241–45
    hypothetical nature of, 243–44
Causation obscured by defendants'
    negligent acts, 258
Causation without fault, 8–11
Comparative causation, 885, 892
Comparative fault, only causal fault
    compared, 336–37
Concurrent causes, 249
Divisible injury, 250
"Duplicative" causation, 251
Duty to preserve plaintiff's small chance of
    life or health, 261–70
Duty to try analysis, 267–68
Element of plaintiff's negligence claim, 241
Epidemiological evidence, 896
Evidence of causation, increased risk as,
    256
Existing injury, aggravation of, 247–48
Increased risk and, 256
Indivisible injury, 250–51, 871–72, 885–86
Inference or burden shifting when injury is
    within the risk, 256, 826, 833
Liability without causation, 248
Loss of chance, 261–70

Market share apportionment technique,
    897–905
Multiple actors, 247
Preemptive causation, 251
Preexisting injury or probability of harm,
    248
Probabilistic or proportionate causation
    Generally, 250–51
    market share compared, 897, 902
Product liability, warnings, causation
    issues, 832–33
Proximate cause and, 246, 273
Relaxed causation requirement, 267
Single indivisible injury, 250
Substantial factor test, 251, 254
Value of the chance
    evaluation of approaches to, 267–68
    increased risk of harm, 270
    loss of chance of better outcome, 261–
        70

FALSE IMPRISONMENT
    Generally, 63
Damages, 66
Duress or threat, by, 66
Exclusion, 66
False arrest compared, 66–67
Instigating confinement, 65–67
Malicious prosecution compared, 1068–69
Physical barriers or force, 64, 66
Police, requests to arrest as, 66
Privileged or not, 64, 100
Shoplifting and, 64

FAMILY MEMBERS
    See also Children; Consortium;
        Prenatal Harms; Sexual Abuse
        or Harassment
Abduction, alienation of affections, criminal
    conversation, 1082–83
Discretionary immunity of parents, death
    of child, 494–95
Domestic abuse
    battery, 491
    child abuse reporting statutes, 162–
        63, 603, 607
    civil rights claims for failure to
        protect, 536
    statute of limitations for continuing
        abuse, 379
Federal Tort Claims Act, *Feres* rule,
    application to, 523
Immunity
    Generally, 489
    family relationship terminated, 491
    foster parents, 496–97
    intentional torts, 490
    negligent supervision immunity, 492,
        495
    rejection of immunities, 491–92
    retention of immunities, parental
        care and authority, 492, 495

violation of duty to larger class injures family, 490
Interference with family, actions for, 1082–83
Mother, duty to fetus or not, 675–80
Negligent supervision, 492, 495
Parental liability, child's tort
    common law, 51
    duty to control known violent child, 616
    statutes, 51
Rejection of immunities, 491
Spousal abuse, see domestic abuse, this topic
Spouse, duty to control known dangers, 615

FAULT
See also Strict Liability
Basis of liability generally, 8–11, 131, 132
Causation distinguished from, 8–11, 127, 244, 336–37, 885, 926–27
Children's liabilities, 8, 46, 50–51, 149–52
Insane persons' liabilities, 42–43, 45, 144–47

FEDERAL TORT CLAIMS ACT
See Governmental Entities

FELA
Comparative fault under, 323
Fellow servant rule abolished in, 976
Railroad workers, federal statutory tort, 185
Wrongful death action under, 689 n.1

FIRE
See also Firefighter's Rule
Assumed risk or comparative fault of victim, 346
Breach of contract to supply hydrant water, 583
Cause in fact, multiple fires, 251
Equipment defective, 833
Governmental failure to fight, 527–28
Negligence in fighting, 527–28
Negligence in setting, 180
Products, 833, 848
Proximate cause
    different risk or not, 278, 290, 295
Public necessity privilege to destroy property in fighting, 120
Rescue, comparative fault, 349
Smoking causing, vicarious liability for, 722
Subrogation by insurer, 180 n.1
Water company's failure to supply water to fight, 583

FIREARMS
See Weapons

FIREFIGHTER'S RULE
Duty to public safety officers limited or not, 437
Expansions, 440–41
Intentional or willful wrongs, 441
Landowners' rule or not, 440
Private rescuers not barred by, 441
Risks to which rule applies, 441

FIRST AMENDMENT
See also Civil Rights
Churches, liability for exploitation, 733
Copyright and, 1098
Defamation and, 1053–67
Emotional harm from speech or exercise of religion, 645
Interference with contract and, 1096
Malicious prosecution and, 1071
Privacy and, 1079–80, 1081–82
SLAPP suits, 1075–76
Trademark and, 1102–03

FORESEEABILITY
See Negligence and Scope of Risk

FRAUD
See Misrepresentation

FREE SPEECH
See First Amendment

GENETIC HARMS
See Prenatal Harms

GOOD SAMARITAN STATUTES
Emergency treatment, immunity, 456–58

GOVERNMENT CONTRACTOR DEFENSE
Compliance with government specifications a defense, 863–64

GOVERNMENTAL ENTITIES
See also Officers
    Generally, 503
911 calls, 525, 536
Administrative agency, failure to follow safety rule, 517
Armed forces, immunity to members of, 519
Assault, battery etc. Immunity, 507
Civil rights claims against states and municipalities, 77–78, 535
Constitutional rights violated
    Feres immunity, 521
    state and local entities, 77–78, 535
Discretionary immunity
    administrative failure to enforce regulations, 516–17
    design vs. implementation test, 509
    firefighting, 527–29
    FTCA, 510
    planning vs. operational level test, 515
    police chase, 530–31
    police decisions, 523
    purposes, 514
    regulations, failure to promulgate, 516–17
    regulations, violations of, 516–17

susceptible of policy analysis, federal
test of, 516
Domestic violence, 536
Eleventh Amendment immunity, 503
Federal Tort Claims Act (FTCA)
Generally, 504
assault, battery and certain other
torts, 507
discretionary immunity, 510
federal court jurisdiction exclusive,
507
Feres rule, see *Feres* immunity for
torts to armed forces, this topic
jury trial denied under, 507
law governing, 504
notice requirement, 507
rules and structure, 504
specific statutory exceptions to
liability, 507
Feres immunity for torts to armed forces,
519
Government contractor complying with
specifications, immunity, 863–64
Government property, 516
High-speed police chase, 530–31
Immunities
abolition, partial, 503
assault, battery and certain other
torts, FTCA, 507
civil rights claims, in, 535
conscious decision, federal, not
required for, 515
federal, 509
funding decisions, federal, 516
government property exception to
immunity, 530
maintenance of property, federal, 516
planning vs. operational level,
federal, 515
qualified immunity, 82–90, 535–36
state-law, 523
traditional, 503
Intentional torts immunity, FTCA, 507
LSD experiments on service persons,
immunity, 521
Municipal immunity, 77, 504, 523
Municipal liability for civil rights
violations, 77, 535
Police
chase, discretionary immunity, 531
constitutional claims, 535
high speed chase, 530–31
public duty doctrine, 532
Private person liability, meaning of
requirement, 77, 504, 506
Promise of police protection, 523
Public duty doctrine, 532
Qualified immunity, 82–90, 535–36
Release of dangerous persons, immunity,
531–32
Reliance on apparent undertaking of, 523
Special relationship controlling duty to act,
524, 560–66

States and local entities
civil rights violations by, 81, 535
immunities or not, 523, 535
Taking of property, no immunity for, 503
Toxic exposures, 523

GROSS NEGLIGENCE
See also Reckless or Wanton
Misconduct
Standard of care defined by
Good Samaritan statutes, 456–58
guest statutes, 406
recreational use statutes, 430

GUEST STATUTES
Limiting duty of care, 406

HEALTH CARE PROVIDERS
See Medical Malpractice

HOSPITALS
See Medical Malpractice

IMMUNITIES
See also Duty; Governmental Entities
Allocating fault of immune tortfeasor, 199,
891
Charities, 497
Contribution against immune tortfeasor,
199
Family members, 489
Governmental entities generally, 503
Indian tribal sovereigns, 503
Judicial and legislative officers, absolute,
509
Local entities, 504, 523
State-law, 523
Teachers, 607
Tribal, 503
United States generally, 504

IMPLIED WARRANTY
See Products Liability

INCAPACITY
See also Disabled Persons; Mentally
Disabled Persons
Alcohol induced, standard of care, 143
Consent, capacity to give, see the topic
Consent
Informed consent rights of incompetent
patients, 462
Statute of limitations, tolling for, 388

INDEMNITY
See Contribution or Indemnity

INDEPENDENT CONTRACTORS
See Vicarious Liability

INFANTS
See Children; Family Members; Incapacity

INFORMED CONSENT
Generally, 458
AIDS doctor treating patient without informing, 464
Battery vs. Negligence theory, 461
Causation requirement, 462
Comparative fault of patient, 466
Disclosure required under materiality approach, what, 458–62
Emergencies affecting, 465
Exceeding consent distinguished, 461
Experiments, not treatment, requiring disclosure, 466
Incompetent patients and, 462
Materiality standard, 458, 461
Medical standard, 460–61
Negligence theory of, 461
Professional standard or patient rule, 461
Surgeon's AIDS not basis of emotional distress claim, 673
Surgeon's cocaine habit not revealed, 464
Surgeon's success rate, duty to reveal or not, 462–63

INJUNCTIONS
Trespass, remedy for, 69–71, 914

INJURIOUS FALSEHOOD
See also Economic Torts
Generally, 1085–88
Defamation compared, 1088
Defined, 1087
Statutory actions, 1088

INSANITY
See also Incapacity; Mentally Disabled Persons; Therapists
Assumption of risk by caregivers, 147
Intentional torts of insane persons, 42, 45
Negligent torts of insane persons, 144–47

INSURANCE
See also Subrogation
Bad faith failure to settle, tort to insured, 949
First-party, 905–06, 1029–33
Intentional torts and, 57
Liability insurance, 905–06
Liability insurance mandated, 1029
Liability insurer's duties, 905–06
No-fault insurance, 1030–39
Private insurance substitute for tort law generally, 1029
Punitive damages, bad faith failure to settle, 949
Types of affecting tort law, 57–58, 905–06
Uninsured motorists insurance coverage, 1029–30
Uninsured motorists undermining tort compensation, 965, 1029–30

INTELLECTUAL PROPERTY
Generally, 1097

INTENT
Battery generally, 37–40, 42–45, 46–50
Child's, 46, 50–51
Dual and single, battery, 42–45
Insanity or mental incapacity and, 42–43, 45
Negligence distinguished, 50
Nuisance cases, 764
Purpose as, 49
Recklessness distinguished, 50
Single and dual, battery, 42–45
Substantial certainty as, 46–50, 1005
Transferred, 56–58, 62
Trespass to land, 67–72
Workers' compensation, 1004–07

INTENTIONAL INFLICTION OF EMOTIONAL DISTRESS
See Emotional Harm

INTENTIONAL TORTS
See Trespassory Torts; and particular torts by name

INTERFERENCE WITH CONTRACT OR PROSPECTS
Boycotts, 1095–96
Burden of proof, 1089
Damages, 1095
Disparagement compared, 1090
Inducing breach of contract, 1088–96
Interference without inducing, 1088–89
Negligent interference not actionable, 1089
Wrongfulness requirement, 1094

INTERFERENCE WITH FAMILY RELATIONSHIPS
See Family Members

INTERVENING CAUSES
See Scope of Risk ("Proximate Cause") Requirement

INTOXICANTS AND INTOXICATED PERSONS
Alcohol provider's duty to protect from, 625–31
Police failure to arrest, leading to injury, 532
Social host providing alcohol, duty to third persons, 630
Standard of care of, 143

JOINT AND SEVERAL LIABILITY
See also Apportionment of Liability; Contribution or Indemnity; Settlement and Negotiation
Abolishing or limiting, 878
Apportionment between negligent and strictly liable actors, 880
Causal apportionment alternative, 248, 336–37, 871, 885, 892
Comparative fault apportionment among tortfeasors, introduced, 197
Concert of action basis, 875

Contribution corollary, see Contribution or
Indemnity
General rules of, 198, 874
Indivisible injury basis for, 247, 251, 258,
876
Insolvent or immune tortfeasors under rule
of, 199, 879
Introduced, 198
Proportionate share systems, 878
Several liability
Generally, 198, 199, 878
market share liability as, 902
Tortfeasor creates risk of tort by second
actor, 876, 885
Vicarious liability basis for, 876

JUDGE AND JURY
Allocation of powers between, 15, 24, 203,
207, 209
Credibility for the jury, 24, 207
Directed verdict standard, 24, 30
Evaluating conduct to be negligence, 212
Expert witnesses, 210, 448
Jury instructions, 25
Summary judgment, 23, 29

LANDLORD AND TENANT
Contract to keep premises repaired, 437,
581
Dangerous tenant or animal, duty to
protect strangers from, 615
Duties of landlord as to premises generally,
434, 615
Guests of tenants, duty to, 613
Tenant-on-tenant violence, 613

LANDOWNERS
See also Landlord and Tenant
Child trespassers
attractive nuisance, 414, 418
common hazards, 418
duty to, 414
tender years, 418
Classification of entrants
abolished, reasonable care adopted,
419
basis for duties, as, 407
changing categories, 411
Duty
limited generally, 407–27
negligence analysis vs. duty analysis,
422–23, 428, 440
Firefighters
duty to, 437–41
intentional or willful wrongs to, 441
other rescuers subject to rule, 441
private rescuers distinguished, 441
risks not inherent in job, 441
Invitees
duty to generally, 407, 410, 596
open, obvious danger, 423
outside scope of invitation, duty to,
407, 410

protection from others, duty to
provide, 596
Lessors, 434
Licensee
danger to discovered, 407
duty to, 407
Open and obvious danger, 423
Outside the land, 412
Police officers and others subject to
firefighters' rule, 441
Reasonable care as duty owed to entrants,
419
Recreational-use statutes, 430
Trespassers
children, 414
danger to discovered, 414
duty to, 414
Willful, wanton standard of care, 407, 412

LAST CLEAR CHANCE
Doctrine avoiding contributory negligence,
349–50

LEGAL CAUSE
See Scope of Liability (Proximate Cause)

LESSORS
See Landlord and Tenant

LIBEL
See Defamation

LITIGATION STATISTICS
See Tort Systems Evaluation

LOSS OF A CHANCE
See Factual Cause

MALICIOUS PROSECUTION
See Tortious Litigation

MARKET SHARE LIABILITY
See also Apportionment of Liability;
Conspiracy
Blood products, 904
Concert of action and, 903
DES, 897
Lead paint, 903
Manufacturer's liability apportioned
according to relative sales of product,
897
Several liability, as, 902
Vaccines, 904

MASTER AND SERVANT
See Vicarious Liability

McDONALD'S COFFEE CASE
Facts vs. Rhetoric, 17

MEDICAL MALPRACTICE
See also Blood or Body Parts or
Products; Informed Consent
AIDS negligently diagnosed, 665
Apology, role of, 451

Assumed risk, consent to negligence exacted as precondition, 358
Avoidable consequences rule, 926
Captain of the ship doctrine, 471
Chiropractors, standard of care, 455
Christian Scientist practitioner, standard of care, 455
Comparative fault of patient, 339–41, 466
"Crisis" and legal change, 474
Customary practice or opinion as standard of care, 445–55
Damages caps, 929–33
Dentists, standard of care, 448
Duty limited by medical custom or opinion, 445, 448, 452
Emergency
    duty to provide screening/treatment, 480–81
    Good Samaritan statutes, 456–58
Expert testimony required to show standard, 445, 448, 452
Good Samaritan statutes, 456–58
Gross negligence, 457
Hospitals
    emergency screening and treatment
        diversion of patient to avoid duty, 481
        duty to provide, 481
    standard of care, 456
    treatment withheld, 481
Incidence of, 474
Incompetent patient, right to refuse life-saving treatment, 462
Independent contractors, 740
Informed consent generally, 458
Institute of Medicine, 474
Instructions, honest mistake, 448
Insurance as reform justification, 474–76
Local standard of care, 452, 453
Malicious prosecution countersuits by physicians sued, 1072–73
Misdiagnosis causing emotional harm to patient or stranger, 665
Mitigation of damages required, 926–27
National standard of care, 454
Non-medical negligence, 450–51
Nonmedical practitioners, 455
Nurses, 455
Nursing homes, see the topic Nursing Homes
Patient's right to refuse life-saving treatment, 462
Pharmacists, duty owed by, 455
Physician-patient relationship basis for claim, 445
Physician's duty to stranger injured from patient's disease, 625
Prevalence of, 474
Protective statutes, 475, 486
Reasonable person standard, 445, 449–50
Referral, duty of, 455
Res ipsa loquitur, 467
Specialists, standard of care for, 454

Standard of care
    chiropractors, 455
    Christian Science practitioners, 455
    dentists, 448
    expert testimony required to establish, 445, 448, 452
    Good Samaritan statutes, under, 456–58
    hospitals, 456
    jury instructions, 448
    local, national or other, 451–55
    medical custom or opinion as, 447–55
    more than one standard, 449
    non-medical negligence, 450–51
    non-medical practitioners, 455
    reasonable care standard distinguished or applied, 450
    specialists, 453
Statute of limitations, 377, 385, 394, 477
Statutory "reforms", 475
Third persons, physician's duty to, 625, 662–64
Ybarra rule, 467

MEDICAL MONITORING DAMAGES
Toxic exposures, recovery for, 387, 672

MENTAL DISTRESS
See Emotional Harm

MENTALLY DISABLED PERSONS
    See also Incapacity; Insanity
Assumed risk by caregiver for harm from, 147
Duties to protect persons from themselves, 338–49
Intentional torts of, liability for, 45
Negligence, liability for, 144–47
Therapist's duty to protect from dangerous patient, 619–24

MISAPPROPRIATION OF COMMERCIAL VALUES
See Trademarks and Unfair Competition

MISREPRESENTATION
    Generally, 1107–35
Accountant or auditor's work communicated to third person, 1117–20
Comparative fault/contributory negligence, 1125
Damages, 1121–23
Disclaimers, 1129
Disclosure of facts, duty to make, 1130
Economic loss doctrine, 1129–30
Future, predictions not actionable, 1128
Knowing or reckless falsehood requirement, 1115
Negligent, 1115–16
Non-party, by, 1116
Nondisclosure of material facts, 1131
Opinion statements, 1126

Present state of mind about the future
misrepresented, 1128
Reliance required, 1124–25
Scienter, 1115
Strict liability for, 1122–24
Third parties, to, 1116

MOTIONS
See Procedure

**MULTIPLE TORTFEASORS OR
CAUSES**
See Apportionment; Cause in Fact; Res
Ipsa Loquitur

MUNICIPALITIES
See Governmental Entities

**NATIONAL CHILDHOOD VACCINE
INJURY ACT**
Liability scheme, 904, 1013–16

NECESSITY
See also Defenses to Intentional
Torts
Private, 124–28
Public, 120–24

NEGLIGENCE
See also Damages; Duty;
Causation in Fact;
Evidence; Negligence Per
Se; Res Ipsa Loquitur;
Risk-Utility Analysis;
Scope of Risk; Standard of
Care; Statutes; and
particular topics such as
Medical Malpractice
Generally, 131
Ability or experience of actor, 149
Actual harm required to establish claim
based upon, 237
Carroll Towing formula, 192–97
Children, 149–52
Compliance with statute as evidence of lack
of, 222
Cost-benefit formula, see Risk-Utility
Analysis
Custom as evidence
Generally, 217
as a shield, 218–21
as a sword, 217–18
defendant's own safety rules, effect,
215–16
industry-wide safety code, 218
non-safety custom, 218
relevant to what issues, 217
Disability, care owed by or to person under,
142–48, 236
Duty analysis vs. Breach analysis, 177,
179–80, 401, 423, 601
Duty of care generally, 135
Elements of the negligence case generally,
133
Emergency, 139–42

Emotional harm, 637–74
Evaluating conduct to determine
negligence, 201
Expert testimony, when not required, 209–
10
Fault and, 131, 132
Foreseeability of harm, 174, 177–78
Hand formula, 192–97
Heart attack or stroke, unforeseeable, 141,
143
Holmes on, 131
Honest mistake, 448
Inferences
Generally, 208
that defendant delayed in remedying
danger, 212
unspecified negligent conduct, of, see
Res Ipsa Loquitur
Institutions of negligence practice, 134
Intent distinguished, 49
Intoxication, 143
Judge and jury roles, see the topic Judge
and Jury
Jury instructions
care commensurate with danger,
135–37
emergency doctrine, 139
honest mistake in medical
malpractice cases, 448
medical malpractice cases, 448
reasonable person standard, 135, 137,
140
res ipsa loquitur, on, see the topic Res
Ipsa Loquitur
Memory, cost-benefit analysis of cost of,
196
Mentally disabled persons, standard, 144–
47
Misrepresentation, 1115–16
Multiple parties negligent
Generally, 197–98
See also Apportionment of
Responsibility; Joint and
Several Liability
Negligent entrustment, 632–34
Objective standard, see Standard of Care
Physical impairment of actor, 142–44
Proving negligent conduct
Generally, 201
circumstantial evidence, 203, 208
credibility rule, 207–08
evidence required to show acts, 201
opinion evidence, 209–10
specific conduct evidence required,
193–94, 201
testimonial accuracy, 206
Reasonable prudent person standard, 135
Recklessness distinguished, 50
Res ipsa loquitur, see the topic Res Ipsa
Loquitur
Risk, negligence as, 131, 133, 171

Risks and costs of avoiding as factors in determining
  costs of avoiding and probability weighed, 192
  formula weighing risks and utilities of conduct, 192–97
  risk improbable because others will provide safety, 180, 187
  risk reasonable because improbable it will eventuate, 177, 180, 187
  usefulness of activity outweighs risk, 171, 191–92
Slip and fall cases, 212–15
Standard of care, see the topic Standard of Care
Statute, compliance with as evidence of lack of, 221–22
Stop, look and listen rule, 156
Sudden incapacitation, 141, 143
Summary judgment inappropriate, 211
Unreasonable risk, as, 50, 131, 133
Weapons, child standard of care, 151

NEGLIGENCE PER SE
  Generally, 152–70
Administrative regulations, 156, 161, 488
Adoption or rejection of statutory standard
  Generally, 161
    class of risk and persons rule and, 160
Breach of duty, and, 162
Defining the standard of conduct
  requirement, 162
Effect of rule, 154
Evidence of negligence alternative, 154
Excused violation, 168 n.9, 169
Licensing statutes, 163
New duties, rejecting statutes that establish, 162
Non-excuses, 170
Nursing home regulations, 488
Ordinances and regulations, 156, 161
Proximate cause limitation on, 160, 163
Statutes creating tort cause of action
  distinguished, 155, 602, 606, 631–32
Statutes protecting public at large, 162

NO-FAULT COMPENSATION SYSTEMS
  Generally, 1029–39
Adoption of, 1038–39
Benefits under, 1031
Compulsory insurance, 1030
Deterrence, 1039
Keeton-O'Connell plan, 1030–31
New York statutes, 1032–33
Pain and suffering excluded, 1030, 1039
Pure vs. Hybrid, 1039
Re-entering the tort system, 1031, 1035
"Serious injury," 1035–38

NONFEASANCE
  See also Contract and Tort; Third Persons, Duty to Protect From
  Generally, 543
Bad Samaritan statutes, 556
Characterizing conduct as, 545
Child, government failure to protect after Contract and, 571
Custodian's duty to act, 560–61
Employer's duty to act, 560
Exceptions to the rule, 553
General rule, 543, 554
Innocently causing harm, duty to assist, 554
Innocently risking harm, duty to assist, 554
Invitor's duty to act, 560
Lessor's duty to act, 560
Making matters worse, 560
Misfeasance compared, 543, 567
Moral obligations and, 553–54, 561, 565
Nonperformance of repair contract, 579
Official nonaction
  constitutional claim denied, 535
  courthouse not protected, 527
  police, 524, 535
Preventing others from assisting, 554, 561
Special relationship creating duty to act, 524, 560–66
Statutes creating duty to act, 553, 556
Taking charge creating a duty to act, 557–60
Undertaking to act or not, 557–61
Worse-off test, 560

NUISANCE
Characteristics of, 764
Coming to the nuisance, 764, 765–66
Fault or not, 763
Public nuisances, 766
Rylands v. Fletcher version, 757
Strict liability or not, 757, 764
Substantial interference required, 764–65
Unreasonable invasion required, 765

NURSING HOMES
  Generally, 484
Abuse of residents, 485–86, 732
Administrative regulations, effect in tort suit, 488
Elder abuse statutes, 488
Inspection or survey reports, 487
Medical standard or not, 486
Res ipsa loquitur, 487

OFFER OF JUDGMENT
Statutes, 241, 906

OFFICERS
  See also Arrest; Governmental Entities
Absolute immunity, judicial and legislative, 509
Civil rights claims against, 77, 535

Qualified immunity, 82–90, 536
Rape or similar sexual attack by, 287, 733

OUTRAGE
See Emotional Harm

PAIN AND SUFFERING
Damages, tort law, see the topic Damages
No-fault, excluded from, 1031, 1039
Social security disability caused by, 1020, 1027
Vaccine injury system, limited recovery of, 1014
Workers' compensation, excluded from, 980

PARENT AND CHILD
See Family Members

PATENTS
Intellectual property in invention protected by, 1097

PETS
See Companion Animals

PHARMACISTS
See Medical Malpractice

PHYSICIANS AND SURGEONS
See Medical Malpractice

POLICE
See Arrest; Civil Rights; Governmental Entities; Officers

POLICY
Role of generally, 4–5

PREEMPTION
Claim, 395, 857–62
Compliance with federal statute eliminating tort, 395
Effect, 399
Express, 400
Products liability
    government specifications for product preempting, 863–64
    tobacco warnings claims, 861
Railroads, 400
Scope, 399
Supremacy Clause, 399

PREMISES LIABILITY
See Landowners

PRENATAL HARMS
    Generally, 675–87
Action against negligent mother for, 675–80
Contemporary rules, 679–80
Damages for wrongful birth, 682, 685
DES children and grandchildren, 681–82
Emotional distress damages in, 680, 686
Healthy children, claims relating to, 686
Live birth after prenatal injury, 679

Mother
    emotional harm claim for injury to fetus, 680
    liability to child for, 675–80
Stillbirth after prenatal injury, 679
Traditional rule denying recovery for, 678
Viability at injury, 679
Wrongful birth, conception, or life, 682

PRISONERS
Civil rights, cruel punishment, 80
Release of dangerous persons, 531–32, 614, 623–24

PRIVACY, RIGHT OF
    Generally, 1076–81
AIDS victims, 625
Constitutional limits on claims based upon publication, 1077, 1080–81
Emotional distress claim compared, 666–67
False light version, 1077
Intrusion on seclusion version, 1077, 1079–81
Private facts version, 1077, 1081–82
Right of publicity version, 1077, 1103–05
Seclusion, intrusion on, 1077, 1079–81
Types of claims, 1077

PRIVATE NECESSITY
See Necessity

PRIVILEGES
See Defenses

PROBABILITY
    See also Risk-Utility Analysis; Statistical Evidence
Damages
    discounting by probability of better outcome, 261–70
    value of life statistically calculated, 925
Factual cause generally, 241
Foreseeability, relation to, 177
Harm, of, see Risk and Risk-Utility Analysis
Informed consent, surgeon's duty to inform of probable life expectancy, 464
    physician's success rate, 462–63
Loss of chance, 261–70
Market share apportionment, 897–905
Negligence, element in determining, 192–97
Preponderance of evidence rule and, 201, 267–69
Res ipsa loquitur, estimates in, 227–28, 232–33
Statistical evidence, occurrence of event, 229

PROCEDURE
    See also Burden of Proof; Evidence
Answer, 23, 28
Appeals, 27, 32
Closing argument, 25, 30

Complaint, 22, 27
Demurrer, 22, 28
Directed verdict, 24, 30, 207–08
Discovery, 23, 28
J.N.O.V., 26, 32
Judgment notwithstanding the verdict, 26, 32
Jury arguments generally, 25, 30
Jury instructions generally, 25, 30
Jury selection, 24
Motion in limine, 24
Motion to dismiss, 22, 28
Narrative summary of a trial, 27–33
New trial motion, 26, 32
N.O.V., 26, 32
Objections to evidence generally, 24
Opening statement, 24
Order of trial, 21–33
Pre-trial conference, 24
Summary judgment, 23, 29, 59, 211

PRODUCTS LIABILITY
Generally, 777–868
Alternative design, what counts as, 818
Amazon, strict liability of, 784, 791
Assumed risk, 843–53
Bullets, talon or hollow point for private use, 820
Burden of proof on design defect, 812–13
Bystanders injured, 807
Causal apportionment, different injuries, 848
Causation, warning defects, 832–33
Combinations of products, 836
Comparative responsibility/contributory negligence, 843–53
Compliance with government specifications as a defense by preemption, 857–62
Compliance with statute
Generally, 857, 863
preemption version, 857–62
Consumer expectation test of defect
abolished, Restatement Third, 802
adopted, Restatement Second, 802
dangerous product intended, 820–24
design defect and, 806–07
food, 804–05
obvious danger and, 832
proof difficulties, 807
retained for food, Restatement Third, 805
Contributory negligence/comparative responsibility, 843–53
Crashworthiness of vehicles, 808, 802
Danger in product inherent, intended, or known, 820–24
Daubert and progeny, 841–43
Decline of strict liability in, 781
Defect
combined tests of, 809–13
consumer expectations test of, 799–805, 812–13, 817

distributional or marketing defect, 824
element of liability, 780, 781, 799
jury question, when, 811
risk-utility test of, 809–23
Defenses and defeats, 843
DES, 897
Design defects
Generally, 806–25
alternative design, what counts as, 818
consumer expectation test with, 806–07, 820–24
danger in product inherent, intended, or known, 820–24
defined, 806
manifestly unreasonable design, 820
negligence, distinguishable or not, 811
reasonable alternative design requirement, 813–20
risk-utility test, 809–23
Disclaimers, 856
Distributors of products, liability, 784, 790–92, 868
Economic, not physical harms, no strict liability, 794–99
Elements of strict products liability, 802
Emotional distress damages, 805
Evidence
comparative risks, 839
Daubert and progeny, 841
expert scientific testimony, admissibility and sufficiency, 841–43
similar accidents, 839
subsequent remedial measures, 840
Firearms, 824
Food containing natural ingredients, 804
General deterrence, 783–84
Government contractor defense, 863–64
Historical development of strict liability, 777–81
Implied warranty, 779
Indemnity, retailer's right to, 782
Learned intermediaries, warnings, 835
Lessors of goods, 792
Manifestly unreasonable design, 820
Manufacturing defect
consumer expectations test, 780, 799, 802
defined, 802
food, 804–05
proof of, 799–805
res ipsa loquitur and, 800, 803
strict liability for, 799–805
Market share liability, 897–905
Marketing technique enhances products danger, 824
Misuse
assumed risk and, 852
compared to no-defect, 852
compared to no proximate cause, 852

foreseeable, 848, 853
superseding cause, as, 852
warnings and, 856
National Childhood Vaccine Injury Act,
    1013–16
Negligence vs. Strict liability, 799, 803–04,
    811
Obvious danger, 826, 832
On-line sellers, liability of, 784, 791
Partial decline of strict liability in, 781
Preemption by federal standards, 857–62
Prescription drugs, 825, 835
Privity's citadel and its fall, 777
Proof, see evidence, this topic
Proximate cause, foreseeable misuse, 848,
    853
Rationales for strict products liability, 781–
    84
Reasonable alternative design
    proof of not required, 817, 819–20
    proof of required, 813–20
    Restatement Third, 817
Recall or repair obligations, 838
Repose, statutes of, 867
Restatement Second § 402A
    consumer expectations test, 802
    historical role, 780
Risk-utility test of design defect, 809–23
Services, 792
Stand-alone economic harm, strict liability
    excluded, 794–99
Statutes of limitation, 865–68
Statutory standards, compliance with, 857,
    863
Strict liability, 780–84, 799–805, 809
Tobacco
    preemption of warning requirements,
        861
    products liability, 861
UCC, disclaimers under, 856
Unavoidably unsafe products, 820–24
Used goods, 792
Warnings
        Generally, 826–38
    at sale, 826–37
    bulk goods, 836
    causation, presumed effect of
        adequate warning, 832–33
    comparative fault and, 831
    consumer expectations and, 832
    content and expression of, 833–34
    design defect, relation to, 832
    English-only warnings, 834, 863
    form and location, 834
    functions of, 826, 831
    heeding presumption, 832–33
    learned intermediaries, 835
    misuse of product and, 856
    nature and seriousness of harm, 834
    obvious dangers, 826, 831–32
    post-sale, duty to give, 837–38
    preemption of standards for by
        federal law, 857–62

prescription drugs, warning to
        physician, 835
    risk-utility balanced warnings, 832
    sophisticated users, 835–36
    Spanish language warnings, 834, 863
    tobacco, federal requirement and
        preemption, 861
    violation of instructions or warnings,
        misuse, 856
Warranty, 779–80
Weapons, bullets, 820

**PROPORTIONATE SHARE LIABILITY
SYSTEMS**
See Apportionment of Responsibility; Joint
    and Several Liability

PROXIMATE CAUSE
See Factual Cause; Scope of Liability
    (Proximate Cause)

PSYCHIATRISTS
See Therapists

PUBLIC NECESSITY
See Necessity

PUBLICITY
Right of, 1103–05

PUNITIVE DAMAGES
See Damages

QUALIFIED IMMUNITY
Civil rights cases, 81–90, 536
Criticisms, 87–88
History, 86

**RECKLESS OR WANTON
MISCONDUCT**
        See also Gross Negligence
Child's willful conduct, parental liability,
    51
Comparative fault, defendant's intentional
    or reckless misconduct, 350–51, 881–
    85
Defamation, reckless or knowing falsehood,
    when required, 1053–67
Defined, 50
Firefighters, landowners' willful risks to,
    441
Guest statute, willful, wanton standard of
    care, 406
Intent distinguished, 49
Landowners' duties to licensees and
    trespassers, 407, 412, 414
Negligence distinguished, 50
Sports, only duty to avoid, 371

RECREATIONAL USE STATUTES
Landowners' duties to recreational users on
    land, 430

RELEASE
See Settlement and Negotiation

RELIGIOUS BODIES OR CLERGY
Emotional harm inflicted, First
    Amendment protection, 645
Medical attention withheld under religious
    doctrine, 455
Sexual exploitation or abuse
    charitable immunity, 500
    punitive damages, 936
    vicarious liability for, 733
Statute of limitations, sexual exploitation
    cases, 389

RES IPSA LOQUITUR
    Generally, 222
Abnormally strong evidence, effect, 226
Attributing fault to defendant, 231
Available evidence not introduced, 229
Burden of proof, 224
Caregivers, nursing home, 236
Cause in fact and, 247
Circumstantial evidence of unknown
    negligent conduct, 222
Common knowledge, probability based on,
    228–29, 472
Comparative fault and, 234–35
Complete explanation of accident and, 231
Control rule, putative, 231–33, 467, 470–71
Direct evidence and, 231
Directed verdict for the plaintiff, 226
Elements, 224–25
Evidence available but not produced, 229
Expert testimony and, 228, 471, 473
Exploding-bottle cases, 233–34
Factual cause and, 247
Falling objects, 222
Fire, 231
Formulating rule of, 225
Inference of negligence
    permitted, not required, 226
    rebuttal of, 227
    required, 226
Instructions on, 225
Instrumentalities accessible to the public,
    233
Jury instructions, 225–26
Medical malpractice, 467
Multiple actors, 235, 467–71
Nursing homes, 488
"Ordinary" accidents, 229
Permissible inference rule, 226
Plaintiff's failure to adduce available
    evidence, 229
Plaintiff's fault, eliminating, 234
Power lines falling, 227–28
Presumption effect, 226–27
Probability estimates
        Generally, 228, 229, 232–33,
            471
    alternative, non-negligent
        explanations, 227–28
    common experience in making, 228–
        29, 471, 473
    experts and, 228–29, 471, 473

necessity of, 228
    statistical evidence, Posner's
        example, 230
Procedural incidents of, 225–26
Products liability and, 799, 802, 803–04
Rebuttal evidence, effect and use of, 227,
    230
Specific evidence of negligence and, 230–31
Statistical evidence of probability, 228
Strict liability and, 799, 802–03
Superior knowledge of defendant, 222, 230
Ybarra rule, medical malpractice, 467

RESCUE DOCTRINES AND RESCUE
Duty to or proximate cause of injury to
    rescuer, 289
Public, professional rescuers, firefighters'
    rule, 437
Rescuer's comparative fault/contributory
    negligence, 349

RESIDENTIAL FACILITIES
See Nursing Homes

RESPONDEAT SUPERIOR
See Vicarious Liability

RISK
See Negligence; Risk-Utility Analysis;
    Scope of Risk ("Proximate Cause")
    Requirement

RISK-UTILITY ANALYSIS
    Generally, 171
Alternatives to, 197–98
Comparative fault cases, in, or not, 330
Estimating costs and benefits of risks, 195
Evaluating, 196
Formula for determining negligence, 192–
    97
Information, costs of, 196
Memory, cost of, 196
Product liability generally, 809–23
Product liability, warnings, 830, 832
Risk of harm to plaintiff
    justified as likely to be avoided by
        plaintiff, 182, 185
    justified as small, 177
    justified because of burden of
        avoidance, 180, 183, 195
    justified by utility of the risky
        conduct, 171, 180, 191–92
    risk-utility formula, 192–97
    unjustified because of extensive harm
        potential, 188

SCHOOLS
See Duty; Teachers, Educators, and
    Schools; Third Persons, Duty to
    Protect From

SCOPE OF LIABILITY (PROXIMATE CAUSE)
Generally, 273
Abnormally dangerous activities strict liability and, 771–72
Alcohol providers, risk of harm done by drinker, 625, 628
Apportionment system, as, comparative fault alternative, 317
Cause in fact and, 246, 273
Comparative fault, disregarding fault outside of, 336–37
"Condition, not a cause" locution, 314–15
Contributory or comparative fault and, 336–37
Crimes, 287, 298–03
Duty analysis alternative to proximate cause analysis, 279
Element of the plaintiff's claim for negligence, 273
Enhancing injury, 296, 892
Extent of harm, 295
Factual cause and, 246, 273
Formulations of the rules
　　duty formulation, 279
　　foreseeability formulation, 278, 287–88
Intervening causes
　　Generally, 297
　　abandonment of doctrine as duplicative, 317
　　crimes, 298–303
　　natural and continuous sequence, 297
　　suicide, 303–06
　　terrorist acts, 303
Jury question, when, 274, 279, 287, 298, 311
Manner of harm affecting, 290
Natural and continuous sequence, 297
Rescue doctrine, 289
Second injury, 298, 314
Strict liability for abnormally dangerous activities and, 771–72
Suicide, 303–06
Superseding causes, see intervening causes, this topic
Termination of the risk or not, 311, 313
Thin skull rule, 296
Type of risk or harm rule, 274, 276–78
Violation of statute and, 160, 163, 290

SELF-DEFENSE
Generally, 91
Assault or imprisonment in, 95
Burden of proof, 91, 94
Deadly force, 95
Defense of others compared, 97
Excessive force, 94
Mistake and, 95
Provocation and, 94
Retreat, when required, 95
"Stand your ground" laws, 96

SEPTEMBER 11, 2001
Damages caps, possible effect on liability in close cases, 933
Death action analogy, 699–703
National victim compensation system, 699–703, 1016–17
Products liability, intended or foreseeable user of aircraft, 854
Report of Special Master, 699
Terrorism as superseding cause, 303

SETTLEMENT AND NEGOTIATION
See also Apportionment of Responsibility; Contribution and Indemnity; Insurance; Joint and Several Liability
Generally, 905–06
Client's rights against own lawyer, 906–07
Compromise, offer of, 241, 906
Ethics rules, 906–07
Factors in, 906
Fraud, coercion and incapacity, 912
Improvident settlement, 907–12
Insurance and, 905–06
Judgment, offer of, 241, 906
Lawyer's obligation in, 906–07
Liability insurer's duty, 905–06
Mistake as to nature or extent of injury, 907–12
Offer of judgment statutes, 241, 906
Release
　　grounds for setting aside, 907–12
　　mistake, avoidance or not, 907–12
Role of in tort law, 132, 906–07

SEVERAL LIABILITY
See Apportionment of Responsibility; Joint and Several Liability

SHIFTING DUTY OR RESPONSIBILITY
See also Assumption of Risk; Nondelegable Duties
Contract or undertaking as shift 556
Contractors and landowners, 745
Products, shifting duty from manufacturer to employer, 852

SLANDER
See Defamation

SLANDER OF TITLE
Injurious falsehood, form of, 1087

SLAPP SUITS
Early dismissal of claims based on free speech rights, 1075–76

SOCIAL SECURITY DISABILITY BENEFITS
Generally, 1018–27
Federal statute on, 1018
Five-step analysis, 1022

Grids, guidelines on impairments and
disabilities, 1022–26
Listings, a schedule of impairments, 1022
Procedures for claim, 1020
Statutory conditions, 1018–21

SOCIAL UTILITY
See Risk-Utility Analysis

SPORTS
Assumption of the risk, 364–71
Baseball Rule, 366
Participants, duty owed to, 368–71
Recklessness standard, 371
Recreational users of land, 430
Spectators, duty owed to, 365, 366–68

SPOUSAL ABUSE
See Family Members

SPRING GUN RULE
Defense of property and, 97

STALKING, STATUTES
Assault and, 62

STANDARD OF CARE
See also Custom; Duty;
Landowners; Medical
Malpractice; Negligence
Generally, 135
Abilities, experience, or knowledge of actor,
149
Children
adult vs. child standard, 149–52
rule of sevens, 152
Custom
medical malpractice cases, 445–55
not the standard generally, 217, 220–
21
Danger high
care commensurate with danger, 136,
137
effect on standard, 136, 137
Defendant's own rules or safety procedures,
215–16
Disability, care owed by or to person under,
144–47, 341–42
Due care standard, see reasonable person
standard, this topic
Emergency, 139–42
Gross negligence standard, guest statute,
406
Health care providers, see Medical
Malpractice
Heart attack or stroke, 141, 143
Insane persons, 144–47
Instructions
emergency, instructions under
attack, 139–42
medical malpractice, 448
reasonable person standard, 137, 140
Intoxication of actor, 143
Knowledge, ability, experience, effect on
standard, 149

Landowners, standards of care for entrants
non-traditional reasonable care
standard, 419
traditional, 407
Medical malpractice, see the topic Medical
Malpractice
Memory, 196
Mentally disabled persons, 144–47
Negligence objective standard, 137, 144–47
Physical characteristics of actor
effect on standard generally, 143
unforeseeable heart attack or stroke,
141, 143
Prudent person standard, see reasonable
person standard, this topic
Reasonable person standard, 135
Reckless, willful, wanton, see the topic
Reckless or Wanton Misconduct
Specific standards or duties
Sports, recklessness standard, 371
Statutory, 152–70

STATES
See Government Entities

STATISTICAL EVIDENCE
Admissibility, *Daubert* and progeny limits
on, 841
Product, causation or capacity for harm,
839, 842
Proof that event occurred by statistical
evidence, 230
Value of chance of better outcome, 261–70

STATISTICS
See Accident Data; Statistical Evidence;
Tort Systems Evaluations

STATUTES
See also Negligence Per Se
Abolishing joint and several liability, 878
Air Transportation Safety etc. Act, 1016–17
Arrest and detention by shopkeepers, 100
Assumption of the risk, 371
Bad Samaritan statutes, 556
Cause of action or defense created by, 155,
602, 606
Charitable immunity, 497
Child abuse reporting statutes, 162–63,
603, 607
Civil rights statute (§ 1983), 77–78
Comparative fault, 323
Compliance with, effect, 396, 857, 863
Compromise, offer of, 241, 906
Coverdell Teacher Protection Act, 607
Crime victim compensation
September 11 victims and survivors,
699–703, 1016–17
Damages capped, 929–33
Death, wrongful death and survival
statutes, 689, 690–707
Detaining or pursuing shoplifters, 106
Dram Shop acts, 631–32
Elder rights, 486, 488

Emergency screening and treatment, hospitals, 480
EMTALA, 480
Federal Employers Liability Act (FELA), see the topic FELA
Fencing districts, cattle, 756
Firefighter's Rule limited or abolished, 437
Free Access to Clinics Entrances Act, 63
Good Samaritan statutes, 456–58
Guest statutes, 406
Health care providers, see medical malpractice, this topic
Hospitals, duty to provide emergency attention, 480–81
Immunities established or abolished
  alcohol providers, 631–32
  charities, 497
  firearms manufacturers and sellers, 824
  Good Samaritan, 456–58
  public entities, 503
  teachers, 607
Intercourse with minor criminalized, effect, 118
Joint and several liability, abolishing, 878
Judgment, offer of, 241, 906
Lead paint in rental premises, 437
Limitation of actions
  negligence claims generally, 378
  products, 865–68
Medical malpractice
  caps on damages for, 929–33
  elder abuse, 486
  Good Samaritan statutes, 456–58
  health care providers special protections, 475, 486
  hospitals, emergency treatment required, 480–81
No-fault automobile statutes, 1032–33
Nursing homes, statutes and regulations, 488
Parental liability, 51
Preemption by federal statute, 395–400, 857–62
Products liability, 824, 838, 853, 855, 857–62
  firearms, claims limited, 824
  known dangerous products, liability ruled out, 820
  recall statutes, 838
Protection of Lawful Commerce in Arms Act, 824
Recreational-use statutes, 430
September 11, 2001 compensation system, 699–703, 1016–17
Several liability, establishing, 878
Shopkeeper's privilege to detain, 100
SLAPP suits, statutes requiring early dismissal of, 1075–76
Social Security disability, 1018–19
Stalking statutes, 2
Standard set by, negligence per se, 152–70

Statutes of limitations, see the topic Statutes of Limitation
Therapists, duties to patient's potential victims, 619–24
Tort reform, see the topic Tort Reform Vaccine, National Childhood Vaccine Injury Act, 904, 1013–17
Violation as negligence per se, 152–70
Weapons, immunity for manufacturers and sellers of, 824
Workers' compensation statutes, general provisions, 977–83

STATUTES OF LIMITATION
  Generally, 378
Accrual of claim
  concealment of defendant's negligence, 391
  discovery rule, 380, 383–85
  injury, at time of, 378–80
Bar before claim accrues, 392–95
Childhood sexual abuse, 389
Concealment of negligence, 391
Continuous treatment, medical cases, 379
Disabilities, tolling for, 388
Discovery rule, 380, 383–85
Equitable tolling, 394–95
Estoppel to plead, 390–92
Exposure without symptoms, 387
Latent potential harms, 380, 386
Medical malpractice, 378–79, 385, 390, 394
Policies of, 378, 394
Pre-accrual bar, 393
Products liability generally, 865–68
Psychological inhibitions to suit, 388
Repose, statutes of, 392–95, 867
Repressed memory, 389
Tolling, 388–89, 394–95
Toxic exposure, latency period, 385
Wrongful death, 706

STRICT LIABILITY
  See also Nuisance; Products Liability; Vicarious Liability
Abnormally dangerous activities
  Generally, 767–75
  elements under Restatement Third, 770
Animals
  cattle, trespass, 755–56
  domestic animal, vicious propensity of, 756–57
  wild, personal injury, 757
Assumed risk, abnormally dangerous activities, 774
Blasting and explosives, 767–72
Case, writ of, 753
Cattle trespasses, 755–56
Common law procedures, 753
Common usage in abnormal danger cases, 770–71

Comparative responsibility under Restatement of Apportionment, 774–75

Contribution between strictly liable and negligent actors, 880

Contributory negligence, abnormally dangerous activities, 774–75

Defenses to, 774–75

Environmental statutes, 767

Escape of non-natural things, 757, 762

Fireworks, 773

Hazardous wastes, 774

History, 10

Impoundments, substances escaping, 757, 762

Land uses mutually risky or harmful, 763

Lateral support, 774

Limited applicability of, 8–11

Misrepresentation, 1122–24

Negligence requirement adopted for direct harms, 754

Nuisance, 757, 764–66

Nuisances today, 764

Plaintiff's involvement in abnormally dangerous activity, 771, 774–75

Poisons, 773

Products liability, see the topic Products Liability

Proximate cause (scope of liability), 771–72

Reasonable care cannot eliminate abnormal danger, 770

Restatement Third on, 770–71

Rockets, 773

Scope of liability (proximate cause), 771–72

Significant risk, abnormal danger, 770

Trespass writ, under, 753

Trespassing animals, 755–56

Writs, early common law, 10, 753

SUBROGATION
Explained, 180 n.1

Insurance, 180 n.1

Interference with contract cases analogous to, 1089

Right to protected, by collateral source rule, 927

Workers' compensation insurer's, 1012

SUBSTANTIAL CERTAINTY INTENT
Sufficiency of generally, 46–50

Workers' compensation, in, 1005

SUICIDE
Comparative fault and, 339

Duty to prevent
foreseeability triggering, 304, 305
no duty, 305
schools' duty, 624–25

Medical care, patient's refusal of, 462

Scope of liability (proximate cause), 303–06

Superseding cause, 303–06

Workers' compensation, compensability, 994

SUMMARY JUDGMENT
See Case Reading; Procedure

SUPERSEDING CAUSE
See Scope of Risk ("Proximate Cause") Requirement

SURVIVAL ACTIONS
See Death

TAKING OF PROPERTY BY GOVERNMENT
Necessity defense and, 123

No immunity for, 503

TEACHERS, EDUCATORS, AND SCHOOLS
Battery by coach alleged, 61

Colleges, duty limits, 609–10

Crossing guards not provided, 608

Discipline, privilege to, 106

Duty to protect students, 603–09

Immunity, 607

Misrepresentation, suitability of school employee, 1113

Sexual abuse
educators' duty to report or control, 603, 607
molesting child, vicarious liability for, 733
school recommending sexually abusive employee, 1113
school's duty to protect students from school employees, 603, 607

Standard of care, sports coach, 149

THERAPISTS
Duty to protect strangers from patient, 619–23

Repression disputes, 389

Sexual exploitation of consenting patients, 114

Sexual exploitation of patient, emotional harm to spouse, 646

Statutes regulating sexual behavior, 114

THIN SKULL RULE
Liability for unforeseeable extent of harm, 296

THIRD PERSONS, DUTY TO PROTECT FROM
Generally, 589

Alcohol provider, duty to drinker's victims, 625–31

Basis for duties, defendant's relationship with attacker, 614

Child abuse investigation and reporting statutes, 162–63, 603, 607

Children, parental duty to control, 51, 616

Colleges, duties to protect students, 609–10

Custody as trigger of, 615

Doctor's duty to protect stranger from patient's disease or other dangerous condition, 625

Dram shop statutes, 631–32

Emotional harm, duty to third person undertaken, 662–64

Employer hiring dangerous persons, 617, 741, 744

Foreseeability and, 596, 597–602, 609

General rule of no duty, 589

Hiring and supervision of potentially dangerous person, 618, 741, 744

Intentional tortfeasor's tort risked by defendant, 885

Landlord, duty to protect stranger from tenant or animal, 615

Landowner's duty to protect invitee, 597

Misrepresentation by non-party, 1116

Negligence, protection of plaintiff from third-party, 597

Negligent entrustment, 632–34

Owner's duty to protect from dangerous vehicle driver, 632–34

Parents' duty to control child, 51, 616

Physicians, duty to stranger injured by patient's condition, 625

Prison release program, duty to protect stranger from releasee, 531–32, 614

Relationship with attacker, 614

School employees, duty to protect from sexual harassment, 603

Schools, protection of students abuse or attack, 603 crossing guards withdrawn, 585

Seller or donor's duty not to provide car to dangerous driver, 633

Social host providing alcohol, duty to protect from drinker, 630

Spouse, duty to control other spouse, 615

Therapist's duty to protect stranger from patient, 619–23

THIRD PERSONS, LIABILITY TO
See also Third Persons, Duty to Protect From

Auditors' or accountants' liability, 1117–20

Intentional trespassory torts, transferred intent, 56–58, 62

Medical, 625, 662

Misrepresentation, 1117–20

Subrogation, see the topic Subrogation

TORT REFORM
See also Tort Systems Evaluation; Damages; Joint and Several Liability

Anecdotes and, the McDonald's case, 17

Criticisms of tort law, 960–63

Damages capped, 476, 929–33

Data on claims, 959, 961–62

Joint and several liability abolished or limited, 878

Medical malpractice, 475

Statutes of limitation, 385, 394, 477

TORT SYSTEMS EVALUATION
Alternative systems, evaluation, 1041–42

Costs, 1042

Criticisms
compensation inadequate, 964–65
delay in payment of loss, 967–68
deterrence inadequate, 968–69
excessive claims or costs, 960, 966–67
inefficiency, 967
limited resources misused, 966–67
lottery effects, 969–70
overcompensation, 965–66
welfare plans alternative, 971, 1027

Disinclination to sue, evidence of under-suing, 961

Judicial process, 1041

TORTIOUS LITIGATION
Abuse of process
Elements, 1074–75
SLAPP suits, 1075–76

Civil suits maliciously prosecuted, 1071

Defamation compared, 1070

Defenses, 1071

Ethics rules, 1073

False imprisonment compared, 1069

Malicious prosecution, elements, 1070–71

SLAPP suits, 1075–76

Special injury rule, civil prosecutions, 1074

TORTS AND TORT LAW
See also Tort Reform; Torts Systems Evaluation; and particular torts, issues, and elements

Alternatives to tort law
evaluation of, 1041–42
no-fault auto insurance, 1030–39
private insurance, 1029–39
public compensation systems, 1013–17
workers' compensation, 975–1012

Compensation objectives, 6–7

Contract and, 3, 567

Corrective justice and, 5

Crime and, 3

Criticisms and evaluations, 959–71

Defined, 3

Deterring unsafe conduct, 7

Fault requirement normally applied, 5–6, 8–11

Justice and policy in, 4–5

Process values, 4

TOXIC TORTS
See also AIDS or HIV; Asbestos; Products Liability

Carcinogen exposure, 668–74

Emotional harm from toxic exposures, 668–74

Fetus exposed in utero, mother's liability, 680

Government-caused exposures, non-testing, discretionary immunity, 517

Government failure to enforce safety
 regulations, 517
Government LSD experiments on service
 persons, 521
Medical monitoring damages, 387, 672,
 925–26
Statute of limitations problems, 386–88
Workers' compensation, 1001–03

TRADE SECRETS
Acquisition tortiously or in violation of
 contract, 1099

**TRADEMARKS AND UNFAIR
 COMPETITION**
Availability of protection, infringement,
 dilution, and free speech rights,
 1099–1103
Competition rights, 1099
Infringement, trademark, 1099–1103
Right of publicity, 1103–05
Trade secrets, 1099

TRANSFERRED INTENT
Application to trespassory torts, 56–58, 62
Assault and, 62
Battery and, 56–58, 62
Extended liability
 limitations on, 71
 reflecting principle of, 57
Intentional infliction of emotional harm,
 principle rejected, 645–46
Limitations on extended liability, 71

TRESPASS TO CHATTELS
Elements, 76

TRESPASS TO LAND
 See also Landowners; Defenses
 Generally, 67
Aerial intrusions, 69
Animal trespass, strict liability for, 755–56
Damages without pecuniary harm, 71
Defending possession against, 97–100
Elements, 68
Extended liability and its limits, 71
Injunctive remedy, 71, 914
Intent required, 69–70
Nuisance and, 70
Possession, interference with, 67
Possessor's duty to trespassers, 407, 412,
 414
Punitive damages for, 71
Remedies, 71
Tangible invasion, 70 71

TRESPASSORY TORTS
 See also Assault; Battery; False
  Imprisonment; Trespass to
  Chattels; Trespass to Land
Common law writ of Trespass and its rules,
 10, 753
Comparative fault rules applicable or not,
 350–51, 881–85
Damages without pecuniary harm, 55, 70

Extended liability for, 56–58, 71
Transferred intent, 56–58, 62

TRIAL PROCEDURE
See Procedure

TROVER
See Conversion

ULTRAHAZARDOUS ACTIVITIES
See Strict Liability

UNDERTAKINGS
Action as, 553–54, 585
Duty derived from, 553–54, 585, 662–64
Emotional distress and, 662–64
Government, by, 523, 532
Reliance and, 525, 527, 585

UNFAIR COMPETITION
Trademark infringement, 1097–1103

UNPUBLISHED OPINIONS
Rules on citing to, 484

VICARIOUS LIABILITY
 Generally, 711–52
Apparent agency, 746
Bailor, not vicariously liability, 751
Battery by employee, 728–30
Borrowed servants, 717–18
Captain of the ship doctrine, 471
Caregivers, scope of employment, 732
Coming and going rule, 719–22
 frolic and detour compared, 726
 workers' compensation laws on, 988–
  89
Concert of action, conspiracy, aiding, 749
Employer's primary negligence
 distinguished, 733
Enterprise liability rationale, 712, 717
Entrustment of a vehicle, 632–34, 750
Family-purpose doctrine, 751
Frolic and detour, 726
Gratuitous service, 718
Imputed comparative/contributory
 negligence, 751–52
Indemnity right of employer, 716–17
Independent contractors
 Generally, 735–48
 apparent or ostensible agency, 746
 completed work causes harm to
  employer's invitee, 745
 control test, 736, 740
 factors in classifying as, 739
 franchisee of restaurant, 716
 incompetent, primary liability for
  selecting, 735, 741
 inherent dangers and peculiar risk,
  744
 negligence of employer distinguished,
  741
 non-delegable duties, 741
 retained control, 741–42

selecting incompetent contractors, 741
Joint enterprise, 748
Loaned servants, 717–18
Medical malpractice cases, 471
Non-delegable duties, 741
Partnership, 748
Police officers off duty, moonlighting, 718
Policy or goal of, 711–16
Punitive damages, employer's vicarious liability for, 935
Rationales of, 711–16
Respondeat superior and scope of employment, 711
Scope of employment
 Generally, 711
 going and coming rule, 719–22
 intentional torts of employee, 715, 728–35
 personal activities of employee, 722–28
 prohibited act of employee, 711, 713, 728–35
 reentry into employment, 726
 sexual torts of employee, 731–33
 temporary deviations, 722, 726
Serving gratuitously, 718
Serving two masters, 717–18
Sexual abuse by employee, 731–33
Tacit agreement as basis for, 750
Unpaid workers, 718

VIOLATION OF STATUTE
See Negligence Per Se; Statutes

WANTON MISCONDUCT
See Reckless or Wanton Misconduct

WARRANTY
See Products Liability

WEAPONS
Bullets (hollow point) sold for private use, 820
Cities' claim for expense resulting from, 824
Federal statute, immunity for sellers of, 824
Immunity for sellers under federal statute, 824
Marketing to encourage criminal use, 824
Minor using, standard of care, 151
Negligent entrustment, 632–34
Protection of Lawful Commerce in Arms Act, 824
Public nuisance, distribution to criminals, 824

WILLFUL MISCONDUCT
See Reckless or Wanton Misconduct

WORKERS' COMPENSATION
Generally, 975–1012
Accident or accidental injury requirement, 993–1001

Arising out of employment requirement, 983–93
Batteries on the job, 992, 1004
Benefits, 979–83
Borrowed servants, 1011
Characteristics, 977–79
Coming and going rule, 988–89
Common-law liability of employers, 975
Company-sponsored recreation, 992
Contribution claim by tortfeasor against negligent employer, 1012
Course of employment requirement, 983–93
Coverage, 978–79
Cumulative stress, 1000
Disability, types and benefits, 981–83
Emotional harm, 999
Exclusive remedy
 Generally, 1003–10
 child injury, parents witnessing barred, 1003
 fetus injured not barred, 1003
 intentional tort to employee, 1004–07
 sexual abuse or harassment, 1007–10
Exposures to disease in different employments, 1001–03
Functional vs. Industrial disability, 981
Going and coming rule, 988–89
Heart attacks, 998
Historical background, 975–76
Horseplay injuries, 900–02
Incidental departures from working, 989
Increased risk, 987
Intentional torts
 co-worker's, 994, 1007
 employer's, 1004–07
Job-related injury, 983–1003
Last-injurious-injury rule, 1002
Lien of employer against recovery from tortfeasor, 1011–12
Mental disorder, 999–1000
Multiple exposure or injury, 1001–03
Occupational disease
 coverage, 1000–01
 exposure in more than one employment, 1001–03
Personal activities causing injury, 983
Positional risks, 987–88
Pre-existing conditions, 999
Recreation, company-sponsored, 992
Scheduled injury, 981
Second-injury funds, 1002–03
Sexual harassment or attack, 1007–10
Statutory employers, 1011
Street risk doctrine, 986
Stress, job-created, 1000
Subrogation rights of employer against tortfeasor, 1012
Suicide or self-inflicted injury, 994
Third parties, claims against, 1010–12
Traveling employees, 989

WRITS
    See also Strict Liability; Trespassory
        Torts
Early common law system, 10, 753

WRONGFUL BIRTH, CONCEPTION,
    OR LIFE
See Prenatal Harms

WRONGFUL DEATH
See Death